HARDPRESS.NET

ISBN: 9781290660174

Published by:
HardPress Publishing
8345 NW 66TH ST #2561
MIAMI FL 33166-2626

Email: info@hardpress.net
Web: http://www.hardpress.net

its ancestor. The mediæval heraldry was growing up in England during the eleventh and twelfth centuries, and it made an extensive use of conventionalized heads of familiar animals, not merely lions, wolves, and bulls, but many kinds of bird and fish, as well as such imaginary creatures as dragons, griffins, and cockatrices. For example, Lucy is the heraldic name for pike, and the shield of the De Lucy family bears on a field gules three lucies or. From this emblem the family surname is likely to have arisen, just as Geoffrey Plantagenet was so called from the sprig of broom or genesta plant worn in his helmet. The familiar name of Pike, as well as that of the Puritan magistrate, Sir Thomas Lucy, who arrested Shakespeare for poaching, has probably come from the heraldic use of pikes or lucies.

The explanation which serves for one of this class of animal surnames might perhaps serve for all; but there is another point to be considered. Heraldic devices were used not only upon banners and coat-of-arms, but also upon signboards, not merely of inns but of other places of business. In days when reading and writing were not common accomplishments, such devices were in general use, and they survived down to a recent time. For tavern signs they are not yet extinct. In old times, as often at the present day in Europe, the shop and the homestead were usually contained in the same building. Thus in the seventeenth century the father of John Milton, who was a solicitor, notary public, and law-stationer, had his office and his home in a certain house known as the Spread Eagle, in Bread Street, Cheapside. Over the front door was the figure of an eagle with outstretched wings. For four or five centuries before Milton's time, in going through any town, you would have passed by a succession of such signs of hawks, cranes, dolphins, salmon, lambs, and bulls, thus finding your way to the particular shop and homestead of which you were in quest. The principle upon which the signs were chosen is not always obvious. Sometimes a family name may have suggested the sign, as if a man named Crow were to paint a black crow over his door; but in early times the sign undoubtedly preceded and suggested the name. The family which dwelt at the sign of the crow came to be called Crow, in the same way that a family which dwelt at a country house called Greenough or Greenhalge (green field) came to be called by the name of the house.

John Fiske.

THE EARLY FORESTERS.

Below will be found the English and Flemish* ancestors of Reginald Foster and undoubtedly of all the other emigrants to Massachusetts in an early day, and in fact every one now bearing this name in the world. The first of the name was:

1. ANACHER GREAT FORESTER of Flanders died in 837, had son.

2. BALDWIN I, OF FLANDERS (Anacher Great Forester), the Forester called "Iron Arm" on account of his great strength, some say on account of his being constantly in armor. He married the Princess Judith, daughter of Charles, the Bald,† King of Aguitenia and Neustria, or in other words the greater part of modern France. He built castles at Bruges and Ghent to defend the country against the Normans. He died at Arras in 877, and was succeeded by his son.

3. BALDWIN II, OF FLANDERS (Baldwin I, Anacher Great Forester), the Forester, married the Princess Alfrith, daughter of Alfred the Great, King of England. He made war against Endes, Count of Paris, who usurped the French crown and defeated him. He died in 919 and was succeeded by his son, Arnulf of Flanders, the Forester, who was succeeded in 988 by his son.

4. BALDWIN III, OF FLANDERS (Baldwin II, Baldwin I, Anacher Great Forester), the Forester, called "of the handsome beard," married the daughter of

---

* See Galway, Ireland, "Vindicator" of Oct. 20, 1866, for genealogical chart of the Blake Forester branch.

† Charles II, the Bald, King of France, was son of Louis I, the Pious, King of France, who was son of Charlemagne, Emperor of the West, who was son of Pepin le Bref, King of France, who was son of Charles I, King of France.

the Count of Luxemborg. He was a great warrior and defended his country against the united forces of the Emperor Henry, King Robert of France and the Duke of Normandy. He died in 1034 and was succeeded by his son.

5. BALDWIN IV (Baldwin III, Baldwin II, Baldwin I, Anacher Great Forester), the Forester called "Le Debonaire," married the Princess Adela, daughter of Robert, King of France, by whom he had issue.

6. i. BALDWIN V the Forester.

7. ii. ROBERT FORESTER, surnamed "the Frislander," from his having conquered the Principality of Frisland.

8. iii. MATILDA or Maud, m. William I, surnamed the Conqueror of England. William, Duke of Normandy, was born in 1024. He was surnamed the Conqueror, from his triumph over Harold at Hastings, on the 14th of October, 1066, and was crowned King of England by Aldred, Archbishop of York, at Westminster Abbey on the 29th of December in the same year. His children were: 1. Robert, surnamed Courthouse, successor to the Duchy of Normandy, d. at Cardiff Castle, Feb. 10, 1134. 2. Richard, killed by a stag in the New Forest, and d. a youth. 3. William Rufus, successor to the crown of England, known as William II, d. Aug. 2, 1100. 4. Henry, successor to the crown of England, after his brother, known as Henry I. He d. from eating too freely of lampreys Dec. 2, 1135. 5. Cicelie, who took the veil at the monastery of Fescamp, and was afterward abbess to the Holy Trinity at Caen, where she d. in 1126. 6. Constantia, m. Alan Fergant, Earl of Brittany, and d. Sept. in 1126. 7. Alice, contracted to Harold. 8. Adela, m. Stephen, Earl of Blois, and had 5 ch. 9. Agatha, d. unm., but betrothed to Alphonzo, King of Galicia. 10. Gundred, m. William de Warren, Earl of Surrey, and d. May 27, 1085.

9. iv. SIR RICHARD FORESTER, called in those days by his Latinized name of Forestarius. Sir Richard and his father, Baldwin IV, passed over to England with his brother-in-law, William the Conqueror, and received the honor of knighthood after the decisive battle of Hastings, being then in his sixteenth year, from whom sprung the Foresters of Etherston and Bamborough Castle in Northumberland, and the Blake Foresters of Ashfield and Knockmoy Abbey, County of Galway and Inchorey Castle, County of Clare.

The Forester family were the principal chieftains in Northumberland and allied by marriage with all the eminent northern families, viz., the Fetherstones, Grays of Chillingham, the Fenwicks, the Lord Barons of Hilton, the Mitfords, Barons of Mitford, from whom the Earl of Redesdale, the Collingswoods of Dislington, the Radcliffes, Earls of Derwentwater, the Haggerstons of Haggerston; the Russels from whom the Duke of Bedford, and others too numerous to mention. Many of the family were distinguished for their deeds of chivalry and warlike actions, and at the siege of Acre, A. D. 1191, a party of Saracens, having sallied forth and surrounded King Richard, he would have been overpowered and made prisoner had not Sir John Forster, who seeing from a distance the danger in which the King was placed, pushed forward with couched lance followed by his retainers shouting, "To the rescue! a Forester! a Forester!" The King then cut down the Saracen leader whose troops retreated before Sir John, who for his bravery and timely assistance received from King Richard a grant to bear a Chevron vert on his shield. There is a monument to his memory in Bamborough Abbey bearing his effigy in full armor. In a song on the battle of Otherbowine, in 1238, the Foresters are placed first of the clans mentioned:

"The Forster, Fenwick, Collingwood, the heroes of Renown,
High in the ranks of Lord Percy, the war axe hewed down,
The Percies in that vengeful fight, both were prisoners taken,
But for the Douglas' dead body were yielded up again."

The Forsters of Bamborough Castle were Lords of Blanchland in Northumberland, and for several generations they were Knights Bannerets, Lords Warden of the Middle Marches, High Sheriffs of Northumberland and hereditary Governors of Bamborough Castle from the reign of James I to that of George I. The Forsters of Etherston—the head of this house—from whom those of Bamborough descended, won their honors on the field of battle; and their descendants, of Huntdon (Hunsdon), by their profound skill in legal knowledge. Sir Richard Forester, the son of Baldwin IV, ,was succeeded by his son.

10. SIR HUGO FORESTURIOUS OR FORSTER (Sir Richard, Baldwin IV, Baldwin III, Baldwin II, Baldwin I, Anacher Great Forester), who marched against Magnus, King of Norway, when he invaded England A. D. 1101. In the battle that ensued King Magnus was slain and his troops routed. Sir Hugo d. in 1121, leaving issue.

11. i. SIR REGINALD. He was knighted by King Stephen for his valiant conduct at the battle of the Standard, fought Aug. 22, 1138. He died in 1156, leaving a son and successor.

12. ii. SIR HUGO, a person of great eminence during the reign of King Stephen, who appointed him Chief Guard of the Royal Forests of England. In 1152 he witnessed a deed in Northumberland in which he is styled Foresturious (the Latinized name of Forster). He bore for arms a shield argant, three bugles or stringed gules.

13. SIR WILLIAM FORSTER (Sir Reginald, Sir Hugo, Sir Richard, Baldwin IV, Baldwin III, Baldwin II, Baldwin I, Anacher Great Forester). He took an active part in suppressing two formidable insurrections that broke out in Wales A. D. 1163 and again in 1165. In 1166 he took his departure for France, the people of Brittany having rebelled against their Duke Conan, but the insurrection was quelled by Henry II with his usual promptitude, and afforded him a pretext for taking the government into his own hands. Sir William was then about returning to England, but Henry becoming involved in hostilities with Louis VII he remained and took part in all the engagements; but the war terminating by the peace concluded at Montmirail, Jan. 6, 1169, he returned to England and d. in 1176. He was succeeded by his son Sir John.

14. SIR JOHN FORSTER (Sir William, Sir Reginald, Sir Hugo, Sir Richard, Baldwin IV, Baldwin, III, Baldwin II, Baldwin I, Anacher Great Forester). He accompanied Richard I to Palestine, where he received the honor of knighthood for his valor. He was one of those who compelled John to sign the Magna Charta in 1215. He d. in 1220 and was succeeded by his son.

15. SIR RANDOLPH FORSTER (Sir John, Sir William, Sir Reginald, Sir Hugo, Sir Richard, Baldwin IV, Baldwin III, Baldwin II, Baldwin I, Anacher Great Forester). He accompanied Prince Richard, brother of Henry III, to France in 1225, the Prince being sent by the King for the purpose of regaining his French provinces. After a year's fighting an armistice was agreed upon, but the French King dying before its expiration, the hostilities were again renewed, but ended in very little result. He d. in 1256 and was succeeded by his son.

16. SIR ALFRED FORSTER (Sir Randolph, Sir John, Sir William, Sir Reginald, Sir Hugo, Sir Richard, Baldwin IV, Baldwin III, Baldwin II, Baldwin I, Anacher Great Forester). He assisted Prince Edward after his escape from the rebel barons in raising an army for the purpose of releasing his father, Henry III and Prince Richard from their confinement, and was appointed one of the King's officers. Having collected his army Prince Edward fought the battle of Eversham Aug. 4, 1265, in which he was victorious. Sir Alfred received the honor of knighthood on the battlefield. He d. in 1284 and was succeeded by his son.

17. SIR REGINALD FORSTER (Sir Alfred, Sir Randolph, Sir John, Sir William, Sir Reginald, Sir Hugo, Sir Richard, Baldwin IV, Baldwin III, Baldwin II, Baldwin I, Anacher Great Forester). He fought at Bannockburn in 1314, and d. in 1328 and was succeeded by his son. His descendants were great chieftains, many being knighted, and being closely allied to the Royalty in Scotland, Ireland, Wales and England. Sixty-one (61) of this family held the offices of mayors or sheriffs of the town of Galway. Frances Blake Forster left five (5) children, two (2) sons and three daughters, who still survived and one of whom, Capt. Blake Forster, J. P. of Forster Street House in this city (Galway) and Bally Keale, County Clare, is the present (1866) head of this (Blake Forster) family. There is a monument to the memory of Sir John Forster (of the time 1190) in Bamborough Abbey, being his effigy in full armor. Sir Reginald's son was:

18. SIR RICHARD FORSTER (Sir Reginald, Sir Alfred, Sir Randolph, Sir John, Sir William, Sir Reginald, Sir Hugo, Sir Richard, Baldwin IV, Baldwin III, Baldwin II, Baldwin I, Anacher Great Forester). He fought at Cricy Aug. 25, 1346, and at Poitiers Sept. 19, 1356. He was knighted for his valor. He d. in 1371, leaving a son.

19. SIR WILLIAM FORSTER (Sir Richard, Sir Reginald, Sir Alfred, Sir Randolph, Sir John, Sir William, Sir Reginald, Sir Hugo, Sir Richard, Baldwin IV, Baldwin III, Baldwin II, Baldwin I, Anacher Great Forster). He took an active part against the French for Henry V, by whom he was knighted He was succeeded by his son.

20. SIR THOMAS FORSTER (Sir William, Sir Richard, Sir Reginald, Sir Alfred, Sir Randolph, Sir John, Sir William, Sir Reginald, Sir Hugo, Sir Richard, Baldwin IV, Baldwin III, Baldwin II, Baldwin I, Anacher Great Forester). He was of Etherston Castle, Knight, b. 1397, married Joan Elwerden, co-heiress to the Earldom of Angus, which is now in abeyance. He was succeeded by his son.

21. SIR THOMAS FOSTER (Sir Thomas, Sir William, Sir Richard, Sir Reginald, Sir Alfred, Sir Randolph, Sir John, Sir William, Sir Reginald, Sir Hugo, Sir Richard, Baldwin IV, Baldwin III, Baldwin II, Baldwin I, Anacher Great Forester). He was knighted, and married the daughter of Fetherstonbaugh, of Stanhope Hall, Durham, Chief of the Fetherston clan. This family is of Saxon origin, and was seated at Fetherston, in Northumberland, before the Conquest; that part of the country having been allotted to its progenitor, a Saxon officer, for his gallant conduct against the Britons. The house in which the family resided was formerly upon a hill, where were two stones—called fether stones. The house was destroyed and a new edifice erected under the hill, which valley was locally denominated a haugh, hence the name Fetherstonehaugh. Sir Thomas' children were:

22. i. SIR THOMAS. He was knighted, was of Etherston, and married the daughter of Lord Baron Hilton, of Hilton Castle. His children were:

24. 1. SIR THOMAS, m. Dorothy Ogle.
25. 2. PATRICK.
26. 3. ROGER.
27. 4. REGINALD.

23. ii. SIR ROGER.

24. SIR THOMAS FORSTER (Sir Thomas, Sir Thomas, Sir Thomas, Sir Thomas, Sir William, Sir Richard, Sir Reginald, Sir Alfred, Sir Randolph, Sir John, Sir William, Sir Reginald, Sir Hugo, Sir Richard, Baldwin IV, Baldwin III, Baldwin II, Baldwin I, Anacher Great Forester). He was of Etherston, Knight, who was High Sheriff of Northumberland in 1564, and also in 1572 married Dorothy, dau. of Ralph, Lord Ogle of Ogle,* and Baron of Bothall of Bothall Castle by Mary his wife, daughter of William Gastroigne of Lawthrop, Knight in Yorkshire. His children were:

28. i. SIR THOMAS FORSTER, m. Feorina Wharton.
29. ii. SIR JOHN FORSTER, Knight of Bamborough Castle.
30. iii. REGINALD, who left only a daughter.
31. iv. ROLLAND, who left only a daughter.
32. v. ROBERT, ancestor of the family of Forsters of York, Baronets.
33. vi. ELIZABETH.
34. vii. AGNES.
35. viii. DOROTHY, who m. Henry Neville, b. of Sir John Neville of Levassy.

28. SIR THOMAS FORSTER (Sir Thomas, Sir Thomas, Sir Thomas, Sir Thomas, Sir Thomas, Sir William, Sir Richard, Sir Reginald, Sir Alfred, Sir Randolph, Sir John, Sir William, Sir Reginald, Sir Hugo, Sir Richard, Baldwin IV, Baldwin, III, Baldwin II Baldwin I, Anacher Great Forester). He was a Knight of Etherston, married Feorina, dau. of Thomas, Lord Wharton of Wharton. He was of Adderstone, High Sheriff of Northumberland. Will dated April 4, 1589, and had children.

36. i. SIR THOMAS FORSTER.
37. ii. CUTHBERT FORSTER, m. Elizabeth Bradford.

37. CUTHBERT FORSTER (Sir Thomas, Sir Thomas, Sir Thomas, Sir Thomas, Sir Thomas, Sir Thomas, Sir William, Sir Richard, Sir Reginald, Sir Alfred, Sir Randolph, Sir John, Sir William, Sir Reginald, Sir Hugo, Sir Richard, Baldwin IV, Baldwin III, Baldwin II, Baldwin I, Anacher Great Forester), m. Elizabeth Bradford. Will dated 1589. His children were:

38. i. SIR MATTHEW FORSTER, knighted April 24, 1617.
39. ii. THOMAS FORSTER of Brunton Esquire, who m. Margaret Forster, dau. of Richard of Zungwell Hall, Esquire, and had one dau., Elizabeth: he married

*The Ogle family is of very great antiquity in the county of Northumberland in England. Sir Robert Ogle, Knight of Ogle, was the eighth in lineal descent from Humphrey Ogle who settled at Ogle at the Conquest; his wife was the daughter of Lord Bothall.

2nd. Elizabeth Carr, dau. of William Carr of Ford, Esquire, and will dated June 19, 1648, and had issue.

40. 1. EPHRAIM FORSTER.

41. 2. JOHN FORSTER.

42. 3. REGINALD FORSTER m. Judith—and Mrs. Sarah Martin.

42. REGINALD FORSTER (Thomas, Cuthbert, Sir Thomas, Sir Thomas, Sir Thomas, Sir Thomas, Sir Thomas, Sir Thomas, Sir William, Sir Richard, Sir Reginald, Sir Alfred, Sir Randolph, Sir John, Sir William, Sir Reginald, Sir Hugo, Sir Richard, Baldwin IV, Baldwin III, Baldwin II, Baldwin I, Anacher Great Forester), b at Brunton, England, about 1595, came to America with wife, Judith, and seven children.

THE FORSTERS OF BAMBOROUGH AND ETHERSTON.

Sir Walter Besant, the celebrated English novelist, has written an intensely interesting novel entitled "Dorothy Forster." Of the family history in his second chapter he has this to say:

There are in Northumberland (one may thank heaven for it) as many Forsters as there are Fenwick's, and more. First it hath been said (but irreverently) the Lord made Adam and Eve; and then he made the Forsters. They are, indeed, as ancient a family as any in the county, as ancient in the county as the Percys, who belong also to Sussex, or the Radcliffes, who came from Cumberland. The ancient and original seat of the Forsters from time immemorial has been at Etherston, which is being interpreted, the Adder's Stone. An old ring of the family, now in possession of John Forster, Esquire, of Etherston, commemorates the origin of the name, being shaped like a twisted viper with tail in mouth, and set with a precious stone. There is a snake or dragon connected with many old and illustrious families. The legend of the Forsters' adder is lost. Mr. Hilyard once made for me a ballad or a song about it, but so full of knights, shepherds, nymphs, and cool grots (of which there are not many in our part of the county), that I thought it fantastical, although ingenious: The shield of the Forsters is: argent: a chevron vert between three bugle horns stringed gules, and for crest a bent arm and a hand bearing a broken lance. The Etherston quartering is also argent: on a bend cottised sable three martlets. The motto is "Si fractus fortis;" but, like the Fenwicks, we have our family legend, namely,—

Let us dearlie then holde
To mynde ther worthines
That which our parents olde
Had left us to posses.

There are branches of the Forsters everywhere; at Bamborough, at Stokesly in Yorkshire, at East Bolton, at Tuggall Hall, at Aldermarston, in Berwick, in Jamaica, descended from Claudius, nephew of Sir Claudius Forster, in London, and I know not where else. With these branches we have nothing here to do, save to mention them with respect as flourishing offshoots of a brave old stock. Especially however to be considered is the noble branch of Bamborough, founded by Sir John Forster, the valiant and trusty Warden of the March, under good Queen Elizabeth for twenty-seven years, and Governor of Bamborough Castle. It was to his son, Sir Claudius, that King James made a grant of the castle and manor. This made him a man of greater importance than his first cousin, Mr. Forster, of Etherston. Yet it is a proud thing to be the head of the house, which will ever be the happiness of the Forster who holds Etherston.

They have always been, like most Northumbrian families, blessed with numerous progeny. One of them had twenty-one sons and a daughter; being unsurpassed in this respect, even in Northumberland, except by Sir William Swinburne's father, who, to be sure, had thirty children. How great a happiness to bring up so many valiant sons to fight England's enemies and maintain the glory of the country! By marriage, especially before the Reformation, into which many noble Houses of the North would never enter, the Forsters were connected with nearly every family of gentle birth in the North; *videlicet*, Lords Crewe, Wharton, Hilton, and Ogle; the Radcliffes, Shaftoes, Swinburnes, Chaytors, Selbys, Herons, Carnabys, Crasters, Ridleys, Fenwicks, Salkelds, Greys, of Chillingham and of Howick; Coles of Brancepeth, and Ordes. By marriage with a Radcliffe, the Forsters of Bamborough acquired the Manor of Blanchland; and by marriage with a

Selby, that of Thornton. One of the Forsters was Lord Chief Justice of England, another was a puisne judge; many of them were sheriffs and knights of the shire. Their history is, in a word, part and parcel of the history of Northumberland itself that is to say, of the great and glorious realm of England.

This book is written for no other purpose than to set forth the true character of a gallant and honorable gentlemen which hath been much defamed; and especially by one who hath eaten his bread, drunk his wine and received many favors at his hands. The name of this gentlemen is Thomas Forster, generally called the Younger. It was he who commanded the princes English forces during the unhappy Rebellion. The hand which writes his history is that of his sister. She is unpracticed in the penman's art, therefore unskilled in the trick of making the false appear the true. Yet she can narrate faithfully the things which happened, she can show hypocrites and villains, stripped of their disguise, the horrid wretches which they are, and she can tell how gallant gentlemen and loyal subjects of the lawful sovereign of these realms (whom may God restore!) were betrayed to their own undoing.

No one should be able to speak of a man so well as his own sister. As for his wife she knows him only when he has arrived at manhood, and has no knowledge of the time when he was a stripling, inexperienced and ignorant, though perhaps full of brave intentions, or a boy at school under ferule and discipline, or a curly-headed laughing child. The sister remembers the growth of her brother's mind; she has watched (if she be an elder sister) the hesitations of the boy, his first doubtful flights , seeming, like the needle when the compass is shaken, to incline now here, now there, until it settle toward a steady north, as toward the straight and narrow path of honor which leadeth to heaven. To a wife a man presents himself completed; at his best; like a finished work, a picture framed, a poem written and printed. As for myself, it is true that I remember not my brother Tom as a child, because he is older than myself, but I knew him as a young man while he wore his own hair still tied up by a ribbon, and went about dressed in gay sagathy and woolen stockings, and great thick shoes for week-day use; with broadcloth and silver buttons, thread stockings, silver buckles in his shoes, and a silk ribbon for his hair on Sundays and holy days. A brave and gallant lad he was, better at hunting than at reading, fonder of sport than of books, hearty with all, ready with a laugh and a friendly word with rich and poor; and gifted with a natural love for friendliness, companionship, and good-fellowship, which made him beloved of all. He is dead now, and his fortunes broken and gone, and his enemies may say, as in the Otterbourne Ballad:—

> Now we have carry'd all Bambroughshire,
> All the welthe in the world have we.

Many have drawn comparisons between Mr. Forster and his gallant companion-at-arms, Lord Derwentwater, who, it must be owned, drew all hearts by qualities as rare as they are admirable. But she makes bold to maintain that if loyalty, fidelity, and courage may command respect, then we must give respect to the memory of Mr. Thomas Forster. These virtues were conspicuous in him, as in all his line. Like a river in a champaign country which runs evenly between its banks, so is the race of Forsters: like the River Coquet, which is now deep, now shallow, now gliding through open fields, now running under rocks, now under high hanging woods, is the race of the Radcliffes: and, like that river, they are most beautiful just before the end.

The father of this Thomas Forster was Thomas Forster, commonly called the Elder, of Etherston. He remained a private gentlemen, taking no office until after the death of his cousins of Bamborough. Then he became sheriff of the county and, between the years 1706 and 1710, knight of the shire. In the House of Commons he made no greater figure than a gentleman of Tory and High Church principles generally desires to make. Thus he was never a prater, nor did he waste the time of the House with idle talk and argument, being always well advised beforehand which side was the right, whose arguments would be the better, and prepared to vote, when called upon, with his friends. He, therefore, acquired the respect which Parliament is always ready to accord to members who sit silent and vote with their party. It would, indeed, have pleased him best could the measures have been brought forward silently, and voted without any speeches at all. It was a poor reward, he said, for the fatigue of a journey from Etherston to Newcastle, and from Newcastle to town, to sit out a long and tedious debate, when one's mind was already made up, and argument can produce no more effect than swanshot on the back of a tortoise. He married, while in his twenty-first year, his second cousin Frances, daughter of Sir William Forster of Bamborough. By her he had issue, namely, Thomas Forster, aforesaid; John, who is now the possessor of Etherston; Margaret, the eldest of the family, married to Sir William Bacon, of Staward; Elizabeth and William, who both died young; and Dorothy. It was the misfortune of these children that their mother, who was as virtuous and prudent as she was beautiful, died while they were all of tender years, and Dorothy, but a little lassie, indeed, too young to feel the blow which fell upon her, and too ignorant to join in the resentment which filled the breasts of her elders when her father, forgetting the incomparable virtues of the wife he had buried, married a second time. This marriage lasted but a short while, ending most tragically in the shooting by accident of madam. Would not one think that any man would plainly see in the death of two wives the plain injunctions of Heaven to wed no more? Yet my father tempted Providence and married a third time, his wife being now a certain Barbara Lawes, from the South Country, whose birth was not such as to warrant this elevation and who understood not the Northumberland people, or their speech or their ways. She brought her husband two children, Ralph, who lived to be thirty years of age, and Mary, now married respectably to Mr. Proctor.

As to my father, he was the easiest and kindest of men; all he asked for in the world was rest and a quiet life; to this he was surely entitled by reason of his birth, his fortune, and his good health. As for his fortune , it was moderate; an estate, some few hundreds a year, and a house as good as any, except the great castles in the county. Etherston Hall is a mile or so from the little hamlet of Lucker and four miles from Bamborough. It is a large, square house, as full of modern conveniences as any gentleman may desire; the sitting-rooms are wainscoted with walnut wood; it has sash windows, glazed with crown glass, which make the rooms light and pleasant in all weathers; there are stoves to burn a coal fire, as well as andirons for wood; in the parlor where we took our meals there was a high-backed chair for madam, and a great oaken settle for my father, who loved the wooden seat of the North Country, with its cupboard below, in which were kept all kind of stores there was a shelf of books if any wanted to read; there were stillroom, dairy, and great cellar well stocked with ale, both small and October, wine, both French, Spanish, and home-made, and whisky, brandy, and Hollands. Outside there was a stately garden full of fruit trees and planted with every kind of flower, fruit and herb; and to screen the house from the cold north and east winds there was a thick plantation, call it rather a small wood or coppice, containing all the trees that afford thick foliage and shelter, as, outside, firs and pines, and within, wych elm, sycamore ash, rowan, and so forth. "Why," my father would say, looking around him, "there is no better house in Northumberland for the entertainment of one's friends, nor, upon my word, doth a pipe of tobacco anywhere taste so well, whether it be in the settle by the fire, or in the garden beneath a tree. Go fetch me one, Dorothy my girl." Seeing how much he loved to be at home it may be thought surprising that he should have endured so long the fatigue of Parliament, the discomforts to a country gentlemen of living in London, and the burden of the long journey to London and back again. Yet a gentleman must not shrink from the duties imposed upon him by his position, and when it became necessary for him to become knight of the shire, he accepted the office with courage.

I have no cause for repentance as regards the Fifth Commandment, and am easy in my conscience concerning my duty to my father. The Fifth Commandment, although it hath been held by some to enjoin submission to all one's superiors in rank,fortune, place, affinity, or age, yet surely was never intended to include stepmothers. If it was, Heaven forgive the Forsters, for they have greatly sinned. Still, without seeking, like Adam in that pitiful excuse of his, to shift the blame upon another, it is not unjust to say that the beginnings of the quarrels were generally made by madam, who desired to rule her step-children, now growing tall and beyond her control, as if they were still little ones, and her own. My sister Margaret, the eldest, a girl of uncommon spirit, was quite able to hold her own. Perhaps madam was wrong when she charged her with inciting the younger ones to disobedience, but I am sure that Tom was right when he, grown too big to be beaten, even by his father, stood between madam and his little sister Dorothy, swearing that he would not let madam lay finger upon her, whether she deserved it or not. Let her go beat her own children as much as she pleased.

"Dame," cried her husband, when madam complained, "must I forever be going about with a whip in my hand, like an overseer in a negro plantation? Do you let the children alone, and they will let you alone."

Then would she sit glum in a corner till Dorothy, went to ask pardon, and all for a time would go well again, and over a pipe of tobacco and a pot of October my father would talk with Tom about his horses and his hounds. When my sister Margret married and went away, the household became more peaceful. Between Tom and Dorothy, she being a child and he a lad who was always ready to promise anything, besides that he regarded his younger sister with singular affection, it was presently arranged and understood that when they grew up they would live together away from Etherston House, and quite apart from madam. The compact was made long before it seemed likely that it would ever be carried out; but then, who knows the decrees of Fate? Nothing, according to the French proverb, is more certain than the unforeseen.

"We will live together," said Tom. "Cheer up, Dorothy. We will go and live somewhere as soon as I come of age to do what I please. Then madam will have no one to flout but Jack—poor Jack!"

It is sad to remember the quarrels which occurred daily between these jealous children and their step-mother. She would rush into my father's presence loud in complaint, scolding like a mad woman, though perhaps it was but a mere trifle, calling loudly for rods and whippings, lamenting the day that ever she came into a house where the children were so disobedient, upbraiding her husband for his lack of severity, and calling on the precepts of Solomon, who is nowhere so clear as on this point of punishing children. (Yet Rehoboam, who was, no doubt, very soundly flogged, did not turn out altogether such a son as the wisest of men and fathers could regard with pride.) On the other side stood Tom and Dorothy, she hanging her head and holding her brother by the hand; he angry, flushed, with fiery eyes, meeting accusation with denial or with charges of his own. When the angry wife flung out of the room, the poor father would turn a perplexed face to his children.

"It is hard," he would say, "that a man cannot come home and hang up his wig and find peace without quarrels and fault-findings. Tom, you villain, why anger madam? Dorothy, child, go ask pardon for both, and then sit down and let us be happy."

Peace was attained presently when, in a happy day, Mr. Hilyard came to the house. No one, before his arrival, understood how to treat the fancies of a whimsical woman, to humor her prejudices, and to keep her in good temper. Of Mr. Hilyard more presently. For the moment, sufficient to note that my father soon learned to trust in him for the maintenance of an unclouded sky at home; my step-mother looked to him for such personal services and attentions as were necessary to keep her in good temper; my brother Tom, for such money (to be begged of my father) as he wanted for his personal pleasure; Jack, for mediation in order to save him from punishment; and Dorothy, for amusement and instruction, combined with the fingering of the spinet, of which she was always fond, and over which she attained, thanks to Mr. Hilyard, a proficiency (she may fairly say) equaled by few. There was never, sure, such a tutor in any family as Mr. Antony Hilyard.

By my mother's side we came from the Bamborough Forsters, a branch of the family more distinguished in the world than the mainstock, and remarkable for the gifts of politeness and love of learning. Madam Frances Forster was the elder daughter of Sir William Forster, of Bamborough and Blanchland, by Dorothy Selby, his wife, daughter of Sir William Selby, and granddaughter of Ferdinando, Lord Fairfax. There were nine children of this marriage, viz., William the eldest, who married his second cousin, Elizabeth Pert Forster, but died in 1698 without issue (she afterward married Lord Stawell, and enjoyed a charge of £350 a year upon the estate); John, the second son, who died unmarried in 1699, aged thirty-one years; Ferdinando, of whom more immediately; Frances, my mother; and Dorothy, the youngest, whose birth caused the death of her mother.

This Dorothy, my aunt, grew up a most incomparable beauty, the equal of whom was not to be seen anywhere in the county. In those days, and until the death of Ferdinando, there was open house kept at Bamborough, with so much company and such prodigality and lavishing of good things as no other house in the county could show. It was ever a distinction between the Forsters of Etherston and those of Bamborough, that the former were quiet gentlemen, lovers of home, and not profuse of expenditure, while the latter were large-handed, hospitable, and never so happy as when they were spending money with open hands and both hands. True, they had a great estate. Sir William first and his sons afterward lived as freely as if they had an endless revenue. They were not spendthrifts, nor did they throw money away in riotous living; but they lived at a great rate; their house was always open for any one who chose to enter; their stables were full of horses; their cellars full of wine; their rooms full of company; grooms and varlets in plenty lived upon them; they even went to London. Madam, I remember, was forever wondering how the Bamborough people could afford, even with their means, this great expense, and looking forward to a sudden end with the satisfaction at other people's misfortunes which makes many women rejoice to play the part of that Trojan princess who constantly foretold disaster. But she was one of those who concern themselves continually with the affairs of other people, and are never so well pleased as when they have some one's fresh misfortune to discuss, or some certain disaster to foretell.

To the beautiful Dorothy the coming and going of fresh company meant the arrival and dismissal of so many lovers, for all men fell in love with her at first sight. Those who were too old lamented their youth; those who were married wished they were single for her sake; those who were rich trusted in their acres; those who were poor hoped she would accept their poverty. In a word, they all with one consent began to ask her in marriage before she was seventeen years of age. But she would have none of them, not from pride, nor from a desire to make a great match (because, being a Forster, she knew that she could marry no one better than a plain Northumberland gentleman), but because she was young and happy, contented to wait single for a while, and because of all the lovers there was none who touched her heart.

"My dear," she said once long afterward, to her niece, "a maid so young is simple and expects more than she can get; this man is too tall, that man too short, another too fat, another is boorish, another drinks too much wine, another has a hasty temper—as if she must needs have a man made on purpose for her. The gentlemen pleased me well enough to converse with, though sometimes they were coarse in their talk (a thing which gentlewomen cannot too strongly reprehend), but I liked not the prospect of spending my whole life with any one of them all. I desired, in short, more than a plain gentleman can be expected to give. Heaven hath granted my desire, save for one small particular, which, perhaps, I forgot to pray for, or I might have had that as well. My husband, most admirable in all other respects, had lost what many young women would prize the most—his youth. Yet he gave me a great place and high rank, with great learning and piety, beyond what may be looked for, even in a bishop; wisdom more than one expects, even in the House of Peers; and, my dear, unfailing love and consideration for woman's weakness, which is as rare as it is delightful." And with that her beautiful eyes filled with tears, but not of sorrow.

For there came to Alnwick when she was staying in their house in that town, being then but just eighteen, the great Bishop of Durham, Lord Crewe, upon a confirmation. Perhaps, but I am not sure, she was herself confirmed by him on that occasion. He was then fifty-six years of age, and, though there is so great a disparity between fifty-six and eighteen, and between a grave bishop and a giddy maiden, his lordship fell in love like any young country squire with Dorothy, and proposed to marry her. To me it seems a truly awful thing to marry a bishop of the English church, and I am not surprised that Dorothy refused him. Being still in her youth, she was naturally inclined to gayety, mirth, laughter, dancing, and the company of the young, which is a quite sufficient reason for her refusal, and we need seek no further. Yet it was a great match, for he was not only Bishop of Durham (that is, a Prince Palatine, with power to appoint his own sheriffs, and almost sovereign in his own diocese), but he was also a great statesman (he had made many enemies in his political career), and, besides this, a peer of the realm by birth and succession, the only member of his sacred profession who could boast of that distinction.

When his lordship found that his suit did not prevail he went away, and presently married a widow—Penelope, the relict of Sir Hugh Tynte. But when, ten years later, she died, he found that he still remembered the beautiful Dorothy—probably he had never forgotten her—and he again offered her his hand and title.

"Child," she told her niece, "when one arrives at twenty-eight, the pleasures of youth have all been tasted. I had been to London, and seen the glories of the Park, the theater, the Row, the gaming-table, and the town of London. Nothing is solid, I had already learned, except the joys of rank, dignity, and wealth. When my lord came to me again he was, it is true, ten years older—he was sixty-six—yet I assure you that he bore himself still with the uprightness and strength which most men show at forty, having no shadow of ailment or weakness, or touch of infirmity. I was, therefore, sensible of the great honor he proposed to me when he asked me again to become his wife. My dear, that venerable hand which I presumptuously rejected at eighteen I accepted with gratitude at eight-and-twenty, and have had no reason since for a single day to regret my decision. Pray Heaven my lord hath continued to regard his marriage with the same feeling of satisfaction!"

Of that, indeed, there could be no doubt, because the bishop remained to the end an ardent lover.

Such then, was the family of the Forsters—a goodly trunk, with many vigorous boughs—their original seat at Etherston, with many stately houses and broad lands, belonging to the off-shoots and younger branches: a house received with the respect due to an equal by all the great Northumbrian families, one which is numbered among those whose origin mounts to the time of the Conqueror or earlier. Their name is not like that of the Fenwicks or the Swinburnes, of territorial origin, but is, perhaps, a corruption of Forester. They were, Mr. Hilyard says, the family who first seized upon the Forest, or they were the King's Foresters. In the old times, when they were always fighting, there was need of as many as could be produced, for the men were mostly doomed to early death fighting on the Border, and the women, more to be pitied, doomed to mourn for husbands, sons, and brothers. So that to both alike fate was unhappy. But that time has passed away. There is peace upon the Marches; and if wicked men stir not up the waters of strife, it is a time for sitting every man beneath his own fig-tree, his wig hung upon one peg, and his sword upon another; his helmet placed beside his forefathers' monuments in the church, above the old coat of mail; a pipe of tobacco in his mouth, a brown tankard of October cider upon the table, with him a friend or two, and talk grave or cheerful, as the time and mood may suggest, while the sun slopes westward, and the shadows lengthen, and the dark crypt of Bamborough Church draweth nearer every hour.

'The way in which Tom Forster, junior, of Etherston, became Tom Forster, of Bamborough, was as follows:

On August the 22d, in the year of grace seventeen hundred and one, Mr. Ferdinando Forster, the youngest and only surviving of the three brothers, Member of Parliament, was entertaining a company of gentlemen to dinner at the Black Horse Tavern in Newcastle. Now, there had been anger (for what reason I know not, and have never heard) for a long time between Mr. Forster and Mr. John Fenwick, of Rock. It has always been maintained that Mr. Forster was a gentleman of easy and cheerful disposition, who bore no malice, and was unfriendly to no one; also that he was ready and willing to an amicable settlement of their differences whatever they might be, hating nothing so much as bad blood, and being ready to forgive private injuries so far as his honor would allow. Unfortunately Mr. Fenwick was of an opposite temperament, being choleric, vindictive, and hot-headed. Also, conceiving that he had been wronged, he went about demanding vengeance, and breathing threats whenever he should meet his adversary. Was it not, therefore, a most unfortunate accident that he should be in Newcastle on that same August morning? And what should be said of the mischievous wretch (reported to be Mad Jack Hall) who informed to this angry man that his enemy was at the Black Horse? Thither he rushed, maddened by his great wrath, and, bursting into the room where Mr. Forster sat with his friends, did assail him with reproaches, insults, curses, and foul names of so outrageous and intolerable a kind that there was nothing for a man of honor to do but (having first called upon his friends to take notice that the quarrel was forced upon him) to rise and follow the aggressor into the open street. At the White Cross they stood, and both drew their swords. Mr. Hall, who had followed Mr. Fenwick, drew his sword as well, with intent to act as second. Just then, before the weapons had crossed, Mr. Forster's foot slipped, and he fell upon the stones. What followed is dreadful to tell, and shows how rage may even make an honorable gentleman blind and mad. For Mr. Fenwick, without awaiting for his adversary to recover, or to be in a position to defend himself, instantly ran him through the heart, so that he fell dead. It has always been said that Mr. Hall should have prevented this cruel murder by striking upon Mr. Fenwick's sword with his own, and there are not wanting those who call him as much a murderer as the unhappy man himself who did the deed. I know not how this may be; but so much is certain, that nothing afterward ever prospered with Mr. Hall; but he was pursued with continual disaster to the day of his violent and untimely end—a clear mark of Heaven's displeasure. They seized Mr. Fenwick red-handed, so to speak, and lodged him in prison. A month later he was led forth and hanged for the murder—a melancholy and disgraceful end for a gentleman of his birth and fortune.

The intelligence of this terrible crime was brought to Etherston by Mr. Hilyard the next day. He lay at Bamborough that night, and so heard the news among the first. Madam was sitting in the garden with the two boys, and Dorothy, Tom being then seventeen and Jack five years younger.

"Alas!" she cried, when she heard the news—the children looking at each other in amazement, not knowing what to say. "Alas! sure some great wickedness, boys, must have been committed by your mother's family. First it is John, then William, and now Ferdinando; all gone in three years. Of nine children there remains but one. These things, we are assured, are visited upon the third and fourth generation. Tom, it would become thee to repent, lest it be visited upon thee as well."

"When I find out what I am to repent of," said Tom, sullenly, because he loved not to hear the least reflection upon his mother's family, "I will repent. My mother's family have brought nothing but honor to us, as far as I know. Meanwhile, there is some credit in being worth notice. Now, a Lawes might steal a pig and be hanged for it, and his grandchildren never a penny the worse."

"With submission, madam," Mr. Hilyard interposed hastily, to prevent further words, "this crime may lead to your step-sons's singular advantage. For, if Mr. Ferdinando had left no will, I mistake much if the estates do not devolve upon him, or upon him and Lady Crewe together."

"Will Tom have Bamborough?" madam asked. "Then he must not have Etherston as well. That," she added, thinking of her own son, not yet born, "should be divided among all the other children, however many there may be. The law is unjust as regards the younger sons. No woman would ever be a second wife did she know how her own children would be served."

"I doubt not, madam," said Mr. Hilyard, "that should the occasion arise, his honor will prove as just and as generous as you would desire."

"Their father," madam replied, tossing her head, "would give all to Dorothy had he his own way. When justice is to be done, Mr. Hilyard, come to me about it."

"As for me," cried Tom, the brave lad, his face suddenly flushing "it will be my business to avenge the death of my uncle. What! The breath only just out of his body, and we are talking of his succession!"

"Nay," said Mr. Hilyard, "as for the murderer, he is in prison; they say that he will be tried for his life. Let me advise you rather to keep this melancholy story before your eyes as an example, never to be forgotten, of the danger of ungoverned wrath, which Lactantius calls a cruel tempest of the mind. Thus, as is recorded, began the madness of Ajax."

They brought the body of Mr. Forster to Bamborough, and buried him in the crypt below the chancel. It was observed that no longer procession had ever been known at the funeral of any one; nay, it is even said that when the coffin was borne into the church, the tail of the long line of mourners was yet a whole mile away from the porch, and they had to wait till all had reached the church, though all could not find room within, before they began the words of the Funeral Service. The chief mourner was my brother Tom, and after him my father, at the head of so great a gathering of Forsters that you might think them an army in themselves. Then came the county gentlemen and private friends, and lastly the tenants and the common people, who wept tears of unfeigned sorrow, for they had lost a landlord and friend of a kind heart, although one who spent at a great rate and lived beyond his income. The foxhunters gave their brother sportsman the last view holloa, as one fires a volley over the grave of a soldier; and the Manor House provided a noble supper for all the mourners, of high and low degree, with as much drink of all kinds as their grief could crave, so that few, indeed, departed sober from that last tribute of respect to the murdered man.

It was proved to be as Mr. Hilyard thought, Mr. Forster had made no will. Therefore, the Bamborough estates fell to Lady Crewe and Tom as co-heirs, each to take a moiety.

"Dorothy," Tom cried, "what we agreed to do shall be done. As soon as I am of age, and can go to live at the Manor House, thou shalt come too, and we will live together."

A noble inheritance indeed, even if one only had a moiety or half part! Not only did it include the manors of Bamborough and Blanchland, but also the rectory and monastery of Shotley, the manor of Thornton, houses at Alnwick and elsewhere, fishing rights on Tweed and Derwent, and presentations to four livings and chapelries. Tom never wearied of enumerating his lands and possessions.

"As to her ladyship," he said, "she may have children and she may not. If she have none, then the whole will be mine. And whatever happens, we shall live in the Manor House, Dorothy, and we will have a noble time—you and I together. She has a dozen palaces and castles; she will surely not grudge me the simple Manor House of Bamborough."

But as yet he wanted three years of twenty-one, and for the present he must needs have patience.

Presently, little by little, there began to leak out uncomfortable reports that all was not as it should be with the estate. For first he heard of a charge of £350 a year in favor of Will Forster's widow—a monstrous and most greedy jointure, truly, when one considers that on many estates as large a poor £40 a year is all that a younger son or daughter may look for. Next he heard of a rent-charge of £500 a year created by the late Sir William Forster to pay for some of his profuse expenditure. This was bought up by Lord Crewe, no doubt at her ladyship's expressed desire, for £10,000. But the bishop was one of the most wealthy men in the kingdom, and could well afford even so great a sum. Here, however, was a goodly cantle cut out of the estate. Half the annual rent gone at once. Tom, for his part, showed little or no concern about it. "There remains," he said, "another £500 a year, beside the houses. There is a good deal to be done with the half of £500 a year. And I am the heir of Etherston as well." He looked on his heritage of Bamborough as a means for living as he wished until the Etherston property fell in.

Yet he ought to have felt that there is a sad falling-off from the £1,600 or so of revenue enjoyed by Sir William to the enjoyment of only a moiety of £800 a year. There were other creditors and claims upon the estate also, of which we knew nothing and, happily as yet, suspected nothing for some time.

The heir of both Bamborough and Etherston was a much more important person than the heir of Etherston alone. Lady Crewe, who, to speak the truth, took little notice of her sister's children while her brothers were living, now showed a very particular interest in Tom, and wrote many letters upon his course of life, both to him and to his father. She begged earnestly that he might go to Cambridge, pointing out that, although her nephew's inclination lay not so much, as she understood, in the direction of books, it would be well for him to make the acquaintance at that ancient seat of learning of the young men, his contemporaries, and to learn how matters of importance are regarded outside Northumberland. Tom went to St. John's College with Mr. Hilyard for his tutor. Here, however, he remained but three or four terms. Then her ladyship pointed out that a country gentleman has to become a magistrate, so that it is most desirable for him to know law, and entreated him to enter at Lincoln's Inn, and reside in London for a part of each year, in order to study the Acts of Parliament and the powers of a justice of the peace. To this, however, Tom objected, saying that his father and his grandfather had been justices without going to Lincoln's Inn, or knowing any law at all, and that, to his mind, a gentleman should not dirty his fingers with the quibbles and shifts of lawyers. In this he continued, although he was reminded that one of his cousins had been Sir Thomas Forster, Justice of Common Pleas under King James I., and another, Sir Robert Forster, no less than Lord Chief Justice of England under Charles I. Then Lady Crewe wrote another letter, in which she clearly told her nephew that his rusticity and that of his friends was such as to unfit him for the posts of distinction open to the owner of Bamborough (her brothers, indeed, especially Ferdinando, had been gentlemen of most courtly and finished manners, acquired in the most polite society of St. James's), and that if he would neither study law nor letters, it behooved him, under proper tutelage, such as that of Mr. Hilyard, to travel into Italy, and so to acquire the manners of the great world. I knew not at the time, and none of us were courtiers enough to discern, that her ladyship, in taking all this trouble, was endeavoring to make her nephew understand that it was her design to make her nephew, the successor of her brothers, no loser by their expenditure, provided only he would show himself worthy of her bounty.

This project she never abandoned, being always most jealous for the honor of the Forsters, although the events which followed prevented her from carrying it into effect. Yet Tom was so foolish as to fall into a great rage upon receiving this letter, alleging that, as for his manners, he was not ashamed of them, and they were those of his father and his friends, that he was not for his part going to become a London beau, and as to traveling in foreign parts, to be sure the prince was in France, but what had an English gentlemean to learn from a set of mangy French and scurvy Italians? And as for distinction and the holding of high posts, he might show her ladyship some day that he was as capable of distinguishing himself as any man in Northumberland rusticity or no rusticity.

"Thou wilt not be guided by the wisest of women, boy," my father said. "She is the wisest of women because she is led by the wisest and most crafty of men. Thou wilt neither to London nor to foreign lands, though here is Mr. Hilyard longing to go with thee. Well, stay-at-homes have litttle wit; ignorance breeds conceit;

I have myself been to London and seen the Court, but as for you, Tom, thou art pure rustic. Besides, though I am a simple and unlearned person, content to stay at home, they will not, I fear, suffer thee the same liberty. For thou hast more to lose, and where the carcass is thither the eagles gather."

Then Lady Crewe privately exhorted Mr. Forster to take care lest his son, through ignorance of the world, should be tempted into some rash enterprise, like that of Sir William Fenwick, who was executed for treason in the year 1696; to remember that fierce spirits were always abroad, endeavoring to stir up immature risings, and to hatch foolish plots for the destruction of unhappy gentlemen; and to be assured that though her own favor and that of her husband would be continued to her nephew should he move prudently, that favor would certainly be withdrawn should rashness plunge him into difficulties with the Government, with much more to the same effect.

"Her ladyship is right," cried my father. "None so hot for the sovereign as my lord bishop till King William comes to the throne. Then he must needs run for it and try the air of France. Running is a very noble exercise when you are young. My lord is out of favor now, and he is getting old, and would fain stay where he is, and I think he would like to taste once more the sweetness of court smiles, but still one who loves the old house. This should be the safest plan, Tom. Be guided by the bishop. He will never go over to the other side, and yet he will never put his neck in the noose. Wherefore my son, remember that conspiracies are hatched by men who have got nothing to lose; it is easy for an Irishman who has got his neck and little else to talk wild and vapor, but for us, who have a name and an estate which we have held together for seven hundred years and perhaps more, the risk is too great. I do not say, neither, that we are to turn Whigs. We who fought for the Stuarts stand by them still. They made my grandfather sheriff and knight; they gave Sir Claudius the Manor of Bamborough; saving our religion—and our estates, Tom—and our estates, boy, mind that—we follow the Stuarts always. When the voice of the country is clearly for the prince, the Forsters will come with the rest. But when thwacks are going, let those who began get first their share of the hammering, while we stand by and see which way the battle is likely to go. Therefore, when thou art of age, Tom, take care to write nothing, to promise nothing, to sign nothing. As for what may happen, we know nothing. The Dutchman hath no children: let us wait; the Princess Anne may follow but we know not. Let us wait, aud meantime lie snug all."

However, there were two years to wait before the coming of age, which was in the year 1702. By consent of Lady Crewe, Tom was allowed during this time to use the Manor House as if it was already his own, and many were the days which we spent in the old place, sometimes with Mr. Hilyard for tutor and companion, spending whole weeks there. The house was not larger than Etherston Hall, but it was, in a way, more splendid. There were portraits on the walls of Sir Claudius his nephew, Sir William, his three sons, the wife of the eldest, my own mother, and the beautiful Dorothy. Truly there never was a more lovely and charming face than that of this portrait, the original of which I had as yet never seen except when a baby. It represented her at the age of twenty or twenty-one. She had a face round rather than oval; a sweet, rounded, dimpled chin; a mouth more like a rose-bud than the lips of a woman; light brown, curling hair, lying in a cluster about her forehead, which, Mr. Hilyard said, was too ample for the Greek idea of beauty, their Venus being low of forehead; the nose was full; the eyes were dark brown, and of a singular brightness. (I reflected with inexpressible joy, when looking upon this sweet face, that my own eyes were of the same color and brightness, and my own hair of the same hue, and the same tendeucy to twist and curl itself about my forehead.) When gentlemen, past the age of thirty or so, came to the Manor House, they gazed at the portrait and sighed, remembering her beauty, and thinking, no doubt, how great a thing it would have been to marry so lovely a woman. When the young men came, they looked upon the portrait with such wonder as they might experience in looking upon that of Helen, Cleopatra, or fair Dido. "She moves," said Mr. Hilyard, "a goddess confessed. Never, since those fair women of old, has there been her like. Sometimes I think that Sappho may have had those eyes, which are yours also, Miss Dorothy; and Lucretia that look, in which you greatly resemble your aunt; and Venus herself that dimpled chin, which I am glad to see remains still in the family."

There were other portraits, but these were the best.

The house itself is of two stories, and is built in the modern fashion, having square sash windows, two on one side the door and one on the other. It looks from the front upon a triangular green, planted with a clump of trees, having a pant at the end, and a field at the base. On the right is the church, and on the left is the broad street leading to the castle. At the back is a garden, not so big or so well provided as that of Etherston, because, by the seaside, everything will not grow; but it has a great store of herbs and fruit trees, with currants, gooseberries, and strawberries in season, lavender and other plants for strong waters and perfumes, and herbs for medicine, though Nature hath been so benevolent as to plant things for suffering man's solace in every hedge, so that, though there is plenty of toothache in the world, there is also plenty of trefoil, yarrow, and groundsel root; and, though none may catch a cough, there is no fear of using up all the ground ivy; and, though men will cut themselves, their wives can gather for nothing as much comfrey, self-heal, and valerian as will cure their wounds.

A goodly garden and ancient, with a trim lawn as well, on which bowls could be played; and a sundial, which had marked the flight of time for many hundreds of years; and a fountain, which was stopped, and would work no longer till Mr. Hilyard set it agoing; and then one marveled how we could have found the garden perfect without the pleasant plash of that jet of water and its rainbow sparkle in the sun.

In every season—summer, winter, or autumn—it was pleasant to walk in the garden, and to look over the low wall at the end of it, and the green meadow beyond it, acrosst he broad sea which stretches away till sea and sky meet. A stormy sea it is when the northeast winds blow, and many have been the wrecks upon the rocks and islets off the shore. To live in the Manor House was in itself a help to cure our rustic ways of thought and speech. For not only were there portraits, but also pictures brought from abroad, pictures of Roman Catholic saints—there was a martyr, I remember, set up as a target for the arrows of his persecutors—of hunting parties, of battles by sea and land. Mr. Hilyard would stand before these pictures and discourse with great learning to me upon the Italian, Spanish, French, and Dutch schools, and the chief merits of each. There was also tapestry, but not much. Mr. Hilyard told me of the famous tapestry wherein is represented the Norman Conquest. There was a cabinet full of curiosities brought home by travelers in foreign parts—among them a stone picked up in the Garden of Gethsemane, and a garland of thorns bought in Jerusalem. This cabinet afforded Mr. Hilyard the opportunity of many a discourse. There were also books—not one shelf only, as we had at Etherston—but many shelves. There were Baker's "Chronicle," Holinshed's "History," Sibbe's "Soul's Conflict," a volume of Jeremy Taylor, Camden's "Britannia," Grey's "Choregraphia," a "History of the Lives, Travels, and Sufferings of the Apostles," with pictures, very moving; Record's "Arithmetic," the "Marrow of Mathematics," Hartmann's "True Preserver of Health," Burton's "Melancholy," Drake's "World Encompassed," Evelyn's "Gardener's Almanack," the "Paradise Lost" of Milton, the Plays of Shakespeare, Bacon's "Essays," Quarles's "Emblems," Butler's "Hudibras," in which Mr. Hilyard greatly delighted—I know not why, because I could never read it with pleasure—and a great many more. I read in most of these books, and, I hope, sucked as much profit from them as was to be expected of a girl. To be sure, I had beside me always a most patient, learned. and kind commentator, who spared no pains to make me understand obscure passages, and to illustrate places which, before he spoke of them, seemed unintelligible. An ignorant reader is like a poor man with empty purse, who walks along a valley strewn with diamonds and precious stones, which he neglects because he knows not how priceless are the stones beneath his feet. Pity it was that Tom would neither read nor listen.

On Sundays, when we all went to church in the morning, there was a great and noteworthy difference after Tom became the half owner of Bamborough. For, as often happens in old churches, this of ours was divided and parceled out among the gentry. The north transept belongs to the Greys of Howick, the south transept to the Radcliffe's, although they are Papists; the north part of the nave belongs to the owners of Lucker, the south to the Forsters of Etherston, and the chancel to the Forsters of Bamborough. While, therefore, my father, with madam and Jack and the children, sat in their pew below the pulpit, Tom, and I with him, and Mr. Hilyard, because he was the tutor, walked proudly into the chancel and sat in a great pew raised three feet above the ground, so that you mounted by steps. The seats were lined with red velvet, very worn. Above us hung our own scutcheon, showing the Radcliffe *fleur-de-lis* among the Etherston martlets; on the other side was the great marble monument of Sir Claudius, who died at Blanchland; and, hanging on the wall, the helmet and iron coat of some other Forster long since dead and gone.

Beside us was the stone effigy, with crossed legs, of Sir Lancelot du Lac, concerning whom Mr. Hilyard had a great deal to say, as to whether he was not a Forster, and thus misnamed from the tradition of some great exploit or deed of arms.

It is an old and crumbling chancel. Among other things it contains an ancient window, through which the unhappy lepers outside could formerly see the elevation of the Host within. Separating chancel from nave is an open screen of carved white stone, a good deal broken. When we stood up for the reading of the Psalms and the singing of the hymn I could see through this screen the back of the vicar at the reading-desk, and in the pew below the pulpit my father's best Sunday wig in the crispest curl, and madam's hat and ribbons. Beyond the pews of the gentlefolk were the seats of the common people, worn black and shiny by generations of the humble worshipers. I suppose that in Heaven there are no velvet-lined pews, with steps to mount, and stoves to keep one warm in winter; but it seems fitting thus to separate gentle and simple, and doubtless even in Heaven there are degrees—one cannot understand that a prince and a scullion will ever sit side by side. As for me, I confess that it was with great pride that I sat beside Tom in the chancel, reflecting that, although my father was the head of the older stock, the noblest and best of the family came from Sir John, the great Warden of the March and Governor of Bamborough Castle—the most splendid possession of his grandchildren.

There was never a day, when I was at the Manor House, but I passed some of it within the old walls, clambering, exploring, and running from one broken chamber to another until I knew every chamber and every vault in the great pile. When I climbed the broken stairs and stood upon the giddy top of the half-roofed keep, I used to look around me with such pride as a Percy should feel at Alnwick or at Arundel. I was prouder even than my brother of the stately place, though he never wearied of rehearsing the greatness of his folk. A noble castle, indeed! This is none other than the Castle of King Ida, called the Royal House. King Edwin lived here; miracles were worked here by saints for the preservation of the castle; William Rufus sat down before it; David Bruce was a prisoner in it; the breaches in the broken walls were caused by the cannon of the Yorkists. Why, whenever I read the history of England in Holinshed or Baker, I turned over the pages and looked out the places where the castle is mentioned, and then my foolish heart would glow with pride. But surely there could be no more delightful place for a young girl's playground and place of meditation. The keep alone remains entire out of all the towers, bastions, forts, and strong places which once stood here; but their ruins still stand. In some places there are broken stone steps leading up to chambers whose floors are gone, windows gaping wide, and roof long since torn off; in others there are deep dungeons, open now to the light of Heaven. At night, I used to think, the groans of dead prisoners still ascend to the sky. From the top of the keep one may look out to sea and behold the Farnes lying beneath one as on a map; to the north is Holy Island, with its ruined church and castle on a hill; to the south is black Dunstanburgh, where the Seeker may be seen nightly by those who look for him; and inland lie the fields and woods belonging to the Forsters. In early summer the rock on which the castle stands, black and terrible in winter, is covered, wherever the least ruggedness affords space for a morsel of earth, with tufts of grass and flowers. There are the thrift, the bell campion, and the trefoil, crimson, white, and blue, very pretty to look upon. Later on, the sandhills, about which the rabbits keep running all the year round in thousands, are covered with flowers of other kinds, the names of which I knew and their properties, thanks to Nurse Judith and Mr. Hilyard.

Often Mr. Hilyard came here with me, telling out of his vast knowledge stories of the days when this place, now so silent and ruinous, was filled with knights and valiant men-at-arms, when the courts resounded with the hoofs of horses, the voices of the soldiers, and the clank of iron heel. He could restore the castle as it used to be, and would mark out for me the inner bailly, the outer bailly, the portcullis, the postern, the outworks, the chapel, the stables, the kitchens, and all, until in imagination I knew the castle as it was when the Percys were its governors. No others came to the old castle except myself and Mr. Hilyard; it was quite lonely and deserted. In stormy weather the waves leaped up to the very walls, while the gulls flew screaming and the wind whistled. In the evening, when the twilight fell, I would sit among the fallen stones, seeing in the shadows of the pile grim spirits of the dead, and hearing in the breeze the voices of departed saints, kings, knights, bishops, and prisoners, brave men, and fair ladies, whose ancient joys and sufferings made this place as sacred as the churchyard.

As for Tom, he cared little about the antiquity of the Castle or its past history, his chief desire being for the time to arrive when he could call the place his own and be out of tutelage, and his principal occupation being hunting of fox and of otter, riding, shooting, fishing, badger-drawing, stalking the wild bulls of Chillingham, cock-fighting, dog-fighting, with the other manly sports in which young men delight. He took great pleasure, in those days, in the wild-fowl shooting on the islands; many a time he has taken me with him when he had no other companion (Mr. Hilyard's stomach being unable to stand the motion of the boat). Then we would sail through the waves to those wild and desolate rocks covered with the nests of the sea-birds which rise screaming from under the feet of the rare visitor. The cries of the birds, the whirr of their wings, the whistling of the wind, the dashing of the waves are the only sounds upon these lonely islands where St. Cuthbert built his hermitage. They are, indeed, a truly fitting place for the gloomy recluse, who (though doubtless a holy man) dared to call the half of the Lord's creatures unclean, and forbade a woman even to set her foot upon the place where he resided. Many pious women have gone into voluntary retreat and hermitage, but one never yet, I believe, heard of a woman thus speaking of man as to call him unholy or unclean. The walls of St. Cuthbert's house yet stand in ruins on his deserted island, but there are now no human beings within their shelter.

I learned to know all the birds by their flight, their cry, and their feathers—the St. Cuthbert ducks, who make nests of the seaweed, the Tom Noddies, the skouts, the guillemots, the shags, the kittiwakes, the gulls, the brockits, the rock pigeons, the sealarks, and the jackdaws who build in the rabbit-holes. In those days, who so brave and handsome as young Tom Forster, leaping lightly from rock to rock, fowling piece in hand, his long hair tied in a ribbon, and blown behind him by the sea breezes, his gray eyes bright, and his cheeks ruddy? What but a great and splendid future could await a lad so gallant? As for the girl that ran behind him, as agile as her brother, dressed in short petticoats and thick shoes with woolen stockings, she was a slip of a thing then, with dark brown eyes (like those of her aunt), and long fair curls flying under her hat. Her brother, though he sometimes swore at his grooms and thrashed the stable boys, never had a harsh or unkind word for her, nor she any thought for him but of tender and true affection. Pity it was that one of natural abilities so good would never read and acquire wisdom.

BAMBOROUGH CASTLE.

The English Home of the Fosters for Many Years—A Description of this Gigantic Medieval Castle—Of Its Interior and Exterior—Bamborough Church and the Buried Fosters—The Farne Islands.

Bamburgh is on the eastern coast of Northumberland, about fifteen miles from Alnwick. The castle stands upon a rising eminence of basaltic rock, which at this point is of great thickness.

By some writers it is thought not unlikely that Bamburg was one of the Roman Stations in the reign of the Emperor Agricoba. But be this as it may, there are no remains about the works of the present castle that will in any way bear out this supposition. It is not till the time of the Saxons that the page of history begins to dawn upon

"Ida's castle, huge and square."

This king began his reign in the year 550, and with his name the castle of Bamburgh has for centuries been associated.

If there are no remains about the castle associating it with the Romans there is equally little to justify us in connecting it with the Saxons. But this is not surprising, as most of the defenses of that period were composed of wood.

It was not till the time of the Normans that a different state of things crept in, and when wood was superseded by stone.

About the earliest mention we have of Bamburgh is by the venerable Bede, who says, "in the year 625 the nation of the Angels, living on the lands northwards of the Humber, with the king, Edwin, received the Christian faith through the mission of Paulinus, by whom the royal convert, with the nobility of his nation, and many

BAMBOROUGH CASTLE—THE ENGLISH HOME OF THE FOSTERS.

people were baptized at York on the 12th April, 627," and that after this event the Holy Bishop tarried with Edwin for more than a month at the northern stronghold.

Bamburgh, "the royal burgh," is supposed to have derived its name from "Bebba," one of the early queens of Northumbria. But its greatness, antiquity and renown is derived from the fact of it having been the place where the good Bishop Aidan spent much of his time.

Oswald had not been long on the throne ere he commissioned Aidan, one of the brethren of the convent of Iona, to instruct the people of his kingdom in the way of religion. Previous to this there was no church or alter in Northumbria.

In 651 the Mercians, under Penda, inflicted great hardships and cruelties upon the inhabitants. The invaders, on arriving before the walls, endeavored to take the place by surprise, but being thwarted in the attempt they next proceeded to encompass the fortress on the land side with wood and thatch, and setting fire to this, the flames suddenly rose above the highest towers and ramparts. Aidan, at that particular time, was upon the island of Farne, where he was wont to resort at particular periods, and anticipating the deadly havoc that would befall those within the walls, at once invoked the divine aid to counteract the subtle machinations of the enemy; nor were the prayers of the bishop allowed to go unheeded, for all of a sudden the wind became changed, which caused the flames to rage violently amongst the besiegers. This was regarded as an intervention on the part of Providence, as it had the effect of causing the seige to be raised.

It was at Bamburgh where one of the first Christian churches in Northumbria was reared, and within this small wooden structure Aidan was peacefully reclining when his spirit was summoned to "the abode of the just."

There can be little doubt but that during the whole of the Saxon rule in this country, the castle of Bamburgh would play a very important part, often will it have shared in victory and adversity. There are instances in its history when its towers, walls and ramparts successfully resisted the attacks of the enemy. Its geographical position would betoken much strength and resistance, and in more recent times this was amply exemplified on the occasion, when for nearly three months it withstood the formidable assaults of the soldiers of Edward IV.

Bamburgh, like other neighboring towns, experienced in the past all the evils attendant upon civil and warlike commotions. On more than one occasion its walls and places of habitation were burnt to the ground, and the inhabitants subjected to the greatest cruelties, but most heroically were those inflictions borne, for as soon as the storm was over there arose from the ruin a fortress stronger and more formidable than the one it supplanted.

During Saxon times the castle was famous for the great advantages it possessed in the shape of a stronghold; this was chiefly owing to its situation. But great as the fortress was in those times, there can be little doubt that the castle at a subsequent period became still more famous for its walls and towers of defense. It is rather remarkable that a place so rich in lore and traditional associations should possess no remains of the sturdy Saxons who first settled within its domain, yet at the same time it must not be forgotten that Bamburgh forms no exception to the general rule, for of all the monuments raised in Northumbria by this brave people, very few now remain to tell of their existence. In the invasion of England, 1091, by Malcolm, King of Scotland, Bamburgh is brought into prominence, for it was here that Mowbray, Earl of Northumberland, took refuge when he refused allegiance to William II. A good deal of the masonry of the castle may be attributed to that period, notably the towers and walls facing the mainland.

The King and his army pursued Mowbray to the outer walls of the castle, but after tarrying a few days, they found it impregnable and consequently resolved to move southwards; but before leaving he took precautionary steps to guard and watch the movements of the insurgents. The King caused a wooden structure to be erected not far from the castle, and this was called "Malvoisin," which signifies the "bad neighbor," and in this town were quartered a number of soldiers. There can be little doubt but that Mowbray was fully aware that due vigilance was exercised by the King's troops over his movements, but he was not only a good soldier, but also fully cognizant of all the strategic qualities which go to make an experienced warrior. Endowed with such qualities he was not slow to take advantage of the position, but in this case he allowed himself to be entrapped in a net of his own making. Mowbray, by means of secret correspondence with the garrison of Newcastle, grew impressed with the idea that by a little effort on his own part he might easily make himself master of that town. Starting from Bamburgh for that purpose, and under cover of night, he had not journeyed far before he ascertained that his movements were watched. Harassed and disheartened, the Earl, by the time he arrived at Newcastle, found the gates of the town closed against him, and being driven to despair he took shelter in the monastry of St. Oswin, at Tynemouth; but the King was so exasperated at his conduct that he wantonly disregarded the sanctity of the asylum by ordering his soldiers to drag him forth.

Mowbray, on his leaving Bamburgh, had committed the custody of the castle to one Moreal, and amongst the inmates was the Earl's wife. After several unsuccessful attempts on the part of the King to induce the garrison to surrender, he resolved upon a last resource, which was to lead Mowbray forth before the walls of the castle, there to be subjected to the torture of having his eyes put out. On this being communicated to the commander, the garrison at once surrendered. Moreal, for his bravery, received a free pardon from the King, but Mowbray was sent to the castle at Windsor.

In the conditions of peace between King Stephen and David I, the Earldom of Northumberland was settled upon Henry, David's son, but the castles of Bamburgh and Newcastle were reserved to the Crown of England. Amongst royal visits we find that King John spent three days at Bamburgh in 1201, and 1213 he again visited this northern stronghold. In the latter year the sum of £117, 8s. 4d. was spent in repairs about the castle, which was probably incurred by reason of the King's visits.

During the reign of Edward I, Bamburgh enjoyed all the privileges of a duly constituted borough. In addition to the holding of fairs, markets and other jurisdictive powers, it returned two members to the Parliament held at Westminster, on the 13th November, 1295, and which was prorogued by Royal Writ to the 27th of the same month.

It was at this castle where John Baliol, King of Scotland, was summoned in 1296 to do homage to the King of England, and it was here in 1312 where the partigans of Henry de Percy induced Henry II to confer upon that nobleman the office of custodian of the castle.

After the battle of Durham, David Bruce, King of Scotland, was confined for a while at Bamburgh; and in 1355 the Earl of Murray, previous to being removed to the castle of Windsor, was retained here as a prisoner. In 1356 a convention was entered into between the King of England and the King of Scotland, and about this time there are several important transactions, all of which are dated Bamburgh.

In the wars of the fifteenth century, between the rival houses of York and Lancaster, Bamburgh is made to form the scene of some of the deadly encounters that were to determine the struggle. After the disastrous battle of Lawton, 1461, Henry VI and his queen sought refuge in Scotland, and although the fortune of the Red Rose was upon the wane in the southern parts of the kingdom, yet for all this, many a heart in the north country beat heavily for the cause of the dethroned monarch, and this is most emphatically shown by the garrisons of the castles of Alnwick, Dunstanburgh and Bamburgh refusing to surrender to the troops of Edward IV, a determination that was not overcome till after the battle of Hexham, when all hope for the cause of Henry was blasted. For nearly three months Sir Ralph Grey, after the battle of Hexham, successfully defended the castle from the fierce attacks that were made against it by the soldiers of the King. It is estimated that at one time King Edward's forces amounted to upwards of 10,000 men, and it was not till the commander of the fortress had been bodily disabled by the falling of one of the towers that the garrison surrendered. The siege to which the castle was subjected during the fifteenth century may justly be regarded as one of the most disastrous that it ever had sustained. After the surrender of the castle by Sir Ralph Grey, it was found that the walls and ramparts had suffered very much from the onslaught; and this is the more apparent by the fact that in the 42d of Edward III we find that commissioners were appointed to examine and repair the great tower and other parts of the building, but from all accounts these repairs only appear to have been of a partial character, for subsequent events all go to prove that the castle after this period began rapidly to sink into decay.

In the time of Queen Elizabeth Sir John Forster, Warden of the Marches, was Governor of Bamburgh Castle, and in the reign of James I, Claudius, a grandson of Sir John, received from the Crown a grant of the castle and manor. After this a good deal of the history of the castle is associated with the Forsters.

Before making any further remarks concerning the Forsters, and their afterwards disposing of the castle and manor, we will give a brief outline of the celebrated fortress.

Of all the castles in the north Bamburgh may be said to be far superior to any other in regard to strength and position. The castle is built upon an overlying mass of basaltic rock, and the whole of the buildings go to form a triangle. Adjoining the mainland the basalt rises very high, and judging from the walls that traverse this part of the line, there are indications that different parts of the masonry have at times undergone repairs, and this may have been caused by parts of the cliff giving way

The principal entrance to the castle is by way of a steep enbankment that runs in a winding direction by the south end of the building. At the latter stands the barbican, or outer gateway. On the northwest side of the walls stood the postern, or sally-port. At stated intervals the walls are strengthened and protected by towers and bastions, some of these being remarkable for their strength, boldness and uniqueness, and this is nowhere seen to greater advantage than in that finely conceived and almost impregnable pass that leads to the keep. As you enter by the barbican you will at once perceive how difficult it would be for an assailant to effect a fooling from this point. Independent of the approach by the keep being protected by a portcullis and two circular towers, it was also strengthened by a deep ditch, which was cut through a narrow gut or strip of rock, and made to communicate with the mainland. If the assailants effected an entrance into the inner baly, they would next find themselves exposed to the greatest danger, for this point was in reality the pass to the keep, and thus formed a second gateway; behind this again was a strong circular tower, constructed in such a way as at the shortest notice to have been used to great advantage against the enemy. The keep, a massive square building, is situated in the miner baly. This part of the castle may be said to differ very considerably, in an architectural point of view, from the whole of our Northumberland Castles. Its chief object has been defense. Situated on a lofty eminence and commanding a wide expanse of sea and inland scenery it could not fail to impart a beauty and grandeur to all around it. At each of the four angles of the keep are exploring turrets, and from the summit of these a wide stretch of country is commandable. In addition to the keep there were in the inner baly several other towers of a miscellaneous character, and in olden times it would be in this part of the castle where the garrison would be quartered. There was also within the walls a small chapel, the remains of which were discovered last century when certain alterations were being effected, but there were no remains amongst them that would warrant the assumption that the building had been older than the early part of the commencement of the twelfth century.

From a recent survey it has been found that the castle occupies eight acres of land, and in addition to this there are within the walls fifty-six acres of rock, warren and hills.

Returning to the Forsters we may state that this family is old origin, dating back to the thirteenth century. For several centuries they have been connected with Northumberland. Sir John, one of the most distinguished of the name, was warden of the Middle Marches in the time of Queen Elizabeth. From Sir John sprang Claudius, who received a grant of the manor from King James. The castle and manor of Bamburgh remained in the hands of the Forsters till 1709, when they were sold to Nathaniel Crewe, Lord Bishop of Durham,* for the sum of £10,000. Lady Crew was the daughter of Sir Wm. Forster, and aunt of Thomas Forster, Esquire, M. P., who was implicated in the rebellion of 1715. Of all the great and renowned names associated with the castle of Bamburgh, none have achieved a greater distinction than that of Lord Crew, thus verifying the words of the poet:—

"Peace hath its victories as great as war."

The Crews were an old family who resided at Stene, in Northamptonshire. John Crew, father of the Bishop, was rewarded with a peerage for the services he had rendered to the restoration of Charles II.

Nathaniel Crew was the fifth son of John Crew, having been born on the 31st January, 1633. At the age of nineteen he went to Oxford, where he was not long before he took his first degree. In due time he became a fellow of the college, and in 1663, after taking his Dr.'s degree, he entered the church, having been ordained by the Bishop of Winchester. It is said that it was about this time that the young cleric first met the King, and report avers that the monarch was so impressed with the amiableness of his character, that he ever afterwards entertained a warm affection for him. Be this as it may, Crew's preferment in the church was not only

* The Right Rev. Nathaniel Crewe, Lord Bishop of Durham, was known as 3d Lord Crewe of Stene. This prelate stood so high in the favor of James II and so strenuously supported that prince's measures that he found it no easy task to make his peace after the Revolution. He did so, however, and the remainder of his life was spent in retirement and devoted to acts of benevolence. He died in 1721 without issue.

rapid, but lucrative. In 1668 he was elected Rector of Lincoln College, and this was followed up by the King appointing him Clerk of the Closet. But these preferments did not suffice, for in 1669 he was made Dean of Chichester, and two years after this (1671) Dean Crewe was promoted to the See of Oxford. There is some doubt as to the exact time that the Bishop was translated to Durham. Hutchinson, a very reliable authority, has given the date 1674. At that time a great deal of jealousy had arisen in regard to the Bishop's preferment. Nor was the this solely confined to the clergy, but the same discontent would seem to have been shared by many of the courtiers of the King. The calumnators of the Bishop did not scruple to aver that this prelate owed his promotion to the Duke of York. In 1675 Bishop Crewe made his customary public entry into the then princely palatinate of Durham. Lord Crew, father of the Bishop, having died in 1679, he was succeeded by his eldest son.

James II having acceded to the throne in 1685, one of his first acts was to make Bishop Crewe a member of the Privy Council. From this date, down to 1689, a great deal of intrigue and jealousy was carried on between the rival factions of the courtiers of James, and which in the end tended much to militate against the actions of the Bishop.

But the Revolution placed Bishop Crewe in a still worse position, and although he voted in convocation that James had abdicated the Kingdom, yet he was excepted by name, so Gibson says, "out of the pardon granted by William, Prince of Orange, and Mary." At this critical moment the Bishop fled to Holland, where his friends said he had gone for a tour, but his enemies entertained different ideas, and not a few were of the opinion that he would never subscribe allegiance to the new Government. Amongst this number was Bishop Burnett. It is said the latter almost counted for a certainty upon being translated to Durham; but in this he was disappointed, as Bishop Crewe arrived in London on the day previous to the expiration of the time prescribed in the proclamation for taking the oath. After this event he was graciously received by the King and Queen. During the reign of the Revolution Government, Bishop Crewe would seem to have retained a passive demeanor, and there are reasons for assuming that at this important period in his life he contemplated retiring from the giddy uncertainties that are ever to be found in the train of political strategies, and this would appear the more certain, as about this time he was about to be married to one Miss Croft, a daughter of Dr. Croft, but the union never took place, as the lady died before the nuptial day. The Bishop next directed his attention to Dorothea Forster, and whom Surtees describes as a "lady of great beauty." She was a daughter of Sir William Forster, who was then one of the members for Northumberland. But the historian asserts that the suit went off, as she refused, being too young. But the next attempt was more successful, as in 1691 the Bishop was married to Lady Tynte, a widow of Sir Hugh Tynte, and daughter of Sir Philip Trowde.

In 1697 Bishop Crewe, who was then in his sixty-sixth year, succeeded his brother Thomas in the title and estates of his family. He was summoned to Parliament as Baron and Bishop. For several years he made it a practice to reside at Stene for a given space.

In the month of March, 1700, Lady Crewe died at Stene, and strange to relate, that in four months from the date of the decease of his first wife, the Bishop was married to the object of his first choice, Miss Dorothea Forster.

For a moment let me revert to the Forsters and their connection with the castle at Bamburgh. It is a remarkable fact that the whole of our local historians have fallen into the grievous error in regard to the time when Lord Crewe purchased the possessions of the Forsters. All of them have fixed the date after the attainder of General Forster, whereas it was six years previous to that event, 1709.

Lord Crewe died at Stene in the year 1722, having attained the patriarchial age of 89. During an active life the Bishop had been no idle looker-on in the conflict that was warred between the rival claims of the Stuarts and the house of Hanover. In every sense of the word he might be termed a partisan of the latter; whilst his sympathies may be said to have been in most cases averse to those opinions held by the bulk of his countrymen. Notwithstanding this, his courtesy, piety and finely cultured mind secured him that respect he so justly deserved.

Lord Crew bequeathed nearly the whole of his personal property to charitable purposes in the Diocese of Durham, for the due administration of which he appointed five trustees. Since the death of the Bishop the property in trust has become very enhanced in value, and after a lapse of 162 years we are able to estimate the great amount of good that has occurred from such a noble benefaction.

On the death of Lord Crewe the duties devolved upon the trustees in devising some scheme for carrying out the trust, and out of this rose the propriety of restoring a part of the castle, and their object was to make it the center for the scheme which they were about to inaugurate. But in order to accomplish this, many obstacles had to be removed, which were not finally overcome till 1758, when Dr. Sharp, Archdeacon of Northumberland, was appointed a trustee in the place of his father.

After disposing of that part of the Bishop's will which related to certain charitable bequests, the trustees next applied themselves to the restoration of the keep, together with some other towers within the walls.

After the fifteenth century, the castle was allowed to get into a dilapidated state. This is confirmed by an inquisition that was made in 1574, when it is stated, "that the drawbridge and gates were then broken down and the castle was only accessible through a breach. Such of the walls as were standing were decayed, and the buildings within the ramparts were for the most part in ruins, except the great tower, and the walls of the massive structure were suffering through the lead having been torn from the roof. Since the time of Sir John Horsley, the then last Governor, the chapel and some turrets had become roofless and ruined."

From the foregoing it will be seen that during the time that the castle was held by the Forsters, they had done little or nothing in the way of repairs, so that when Dr. Sharp resolved to grapple with the work of restoration the prospect would be anything but encouraging, as at that time the whole of the towers were not only in a dilapidated state, but what was nearly as bad, every chamber was completely filled with soil.

Archdeacon Sharp possessed a warm attachment for the great northern fortress, and in order to give effect to this he was anxious that the castle should be one of the principal mediums in transmitting to future generations the noble and philanthropic deeds of one of the greatest of the many prelates that have adorned the princely palatinate of Durham. Actuated by such laudable motives, the Archdeacon and the other trustees resolved upon restoring the keep, so that it might be used as a temporary residence of the trustees, whose business demanded their attendance. But before this part of the work could be accomplished, a good deal else of a miscellaneous character would have to be attended to. At that time the keep was the most entire part of the whole building, and if this was to be attended to, then it was necessary that the gateway, towers and ramparts should be all examined, and if necessary, utilized and made subservient to the wants of the newly formed trust. Thus Bamburgh, grim and mighty in the past, was in the future to become still more glorious in becoming the asylum for all that is great, noble and good.

The amount of interest Dr. Sharp took in the charity will be best gathered from Hutchinson, who writing in 1776, says: "He resides for many months in each year in the castle of Bamburgh, superintends the charity, and he has his eyes upon every new channel by which he may give relief or consolation to his suffering fellow creatures. The shipwrecked and diseased are comforted by his visitation, and the cal amities are alleviated by his care; and his residence there diffuses blessings over the neighboring coast." After the approaches to the castle had been opened out, the chambers and buildings in the inner baly cleared of the sand that had accumulated in and about them, and the breaches in the walls were repaired, the general appearance of the entire structure began to assume something of its former greatness.

In adapting the charity to the requirements of the times the trustees were actuated by the most disinterested motives. They caused a considerable sum to be set aside for education and other benevolently organized schemes. At the castle, apartments were furnished and set apart as a surgery and dispensary. On certain days in each week the poor in the neighborhood are allowed medicine gratuitously, and the privilege of consulting a duly qualified medical practitioner. Formerly meat, flour, coals, and other gratuities, were, with the consent of the trustees, distributed at stated times amongst the sick and deserving poor. To guard against shipwrecks and other casualties that are constantly occurring on our coast, great care and provision was observed, but amongst the most laudable objects inaugurated was that which provided for the cause of education. In addition to a regular school for the use of boys and girls in the village, there was another set apart at the castle for clothing and educating thirty poor girls. By means of these agencies a great and lasting good has been accomplished, for it is only by acts such as these that you practically assist the poorer classes of the community.

In 1778 a public library was established within the castle. In that year the whole of the valuable books belonging to the Rev. Thomas Sharp, incumbent of

Bamburgh, were purchased by the trustees, and went to form the nucleus of what is now a very extensive collection.

Dr. Sharp, by his will, bequeathed the whole of his books to the newly formed library at Bamburgh, which was available to residents within a radius of twenty miles.

The works about the castle which are associated with the name of Dr. Sharp, are to a certain extent scattered over a large portion of the entire range of the building. But it was to the keep where he directed his main efforts, and unfortunately it is here where the greatest mischief was done. Externally, there was little opportunity afforded for changing the general character of the keep; but not so when they came to gut and mutilate the interior. The remodeling of the areas of the principal chambers is the point where the evil commenced. In order to give the apartments a more lofty and imposing aspect, every sacrifice was made, whereby the harmony and grandeur of the interior was likely to be lessened, but this was the one prevailing idea of the eighteenth century. Time accomplishes much, and let us hope that ere long something may be done that will cause this fine old mediaeval structure to stand forth as in the days of yore

"To tell the soul of all that once hath been."

The restoration of the castle was commenced by Archdeacon Sharp in 1770, and the internal arrangements of the present keep may be said to date from that period. The several apartments may be enumerated as follows: Entrance Hall, Waiting or Servant's Hall, Court Room, Armory, Kitchen, Library, and Twelve Bedrooms, two of the latter only dating from the late Archdeacon Sharp's time. Access to the upper apartment is gained by the principal staircase, whilst a third communicates with the north turret. As an instance of the strength and solidity of this part of the building, we may state that the thickness of the walls varies from eleven to nine feet. The staircases pierce through a mass of solid masonry, and thus communicate with the whole of the apartments. It is very probable that previous to the alterations in the last century, the whole of the turrets possessed auxiliaries similar to the north turret.

Within the curtain wall are still to be seen the ruins of a small church dedicated to St. Peter.

Several of the towers within the baly are now used for the following purposes, viz.: dispensary, offices and household accommodation for the resident agent, and school house in which thirty poor girls are educated, boarded and trained in domestic duties.

About ten years ago certain changes were introduced into the management of the trust by order of the Court of Chancery.

Amongst the changes made was that every boarder should contribute £5 annually towards her maintenance; another was the power of the trustees to let the keep for stated periods, subject to the approval of the said trustees; the application to be made to C. Rowlandson, Esq., agent to the trustees.

Description of the Interior of the Keep—Entrance Hall.

The chief attractions in this chamber are two large massive chains, which are described as "King Ida's Watch Chains." These were formerly used for the raising of sunken vessels. A Sedan chair, covered with leather and studded with nails, was the one used to carry the good and amiable Archdeacon Sharp from the castle to the church.

There is also in the chamber a genealogical map, or tree, of the Kings of Scotland from the earliest times. In the chamber now used as a Servant's Hall is a very good portrait of Lord Crewe, Bishop of Durham. Another portrait of interest is that of the old man who discovered the well in the interior of the castle during the alterations that were carried out in 1770 by Archdeacon Sharp, the depth of which was upwards of 150 feet, and this was carried through a rock of basalt, measuring in thickness about 75 feet.

Court Room.

The paintings in this apartment are nearly all of a local character. Over the fire-place are two finely executed portraits, one of Lord Crewe, and the other of his noble consort Lady Crewe. Over the doorway that leads to the Armory is a portrait of the venerable Archdeacon Sharp. The next picture that commands attention is a very clever portrait of the Reverend Sir George Wheeler, Knight. Near to the latter we have a portrait of another eminent north country divine, the most Rev. Dr. John Sharp, Lord Archbishop of York, grandfather of Dr. Sharp. Another picture of interest is that of Thomas Sharp, D. D. He was son of Archbishop Sharp, and was Archdeacon of Northumberland, Rector of Rothbury, and Prebendary of Durham. He died in 1758. The next two portraits are those of ladies, but neither of the subjects are known, although it is supposed, by some, that they are relations of the Forster family. We have in this apartment a beautiful piece of statuary miniature representing Archdeacon Sharp. There is also a rare and valuable collection of engravings. Among other objects of interest will be found

THE TAPESTRY

consisting of four pieces, which are intended to illustrate some of the principal incidents in the life of the Emperor Justinian. They were brought about the year 1788, from the Deanery of Ripon. They are of considerable dimensions, the two largest measuring 15 feet by 8 feet, and containing several figures as large as life. The colors at one time have been extremely vivid, but are now faded in some degree from age; upon the whole, however, they are in excellent preservation and exhibit such correct drawing and good composition that it is evident the paintings or designs from which they were worked must have been the production of no common master. The first of the series I imagine to represent the Emperor Justinian, seated at a large table and engaged with his compeers in forming the celebrated Digest of Roman Law. A remarkable figure standing behind his chair may probably represent Trebonianus. Two of the lawyers are in oriental costume, and one of the two may be supposed to be Basilides, who had been Prefect of the east. In the second the Emperor is seen advancing in royal apparel to an open temple of Janus. Slaves newly manumitted are crowding round him, and kissing the hem of his garment. Other persons are also introduced as spectators of the scene. Justinian may here be conjectured to be in the act of proclaiming, immediately after one of the great victories gained by Belisarius, the "eternal peace." which by the way lasted two years. The third is a coronation: the Emperor kneels on a cushion with the scepter in his right hand, while a stately figure on a scarlet robe is placing a crown upon this head, before him stand two Flamens holding an open book, on which may be distinguished the words "Lex Romanas." Between the priests and the Emperor lies a naked sword wreathed with olive. On another cushion, and beside it, a kneeling page throws the light of a torch on the open volume. This transaction is represented as taking place at night on a terrace, and the populace are gathered in a court below. In the fourth piece of tapestry, Justinian appears, not exactly in a hunting dress, but with a hunting spear in his hand, in a wild country, with only two attendants; he has come suddenly upon two of his hounds, which lie dead, and apparently poisoned, on the ground. A chased bowl stands near them, and a stream of water gushes from the rock at a small distance. The countenance and attitude of the Emperor are strongly expressive of surprise and regret.

A good deal of the furniture is very old and curious. Among this will be found several pieces of carved. One piece deserves special mention, and this is an old sofa "covered with work in tent stitch."

THE ARMORY

occupies the entire length of the keep, and upon the walls are displayed some very good examples of pictures, swords, halberts, guns, pistols, and other specimens of ancient armory.

Among the pictures probably none attracts the attention of the visitor more than an oil painting of "Bamburgh Castle, by Moonlight," by James Wilson Carmichael, taken in 1863, and presented to the trustees by Mrs. Bland, wife of Archdeacon Bland. For effect and coloring the picture may be said to be unique, and a fine example of the work of one of England's greatest marine painters. Another very interesting picture in oil of Bamburgh Castle in 1788, is by G. Sykes. There is also a very fine lot of old engravings in this part of the castle, and along with these may be mentioned a complete list of Lord Crewe's trustees, from the date of the Bishop's death down to the present time. A rare engraving of the right Hon. James, Earl of Derwentwater, will be found in this room. James, or as he is more aptly termed the last Earl of Derwentwater, having been implicated in the Rebellion of 1715, was beheaded on Tower Hill in 1716.

THE OLD BANQUETING HALL

is supposed to have been on the flat, now partly used as a kitchen, for there is still to be seen the gallery of the minstrels. Scott, in his "Lay of the Last Minstrels," gives a fine portrayal of the last of the ancient Border Minstrels.

THE LIBRARY.

In this apartment there is an admirable portrait of "General Thomas Foster," who was implicated in the Rebellion of 1715. Another portrait is that of "Miss Dorothea Foster," sister of General Foster.

Thomas Foster, the Rebel General, was the eldest son of Francis Forster. It is stated that General Forster owed his escape from Newgate to his sister Dorothy. The latter is reported to have ridden from Adderstone in company with one Purdy, a blacksmith. On her arrival in London and after an interview with her brother, she managed to array the General in the clothes she was then wearing, and by this means he escaped to France, where he remained to the time of his death in 1738, when his body was brought to England and buried in the family vault in Bamburgh church, where the bodies of sixty other Forsters are interred.

In all, the number of books in library amounts to about 4,000, which are divided into two sections, one known as the "modern library," which is in the keep, and the "old library" is in that part of the building now occupied by the charity children. The books in the library at Bamburgh are a fine collection, embracing many hundreds of rare and valuable works, and to the student and antiquary are of immense importance; but this valuable depository of learning is not sufficiently taken advantage of in Northumberland. I am sure that the librarian, the vicar of Bamburgh, would only be too glad to give any information respecting the class of books on the shelves, as well as the conditions on which they are issued.

TRUSTEES.

The present trustees of Lord Crewe's Charity are: Rev. Dixon Brown, M. A., Chairman, Unthank Hall, Haltwhistle. Rev. Canon Mason, M. A., Rector of Whitfield. Rev. Canon Chester, M. A., Rector of Easington. Rev. Wm. Walter Merry, D. D., Rector of Lincoln College, Oxford. The agent is C. Rowlandson, Esq. The College, Durham, sub-agent, Mr. R. G. H. Hutchinson, Bamburgh Castle.

In a sense, all the ground about Bamburgh may be termed "classic," for every step unveils some hidden treasure, reminding us of the time when the Saxon, Dane and Norman met in open feud and deadly combat. From the castle and embankments the scenery is magnificent and full of interest; upon a fine day when the sky is clear the different islands, which are so familiar to he mariners who frequent our coast, are seen to advantage. To the south in mellow decay are the crumbling walls of "Dunstanburgh's cavernous shore," and beyond there again stand

"Warkworth, proud of Percy's name.'

To the north the prospect is of the same pleasing description, embracing Lindisfarne, with its many memories and hallowed associations, and to the north of this again is the good old border town of Berwick, around whose history still hovers much that relates to ancient lore and reminiscence; while on the west a wide expanse of beautiful country imparts a charm to the landscape, and combines in casting a halo around a scene already rich in valiant deeds and historic associations.

Few watering places in the north of England afford a more pleasing aspect than Bamburgh. Great and illustrious in the past on account of its historic associations, it has in modern times become the favorite resort of the tourist, the pleasure seeker, and those in quest of health. From a geographical point of view, the situation of the village may be termed exceptionally good. It is built on the brow of a hill, which gradually slopes from the sea embankments upwards. To the west it is sheltered by a beautiful grove of trees which greatly enhance the entrance to the principal street. To the east it lies nestled, as it were, under the shadow of the great Norman Fortress. On the north and south sides of the castle a fine stretch of sandy beach can hardly fail to please the most fastidious taste. This place is most frequented during the summer months, by numbers of visitors who never tire in exploring a locality almost inexhaustive in its associations of the past.

OLD MANOR HOUSE.

The Old Manor House, formerly the residence of the Forsters, stood on the site of what is now known as the "Hall," and which adjoins the parish church. The old building was anciently used as a religious house, but after the Dissolution it became the adopted home of the Forsters. Several of the pictures which grace the walls of this house, together with much valuable furniture, were removed in 1709, thus verifying an old saying, "that the Manor House shared the vicissitudes of a once powerful family." In prosperity as well as in adversity, the castle and manor of Bamburgh have become interwoven with the history of the Forsters. The

Church, as dedicated to St. Aidan, first Bishop of Lindisfarne, and may justly be termed a fine structure of the early part of the thirteenth century. It is bold in design, chaste in proportion and arrangement, and the same characteristic runs throughout the entire structure. Before attempting to deal with the architecutural features of this great historic church, let me briefly state that it was at Bamburgh where one of the first Christian Temples in ancient Northumbria was reared. Shortly after Aidan's appointment, in 635, to the see of Leindisfarne, he appears to have made Bamburgh one of his chief places of resort. Previous to that time, Bede says, "There was no altar throughout the Kingdom of Northumbria." It was through Oswald's influence that the Bishop was induced to leave the "sea-girl island of Iona" with the view of converting the natives from heathenism to Christianity. For nine years Aidan labored in the northern kingdom, and it was during those short eventful years that a church, chiefly composed of wood, was first built at Bamburgh. At the west end of the structure was a small apartment, and it was here where the Bishop was reposing, his head reclining against a buttress which supported the erection, when the news arrived of the death of Oswin. St. Aidan felt the blow so keenly that he soon sickened and died. That a church dating from Saxon times existed at Bamburgh at the time of the Conquest is certain, but there are no remains about the present structure that can be associated with those times. In the absence of any I am led to infer that the ancient church was composed principally of wood. This opinion would almost apply to what is known as the Norman period; for if there are no existing proofs of a Saxon church, neither is there any trace of Norman remains. If this conjecture is right then we may readily conclude that the Saxon church did duty down to the time of the twelfth century, when it was superseded by the present graceful edifice.

One of the most interesting objects connected with this church is the small Crypt which exists under the floor of the chancel. For many years all trace of this fine mediaeval remain was hidden, and it was not till 1837, when certain repairs were being carried out about the chancel, that some workmen engaged came upon an opening in the floor which led to chambers underneath. After an entrance had been affected, the apartments were found to be filled with rubbish, this device having no doubt been resorted to shortly after the death of Mr. B. Foster, who is reported as having been the last of the name buried in this part of the church.

The date of the Crypt is undoubtedly co-eval with the chancel. The discovery of this chamber in 1837 led to further excavations being made, which resulted in a passage being exposed at the east end of the structure that led to the underground chamber. This approach, which is in close contiquity to the chancel, may be described as a narrow passage, and being a good depth under the surface of the churchyard, is almost unique in style and arrangement. At the terminus of the passage a beautiful pointed doorway opens into the chamber.

There is evidence about this interesting remain to show that in ancient times when border feuds and state intriques were constantly being fermented, it would be used by the brethren at the adjoining monastry as a chapel or alter, and it was not till more recent times that it came to be used as a charnel house for the dead.

As much interest is centered in the Crypt, not only from an architectural point of view and the use for which it may have been intended, but more especially as being so closely connected with the Forsters of Northumberland. We have, through the kindness of the Rev. Arthur Octavius Medd, formerly vicar of Bamburgh, been fortunate in getting access to some papers in the possession of Miss E. Carr of Bamburgh, which belonged to her father, the late Mr. Wm. Carr, who died in 1861, aged 76 years. Of course, architecturally, the documents are not of much value, but historically they are full of local interest, especially the following, showing the state of the Crypt and its contents as discovered on Tuesday, July 25, 1837.

"Examined the vaults beneath Bamburgh Church, sometime called the Death House, and sometime the vault of the Forsters."

"The oak planks which supported the floor were entirely decayed, and on their removal there appeared a flight of stone stairs, leading to the apartments below. On examination this was found to pass through the original wall of the vaults and terminate in a long-arched chamber, like a passage of worked stone, the arch having been finished with plaster resting on a cornice, and with a narrow window at the east end."

"The different proofings of the floor, apparently through light rubbish, under and near the window, seem to favor the tradition current at Bamburgh that there was a subterranean passage from the religious house, directly opposite to the east end of the chancel."

"At the foot of the steps was a square opening which led to a second chamber, the sides of which had been rudely broken, and which had the appearance of having been a doorway. This apartment, which possessed a groined stone roof, and other peculiarities of the gothic period, may justly be termed a fine chamber. At the east end on a stone platform were laid five coffins which were made to rest from north to south. Between the south wall and the columns there was an intermediate space of about two and a half feet. In the south wall was a piscina, which was lighted by a narrow lancet window. At the east end are two other windows of a similar character, and on the south side was a large doorway, traces of which may be seen on the walls of the chancel. In the roof was a staple, probably for suspending a lamp. We could not find a floor, and sticks went down three feet without interruption. This apartment has undoubtedly been a chapel. The chambers and passage are well ventilated and entirely free from dampness."

The foregoing coffins are enumerated as follows:—

1. Mr. B. Forster, of Adderstone, 1765; the body of John or Wm. had been removed so as to make room for this coffin.

2. Fernando Foster, murdered at Newcastle Aug. 22, 1701, by John Fenwick, of Rock.

3. John or Wm. Forster, 1700.

4. General Forster, implicated in the Rebellion of 1715. This distinguished individual would seem, after his escape from Newgate, to have settled down in France. He died in 1738, and his remains were brought to England. His funeral was entirely private. In addition to the hearse drawn by one horse, a confidential servant of the deceased was all that made up the funeral cortege when the remains of the rebel General were consigned to their last resting place in Bamburgh church.

5. Dorothy Forster, married in 1739, to one of the name of Armstrong. The latter is described as having been a man of "inferior person." Mr. Armstrong and his wife lived for a while at Bamburgh Friars. Dorothy died at Crookham, in this county, on the 5th of May, 1771.

The first coffin was perfect; the second, of wood only, had fallen to pieces, but there remained the whole trace of a figure, the legs and thigh bones entire, and in place of the skull, on which the coffin lid had fallen, was mass of white dust, like lime. The third was in much the same state, but in this case the skull of the figure had not crumbled to dust. The fourth was perfect, except only the cloth covering the outer coffin of elm, and was entire and strong. It is reported that thirty years previous to this an opening had been made near the foot to ascertain the presence of this body, which had been disputed. It rested in sawdust closely packed; the linen clothes were there, and the legs were fleshy and perfect. No further examination at that time was made. Mr. Embleton thought he detected the smell of hartshorn near this coffin. The fifth was in a bad state, having fallen to pieces, so the remains were not exumed. A few years ago a coffin was dug up in the chancel, it never having had a body in it, which strengthened the supposition that General Forster's body was not in the vault. This said General Foster was condemned to death, and only delivered from prison by the intrepid devotion of his sister Dorothy, who now lies by his side in the vault. It is generally averred that a mock funeral took place at Bamburgh some few years previous to the death of General Forster in 1738, and the coffin discovered in the chancel, and alluded to in Carr's notes, most probably points to this event. A somewhat similar report to this is given by Amelia, Countess of Derwentwater, as she styled herself after the death of the only son of James, the last Earl of Derwentwater. This lady alleged that the reported death of the Earl's son was a complete fabrication, and only intended to divert the animosity that was in those days evinced against those who espoused the cause of the Stuarts. This good lady further alleged that the young scion of "Radcliffe's fair domain," ultimately banished himself to a foreign land, where he lived to an old age, and died in the greatest obscurity. With regard to the murder of Fernando Forster, one of the members of Parliament for the county of Northumberland, we get a very accurate account of the quarrel from Alderman Hoarby's manuscript notes to Brand: "He says he takes for his authority Edward Collingwood, Esq., Recorder of Newcastle, who informed me that his father was present when the quarrel happened. The company consisted of the whole or part of the Grand Jury of Northumberland, and probably during that state of conviviality which prevailed much on these occasions about that period, Mr. Fenwick came in singing a favorite party song, the burthen of which was, "Sir John Fenwick, the flower among them." This brought on some altercation betwixt him and Mr. Forster, but the company interfering, the matter was supposed to be quite settled. The next morning the parties met accidentally near the White Cross, the altercation was renewed, swords were drawn, and Mr. Forster killed."

One of the windows at the west end of the church contains full length figures of St. Aidan, the apostle of Northumbria, and St. Cuthbert. Both of the saints are arrayed in their episcopal robes. In the arms of St. Cuthbert is the head of St. Oswald. This window was manufactured by Messrs. Hardman, of Birmingham, and was the gift of Mrs. Forster, of Tuggal. In the interior are several chaste and beautiful tablets, monuments, and tombstones. On the north side of the chancel and within the altar rails is a tablet to the memory of Sir Claudius Forster, Bart. He was created a baronet on the 7th of March, 1619, and it was to this same Sir Claudius that the castle and manor were granted in the reign of James I. The following inscription in Latin appears upon the tablet:—

Scio quod Redemptor M' : vivit in Cœlo Sta : Sal : D.

Claudius Forsterus, Esques Aurat et Baronetlus antiqua numerosa et noble Forsteroru familia in Com. Northumb oriundus Dno. Nicolas Forster, qui 37 Anos Mediar Marchiar: Scotia vers Dns Guardian extitil filiet haeres Horvoratiss etiam Dns. Cumbriæ et Bedf: Comitibus neceron insigni et illustri Fenwicoru progenie, totique sanguine conjunct; Castridenque Bamburg Dns. Senescal et summ: Constabulari; Obüt in manerio suo de Alba Terra in Comit: Northumb: Anno Sal: Nost 1623.

Memoriæ sacrum lugens posuit uxor egies Dwa: Elizabetha.

Guliebma Fenwick d Wallingtonia, Equitis Aurati.

The following inscription will be found on a monument to the Forsters in the chancel: "In the vault below lie buried the bodyes of William, John and Ferdinand, sons of Wm. Forster* of Bamburgh, Knt., by Dorothy,† daughter of Sir Wm. Selby, of Twisdale, Bart., and Elanor, daughter of Ferdinand, Lord of Fairfax, of Denton. William was born 28th July, 1666; married Elizabeth, dau. of Wm. Pert, Esq.; died 1st September, 1700, without issue. John was born 21st September, 1668; died 15th November, 1669. Ferdinand, born 14th February, 1699; died 22d August, 1701. Both unmarried."

They had another brother, Nicolas, who died young, and was buried in the Church of Saint Mary in the South Bailey at Durham. So also five sisters: Elanor and Dorothy, who died young; Frances married Thomas Foster, of Etherstone, Esq., by whom she had several children; Mary who died unmarried; and Dorothy, wife of the Right Hon. Lord Crewe, Lord Bishop of Durham, of whom their mother died. She being the only one remaining of the family, set up this monument in memory of her dear brothers, as a last respect that could be paid them for their affection to the church, ye monarchy, their country, and their sister, A. D., 1711; this being the burying place of their ancestors.

On the north side of the chancel, and within the enclosure, is hung the helmet, breastplate, sword and glove of Ferdinando Forster, Esq.

In 1857 a paper was found in the helmet of the aforesaid Ferdinando Forster, Esq., and upon it was written the following: "Prayer and blessing to you and your wife, your son Dawson and his wife, hoping these few lines will find you in good health at present, praised be God for it. I have it to testifie of, I have sent you some hose yarn and a yard of —— and I desire you to send me money of —— butter—— comes to 10s for having to —— money for my husband left me betwixt 5 —— to pay when he died, and I do intend a deed (or gift) of all I am of, &c."

Before leaving the structure, there are certain legends and traditions about the building to which I will allude. The first of these is concerning the slight deflection in a southerly direction of the chancel arch; a similar divergence also exists in one of the transept arches. Mr. Wilson, in his "Churches of Lindisfarne," says: That some authorities regard the deflection as depicting the 'head of Christ as He hung upon the cross.' "Others again imagine that it is intended to mark a spot in the sky, at which the sun rose on the day of the death of St. Aidan. To those who are fond of ancient and legendary lore, few ideas can be more congenial than these here advanced; but in most cases wherever deflections exist, either in arches or main walls, they may possibly be found to have been caused by some temporary derangement, such as the making of vaults and graves in close contiguity to the principal walls of the building. Concerning the lychnoscopes on the north and south sides of the chancel, which are marked by a low narrow window with trefoil

* Born Nov. 12, 1624, P. R.

† Ob 26th September; B. 30, 1672, P. R.

heading, there are some who think that the openings may have been intended to emit the light which burned before the altar, in order that it might scare the evil spirits from the graves of the newly buried in the churchyard. Another tradition exists, which is that a subterranean passage connected the monastery with the church; but up to the present have been found about the building to favor such a conjecture.

Only once, between the reign of Henry I., and that of John, 1197, is there any mention of the church, and this is during the time of Richard Coeur de Lion, when Bamburgh contributed five marks toward the exchequer.

In 1725 the church was still in a bad state, the following document, supplied by the Rev. Canon Carr, of Whickham, and Rural Dean of Ryton, which bears upon the state of the church during the early part of last century will read with interest. Canon Carr procured a copy of the report from one in the possession of the Rev. G. Wilkinson, of Harperley Hall, in the county of Durham. The survey was made in the above year by the Rev. Dick, or Dickson, who was Vicar of Norham. In this report it is stated that "Bamburgh is a curacy, and that the income from all sources amounted to £125, 3s. 4d." It is further stated "that the living is endowed, and has belonging to it a chapel of ease, four miles from the mother church, called Beadnell, where there is divine service once a month only, in the afternoon. It is in the gift of the five trustees." "The Church of Bamburgh was in a very bad condition, a great part of it being uncovered and lying exposed to any profanation; but since this Archdeacon's visitation, the isles that were down are rebuilt, and cover'd with lead, the floor is new flag'd, and the walls plaster'd and whitewash'd, and all things therein are decent and becoming. The church is large, and the chancel very spacious, wh was some yrs ago repaired and beautified by the late Ld Rp of Durham. There is also in the vestry a small parochial library, consisting of about 60 vols., wh was lately begun, and is now increasing by the voluntary subscriptions of the gentlemen of the parish." "The parish is of gt extent, and very populous, and as wealthy. There are few Dissenters in it of any denomination. There is a small glebe, and no means remaining, for wh reason the gentlemen of the vestry, from time to time, and now, have settled upon the curate a commodious farm, with a good house upon it, for wh he is to pay 12lb per annm into the vestry for the repairs of the Ch and procuring the elements for the H. Communion

The gt Tythes are in the possession of the
Earl of Tankerville,
Mr. Henry Neville Grey,
Mr. Forster, of Adderstone,
And some other gentlemen."

The document is interesting, as it gives a good deal of information upon the state of the church during the early part of the eighteenth century. From this record we gather that the building was rescued from the dilapidated state it had fallen into through the munificence of Lord Crewe. Previous to the time of this Bishop, the church had got into a bad and ruinous condition. That the Forsters would take a great interest in the building is only natural, so that after Lord Crewe's marriage with Miss Dorothea Forster, it is not surprising that one of his first acts in the parish was to restore the ancient structure. In the year following his marriage he strengthened the family ties when he purchased a rent charge of £500 a year on the estates of the Forsters, and for which he paid the sum of £10,000. This bill was sanctioned by the Court of Chancery for the payment of certain debts that had been secured on the property. And this was followed up in 1704 by several creditors presenting another bill, in which they petitioned the court to have the whole of the estates sold for the payment of debts incurred by William and Ferdinando Forster. The court complied with the petition, and the whole of the property was offered for sale, whereupon Lord Crewe was declared to be the purchaser, for the sum of £20,679 10s. In the latter sum was included in the purchase a life rent charge of £350 a year, payable to Elizabeth, widow of Wm. Forster. It was not till 1709 that the deed confirming the sale was enrolled in Chancery, and that after all debts had been paid there only remained for Lady Crewe and Thomas Forster, the rebel general, the sum of £1,028, 15s. 7d. Thus it will be seen that six years previous to the Rebellion of 1715, the Forsters had nearly exhausted the whole of their once wide possessions.

How the church acquired possession of the Fowberry estate, there appears to be no record. But as this would form part of the ancient manor, it is not improbable that it would be conferred by Lord Crewe about the time that he became the purchaser of the estates of the Forsters.

There were two chantries in Bamburgh Church, one of which was endowed by the ancient Earls of Devilstone or Derwentwater, from lands held by them at Spindlestone. This altar stood in the north transept, and for several years was the burying place of the Greys of Shoreston Hall. The registers of Bamburgh Church commenced in 1653, and from this time down to 1760 are very imperfect. Among Miss Carr's papers the following occurs: "Thos. Forster of Edderstone had a daughter bap. Eliz., Aug. 14, 1684. Godfather was Mr. Ralph Forster of Halton's son who stood up for Mr. John Forster. Godmothers were Mrs. Betty Forster, Mr. Francis Forster's daughter, of Durham, and Mr. Grey's younger daughr. Thos. Forster of Adderstone had son bap., Willm., Nov. 1, 1685. Godfathers were Esq. Forster of Balmbro, Mr. Robt. Hebburn of Hebburn, and Mrs. Mary Forster, Mr. Ralph Forster, Halton's daughr. Thomas Forster of Etherston Esqe had a daughter baptzd Dorothy, Mr. Ralph Forster of Halton, Mrs. Mary Forster, his Lady's sister, her aunt Mrs. Grey of Durham, and Mrs. Magdalen Grey's daughter of Howick were the Gossip's. Feb. 3, 1686, Thomas Forster of Etherston, Esquire, had a son born, John, bap. fifth of July, 1688, Mr. John Forster, Mr. Ferdinando Forster, his lady's brothers were Godfathers, and Madam Margaret of Durham, Godmother."

FARNE ISLANDS.

These islands are situated to the southwest of Bamburgh, and at a distance of two miles from the latter place, while from Monkshouse, which is the nearest point from the mainland, the distance is about one and a half miles. It is estimated that the number of islands vary from fifteen to twenty-five; this, in a measure being due to the flow and ebb of the tide. It is remarkable the effect that this evolution has upon these tiny spaces of land. At full tide several of them are covered with water, but when the tide begins to recede they are again united, and form one distinct island. But the transformation is perhaps more apparent at full tide, for then the several islands are reduced to three or four. There are two groups of islets, separated from each other by the Ox Scar Road, which is one mile in breadth, and from five to eight fathoms deep, affording facilities to vessels of almost any size to pass, but not without danger. Several of the names associated with the island are of ancient origin, and may be traced back to Saxon times. Amongst these are Farne, Wedum, Staple, Brownsman, South Wamses, North Wamses, Harcar Scarcar, Crumstone, Longstone, Megstone, Noxes, Nivestone, Clive Car, Swedman, Outcarres, Nameless Rock, Roddam, and Green, Northern Hares, etc.

Farne is derived from the German word "Ferhern," signifying, as Raine says, to "rest from labor, and thus applicable to the early recluses, who repose from the labors and struggles of the world."

Farne is very frequently applied to the whole of the islands, and probably this is the most correct way of designating them, as in Saxon times they were only known as Farneland. In several charters and documents the inner island is termed the "House Island." In the twelfth century it was styled the "Stapol-i-land," and in more recent times it occurs as "Stapleland" and "Staple."

There can be little doubt that the inner island owes much of its greatness to St. Cuthbert, although previous to this time it had been the resort of St. Aidan. During the time that St. Cuthbert was connected with Lindisfarne he often visited Farne, and his example in after years was followed by Ethelwold, who at one time was a monk at Ripon. He came to Farne in 687, and continued there to his death in 699. After Ethelwold came Felgeld, Elwin, Bartholomew and Thomas ex-Prior of Durham.

The greater portion of Bamburgh Estate, including the Castle, has been purchased by Lord Armstrong, C. B., of Cragside, Rothbury, from the trustees of Lord Crewe.

It was in the early part of the year 1894 that the public first learned that this historic domain was likely to change hands. But sudden as the announcement was, public anxiety was relieved when the name of the popular purchaser became known. At the Audit dinner held in connection with the Court Leets of the Manor of Bamburgh and Bamburgh Castle on April 24, 1894, at which several of the trustees were present, the following letter was read by the chairman, the Rev. Dixon Brown, from which may be gathered to a large extent, the particular use that his lordship was intending to make of the Castle:—

Extract from Lord Armstrong's letter:—

"The preservation of Bamburgh Castle as a historic monument, and its restoration to a more dignified position than it at present holds, are the chief inducements that have led me to contract for its purchase. I therefore have no objection to enter into a covenant to run with the land, that I will do nothing to change the historic character of the Castle. But it seems difficult to define what would and what would not be a change. I think it would be desirable to put on record what I intend to do. First, I intend to restore the Great Hall of the Castle, in the style of the period in which it was built. Second, I intend to convert the adjoining buildings into a charitable institution, to be approved of by Lord Crewe's trustees. These buildings have only of late years been used as a boarding school for girls, and are now used for seaside lodgings. The institution will most probably be for the benefit of convalescent patients, who will have the advantage of using the restored Great Hall for exercise and recreation."

From the foregoing may be gathered the motives of this generous benefactor. In addition to alterations to the Castle, Lord Armstrong contemplated doing a great deal for the entire estate. But our aim on the present occasion is to deal more particularly with the Castle. Those who are familiar with the architectural features of this fine old stronghold, will be aware that during the early years of the Trust, nearly the whole of the building was subjected to many violent changes, and that while the mere outlines may not have been much interfered with, this does not apply to several internal alterations that were carried out. Such being the case it was only natural that Lord Armstrong should seize the first opportunity for having the fortress restored to what it was in pre-historic times. Owing to certain arrangements a start has first been made with some of those towers and chambers situated on the southeastern part of the wall, and in close proximity to the eastern part of the keep. At this juncture it is rather difficult to give a foreshadowing of all that is contemplated. But this to a certain extent may be gathered from the remarks of that eminent architect, Mr. C. J. Ferguson, F. S. A., who only last year at a meeting at Bamburgh, said "that with the help of Mr. Gibbings and Mr. Hart, he was endeavoring to disqualify himself for either classification, and had commenced his education by making a careful plan and drawings of the Castle as it now existed, for nothing unfolded the history of a building so thoroughly as a careful plan. All great variations in the style of building arose from some new or improved method of construction. The mediæval art was a transition from concrete to masonry, as the walls got thinner and thinner and the masonry better in quality and finish. The greater part of the outer walls of Bamburgh Castle and the towers which stand upon them were ancient. The muniment tower was a fine example of a thirteenth century tower, and had two original windows of great interest, but it had unfortunately been partially refaced, but great care would be taken to preserve as much of the old work intact as possible. The kitchen, though somewhat hidden under modern additions, was the old kitchen of the Castle, and had the peculiar feature of having vents or flues for ventilation formed over each of the windows. To the west of it stood the old King's Hall, the site now being occupied by a laundry, wash house, and other offices. These would be taken down and the hall rebuilt, probably the same size, seventy feet by thirty feet. It would not be the old hall, but would occupy the site, and be a lasting monument of its predecessor. The lower parts of the old walls had unfortunately been refaced some time ago, and so had lost some of their original expression. Great care, however, would be taken to preserve whatever of it was left. From the foregoing it will be seen that the ancient King's Hall was on the east side of the keep and to west of the old kitchens. After its demolition the site was utilized by the erection of a dairy, laundry, and other offices. These are all being swept away, and the walls of a new hall, almost on the identical lines of the old one, are being erected. Of the history of this particular part of the Castle, Mr. Bates says it was in existence at the time of the Conquest, and may be said to have witnessed much of the chivalry and martial achievements that are associated with its history. "It," as this same authority facetiously remarks, "may have been associated with one of the most distinctive Northumbrian tenures in supplying logs for its hearth." Nor is it at all unlikely "that it was probably at this hearth that the Countess Judith tested the miraculous properties of St. Oswin's hair. The history of Ida's Castle at Bamburgh carries our minds back to the days of feud, war, and turmoil, and it was not till the time of Oswald that better things were ushered in, when the godly influences of Aidan and that noble band of Iona Missioneris caused the glad tidings of the gospel to be felt. At the present time there are nearly 200 workmen employed about the building, and as the work progresses we may expect to see this number still more augmented. Some of the alterations in progress at the present time are formidable difficulties, especially where the basalt has to be excavated for specific purposes. One of the most arduous undertakings has been the cutting out of a passage that will afford communication between the kitchens and the keep, and where by means of a hydraulic lift erected under the floor of the latter every facility will be afforded for rapidly supplying the good store for "my lord's table." The stones for the work of reconstruction are being brought from Lord Armstrong's quarries at Craigside, and judging from the color and nature of the dressed ashbars, they will assist in imparting a still bolder effect to the exterior. The whole of the works are being executed from plans specially prepared by Mr. Ferguson, and we may say that in the hands of such a competent authority, full justice will be done to the undertaking. The Clerk of the works is Mr. Laidler, who is imbued with a keen relish for the project before him.

During the last twelve months a considerable amount of expense has been incurred over certain repairs and alterations that are going on at the Church This was caused in a great measure by the roof of the chancel having gotten into a dilapidated state. For some time past the present Vicar who had under consideration a plan for raising both the roof of the chancel and the nave to their original height, such as existed previous to the fifteenth century. Bamburgh Church, like a good many more in Northumberland, joined in the transition from the high pitched roof to the low flat-roof, and the change was no doubt brought about by the fact that the low roof was better adapted to our northern climate than the other. It is a somewhat knotty point, and one over which a great difference of opinion exists. Be this as it may, the architect, Mr. Wm. Searles Hicks, is to be congratulated on the manner in which the work is being executed. The Church is worthy of careful study. There are no traces about the present building that can be associated with the early Saxon Church, but in the absence of such we are almost safe in assuming that the pre-existing structure would be chiefly composed of wood. There is no part of the present building that dates earlier than the middle of the thirteenth century, whilst the chancel and crypt are both somewhat later. The transepts which show indications of an extension, date from about the early part of the fourteenth century. The small pointed doorway at the southwesternmost part of the south facade has often led to a good deal of conjecture. Judging from the importance of the place, and with a monastery of no mean significance close at hand, it is not improbable that the western part of the nave and a portion of the south aisle may have served as an altar. These were formerly to be found oftener at the east end of our churches, but we have instances, as at Durham, where the west end was occasionally resorted to.

BAMBOROUGH CASTLE.

As It Appeared in 1896 when Visited by Mrs. Sophie Foster Symes—An Interesting Account of the Early Home of the Family.

'Twas in making a tour of the Cathedral towns in the summer of '96 that we came to Northumberland. We had spent the Sunday at York and at noon of a beautiful August day—quite like our own September ones—we alighted from the train at Belford. With another party bent upon visiting the famous old Bamboro' Castle we occupied a wagonette and made the distance of eight miles in time almost too quick for any lingering enjoyment of the landscape, diversified by an occasional glimpse of the North Sea, very fierce and wild at that point of the coast.

Arriving at the village of Bamboro', neither the Victoria Inn nor the Crewe Arms, could afford us accommodation, so we sought and found refuge in a cottage within the shadow of the Castle walls. In the absence of the family, we were attended by the care-taker of the domicile, a maiden who bore the name of Short, but who at the same time was possessed of a face so long and of a nature so melancholy, that we only endured her serving of the goose-berries and mushrooms—abundantly bestowed by kind neighbors—for two meals of the day, taking our dinners at the Inn, patronized by H. R. H. the Prince of Wales, so the sign board read.

Bamboro' village is a typically English one, of primitive aspect, two streets, one leading to the stage road and the other to the Manor house and the Church, uniting in one, and terminating at the Castle. Then, like any other well regulated English village, it has a "Lord of the Castle" and a "gray haired Vicar" and the "Squire" —the rest of the inhabitants seemed like simple honest folk, many of whom live their short, or their long lives—it matters little which—with never going from the boundary of their native hamlet; yet the history that events have made in this remote corner of England I can only refer to—for does it not take the greater part of the seven gigantic volumes of the History of Northumberland to record?

As the roads, so does interest, center at the Castle, one of the most ancient in all England. King Ida's reign began in the year 550 and prior to that "a castle huge and square" existed; to the antiquarian and student of architecture, the various epochs in building, Roman, Saxon and Norman, afford an interesting study.

Bamboro' derives its name from Babba, one of the early Queens of Northumbria. It was by a grant from William the Norman that the Forsters became possessed of this splendid fortress, retaining it until 1709. In the spring of 1895 the property was purchased by Lord Armstrong, of Armstrong gun fame, and he has by this time, I presume, completed the restoration to its old time splendor, this castle "superior to any other in strength and position."

As the Forsters were so identified with all pertaining to Bamboro' it was with no ordinary interest our little party of four climbed the winding path that morning, when, by Lord Armstrong's courtesy we were to have entrance within the Castle walls. Eight acres are enclosed and the principal gate of Norman build is very imposing. On this our first visit, we passed in quick review the moat, the portcullis, the towers and bastions, all remarkable for their impregnability, and hastened to the keep, a massive square building outwardly, and its interior of grand proportions. In the year 1700 some efforts at repair were made, but since then, till the more recent ownership, it has been somewhat neglected. Much of the elegant forniture remained, also the famous Justinian tapestries, the armor, plate, and china, (Oh, how we coveted the possession of one cup). The family portraits were most interesting, especially that of Sir Walter Besant's heroine, Dorothy Forster, and that of her revolutionary brother, General Tom Forster. We peered down the well 150 feet deep, accidentally discovered in 1770 and located in a small passage way. . We only had, it seemed to us, a brief time in the library, with its many priceless volumes, its missals and illuminated texts, centuries old. We had to carefully pick our way down the old worn stone steps at the further end from that we entered, viewing, on the ocean side of the Castle's domains, the scene of Grace Darling's exploits.

The Vicar of the parish, dear old Canon Long, welcomed us as long wandering children returning to their native heath and 'twas at once our privilege and pleasure to go to the rectory for our afternoon tea and hear him tell of Bamboro' and of the brave, adventurous Forsters; then to walk with him through the high walled garden, once belonging to a convent, but destroyed by Cromwell—and along the same paths trod by the gentle nuns centuries before, and later on by beautiful Dorothy Forster and her handsome, chivalrous lover, the Earl of Derwentwater and who, because one would not give up the Protestant religion and the other his Roman Catholic faith, were never wed. This garden is directly across from the Manor House included in the original grant to the Forster family, now the home of "the Squire," and where we were most hospitably entertained, meeting many of the Bamburghers.

One of the first Christian churches in that part of England was built in Bamboro' in 635, the present one is believed to have been erected in the twelfth century and has many fine, unusual features. Some of the windows are exquisite in color. The young lady of our party went to the crypt "the graveyard of the Forsters" 'tis called, where sixty-six of that name are buried. This was only discovered and opened within a few years.

On the following Sunday the American descendants of this once famous family were accorded seats in the Forster pew and over the ashes of her ancestors, they listened to a memorial sermon to a fair, sweet girl called to another world the year before. After service we lingered in the little churchyard reading the quaint inscriptions on many of the monuments, especially that of Grace Darling's, whose memory is justly held in great reverence, love and pride.

And then the little old caretaker of the church asked us to go and see her yet older and crippled mother, who would tell us so much of the Forsters and show us some gifts that had been held in her family for generations.

From time immemorial Bamboro' has been visited by the grandest and the greatest of the realm on hostile and peaceful intent bent, happily only of the latter kind for many a year now, and there are many who in the summer seek this retired spot for the rest it affords. In the days of our stay there Sir Henry Irving was wont to pace the beach or country road, book in hand, studying the lines of Cymbaline.

How vividly does the last night of our stay at Bamboro' come to mind! At low tide we wandered far out on the sands and looking backward viewed for the last time, this grand old Castle and fortress, the scene of so many struggles, fierce and destructive, by sea and by land, yet like a mighty Sphinx immovable, calm and majestic with the rays of the setting sun resting in glory upon tower and turret. As for centuries it has stood, so it will stand, when we, like those whose memory we came to reverence, have passed on and generations will have followed us.

ST. AIDAN'S CHURCH.

A Description of the Old Parish Church of the Forster Family in Bamburgh, Northumberland Co., England—The Chancel and Crypt Cover the Remains of Sixty-three of the Forsters.

The Glebe, Bamburgh, Belford, Northumberland, England—March 30, 1895.

Bamburgh is now a small place, inhabited chiefly by agricultural laborers, and the distressed state of the land in England renders owners incapable of doing much for church restoration—especially as the old churches have required so much repair of late years. Lord Armstrong has purchased Bamburgh Castle, and will live there part of the year—partly as a change from his property at Craigside, Rothberry, and partly to overlook a Convalescent Home for decayed gentlefolks, which he will raise on the Castle Hill at Bamburgh. Will you tell your friends that all the armor belonging to the Forsters, with family pictures, and other relics, have been in the hands of the "Crewe Trustees"—five clergymen elected for the purpose of Lord Crewe's charities under his will. Lord Crewe was the Bishop of that name who married Dorothy Forster, the aunt of the Dorothy, Walter Besant's heroine. The Crewe Trustees have been forced in these bad times to part with Bamburgh Castle and some farms near it to Lord Armstrong, but they retain the family pictures, etc., and the valuable library, which contains some early printed books of the greatest rarity and value.

Your ancestors' name is highly thought of in this part of England (and everywhere amongst educated people). Lord Armstrong, I am sure, would give people leave to go through the old buildings, as well as Adderstone Hall, five miles from Bamburgh, where the Forsters partly lived. He has recently restored the Hall and has presented it to some members of his family. This whole part is very full of historical interest, and would, I am sure, afford great delight. Allow me to add that nothing touches the hearts of Englishmen so much as the love of the American people for the old country and its antiquities.

The old Castle still under restoration; but nothing has been done to impair its character—and the drawings of the restored buildings will assure you of Lord Armstrong's reverence for antiquity. The chief architect, Mr. Ferguson, of Carlisle, is the famed restorer of Haworth Castle, the seat of Lord Carlisle. That work of restoration is a most skillful and successful attempt to harmonize new and old. The old characterizes the building and the new looks old.

We are engaged in the work for the restoration of Bamburgh Church. The chancel is approaching completion—so far as the roof goes—but the interior will require a large outlay. The chancel and crypt cover the remains of sixty-three Forsters.

H. F. LONG.

ST. AIDAN'S CHURCH, EXTERIOR.

Bamburgh, on the mainland, with Holy Island and the Farne Islands off the coast, is the chief source of English Christianity. Bamburgh Crag, a natural fortress of volcanic rock, formed, in Saxon times, the seat of a Kingdom which stretched from the Humber to the Forth, with a protectorate or ascendancy over almost the whole Heptarchy. Ida, the founder of the Kingdom, landed with his followers, the Angles, above the Tweed, and seized the magnificent rock known to the Britons as Dingueroy, and afterwards to the Anglians as Bebbanburgh, or Bamburgh, from Bebba, the wife of Ida's grandson. Here dwelt Oswald, the Royal Saint, to whose zeal and guidance we owe the rise and march of English Christianity—as distinct from foreign importations. Not long after his accession, Oswald invited S. Aidan from the island monastery of Iona, and gave him a commission to evangelise his realm. And so it was, remarks Professor Bright, that, in the summer of 635, S. Aidan approached his task. From the outset, the Saint maintained his Celtic views and practices—the Celtic Easter, Celtic monasticism, Celtic discipline, the Celtic tonsure, and the Celtic form of Baptism. His first settlement, indeed, betrayed his preferences; for he carried with him the remembrance of Iona, his island home, reproducing it in Lindisfarne or Holy Island. Here his position corresponded with his origin: he became a Missionary Bishop, of the same type as the Monks of Iona, and was sent without foreign authority from the neighboring Scottish Church, at the summons of the Northumbrian King.

As the friend of S. Oswald, the Saint spent much of his time at Bamburgh, where he raised a Church of wood, as the Anglian manner was, and died in a small cell at the west end, in view, tradition says, of the Altar, and within hearing of the Vesper Service.

The above Church, passing through Norman and later stages, is the successor of the wooden church, occupies the same site, and perpetuates the same associations. Its Christianising influence was great. From the group of Lindisfarne, the Farne Islands, and Bamburgh—all united in religious work—missionaries flowed over most of the Heptarchy. The same spirit of independence which marked S. Aidan and the Celtic school characterised their work; and thus the whole of England bears witness to S. Aidan's impress.

In this view, the Church of S. Aidan, at Bamburgh, is a center of national interest; and Churchmen in every part of the Anglican world have a right to share in its history, by contributing to the preservation and increasing the beauty of this great Church memorial.

The Church is a noble structure many feet in length, and stands on a slope rising towards the Budle Hills, in view of Holy Island and the Farnes, with which it forms a group of sacred places. The site dips eastwards, and in the hollow is a Crypt, probably built at first at the eastern extremity of the Saxon Chancel. The present Chancel, 60 feet in length, was built over the Crypt and over the site of the older Chancel. The authors of this change were the Augustinian Canons from the Priory of Nostell, in Yorkshire, to which, as the parent of similar institutions in the North, Henry I. assigned the Church and land in Bamburgh. These Canons raised for themselves a monastery east of the Churchyard (on the site afterwards belonging to the Forsters, and associated with the life of Dorothy Forster), and carried out the subsequent alterations in the church—such as the enlargement of the transepts for Chantry Chapels, and the widening of the South Aisle for parochial purposes.

The internal walls of the Chancel are adorned with a beautiful arcade which frames 13 lancet windows of exquisite design; but the eastern windows were, at some time, dwarfed to suit the low roof which now remains and needs renovation. It is proposed to restore the windows to their original height, as shown by existing traces, and to raise the roof to its ancient pitch.

The effect will be a great accession of dignity to the Church, and the improvement of the building for acoustic purposes. In place of the plaster-work on the inner wall at the east end of the Chancel, it is intended to erect canopies of Caen stone, enclosing historical figures of S. Aidan, S. Oswald, S. Cuthbert, and other missionaries who spread Christianity from this part of Northumberland. or contributed to its annals.

A Faculty has issued from the Bishop's Court authorising the above alterations in the Church.

In the Churchyard, it is proposed to raise a bronze canopy over Grace Darling's monument, in place of the stone cover which was blown down in the terrible gale of November, 1893. The monument is a raised tomb, supporting a recumbent figure of the heroine, whose character is beautifully expressed in the humble modesty and Christian strength of the face and mien:

> "Pious and pure, modest, and yet so brave;
> Though young, so wise; though meek, so resolute."

ST. AIDAN'S CHURCH, INTERIOR.

OTHER ENGLISH FORSTER BRANCHES.

The name Forster, Foster is by high and most competent authority identified with Forester, which, in English opinion, is quite an aristocratic surname. A Reginaldus le Forester was in the House of Commons in 1347.

The Forsters in England were a very numerous family and besides occupying many large estates in that country emigrated to Ireland and the Island of Jamaica. We give below a few of the prominent branches:

FOSTERS OF SHOPSHIRE—This ancient Shopshire family springs from Richard Forestarius, who lived in the reign of Henry III. John Forester, of Walling Street, Co. Salop, held from Henry VIII. a grant of the privilege of wearing his hat in the royal presence, the original of which grant is now in possession of Lord Forester. From this John lineally descended, Francis Forster, of Dothill, Co. Salop, who m. Mary, dau. of Richard, Lord Newport, of Ercall. His son, Sir Wm. Forester, Knt., of Dothill, m. Cecil, dau. of James, 3d Earl of Salisbury, and was s. by his son, Wm. Forester, Esq., who m., 1714, Catherine, dau. of Wm. Brooke, Esq., and had issue: Brook Forester, Esq., who m. in 1734 Elizabeth, only dau. and heir of Geo. Weld, Esq., of Welley Park, Co. Salop, by whom he had two sons, Geo. (who d. unm. in 1811, and devised his fortune to his nephew, the late peer) and Cecil Forester, Esq., who m. dau. and co-heir of Robert Townsend, Esq., by whom (who died at an advanced age, 24th May, 1825) he had Cecil Weld Forester, Esq., who inherited the estates of his uncle, and was elevated to the peerage, as Baron Forester, of Willey Park, Co. Salop, 17th July, 1821. His lordship m. 16th June, 1800, Katherine Mary, second dau. of Charles, 4th Duke of Ruthland, by whom (who d. 10th May, 1820) he had issue, John George Weld, present peer. Geo. Cecil Weld, M. P., b. 10th May, 1807, an officer in the horse guards. Chas. Robert Weld, b. 28th December, 1811, lieutenant of the Twelfth Lancers. Orlando Watkin Weld, b. 18th April, 1813, in holy orders. Emilieus John, an officer in the army. Henry Townsend, b. 19th January, 1821, in the guards. Anne Elizabeth, m. 1802, to the Earl of Chesterfield. Elizabeth Katherine, m. 1822, to the Hon. Robert John Smith, and d. 22d July, 1832. Isabella Elizabeth Annabella, m. 30th November, 1830, to the Hon. George Anson. Henrietta Maria, m. 6th July, 1833, to Lord Albert, Co. Selina Louisa. The baron d. 1828. Creation 17th July, 1821. Arms Quarterly: first and fourth, quarterly, perfesse, dancettee, ar and sa, in the first and fourth quarters, a bugle horn of the last, garnished, or for Forester; second and third, az a fesse embattled, between three crescents, two and one, erm. for Weld. Crest of Foresters, a talbot, passant, ar, collard, sa and line reflexed, ar. Crest of Weld, a wivern, sa., gutte's-d'or, collard, and interior of the wings of the last line reflexed over the back, gu. Supporters, two talbots, ar., collard, sa therefrom pendant a bugle horn, as in the arms, line reflexed over the bark, erm. Motto, semper eadem. Seal, Willey Park, Shopshire.

FOSTER OF LYSWAYS HALL—Foster, Charles, of Lysways Hall, Co. Stafford, M. P. for Walsall, D. L. and J. P. Co. Stafford, m. August, 1840, Frances, dau. of the late John Surtus, Esq., of Durham, and of Chalean La Colinois, in Brittany, cousin of the Earl of Elden and has three sons: i. Charles, b. 1841; ii. John Henry, b. 1843; iii. Villius Francis, b. 1850.

Lineage.—Until a century back the Forsters were settled in Worcestershire. William Foster, of Birtsmorton in that county, m. Margaret Smith, a descendant and co-representative of Capt. John Smith who 1603 was in the service of Sigismond, Duke of Fransylvania, and left one son, Charles Foster, Esq., who d. at Walsall, in Staffordshire, 28th June, 1815, leaving issue, Charles Smith, his heir; John of Hanch, Co. Stafford. The elder son Charles Smith Foster, of Lysways Hall, Co. Stafford, J. P. and D. L., M. P. for Walsall, high sheriff 1845, m. Elizabeth, dau. of Richard Emery, Esq., of Burcott, House Shropshire, and left at his decease, 17th November 1850, one son, Charles, now of Lysways Hall, and one dau., Ellen Catherine, m. to Richard Dyott, Esq., of Freeford.

FOSTER OF JAMAICA, EGHAM AND KEMPSTONE.—Foster, the Rev. Frederic Adolphus La Trobe, of Kempstone, Bedfordshire and of the Boym and Lancaster Estates, Jamaica, Rector of Little Munden Herts, b. 12th October, 1820; m. 2d May, 1849, Annie Hulbert, dau. of the Rev. William Reed, of Stone Easton,

Co. Somerset, domestic chaplain to His late R. H. the Duke of Kent; and his issue: i. Frederick La Trobe, b. 31st July, 1853. ii. Henry Reed, b. 25th January, 1860. v. Annie Louisa; vi. Caroline Nora; iii. Hellen Mary; iv. Lelia Kate.

Lineage.—This family claims to be descended from the ancient and distinguished house of Forster or Foster of Etherston Castle, Lucker and Bamborough Castle, Northumberland, the ancestor of which, according to tradition, was De Forestier, a Norman cavalier who came over with William the Conqueror. Thomas Foster, of Etherston, b. 1397, d. 1425, was father of Thomas Forster, who m. a Featherstonhaugh. His son, Thomas Forster, m. the sister of the Blind Baron of Hilton. His son, Sir Thomas Forster, was high sheriff of Northumberland 1564 and 1572; and m. Dorothy, dau. of Lord Ogle. His son, Sir Thomas Forster, b. 1518, m. Frances, sister of Thomas, Lord Wharton. His brother, Sir John Forster, was a distinguished military leader in the fueds between the English and Scottish Borderers, and was governor of Bamborough, and warden of the Middle Marches; he signed the treaty concluded in 1563 between Queen Elizabeth and Mary Queen of Scots. He m. Jane, widow Robert 5th Lord Ogle and eldest dau. of Sir Cuthbert Radclyffe and Margaret his wife, dau. of Henry, Lord Clifford. He d. 1602, leaving (with a dau., Eleanor, m. to Sir Francis Russell whose son was 1st Earl of Bedfordshire) a son, Sir Nicholas Forster, governor of Bamborough, Lord of Blanchland. He m. Jane, dau. of Sir Anthony Ratcliffe, and d. 22d July, 1613. His son, Sir Claudius Forster, Bart., m. Elizabeth, dau. of Sir William Fenwick; d. 1623, and was father of Sir William Forster, who m. first Dorothy, dau. of Sir William Selby, Bart. of Twisdal, and secondly Eleanor, dau. of Ferdinand, Lord Fairfax, and had issue: William, d. s. p.; John, M. P. for Northumberland, d. unm.; and Ferdinand, M. P. for Northumberland, d. unm. His nephew, Thomas Forster, of Etherston and Lucker, b. 1659, m. his cousin, Francis, dau. of Sir William Forster of Bamborough Castle. He was high sheriff of Northumberland, and d. 1723. His son, Thomas Forster, b. 1683, by whom and from whose time the spelling of Foster has been used, was M. P. for Northumberland. His estates forfeited for the part he took in the rebellion of 1715, and were granted to Lord Crewe, Bishop of Durham, who had m. Dorothy Foster, the aunt of the said Thomas Forster. In 1715 he surrendered, together with Lord Derwentwater and others, and was sent to London and committed to Newgate on the charge of high treason, whence he afterward escaped through the aid intrepidity of his sister Dorothy, and fled to the continent. He d. leaving no male representative of this branch of the family, but the descent is traced in the Harl MSS. from Roger Forster, the brother of Thomas Forster above mentioned, as having m. the sister of the Blind Baron of Hilton. Roger Forster m. a dau. of ——Hursey; his son, Thomas Forster, of Hunsdon Herts, yeoman of the great chamber to Queen Elizabeth, m. Margaret Browning, and d. 1571. His son, Sir Thomas Forster, of Hunsdon, b. 1548; m. Susan, dau. of Thomas Forster of Iden, Co. Sussex. He was chief justice of the Court of Common Pleas, and d. 1612. His second son, Sir Robert Foster, of Great Fosters Egham, b. 1589, was chief justice of the Court of King's Bench, and d. 1665. Thomas Foster, eldest son of Sir Thomas, m. Ann Baskerville, and had issue. His second son, Col. John Foster, of Egham, held a military command in the expedition to Jamaica under Penn and Venables, 1655. He received a grant of extensive estates in the parish of S. Elizabeth in that island, the greater part of which are still in the possession of the family. His son, Thomas Foster, perished in the earthquake at Port Royal, 1692. His son, Col. John Foster, of Egham, Surrey and of Elim, the Bogue, Two Mile Wood, Lancaster, Waterford, The Island and other estates in Jamaica, resided in Elim in that island. He was b. July, 1681, and d. 30th August, 1731. He m. Elizabeth Smith of Barbadoes, and by her (who m. secondly Dr. Henry Barham of Jamaica) had issue: i. Thomas, b. 1720, d. s. p. He resided upon the family estate at Egham, Co. Surrey, and was M. P. for Dorchester. His will give rise to a lengthened litigation. ii. William, of whom presently. iii. John, b. 1723, d. unm. 1744. iv. Samuel, b. 1725, m. and had issue: 1. John of Egham, Surrey, and of Elim, Lancaster and Two Mile Wood, Jamaica, m. and had issue: George, who m. and had issue, a son, George John Henry, capt. Twenty-third regt., m. and had issue: Henry, rector of Col. Rogers, Gloucestershire canon of Gloucester, m. Ellen, youngest dau. of the late Rear-Admiral Sir Michael Seymour, Bart., K. C. B., and had issue: John, Her Majesty's chaplain of the Savoy, rector of Stambourne, m. Laura, dau. of Col. Lapsley, R. A., and d. 1868, having had issue. 2. Samuel Warren, had issue; 3. Richard, d. unm. 1. Elizabeth, m. to John Venner, Esq.; 2. Flora, m. to her cousin, John Foster, Esq., of Brickhill House, Beds. v. Joseph b. 1729, afterward took the name Barham in addition to that of Foster, and had issue: 1. Mary, m. Florentius Vassal, Esq., whose granddau., Elizabeth Vassal, m. first Sir Godfrey Webster, Bart., and afterwards Henry Richard, 3d Baron Holland; 2. Margaret, m. to Conlin Campbell, Esq.; 3. Elizabeth, d. 1729. vi. Sarah, m. William Mathew Burt, governor of Shanta Cruz, captain-general and governor-in-chief of the Leeward Islands. The second son, William Foster, b. 1722, d. 1768; he m. first Elizabeth Vassal, but by her had no issue, and second, 8th February, 1743, Dorothy Gale, of Acomb, near York, and of Lucena in the Island of Jamaica, of an old distinguished family, and by her had issue: 1. Thomas of Grove House, Chalfont, St. Giles, Buckinghamshire and St. Pol in the Pyrennese, b. 19th August, 1752, had issue by his first wife, Deborah Senior: i. Thomas, and second, William, both d. unm. 1. Elizabeth Deborah m. to Rear-Admiral Sir Thomas Ursher, K. C. B. and K. G. H.; 2. Maria Catharine, m. to William Pennefather, Esq.; 3. Dorothy Valina, m. first to Capt. Fergus, R. N., secondly to Robert Strong, Esq., and thirdly to Baron d' Eisendecker; 4. Emma Louisa Keith, m. to James Esdaile Hammet, Esq. By his second wife, Elizabeth Overend, the above named Thomas Foster, of the Grove, had issue: 1. Marianne, m. to her cousin, Herman Von Zezschwitz, capt. in the Saxon cavalry; 2. Harriet, m. to her cousin, Edward Von Zezschwitz, major in the Saxon army chamberlin to the King Saxony. The male line in this the eldest surviving branch thus became extinct. ii. Frederic William, of the Bouge Estate, Jamaica, a bishop of the Moravian Church, b. 1760, m. 1791 Anna Louisa Eleanor La Trobe, of a noble refugee family from Languedoc, and d. at Ockbrook, Co. Derby, 1835, having had issue: 1. John Frederic, of whom presently; 2. William of Ockbrook, Co. Derby, b. 1797, m. Marianne, second dau. of Sir William Bayshawe of the Oaks and Wornahill Hall, Derbyshire, and d. 1829, having had issue, one son, Fredrick William, b. June, 1818, d. April, 1838; 3. Isaac Henry, b. 1800, d. unm. 1827. 1. Anna Dorothy, m. to John Amery, Esq., banker at Stonebridge; 2. Mary Louisa, m. to her cousin, the Rev. P. La Trobe of Ely Place, London, secretary to the Moravian Missions; 3. Margaret Eleanor, d. unm. 1833. iii. John, of the Bogue Estate, Jamaica, and of Brickhill House, and Lord of the Manor of Marston, Co. Bedford (see Foster of Brickhill). 1. Elizabeth Dorothy, m. to W. H. Weber, Esq.; 2. Sarah, m. to Baron Christlieb, Frederick Von Zezschwitz of Taubenhem and Deutsch Baslitz in Upper Lusatia, an ancient distinguished Saxon family, and had issue. iii. Anna Benigna, b. 1758, d. unm.; iv. Mary Helden, m. to John Roederer, Esq., of Neuwied on the Rhine. The eldest son of Fredrick William Foster, John Frederic Foster, Esq., of the Bogue Estate, Jamaica, and of Kempstone, Co. Bedford, barrister-at-law, J. P. for Lancashire and Cheshire, and D. L., chairman of the Quarter Sessions for the hundred of Salford, Co. Lancaster, b. 18th June, 1795, m. 13th May, 1817, Caroline, eldest dau. of the late Sir William Chambers, Bagshawe of the Oaks and Wormhill Hall, Co. Derby, and of Coats Hall, Co. York, and had issue: i. John William Bagshawe, b. 1818, d. 1828; ii. Fredric Adolphus La Torbe, now of Kempstone; iii. Thomas Barnham, civil engineer, b. 8th July, 1827, m. 15th September, 1858, Mary Anne, dau. of Samuel Taylor, Esq., J. P. and D. L of Ibbotsholme, Co. Westmoreland, and Eccleston, Co Lancaster, and had issue, Fredric Barnham, b. 27th June, 1859. iv. William Henry, commissioner of crown lands, warden of the gold fields, and protector of the Chinese, and J. P in the colony of Victoria, b. 25th April, 1832, m. 2d September, 1858, Catharina McLean, dau. of Alexander Patterson, Esq , and has issue, John Frederick, b. July, 1859. i. Caroline Louisa, m. to Edward Loyd, Esq., banker, of Prestwick Lodge, Co. Lancaster, and Lillisden, Kent, J. P and D. L.; ii. Mary Eleanor, m. 29th April, 1851, to James Collier Harter, Esq., of Oak End, Co. Lancaster, and d. 24th December, 1857; iii. Margaret Helen, m. to Arthur, son of Sir Benjamin Heywood, Bart. Mr. Foster d. 9th April, 1858.

FOSTER OF BRICKHILL.—Foster, Morgan Hugh, Esq., of the Bogue, Lancaster and Two Mile Wood Estates, Jamaica, and of Brickhill near Bedford, Companion of the Order of the Bath, b. 1815, m. 1838 Mary, dau. of George Flint, Esq., and has surving issue: i. Algernon Craufurd, b. 1st December, 1839; ii. Edward, b. 1841, d. young; iii. Arthur, b. 21st July, 1843; iv. William Erskine, b. 21st October, 1847; i. Alice, d young; ii. Edith Margaret; iii. Florence Amelia.

Lineage.—The same as the preceding family down to John Foster of the Bogue Estate, Jamaica, and of Brickhill House, Bedfordshire, Lord of the Manor of Marston in the same county, a magistrate in England and in Jamaica, for many years chairman of the Central Agricultural Society in London, b. 21st June, 1831. In consequence of the eminent services he had rendered to agriculture, as well by his speeches as by his writings, he was presented with two magnificent pieces of plate, one by the agriculturists of Co. Bedford and the other by the agriculturists of the whole of England. He m. first Margaret, dau. of Thomas Place, Esq., recorder of York, and had issue: William, who d. unm.; Thomas, d. young; Edward, d. young; Margaret, m. to the Rev. Maurice Farrel, rector of Woughton Bucks. John Foster, m. secondly his cousin, Flora Foster, but by her had no issue; thirdly Amelia, dau. of John Morgan, Esq., barrister-at-law, recorder at Maidestone, and sister of the Countess of Carhampton. Of this last marriage there was issue Algernon, b. 1811, d. 1821; Arthur Fitz John, heir to his father; Morgan Hugh, now of Brickhill House; Mary Amelia, m. to the Rev. Henry Fuller, rector of Thornhaugh and Wansford, Northamptonshire; Flora, m. to the Rev. Alfred Dawson, rector of Flitwick, Bedfordshire. The eldest surviving son, Arthur Fitz John Foster, Esq., of the Bogue Estate and of Brickhill, barrister-at-law, and member of the House of Assembly, Jamaica, b. 1813, d. unm. 1842, and was s. by his brother, the present Morgan Hugh Foster of Brickhill, near Bedford.

FOSTER, BARHAM BRANCH.—Joseph Foster, Esq. (youngest son of Col. John Foster), b. 1729, d. 1789. He took the name of Barham, and m. first Dorothea, dau. and eventual heir of Erasmus Vaughn, Esq., of Treecwn, Co. Pembroke; secondly Lady Hill of Hawkstone. The eldest son of the first marriage, Joseph Foster Barham, Esq., of Trecwn and of Stock bridge Hants, b. 1760, M. P. for that borough, m. 1792 Lady Caroline Tufton, dau. of Sackville 8th Earl of Thanet, and had issue, several sons and daus. The eldest son, John Foster Barham, who was M. P. for Stockbridge and afterwards for Kendal, m. Lady Katharine Grimston, dau. of the Earl of Verulam, who survived her husband, and is the present Countess of Clarendon. The second son, William Foster Barham, d. unm. The third son, the Rev. Charles Henry Barham, how of Trecwn, nephew and sole representative of Henry, last Earl of Thanet, m. first Miss Ince, and secondly Miss Massey, but has no issue. There are also two daus., Mary who m. Count Gaggiotti, and Caroline who m. the Rev. Sanderson Robins, rector of Shaftesbury.

FOSTER OF BALLYMASCANLAN.—Foster, Fredrick John, Esq., of Ballymascanlan House, Co. Louth, J. P. and D. L., High Sheriff 1845, m. 22d October, 1827, Isabella, fourth dau. of Peter Vere, Esq.

Lineage.—William Foster, Esq., M. P. for Dunlier (second son of the Rev. Thomas Foster, D. D., and nephew of the Right Hon. Anthony Foster, lord chief baron of Ireland, father of John Foster, speaker of the Irish House of Commons, afterward Lord Oriel), m. 1743 Patience, dau. of John Fowke, Esq., and had issue: i. John William, M. P. for Dunlier, who m. 1788 Rebecca, only child of Hamilton McClure, Esq., of Dublin, and d. 1809, having had issue: 1. Fredrick John of Ballymascanlan House; 2. William Hamilton, d. 1813; 3. Henry, d. 1820; 4. Charles Thomas, d. 1822. 1. Elizabeth Susan; 2. Louisa Jane, m. 26th October, 1819, to Thomas, Lord Plunkett, D. D., Bishop of Tuam; 3. Emily Anna. ii. Henry. i. Patience, m. 1766 to John McClintock, Esq., M. P.; ii. Elizabeth, m. to John Longfield, Esq., M. P.

FOSTER OF WADSWORTH BANKS.—Foster, Henry, Esq., of Wadsworth Banks and Tolling Royd, Co. York, J. P., b. 29th May, 1795.

Lineage.—The ancestors of this family came from Wensleydale, N. R of Yorkshire, about 400 years ago, to the Slack near Heptonstall, which they obtained by purchase. The Slack estate is still retained by a branch of the same family, and the present occupier and owner is John Foster, Esq., who m. the only dau. and heir of Henry Lord, Esq., of Bacup, Lancashire. John Foster, Esq., of Slack, and son of Thomas Foster, Esq., of the same place, m. Elizabeth, dau. of Thomas Greenwood, who erected the chapel at Slack at his own expense and preached in it gratuitously; by this lady Mr. Foster had, with a dau., three sons: John, from whom the present John Foster, Esq., of Slack; Henry, of whom presently; and William, who d. s. p. The second son, Henry Foster, Esq., removed from Slack to his own estate at Wadsworth Banks, about the year 1870. He m. Ann Townsend of Heptonstall, and had, with a dau. Mary, who d. s. p., aged 73, a son, John Foster, Esq., of Wadsworth Banks, who m. 23d December, 1790, Sarah, dau. of William Howorth Gent of White Lee, and had (with dau. Elizabeth who d. young) an only son, the present Henry Foster, Esq., of Wadsworth Banks. Mr. Foster d. 12th September, 1812, aged 51.

FOSTER OF THURNBY.—Foster, Hon. William John, of Thurnby, Newton, New South Wales, prime Judge of the Supreme Court of N. S. W., b. at Rathescar, Co. Louth. 13th January, 1831, m. 8th August, 1854, Matilda Sophia, dau. of John Williams, Esq., of Landigige, Pembrokeshire, South Wales, by Jane Makeig his wife, and has issue: i. Arthur William John, b. 24th June, 1855; ii. William Henry, b. 24th May, 1856, m. 1886 Ella, dau. of George Clift, Esq., and has issue, a daughter; iii. Thomas Chichester James, b. 5th September, 1858; iv. Edward Pokenham, b. 25th June, 1860; v. Frederick Leopold, b. 18th April, ——; vi. Charles Ernest, b. 1st December, 1871; vii. Rodolph Wellesley, b. 26th Sepetember, 1874. i. Catharine Jane, m. 1st August, 1882, Lieut. Henry John Jeffreys, R. N.; ii. Welhelmina Rosalind, m. 29th September, 1886, William McIntyre St. Clair Maclardy, Esq., of Sydney; iii. Helen Mary Elizabeth, unm. Mr. Justice Foster was educated first at Cheltenham College; settled in Victoria in 1854 (having visited the colony two years previously), and engaged for a short time in agricultural pursuits; subsequently studied for the bar and was admitted 13th May, 1858; the following year was appointed crown prosecutor for the northern district, and in 1870 crown prosecutor for Sydney, which office he resigned December, 1877, and became attorney-general under the Farnell administration, with a seat in the Legislative Council, which he resigned in 1880; afterward became M. P. for Newton; in 1881 minister of justice in the Parke's ministry; and again in 1887 attorney-general, which office he subsequently resigned in February, 1888, was appointed a judge of the Supreme Court of N. S. W. Mr. Justice Foster has written a treatise on the District Courts Act, which is still regarded as the standard work on that subject. He has been a member of every diocesan provincial and general synod of the Church of England constituted in New South Wales.

Lineage.—Mr. Justice Foster traces his discent through the families of Fortescue, Chichester and Bonchier, back to King Edward III. According to tradition his paternal ancestors were formerly seated in Berkshire, whence they migrated to Ireland. John Foster, Esq., of Dunlier, Co. Louth, for many years M. P. for that borough, m. 10th December, 1704, Mary, youngest dau. of William Fortescue, Esq., of Newarth, Co. Louth, who was grandfather of William Henry, first Earl of Clermont and son of Sir Thomas Fortescue, Knt. of Dromeskin, Co. Louth, lieutenant-colonel of Prince Charles' Horse Guards, and governor of the Castle of Carrickfergus, and by her (who d. 29th October, 1762, aged 77 years) left at his decease, 16th May, 1747: i. Anthony (Right Hon.), of whom hereafter; ii. Thomas (Rev.), D. D., rector of Dunlier, b. 16th November, 1709, m. 1740 Dorothy, dau. of William Burgh, Esq., of Bert, Co. Keldare, and was s. by his son, John Thomas, of Dunlier, some time M. P., who m. 2d April, 1776, Lady Elizabeth Hervey, dau. of Fredrick Augustus, fourth Earl of Bristol, Lord Bishop of Derry, and d. 1795, having had by her (who m. secondly, 19th October, 1809, William, fifth Duke of Devonshire, K. G., but d. s. p. by him 20th March, 1824): 1. Fredrick Thomas, b. 2d October, 1777, M. P.; 2. Augustus John (Right Hon. Sir), Bart., P. C., G. C. H. of Stonehouse, Co. Louth, b. December, 1780, was appointed envoy extraordinary and minister plenipotentiary to the United States 1812, and subsequently to Sweden, Denmark and Sardinia. He was created a baronet 30th September, 1831; he m. 18th March, 1815, Lady Albina Jane, dau. of the Hon. George Vere Hobart, second son of George, third Earl of Buckinghamshire, and d. 1st August, 1848 (his widow dying 28th May, 1867) having had: i. Fredrick George (Sir), who s. as second baronet, b. 3d January, 1810, and d. unm. 25th December, 1857; ii. Cavendish Hervey (Rev. Sir) of Glyde Court, Ardee, Co. Louth, rector of Theydon Garnow, Epping, Co. Essex, 1843 to 1857, b. 7th May, 1817; educated at Eton and Magdalene College, Cambridge (B. A. 1841); s. his brother as third baronet 25th December, 1857; m. 15th January, 1844, Isabella, youngest dau. of the Rev. John Todd, curate of Frankley and S. Kenelm, Halesowen, Co. Salop, and by her (who d. 3d June, 1881) has: 1. John Frederick, J. P. and D. L., high sheriff Co. Louth 1875, late major Sixth battalion Royal Irish Rifles (Louth militia) and formerly of the Thirteenth Hussars, b. 18th January, 1847, educated at Marlborough and Magdalene College, Cambridge; m. 20th April, 1871, Caroline Emily, eldest dau. of Thomas Coxhead Chesendale Marsh, Esq., of Gaynes Park, Co. Essex, and has issue: Augustus Vere, b. 30th March, 1873; Emily Albinea, Mary Isabella and Alice Jane Blanche. 2. Hervy, lieutenant Royal Irish Rifles, b. 20th June, 1851, d. unm. 31st March, 1887. 1. Jane Vere, m. 2d October, 1872, to Robert Boothby Heathcote, Esq., of Friday Hill Chingford, Co. Essex. iii. Vere Henry Louis, b. 25th April, 1819. iii. William, M. P. for Dunlier, who m. 1743 Patience, dau. of John Fowke, Esq., of Dublin, and d. 24th August, 1783, leaving issue: 1. John William of Casterling, Co. Louth, D. L., M. P. for Dunlier, b. 1745; m. 1788 Rebecca, only child of Hamilton McClure, Esq., of Dublin, and d. 1809, having had issue: i. Fredrick John of Casterling and Ballymascanlan, Dundalk, Co. Louth, J. P. and D. L., high sheriff Co. Louth 1845, b. 1799, m. 22d October, 1827, Isabella, fourth dau. of Peter Vere, Esq., of Carltonian, Trent, Co. Nottingham; ii. William Hamilton, d. 1813; iii. Henry, d. 1820; iv. Charles Thomas, d. 1822. i. Elizabeth Susan; ii. Louisa

Jane, m. 26th October, 1819, Thomas Span, second Baron Plunket, P. C., D. D., Lord Bishop of Tuam, Killalu and Achonry, being so consecrated in 1839; and had issue, female (see Burkes Peerage); iii. Emily Anna, d. 1874. 2. Henry. 1. Patience, m. 1866 to John McClintock, Esq., M. P.; 2. Elizabeth, m. to John Longfield, Esq., M. P. i. Margaret, m. to Stephen Sibthorpe, Esq., of Brownston; ii. Charlotte, m. 1738 to Nicholas Forster, Esq., of Tullaghan, great grandfather of Sir Thomas Oriel Forster, Bart. of Coolderry, Co. Monaghan, Ireland. The eldest son, the Right Hon. Anthony Foster, Lord Chief Baron of the Exchequer, Ireland, from 1776 to 1777, b. 12th December, 1705, m. first 25th February, 1736, Elizabeth, dau. of William Burgh, Esq., of Bert, Co. Kildare, and by her (who d. 30th July, 1744) had: 1. John (Right Hon.) Baron Oriel, so created 17th July, 1821, P. C. Great Britain, chancellor of the exchequer, and last speaker of the Irish House of Commons from 1785 to 1801, barrister-at-law of the Middle Temple, b. 28th September, 1740, m. 14th December, 1764, Margaret Amelia, dau. of Thomas Burgh, Esq., M. P. of Bert, Co. Kildare. She was created a peeress of Ireland as Baroness Oriel in 1790 and Viscountess Ferrard 1797. Lord Oriel d. 16th August, 1828, having had issue, besides a dau., Anne Dorothea who m. James Blackwood, Esq., an only son, Thomas Henry, afterward Thomas Henry Foster Skeffington, Viscount Forard, who m. 29th November, 1810 Harriet (nee Skeffington), Viscountess Massereene, only dau. Chichester, fourth Earl of Massereene, and d. in 1843 The Viscountess d 2d January, 1831, leaving issue. Their eldest son, John Skeffington, became Viscount Massereene, Viscount Farrard and Baron Oriel (see Burkes Peerage, Massereene Viscount). ii. William (Right Rev.) of whom presently. 1. Margaret, b. 1737, m. 1759 the Hon. and Right Rev. Henry Maxwell, D. D., Bishop of Dromose, 10th March, 1765, and of Meath 15th April, 1776, third son of John, first Baron Farnham of Farnham, Co. Cavan, Ireland, and father of John, fifth Lord, and of Rev. Henry, sixth Baron Farnham. She d. 7th October, 1798 The Lord Chief Baron m. secondly 1749 Dorothea, dau. of Thomas Burgh, Esq., of Oldtown, Co. Kildan (see Burke's Landed Gentry, De Burgh of Oldtown), and d. 3d April, 1778. His second son, Right Rev. William Foster, D. D., Bishop of Clogher, Ireland, was consecrated 14th June, 1789, Bishop of Cork and Ross, translated to Kilmore 1790, and to Clogher 1796, b. 1774, m. Catharine Letitia, dau. of Rev. Henry Leslie, D. D., of Ballybay, Co. Monaghan, prebenday of Tullycorbet Clogher, and afterward prebenday of Tandragee in the Cathedral of Armah (see Leslie of Ballibay in Burke's Landed Gentry), and d. November, 1797, having by her (who d. 1814) had issue: John Leslie (Right Hon.) of Rathescar, Co. Louth, M. P. for that county for nearly twenty years, baron of the exchequer of Ireland, m. 1814 Hon. Letitia Vesey Fitzgerald, dau. of the Right Hon. James Fitzgerald, P. C., by Catharine his wife first Baroness Fitzgerald and Vesey, and sister of Lord Fitzgerald and Vesey, and d. 1842 having by her (who upon the death of her brother Henry, third Lord Fitzgerald and Vesey in 1860 in accordance with the will of her brother William, second Lord Fitzgerald and Vesey, assumed for herself and her issue the surnames of Vesey Fitzgerald after that of Foster, and d. 1866), had issue: 1. William Foster Vesey Fitzgerald of Moyvane, Newton, Sandes, Co. Kerry, Kilmurry, MacMahon, Kilmihill, Co. Clare, and Mullacloe, Co. Louth, J. P., Cos. Clare and Kerry, b. 12th July, 1815, educated at Trinity College, Dublin (B. A. 1839), m. 27th April, 1847, Sarah Anne, only child of Henry Quilter, Esq., of Monken Hadley, Co. Middlesex, and had issue: i. John Vesey, barrister-at-law, b. 25th February, 1848, educated at Eton and Balliol College, Oxford; ii. William Vesey, b. 25th March, 1850; iii. Henry Martin, b. 1st April, 1852. 2. John Foster Vesey Fitzgerald (Hon.), J. P., b. in Dublin 1818, educated at Trinity College, Dublin, and emigrated to Australia in 1840. He was twice colonial secretary of Victoria, Australia; acting governor of Victoria in 1854; the following year was elected to the first legislative assembly under the new constitution, and held office as treasurer in the first O'Shanassy ministry in March, 1857; finally leaving the colony for Europe. He m. 1850 Emily, dau. of Rev. John Joseph Fletcher, D. D., of Dunran, Co. Wicklow, and has issue: i. John, b. 1864; ii. Emily Henrietta Louisa; iii. Anna. 3. James Foster Vesey Fitzgerald of Moyriesk Quin Co. Clare, J. P. Cos. Clare and Galaway, D. L. Co. Clare, and high sheriff of Clare 1868, b. 8th May, 1821, educated at Trinity College, Dublin (B. A. 1842), m. 4th December, 1845, Henrietta Louisa, dau. of the late Sir Ross Mahon, Bart. of Castlegar, Co. Galaway, by his third wife the Hon. Maria Geraldine Fitzgerald, dau. of the Right Hon. James Fitzgerald of Incheronan, Co. Clare, prime sergeant in Ireland, by Catharine, his wife, Baroness Fitzgerald and Vesey, and had issue: i. James, B. A. of Trinity College, Dublin, barrister-at-law, b. 1846; ii. George, captain Clare artillery, b. 1849. i. Henrietta Mary Emily, m.

1870 George Barrington Godbold, Esq., late captain Twenty-seventh regiment, and d. 24th December, 1877; ii. Geraldine Sophia, m. 1872 Robert Hume Crowe, Esq., Toorah, J. P. Co. Clare. i. Letitia; ii. William Henry, Rev., of whom hereafter. i. Catharine, m. 1805 William Drumond Delap, Esq.; ii. Anna, m. Jonas Stowell, Esq., of Old Court, Co. Cork, and had amongst other issue a son, afterward Sir William Foster Stowell, K. C. M. G. of D' Estaville, Kew, Melbourne, ex-Chief Justice of the Colony of Victoria, second son, who was b. in Co. Cork June, 1815; educated at Trinity College, Dublin (B. A. 1837), called to the Irish bar 1839; emigrated to Victoria, arriving in Melbourne 1843, and afterward held large squatting interests near Avoca and between Lake Wallace and Glenely; appointed attorney-general of Victoria 1851; returned to the legislative assembly of Victoria for Melbourne in 1856, and succeeded Sir William A. Becket as chief justice in 1857. remaining in that office until 1886, when he was appointed lieutenant-governor of the colony of Victoria. Sir W. F. Stowell was knighted in 1857, and created K. C. M. G. in 1886. In 1873 the University of Dublin conferred upon him the degree of LL.D. He m. January, 1856, Mary Frances Elizabeth, only dau. of the late William Pomeroy Greene, Esq., of Collen House, Collen, Co. Louth, Ireland, and afterward of Woodlands, Victoria, Australia, formerly lieutenant, R. N. (see Greene of Greystone), and had issue: 1. Jonas Molesworth; 2. William; 3. Charles Leslie; 4. George Cooper; 5. Richard Rawdon; 6. Rodolph de Salis. 1. Anne Catharine; 2. Mary Letitia; 3. Henrietta; 4. Melian. iii. Henrietta, m. 1810 Jerome Fane, Count de Salis, and d. 1856, leaving issue: William Fone de Salis, who emigrated to Victoria, but afterward returned to England and became chairman of the board of directors of the Peninsular and Oriental Steam Navigation Company; and the Hon. Leopold Fane de Salis, member of the Legislative Council of New South Wales. iv. Elizabeth, m. Rev. James McCreight, and had issue, a dau., Letitia, m. Edward Jeffreys, Esq.; v. Letitia, m. John Henry North, Esq., Q. C., sometime M. P. for the University of Dublin, and d. s. p. The second son, Rev. William Henry Foster, Lough Gilly, Co. Armah, and of Altamenah, Donegal, Ireland. rector of Lough Gilly, Co. Armah, and formerly midshipman, R. N., m. 18th December, 1821, Catharine, dau. of James Hamilton, Esq., of Brown Hall, Ballintra, Co. Donegal (who was maternally descended from the Scottish royal house of Stewart), by the Hon. Helen Pakenham, his wife, sister of Thomas, Earl of Longford, Major-General Sir Edward Michael Pakenham, G. C. B., Lieutenant-General Sir Hercules Robert Pakenham, K. C. B., and Catharine, wife of Arthur, the first and great Duke of Wellington, and d. 1861, having had by her (who was b. 1803 and d. 1873): i. Arthur Hamilton William, of Bell Isle and St Ernan's, Co. Donegal, J. P. Co. Donegal, b. 1824; educated at Trinity College, Cambridge; m. Arabella Rose, dau. of John Hamilton, Esq., of St. Ernan's and Brown Hall, Co. Donegal, J. P. and D. L., high sheriff 1826 (see Burke's Landed Gentry, Hamilton of Brown Hall), and has issue, four daughters: ii. William John (Hon.) of Thurnby, Newton. i. Catharine Helen, m. 1849 John James Verschoyle, Esq., of Tassaygard Saggard, Co. Dublin, and of 36 Upper Mount street, Dublin, Ireland, J. P. Co. Dublin, who was educated at Trinity College, Dublin; third son of the late John Verschoyle, Esq., of Stillorgan House, Co. Dublin (who d. 1840), by Margaret his wife, dau. of John Stuart, Esq., of Dromespil, Co. Tyrone, and has issue, besides five daughters, two sons, the elder of whom is the Rev. John Stuart Verschoyle, B. A., of Pembroke College, Cambridge, curate of Holy Trinity, St. Marylebone, London, b. 1858; ii. Catharine Wilhelmina, unm.; res. Thurnby Newton, New South Wales, Australia.

FOSTER.—Foster, the Rev. Sir Cavendish Henry, of Stonehouse, Co. Louth, rector of Thoydon, Garnon, Essex, b. 7th May, 1817; s. his brother as third bart. 25th December, 1857; m. 15th January, 1844, Isabella, youngest dau. of the late Rev. John Todd, curate of Frankley and St. Kenelm Halesowen, and by her, who d. 3d June, 1881, has: i. John Fredrick, D. L., late Thirteenth Hussars, major Sixth battalion Royal Irish Rifles, b. Jan. 18, 1847, m. 20th April, 1871, Caroline Emily, eldest dau. of T. C. Chirenhale Marsh Augustus Vere, b. 30th March, 1873: Emily Albina, Mary Isabella, Alice Jane Blanche; ii. Hervy, lieutenant Royal Irish Rifles; b. 20th June, 1851, d. unm. 31st March, 1887. 1. Jane Vere, m. 2d October, 1872, to Robert Boothby Heathcote, Esq., of Friday Hill, Chnegford, Essex.

Lineage.—John Foster, Esq., M. P. of Dunlier, Co. Louth, m. 10th December, 1704, Elizabeth, youngest dau. of William Fortescue, Esq., of Newarth, Co. Louth, and d. 16th May, 1747, leaving issue: 1. Anthony (Right Hon.), Lord Chief Baron of the Exchequer, Ireland, m. first 1736 Elizabeth, dau. of William Burgh, Esq., of Bert, Co. Kildan, and had issue: 1. John, Baron Oriel, so created 1821, Chancelor of the Exchequer and last Speaker of the Irish House of Commons, m. Margaret, dau. of Thomas Burgh, M. P. of Bert, who was created a Peeress of Ireland as Baroness Oriel in 1790, and Viscountess Ferrord 1797 (see Massereene v); 2. William (Right Rev.), Bishop successively of Cork, Kilmore and Clogher, m. Catharine Letitia, dau. of Rev. Charles Leslie, D. D., of Ballybay, Co. Monaghan, and d. 1797, having by her (who d. 1814), had issue: John Leslie, M. P. Co. Louth, Baron of the Exchequer, Ireland, m. 1814 Hon. Letitia Vesey Fitzgerald, sister of Lord Fitzgerald and Vesey, and d. 1842, having by her (who assumed the additional surname of Vesey Fitzgerald, aud d. 1866), had issue: 1. William Foster Vesey Fitzgerald, m. Sarianne, only child of Henry Quilter, Esq., of Monken Hadley, Middlesex, and has issue; 2. John Foster Vesey Fitzgerald, m. Emily, dau. of Rev. John Joseph Fletcher, D. D., of Dunran, Co. Wecklow, and has issue; 3. James Foster Vesey Fitzgerald, of Moyriesk Quin, Co. Clare, J. P., D. L., b. 8th May, 1821, m. 4th December, 1845, Henrietta Louisa, dau. of Sir Ross Mahon, Bart. of Castlegar, Co. Galaway, and has issue (see Burke's Landed Gentry); 4. Letitia. William (Rev.) rector of Loughgilly, Co. Armagh, m. Catharine, dau. of James Hamilton, Esq., ot Brownhall, Co. Donegal, and had issue. Catharine, m. 1805 to William Drumond Delap, Esq. Anna, m. to Jonas Stowell, Esq. Henrietta, m. Jerome Fane, Count de Salis, and d. 1856, leaving issue. Elizabeth, m. to Rev. James Mereight. Letitia, m. John Henry North, Esq., Q. C., M. P. 1. Margaret, m. Most Rev. Henry Maxwell, Bishop of Meath (see Farnham B), and d. 1792. The Lord Chief Baron m. secondly Dorothea, dau. of Thomas Burgh, Esq., of Oldtown, and d. 1778. ii. Thomas, of whom presently; iii. William, M. P. of Dunlier, who m. Patience, dau. of John Fowke, Esq., of Dublin, and d. 24th August, 1783, leaving issue, two daus., Patience, m. to John McClintock, Esq., M. P., and Elizabeth, m. to John Londfield, Esq., M. P., and two sons of whom the elder, John William, M. P., b. in 1745, m. Rebecca, dau. of Hamilton McClure, Esq., of Dublin, and had Fredrick John of Ballymascanlan, Co. Louth, J. P. and D. L.; Louisa Jane m. to Thomas, second Lord Plunket; Elizabeth and Emily. i Margaret, m. to Stephen Sibthorpe, Esq., of Brownston; ii. Charlotte, m. to Nicholas Foster, Esq., of Tullaghan. The second son, the Rev. Thomas Foster, D. D., rector of Dunlier, b. 16th November, 1709, m. 1740 Dorothy, dau. of William Burgh, Esq., of Birt, Co. Kildare, and was s. by his son, John Thomas Foster, Esq., of Dunlier, sometime M. P., who m. 2d April, 1776, Lady Elizabeth Hervy, dau. of Fredrick Augustus, fourth Earl of Bristol, Bishop of Derry, by whom (who m., after his decease, William, fifth Duke of Devonshire, and d. in 1824) he had issue: Fredrick Thomas, b. Oct. 2, 1777, M. P.; Augustus John. Mr. Foster d. in 1795. His second son, the Right Hon. Augustus John Foster, P. C., G. C. H., b. December, 1780, was appointed envoy extraordinary and minister plenipotentiary to the United States 1812, and subsequently to Sweden, Denmark and Sardinia. He was created a baronet 30th September, 1831; he m. 18th March, 1815, Albina Jane, dau. of the Hon. George Vere Hobart, second son of George, third Earl of Buckinghamshire, and by her (who d. 28th May, 1867) had: Fredrick George, second bart.; Cavendish Hervey, present bart.; Vere Henry Louis, b. 25th April, 1819; Sir Augustus John, d. Aug. 1, 1848, and was s. by his eldest son. ii. Sir Fredrick George, who was b. 3d January, 1816, and d. unm. 25th December, 1857.

FOSTER.—Foster, Sir William, of the city of Norwich, D. L. for Co. Norfolk, b. March, 1825, late capt. Eleventh Hussars, m. first in 1854 Georgiana, second dau. of Richard Armit, Esq., of Monkstown, Co. Dublin, and by her (who d. in 1861) had issue: i. William Yorke, b. 1st April, 1860, lieut. R. H. A., m. 10th October, 1885, Aileen Ethel, dau. of Lieut.-Col. Augustus Berkley Portman, Bombay Staff Corps (see Portman v), and had issue, Aileen Cavendish, b. 1886. i. Emily Georgiana; ii. Mary, and iii. Diana, twins. He m. secondly 25th June, 1864, Harriet, youngest dau. of Capt. Thomas George Wills, R. N., and had issue. ii. Thomas Hudson, R. H., b. 31st December, 1867; iv. Harriet; vi. Lucy, m. 1886 Lucas Temple Cobbold, Esq.; vii. Amy.

Lineage.—William Foster, Esq., of Norwich, b. in 1762 (son of William Foster of the same place by Sarah his wife, dau. of Robert Pratt also of Norwich), m. first 24th August, 1787, Mary, dau. of Jehosephat Postle, but by her had no issue; and secondly in June, 1794, Anastatia, dau. of John Beevor, M. D., of Norwich, by whom he left at his decease in 1821: i. Lambert Blackwell of Brundal, Norfolk, in holy orders, b. 27th June, 1795, m. 22d November, 1821, Mary Greene, dau. of the Rev. R. E. Browne of Elsing, and d. 16th March, 1863, having by her (who d. June, 1870) had issue: 1. Lambert Blackwell, b. Feb. 1, 1824; 2. William, b. 24th July, 1828. 1. Mary, d. unm. 29th November, 1842; 2. Anastasia, d. unm. 14th December, 1845; 3. Charlotte Frances. ii. William, created a baronet in 1838. 1. Anastasia, m. first

20th April, 1829, Giovani Pietro Guillo Francesco Cucchi Piedemonte, who d. 11th August, 1835, and secondly in 1841 to Emesto Baldassare Luigi Penotts Piedemonte. She d. July, 1855. The second son, 1. William Foster, Esq., of the city of Norwich, b. 16th June, 1798, was created a baronet 3d August, 1838. He m. 14th June, 1821, Mary Anne, dau. of Starling Day, Esq., of Norwich, banker, and by her (who d. 28th December, 1885) had issue: i. William, present bart.; ii. Charles (Thorpe Norwich), b. 12th November, 1828, m. 18th May, 1858, Charlotte, third dau. of Capt. T. G. Willis, R. N.; iii. Frances Gostling (Norwich), b. 3d July, 1830, m. first 16th August, 1853, Lucy, third surviving dau. of Capt. William Gwyn, R. N., of Tasburg Lodge, Norfolk, and by her (who d. 1864) had issue: Herbert Francis, b. July 10, 1860; Charles Blackwell, b. 13th September, 1861; Lucy Maude, m. 1886; Lucas Temple Cobbold, Esq., of Ipswich; and Alice Mary. He m. secondly 5th September, 1865, Bertha, second dau. of the late Timothy Steward, Esq., of Hugham Lodge, Norfolk, and has a son, Reginald Stewart, b. 8th January, 1867; and two daus., Winifred Bertha and Eveline Margaret. 1. Emily, d. in 1846; 2. Julia, m. 11th April, 1867, Herbert William Day, Esq., of the Heath, East Durham. Sir William d. 2d December, 1874; creation 3d August, 1838.

FOSTER OF BRICKHILL.—Foster, Arthur Fitz John, Esq,. of Brickhill Co. Bedford, b. 14th January, 1813, s. his father 30th June, 1831.

Lineage.—There is a strong presumptive evidence of the descent of this family from the Fosters of Bamborough Castle in Northumberland, but the link of connection has not been precisely ascertained. The immediate ancestor of the branch before us having forfeited his estates in England during the political troubles of the period in which he lived, joined the expedition of Pennand Venables in 1655, and obtained a grant of a considerable tract of land in the Island of Jamaica, which is now enjoyed by his descendants, the Fosters and Barhams. His son and successor, Col. John Foster, of the Island of Jamaica, d. there 30th August, 1731, aged 50, leaving four sons and three daus; viz.: i. Thomas of the Grange; ii. William, of whom presently; iii. Samuel, who m. twice; iv. Joseph, who assumed the additional surname of Barham. He m. and had issue: 1. Joseph, his heir, of Stockbridge Hants, M. P., m. in 1793 Lady Caroline Tufton, dau. of the eighth Earl of Thanet, and d. having had issue. 1. John of Trecwn, Co. Pembroke, and Stockbridge Hants, J. P. and D. L., high sheriff for Co. Pembroke in 1834, and M. P. for Kendal, b. in 1800, m. in 1834 Lady Katharene Grimston, but d. s. p. in 1838; 2. William; 3. Charles; 4. Mary, m. in 1839 to the Rev. Mr. Robins.

F. H. Foster, cashier of the Claremont, N. H., National Bank, in writing to the author, in March, 1898, says:—

In response to your request I enclose extracts which I made of data given in "Fosters and Forsters of No. of Eng.," about which I wrote you. You will notice that this particular line which I traced in the above work ends in one Reynold, fourth child of Thos. of Brunton, whose (Thos.) will was dated June, 19, 1648. The possibility occurred to me that this Reynold might have been our Reginald as the name in N. E. is spelled in various ways, viz.: Renall, Rennoll, Renol and Reginal, and there would seem from the date of his father's will that there would be no anachronism in the way. The book gives no data other than those quoted and I am absolutely without any clue or evidence which would serve to support a hypothesis upon the matter. The only tangible clue I found in my search in Boston Library was a note in Emerton and Water's gleanings from Eng. records about N. E. Families—Salem Press, 1880, p. 40, viz.:—

"Margaret Foster of Shrewsbury, Salop, May 15, 1629, widow of Thos., late of Reddington aged —. Grandchildren Reginald and Leighton Foster. Estate at Edmonton, Middlesex. D. Newell Foster, dau. Judith Hosier. The name of Judith Hosier occurs as witness to the will of Isabella Forster in 1631."

Also another note, p. 82, Part I, Vol. I, of same work, has extracts from will of Elizabeth Hailes of lower Shadwell at Stepney, in County of Middlesex, widow, 28th September, 1664. Proved March 22, 1664. "To my cousin John Foster at Tower Hill. . . . . . To my cousin William Foster at New England the full sum of ten pounds. . . . . . To my cousin Isaac Foster's daughter. . . . . ."

As you will see, neither of these "gleanings" has any apparent connection with the line which I traced from "De Buckton." The "cousin William at New England" might be the third son of Reginald, who would have been about 31 years old at the date of Elizabeth Haile's will above mentioned. This seems to me the most tangible clue of anything I have been able to find, but I do not know just how any one could follow it out without the assistance of some one on the other side.

Extracts from the "Fosters and Forsters of the North of England," Boston Pub. Library: 1. John, son of Gilbert de Buckton, called Forster, alias Forrester, who was chief game keeper and a forrester to the Bishop ot Durham, 1342. 2. John Forster of Buckton, Forrester to the Bishop of Durham, aged 26 at the death of his father. Did homage Jan. 26, 1342. 3. John Forster of Buckton, No. Durham, wf. Elizabeth. 4. Thos. Forster of Buckton, lived temp. Richard second, wf. Jean de Elmedon, co-heir to Gilbert, Earl of Angus. 5. Thos. Forster of Etherstone, liv. temp. Henry IV and wife Elizabeth heiress to her brother Roger de Etherstone, Lord of Etherstone, temp. Henry IV. 6. Thomas Forster of Etherstone,

living temp. Henry V and wife Elizabeth. 7. Thomas Forster of Etherstone, Co. Northumberland, living temp. Henry VI, wife Joan, dau. of Sir Wm. De Hylton, Knt. of Hylton Castle. Sec. to "Blind Baron." 8. Sir Thomas Forster, Knt., Marshall of Berwick on Tweed, will dated 3d March, 1526, wife Dorothy, dau. of Robert, Lord Ogle. 9. Thos. Forster of Adderstone, high sheriff of Northumberland, 5th and 14th, Elizabeth. Will dated 4th April, 1589. Wf. Florence, sister of Thomas, Lord Wharton. 10. Cuthbert Forster of Brunton, Gent, and wife Elizabeth Bradforth; will dated 1589. 11. Thomas Forster of Brunton 1615; will dated June 19, 1648. 12. Reynold Forster, fourth child of above.

Extract from "America Heraldica," Page 137. Boston Pub. Library. Bates Hall Genealogical reference books, No. 1002-4. Published in 1886. Foster.—Reginald Foster of Little Badow, Co. Essex, Eng., landed at Ipswich, Mass., 1638. He belonged to the Foster family of Bamborough and Etherstone Castle, Co. Northumberland. Reginald brought with him five sons and two daughters. We find also in the old burial ground at Charlestown, Mass., the tombstone (with the arms we give) of the wife of Richard Foster, Jr., 1724. He was the grandson of Wm. Foster, known to have been in Charlestown about 1650. These arms are those of the Fosters of Brickhill, Co. Bedford, and the Bogue, Co. Lancaster. Also represented by the Fosters of Jamaica in the West Indies. Various ancient silver articles with the Foster arms are preserved in America. Among others a large tankard with the arms beautifully engraved and the tinctures clearly indicated. It is in the possession of Edward Ingersoll Browne of Boston, the lineal descendant of the Browns of Watertown. Crest, an arm in armor embowed holding in the hand a broken tilting spear, proper.

References: Joseph Foster, Foster Genealogy, 1886. Heraldic Journal—1—56. Wyman's Charlestown Mass. Genealogies, N. E. H. and G. Reg. 1—20—25—30. (Concerns also several other branches of the Foster stock.) Sir Bernard Burke. The General Armory of England, 1884. Page 165 of above work (America Heraldica) has arms: Argent, a chevron vert between three bugle horns, sable, stringed gules. Same arms as the Fosters of St. Andrews, Co. Bedford, (Walfords Co. Families.)

Col. I. L. Vivian of London, England, in 1891 and 1892 made a search for the ancestry of the emigrant Reginald Foster, but it proved unsuccessful.

Col. Chester of London, recently deceased, was employed at one time by, I think, John Foster of Boston, but failed to accomplish anything in this direction. Col. Vivian's researches were made in both Devonshire and Suffolk. Later he writes: "I have given up Devonshire as being in no way connected with your family." Col. Vivian writes that Harlow records have been stolen or destroyed. He examined as to Bocking in Essex, whence came the Whipples of Ipswich, and where Rev. Nathaniel Rogers of Ipswich settled. Later he reports that the "Registers of Bocking prior to 1655 are lost." "The Ipswich Registers all begin before 1600, but a general search through them has proved useless." "The births also have been examined at Norwich for Essex births, but nothing can be found to give any clue to Reginald Foster who emigrated to New England." He writes 27th April, 1892, "It struck me suddenly on finding the loss of certain Parish Registers in Essex, that I might get something from the Subsidy Rolls. I therefore yesterday looked up the Hundred of Hinkford which has forty-nine parishes, all of which I most carefully examined with this result, that Foster was a family living at Felstead in the reign of King James I. and King Charles I."

"1 Essex, 21, James I, Parish of Felstead, Michael Foster on lands valued £3 paid 8s tax." "2 Essex, 3 and 4, Charles I. Parish of Felstead, Andrew Foster on lands £1, paid 4s tax."

"I chose the above period as being near Reginald Foster and it is clear there were Fosters at Felstead holding land between 1600 and 1630." Col. Vivian, however, felt that he was on the right track, writing: "Felstead is in the same hundred as Bocking and Harlow, all within a circle of about twelve miles in diameter. I looked up ninety-nine (99) parishes. Felstead was the only one that had the name of Foster." Col. Vivian interviewed Joseph Foster of London. He writes: "Mr. J. Foster of London has not printed anything to help you, he told me he felt no interest whatever in Reginald Foster." Col. Vivian also interviewed Mr. Waters, and writes: "I understood Mr. Waters to say last week when I saw him that the great difficulty was there are too many Reginald Fosters about the period named, and that it would cost a lot of money to look them up."

FOSTER.

West of England, 1395-1419.

John Forster became rector of Blackborough, Devonshire, 25th February, 1413.
Walter Foster, details not noted.
Reginald Foster, d. at Trenoglos, Cornwall, in 1409.

FOSTER.

The name Reginald Foster occurs as one of those who during the Great Rebellion compounded for his property. The particulars, easily to be ascertained, would disclose his place of abode and other matters.

"Fosters of Dowsby and Moulton, Co. Lincoln," compiled by Everard Green, Esq., F. S. A. Reprinted from the 'Miscellaneous 'Genealogica et Heraldica,' of November, 1875, for W. E. Foster, Esq., London. Mitchell & Hughes, Printers, 24 Wardow Street, W., 1875.

Arms.—Sable, a chevron engrailed ermine, between three broad arrows, or feathered argent.

Crest.—An antelope's head, erased argent, attired or colored and chained of the last.

Motto.—"Inconcusser Fides."

FOSTER LAND GRANTS IN NOVA SCOTIA.

List of all grants of land issued to the name of Foster; from the Index to Grants of Nova Scotia from 1707 to 1854 (inclusive). N. B.—New Brunswick was a part of Nova Scotia until 1785.

DATE	NAME OF GRANTEE.	NO. OF ACRES.	LOCALITY.	COUNTY.
27 June, 1759	Foster, Jeremiah and many others.........	100,000	Tp. of Granville....	....
18 Oct., 1759	Foster, Hugh and others	100,000	Tp. of Shoreham...	....
1 Sep., 1759	Foster, Thomas, and others................	100,000	Tp. of Liverpool....	....
4 Mar., 1761	Foster, William.......	1,000	Tp. of Horton......	....
12 Oct., 1763	Forster, Christian......	1,000	Windsor Road.....	....
22 Nov., 1764	Foster, Edward, William, John, Thomas, and many others.....	100,000	Tp. of Liverpool....	....
12 Oct., 1763	Foster, Christian, and another..............	1,000	Sackville Road.....	....
30 Oct., 1765	Foster, Isaac, Isaac Jr., Jacob; Forster, Isaac, Ezekiel, Jeremiah, Joseph and others ...	100,000	Tp. of Granville....	....
3 July, 1766	Foster, Jacob, license to alienate to T. Buck ..	500	Tp. of Granville....	....
11 Jan., 1768	Foster, Robert, and others...............	47,000	Tp. of Sackville....	....
22 July, 1774	Foster, Robert and John	12,250	Tp. of Sackville....	....
22 July, 1774	Foster, Robert and Andrew and others......	12,250	Tp. of Sackville....	....
15 July, 1783	Foster, Edward, Senr., Foster, Edward, Jr....	1,550	Twn. plt. Dartmouth	....
14 July, 1784	Foster, Jacob, and others	10,866	Town plat of Gage..	Sunbury
14 July, 1784	Foster, Lawrence, and others................	21,892	Twn. plt. Kingston..	"
14 July, 1784	Foster, Elias, and others....	4,500	Kennebeccasius Riv. Twn. of Kingston...	"
14 July, 1784	Foster, Josiah, and others...............	38,450	Tp. of Sunbury.....	"
3 Aug., 1784	Foster, Joshua, and others...............	7,600	St. John River......	"
2 June, 1785	Forster, William, and others	53,850	Twn. Guysborough.	Halifax
16 June, 1785	Foster, William, and others...............	20,300	Rhemsheg..........	Cumberland
4 Feb., 1789	Foster, William, and others...............	17,150	Sable River........	Shelborne
7 Aug., 1790	Foster, William, and others...............	Town lots	Tp. of Guysborough.	Sydney

FOSTER LAND GRANTS IN NOVA SCOTIA—Continued.

DATE.	NAME OF GRANTEE.	NO. OF ACRES.	LOCALITY.	COUNTY.
21 Sep., 1790	Foster, John, and others in trust for a common	384	Tp. of Wilmot.......	....
1 May, 1797	Foster, Edward........	11	Tp. of Dartmouth...	Halifax
1 May, 1797	Foster, Benjamin, and another................	Water lots	Town of Granville..	Annapolis
26 Oct., 1821	Foster, Joseph, and others...............	200 Foster's share	New Annapolis Rd..	"
19 Aug., 1822	Foster, William.......	Lot	Town of Dartmouth.	Halifax
21 Jan., 1828	Foster, John...........	200	Brookfield Road....	Queens
18 Oct., 1830	Foster, William.......	Water Lot	Dartmouth..........	Halifax
25 Apl., 1845	Foster, George.........	100	Sissiboo River......	Digby
25 May, 1845	Forster, Avard.........	142	New Germany......	Lunenburg
2 Mch., 1853	Foster, Ezra...........	200	Lake Spry..........	Annapolis

FOSTERS IN AMERICA.

ALLEN FOSTER'S SONS. Early in the 17th century four sons of Allen Foster, of England, viz., Jonathan, David, Ephraim and Samuel, came to this country. One settled in Maine, another on Long Island, another in northern New Jersey, and Samuel in Cape May, south New Jersey, from whom sprang most all the Fosters in the lower county of West Jersey. One of Samuel's sons was Nathaniel, who had a son Salathiel, who had a son Reuben, who had a son Reuben, Jr. He m. Nov. 20, 1804, in Cape May, N. J., Nancy Edmunds, who died in her 74th year, Aug. 6, 1855. He d. in his 90th year June 24, 1870, leaving Robert Edmunds Foster and Downs E. Foster. The latter was b. Oct. 20, 1807; m. Ann Lawrence Hughes, b. Nov. 9, 1817; d. Feb. 26, 1865. He was a contractor and builder, and d. Oct. 20, 1886.

Ch. 1. JANE ANN FOSTER; res. Cape May, N. J.
2. SAMUEL L. FOSTER; P O. address, Norfolk, Va.
3. DOUGLASS FOSTER; res. Baltimore, Md.
4. ELLA FOSTER; res. Cape May, N. J.
5. RHODA FOSTER; res. Cape May, N. J.
6. MARY C. FOSTER; res. Cape May, N. J.
7. REUBEN FOSTER, b. Cape May Co., N. J., Oct. 28, 1839; m. there Nov. 6, 1866, Sarah L. Head. He is general manager for the Chesapeake and York river lines of steamboats. Res. 2301 Charles St., Baltimore, Md.

Ch. 1. ENOCH EDMUNDS FOSTER, b. Sept. 2, 1867; m. Oct. 25, 1894.
2. ARTHUR D. FOSTER, b. Nov. 9, 1872; m. Nov. 30, 1898.
3. REUBEN CARL FOSTER, b. July 10, 1875.
4. FRED FOSTER, b. Oct. 5, 1879.

ANDREW. He died in Andover May 7, 1685, ae. 106. See notice of descendants in this book.

CHRISTOPHER. Coming from England he first located in Lynn, but soon removed to Long Island, where he was an early settler. Descendants in this work.

HON. EDWARD. Born in Devonshire, England, son of Timothy. Settled in Scitnate. See notice of descendants in following pages.

CAPT. HOPESTILL. Son of Richard, and grandson of Rev. Thomas; born in Biddenden, England; settled in Dorchester. Descendants in this book.

EDWARD. Born in England, came to America about 1650, m. in Springfield, Mass., Dec. 26, 1661, Esther Bliss, who lived with John Pynchon. She d. June 12, 1683; m. second Jan. 17, 1683, Mrs. Sarah Miller, who d. Mar. 9, 1708. He was a freeman in 1690, and d. in Springfield Feb. 22, 1720, s. p.

CAPT. THOMAS. Son of John, b. in Kingsware, England, about 1642, m. in New London, Conn. Was a master mariner and sailed between Boston, New London and the Barbadoes. See notice elsewhere.

EDWARD. Brother of Capt. Thomas; res. in Marblehead, Mass., Middletown and Guilford, Conn. His descendants are given in this work.

BARTHOLOMEW. Brother of Capt. Thomas, resided in Gloucester, Mass. Was engaged in maritime pursuits like his brothers. See notice in following pages.

SERGT. THOMAS. Son of Rev. Thomas, b. in England, came to America, resided in Boston, Weymouth, Woburn, Braintree and Billerica. Was one of the early Baptists. Descendants in this work.

CAPT. WILLIAM. Brother of Sergt. Thomas, b. in England, resided in Charlestown, Mass.; was a master mariner, was captured with his son by the Turks, while enroute to Bilboa. See descendants elsewhere.

HON. SAMUEL. Born in England, came to America, located in Dedham, married there, moved to Wenham and finally settled in Chelmsford. Was the ancestor of a large family. See descendants in this book.

JOHN, SR. Came from England and settled in Salem, Mass. It is said he was closely related to Samuel of Chelmsford and Andrew of Andover, but I do not think so. See descendants in these pages.

REGINALD. Born in Brunton, England, came to America, settled in Ipswich, Mass., and was the ancestor of a numerous posterity. His ancestry is traced back to 837, and his descendants fully given in this work.

WILLIAM. Born in England, was of Ipswich, Mass., and Newport, Rhode Island; may have been brother or relative of Reginald. He had land granted him in Ipswich in 1635, says Felt. He was disarmed Nov., 1637, as a follower of Wheelwright, and supporter of Mrs. Hutchinson. "Yet he was a man with the prefix of respect; and was in Sept. foll. informed that we conceive him not fit to live with us; therefore he was wished to depart bef. the Gen. Court in Mar. next. Yet he may have, like not a few of his associate misbelieve, made his peace or been too much respected for his est. and thot. less dangerous soon after." I think on account of his religious difficulties he moved to Newport, R. I., in 1639. In the earlier records we find the name spelt indifferently Foster and Forster—the former spelling being the more common. The "r" has now been entirely dropped, except by the descendants of Jacob Forster, of Charlestown, Mass., who was the first I believe, to write the name always in this manner.

COL. JOHN. Born Alesbury, Bucks Co., England, came to America, located in Boston; m. Lydia ——, who d; m. second Abigail ——, who d. Aug., 1711. He d. Feb. 9, 1711. He was one of the wealthiest merchants in Boston, and one of the most influential men of his day. John, Boston, an emin. merch. from Alesbury Co., ar. co. 1679, of the council of safety 1689, rep. 1690, at May session, for Portsmouth, where the inhab. earnestly desir. to continue the union with Mass. after the overthrow of Andros; Col. of Boston reg. named in the Chart. of William and Mary by approb. of Increase Mather, a couns.—Savage. John Foster (1679), of Boston, was an eminent merchant from Alesbury, Bucks county, England, and was admitted a freeman in 1682. He joined the artillery company immediately after his arrival, and became very prominent in the affairs of the company from 1690 to 1695. He was of the Council of Safety in 1689; was representative for Portsmouth in 1690; one of Gov. Dudley's (1677) councillors; named in the charter of William and Mary in 1692; one of the first council under it, in which office he continued until his death. He is mentioned in the Boston records, the first time, March 15, 1679-80, when being elected constable, he was fined for refusing to serve; and was selectman in 1690, 1691 and 1692. On the 7th of December, 1692, he was appointed a justice of the inferior court of Common Pleas for Suffolk county, and served in that office until his decease. He is called "Capt." in the Boston town records, 1696-8, and Mr. Savage says he was colonel of the Boston regiment, a wealthy merchant and of a most fair and unblemished character.

John Foster. Adm. to estate of Col. John Foster, late of Boston, dec'd, granted to son-in-law, Thomas Hutchinson, merchant of Boston, Mar. 26, 1711. Lib. 17, Fol. 220.

Will—Abigail Foster, relict widow of John Foster late of Boston—niece Mrs. Hannah Ruck wife of Mr. John Ruck, Merchant—Abigail Ruck, daughter of said John and Hannah—Peter, Hannah and Elizabeth, three other children of said John and Hannah Ruck—niece Mrs. Elizabeth Hutchinson—Mrs. Lydia Hutchinson daughter of my aforenamed husband, and now wife of Mr. Edward Hutchinson—Mr. John Foster Mariner—and my kinswoman his present wife—Abigail Salter wife, of Jabesh Salter, Jr. and Mary Foster the two daughters of my aforesaid kinswoman Sarah Foster—John Richardson, Woodmansey Richardson, Elizabeth Richardson the three children of my cousin John Richardson, dec'd—and to his Widow, Mrs. Margaret Richardson my kinswoman, Mrs. Johanna Perry

widow—nephew Capt. Thomas Hutchinson—and his son Foster Hutchinson—
Thomas Hutchinson, Exec.

Dated Mar. 1, 1710-11.

Prob. Sept. 1, 1711. Lib. 17, Fol. 296-7.

Ch: i. MARY, b. Mar. 13, 1678.

ii. LYDIA, b. Oct. 22, 1680, d. in infancy.

iii. JOHN, b. Feb. 5, 1681, d. in infancy.

iv. JOHN, b. July 27, 1684, m. Sarah ——, was a mariner. Had two daughters.

v. SARAH, b. Jan. 29, 1686, m. Gov. Thomas Hutchinson. He was the eldest son of Col. Elisha, whose father, Capt. Edward, was wounded in King Philips war in 1675, at Brookfield, and died in a few days at Marlboro. Thomas was born Jan. 30, 1674, and was bred to mercantile pursuits. He was early a member of the provisional legislature, and thirty years a member of the council. He was distinguished for independence of character, in times of great party excitement; was much esteemed for his integrity and for his liberal benevolence on all occasions when the public exigencies required his aid. Snow says that in 1713 he built at his own charge the Grammar school in Bennet street, and he was a liberal contributor to Harvard College. He died Dec. 3, 1739, much lamented. His eldest son, 1, Foster Hutchinson, who was graduated at Harvard in 1721 died early; 2, Thomas, b. 1711, governor of Massachusetts; 3, Foster; and daus., 4, Mrs. Rev. William Welsteed; 5, Mrs. Rev. Samuel Mather; 6, Mrs. Rev. Rogers, and 7, Mrs. Davenport.

Gov. Thomas Hutchinson, of Massachusetts Bay, under the second charter, as stated above, was b. in 1711. He was admitted to Harvard College when only twelve years of age. His progress in study was a subject of particular notice and applause. In 1727 he received his bachelor's degree, but instead of entering a learned profession, he engaged in mercantile pursuits. Not being successful, he studied law and was elected a selectman in 1738. He visited London and effected the settlement of important matters for Boston. On his return he was elected to the legislature and annually re-elected for ten years, three of which he was speaker. In the assembly he possessed the charm of oratory beyond any man in that body. There was with him fluency and pathos. He could argue as well as declaim. He took an important part in that body; later he was Judge of Probate. In 1758 he was appointed lieutenant-governor, and in 1760 Chief Justice of the State. The governor having the precedence, Lieutenant-Governor Hutchinson presided as Chief Magistrate and at this time held the offices of Judge of Probate, Councillor, Chief Justice and Lieutenant-Governor. He was a friend of England, sympathized with the mother country, and just prior to the Revolution was particularly obnoxious. Aug. 26, 1765, a drunken mob visited his residence, split the doors of the house to pieces, destroyed or cast into the streets everything which was in the house and kept possession of it until daybreak. He was that night at the castle. The damage was estimated at £2,500, besides many public and private papers. He was paid by the government £3,194, 17s. 6d. for his damage and loss. In 1768 British troops arrived in Boston and intensified the feeling against Mr. Hutchinson. The following year, the governor leaving the province, the administration devolved upon Mr. Hutchinson as lieutenant-governor. The following year occurred the Boston Massacre, and this further inflamed the public mind. A long discussion with the assembly followed on proroguing that body to Cambridge by order of the King. The council was opposed to him. In March, 1771, his commission as governor was received from England. He accepted it, and from that time until his departure for England, in 1774, he was in constant dispute with the assembly and council. While he was governor, Dec. 14, 1773, occurred the Boston Tea Party, when a number of citizens, disguised as Indians, threw three hundred and forty-two chests of tea from the ships into the sea. The King intended to re-appoint Mr. Hutchinson governor, but he left for England where he afterward resided, receiving a pension for life from the British government. He was a man of good character unwearied industry and highly respectable talents. As a judge he was irreproachable and evinced great ability. But it was his fortune to live at the time of that revolution, and in the very center of popular excitement. He was on the wrong side, and fell a martyr to the cause in which he was engaged. He published many volumes of an historical character, and after his death his grandson, Rev. John Hutchinson, published his third volume of Massachusetts history. He died at Broughton June 9, 1780. His daughter died Sept. 21, 1771; his son William Feb. 20, 1780. His son Thomas died at Heavitree, near Exeter, in 1811, ae. 71, and his son Elisha at Blurton Parsonage, Trentham, Staffordshire, in 1824, ae. 80.

vi. LYDIA, b. Feb. 25, 1687, m. Col. Edward Hutchinson. He was born in 1678, bred a merchant. He was much in public business, was selectman of Boston, representative in the legislature, colonel of a regiment, judge of the court of common pleas, judge of probate of Suffolk county, and for thirty years treasurer of Harvard College. He was highly respected, and died in 1752. He left three children: 1, Edward, who graduated at Harvard in 1748, lived a great invalid for many years and died unmarried; 2, Sarah, who lived to a great age unmarried; 3, Elizabeth, who m. in 1757 Rev. Nathaniel Robbins, of Milton, who was father of Hon. Edward Hutchinson Robbins, who graduated at Harvard College in 1775, speaker of the house of representatives, judge of probate court and lieutenant-governor.

JAMES was b. in England. He was a mariner and d. unm. in Yarmouth. Barnstable Co., Mass., in 1685. His will, which is the first one entered on the Barnstable records, is found in Vol. 1, Page 1, and is as follows:

From Probate Records of Barnstable Co., Vol. 1, Page 1.

In the Name of God, Amen. I, James Foster late of London being weake in body but of disposing mind and memory, Blessed be God and not knowing how soone it may please Almighty God to calle me hence by death, do therefore make and ordain this my last will and testament, as followeth:

First I bequeath my soule to God that gave it me, and my body to the dust from whence it was, in deasent burial, and for that outward and temporal estate which God of his goodness hath given me my will is that my funeral charge be paid and al other charges and reasonable dues belonging to any person by reason of my sickness and board since I came to New England be also paid by my Executors hereafter named.

I give to Mr. Robert Goss my hoope ring and to each person whose turne it hath been to watch with me in this time of my sickness I do give five shillings, I do give to Elisha Hedg Jur. ten shillings and I do give Charles Knight his freedom and whereas I have bought the liberty of purchas of an island called Quitneset being in or near Manomoyet and have been at considerable charge about the same, my will is that purchas of sd island be made if it may be obtained for eighteen pounds in money, and all the writings and conveyances of it to be entered in the Court Rowles at New Plymouth; and said Quitneset Island I do give to my sister Elizabeth Wopshot the daughter of Elizabeth Torlton lately living in Jacobs Streete in Southworke near London and to the heirs of her body but in case shee die without issue then I give it to my honnoured mother Elizabeth Torlton the wife of Mr. John Torlton living in Jacobs Street, and I do give to my servant Edward Ames the one half of the price I am to have for him which part is five pounds in shooes at money price, and to my other two servants Larrance bustob and Christopher West I do give twenty shillings apiece.

Concerning my debts that lie in Antego for the receiving of which Mr. John Norman is my attorney with order to shipe them for Bostown in New England, and my will is that the produce of what he sends to Boston (after the charge thereabout is paid) be sent home to England to Mr. Robert Torlton lately living in Pewter Hall in Lime Streete in London to be disposed according to former order given to him. And to my well beloved friends Capt. John Thacher and Mr. Elisha Hedge both of Yarmouth I do give two guinnes to make each of them a ring. And in defect of the gould the vallue thereof in silver, and lastly I do ordain and appoint the said Capt. John Thacher and Mr. Elisha Hedge Executors to this my last Will and Testament.

In witness whereof I the said James Forster have hereunto set my seale and made my marke (my hands being so weake I cannot write,) this eleventh day of February 1685

the marke of and × a (seale)
James Foster.

Signed sealed and declared
in presence of
Joseph Rider,
Samuel Howes.
Proved July 13, 1686.
A true copy ot the record.

COLLEGE GRADUATES BY NAME OF FOSTER.

Below will be found a list of persons by the name of Foster who have been graduated at the various colleges in this country:

HARVARD UNIVERSITY, CAMBRIDGE, MASS.—The following is a list of graduates of Harvard College by the name of Foster. The first date is the year of graduation and the second the date of death. The residences of the living are given where known: John, 1667; Isaac, 1671, 1682; Jedediah, 1744, 1779; Thomas, 1745, 1777; George, 1752, 1759; Jacob, 1754, 1798; Abiel, 1756, 1806; Isaac, 1758, 1781; Dwight, 1784, 1823; Edmund, Yale 1778, 1784, 1826; Daniel, Dart 1777, 1785, 1795; Bossenger, 1787, 1816; John, 1787, 1829; Freeman, 1799, 1863; Andrew, M. D., 1800, 1831; John, 1802, 1836; Thomas, M. D., 1805, 1831; Jacob, 1806, 1817; John, 1813, 1836; Alfred Dwight, 1819, 1852; Charles Phinehas, 1825, 1879; George Emerson, 1829, 1842; Andrew, 1833, 1879; Samuel Conant, M. D., 1834; Charles Francis, M. D., 1838, 1865; Jacob Collier, 1841; Francis Charles, 1850, 15 Oxford, Cambridge, Mass.; Jacob Post Girard, 1847; Charles Amos, 1853; Charles Marsh, 1863, Topeka, Kans.; Charles Mattoon, 1867; Hubbard Aug., 1871; Alfred Dwight, 1873, 87 Milk St., Boston; Francis Hugo, Prof., Rev., 1873, Pres. Theo. Sem., Oakland, Cal.; George Russell, 1875; Charles, 1877; Jacob Richards, 1877; Charles Chauncey, M. D., 1880, 5 Riedesel Av., Cambridge, Mass.; Charles H. W., 1881, Upland Road, Brookline, Mass.; John McGraw, Rev., 1882, Boston, Mass.; Warren Worden, 1882; Samuel Lynde, A. B., 1885; Burnside, M. D., A. B., Yale 1882, 1886; Eugene Hiawatha, A. M, A. B., Antioch 1878, 1886; Chauncey Charles, A. B., 1887; George Waldo, A. B., 1887; Clarendon Atwood, M. D., 1889; Arthur Fay, LL. B., 1889; Stephen Austin, LL. B., A. B., Tufts, 1887, 1891; Herbert Darling, A. M., A. B., Dart. 1885, 1892; Sumner Hatherly, LL. B., 1895; Herbert Baldwin, A. B., 1895; Benjamin Oliver, A. M., 1897; Herbert Ira, A. B., 1898; Lindsey King, A. B., cum laude, 1898; William Albert, LL. B., S. B., Dart. 1895, 1898.

YALE COLLEGE, NEW HAVEN, CONN.—The list of graduates by the name of Foster from this institution is as follows: Isaac, M. A., 1770, 1807; Benjamin, M. A. 1781, 1774; Brown, 1786, D. D. Brown 1792, 1798; Dan, M. A., Dart., 1774, 1809; Isaac, M. A., Dart. 1778, 1776, 1794; Edmund, M. A., 1778, 1826; Eleazer, M. A., 1802, 1819; Lemuel, 1828, 1872; Lewis, 1831, 1839; Eleazer Kingsbury, 1834, 1877; Stephen Clark, 1840; Thomas Edwin, M. A, 1840, 1851; Charles, 1844, 1877; Dwight, M. A., LL. D. 1871, 1848, 1884; William Edward, 1860; Henry W. W., 1861; Eleazer Kingsbury, Judge Cir. Ct. Florida, 1863; William L., lawyer, 1865; John Pierrpont Coddington, M. D., 1869; Lauren M., 1871; Frank Wade, 1874; William, LL. B., 1874; Roger, LL. B., Columbia 1880, M. A. 1883, 1878; George Forris, 1879; Samuel Monell, 1879; Burnside, M. D., 1882; Reginald, LL. B., 1884; Lambert, 1885, 1890.

BROWN UNIVERSITY, PROVIDENCE, R. I.—The following are the graduates by the name of Foster from this institution:

Henry Foster, A. M.; A. B. Oxford university. Clergyman Church of England; curate and lecturer St. Andrew Wardrobe, Blackfriars 1769-89; curate St. James, Clerkenwell 1804-14. Author Grace displayed and Saul converted, 1814; The Bible preacher, 1824. Born 1745; died 1814. Darling's cyc. bib., Manning and B. U.

Daniel Foster, A. M.; A. B. Dartmouth college 1777; A. M. 1780; Harvard university 1785. Ordained Congregational 1778; pastor, New Braintree, Mass.,

1778-95. Author Sermon at ordination of Joshua Crosby; Mass. election sermon, 1790. Born Warren, Mass., 1751; died Sept. 4, 1795.

Dwight Foster, A. M.; Harvard university 1774. Admitted to bar 1778; lawyer Providence, R. I., 1778-79; justice of peace 1779; lawyer, Brookfield, Mass, 1779-1823; delegate, Mass. constitutional convention 1779, '99; justice of peace Worcester co. 1781; special justice Court of common pleas 1792; high sheriff Worcester co. 1792; member Mass. house of representatives; Mass. senate; U. S. house of representatives 1793-99; U. S. senate 1800-03; chief justice Court of common pleas, Worcester co. 1801-11; member Mass. executive council 1818. Born Brookfield, Mass., Dec. 7, 1757; died Brookfield, April 29, 1823. Cyc. Am. biog., Cong. direct.

Theodore Foster, A. M.; Dartmouth college 1786. Lawyer, Providence, R. I.; member R. I. house of representatives 1776-82, 1812-16; town clerk, Providence many years; judge Court of admiralty 1785; member U. S. senate 1790-1803; trustee Brown university 1794-1822; antiquary, collecting materials for history of R. I. Born Brookfield, Mass., April 29, 1752; died Providence, R. I, Jan. 13, 1828. R. I. cyc., Cyc. Am. biog., Cong. direct.

Benjamin Foster, A. M.; D. D. 1792; A. B. Yale college 1774; A. M. Yale college 1781. Ordained Baptist 1776; pastor, Leicester, Mass., 1776-85; First church, Newport, R. I., 1785-88; First church, New York, N. Y., 1788-98; trustee Brown university 1786-98. Author divine rite of immersion; Primitive baptism defined: Dissertation on the seventy weeks of Daniel, 1787. Born Danvers, Mass., June 12, 1750; died New York, N. Y., Aug. 26, 1798. Cyc. Am. biog., Bapt. encyc.

Theodore Dwight Foster, A. M. Died 1802.

Theodore Adelphidos Foster, A. M.

Lafayette Sabine Foster, LL. D 1851. Teacher, Providence, R. I.; principal academy, Queen Anne co., Md., 1829-30; admitted to bar 1831; lawyer, Norwich, Conn., 1831-33, '35-80; Hampton, Conn., 1833-35; member Conn. house of representatives 1839-41, '46-48, '54-55, '70; speaker three terms; mayor Norwich 1851-53; member U. S. senate 1855-67; president pro tempore 1865-67; appointed professor Yale college 1869, but declined; justice Conn. supreme court 1870-76; commissioner from Conn. to settle boundary with N. Y. 1878-79; one of three commissioners to negotiate with N. Y. for purchase of Fisher's Island; member commission on simpler procedure for the state courts 1878; vice-president American Bible society. Born Franklin, Conn., Nov. 22, 1806; died Norwich, Conn., Sept. 19, 1880. Cyc. Am. biog., Cong. direct., Nec. 1881.

George Foster. From Cambridge, Mass.; died 1817.

James Milton Foster. From Springfield, Mass.

Joseph Coggin Foster, A. M.; D. D. Central university of Iowa 1883. Baptist clergyman; pastor, Brattleboro, Vt., 1843-56; First church, Beverly, Mass., 1856-73; Randolph, Mass., 1873-82; associate editor Watchman, Boston, Mass., 1882; member school committee Brattleboro 1843-56; Beverly 1856-73; Boston correspondent Watch tower, New York, N. Y., 1879-81. Author Uncertainty of Life, obituary discourse, 1849; Baptism and communion, tract, 1860; Providence illustrated, historical discourse, dedication of Baptist meeting house, Brattleboro, Vt., Dec. 28, 1870; Accountableness for evils of intemperance, tract, 1871; Lowliness of Christ, sermon, 1892. Address, South Main St., Randolph, Mass. Died 1899.

Louis Tucker Foster. Cotton manufacturer. Address, 6 Olive St., Providence R. I. P.

William Eaton Foster, A. M. Librarian public library, Hyde Park, Mass., 1873-76; cataloguer Turner free library, Randolph, Mass., 1876-77; librarian public library, Providence, R. I., 1877. Author Literature of civil-service reform in the U. S., 1881; The civil-service reform movement, 1881; Libraries and readers, 1883; Stephen Hopkins, a R. I. statesman, 1884; Early attempts at R. I. history, comprising those of Stephen Hopkins and Theodore Foster, edited, in Collections of the R. I. historical society, vol. 7, 1885; References to political and economic topics, 1885; References to the history of presidential administrations, 1789-1885, 1885; Town government in R. I., 1886; References to the constitution of the U. S., with an appendix, 1890; Public support of public libraries, 1891; Address before R. I. society of the Sons of the American Revolution, 1891, 1892; Some R. I. contributions to the intellectual life of the last century, 1892; besides various periodical articles, partially enumerated in Annual report of the American historical association, 1889. Address, Public Library, Providence, R. I. Am. hist. assoc., P.

Austin Powers Foster, A. M. Principal high school, Candia, N. H.; classical department, Grove school, Dallas, Tex.; examiner public school teachers Dallas; publisher and wholesale book dealer. Address, 312 Main St., Dallas, Tex. P.

Irving Lysander Foster, A. M. upon examination 1894. Instructor French, Brown university 1893-94; student, Leipsic, Germany. Address, care Fr. Dr. Buch, Leplay Str. 8 [2], Leipsic, Germany.

Theodore Clyde Foster. 78 Waterman St., Providence, R. I.

Albert Orson Foster. 86 Lansing St., Utica, N. Y.

Marsden Rhodes Foster. In charge of Methodist Episcopal Church, Drownville, R. I. Address, Drownville, R. I.

DARTMOUTH COLLEGE, HANOVER, N. H.—The following Fosters were graduated from this institution: Aaron Foster, Rev., A. M., and Theo. Sem. 1825, 1822, 1870, ae. 76; Amos Foster, Rev., A. M , 1822, 1884, ae. 87; Asa Emerson Foster. A. M., 1822, 1875, ae. 80; Abiel Foster, 1823, 1869, ae. 70; Addison H. Foster, A. M., M. D., 1863, Chicago; Charles Foster, major 11th Iowa vols., 1840, 1864, ae. 44; Charles Heselton Foster, M. D., 1875, Lisbon, Me.; Charles Lee Foster, 1860, 1863, ae. 27; Clarence Marion Foster, Columbia 1875, 1873, New York, N. Y.; Dan Foster, A. M., Hon. Deg., Yale 1774, 1774, 1810, ae. 62; Daniel Foster, Rev., A. M., Harvard 1785, Brown 1787, 1777, 1795, ae. 44; Daniel Foster, Rev., A. B. 1845, Capt. 37th U. S. C. T., 1841, 1864, ae. 47; David J., lawyer, 1880, Burlington, Vt.; Davis, Rev., and Theo. Sem. 1855, D. D. 1885, 1849, Winchendon, Mass.; Eden Burroughs, D. D. Wms. 1861, 1837, 1882, ae. 68; Emerson, Rev. A. M., 1773, 1814, ae. 67; Frederick, Rev., 1840, 1865, ae. 51; Frederick Fairfield, 1865, Weare, N. H.; Geo. Vickery, m., 1882, New York, N. Y.; Henry Richard, Rev., Ct. Teo. Md. 1885, 1882, 1887, ae. 28; Herbert Darling, A. M., 1885, Worcester, Mass.; Herman, lawyer, Pres. senate N. H. 1861, 1861, 1875, ae. 74; Horace K., A. M., M. D., 1879, Peabody, Mass.; Isaac, Rev., A. M., A. B. Yale 1776, 1778, 1794, ae. 39; Isaac, A. M., 1828, 1877, ae. 71; Joel, Rev., A. M., 1777, 1812, ae. 57; John, Rev., A. M., Harvard 1787, D D. Harvard 1815, 1783, 1829, ae. 66; John, 1858, Faribault, Minn.; John, lawyer, 1876, Manchester, N. H.; John Hilbert, 1821, 1874, ae. 78; John Luther, lawyer, 1864, 1890, ae. 52; Moses, 1841, Andover, Mass., died; Nahum Parker, Rev., D. D., Cent. Univ. Iowa 1875, 1834, 1876, ae. 62; Richard Baxter, Rev., A. B. 1867, 1st Lt. 62d U. S. C. T., 1851, Cheney, Kans.; Roswell, Rev., and Theo. Sem. 1853, 1849, Phillipston, Mass.; Stephen, Rev., and Theo. Sem. 1824, Pres. Univ. Tenn., 1821, 1835, ae. 36; Stephen Symonds, 1838, 1881, ae. 71; Sylvester M., 1884; Theodore, A. M., A. B. Brown 1770, U. S. senate 1790-1803, 1786, 1828; Walter Henry, 1874, 1878, ae. 25; Warren William, lawyer, A. M., LL. B. Columbia 1883, 1881. New York, N. Y.; William Cowper, Rev., Theo. Sem. 1844, 1841, Middletown. Conn.; William Hamilton, 1885, Concord, N. H.; William Lawrence, lawyer, A. M., judge Sup. court N. H. 1869-74, chief justice N. H. 1874-6, judge Sup. court 1876-81, 1860, Concord, N. H.; Willie Hudson, 1879, 1880, ae. 23.

CORNELL UNIVERSITY, ITHACA, N. Y.—Alla Wright Foster, 1872-3, A. M. 1877, A. B. Vassar 1872, Hotel Eliot, Roxbury, Mass.; Charles E., 1877-8, Ithaca, N. Y.; Geo. Emett, 1870-2, Milford, N. H ; Henry Ward, 1873-7, Ithaca, N. Y.; Lucy Allison, 1868-72, d. in Denver, Colo., Mar. 29, 1882; Lottie A., 1884-8, Ithaca, N. Y.; Dr. Newel Kelley, 1869-73, Canterbury, N. H., 335 E 12th St., Oak land, Cal.; Reuben Burdick, 1870-4, So. Lake Weir, Fla.

UNIVERSITY OF MICHIGAN, ANN ARBOR, MICH.—The following are the graduates of this college of persons by the name of Foster: E., engineering; B. L., bachelor of letters; Ph. B., bachelor of philosophy; LL. B., bachelor of laws; B. S., bachelor of science. Burt Lewis Foster, Ann Arbor, Mich., '96, E. (Mech. E.); Charles Woodworth Foster, '95, B. L., '96, LL. B., Lansing, Mich; Elijah C. Foster, '67, LL. B., Dept. of Justice, Washington, D. C. (1890); Emory Arthur Foster. Law, '86-'87, registered from Independence, Kans.; Francis Alma Foster, '97, B. L., Detroit, Mich.; Francis Albert Foster, '85, M. D., East Jordan, Mich.; Frank Albert Foster, '79, M. D., Waltham, Mass.; Frank Augustus Foster, non-grad., Lit., '77-78, Ludington, Mich.; Frank Henry Foster, '82, LL. B., 623 Kansas Ave., Topeka, Kans.; George A. Foster, '61, LL. B.; George Forris Foster, non-grad., Lit., '74-76, A. B. (Yale) 1879, 182 Fifth Ave., New York, N. Y.; Homer Redfield Foster, '97, Ph. B., Seattle, Wash.; Irving Charles Foster, Med., '82-83, M. D. (Coll. of Phys. and Surg., Chicago), '84, Albion, Mich.; Isaac Foster, '95, LL. B., Gladwin, Mich.; John Reynolds Foster, '67, LL. B., A. B (Hillsdale Coll.), 1865; Joseph Foster, '94, M. D., Lansing, Mich.; Mary Celinda Foster, '85, M. D. (Mrs. Wm. H. Brenton), Green Mountain Falls, Colo. (1890); (Mrs.) Mary E. Foster, '76, LL. B.; Morris Bishop Foster, '70, B. S., Hector, Minn.; Newell Kelley Foster, Med. '77-78, B. S. (Cornell Univ.), 1873, Oakland, Cal.; Riley Foster, '72, B. S., (brother of Morris B. Foster above); Sidney Foster, Law, '81-82, registered from Toledo, O.; Stephen Foster, non-grad., Lit., '70-72;

Stephen Olin Foster, '77, LL. B., Turin, N. Y.; Thomas Reese Foster, '91, M. D., St. Peter, Minn.; William Henry Foster, '90, LL. B., Hamilton Milliken Blk., Traverse City, Mich.

The following are deceased: George Adelbert Foster, '67, A. B., '70, A. M., died at Ann Arbor Mich., Sept. 5, 1881; Gustavus Lemuel Foster, '63-65, Lit., died at Dansville, N. Y., Feb. 14, 1891; Newton Trumbull Foster, '67, LL. B., died at Paw Paw, Mich., Oct. 8, 1877; Leroy Allison Foster, '67-68, Lit., died at Denver, Colo., March 29, 1882; Sidney Hiram Foster, '73-74, Med., died at Malone, N. Y., May 19, 1891.

WILLIAMS COLLEGE, WILLIAMSTOWN, MASS.—The following are the Foster graduates from this college with the year of graduation: Festus, 1800; John, 1834; Joseph Crane, 1857; Addison Pinneo, 1863; Russell Burroughs, 1869; Arthur Lewis, 1870; Mathias Lancton, 1881; William James, 1884; Harold (Harry?) Ernest, 1895.

Joseph Crane Foster was born in Carmel, N. Y., July 20, 1822. After his graduation at Williams he studied theology at Andover, and was licensed to preach by the Presbytery at Bedford, and installed pastor of the church at Red Mills, N. Y., in ——, and remained there until 1859. He d. July 23, 1860, ae. 38.

AMHERST COLLEGE, AMHERST, MASS.—The graduates of Amherst college by the name of Foster are: Benjamin Franklin, 1829, d. 1868, aet. 65; Galen, 1831, d. 1895, aet. 87; John Phelps, 1834, d. 1851, aet. 44; Andrew Butler, 1840, d. 1891, aet. 71; Edgar Lowell, 1864, d. 1872, aet. 34; George Byron, 1883; Edgar Lowell, 1897; Nellis Barnes, 1898.

Non-graduate students: George Emery, 1867; William Phillips, 1879, d. (?); George Wilson, 1883.

Andrew Butler Foster, who graduated in 1840, was son of Andrew Butler and Clariesa (Davenport) Foster; was born in Brookline, Dec. 6, 1819, and was fitted for college at Phillips, Andover Academy. He studied theology at Andover Theological Seminary and East Windsor, now Hartford Theological Seminary, 1840-43. He was ordained at Orford, N. H., in 1844, and was pastor there until 1847; was pastor at Petersham, N. H., 1853-5, and preached after that at Westminster, Vt., and at Orange, Mass. In 1870 on account of infirm health he retired from the ministry and became a druggist at Orange. He retired from business in 1889 and devoted the remainder of his life to traveling for his health. He d. of cancer of the stomach at Orange, Feb. 25, 1891. He was m. Oct. 3, 1843, to Irene C. Cooley, dau. of Moses D., of Amherst, who d. Aug. 12, 1884. They had two ch., both deceased.

PHILLIPS EXETER, EXETER, N. H.—The following are the graduates here by the name of Foster: David Foster, 1791, Canterbury, N. H.; Wm. Emerson Foster, 1824, H. U. 1829, A. M., M. D, Boston, Mass., d. 1842; John Foster, 1852, Dart. Coll., 1858, teacher, Faribault, Minn., Dublin, N. H.; Wm. Rice Foster, 1863, Stafford Springs, Conn.; Wm. Russell Foster, 1870-71, H. U. 1875, lawyer, Portsmouth, N. H., d. 1883; John McGraw Foster, 1876-77, H. U. 1882, Boston, Mass.; Herbert Darling Foster, 1879-81, Dart. Coll., instructor, Dartmouth Coll., Winchendon, Mass.; Wm. Elliott Foster, 1883, Middletown, Conn.

BELOIT COLLEGE, BELOIT, WIS.—There was only one graduate of Beloit by the name of Foster, viz: George T. Foster, M. A., class of '75, who d. at Cherokee, Ia., Feb. 23, 1895.

FOSTERS IN THE REVOLUTIONARY WAR.

FOSTERS FROM MASSACHUSETTS.

During the past few years it has been quite the thing to join one of the patriotic-hereditary societies. Following is the list of those by the name of Foster who took part in the struggle for American Independence from Massachusetts:

—— FOSTER, Ipswich (West Parish). Drummer on Lexington Alarm Roll of Capt. Abram How's co., which marched on alarm of April 19,17 75, from Ipswich (West Parish); service 2 days.

—— FOSTER, Plymouth. Sergeant, on Pay Abstract of Capt. Samuel N. Nelson's co., Col. Willard's regt., for travel allowance from Fort Edward to Plymouth via Albany, dated in council Jan. 28, 1777; also for travel from Plymouth to Skeenesborough by way of No. 4 (Charlestown), dated Boston, Jan., 1777.

——— FOSTER. Lieutenant. On list of men drafted from companies commanded by Capts. Gore, Mayo, White and May, who served at Nantasket in June, 1776, under Lt. James Morton, driving ships from Boston harbor; service 3 days.

——— FOSTER. Private, on muster and pay roll of Capt. Amos Foster's co., Col. Cyphrian How's regt.; detached from 7th Middlesex co. regt.; enlisted July 28, 1780; discharged Oct. 10, 1780; service, 2 mos.; 13 days travel included.

AARON FOSTER, Ipswich. Clerk, on Lexington Alarm Roll of Capt. Johnathan Cogswell Jr.'s co.; marched on alarm of April 19, 1775, from Ipswich; service, 3 days.

AARON FOSTER. Rank not given; on warrant to pay officers in Capt. Richard Dodge's co., Col. Putnam's regt.; 3 mos. service in 1781 at West Point; roll dated Feb. 22, 1785.

ABEL FOSTER, Townsend. Private, on Lexington Alarm Roll of Capt. Samuel Douglass' co., Col. James Prescott's regt., which marched on alarm of April 19, 1775, from Townsend; service, 5 days. On muster roll of Capt. Henry Farwel's co., Col. Wm. Prescott's regt.; dated Aug. 1, 1775; enlisted April 25, 1775; service, 98 days. Reported enlisted April 19, 1775, on return of Capt. Hugh Maxwell's co.,—Col. John Bailey's regt. in service before Aug. 15, 1775—Corporal on return of Capt. Mawxell's co.—in camp near Valley Forge, Jan. 24, 1778. On Continental army pay accounts of Col. Bailey's regt.; service, from June 1, 1777, to Dec. 31, 1779; credited to Fitchburg; reported 3 mos., 4 days service as private, and 27 mos., 26 days as corporal.

*ABIAL FOSTER, Billerica. On list of men enlisted into Continental Army from Capt. Wm. Thurlo's co.; dated Fitchburg Dec. 20, 1777; enlisted for Fitchburg for 3 years; joined Capt. Fox's co., Col. Henley's regt.; on receipt for bounty paid by town of Billerica, to serve 3 years, dated April 8, 1782.

ABIJAH FOSTER. Private, Capt. Stephen Smith's co; enlisted Sept. 13, 1775; service, 3 mos., 25 days; discharged Dec. 31, 1775; stationed at Machias; also on muster and pay roll of Capt. Joseph Seavey's co., Col. Benj. Foster's (Lincoln co.) regt.; enlisted June 22, 1777; discharged July 16, 1777; 23 days service; ordered on duty for defence of Machias; also from July 16 to Oct. 10, 1777; 2 mos., 24 days; also 1 day in Dec., 1778.

ABIJAH FOSTER. Private, on pay roll of St. John Scott's co., for 1 mo., 8 days service at Machias, between Aug. 31 and Nov. 20, 1779; 6th Lincoln co. regt.

ABNER FOSTER. Private, Capt. Benj. Adams' co., Col. Johnson's regt.; enlisted Aug. 15, 1777; discharged Nov. 30, 1777; service, 4 mos. in northern army.

ABRAM FOSTER. Private, on return of Capt. Thomas Wighill's co., Col. L. Baldwin's regt.; service in 1775, wages for month of August also for service in January, 1776.

ABRAHAM FOSTER (or FORSTER), Reading. Rank not given on roll of Capt. John Flint's co., Col. David Green's regt.; 10 days service; roll dated Reading, Dec. 19, 1775; also on muster roll of Capt. John Bacheller's co., Col. Bridge's regt., as sergeant, dated Aug. 1, 1775; enlisted April 24, 1775; service, 3 mos., 14 days; also on order for advance pay—roll dated Cambridge, June 22, 1775.

ABRAHAM FOSTER. As sergeant in the Training band, in Reading, under Capt. Thomas Eaton.

ABRAHAM FOSTER. On list officers chosen by their respective cos. and field officers; 1st lieut. in James Bancroft's (4th) co. of 2d Middlesex co. regt.; commissioned by council May 6, 1776; dated Woburn March 26, 1776; a Reading co.

ABRAHAM FOSTER. Commissioned Capt. in 4th co. of 2d Middlesex co. regt. August 20, 1777; on muster and pay roll Capt. A. Foster's co., Col. Jonathan Fox's regt.; dated Woburn Aug. 31, 1777; enlisted Aug. 1, 1777; marched to Bennington; also in Col. Samuel Bullard's regt.; enlisted Aug. 14, 1777; discharged Nov. 30, 1777; 3 mos., 28 days service; travel allowed; service near Stillwater under Gen. Gates; on abstract of rations due men Col. Bullard's regt. from Aug. 14 to Dec. 11, 1777; and on list of officers claiming traveling expenses for his company of 62 men in Col. Samuel Bullard's regt. from Scarsdale to their home, in council, Nov. 4, 1778.

ABRAHAM FOSTER. Corporal, on pay abstract of Capt. Pettengill's co., Col. Baldwin's regt.; for service in Feb., 1776; dated New York April 19, 1776; also for service in March, June, 1776; also in service Nov. 29, 1776; reported advanced to sergeant May 8, 1776; on list of men having lost goods on evacuation of New York, Sept. 14, 1776.

---

*Also called Abel and Abiel.

ALEXANDER FOSTER, Attleborough. 1st lieutenant on Lexington alarm roll of Capt. Stephen Richardson's co., which marched on alarm of April 19, 1775, from Attleborough; service 9 days; on list of officers ordered to be commissioned in council March 21, 1776; chosen by the 4th regt., March 18, 1776, as 1st lieutenant in Capt. Stephen Richardson's co., Col. John Daggett's (4th) Bristol co. regt.; on an order dated July 5, 1776, for wages, etc., on Ephraim Newell, town treasurer of Attleborough; service on alarm caused by battle of Bunker Hill; on muster and pay roll of Capt. Elisha May's co., Col. John Daggett's regt., for service at Rhode Island; enlisted Aug. 23, 1778; discharged Sept. 2, 1778; service, 11 days.

ALEXANDER FOSTER. Captain. On muster and pay roll of Capt. Alexander Foster's co., Col. John Daggett's regt.; service in R. I. on alarm of Dec. 8, 1776; service, 25 days; warrant allowed in council June 5, 1777; also in Col. Thomas Carpenter's regt. For service on alarm in R. I. enlisted July 27, 1778; discharged Aug. 12, 1778; service, 17 days. Also enlisted July 27, 1780; service, 7 days. Reported marched to Tiverton, R. I., on six days campaign. Also on pay roll of Col. Isaac Dean's regt.; enlisted July 31; discharged Aug. 8, 1780; service, 10 days. On list of officers of Massachusetts militia as captain of the 4th Bristol co. regt; commissioned July 31, 1777.

ALEXANDER FOSTER, Attleborough. Private, on muster and pay roll, Capt. Samuel Robinson's co., Col. Wales' regt.; service in R. I.; enlisted June 21, 1778; discharged July 13, 1778; service, 22 days.

ALLEN FOSTER, Ipswich (West Parish). Private, on Lexington alarm roll of Capt. Abraham How's co.; marched on alarm of April 19, 1775, from Ipswich (West Parish); service, 2 days.

ALLMA FOSTER. Private, on muster and pay roll of Capt. Enoch Robinson's co., under Capt. Commandant Samuel Fisher; enlisted Aug. 12, 1779; discharged Sept. 12, 1779; service at R. I., 1 mo., 2 days; roll sworn to at Attleborough.

AMOS FOSTER, New Salem (possibly). Private, on Lexington alarm roll of Capt. Ebenezer Goodall's co., Col. Woodbridge's regt.; marched on alarm of April 19, 1775, from (possibly New Salem); service, 4 days.

AMOS FOSTER. Private, on list returned as having served on main guard at Prospect Hill July 16, 1775, under Col. L. Baldwin.

AMOS FOSTER, JR. Private, on pay abstract of Capt. Zachariah Fitch's co., Col. Samuel Brewer's regt., for service from Aug. 23 to Sept. 30, 1776; 1 mo., 9 days.

AMOS FOSTER, Tewksbury. Private, on Lexington alarm roll of Capt. John Trull's co., Col. Ebenezer Bridge's regt.; marched on alarm of April 19, 1775, from Tewksburg; service, 9 days. Also on muster roll of Capt. Benj. Walker's co., Col. Ebenezer Bridge's regt.; dated Aug. 1, 1775; enlisted April 28, 1775; service, 3 mos., 11 days, and on order for advance pay, dated Cambridge June 6, 1775.

AMOS FOSTER. Private (probably), on muster and pay roll of Capt. Edward Farmer's co., Col. Jonathan Reed's regt.; enlisted Sept. 29, 1777; discharged Nov. 8, 1777; service, 41 days; marched to reinforce the northern army by resolve of Sept. 22, 1777.

AMOS FOSTER, Beverly. Private, on muster roll Capt. Trescott's co., Col. J. Brewer's regt., dated Aug. 1, 1775; enlisted July 6, 1775; service, 25 days. Also on return dated Prospect Hill Oct. 6, 1775, and on order for bounty coat or equivalent due for the 8 mos. service in 1775 in above co. and regt., dated Prospect Hill Oct. 25, 1775, payable to Lt. Nathaniel Cushing.

AMOS FOSTER, Boston. On discriptive list; age, 54 years; 5 ft., 8 inches, light complexion; arrived at Springfield Aug. 1, 1780, 32d division marched to camp Aug. 2, 1780, under Lieut. Benj. Pike.

AMOS FOSTER, Tewksbury. Ensign, on Lexington alarm roll of Capt. Jonathan Brown's co., Col. David Green's regt.; marched on alarm of April 19, 1775, from Tewksbury; service, 7 days. On list of officers of Massachusetts militia, chosen by company and accepted by council May 31, 1776, as 2d lieutenant in Joshua Baldwin's co., Tewksbury East co. (8th) of Simeon Spaulding's regt, 7th Middlesex co. regt. On list of officers of Massachusetts militia as captain in the 8th co. of the 7th Middlesex co. regt.; commissioned June 29, 1780; commanded by J. Brown. Captain on muster and pay roll of Capt. Amos Foster's co., Col. Cyprian How's regt., 7th Middlesex co. regt. for service at R. I. on alarm by a resolve of June 22, 1780; enlisted July 4, 1780; discharged Oct. 30, 1780; service, 4 mos., 10 days.

ANDREW FOSTER, Freetown. On descriptive list of men raised on resolve of Dec. 2, 1780; received at Taunton March 8, 1781, by Sergeant Ebenezer Crocker to be conducted to Springfield and delivered to Col. Wm. Shepard; age, 21 years;

stature, 5 ft. 3¾ inches; complexion, light, eyes blue, hair light, occupation farmer; served in Norton's co.; enlistment during war.

ANDREW FOSTER, Lynn. Private, Lexington alarm roll of Capt. Ezra Newhall's co.; marched on alarm of April 19, 1775, from Lynn; service, 21 days.

ANDREW FOSTER, Lynn. Private, on Lexington alarm roll of Capt. Nathaniel Bancroft's co.; marched from Lynn on alarm of April 19, 1775; service, 2 days.

ANDREW FOSTER, Andover. On list of men enlisted into Continental army from Capt. James Gates' co. of 8th Worcester co. regt; enlisted for Ashburnham for 3 years; joined Capt. Summers' co., Col. Greaton's regt; enlisted before May 26, 1777. On return from service from Jan. 1, 1777, to May 1, 1777; credited to Reading as 15 mos service as sergeant and 13 mos as private; reported deserted.

ANDREW FOSTER, Cambridge. Appears on descriptive list of men enlisted from Middlesex co. under resolve of Dec. 2, 1780; age, 14 years; stature, 4 ft. 6 in., complexion light, hair light, blue eyes; laborer: enlisted July 1, 1781, for 3 years; reported rejected.

ANDREW FOSTER, Newton. On list of men enlisted into Continental army from co. of Middlesex; enlisted for Newton.

ANDREW FOSTER. Seaman, on pay roll of officers and crew of Ship Protector, John F. Williams commander; enlisted March 25, 1780; discharged Aug. 17, 1780; service, 4 mos., 23 days.

ANDREW FOSTER. Private, on muster roll of Capt. Francis Green's co., Col. Joseph Vose's (1st) regt. for Feb. and March, 1781; enlisted Feb. 15, 1781, for during the war; on roll dated West Point April —, 1781; reported joined April 3, 1781; confined for desertion; on another roll, dated at West Point, in April, he was reported dead.

ANDREW FOSTER, Concord. On descriptive list of enlisted men; age, 19 years; stature, 5 ft.; complexion, light; occupation, farmer; mustered by Ensign Phelon; return made by Nathaniel Barber, Muster Master, Suffolk co., Boston, Sept. 25, 1780, Col. Henry Jackson's regt.

ANTHONY FOSTER, Marblehead. Private on muster roll of Capt. Haynes' Co., Col. J. Brewer's regt., dated Aug. 1, 1775; service, 15 days. Also on order for bounty coat due for the eight months service in 1775, dated Cambridge Oct. 25, 1775, payable to Capt. Haynes'.

ANTHONY FOSTER, New Gloucester. Private on company return of Capt. Haynes' co., Col. Brewers' regt., dated Prospect Hill Oct. 6, 1775.

ANTHONY FOSTER. Private, in Capt. Aaron Haynes' co., Col. Asa Whitcomb's regt., at Ticonderoga, roll dated Dec., 1776; reported discharged Jan. 1, 1776; service, 11 mos.

ASA FOSTER, Ware. Private on muster and pay roll of Capt. Samuel Fairfield's co., Col. Nathan Sparhawk's regt.; enlisted Oct. 1, 1778; service, 2 mos., 17 days, at Dorchester.

BARTHOLOMEW FOSTER. On order for bounty coat, or equivalent in money, given by Mary Foster (widow), adminx, dated Boston Nov. 26, 1776, payable to Jabez Fisher; bounty due for service in Capt. John Boyd's co., Col. John Greaton's regt.; service certified to by Lieut. Ebenezer Dean; reported as having marched to Quebec in Capt. Hubbard's co, Col. Arnold's regt.

BARTHOLOMEW FOSTER. Prize Master. On muster and pay roll of officers and crew of the brigantine "Tyranicide," commanded by Capt. Jonathan Hearaden; enlisted March 26, 1778; service, 1 mo., 9 days; reported died May 5, 1778.

BENJAMIN FOSTER. On list of officers of Massachusetts militia, appointed by Brig.-Gen. Michael Farley as quartermaster of Col. Cogswell Jr.'s regt., in Brig.-Gen. Farley's brigade; drafted from training band and alarm list of Essex co. militia, and ordered to march to Horse Neck under resolve of Sept. 12, 1776; dated Ipswich Sept. 30, 1776.

BENJAMIN FOSTER, Boxford. Sergeant. On muster and pay roll of Capt. Jonathan Evan's co., Col. Nathaniel Wade's regt., for service in Rhode Island (North Kingstown); enlisted July 1, 1778; discharged Jan. 1, 1779; service, 6 mos., 7 days.

BENJAMIN FOSTER, Wilmington. Private, on Lexington alarm roll of Capt. Timothy Walker's co., Col. Green's regt., which marched from Wilmington on alarm of April 19, 1775; service, 7½ days. Also on receipt for advance pay, dated camp at Cambridge, June 22, 1775, payable to himself for services in Capt. Harnden's co., Col. Bridge's regt; autograph signature; reported corporal.

BENJAMIN FOSTER. Corporal. On muster and pay roll of Capt. John

Crawford's co., Col. James Convers' regt. for service in R. I. on alarm; enlisted July 23, 1777; discharged July 26, 1777; service, 4 days. Also in same co. marched to Bennington on alarm of Aug. 20, 1777; enlisted Aug. 20; discharged Aug. 23, 1777; service, 5 days (travel included). Also on pay roll of Capt. Crawford's co., Col. Job Cushing's regt.; enlisted Sept. 7, 1777; discharged Nov. 29, 1777; service, 3 mos., 3 days, travel included.

BENJAMIN FOSTER, Leicester. Chaplain. On muster roll of Col. Samuel Denny's regt., which marched to reinforce northern army Aug. 19, 1777; service, 5 days.

BENJAMIN FOSTER, Oakham. Private, on a pay abstract of Capt. Nathan Hamilton's co., Col. Samuel Brewer's regt.; service, from Aug. 3 to Sept. 30, 1776; 1 mo., 29 days. Also on receipt for wages for Oct., 1776, dated Ticonderoga Mills, Nov. 3, 1776, in above company. Also on pay abstract for mileage from Fort Edward to his home in Oakham, dated Brookfield, Feb. 6, 1777.

BENJAMIN FOSTER, Reading. On return for equipments made by Capt. Amos Upton dated at Reading, April 21, 1775; John Flint captain instead of said Upton. Also on roll of Capt. Flint's co., dated Dec. 19, 1775; service, 4 days.

BENJAMIN FOSTER. Private, on muster and pay roll of Capt. John Dodge's co., Col. Jacob Gerrish's regt., from April 1, 1778, to July; also from July 2, 1778, to July 12, 1778; guard duty at Cambridge; autograph signature for wages for 2 mos. service in April and May, dated camp Winter Hill, June 21, 1778. Also on muster and pay roll Capt. Samuel Huse's co., Col. Jacob Garrish's regt. of guards; enlisted July 26, 1778; discharged Dec. 14, 1778; guards at Cambridge, 4 mos. 21 days.

BENJAMIN FOSTER. On list of men on return of Capt. John Harendel's co., May 11, 1775. (Nothing more.)

BENJAMIN FOSTER. Private on pay abstracts for service for months of February, March, April, May, June, July and August, 1776, in Capt. Moses Brown's co., Col. John Glover's (14th) regt.; enlisted Jan. 29, 1776.

BENJAMIN FOSTER, Machias. Private, on muster and pay roll of Capt. Jabez West's co. (raised at Machias for expedition against St. Johns); enlisted May 22, 1777; discharged July 17, 1777; service, 1 mo. 25 days.

BENJAMIN FOSTER. Appears on list of officers of the Massachusetts militia, chosen by the legislature Jan. 30, 1776, as colonel of 6th Lincoln co. regt.; concurred in council Feb. 8, 1776. On a return, dated Gouldsborough, March 20, 1777. Also on pay roll, date not given; service at Machias between May 20, 1777, and Aug. 20, 1777; service, 1 mo. 11 days. Also service at Machias, as engaged, Aug. 20, 1777; discharged Oct. 10, 1777; 1 mo. 21 days.

BENJAMIN FOSTER. Private, on muster and pay roll of Capt. Wm. Green's co., Col. Cyprian How's regt: for service in R. I.; enlisted July 30, 1780; discharged Nov. 1, 1780; service, 3 mos. 7 days.

BENJAMIN FOSTER. On list of field officers of Massachusetts militia as quartermaster of Col. James Frye's regt.

BENJAMIN FOSTER, Boxford. Drummer, on Lexington alarm roll of Capt. Wm. Pearley's co., Col. James Frye's regt., which marched on alarm of April 19, 1775, from Boxford; service, 7 days; enlisted Feb. 16, 1775. On muster roll of above co., dated Aug. 1, 1775, his time of enlistment is given as April 26, 1775; service, 1 mo. 1 day. Also on receipt for advance pay, dated Cambridge camp, June 22, 1775. On order for bounty coat, dated Cambridge Nov. 14, 1775. As quartermaster sergeant on return dated at Cambridge camp, May 17, 1775, was appointed quartermaster Jan. 23, 1776; commissioned March 13, 1776, Col. Isaac Smith's regt.

BENJAMIN FOSTER, JR., Machias. Private, on muster and pay roll of Capt. Stephen Smith's co., stationed at Machias; enlisted Sept. 13, 1775; service, 3 mos., 25 days; discharged Dec. 31, 1775. Also private in Capt. John Scott's co.; enlisted Nov. 28, 1776; discharged Dec. 21, 1776—24 days. Also on muster and pay roll of Capt Joseph Sevey's co., Col. Benjamin Foster's regt.; enlisted June 23, 1777; discharged July 16, 1777—23 days. As corporal in Capt. Sevey's co; enlisted July 16, 1777; discharged Oct. 10, 1777; service, 2 mos. 24 days. Also one day's service between Dec. 5 and 25, 1778.

BENJAMIN FOSTER, JR. On list of men in the training band in Reading under Capt. Thomas Eaton.

BENNET FOSTER, Cambridge. Private, on muster roll of Capt. Abijah Child's co., Lieut. Wm. Bond's regt.; in camp at Prospect Hill for Aug and Sept., 1775; reported as having supplied the place of George Wellington, who was discharged July 28, 1775; enlisted July 28, 1775. Also on a pay abstract of Capt. John Minott's co., Col. Dike's regt., for equipments for Dec., 1776, and Jan. and Feb., 1777, on return of this co. from Jan. 9, 1777, to March 1, 1777.

BENNETT FOSTER, Menotomy. Matross, on Continental pay accounts of Capt. John Wells' co., Col. John Crane's (artillery) regt; service, from March 1, 1777, to Dec. 31, 1779; enlisted for 3 years: credited to Capt. David Allen's co. on muster rolls for Sept., 1777, and Jan. 1, 1778. Also on pay accounts of Capt. Jackson's co., Col. Crane's regt.; service, from Jan. 1, 1780, to March 1, 1780.

BENNETT FOSTER. Marine. On list of officers and crew of the state ship Tartor, commanded by John Cathcart; enlisted Aug. 3; discharged Nov. 21, 1782; service, 3 mos. 18 days; autograph signature.

*BENNING FOSTER. Private. Served in Capt. Dyer and West's co., that marched to St. Johns May, 1777; service, 1 mo. 25 days. On another roll enlisted July 15, 1777; discharged Dec. 13; service, 4 mos. 28 days. Also enlisted Dec. 13, 1777; discharged June, 1778,—5 mos. 18 days. —A company of artillery. Service under Col. John Allen, commander-in-chief of the Indians, eastern department. On pay roll of artillery co. under Col. John Allen, entering June 1, 1778; discharged Dec. 1, 1778; 6 months stationed at Machias.

BENONIA FOSTER, Concord. Private, on muster roll of Capt. Joseph Butler's co., Col. John Nixon's regt.; dated Aug. 1, 1775; enlisted April 29, 1775; service, 3 mos. 9 days. On Sept. report is reported sick in hospital. Also on order for bounty coat, or equivalent, due for the 8 months' service in 1775, dated Winter Hill, Dec. 20, 1775.

BENONI FOSTER. Private, on muster and pay roll of Capt. Joseph Seavey's co., Col Benj. Foster's regt.; on duty at Machias between Dec. 5 and 25, 1778; service, 13 days.

BENONI FOSTER. Seaman. On muster and pay roll of officers and crew of Brig. Hazard, commanded by Capt. John F. Williams; enlisted May 12, 1779; service, 1 mo. 9 days; reported as one of the crew placed on board the Ship Putnam, or who left the brig on her arrival at Boston.

BOSTON FOSTER, Boston (probably). Appears on an enlistment agreement, dated Boston, June, 1780; signed by said Foster and others, engaging themselves to serve in Continental army for the term of 6 months from time of arrival at place of rendezvous—Capt. Wells' co.—age, 36; stature 5 ft. 8 in.; complexion, black. Received bounty of Edward Proctor, colonel of Boston regt. On descriptive list given on his arrival at Springfield, July 2, 1780; age, 32; complexion, negro. He also enlisted July 22, 1780, to serve in the militia under Brig.-Gen. John Fellows. Was private on muster and pay roll of Capt. Alexander Hodgdon's co., Col. Ebenezer Thayer's regt., for service in R. I.; enlisted July 31, 1780; discharged Oct. 30; service, 3 mos. 3 days (3 days' travel included).

C. FOSTER. On a receipt, dated March 25, 1782, for £6 given by Isaac Burnham, sergt.

CALEB FOSTER. Private, on muster and pay roll of Capt. John Kettell's co., Maj. Heath's regt. of Guards doing duty in and about Boston; enlisted Aug. 21, 1779; discharged Sept. 30, 1779; service, 1 mo. 12 days.

CATO FOSTER, Andover. On pay abstract of Capt. Benjamin Farnum's co., Col. Ebenezer Francis' regt.; rations allowed from date of enlistment, March 8, 1777, to time of arrival at Bennington; credited with allowance to March 28, 1777 —33 days, including 11 days for 220 miles travel. On muster return of Capt. Farnum's co., Col. Benj. Tupper's regt., dated Jan. 24, 1778, was reported unfit for duty for want of clothes. On return of enlisted men, dated Andover, Feb. 16, 1778, enlisted for 3 years; on pay accounts of Capt. Stephen Abbot's co., Col. Tupper's regt.; service from March 8, 1777, to Dec. 31, 1779; reported enlisted April, 1778, for during the war.

CATO FOSTER, Andover. On descriptive list of men belonging to Andover; age, 22 yrs.; stature, 5 ft. 5 in.; complexion, black; hair, black; enlisted May 12, 1779, for during the war; joined Capt. Daniel Lunt's co., 10th regt., rank of Drummer; enlisted by Capt. Abbot; on pay accounts of Capt. Abbot's co., for service from Jan. 1, 1780, to Dec. 31, 1780; service, 9 mos. as Private, and 3 mos. as Corporal; also on roll from Jan. 1, 1781, to Jan. 1, 1782, as Private.

CATO FOSTER, Salem. On list of men of the 1st regt.; entitled to 200 acres of land or $20 in money, by resolve of court, March 5, 1801.

CHANDLER FOSTER. Private, on muster and pay roll of Capt. Isaac

*Name Benen on roll.

Marsh's co., Col. Sear's (Berkshire co.) regt.; enlisted July 21, 1781; discharged Nov. 2, 1781; service, 3 mos. 12 days; stationed at Fort Plains, Tryon co., under Brig.-Gen. Starks.

CHARLES FOSTER, Kingston. Appears among a list of prisoners on board the Guard Ship "Adams," by the Board of War as returned by Joseph Dobel, Sept. 8, 1777; reported received Aug. 26, 1777.

CHILLINGSWORTH FOSTER. Private, on muster and pay roll of Capt. Benj. Berry's co., Maj. Zenas Winslow's regt. (Harwich militia); 3 days' service; service at Bedford and Falmouth, on alarm of Sept. 7, 1778.

DANIEL FOSTER, Groton. Private, on muster roll of Capt. Henry Farwell's co., Col. Wm. Prescott's regt., dated Aug. 1, 1775; enlisted April 25, 1775; service, 98 days. Is also on the October return, and on order for bounty coat or equivalent in money due for the 8 months' service, dated Sewall's Point, Nov. 16, 1775.

DANIEL FOSTER. Sergeant, on muster and pay roll of Capt. Zadock Buffington's co., Col. Samuel Johnson's regt.; enlisted Aug. 15, 1777; discharged (at Cambridge) Nov. 30, 1777; 3 mos. 16 days' service at the Northward.

DANIEL FOSTER, Rutland. Private, autograph signature for advance pay, dated July 13, 1775, due for services in Capt. Adam Wheeler's co., Col. Doolittle's regt; on the company return, dated Winter Hill, Oct. 6, 1775; also in Capt. Joseph Livermore's co.; enlisted July 7, 1779; discharged Oct. 2, 1779; 2 mos. 26 days' service as Guard at Rutland.

DANIEL FOSTER. Private, on pay abstract of Capt. Barnabas Dodge's co., Col. Baldwin's regt., for service in Nov., 1775; reported enlisted Nov. 22, 1775; also for service in Dec., 1775; enlisted Dec. 1, 1775; also reported as enlisted for 1 year from last of Dec., 1775; also on list of men who did not pass muster, dated at Chelsea, Jan. 3, 1776; on list of men who received ammunition Jan. 24, 1776; on return of men receiving advance pay for Jan., 1776; on pay abstract for service in April, 1776, also for May, June and July, in camp at New York; also on list of men agreeing to serve 6 weeks from Dec. 31, 1776, dated at Trenton; also on list of those returning guns into public store at Chatham, Feb. 12, 1777.

DANIEL FOSTER. Private, on muster roll of Capt. Joseph Bates' co., Lieut.-Col. John Brooks' regt., for Aug., 1781; enlisted July 25, 1781, for 6 months, dated in camp at Peekskill; also on the Sept. report; also Oct. and Nov. reports, dated at "York Hutts;" on Dec. report, dated at "York Hutts," reported deserted, Jan. 11, 1782.

DANIEL FOSTER. Seaman, on muster and pay roll of the Frigate Boston; enlisted June 27th (year not given).

DANIEL FOSTER, Ipswich. Private on muster and pay rolls of Capt. Jeremiah Putnam's co., Col. Nathaniel Wade's regt.; enlisted July 15, 1778; service to Dec. 31, 1778, 5 mos. 21 days in R. I.; also served as Corporal in Capt. Putnam's co., Col. Nathan Tyler's regt. from Dec. 1, 1779, to Jan. 1, 1780; service, 1 mo. 5 days; also from July 8, 1779, to Dec. 1, 1779, 4 mos. 23 days.

DANIEL FOSTER, Ipswich. On descriptive list of 6 months' men to reinforce Continental army, by resolve of June 5, 1780; age, 18 yrs ; stature, 5 ft. 9 in.; complexion, ruddy; arrived at Springfield July 5, 1780; marched from Ipswich June 22, 1780; discharged Jan. 9, 1781; service, 7 mos.

DANIEL FOSTER. On muster and pay roll of Capt. Joseph Bates' co., as Sergeant; enlisted July 9, 1780; discharged Jan. 9, 1781, dated at West Point.

DAVID FOSTER, Boxford. Private, on Lexington alarm roll of Capt. Jacob Gould's co., Col. Samuel Johnson's regt.; marched on alarm of April 19, 1775, from Boxford; service, 6 days; also on a pay abstract of Capt. Richard Peabody's co., Col. Edward Wigglesworth's regt., for service in 1776 for travel allowance from Ticonderoga home to Boxford.

DAVID FOSTER, Gloucester. On descriptive list, dated June 9, 1780, of officers and crew of Ship America, commanded by John Somes; age, 37 yrs.; stature, 5 ft. 4 in.

DAVID FOSTER, Watertown. Private, on muster roll of Capt. Asa Prince's co., Col. Mansfield's regt., dated Aug. 1, 1775; enlisted May 8, 1775; service, 3 mos.; also on order for bounty coat or equivalent for the 8 months' service, 1775, Capt. Prince's co., Col. Hutchinson's regt.

DAVID FOSTER. Private, on muster and pay roll of Capt. John Dix's co., Col. McIntosh's regt.; service in R. I.; enlisted Aug. 1, 1778; discharged Sept. 12, 1778; service, 1 mo. 15 days, 4 days' travel allowed.

DAVID FOSTER, Winthrop, Me. Private, on muster roll of Capt. Samuel McCobb's co., Col. Nixon's regt., dated Aug. 1, 1775; enlisted June 1, 1775; service,

2 mos. 5 days; also on receipt for advance pay, dated Cambridge, July 26, 1775; at Winter Hill, Oct. 7, 1775. Is on a list of men returned with a petition of inhabitants of Winthrop, dated March 10, 1777, asking consideration on account of their exposed condition, as having voluntarily enlisted in the army in 1775.

DAVID FOSTER. On a list of men returned as having served on Main Guard at Prospect Hill, July 16, 1775, under Col. L. Baldwin; rank, Private.

DAVID FOSTER, Westminster. Corporal, on Lexington alarm roll of Capt. Noah Miles' co., Col. John Whitcomb's regt., which marched on alarm of April 19, 1775, from Westminster to Cambridge; service, 5 days; then enlisted into the army; commissioned Ensign, June 12, 1775, of Capt. Edward Bemis' co., Col. Asa Whitcomb's regt.; given as 2d Lieutenant on the Oct., 1775, return.

DAVID FOSTER, Harwich. On list of officers of Massachusetts militia; chosen by election of the company, 1st Lieutenant in Abijah Bang's co., of 2d Barnstable co. regt.; consented to in Council, April 20, 1776; 7 days' service performed during Sept., 1778, on alarm at Bedford and Falmouth; also on pay abstract, dated Nov. 7, 1778; 2 days' service guarding prisoners from Ship Somerset at Harwich, and thence to Yarmouth.

DAVID FAUSTER (or FOSTER). Mariner, on descriptive list, dated May 16, 1780, of officers and crew of schooner Betsey, commanded by George West, Jr.; age, 29 yrs.; stature, 5 ft. 7 in.; complexion, dark.

DAVID FOSTER, 2d Attleborough. Private, on Lexington alarm roll of Capt. Stephen Richardson's co., which marched on alarm of April 19, 1775, from Attleborough; service, 6 days.

DAVID FOSTER. On list of Massachusetts State Pensioners, pensioned June 12, 1800, for life, amount $70; reported dead, last warrant June 7, 1801.

DAVID FOSTER. (Rank not given, probably Corporal), on muster and pay roll of Capt. Miles Greenwood's co., Col. Jacob Gerrish's regt. (of guards); enlisted Nov. 11, 1777; discharged Feb. 2, 1778; service, 2 mos. 22 days; also enlisted Feb. 3, 1778; discharged April 3, 1778; service 2 mos. 1 day; dated, camp at Winter Hill.

DAVID FOSTER. Private, on muster and pay rolls of Capt. Cadwalladar Ford's co., Col. Brook's regt. (guards at Cambridge); enlisted Nov. 5, 1777; discharged Feb. 3, 1778; service, 2 mo. 29 days. On Nov. report, reported sick—absent; enlisted Feb. 2, 1778; discharged April 3, 1778; service, 2 mos.; order for wages, dated Reading, Feb. 26, 1778.

DUDLEY FOSTER, Boxford. Private, on Lexington alarm roll of Capt. William Pearley's co., Col. James Frye's regt.; marched on alarm of April 19, 1775, from Boxford; service, 7 days; enlisted Feb. 16, 1775; on muster roll dated Aug. 1, 1775; enlisted April 26, 1775; service, 3 mos. 8 days; on order for bounty coat or equivalent in money due for the 8 months' service, dated Cambridge, Nov. 14, 1775.

EBENEZER FOSTER, Oakham. Appears on list of officers of Massachusetts militia; recommended by field officers and accepted by Council, May 31, 1776, as Adjutant in James Converse's regt. (4th Worcester co. regt.), dated Brookfield, May 14, 1776; commissioned in Council, May 31, 1776, also given as June 4 and 5, 1776.

EBENEZER FAUSTER (FOSTER), Rochester. Private, on muster roll of Capt. Earl Clap's co., Col. Theophilus Cotton's regt., dated Aug. 1, 1775; enlisted May 2, 1775; service, 3 mos. 6 days; also on a return of men enlisted into the Continental army from above regt., dated Feb. 19, 1778, to serve 3 years; joined Capt. Turner's co., Col. Bradford's regt.; reported commissioned Ensign, June 1, 1777; reported killed, Sept. 19, 1777.

EBENEZER FOSTER, Westford. Private, on Lexington alarm roll of Capt. Timothy Underwood's co., Col. Wm. Prescott's regt.; marched on alarm of April 19, 1775, from Westford; service, 8 days. On muster return of Capt. Solomon Kidder's co., Col. Brook's regt., for service at White Plains, year not given, possibly 1776; on pay accounts of Capt. W. H. Ballard's co., Col. Brooks' regt.; service from May 1, 1777, to Oct. 1, 1777; reported died Oct. 1 or 7, 1777.

EBENEZER FOSTER, Wilmington. Private, on Lexington alarm roll of Capt. Timothy Walker's co., Col. Green's regt., which marched on alarm of April 19, 1775, from Wilmington; service, 3½ days.

EBENEZER FOSTER, (probably Wilmington). On list of men, dated July 8, 1776, who hired men to serve on Crown Point expedition; hired John Gowing, Jr.

EBENEZER FOSTER. Private, on return of Capt. Jonathan Poore's co.; receipt for wages for 6 weeks' service. On reverse of roll, dated Newbury, March 18, 1777.

EDMUND FOSTER, Reading. Private, on Lexington alarm roll of Capt.

John Bacheller's co., Col. Ebenezer Bridge's regt.; marched on alarm of April 19, 1775, from Reading; service, 11 days.

EDMUND FOSTER, Wrentham. Sergeant, on muster roll of Col. Joseph Read's regt., dated Aug. 1, 1775; enlisted April 27, 1775; service, 3 mos. 12 days; on order for bounty coat due for the 8 months' service in Capt. Oliver Pond's co., Col. Read's regt., dated Roxbury, Dec. 27, 1775.

EDWARD FOSTER, Beverly. Private, on muster roll of Capt. John Low's co., Col. Mansfield's regt.; enlisted May 12, 1775; service, 2 mos. 25 days; autograph signature on receipt for advance pay, dated Cambridge, June, 30, 1775; on order for bounty coat due for 8 mos. service, dated Winter Hill, Oct. 21, 1775.

EDWARD FOSTER, Dorchester. Sergeant, on muster rolls of Maj. Thomas Pierce's co., Col. Gridley's (artillery) regt., dated Aug. 1, 1775; enlisted May 8, 1775; service, 3 mos. 1 day. On order for bounty coat or equivalent in money, dated Roxbury, Dec. 30, 1775; also on muster and pay roll of Capt. Hopestill Hall, Col. Robinson's regt.; enlisted Jan. 29, 1776; service, 23 days; roll dated Roxbury, March, 30, 1776; also on muster and pay roll of Capt. Seth Sumner's co., Col. Benjamin Gill's regt.; enlisted June 12, 1776; service, 3 mos; also on Lieut. Wm. Foster's co., Col. Pierce's muster and pay roll; enlisted March 1, 1778; discharged April 8, 1778; service, 1 mo. 9 days; stationed at Moon Island.

EDWARD FOSTER, Milton. Matross, on Lexington alarm roll of Capt. Daniel Vose's co., Col. Robinson's regt., which marched from Milton to Roxbury; service, 14 days; at battle at Concord before standing army was completed.

EDWARD FOSTER, Sturbridge. Corporal, on Lexington alarm roll of Capt. Timothy Parker's co., Col. Warner's regt., which marched on alarm of April 19, 1775, from Sturbridge; service, 14 days; also on muster and pay roll of Capt. Abel Mason's co., Col. Jonathan Holman's regt.; service, in R. I. on alarm; enlisted Dec. 10, 1776; discharged Jan. 20, 1777; service, 1 mo. 14 days, 3 days travel included; also on muster and pay roll of Capt. Benj. Freeman's co., Col. Holman's regt.; enlisted Sept. 26, 1777; discharged Oct. 18, 1777; service, 1 mo.; service at Northern Dept., rank given both as Clerk and Sergeant.

EDWARD FOSTER, Beverly. 2d Mate, on descriptive list of officers and crew of the privateer brig, Stark, commanded by Ezra Ober, dated June 14, 1780; age, 23 yrs.; stature, 5 ft. 8 in.; complexion, dark; also on a list dated Aug. 22, 1780, as 2d mate of the brigatine Fanny, commanded by Herbert Woodbury; no description.

EDWARD FOSTER, JR. On a return of Capt. S. Richardson's 4th co. (2d Attleborough co.), in service as 2 mos. men at York in 1776; reported "did ½ a turn."

ELIAS FOSTER. Private, on a pay abstract of Capt. Jonathan Minott's co., Col. Baldwin's regt., for travel allowance, dated Cambridge, Jan. 12, 1776.

ELIJAH FOSTER, Ipswich (W. Parish). Private, on Lexington alarm roll of Capt. Abraham How's co., which marched on alarm of April 19, 1775, from Ipswich (W. Parish); service, 2 days.

ELIJAH FOSTER, Bolton. Private, on Lexington alarm roll of Capt. Benjamin Hastings' co., Col. John Whitcomb's regt.; marched on alarm of April 19, 1775, from Bolton to Cambridge; service, 13 days.

ELIJAH FOSTER, JR., Bolton. On return of men enlisted into the Continental army from Capt. David Nurse's co., Col. Whitney's regt., dated Jan. 2, 1778; enlisted for Bolton for 3 yrs.; joined Capt. Daniel Barns' co., Col. Bigelow's regt.; also on pay accounts for service from May 15, 1777 to July 5, 1779; reported deserted on muster rolls, dated Van Schaick's Island, Sept. 1, 1777; enlisted May 15, 1777; reported sick in General Hospital for March and April, 1779, dated Providence, reported sick in General Hospital.

ELIPHALET FOSTER, Winthrop, Me. Sergeant, on muster roll of Capt. McCobb's co., Col. Nixon's regt., dated Aug. 1, 1775; enlisted June 1, 1775; service, 2 mos. 5 days; on return for cartridge boxes, dated Cambridge, June 24, 1775; autograph signature on receipt for advance pay June 26, 1775; at Winter Hill, Oct. 7, 1775; returned with a petition of inhabitants of Winthrop, dated March 10, 1777, asking consideration on account of their exposed condition as having voluntarily enlisted in the army in 1775; lieutenant, on muster and pay roll of Capt. John Blunt's co., Col. Samuel McCobb's regt.; enlisted June 28, 1779; discharged Sept. 28, 1779; service, 3 mos.; 2d lieutenant, on muster and pay roll of Capt. Timothy Foster's co., Maj. William Lithgow's regt.; service, 1 mo. 7 days, between Sept. 1st and Nov. 4, 1779; service in Lincoln co.

ELISHA FOSTER. On list of men mustered in Worcester co. to serve in Capt. Harwood's co., Col. Nixon's regt.; on return made by Thos. Newhall, muster master; mustered April 4, 1777; enlisted for 3 yrs.

ELISHA FOSTER, Brookfield. Enlisted out of Col. Converse's regt. for western; list dated Brookfield, Sept. 15, 1777.

ELISHA FOSTER, Brookfield. Enlisted into army out of Capt. Daniel Gilbert's co., list dated Feb. 17, 1778; enlisted in 1777 for town of Brookfield for 3 yrs; on pay accounts of Col. Nixon's regt., for service from Feb. 25, 1777, to Dec. 31, 1779; on muster roll, dated Peekskill, Feb. 16, 1779; roll for May, dated Highlands; enlisted Feb. 15, 1777; on pay accounts for service from Jan. 1, 1780, to Dec. 31, 1780; reported Sergeant; commissioned in council as Ensign, June 15, 1781; on descriptive list of men belonging to Brookfield, dated West Point, Jan. 29, 1781; age, 21 yrs.; stature, 5 ft. 9 in.; complexion, light; hair, light; eyes, light. Enlisted Dec. 23, 1779, during war; joined Capt. Pike's co., Lieut.-Col. Smith's regt.; also given Col. Thos. Nixon's regt.; reported Sergeant; autograph signature on pay abstract, dated Boston, June 22, 1781, for service for October to December, 1780. On return for wages for service for Jan. to Dec., 1781, reported appointed Ensign, June 14, 1781; also on return for wages for January to December, 1782, with rank of lieutenant.

ELISHA FOSTER, Harwich. Private, on muster and pay roll of Capt. Bangs' co., Col. Nathaniel Freeman's regt., for service on alarm in R. I.; enlisted Oct. 1, 1777; discharged Nov. 1, 1777; service, 31 days.

ELISHA FOSTER, Holden. On list of men mustered in Worcester Co., to serve in Capt. Hubbard's co., Col. Denny's regt.; on return made by Thomas Newhall, muster master; enlisted for 9 mos; mustered July 2, 1779. On descriptive list returned by Seth Washburn, supt. for Worcester Co.; age, 20 yrs.; stature, 6 ft.; complexion, light. Division of militia marched to Springfield July 8, 1779.

ELISHA FOSTER. Private, on muster and pay roll of Capt. Daniel Grout's co., Col. John Rand's regt.; enlisted July 7, 1780; discharged Oct. 9, 1780; service, 3 mos. 11 days, travel allowed; marched to Claverack; discharged at West Point.

ELISHA FOSTER, Worcester. Private, on muster and pay roll of Capt. John Cutler's co., Col. Luke Drury's regt.; enlisted Aug. 20, 1781; discharged Nov. 28, 1781; service, 3 mos. 16 days, travel included; joined regt. at West Point, Aug. 28, 1781.

ELISHA FOSTER, Scituate. Private, on pay abstract of Capt. William Turner's co., Col. Bailey's regt., for travel allowance; joined Col. Bailey's regt., Dec. 10, 1775.

ELISHA FOSTER, Scituate. Sergeant, on Lexington alarm roll of Capt. Galen Clapp's co., Col. Anthony Thomas' regt., which marched on alarm of April 19, 1775, from Scituate; service, 4 days. Also on muster and pay roll of Capt. Joseph Stetson's co., Col. Thomas' regt.; enlisted March 24, 1776; discharged March 29, 1776; service, 5 days; marched on alarm from Scituate to Hingham after taking of Dorchester Heights. Commissioned 2d Lieutenant May 10, 1776. Lieutenant, on muster and pay roll of Lieut. Anthony Waterman's co., Col. John Cushing's regt.; enlisted Dec. 10, 1776, on alarm at R. I.; marched to Bristol, R. I.; service, 15 days. Also on pay abstract of Capt. Hayward Peirce's co., Col. Cotton's regt.; service, 1 mo. 1 day, between September and November, 1777; expedition to Tiverton, R. I.

ELISHA FOSTER, Dorchester. On order for bounty coat or equivalent in money given by Thomas Foster (father), dated Dorchester, April 10, 1776, payable to Capt. Ebenezer Withington; bounty due on account of service in Capt. Elijah Vose's co., Col. Heath's (later) Col. Greaton's regt.; service, certified to by the selectmen of Dorchester; reported enlisted in April, 1775, and died in Dec., 1775.

ELISHA FOSTER. Seaman, on muster and pay roll of officers and crew of brigantine "Independence;" enlisted July 18, 1776; discharged Sept. 22, 1776; service, 2 mos. 4 days. Also on another roll as discharged Jan. 20, 1777; date of enlistment not given; service, 3 mos. 28 days; crew sent to convey prize brigantine Nancy to Plymouth; rolls dated Plymouth.

EPHRAIM FOSTER, Boxford. Private, on Lexington alarm roll of Capt. John Cushing's co., Col. Samuel Johnson's regt.; marched on alarm of April 19, 1775, from Boxford; service, 4 days.

EZEKIEL FOSTER, Bernardston. Private, on muster roll of Capt. Agrippa Wells' co., Col. Asa Whitcomb's regt.; enlisted May 1, 1775; service, 3 mos. 8 days.; on receipt for wages for Sept., 1775, dated Prospect Hill, Nov. 17, 1775. Also on October return as Private; on order for bounty coat or equivalent, due for the 8 mos. service, dated Prospect Hill, Dec. 22, 1775; payable to Capt. Wells.

EZEKIEL FOSTER, Bernardston. Ensign, on list of officers in Col. Asa Whitcomb's regt.; commissioned June 12, 1775; 2d Lieutenant, on muster roll dated Aug. 1 1775; enlisted May 1, 1775; service, 3 mos. 8 days; on report dated Prospect Hill, Nov. 17, 1775, reported Lieutenant.

EZEKIEL FOSTER, Greenfield. Lieutenant, on Lexington alarm roll of Capt. Agrippa Wells' co., Col. Samuel Williams' regt., which marched from Greenfield on alarm of April 19, 1775 (marched April 20th); service, 10 days; enlisted into the army May 1, 1775.

EZEKIEL FOSTER. 2d Lieutenant, on muster and pay roll of Capt. Daniel Pomroy's co. (a detachment from a Hampshire Co., regt. serving under Gen. Starks in Northern Dept.); enlisted July 1, 1778; discharged Oct. 31, 1778; service, 4 mos.

EZEKIEL FOSTER. 2d Lieutenant, on list of officers of Massachusetts militia of 6th Lincoln Co. regt., commissioned July 11, 1776. Lieutenant, on muster and pay roll of Capt. Joseph Sevey's co,, Col, Benjamin Foster's regt,; enlisted July 16, 1777; discharged Oct, 10, 1777; service at Machias, 2 mos., 24 days.

EZEKIEL FOSTER, (perhaps) Greenfield. Sergeant, on muster and pay roll of Capt. Timothy Child's co,, Col, David Leonard's regt,; enlisted Feb, 24, 1777; discharged April 10, 1777; service, 1 mo. 17 days.

EZEKIEL FOSTER. Private, on muster and pay roll of Capt. Amasa Sheldon's co., Col. Elisha Porter's regt.; enlisted July 10, 1777; discharged Aug. 8, 1777; service, 1 mo. 4 days.

EZEKIEL FOSTER. Private, on muster and pay roll of Benjamin Larrabee's co., Col. Mitchel's regt., which marched on expedition to Penobscot; enlisted July 9th; discharged Sept. 12, 1779; service, 2 mos. 3 days.

EZEKIEL FOSTER, JR., Greenfield. Private, on Lexington alarm roll of Capt. Agrippa Wells' co., Col. Samuel Williams' regt.; marched (April 20th) on alarm of April 19, 1775, from Greenfield; enlisted into the army May 1, 1775.

EZEKIEL FOSTER, JR. Corporal, on muster and pay roll of Capt. Amasa Sheldon's co., Col. Elisha Porter's regt.; enlisted July 10, 1777; discharged Aug. 8, 1777; service, 1 mo. 4 days, travel included; service in Northern Dept.

EZRA FOSTER, Tewksbury. Private, on muster and pay roll of Capt. Samuel Tay's co., Lieut.-Col. Webb's regt.; enlisted Sept. 12, 1781; discharged Dec. 1, 1777; service, 3 mos. 11 days, travel included.

EZRA FOSTER appears on receipt for bounty paid him by Capt. John Trull, for class No. 3, for town of Tewksbury, to serve in Continental army for 3 yrs.; receipt dated Boston, June 14, 1782.

EZRA FOSTER. Private, on muster and pay roll of Col. Benjamin Tupper's (10th) regt.; enlisted May 29, 1782; service, 7 mos. 3 days; roll made up to Jan. 1, 1783.

EZRA FOSTER. Private, on return of Capt. Matthew Chamber's co., Lieut.-Col. Calvin Smith's regt. (6th); in service for December, 1782, for wages.

EZRA TRASK FOSTER, Beverly. Private, on Lexington alarm, roll of Capt. Larkin Thorndike's co., which marched on alarm of April 19, 1775, from Beverly to Concord; service, 2½ days.

FLETCHER FOSTER, Sturbridge. Private, on Lexington alarm roll of Capt. Timothy Parker's co. of minute men, Col. Warner's regt., which marched on alarm of April 19, 1775, from Sturbridge; service, 14 days.

FLETCHER FOSTER. Private, on muster and pay roll of Capt. Abel Mason's co, Col. Jonathan Holman's regt.; service in R. I. (stationed at Providence); enlisted Dec. 10, 1776; discharged Dec. 28, 1776; service, 22 days, 3 days travel included.

FENNER FOSTER, Granville. Private, on Lexington alarm roll of Capt. Lebbens Ball's co. of minute men, which marched April 20th, on alarm of April 19, 1775, from Granville; service, 9 days; reported "Enlisted" into army April 29, 1775. Private, on muster roll of Capt. Ball's co., Col. Danielson's regt.. dated Aug. 1, 1775; service, 3 mos. 10 days; on order for bounty coat or equivalent due for the eight mos. service, dated Roxbury, Dec. 22, 1775. On muster roll of Capt. Aaron Coe's co., Lieut.-Col. Timothy Robinson's regt., dated in garrison at Ticonderoga, Feb. 24, 1777; enlisted Dec. 25, 1776. On list of men enlisted out of Capt. Coe's co., list dated March 31, 1779; enlisted for 3 yrs.; joined Capt. Keep's co., Col. Shepherd's regt. On muster roll of Lieut. John Wright's co. (formerly Capt. Keep's) for July and Aug., 1778; reported with the guard. On roll dated Providence, Nov. 13, 1778, reported with the commissary; on Dec., 1778, roll, as butcher; on Continental army pay accounts of Capt. Keep's co., for service from April 5, 1777, to Dec. 31, 1779; on pay accounts of Capt. Webb's co., Col. Shepherd's regt., for service from Jan. 1, 1780, to April 4, 1780.

GEORGE FOSTER, Hubbardston. Autograph signature on order for advance pay, dated July 13, 1775, Charlestown camp, due on account of service in Capt. Adam Wheeler's co., Col. Doolittle's regt.

GEORGE FOSTER, Sutton. Private, on Lexington alarm roll of Capt. Arthur Daggett's co., Col. Larned's regt.; marched on alarm of April 19, 1775, from Sutton; service, 15 days. On petition, dated Roxbury, June 21, 1775, signed by said Foster and others, who had enlisted to form an artillery company, stating their unwillingness to serve under John Wiley as captain, owing to their belief in his incompetence; petition addressed to the Provincial Congress. Matross, on muster roll of Capt. Ezra Badlam's co., Col. Richard Ridley's regt.; enlisted May 11, 1775; also on roll dated Sewall's Point, Oct. 8, 1775; also on order for bounty coat or equivalent, dated same place, Dec. 26, 1775, due for the 8 mos. service. On list of men mustered in Worcester Co. to serve in Capt. Burbank's co., Col. Crane's regt.; enlisted during the war; mustered April 30, 1777. Sergeant, on rolls of Capt. Jonathan Drury's co., Col. Crane's regt., from Sept., 1777 to Jan. 1, 1778; on muster roll of Capt. David Cook, dated Feb. 5, 1779, reported on furlough; on roll dated April 7, 1779, reported sick—absent; on pay accounts of Capt. Cook's co., for service from March 8, 1777, to Dec. 31, 1779, credited to Sutton, res. Plymouth. Reported served 33 mos. 23 days, as Sergeant. On pay accounts for service from Jan. 1, 1780, to April 1, 1780; reported deserted April 1, 1780.

GEORGE FOSTER. Private, on company return of Capt. Nathan Peter's co., Col. Timothy Danielson's regt., dated Oct. 6, 1775; reported deserted.

GEORGE FOSTER. On list of prisoners sent from Newport on the Lord Sandwich prison ship, and landed at Bristol, March 7, 1778.

GEORGE FOSTER. Private, on muster and pay roll of Capt. Samuel Sloper's co., Col. Israel Chapin's regt.; enlisted Nov. 5, 1779; discharged Nov. 22d; service, 22 days, 5 days travel included; stationed at Claverack.

GERSHOM FOSTER, Middleborough. Private, on Lexington alarm roll of Capt. Isaac Wood's (2d) co.; marched on alarm of April 19, 1775, from Middleborough to Marshfield; service, 3 days. Private, on company return of Capt. Isaac Wood's co., Col. Theophilus Cotton's regt., dated Oct. 6, 1775; on muster and pay roll of Capt. Abner Brown's co., Col. Ebenezer White's regt.; service in R. I., on an alarm; marched Aug. 1, 1780; discharged Aug. 9th; service, 9 days.

GERSHOM FOSTER. Lieutenant, on muster and pay roll of Capt. Timothy Ingraham, from March 1st to May 1, 1778, 61 days; stationed at Dartmouth at the fort.

GIDEON FOSTER, Andover. Private, Lexington alarm roll of Capt. Joshua Holt's co.; marched on alarm of April 19, 1775, from Andover to Cambridge; service, 1½ days.

GIDEON FOSTER, Danvers. 2d Lieutenant, on Lexington alarm roll of Capt. Samuel Epes' co., Col. Pickering's regt.; marched on alarm of April 19, 1775, from Danvers; service, 2 days; enlisted as Capt. in Col. John Mansfield's regt., May 6, 1775; commissioned May 27, 1775; commissioned Capt. of 3d co., 8th Essex co. regt. of Massachusetts militia, May 3, 1778.

HACHALIAH FOSTER (credited to Granville, residence not given). On list of men enlisted into army out of Capt. Aaron Coe's, John Hamilton's and William Coolidge's co's., dated March 31, 1779; enlisted for 3 yrs; joined Capt. Keep's co., Col. Shepherd's regt. Sergeant of Lieut. Wright's co., for July and August, 1778, reported wounded; also on October return, dated Providence, Nov. 13, 1778; and on pay accounts of Capt. Keep's co.; service, from March 1, 1777, to Jan. 1, 1779. Name spelled Hakaliah on this roll.

HETHERLY FOSTER, Georgetown. 2d Lieutenant, Capt. John Berry's co., Col. McCobb's (1st) Lincoln co. regt.; commissioned July 1, 1776; roll dated Georgetown, Nov. 19, 1779.

ISAAC FOSTER, Tewksbury. Private, on muster roll of Capt. Furbush's co., Col. Bridge's regt., dated Aug. 1, 1775; enlisted May 25, 1775; service, 2 mos. 12 days,; on order for bounty coat or equivalent due for the 8 mos. service in 1775, dated Cambridge, Nov. 21, 1775. Corporal, on muster and pay roll of Capt. Moses Barn's co., Lieut.-Col. Pierce's regt.; service in R. I.; enlisted May 17th; discharged July 1, 1779; service, 1 mo. 14 days.

ISAAC FOSTER, Tewksbury. Private, on muster and pay roll of Capt. Thomas Hovey's co., Col. Nathan Tyler's regt.; service in R. I.; enlisted July 10, 1779; discharged Dec. 1, 1779; service, 4 mos. 21 days, also 27 days in December. On descriptive list of men raised to reinforce Continental army, for term of 6 mos., on resolve of June 5, 1780. Age, 19 yrs; stature, 5 ft. 7 in.; complexion, light. Arrived at Springfield July 9, 1780; marched July 4, 1780; discharged Jan. 8, 1781; service, 6 mos. 16 days.

ISAAC FOSTER. Private, on muster and pay roll of Capt. John Joslin's co., Col. Job Cushing's regt.; marched from Loeminster to Bennington, last of July, 1777, to join Col. Seth Warner; no service given; reported deserted; roll dated Leominster, Dec. 29, 1777.

ISAAC FOSTER, Tewksbury. Descriptive list of men from Middlesex co., under resolve of Dec. 2, 1780. Age, 18 yrs.; stature, 5 ft. 8½ in.; complexion, light; hair, brown; eyes, gray· farmer; enlisted Jan. 1, 1781 or 82, enlisted for 3 years.

ISAAC FOSTER, Chelmsford. Private, on Lexington alarm roll of Col. Moses Parker's co.: marched on alarm of April 19, 1775, from Chelmsford: 16 days' service: marched under command of Lieut. Benjamin Walker. Corporal, on return of Capt. John Minott's co., Col. Dike's regt.: service, from Dec. 13, 1776, to March 1, 1777. Sergeant, on muster and pay roll of Capt. Minott's co., Col. Josiah Whitney's regt.; service in R. I.; arrived at Providence May 10, 1777; discharged July 9, 1777: service, 2 mos. 9 days.

ISAAC FOSTER, Pembroke. Private, on muster roll of Capt. Isaac Pope's co., Col. William Shepard's regt.; enlisted for 8 months: on return made by James Hatch, muster master, dated Oct. 7, 1777.

ISAAC FOSTER. On list of men who delivered firelocks, dated Jan. 1, 1776.

ISAAC FOSTER, Greenfield. Private, on muster and pay roll of Capt. Daniel Winchester's co., Col. Ruggles Woodbridge's (Hampshire co.) regt.; enlisted Aug. 17, 1777; discharged Nov. 29, 1777, 8 days travel included; service in Northern Dept. On muster and pay roll of Capt. John Wells' co., Col. Timothy Robinson's regt.; enlisted Dec. 23, 1776; discharged April 1, 1777; 100 days detached and marched to Ticonderoga. On muster and pay roll of Capt. Timothy Child's co., Col. David Field's regt.; enlisted Aug. 14th; discharged Aug. 18, 1777; service, 4 days, on alarm at Bennington.

ISAAC FOSTER. Private, on muster and pay roll of Capt. Abijah Bang's co. (Maj.) Zenas Winslow's (2d Barnstable co.) regt; 5 days' service during Sept., 1778; marched on alarm at Bedford and Falmouth.

ISAAC FOSTER. Private, on muster and pay roll of Capt. Abram Washburn's co., Col. Jacob Gerrish's regt.; enlisted July 27th; discharged Dec. 14, 1778; service, 4 mos. 18 days; service at and near Boston.

ISAAC FOSTER. Deputy Director General in the Eastern Hospital on Continental army pay accounts, for service from April 10, 1777, to Dec. 31, 1779, and from Jan. 1st to Sept. 30, 1780.

ISAAC FOSTER. On an abstract from Col. Hatch's book, on account dated Jan. 20, 1781.

*ISAAC FORSTER. On return of 4th Massachusetts regt. in New Windsor Hospital, Feb. 1783.

ISAAC FOSTER. Probably Sergeant, on muster and pay roll of Capt. Simon Hunt's co., Col. Gerrish's regt.; enlisted July 14, 1778; discharged Dec. 16, 1778; service, 5 mos. 3 days; roll dated Winter Hill, regt. of Guards.

ISAAC FOSTER. Private, on muster and pay roll of Capt. Edmund Longley's co., of Col. Cogswell's regt.; enlisted Oct. 1, 1778; discharged Dec. 31, 1778; service, 3 mos. 1 day; Guards near Boston.

ISAAC FOSTER. Corporal, on muster and pay roll of Capt. Moses Barn's co., Lieut.-Col. Solomon Pierce's regt.; enlisted May 17, 1779; discharged July 1, 1779; service, 1 mo. 14 days.

ISAAC FOSTER. Private, on muster and pay roll of Capt. Isaac Parson's co., Col. Prime's regt.; enlisted June 2, 1780; discharged Dec. 11, 1780; service, 6 mos. 10 days; roll dated North Yarmouth; service at Eastward, under Brig.-Gen. Wadsworth.

ISAAC FOSTER, JR., Greenfield. Private, on muster and pay roll of Capt. Child's co., Col. Field's regt.; enlisted Aug. 14, 1777; discharged Aug. 18th; service, 4 days; on alarm at Bennington.

ISAAC FOSTER, JR., Lunenburg. On list of men drafted from Worcester co. militia to go to Horse Neck under Col. Converse, who did not join regt.; drafted to Capt. William Edgell of Westminster.

*ISAIAH FOSTER, Chelmsford. On descriptive list of enlisted men. Age, 22 yrs.; stature, 6 ft.; complexion, light; occupation, farmer. Enlisted April 25, 1775; joined Capt. John Ford's co., Col. Bridge's regt. Private, on roll dated Aug. 1, 1775; service, 3 mos. 14 days; on receipt for wages from Feb. 5th to April 1, 1776, dated Chelmsford, April 19, 1776; on return of men in Capt. Solomon Kidder's co., Col. Brook's regt.; service at White Plains; endorsed 1776.

* Probably Jr.

ISAIAH FOSTER, Pepperellborough. On receipt for bounty for 2d class, paid by Samuel Booth for Pepperellborough, to serve in Continental army for 3 years; receipt dated Pepperellborough, April 13, 1782. On descriptive list; age, 47; stature, 5 ft. 9 in.; complexion, light; hair, light; eyes, blue; occupation, carpenter; enlisted April 13, 1782, for 3 years; joined Capt. James Tisdale's co., 3d Massachusetts regt., dated Hutts, New Boston, May 13, 1782. Private, on muster rolls dated Nov. 9, 1782, Feb. 24th, March 11th and Oct. 14, 1783; on accounts of clothing delivered, dates from Nov. 20, 1782, to Dec. 16, 1783.

ISAIAH FOSTER, JR., Chelmsford. Private, on Lexington alarm roll of Capt. Oliver Barron's co., Col. David Green's regt, which marched on alarm of April 19, 1775, from Chelmsford; service 6 days.

ISRAEL FOSTER, Bolton. Private, on Lexington alarm roll of Capt. Robert Longley's co., Col. Asa Whitcomb's regt., which marched on alarm of April 19, 1775, from Bolton; service, 3 days; discharged April 20, 1775.

ISRAEL FOSTER, Beverly. Appears on a petition dated Beverly, July 15, 1778, signed by Joseph Wood, Town Clerk, in behalf of selectmen of Beverly, asking consideration on account of men who have moved into or from said town or have died since return, under resolve of Dec. 9, 1776, or are unable to contribute toward raising the town's quota. Reported: moved from Marblehead and is unable to contribute; reported: Israel Foster moved out of town.

JACOB FOSTER, Andover. Private, on Lexington alarm roll of Capt. Henry Abbott's co., which marched on alarm of April 19, 1775, from Andover; service, 1½ days.

JACOB FOSTER, Berwick, Me. Chaplain, on company return of Col. James Scammon's (30th) regt., not dated, probably October; return reported: enlisted May 31, 1775: on muster roll of Col. Edward Phinney for Nov., 1776, dated Fort George, Dec. 8, 1776; appointed Jan. 1, 1776; reported, resigned Feb. 28, 1776.

JACOB FOSTER. Bridgewater. Matross, on muster and pay roll of Capt. David Lothrop's co., Col. John Bailey's regt., from April 10, 1775, to May 2, 1775; service, 3 weeks 2 days Gunner, on muster roll of Maj. Thomas Pierce's co., Col. Gridley's regt.; enlisted May 26, 1775, on October return of Capt. Lothrop's co. is ranked private; reported, enlisted in the artillery May 30, 1775; enlisted as Private in Capt. Abram Washburn's co., Col. Abijah Stearn's regt., April 11, 1778; service, 2 mos. 24 days, at Castle Island.

JACOB FOSTER, Lincoln. Private, on Lexington alarm roll of Capt. William Smith's co., Col. Abijah Pierce's regt., which marched from Lincoln on alarm of April 19, 1775; service, 8 days; on muster and pay roll of Capt. John Hartwell's co., Col. Eleazar Brook's regt.; service, 5 days; date of enlistment not given; called March 4, 1776, to fortify Dorchester Hills.

JAMES FOSTER, Boston (probably). On an enlistment agreement, dated Boston, June, 1780, signed by said Foster and others, engaging themselves to serve in the Continental army for the term of 6 months from the time of arrival at place of rendezvous, Capt. Hodgdon's co.; age, 44 yrs.; stature, 5 ft. 8 in.; complexion, light; received bounty of Edward Proctor, colonel of Boston regt.

JAMES FOSTER, Harwich. Private, on pay abstract of Capt. Abijah Bangs' co, Col. Dike's regt., for gun and blanket money, dated Boston, Feb. 24, 1777; on return for service, from Dec. 13, 1776, to March 1, 1777; pay abstract service, Nov. 7, 1778, 2 days guarding prisoners from Ship Somerset, at Harwich, from thence to Yarmouth.

JAMES FOSTER, Rockingham, N. H. Autograph signature on receipt for advance pay given by company, dated Cambridge, June 10, 1775, on account of service in Capt. Joseph Butler's co, Col. Nixon's regt. Private, on muster roll dated Aug. 1, 1775; enlisted May 23, 1775; service, 2 mos. 13 days; also on return dated Winter Hill, Sept. 30, 1775; reported, discharged; on order for bounty coat or equivalent due for the 8 months' service, dated Winter Hill, Dec. 20, 1775.

JAMES FOSTER, Reading On list of men in Capt. Amos Upton's co., showing equipments, dated Reading, April 21, 1775; on list of men in Capt. John Flint's (3d) co., Col. Baldwin's regt, dated May 15, 1775; also on roll of Capt. Flint's co., dated Reading, Dec. 19, 1775; service 6 days.

JAMES FOSTER. Appears on a report of the Enlistment Committee of Worcester co., of men raised to reinforce the Continental army at Canada. As captain, marched with his company under Col. Jona Smith, July 22, 1776, report dated Watertown, Sept. 6, 1776.

JAMES FOSTER, Machias. Private, on muster and pay roll of Capt. Stephen Smith's co., enlisted Sept. 15th; discharged Dec. 31, 1775; service, 3 mos. 23 days.

at Machias; also on pay roll of Capt. Jabez West's co.; enlisted May 22, 1777; discharged July 17, 1777; service, 1 mo. 25 days; expedition against St. Johns, N. S. Also on muster and pay roll Capt. West's co., as enlisted July 15, 1777; discharged Aug. 15, 1777; service, 1 mo. On a certificate (year not given) signed by Capt. Jabez West, stating that Capt. Stephen Smith, muster master for Lincoln co., paid said James Foster, and other men belonging to Capt. West's co., the bounty allowed them for engaging to serve on expedition against St. John.

JAMES FOSTER, Marblehead. 2d Sergeant, on company return of Capt. Curtis' co., Col. Glover's regt., probably October return. 1775; on order for bounty coat or equivalent in money due for the 8 months' service in 1775, dated Cambridge, Dec. 21, 1775.

JAMES FOSTER. Private, on muster and pay roll of Capt. Joseph Roe's co.; enlisted Aug. 5, 1776; service, 2 mos. 23 days; roll dated Beverly; ordered to serve at the lines at Beverly, July 20, 1776.

JAMES FOSTER. Private, on muster and pay roll of Capt. William Cooley's co., Col. John Mosley's regt.; enlisted Aug. 17th; discharged Aug. 19, 1777; service, 4 days. A Hampshire co. regt. marched on alarm toward Bennington; roll sworn to at Granville.

JAMES FOSTER. Private, on muster roll of Capt. Samuel Foster's co., Col. John Greaton's regt.; enlisted Feb. 1, 1778, for during the war; reported on command at Kinderhook. On return dated White Plains, July 20, 1778. On return dated Sept. 1, 1778. Reported transferred to Col. Chandler's regt.

JAMES FOSTER. Private, on muster and pay roll of Capt. Barnabas Doty's co., Col. Ebenezer Sprout's regt.; enlisted Sept. 13, 1778; discharged Sept. 17, 1778; 5 days' service on alarm at Falmouth, Barnstable co.

JAMES FOSTER. Appears on an order, dated Cambridge, Sept. 23, 1778, signed by Capt. John Walton, directing Sergt. Samuel Butterfield to detach said Foster and others from Capt. Walton's co., to join Capt. Frost the following day at Cambridge and to march thence to Boston to serve there or elsewhere, as directed by the Council, until Jan. 1, 1779, unless sooner discharged.

JAMES FOSTER. Private, on Continental army pay accounts of Capt. McFarland's co., Col. Nicholas' invalid corps, for service from June 2, 1780, to July 17, 1780; reported discharged, July 17, 1780.

JEDEDIAH FOSTER. On a receipt, dated June 26, 1776, for 2 months' wages; service in the winter of 1775-6, in Capt. Selah Heart's co., Col. Erastus Woolcot's regt.

JEREMIAH FOSTER, Suffield Ct. Private, on muster roll of Capt. Nathan Peters' co., Col. Timothy Danielson's regt., dated Aug. 1, 1775; enlisted April, 26, 1775; service, 3 mos. 13 days; also on October, 1775, return; and on order for bounty coat or equivalent due for the 8 months' service, dated Roxbury, Nov. 20, 1775.

JEREMIAH FOSTER. Corporal, on muster and pay roll of Capt. Joseph Rae's co.; enlisted July 25, 1776; service, 3 mos. 3 days; roll dated Beverly.

JEREMIAH FOSTER. Sergeant, on muster and pay roll of Capt. John Lane's (Seacoast) co., Col. Joseph Foster's regt.; enlisted Jan. 10, 1776; discharged Feb. 15, 1776; service, 1 mo. 5 days; enlisted in Capt. Giddings' co., Col. Foster's regt., Feb. 15. 1776; service, ½ mo.; service to March 1, 1776. 2d Lieutenant, on muster and pay roll Capt. Giddings' co. from Feb. 29, 1776; service, 3 mos.; stationed at Gloucester; commissioned March 18. 1776; reported as serving in the room of Moses Atkinson; also on pay roll for service from June 1, 1776, 3 mos., and from Sept. 1, 1776, 2 mos. 18 days; discharged Nov. 18, 1776.

JEREMIAH FOSTER. Corporal, on muster and pay roll of Capt. Samuel Clark's co., Col. John Brown's regt.; enlisted June 30, 1777; discharged July 26, 1777; service, 27 days. Also enlisted Sept. 7, 1777; discharged Sept. 30, 1777; service, 24 days in same co., but Col. Benjamin Symond's regt.; Col. Brown's regt., enlisted July 18, 1780; discharged Oct. 23, 1780; Capt. John Spoor's co.; service, 3 mos. 10 days, 4 days travel included; a Berskire co. company.

JEREMIAH FOSTER. Appears on a petition, dated Boston, Feb. 2, 1781, as 1st Lieutenant on board the ship "Betsey," commanded by Philemon Haskell; age, 23 yrs; height, 5 ft.; complexion, dark; black hair.

JEREMIAH FOSTER, JR., Boxford. Private, on Lexington alarm roll of Capt. Jacob Gould's co., which marched on alarm of April 19, 1775, from Boxford; service, 3 days.

JEREMIAH FOSTER, JR., Williamstown. Private, on muster and pay roll of Capt. John Spoor's co., Col. John Brown's regt.; enlisted July 18, 1780; discharged Oct. 23, 1780; service, 3 mos. 10 days, 4 days' travel included. On descriptive list of enlisted men; age, 17 yrs.; stature, 5 ft. 4 in.; complexion, dark; hair, black; occupation, laborer. Enlisted for 3 years; joined Capt. Whipple's co., Col. Simond's regt.; dated Lenox, Aug. 20, 1781. On muster roll of Capt. Luke Day's co., Lieut.-Col. John Brook's regt.; at West Point from June to July, 1781. On roll dated Camp Continental Village, Oct. 1, 1781; enlisted April 1, 1781; reported confined; also appears on rolls for Oct., Nov., Dec., 1781, to April, 1782.

JOB FOSTER, Plymouth. Private, on muster rolls of Capt. Mayhew's co., Col. Cotton's regt., dated Aug. 1 and Oct. 7, 1775; enlisted July 18, 1775; and on order for bounty coat or equivalent due for the 8 months' service, dated Roxbury, Nov. 8, 1775.

JOHN FOSTER, Ashby. Private, on Lexington alarm roll of Capt. John Jones' co., Col. James Prescott's regt., which marched on alarm of April 19, 1775, from Ashby; service, 7 days.

JOHN FOSTER, Andover. Private, on Lexington alarm roll of Capt. Joshua Holt's co., which marched on alarm of April 19, 1775, from Andover to Cambridge; service, 1½ days. On muster and pay roll of Lieut. William Foster's co., Col. Pierce's regt.; enlisted March 1st; discharged April 4, 1778; service, 35 days. Lieutenant, on muster and pay roll of Capt. Amos Foster's co., Col. Cyprian How's regt., for service in R. I., on alarm; appointed Oct. 11th; discharged Oct. 30, 1780; service, 25 days.

JOHN FOSTER, Barnstable. Private, on Lexington alarm roll of Capt. Micah Hamilton's co., which marched on alarm of April 19, 1775, from Barnstable to Marshfield; service, 2 days. On muster and pay roll of Capt. Micah Hamblin's co.; enlisted July 10, 1775, to Dec. 31, 1775. Corporal, on muster and pay roll of Capt. Benjamin Godfrey's co., Col. John Cushing's regt.; service in R. I., from Sept. 30, 1776, 1 mo. 24 days; roll dated Newport, and of Capt. Abijah Bangs' co., Maj. Zenas Winslow's regt.; 5 days' service in Sept., 1778, on alarm at Falmouth.

JOHN FOSTER, Attleborough. Private, on Lexington alarm roll of Capt. Moses Willmarth's co., Col. John Daggett's regt.; marched on alarm of April 19, 1775, from Attleborough; service, 9 days. On order, dated July 5, 1776, for wages on Ephraim Newell, town treasurer of Attleborough; service on alarm caused by battle of Bunker Hill.

JOHN FOSTER, Billerica. Private, on Lexington alarm roll of Capt. Jonathan Stickney's co., Col. Bridge's regt.; marched on alarm of April 19, 1775, from Billerica; service, 6 days; regt. of minute men. Also on rolls dated Aug. and Sept., 1775, and on order for bounty coat or equivalent due for the 8 months' service, dated Cambridge, Nov. 16, 1775. On a return of men enlisted into Continental army from Capt. Edward Farmer's co., 7th Middlesex regt., dated Feb. 16, 1778; joined Capt. Elijah Danforth's co., Col. Nixon's regt. Corporal, on return dated camp near Peekskill; in service Aug. 15, 1777; on muster roll of Lieut.-Col. C. Smith's co., Col. Nixon's regt., dated Highlands, June 12, 1779; enlisted April 7, 1777; service, 2 yrs. 2 mos. 5 days; reported enlisted for 3 years. Also on rolls for Aug., Sept., Oct., Nov., Dec., 1779; on pay accounts for service from April 9, 1777, to Dec. 31, 1779; on pay accounts, service from Jan. 1, 1780, to April 7, 1780; discharged April 7, 1780; autograph signature on receipt for clothing, etc., dated Peekskill, Dec. 5, 1780.

JOHN FOSTER, Boston. On list of men enlisted into Continental army; enlisted for Northbridge for 3 years; return made by Col. Benjamin Gill, June 27, 1777; enlisted from Capt. Josiah Woods' co., of Worcester co. regt., dated Northbridge, Feb. 13, 1778; joined Capt. Dolliver's co., Col. H. Jackson's regt.; enlistment to end June 5, 1780. Drummer, on pay roll of Capt. Nathaniel Jarvis' co., Col. Jackson's regt.; service from Jan. 31, 1778, to March 1, 1780.

JOHN FOSTER, Boston. Gunner, on muster roll of Capt. Burbeck's co., Col. Gridley's regt., dated Aug. 1, 1775; enlisted June 9, 1775; service, 1 mo. 24 days. Also on Sept. return and on order for bounty coat or equivalent due for the 8 months' service in 1775, dated Jan. 6, 1776.

JOHN FOSTER, Boston (probably). On an enlistment agreement, dated Boston, July 22, 1780, signed by said Foster and others, engaging themselves to serve in the militia under Brig.-Gen. John Fellows for term of 3 months from time of arrival at rendezvous, Capt. Loring's co.; age, 15 yrs.; stature, 5 ft. 3 in.; complexion, light. Received bounty of Edward Proctor, Col. of Boston regt. Drummer, on muster and pay roll of Lieut. William Bird's co., Col. Thayer's regt.; enlisted July 19, 1780; discharged Oct. 10, 1780; service, 3 mos. 3 days; stationed at West Point.

JOHN FOSTER, Needham. On descriptive list of men raised to reinforce Continental army, for term of 6 months, by resolve of June 5, 1780; age, 46 yrs.; stature, 5 ft. 8 in.; complexion, light; arrived at Springfield July 16, 1780; marched to camp same day, under command of Sergeant Thomas Kench.

JOHN FOSTER, Dudley. On descriptive list of enlisted men belonging to Dudley, Worcester co.; age, 37 yrs.; stature, 5 ft. 5 in.; complexion, dark; occupation, baker; enlisted Jan. 2, 1781, for 3 years, Capt. Coburn's co., Col. Grout's regt.; on receipt for bounty, dated Dudley, April 18, 1781.

JOHN FOSTER, Dorchester. Private, on Lexington alarm roll of Lieut. Hopestill Hall's co.; marched on alarm of April 19, 1775, from Dorchester; service, 7 days. On muster roll of Capt. Edward Webber's co., Col. John Fellows' regt., dated Aug. 1, 1775; enlisted May 10, 1775; service, 3 mos. 25 days. Also on return dated Oct. 7, 1775, and on order for bounty coat or equivalent, dated in camp at Dorchester, Dec. 25, 1775. Also on pay roll of Capt. John Robinson's co., Col. Benjamin Gills' regt.; 2 days' service in March, 1776, guarding lines near Dorchester Heights. On muster and pay roll of Capt. Seth Sumner's co., Col. Gill's regt., ordered to march to Moon's Island June 12, 1776, 3 days' service. On pay abstract of Capt. Isaac Tuckerman's co., Col. Ebenezer Francis' regt., for mileage; dated Nov. 28, 1776. On return of Capt. Oliver Lyman's co., Col. Dike's regt.; service from Dec., 1776, to March 1, 1777. On muster and pay roll of Capt. Sumner's co., Col. Gill's regt.; service in R. I.; marched April 17, 1777; service, 25 days. On muster and pay roll of Capt. John Bradley's co., Col. Gill's regt.; enlisted Aug. 14, 1777; service, 3 mos. 28 days (12 days' travel allowed); marched to Manchester, Vt., to join Northern army. On list of men enlisted to serve 9 months in Continental army under Gen. Washington, dated Dorchester, May 19, 1778; autograph signature. On descriptive list of enlisted men; age, 44 yrs.; stature, 5 ft. 7 in.; complexion, dark; hair, dark; eyes, gray; occupation, weaver; enlisted June 14, 1778, to serve 9 months from arrival at Fishkill, from Capt. Sumner's co., Col. Gill's regt.; received from Maj. Stephen Badlam and delivered to Brig.-Gen. Jonathan Warner at Fishkill by Capt. Robert Davis, under resolve of April 20, 1778, dated Roxbury, June 5, 1778.

JOHN FOSTER, JR., Dorchester. Fifer, on Lexington alarm roll of Capt. Abraham Wheeler's co. of minute men, Col. Lemuel Robinson's regt., which marched on alarm of April 19, 1775, from Dorchester; service, 12 days. On muster and pay roll of Capt. Hopestill Hall's co., Col. Lemuel Robinson's regt.; enlisted Jan. 29, 1776; service, 23 days; also 12 days' service in March, 1776, in Capt. John Robinson's co., Col. Benjamin Gill's regt. On muster and pay roll of Capt. Sumner's co., ordered to march to Moon Island June 12, 1776; service, 3 days. On muster roll of Capt. Thomas Wellington's co., Col. Asa Whitcomb's regt., dated in camp at Ticonderoga, Nov. 27, 1776; enlisted Oct. 1, 1776; service, 1 mo. 26 days. On muster and pay roll of Capt. Sumner's co., Col. Gill's regt.; service in R. I.; marched April 17, 1777; service, 25 days. Muster and pay roll of Capt. Lemuel Clap's co.; enlisted May 19, 1779; discharged Aug. 10, 1779; service, 2 mos. 23 days. A detachment of Guards under Maj.-Gen. Nathaniel Heath, at Dorchester Heights: also from Aug. 11th to Oct. 31, 1779—2 mos. 21 days; also from Nov. 1, 1779, to Jan. 31, 1780—3 mos.; also from Feb. 1, 1780, to May 1, 1780—3 mos.

JOHN FOSTER, Littleton. On descriptive list of men raised in Middlesex co. to reinforce Continental army, for 9 months, by resolve of April 20, 1778; age, 35 yrs.; stature, 5 ft. 6 in.; belonged to Col. Reed's regt.; arrived at Fishkill June 23, 1778.

JOHN FOSTER, Gloucester. 3d Sergeant, on muster and pay roll of Capt. William Pearson's co., stationed at Gloucester; enlisted Jan. 9, 1776, to May 31, 1776; also 1 mo. 25 days between June 1st and Aug. 31, 1776. Commissioned 2d Lieutenant of Capt. Samuel Page's co., Col. Ebenezer Francis' regt., Feb. 3, 1777. On a petition as lieutenant, dated Van Schaick's Island, Aug. 31, 1777. Autograph signature on an order, dated camp near Valley Forge, April 8, 1778, on Board of War for clothing to replace that lost on retreat from Ticonderoga in Col. Benjamin Tupper's regt., Gen. John Paterson's brigade; also on order for clothing, order dated Danbury, Oct. 12, 1778; name cancelled from roll. Lieutenant, on muster roll of Maj. William Lithgow's co., Col. Tupper's regt., dated West Point, April 5, 1779, for March, 1779; appointed or enlisted Nov. 6, 1776; service, 2 yrs. 4 mos. 29 days; reported, transferred to light infantry co., April 1, 1779. On Continental army pay accounts of Col. Tupper's regt., for service from Jan. 1, 1777, to July 14, 1779; reported, resigned July 14, 1779.

JOHN FOSTER, Machias. On muster and pay roll of Capt. Stephen Smith's co.; enlisted Sept. 13, 1775; discharged Dec. 31, 1775; 3 mos. 25 days' service, stationed at Machias. Reported advanced to Corporal, Oct. 25, 1775. Sergeant, on muster and pay roll of Capt. Jabez West's co.; enlisted May 21st; discharged July 19, 1777; service on expedition against St. Johns, 1 mo. 28 days.

JOHN FOSTER, Marblehead. Private, on muster roll of Capt. Francis Symonds' co., Col. John Glover's regt., dated Aug. 1, 1775; enlisted June 15, 1775; 1 mo. 19 days' service.

JOHN FOSTER, Marblehead. Private, on muster roll of Capt. Haynes' co., Col. J. Brewer's regt., dated Aug. 1, 1775; enlisted July 17, 1775; service, 15 days. On company return, dated Prospect Hill, Oct. 6, 1775, says he belonged to Newburyport. On order for bounty coat or equivalent due for 8 months' service, dated Cambridge, Oct. 25, 1775.

JOHN FOSTER, Plymouth. Private, on Lexington alarm roll of Lieut. Stephen Churchill's co., which marched (April 20th) on alarm of April 19, 1775, from Plymouth to Marshfield; service, 7 days. On return of men enlisted into Continental army from Capt. Sylv. Harlow's co., 1st Plymouth co. regt., dated Plymouth, Feb. 21, 1777, for 3 years; joined Capt. Donham's co., Col. Bailey's regt. Sergeant, on Continental army pay accounts of said regt.; service, from Feb. 10, 1777, to June 13, 1778; reported, died June 13, 1778.

JOHN FOSTER, Roxbury. Private, on Lexington alarm roll of Capt. Lemuel Child's co., Col. William Heath's regt.; marched on alarm of April 19, 1775, from Roxbury; service, 15 days; dismissed May 3, 1775.

JOHN FOSTER, Roxbury. Private, on company return of Capt. Williams', Col. Heath's regt., dated Oct. 5, 1775; encamped at Fort No. 2. On order for bounty coat or equivalent, dated Cambridge, Dec. 22, 1775, payable to Capt. Williams.

JOHN FOSTER, Rutland. Private, on Lexington alarm roll of Capt. David Bent's co., Col. Nathaniel Sparhawk's regt.; marched on alarm of April 19, 1775, from Rutland to Cambridge; service, 6 days; marched April 20th. Also on muster and pay roll, same regt. detached, Aug. 20, 1777; marched from Rutland to Bennington on alarm; service, 11 days.

JOHN FOSTER, St. George or Vassalborough. On list of men enlisted into Continental army from Capt. T. Nash or S. Ward's cos., dated Weymouth, Jan. 2, 1778; enlisted for Weymouth for 3 years; joined Benjamin Burton's co., Col. Sherburne's regt. Also on a list dated Gardnerstown, Feb. 2, 1778, as belonging to Winthrop, and drafted from Col. Joseph North's (2d Lincoln co.) regt. On return of men mustered in Suffolk co., dated Boston, June 8, 1777; received £20 bounty. On return of men in Col. Henry Sherburne's regt., certified to in Boston, June 15, 1779, by Capt. Benjamin Burton; enlisted April 18, 1777, for 3 years or during war. Private, belonged to Vassalborough. On pay accounts of Col. Sherburne's regt.; service from March 8, 1777, to Dec. 31, 1779; also from Jan. 1, 1780, to March 17, 1780; reported discharged March 17, 1780.

JOHN FOSTER. Appears on a petition dated Boston, Sept. 4, 1777, requesting that he be appointed 1st Lieutenant of a sloop called the Revenge, commanded by Nathaniel Coit Webb.

JOHN FOSTER. Private, on muster and pay roll of Capt. Joseph Seavey's co., Col. Benjamin Foster's regt. (Lincoln co.); enlisted July 16, 1777; discharged Oct. 10, 1777; service, 2 mos. 24 days; service at Machias when British ships lay without the harbor.

JOHN FOSTER. Private, on muster and pay roll of Capt. John Oliver's co., Col. Nathan Sparhawk's regt., from Sept. 28, 1777, to Oct. 18, 1777; service, 28 days; marched to reinforce Northern army at the reduction of Burgoyne.

JOHN FOSTER. Private, on muster and pay roll of Capt. John Crawford's co., Col. Job Cushing's regt.; enlisted Sept. 7th; discharged Nov. 29, 1777; 2 mos. 23 days' service, travel allowed.

JOHN FOSTER. Sergeant, on muster and pay roll of Capt. Alexander Foster's co., Col. John Daggett's regt.; service in R. I., on alarm of Dec. 8, 1776; service 25 days.

JOHN FOSTER, Marblehead. On list of men who delivered firearms, dated Feb. 23, 1776; reported, "Of the selectmen of Marblehead."

JOHN FOSTER. Private, on muster and pay roll of Capt. John Hartwell's co., Col. Eleazar Brook's regt., called March 4, 1776, to fortify Dorchester Hills; 5 days' service; marched from Lincoln. On receipt dated Lincoln, Sept. 21, 1776, for wages due, signed by self and others in above co.

JOHN FOSTER. Private, on muster and pay roll of Capt. Abram Washburn's co., Col. John Cushing's regt., stationed at Newport, R. I.; enlisted Sept. 20, 1776; service, 59½ days. Roll dated Bridgewater, Nov. 28, 1776; also on muster and pay roll of Capt. Francis Cushing's co., Col. John Cushing's regt.; 11 days' service, marched to Bristol, R. I., on alarm of Dec., 1776.

JOHN FOSTER. Sergeant, on pay abstract of Capt. James Prentiss' co., Col. Samuel Brewer's regt., for travel allowance from place of discharge, Saratoga, home; allowed in council, Feb. 3, 1777, roll indorsed "travel from Fort Edward."

JOHN FOSTER. Sergeant, on muster and pay roll of Capt. John Stutson's co., detached Dec. 10, 1777; discharged March 1, 1778; service, 2 mos. 22 days; Maj. Edward Proctor's detachment of guards at Boston, under Maj.-Gen. Heath.

JOHN FOSTER. Seaman, on list of prisoners sent from Newport, R. I., on the Lord Sandwich prison ship and landed in Bristol, March 7, 1778.

JOHN FOSTER. Private, on muster and pay roll of Capt. Adam Henry's co., enlisted Jan. 5th; discharged March 31, 1779; service, 2 mos. 29 days; a company of guards detached to guard troops of Convention at Rutland, detached from militia.

JOHN FOSTER, Salem. Seaman, on descriptive list dated June 17, 1780, of officers and crew of Privateer Brigantine Addition, Joseph Pratt commander; age, 21 yrs.; stature, 4 ft. 6 in.; complexion, dark.

JOHN FOSTER, Coxhall. On list of men in an account of bounties paid to soldiers, raised by town of Coxhall, by resolve of court, Dec. 2, 1780.

JOHN FOSTER. Private, on muster roll of Capt. Charles Parson's co., Col. Goose Van Schaick's (1st N. Y.) regt., for Jan.-March, 1781, dated West Point; enlisted for during war.

JOHN FOSTER, Wells. On receipt for bounty paid by Paul Chadburn for a class for town of Wells, dated Wells, Aug. 20, 1782.

JOHN FOSTER. Private, on a return of Capt. Caleb Chapin's co., for clothing.

JOHN FOSTER, JR., Dorchester. Private, on pay abstract of Capt. Isaac Tuckerman's co., Col. Ebenezer Francis' regt., for mileage, etc., dated Nov. 28, 1776.

JOHN FOSTER. Private, on muster and pay roll of Capt. Abel Richard's co., Col. Benjamin Hawes' regt.; enlisted Sept. 25th; discharged Oct. 28, 1777; service, 1 mo. 7 days; marched on secret expedition to R. I., 3 days' travel allowed; roll sworn to at Dedham.

JOHN WOODEN FOSTER, Machias. Private, on muster and pay roll of Capt. Stephen Smith's co.; enlisted Sept. 13, 1775; discharged Dec. 31, 1775; service, 3 mos. 24 days; stationed at Machias. On muster and pay roll of Capt. John Scott's co.; enlisted Nov. 29, 1776; discharged Dec. 21, 1776; service, 23 days; raised to reinforce Col. Jonathan Eddy at Cumberland, against British garrison there. On muster and pay roll of Capt. Joseph Sevey's co., Col. Benjamin Foster's regt.; enlisted June 23, 1777; discharged July 16, 1777; 23 days' service. Also enlisted same co. July 16th; discharged Oct. 10, 1777; service, 2 mos. 24 days. Corporal (on roll as John W.), on muster and pay roll, 1 day's service at Machias, between Dec. 5 and 25, 1778; also 6 days' service between Aug. 31st and Nov. 20, 1779. Note, his middle name is also given Woodin and Wooding.

JONATHAN FOSTER, Ashby. Private, on Lexington alarm roll of Capt. John Jones' co., Col. James Prescott's regt.; marched on alarm of April 19, 1775, from Ashby (marched April 20th); service, 7 days.

JONATHAN FOSTER, Rowley. On return of men raised under resolve of Dec. 2, 1780; raised March 17, 1781; enlisted for 3 years. On receipt for bounty paid him by Daniel Mighill and others; receipt dated Rowley, Jan. 20, 1781.

JONATHAN FOSTER, Shirley. On descriptive list; age 23 yrs.; stature, 5 ft. 9 in.; complexion, dark; hair, dark; occupation, yeoman; birthplace, Shirley; enlisted April 28, 1782, for 3 years; joined Capt. Benjamin Heywood's co., 6th regt. Private, on muster and pay roll of Col. Benjamin Tupper's (10th) regt.; enlisted April 28, 1782; service, 8 mos. 3 days; roll made up to Jan. 1, 1783; transferred to 6th regt., Dec. 17, 1782.

JONATHAN FOSTER, S. E. Tewksbury. Private, on Lexington alarm roll of Capt. Jonathan Brown's co., Col. Green's regt.; marched on alarm of April 19, 1775, from Tewksbury; service, 1 day.

JONATHAN FOSTER, Tewksbury. On list of men raised for 6 months' service, returned by Brig.-Gen. Paterson as having passed muster, return dated Camp Fotoway, Oct. 25, 1780. On pay roll of 6 months' men raised by Tewksbury for service in Continental army during 1780; marched July 4, 1780; discharged Dec. 9, 1780; service, 5 mos. 17 days.

JONATHAN FOSTER, Lenox. 1st Lieutenant, on list of officers of Massachusetts militia in Capt. Oliver Belding's co., 2d Berkshire Co. regt.; commissioned May 3 or 4, 1776. Also on muster roll of Capt. Erastus Sergeant's co., Col. Benjamin Simond's regt., dated in camp at Ticonderoga, Feb. 25, 1777; appointed or enlisted Dec. 16, 1776. On a return dated Sheffield, May 1, 1777, signed by John Fellows of a detachment from said Fellows' (Berkshire co.) brigade, made agreeable to order of General Court to reinforce Continental army and which marched the beginning of Jan., 1777. On muster and pay roll of Capt. Jesse Bradley's co., Col. John Brown's regt.; entered service June 30th; discharged July 26, 1777; 27 days' service. Autograph signature on list of officers who petition to General Court, dated Camp above Stillwater, Sept. 15, 1777, requesting that clothing may be furnished them to replace that lost on retreat from Ticonderoga. On muster and pay roll of Capt. Oliver Belding's co., Col. Brown's regt.; enlisted Sept. 21st; discharged Oct. 14, 1777; service, 24 days, service at Northward. Also on muster and pay roll of Capt. Charles Dibble's co., Col. Rossiter's (3d) regt.; enlisted Oct. 14, 1780; discharged Oct. 17th; service, 3 days on alarm to the Northward. Also on list of officers in Massachusetts militia; 1st Lieutenant in Capt. Samuel Goodrich's co. of 3d Berkshire co. regt.

JONATHAN FOSTER, Ashby (?). On a list* of men draughted Aug. 19, 1777, to serve 3 months.

JONATHAN FOSTER. Appears on a receipt for advance pay, dated Cambridge, June 30, 1775, due on account of service in Capt. John Low's co., Col. Mansfield's regt.

JONATHAN FOSTER, Beverly or Berwick. Private, on muster roll of Capt. John Low's co., Lieut.-Col. Hutchinson's regt., dated Aug. 1, 1775; enlisted May 12, 1775; service, 2 mos. 25 days. On company return of Capt. Low's co., Col. Mansfield's regt., given as belonging to Berwick. On order for bounty coat due for 8 months' service in 1775, dated Winter Hill, Oct. 21, 1775. On pay abstracts of Capt. Moses Brown's co., Col. John Glover's regt; service in Feb., Oct., 1776; enlisted Jan. 11, 1776.

JONATHAN FOSTER, Beverly. Mate, on descriptive list, sworn to Sept. 11, 1780, of officers and crew of the brigantine Freedom, commanded by Benjamin Ober; age, 24 yrs.; stature, 5 ft. 9 in.; complexion, dark.

JONATHAN FOSTER, Boxford. Lieutenant, on Lexington alarm roll of Capt. John Cushing's co. (of minute men), Col. Samuel Johnson's regt., which marched on alarm of April 19, 1775, from Boxford; service, 6 days. Commissioned Feb. 3, 1776, captain in Col. Huntington's regt. of Massachusetts militia. Also on list of an Essex Co. regt. commanded by Col. Wade, detached for Providence; commissioned July 24, 1778; enlisted July 1st; discharged Oct. 17, 1778; service, 109 days. On roll made up to Jan. 1, 1779; reported, stationed at Middletown, R. I., for 6 months.

JONATHAN FOSTER, Douglas. Corporal, on Lexington alarm roll of Capt. Benjamin Wallis' co. (minute men), Col. Arnold's regt., which marched on alarm of April 19, 1775, from Douglas; service, 11 days; roll dated Roxbury Camp. On roll dated same place, Oct. 6, 1775, as Private on late Capt. Arthur Daggett's co., Col. Ebenezer Lerned's regt.

JONATHAN FOSTER, Dudley. Private, on Lexington alarm roll of Capt. Nathaniel Healy's co. (minute men), Col. Ebenezer Larned's regt.; marched on alarm of April 19, 1775, from Dudley; service, 8 days. Also on muster roll, same co., dated Aug. 1, 1775; enlisted April 27, 1775; service, 3 mos. 1 week, 4 days. Also on October return; on order for bounty coat or equivalent due for the 8 months' service in 1775, dated Roxbury, Nov. 2, 1775.

JONATHAN FOSTER, Ipswich. Private, on Lexington alarm roll of Capt. Nathaniel Wade's co., which marched on alarm of April 19, 1775, from Ipswich to Cambridge; service 21 days; April 19th, marched to Mystic; on April 20th, ordered to Salem; on 21st, to Ipswich; from there to headquarters at Cambridge. Corporal, on return of same co.; in service June 5, 1775. On muster roll, same co., Col. Little's regt., dated Aug. 1, 1775; enlisted May 10, 1775; service, 11 weeks, 5 days. On order for bounty coat or equivalent, dated in camp, Dec. 21, 1775. Sergeant, on a return of above co. (not dated); enlisted Nov. 21, 1775. On pay abstracts of said regt., for wages for Feb. and March, 1776. Autograph signature on receipt dated Long Island, June 9, 1776, for allowance to April 30, 1776. Also on receipt dated same place, July 14, 1776, for provisions from April to July 3d, given by company,

* This list was found among old papers in town of Ashby.

received of Capt. Wade. On list of men who sent letters by Port, July, 1776. On pay abstract for arms, etc., dated Prospect Hill, 1776. On receipt dated Ipswich, Feb. 24, 1777, wages and travel allowance; autograph signature.

JONATHAN FOSTER, Ipswich. Private, on muster and pay roll of Capt. David Low's co., 3d Essex Co. regt.; engaged Sept. 30, 1777 (marched Oct. 2, 1777); discharged at Cambridge, Nov. 7, 1777; service, 40 days; service in a regt. commanded by Maj. C. Smith, in Northern Dept., and guarding Gen. Burgoyne's army to Prospect Hill. On descriptive list of enlisted men; age, 29 yrs.; stature 5 ft. 10 in.; complexion, light; hair, light; engaged for Ipswich for 9 months; Col. Jonathan Cogswell's regt., raised by resolve of Gen. Assembly of April 20, 1780; arrived at Fishkill June 12, 1778. On list of deserters from 5th Massachusetts regt., Col. Rufus Putnam, dated Nov. 20, 1780; age, 28 yrs.; stature, 5 ft. 8 in.; complexion, light; hair, brown; enlisted for 3 years; deserted March, 1779.

JONATHAN FOSTER, Medford. On a list of men in Medford, who paid money to persons to go to Canada, dated Oct. 8, 1776.

JONATHAN FOSTER, Reading. Private, on Lexington alarm roll of Capt. John Walton's co., Col. David Green's regt.; marched on alarm of April 19, 1775, from Reading; service, 1 day. Private, on list of men in the Reading Training Band, under Capt. John Walton, May 13, 1775.

JONATHAN FOSTER, Winchendon. Private, on Lexington alarm roll of Capt. Moses Hale's co., Col. Nathan Sparhawk's regt., marched on alarm of April 19, 1775, from Winchendon to Cambridge; service, 14 days.

JONATHAN FOSTER. Sergeant, on muster and pay roll of Capt. Isaac Martin's co., Col. Ezra Woods' regt.; marched to R. I. on alarm of Dec. 8, 1776; service, 9 days.

JONATHAN FOSTER. Private, on muster and pay roll of Lieut. Josiah Wilson's co., Col. Porter's (Hampshire co.) regt.; enlisted Sept. 23d; discharged Oct. 17, 1777; service, 1 mo. 2 days, 7 days' travel included; marched on alarm to reinforce Maj.-Gen. Gates at the Northward.

JONATHAN FOSTER. Private, on pay roll of Capt. Job Shattuck's co., Col. John Robinson's regt., dated Cambridge, March, 1776; service, 6 days; service from enlistment to date of marching to camp. Also on muster and pay roll of Capt. Aaron Jewett's co., Col. Samuel Bullard's regt.; enlisted Aug. 15, 1777; discharged Nov. 29, 1777; service, 3 mos. 26 days, 11 days travel included; marched to Saratoga; roll dated Littleton.

JONATHAN FOSTER, Dracut. Private, on muster and pay roll of Capt. Joseph Bradley Varnum's co., Col. McIntosh's regt.; enlisted Aug. 1, 1778; discharged Sept. 11, 1778; service, 1 mo. 15 days; expedition to Rhode Island, 5 days' travel included.

JONATHAN FOSTER, JR., Ipswich (W. Parish). Private, on Lexington alarm roll of Capt. Abram How's co.; marched on alarm of April 19, 1775, from Ipswich (W. Parish); service, 2 days.

JOSEPH FOSTER, Andover. Appears on a list of men enlisted into Continental army from Jonathan Glover's regt., dated Nov. 7, 1777; enlisted for Marblehead for 3 years, or during war; joined Col. Benjamin Tupper's regt. On muster roll of Capt. Stephen Abbot's co., said regt., dated West Point, April 5, 1779; Private, reported transferred to Capt. Samuel Page's co., light infantry, April 1, 1779. On muster roll of said co., dated West Point, April 5, 1779; service, 2 yrs. 22 days. On pay accounts of Capt. Abbot's co., for service from March 13, 1778, to Dec. 31, 1779. Sergeant, on pay account; service from Jan. 1, 1780, to Dec. 31, 1780; reported 1 mo. 20 days as Private, 10 mos. 10 days as Sergeant. On descriptive list of enlisted men; age, 21 yrs.; stature, 5 ft. 8 in.; complexion, light; hair, light; occupation, husbandman; enlisted Oct. 26, 1779, during war; birthplace, Andover; enlisted by Capt. Abbot at West Point. On muster and pay roll made up from Jan. 1, 1781, to Jan. 1, 1782; 12 mos service; reported, Feb. 1, 1782, reduced; May 1, 1782, promoted to Sergeant. On an account of rations, small stores, etc., delivered officers and soldiers of 10th Massachusetts regt., by E. Lunt, state commissary, year not given.

JOSEPH FOSTER, Becket. Sergeant, on Lexington alarm roll of Capt. Peter Porter's co. (minute men), Col. Paterson's regt., which marched on alarm of April 19, 1775, from Becket to Cambridge (marched April 23d); service, 1 mo. 1½ days.

JOSEPH FOSTER, Beverly. Private, on Lexington alarm roll of Lieut. Peter Shaw's co., of minute men; marched on alarm of April 19, 1775, from Beverly; service, 2 days. Autograph signature on receipt for advance pay given by company, dated Cambridge, July 1, 1775, payable to himself, pay due on account of service in Capt. John Low's co., Col. John Mansfield's regt. On muster roll of Capt. John Low's co., dated Aug. 1, 1775; enlisted May 12, 1775; service, 2 mos. 25 days; also on October, 1775, return, and on order for bounty coat or equivalent due for the 8 months' service, dated Winter Hill, Oct. 21, 1775.

JOSEPH FOSTER. Private, on list of men enlisted in Seacoast co., of Beverly, as returned by Lieut. Joseph Wood; enlisted Nov. 25, 1776. Also on muster and pay roll of said co., as enlisted May 12, 1777, stationed at Beverly.

JOSEPH FOSTER, Attleborough. Corporal, on Lexington alarm roll of Capt. Stephen Richardson's co., minute men; marched on alarm of April 19, 1775, from Attleborough; service, 9 days. On order, dated July 5, 1776, for wages, etc., on Ephraim Newell, town treasurer of Attleborough, for service on alarm caused by battle of Bunker Hill. On return of Capt. Stephen Richardson's co., Col. Daggett's regt., in service as 5 months' men, at Dorchester in 1776. On receipt for wages, dated Dorchester, Oct. 9, 1776, given by Capt. Hodge's co., from Aug. 12th to Oct. 1, 1776; also for months of October, Nov., 1776. On muster and pay roll of Capt. Alexander Foster's co., Col. Daggett's regt.; marched to Rhode Island on alarm of Dec. 8, 1776; service, 25 days. On muster and pay roll, same co., Col. Thomas Carpenter's regt.; service in campaign at R. I., from July 27th to Aug. 12, 1778, 17 days. Also on muster and pay roll of same co., Col. Isaac Dean's regt.; marched on alarm to Tiverton, R. I., July 31, 1780; discharged Aug. 8, 1780: service, 10 days.

JOSEPH FOSTER, Beverly. Appears on a return of men enlisted into Continental army from 2d Beverly co. of Essex co. regt., dated Beverly, Feb. 13, 1778; enlisted for Beverly for 3 years; joined Capt. William Porter's co., Col. Francis' regt. On pay abstract of said regt., for subsistence money from time of enlistment, Feb. 17th, to time of arrival at Bennington, 36 days' travel included; roll sworn to March 6, 1777.

JOSEPH FOSTER, Billerica (probably). Private, on Lexington alarm roll of Capt. Jonathan Stickney's co. of minute men, Col. Bridge's regt.; marched on alarm of April 19, 1775, from Billerica (probably); service, 8 days. Also on muster and pay roll of Capt. Edward Farmer's co., Col. Jonathan Reed's regt.; enlisted Sept. 29th; discharged Nov. 8, 1777; service, 41 days; company marched to reinforce Northern army, by resolve of Sept. 22, 1777.

JOSEPH FOSTER, Chelmsford or Kittery. Private, on Continental army pay accounts of Col. Sprout's regt; service from Jan. 1, 1777, to July 6, 1777; enlisted for during war; reported prisoner since July 6, 1777, also reported dead.

JOSEPH FOSTER, Dorchester. Matross, on muster roll of Maj. Thomas Pierce's co., Col. Gridley's regt., dated Aug. 1, 1775; enlisted July 15, 1775; service, 2 weeks 3 days. Also on return dated Sept. 29, 1775. On order for bounty coat or equivalent due for the 8 months' service, dated Roxbury, Dec. 27, 1775. Also on return, dated Roxbury Camp, Dec. 16, 1775, of men enlisted for the ensuing year under the new establishment; Capt. Thomas Pierce's co., Col. Knox's artillery regt.

JOSEPH FOSTER, Danvers. Appears on a return of men raised under resolve of Dec. 2, 1780; raised March 12, 1781, for 3 years.

JOSEPH FOSTER, Dudley. Private, on muster and pay roll of Capt. David Batcheller's co., Col. Ezra Wood's regt., enlisted June 5, 1778; discharged Jan. 29, 1779; service, 8 mos. 13 days; raised for 8 months, service at North River. Autograph signature on order, dated Dudley, April 12, 1779, for wages, etc. On muster and pay rolls of Capt. Thomas Fish's co., Col. Nathan Tyler's regt.; enlisted July 1, 1779, to Dec. 1, 1779; 4 mos 20 days' service in R. I.; also from Dec. 1 to 25, 1779, 28 days; also from Nov. 30, 1779, to Jan. 1, 1780, 1 mo. 3 days, travel allowed.

JOSEPH FOSTER, Dunbarton, N. H. Matross, on muster roll of Capt. Callender's co., Col. Gridley's regt., dated Aug. 1, 1775; enlisted June 30, 1775; service, 1 mo. 4 days. Also on order for bounty coat or equivalent, due for the 8 months' service in 1775 in Capt. William Perkin's co., Col. Richard Gridley's regt., dated Nov. 6, 1775, payable to Capt. Perkins.

JOSEPH FOSTER, Ipswich. On order for advance pay, dated Cambridge, June 8, 1775, payable to Lieut. Billy Porter, pay due on account of service in Lieut. Billy Porter's co, Col. Mansfield's regt., autograph signature. Private, on muster roll of Capt Francis' co., dated Aug. 1, 1775; enlisted May 4, 1775; service, 3 mos. 5 days; belonged to Beverly. On roll dated Oct. 6, 1775, given, belonged to Ipswich. On order for bounty coat or equivalent, due for the 8 months' service in 1775, dated Winter Hill, Oct. 26, 1775, payable to Capt. Francis.

JOSEPH FOSTER, Kittery. On list of men enlisted in York co., to serve in Capt. James Donnel's co., Col. Samuel Brewer's regt.; return made by Joseph Bragdon, muster master, March 31, 1777; enlisted for 3 years. Received State and Continental bounty; on muster return, dated Camp at Valley Forge, Jan. 25, 1778; on Continental army pay accounts of Col. Sprout's regt.; service from Feb. 20, 1777, to Dec. 31, 1779, and from Jan. 1, 1780, to Feb. 20, 1780.

JOSEPH FOSTER, Lunenburg. Private, on Lexington alarm roll of Capt. George Kimball's co.; marched (April 20th) on alarm of April 19, 1775, from Lunenburg; service, 6 days. On muster roll of Capt. John Fuller's co., Col. Asa Whitcomb's regt., dated Aug. 1, 1775; enlisted April 25, 1775; service, 3 mos. 1½ days. Also on receipt dated Prospect Hill, Oct. 4, 1775, for wages from Aug., 1775; also on receipt dated same place, Nov. 17, 1775, wages for Sept., 1775; also on the October return.

JOSEPH FOSTER, Sudbury. On return of men enlisted into Continental army from Capt. Maynard's co., Col. Ezekiel Howe's regt., to serve during war; not dated.

JOSEPH FOSTER, Ware (probably). Captain, on Lexington alarm roll of Capt. Joseph Foster, Col. Ruggles Woodbridge's regt., which marched (April 20th) on alarm of April 19, 1775; service, 25 days.

JOSEPH FOSTER, Rehoboth. Appears among a list of men raised agreeable to resolve of Dec. 2, 1780; received at Taunton, Dec. 24, 1781, by Oliver Sooper to be conducted to Boston and delivered to Maj. Pettingall; age, 25 yrs.; stature, 5 ft. 8 in.; complexion, light; occupation, farmer; enlisted Dec. 19, 1781, for 3 years; reported deserted Dec. 22, 1781. Appears on receipt for bounty paid him by Philip Miller for town of Rehoboth.

JOSEPH FOSTER, Tewksbury. On descriptive list, age, 19 yrs.; stature, 5 ft. 6 in.; complexion, dark; enlisted for 9 months; joined Capt. Trull's co., 7th Middlesex co. regt., dated Lincoln, July 21, 1779.

JOSEPH FOSTER, Ware. Sergeant, on pay abstract of Capt. Elijah Dwight's co., for billeting money to and from camp. On list of officers, dated March 16, 1776, as returned by Col. Samuel Howe, rank 2d lieutenant, Capt. William Brakingridge's (Ware) co.; commissioned April 1, 1776. Lieutenant, on muster and pay roll of said co.; engaged July 9, 1777; discharged July 29, 1777; service, 26 days. Also on muster and pay roll of Capt. Samuel Fairfield's co., Col. Nathan Sparhawk's regt.; entered Sept. 22, 1778; 2 mos. 24 days' service at Dorchester.

JOSEPH FOSTER. Surgeon, on list of officers in Cambridge Hospital, approved of by a committee of Congress, July 5, 1775.

JOSEPH FOSTER. Private, on pay abstracts of Capt. Moses Brown's co., Col. John Glover's regt., from April to Aug., 1776; enlisted June 15, 1775.

JOSEPH FOSTER. Private, on muster and pay roll of Capt. Joseph Rae's co.; enlisted July 25, 1776; service, 3 mos. 3 days; roll dated Beverly; service at Beverly.

JOSEPH FOSTER. On list of men enlisted into Continental army by Maj. John G. Fraizer and turned over to Capt. Nathaniel Cushing. Commanded to join Col. Paterson's regt., by order dated Headquarters, Nov. 17, 1776, signed by D. Adjt.-Gen. J. Trumbull, Capt. Dodge's co., Col. Willard's regt.

JOSEPH FOSTER. Private, on muster roll of Capt. William Hudson Ballard's co., Col. Asa Whitcomb's regt.; taken to, Nov., 1776, dated in camp at Ticonderoga, Nov. 27, 1776; enlisted Jan. 1, 1776. Reported re-engaged Nov. 15, 1776, to serve during war as Private in Capt. Brewer's co., Col. Brewer's regt., but to serve in Whitcomb's regt. until Dec. 31, 1776.

JOSEPH FOSTER. Private, on muster and pay roll of Capt. Peter Porter's co., Col. Benjamin Simonds' regt.; entered service April 26, 1777; left service May 20, 1777, 25 days; company marched to Saratoga; Berkshire co. regt.

JOSEPH FOSTER. Marine, on muster and pay roll of officers and crew of brigantine Hawk, commanded by Capt. Jonathan Oakes; service with fleet under Com. John Manley; enlisted May 3d; discharged June 1, 1777; service, 1 mo.

JOSEPH FOSTER. Private, on muster and pay roll of Capt. John Thompson's co., Col. Leonard's regt. (Hampshire co.); enlisted May 7th; discharged July 8, 1777; service, 2 mos. 10 days, 9 days' travel included; marched to reinforce Northern army.

JOSEPH FOSTER. Private, on muster and pay roll of Capt. Ebenezer Goodale's co., Lieut.-Col. Samuel Williams' regt.; enlisted July 1, 1777; discharged Aug. 12, 1777; service, 1 mo. 9 days, travel allowed; marched to join Northern army.

JOSEPH FOSTER. Private, on muster and pay roll of Capt. John Moore's co., Col. Jonathan Reed's regt., from enlistment April 2, 1778, to July 3, 1778; service, 3 mos. 2 days, guards stationed at Cambridge.

JOSEPH FOSTER. Appears on instructions of council to commissary of prisons, dated Dec. 20, 1777, to permit James Coates, master of the brigantine Fame, to proceed to Providence, R. I., to go in a flag of truce from thence to Newport, provided Maj.-Gen. Spencer shall allow him one for that purpose, he giving his parole upon his arrival at Newport or New York, to procure the liberation of said Foster taken in the brigantine "Defence," commanded by Capt. Pickering, and then detained as a prisoner in New York; or in case said Foster should have been released to return a prisoner of equal rank, or to return personally in one month's time. Also appears on a petition, dated Boston, Dec. 19, 1777, signed by his brother, William Foster, requesting that the above Joseph may be released from the guard-ship at New York where he has been a prisoner since April, 1777. Also on list of prisoners, dated Feb. 24, 1778, to be exchanged for British prisoners, under parole to be returned by Col. Johonnott, said Joseph Foster to be exchanged for James Coates, Master Brig. "Fame."

JOSEPH FOSTER. Private, on muster and pay roll of Capt. Moses Willmarth's co., Col. John Daggett's regt.; service, 2 mos. 25 days; service at R. I.; enlisted for 3 mos., Jan. 1, 1778.

JOSEPH FOSTER. Private, on muster and pay roll of Capt. Samuel Merriman's co., Col. Israel Chapen's regt.; enlisted Oct. 15th; discharged Nov. 21, 1779; service, 1 mo. 14 days, travel included.

JOSEPH FOSTER. Appears on a list of officers of Massachusetts militia, as 1st Lieutenant of the 2d (Leominster) co., 8th Worcester Co. regt., commissioned July 6, 1780.

JOSEPH FOSTER. Appears on a pay roll for wages for services as Commander of the troops stationed at Gloucester for defense of the sea coast for 11 months and 7 days, dated Gloucester, Nov. 26, 1777; service from Dec. 13, 1775, to Nov. 19, 1776. Also on a petition dated Boston, Oct. 10, 1778, given by Winthrop Sargent and others, asking for the commission of the above named "Foster" as Commander of the brigantine "General Mercer;" commissioned by council Oct. 11, 1780. Also on a petition dated Boston, Feb. 19, 1781, signed by Winthrop Sargent in behalf of himself and others asking that said Foster be appointed Commander of the "Polley"; granted in council Feb. 20, 1781.

JOSEPH FOSTER. Private, on muster and pay roll of Capt. Samuel Johnson's co., Col. Johnson's regt.; enlisted Aug. 14th; discharged Nov. 30, 1777; service, 4 mos. 13 days, travel included; service with Northern army; roll sworn to at Andover.

JOSEPH FOSTER. Ensign, on return of officers in Col. Wigglesworth's regt.; allowed by order of court of March 13, 1778.

JOSEPH FOSTER. Corporal, on muster and pay roll of Capt. Elias Parkman's co. (a detachment of guards); engaged July 2d; discharged July 17, 1778; service, 15 days.

JOSEPH FOSTER. Seaman, on list of prisoners sent to Boston in the Cartel Snow Swift, from Halifax, Sept. 30, 1778.

JOSEPH FOSTER. Private, on muster and pay roll, Capt. not given; enlisted Aug. 1st; discharged Oct. 31, 1779; service, 3 mos., stationed at Beverly.

JOSEPH FOSTER. Private, on muster and pay roll of Capt. Adam Henry's co.; enlisted Jan. 6, 1779; discharged April 4, 1779; service, 3 mos.; a company of guards detached from militia to guard troops of Convention at Rutland.

JOSHUA FOSTER—Private, on muster and pay roll of Capt. Jonathan Ayer's co., Col. Nathaniel Wade's regt.; enlisted July 14th; discharged Oct. 10, 1780; service, 3 mos. 8 days; roll dated Haverhill, April 10, 1781.

JOSHUA FOSTER, Westford. Appears on list of men from county of Middlesex; enlisted into the Continental army for Westford.

JOSIAH FOSTER, Beverly. Sailor, on descriptive list, dated June 6, 1780, of officers and crew of sloop Fish Hawk, commanded by Samuel Foster: age, 21 yrs.; stature, 5 ft. 4 in.; complexion, dark. Also on list of officers and men of brigantine Fanny, commanded by Herbert Woodbury, dated Aug. 22, 1780.

JOSIAH FOSTER. Private, on muster and pay roll of Capt. Jonathan Proctor's co., Col. Jacob Gerrish's regt.; enlisted Nov. 12, 1777; discharged Feb. 3, 1778; service, 2 mos. 21 days, as guards at Charlestown.

JOSIAH FOSTER, Dracut. Lieutenant, on Lexington alarm roll of Capt. Peter Coburn's co. of minute men in Col. Bridges' regt., which marched on alarm of April 19, 1775, from Dracut; service, 7 days. On list of officers in Col. Bridges' regt. to be commissioned May 27, 1775; rank, Lieutenant in Capt. Coburn's co. On muster roll, dated Aug. 1, 1775; enlisted April 26, 1775; service, 3 mos. 13 days. Also on receipt for pay, dated Cambridge, Nov. 6, 1775, and on a receipt dated Dec.

29, 1775. On a certificate of services dated Dracut, Oct. 14, 1776, given by Peter Coburn, Capt., in which he certifies that said Foster was a Lieutenant in his company in Col. Bridges' regt., at the battle of Bunker Hill, June 17, 1775, where he lost some articles; money for losses allowed in council, Oct. 25, 1776. Also on return of Capt. Joseph B. Varnum's co., Col. Simeon Spaulding's regt., for equipments for 1777, for alarm list.

JUDE FOSTER, Western. Private, on Lexington alarm roll of Capt. Josiah Putnam's co., Col. Jedediah Foster's regt., which marched on alarm of April 19, 1775, from Western to Roxbury; service, 8 days. Private, on muster roll of Capt. John Grainger's co., Col. Learned's regt., dated Aug. 1, 1775; enlisted April 29, 1775; service, 3 mos. 1 week 3 days. Also on return, dated Oct. 7, 1775. On muster roll of Capt. Jonathan Danforth's co., Col. Asa Whitcomb's regt., dated in Camp at Ticonderoga, Nov. 27, 1776; enlisted Jan. 1, 1776; service, 10 mos. 26 days; reported sick in hospital. On muster and pay roll of Capt. Daniel Gilbert's co., Col. Job Cushing's regt., from July 30, 1777, to Sept. 2, 1777; 1 mo. 4 days' service at Bennington; marched from Brookfield to Bennington and Half Moon. (Probably) Corporal, on muster and pay roll of Capt. Thomas Whipple's co., Col. Abijah Stearns' regt., from March 30 to July 2, 1778; service, 3 mos. 3 days, guarding Convention troops.

LEVI FOSTER, Machias. Private, on muster and pay roll of Capt. Jabez West's co.; enlisted May 21st; discharged May 30, 1777; service, 9 days. Also on muster and pay roll of Capt. Joseph Sevey's co., Col. Benjamin Foster's regt.; enlisted July 16th; discharged Oct. 10, 1777; service, 2 mos. 24 days; also 5 days' service in December, 1778, and 15 days' service in Lieut. John Scott's co., between Aug. 31st and Nov. 20, 1779.

LEMUEL FOSTER, Dudley. Private, on list of men in Capt. Reuben Davis' co., which marched to join regt. Aug. 5th; joined Aug. 20th (year not given). On warrant for pay, dated Aug. 20, 1783. Also on muster and pay roll of Capt. Benjamin Allton's co., Col. John Rand's regt.; enlisted July 9th; discharged Oct. 10, 1780; service, 3 mos. 11 days.

LEMUEL FOSTER. Private, on muster and pay roll of Capt. Elias Pratt's co.; enlisted April 13, 1779; discharged July 1, 1779; 2 mos. 18 days' service, as guards at Rutland.

LEMUEL FOSTER. Private, on muster and pay roll of Capt. Timothy Paige's co., Col. John Rand's regt.; enlisted July 20, 1780; discharged Oct. 10, 1780; 3 mos. service, 9 days' travel allowed; service at West Point.

LUNEY FOSTER, Attleborough. Private, on muster and pay roll of Capt. Samuel Robinson's co., Col. Wade's regt., for service in R. I.; enlisted June 21, 1778; service, 22 days. "Lune," on muster and pay roll of Capt. Alexander Foster's co., Col. Thomas Carpenter's regt.; service in R. I.; enlisted July 27th; discharged July 31, 1780; service, 7 days; marched to Tiverton. On roll of same company as marched July 31, 1780; discharged Aug. 8, 1780; service, 10 days.

LEONARD FOSTER, Pepperell. Private, on muster and pay roll of Capt. Aaron Jewett's co., Col. Job Cushing's regt.; enlisted July 27, 1777; discharged Aug. 29, 1777; service, 1 mo. 10 days; marched to Bennington on alarm; 7 days' travel included. On descriptive list: age, 19 yrs.; stature, 5 ft. 9 in.; complexion, dark; enlisted for 9 months, Capt. Lakin's co., Col. Read's regt.; received of Justin Ealy, Commander at Springfield, Aug. 23, 1779, by Capt. James Tisdale. On receipt, dated Springfield, Aug. 22, 1779, for equipments; and on list of 9 months' men entering service Aug. 8, 1779, discharged May 8, 1780.

LINCOLN FOSTER. Private, on muster and pay roll of Capt. Simeon Fowler's co., Col. Jonathan Reed's regt.; enlisted April 23, 1778, to July 8, 1778; service, 2 mos. 16 days, served as guard at Cambridge.

LINCOLN FOSTER. Seaman, on muster and pay roll of officers and crew of brig Hazard, commanded by John F. Williams; enlisted Dec. 4, 1778; discharged April 20, 1779; service, 4 mos. 16 days.

LINE FOSTER. On list of prisoners sent from Newport, R. I., in the Lord Sandwich prison ship, and landed in Boston, March 7, 1778.

MICAH FOSTER, Pembroke. Corporal, on Lexington alarm roll of Capt. Thomas Turner's co., Col. Anthony Thomas' regt., which marched on alarm of April 19, 1775, from Pembroke; service, 3 days. Private, on muster and pay roll of Capt. Freedom Chamberlain's co.; marched on alarm (of the taking of Dorchester Heights), March 5, 1776; service, 5 days.

MICHAEL FOSTER, Sturbridge. Private, on muster and pay roll of Capt. Samuel Hamant's co., Col. Nathaniel Wade's regt.; enlisted June 26, 1778, enlistment to expire Jan. 1, 1779; roll dated Middleton, R. I., Aug. 27, 1778. Also on muster and pay roll of Capt. Abel Mason's co., Col. Jacob Davis' regt.; enlisted July 30th; discharged Aug. 8, 1780; service, 13 days, travel included; marched to Tiverton, R. I.

MOSES FOSTER, Bridgton. Private, on pay roll of 6 men sent by town of Bridgton to act as guards at Sudbury, Canada, and who joined guards sent by the selectmen of Fryeburg.

MOSES FOSTER, Ipswich. On descriptive list, dated May 27, 1780, of officers and crew of the ship Rambler, commanded by Benjamin Lovett: age, 19 yrs.; stature, 5 ft. 8 in.; complexion, light.

MOSES FOSTER, Ipswich (W. Parish). Private, on Lexington alarm roll of Capt. Abram How's co., which marched on alarm of April 19, 1775, from Ipswich (W. Parish); service, 2 days. Also on muster roll of Capt. John Baker's co., Col. Little's regt., dated Aug. 1, 1775; enlisted May 11, 1775; service, 2 mos. 26 days. On order for bounty coat or equivalent in money, due for the 8 months' service in 1775, dated Dec. 11, 1775, payable to Capt. Baker. Corporal, on muster and pay roll of Capt. Robert Dodge's co., Col. Jonathan Titcomb's regt.; marched from home April 25, 1777; service, 2 mos. 8 days; roll dated Warren, June 28, 1777. Also on muster and pay roll of Capt. David Low's co., 3d Essex Co. regt.; engaged Sept. 30, 1777 (marched Oct. 2d); discharged Nov. 7, 1777; service, 40 days; service in regt. commanded by Maj. C. Smith, in Northern Dept., and guarding Gen. Burgoyne's army to Prospect Hill; discharged at Cambridge. Sergeant, on muster and pay roll of Capt. Jeremiah Putnam's co., Col. Nathaniel Wade's regt., for service at R. I.; enlisted July 15, 1778, to Dec. 31, 1778; service, 5 mos. 21 days; also January to November, 1778; enlisted to serve 12 mos. from Jan. 1, 1778; certificate of service, dated Ipswich, Jan. 18, 1779, given by Col. Nathaniel Wade, that said Foster served to credit of town of Ipswich in Capt. Simon Brown's co., at Providence, until Jan. 1. 1779; raised by resolve of June 10, 1778.

MOSES FOSTER, Sturbridge. Private, on muster and pay roll of Capt. Adam Martin's co., Col. Learned's regt., dated Aug. 1, 1775; enlisted May 1, 1775; service, 3 mos. 8 days; also on return dated Oct. 7, 1775.

MOSES FOSTER. Private, on muster and pay roll of Capt. John Dodge's co., Col. Jacob Gerrish's regt. (of guards), from April 1, 1778, to July 1, 1778; service, 3 mos. 4 days. Also on order for wages due for months of April and May, autograph signature.

MOSES FOSTER. Private, on muster and pay roll of Lieut. John Scott's co., for 9 days' service at Machias, between Aug. 31st and Nov. 20, 1779.

MOSES FOSTER, JR., Ipswich. On list of men enlisted into Continental army from 3d Essex Co. regt., dated Ipswich, Feb. 17, 1778; enlisted for 3 years; joined Capt. Burnham's co., Col. Jackson's regt. On pay accounts of above regt. for service from March 1, 1777, to Dec. 31, 1779. Private, also from Jan. 1st to Feb. 21, 1780.

NATHAN FOSTER, Reading. On list of men in Capt. Amos Upton's co., showing equipments, roll dated Reading, April 21, 1775. Also on list of men in Capt. John Flint's co., Col. Baldwin's regt., dated May 15, 1775; and on roll of same company, dated Dec. 19. 1775, for 12 days' service.

NATHAN FOSTER. Private, on muster and pay roll of Capt. Caleb Turner's co.; enlisted July 13, 1775, to Dec. 31, 1775; service, 6 mos. 3 days. Autograph signature on order for one month's pay, dated Bristol, Nov. 18, 1775. On muster and pay roll; enlisted March 26, 1776, to June 10, 1776; service, 2 mos. 15 days; also 3 mos. service between June 10th and Sept. 10, 1776, and from Sept. 10, 1776, to Dec. 7, 1776; service, 2 mos. 27 days; stationed at Boothbay, seacoast defense· all the rolls dated at Bristol.

NATHAN FOSTER. Private, on muster and pay roll of Capt. John Wells co., Col. Timothy Robinson's regt.; enlisted Dec. 23, 1776; discharged April 1, 1777; service, 100 days. A Hampshire Co. regt. marched to Ticonderoga; enlisted to serve until March 23, 1777. Also on muster and pay roll of Capt. John Wells' co., Col. David Wells' regt.; enlisted Sept. 22, 1777; discharged Oct. 23, 1777; service, 1 mo. 2 days; roll dated Shelburne, Nov. 21, 1777. Also on receipt dated Shelburne, Sept. 22, 1777, for mileage, etc., from Shelburne to Stillwater, 112 miles, given by said Foster and others to the selectmen of Shelburne; Capt. John Wells certifies that the men whose names appear upon the receipt went out of the town with him.

NATHAN FOSTER, JR. Appears on a receipt dated Dorchester Camp, Feb. 15, 1776, for ammunition received from Capt. Barnabas Sears.

NATHAN FOSTER, JR. Private, on muster and pay roll of Capt. Caleb

Turner's co.; enlisted March 26, 1776, to June 10, 1776; service, 2 mos. 15 days, in seacoast defense; roll dated Bristol; also 3 mos. service between June 10th and Sept. 10, 1776, and from Sept. 10th to Dec. 7, 1776; service, 2 mos. 27 days, at Boothbay.

NATHANIEL FOSTER, Chelmsford. Private, on Lexington alarm roll of Col. Moses Parker's co., which marched on alarm of April 19, 1775, from Chelmsford under command of Lieut. Benjamin Walker; service, 7 days. On descriptive list of enlisted men: age, 20 yrs.; stature, 6 ft.; complexion, dark; occupation, farmer; enlisted April 26, 1775; joined Capt. Ford's co., Col. Bridge's regt. Autograph signature on order for advance pay, dated Cambridge, June 6, 1775, payable to Lieut. Isaac Parker. Also on muster roll, dated Aug. 1, 1775; service, 3 mos. 13 days. Also on company return, dated Sept. 25, 1775.

NATHANIEL FOSTER, Ipswich. Private, on muster and pay roll of Capt. Charles Smith's co.; enlisted July 18, 1775, to Nov. 1, 1775; service, 3 mos. 22 days; also from Nov. 1, 1775, to Jan. 1, 1776, 2 mos. 6 days. Sergeant, on muster and pay roll of Capt. Daniel Gidding's co., Col. Foster's regt.; enlisted April 5, 1776; service to May 31, 1776, 1 mo. 27 days, at Gloucester; also from June 1st to Aug. 31, 1776, 3 mos; and from Sept. 1st to discharge, Nov. 18, 1776, 2 mos. 18 days, seacoast defense.

NATHANIEL FOSTER, Middleborough. Fifer, on Lexington alarm roll of Capt. Abiel Peirce's co., which marched on alarm of April 19, 1775, from Middleborough to Marshfield; service, 2 days.

NATHANIEL FOSTER, Woolwich. On return of men enlisted into Continental army from Essex Co., of Col. Jonathan Cogswell's regt., dated Ipswich, Feb. 17, 1778; enlisted for Ipswich for 3 years; joined Capt. John Bailey's co., Col. Jackson's regt. On muster and pay roll of said co.; enlisted April 30, 1777; discharged May 26, 1777; service, 27 days. On army pay accounts of Capt. John Burnam's co., Col. Jackson's regt.; service, from April 30, 1777, to Dec. 31, 1779; also from Jan. 1, 1780, to April 21, 1780.

NATHANIEL FOSTER. Private, on muster and pay roll of Capt. Abijah Bangs' co., Maj. Zenas Winslow's regt.; service, 5 days in Sept., 1778, on alarm at Bedford and Falmouth. Also on pay abstract dated Nov. 7, 1778; service 2 days guarding prisoners from Ship Somerset, at Harwich, and thence to Yarmouth.

NATHANIEL FOSTER. Appears on a receipt dated Nov. 2, 1781, for £9 for Sergt. Asa Graves of Col. Smith's regt., signed by himself.

NATHANIEL FOSTER, JR. Private, on muster and pay roll of Capt. Abner Bourn's co., Col. Ebenezer White's regt., for service in R. I., on alarm of Aug. 1, 1780; marched Aug. 1, 1780, discharged Aug. 9, 1780, service, 9 days; roll sworn to at Middleborough, Jan. 22, 1781.

NOAH FOSTER, Chelmsford. On descriptive list of enlisted men age, 18 yrs.; stature, 5 ft. 6 in.; complexion, light; occupation, farmer; enlisted April 27, 1775; joined Capt. John Ford's co., Col. Bridge's regt. Autograph signature on order for advance pay, dated Cambridge, June 6, 1775, payable to Lieut. Isaac Parker. On muster roll of above co., dated Aug. 1, 1775; service, 3 mos. 12 days; also on roll dated Sept. 25, 1775. Private, on army pay accounts of Capt. William Hudson Ballard's co., Col. John Brooks' (late Ichabod Alden's) regt., for service from March 10, 1777, to Oct. 7, 1777; reported killed Oct. 7, 1777.

OBADIAH FOSTER, Andover. Private, on Lexington alarm roll of Capt. Joshua Holt's co., which marched on alarm of April 19, 1775, from Andover to Cambridge; service, 1½ days.

PARKER FOSTER, Kittery, Me. Ensign, on muster roll of Capt. Tobias Fernald's co., Col. James Scammon's regt., dated Aug. 1, 1775; enlisted May 12, 1775; service, 2 mos. 24 days; also 2d Lieutenant, on return (not dated), probably Oct., 1775.

PARKER FOSTER, Kittery, Me. Private, on muster and pay roll of Capt. Samuel Grant's co., Col. Titcomb's regt., for service and travel allowance to and from camp at R. I.; service, 2 mos. 12 days; council date, July 21, 1777. Also on descriptive list of enlisted men: age, 18 yrs.; stature, 5 ft. 7 in.; complexion, light; enlisted for 9 months in 1779. On receipt dated Springfield, Aug. 22, 1779, for equipments given to Capt. James Tisdale by himself and others. On list of 9 months' men entering service Aug. 23, 1779; time of discharge, May 23, 1780; arrived at Springfield Aug. 1, 1780; marched to camp Aug. 2d, under command of Lieut. Benjamin Pike. On pay roll of 6 months' men; enlisted as Private Aug. 1, 1780; discharged Feb. 1, 1781; service, 6 mos. 15 days. On order dated Oct. 26, 1783, for 2 months' pay as Sergeant, given in a memorandum of orders accepted on account of wages.

PAUL FOSTER. Private, on muster and pay roll of Capt. Moses Brown's co.; enlisted July 15, 1775; service, 6 mos. 2 days; stationed at Beverly. Also on list of men's names signed to a receipt for advance pay given by Rev. Daniel Hopkins, dated Beverly, Sept. 25, 1775, for service guarding the sea coast.

PAUL FOSTER. Prize Master, on descriptive list sworn to June 17, 1780, of officers and crew on board the Eagle, commanded by William Groves; stature, 5 ft. 8 in.; complexion, dark.

PEREGRINE FOSTER, Brookfield. Private, on muster and pay roll of Capt. Daniel Gilbert's co., Col. Job Cushing's regt., from July 30th to Sept. 2, 1777; 1 mo. 4 days' service at Bennington; marched from Brookfield to Bennington and Half Moon. Sergeant, on muster and pay roll of Capt. Asa Danforth's co., Col. Convers' regt.; marched Sept. 23, 1777; service, 31 days; marched to join Gen. Gates' army. Sergeant, on muster and pay roll of Capt. Gilbert's co., Col. Josiah Whitney's regt., for service in R. I., from Aug. 2d to Sept. 13, 1780: 1 mo. 16 days.

PERLEY FOSTER. Private, on muster and pay roll of Lieut. Solomon Jackson's co., Col. John Ashley's regt.; enlisted Oct. 13, 1781; discharged Oct. 20, 1781; service, 12 days; a Berkshire Co. regt. which marched on alarm at the Northward, under Lieut.-Col. John Collar, by order of Col. John Ashley; roll dated Tyringham, 4 days' travel included.

PETER FOSTER. Private, on muster and pay roll of Capt. Nathaniel Woods' co., Col. Ebenezer Sprout's regt.; enlisted Sept. 6, 1778; discharged Sept. 12th; service, 6 days, on 2d alarm at Dartmouth; roll dated Middleborough. On muster and pay roll of Capt. Edward Sparrow's co., Col. John Jacobs' regt.; enlisted July 23d; discharged Oct. 27, 1780; service, 3 mos. 5 days; detached to reinforce Continental army by order of council June 22, 1780; 3 mos. service; roll sworn to at Middleborough.

PETER FOSTER. Private, on muster and pay roll of Capt. John Kettell's co.; enlisted Aug. 14th; discharged Sept. 30, 1779; service, 1 mo. 18 days; Maj. Heath's detachment of guards doing duty in and about Boston, by resolve of June 18, 1779.

PETER FOSTER. Private, on muster and pay roll of Capt. John Abbot's co., Col. Nathaniel Wade's regt.; enlisted July 10th; discharged Oct. 10, 1780; service, 3 mos. 11 days; raised for 3 mos. service at West Point, by resolve of June 22, 1780.

PHILEMON FOSTER, Ipswich (W. Parish). Private, on Lexington alarm roll of Capt. Abraham How's co. of minute men, which marched on alarm of April 19, 1775, from Ipswich (W. Parish); service, 2 days. Sergeant, on muster and pay roll of Capt. John Dodge's co., Col. Jacob Gerrish's regt.; enlisted Nov. 12, 1777, to Feb. 3, 1778; service, 2 mos. 21 days (a regt. of guards serving at Charlestown); enlisted Feb. 3, 1778; discharged April 3, 1778; service, 2 mos. 1 day. Also on roll for Feb., 1778, dated Winter Hill, April 17, 1778, detached Nov. 5, 1777, to guard Burgoyne's army.

PHILEMON FOSTER. Private, on muster and pay roll of Capt. William Weston's co.; enlisted Sept. 27, 1776; discharged Nov. 19, 1776; roll made up from Oct. 1, 1776; service, 1 mo. 18 days; stationed on Gurnet for defense of Plymouth harbor.

PHINEAS FOSTER. Private, on muster and pay roll of Capt. James Mallon's co. (raised in Essex and Plymouth Cos.), Lieut. Putnam's regt.; enlisted Aug. 26, 1781; discharged Dec. 4, 1781; service, 3 mos. 20 days, travel included.

REUBEN FOSTER, Chelmsford. Private, on Lexington alarm roll of Col. Moses Parker's co., which marched on alarm of April 19, 1775, from Chelmsford; service, 8 days. On descriptive list of enlisted men: age, 23 yrs.; stature, 6 ft. 1 in.; complexion, light; occupation, farmer; enlisted April 27, 1775; joined Capt. John Ford's co., Col. Bridge's regt. Private, on muster roll of said co., dated April 27, 1775; service, 3 mos. 12 days; also on company return, dated Sept. 25, 1775.

REUBEN FOSTER. Private, on pay abstract of Capt. James Russel's co., Col. Eleazar Brooks' regt.; service, 5 days; marched to Dorchester, March 4, 1776, to reinforce the army.

RICHARD FOSTER. Seaman, on muster and pay roll of officers and crew of ship "Protector," commanded by Capt. John F. Williams; enlisted March 5, 1780; discharged Aug. 17, 1780; service, 5 mos. 12 days.

RICHARD FOSTER, Massachusetts. Seaman, on descriptive list sworn to at Boston, Sept. 9, 1780, of officers and crew of ship General Mifflin, commanded by George Wait Babcock; age, 22 yrs.; complexion, light.

RICHARD FOSTER, Amesbury. On descriptive list of men enlisted from Essex Co., for term of 9 months from arrival at Fishkill; age, 17 yrs.; stature, 5 ft. 4 in.; complexion, dark; arrived at Fishkill June 17, 1778.

RICHARD FOSTER, Boxford. Private, on Lexington alarm roll of Capt. Jacob Gould's co., Col. Samuel Johnson's regt., which marched on alarm of April 19, 1775, from Boxford; service, 6 days.

RICHARD FOSTER, New Salem. Corporal, on muster roll of Capt. Nathaniel Healey's co., Col. Learned's regt., dated Aug. 1, 1775; enlisted May 10, 1775; service, 2 mos. 3 weeks, 5 days; also on return of said co., dated at Roxbury Camp, Oct. 6, 1775.

RICHARD FOSTER, Salem. On descriptive list of men raised to reinforce Continental army for term of six months, by resolve of June 5, 1780: age, 18 yrs.; stature, 5 ft. 8 in.; complexion, light; arrived at Springfield, July 22, 1780; marched to camp same day under command of Capt. William Scott. On list of 6 months' men having passed muster, dated Camp Totoway, Oct. 25, 1780. On pay roll of 6 months' men raised by town of Salem; marched July 23, 1780; discharged Dec. 5, 1780; service, 4 mos. 25 days.

ROBERT FOSTER. Appears on list of officers of the Massachusetts militia chosen by their respective companies, agreed to in council June 6, 1776, as Captain of 7th co., in Col. Timothy Pickering, Jr.'s 1st Essex Co. regt., dated Salem, May 15, 1776; commissioned June 6, 1776. Also on a petition dated Salem, May 19, 1778, signed by himself, asking for a discharge from his commission as captain in the 7th co., of Col. Pickering's (1st) regt., in the county of Essex; accepted by council May 20, 1778.

ROBERT FOSTER. Appears among a list of officers of Massachusetts militia as 2d Lieutenant in the volunteer co. (from Salem), Capt. Samuel Flagg's (Essex Co.) regt.; commissioned July 25, 1778.

ROBERT FOSTER. Quarter Master, on pay roll, commenced July 31, 1778; discharged Dec. 1, 1778; rations allowed for 4 mos.; service under Col. John Allan at Machias; also from Dec. 1, 1778, to June 1, 1779: 6 months. Also on pay accounts from July 4, 1777, to June 1, 1779, and from June 1, 1779, to Dec. 1, 1779, also from Dec. 1, 1779, to June 1, 1780. Assistant to Deputy Quartermaster General, on pay abstract, for service at Machias, from May 5, 1780, to Jan. 31, 1781; service, 8 mos. 26 days.

ROWLAND FOSTER, Boxford. Private, on a pay abstract of Capt. Richard Peabody's co., Col. Edward Wigglesworth's regt., for service in 1776, and travel allowance from Ticonderoga home.

RUFUS FOSTER. Private, on a return of Capt. Caleb Chapin's co., for clothing.

RUFUS FOSTER, Bernardston. Private, on muster and pay roll of Capt. Lawrence Kemp's co., Col. David Wells' regt.; enlisted May 10, 1777; discharged July 17, 1777; service, 2 mos. 9 days, at the Northward. Also on muster and pay roll of Capt. James Walsworth's co., Col. Elisha Porter's regt.; enlisted July 22, 1779; discharged Aug. 27, 1779; service, 1 mo. 11 days, at New London, Conn., 6 days' travel allowed. On descriptive list of men belonging to Hampshire Co.: age, 19 yrs.; stature, 5 ft. 8 in.; complexion, light; hair, light; eyes, light; joined 5th Hampshire Co. regt.; dated Deerfield, July 24, 1780. Private, on muster and pay roll of Capt. Isaac Newton's co., Col. S. Murray's regt.; enlisted July 22, 1780; discharged Oct. 10, 1780; service, 2 mos. 28 days, 9 days' travel allowed.

REYNOLD, RUNNEL, or RUNNELS FOSTER, Bradford. On descriptive list of enlisted men: age, 32 yrs; stature, 5 ft. 8 in.; enlisted for 9 months from arrival at Fishkill, June 19, 1778. On receipt for bounty paid him by Lieut. Abel Kimball, class No. 4, for town of Bradford, to serve in the Continental army for 3 years; dated Boston, May 29, 1782.

SAMUEL FOSTER, Billerica. Private, on a return of men in Capt. Solomon Kidder's co., Col. Brook's regt.; in service at White Plains; endorsed 1776. Private, on muster and pay roll of Capt. Fox's co., Col. Johnson's regt.; enlisted Aug. 6, 1777, for 3 years; enlisted for Marlborough; reported promoted to Sergeant, May 30, 1778, to Sergeant-Major Aug. 1, 1778, reduced to Sergeant April 9, 1779. On list of men enlisted into Continental army from Capt. Edward Farmer's co., 7th Middlesex regt., dated Feb. 16, 1778; joined Capt. Fox's co., Col. Hanly's regt. On pay roll of Capt. Lemuel Trescott's co., Col. David Henley's regt.; dated Providence, Sept. 11, 1778: service from April 1st to May 1, 1778: 1 mo. Private Sergeant, on roll dated Pawtuxet, May 4, 1779. On muster roll of Capt. Fox's co.,

Col. Henry Jackson's regt., dated Providence, Nov. 1, 1779, for Oct., 1779; also on pay rolls to Aug. 6, 1780.

SAMUEL FOSTER, Haverhill. On descriptive list of men raised for 6 months, agreeable to resolve of June 5, 1780: age, 17 yrs.; stature, 5 ft. 2 in.; complexion, light; arrived at Springfield July 1, 1780; marched to camp July 2, 1780. On list of men who passed muster, return dated Camp Totoway, Oct. 25, 1780. On pay roll of 6 months, men raised by Haverhill; marched June 29, 1780; discharged Dec. 16, 1780; service, 5 mos. 25 days.

SAMUEL FOSTER, Beverly. On a petition dated Boston, Nov. 29, 1779, signed by Josiah Batchelder, Jr., on behalf of himself and others, requesting that said Foster be appointed commander of sloop "Fish Hawke;" granted by council Nov. 30, 1779. Master, on descriptive list dated June 6, 1780, of officers and crew of sloop Fish Hawke, commanded by Samuel Foster: age, 32; stature, 5 ft. 5 in.; complexion, dark. On a petition dated Boston, May 2, 1781, signed by Samuel Foster in behalf of Josiah Batchelder and others of Beverly, asking that said Foster be appointed commander of sloop "Fish Hawke;" granted in council May 2, 1781. Also on a petition dated Boston, Aug. 23, 1781, signed by Samuel Foster in behalf of Nathaniel Silsby and others of Salem, asking that said Foster be appointed commander of schooner "Surprise;" granted in council, Aug. 23, 1781.

SAMUEL FOSTER, Kingston. On list of prisoners sent on board the guard ship "Adams," by the Board of War as returned by Joseph Dobel, Sept. 8, 1777; reported received Aug. 26, 1777.

SAMUEL FOSTER, Newburyport. Corporal, on Lexington alarm roll of Capt. Moses Nowell's co.; marched on alarm of April 19, 1775, from Newburyport; service, 4 days. Sergeant, on muster roll of Capt. Benjamin Perkins' co., Col. Moses Little's regt., dated Aug. 1, 1775; enlisted May 9, 1775; service, 12 weeks. On company return (not dated), probably Oct., 1775: age given as 24 yrs. On order for bounty coat or equivalent, due for the 8 months' service in 1775, dated in camp, Dec. 27, 1775, payable to Capt. Perkins.

SAMUEL FOSTER, Manchester. Lieutenant, on Lexington alarm roll of Capt. Andrew Marster's co.; marched on alarm of April 19, 1775, from Manchester to Medford; service, 3 days.

SAMUEL FOSTER. Appears on list of men's names signed to receipt for advance pay, given by Rev. Daniel Hopkins, dated Beverly, Sept. 25, 1775; service, guarding the sea coast. Sergeant, on muster and pay roll of Capt. Moses Brown's co.; enlisted July 15, 1775; service, 6 mos. 2 days. Also on pay abstract of above co., Col. Glover's regt., for service in Feb., 1776; enlisted Jan. 8, 1776; also in service to Sept., 1776, inclusive.

SAMUEL FOSTER, Roxbury. Sergeant, on Lexington alarm roll of Capt. Moses Whiting's co., Col. John Greaton's regt., which marched on alarm of April 19, 1775, from Roxbury; service, 5 days. Lieutenant, on list of officers in Capt. Edward P. Williams' co., Gen. Heath's regt., dated Roxbury Camp, May 20, 1775. Also on return dated Oct. 5, 1775. Captain, on muster roll of 2d Massachusetts regt., Col. John Greaton's, for Dec., 1777, dated Albany, Jan. 2, 1778; commissioned Jan. 1, 1777; reported on furlough for 6 months with Gen. Gate's leave, granted Dec. 25, 1777. On Continental army pay accounts of Col. Greaton's regt., for service from Jan. 1, 1777, to May 6, 1778; reported: deceased May 6, 1778. On list of officers whose widows or orphans received half pay for 7 years (to May 6, 1785), by resolve of Aug. 24, 1780.

SAMUEL FOSTER, Westminster. Private, on Lexington alarm roll of Capt. Elisha Jackson's co., Col. Asa Whitcomb's regt., which marched on alarm of April 19, 1775, from Westminster to Cambridge; service, 9½ days. Private, on pay abstract of Capt. Jackson's co., dated Aug. 22, 1777; service, 10 days, on alarm at Bennington; marched from Westminster to East Hoosac, and there dismissed.

SAMUEL FOSTER, Wilmington. Private, on Lexington alarm roll of Capt. Timothy Walker's co., Col. Green's regt., which marched on alarm of April 19, 1775, from Wilmington; service, 4½ days.

SAMUEL FOSTER, Wrentham. Private, on Lexington alarm roll of Capt. Samuel Powell's co., Col. John Smith's regt., which marched on alarm of April 19, 1775, from Wrentham; service, 11 days. Also on muster roll of Capt. Oliver Pond's co., Col. Joseph Read's regt., dated Aug. 1, 1775; enlisted May 2, 1775; service, 3 mos. 7 days; also on company return, dated Sept. 25, 1775.

SAMUEL FOSTER. Appears on list of men who received money from the public treasury for losses at battles of Lexington and Bunker Hill; allowed by council, June 13, 1776.

SAMUEL FOSTER. Prize Master, on muster and pay roll of officers and crew of the brigantine "Tyranicide," commanded by Capt. Jonathan Haraden; enlisted March 13, 1777; discharged Aug. 29, 1777; service, 5 mos. 16 days.

SAMUEL FOSTER. Lieutenant, on muster and pay roll of Capt. John Blunt's co. (Lincoln Co. regt.); enlisted March 6, 1780; discharged Sept. 6, 1780; service, 6 mos.

SAMUEL FOSTER. Private, on muster and pay roll of Capt. Nathaniel Carter's co., Col. Job. Cushing's regt.; enlisted Sept. 7, 1777; discharged Oct. 22, 1777; service, 1 mo. 24 days.

SAMUEL FOSTER. Private on muster and pay roll of Capt. Thomas Whipple's co., Col. Abijah Stearns' regt. from March 30, 1778, to July 2, 1778; 3 mos. 3 days; service guarding convention troops.

SAMUEL FOSTER. Private, on muster and pay roll of Capt. Elijah Deming's co., Col. Ashley's regt.; enlisted June 4; discharged July 15, 1778; service, 1 mo. 11 days. Also from July 19, 1779, to Aug. 27, 1779, in Capt. Collar's co, 1 mo. 9 days.

SAMUEL FOSTER. Appears in a petition dated Boston, May 7, 1782, given by himself and others, asking for the commission of the above as commander of the schooner Penguin; approved in council May 7, 1782.

SETH FOSTER. Private on pay abstract of Capt. Abijah Bangs' co., Maj. Zenas Winslow's regt.; service on alarm at Bedford and Falmouth in September, 1778; 5 days. Also on muster and pay roll of Capt. Elijah Smalley's co., Col. Winslow's regt.; 4 days' service on alarm at Bedford and Falmouth in September, 1778.

SETH JEWETT FOSTER. Private, on muster and pay roll of Capt. John Robinson's co; service in R. I.; enlisted Aug. 4, 1781; discharged Dec. 1, 1784; service, 4 mos. 1 day (5 days' travel allowed). Also on a warrant to pay men in above company, dated April 11, 1783.

SILAS FOSTER, Acton. Private, on pay abstract of Capt. David Wheeler's co., Col. Nixon's regt., for travel allowance, dated Winter Hill, Jan. 15, 1776; Sergeant on pay abstract of Capt. Zachariah Fitch's co., Col. Samuel Brewer's regt.; service, from Aug. 23 to Sept. 30, 1776; 1 mo. 9 days.

SIMEON FOSTER, Andover. Private on Lexington alarm roll of Capt. Nathaniel Lovejoys' co. (minute men), Col. Samuel Johnson's regt., which marched on alarm of April 19, 1775, from Andover to Cambridge via Billerica; service, 3½ days.

SIMEON FOSTER, Andover. On decriptive list of men raised for six months, agreeable to resolve of June 5, 1780; age, 24 years; stature, 5 ft. 5 in; complexion, light; arrived at Springfield July 1, 1780; on list dated camp Totoway, Oct. 25, 1780, as having passed muster; on pay roll for six months' men; marched June 26, 1780; discharged Dec. 18, 1780; service, 6 mos. 3 days.

SIMEON FOSTER, Groton. Private on Lexington alarm roll of Capt. John Nutting's co., Col. William Prescott's regt., which marched on alarm of April 19, 1775, from Pepperell; service, 6 days. Also on return of the above company, dated Aug. 1, 1775, enlisted April 25, 1775; service, 3 mos. 8 days. On order for county coat, or equivalent, due for the eight months' service, dated Cambridge, Jan. 1, 1776. On descriptive list of men raised in Middlesex Co. to reinforce Continental army for nine months by resolve of April 20, 1778: age, 43 years; stature, 5 ft. 9 in. Also on list returned as arrived at Fishkill, Aug. 5, 1778; reported detained by an accident which happened after his march.

SIMEON FOSTER. Private, on muster and pay roll of Capt. Joseph Eaton's co., Col. Samuel Johnson's regt.; enlisted Aug. 15, 1777; discharged Nov. 30, 1777; service, 3 mos. 16 days; marched on expedition to the northward.

SIMEON FOSTER. Private, on muster and pay roll of Capt. Samuel Russell's co., Col. Samuel Bullard's regt.; enlisted Aug. 15, 1777; discharged Nov. 30, 1777; service, 3 mos. 28 days; roll dated Danvers (12 days' travel included).

SKELTON FOSTER. Private, on muster and pay roll of Capt. John Crawford's co., Col. James Converse's regt.; enlisted Aug. 20; discharged Aug. 23, 1777; service, 5 days, travel included; marched on alarm at Bennington.

SMITH FOSTER, Westford (also given as Billerica). Private, on return of Capt. John Minot's co., Col. Dike's regt.; service from Dec. 13, 1776, to March 1; 1777; discharged Feb. 18, 1777. On return of men enlisted into army from Capt. Wright's co., 6th Middlesex co. regt., dated Littleton Sept. 17, 1777, for three years. joined Cap. William H. Ballard's co., Col. Ichabod Alden's regt. On muster roll of said co., dated Cherry Valley May 14, 1779; enlisted May 17, 1777. On roll of

Lieut. John Brook's co.; made up to Dec. 31, 1779, 2 years, 7 mos., 15 days' service (is given as belonging to Acton). Reported as enlisted for during war Dec. 20, 1779. On pay accounts of Capt. Ballard's co.; service from May 17, 1777, to Dec. 31, 1779; reported transferred to Col. Crane's regt. On pay accounts of Capt. Treadwell's co., Col. Crane's regt.; service from Jan. 1, 1780, to Dec. 31, 1780. Matross on list of men in 1st artillery regt., who did not receive gratuity granted by resolve of Jan. 15, 1781. Matross on muster roll of Capt. Treadwell's co. for Feb. and March, 1781, dated at West Point; reported on furlough. On muster roll for April, 1781.

STEPHEN FOSTER, Dorchester. Private, on muster and pay roll of Capt. Lemuel Clap's co., Col. Benjamin Gill's regt.; enlisted March 14, 1776; discharged March 26, 1776; service, 12 days. Also enlisted June 13; discharged June 16, 1776; service, 3 days. On pay abstract of Capt. Richard Mayberry's co., Col. Ebenezer Francis' regt., for travel allowance from Dorchester Heights home; allowed in council Nov. 29, 1776.

STEPHEN FOSTER, Groton. Private, on muster roll of Capt. Lawrence's co., Col. Prescott's regt., dated Aug. 1, 1775; enlisted April 25, 1775; service, 3 mos. 8 days. On company return, dated Oct. 6, 1775, reported either killed in battle or taken prisoner, June 17, 1775. On order for bounty coat, or equivalent in money, due for the eight months' service in 1775, dated Cambridge, Oct. 30, 1775, payable to Captain Lawrence.

STEPHEN FOSTER, Oakham. Private, on muster roll of Capt. Simeon Hazleton's co., Col. Fellows' regt., dated Aug. 1, 1775; enlisted May 2, 1775; service, 3 mos. 7 days. Also on return dated Oct. 7, 1775.

STEPHEN FOSTER. Private, on muster roll of Capt. Aaron Haynes' co., Col. Aas Whitcomb's regt., dated in camp at Ticonderoga, Dec. 1, 1776; enlisted Jan. 1, 1776; service, 11 mos.; reported died Sept. 28, 1776.

STEPHEN FOSTER, Topsfield. Private, on Lexington alarm roll of Capt. Stephen Perkins' co. of minute men, which marched on alarm of April 19, 1775, from Topsfield; service, 1 day.

STEPHEN FOSTER. Private, on muster and pay roll of Capt. Joseph Eaton's co., Col. Samuel Johnson's regt.; enlisted Aug. 15, 1777; discharged Nov. 30, 1777; service, 3 mos. 29 days (13 days' travel included); on expedition to the northward.

STEPHEN FOSTER. Private, on muster and pay roll of Capt. Timothy Foster's co.; enlisted Sept. 1, 1779; discharged Nov. 1, 1779; service, 2 mos.; defending frontiers of Lincoln co.

STUART FOSTER, Winthrop. Private, on muster and pay roll of Capt. Oliver Colborn's co., Col. Arnold's regt.; enlisted July 25, 1775; service, 20 days.

THEOPHILUS FOSTER, Brookfield. Private, on Lexington alarm roll of Capt. Ithamer Wright's co., which marched on alarm of April 19, 1775, from Brookfield; service, 8 days, travel included; returned home April 23, 1775.

THOMAS FOSTER, Dorchester (possibly). Private, on Lexington alarm roll of Capt. William Holden's co., Col. Robinson's regt., which was mustered on alarm of April 19, 1775, and marched under command of Lieut. Preserved Baker; service, 10 days.

THOMAS FOSTER, Middleborough. On return of men enlisted into Continental army from Capt. Nathaniel Wood's co., 4th Plymouth co. regt., dated Feb. 19, 1778; enlisted for during war; joined Capt. Wadsworth's co., Col. Bradford's regt. On roll dated at Boston made up for billeting allowance; enlisted March 6, 1777; 64 days. On muster return dated Valley Forge Jan. 28, 1778, reported on furlough. On pay accounts of said regt., private; service, from March 6, 1777, to Dec. 31, 1779. Also for service from Jan. 1, 1780, to Dec. 31, 1780; rank, Sergeant. On register of furlough of Lieut.-Col. J. Brooks' 7th regt. since Jan. 1, 1781; rank, Sergeant, in Capt. King's co., leave given by Major Porter to go from West Point to Middleboro, Jan. 25, 1781, for 40 days; overstayed 72 days. Reported on duty on muster roll for May, 1781. On muster rolls from June to November, 1781; reported as on extra duty as armorer; reported reduced to private June 1, 1781. On muster rolls dated York Hults, December, 1781, and February, 1782, reported on furlough. On a list of men dated Boston Jan. 28, 1803, returned by John Avery, secretary, and J. Jackson, treasurer, who had enlisted into the Continental army and actually served three years, and were accordingly entitled to gratuities under resolves of March 4 and June 19, 1801; credited with $20.

THOMAS FOSTER. Private, on muster roll of Capt. Jonathan Allen's co., Col. John Fellows' regt., dated Aug. 1, 1775; enlisted May 1, 1775; service, 17 days. Residence not given—marked "transient."

THOMAS FOSTER. Private, on muster and pay roll of Capt. Nathaniel Goodwin's co., Col. Theophilus Cotton's regt., detached Sept. 25, 1777; discharged Oct. 10, 1777; service 15 days; on secret expedition to Newport, R. I.

THOMAS FOSTER. Private, on muster and pay roll of Capt. Nathaniel Carter's co., Col. Job Cushing's regt.; enlisted Sept. 7, 1777; discharged Nov. 29, 1777; service, 3 mos. 4 days.

THOMAS FOSTER. Surgeon's Mate, on muster and pay roll of officers and crew of the brigantine Hazard, dated Boston, June 6, 1778; enlisted Nov. 22, 1777; discharged May 11, 1778; service, 5 mos. 19 days. Deceased.

THOMAS FOSTER. Private, on muster and pay roll of Capt. John Dodge's co., Col. Jacob Gerrish's regt. (guards serving at Charlestown); enlisted Nov. 23, 1777, to Feb. 3, 1778; 2 mos. 10 days. Also on roll dated April, 1778, for February, 1778, reported on guard. On muster and pay roll; enlisted Feb. 3, 1778; discharged April 3, 1778; service, 2 mos. 1 day. Also between April 1 and July 1, 1778; 2 mos. 27 days. Also on receipt, dated Camp Winter Hill, June 21, 1778, for wages for service in April and May; service, 23 days in April and the month of May; autograph signature.

THOMAS FOSTER. Private, on muster and pay roll of Capt. Ward Swift's co., Col. Freeman's regt.; 8 days' service on alarm at Dartmouth and Falmouth, Sept. 6, 1778.

THOMAS FOSTER, Gardnerstown. Private on muster and pay roll of Capt. Oliver Colborn's co., Col. Arnold's regt.; enlisted July 25, 1775; service, 20 days. Also on a return of men enlisted into the Continental army from Captain Swan's co.,Col. Benjamin Gill's regt. (also given Col. Joseph North's 2d Lincoln Co. regt.), dated June 27, 1777, for town of Stoughton, for three years; joined Capt. Burton's co., Col. Sherburne's regt. On a return of officers and men belonging to Massachusetts in Col. Henry Sherburne's regt., certified at Boston, June 15, 1779, by Capt. Benj. Burton; enlisted March 18, 1777, for three years or during war. Residence, Vassalboro. On Continental army pay accounts of Col. Sherburne's regt. for service from March 18, 1777, to Dec. 31, 1779; reported deserted Feb. 3, 1780.

THOMAS FOSTER, Ipswich (W. Parish). Lieutenant, on Lexington alarm roll of Capt. Abram How's co., which marched on alarm of April 19, 1775, from Ipswich (W. Parish); service, 2 days. Also on list of officers of Massachusetts militia, chosen by their respective companies and field officers as captain in 8th co. of Essex Co. regt.; commissioned by council May 7, 1776.

THOMAS FOSTER, Ipswich. Private, on Lexington alarm roll of Capt. Jonathan Cogswell Jr.'s co., which marched on alarm of April 19, 1775, from Ipswich; service, 3 days. Also on muster and pay roll of Capt. Abraham Dodge's co., Col. Moses Little's regt., dated Aug. 1, 1775; enlisted May 3, 1775; service, 12 weeks 6 days. On company return, dated Oct. 9, 1775, his age given 20 years. On order for bounty coat, or equivalent, due for the eight months' service in 1775, dated in camp, Dec. 21, 1775, payable to Lieut. James Lord. Also on muster and pay roll of Capt. Daniel Giddings' co., Col. Foster's regt.; enlisted March 12, 1776; service to May 31, 1776; 2 mos. 20 days; stationed at Gloucester. Also from June 1 to Aug. 31, 1776; service, 3 mos. Also from Sept. 1, 1776; 2 mos. 18 days; discharged Nov. 18, 1776. On a return of men enlisted into Continental army from 3d Essex Co. regt. for three years; joined Capt. Burnham's co., Col. Jackson's regt. On a list of officers in Col. Michael Jackson's regt., dated West Point, Nov. 8, 1779; rank, Ensign; commissioned Nov. 26, 1779. On pay accounts of above regt. for service from March 18, 1777, to Dec. 31, 1779. On list of officers in said regt. as Ensign; recommended as Lieutenant; commission to date from Oct. 6, 1780, in place of Lieut. Jackson, promoted; dated Camp Totoway, Oct. 15, 1780. On army pay accounts for service from Jan. 1, to Dec. 31, 1780; reported served 9 mos. 24 days as Ensign; 2 mos. 6 days as Lieutenant. On list of officers in Lieut.-Col. Badlam's (8th) regt., dated Philipsburg, July 18, 1781; lieutenant commissioned Oct. 6, 1780.

THOMAS FOSTER, JR., Ipswich. On a descriptive list of men raised to reinforce the Continental army for six months, agreeable to resolve of June 5, 1780: age, 18; stature, 5 ft. 10 in; complexion, dark; arrived at Springfield July 5, 1780; marched to camp same day; passed muster at Camp Totoway; return dated Oct. 25, 1780. On pay roll of six months' men as marched June 17, 1780; discharged Dec. 3, 1780; 5 mos., 28 days. Also on list of three years' men, raised by resolve of Dec. 2, 1780; raised March 14, 1781. On receipt for bounty, class No. 31, dated Ipswich, March 23, 1781. Corporal on pay roll of Col. Benjamin Tupper's regt.; 9 mos. 18 days; roll made up from Jan. 1, 1781, to Jan. 1, 1782; reported promoted from Private to Corporal Nov. 16, 1781. Also on pay roll from Jan. 1, 1782; service, 12 mos.

THOMAS FOSTER, Lenox. Drummer on muster and pay roll of Capt. Caleb Hyde's co., Col. James Easton's regt., which marched from Lenox on alarm at Ticonderoga May 10, 1775; service, 5 days.

THOMAS FOSTER, Middleborough. Private, on muster and pay roll of Capt. Joshua Benson's co., Col. Theophilus Cotton's regt., dated Aug. 1, 1775; enlisted June 1, 1775; service, 2 mos. 4 days. Also on order for bounty coat, or equivalent, due for the eight months' service in 1775, dated Roxbury, Nov. 14, 1775, payable to Lieut. William Tomson.

THOMAS FOSTER, Middleborough. On list of men mustered in Plymouth Co., to serve in Capt. Joseph Tupper's co., Col. Bigelow's regt.; mustered between March 5 and March 22, 1777; age, 42 years.

THOMAS FOSTER, Middleborough. Private, on pay abstract of Capt. Matthew Randall's co., Col. Marshall's regt., for advance pay, dated camp at Hull, June 18, 1776. On muster and pay roll of said regt.; enlisted June 1, 1776, to Aug. 1, 1776; 2 mos. Also on return as in service from Aug. 1 to Nov. 1, 1776; 3 mos. Also on pay roll for November, 1776; 1 mo. 2 days.

THOMAS FOSTER. Private, on muster and pay roll of Lieut. Jonah Washburn's co., Col. Ebenezer Sprout's regt., which marched from Middleboro on alarm of Dec. 8, 1776, at R. I.; service, 5 days; roll dated Middleborough March 28, 1777.

THOMAS FOSTER, Winthrop. On list of men enlisted or drafted into Continental army out of Col. Joseph North's (2d Lincoln Co.) regt., dated Gardnerstown, Feb. 2, 1778; enlisted for three years; joined Capt. Langdon's co., Col. Jackson's regt. On list of men returned with a petition of inhabitants of Winthrop, dated March 10, 1777, asking consideration on account of their exposed condition as having voluntarily enlisted in the army in 1776.

THOMAS FOSTER. Private, on muster and pay roll of Capt. Nathaniel Wood's co., Col. Simon Cary's regt.; service, 5 days; roll dated Roxbury, April 1, 1776.

THOMAS WAITE FOSTER, Hadley. Captain, on list of men in Col. Woodbridge's regt., dated Cambridge, April 25, 1775. Also in a letter regarding sending a cannon to Cambridge from Com. Gen. John Pigeon to Major Baldwin, dated April 25, 1775. Also on muster roll of Col. Richard Gridley's regt., dated Aug. 1, 1775; enlisted April 19, 1775; 3 mos. 20 days. Also on the October, 1775, return.

THOMAS WAITE FOSTER. Appears in a letter written by himself, a gunner in the ship Warren, on the Penobscot expedition, asserting that Paul Revere had apparently been consistent in action at above expedition; sworn to before court Nov. 11, 1779.

TILLA FOSTER, Greenwich. Private, on muster and pay roll of Capt. Oliver Coney's co., Col. Sears' regt.; marched Aug. 12, 1781; discharged Nov. 15, 1781; service, 3 mos. 10 days.

TILLEY FOSTER, Rochester. Private, on Lexington alarm roll of Capt. Earl Clap's co., Col. Theophilus Cotton's regt., which marched in consequence of alarm of April 19, 1775; service, 12 days. Also on muster roll of above co., dated Aug. 1, 1775; enlisted May 2, 1775; service, 3 mos. 6 days. Also on return dated Oct. 7, 1775, and on muster and pay roll of Capt. Elisha Haskell's co., Col. Benjamin Hawes' regt.; service in R. I. from July 29 to Sept. 11, 1778; 1 mo. 15 days.

TIMOTHY FOSTER, Dorchester (probably). Sergeant, on Lexington alarm roll of Capt. William Holden's co., Col. Robinson's regt., which was mustered April 19, 1775, and marched under command of Lieut. Preserved Baker; service, 10 days.

TIMOTHY FOSTER, Dudley. Sergeant, on Lexington alarm roll of Capt. Nathaniel Healey's co. (minute men), Col. Ebenezer Learned's regt., which marched on alarm of April 19, 1775, from Dudley; service, 6 days.

TIMOTHY FOSTER, JR., Dudley. Ensign, on muster roll of Capt. Nathaniel Healey's co., Col. Learned's regt., dated Aug. 1, 1775; enlisted April 24, 1775; service, 3 mos. 2 weeks. Also on list of officers of Massachusetts militia as 2d Lieutenant in 3d co. of 5th Worcester Co. regt.; commissioned April 4, 1776. Lieutenant on muster and pay roll of Capt. Healey's co., Col. Jonathan Holman's regt., dated Providence, R. I., Jan. 21, 1777; service, 21 days; on alarm of December, 1776. Also on pay abstract, dated Fort Edward Oct. 17, 1777; engaged Sept. 26; discharged Oct. 6, 1777; service, 30 days. On list of officers of Massachusetts militia as 2d Lieutenant, Capt. David Keith's co., Col. Holman's regt., commissioned Sept. 25, 1778; commissioned Feb. 19, 1780, 1st Lieutenant in Capt. Lemuel Corbin's co., Col. Davis' (5th) regt.

TIMOTHY FOSTER, Taunton. Matross, on muster and pay roll of Capt. Samuel Fale's co., Col. G. Williams' regt., for time and travel to Slade's Ferry in Swazey, R. I., on alarm of Dec. 8, 1776; service, 4 days.

TIMOTHY FOSTER. Appears among a list of men's names signed to a receipt for advance pay, given by Rev. Daniel Hopkins, dated Beverly, Sept. 25, 1775; service, guarding the sea coast. Fifer on muster and pay roll of Capt. Moses Brown's co.; enlisted July 15, 1775; service, 6 mos. 2 days; stationed at Beverly.

TIMOTHY FOSTER. Appears in a pay roll of Sergt. Enos Dean's detachment of guards; service, 14 days; by order of committee of correspondence, etc., in order to prevent escape of Highlanders and other prisoners from Taunton jail during the alarm of Dec. 8, 1776.

TIMOTHY FOSTER. Private, on muster and pay roll of Capt. Nathaniel Clap's co., Col. Benj. Hawes' regt.; service at R. I.; enlisted July 26, 1778; discharged Sept. 11, 1778; service, 17 days.

TIMOTHY FOSTER. Private, on muster and pay roll of Capt. John Blunt's co., Col. Samuel McCobb's regt.; service, 1 mo, between June 28 and Sept. 28, 1779; on expedition against Penobscot.

TIMOTHY FOSTER. Captain, on list of officers of Massachusetts militia in 7th co. of 2d Lincoln Co. regt.; commissioned July 23 (or Aug. 23), 1776. On muster and pay roll of his company in Major Lithgo's detachment; enlisted Sept. 1, 1779; discharged Nov. 2, 1779; service, 2 mos. 2 days, defending the frontiers of Lincoln Co.

TIMOTHY FOSTER. Private on muster and pay roll of Capt. Joshua Wilbore's co., Col. Mitchell's regt., for service in R. I. on alarm of Aug. 2, 1780; marched Aug. 2, 1780, to Tiverton, R. I.; service, 8 days.

WARHAM FOSTER. Sergeant-major, on muster roll of Capt. Abijah Savage's co., Col. Henry Sherburne's regt., dated Rhode Island, Aug. 21, 1778; enlisted May 6, 1777, for 3 years.

WILLIAM FOSTER, Andover. First Lieutenant, on Lexington alarm roll of Capt. Henry Abbot's co., which marched on alarm of April 19, 1775, from Andover; service, 1½ days.

WILLIAM FOSTER, Attleborough. Private, on muster and pay roll of Capt. Samuel Robinson's co., Col. Wade's regt., for service at R. I.; enlisted June 21, 1778; service, 22 days.

WILLIAM FOSTER, Attleborough. On list of men mustered in Bristol Co., by return made by James Leonard, muster master, Oct. 28, 1779; enlisted for three years. Drummer on muster and pay roll of Capt. Joseph Franklin's co., Col. Nathan Tyler's regt.; service in R. I.; enlisted Aug. 24, 1779, to Dec. 31, 1779; service, 4 mos. 7 days. Also from Dec. 1 to Dec. 31; 1 mo. 2 days; travel included.

WILLIAM FOSTER, Boxford (probably). Private, on Lexington alarm roll of Capt. John Cushing's co. (minute men), Col. Samuel Johnson's regt., which marched on alarm of April 19, 1775, from Boxford (probably); service, 2 days.

WILLIAM FOSTER, Mendon. On descriptive list of men enlisted from Worcester Co., dated Leicester, June 2, 1778; enlisted for nine months from time of arrival at Fishkill, June 7, 1778; age, 18 years; stature, 5 ft. 9 in; complexion, dark; hair, dark brown; eyes, light; belonged to Capt. Cragin's co., Col. Ezra Wood's regt. On muster and pay roll of Capt. Philip Ammidon's co., Col. Nathan Tyler's regt., which marched to R. I. on alarm of July 27, 1780; enlisted Aug. 2, 1780; discharged Aug. 8, 1780; service, 10 days. Also on certificate of enlistment dated Mendon, Aug. 2, 1781, given by selectmen of Mendon, certifying the above enlisted in the Continental army for three years, in March, 1781.

WILLIAM FOSTER, Monson. Private, on Lexington alarm roll of Capt. Freeborn Moulton's co., Col. Danielson's regt., which marched on alarm of April 19, 1775, from Monson to Cambridge; service, 20 days; left Cambridge May 5, 1775.

WILLIAM FOSTER, Northbridge. Corporal, on Lexington alarm roll of Capt. Josiah Wood's co. (minute men), which marched on alarm of April 19, 1775, from Northbridge to Roxbury; service, 9 days. Sergeant, on muster and pay roll of Capt. Peter Penniman's co., Col. Wood's regt.; service at R. I. from April 18 to May 7, 1777; 21 days.

WILLIAM FOSTER, Newbury. Private, on Lexington alarm roll of Capt. Thomas Noyes' co., which marched (April 20) on alarm of April 19, 1775, from Newbury to headquarters at Cambridge; service, 4 days.

*WILLIAM FOSTER, Cape Ann. Sergeant, on muster roll of Capt. John

*Reported served for his brother, Job Foster.

Row's co., Col. Eben Bridge's regt.; dated Aug. 1, 1775; enlisted May 29, 1775; service, 2 mos. 8 days. Also on order for bounty coat, or equivalent, due for the eight months' service in 1775, dated Cambridge, Nov. 9, 1775; payable to Lieut. Mark Pool. Also on an order, dated Gloucester, Oct. 16, 1776, for losses at Bunker Hill, given by himself and others on Henry Gardner, treasurer; payable to Samuel Whittemore.

WILLIAM FOSTER, Dudley. Private, on muster and pay roll of Capt. Nathaniel Healey's co., Col. Jonathan Holman's regt., which marched to R. I. on alarm in Dec., 1776; service, 43 days. Corporal, on muster and pay roll of Capt. Lemuel Corbin's co., Col. Jacob Davis' regt; detached for service in R. I., on alarm of July 30, 1780; service, 13 days.

WILLIAM FOSTER, Ipswich. Private, on receipt for advance pay, dated Cambridge, July 2, 1775, due on account of service in Capt. Gideon Parker's co., Col. Little's regt.; autograph signature. On muster and pay roll of said co., dated Aug. 1, 1775; enlisted May 15, 1775; service, 2 mos, 22 days. Also on company return, dated Oct. 8, 1775; age, 39 years. On order for bounty coat, or equivalent in money, due for the eight months' service in 1775, dated Prospect Hill, Dec. 28, 1775; payable to Capt. Parker.

WILLIAM FOSTER, Oxford. Private, on Lexington alarm roll of Capt. John Town's co., which marched on alarm of April 19, 1775, from Oxford to Roxbury; served 6 days and "enlisted into the army." Private, on muster roll of Capt. Campbell's co., Col. Learned's regt., dated Aug. 1, 1775; enlisted April 26, 1775: service, 3 mos., 1 week 5 days. Also on return, dated Oct. 7, 1775, and on order for bounty coat, or equivalent, due for the eight months' service, dated camp at Roxbury, Oct. 26, 1775. Private, on muster roll of Capt. Thomas Fish's co., Col. William Shepard's regt., for July and August, 1778, dated Sept. 5, 1778; enlisted for three years. On October return, dated Providence, Nov. 13, 1778, reported on duty. On pay accounts of Capt. Moore's co., Col. Shepard's regt., for service from March 11, 1777, to Dec. 31, 1779; reported 13 months' service as Corporal, and 20 months 20 days as Private. Corporal on return of Capt. Moore's co., dated Mountain Hutts, West Point, Jan. 23, 1780 (?), made up from Jan. 1 to Dec. 31, 1780; enlisted March 7, 1777; service, 2 mos. 7 days; reported discharged March 7, 1780.

WILLIAM FOSTER, Reading. Private, on Lexington alarm roll of Capt. Thomas Eaton's co., Col. Green's regt., which marched on alarm of April 19, 1775, from Reading; service, 8 days. Also on list of men in the training band under Capt. Eaton.

WILLIAM FOSTER. Roxbury (also given Boston). Private, on a return of Capt. Edward P. Williams' co., Col. John Greaton's regt., dated Oct. 5, 1775, and on order for bounty coat, or equivalent, due for the eight months' service, dated Cambridge, Dec. 22, 1775, payable to Capt. Williams. On a return of men enlisted into Continental army, from Capt. Edward Cobb's co. of 3d Plymouth Co. regt., dated May 15, 1777; enlisted for Abington, for during war. Joined Capt. Foster's co., Col. Greaton's regt. Also on roll, dated Albany, Jan. 2, 1778; enlisted March 3, 1777. Also on returns, dated White Plains, July 20, and Sept. 1, 1780. And on muster roll of March, 1779, dated Cortlandt Manor, April 7, 1779; reported transferred to Major Oliver's co. On pay accounts of Col. Greaton's regt.; service from Jan. 1, 1780, to Dec. 31, 1780. On descriptive list of men belonging to Roxbury: age, 33 years; stature, 5 ft. 9 in; complexion, dark; hair and eyes, dark; enlisted Feb. 16, 1777, for during war, dated West Point, Jan. 25, 1781.

WILLIAM FOSTER. Private, on Lexington alarm roll of Capt. Ebenezer Withington's co., which was mustered April 19, 1775; service, 3 days.

WILLIAM FOSTER. On list of men who received money from public treasury for losses at battles of Lexington and Bunker Hill; allowed by council June 13, 1776.

WILLIAM FOSTER. Private, on muster and pay roll of Capt. Noah Lankton's co., Col. John Ashley's regt.; enlisted July 8, 1777; discharged Aug. 14, 1777; service, 1 mo. 8 days; marched to Kingsbury; roll dated Tyringham.

WILLIAM FOSTER. Drummer, on muster and pay roll of Capt. Samuel Clark's co., Col. Benjamin Symonds' regt.; enlisted Sept. 7, 1777; discharged Sept. 20, 1777; service, 14 days; marched to Paulett by order of Major-General Lincoln. Also on muster and pay roll of Capt. Israel Harris' co., Col. Simonds' regt.; enlisted Oct. 12; discharged Oct. 19, 1780; service, 11 days; 4 days' travel allowed; marched on alarm to the northward.

WILLIAM FOSTER. Appears on a petition, dated Boston, Dec. 19, 1777, for his brother Joseph Foster, who is a prisoner on the guard vessel at New York, and whom he would like to have released by sending some one to take his place.

WILLIAM FOSTER. Lieutenant, on muster and pay roll of Lieut. William Foster's co., Col. Pierce's regt.; joined March 3, 1778; discharged April 8, 1778; service, 37 days; stationed at Long Island.

WILLIAM FOSTER. Sergeant, on a warrant to pay officers and men on a roll bearing date Nov. 12, 1784, Capt. Toy's co., Col. Webb's regt.

BILLY FOSTER (also William on one roll), Winthrop, Me. Corporal, on return of Capt. Samuel McCobb's co., Col. Nixon's regt., for cartridge boxes received, dated Cambridge, June 24, 1775; autograph signature on receipt for advance pay, dated Cambridge, June 26, 1775. On muster roll dated Aug. 1, 1775; enlisted June 1, 1775; service, 2 mo. 5 days. Also on Oct., 1775, return, dated Winter Hill. Autograph signature on order for bounty coat, or equivalent, dated Winter Hill, Dec. 20, 1775. Also on list of men returned with petition of inhabitants of Winthrop, dated March 10, 1777, asking consideration on account of their exposed condition, as having voluntarily enlisted in the army in 1775.

WILLIAM FOSTER. On list of men mustered in Suffolk Co. to serve in Capt. Nathaniel Cushing's co., Col. John Peterson's regt., by return made by Nathaniel Barber, dated Boston, Feb. 2, 1777; enlisted for three years; received £20 bounty.

WILLIAM FOSTER. Appears on list of men who signed oath of allegiance, dated Feb. 24, 1777.

WILLIAM FOSTER. On list of men mustered in Worcester Co. to serve in Capt. Foster's co., Col. Nixon's regt. by return made by Thomas Newhall, muster master; enlisted for three years; mustered April 21, 1777.

WILLIAM FOSTER. Second Lieutenant, on list of officers of Massachusetts militia, chosen by the 1st company and accepted by council May 10, 1776, Capt. Ebenezer Gore's co., Col. William McIntosh's regt. On muster and pay roll of Capt. Abel Richard's co., Col. Benjamin Hawes' regt.; enlisted Sept. 25; discharged Oct. 28, 1777; service, 1 mo. 7 days; 3 days' travel allowed; secret expedition to R. I. Also on muster and pay roll of Capt. Caleb Whiting's co., Col. Hawes' regt.; entered July 28; discharged Sept. 12, 1778; service on expedition to R. I. On a petition, dated Roxbury, May 2, 1779, of resignation from militia; granted in council May 7, 1779.

WILLIAM FOSTER. Private on muster and pay roll of Capt. Lemuel Clap's co.; enlisted May 11; discharged Aug. 10, 1779; service, 3 mos.; guards at Dorchester Heights.

WILLIAM FOSTER. Sergeant, on muster and pay roll of Capt. David Batcheller's co., Lieut.-Col. Nathan Tyler's regt.; for service in R. I., on alarm of Dec. 8, 1776; enlisted Jan. 8, 1777; service, 12 days. Also enlisted in same company July 28, 1780; discharged Aug. 8, 1780; service, 15 days.

WOODEN FOSTER. Private, on muster and pay roll of Capt. Joseph Sevey's co., Col. Benjamin Foster's (Lincoln Co.) regt.; enlisted June 23, 1777; discharged July 16, 1777; service, 23 days, at Machias. Also enlisted July 16; discharged Oct. 10, 1777; 2 mos. 4 days, and 1 day's service between Dec. 5 and 25, 1778, at Machias.

ZEBULON FOSTER, Beverly. Private, on muster roll of Capt. Lemuel Trescott's co., Col. J. Brewer's regt., dated Aug. 1, 1775; enlisted July 6, 1775; service, 25 days. Also on return, dated Prospect Hill, Oct. 6, 1775, and on order for bounty coat, or equivalent, due for the eight months' service in 1775, dated Prospect Hill, Oct. 25, 1775.

ZEB. FOSTER. Seaman, on muster and pay roll of officers and crew of brigantine Tyranicide, commanded by Capt. Jonathan Haraden; enlisted Feb. 26, 1777; discharged Aug. 29, 1777; service, 6 mos. 3 days.

FOSTERS FROM CONNECTICUT.

JOSEPH FOSTER, of Chaplin, Conn; pension granted 1840; ae. 78.

ADONIJAH FOSTER, enlisted April 11, 1778; three years; Windham; Capt. Wm. Sizer.

ALPHEUS FOSTER; pension granted 1832; Middlesex Co.

AMAN FOSTER, enlisted July 11, 1780; discharged Oct. 25, 1780; 4th Conn. regt.

ASA FOSTER, enlisted Feb. 6, 1777, for three years; discharged Feb. 16, 1780; Capt. Hait.

ASA FOSTER, of Connecticut; residing in Ohio; granted a pension in 1818.

ASA FOSTER; Sergeant; in service 2 days; town of Stafford.

ASA FOSTER, joined April 7, 1777; Lieutenant Smith's company; discharged May 19, 1777.

BENJAMIN FOSTER, enlisted May 10, 1775; discharged Dec. 15; Capt. Manning 7th company; Woodstock.

BENJAMIN FOSTER, enlisted July 12, 1775; Capt. Wm. Hubbell; New Fairfield; discharged Dec. 23.

BENJAMIN FOSTER, of Sharon, was in Capt. Woodbridge's company for three years; was discharged in 1780.

BENNETT FOSTER, enlisted July 20, 1780; discharged Dec. 25.

CHARLOTTE FOSTER, of Ellington; ae. 74; in 1840 was a revolutionary pensioner.

CHAUNCY FOSTER, of Windsor, was in Capt. Blackman's company in 1777 to 1780; he also served in the R. I. militia.

CHRISTOPHER FOSTER, from near New London, was sick in hospital at Stamford as a discharged revolutionary soldier, in 1776.

DANIEL FOSTER, was Ensign in Capt. Daniel Clark's company in 1777; was Ensign in Capt. Nathan Wales' 3d company in 1780.

DAVID FOSTER was pensioned in 1818; was then residing in New York state.

EDWARD FOSTER, of Colonel Wylly's regiment, was sick in hospital at Stamford, Nov., 1776; he was of Weathersfield, and was of Capt. Throop's company; was in Capt. Shephard's company in 1777; he was pensioned in 1818.

ELIJAH FOSTER, of Sharon, was second Lieutenant in Benj. Mills' company. in 1776.

EPHRIAM FOSTER, of East Haddam, was in Capt. Holmes' company; later in Capt. Jones' company.

FRANCIS FOSTER, from near Bethlehem, was in Capt. Beardsley's company and later in Capt. Watson's company.

GEORGE FOSTER, of Killingly, was in Capt. Warren's company; later in Capt. Trowbridge's company, and after the battle of Long Island, Aug. 27, 1776, was reported missing; was captured, however, and paroled Aug. 30. He d. at Milford about Jan. 1, 1777.

HACHALIAH FOSTER, of East Windsor, was at siege of Boston in 1775 in Capt. Parson's company; later in Capt. Wolcott's company, and was reported missing Sept. 15, 1776.

ISAAC FOSTER was Sergeant Major of Col. Wm. Douglass' regiment; was in battle at White Plains Oct. 28, 1776.

SERGT. ISRAEL FOSTER was in Capt. Mills' company. He was from Sharon; was in the defence of Ft. Washington in N. Y.

CORP. JABEZ FOSTER, of Lebanon, was in Capt. Tildens' company at the Lexington alarm; was at battle of Bunker Hill in Capt. Clark's company in Col. Israel Putnam's regiment; was a Corporal in Capt. Tilden's company in 1778.

JAMES FOSTER, of Saybrook, was in Capt. Mattock's company in 1777 from Hartford; was transferred to invalid corps; was in Capt. Wylly's company and again transferred to invalid corps in 1781. In 1781 he was drummer in Capt. Hopkins' company from Hartford.

JEDEDIAH FOSTER, of Farmington, was in Capt. Heart's company in 1776.

JEREMIAH FOSTER, of Suffield, was in Capt. Hanchett's company in 1775.

JESSE FOSTER, of Danbury, was in Capt. Doolittle's company in 1775; was later in Capt. Pendleton's company; then in Capt. Benedict's company at Ft. Washington.

JOHN FOSTER, of Wyoming Valley, Pa., was in Capt. Durkee's company in 1776. This was settled by people from Conn., and known as Westmoreland County; was in battles at Bound Brook, N. J., Brandywine and Germantown and wintered at Valley Forge. He d. Jan. 1, 1778.

JOHN FOSTER, of Middletown, was in service in Capt. Beebe's company at siege of Yorktown in 1781. Beebe was from Stratford. This company was the corps of lappers and miners.

JOHN FOSTER, of East Windsor, was in Capt. Prior's company until Nov., 1776; was in Capt. Hedgwick's company until Dec., 1776; in 1777 in Capt. Grant's company; was later pensioned in 1840 while living in New London Co. at Norwich; ae. 78.

JOHN FOSTER, of East Haddam, Middlesex county; was pensioned in 1840; ae. 92.

JONAH FOSTER, of Ridgefield, was in Capt. Beardsley's regt., in July, 1779, to repel Tryon's invasion; was recruiting officer for Continental army in 1781; was in Capt. Hait's company in 1776.

JOSEPH FOSTER, served from July to Dec. 1780 in the 3d regiment.

JOSEPH FOSTER, of Windham Co., was fifer in Capt. Chandler's company in 1776; in 1832 he res. in Windham Co., and was granted a pension. He was b. in 1761.

MICHAEL FOSTER, of Westmoreland, Pa. (then of Conn.); was in Capt. Spaulding's company in 1779.

CORP. NATHANIEL FOSTER, from near Danbury, was in Capt. Walbridge's company in 1777, and was a prisoner June 30 of that year.

NATHAN FOSTER was in Capt. Doolittle's company in 1775; he was about Fairfield.

OZIAS FOSTER, of Sharon, was in Capt. Martin's company in 1778; was at West Point.

PETER FOSTER, from near Windham, was in Capt. Durkee's company in 1781.

SAMUEL FOSTER was in 1777 and 1778 in Capt. Hait's company of Stamford; was a farmer; was in the 1st Conn. troop in 1780; in 1776 was in Capt. Benedict's company.

SAUL FOSTER, of New Haven, Co., was granted a pension in 1832. He resided in Madison, Conn., in 1840, and was ae. 85, having been b. in 1755.

STEPHEN FOSTER, of Ashford, was in Capt. Thos. Knowlton's company in 1775.

THOMAS FOSTER was in service in 1779-80 in the 2d Conn. regt.; was in Capt. Branch's company in 1778.

TIMOTHY FOSTER, of Ridgefield, was in Col. Canfield's regiment at West Point in 1781.

SERGT.-MAJOR WARHAM FOSTER, of East Windsor, was in Capt. Elsworth's company in the Lexington alarm; was in company of Capt. Pitkin, of Hartford in 1775; Sergeant-Major 1777-78-80 in Col. Meig's regiment; in 1776 was in Capt. Simons' company.

SERGT. WILLIAM FOSTER, of Canterbury, was Sergeant in Capt. Cleveland's company at Lexington alarm.

ZEPHANIAH FOSTER, of Lebanon, was in Capt. Fitch's company in 1777-78.

8

A LIST OF REVOLUTIONARY PENSIONERS.

Collected from Various Government Publications.

Name, County and Page of Revolutionary Pension Reports.	Grade.	Allowance.	Sum Received.	Description of Service.	When Placed on Pension Roll.	Commencement of Pension.	Age and Death.
MAINE.							
Jonathan Foster, Hancock, page 36	Private	$ 96.00	$1,159.90	Massachusetts line	Nov. 20, 1817	April 10, 1817	85. 1732.
David Foster, Kennebec, page 35	Private	96.00	168.20	Rhode Island line	Jan. 28, 1819	Aug. 14, 1818.	82, Apr. 7, 1825.
Samuel Foster, Kennebec, page 35	Private	96.00	638.13	Rhode Island line	Jan. 28, 1819	Aug. 14, 1818.	82, Apr. 7, 1825.
Parker Foster, York, page 77	Sargeant	96.00	1,528.80	Massachusetts line	March 30, 1819.	April 1, 1818.	73. 1746.
Stephen Foster, Kennebec, page 107	Private	30.00	90.00	Massachusetts Mil.	April 26, 1833.	Mch. 4, 1831.	78. 1745.
William Foster, Lincoln, page 117	Sargeant	40.00	....	Mass. State troops	July 22, 1834	Mch. 4, 1831.	84. 1750.
Benan Foster, York, page 150	Private	100.00	300.00	Mass. State troops	May 15, 1833	Mch. 4, 1831.	74.- 1759.
NEW HAMPSHIRE.							
James Foster, Cheshire, page 32	Private	96.00	1,429.06	N. H. Contl. line	March 23, 1819.	April 15, 1818	70.
Abiel Foster, Cheshire, page 32	Private	96.00	494.66	Mass. Contl. line	July 9, 1819	May 28. 1818.	59. July 23, 1823.
Andrew Foster, Cheshire, page 32	Sargeant	96.00	326.13	Mass. Contl. line	Oct. 29, 1819	April 11, 1818	69.
Ezra Foster, Grafton, page 39	Private	96.00	1,428.00	Mass. Contl. line	Sept. 17, 1819	April 4, 1818.	77.
Jonathan Foster, Grafton, page 39	Private	96.00	172.80	Mass. Contl. line	Oct. 5, 1819	May 1, 1818	99.
Jeremiah Foster, Merrimac, page 57	Private	96.00	990.13	N. H. Contl. line	Jan. 18, 1820	May 11, 1818.	76.
Samuel Foster, Rockingham, page 62	Private	96.00	746.13	Mass. Contl. line	April 13, 1819	April 7, 1818.	68, January 15, 1826.
Abner Foster, Cheshire, page 80	Private	30.00	90.00	Mass. Contl. line	April 23, 1833	Mch. 4, 1831.	73.
Luna Foster, Cheshire, page 80	Private	30.00	....	N. H. Contl. line	June 16, 1834	Mch. 4, 1831.	69.
MASSACHUSETTS.							
David Foster, Essex, page 72	Artificer	96.00	182.00	Massachusetts line	June 30, 1818	April 10, 1818	66.
Nathaniel Foster, Essex, page 72	Private	96.00	1,528.26	Massachusetts line	March 10, 1819.	April 3, 1818.	74.
Abraham Foster, Essex, page 72	Private	96.00	162.93	Massachusetts line	May 1, 1819	June 23, 1818	....
Gideon Foster, Essex, page 92	Captain	150.00	480.00	Mass. State troops	April 10, 1833	Mch. 4, 1831.	89.
Daniel Foster, Essex, page 92	Private and Sargeant.	80.00	198.00	Mass. State troops	Jan. 29, 1833	Mch. 4, 1831.	70, August 29, 1833.
William Foster, Middlesex, page 167	Private	48.00	924.00	3d Regt. N. H. militia	March 25, 1820.	Nov. 29, 1814.	....
Leonard Foster, Middlesex, page 177	Private	96.00	730.93	Massachusetts line	June 11, 1818	April 24, 1818	80.
John Foster, Middlesex, page 177	Private	95.00	1,133.59	Massachusetts line	June 30, 1818	April 6, 1818	94.
Nathan Foster, Middlesex, page 177	Private	96.00	1,526.93	New Hampshire line.	Feb. 4, 1819	April 8, 1818	71.
Smith Foster, Middlesex, page 177	Private	96.00	392.00	Massachusetts line	June 21, 1819	July 18, 1818.	66, August 16-22.
Joseph Foster, Middlesex, page 194	Private	96.00	184.26	Mass. Contl. line	July 31, 1818	April 3, 1818.	....
Amos Foster, Middlesex, page 194	Private	54.88	137.20	Massachusetts Mil.	June 12, 1833	Mch. 4, 1831.	80.
Edward Foster, Norfolk, page 223	Private and Sargeant	35.72	107.16	Massachusetts Mil.	July 1, 1833	Mch. 4, 1831.	81.
Jude Foster, Worcester, page 288	Corporal	44.00	2.88	Revolutionary army.	Unknown	Mch. 4, 1789.	March 28, 1789.
Ephriam Foster	Private	....	....	....	....	....	....
RHODE ISLAND.							
Anthony Foster, Providence, page 5	Private	48.00	480.00	....	....	Mar. 4, 1789	....
George Foster, Washington, page 43	Private	80.00	240.00	Rhode Island militia.	Nov. 18, 1833	Mar. 4, 1831.	84.
Gardner Foster	Sargeant	96.00	1,556.26	Revolutionary army.	Jan. 22, 1818	Dec. 18, 1817	....

A LIST OF REVOLUTIONARY PENSIONERS—Continued.

VERMONT.

Name, County and Page of Revolutionary Pension Reports.	Grade.	Allowance.	Sum Received.	Description of Service.	When Placed on Pension Roll.	Commencement of Pension.	Age and Death.
Gardner Foster, Essex, page 7	Sargeant	96.00	1,556.26	R. A., 6th R. U. S. Inf.	Jan. 22, 1818	Dec. 18, 1817.	
*Samuel Foster, Franklin, page 21	Private	48.00	240.00	3rd Reg. artillery	August 3, 1818.	Feb. 17-15	† May 10, 1833.
Simeon Foster, Franklin, page 43	Private	96.00	821.21	N. H. Contl. line	May 24, 1820	March 25-19.	94, Dec. 14, 1827.
Joseph Foster, Orange, page 51	Private	96.00	1,526.44	Mass. military	Dec. 19, 1819	April 10 18	
Abel Foster, Rutland, page 61	Corporal	96.00	1,527.48	Mass. Contl. line	Sept. 24, 1818	April 6-18	80.
Jonathan Foster, Windsor, page 78	Private	96.00	996.05	N. H. Contl. line	May 15, 1819	April 9-18	68, August 21-28.
Thomas Foster, Washington, page 133	Private and Sargeant.	70.00	93.30	Connecticut military.	Nov. 29, 1833	March 4-31	74, July 9, 1852.
Jacob Foster, Windsor, page 149	Private	36.00	108.99	Conn. Contl. line	June 21, 1833	March 4-31	78.
Rufus Foster, Windsor, page 149	Private	56.66	169.98	Mass. military	May 14, 1833	March 4-31	78.
William Foster, Rutland, page 163	Private	80.00	524.22	3rd Regiment	Jan. 12, 1829	R.Temple,A.	September 21-32.

CONNECTICUT.

Name, County and Page of Revolutionary Pension Reports.	Grade.	Allowance.	Sum Received.	Description of Service.	When Placed on Pension Roll.	Commencement of Pension.	Age and Death.
Jesse Foster, Fairfield, page 33	Private	96.00	225.05	Connecticut line	Sept. 18, 1818.	April 2, 1818.	75, Aug. 9, 1820.
John Foster, Fairfield, page 33	Private	96.00	1,413.61	Connecticut line	Nov. 16, 1818	Mar. 23, 1818.	74.
Edward Foster, Middlesex, page 55	Private	96.00	463.73	Connecticut line	May 15, 1819	Oct. 26, 1818.	63, Aug. 21, 1823.
Chauncey Foster, Tolland, page 74	Private	96.00	125.03	Rhode Island line	May 17, 1819	Nov. 16, 1818.	60.
Alpheus Foster, Middlesex, page 117	Private	30.00	90.00	Conn. Continental	August 11, 1833	Mar. 4, 1831.	73.
Samuel Foster, New Haven, page 125	Private	26.66	79.98	Conn. Continental	March 28, 1834.	Mar. 4, 1831.	77.
John Foster, New London, page 134	Private	39.88	119.64	Connecticut military.	April 1, 1833	Mar. 4, 1831.	74.
Joseph Foster, Windham, page 198	Private and Fifer	78.99	236.97	Conn. Continental	July 15, 1833	Mar. 4, 1831.	72.

NEW YORK.

Name, County and Page of Revolutionary Pension Reports.	Grade.	Allowance.	Sum Received.	Description of Service.	When Placed on Pension Roll.	Commencement of Pension.	Age and Death.
Samuel Foster, New York, page 42	Private	64.00	214.69	6th Reg. U. S. I.	May 21, 1816	April 27, 1815	
Edward Foster	Captain	120.00	1,738.66	9th Reg. U. S. I.	Jan. 8, 1818	Nov. 1, 1811.	
Edward Foster, Queens, page 71	Captain	180.00	783.50	9th Reg. U. S. I.	May 28, 1829	April 17, 1829	‡
Hackaliah Foster	Sargeant	30.00	679.10	Sheperd's Reg. U. S. I.	Sept. 1793	Sept. 4, 1793.	
Hackaliah Foster, Saratoga, page 74	Sargeant	48.00	209.33	Sheperd's Reg. U. S. I.	Sept. 1793	Aug. 24, 1816.	September 4, 1820.
Joseph Foster, Seneca, page 77	Private	96.00	1,766.98	1st Reg. N. Y. Mil.	May 11, 1816	Oct. 10, 1815.	
Daniel Foster, Cayuga, page 119	Corporal	96.00	1,175.72	New Hampshire line.	April 28, 1820	June 6, 1818.	79.
Daniel Foster, Genesee, page 118	Private	96.00	65.61	Massachusetts line	Oct. 12, 1818	April 23, 1818	62, Dec. 29, 1818.
David Foster, Greene, page 153	Private	96.00	1,475.99	Connecticut line	Dec. 23, 1818	April 20, 1818	77.
Nathaniel Foster, Saratoga, page 230	Private	96.00	974.22	New York line	Jan. 22, 1821	July 12, 1823.	88.
Erastus Foster, Steuben, page 240	Private	96.00	1,478.66	Massachusetts line	July 14, 181	April 10, 1818	74.
Parla Foster, Columbia, page 293	Private	25.19	52.38	Massachusetts Mil.	May 21, 1833	Mch. 4, 1831.	74.
Samuel S. Foster, Genesee, page 212	Midshipman	111.00		United States Navy	Jan. 18, 1833	Mch. 4, 1831.	69.
Benjamin Foster, Genesee, page 212	Corporal & Sargeant.	100.00	300.00	Massachusetts Mil.	April 5, 1834	Mch. 4, 1831.	79.
Samuel Foster, Greene, page 318	Private	80.00		Connecticut Contl.	June 18, 1833	Mch. 4, 1831.	72.
Giles Foster, Lewis, page 332	Private	46.66		New York Mil.	Aug. 10, 1833	Mch. 4, 1831.	76.
Timothy Foster, Oneida, page 360	Private	47.00		Connecticut Mil.	April 20, 1834	Mch. 4, 1831.	79.
Vincent Foster, Saratoga, 413	Private	40.00	100.00	New York Contl.	June 26, 1833	Mch. 4, 1831.	79.

*His heirs were Sally, Daniel, Jacob, Polly and Lydia Foster. †Pension ended February 17, 1820. ‡Raised to this rate by Inc. Dis.

A LIST OF REVOLUTIONARY PENSIONERS—Continued.

Name, County and Page of Revolutionary Pension Reports.	Grade.	Allowance.	Sum Received.	Description of Service.	When Placed on Pension Roll.	Commencement of Pension.	Age and Death.
OHIO.							
Ephraim Foster, Washington, page 97	Private	$96.00	$217.29	N. H. Contl	Oct. 10, 1818	April 14, 1818	85.
Scioto Foster, Scioto, page 159	Private	60.00	180.00	Virginia Contl	May 10, 1833	Mch. 4, 1831.	78.
INDIANA.							
James Foster, page 6	Sargeant	48.00	616.40	Ohio volunteers	Feb. 22, 1817	May 8, 1813	
Alexander Foster, Montgomery, page 60	Private	36.66	109.98	Penn. State troops	Nov. 12, 1833	Mch. 4, 1831.	74.
PENNSYLVANIA.							
Thomas Foster, Luzerne, page 101	Private	96.00	1,280.28	Rhode Island Contl	Oct. 22, 1819	May 4, 1818	78.
John Foster, Huntington, page 159	Private	50.00	150.00	Pennsylvania militia.	May 11, 1833	Mch. 4, 1831.	78.
Robert Foster, Union, page 186	Private	80.00	232.21	Pennsylvania militia.	Feb. 4, 1833	Mch. 4, 1831.	76.
MARYLAND.							
Thomas Foster, Baltimore, page 30	Private	96.00	577.06	Pennsylvania line	Nov. 9, 1819	Sept. 1, 1819.	77.
VIRGINIA.							
Crosby Foster, page 36	Private	50.00	1,212.00			Sept. 4, 1789.	
Thomas Foster, Fluvania, page 59	Artificer	96.00	41.54	Virginia line	Nov. 21, 1818	Mch. 30, 1818	80, Nov. 26, 1818.
James Foster, Munroe, page 83	Private	96.00	552.12	Virginia line	Mch. 5, 1819	Aug. 19, 1818	77, March 3, 1824.
Larkin Foster, Amelia, page 110	Private	31.66		Virginia Contl.	April 30, 1834	Mch. 4, 1831.	73.
James Foster, Berkely, page 116	Private	20.00	60.00	Pennsylvania militia.	April 1, 1833	Mch. 4, 1831.	77.
James Foster, Frederick, page 138	Private	80.00	240.00	Virginia militia	Nov. 26, 1832	Mch. 4, 1831.	72.
John Foster, Munroe, page 172	Private	80.00	240.00	Virginia Contl	Mch. 22, 1832	Mch. 4, 1831.	75.
Peter Foster, York, page 212	Lieutenant	320.00	2,248.00	Gibson's Virginia	Sept. 14, 1831	*	March 11, 1833.
SOUTH CAROLINA.							
Joshua Foster, Dist. of Marion, page 28	Private	96.00	148.64	Virginia Contl. line	April 6, 1820	Aug. 18, 1818	67.
KENTUCKY.							
John Foster, Barren	Private	96.00	867.03	Virginia line	May 6, 1825	Feb. 22, 1825.	79.

*John Nicholas, agent; Edwin Shelton, Adm

SUSPENDED AND REJECTED CLAIMS—1850.

Report of 32d Congress at Washington, D. C., 1852.

NAMES.	RESIDENCE.	REASONS FOR SUSPENSION.
John Foster	Bristol, Lincoln Co., Me.	Not on rolls, no such corps as he alleges was maintained in 1777, he did not serve six months.
Joseph Foster (deceased), by John L. Wilson, administrator.	West Fairlee, Orange Co., Vt.	Entitled to full pension as a sergeant of infantry upon the return of his certificate, under the act of 1848.
Priscilla Foster, widow of John Foster.	Reading, Hartford Co., Conn.	Suspended for further proof of the date of the marriage. Proof of service admitted.
Lucretia Foster, widow of Wareham Foster.	Ellington, Tolland Co., Conn.	A definite statement of the soldier's service, grade, officers, and duration is required in order to an inspection of the rolls.
Esther Foster, widow of Isaac Foster.	Milford, New Haven Co., Conn.	No proof that he was a soldier of the revolution.
Isaac Foster.	Riverhead, Suffolk Co., N. Y.	No proof of service.
Anna Foster, formerly widow of John Poppino.	Goshen, Orange Co., N. Y.	He did not serve six months.
Susannah Foster, widow of William Foster.	Albany, Albany Co., N. Y.	Not a widow at the date of the act.
Sarah Foster, formerly widow of James Follingsly.	Carlton, Orleans Co., N. Y.	He did not serve six months.
Sidney Foster, widow of John Foster.	Spartansburg, S. C.	For proof of identity that he was the person referred to on one or other of the auditor's certificates of soldiers of the same name.
George Foster.	Vernon, Hickman Co., Tenn.	Not six month's service.
Samuel Foster.	Indianapolis, Marion Co., Ind.	Not under competent military authority or organization.

N. Y. PROVINCIAL TROOPS 1760.

ABRAHAM FOSTER, b. 1740; Suffolk county, N. Y.
CHRISTOPHER FOSTER, b. 1743; Suffolk county, N. Y.
ALEXANDER FOSTER b 1723; Ireland.
ELNATHAN FOSTER, Southhold, N. Y.
JEREMIAH FOSTER, carpenter, b. 1738; Suffolk county, N. Y.
OBEDIAH FOSTER.
DAVID FOSTER, shoemaker b. 1740; Suffolk county, N. Y.
GILBERT FOSTER, weaver, b. 1739, Hempstead, N. Y.
JAMES FOSTER, b. 1740, Scotland.
JOHN FOSTER, b. 1739; Westchester, N. Y.
NATHANIEL FOSTER.
ROWLAND FOSTER, b. 1755.
SAMUEL FOSTER, b. 1755.
WILLIAM FOSTER, b. 1742; Gloucester, N. J.

CONNECTICUT MEN IN WAR OF 1812.

ELEAZER FOSTER, of Hartford, was in Maj. Daniel Ketchum's command, 25th infantry, in war of 1812.

SAMUEL FOSTER, of Middletown, was in 37th infantry, Capt. Brown, in war of 1812.

JOHN FOSTER, of New London, was in the artillery of Capt. McKeon, in war of 1812.

WILLIAM FOSTER, of New London, was in 37th infantry, Capt. Gaylord, in war of 1812.

CHARLES FOSTER, musician, Capt. Copeland's co.

CHARLES FOSTER, private, Capt. Clark's co., of New London.

CLARK FOSTER, first lieutenant, Capt. Adams' co., of New London.

EDWARD FOSTER, private, Saybrook, Capt. Andrews' co.

EDWARD FOSTER, private, Saybrook, Capt. Webber's co.

FLETCHER FOSTER, New London, Saybrook, Capt. Sabin's co.

JOSEPH FOSTER, corporal, Capt. Phelps' co.

LABAN FOSTER, private, Capt. Abell's co., of New London.

LYMAN FOSTER, of New London, private, Capt. Swift.

LYMAN FOSTER, New London, musician, Capt. Strong.

MAHLON FOSTER, private, Capt. Hall.

MATHEW FOSTER, sergeant, Capt. Butler.

RUSSELL FOSTER, corporal, Capt. Webster.

THOMAS FOSTER, private, New London, Capt. Middleton.

WILLIAM FOSTER, private, Capt. Wilson.

REGINALD FOSTER, OF IPSWICH, MASS.

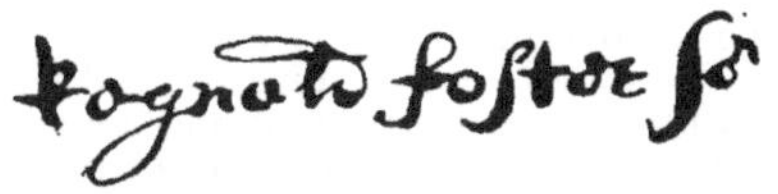

was born in Brunton, England, and was a descendant of an ancient and respectable family of that section, which was identified with those families in the northern counties of England, who were known by the name of Forster, and had distinguished themselves in their successful achievements against their Scottish foes, and are mentioned in the 'Lay of the Last Minstrel,' and 'Marmion.'* He came to America in one of the vessels embargoed by King Charles I., accompanied by his wife, Judith, five sons and two daughters, and settled in Ipswich, Mass., about the year 1638, and was one of the earliest inhabitants of that town.

"A proclamation was issued 30 April, 1637, to prevent the emigration of Puritans" from England; "the king," Charles the First, "refused his dissenting subjects the security of the wilderness." "In England the proclamation was but little regarded. The Puritans, hemmed in by dangers on every side, and at that time having no prospect of ultimate success, desired at any rate to escape from their native country. The privy council interfered 1 May, 1638 [in April, 1638], to stay a squadron of eight ships, which were in the Thames, preparing to embark for New England." "The fleet," however, "was delayed but a few days; on petition of the owners and passengers King Charles removed the restraint," and "there came over during this summer, twenty ships, and at least three thousand persons." Within the first fifteen years after the settlement of New England, and before the assembling of the Long Parliament, in 1640,—and there was never afterwards any considerable increase from England,—there came over from England twenty-one thousand two hundred persons, or four thousand families, coming in two hundred and ninety-eight ships. These twenty-one thousand English Puritans, who came over to New England before the meeting of the Long Parliament, have now increased to nearly thirteen million. According to the most careful estimates, at least one fourth of the whole population of the United States at the present moment is descended from these men.

Nothing certain, however, was known until recently of Reginald Foster's birthplace, or of his English ancestry. Some information as to families in England of the same name will be found in A Pedigree of the Forsters and Fosters, of the North of England, and of some of the families connected with them, 4to, illustrated, published by John Camden Hotten, 74 and 75 Piccadilly, London, 1871. The book was also printed as a folio, illustrated, xlvi. 66 pages. It was compiled by the distinguished genealogist, Joseph Foster, of London, who printed in Sunderland, in 1862, a first edition of this work, under the title of "Some Account of the Pedigree of the Forsters of Cold Hesleden, County Durham, 4to. He had, in 1888, in preparation an exhaustive history of the Forster, Foster and Forester families, to include the branches in England and America; the first volume of his "Foster's Family History Library." A record of the "Will of Reynowld Foster, of Harlowe, in the County of Essex, yeoman," dated 18 September, 1622, proved 7 January, 1622 (O. S.) and mentioning wife "Margaret," sons "Reynold," "William," and "Peter," and daughters "Sara" and Elizabeth," has been discovered in England by Henry F. Waters, of Salem, Mass., the eminent genealogist, who also found several mentions of deeds, etc., to and from Reginald or "Reynowld" Foster in the same locality. As Reginald Foster had children bearing three of the names mentioned, "Reynold" "William," and "Sara," it has been suggested that he himself may have been the son "Reynold," naming three of his children for his brother, sister and himself, and that William Foster, the early settler in Ipswich, who went from Ipswich to Newport, R. I., in 1638, may have been the son "William." and that both came to America from Harlow, Essex County, England. No

* "There was mounting 'mong graemes of the netherby clan;
Forsters, Fenwicks, and Musgraves, they rode and they ran;"
Marmion, Canto 5, XII.

evidence in support of this theory has, however, yet been discovered, but Harlow is only about forty-five miles from Ipswich, England, after which Ipswich in New England was called in acknowledgment of the great honor and kindness done to our people, who took shipping there, as stated in "Felt's History of Ipswich." No mention of Reginald Foster can be found in the parish records of Exeter, England, it is said, perhaps unadvisedly; but the records of Harlow prior to 1795, relied on for positive evidence, have unfortunately been stolen or destroyed. The historical novel "Dorothy Forster," by Walter Besant, New York, 1887, No. 384 of Lovell's and No. 696 of Munro's Library, a story of the Rebellion of 1715, when Thomas Forster commanded the English forces of the Pretender, is of interest to all who bear the name, as it describes the Forsters as a numerous, prominent and ancient family of Northumberland, whose "history is, in a word, part and parcel of the history of Northumberland itself, that is to say, of the great and glorious realm of England."

The name of Foster was probably originally Forester, which "Webster's Dictionary," after mentioning its equivalents of "French and Provençal, forestier, Low Latin, forestarius, Spanish, florestero, New High German, förster, Old High German, forstari," defines as. "One who has charge of a forest, an officer appointed to watch a forest and preserve the game," and says that it was used by Shakespeare, 1564-1616, for "An inhabitant of a forest, a sylvan." This origin of the name is confirmed by the different Foster Arms, many of which bear three hunting horns, and others different sylvan emblems. For while no particular one of these arms (two of which may be seen in the "Heraldic Journal," Boston, 1865-1868, pages 27 and 55, and a third in the "Curio," New York, October, 1887, page 68) can be fairly claimed by any of Reginald Foster's descendants, until his English ancestry is clearly established, they are collectively good evidence of this derivation of the family name; which is further confirmed by the fact, mentioned by Webster, that, "Foster," contracted from forester, and meaning "a forester," was so used by Spenser, 1553-1599, though the word is now obsolete. Further evidence of this derivation of the name will be found in the following extract from page 216 of "An Etymological Dictionary of the English language," by Rev. Walter W. Skeat, M. A., Oxford, 1882. "Forest, a wood, a wooded tract of land (French. derived from Latin). Middle English, forest, King Alisaunder, 3581 [A metrical romance of Early English literature, line 3581], derived from Old French, forest, 'a forrest,' Cot. [Cotgrave's "French and English dictionary"], derived from Low Latin foresta, a wood; forestis, an open space of ground over which rights of the chase were reserved, * * * document quoted in Brachet, q. v. (Brachet's "Etymological French dictionary," which see], derived from Latin foris, out of doors, abroad; whence forestis, lying open, derived from Latin fores, doors; see Foreign. Derivatives, forest-er, contracted to forster, Chaucer, C. T. 117 [Caterbury Tales, line 117 (of the Prologue)]; and to foster, Spenser, F. Q. iii, 1. 17 [Faery Queen, iii, i, 18.]."

The references to Chaucer and Spenser are as follows:

"A forster was he sothely as I gesse."

(Chaucer, born 1328, died 1400.)

"But after the foule foster Timias did strive."

(Spenser, born 1553, died 1599.)

"Previous to 1752 the year commenced in March, which was consequently the first month, and February, which is now the second, was the twelfth. Ten days must be added to any date in the sixteenth century, and eleven days in the seventeenth, to bring them up to the present style of reckoning."

About the end of the year 1632, was discovered a very desirable tract of land, ten miles to the northeastward of Salem, called by the Indians, Agawam, afterwards called "Ipswich." Fearing that the French might occupy Agawam, the son of the Governor of Massachusetts (Winthrop) was sent in the Spring of 1633, with twelve men, to "begin a plantation there," "but it was not long before many others came." "Hubbard's History of New England."

"Aprill 1th, 1633. It is ordered, that noe pson wtsoeuer shall goe to plant or inhabitt att Aggawam, withoutt leave from the Court, except those that are already gone, vz: Mr. John Winthrop, Jun'r, Mr. Clerke, Robte Coles, Thomas Howlett, John Biggs, John Gage, Thomas Hardy, Willm Perkins, Mr. Thornedicke, Willm. Srieant [Three names are wanting to make up the number before mentioned].

June 11, 1633. There is leave graunted to Tho. Sellen to plant att Aggawam.
5 August, 1634. It is ordered that Aggawam shal be called Ipswitch."

"At Ipsidge a plantation made upe this yeare. Mr. Ward P. Mr. Parker T.—

James Cudworth, 1634" ("Early Records," Ipswich Antiquarian Papers, February, 1880).

"1638-9, Mch 13. Maschanomet, the sagamore of Agawam, ackowledged that hee had received 20£ of Mr. John Winthrope, Iunior, for all his land in Ipswich, for wch hee acknowledged himselfe fully satisfied" (Ipswich Antiquarian Papers, June, 1880).

"The famous Captain John Smith, sailing along the New England coast in 1614, was struck with 'the many rising hills of Agawam.' The Pilgrim Fathers heard of it in 1620 as a desirable locality where to found a settlement. Governor John Winthrop declared in 1632 that it was 'the best place for cattle and tillage in the land.' Wood, in his 'New England's Prospect,' written shortly after, described it as 'abounding in fish and flesh, meads and marshes, plain ploughing-ground, and no rattlesnakes;' and Johnson, in his 'Wonder Working Providence' in 1646, referred to it as situated on 'a faire and delightful river,' and as having 'very good land for husbandry.'" "John Winthrop and his twelve companions in 1633, a hundred others with their families a year after, and at the end of fifteen years a thousand in all" settled in Ipswich. "Houses were rapidly put up. Johnson speaks of them in 1646 as 'very faire-built with pleasant gardens.'" ("Historical Address," Ipswich's 250th Anniversary Celebration, Boston, 1884, pp. 29, 32-33, and 49.) "In 1675, forty-two years after the settlement of Ipswich, there were four hundred houses in town." (Ipswich Antiquarian Papers, July, 1884.) "In forty years its population had increased to fourteen hundred. During the Revolution it was forty-five hundred. In 1670 it was spoken of, side by side with Boston, as 'one of our maritime towns'; and at the end of its first hundred years its county valuation was second only to that of Salem. Then followed its long period of stagnation," "which lasted till the end of its second hundred years. Then came the railroad train skilfully flanking the bar to commerce Nature had placed at the mouth of its river, and opening a new artificial port on dry land right at its heart; then with it all the wonders of modern discovery and invention, sending into its veins their quickening life. And to-day, with two hundred and fifty years on its brow, it stands forth, not a city, not a commercial metropolis, not a large manufacturing place, but an active, healthy, up-with-the-times New England town, radiant with all the combined beauty of ripened age and vigorous youth." "Its population in 1860 was 3,349; in 1870, 3,674; in 1880, 3,699; in 1884, about 3,900." ("Historical Address," Ipswich's 250th Anniversary Celebration, Boston, 1884, pp. 50-51).

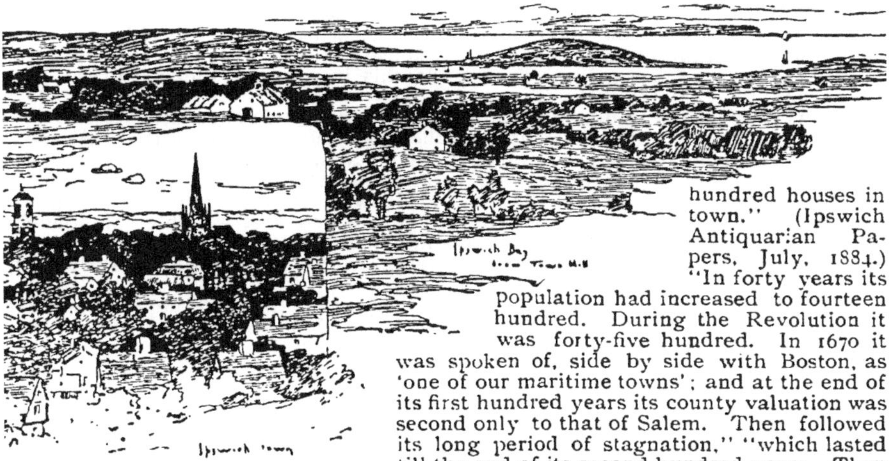

VIEWS IN IPSWICH, MASS.

"Before Europeans came to this country, Agawam reached from Merrimack River on the north, to Naumkeag River, now of Salem, on the south; from Cochichawick, afterwards named Andover, on the west, and to the sea-side on the east. When it was settled by Mr. Winthrop and others, its boundaries on the north and west remained the same; but those on the east, were its own bay and that of Squam, and the town of Gloucester; and on the south were Manchester, Wenham, and Danvers, all four of which latter places were then villages belonging to Salem. Johnson remarks on this territory, 'The Sagamoreship or Earldom of Agawam, now by our English nation called Essex.' 1636. Wessacumcon, or Newbury, being settled, the court order, that Ipswich shall run six miles into the country. As population flowed in and spread over its surface, as corresponding necessities arose and reasons for separation successively prevailed. this town became reduced to its present size. The latitude of Ipswich, as taken at the Court-House, is 42° 41′ north, and longitude, at the same place, 70° 50′ west. This place, now having Rowley on the north, Boxford and Topsfield on the west, Hamilton and Essex on the south, and the ocean on the east, has an area of 25,478 acres. Of this 3,579 acres are water, 1,509 sand on Castle Neck and Plumb [Plum] Island. There are 72 miles of roads" ("Felt's History of Ipswich, Cambridge," 1834, pp. 1-2).

Reginald Foster "lived near the 'East Bridge,' which stood where the stone bridge is now. It is supposed that the remains of what is known as the 'old Foster house,' may have been the site of his residence. This seems probable, for 6 April, 1641, there was 'granted Reginald Foster, eight acres of meadow in the west meadow, if any remain there ungranted, in consideration of a little hovel that stood at the new bridge, which was taken away for the accommodating of the passage there,' and '4th 11mo., 1646,' he with others 'promise carting voluntary toward the East Bridge beside the rate a day work a piece'' "The Descendants of Reginald Foster," Boston, 1876, p. 3."

In the "Ipswich Antiquarian Papers," for December, 1880, will be found a picture of "the ancient house, which stood about half way between the Town Hall and the residence of the late Miss Sally Choate, now the office of George Haskell, Esq. For many years its easterly end was but a heap of ruins. It was called 'the Rust house,' and 'the Foster house.' It was entirely taken down about twenty years ago. In its prime it was a handsome and substantial mansion. Some years ago a writer in the "Historical Genealogical Register" (probably Mr. Hammatt) thought it might have been the first house built by Reginald Foster: which he gave to his son Deacon Jacob Foster. If this is correct,* the house was built about 1638."

A view of Choate bridge built in 1764, "the stone bridge" mentioned above, is given at page 148 of "The Celebration of the Two Hundred and Fiftieth Anniversary of the Incorporation of the Town of Ipswich, Mass., August 16, 1884, Boston, 1884; which contains other views of Ipswich, and an interesting record of the celebration.

"The Dennison Memorial," printed at Ipswich, in 1882. referring to "primitive Ipswich," relates that "At Choate bridge, we find first a lighter or gondola, and then logs and planks to carry men and horses over, and land them just before the door of Mr. Manasseh Brown's residence, which in that day was Reginald Foster's."

Of his [Reginald Foster's] life we know very little; the following facts, gleaned from town and county records, indicate however that he was an active citizen. The danger from Indians in these early times was such that in the year 1645 a law was passed requiring the 'youth from ten to sixteen years to be exercised with small guns, half pikes, bows and arrows,' and also that 'every town is to have a guard set a half hour after sunset, to consist of a pikeman and musketeer, and to prepare for any sudden attack from the Indians.' Our ancestor, on the 19th December, 1645, subscribed with others his proportion of three shillings toward the sum of £24. 7 shillings 'to pay their leader, Major Dennison,' who then commanded the military forces of Essex and Norfolk Counties'' "The Descendants of Reginald Foster," Boston, 1876, p 3 Such was the danger arising from this source, that in 1637 a law was passed in Ipswich, that 'no person is allowed to travel alone above one mile from his house, except where houses are near together, without arms.' " "One Line of the Descendants of William Foster," p. 5. Reginald Foster "bought of Ralph Dix, of Ipswich, 8 March, 1647-8, 'all his six acre lott he '(Dix)' bought of William White [same day], lying in the common field on the north side of the river, bounded on land of Thomas Smyth, Humphrey Broadstreet and Robert Lord.' We find no mention of him again until 1652, when it was 'Granted Thomas Clark and Reginald Foster, that when they shall have cut through a passage from this river into Chebacco river of ten feet wide and soe deepe as a lighter may pass through laden, and to make a ford and footebridge over, that then the town have given unto them £10 towards said passage.' On 3 June of the same year [1652] he was a witness to the will of William Averill, of Ipswich. He bought of Roger Preston, 11 March, 1657-8, for £50, his dwelling house, house lot, barn and other buildings, also another house lot, with gardens, orchards, etc., which Preston bought of Robert Wallis, situated on the north side of the river, and one planting

*It is correct—see will and inventory of Reginald Foster, and the record of his son, Jacob Foster.

lot of three acres, on the north side of Town Hill, bounded on land of widow Rose Whipple, Andrew Hodges, John Morse and Thomas Treadwell. The houses were on 'the High Street,' probably at the east end—and in the vicinity of the ancient dwelling house of Rev. Mr. Norton, which [in 1876] yet stands. He had also a house lot near the 'meeting house green.'

On 29 September, 1663, he was an appraiser of the estate of Robert Roberts."—"The Descendants of Reginald Foster," pp. 3-4.

In "1661, he was a surveyor of highways; his name with the names of his sons, Abraham, Reginald, Isaac and Jacob, are in a list of the inhabitants [of Ipswich] that have shares in Plum Island, etc., 14 February, 1664. The same names are on a list of those that by law are allowed to have their votes in Town affairs, 2 December, 1679."—The Hammatt Papers, Ipswich, Mass., 1880—188-, No. iii, p. 105.

"In the grant of King James, 1621, to Captain John Mason, of land between Naumkeag and Merrimack rivers, there is the subsequent clause: 'The great Isle, henceforth to be called, Isle of Mason, lying near or before the bay, harbour or river of Agawam.' This must have been Plumb [Plum] Island, part of which was set off to Ipswich by the General Court, 1639 [1649]."—"Felt's History of Ipswich," Cambridge, 1834, p. 36.

"Plum Island bears north and south, and is between eight and nine miles in length, and less than a mile in width." Plum Island was so called from the "small beach plum" which is indigenous there, and "was extensively used for many years as a winter resort for cattle, and from the value which the early settlers seemed to place upon it, we should infer that it was somewhat more prolific of herbage than we find it at the present day."

The northern half of it was originally owned by the town of Newbury," though sold in 1827 to Moses Pettengill, of Newburyport, the island having been divided in 1649 by the General Court "to Ipswich two-fifths, Newbury two-fifths, Rowley one fifth. The southern part of the island belongs to Ipswich and Rowley, and contains a few dwelling-houses and farms; but the northern part is entirely composed of sand, which is thrown by the wind into hillocks of various heights and forms, and on the eastern shore is continually the sport of the Atlantic billows, which change its outline from year to year, making its shores a new study to the lover of nature, who might here revel in one of her wildest and most fantastic forms, an ever new delight.

"In the earlier records we find the name spelt indifferently Foster and Forster, —the former spelling being the more common. The 'r' has now been entirely dropped, except by the descendants of Jacob Forster, Sen., [Jacob Forster[6] (Jacob,[5] Jacob,[4] Isaac,[3] Reginald,[2] Reginald[1])] of Charlestown, Mass., who was the first, I believe, to write the name always in the same manner."—"The Pedigree and Descendants of Jacob Forster, Sen., of Charlestown, Mass.," Charlestown, 1870, p. 3. Reginald Foster's "name is variously written in an abbreviated form; viz.:—Renald, Regnold, Rejnald, Ringdell, Reginold. He signed his will, Renold ffoster.

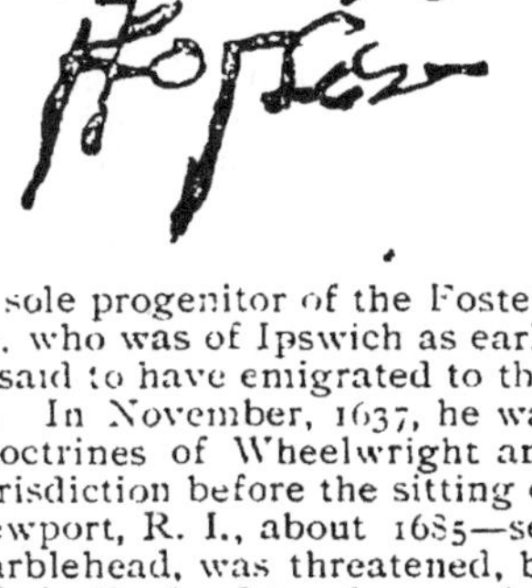

It is erroneously supposed by many that he is the sole progenitor of the Fosters of America. There is an account of a William Foster, who was of Ipswich as early as 1635, and had land granted him that year, and is said to have emigrated to this country from England in 1634, in the ship Hercules. In November, 1637, he was disarmed for entertaining the peculiar views and doctrines of Wheelwright and Ann Hutchinson, and warned to depart from the jurisdiction before the sitting of the general court in March following [he died in Newport, R. I., about 1685—see elsewhere]. A William Foster, living in 1652, at Marblehead, was threatened, by court, with a fine of £20, for 'living heare and his wife in England,' and warned to 'go to her before the end of the 7th mo., 1652' (County Court Records).

"Andrew Foster, an early settler of Andover, died 7 May, 1685, at the very advanced age of 106 years. His wife, Ann Foster, was condemned for supposed witchcraft (see 'Abbott's History of Andover,' page 154), but died in prison. [Her daughter, Mary (Foster) Lacey, wife of Lawrence Lacey, and her granddaughter, Mary Lacey, jr., were also accused of witchcraft in 1692, and tried, the former being condemned, though not executed, and the latter acquitted (see 'Bailey's Historical Sketches of Andover, Mass.,' Boston, 1880, pages 200, 201 and 207).] Her son Abram petitioned, 13 September, 1710:—

"The honorable committee now sitting in Salem * * * that the attainder may be taken off * * *. The charges which I was forced to pay the keeper before I could have the dead body of my mother to bury her was £2 10s; money and provisions expended while she was in prison, £4. Total expenses six pounds ten shillings.

ABRAM FOSTER, Son of the Deceased.'

"Andrew Foster appears in no way identified with the Fosters of Ipswich. An account of his descendants, by Edward Jacob Forster, M. D., may be found in the 'New England Historical and Genealogical Register,' vol. xx, page 227. There were, besides, Bartholomew of Gloucester, Christopher of Lynn, Edward of Scituate, William of Charlestown (of whose family an account was published in the N. E. H. and G. Register for January, 1871 [vol. xxv, page 67]), Hopestill of Dorchester, and several others contemporary with him; but between whom it is not known that any relation existed."—"One Line of the Descendants of William Foster," pp. 6-8.

Reginald Foster "was twice married. First to Judith ——, in England, who died in Ipswich, October, 1664 [she was the mother of all the children]; second, September, 1665, to Sarah Martin, of Ipswich, who, after her husband's decease, married, 21 September, 1682, William White, of Haverhill, whose first wife, Mary, died 22 February, 1681."

"The exact date of Reginald Foster's death is unknown. [He died between 5 March and 30 May, 1681, aged over eighty years.] His will was proved 9 June, 1681."

Sarah Martin, his second wife, was the "widow of John Martin, of Ipswich. She survived Reginald, and 21 September, 1682, she became the second wife of William White, of Haverhill (as already stated). She died 22 February, 1682-3."

"The will of Reginald was made 30 April, 1680, a codicil attached, signed 5 March, 1680-1 and approved 9 June, 1681. He appears to have been a large owner at Plum and Hog Islands; and among his bequests, he gives to his son William 'my six acres of land I had of Thomas Smith, and six acres of marsh at Hog Island.' He also mentions his wife Sarah, sons Abraham, Renold, Isaac, Jacob, and daughters Sarah, wife of William Story, Mary, wife of Francis Peabody, and grandchild Hannah Story. He left an estate valued at £744-16, including real estate at £671. Inventory taken 30 May, 1681, by John Whipple and Simon Stace.

The originals of the Will and Inventory of the Estate of Reginald Foster cannot be found. The following are official copies from the Records in the Registry of Deeds, at Salem, Mass.

Will of Reginald Foster. "Book 4, Leaf 402, Ipswich Records.—The last Will and testament of Renol ffoster Senr. of Ipswich in the County of Essex in New England, made the last day of Aprill, Anno Dom. one thousand six hundred & 80, being this day by Gods good providence of perfect understanding, tho, through infirmatyes of body, dayly mindfull of my mortality. Therefore for the setting my house in order I make and apoynt this my last Will and testament as followeth.

In the name of God Amen my soule I committ into the hands of Jesus Christ, my blessed redeemer, In hope of a joyfull resurrection at the last day my body to a decent comly buriall, And for my outward estate which the Lord hath graciously given me, I thus dispose of it in manner following:

Imp. To my beloved wife Sarah I give the use of the house I now dwell in, and the orcyards [orchards], and gardens and five pound yearly, dureing her naturall life, and two cowes, which she shall chuse out of my stock, and the keeping of them both summer & winter yearly, also I give her the bedstead with beding in the parler, and the rest of the linnen & woollen yarne that she hath made and prvided into the house, also the use of a bras pot, and cheespres, and kneading trough, with the utensils in the Leantoo, and the great kettle & two skillets dureing her naturall life, Also I give her three sheepe to be kept winter & summer, also two piggs, and what provisions shall be in the house at my decease, also the table and forme for her naturall life, ffurther my will is that the household stuff & things that my wife brought into the house when I marryed her be at her dispose in life and at death.

I give and bequeath unto my son Abraham ffoster my now dwelling house and orchard and ground about it, three acres more or less & halfe the barne, and halfe that land in the field lyeing betweene the land of John Denison & Philip ffowlers, and ten acres on this syde the River caled Muddy River by Major Denisons & John Edwards land, and six acres of salt marsh, All which I give him after my wives decease, I give him four acres of marsh at Plumb Island and the six acres at Hogs Island.

I give and bequeath unto my son Renol ffoster all the land which he possesses of myne at the ffalls, that he hath built a house upon both upland & marsh be it fifty acres more or less, only to pay out of it within a yeare after my decease to Sarah my daughter Story, the sum that I have given her, except wt ye sheets & pillo cases amounts to.

I give and bequeath unto my son Isaack ffoster my eight acres of fresh meadow at the west meadows joineing to meadows of his, and four acres of salt marsh at Hogs Island, Jacob to have the use of the salt til the decease of my wife.

I give and bequeath unto my son William ffoster my six acres of land I had of Thomas Smith, & six acres of marsh at Hog Island, the marsh to Jacob till my wives decease.

I give and bequeath unto my son Jacob ffoster the house he lives in & ground about it, and my two lotts beyond Muddy River ten acres more or lesse and the remainder of salt marsh att Hog Island, further my will is that my son Jacob have my land at home and barne dureing my wives naturall life, further I give him my pasture on the south syde of the river by Simon Tompsons, and the pasture by Caleb Kimballs, also I give him a feather bed, only my will is that he pay what I have given my wife & keepe in repaires for her yearly, what I have allowed her and given her in my will.

I give and bequeath to my daughter Sarah, William Storeys wife the sum of ten pounds vizt. a payre of sheets and a paire of pillow cases, and what they amount not to of the sum, the rest in the hands of my son Renol, which I have willed him to pay as appeares above.

I give and bequeath unto my daughter Mary the wife of ffrancis Peabody the summ of ten pound, part of it to be payd in a payre of sheetes and a paire of pillo cases & a fether bed, the bed after my wives decease.

I give my granchild Hanah Story the sum of six pound vizt a bed bolster pillow and paire of sheetes and blanketts, which are of my now wives makeing, the rest to be payd by my executors if she carry it well to my wife while she lives with her as she hath done to us hitherto.

My will is that my son Jacob have the implements of husbandry.

My will is wch I desire and apoynt my two sonns Abraham ffoster and Jacob ffoster, to be my executors of this my last will and testament, and request and desire my beloved ffriends Simon Stace & Nehemiah Jewett to be my overseers to this my will fullfild by my executors, and if any difference arise amongst my wife and children, or amongst them, about any perticular in my will, my will is that my two overseers shall end it, and they rest satticefied as they two shall agree, and if they two differ, then as a third man, who they shall choose joyning with either of them.

In wittnes whereof I have sett to my hand & seale, read, signed, sealed and declared to be the last will and testament of me Renol ffoster Senr. the day and yeare above written 1680, as wittnes my hand & seale

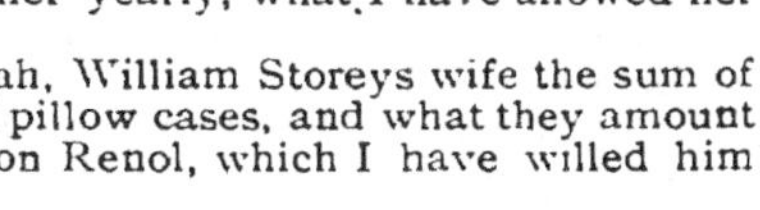

Wittnesses.
John Starkweather
Nehemiah Jewett

Memorandum. The things given my wife for her naturall life be soe exsept she marry againe and what debts shee shall have due for labor & worke shall be for her proper use & sole benifitt, and that the repaires of the house be out of her estate, and dureing her abode in it, and that my wife shall have liberty to cutt & procure what woood she needeth from of [off] my land at Muddy River, this declared the 5 of March 16$\frac{80}{81}$ to be his last will.

In presence of wittnesses — Renol ffoster
John Starkweather
Nehemiah Jewett.

The 9th June 1681 Nehemiah Jewett & John Starkweather appeared before our Honered majestrates Major Genll Denison Esqr. and Major Samuell Appleton Esqr.

& the clerke present and made oath that they were present and saw Renol ffoster signe, seale & publish this to be his last will & testament and they know of no other and that he was of a disposeing mynd.

As attest. ROBERT LORD, Cler.

Essex Registry Deeds, So. Dist. Salem, Dec. 16, 1887.

The foregoing is a true copy of record in this office.

Attest. CHAS. S. OSGOOD, Reg."

The following notices of Reginald Foster's "beloved ffriends Simon Stace and Nehemiah Jewett," the overseers of his will, are taken from "Felt's History of Ipswich," Cambridge, 1834.

"1699, October 27th. Simon Stacey died. He was Selectman, often entrusted with town affairs, Captain of a company, and Representative to the General Court in 1685, 1686, 1689. He left a wife, Sarah, who died 29 November, 1711. Estate £660 8s. 1d."

"1720, January 20th. Nehemiah Jewett died lately, son of Jeremiah, who died 1714. His wife's name was Exercise, and was alive 1685. He left children, Nehemiah, Joseph, and Benjamin; and son-in-law, Daniel Dow, and grandson, Nehemiah Skillion. He sustained various trusts in the town; was Representative 1689, 1690, 1692, 1693, 1694, 1695, 1696, 1697, 1701, 1702, 1703, 1704, 1705, 1706, 1707, 1709, and Speaker of the House 1693, 1694, 1701; was Justice of the Sessions Court. 1711-12, he was on a Committee to compensate individuals, who were damaged by prosecutions for witchcraft, or the heirs of such among these individuals as had died. Mr. Jewett was a highly respected member of the Legislature and esteemed in every walk of his life."

Inventory of the Estate of Reginald Foster. Book 4, Leaf 403, Ipswich Records.—An Inventory of all the goods and chattells of Renol ffoster, late of Ipswich deceased, taken & aprised by us whose names are under written this 30 May 1680 [1681].

Imprimis. The house and barne with homstead with all previledges... [£]	150-00-00
The house Jacob ffoster liveth in with ye homstead & previledges	100-00-00
Ten acres of land at Muddy River	035-00-00
4 acres & a halfe in the comon field	020-00-00
29 acres of salt marsh	084-00-00
8 acres of fresh meadow	16-00-00
12 acres of pasture lands	40-00-00
20 acres of land in the common field	76-00-00
by 50 acres of upland and marsh	150-00-00
One ox, 4 cowes, 2 steers 2 years old	21-00-00
One calfe, 10 sheepe, three lambes	05-00-00
Three swine	01-10-00
A bed in the chamber with beding upon it	05-00-00
20 bushells of Indian corne & rye	03-05-00
Two boxes & severall old tubbs	01-00-00
A coslet [corselet], 2 pikes, old rapier 20^s and money 20^s	02-00-00
A ffeather bed of 2 sheets 2 pillow cases	05-00-00
A paire of sheets & a paire of pillow cases	00-16-00
A bedstead in the parlour with beding and curtaines	02-00-00
A trundle bed with beding	00-15-00
A flock bed, 1 pillow, 1 bolster a paire of sheets 2 blankets	03-06-00
Sheets, pillow cases, table linnen	03-00-00
3 paire of sheets & one sheet	01-10-00
2 table cloths, two napkins	00-16-00
Two chests, one old trunke, one box	00-12-00
His weareing apparrell, woollen *woollen* and linnen	06-10-00
A table forme, a chayer	00-10-00
Pewter & brass 2$^£$ tubbs, keeler pailes barrells 1$^£$	03-00-00
in porke, a cheespres and kneading trough	01-08-00
A paire of cobirons, a tramell, a warming pan, frying pan, long Spit & other small things	01-00-00
Ten pound of yarne 1$^£$ Utencills of husbandry 1 £ 10$_s$	02-10-00
An old iron pot & kettle 10^s. A pitt saw & milk vessells and churne 15^s.	01-05-00

Sixteen pound of sheeps woole 16s. A trowell, halfe bushell, four Hammers [7s] 001-03-00

[£] 744-16-00

JOHN WHIPPLE.
SIMON STACE.

The 9th of June 1681 Abraham ffoster and Jacob ffoster Executors made oath that the above written is a full and true inventory of there ffathers estate to the best of there knowledge and if more appeare to add the same before the worshipfull Major Genell Denison Esqr. Major Samuell Appleton Esqr. and the clerke being present.

As attest. ROBERT LORD, Cler.

Essex Registry Deeds, So. Dist. Salem, Dec. 16, 1887.

The foregoing is a true copy of record in this office.

Attest. CHAS. S. OGSOOD, REG."

The first printed notice of Reginald Foster which has been found, is contained in an extract from the Boston Gazette of 9 November, 1779; reprinted in the appendix, page 33, of the sermon preached on the occasion of the death, 17 October, 1779, of Hon. Jedediah Foster (Ephraim, Ephraim, Abraham, Reginald) of Brookfield, Mass., by Nathan Fiske, D.D. This account was doubtless furnished by his son, Senator Theodore Foster, of Rhode Island, and the pamphlet was, in fact, printed at Providence, R. I., apparently under his supervision. The notice was as follows:

"He [that is, Jedediah Foster] was born at Andover, on Merrimack River, October 10, 1726, descended from an antient and reputable Family (Reginald Foster's) who came from England A. D. 1636, on Account of the Troubles in the Reign of Charles I."

The following note is added at the foot of the page.

"This Gentleman Reginald Foster was born in the Reign of Queen Elizabeth, in England, in the latter End of the Fifteenth Century, and was descended of the same Family with Sir Reginald Foster, who was made a Baronet of England July 21st, A. D. 1661, mentioned in the 30th Edition of Chamberlayne's Present State of Great-Britain, and in the Heraldry Books of the English Peerage.—He brought with him to America his Wife, with five Sons and two Daughters, with whom he settled at Ipswich, Eastward of Boston.—All his children, as well as himself, lived to old Age.—All married and had large Families, from whom have risen a numerous Progeny, now settled in different Parts of the United States of America."

The first genealogical record of Reginald Foster and his descendants, known to exist, is contained in the "Foster Papers," now in the possession of the Rhode Island Historical Society. These papers, both originals and copies, amount to about one thousand, and are preserved in sixteen bound volumes; they relate generally to the history of Rhode Island, and were left to the Society in 1828 by the late Senator Theodore Foster (Jedediah, Ephraim, Ephraim, Abraham, Reginald), of that State.

One of these volumes, the largest, is nearly twenty-four inches high, and is lettered "Foster Papers, Vol 8.—Genealogies." It contains genealogies of the following families: Pyncheon, Foster, Williams, Olney, Dexter, Crawford, Arnold, Westcott, Dwight, Harris, Fenner and Cranston. The Foster genealogy is on one large sheet (made however of several pieced together), about 39 by 23¾ inches. In order to shut into the book, it has to fold over twice. The genealogy is in the well-known form of using connecting lines. Across the top is written this heading, the whole, without the parentheses, forming only two lines, but very long ones:

"A Genealogical Table of the Posterity of Reginold (Rennold) Foster who was born in the reign of Queen Elizabeth at (or near) Exeter in England the latter End of the Fifteenth Century was married and Settled at (or near) Exeter where he had born Five Sons and Two Daughters with whom he removed to New England in the Year 1638 and settled at Ipswich in the State of Massachusetts Bay (Massachusetts). He removed from England a little before the Commencement of the Civil Wars in the Reign of Charles the First) and with his Family was on Board one of the Vessels embargoed by a Proclamation of the King and Council issued in April 1638, copied into "Rushworth's Memorials".)"

The chart shows that it was originally prepared by Theodore Foster, sometime between 20 March, 1777, and 17 October, 1779; and probably the words in parenthesis were added by him on or about 13 January, 1803, when he copied on pages 65–68 of "Foster Papers, Vol. 9," the extracts from "Rushworth's Historical

Colections," vol. ii, for 1637-1638, referred to in the last parenthesis (see London edition, 1680, page 409) following them with this entry:

"N. B. My Ancestor Reginald Foster, came from the West of England, with a Wife, Five Sons, and Two Daughters in the Year 1638 and settled in Ipswich eastward of Boston in Massachusetts and is supposed to have been on Board of one of the Eight Vessels mentioned in the foregoing order, and among those whom 'His Majesty was graciously pleased at this Time (6 April 1638) to free from a late Restraint and to set at Liberty to proceed in their intended Voyage."

It will be seen that Theodore Foster in the last paragraph, while fixing 1638 as the year in which Reginald Foster came to America, leaves uncertain the exact locality of his English birthplace and home, which in his earlier printed and written statements, he placed first as "at" and afterwards as "at or near," Exeter, England.

Some of the following information of the descendants of Reginald Foster, as well as of Reginald Foster, John Foster, and Jeremiah Foster, the direct ancestors of Colonel Joseph Foster, and their descendants, has been taken from "The Descendants of Reginald Foster, who settled in Ipswich, Essex County, Mass.," A.D. 1638, by Edward Jacob Forster, M. D., Boston, 1876, pages 24; originally printed in the "New England Historical and Genealogical Register," volume xxx, pages 83-102, as already mentioned on page 12; which furnishes a record of the first four generations of the family; or has been furnished from his manuscripts by Dr. Forster (Jacob, Jacob, Jacob, Jacob, Isaac, Reginald, Reginald), who was a resident of Charlestown District, Boston, Mass.

Further information in relation to Jacob Forster (Jacob, Jacob, Isaac, Reginald, Reginald), of Charlestown, Mass., his direct ancestors, and his descendants, may be obtained from Dr. Forster's pamphlet, The Pedigree and Descendants of Jacob Forster, Sen., of Charlestown, Mass., by Edward Jacob Forster, M. D., Charlestown, 1870, pages 25.

Much valuable information has also been drawn from One Line of the Descendants of William Foster, son of Reginald Foster, of Ipswich, Mass., by Perley Derby, of Salem, Mass., Boston, 1872, pages 35, which furnishes an account of Reginald Foster, and his children, but relates more particularly to the direct ancestry and descendants of John Foster (Obadiah, John, William, William, Reginald), of Warner, N. H., and was privately printed for his son John Foster, of Boston, to whom the compiler is indebted for a copy. Extracts have already been given. Perley Derby, Esq., of Salem, placed his Foster manuscripts at the disposal of Col. Joseph Foster, kindly aided in his research, and the changes in the heretofore published order of birth of the children of Reginald Foster were made with his approval.

A notice of Reginald Foster, of Ipswich, and the descendants of his son Abraham Foster, by the late Hon. Alfred Dwight Foster (Dwight, Jedediah, Ephraim, Ephraim, Abraham, Reginald), of Worcester, Mass., in the New England Historical and Genealogical Register, for October, 1847, vol. i, pages 352-354, has also been consulted. This is the first published record of the Foster family knownto the compiler; its author doubtless had access to the "Foster Papers" already mentioned.

The account of Reginald Foster and his descendants in "Savage's Genealogical Dictionary of New England," Boston, 1860-1862, has been examined, and found to contain many errors.

Additional information as to Hon. Jedediah Foster (Ephraim, Ephraim, Abraham, Reginald) of Brookfield, Mass., mentioned above and on other pages in this book, and his descendants, may be obtained from "The History of the Descendants of John Dwight, of Dedham, Mass.," by Benjamin W. Dwight, New York, 1874, vol. ii, pages 633-680.

The compiler is indebted to Col. Joseph Foster, of Portsmouth, N. H., for information for the interesting extracts and other valuable information.

A manuscript record of the descendants of Jacob Foster, son of Reginald Foster, "from whom descended Archibald Foster, Esq., formerly cashier of Granite Bank, Portuguese and Brazilian Consul, Boston," is referred to in "One Line of the Descendants of William Foster," page 2, but the compiler has no other knowledge thereof. A record of some of the descendants of his daughter, Sarah Foster3, wife of John Caldwell, with a notice of the Foster family, will be found in the Caldwell Records, by Augustine Caldwell, of Ipswich, Mass., Boston, 1873, pages 80.

Many town histories of New England have published short notices of the Fosters residing in their respective towns, but not until this publication has there any attempt been made at a complete history and genealogy.

1. REGINALD FOSTER* (see English Fosters elsewhere for his ancestors), b. England abt. 1595; m. there ——; m. 2d, Judith ——; d. Oct., 1664; m. 3d, Sept. 19, 1665, Mrs. Sarah (White) Martin, wid. of John. She was widow of John Martin, of Ipswich. After Reginald's death she m. a third time, Sept. 21, 1682, William White, of Haverhill. She was his second wife. She d. Feb. 22, 1683. Sarah Martin was the second wife of John Martin, of Charlestown, a ship-carpenter, who was a nephew of Priscilla Upham.

From an other authority we have this. "Reginald Foster, of Little Badow, Co. Essex, England; landed in Ipswich, Mass., in 1638. He belonged to the Foster family of Bamborough and Etherstone Castle, Co., Northumberland. Reginald brought with him five sons and two daughters."

Savage says. "Now this unusual blessing of fruit in old age, when the last ch. came fifty-six years after the first, I doubted, might have arisen from mistake, and that both the last ws. and their offspring should really belong to his s. Reginald, wh. might well have had Judith to w. bef. he took Eliz Dane, and after d. of the latter have m. Sarah Martin, inasmuch as Sen. and Jr. are changeable characters, and he wh. was Jr. on the d. of his f. would be call. Sen. But this explanat. is not receivab. bec. the first Reginald d. 1681, as we infer from the date of inv. 30 May in this yr., and the Prob. rec. of his will of 30 Apr. bef. proving that he left w. Sarah, and ch. Abraham, Renold, Sarah, w. William Story, Isaac, Jacob, William, and Mary, w. of Francis Peabody."

He came from England, it is said, in 1638, and had a grant of land in Ipswich, April 6, 1641. He brought with him his seven children by his first wife. At his death, in 1681, his wife's name was Sarah. This fact is mentioned, as it is stated by some historians, that he did not marry a third time. At his death his children mentioned in the will were Abraham, Renold, Sarah, wife of Wm. Story, Isaac, Jacob, William, and Mary, wife of Francis Peabody. It is remarkable of this family that they all lived to extreme old age, all married and all had large families, from which are descended a very numerous progeny, which in every case has been highly respected.

In the Ipswich records we find Goodman Foster, referring to Reginald, whose name is somtimes abreviated Renald. He resided near the "East Bridge," which was where the stone bridge now is, but whether his residence was where the ruins of the "Old Foster House" yet stood, I have not learned. Under date of April 6, 1641, is "granted to Reginald Foster eight acres of meadow in the west meadow if any remain there ungranted, in consideration of a little hovel that stood at the new bridge, which was taken away for the accomodation of the passage there." Whatever facts we have of them are gleaned from the town and county records, which show him to have been a very active man. The danger from Indians in those early days was such that in the year 1645 a law was passed requiring the "youth from ten to sixteen years to be experienced with small guns, half pikes, bows and arrows, and also that every town is to have a guard set a half hour after sunset, to consist of a pikeman and musketeer, and to prepare for any sudden attack from the Indians. Reginald Foster, Dec. 19, 1645, subscribed with others his proportion of three shillings towards the sum of £24, 7sh "to pay their leader, Major Dennison," who then commanded the military forces of Essex and Norfolk counties. He bought of Ralph Dix, of Ipswich, 8 March, 1647-8, "all his six acre lott he" (Dix) "bought of Wm. White, lying in the common field on the north side of the river, bounded on the land of Thomas Smyth, Humphrey Broadstreet and Robert Lord." We find no mention of him again until 1652, when it was granted Thomas Clark and Reginald Foster, that when they shall have cut through a passage from this river into Chebacco River of ten feet wide and soe deepe as a lighter may pass through laden, and to make a ford and footbridge over, that then the town have given unto them £10 towards said passage." On 3 June of the same year he was a witness to the will of William Averrill, of Ipswich. He bought of Roger Preston, 11 March, 1657-8, for £50, his dwelling house, house lot, barn and other buildings, also another house lot, with gardens, orchards etc., which Preston bought of Robert Wallis situated on the north side of the river, and one planting lot of three acres, on the north side of Town Hill, bounded on the land of widow Rose Whipple, Andrew Hodges, John Morse, and Treadwell. The houses were on "the High Street" probably at the east end—and in the vicinity of the ancient dwelling house of Rev.

*In the earlier record we find the name spelt Foster and Forster—the former spelling being the more common. The "r" has now been entirely dropped, except by the descendants of Jacob Forster, Sen., of Charlestown, Mass., who was the first, I believe, to write the name always in this manner—Edward Jacob Forster, M. D.

Mr. Norton, which yet stands. He had also a house lot near the "meeting-house green." On 29 September, 1663, he was an appraiser of the estate of Robert Roberts. Reignald Foster was married when he came to this country. He d. in 1681; res. Ipswich, Mass.

2. i. MARY, b. England, abt. 1618; m. ——, Wood and Lieut. Francis Peabody, b. 1614 He was from St. Albans, Wertfordshire, England, and came to New England in the ship "Planter," Nicholas Trarice, master, in 1635. He was a husbandman and was then twenty-one years of age. He was one of the original settlers in Hampton, N. H., with Rev. Stephen Bachiler*
and resided there for many years, finally removing to Topsfield, Mass. He was chosen to "ende small causes" by the people of Hampton, and confirmed in that office by the justices of the court. He was a large land owner in Topsfield, Boxford and Rowley. He d. Feb. 19, 1697. She d. April 9, 1705. They had fourteen ch. 1. John, b. in 1642; m., first, 23 November, 1665, Hannah Andrews,† and second, 26 November, 1703, Sarah Mosely; will proved August, 1720. A descendant was George Peabody (Thomas, David, David), of London, England, b. 18 February, 1795; the famed London banker and philanthropist; d. in 1869. 2. Joseph, b. in 1644; m. 26 October, 2668, Bethiah Bridges; d. in 1721. Descendant is Andrew Preston Peabody (Andrew, Andrew, Zerubabel, Joseph), of Cambridge, Mass., b. 19 March, 1811, in Beverly, Mass.; Harvard University, 1826; D. D., 1852; minister of the South Church in Portsmouth, N. H., 1833-1860; appointed Plummer Professor of Christian Morals, Harvard University, 1860; the distinguished Unitarian divine. 3. William, b. in 1646; m. 14 August, 1684, Hannah Hale; d. March, 1699. Descendants are: a. Oliver Peabody, of Natick, Mass., b. 7 May, 1698; Harvard University, 1721; minister of Natick, for about thirty years; d. 2 February, 1752. b. John Peabody (John), of Andover, Mass., b. 20 August, 1732; at siege of Louisburg, 1758; and captain of an Andover company in the Revolution (see "Bailey's Historical Sketches of Andover, Mass.," Boston, 1880, pages 160-161, and 284-285); d. 12 June, 1820. c. Stephen Peabody (John), of Atkinson, N. H., brother of the preceding, b. ——; Harvard University, 1769; minister at Atkinson, 1772-1819; a man of eminence among the clergy of New Hampshire at that time; m., second, Elizabeth (Smith) Shaw, a widow, sister of the wife of President John Adams; d. 23 May, 1819. His son, Hon. Stephen Peabody, of Bucksport, Maine, b. 6 October, 1773, Harvard University, 1794, judge of the Court of Common Pleas of Hancock County, Maine; d. 12 April, 1851. d. Oliver Peabody (Oliver, John), of Exeter, N. H., b. 2 September, 1753; Harvard University, 1773;

---

*See Batchelder Genealogy, by Fred C. Pierce.

†Their dau. Mary m. Lieut. Richard Hazen. His son Lieutenant Moses m. Abigail White; their dau. Abigail m. Benjamin Mooers; their dau. Abigail, b. Jan. 6, 1754, m. James Hazeltine, b. March 27, 1750, of Haverhill. James' brothers and sisters were: 1. Samuel Haseltine, b. June 28, 1740; m. Elizabeth Haseltine, his cous. 2. Mary Haseltine m. Rev. Stephen Peabody. 3. John d. y. 4. Eben d. y. 5. James, b. March 27, 1750. 6. Bille, b. March 10, 1751, d. unm. 7. Sarah, d. y. 8. Dea John, b. Nov. 8, 1756; m. Rebecca Barton. James and Abigail had John, b. Feb. 28, 1793; m. Mar. 11, 1830, Elizabeth Stanley Shinn, b. April 22, 1811; d. June 29, 1882. He d. Dec. 11, 1871. Ch: 1. Caroline Augusta, b. Philadelphia, Dec. 17, 1830; m. Feb. 7, 1855, Emile Marquize, b. at Ortez, France, May 20, 1820; had 3 ch. 2. Mary White, b July 17, 1832; d. y. 3. Major James Henry, b. Nov. 2, 1833; m. July 5. 1881, Maria Nazarena Filamena Trombetti; b. Ferracina, Italy, Feb. 21, 1846. They live in Italy. He is a sculptor. Served through the rebellion as major of 6th Penn. cavalry 4. William Stanley, b. June 11, 1835; m. 1st, Helen Lane, Oct. 9, 1860. She d. June 11, 1864. M. 2d, Feb 28, 1866, in N. Y., Helen Wykoff Marshall, b. March 4, 1837. 1 ch. by 1st wf. and 4 by 2d wf. 5. Elizabeth Stanley, b. April 22, 1837; m. May 30, 1860, Wm. Poultney Smith, (now Pres. of the Commercial Nat. Bk. of Phila.), b. March 9, 1835 (7 ch.). 6. Capt. John White b. Sept. 6, 1838; m. Rose Idler, June 9, 1869. He was captain in the 2d Penn cavalry all through the war. 1 ch m. 7. Charles Field, b. July 29, 1840; m. in Pittsburg Sept. 6, 1863, Elizabeth Holmes Patterson, b. Dec. 15, 1840; d. at Corronnado Beach, Sar Diego, Cal., March 29, 1891. 3 ch. Was for a time first lieutenant of artillery. 8. Lucy, b. Sept. 28, 1841, d. y. 9. Albert Chevalier, b. Jan. 16, 1843; unm., lives in France; grad. of Harvard University, Cambridge; as was also (4) William Stanley (above). 10. Child, d. y. 11. Marianne Lucy, b. June 9, 1846; m. Oct. 11, James S. Dumaresq; she d. in Boston, July 16, 1881. John. b. 1793; had brothers and sisters: 1. James; m. Susanna West. 2. Capt. William; b. Sept. 13, 1783; d. Oct 25, 1841; m. Susan Badger. 3. Benjamin, m. Betsey Hardy. 4. Abigail, b. Mar. 27, 1780; d. April 27, 1875: m. Daniel Haddock; 5. John (my father (see above). 6. Mary, m. Richard West. 7. Elizabeth, m. Stephen Kimball. 8. Sarah, m. Warner Whittier, of Haverhill, Mass., for 1st wife. 7. Charles Field, ad. 1720 Chester St., Philadephia, Pa. Ch: 1. Esther Holmes Haseltine, b. Phila., April 29, 1864; m. Jan. 14, 1886, her cous. Charles Stewart Carstairs; has 4 ch., Charles Haseltine, Carol., James Stewart, and Elizabeth Holmes. 2. Elizabeth Stanley Haseltine, b. Dec. 28, 1867; d. Feb. 9, 1881. 3. Caroline Marquize Haseltine, b. Oct. 29, 1873.

judge of the Court of Common Pleas of Rockingham County, N. H.; d. 3 August, 1831. Out of his twelve children three may be named. Lucretia Orne Peabody, b. 4 July, 1786; m. 21 October, 1816, Alexander Hill Everett, diplomatist and author, brother of Edward Everett, orator and statesman, Rev. William Bourn Oliver Peabody and Rev. Oliver William Bourn Peabody, twins, b. 7 July 1799; Harvard University, 1816; the former d. 28 May, 1847; the latter d. 5 July, 1848. e. Charles Augustus Peabody (Samuel, Richard, Stephen), of New York, b. 10 July, 1814; judge of the Supreme Court of the State of New York, 1856—1857; delegate from the United States to the International Code Conference at Cologne, in 1881. f. John Appleton (Elizabeth (Peabody) Appleton, Ephraim Peabody, Thomas, Ephraim), of Bangor, Maine, b. ——; Bowdoin College, 1822; LL. D., 1869; Chief Justice of the Supreme Court of Maine, 1869. 4. Isaac, b. in 1648; m. Sarah ——; will proved 2 January, 1727. Descendants are: g. Joseph Peabody (Francis, Francis), of Salem, Mass., b. 12 December, 1757; an eminent ship owner and merchant. His daughter, Catherine Elizabeth Peabody, b. 23 June, 1808; m. October, 1826, John Lowell Gardner, of Boston. His granddaughter, Mary Peabody (George, Joseph), m. Hon. William C. Endicott, of Salem, Secretary of War, and their daughter, Mary Endicott, m. 15 November, 1888, in Washington, D. C., Hon. Joseph Chamberlain, M. P., of England. h. Nathaniel Peabody (Isaac, Matthew), of Salem, Mass., b. 30 March, 1774; Dartmouth College, 1800; a teacher and physician; m. 3 November, 1802, Elizabeth Palmer (see "Bailey's Historical Sketches of Andover, Mass.," Boston, 1880, pages 553-554). Three of their seven children may be named. Elizabeth Palmer Peabody, b. 16 May, 1804; d. about 1886. Mary Tyler Peabody, b. 16 November, 1806; m. Horace Mann, b. in 1796, d. in 1859, Secretary Massachusetts Board of Education. Sophia Amelia Peabody, b. 21 September, 1809, m. 30 June, 1842, Nathaniel Hawthorne, the author, b. in 1804, d. in 1864; she was the author of "Notes in England and Italy," written when her husband was consul at Liverpool; children, Una Hawthorne, Julian Hawthorne, who like his father has gained distinction as a novelist, and Rose Hawthorne, who m. George Parsons Lathrop, the novelist, essayist and poet. 5. Sarah, b. in 1650; m.—— How, of Ipswich. 6. Hepsibah, b. in 1652; m. ——Rea, of Salem Village. 7. Lydia, b. in 1654; m. Jacob Perley. 8. Mary, b. in 1656; m. John Death, of Framingham. 9. Ruth, b. 22 May, 1658; d. before 1698. 10. Damaris, b. 21 January, 1660; d. 19 December, 1660. 11. Samuel, b. 4 January, 1662; d. 13 September, 1677. 12. Jacob, b. 28 July, 1664; m. 12 January, 1686, Abigail Towne; d. 24 November, 1689. A descendant is: i. Nathaniel Peabody (Jacob, Jacob), of Atkinson, N. H., b. 18 February, 1741; colonel in the revolutionary army; member of the Continental Congress, from New Hampshire, 1779; d. in 1823. 13. Hannah, b. 28 May, 1668; d. before 1698. 14. Nathaniel, b. 29 July, 1669; m. Frances ——; d. in 1715.

3. ii. ABRAHAM, b. Exeter, England, 1622; m. Lydia Burbank.
4. iii. REGINALD, b. England in 1636; m. Elizabeth Dane.
5. iv. WILLIAM, b. England in 1633; m. Mary Jackson.
6. v. ISAAC, b. England in 1630; m. Mary Jackson, Hannah Douring, and Martha Hale
7. vi. JACOB, b. England in 1635; m. Martha Kinsman and Abigail Lord.
8. vii. SARAH, b. England in 1620; m. about 1640 William Storey, of Ipswich. He was b. in 1614, in Norwich, Norfolk County, England, embarked for America 8 April, 1637, at the age of twenty-three, and settled in Ipswich. He was a carpenter. In 1671 he erected a saw-mill on Chebacco River. Sarah (Foster) Story was living in 1668, aged forty-eight, as stated in her disposition in the Court Records, November term, 1668, in case of a complaint against Thomas Wells and others, of Ipswich, for reproaching Major-General Denison. In volume v, page 596, Essex County Deeds, it is recorded that William Story, senior, deeded 31 March, 1693, to his son Seth Storys, "all my housing, lands, fences, orchards, &c. belonging to my lands in Chebacco, in Ipswich, adjoining to Chebacco Falls River, having the latter on the E. and S. E., and land of Thos. Low on E. & N. E., and

land of Renold Foster [Reginald Foster2] on S. & S. W., and Ipswich common on W. & N. W." The Story estate in Chebacco was originally a large tract of land and extended "from the southern part of Belcher's lane to the river, bounded on the east by White's Hill, and land of Deacon Thomas Low, on the south-west and west by land of Reynold Foster, on the west and north-west by common land belonging to Ipswich ("Crowell's History of Essex," Essex, 1868, pp. 236-237). Referring to William Story, senior, it is also stated in "Crowell's History of Essex," page 237, that "William's son, Seth, was married and lived with him, and on condition of his maintaining him the rest of his days, he conveyed to him by deed of gift the farm, which he" occupied. "This deed is dated 13 April, 1693 [31 March, 1693]. This same year his grandson, Seth, was born, who lived nearly a hundred years on a part of the same farm, filled the office of elder in the same church in which his father had been deacon, and in which his brother Zechariah was deacon during the time that he was an elder." It is not believed that Andrew Story, who came from England and settled in Ipswich as early as 1636, was the father of William Story, as stated on page 236, or his brother as suggested on page 478, of the "History of Essex." He was probably no relative. Andrew Story served in the Ipswich quota in the Pequot war of 1637, and most of the many Storys in Essex are descended from him. William Story made a deed of gift, 3 April, 1693, to his son Samuel3, of all his upland and swamp at south side of Chebacco Falls River; also one-half his salt marsh he formerly bought of Henry Archer, "said son Samuel paying to my daughter Susanna Browne 40s, and to my granddaughter Ruth Walker 40s within 2 years after my decease," also "I doe give to my granddaughter, my sd. son's daughter Elizabeth a little iron Kettle & a pewter bowle and a broad box that useth to stand in ye bed Leantow." This deed was witnessed by Thomas Wade and Richard Walker, senior. William and Sarah (Foster) Story were not the ancestors "of Dr. Story, formerly of Boston, and of the late Judge Story," as has been somtimes stated. Mr. Justice Joseph Story of the United States Supreme Court, born 1779, died 1845, was the "son of Dr. Elisha and Mehitable (Pedrick) Story" ("Historical Collections Essex Institute," vol. xv, page 283) and his emigrant ancestor, Elisha Story, of England, was born about 1681, arrived in Boston, with his only sister Sarah Story, in 1700, was a member of the Old South Church in 1704, and died before 30 September, 1725, when his will was proved. William Story d. January, 1702-3. Administration on his estate was granted to his eldest son, Seth Story3, 20 January, 1702-3. William and Sarah (Foster) Story had seven children; Sarah, Seth, William, Abigail, Samuel, Hannah and Susanna. Children: Sarah, b. about 1641; m. 29 October, 1661, Richard Walker, who was living in 1693. Ch. i. Hannah, b. 10 September, 1663. ii. Sarah, b. 29 November, 1666. iii. Richard, b. 6 February, 1674. iv. Ruth, b. ——; named in before mentioned deed of gift, 3 April, 1693, from her grandfather, William Story. 2. Seth, b. in 1646; m. ——. Residence, Chebacco, Ipswich. He was Deacon of the church at Chebacco, otherwise known as the "Second Church in Ipswich." He d. 9 October, 1732, aged eighty-six. Ch: i. Zechariah, b. in 1684; m. ——. Residence, Chebacco, Ipswich. He also was Deacon of the "Second Church." He d. 16 February, 1774, aged ninety. 1. Jeremiah, b. ——. 2. Nathaniel, b. ——. 3. Isaac, b. ——. 4. Jesse, b. 1730; m. ——; d. 27 May, 1824, aged ninety-four. "In the House of Representatives [of Massachusetts]—'Resolved that there be paid out of the public Treasury of this State to Jesse Story of Chebacco in Ipswich (father of Jesse Story, Jr., under 21 years of age) the sum of £5. 15s. in full for the loss he sustained in arms, ammunition and wearing apparel by the death of his said son who was killed at the battle of Bunker's Hill, as will appear in the account and certificate.'– Records of General Court" (Crowell's Essex, Essex. 1868, p. 206). Ch. a. Jesse, b. after 17 June, 1754; killed, a minor, at Bunker Hill. b. Parker, b. ——. c. Ephraim, b. ——. 5. Lucy, b. ——. 6. Rachel, b. ——. 7. Deborah, b. ——. 8. Jerusha, b. ——. 9. Lois, b. ——. ii. Seth, b. in 1693; m. ——; Residence, Chebacco, Ipswich. He was also Deacon, and afterwards Elder of the "Second Church." He d. 11 August, 1786, aged ninety-three. Ch: d. John, b. ——. e. Ebenezer, b. ——, m. ——; and had i. Jonathan, b. ——. 3. William, b. in 1650; nineteen years old in 1669; living in 1693. 4. Abigail, b. in 1654; fifteen years old in 1669; d. before 1703. 5. Samuel, b. ——; m. Mary ——; named in before mentioned deed of gift, 3 April, 1693, from his father, William Story; he was of Norwich, Conn., before 1723; d. in 1726. i. Elizabeth, b. ——; named in before mentioned deed of gift, 3 April, 1693, from her grandfather, William Story. 6. Hannah, b. 19 August, 1662; named in will of Reginald Foster. 7. Susanna, b. —— probably identical with an unnamed daughter, b. 4 March, 1664; m. —— Browne; named in before mentioned deed of gift, 3 April, 1693, from her father, William Story.

3. ABRAHAM FOSTER (Reginald), b. Exeter, Devonshire, England, 1622; m. 1655, Lydia Burbank, dau. of ~~Caleb~~ and ~~Martha~~ of Rowley. He came from England with his father when sixteen years of age and located in Ipswich. He d. Jan. 25, 1711. Res. Ipswich, Mass. Caleb Burbank was of Rowley, in 1691, and had children, John and Lydia, and perhaps others; he is supposed to have been the son of John Burbank, who was made freeman in Rowley, 13 May, 1640, and who in his will 5 April, 1681, mentions wife Jimima, and children, John, Caleb and Lydia. Foster joined the church in full communion 12 April, 1674; and was seventy-six years of age, 26 September, 1698, when he gave his deposition concerning Rev. John Norton's land. He was a yeoman. There is no will or administration of his estate, as he distributed it among his family by deed, 21 Dec., 1698 (Essex Deeds, lib. 13, p. 206).

9. i. EPHRAIM, b. Oct. 9, 1657; m. Hannah Eames and Mary West.
10. ii. ABRAHAM, b. Oct. 16, 1659; m. Mary Robinson.
11. iii. JAMES, b. Jan. 12, 1662; d. before 1698; not mentioned in his father's distribution of real estate.
12. iv. BENJAMIN, b. in 1670; m. Ann ——.
13. v. EBENEZER, b. July 15, 1672; m. Mary Borman.
14. vi. MEHITABLE, b. Oct. 12, 1675; m. Dec. 31, 1700, Ebenezer Averill.
15. vii. CALEB, b. Nov. 9, 1677; m. Mary Sherwin.
16. viii. ISAAC, b. 1668; d. s. p. Feb. 13, 1717. 1717 made his will "upon going out upon his country's service." Upon a chart sent me by Moses Foster, cashier National Bank, Andover, I find the following: "Had one son, Ebenezer, who settled Rowley," but I think this must be wrong
17. ix. A little child, b. Dec. 27, 1668.
18. x. RUTH, b. ——; m. April 16, 1702, Jeremiah Perley, of Boxford, son of John and Mary (——) Perley, of Boxford; baptized 10 July, 1680. She d. ——. He m., second, 20 December, 1710, Alice Hazen, daughter of Thomas and Mary (Howlett) Hazen, b. 10 June, 1686, in Boxford, who d. 17 October, 1740; and third, 10 November, 1741, Sarah Hale, of Newbury, who d. before 1758. He d. before 26 June, 1758, when his will was proved. Jeremiah Perley had three children, but by which wife or wives is uncertain. Sarah m. Daniel Black, of Boxford. Hannah m. Paul Prichard, of Boxford. Abigail m., first, 15 March, 1750, William Spofford, son of Capt. John and Dorcas (Hopkinson) Spofford, who d. in the army; and second, Rufus Wheeler, of Maine.

4. REGINALD FOSTER (Reginald), b. England in 1636; m. Elizabeth Dane, dau. of John Jr. and niece of Rev. Francis. Reginald, of Chebacco, Ipswich, married Elizabeth, daughter John Dane. He died leaving an estate of about £350. His will was dated 11 July, 1704, and proved 10 Jan., 1708. Daniel Warner, in his Record, "mentions the above children and no more," saying his "aunt Foster had," etc—N. E. H. G. Register, vol. xv, p. 50.

He left a will, wherein he speaks of his extreme old age, "the craziness and weakness of his body." Inventory of his estate, £326 16s. 7d., 1s. 6d. were for rum, sugar, spice, gloves and cider, for the funeral, a custom quite prevalent in those days.

Elizabeth (Dane) Foster was a niece of Rev. Francis Dane, forty-eight years minister at Andover, Mass., who boldly denouncing the witchcraft delusion of 1692, was prominently connected with the trials at Salem when almost every member of his family was under arrest on suspicion, and a daughter and granddaughter were tried and condemned to death. See Bailey's Historical Sketches of Andover, Boston, 1880, pp. 199 and 423.

Reginald Foster, fourth child of Reginald and Judith (——) Foster, was born in England, as stated in the "Foster Papers" already mentioned. Residence, Chebacco, Ipswich. He married about 1652, Elizabeth Dane, daughter of John Dane, jr., of Ipswich, New England, author of "A Declaration of Remarkable Providences in the Course of my Life, By John Dane, of Ipswich," 1682, Boston, 1854; and granddaughter of John Dane, senior, of Berkhampstead and Bishops Stortford, Herts, England, and of Ipswich and Roxbury, New England as, mentioned on page 12, and to be related on later pages. Reginald Foster was the third signer of the following petition in favor of John Proctor and his wife, Elizabeth Procter, condemned to death for witchcraft, 5 August, 1692 at Salem; which, however, was of no avail, as John Procter was executed 19 August, 1692. His wife gave birth to a child about a fortnight after his execution. This indicates to what alone she owed her life. The petition, signed also by Isaac Foster, probably the eldest son of Reginald Foster[2], is taken from "Upham's History of Witchcraft," Boston, 1867, where, volume ii, pages 304 and 307, the following tributes to the signers will be found. "Notwithstanding the danger to which any one was exposed who expressed sympathy for convicted or accused persons, or doubt of their guilt, a large number had the manliness to try to save this worthy and honest citizen. John Wise, one of the ministers of Ipswich, heads the list of petitioners from that place. The document is in his handwriting. Thirty-one others joined in the act, many of them among the most respectable citizens of that town."

"I have given the names of the men who signed this paper, as copied from the original. It is due to their memory; and their descendants may well be gratified by the testimony thus borne to their courage and justice."

"The Humble and Sincere Declaration of us, Subscribers, Inhabitants in Ipswich, on the Behalf of our Neighbors, John Procter and his Wife, now in Trouble and under Suspicion of Witchcraft.

To the Honorable Court of Assistants Now Sitting in Boston:

Honored and Right Worshipful,—The aforesaid John Procter may have great reason to justify the Divine Sovereignty of God under these severe remarks of Providence upon his peace and honor, under a due reflection upon his life past; and so the best of us have reason to adore the great pity and indulgence of God's providence, that we are not exposed to the utmost shame that the Devil can invent, under the permissions of sovereignty, though not for that sin forenamed, yet for our many transgressions. For we do at present suppose, that it may be a method within the severer but just transactions of the infinite majesty of God, that he sometimes may permit Sathan to personate, dissemble, and thereby abuse innocents and such as do, in the fear of God, defy the Devil and all his works. The great rage he is permitted to attempt holy Job with; the abuse he does the famous Samuel in disquieting his silent dust, by shadowing his venerable person in answer to the charms of witchcraft; and other instances from good hands,—may be arguments. Besides the unsearchable footsteps of God's judgments, that are brought to light every morning, that astonish our weaker reasons; to teach us adoration, trembling, dependence, &c. But we must not trouble Your Honors by being tedious. Therefore, being smitten with the notice of what hath happened, we reckon it within the duties of our charity, that teacheth us to do as we would be done by, to offer thus much for the clearing of our neighbor's innocency; viz., that we never had the least knowledge of such a nefandous wickedness in our said neighbors, since they have been within our acquaintance. Neither do we remember any such thoughts in us concerning them, or any action by them or either of them, directly tending that way, no more than might be in the lives of any other persons of the clearest reputation as to any such evils. What God may have left them to, we cannot go into God's pavilion clothed with clouds of darkness round about; but, as to what we have ever seen or heard of them, upon our consciences we judge them innocent of the crime objected. His breeding hath been amongst us, and was of religious parents in our place, and, by reason of relations and properties within our town, hath had constant intercourse with us. We speak upon our personal acquaintance and observation; and so leave our neighbors, and this our testimony on their behalf, to the wise thoughts of Your Honors.

Jno. Wise.	Nathanill Perkins	Benjamin Marshall
William Story Senr.	Thoms Lovkine.	John Andrews Jur.
Reinalld Foster	William Cogswell.	William Butler.
Thos. Chote.	Thomas Varny.	William Andrews.
John Burnum Sr.	John Fellows.	John Andrews.
William Thomsonn.	William Cogswell Jur.	John Chote Ser.
Tho. Low Senr.	Jonathan Cogswell.	Joseph Procter.
Isaac Foster.	John Cogswell Ju.	Samuel Gidding
John Burnum junr.	John Cogswell.	Joseph Evleth
William Goodhew.	Thomas Andrews.	James White."
Isaac Perkins.	Joseph Andrews.	

Reginald Foster died 28 December, 1707, aged seventy-one years. He left an estate inventoried at £326. 19s., with debts amounting to £19. 16s. 7d., of which £4. 1s. 6d. was for rum, sugar, spice, gloves and cider for the funeral, a custom quite prevalent in those days.

His will dated 11 July, 1704, and proved 19 January, 1707-8, is as follows:

Will of Reginald Foster.

In the name of God. Amen. I, Reginald Foster of Chebacco, in Ipswich, in ye County of Essex in New England being att this time thro ye goodness of God in prfect understanding & memory tho very crazy & weak of Body by reason of old age & other infirmities we attend mee. In ye first place I committ my Imortall soul into ye hands of Almighty God who gave itt & In ye hopes of a blessed Resurrection to Life eternall thro Jesus Christ my blessed Redeemer. And my Body to ye earth from whence it was taken to be decently Buryed by my Executors hrafter mentioned. And wt worldly estate the Lord hath been plased to bless mee with I give & bequeath as hereafter followeth

I give & bequeath unto my beloved wife Elizabeth Foster the parlour yt I now enjoy & also wt use of ye cellar shee needeth & half ye Orchard also ye keeping of a cow & two sheep Winter & Summer & firewood fetched home & cutt fitt for ye fire so much as shee needeth for her use and a horse & one to ride before her to carry her to meeting and this Nathaniel Foster my son shall doe.

Item. I doe appoint my two sons Isaac & John Fosters to pay ye mother five & forty shillings apiece yearly In provision such as she needs & requires wc is four pounds ten shillings but If shee desires to remove to Billerica they shall carry wt was brought to Andover & yn pay yearly in Specie wt. was agreed upon—and my will is yt. all be done honestly according to truth.

Item. I Doe will unto my son Isaac Foster the house he hath lived in since he marryed Also nine acres of Land in my upper pasture joyneing to itt from Seth Stores Land & so Downward also my upland by ye widow Martins But I Reserve a convenient cart way thro it to fetch up hay or what may be needfull—Also I will my said son Isaac a third part of ye meadow about ye Ditch equally divided and Isaac his part shall Lye next Goodm Kinsmans Also a third part of my Low Meadow or Salt Marsh being divided from Deacon Goodhue meadow to Procters Creek and Isaac shall have his next Deacon Lows and his Brethren shall have a way through that to Theirs.

Item. I give to my son John Foster ye house he lives in & ye orchard—and ye upper pasture except what I shall otherwise dispose of and all that part of ye corn feild next Mr. Wades mill excepting one acre joyneing to ye high way next my house also I will to him one third part of both ye parcells of meadow or salt marsh above named excepting yt meadow given to Nathaniel betwixt ye Ditch & ye upland.

Item. I give to my son Nathaniel Foster my now dwelling house & half ye Orchard & Barn & yt part of ye corn feild next Seth Storeys & the Lower pasture all within ye stone wall & one acre of ye other feild next my house & two acres of my upper pasture to water his cattle and ye meadow betwixt ye Ditch & ye upland next ye widow Martinns & Nathaniel shall have a way to his corn feild thro his brother John's & his brother John thro his to carry wt is needfull Also John & Nathaniel shall equally divide ye meadow above ye Ditch between them & settle ye Bounds as they shall agree or as they may Chose Indifferent men to doe it for them & and so with ye Lower meadow & if John will take a part of my Barn away & he halfe ye cost to sett up a Lentoo he may doe it if he will.

Item. I give & bequeath to my eldest daughter Elizabeth ten pounds to be payd to her a Legacy out of my estate by my son Isaac above named within a year after my decease.

Item. I give to my Daughter Judith ten pounds for a legacy to her to be payd out of my Estate by my son John before named within a year after my Decease also I give further to my Daughter Judith my bed & bedsted boulster & 2 pillows curtains & coverlid belonging to it and also my table that stands in the parlour.

Item. I give & bequeath to my daughter Elenour eight pounds to be payd to her for her legacy out of my estate by my son Nathaniel Foster aforenamed within one year after my decease and my son Nathaniell Fosters hall have the other halfe of ye Orchard after my wife's decease or removal.

Ult. I constitute & appoint my loving son John Foster to be my Executor of this my last will & testament together with my beloved wife and my son Nathaniel Foster and for confirmation that this is my last will & testament and yt I hereby will & make void all former wills yt I have heretofore made. I ye aforesaid Reginold Foster have hrunto sett & affixed my hand & seal this eleventh day of July Anno Domini one thousand seven hundred & four In ye Third year of ye Reigne of Queen Anne

Reginold Foster (seal)

Signed and sealled in ye presence of us three witnessess

Joseph Eveleth
Nathaniel Rust junr.
Umphrey Clark

Will proved 19 Jan. 1707-8. Rec. B. 309, Page 278.
Essex, ss. Probate Office, 27 April, 1885.
A true copy of record.
Attest J. T. Mahoney Register

Daniel Warner in his "Record" mentions the following children and no more, saying his "aunt Foster had," etc.—(N. E. H. G. Register, vol. xv., p, 50.)

Reginald and Elizabeth (Dane) Foster had twelve children; Elizabeth, Isaac, Judith, Sarah, Mary, John, Rebecca, Naomi, Ruth, Eleanor, Hannah and Nathaniel. He d. Dec. 28, 1707. Res., Chebacco Parish in Ipswich, Mass.

19. i. REBECCA, b. Feb. 26, 1667; d. July 1, 1684.
20. ii. NAOMI, b. May 6, 1669; d. before 1707.
21. iii. RUTH, b. Dec. 17, 1671; d. Jan. 1, 1677.
22. iv. HANNAH, b. Oct. 5, 1675; d. before 1707.
23. v. ISAAC, b. in 1656; m. Abigail ——.
24. vi. JOHN, b. July 15, 1664; m. Mary ——.
25. vii. NATHANIEL, b. Sept. 19, 1678; m. Joanna Marshall.
26. viii. ELIZABETH, b. ——, 1653; m. Aug. 8, 1674, Simon Wood, of Ipswich.
27. ix. JUDITH, b. Jan. 20, 1659.
28. x. MARY, b. June 18, 1662; prob. d. before 1707.
29. xi. SARAH, b. ——; prob. d. before 1707.
30. xii. ELEANOR, b. June 14, 1673.

5. WILLIAM FOSTER (Reginald), b. England in 1633; m. May 15, 1661, Mary Jackson, b. Feb. 8, 1639; dau. of William and Joanna. William Jackson lived on Bradford Street, where, in 1643, a house lot, containing one acre and a half, was laid out to him not far from the meeting-house. He gave 6 December, 1680, to his daughter Mary Foster, out of his estate, two acres of meadow in the common field, one ox and a heifer, all of the value of £11, and "20s. of which is for her daughter's paines with me and my wife;" or, in other words, for the great care and comfort she had bestowed upon them in their old age, while abiding under their roof. William Jackson d. 1 May, 1688. William Foster was a yeoman, lived first in Ipswich, and afterwards removed to Rowley, where he was received as an inhabitant in 1661. He settled in that section of the town known as Rowley Village, which was afterwards incorporated under the name of Boxford. Before his removal he purchased of Joseph Jewett, of Rowley, for £11s. 13. 4d., a seventy-second part of the village lands in said town; but Mr. Jewett d. ——, before he gave him a deed of it, and he afterwards received one from the executors, bearing date of 30 May, 1661, witnessed by Thomas Dorman, Francis Peabody and Gershom Lambert. About the year 1666-7 the village lands were laid out by John Pickard and Ezekiel Northend. Of this land, William Foster, Francis Peabody, husband of his sister Mary Foster, Joseph Bixbie and Abraham Reddington, received eight hundred acres, bounded north by land of Messrs. Dorman, Cummins and Stiles, west by Andover line, south

by Wade's brook, etc., and east by various other lots. This grant consisted of upland, meadow and swamp. It is recorded in Essex Registry of Deeds, under date of 27 February, 1706-7, that he gave his son Samuel Foster one half of his right in this land, describing the same bounds and parties to whom it was laid out. He bought, 3 April, 1695, with his sons William and Jonathan, and John Kimball, all of Boxford three hundred acres of land of Robert and Bethiah Eames, "lying between Five Mile Pond and Moses Tyler's house, on both sides of Ipswich road." By deed, bearing date 25 August, 1710, he gave to his "son David, of Haverhill, all that right which falleth to us in lands, orchards, &c., which our Hon'd Father Wm. Jackson, formerly of Rowley, dec'd did give to his son John Jackson and John Jackson's son John, William Jackson's grandson, and in case his grandson John died childless, then . . . the estate mentioned in said deed . . . to return to our father's three daughters or their children. William Jackson's grandson John dying childless, said lands are divided among said daughters; viz., Elizabeth How (of witchcraft fame). Eizabeth (Jackson) How, wife of James How Jr., grandson of John Dane senior, was executed 19 July, 1692, in Salem, for witchcraft. John Dane senior was the grandfather of Elizabeth (Dane) Foster, wife of Reginald Foster (Reginald), Mary Foster my wife, and Deborah Trumbull; which land in my right (Mr. Jackson's deed bearing date in Rowley 6 December, 1680,) I give to my son David. Mr. Foster was one of the leading men in the town of Rowley, holding many offices of trust, and frequently serving on committees in matters of importance, with great acceptance. In 1675, he, with Joseph Peabody and John Kimball, were appointed collectors of taxes. In 1677 and 1680 John Peabody and he were appointed on the part of the village to enforce the strict observance of the Sabbath, "and to have the special inspection of those families nearest their house on either side of them," according to the provisions of a law of the General Court, passed 23 May, 1677. Up to the year 1685, Rowley Village had been subject to the control and government of the town proper, which was contrary to the expectations of the settlers when the Village lands were allotted them, who considered themselves "free from any engagement to the town of Rowley else we had not purchased it." According to the records, the Village, in 1673, was composed of but sixteen families, living nine miles distant from the town, and near to the bounds of Topsfield. In 1685 they had increased to forty families, and the lands, containing about eighteen thousand acres, they thought "would comfortably setuate one hundred families;" and considering the distance from town, and the general difficulties under which they continually labored in their governmental affairs, and other matters owing to their remote situation, they conceived the importance of petitioning the General Court for leave to settle a minister, and grant them "township prevelig, that so wee might the more comfortably carry on so needfull a work, for the betor edication of our children that cannot gooe fouer mieles to meting" (to Topsfield). This petition was signed by "Abraham Reddington, Sen., Joseph Bixbee, Sen., Samuel Busbee, Sen., William Foster and John Peabody." It was dated "27: 3 mo. 1685." The petition was granted 5 June, 1685, "Provided it may be with the consent of the Selectmen of Rowley," and which finally resulted in the incorporation of the town of Boxford; for shortly after the above grant two committees were appointed, one on the part of Rowley Village, of which William Foster was a member, and the other on the part of Rowley, which met together 7 July, 1685, and agreed upon "a parting line betwixt the town of Rowley and the village," that all the common undivided village land except the ministers farm. shall belong to Rowley, and "that the inhabitants shall be free from all rates to the town, excepting 20s. in silver, to be paid Joseph Bixbee, Sen., John Peabody, William Foster, Samuel Symonds and Moses Tyler, yearly . . . while [or until] they have an orthodox minister settled in the village."

The following is a copy of a paper found among the Court files: "Theas few Liens may Sertify anney gentilmen whome it may Consern that the Town of Boxford have with the Consent of the Selectmen of Boxford chosen William Foster, Sener, to be thaier ordenary Keepper for this year '93 and doe desier that hee may have a Lisenc for the aboue said purpos this 13th of June 1693

as a test

(sd) John Pebody
Clark."

William Foster made his will 3 September, 1711, when seventy-eight years of age. as stated in the will. He d. 17 May, 1713, in Boxford. His will was proved 15 June, 1713. In his will he gave his five sons, Jonathan, William, Timothy, David and Samuel, all his salt marsh he had of his father Foster, lying in Ipswich, which was to be enjoyed by his wife Mary and son Joseph during her widowhood, his "son Samuel to keep son Joseph at his house to look out for him." He appointed his sons Jonathan and Samuel executors. The following extract from Essex Deeds, Book 43, page 279, under date of 11 February, 1723-4, enumerates his children and sons-in-law:

" . . . we Jonathan Foster, Timothy Foster and Samuel Foster of Boxford, William Foster of Andover, David Foster of Haverhill, Mary Kilburn [Mary Foster] and John Platts [who m. Judith Foster], Theophilus Rix and Hannah Rix his wife [Hannah Foster], of Wenham . . . for . . . the sum of thirty pounds . . . paid . . . by John Perkins of Andover . . . have sold . . . said John Perkins, his heirs, &c., a certain piece . . . of meadow lying in Andover and Salem, containing by estimation five acres . . . ."

William and Mary (Jackson) Foster had nine children: Mary, Judith, Jonathan, William, Timothy, Hannah, David, Samuel and Joseph.

History of Boxford, Mass., says: "William Foster, from Ipswich, settled in Rowley Village in 1661. The old house that stood some years ago on the site of the late residence of Mr. Dean Andrews, deceased, was undoubtedly his residence. The first town meetings were held in his house; and in it was also kept for several years after the incorporation of the town, a kind of tavern called in the language of those days, an ordinary. Mr. Foster was one of the principal men in the Village, as the numerous offices of trust of all kinds held by him fully prove." He d. May 17, 1713. Res., Boxford, Mass.

31. i. MARY, b. Nov. 16, 1662; m. Nov. 20, 1682, Samuel Kilburn, of Rowley.
32. ii. JUDITH, b. June 19, 1664; m. 13 April, 1693, John Platts. Five children: 1. Mary Platts. 2. James Platts. 3. John Platts. 4. Ebsaba Platts. 5. Jonathan Platts.
33. iii. HANNAH, b. Nov. 23, 1673; m. May 11, 1709-10, Theophilus Rix, of Wenham, who died July 5, 1726. She was his second wife. Two children: 1. Samuel Rix, b. April 7, 1711. 2. Hannah Rix, b. May 4, 1717.
34. iv. JONATHAN, b. 6 March, 1667-8; m. Abigail Kimball.
35. v. WILLIAM, b. 1670; m. Sarah Kimball and Margaret Gould.
36. vi. TIMOTHY, b. 1672; m. Mary Dorman and Ruth Andrews.
37. vii. DAVID, b. 9 May, 1679; m. Mary Black.
38. viii. SAMUEL, b. 20 February, 1681; m. Mary Macoon.
39. ix. JOSEPH, b. 168—; bap. May 21, 1682; living in 1711, but probably never m. See his father's will.

6. ISAAC FOSTER (Reginald), b. England 1630; m. May 5, 1658, Mary Jackson. She d. Nov. 27, 1677; m. 2d, Nov. 25, 1678, Hannah Downing, who d. Nov. 27, 1678; m. 3d, March 16, 1679, Martha Hale, who survived him. He lived in Ipswich, near Topsfield, at the east end of "Symond's Farm," the town line dividing the farm. He was sixty-two years old when he made his will; proved March 29, 1692. Isaac Foster had fourteen children; eleven by his first wife, and three by the second: Jonathan, Mehitable, Jacob, Benjamin, Elizabeth, Mary, Daniel, Martha, Ruth, Prudence, Hannah,—second wife—Hannah, Eleazer and Sarah.

He d. March, 1692. Res., Ipswich, Mass.

40. i. JONATHAN, b. 9 January, 1658-9; d. May 15, 1661; not mentioned in father's will.
41. ii. MEHITABLE, b. 19 September, 1660; d. February, 1660-1.
42. iii. JACOB, b. 9 February, 1662-3; m. Sarah Wood and Mary Edwards.
43. iv. BENJAMIN, b. June, 1665; m. ——— ———.
44. v. ELIZABETH, b. 20 April, 1667.
45. vi. MARY, b. 26 June, 1669; m. Richard Grant, 27 February, 1688.
46. vii. DANIEL, b. 14 November, 1670; m. Katherine Freese and Mary Dresser.
47. viii. MARTHA, b. 1 August, 1672; m. Thompson Wood, 8 December, 1691.
48. ix. RUTH, b. 20 February, 1673-4; m. ——— Groue.
49. x. PRUDENCE, b. 23 May, 1675; m. Joseph Borman, 17 February, 1696-7.
50. xi. HANNAH, b. 24 October, 1676; d. before 1681.
51. xii. ELEAZER, b. April, 1684; m. Eliza Fiske.
52. xiii. SARAH, b. 19 March, 1687.
53. xiv. HANNAH, b. February 16, 1681.

7. DEA. JACOB FOSTER (Reginald), b. England in 1635; m. Jan. 12, 1658, Martha Kinsman, dau. of Robert (r. of Ipswich), who d. Oct. 15, 1666; m. 2d, Feb. 26, 1667, Abigail Lord; d. June 4, 1729.

Jacob was a resident of Ipswich, in which place he died. He was deacon of the first church. He married, first, Martha Kinsman, who died. He married secondly, Abiagal, daughter of Robert and Mary (Wait) Lord. She survived him. The grave of Deacon Foster is marked by a stone rudely carved; the inscription is "Here lies Dec'n Jacob Foster, who died July ye 9th 1710, in ye 75 yr of his age." Deacon Foster lived in the first house built by his father Reginald. It stood on the south side of Ipswich river, near the stone bridge; and on a portion of what is now the Heard Estate. The house lots as they were granted from the bridge, were given as follows:—to John Proctor, House, built in 1635, yet stands; and is now owned by the venerable Capt. Samuel Baker. 2. Thomas Wells, probably a physician, as he had "phissic," books. In 1677 mention is made of "the house that Thomas Wells built." 3. Samuel Younglove. The house he doubtless built was taken down in 1862. 4. The Foster lot. An old "Foster House" remained on this lot till within the recollection of the present generation. Its last Foster occupant was an aged woman known as "Molly Foster." The house was called in Ipswich the old Foster house, as long as it stood. It was given by Reginald Foster at his death to Deacon Jacob, his son, and the Deacon lived on it. The deacon also owned another house which he sold to Abraham Perkins—son of John, and grandson of Elder John Perkins. For in the will of Hannah (Bernsley) Perkins, widow of Abraham, she bequeaths the house her husband bought of "Deacon Foster, dec'd," to the three of her grandsons. He d. July 7, 1710. Res., Ipswich, Mass.

54. i. JUDITH, b. 20 October, 1659; d. 27 January, 1659-60.
55. ii. JOHN, b. 1660; d. 1660.
56. iii. JACOB, b. 15 May, 1662; d. June, 1662.
57. iv. MARY, b. ——; d. 11 January, 1666-7.
58. v. SARAH, b. 3 August, 1665; m. John Caldwell. She d. July 11, 1721.
59. vi. ABRAHAM, b. 4 December, 1667; m. Abigail Parsons.
60. vii. JACOB, b. 25 March, 1670; m. Mary Caldwell, Martha Graves and Mary Willis.
61. viii. AMOS, b. 15 August, 1672; d. 12 October, 1672.
62. ix. ABIGAL, b. 3 July, 1674; d. before 1710.
63. x. NATHANIEL, b. 7 October, 1676; d. previous to 1710.
64. xi. SAMUEL, b. 10 September, 1678; d. previous to 1710.
65. xii. JOSEPH, b. 14 September, 1680; m. Elizabeth Goodwin, Mary Cressy and Sarah Brown.
66. xiii. JAMES, b. 12 November, 1682; m. Anna Cross.
67. xiv. MARY, b. 25 December, 1684; not mentioned in father's will; d. before 1710.

9. EPHRAIM FOSTER (Abraham, Reginald), b. Ipswich, Mass., October 9, 1657; m. ——, 1677, Hannah Eames, dau. of Robert, b. 1661, d. July 8, 1731; m. 2d, Jan. 8, 1732, Mary West, of Bradford, wid. of John West. He was a blacksmith.

"One of the prominent names in the early town history [of Andover, Mass.,] was Ephraim Foster. He was a grandson of Reginald Foster, a citizen of Ipswich of some consideration, and who is said by genealogists to have been descended from an ancient family of Forsters, mentioned by Walter Scott in his tales and ballads of Scottish border warfare. Ephraim Foster was a man conspicuous in the town matters of Andover, although not connected prominently with the military or the civil history. He seems, judging from the numerous documents in his handwriting, to have excelled as a scribe, and to have been versed in the art of punctuation, then little known to the majority of our town officials. His favorite point was the colon, with which his papers are plentifully besprinkled, without regard to the grammatical or rhetorical construction. This characteristic appears in the 'Proprietor's Records,' where his handwriting occurs. Some of the family estates were in the east part of North Andover, one of the ancient homesteads (that afterward occupied by J. M. Hubbard, Esq., and noted for the large and beautiful elm tree, still vigorous) was Ephraim's residence. He d. September 21, 1746. Res., Andover, Mass., in that part now North Andover.

Ephraim Foster seemed to put some faith in his townsman's prophecies. He testified that Wardell had made some predictions in regard to the birth of his (Foster's) children, that there would be five girls in the household before a son should be born. This had proved true. The witness had also often seen Wardell "tell fortins," and he observed that in doing so the fortune teller always "looked first into the hand of the person, and then cast his eyes down on the ground." This was proof of his being in league with Satan, though the connection is not obvious.

68. i. ROSE, b. May 9, 1678; d. unm. Feb. 25, 1693.

John Hawthorne, Jona Corwin, Assistants.

The examination and confession (September 8, 1692,) of Mary Osgood, wife of Capt. Osgood, of Andover, taken before John Hawthorne and Majesties' justices. She confesses, that about eleven years ago, when she was in a melancholy state and condition, she used to walk abroad in her orchard; and upon a certain time she saw the appearance of a cat at the end of the house, which yet she thought was a real cat. However, at that time, it diverted her from praying to God, and instead thereof she prayed to the devil, about which time she made covenant with the devil, who, as a black man, came to her and presented her a book, upon which she laid her finger, and that left a red spot; and that upon her sinning the devil told her he was her god and that she should serve and worship him; and she believes she consented to it. She says further, that about two years ago she was carried through the air in company with Deacon Frye's wife, Ebenezer Barker's wife and Goody Tyler, to Five Mile Pond, where she was baptized by the devil, who dipped her face in the water, made her renounce her former baptism, and told her she must be his, soul and body, forever, and that she must serve him, which she promised to do.

She says the renouncing her first baptism was after her dipping, and that she was transported back again through the air in company with the aforenamed persons, in the same manner as she went, and believes they were carried upon a pole.

Q. How many persons were upon the pole?

A. As I have said before; viz.: four persons and no more, but whom she had named above. She confesses she has afflicted three persons: John Sawdy, Martha Sprague and Rose Foster; and that she did it by pinching her bed clothes, and giving consent, the devil should do it in her shape, and that the devil could not do it without her consent. She confesses the afflicting persons in the court by the glance of the eye. She says, as she was coming down to Salem to be examined, she and the rest of the company with her stopped at Mr. Phillip's to refresh themselves up, and the afflicted persons, being behind them upon the road, came just as she was mounting again, and were then afflicted and cried out upon her, so that she was forced to stay until they were all passed, and said she only looked that way toward them.

Q. Do you know the devil can take the shape of an innocent person and afflict?

A. I believe he cannot.

Q. Who taught you this way of witchcraft?

A. Satan; and that he promised her abundance of satisfaction and quietness in her future state, but never performed anything, and that she has lived more miserably and more discontented since than ever before. She confesses further that she herself, in company with Goody Parker, Goody Tyler and Goody Dean, had a meeting at Moses Tyler's house last Monday night, to afflict, and that she and Goody Dean carried the shape of Mr. Dean, the minister, between them, to make persons believe that Mr. Dean was afflicted.

Q. What hindered you from accomplishing what you intended?

A. The Lord would not suffer it so to be; that the devil should afflict in an innocent person's shape.

Q. Have you been at any other witch meetings?

A. I know nothing thereof, as I shall answer in the presence of God and his people, but said that the black man stood before her and told her that what she had confessed was a lie; notwithstanding she said that what she had confessed was true, and thereto put her hand. Her husband, being present, was asked if he judged his wife to be any way discomposed. He answered that, having lived with her so long, he doth not judge her to be any way discomposed, but has cause to believe what she has said is true. When Mistress Osgood was first called, she afflicted Martha Sprague and Rose Foster by the glance of her eyes, and recovered them out of their fits by the touch of her hand. Mary (Foster) Lacey and Betty Johnson and Hannah Part saw Mistress Osgood afflicting Sprague and Foster. The said Hannah Post and Mary Lacey and Betty Johnson, Jun., and Rose Foster and Mary Richardson were afflicted by Mistress Osgood, in the time of their examination, and recovered by her touching of their hands.

'I,' underwritten, being appointed by authority to take this examination, do testify upon oath, taken in court, that this is a true copy of, the substance of it, to the best of my knowledge, January 5, 1692-3. The within Mary Osgood was examined before their majesty's justice of the peace in Salem.

[ATTEST.] John Higginson, Just. Pac."

69. ii. HANNAH, b. May 28, 1681; d. young.

70. iii. HANNAH, b. May 15, 1684; m. March 5, 1701, Timothy Stiles, of Boxford. He was son of Robert; was b. Boxford Oct. 1, 1678; with his wife admitted to the church June 27, 1703; was selectman in Boxford 1724-8-34-5. He d. Dec. 7, 1751. Ch: 1. Jacob, b. Feb. 6, 1702; m. Sarah Hartwell. 2. Hannah, b. April 12, 1704; m. Abial Barker, of Andover. 3. Keziah, b. March 30, 1707; m. Moses Walton, of Boston. 4. Ephraim, b. Dec. 27, 1708; m. Elizabeth Louksford. 5. Gideon, b Feb. 26, 1711; m. Sally Faulkner. 6. Mary, b. Feb. 11, 1713; m. Thomas Clark. 7. Ezra, born July 2, 1715; m. Mary Warren and Mrs. Sarah Johnson. 8. Jeremiah, b. Oct 5, 1722; d. Dec. 17, 1727. 9. David, b. July 1, 1724; d. April 13, 1725.

71. iv. JEMIMA, b. Feb. 25, 1686; m. Ezekiel Ladd; b. Feb. 14, 1686; res. Boxford. She d. s. p.

72. v. EPHRAIM, b. March 12, 1688; m. Abigail Poor.

73. vi. JOHN, b. March 26, 1690; m. Rebecca Rowland and Dorcas Hovey.

74. vii. GIDEON, b. May 13, 1692; d. June 25, 1707.

75. viii. DAVID, b. April 18, 1694; m. Elizabeth Abbott and Lydia Farnum and Judith Norton.

76. ix. MOSES, b. Sept. 27, 1696; m. Elizabeth Rogers and Mary Gray.

77. x. AARON, b. Apr. 21, 1698; m. Martha Smith.

78. xi. JOSHUA, b. March 13, 1702; m. Mary Barker and Mary Town.

79. xii. RUTH, b. March 9, 1704; m. May 11, 1722, Capt. Jacob Abbott, of Brookfield. She d. 1774, s. p.

10. ABRAHAM FOSTER (Abraham, Reginald), b. Ipswich, Mass., Oct. 16, 1659; m. Nov. 15, 1693, Mary Robinson, dau. of Robert, of Newberry. He was a soldier in the military service of the colony "and was wounded in the public service and is to receive £8 out of the public treasury 'for smart money.'" He d. May 23, 1741. Res. Ipswich and Topsfield, Mass.

80. i. ABRAHAM, b. June 12, 1696; m. Sarah Dunnell.

81. ii. NATHAN, b. May 17, 1700; m. Hannah Standish.

82. iii. DANIEL, b. April 13, 1705; m. Hannah Black and Elizabeth Davis.

12. BENJAMIN FOSTER (Abraham, Reginald), b. Ipswich, Mass., in 1670; m. Ann ——. After his death she resided in Billerica in 1739. Benjamin was born in Ipswich; removed to Topsfield, then to Boxford, finally to Lunenberg, where he died. He was a weaver. While of Boxford, he sold to Thomas Potter one half of one of the two rights granted to the heirs of Abraham Foster by his father, Renold, in Bush Hill and Turners 8ths, so that the one half of one I have sold depended from my grandfather Renold to my father Abraham and from him to me 29 May, 1727.—(Essex Deeds, v. –, p. 50.) The last two children were born in Boxford. Widow Ann Foster, Kezia and Isaac cautioned at Billerica 1739. He d. Sept. 12, 1735 in L. Res. Ipswich, Topsfield, Boxford and Lunenburg, Mass.

83. i. BENJAMIN, b. 25 Nov., 1700; bapt. 27 Nov. ———; m. Mrs. Sarah Low.

84. ii. AMOS, b. 28 April, 1702; bapt. 10 May; m. Elizabeth Kitteredge.

85. iii. DEBORAH, b. 7 May, 1704.

86. iv. KEZIA, b. 4 May, 1707; m. in L. Sept. 5, 1741, Jacob Corey, Jr., of Tewksbury.

87. v. GIDEON, b. 10 Oct. 1709; m. Lydia Goldwait and Deborah ——
88. vi. JEMIMA, b. 24-12 Feb. 1711-12; d. young. The above were born in Ipswich.
89. vii. ISAAC, b. 3 Dec., 1722; bapt. Dec. 1722; m. Mary Rice.
90. viii. JEMIMA, bapt. Dec. 1725; m. July 28, 1738, Jonathan Fisk, Jr.; res. Lunenburg, Mass. He was b. Watertown, Oct. 29, 1753; admr of his estate granted to Jemima, his widow; she m. 2d, in 1754, —— Cragan. Ch: 1. Jemima, b. Feb. 8, 1739. 2. Benjamin, b. Nov. 4, 1744.

13. EBENEZER FOSTER (Abraham, Reginald), b. Ipswich, Mass., July 15, 1672; m. June 23, 1705, Mary Borman, who d. June 19. 1716. Ebenezer was born in Ipswich, here moved to Rowley, where he married. He was a husbandman. His will, dated 5 June, 1717, was proved 14 April, 1718. Caleb and Isaac, his brothers, were executors. He d. Feb. 25, 1718. Res., Rowley, Mass.

91. i. JEMIMA, b. and bapt. 6, 1706-7; d. 12 March, 1706-7.
92. ii. RUTH, b. 23 Jan. 1709-10; bapt. 5 Feb., 1709-10; m. before May 3, 1736, Jacob Wildes, of Arundel, Me., and Kennebunk Port. Their ch. were: 1. Jacob. 2. John. 3. Ephraim. 4. Mary; m. Eben Simmons. 5. Ruth; m. Jacob Rhodes. 6. Dorothy; m. Gideon Merrill.
93. iii. MOSES, b. 5 Oct., 1713; m. Hannah Andrews.

15. CALEB FOSTER (Abraham, Reginald), b. Ipswich, Mass., Nov. 9, 1677; m. June 2, 1702, Mary Sherwin, of Ipswich. Res., Ipswich. In 1700 he had a seat assigned to him "behind ye pupit," in the meeting house then recently built. He d. Jan. 25, 1766. Res., Ipswich, Mass.

94. i. LYDIA, b. 14 May, 1703; bapt. 16 May; pub. April 21, 1724, Nathan Dresser.
95. ii. JONATHAN, of Boxford, b. 30 Nov., 1704; bapt. 3 Dec.; m. Jemima Cummings and Dorcas Porter.
96. iii. SARAH, b. 3 (Sept.), 1706; bapt. 8 Sept.; d. young.
97. iv. CALEB, b. 5 June, 1708; m. Priscilla Buxton.
98. v. STEPHEN, b. 24 April, 1710; bapt. 30 April; m. Rebecca Peabody.
99. vi. MARY, bapt. 30 Dec., 1711; d. unm. Dec. 19, 1780.
100. vii. SARAH, bapt. 11 Sept., 1715; admitted to Topsfield Ch. June 27, 1736.
101. viii. PHILEMON, b. 2 June, 1713; bapt. 6 June; d. 1737.
102. ix. JOHN, bapt. 10 Nov., 1717; d. previous to 1766.

In deeding in 1766, his property to his sons, as he does not mention Philemon or John, it is to be presumed that they died before that date.

23. CORP. ISAAC FOSTER (Reginald, Reginald), b. Ipswich, Mass., in 1656; m. Nov. 25, 1678, Abigail ——. She d. Oct. 4, 1749. He was styled "corporal." Administration on his estate was granted to son Jonathan, 15 Dec., 1741, (Essex Probate Records, Vol. xxiii, p. 41. Estate, £124.15). Jonathan was appointed administrator of the estate of his mother, Abigail, 30 Oct., 1749 (Essex Probate Record, Vol. xxix, p. 28.) The signatures and other evidence show that these two Jonathan's are the same person, and consequently son of Isaac and Abigail. As I intend to trace the son Jacob, it seems necessary that I should give my authority for considering him a son of Isaac, as there appears to be no record of his birth extant. Among the early series of Middlesex wills are preserved two letters, both addressed to the Hon. Samuel Danforth Esq.,—the first dated 7 March, 1757, and signed Jonathan Foster, in which he speaks of his brother Jacob of Holliston; the second dated 18 April, 1757, is signed by Jacob Foster of Holliston, and mentions his brother Jonathan of Ipswich. The latter is indorsed "Capt. Jacob Foster's Letter," etc. Jonathan's signature agrees with those on the two letters of administration mentioned above.

[I have two old account books, containing the personal and family accounts of Isaac Foster, last mentioned, and of his son Jonathan Foster, and of Jonathan's son Jacob Foster, who was my great-grandfather. These accounts are consecutive and cover a period from 1705 to 1790, and they contain many entries, showing relationships between persons therein named, and giving interesting glimpses of conditions of life during three generations. In the back part of the older book are the original family records of the families of Isaac, and his son Jonathan, and Jonathan's son Jacob, beginning with the record of a marriage November 25, 1678, and giving dates of births, marriages and deaths for these three generations. Some of the oldest entries are quite faded, but most of the records are very plain and legible. These enable us to make important corrections of errors into which Judge Savage was easily led by the contemporaneous existence of so many "Abrahams," "Isaacs," and "Jacobs" in the different families. I have not time now to consider these matters at length, nor to review these old books and records; but what follows is based upon the old records of the three generations mentioned. Some facts relating to Jonathan Foster are from Dr. Edward Jacob Forster's compilation above referred to. Other authorities have also been consulted. It is my intention, when I can find time to devote to the work, to publish a review of and extracts from these old accounts and family records, for the benefit of those who may be interested in them.

Akron, Ohio, February 6, 1899. George M. Wright.]

He d. April 11, 1741. Res., Ipswich, Mass.

103. i. HANNAH, b. 16 Feb., 1681.
104. ii. JONATHAN, b. May 2, 1705; m. Elizabeth Storey.
105. iii. ISAAC, b. ——; m. —— ——, and Rachel ——.
106. iv. JACOB, b. ——, 1703; m. Mary Suffield.
107. v. ABIGAIL.
108. vi. FREEBORN, bapt. 28 Jan., 1727-8; m. Isaac Balch. She d. April 22, 1749.

24. SERGT. JOHN FOSTER (Reginald, Reginald), b. Ipswich, Mass., July 15, 1664; m. Mary ——. He d. Dec. 9, 1736. Res., Chebacco Village, Mass.

109. i. JEREMIAH, b. 1691; m. Dorothy Rust.
110. ii. MOSES, b. 1697; m. Mary Rust, Mary Blodgett and Ann Varney.
111. iii. JOHN, b. ——; m. Mehitable Burnham.
112. iv. JOSHUA, d. unm.; a mariner.
113. v. MARTHA, m. Jonathan Burnham.
114. vi. ELIZABETH, m. Daniel Smith.

25. NATHANIEL FOSTER (Reginald, Reginald), b. Ipswich, Mass., Sept. 19, 1678; m. April 19, 1704, Joanna Marshall. His will is dated Dec. 9, 1756, and was proved June 21, 1762. He d. Dec., 1756. Res., Chebacco Parish, Mass.

115. i. DINAH, b. 17—; d. 23 July, 1781, aged about 78 years.
116. ii. SARAH, b. 18 March, 1706; m. William Holmes.
117. iii. HANNAH, b. 27 April, 1710; d. 5 Aug., 1794, unm.
118. iv. MARY, b. 18 Aug., 1716; d. 24 Sept., 1733, unm.
119. v. JEMIMA, b. 29 May, 1721; d. 22 July, 1797.
120. vi. NATHANIEL, b. in 17—; m. —— Low.

34. JONATHAN FOSTER (William, Reginald), b. Boxford, Mass., Mar. 6, 1667; m. Dec. 14, 1693, Abigail Kimball (sister of William's wife), dau. of John and Sarah, b. April 29, 1667. No will or settlement of estate on record. They were admitted to the church Sept. 21, 1703. He d. May 21, 1730. Res., Boxford, Mass.

121. i. JONATHAN, b. Sept. 15, 1693; m. Hannah Peabody.
122. ii. ABIGAIL, b. Nov. 22, 1697; m. July 13, 1727, Jacob Tyler, of Andover.
123. iii. ZEBADIAH, b. Sept. 28, 1702; m. Margaret Tyler.

35. WILLIAM FOSTER (William, Reginald), b. Rowley Village, Mass., afterward Boxford, 1670; m. July 6, 169—, Sarah Kimball, dau. of John and Sarah; b. Sept. 19, 1669; d. Nov. 6, 1729; m. 2d, Nov. 13, 1744, Margaret Gould. Removed to Andover 1697-8, and died there in his 86th year. He was a weaver, and in his will he gave to his son Asa his "Weaver's loom." He was at first a member of the north Parish in Andover, but in 1711 he was one of the thirty-five who was dismissed. An account of his real estate transactions can be found in "One Line of the Descendants of William Foster," by Pertey Derby, p. 20. Sept. 3, 1697, while of Boxford he bought of William and Eleanor Chandler, of Andover, their homestead of sixty acres, consisting of house, barn, orchard, upland and swamp, lying in Andover; and it must have been soon after this date that he removed there, for we find Nov. 21, 1699, that William Foster, of Andover, weaver, bought of John Russ one half of his upper meadow, and afterward, June 5, 1711, he bought of Stephen Osgood, Andover and Hooker Osgood, of Lancaster, all their right and proprietorship in Andover, derived by heirship, from their father, Stephen Osgood, of Ando-

ver. April 3, 1695, before his removal, he with his father, William, brother Jonathan and John Kimball, all of Boxford, bought of Robert and Bethiah Eames, 300 acres of land "between Five Mile Pond and Moses Tylers' house, on both sides of Ipswich road." The following item appears in the registry of deeds for Essex county, book 43, p. 279: ". . . we Jonathan Foster, Timothy Foster and Samuel Foster of Boxford, William Foster of Andover, David Foster of Haverhill, Mary Kilburn and Platts" (who married Judith, daughter of William Sen. of Boxford), "Theophilus Rix and Hannah Rix, his wife, of Wenham . . . for . . . the sum of thirty pounds . . . paid . . . by John Perkins of Andover . . . have sold . . . said John Perkins his hus., etc., a certain piece . . . of meadow lying in Andover and Salem, containing by estimation five acres . . . Feb. 11, 1732-4. It will be seen by the family record that the foregoing enumerates the children and sons-in-law of said William Sen., of Boxford. Feb. 1, 1714-15, 'William Foster, Andover, weaver,' bought of John Lovejoy 50 acres of upland in Andover, bounded by land of John Frye and meadow of Stephen Barnard, and also by Pond meadow. Also one right in common land Jan. 20, 1715-16, he buys of Hephsibah Frye "30 acres, a part of the great division which said Frye's grandfather John Frie, gave to her father, Benjamin Frie, dec'd." In this deed he is styled "weaver," his identity being preserved from the fact of a bequest made to his son Asa, of his "weaver's loom" before referred to. Jan. 15, 1717-18, he and Christopher and Ebenezer Lovejoy bought of James Frye of Andover, eight acres of land on the west side of Shawshine river. Dec. 23, 1729, he sells to his son John Foster several parcels of land, bounded on John Dane, Marbles meadows and Crane meadow dam. Dec. 20, 1731, he sold to Moses Foster, carpenter, a ten rods right in Capt. Stephens' dam at Deer meadow; Robert Walker and Asa Foster, witnesses. Sept. 1, 1744. he gives to his son Asa five tracts of land, including the homestead and afterward, June 3, 1746, he gave to him thirty-five acres, bounded on Pond meadow dam, and the parsonage land. Mr. Foster settled in South Andover, and was at first a member of the church at the North Parish, and was one of the thirty-five members who were subsequently dismissed to form and establish the South church in 1711. He left a will, made 9 February, 1754, and proved 8 September, 1755, wherein he mentions his wife Margaret, daughters Sarah (Abbot), Mary (Abbot), Hannah (Lovejoy), granddaughter Lydia (Blunt), son Asa, to whom he gives £13 6s. 8d., his "weaver's loom," a piece of land near Billerica line, and all his right at Wood hill; son John, to whom he gives all the remaining land he bought of Hephsibah Frye, and nine acres in Marble's meadow; grandson Daniel, son of son Asa, to whom he gives his "Great Bible."He d. Aug. 29, 1755. Res., Andover, Mass.

124. i. SARAH, b. 20 April, 1693, in Boxford; bapt. 15 July, 1693, in Topsfield; m. Nehemiah Abbott, Nov. 2, 1714. Had ch: Bigsly Abbott. Abigail Abbott; m. 1699. Amos Lawrence, Groton. Had ch: Samuel Lawrence, b. in Groton, 1754; m. Susannah Parker. Had ch: Abbot Lawrence, b. 1792; m. Katherine Bigelow. Amos Lawrence, b. 1786; m. Sarah Richards. Luther Lawrence, b. 1778; m. Lucy Bigelow. William Lawrence, b. 1783; m. Lucy Bigelow. Samuel Lawrence, b. 1801; m. Alis Trumbull. He d. Aug. 29. 1755. Res., Andover, Mass.

125. ii. MARY, b. 2 Jan., 1698, in Boxford; m. Dec. 9, 1717, Timothy Abbot. Timothy was son of Timothy, and gr.-son of George, the immigrant. Timothy Jr. had a son Asa, who m. Elizabeth Abbot; their son was Caleb, who m. Sarah Ames; he was for seven years a soldier in the Revolutionary war; was at Lexington, Bunker Hill, Trenton, Princeton, Saratoga. Their dau. Clarissa m. Rev. Ebenezer Poor; their son Edward P. m. Marietta Allen; res., Lawrence, Mass ; their son is Abbot A. Clarissa is now living in her 94th year and is a Daughter of the American Revolution.

126. iii. JOHN, b. 27 Sept., 1701, in Andover; m. Nancy Osgood.

127. iv. HANNAH, m. June 25, 1722, John Lovejoy, son of Ebenezer.

128. v. LYDIA, b. May 6, 1708; m. Feb. 14, 1728, David Blunt, a son of William and Sarah Blunt, b. Nov. 18, 1699. Two ch: 1. David Blunt, b. March 9, 1729. 2. Lydia, b. April 6, 1731.

129. vi. ASA, b. 16 June, 1710; m. Elizabeth Abbott and Lucy Rogers.

36. TIMOTHY FOSTER (William, Reginald), b. Boxford, Mass., in 1672. He married 1st, Mary, daughter of Ephraim and Martha Dorman. He received

from his father-in-law 4 Sept., 1718, 100 acres of land for the benefit of his children by Mary, she being then deceased; said land being formerly in Coxhall, now Swanville, Me. He was selectmen and postmaster. He married 2d, before 1722, Rutn Andrews. He d. 1751. Res., Boxford, Mass. His children were:

130. i. JEREMIAH, b. 4 May, 1701; m. Abigail Wood and Mrs. Bridget Pemberton.
131. ii. DAVID, b. 17 Aug.; bapt. 20, 1704; m. Mrs. Hannah Senious.
132. iii. AMOS, bapt. 1 Feb., 1713; m. Mary Dorman.
133. iv. MARY, b. 21 June, 1718; d. young.
134. v. REBECCA, bapt. June, 1710; m. Samuel Gould.
135. vi. MARY, b. June, 1720.

37. DAVID FOSTER (William, Reginald), b. May 9, 1679; m. in Haverhill, Mary Black. He removed from Haverhill after the birth of his second child, where he was living in 1775. He married there Mary Black. There is no will or settlement of his estate on record. He was a joiner and a yeoman. Res. Haverhill, Mass. His children were:

136. i. ABIAL, b. 2 May, 1702; m. Ruth Clement and Hannah Russell.
137. ii. PHINEAS, b. 5 June, 1704.
138. iii. SIMON, b. 17 June, 1707; m. — — — —.
139. iv. HANNAH, b. 29 Oct., 1709.
140. v. LYDIA, b. 28 Feb., 1712.
141. vi. GRACE, b. 20 May, 1714.
142. vii. DORCAS, b. 1 April, 1717.

38. SAMUEL FOSTER (William, Reginald), b. Boxford, Mass., Feb. 20, 1681; m. Sept. 2, 1703, Mary Macoon, of Cambridge. She d. Oct. 6, 1740. He d. Aug. 30, 1747. Res., Boxford, Mass.

143. i. SAMUEL, bapt. 27 Jan., 1705; d. young.
144. ii. THOMAS, bapt. 23 May, 1708; m. Alice Pearly.
145. iii. MERCY, b. 23 Oct.; bapt. 30 Oct., 1711; m. 11 Jan., 1738, Elisha Towne, of Topsfield.
146. iv. WILLIAM, b. 22 July; bapt. 2 Aug., 1711; m. ——— ——— and Mary Clarke.
147. v. MARY, b. 5 May; bapt. 5 July, 1719.
148. vi. SAMUEL, bapt. Jan. 1721-2; d. 15 Feb.,1748.

42. JACOB FOSTER (Isaac, Reginald), b. Ipswich, Mass., Feb. 9, 1662; m. Sept. 12, 1688, Sarah Wood, dau. of Isaiah, who d. Sept. 27, 1697; m. 2d, May 20. 1700. Mary Edwards. Jacob was born in Ipswich; removed to Topsfield as early as 1686, where all of his children were baptized. In 1718 he removed to Lebanon, Conn. He married, 1st, Sarah, daughter Isaiah Wood; 2d, Mary Edwards. Jacob and his wife, Mary, were dismissed from the church at Topsfield 29 Jan., 1718, and admitted to the church at Lebanon 6 July, 1718. An administrator was appointed for his estate in 1745. It is said he had a son, Israel, according to probate records. He d. in 1745. Res. Lebanon, Conn.

149. i. BENJAMIN, bapt. 6 Oct., 1689; m. Sarah Woodward.
150. ii. MARY, b. 13 May; bapt. 17 May, 1691.
151. iii. ISAAC, b. 13 Mar.; bapt. 16 Mar., 1701; d. 27, Dec. 1703.
152. iv. JOHN, b. 11 Sept.; bapt. 13 Sept., 1702; m. Hannah Thorp.
153. v. EZEKIEL, bapt. 31 Dec., 1704; d. Lebanon, 20 Oct., 1727.
154. vi. MARTHA, bapt. 24 ——, 1709; d. before 1745; not mentioned in probate.
155. vii. DAVID, bapt. 29 April, 1711; m. Althea Cogswell.
156. viii. JONATHAN, b. 3 June, 1714. The same as Martha.
157. ix. ISRAEL, b. ——; m. at Lebanon, Conn., Apr. 10, 1733, Ruth Bridges.

43. BENJAMIN FOSTER (Isaac, Reginald), b. Ipswich, Mass., June, 1665; m. — — ——. He died in 1700, and the administration of his estate was granted to his brother Daniel Nov. 20, 1700.

He died in 1700. Res., Ipswich, Mass.

158. i. BENJAMIN, b. about 1699; m. ——— ———.

46. DANIEL FOSTER (Isaac, Reginald), b. Ipswich, Mass., Nov. 14, 1670; m. Mar., 1693, Katherine Freese, of Topsfield, who d. Mar. 3, 1694; m. 2d, Dec. 4,

1696, Mary Dresser, b. 1670; d. Lebanon, Conn., Jan. 24. Daniel was born in Ipswich; resided in Topsfield, where his children were born, until 1718, when he removed to Lebanon, Conn., where, in company with his brother, Jacob, and his wife, Mary, were admitted to the church there at the same time. His will, dated 4 May, 1746, was proved 19 Nov., 1753. [Windham Probate Records, Vol. 4, page 396.] He married, 1st, Katharine Freese, of Topsfield; 2d, Mary, daughter of Samuel and Mary Seaver Dresser, of Rowley. He d. Nov., 1753. Res., Lebanon, Conn.

159. i. KATHARINE, b. 21 Aug.; bapt. 23 Aug., 1696.
160. ii. MARY, b. 24 Feb., 1697; d. 23 Jan., 1698-9.
161. iii. HEPSIBAH, b. 7 May, 1700.
162. iv. MEHITABLE, b. 16 Oct.; bapt. 19 Oct., 1701; m. Daniel Dennison at Lebanon, Conn., Apr. 7, 1722.
163. v. PHINEAS, b. 19 July; bapt. 25 July, 1703; m. Lydia Hills.
164. vi. HANNAH, b. 29 Apr.; bapt. 6 May, 1705; d. young.
165. vii. JEREMIAH, b. 16 June, 1707; bapt. 15 Jan., 1707-8; m. Mary Skinner.
166. viii. HANNAH, bapt. 5 Jan., 1709; unm.; d. 1746.
167. ix. ASA, b. (15, 11, 1710, 15 Jan., 1710-11); bapt. 21 Jan. 1710-11; m. Hannah White.
168. x. CATHERINE, b. Lebanon, Conn.; m. there Daniel Calkins. Res., Lebanon, Conn.

51. ELEAZER FOSTER (Isaac, Reginald), b. Ipswich, Mass., Apr., 1684; m. Dec. 6, 1703, Elizabeth Fiske; b. Oct. 9, 1679; d. Feb. 19, 1758. He was a weaver. He d. Nov. 15, 1771. Res., Ipswich, Mass.

169. i. ELIZABETH, b. Feb. 17, 1705.
170. ii. HABIJAH, bapt. Jan., 1707; m. Mary Knowlton.
171. iii. JOHN, b. May 20, 1714; m. —— ——.

59. ABRAHAM FOSTER (Jacob, Reginald), b. Ipswich, Mass., Dec. 4, 1671; m. July 2, 1699, Abigail Parsons; d. Oct. 8, 1732. Administration on his estate was granted his widow, 27 Jan., 1720-1. He was a carpenter. From one —— I have date of his will, Dec. 23, 1735. He d. Dec. 25, 1720. Res., Ipswich, Mass.

172. i. JEREMIAH, b. 1700; m. Mrs. Rebecca Metcalf.
173. ii. ABRAHAM, b. 5 July; d. 20 May, 1702.
174. iii. NATHANIEL, b. 11 (2) Feb., 1702; d. young.
175. iv. ABRAHAM, b. 5 (16) June, 1716; m. Elizabeth Davis.
176. v. NATHANIEL, b. 9 Aug., 1719; m. Sarah Deland.
177. vi. JUDITH, b. 15 Mar., 1713; d. unm. before 1735.
178. vii. ABIGAIL, m. Daniel Safford; 2 ch: Daniel and Abraham.
179. viii. MARY, b. 15 May, 1715.
180. ix. SARAH, m. John Rust, and 2d, Jacob Parsons. Ch. Rust. 1. John, b. 22 May, 1732. 2. Sarah, b. 25 Sept. 1735. 3. Henry, b. 23 Aug. 1737. 4. Mary, b. 16 July, 1738. 5. Abigail, b. 6 Nov. 1742. 6. Daniel, b. 24 June, 1747.

60. JACOB FOSTER (Jacob, Reginald), b. Ipswich, Mass. Mar. 25, 1670. He was a blacksmith. He was thrice married, first to Mary, dau. of John and Sarah Caldwell, 5 March, 1697. She was born 26 Feb. 1672; d. 2 April, 1709; secondly to Martha Graves to whom he was published 10 Dec. 1709; thirdly, to Mary Willis to whom he was published 14 Oct. 1742. He d. Mar. 6, 1758. Res. Ipswich, Mass.

181. i. JACOB, b. 9 May, 1697; d. young.
182. ii. WILLIAM, b. 11 May, 1699; m. Elizabeth Clarke.
183. iii. MARY, b. 19 March, 1700; m. Jacob Loudon.
184. iv. ABIGAIL, b. 27 Sept., 1703; m. William Holland.
185. v. ISRAEL, b. 3 March, 1706-7; not mentioned in father's will.
186. vi. NATHANIEL, b. 14 Dec., 1712; m. Elizabeth Leatherland.
187. vii. ANNE, b. April 1715; m. Robert Mitchel. Res. Newbury.
188. viii. MARTHA, m. Richard Harris. In company with Jeremiah Foster of Ipswich in 1743, Harris purchased of Benjamin Morse a farm of one hundred and twenty acres in Harvard. Harris took the west sixty acres with the buildings. He was a weaver by trade and went to Harvard to keep his sons from being sailors. He died in 1776 and his heirs disposed of his estate near the close of the century to Oliver Hill. In 1752 he was a member of the board of assessors. Res. Harvard, Mass. Ch: 1. John, b. Oct. 13, 1745. 2. Rebecca, Mar. 25, 1748.

3. Anna, b. Apr. 23, 1750. 4. Nathaniel, b. Apr. 4, 1752. 5. William, b Oct. 8, 1754. 6. Richard Jr., was deacon of the church; Corporal in Revolutionary war in Capt. Asa Houghton's company; town clerk 1780-5; selectman 1778-9-80-1-3-4-5-94-7. He married Lydia Atherton. One of his sons was John, b. Oct. 13, 1769. Graduated at Harvard College, A. M. 1791. He studied law with Hon. Steven Strong of Amherst, N. H., and Hon. Timothy Bigelow of Groton. Admitted to the bar at Hopkinton, N. H., 1794; Judge of Probate for Hillsborough Co. 1812-1823; of Merrimack Co. 1823-1843; trustee of Dartmouth College; appointed associate justice of the Supreme Court of N. H. in 1846, when he declined the office; but accepted it again when appointed, and served 1823-33 to Apr. 23, 1845 in Hopkinton N. H.; m. Sept. 1, 1799, Mary Poor; had a son George and three daus. He was a mason and attained the highest honors in that body.

65. JOSEPH FOSTER (Jacob, Reginald), b. Ipswich, Mass. Sept 14, 1680. He was a cordwainer. He attended the South Meeting House owning one half of a gallery pew. His estate was valued at £215 11 7. He married first Elizabeth Goodwin, 23 Jan., 1704; secondly, Aug. 13, 1712, Mary Cressy of Salem to whom he was published 20 July, 1712; thirdly, Sarah, dau. of Nicholas and Mary (Linforth) Brown to whom he was published 30 (11) 1714. She was born in Haverhill, 3 March, 1685-6; d. May, 1761. He d. Feb. 22, 1755. Res. Ipswich, Mass.

189. i. ELIZA, b. 23 (12), 1706; not mentioned in father's will.
190. ii. SAMUEL, b. 16 April, 1709; d. 5 Sept., 1730.
191. iii. JOSEPH, b. 14 Feb., 1714; m. Hannah Trask.
192. iv. JAMES, b. 4 March, 1716; m. Sarah Hart.
193. v. NATHAN, b. 19 Feb., 1717-8; m. Mary Hart.
194. vi. SARAH, bapt. 13 Jan., 1722; d. 24 March, 1722.
195. vii. ISAAC, b. 21 Aug., 1720; m. Sarah Brown.
196. viii. SARAH, bapt. 23 Feb., 1732; d. 30 April, 1739.
197. ix. JACOB, b. and bapt. 27 March, 1726; m. Sarah Kimball.
198. x. EBENEZER, bapt. 6 Nov., 1720; not mentioned in father's will.
199. xi. ABRAHAM, bapt. 27 Oct., 1728; m. Susannah Sumner.

66. JAMES FOSTER (Jacob, Reginald), b. Ipswich, Mass., Nov. 12, 1682. His will dated 20 April and proved 6 May, 1715, gives the use of his estate at £165: 17:6, to his wife Anna during her life, afterward to the children of his brothers Jacob, Abraham and Joseph and brother-in-law John Caldwell. He married Anna Cross 15 May, 1706-7 but left no issue. His widow was published to Benjamin Fowler of Rowley 23 July, 1756. He d. Apr. 1751. Res. s. p. Ipswich, Mass.

72. EPHRAIM FOSTER (Ephraim, Abraham, Reginald), b. Andover, Mass. Nov. 12, 1687; m. Jan. 17, 1716, Abigail Poor of Newbury, dau. of Joseph Poor of Newbury. She m. 2d, 1739, Capt Nathaniel Frynd. He was a blacksmith. She d. Aug. 28, 1747 in Brookfield, Mass. while on a visit to her son. He d. Apr. 8, 1738. Res. Andover, Mass.

200. i. JEDEDIAH, b. 16 Oct. 1717; d. young.
201. ii. SALLY. d. young.
202. iii. HANNAH, b. 2 Aug. 1725; d. 7 March, 1725-6.
203. iv. JEDEDIAH, b. 10 Oct., 1726; m. Dorothy Dwight.
204. v. NAOMI, d. young.
205. vi. HANNAH, b. 23 March, 1729; d. 18 Dec. 1736.

73. CAPT. JOHN FOSTER (Ephraim, Abraham, Reginald), b. Andover, Mass., Mar. 26, 1690; m. Jan. 17, 1715. Rebecca Rowland of Boxford. She d. and he m. 2d (pub.) Sept. 17, 1732, Dorcas Hovey of Boston, dau. of Lake. He d. Dec., 1778. His will was proved Dec. 7, 1778. Res. Andover, Mass.

206. i. JOHN, b. 17 Feb. 1716; m. Deborah Barker.
207. ii. JEMIMA, b. 24 April, 1717; d. 24 Jan., 1736-7.
208. iii. STEPHEN, b. 14 Aug., 1720; m. Abigail Smith.
209. iv. NATHAN, b. 4 July, bapt. 7 July, 1734; d. young.
210. v. REBECCA, b. 20 Nov., 1735; d. 18 Jan., 1736-7.
211. vi. JEMIMA, b. 1741; d. 1757.

75. DEA DAVID FOSTER (Ephraim, Abraham, Reginald), b. Andover Mass. Apr. 18, 1694; m. Nov. 25, 1714, Elizabeth Abbott. She d. Aug. 1, 1715; m. 2d, Aug. 29, 1716, Lydia Farnum, who d. Mar. 21, 1745; m. 3d, Sept. 17, 1748, Judith Norton. She m. Jan. 14, 1760, Nehemiah Carleton of Bradford. She was from Salisbury. He d. June 22, 1759. Res. Andover Mass. He was deacon of the Andover church.

The following order for gravestones for the old burying ground is found among some ancient manuscripts preserved in the family of the persons who ordered them:

Mr. Robert Mulican of Bradford: Ser pray make; for me Two Grave Stones; one for David Foster jeuner of Andover who died the 22; day of Dec; in the year of our Lord; 1736, in the 20th year of his age; the son of David and Lidea Foster of Andover.

And one for Lidea Foster the daughter of David and Lidea Foster of Andover who died in the 17th year of her age in the year of our Lord 1736 and, when they are made; send me word; and I will come and pay you for them.

David Foster.

And one for Isaac Foster; the son of Joshua and Mary Foster of Andover who died in the third year of her age in the year 1738. Pray send me word when it is made; and I will satisfye you for it.

Joshua Foster.

Let them all be made; before you send us word the 3rd day of April, 1739.

212. i. EBENEZER, b. Nov. 23, 1715; prob. d. young.
213. ii. DAVID, b. Dec. 20, 1717; d. Dec. 22, 1736, "only son."
214. iii. LYDIA, b. July 21, 1720; d. Aug. 24, 1736.
215. iv. MEHITABLE, b. May 21, 1730; m. Apr. 32, 1751, Nathaniel Andrews of Boxford.
216. v. REBECCA, b. July 25; bapt. July 30, 1732; m. —— Johnson of Andover.
217. vi. ELIZABETH, m. Jan. 11, 1739, Benjamin Stiles of Boxford.
218. vii. RUTH, 1722; m. Nov. 8, 1744 Benjamin Foster Jr., who d. before 1779. One ch. was David Foster Porter.
219. viii. DAVID, b. after Dec. 22, 1736; d. young. Benjamin Foster was appointed his guardian.
220. ix. GIDEON, b. ——; prob. d. young.
221. x. LYDIA, b. after Aug. 24, 1736; prob. d young.

76. MOSES FOSTER (Ephraim, Abraham, Reginald), b. Andover, Mass., Sept. 27, 1696; m. (prob.) Nov. 27, 1719, Elizabeth Rogers of Boxford. She d. Oct 2, 1729; m. 2d Nov. 26, 1730, Mary Gray, According to the records of the Andover South Church she was dismissed to the church in Boxford. He removed to New Hampshire living in Suncook and Pembroke, Merrimack Co. He was in the latter place as early as 1746. His will dated, March 12, was proved Dec. 7, 1766, at Exeter, N. H. The history of Pembroke, N. H., says: "He came to Pembroke prior to 1743, having bought of Samuel Gray, July 5, 1742, the southerly half of lot No. 62 in the west, with two other pieces of land; commanded the garrison in the fort on the site of Moody K. Wilson's house; June 14, 1748, deeded to his son Asa, two pieces of land, and Dec. 1, 1750, to his son Moses, three pieces; had a brother Ephraim b. 1687, and John born 1690, who settled in Concord; and died 1773. Children born in Andover, Mass. He d. Nov. 1766. Res. Andover, Mass., and Pembroke, N. H.

222. i. ASA, b. April 15, 1720; m. Mary Barr.
223. ii. MOSES, b. March 25, 1723; d. young.
224. iii. DANIEL, b. Jan. 7, 1726; m. Ann Ingalls.
225. iv. MOSES, b. March 26, 1728; m. Rachel Whittemore.
226. v. EPHRAIM, b. Aug. 30, 1731; m. —— ——.
227. vi. HENRY, b. July 23, 1733; d. Jan. 16, 1736-7.
228. vii. MARY, b. March 21, 1736; Jan. 29, 1736-7.
229. viii. MARY, b. Dec. 27, 1737; m. Col. Samuel Conner of Pembroke, N. H. He was killed in the battle of Bennington in 1777.
230. ix. ELIZABETH, b. March 3, 1740.
231. x. HENRY, b. March 8, 1742.
232. xi. CALEB, —47; m. Hannah ——.
233. xii. SARAH, b. March 25, 1723; m. (pub.) March 26, 1743, Francis Carr.
234. xiii. ANNE, b. in Pembroke, N. H. (see town history) m. Col. Jonathan Elkins. Col. Jonathan was b. in Hampton, N. H., Aug. 3, 1734,

was son of Jonathan and Rachel (Page) gr.-son of Jonathan and Joanna (Roby) gt. gr.-son of Dea Gersham and Mary (Sleeper) and gt. gt. gr.-son of Henry, the emigrant who moved to Peacham, Vt. where he was the first settler. He served in the French and Indian war. The following is copied from the N. H. records. "Jona Elkins came into ye house of representatives and represented that he was a soldier in the Crown Point Expedition in the year 1755; that he was discharged in the muster roll ye 21st of October which was 21 days short, he being left to the care of the sick at Albany which place he did not leave till ye 28th of said month and prayed further allowance"—which was granted.

77. AARON FOSTER (Ephraim, Abraham, Reginald), b. Andover, Mass., April 21, 1699; m. Mar. 13. 1721, Martha Smith; she d. before Feb. 1775 for Mar., 1775 he m. Anna Knight of Bolton. According to the Worcester Co. probate records, Aaron died in 1777. for his widow Anna was admr. of her husband's estate, he having died intestate. She d. in 1823, according to Bolton, Mass. town records. Aaron was a prominent citizen in Bolton and for many years he was town clerk. He d. in 1777. Res. Andover and Bolton, Mass.

235. i. PENELOPE. b. Jan. 6, 1723; d. Aug. 21, 1724.
236. ii. MARTHA, b. March 12, 1724; d. July 7, 1735.
237. iii. ELIJAH, b. April 11, 1726; m. Elizabeth Knight.—
238. iv. ISRAEL, b. July 17, 1729; said to have d. young.
239. v. ELEANOR.
240. vi. PENELOPE, b. Jan. 30, 1732.

Robert Parker, of Andover, b. 1732, son of the Nathan, Joseph, James or Joseph I forget which now—, anyway, he the elder takes his portion and disappears from view. Before the Revolution a Robert Parker and wife, Penelope, drop down on Amherst, N. H. and live and die there and a grandson Carleton Parker returns to Andover and the descendants still live here. We have thought Robert, whose father bought out his neighbor Aaron Foster, when he moved to Bolton about 1732, may have followed them out to Bolton and married this infant, Penelope. He died in Amherst at the age which placed his birth in 1732. Her death I did not obtain.

78. JOSHUA FOSTER (Ephraim, Abraham, Reginald), b. Andover, Mass., Mar. 13, 1702; m., May 7, 1730, Mary Barker; m 2d Aug. 17, 1769, Mary Town, of Boxford; d. July, 1769 Res. Andover, Mass.

241. i. JOSHUA, b. May 19, 1731; m. Mary Farnum.
242. ii. NATHAN, b. Aug. 11, 1733; d. Oct. 20, 1752.
243. iii. ISAAC, b. May 25, 1736; d. Sept. 7, 1738.
244. iv. HANNAH, b. April 9, 1739; m. Feb. 14, 1758, Phinehas Tyler of Andover. A son Phinehas was born Feb. 14, 1765.
245. v. MARY, b. Nov. 23, 1741; d. Dec., 1747.
246. vi. ISAAC, b. Feb. 11, 1745; d. Jan. 12, 1747-8.
247. vii. MARY, b. March 22, 1750; m. Bradstreet Tyler of Boxford, April 13, 1769 in Atkinson, N. H., having been published in Andover March 29, 1769 and forbidden by her father. They had 5 ch:
248. viii. SUSANAH, b. Nov. 17, 1747; m. Samuel Barker. They had Nathan, Susannah and Elizabeth, who was b. July 1, 1776.

80. ABRAHAM FOSTER (Abraham, Abraham, Reginald), b. Ipswich, Mass., Jan. 12, 1696; m. (pub.) Apr. 5, 1718, Sarah Dunnell, b. 1696; d. Apr. 10, 1732. He was a carpenter. Administration on his estate was granted to his son Thomas June 20, 1767. He was published at Topsfield to Sarah Dunnell. She was admitted to the church at Topsfield July 2, 1732. He d. Apr. 23, 1767. Res. Topsfield, Mass.

249. i. ABRAHAM, b. May 4, 1719; m. Priscilla Todd.
250. ii. SARAH, b. May 4, 1721; m. Abraham Adams, who d. Sept. 18, 1771.
251. iii. THOMAS, b. Aug. 11, 1724; m. Mehitable Peabody.
252. iv. HANNAH, b. Sept. 18, 1726; d. 1802, unm.
253. v. AMOS, bapt. Dec. 22, 1728. He bought land in Rowley in 1758.
254. vi. RUTH, bapt. March 17 1734; d. 1806, unm.
255. vii. ABIGAIL, bapt. April 3, 1737.

81. NATHAN FOSTER (Abraham, Abraham, Reginald), b. Ipswich, Mass., May 17, 1700; m. Nov. 3, 1724, Hannah Standish, dau. of Dea. Josiah and Sarah Standish and gt. gr.-dau. of Capt. Myles Standish, b. 1706. At the time of his death he was "something over 50 years of age." He d. May 26, 1753. Res., Stafford, Conn. He was born in Ipswich, Mass., and removed about 1720 to Stafford, Conn., where he ever after resided and where he died. Standish Genealogy, up to marriage of Hannah Standish to Nathan Foster—Myles, b. Duxbury Hall, Lancashire, England, 1586. Came in Mayflower, 1620, with wife Rose, who d. Jan. 29, 1621. They had no children. In 1623 he m. his cousin Barbara, who came in the Ann. He d. Oct. 3, 1656. They had: 1. Alexander; d. 1702; he m. 1st, Sarah Alden; 2d, Mrs. Desire Sherman. 2. Charles; alive in 1627. 3. John; alive in 1627. 4. Myles B., d. April, 1663. 5. Josiah, b. 1634. 6. Lora. 7. Charles. Josiah, of Duxbury, Norwich and Preston, b. 1634; m. 1st. Dec. 19, 1654, Mary Dingly, of Marshfield; 2d, Sarah Allen, of Braintree. By first and second wives he had: 1. Myles; m. Mehitable Adams. 2. Josiah; m. Sarah. 3. Samuel; m. Deborah. 4. Israel; m. Elizabeth Richards. 5. Mary; m. Cary. 6. Lois; m. Hugh Calkins. 7. Mehitable. 8. Martha. 9. Mercy. Josiah, Deacon Josiah, of Stafford, Conn., d. March 26, 1753; m. Sarah ——; no last name on tombstone. She d. January or June 16, 1741. They had: 1. Eleazer. 2. Jehoden. 3. Mehitable; m. —— Rood. 4. Sarah; m. —— Howard. 5. Hannah; m. Nathan Foster. 6. Mercy; m. —— Perkins.

March 19, 1761, Nathan Foster, of Stafford, for £140 bought of Jos. Gray, of Brimfield, 140 acres, located in Western, Mass. (Worcester Co. deeds.) April 20, 1761, Nathan, of Stafford, bought of Samuel Wheeler Jr., of Western, 35 acres, in said town. (Ibed.) April 14, 1749, Nathan, of Stafford, administrator of his father, Nathan, sold land to Josiah Standish Read (or Rood).

Hartford, Conn., Probate: At a Court of Probate, Holden at Hartford, for the District of Hartford, on the 6th Day of December, 1763, we the subscribers, Daniel Alden, Jr., Daniel Bloggett and Seth Johnson, being appointed to Distribute the estate of Nathan Foster, late of Stafford, Deceased, and being under Oath, according to the Court Order, we sett off to Nathan Foster, eldest son a Double Share; to Daniel Foster, a single share; to Standish Foster, a single share; to Mary Rood, a single share; to Hannah Alden, a single share; to Louis Palmer, a single share; to Eunice Parish, a single share; to Mehitable Lillie, a single share; to Phebe Foster, a single share; to Sarah Lillie, a single share.

Signed

Daniel Alden Jr.
Daniel Bloggett
Seth Johnson
Distributors.

Return 9 December 1763

256. i. MARY, b October 12, 1725; m 8 May, 1749, Josiah Standish Rood. Res. Ashfield.

257. ii. NATHAN, b. May 27, 1728; m. Elizabeth Lansford.

258. iii. HANNAH, b. April 15, 1730; m. —— Alden, of Stafford, Conn.

259. iv. LOIS, b. January 7, 1732-3; m. Nathan Palmer. They had numerous descendants, and there were several Nathan Palmers among them. One was named Strange Nathan Palmer—not a nickname as one would suppose, but his real name. Another of their children was named Elihu, he studied Divinity, but fell from the faith of his father's, and became Diest; was the author of many deistical works, and was a man of talent and irreproachable character. He became blind by a severe attack of yellow fever, which nearly cost him his life. A number of Lois' children settled in New Jersey, and some of her grand-children resided at Mount Holly, and one grandson published a newspaper there. One descendant of their's was Mrs. M. Louise Thomas, Tacomy, Philadelphia, Pa.

260. v. EUNICE, b. February 29, 1733-4; m. Elijah Parish. He was b. prob. in Canterbury, Conn.; was a farmer at Lebanon and Windham, Conn. She d. Dec. 13, 1799. Ch: 1. Asa, b. 1769; d. Feb. 20, 1772. 2. Elijah, b. Nov. 7, 1762; m. Nov. 7, 1796, Mary Hale, dau. of Dea. Joseph; b. 1767; d. May 30, 1831. He d. Oct. 15, 1825. Was graduated at Dartmouth in 1785, an eminent divine nearly all his ministerial life, D. D. 40 years, pastor of the Byfield, Mass., church. Had 3 ch., one grandson was Rev. Daniel Parish Noyes, pastor at Wilmington, Mass. 3. Ariel, b.

Nov. 29, 1764; m. July 7, 1792, Hannah Chute; b. April, 1765. He d. May 20, 1794. She d. April 28, 1842. He was graduated at Dartmouth in 1788, ordained pastor Congregational church at Manchester-by-the-Sea, in 1792, a man of remarkable cheerfulness and vivacity, loved by all. Only two ch: i. Philomela, b. 1793; d. ae. 2 weeks; ii. Amelia, b. Sept. 18, 1794; m. June 18, 1819, Rev. Ebenezer Perkins; res., Royalston, Mass. 4. Philomela, b. Dec. 4, 1768; m. June 26, 1794, Dea. Stephen Thurston (see the excellent Thurston Genealogy). She was b. Jan 2, 1770. Died after marrying three times, in Bedford, N. H., Sept. 13, 1833. She d. July 24, 1818. Ch. by Philomela: a. Philomela, b. 1795; m. Rev. Samuel Newell. b. Delia, b. 1796; d. 1823. c. Clarissa, b. 1801; was celebrated teacher; killed by cars in Elmira, N. Y., 1884. d. Lucinda, b. 1805; d. 1806. e. Mary C., b. 1806; d. Eatonton, Ga., 1825. f. Ariel G., b. June 11, 1810; m. Julia Clark Hart, Cornelia G. Hull and Georgianna Gibson. g. One ch. by 3d wife.

261. vi. MEHITABLE, b. 20 February, 1737-8; m. Nov. 10, 1763, Silas Lilly. He was descended from George Lilly, of Reading, 1658 through George, and Reuben who m. Mary Brewster, a des. of Elder William Brewster.

262. vii. PHEBE, b. March 1, 1739-40; m. —— Crittenden, of Ashfield, Mass.

263. viii. SARAH, b. January 4, 1742; m. 1761, Jonathan Lilly. They were married at Stafford, Conn. He was son of Samuel, of Sutton, Woodstock and Stafford; gr.-son of George Jr. Jonathan had a son Foster who had a son Jonathan who had a son Julius W., b. 1842, who res. 620 W. 66th, Chicago. H. Ivah Thomsen, who in 1892 res. at 16 Madison St., West, Baltimore, Md., is a direct decendant of Sarah.

264. ix. DANIEL, b. July 22, 1744; m. Kezia Sawyer and Welthea Almira Ladd.

265. x. ASA, b. July 15, 1746; m. Huldah Wheeler and Eliza Thompson.

266. xi. STANDISH, b. Feb. 24, 1749; m. Sarah Spaulding.

82. DANIEL FOSTER (Abraham, Abraham, Reginald), b. Ipswich, Mass., April 13, 1705; m. (pub.) Jan. 1, 1724, Hannah Black (or Clark), of Rowley; m. 2d, (pub.) May 16, 1733, Elizabeth Davis, of Rowley. He d. Harvard, Mass., April 30, 1752. Res., Rowley and Ipswich and Harvard, Mass. He lived in Rowley in 1724, and was in Ipswich as late as 1746. He was granted the adm. of his father's estate April 5, 1742.

Will of Daniel Foster, of Harvard: In Name of God Amen This twenty second Day of November in the Twenty second year of his majesties Reign Anno Domini 1748 I Daniel Foster of Harvard In the County of worcester and Provance of the massachusetts bay in New England, yeoman Being well in Health and of Perfictt mind and memory. (Praise be given to Almighty God for the same) and calling to mind the mortallity of my Body and Knowing it is appointed For all men once to Die. Do therefore make and ordain this and No other to be my Last will and Testament hereby making Null and voide all othere and former wills and Testaments by me made and signed and Princapley and First of all my soul I Recomend Into the hands of Almighty God that gaive it, my Body I Recomend to the Earth to be Decantely Buried at the Descerition of my Estatt or hereafter Named Nothing Doubting but at ye generall Reseriction I shall Receive the same again by the mighty Power of God, and as to such wordly estate as it hath Pleased God to Bless me with all I Give Demiss Disspose of the same in the Following manner (viz)

Item, my will is that my Debts and Funerall Charges be First Paid. Item, I give and Bequeath to Elizabeth my Beloved wife the whole use and Improvement of my Dwelling house while she shall Remain my widow also the use and Improvement of all my moveable Household Goods (Except what I shall herein give away) During the Time she shall be my widow, and the use of a cow summer and winter while she is my widow and of a horse to Ride to meetting and elsewhare as she hath need while my widow, also ananuelly while she is my widow she shall haive six Bushell of Indian corn, and four bushells of Rye, and a bushell and a halfe of malt, and one hundred and forty Pounds of Beefe yearly and wood sufficant for one fire. Brought to the Door and cut fitt for the fire and every thing Else that she shall stand in nessity of while she is my widow for her own supporte while my widow all to be found and provided for her and Brought to the said House by my son Isaac his heirs executors or administrators and if she Dies my widow then he shall give her a Christiain Buriall and my will is that, that parte of the moveable Estate that my said wife Brought to me when I married her the Children of her sister Sarah Platts shall have so much of them as Remains after my wife hath Done with them. Item. I give and Bequeath unto my Daughter morey whitman or her heirs ten Cows and four sheep and a silver spoon marked with A. M. F. and one half of my Books (Excepting Burketts Esrositions) which with what I have allready given her is in full of her Porition of my Estate. Item, I give and Bequeath unto my grandson Dan Foster a silver spoon marked D. F. Item all the remaining Parte of my Estate that I shall Die sisesed off and the Reversion thereoff Both Real and Personall wheresoever. I give and Bequeath unto my son Isaac Foster his heirs and Asigns Forever Constituting and appointing my son Isaac Foster to be sole executtor of this my last will and testament In wittness whereof I haive hereunto affixed my hand and seal the Day and year First and aforewritten

Daniel Foster

Signed, sealed, Published Pronounced and Declared by the said Daniel Foster as his Last will and testament In the Presence of us wittnesses

John Laughton
her
Sarah O Laughton
mark
Jeremiah Laughton

Joseph Wilder, Judge of Prob.

267. i. ISAAC, b. Feb. 19, 1725; m. Elizabeth Emerson.

268. ii MARY, b. Aug. 14, 1727; m. Feb. 6, 1747, Dea. John Whitman. He was b. Stow, Mass., Sept. 21, 1717 (John, Zechariah, John). She d. Dec 24, 1812 near Annapolis, Nova Scotia. In 1755 the English government having dispossed of a large number of French settlers in Nova Scotia, the governor of the Province issued a proclamation invit ng settlers; in company with forty-five others John and wife arrived in Annapolis, N. S., in June, 1761, in the sloop "Charming Molly," bringing their families with them, their household goods and stock; a full list of their possessions is to be found in the diary of Felsh, Evans and Bent, who were appointed a committee to wait on the governor and obtain the promised land; a grant was finally issued to about one hundred of a tract extending along the south line of the Annapolis river from Saw Mill creek to Wilmont line, and seven and one-half miles in depth. John did not survive to receive his share, which was distributed among his sons. He died Sept. 12, 1763, leaving considerable property and the foundation for a handsome establishment; his widow was left with eleven children, all under fifteen years of age. This was to them truly afflicting dispensation, situated as they were in a strange land, and remote from all their connections; the widow, however, was a woman of superior intellect and of no ordinary share of resolution; she kept the family together, nurtured and educated her children and lived to see nine of them—two having d'ed young—eligibly and comfortably situated in the world. For many years she enjoyed the remuneration of her toil, perplexity and solicitude in their dutiful gratitude, love and veneration. John, though a young man, had been chosen Deacon of the church at Stow, and had he lived would have become a prominent character in the Province. Mrs. (Foster) Whitman m. 2d, Judge Samuel Bancroft, brother of Rev. Aaron Bancroft, of Worcester, Mass. Samuel was b. in Reading, Mass., in 1736; m. Sarah Holt for first wife. He was a judge in Nova Scotia. Ch: 1. Dorcas, b. May 5, 1749; m. Capt. Ebenezer Perry and Samuel McIntire; res., Upper Canada. 2. Daniel, b. June 5, 1750; m. Sarah Kendall; 11 ch; res., Rosette, N. S. 3. Hannah, b. Aug. 12, 1751; m. Wm. Ellery Tufts; res., Albany, N. S. 4. Edward, b. Aug. 6, 1752; m. Dorothy Gates; res., Annapolis, N. S. 5. John, b. Sept. 25, 1753; m. Elizabeth Rice, of Stow, Mass; res., Round Hill, N. S. 6. Salome, b.

March 29, 1755; m. Major Ezekiel Cleveland and Nathaniel Parker; res., Nictaux, N. S. 7 Elnthan, b. April 16, 1756; d. March 1, 1765 8. Jacob, b. Oct. 14, 1757; m. Annie Spinney; res., Rosette, N. S. 9. Isaac, b. Nov. 3, 1758; d. July 20, 1777. 10. Abraham, b. Sept. 10, 1761; m. Hannah Webber; res., Chester, N. S. 11. Nancy, b. March 26, 1763; m. Nelson Freeman; res., Milton, N. S.

269. iii. DANIEL, b. Aug. 28, 1729; m. —— ——.

270. iv. HANNAH, b. Sept. 20, 1731.

271. v. ELIZABETH, b. March, 1733.

83. DR. BENJAMIN FOSTER (Benjamin, Abraham, Reginald), b. Ipswich, Mass., Nov. 25, 1700; m. —— ——; m. 2d, June 22, 1761, Mrs. Sarah Low. He died of asthma. He was a physician. Felt in his History of Ipswich, says of him: "He had been in the practice of his profession over fifty years, was distinguished botanist, a skilful and successful physician." He d. Dec. 19, 1775. Res., Ipswich and Boxford, Mass.

84. AMOS FOSTER (Benjamin, Abraham, Reginald), b. Ipswich, Mass., April 28, 1702; m. Oct. 8, 1725, Elizabeth Kittredge, of Haverhill. She d. Nov. 29, 1756. He removed to Boxford with his father, thence to Tewksbury, where he was in 1730. His will was proved June 17, 1754. He died April 28, 1754. Res., Tewksbury, Mass.

Amos Foster's will:—In the Name of God Amen: The Twenty fifth Day of April A. D. 1754 I Amos Foster of Tewksbury in the County of Middlesex and Province of ye Massachusetts Bay in New England yeoman being sick and weak of body, but of perfect mind and memory. Thanks be given to God therefor, therefore calling to mind ye Mortality of my body, and knowing that it is appointed for all men once to die do make and ordain this my last will and testament: that is to say Principally and first of all I recommend my Immortal Soul in the hand of God that and my body I recommend to the Earth to be Buried in decent Christian Burial at the Discretion of my Executor hereafter named. And as touching such worldly Estate wherewith it hath pleased God to bless me with in this life I give demise and dispose of the same in the following manner and form vis

Item. My will is that all my Just Debts and funeral Charges be well and truly paid out of my Estate by my Executor—I give unto Elizabeth Foster my well beloved wife the use and Improvement of ye East End of my Dwelling house being in Tewksbury and all my goods or personal Estate in ye house. (excepting one bed guns and swords and grain) and fire wood brought for ye house and eight bushels of Indian Corn and six bushels of ry e?] and seven schore wait of pork and Twenty one Shillings and four pence to be paid and allowed Annually. All the above said goods and allowance to be granted and allowed her so long as she shall Remain my widow and a Cow to be kept for her use.

Item. I give and Demise unto my son Jonathan Foster all my Lands and Buildings (except ye improvement of part of my house as aforesaid) they lying and being in Tewksbury afores'd, and bounded as the same are in Deeds to him the Jonathan his heirs and assigns ?] forever To enable him to pay my Debts and Legacies and to do for and to take care of my wife according as above ordered

I give unto my Eldest son James Foster the sum of Thirteen pounds Six Shillings and Eight pence it being his full portion out of my estate.—

I give unto Amos Foster my son ye sum of Thirteen pounds Six Shillings and Eight pence it being his full portion of my estate.

I give unto my daughter Mary Foster the sum of Thirteen Pounds six Shillings and Eight pence it being her full portion of my Estate. And to be paid by my son Jonathan in two years after my Decease. And I do hereby constitute and ordain my son Jonathan Foster to be sole Executor of this my last will and testament—and hereby I do revoke and disanul all other wills and testaments by me made or bequeathed ratifying and comfirming this and no other to be my last will and testament. In witness whereof I have hereunto set my hand and Seal ye day and year above written

Amos Foster

Signed sealed published pronounced and declared by said Amos Foster as his last will and testament in presence of us the subscribers

Prob. June 17, 1754.

Thomas Kittredge
her
Betty X Peacock
mark
Thos. Kidder

272 i. JAMES, b. Aug. 15, 1736; m. Dolly ——, Betty —— and Lydia —.
273. ii. JONATHAN, b. Aug 23., 1732; m. Lydia ——, Sarah Allen and Mrs. Olive Harwood.
274. iii. AMOS, b. Nov. 30, 1727; m. Hannah —— and Sarah ——.
275. iv. MARY, b. Oct. 7, 1734; m. 13 June, 1770, James Kitteridge.

87. GIDEON FOSTER (Benjamin, Abraham, Reginald), b. Ipswich, Mass., 10 Oct., 1709; m. Feb. 10, 1732, Lydia Goldwait; b. 7 May, 1710; d. ——; m. 2d, Deborah ——. He was a mason. He d. 1772. Res., Danvers, Mass.

276. i. LYDIA, b. May 22, 1733; d. 23 May, 1741.
277. ii. GIDEON, b. May 23, 1741; d. 13 June, 1741.
278. iii. LYDIA, b. April 12, 1747; m. in Danvers, Jan. 25, 1770, Abel Osborn.
279. iv. GIDEON, b. Feb. 13, 1748; m. Mercy Jacobs and Mary Tapley.
279x. v. ASAHEL, b. July 16, 1749; m. Joanna Symonds.
280. vi. BENJAMIN, b. June 12, 1750; m. Elizabeth Green Young and ——

89. ISAAC FOSTER (Benjamin, Abraham, Reginald), b. Boxford, Mass., Dec. 3, 1722; m. (pub. Sept. 28) Dec. 1745, Mary Rice. Res. Tewksbury and Lunenburg, Mass.

281. i. MARY, b. Nov. 8, 1746.
282. ii. BENJAMIN, b. May 26, 1748.
283. iii. ISAAC, b. Aug. 15, 1751.
284. iv. KEZIAH, b. Feb. 10, 1753.
285. v. RICHARD, b. July 31, 1756.

93. MOSES FOSTER (Ebenezer, Abraham, Reginald), b. Rowley, Mass., Oct. 5, 1713; m. Mar. 10, 1737, Hannah Andrews of Boxford. He removed to Arundel (now Cape Porpoise) York Co. Me., where he was living in 1735. He was married at Ipswich to Hannah Andrews of Boxford. Res. Cape Porpoise, York Co. Me., and Arundel and Kennebunk Port, Me.

286. i. MOSES, b.
287. ii. HANNAH, b.
288. iii. MOLLY, b. ——; m. Benjamin Thompson.
289. iv. ELIZABETH, b. ——; m. 1781, Asa Burbank, his third wife and had by her Ebenezer and Moses.

95. JONATHAN FOSTER (Caleb, Abraham, Reginald), b. Ipswich, Mass. Nov. 30, 1704; m. Jan. 1, 1733, Jemima Cummings; m. 2d, Dec. 17, 1751, Dorcas Porter at Topsfield. He d. May, 1779. Res. Ipswich, Mass.

290. i. AFFE, b. Dec. 4, 1734.
291. ii. PHILEMON, b. June 11, 1737; m. Ruth Perley.
292. iii. APPHIA, b. Jan. 16, 1739.
293. iv. JEMIMA, b. April 1, 1742; d. unm.
294. v. OLIVE, b. Aug. 20, 1744; m (pub.) Aug. 3, 1776, Amos Chapman.
295. vi. JONATHAN, b. Sept. 16, 1753.
296. vii. MOSES, b. Dec. 18, 1735; m. Mary Fuller.
297. viii. DORCAS, b. Dec. 18, 1756; m. July 3, 1800, Daniel Ellsworth, of Rowley, son of Jonathan and Eunice Ellsworth, b. May 12, 1767, to whom she was published April 12, 1800. Ch. 1. Hiram, b. October 22, 1801. 2. Jeremiah, b. May 16, 1803. 3. Elbridge, b. September, 20 1805. 4. Daniel, b. January 13, 1808. 5. Dorcas, b. December 13, 1816.
298. ix. MARY, b. June 10, 1759; d. unm.
299. x. CALEB, b. Dec. 8, 1760; m. Hepsibah ——.
300. xi. MERCY, b. Jan. 20, 1764; m. (pub.) Aug 1, 1785, Isaac Plummer of Newbury.
301. xii. SALOME, b. Nov. 4, 1766; m. first, September 14, 1791, Nathaniel Foster, (Stephen, Stephen, Caleb, Abraham, Reginald) as stated below; and 2d, Nathaniel Gould, to whom she was published April 23, 1806. Res., Topsfield.

97. CALEB FOSTER (Caleb, Abraham, Reginald), b. Ipswich, Mass., June 5, 1708; m. at Rowley, Nov. 4, 1729, Priscilla Buxton. Caleb Foster Jr. and wife Priscilla make deed to Thomas Foster, Ipswich Jan. 14. 1763; This is the latest we

find any account of him. There is no record of any children at Ipswich. Res. Ipswich, Mass.

302. i. JOHN, b.——; m. ——Kilmer.
303. ii. REGINALD, b. ——; m. ——Conant.
304. iii. NATHAN, b. ——; m. Miriam ——.

98. STEPHEN FOSTER (Caleb, Abraham, Reginald), b. Ipswich, Mass., Apr. 24, 1710; m. Apr. 21, 1736, Rebecca Peabody. Rebecca (Jacob, Jacob, Mary (Foster) Peabody, Reginald Foster) was daughter of Deacon Jacob and Rebecca (Barker) Peabody; b. 3, February, 1715, in Topsfield. She d. March 23, 1790. He lived in Topsfield, where he d. January 15, 1781. There is no settlement of his estate on record. He d. Jan. 15, 1781. Res. Ipswich, Mass. and Topsfield, Mass.

305. i. STEPHEN, b. July 13, 1741; m. Abigail Boardman and Sarah Dorman.
306. ii. NATHANIEL, b. Jan. 9, 1743-4; d. Jan. 23, 1743-4.
307. iii. ABIGAL, b. Feb. 25, 1746; m. Dec. 14, 1769, Philemon Perkins. 1 Jacob, b. ——. 2. Dudley, b. ——. 3. Stephen, b. ——. 4 Jonathan. b. ——.
308. iv. JACOB, b. July 26, 1749; d. Jan. 28, 1770, a young man.

104. JONATHAN FOSTER (Isaac, Reginald, Reginald), b. Ipswich, Mass. May 2, 1705; m. July 5, 1733, Elizabeth Storey. He was born in Ipswich; removed to Lincoln and was there Nov. 1, 1764, for at that time with wife Elizabeth he sold two wood lots to Jeremiah Burnham and son Jeremiah of Ipswich. Again 19 April, 1765, they sold to Moses Foster of Ipswich one-third of wood lot in Chebacco. He d. May 8, 1782. Res. Lincoln, Mass.

309. i. JONATHAN, b. April 23, 1734; d. Oct, 12, ——. (The edge of leaf of the old family record is worn so that part of this date is illegible, but it follows the record of a death Oct. 28, 1772).
310. ii. MARTHA, b. July 15, 1735; baptized July 20, 1735; m. Aaron Burnham, Oct. 26, 1756.
311. iii. JOSHUA, b. Feb. 18, 1736-7; d. Feb. ——, 1739-40.
312. iv. ELIZABETH, b. Dec. 11, 1738; m. Nathan Page, of Newbury, April 19, 1758.
313. v. ABIGAIL, b. Feb. 17, 1740-1; bapt. Feb. 22, 1740-1; d. May 18, 1770, "in the 30 year of her age."
314. vi. ISAAC, b. Feb. 10, 1742-3; d. Oct. 28, 1772, "in the thirty year of his age."
315. vii. EUNICE, b. Aug. 22, 1744.
316. viii. JACOB, b. July 15, 1746; m. Sarah Wheeler, of Lincoln, Mass., April 18, 1780; d. Nov. 8, 1791.
317. ix. SUSSANNA, b. March 6, 1749 50.

The old family record shows the following entries in the handwriting of Jonathan Foster:—"1741 my father died April the 11." "April the 22 sister Free [Freeborn] died the same month." "October the 4, 1749, mother dide."

105. ISAAC FOSTER(Isaac, Reginald, Reginald), b. Ipswich, Mass.; m. —— ——; m. 2d, Rachel ——. He married twice; first ——, secondly, Rachel ——. Removed to Holliston where he was Jan. 16, 1756. Administration on his estate was granted Timothy Townsend of Holliston Jan. 24, 1764. He d. 1763. Res. Holliston, Mass.

318. i. STEPHEN, b. ——. Stephen of Holliston letter date March 16, 1779; inventory ex. September 3, 1783 incomplete.
319. ii. HANNAH.
320. iii. SARAH.
321. iv. ABIGAIL.

106. CAPT. JACOB FOSTER (Isaac, Reginald, Reginald), b. Ipswich, Mass. in 1703; m. Apr. 10, 1728, Mary Suffield. He removed to Holliston, Mass. On various deeds, etc., he is styled "Captain" although of what I failed to discover. On other documents his name appears as "Jacob Foster, Gentleman." He was married by the Rev. Daniel Baker, to Mary, daughter of William and Hannah (Ballard) Suffield, of H. He d. in Canterbury, Conn., Jan 17, 1779. Res. Holliston, Mass.

322. i. MARY, b. Nov. 3, 1729; m. Moses Twitchel.
323. ii. JACOB, b. March 10, 1732; m. Hepsibah Prentice.

324. iii. WILLIAM, b. April 29, 1734; m. Hannah Durkee.
325. iv. SHEFFIELD, b. Oct. 10, 1738; d. young.
326. v. HANNAH, b. May 14, 1740.
327. vi. ISAAC, b. Sept. 27, 1741; d. Dec., 1741.
328. vii. ISAAC, b. March 18, 1743-4; m. Patience ——.
329. viii. ABIGAL, b. 1749-50.
330. ix. REBECCA, b. Dec. 7, 1753.

109. CAPT. JEREMIAH FOSTER (John, Reginald, Reginald), b. Ipswich, Mass., in 16[illegible]; m. Dorothy Rust, dau. of Nathaniel and Joanna (Kinsman). She d. May 14, 1745. He was a mariner and also had a sawmill in Ipswich, 1730-69. He d. Mar. 25, 1769. Res., Ipswich, Mass. Crafts' Journal, at Louisbury, 1745: He appears to have been in Capt. Jeremiah Foster's Co. (John, Reginald, Reginald), who is mentioned. Crafts writes, Oct. 13, 1745: "I believe that ye Captain and Lieut. Gidding will be discharged" and I will send money by them. Louisbury, July 16, 1745: Ensign Goodhoe and ten men, among them Jeremiah Foster, Jr., left for home. Aaron Foster too sick to go.

331. i. JEREMIAH, b. ——; was in the French and Indian war, 1745.
332. ii. MOSES.
333. iii. JOHN.
334. iv. JOANNA, bapt. June 12, 1726.
335. v. EPHRAIM, bapt. July 7, 1728.
336. vi. JOSEPH, bapt. July 19, 1730; m. Lydia Giddings and Mrs. Hannah Somes.
337. vii. MARTHA, bapt. July 30, 1732.
338. viii. DOROTHY, pub. Jno. Emerson, Oct. 19, 1754.
339. ix. BENJAMIN, b. Jan. 5, 1734-5.
340. x. MARY; m. John Emerson, Jan. 12, 1756.
341. xi. ELIZABETH, bapt. Dec. 5, 1736.
342. xii. JOSHUA, bapt. Sept. 16, 1739.
343. xiii. MIRIAM, bapt. Oct. 11, 1741.

110. DEA. MOSES FOSTER (John, Reginald, Reginald) b. Ipswich, Mass., in 1697; m. Jan. 18, 1732, Mary Rust; b. 1702. She d. May 2, 1732; m. 2d, Jan. 18, 1733, Mary Blodgett; b. 1702; d. Nov. 11, 1777, in Ashburnham; m. 3d, Mrs. Ann Varney; b. 1700; d. Feb. 21, 1787.

The first meeting of the proprietors of Dorchester, Canada (Ashburnham), was held Feb. 20, 1749. At this writing and mingling with them was Moses Foster, then about 60 years of age. For some years he had resided a portion of the time at least in that place. He brought them tidings of the wilderness, and gave an account of what had happened there. He had purchased one first and one second division lot, lying adjacent in the northeast part of the town now in Ashby. The title of one of these lots was in dispute, and the proprietors at this meeting made him a grant of fifty acres. Not content with this measure of kindness to their aged guest, the proprietors voted him £5 "for being one of the first settlers." There is no record of this payment, but a few years later a tract of about fifty acres was granted to "Mr. Moses Foster one of the first settlers," on condition he "shall come personally and settle and inhabit there and continue there for several years, provided his life be spared him." This grant was located adjacent to and east of the common, and for many years was known as the Deacon Foster grant. Permission was also given Mr. Foster to throw up his house lot No. 51 and lay out another, which he did, selecting a tract extending north from the land granted to him, but not extending so far westward. He probably first resided in Ashburnham about 1750, the date, however, is not definately known, but in 1750 he moved to the common, and in 1751 was a licensed inholder, and for a number of years kept a public house. He was one of the original church members and the first deacon. His pew in the meeting house in 1760 was the one nearest the pulpit, which showed in "seating the meeting house" he was the most prominent resident in the place. In his extreme old age he returned to Ipswich.

He was a husbandman. His will was dated March 28, 1782. He died at Chebacco, Ipswich, Sept. 27, 1785. He married, first, Mary, daughter of Nathaniel Rust. He d. Sept. 27, 1785. Res., Ipswich, Ashburnham and Ipswich, Mass.

344. i. MIRIAM, bapt. Aug. 14, 1726.
345. ii. ZEBULON, bapt. Sept. 22, 1728; m. Anna Knowlton.
346. iii. MOSES, b. 1730; m. Mary ——.

347. iv. AARON, b. 1723; m. Ruth Lowe.
348. v. JANE, b. abt. 1731; m. June 3, 1756, in Ashburham, Zimri Haywood, of Lunenburg. He was son of Nathan, b. Sept. 5, 1731. He resided in Ashburham, and was an early settler there. When Ashby was incorporated in 1767 his farm and mill were included in that town, and later removed to Winslow, Me., where he died. Ch: 1. Rebecca Willis, b. Jan. 9, 1757. 2. Eunice, b. June 16, 1760. 3. Nathan, b. Mar. 15, 1762. 4. Elizabeth, b. May 20, 1764. 5. Thomas, b. May 5, 1766.

111. JOHN FOSTER (John, Reginald, Reginald), b. Ipswich, Mass.; m. Dec. 27, 1732, Mehitable Burnham. Administration was granted on his estate to widow Mehitable Oct. 28, 1766; it was valued at £196. He d. 1766. Res., Ipswich, Mass.

349. i. JACOB, bapt. July 14, 1734; d. young.
350. ii. MARY, bapt. Dec. 3, 1738.
351. iii. LUCY, bapt. May 3, 1741; d. young.
352. iv. JOHN, bapt. May 29, 1743.
353. v. LUCY, bapt. Oct. 27, 1745.
354. vi. JOANNA, bapt. June 19, 1748.
355. vii. ELIZABETH, bapt. Sept. 9, 1750.
356. viii. SARAH, bapt. April 15, 1753.
357. ix. JACOB, bapt. Oct. 5, 1775.

120. NATHANIEL FOSTER (Nathaniel, Reginald, Reginald), b. Ipswich, Mass., 17—; m. (pub.) Nov. 26, 1726, Mabel Low. He removed to Newbury, being dismissed from the church at Chebacco to the third church there 20 May, 1744. He was a shipwright. Nov. 5, 1762 he deeded 10 rods of land and a house to his son Nathaniel Jr., shipwright. He married daughter of Thorndike Low. They were both admitted to the church at Chebacco in Jan., 1727-8. He d. ——. Res., Chebacco and Newbury, Mass.

358. i. MARY.
359. ii. DEBORAH, bapt. April 16, 1729.
360. iii. ISAAC, bapt. July 19, 1730.
361. iv. NATHANIEL, bapt. March 19, 1731-2.

121. COL. JONATHAN FOSTER (Jonathan, William, Reginald), b. Boxford, Mass., Sept. 15, 169—; m. Hannah Peabody; b. 1693; d. June 1, 1769. He d. ——. Jonathan Foster, of Boxford, sold land in Chester, N. H., in 1762; witnesses, Oliver and Richard Foster. Exeter deeds. Res., Boxford, Mass.

362. i. OLIVER, b. Aug. 17, 1719, in Boxford.
363. ii. HANNAH, b. Dec. 15, 1721, in Boxford; d. in Boxford, Jan., 22 1760, unm.
364. iii. JONATHAN, b. Oct. 11, 1727, in Haverhill; m. Rebecca Dorman.
365. iv. WILLIAM, b. Nov. 9, 1729, in Haverhill.
366. v. RICHARD, b. Feb. 20, 1732-3, in Boxford; m. Elizabeth Kimball.

123. ZEBADIAH FOSTER (Jonathan, William, Reginald), b. Boxford, Mass., Sept. 28, 1702; m. (pub.) Jan. 12, 1723, Margaret Tyler. He was born in Boxford, with his wife was admitted to the church there Jan. 28, 1728. He was living there in 1771. He married Margaret Tyler to whom he was published Jan. 12, 1732-4. He d. Feb. 21, 1772. Res., Boxford, Mass.

367. i. MARGARET, b. July 13, 1724.
368. ii. LYDIA, b. Feb. 24, 1725-6.
369. iii. ANNE, b. May 13, 1728; d. 9 April, 1748.
370. iv. ZEBADIAH, b. Dec. 14, 1730; d. 8 Nov., 1734.
371. v. ABNER, b. April 23, 1733; m. —— ——.
372. vi. ZEBADIAH, b. Aug. 25, 1735.
373. vii. DUDLEY, b. Feb. 21, 1737.
374. viii. ABIGAL, b. June 25, 1740; m. Nathan Kimball Jr., of Boxford.
375. ix. LUCY, b. March 25, 1747.

126. CAPT. JOHN FOSTER (William, William, Reginald), b. Andover, Mass., Sept. 27, 1701; m. Jan. 13, 1724, Mary Osgood. She d. April 6 1772. He was a yeoman and possessed considerable land. In the history of Andover he is styled "captain." He appears to have been a man of influence, and with his brother, Capt. Asa, was appointed on a committee to instruct the representative

at the General Court to enter a protest against the Stamp Act. Again in 1768 the two brothers were on a committee to frame resolutions to induce the inhabitants to ignore extravagance, idleness and vice and to promote manufacturers, industry, economy and good morals in the town, and discountenance importation and the use of foreign superfluities.

He is not a descendant from Andrew, as it is suggested he may be in the N. E. Historical and Genealogical Register, Vol. xx, p. 308. March 13, 1728-9, he bought of Caleb Johnson twenty-five acres of land on the west side of Shawshine river, bounded by the land of William Foster. Feb. 7, 1731-2, he and his brother Asa bought of Samuel Peters thirty-one acres and thirty-three poles of land on Blanchard's plain. Sept. 24, 1733, he again purchased of said Peters twenty-five acres more on west side of Shawshine river, which was a part of Allen's farm. In the history of Andover he is styled "Capt. John Foster." He and his brother Capt. Asa were men of sound moral and intellectual attainments and influence. Oct. 21, 1765, they with others were appointed a committee to draw up instructions for the Representative of the town at General Court, to enter a protest against the support of the Stamp Act. The inhabitants of Andover and other towns had already begun to experience the harassing effects of that unwelcome measure. March, 1768, the two brothers were appointed on another committee to frame resolutions "to induce the inhabitants to ignore extravagance, idleness and vice and to promote manufactures, industry, economy and good morals in the town, and discountenance importation and the use of foreign superfluities," and the said committee to make themselves prominent in the moral enforcement of the foregoing suggestions, by their consistent example. The report was adopted.

"Capt. John bought of Sherebia Ballard, the estate where the present heirs still reside near the South church, for £3800, containing the homestead and meadow, the finest on the Shawshine, west side of the road from South Meeting House to Boston (still taking its way east of Spring Grove Cemetery) and the road from the meeting house lay formerly over the top of the high ridge behind the house, that seems to have faced the west, and a bridle path cut across the grounds between the estate and the old road. The land included the triangle on the west side of the river, up to George Baker's Little Hope Brook, now crossed by the B. & M. R. R. Just where the house stood then is not known. The tradition is that Capt. John brought part of the old home of William from the West Parish and set it up against that of the Ballard building. It is the south section of the present house. Old David Baker could recall a huge door on the east side that allowed logs at full length to be taken through to the ample fire-place in what is now the dining-room of the summer residence of Mrs. Green. William evidently helped John to this bit of luck, for he says, 'I have given him a large part of my estate and allowed him several other advantages of no small value; and inasmuch as he has the nine acre meadow near his house, called Marble's meadow, besides what was left of Hephziba Frye's purchase, because it would be inconvenient for him to have this meadow and upland disposed of to other persons, I could not in justice ask any of the others to pay legacies, debts and expenses.' So Capt. John went over there to live near his sisters, and Asa kept a tavern somewhere now undecided either on the Concord Road near the West Parish Meeting House, or on some estate he purchased in our Moose Country in the trail nearer the North Meeting house."—Miss Abbott. He d. June 17, 1772. Res., Andover, Mass.

376. i. WILLIAM, b. Sept. 24, 1727; d. 8 April, 1729.
377. ii. JOHN, b. March 22, 1729; d. April 7, 1729.
378. iii. WILLIAM, b. March 4, 1730; d. Sept., 1803; m. Hannah Abbott.
379. iv. A SON, b. and d. Jan. 13, 1732.
380. v. JOHN, b. Feb. 14, 1733; m. Hannah Ballard.
381. vi. MARY, b. Jan. 12, 1735; d. Dec. 7, 1763.
382. vii. ISAAC, b. April 28, 1737; m. Dorcas Jewett.
383. viii. GIDEON, b. Aug 21, 1739; m Elizabeth Russell.
384. ix. OBEDIAH, b. May 25, 1741; m. Hannah Ballard.
385. x. SOLOMON, b. April 14, 1743; m. Rebecca Brown.
386. xi. OSGOOD, b. Nov. 10; d. Nov. 15, 1745.

129. CAPT. ASA FOSTER (William, William, Reginald), b. Andover, Mass., June 16, 1710; m. Oct. 26, 1732, Elizabeth Abbott, dau. of John; b. Oct. 21, 1712; d. July 4, 1758; m. 2d, (pub.) Dec. 10, 1763, Lucy Rogers Wise, of Ipswich; b. 1723; d. Oct. 17, 1787. She was dau. of Major Ammi Rohammie Rogers, of Ipswich. In 1758 he was commissioned by Thomas Pownall (Capt., Gen. and Vice Admiral of

Mass. Province under Geo. II) as captain in Col. Ebenezer Nichols' regiment, raised for the invasion of Canada. This commission was signed by Col. Ebenezer Nichols and Gen. Thomas Gage. Oct. 21, 1765, the citizens of Andover voted to select a committee to draw up instructions to the representative of the town at the General Court of the Province in relation to opposing the arbitrary measures of the British government. Capt. Asa Foster was one of this committee. Again in 1768 he was one of a committee to prepare a report to submit to the town to consider some measures that may tend to encourage prudence and manufactures and to lessen the use of superfluities in the town. In 1776 he was elected one of the committee on correspondence, inspection and safety. He left an estate valued at £830. 16s. 7d. He owned 160 acres of land in Canterbury, N. H., besides large tracts of upland, meadow, etc., in Andover.

"Capt. Asa owned the upland back of George Baker's, which he sold to Thomas Abbott in 1764. For David Blunt had lost his wife and married again, and little Lydia Blunt had grown up, the heiress of Grandsir Foster and father David, and married young Thomas Abbott, whose home was in the Baker House. When her son moved away in 1794, the old lady kept her dower room, and staid on four years longer, dying in 1798, probably the one who passed along the Foster tales to the Baker children of Dr. Symonds Baker and his wife Lydia Gray, kin to her and the new proprietors of the old homestead. Bailey's History gives the site of the tavern of Capt. Asa, I find, near the present residence of Charles Shattuck. Asa commanded an expedition to Canada in 1758, and looked well after his men, and was willing to own he could make a mistake in muster rolls. He lived through the Revolution, giving his encouragement and influence in various ways. He did not get a very complimentary notice from the Frenchman who stopped at his inn (see p. 406, Bailey). but perhaps, like his neighbor, Dr. Baker, he had sent all supplies to feed the Bostonese. His first wife, Elizabeth Abbott, was a daughter of Dea. John and Elizabeth (Harnden). Her young brother Abiel, a man of promise, died after he graduated from Harvard, but his mantle fell upon his namesake, Abiel Foster, son of Capt. Asa. Elizabeth died before the Revolution, so the bad management of the tavern kitchen must be attributed to Lucy Rogers, the second wife from Ipswich, a widow with a daughter Mary, who married the ambitious young Abiel. He left Harvard for the ministry at Canterbury, N. H., was drawn into politics and served in the provincial and continental Houses of Congress, also offices high in Court and state of N. H."—Miss Abbott. He d. July 17, 1787. Res., Andover, Mass.

387. i. ASA, b. Sept. 11, 1733; m. Hannah Symonds and Hannah Peters.
388. ii. ABIEL, b. Aug., 8, 1735; m. Hannah Badger and Mary W. Rogers.
389. iii. DANIEL, b. Sept. 25, 1737; m. Hannah Kittridge.
390. iv. DAVID, b. May 7, 1740; d. Oct., 1740, at Canterbury, N. H.
391. v. DAVID, b. Dec. 24, 1741; m. Sarah Foster.
392. vi. ELIZABETH, b. April 14, 1744; m. Nov. 7, 1768, Gen. Nathaniel Lovejoy. She d. April 24, 1775. He was general in Rev. war. H. U. gr. 1766.
393. vii. JONATHAN, b. July 28, 1747; m. Lucy Rogers.
394. viii. SARAH, b. Feb. 15, 1750; m. Dec. 23, 1772, Timothy Bradley. Timothy Bradley Jr., b. Oct. 13, 1743, son of Timothy and Abiah Bradley, of Concord, N. H. Their ch. were: 1. Elizabeth, b. Jan. 9, 1775. 2. Asa, b. Dec. 13, 1776. 3. Sarah, b. April 26, 1779. 4. Abiah, b. Aug. 7, 1781. 5. Hanna. 6. Peters, b. Jan. 1, 1784. 7. Timothy, b. Jan. 24, 1786. 8. Foster, b. May 3, 1788. 9. Abiel, b. May 6, 1790. 7. Timothy and his wife, Annie Morrill, had sons: 1. Asa F. 2. Cyrus P. 3. David M. 4. Timothy. 5. Seth E.; all of whom settled in or near Chicago, Ill., and left families. 5. Seth E. lives at Willamette, a suburb of Chicago. A son of David M., whose name is David E. Bradley, is a merchant, Chicago, Ill. His address is 300 Ft. Dearborn Bldg., 134 Monroe St. There are many descendants of Timothy Bradley in Chicago and vicinity.

Abiel Bradley, son of Timothy Bradley Jr. and Sarah, daughter of Capt. Asa Foster, of Andover, Mass., b. May 6, 1790. He served in the war of 1812. Timothy Bradley Jr. was a son of Timothy Bradley, who served in Col. Poore's regiment under Capt. Ebenezer Eastman, in the war of the Revolution. His father was one of the first settlers at Concord, N. H. His brother

Benjamin was with Col. Rogers' rangers in 1759, and he perished in the service. His two uncles were killed by Indians at Concord in 1746. Abiel m. Nancy Curry, of Canterbury, N. H. Their children were: 1. Thomas Curry, m. Martha Clough Chamberlain April 5, 1820, dau. of Capt. John A. and Mary Rogers (Clough) Chamberlain, of Canterbury, N. H. He was a master mariner and followed the seas for some years, spent a few years in Australia, and settled in Three Oaks, Mich., in 1857. He was first lieutenant in Twelfth Michigan Vols.; was wounded at Shiloh; served the government in various capacities until the close of the war in 1865. He died at Three Oaks, Mich. (his widow and daughter Grace live there). Their children were: Grace Elizabeth, a successful teacher and matron over dependent children. 2. John Chamberlain, merchant, Cleveland, Ohio, m. Amelia Burrell, of Buffalo, N. Y., and have five children. 3. Martha Ann, m. Merritt Wilson, yardmaster, Kensington, Ill.; three children. 4. Charles Henry, traveling salesman; residence, Three Oaks, Mich.; b. March 24, 1861; m. Winnifred Sherrill, of Three Oaks, Mich.; four children. 5. Hannah Robertson, m. Alfred Eastman, of Concord, N. H.; master mechanic, Buffalo, N. Y.; three children. 6. William, m. Philusia Barnes; died on Whidleys Island, Puget Sound, 1867; no children. 7. Charles Eastman, b. in 1828; m. Abby Bacheldor, of Canterbury, N. H.; was conductor on R. R. for many years; died in 1873; one son, Frank, who lives in Columbus, Ohio.

395. ix. LUCY, b. Feb. 1, 1765; m. —— Wilson; d. Nov. 1, 1845.

130. LIEUT. JEREMIAH FOSTER (Timothy, William, Reginald), b. Boxford, Mass., May 4, 1701; m. (pub.) Oct. 31, 1731, Abigail Wood; d. July 27, 1750; m. 2d, Aug. 14, 1755, Mrs. Bridget Pemberton in Andover. He d. Aug. 15, 1785. Res. Boxford, Mass.

396. i. JEREMIAH, b. Nov. 11, 1732.
397. ii. EZRA, b. Oct. 22, 1734.
398. iii. HULDAH, b. Jan. 12, 1736; m. May 3, 1759, Amos Gould and 1784, Capt. Benjamin Kimball of Bridgton, Me.
399. iv. MOSES, b. March 9, 1738-9.
400. v. RUTH, b. Sept. 15, 1741.
401. vi. HANNAH, b. Sept. 14, 1742; d. young.
402. vii. HANNAH, Sept. 4, 1744; m. Deacon Moses Peabody.*
403. viii. PHEBE, bapt. July 12, 1747; d. April 9, 1749.
404. ix. RACHEL, b. Oct. 25, 1749.
405. x. DAVID, b. Aug. 23, 1756
406. xi. ABIGAIL, b. Aug. 27, 1758.
407. xii. SARAH, b. Sept. 2, 1760.
408. xiii. JOSHUA, b. Oct. 20, 1762.

131. DEA. DAVID FOSTER (Timothy, William, Reginald), b. Boxford, Mass., Aug. 17, 1704; m. May 31, 1750, Mrs. Hannah Sessions of Andover. One of the settlers and original proprietors of Keene; clerk of the proprietors for thirty years, fought in the Indian wars of 1748-49; member of the committee of safety 1776. He d. 1779. Res. Pomfret, Conn., and Keene, N. H.

409. i. DAVID, b. Mar. 9, 1755; m. Mary Dassance.
410. ii. HANNAH, b. Apr. 3, 1751.
411. iii. REBECCA, b. June 9, 1735.

132. AMOS FOSTER (Timothy, William, Reginald), b. Boxford, Mass., Feb. 1, 1713; m. Dec. 22, 1751, Mary Dorman. She d. before 1761 s. p. His will was proved Nov. 25, 1761. He d. Feb., 1761. Res. s.p. Ashuelot and Keene, N. H.

136. ABIAL FOSTER (David, William, Reginald), b. Boxford, Mass., May 2, 1702; m. July 11, 1728, Ruth Clement; d. Feb. 4. 1740; m. 2d, Nov. 26, 1741, Hannah Russell, d. Mar. 30, 1803. Res. Haverhill, Mass.

*Dea. Moses and Hannah (Foster) Peabody had Nathan and Hannah (Stickney) Peabody; had Amasa and Hannah (Peabody) Wilder; had Charles Peabody, and Eloise (Walker) Wilder; had W. F. and Fanny R. (Wilder) Winchester. Res. 2031 No. Illinois St. Indianapolis, Ind.

412. i. ELIZAH, b. June 9, 1729; d. July 15, 1736.
413. ii. SARAH. b. Sept. 12, 1731; d. July 5, 1736.
414. iii. RUTH, b. Jan. 26, 1733.
415. iv. MIRRIAM, b. Feb. 13, 1735-6; d. April 22, 1737.
416. v. SAMUEL, b. Feb. 16, 1737-8.
417. vi. MOSES, b. Jan. 27, 1739-40; d. 16 March, 1739-40.
418. vii. JOSHUA, b. 27 Jan, 1739-40; d. March 16, 1739-40.
419. viii. ABIGAIL, b, April 6, 1745.

138. SIMON FOSTER (David, William, Reginald), b. Haverhill, Mass., June 17, 1707; m. ——— ———. He was a soldier in 1725.. Res. Haverhill, Mass.

420. i. JOHN, bapt. July, 1732.

144. THOMAS FOSTER, (Samuel, William, Reginald), b. Boxford, Mass, May 23, 1708; m. July 14, 1731, Allis Pearly. She m. (pub.) Aug. 25, 1734, Benjamin Rogers in Boxford. He d. before 1734. Res. Boxford, Mass.

421. i. JOHN, bapt. July, 1732.

146. WILLIAM FOSTER (Samuel, William, Reginald). b. Boxford, Mass., July 22, 1711; m. ——— ——— ———; m. 2d (pub.) Feb. 7, 1747, Mary Clarke of York, Me. He was a tailor, seaman and inholder. He removed to Newbury between March, 1756 and Jan., 1758 and was living there in 1763. There is no settlement of his estate to be found. He first married ———, who was the mother of his son William as per Essex Deeds, Vol. 105, p. 74. Res. Newbury, Mass.

422. i. WILLIAM.
423. ii. HANNAH, b. May 27, 1749.
424. iii. SAMUEL, b. Nov. 22, 1750.

149. BENJAMIN FOSTER (Jacob, Isaac, Reginald), bapt. Ipswich, Mass., Oct. 6, 1689; m. in Ipswich, Mass., Mar. 15, 1725, Sarah Woodward, dau. of Ezekiel Jr., and Abigail, b 1701, d., 1805 ae. 104. He was born in the old town of Ipswich, Mass., married there, went to Lebanon, Conn. and later to Rockingham county, N. H., probably soon after 1740. The children were all born in Mass., four of them married in N. H. at Hampstead. With two sons and two daughters and their families the parents moved to Granville, Annapolis Co , Nova Scotia in 1760. The day following their arrival the father died. The widow lived for 45 years afterward and died there at the advanced age of 104 years. She was a very quiet and industrious old lady, always spinning flax on her wheel and when she was tired and faint would make a little hasty pudding in the skillet over some coals on the hearth of the old fire place saying she "only wanted a few bites to content nature."

A. W. Savary, Judge of County Court, Annapolis, N. S., author of the Savary Genealogy and editor of Calnek's History of Annapolis, says: "No individual family (Foster) has done more than this in the planting of orchards and changing the wilderness landscapes of a century ago into objects of value and beauty. Monuments of their industry and intelligence are conspicuous in every township and hamlet of the county." Their common ancestor was Benjamin Foster, of Hampstead, N. H., b Oct. 6, 1689; supposed to be a great-grandson of Reginald, im. from Exeter to Ipswich, Mass., in 1638. He died either in New Hampshire or immediately after his arrival in Nova Scotia. In 1760, his widow Sarah, (dau. of Ezekiel Woodward,) with sons Isaac and Ezekiel, settled in Granville, N. S., where she died in 1805, aged 104. Jeremiah, another son who came later, returned to the old colonies, and is perhaps the ancestor of the Fosters of Machias, Me. Isaac and Ezekiel became permanent residents of Annapolis county, as did also their three sisters. He d. 1760. Res. Lebanon, Conn., Hampstead, N. H. and Granville, Nova Scotia.

425. i. JUDITH. b. 1726; m. Nov. 26, 1745, John Chute. He was son of Lionel (Jones, Jones, Lionel) had 10 ch. They went to Nova Scotia in 1759 and resided in Granville. He d. in Nov. 1791 ae, 72. She d 1808 ae. 83 Ch. 1. Samuel b. Feb. 16, 1746; m. Sarah Barnes. Res. G. 2. John, b Apr. 7, 1748; d. May 7, 1748. 3. Hannah, b. Sept. 16, 1749; d. Nov. 1, 1749. 4. John, b. Apr. 9, 1752; m Mary Croker; was a captain of militia. Res. Digby, Joggins, N S. 5. Benjamin, b Sept. 27, 1754; m. Martha Foster dau. of Ezekiel and Mary (Roberts). 6 Thomas, b. Mar. 13, 1757; m. Sybil Marshall and Sarah McKenzie. Res. G. 7. Sarah, b. Nov.

3, 1758; m. Thomas Hicks. Res. Falmouth, N. S. 8. James. b. Jan. 22, 1762; m. Elizabeth Morse and Elizabeth Wright. 9. Hannah b. Dec. 25, 1764; m. Obadiah Morse. Res. Bridgetown, N. S. 10. Susan. b. Dec. 10, 1767; m. Rev. Thomas H. Chipman. Res. Granville, N. S.

426. ii. ISAAC b. Feb. 18, 1728; m. Mehitable Worthing.

427. iii. EZEKIEL. b. 1730; m. Mary Roberts and Ruth Farnsworth.

428. iv. ELIZABETH. b. 1733; m. 1761, Francis B. Le Cain. They had four ch. and lived in Annapolis Royal, N. S. where LeCain died 1806, aged 84. Le Cain's children were: Francis. b. 1762; m. Margaret, daughter of Andrew Ritchie. Benjamin, b. 1764; m. Mary, daughter of Nath Winchester. Nicholas, b. 1765; m. Catharine ——. William, b. 1767; m. Sarah Henshaw, d. 1830. Francis J., d. 1843.

429. v. SARAH, b. 1736; m. Hampstead, N. H., Apr. 26, 1764, Abel Wheelock. He was b. in Lancaster, Mass., June 29, 1739. Res. Granville, N. S.; ch:
1. Benjamin. b. Jan. 26, 1765; m. Elizabeth Jacques. Res. G. 2. Joseph. b. July 7, 1767; d. young. 3. John, b. Apr., 1769; m. Mary Gilliott and Mittie Parker. Res. Tarbrook, N. S. 4. Sarah, b. Feb. 24, 1771; m. Thomas Wheeler Banks. 5. Samuel, b. Jan. 6, 1773; m. Mary Wilkins. Res. Tarbrook. 6. Elizabeth, b. 1775; m. Major Ezekiel Cleveland. 7. Abel. b. Apr. 23, 1777; m. Parney Parker. Res. Nictaux, N. S. 8. Abigail, b. 1779; m. Samuel Felch. 9. Oliver, b. 1782; d. young.

430. vi. JEREMIAH, b. 1740; m. Jemima Kent.

152. SERGT. JOHN FOSTER (Jacob, Isaac, Reginald), b. Ipswich, Mass. Sept 11, 1702; m. in Lebanon, Conn., Aug. 26, 1724, Hannah Thorp. Removed to Topsfield, and afterward with his father to Lebanon, Conn., where he married Hannah, daughter of Peter and Abigail (Higley) Thorp of Widham. Owned covenant Dec. 3, 1727, Lebanon. About 1741 he removed to Deerfield, Mass. Was a soldier in French and Indian war 1747-8 and 9, serving as sergeant in Capt. Samuel Child's company. Also served in later French war 1754-56. Settled at Bernardston. Sergeant Foster died in Burke Fort and was buried in the old cemetery of the place. This death occurred about 1755-1758. He d. abt. 1758. Res. Lebanon, Conn., Deerfield and Bernardston, Mass.

431. i. ISAAC, b. 1725; bapt. Dec. 3, 1727; m. Irene Allen and Edatha Miller.

432. ii. EZEKIEL, b. 1727, bapt. July 7, 1728; m. Margaret Henry.

433. iii. JOHN, b. abt. 1744; m. Mindwell Atherton and Lydia Foster.

155. HON. DAVID FOSTER (Jacob, Isaac, Reginald), bapt. Topsfield, Mass., Apr. 29, 1711; m. in Lebanon, Conn., Mar. 23, 1731, Althea Cogswell. David Foster was in Topsfield, Mass., and before he attained his majority emigrated to Connecticut, locating in Lebanon. which was an incorporated town before 1700. There he was married, followed farming, and remained until 1750, when there was quite an exodus to the new town of Sharon in the extreme western part of the state in which he joined. In Sharon he resided on the place which was afterward occupied by his daughter, Mrs. Jackson. David Foster was one of the leading men of the town and held all the principal offices. He was a member of the Connecticut general assembly at the sessions of 1763-64 and was selectman for eight years. He d. in Sharon, 1793. Res. Lebanon, Conn. and Sharon, Conn.

434. i. RUBIN, b. April 3, 1733.

435. ii. ELIJAH, b. Feb. 26, 1734-5; m. Deborah Holley.

436. iii. ELIAB, b. Apr. 18, 1737.

437. iv. LUCY, b. Sept. 14, 1740; m. in Sharon, Conn., John Jackson. He d. before 1842.

158. BENJAMIN FOSTER (Benjamin, Isaac, Reginald), b. Ipswich, Mass., about 1699; m. ———b. —. She d. E. Machias, Me. He d. in Scarboro, Me., about 1763. Res. Ipswich, Mass., in Conn., Greenland and Portsmouth N. H., and Scarboro, Me.

438. i. BENJAMIN, b. 1726; m. Abigail Milliken and Elizabeth Scott.

439. ii. SARAH, b. ——; m. May 17, 1750, Joseph Milliken, bapt. May 29, 1729. He was a grantee of Trenton on Union river in 1763. His second wife was Miss Berry.

440. iii. ISAIAH, b. ——; m. Lydia Fogg.
441. iv. WOODEN, b. ——; m. Francis Scott.
442. v. EZEKIEL, b. abt. 1734; m. —— ——.

163. PHINEAS FOSTER (Daniel, Isaac, Reginald), b. Topsfield, Mass., July 16, 1703; m. in Lebanon Conn., May 1, 1735, Lydia Hills. Res. Lebanon, Conn., and then to Sharon.

443. i. PHEBE, b. Apr. 5, 1736; m. Aug. 7, 1754, Elias Bakom of Mansfield.
444. v. PHINEHAS, b. Aug. 15, 1754.
445. ii. SARAH, b. Nov. 19, 1738; m. Mar. 25, 1756, Judah Bill. Res. Sharon.
446. iii. DAVID, b. Feb. 2, 1742.
447. iv. PHINEAS, b. —— ; d. Feb. 17, 1746.

165. JEREMIAH FOSTER (David, Isaac, Reginald), b. Topsfield, Mass., June 19, 1707; m. in Lebanon, Conn., Mary Skinner. Res. Lebanon, Conn., and Sharon, Conn.

448. i. SAMUEL, b. Feb. 13, 1731-2; d. 23 Feb., 1731-2.
449. ii. MARY, b. July 3, 1733.
450. iii. JEREMIAH, b. May 9, 1735.
451. iv. NATHANIEL, b. Feb. 27, 1738; d. Sharon, Conn., Sept. 15, 1741.
452. v. ZERVIAH, b. July 11, 1740; d. Sharon, Jan. 8, 1741.

167. ASA FOSTER (Daniel, Isaac, Reginald), b. Topsfield, Mass., Jan. 15, 1710; m. Sharon, Conn., Feb. 4, 1744-5, Hannah White. Res. Lebanon, Conn.

453. i. MARY, b. May 20, 1745; d. June 25, 1751.
454. ii. SAMUEL, b. and d. April 5, 1747.
455. iii. DANIEL, b. Feb. 26, 1747-8.
456. iv. ASA, b. April 22, 1750.
457. v. MARY, b. Sept. 24, 1755.
458. vi. WILLIAM, b. Oct. 24, 1755.
459. vii. HANNAH, b. May 5, 1757.

170. ABIJAH FOSTER (Eleazer, Isaac, Reginald), bapt. Ipswich, Mass., Jan., 1707; m. Dec. 13, 1733, Mary Knowlton of Ipswich, dau. of Robert. He was baptized in Ipswich. Removed to New Ipswich, N. H., probably being sent there by the grantees about 1734. He was the first that went and he soon returned, for his son Ebenezer, was the first child born in New Ipswich. In 1758 or 9 with his son Ebenezer, enlisted in the army against the French and Indians. While encamped near Crown Point both father and son died of the smallpox. He married Mary Knowlton of Ipswich. During the revival of 1786 she joined the Rev. Mr. Farrar's church.

This is what the history of New Ipswich says: Abijah Foster was from Ipswich; he was great grandson of Reginald Foster, who came to New England in 1638, and with his five sons settled in Ipswich. He was of a very respectable family of Exeter in England, and d. at Ipswich in extreme old age.

"Abijah Foster was born in 1707, and no doubt was sent here in the employ of the Ipswich grantees. His was the first family which came here, and he must be regarded as the first settler in town, but it is not so easy to fix the time of his advent. After a very thorough examination of the records of Ipswich, and almost everything that could throw any light on the subject, it would seem that his location here was in the spring of 1738. It is certain he was there in the fall of 1736 and was not there in the fall of 1738. He was accompanied by his wife and daughter. He undoubtedly had his choice of a lot for a farm, and fixed on what was known for a long time as the Hill's Farm, a considerable part of which is now occupied by Joseph Barrett, Esq. His house, which was built of logs, stood near the present Bank building; the old cellar hole was visible within a few years.

"Mr. Foster was a man of an unsettled disposition; he disposed of his farm in 1750 to Joseph Bates and removed to what was formerly known as the Fletcher Farm, now owned by Mr. Joseph Davis; some vestiges of his cellar still remain. This farm he disposed of in 1755, to Capt. Thomas Fletcher, and removed his family to the land now owned by Caleb Campbell. His house there stood a few rods east of Mr. Campbell's barn; the side of it can still be traced.

"Mr. Foster was in town in June 1758, but either in that or the succeeding year he enlisted in the army then employed in a campaign against the French and Indians; he was accompanied by his eldest son Ebenezer, the first child born in town, who was then about 19 years old. While the army was encamped near

Crown Point, they both took the smallpox and died. His widow continued to reside in the house he last erected for many years. She joined the Rev. Mr. Farrar's church in the great revival in 1786 and was baptized by immersion at her request. It is supposed she removed from town with her son Daniel.

"The name of the first permanent resident, with his family, has been determined, so as to leave no question on that point; but the precise date of his advent is less positively settled. From extensive researches into the history of his family, and from other collateral circumstances we have been able to arrive at a conclusion which admits of but very little controversy. Abijah Foster with his wife and daughter Mary, then one year old, came from old Ipswich some time during the summer of 1738 and became the pioneer settler in this place. His wife was the first woman in town, and his son Ebenezer was the first mail child born in town. He first located himself on the lot in the center village." [History New Ipswich, N. H.] He d. 1759. Res. New Ipswich, N. H.

460. i. MARY, b. in Ipswich Aug., 1736.

461. ii. EBENEZER, b. in New Ipswich about 1739. The first child born in New Ipswich; a soldier in the French and Indian war; d. in 1759 of smallpox while encamped near Crown Point.

462. iii. ELIZABETH, b. in New Ipswich about 1741; m. 1759, John Fletcher and 2d, William Hodgkins. They had 6 ch. She d. Feb. 27, 1800. John Fletcher was born in Concord, Mass., where he learned the cooper trade. He went to New Ipswich in 1758 and married the next year. His wife was the first female child born in that town. He settled near what is called the Hodgkin corner about one-half mile S. W. of the meeting house and there he erected a residence and planted an orchard. He was killed by the falling of a tree near his own house Jan. 14, 1763. The family was attracted to the spot by the peculiar noise made by the cat which came into the house. His only son, Joseph, b. 1763, d. in his 19th year.

463. iv. SAMUEL, b. ——; m. Tabitha Hodgkins. He d. in 1780. He erected a house in Mill Village, was a soldier in the Revolutionary war and died in the service.

464. v. DANIEL, b. ——; m. ——. Res. Nelson, N. H., 1802. He was a soldier in the Revolutionary war for 3 years; was a carpenter by trade and built a residence.

465. vi. EPHRAIM, b. ——. He was in the Revolutionary army for 3 years and d. in service in 1780.

466. vii. HIPSEY, b. 1759; m. —— Twichell; m. 2d, Isaac Appleton June 2, 1791. She d. New Ipswich, N. H., 1839.

171. JOHN FOSTER (Eleazer, Isaac, Reginald), b. Ipswich, Mass., May 20, 1714.; m. —— ——. He was probably a weaver for that was his father's occupation and Essex Deeds 83, 105, Dec. 1, 1741, Eleazer Foster, Ipswich, weaver, sells to John Foster, weaver, one-quarter acre land bounding on that of John Manning. Res. Ipswich, Mass.

172. JEREMIAH FOSTER (Abraham, Jacob, Reginald), b. Ipswich, Mass., about 1700; m. (pub.) June 21, 1735, Mrs. Rebecca Metcalf. She d. Feb. 6, 1776. May 26, 1743. Jereih Foster and Rich'd Harris of Ipswich bought of Benjamin Morse of Harvard, Worcester Co. 112 acres land situated on Stow on west side of the river, bounding on Lancaster and Lunenburg lines. Foster resided in the eastern half. Each occupied the other farm buildings together. In 1750 he sold his property to John Millard.

Jan. 13, 1750, Jere Foster and wife Rebecca of Dorchester, Canada, Worcester Co. to Josiah Haynes of Sudbury, Middlesex Co. (Middlesex Deeds). In 1749 in seating the Harvard meeting house he was given the fifth seat below. Immediately after the final conquest with Canada, which forever relieved New England from fear of French invasion, the landless and the adventurous began swarming from the older towns of Massachusetts into the wilderness where land could be had for the clearing. There happened a noteworthy exodus from Harvard. Nearly one tenth of her citizens sought homes in the newer towns. Most of these emigrants by chance found their promised land in Dorchester, Canada, which was incorporated as Ashburnham in 1765. Jeremiah Foster was the first of those from Harvard to reach that settlement, having with him through the woodland paths, upon an ordinary farm cart drawn by oxen, his family and worldly possessions. In Ashburnham he settled on land west of Lake Naukeag still known as Foster Hill. He was a man of exemplary character, reserved in manner, industrious, honest, a kind neighbor and an excellent citizen. He d. Dec. 12, 1788. Res. Ipswich, Harvard and Ashburnham, Mass.

467. i. JEREMIAH, bapt. Aug. 8, 1736; d. young.
468. ii. ABIGAIL, bapt. Feb. 17, 1737-8.
469. iii. JEREMY, bapt. Jan. 6, 1739-40; m. Sarah Fellows.
470. iv. SAMUEL, bapt Jan. 8, 1741; m. Susanna Wood.
471. v. SARAH, b. July 28, 1744.
472. vi. JUDITH, b. Mar. 2, 1747; m. Nov. 14, 1769, Dr. Peter Brooks. She d. Mar. 9, 1824. His lineage is not known. He was the first resident physician in Ashburnham, Mass. Between 1790 and 1800 he left his family and the town. It is not known where he died. Ch: 1. Calvin, b. Mar. 25, 1770; res. south. 2. Luther, b. Feb. 15, 1772; m. Lucy Gates, rev. to Ohio; 11 ch. 3. John Swift, b. and d. 1774. 4. Sewell, b. Feb 4 1777; m. Sally ——; 7 ch. Res. A. 5. Peter, b. Jan. 11, 1780 6. Dorcas, b. Jan. 24, 1782. 7. Lydia, b. Sept. 23, 1784; d unm. June 30, 1851. 8. Dickerson, b. Oct. 13, 1787; m. Hannah Kemp of Groton; res. A; 6 ch.
473. vii. REBECCA, b. Oct. 29, 1750; m. Jan. 22, 1772, Caleb Ward, b. Waltham, Nov. 22, 1748. He died June 20, 1813. She d. Mar. 22, 1831. He was a selectman in Ashburnham and his name was frequently on the town records. His wife resided in A. for 77 years and 60 years in the house in which she died. Ch: 1. Samuel, b. Dec. 22, 1772 (Deacon); m. Ruth Townsend; res. A; 2 ch. 2. Sarah, b. Oct. 27, 1774; m. Thomas Piper; res. Weston, Vt. 3. Rebecca, b. 1776; d. Nov. 23, 1780. 4. Caleb, b. Aug 6, 1778; m. Mary Rice; res. A.; 6 ch. 5. Nahum, b. Aug. 7, 1780; res. Peterboro, N. H. and joined the Mormons. 6. Jacob, b. Nov. 22, 1782; m. Sally Whittmore. He was in the war of 1812; res. A, 14 ch. 7. Jonas, b. Feb. 15, 1785; m. Susan F. Thurston; res. Oxford, Mass. 8. Rebecca, b. Sept. 14, 1788; m. Ezra Lawrence. 9. Lucy, b. July 28, 1790; m. Samuel Wilson; res. Nelson, N. H.

175. ABRAHAM FOSTER (Abraham, Jacob, Reginald), b. Ipswich, Mass., July 5, 1716; m. Nov. 5, 1742, Elizabeth Davis of Charlestown, b. Nov. 3, 1720, dau. of Barnabas; d. Jan. 19, 1795. 5 (6), 1716. Mark Haskell was appointed his guardian April 3, 1733, he then being seventeen years old. He was a joiner and resided in Boston and Charlestown and died before 1750. In 1744 with B. Davis, etal, he sells to R. Miller an estate. He d. prior to 1749. Res. Boston and Charlestown, Mass.

474. i. ELIZABETH, bapt. Nov. 18, 1744; m. May 21, 1762, John Rogers.
475. ii. ABRAHAM, bapt. Dec. 2, 1744; m. —— ——.

176. NATHANIEL FOSTER (Abraham, Jacob, Reginald), b. Ipswich, Mass. Aug. 9, 1719; m. May 6, 1741, Sarah Deland; bapt. July 12, 1724; d. Aug., 1796. He removed to Salem where he pursued the occupation of a tailor and died. He married Sarah, daughter of George and Bethia (Peters) Deland of Salem. She was bapt. 1st church Salem. He d. Oct. 1808. Res. Salem, Mass.

476. i. NATHANIEL, bapt. 1st church Nov. 7, 1742; m. Elizabeth Yell.
477. ii. SARAH, bapt. 1st church, Jan. 13, 1744-5.
478. iii. ABRAHAM, bapt. 1st church, March 1, 1746-7.
479. iv. ABIGAIL, bapt. 1st church, March 26, 1749.
480. v. GEORGE bapt. 1st church, J. 13, 1750-1.
481. vi. JOSEPH, bapt. 1st church, Nov 11, 1753.
482. vii. SAMUEL, bapt. 1st church, Nov 6., 1757.
483. viii. JOHN, bapt. 1st church, May 11, 1760; d. young.
484 ix. JOHN, bapt 1st church, May 2, 1762.
485. x. DAUGHTER, bapt. 1st church, April, 1764.

182. WILLIAM FOSTER (Jacob, Jacob, Reginald), b. Ipswich, Mass., May 11, 1699; m. (pub.) Sept. 7, 1734, Elizabeth Clark. She d. Feb., 1767. Administration was granted on his estate to Isaac Dodge who gave bonds with Nathan Foster Jan. 1., 1776. April 30, 1760, Wm. Foster, cordwainer and wife Elizabeth sell to Isaac Dodge Miller 1 upland right in Jeffery Neck. He d. 1775. Res. Ipswich, Mass.

486. i. WILLIAM, bapt. Aug 17., 1735.
487. ii. ELIZABETH, b. March 19, 1737; living 1776, unm.
488. iii. SARAH, bapt. May 12, 1740; pub. Nathaniel Hodgkins.
489. iv. MARY, bapt. July 25, 1742; m. —— Kimball.
490. v. HANNAH, bapt. Feb. 2. 1745; d. before 1776.
491. vi. ABIGAIL, bapt. March 20, 1747; d. young.
492. vii. ABIGAIL, bapt. March 18, 1749.
493. viii. REBECCA, bapt. 1753.

186. NATHANIEL FOSTER (Jacob, Jacob, Reginald), b. Ipswich, Mass. Dec. 14, 1712; m. (pub.) Nov. 29, 1735, Elizabeth Leatherland. She m. before 1758, Benjamin Brown 3d. He was a blacksmith. He d. Aug. 16, 1747. Res. Ipswich, Mass.

494. i. ELIZABETH, b. Feb. 5, 1736; pub. to Richard Sutton.
495. ii. NATHAN, b June 20, 1737.
496. iii. MARTHA, b. May 6, 1739; d. young.
497. iv. MARTHA, b. April 13, 1740.
498. v. MARY, b. April 13, 1740.
499. vi. SARAH, bapt. Aug. 1, 1742.
500. vii. NATHANIEL, bapt. Dec. 22, 1745; d. Aug. 23, 1747.

191. DEA. JOSEPH FOSTER (Joseph, Jacob, Reginald), b. Ipswich, Mass., Feb. 14, 1714; m. there Nov. 12, 1735, Hannah Trask. She d. Aug. 11, 1778. Dea. Joseph Foster died Feb. 27, 1767, aged 53 years and 13 days. At selectmen's meeting March 16, 1767, ordered £5.2.0 paid to widow Hannah Foster in full for services of her late husband Dea. Joseph Foster as town clerk, selectman and overseer. March 3, 1761 Joseph Foster received £3 for his disbursements for the French neutrals. Hannah, widow late Dea. Joseph Foster died Aug. 11, 1778. He d. Feb. 27, 1767. Res. Beverly, Mass.

501. i. THOMAS, b. Oct. 18, 1736; d. July 26 1794.
502. ii. JOSEPH, b. Dec. 25, 1739; m. Elizabeth Hilton.
503. iii. MARY, b. Jan. 18, 1741; m. Henry Herrick, Nov. 21, 1765.
504. iv. HANNAH, b. March 4, 1743-4; m. first, Jonathan Ellingwood, May 5, 1767; 2d, Nehemiah Smith, Apr. 12, 1774.
506. v. DANIEL, b. Feb. 14, 1745-6; m. Judith Woodbury.
507. vi. ELIZABETH, b. April 7, 1748.
508. vii. SARAH, b. Dec. 29, 1750; m. Feb. 11, 1772, Ebenezer Tuck.
509. viii. EZRA-TRASK, b. Sept. 29, 1752; m. Sarah Stickney.
510. ix. MERCY, b. Dec. 9, 1754; d. Dec. 1, 1755.
511. x. JEREMIAH, b. April 21, 1756.
512. xi. LYDIA, b. March 8, 1757.
513. xii. JAMES, b. Aug. 31, 1759.

192. DEA. JAMES FOSTER (Joseph, Jacob, Reginald), b. Ipswich, Mass. Mar. 4, 1716; m. (pub.) June 25, 1746, Sarah Hart. Removed to Boston where two of his children were born. Returned to Ipswich, being admitted in 1766 to the South Church at Chebacco from the Brattle street church, Boston. His wife was Sarah Hart to whom he was published in Ipswich. She was living in 1803. He was postmaster in Ipswich, being succeeded by Daniel Noyes, June 23, 1775. He gave a deed Oct. 10, 1807, being then 91 years of age. His will dated May 29, 1786 was disproved Dec. 9, 1807 as one of the witnesses, Mary Foster, had no recollection of being present at the signing and the others, Sarah Lowater and Nathan Foster were deceased. Administration was afterward granted Nathaniel Lord, 3d, Nov. 2, 1807. The will mentions wife Sarah, only son James and only daughter Sarah. He d. Oct. 10, 1807. Res. Ipswich, Mass. Dea. Joseph Foster was the first postmaster at Ipswich. He was appointed by the Provisional Congress and before this time the mail had been brought through that town on horseback. Sarah Hart was born Oct. 2, 1715, daughter of Ensign Nathaniel and Sarah (Rust) Hart of Ipswich, Mass.

514. i. SARAH, b. in B., Dec. 25, 1747.
515. ii. JAMES, b. in B., Aug. 30, 1749.
516. iii. JOHN, bapt. in I., March 29, 1752; d. young.
517. iv. JOSEPH, bapt. in I., June 3, 1753; d. young.

193. NATHAN FOSTER (Joseph, Jacob, Reginald), b. Ipswich, Mass., Feb. 19, 1717; m. Dec. 27, 1743, Mary Hart, dau. of Nathaniel and Sarah, b. Jan. 20, 1718; d. Apr. 10, 1778. He d. Oct., 1795. Res. Ipswich, Mass.

518. i. MARY, b. — Nov., 1744; d. unm. March, 1828.
519. ii. SAMUEL, b. Oct. 23, 1746; m. Lucy Farrington of Cambridge, Mass. Res. Stratham, N. H.
520. iii. JAMES, b. Dec. 18, 1747; m. Elizabeth Hiller.
521. iv. NATHANIEL, b. Nov. 30, 1752: m. Susanna Hiller.
522. v. WM. HART, bapt. July 24, 1757; d. young.

195. ISAAC FOSTER (Joseph, Jacob, Reginald), b. Ipswich, Mass., Aug. 21, 1720; m. Nov. 8, 1744, Sarah Brown, dau. of John. His will is dated Feb. 1, 1783 and proved April 10. He died Mar. 12, 1783. He gave his son John a cow and clothes but I cannot trace him. Isaac of Billerica, 1783-5684, Middlesex, Court, appraisers Dea. Joshua Abbott: Major Edw. Farmer, Jacob Manning, to act Apr. 10, 1783. Joseph and Sam already have a deed of estate they improve and they are to have the residue to finish up some business agreed on in the papers named. This Isaac had surveying instruments in his inventory. Isaac Foster's will.—1783. In the name of God, Amen, I, Isaac Foster of Billerica in County of Middlesex and Commonwealth of Massachusetts, yeoman, being very sick and weak of body, but of sound and dispoising ?] mind, do make this my last will, and first I would give my Soul unto God who gave it, my body I recommend to the Earth to be buried in a decent manner, at the discretion of my Executor hereafter named, as to such worldly Estate as I have I give and dispoise ?] of the same in the following manner:

1st, my will is that all my debts and funeral charges be paid by my Executor out of my Estate.

2nd. I give and bequeath unto my beloved wife Sarah all my household Suff ?] and indoor movable ?]. I also give unto her one cow, two sheep, my stock of bees, all to her own Disposal forever. I give my wife the improvement ?] of sufficient rooms in my Dwelling house as long as she shall remain my widow. I also give unto my wife one-third part of the income of my Real Estate during her natural life. My will is that the movabls ?] within doors given to my wife be apprized into my estate.

3rd. All my wearing apparril ?] I give unto my sons Isaac, Jacob and John my will is my son Isaac have my best Sute ?] throughout and if that do not amount to one full third of s'd clothing that he have some other things to make up one-third, that the remainder be equally divided between the other two, viz.: Jacob and John.

4th. I give unto my sons Joseph and Samuel all my shop tools to be Equally divided.

5th. I give unto my son Samuel all my husbandry tools and my surveying implements. My will is that the remainder of my Live Stock not given away be to enable my Executors to pay Debts and give unto my son John one cow or money equivalent to be paid within one year after my Decease.

6th. The remainder of my Estate, Real, personal or mixed I give unto my sons Joseph and Samuel (and whereas I have sometime since given to them a Deed of all my Real Estate, they being obliged by Bond, having given date with said Deed to perform certain matters and things therein mentioned, which bond together with this Presence ?] must be the Rule of their administration of my Estate, I constitute and appoint my said sons Joseph Foster and Samuel Foster my Executors of this my last will and testament, hereby revoking all other wills, or Executors by me maid ?] or named, confirming this to be my last will in witness whereof I have hereunto set my hand and seal this first day of February, A. D. One Thousand Seven Hundred Eighty Three.

Signed, sealed, published and declared by the said Isaac Foster to be his last will in Presence of

William Baldwin.
Timothy Foster. Isaac Foster.
-Risza [?] Baldwin. (Clarissa).

Prob. April 10, 1783. Res. Billerica, Mass.

523. i. ISAAC, b. Mar. 8, 1745; m. Lydia Bacon.
524. ii. JACOB, b. Dec. 20, 1747; m. Hannah Frost.
525. iii. SARAH, b. Mar. 4, 1749; d. Apr. 4, 1750.
526. iv. JOSEPH, b. Mar. 21, 1750; m. Sarah Baldwin and Lucy Hill.
527. v. SARAH, b. May 29, 1753; d. bef. 1783.
528. vi. JOHN BRAINARD, b. June 28, 1755; m. Sarah Taylor and Lydia Foster.
529. vii. SAMUEL, b. Mar. 31, 1758; m. Mary Colcord.
530. viii. ABIGAIL, b. Feb. 21, 1761; d. before 1783.

197. JACOB FOSTER (Joseph, Jacob, Reginald), b. Billerica, Mass., March 27, 1726; m. (pub.) Aug. 25, 1750, Sarah Kimball. His will was made Aug. 4, 1760; proved Oct. 19, 1761.

Jacob Foster's will. 1760.—In the name of God Amen, I Jacob Foster of Billerica in the county of Middlesex and Province of the Massachusetts Bay in New England Cordwainer being indisposed in body but of perfect mind and memory thanks be given to God therefor. Do made and ordain this my Last will and testament principally and first of all I give and recommend my Soul unto the hands of God that gave it hoping through the mercy of God and merit of our glorious Reedeemer to obtain the full Pardon of all my sins and to inherit Eternal Life and my Body when Dead to the Earth to be Buried in Christian-life and Decent Burial at the Discretion of my Executrix hereafter named and that small Portion of this worlds goods with which it has Pleased God to Bless me with I give [demiss ?] and Dispose of the same in the following manner and form—

Item my will is that all my just debts and funeral Charges be paid by my Executrix hereafter named out of my Estate—

Item I give to Sarah my Beloved wife the whole of my Estate that I have in [possestion ?] Both Real and personall (except somethings (particularly ?) mentioned hereafter) to enable her to pay my just Debts and to bring up my Children and for her own maintainance.

Item I give to my only Son Timothy that part and [potion ?] of my Hon'd father (Joseph Foster [lait?] of Ipswich deceased) his Estate which he gave me in his last will and testament after my Hon'd mother's decease. I also give to my said Son three of my Books viz. Baileys Dictionary, Salmons geographical and Historical Grammar and modern gazeteer. I also give to my s'd son my millitary armor.

Item I give to my only Daughter Sarah twenty pounds in money or good house hold stuf Shuch?] as is necessary to keep house with to be paid by my Executrix out of my Estate when she shall come to the full age of twenty one years or if she shall be married sooner upon her marriage Day—

Item my will is that if my son or daughter should deceas?] before they arrive to the age of twenty one years the survivor inherit the whole of what I have given to Both—

Item my will is that my said wife take the whol?] care of the portion I have given to my said son and that she joyn?) with my Brother in deviding or selling my fathers Estate after my Mothers deceas?] and that she receive my s'd. sons part and put it out to the best advantage for him til he be capable to take care of it for him self, and I do hereby constitute and appoint Sarah my Beloved wife only and sole Executrix of this my last will and testament and I do hereby utterly revoke make void and disanull?] any other or former will or Executr by me in any way made or named. Rattifiing?] and confirming this and no other to be my last will and testament in witness where of I, the said Jacob Foster have set my hand and seal this fourth day of August in the year of our Lord One Thousand seven hundred and sixty.

Jacob Foster

Signed sealed and published pronounced and declared by the said Jacob Foster as his last will and testament in presents?] of us the subscribers

Prob. Oct 19-1761

Isaac Foster
Solomon Pollard
Hannah Stickney.

He d. Oct., 1761. Res., Billerica, Mass.

531. i. SARAH, b. April 27, 1752; d. June 7, 1752.
532. ii. SARAH, b. June 5, 1753; m. Dec. 12, 1774, John Bell, of Charlestown.
533. iii. TIMOTHY, b. July 19, 1755; d. Nov. 23, 1756.
534. iv. ELIZABETH, b. Oct. 27, 1757; d. Jan. 12, 1758.
535. v. TIMOTHY, b. Nov. 4, 1759; m. Sally Crosby.

199. ABRAHAM FOSTER (Joseph, Jacob, Reginald), bapt. Ipswich, Mass., Oct. 27, 1728; m. Boston, Nov. 1, 1753,* Susannah Sumner. Removed to Boston where he settled. He was a cabinetmaker. His wife was Susannah Sumner. He had six children. Oct., 1761, he bought of Jno. Downe for £230.14.4. parcel of land, house and buildings on First street, in the north end of Boston. Aug. 16, 1773,

*Boston records say Ephraim Foster m. Susannah Sumner Nov. 1, 1753.

Abraham Foster and wife, Susannah, mortgaged this estate to John White for £133.

Joseph Foster, of Boston, goldsmith, admitted adm. on estate of Abraham Foster, late of Boston, cabinetmaker, dec'd. James Foster Jr. and Nathaniel Foster, gentlemen, both of Boston, bound with said Joseph Foster. Aug. 9, 1796. Lib 94, Fol. 454-487-8-491. He d. in 1796. Res., Boston, Mass.

536. i. ELIZABETH, b. ——.
537. ii. SUSANNAH, b. ——
538. iii. JOSEPH, b. ——; m. —— — —.
539. iv. MARY, b. ——
540. v. SARAH, b. ——.
541. vi. RACHEL, b. ——.

James Foster, of Boston, married one of the above girls, as will be seen by the following from Suffolk Pub.: Joseph Foster, of Boston, goldsmith, adm. on estate of James Foster, late of Boston, scrivener, his brother-in-law, dec'd. Nov. 9, 1818. Lib. 191, Fol. 151. Lib. 170, Fol 15. Lib. 312, Fol. 13.

Bond—Joseph Foster, goldsmith; Moses Brown Foster, copper plate printer and Joseph Foster 2d, scrivener of Boston, bound with him. Lib. 205, Fol. 160. Inventory mentions Samuel Foster, Nathaniel Foster, appraisers. Dec. 23, 1818. Joseph Foster, adm. Lib. 116, Fol. 727.

203. HON. JEDEDIAH FOSTER (Ephraim, Ephraim, Abraham, Reginald), b. Andover, Mass., Oct. 10, 1726; m. May 18, 1749, Dorothy Dwight, dau. of Brig.-Gen. Joseph Dwight; b. Nov. 13, 1729; d. Jan. 12, 1818.

Gen. Dwight was son of Henry, of Dedham and Hatfield. Was b. Oct. 16, 1703; was graduated at Harvard in 1722. His father purchased large tracts of land in Brookfield, about 1,400 acres, and Joseph settled there on Foster Hill in 1728; was representative in 1731, and in all eleven years; was speaker of the House in 1748-9; was admitted to the bar in 1733; judge court of Common Pleas of Worcester county in 1739; was colonel of the Ninth Mass. Regt. in the expedition against Cape Breton, 1744; commissioned brigadier-general 1745; appointed judge of the Court of Admiralty 1745; commanded the Mass. Regt. of artillery at the reduction of Louisburg and was distinguished and commended by Gen. Pepperell. He commanded a brigade in the Crown Point expedition of 1756. At the close of the French and Indian war he removed to Great Barrington and was appointed judge of Berkshire county Court and Probate. His wife was Mary Pynchon.

Mr. Foster was graduated at Harvard college in 1744, and soon after went to Brookfield and engaged in business with Brig.-Gen. Joseph Dwight. He was a man very much trusted and respected. He retained various offices; was deacon of the church in the First Parish; was judge of the Probate Court; judge of the Supreme Judicial Court of Massachusetts. Rev. Nathan Fisher, D. D., preached his funeral sermon, in which he gave him a very high character. In 1753 he headed a petition to the selectmen to lay out the First parish into two parishes. In 1774 he was elected delegate to the Provincial Congress at Cambridge. He was often moderator of the town meetings, and often served on important committees. During the Revolutionary war he was a colonel. In 1775 there was a prevalent prejudice against inoculation as a guard against violent disease, especially smallpox. Col. Foster went to Esopus, N. Y., and was there inoculated, had the disease and returned in health. He was representative in the legislature 1761-2-3-4-5-6-7-8-9-'70-1-2-3-4-5-9. He was a deacon in the church. He held various military offices, from captain of a company to major of a regiment, under Major-General Winslow, by commission from Gov. Shirley. In 1754 he was commissioned justice of the peace and of the quorum for Worcester county. He was also judge of probate, and afterward one of the judges of the Superior court of Massachusetts. He was a representative of the town in the General Council for 15 years (1761-76), and a member of all the Provincial Congresses of Massachusetts. In 1779 he was a member of the convention for forming a State constitution and of the committee itself appointed to draft it; during the session of which committee he died. He was a man of thorough integrity and honor and of large benevolence, an active Christian and a zealous patriot. "Blessed with a happy steadiness and presence of mind" he always studied to be useful, "being of the fixed opinion that no one should desire to outlive his usefulness." He was especially hopeful, determined and active in that part of the Revolutionary war in which he had an opportunity to take any share of duty or service.

Mrs. F.'s personal appearance was thus described by her grandson, Alfred Dwight

Foster Esq., in a letter addressed by him to Fredric A. Foster Esq., of Lancaster, O.: "She had always, within my memory, a head of perfectly white hair and very black eyes, although the Dwights almost without exception have light complexion and blue eyes, as my father and uncles Theodore and Theophilus had." He d. Oct. 17, 1779. Res., Brookfield, Mass.

542. i. PAMELA, b Aug. 12, 1750; d. Jan. 19, 1751.

543. ii. THEODORE, b. April 29, 1752; m. Lydia Fenner and Esther Bowen Millard.

544. iii. THEOPHILUS, b. Mar. 16, 1754; m. Susanna Packard and Hannah Crosby.

545. iv. ABIGAIL, b. Jan. 10, 1756; d. July 25, 1779; unm. She is described as having been "a lady of superior talents and accomplishments, of a sweet attractive disposition, and full of faith in God, and of the spirit of duty, and of patient endurance under severe trials."

546. v. DWIGHT, b. Dec. 7, 1757; m. Rebecca Faulkner.

547. vi. PERGRINE, b. Dec. 28, 1759; m. Mrs. Polly (Parkman) Bradshaw.

548. vii. RUTH, b. Sept. 11, 1766; m. Mar. 2, 1786, General Thomas Ives, of Great Barrington, Mass. She d. Feb. 15, 1852; ae. 85. Gen. Thomas Ives, b. in New Haven, Conn., Feb. 2, 1753, (son of Thomas Ives Jr., b. in 1712, and d. Nov. 17, 1752. Anna Heaton, b. in 1711, who d. ae. 81, June 22, 1795). He was grad. at Yale 1777, and studied law at Litchfield, Conn., with Tappan Reeve Esq., and became a lawyer as well as large farmer at Gt. Barrington, Mass. He was distinguished in his profession and was greatly esteemed as an upright and honorable man. He held at different times various military offices, from that of a captain to that of a major-general of militia. He was also a man of much public spirit. He was successively a member of both houses of the State legislature—of the senate in 1797. He d. March 8, 1814, ae. 61, at Gr. Barrington, where she also d. Feb. 15, 1852, ae. 85, having been a widow for 38 years. "Possessing a benevolent disposition, a well-cultured mind and sprightly manners, together with an unusual degree of intelligence, she endeared herself to young and old. Ch: 1. Harriet Ives, b. Feb. 12, 1787; d. unm. Sept. 24, 1815, ae 28. 2. George Heaton Ives, b. April 15, 1789; d. unm. April 29, 1825, ae. 36. He was a lawyer at Gt. Barrington. 3. Alma Cornelia Ives (twin), b. March 17, 1791; d. Oct. 1, 1792. 4. Anna Maria Ives (twin), b. March 17, 1791; m. May 29, 1816, Philo Parks, of Salisbury, Conn.; d. Feb. 25, 1863. i. Alma Cornelia Parks, b. April 27, 1817; m. March 28, 1844, Thomas Warner, of Kalamazoo, Mich. They have several children. ii. Elizabeth Parks, b. Dec. 21, 1818; d. Feb. 26, 1835. iii. James William Parks, b. Oct. 14, 1822; m. Dec. 2, 1846, Caroline Jewell, who d. Feb. 2, 1850; and he m. afterward Maria Jewell, her sister. No children. iv. Ruth Foster Parks, b. Feb. 7, 1827; m. a Judson. She d., leaving one child. v. Amanda Maria Parks, b. Sept. 12, 1829; is unm. vi. Foster Ives Parks, b. May 20, 2831; resides in Mich.; has a family. 5. Alma Cornelia Ives, 2d, b. April 14, 1793; m. April 17, 1821, Benoni C. Wells; d. Sept. 8, 1856. Wells, b. Jan. 8, 1789 (son of Ashbel Wells, of W. Hartford, Conn. and Britty Chancer, an English lady), a farmer in Stockbridge, Mass., where he d. Sept. 10, 1845, and she d. Sept. 8, 1856, ae. 63. Ch: i. Thomas Wells, b. Feb. 12, 1822; m. Oct. 20, 1847, Gertrude Perrine (dau. of Humphrey Mount Perrine, b. May 20, 1785, and Fanny Dodd, b. April, 1791, whom he m. Feb. 15, 1813). They reside in Stockbridge; he is a farmer; four children. 6. Nancy Ives, b. June 13, 1795; m. Solomon Pitkin; m. Oct. 8, 1820, Pitkin, b. Sept. 15, 1797 (son of Timothy Pitkin, of East Hartford, Conn., and Jerusha ——), a merchant at Ellington, Ct., and afterward at Amherst, Mass., where he was also pres. of a bank. He d. at Memphis, Tenn., of consumption about 1851. She d. at Gr. Barrington, Aug. 4, 1872. ae. 77. Ch: i. Rev. Solomon Dwight Pitkin, b. June 20, 1822; grad. at Amherst in 1843, and at New Haven Theol. Sem. in 1846; a Presb. clergy-

man at Benton, Wis. (1847-50), and Battle Creek, Mich., 1850-8. He d. Sept. 30, 1858. He was a man of industry and polish, and of graceful, effective elocution He m. (whom not ascertained) and had two ch. that d young. ii. Charles Fredric Pitkin, b. Aug. 22, 1824; was drowned at Gr. Barrington, Mass., July 10, 1846, ae. 22; a very interesting man and remarkable for his talents and piety. iii. George Edward Pitkin, b. July 2, 1826; resides in Kansas City, Mo., and is engaged in the auditor's department of the Missouri River, Fort Scott & Gulf railroad. He is married and has a family of children. iv. James Francis Pitkin, b. March 11, 1832; d. April 11, 1836. v. Louisa R. Pitkin, b. Dec. 20, 1835; resides, unm., in Chicago. vi. Thomas Ives Pitkin, b. July 18, 1837; d. May 26, 1838. vii. William Pitkin, b. Oct. 8, 1840; d. in Chicago about 1860. 7. Elizabeth Ives, b. June 7, 1797; m. John Chatfield, June, 1817. Chatfield, b. May 30, 1793 (son of Isaac Chatfield, of Oxford, Conn., and Sarah Whittmore), a carpenter and builder at Gr. Barrington, who removed in 1856 to Owego, N. Y., where he lived on a farm, and where he d. Aug. 9, 1865, ae. 72. 1. Hon. Thomas Ives Chatfield, b. Sept. 16, 1818; in Gr. Barrington, removed May, 1839, to Owego, N. Y., where he was at first a baker (1839-45), but has been since 1845 engaged in the grocery business, and now in a large wholesale way. He was in 1852 a (republican) member of the State legislature, and later (since 1871) a member of the State Senate. He has been also at different times Pres. of the village of Owego, civil justice and town supervisor, and was a delegate to the National republican convention at Chicago, which nominated Grant for the presidency (in 1868). He m. Nov. 9, 1841, Mary Purdy Bundy, b. in Owego, March 24, 1822 (dau. of David Bundy and Sarah Whipple). She d. Sept. 18, 1857. He m. for 2d wife, June 22, 1858, Lucy Goodrich, b. July 15, 1830, in Tioga, N. Y. (dau. of Erastus Goodrich, of Owego—b. in Glastonbury, Conn., June 10, 1787—and Hope Talcott, b. there May, 1785, who were m. in Owego, Feb. 27, 1812). His ch: 1. John James Chatfield, b. April, 7, 1845; d. of croup, Jan. 25, 1852. By second wife: 2. A son unnamed, b. Jan. 1 and d Jan. 2, 1869. 3. Thomas Ives Chatfield, b. Oct. 4, 1871. 2. Charles James Chatfield, b. Aug. 23, 1820; m. Aug. 15, 1843, Sarah Delia Foster, b. Feb. 2, 1826 (dau. of Robert Wallis Foster and Tammason Smith). He was a merchant at Painted Post, N. Y., where he d. March 23, 1864, ae. 43, and where his widow resided. He had four children: 1. Charles James Chatfield, b. Aug. 4, 1844; m. Dec. 27, 1869, Mary Ada Blake, and lives in Rye, N. Y. He had two children; viz.: Mary Ada, b. Sept. 7, who d. Sept. 23, 1871, and a son unnamed, b. June 21, 1873. 2. Frank Albert Chatfield, b. Aug. 24, 1848. 3. Ida Elizabeth Chatfield, b. Oct. 8, 1850. 4. Lillian Foster Chatfield, b. Jan. 18, 1859. 3. John R. Chatfield, b. at Gr. Barrington, Jan. 28, 1823; m. there Oct. 8, 1845, Abby Eunice Smith, of Gr. Barrington, b. Feb. 11, 1827, in Bridgewater, Conn. (dau. of Orange Smith, now of Owego, and Martha Morris). He is a hardware and stove merchant at Owego—(Storrs & Chatfield). He has had five children. 1. George Smith Chatfield, b. at Great Barrington, Aug. 1, 1847; m. Sept. 14, 1869, Ella Gertrude Fritcher, b. in Athens, Pa., Sept. 14, 1848 (dau. of George Fritcher, of Owego, and Lucy Loomis). He is a clerk in his father's store. One child: 1. Clara Chatfield, b. Jan. 16 and d. Jan. 18, 1873. 2. Frank Edward Chatfield, b. at Owego, Jan. 1, 1859; d. March 24, 1860. 3. Harry Ives Chatfield, b. there July 1, 1862. 4. George Albert Chatfield, b. Oct. 19, 1827; d. July 9, 1829. 5. Mary Elizabeth Chatfield, b. Oct. 29, 1829; m. Jan. 2, 1854, Thomas Pest, b. in Spencer, N. Y., March 10, 1829 (son of Thomas Pest and Amanda Dakin), a clerk in Owego. Two children: 1. Fred Chatfield Pest, b. Dec. 28, 1858. 2. Willis Ives Pest, b. May 27, 1866. 8. Dwight Foster Ives, b. June 6, 1799; was drowned Sept. 30, 1820. 9. Amanda Ives, b. July 24, 1800;

m. Ralph Taylor. 10. Thomas Earle Ives, b. Sept. 30, 1802; d. Nov. 30, 1843, ae. 41. 11. David Ives, b. Sept. 21, 1805; d. Jan. 1, 1850. 12. Charles J. Ives, b. Feb. 8, 1807; d. Feb. 23, 1816.

206. JOHN FOSTER (John, Ephraim, Abraham, Reginald), b. Andover, Mass., Feb. 11, 1716; m. there June 25, 1740, Deborah Barker, of Andover, b. 1716. He was a blacksmith and was killed by lightning. He d. in 1773. Res., Andover, Mass.

549. i. JEMIMA, b. Nov. 22, 1741; m. bef. 1773, William Foster, of Boxford. She d. bef. 1773; only one mo. after her marriage, s. p.
550. ii. WILLIAM, b. Oct. 3, 1743; m. Mehitable Fuller.
551. iii. EPHRAIM, b. Nov. 13, 1745; m. June 28, 1770, Sarah Town, dau. of Joseph and Sarah; d. s. p. Sept. 1, 1807.
552. iv. DORCAS, b. Aug. 26, 1747; m. (pub.) Feb., 1775, Mark Avery. Ch. one: John.
553. v. JOHN, b. Jan. 8, 1750; d. Sept. 11, 1755.
554. vi. DEBORAH, b. Feb. 2, 1752; m. Mar. 10, 1772, Paul Avery. One ch., d. young and 2 Deborah.
555. vii. JUDITH, b. July 29, 1755; unm.; d. Aug. 8, 1828.
556. viii. JOHN, b. Oct. 24, 1760; m. Dorcas Town.

208. STEPHEN FOSTER (John, Ephraim, Abraham, Reginald), b. Andover, Mass., Aug. 14, 1720; m. (pub.) May 12, 1744, Abigail Smith of Danvers. His will was proved Oct. 2, 1787, and heirs Sept. 9, 1807. He d. 1787. Res. Andover, Mass.

557. i. DAVID, b. Mar. 5, 1745; m. Ruth Peabody.
558. ii. REBECCA, b. Mar. 11, 1746; m. May 3, 1768, William Reynolds. A son Stephen was bapt. 1771. Res. New Salem, N. H.
559. iii. ABIGAIL, b. Aug. 23, 1749; m. June 23, 1774, Phinehas Barker. Res. A.
560. iv. STEPHEN, b. July 3, 1751; m. Rebecca Wood.
561. v. EUNICE, b. Apr. 15, 1753; m. (pub.) May 2, 1778, Jeremiah Pearley of Boxford; she m. 2d, before Sept. 9, 1807, Rev. Dr. Daniel Gould. She joined the Boxford ch. Sept. 21, 1777. Rev. Daniel Gould was b. in Topsfield, Mass., Dec. 8, 1753. He was the son of Daniel and Lucy (Tarbox) Gould, and the fifth in descent from Zaccheus Gould, who was born in England about 1589, came to this country in 1638, and settled in Topsfield. He graduated at Harvard College, and before entering College and while a student at Dummer Academy he served a term in the continental army. Returning he studied Theology with Rev. Mr. Moody of Byfield. He was admitted to the church in Topsfield Dec. 7, 1783. He came to Bethel and preached as a candidate in 1798-9, and was installed as the first settled minister in Bethel in Oct., 1799. He remained here until 1815, when having received a call, he became the pastor of the church in Rumford and moved there. He was installed as such May 31, 1815. He brought the first chaise into Bethel and was himself a conspicuous figure in his cocked hat, black silk gown and breeches which was the ministerial dress of that day. He was very social in his habits and popular with all classes. His fund of anecdotes was inexhaustible. He wrote his sermons and when reading them held the manuscript near his eyes. In his will he left a small sum to Bethel Academy on the condition that the institution should take his name, which was agreed to by the trustees. An oil portrait, said to be a correct likeness has also been presented to the Academy by Miss Mary Hurd of Topsfield, a niece of Mr. Gould. Mr. Gould married for his first wife, Dec. 24, 1782, Mary, eldest daughter of Geo. Booth of Hillsboro, N. H. She d. Oct. 1, 1785. They had one daughter, Molly, b. Sept. 28, 1785, and died the Dec. following. Dec. 25, 1788, he married Mrs. Eunice Perley, daughter of Stephen Foster of Andover, Mass., and relict of Jeremiah Perley of Topsfield. She came with him to Me. and died in this town.
562. vi. SIMEON, b. Aug. 14, 1755; m. —— Harriman.
563. vii. ELIZABETH, b. Aug. 9, 1757; d. unm. Andover, June 27, 1843.

564. viii. JOHN, b. Dec. 10, 1759; m. Sarah Ingalls.
565. ix. NATHAN, b. Nov. 23, 1761; m. Susanna Barker.
566. x. DANIEL, b. Apr. 26, 1765; m. Hannah Swan

222. ASA FOSTER (Moses, Ephraim, Abraham, Reginald), b. Andover, Mass., Apr. 15, 1721; m. (pub) Dec. 1, 1744, Mary Barr. He may have married a second time which I think quite likely. The records of Pembroke, to which he moved with his family, state his wife's name was Lydia.. Res. Pembroke, N. H.

567. i. BETTY, b. 1750, Sept. 29; d. Sept 16, 1768.
568. ii. ASA, b. 1752, June 15.
569. iii. SARAH, b. 1755, Jan. 26.
570. iv. SUSANNAH, b. 1757, Feb. 2.
571. v. ACHSAH, b. 1758, Oct. 21.
572. vi. FREDERICK, b. 1760, Aug. 23; m. Mary Eastman.
573. vii. HANNAH b. 1762, July 11; m. Dec. 13, 1782, John Hall of Warner.
574. viii. MOSES, b. 1764, Oct. 2; d. Jan. 25 1765.
575. ix. LYDIA b. 1766, Oct. 3.
576. x. HITTY, b. 1770, Jan. 11.

224. DANIEL FOSTER (Moses, Ephraim, Abraham, Reginald), b. Jan. 7, 1726, in Andover, Mass.; m. there Feb. 14, 1754, Ann Ingalls. At the time of this marriage he was from Suncook, N. H. He went to Hiram, Me., in 1774, with his brother-in-law Ingalls and was the second settler in that town. He located on the Saco river, not far from the bend on Foster's Hill. He died in 1780 without leaving issue. It was the first death after the settlement of the town. His grave is in the Pines by the roadside and a monument has been erected there. His wife was the daughter of Moses and Maria of Andover, Mass. He died in 1780. Res. Suncook, N. H. and Hiram, Me.

225 MOSES FOSTER (Moses, Ephraim, Abraham, Reginald), b. Andover, Mass., Mar. 26, 1728; m. Rachel Whittemore; b. Aug. 1734; d. Feb. 16, 1817. He d. Jan. 21, 1823. Res. Pembroke, N. H.

577. i. RUTH, b. 1757; m. Amos Gile; Res. Pembroke. He was b. June 10, 1749; d. Sept. 25, 1833. She d. Nov. 26, 1836. Ch: 1. Timothy, b. Sept. 27, 1788; m. Lydia Carling. 2. Rhoda, b. 1790; d. Apr. 13, 1871. 3. Moses F. b. 1792; n. f. k. 4. Ruth, b. June 18, 1793; m. Ephraim Osgood of Chester. She d. Apr. 5, 1865. 5. Daniel, b. Mar. 7, 1796; m. Mary J. Sherwell. Res. Sandown. 6. Mary, b. Nov. 20, 1799; d. Apr. 6, 1815.

226. CAPT. EPHRAIM FOSTER (Moses, Ephraim, Abraham, Reginald), b. Andover, Mass., Aug. 30, 1731; m. —— ——. Captain Ephraim Foster, came from Connecticut, so his descendants say, at the close of the Revolutionary war, and, it is said obtained a grant from the Continental Congress of a tract of land in the central part of Vermont, which is now the town of Peacham. He d. in Peacham, Vt., 1803. Res. at the Bow, N. H.

578. i. ENOCH, b. Apr. 27, 1770; m. Polly Guy and Mrs. Susannah (Mudgett) Gould.
579. ii. EPHRAIM, b. 1767; m. Jerusha Miner and Sarah Herrick.
580. iii. —— b. ——; m. —— Clark.
581. iv. ——, b. ——; m. Moody Morse.
582. v. DANIEL, b. ——.
583. vi. MOSES, b. ——.

232. CALEB FOSTER (Moses, Ephraim, Abraham, Reginald), b. Andover, Mass., in 1747; m. Hannah ——; b. 1737; d. Apr. 28, 1811. He d. May 3, 1821. Res. Pembroke, N. H.

584. i. CALEB, b. Feb 3, 1777; m. Mar. 6, 1798, Betsey Foster. They res. in Pembroke, N. H.
585. ii. HANNAH, b. Aug. 16, 1768.
586. iii. ELIZABETH, b. Dec. 10, 1770.

237. ELIJAH FOSTER (Aaron, Ephraim, Abraham, Reginald), b. Bolton, Mass., Nov. 11, 1727; m. Dec. 4, 1749, Elizabeth Knight. He was in the Revolutionary war. He d. —. Res. Bolton, Mass.

587. iii. ABNER, b. Sept. 10, 1770; m. Judith Wetherby.

588. i. ISRAEL, b. Dec. 26, 1752; m. Susanna ——.
589. ii. ELIJAH, b. June 23, 1758..
590. iv. AARON, b July 19, 1773.
591. v. JEDEDIAH, b. Apr. 30, 1772; m. Linda Demary.

249. ABRAHAM FOSTER (Abraham, Abraham, Abraham, Reginald), b. Topsfield, Mass., May 4, 1719; m. May 10, 1744, Priscilla Todd of Rowley. He d. Oct. 27, 1796. Res. Topsfield and Rowley, Mass.

592. i. MEHITABLE, b. Apr. 2, 1745; m. Samuel Burbank of Rowley who d. Feb. 4, 1771.
593. ii. MARTHA, b. Sept. 15, 1746.
594. iii. AMOS, b. Aug. 28, 1748; d. Dec. 21, 1821.
595. iv. MOLLY, b. Aug. 31, 1751; m. Dec. 15, 1774 Joseph Plummer of Newbury. She was "a beautiful and very agreeable woman." Ch: Hannah, b. Mar. 20, 1777.
596. v. ABRAHAM, b. Feb. 24, 1755; m. May, 1783, Abigail Ames of Bradford. Res. Bradford, Mass.
597. vi. PRISCILLA, b. Aug. 4, 1753; m. June 11, 1777, William Dickinson of Rowley.
598. vii. RACHEL, b. Sept. 23, 1756; m. Nov. 23, 1777, Jonathan Hobbs.
599. viii. CHILD, b. Oct. 4, 1758; d. Oct. 21, 1758.
600. ix. ABNER, b. Oct. 8, 1760.
601. x. ABIJAH, b. Sept. 12, 1762; m. Artemiria Blake.
602. xi. ASA, b. Aug. 20, 1766.
603. xii. CHILD, b. Nov. 20, 1764; d. Nov. 20, 1764.

251. CAPT. THOMAS FOSTER (Abraham, Abraham, Abraham, Reginald), b. Aug. 11, 1724, Topsfield, Mass; m. Apr. 5, 1748, Mehitable Peabody, daughter of Matthew and Mehitable Peabody, b. Dec. 24, 1728, to whom he was published Nov. 21, 1747. She was admitted to the church April 29, 1750. He was captain in the militia. Res. Ipswich. Administration was granted on his estate, Dec. 8, 1789.

604. i. ELIJAH, b. Feb. 19, 1749.
605. vii. THOMAS, b. March 27, 1766; m. April 14, 1787, Lydia Batchelder.
606. ii. ALLEN, b. April 24, 1751; m. Lucy Potter.
607. iii. ABIGAIL, b. April 19, 1753; published 13 March, 1773, to Moses or Thomas Palmer.
608. iv. EBENEZER, b. March 24, 1755.
609. v. MEHITABLE, b. March 24, 1760.
610. vi. DANIEL, b. March 12, 1762; m. Dorothy Pingree.

257. NATHAN FOSTER (Nathan, Abraham, Abraham, Reginald), b. Stafford, Conn., May 27, 1728; m. Nov. 19, 1750, Elizabeth Lansford. He moved to Warren, Mass. from Stafford, Conn., in 1761. Aug. 19, 1791, Nathan Foster of Western, now Warren, Worcester, Co., sold land to George Gleason of Rowe, witnessed by Lydia and Joel Foster. The town of Western was incorporated June 16, 1741 and name changed to Warren, Mar. 13, 1834.

"Dec. 13, 1763. Nathan of Western, Mass., deeds to his brothers Daniel, Asa and Standish Foster, land, formerly of father Nathan's in Stafford. Between Apr. 1761 and above date he removed to Western.

I find no definite date of his death, but on the Worcester Co. records of Probate is found his inventory, presented Nov. 6, 1809, $1176.76.

Oct. 18, 1811, his widow Betsey's dower was set off, and Asa Patrick named as guardian of minor children. He d. Oct., 1809. Res. Warren, Mass.

611. i. ASA, b. May 17, 1764; m. Elizabeth Thomas.
612. ii. JOEL, b. Apr. 8, 1755; m. Priscilla Foster and Mrs. Mary Winship.
613. iii. JOHN, b. Apr. 19, 1763; m. Hannah Von Webster.
614. iv. NATHAN, b. July 5, 1753; m. Abigail Seeley.
615. v. JUDE, b. Warren, Mass.; m. Sarah Goodnough of Princeton and Lydia M. ——.
616. vi. TIRZA, b. ——; m. —— Rogers.
617. vii. ELIZABETH, b. ——; m. —— Woodther.
618. viii. LYDIA, b. ——; m. —— Bellows; res. Western, Mass; m. 2d. —— Fairbanks; res. Warren, Mass., on old homestead.
619. ix. AZUBAH, b. Apr. 4, 1751.

264. CAPT. DANIEL FOSTER (Nathan, Abraham, Abraham, Reginald), b. Stafford, Conn., July 22, 1744; m. Coventry, Conn., Apr. 1, 1765, Kezia Sawyer. She d. and he m. 2d, Feb. 12, 1803, Welthea Almira Ladd, b. Feb. 19, 1763; d. Feb. 11, 1851. She was connected by lineage with some of the principal colonial families in eastern Connecticut and was a woman of great energy and shrewdness of more than common intellectual ability and highly gifted in conversational powers. He was an officer in the Revolution and was descended on his mother's side from Capt. Myles Standish. He served with distinction at the battles of White Plains, Stillwater and Saratoga. He removed after his father's death, about 1753, to Windham, Conn., where a married sister lived. He afterward resided in Franklin, Conn. He was a blacksmith, and a captain in the Revolution, being in the army at the taking of Burgoyne, in 1777. He d. ——. Res. Canterbury, and Franklin, Conn.

620. i. LAFAYETTE SABINE, b. Nov. 22, 1806; m. Joanna Boylston and Martha Prince Lyman.

621. ii. FIDELIA WELTHEA, b. Aug. 25, 1804; m. Augustus Hyde of Norwich, Conn. Eugene, b.——; m. ——. He d. ——. Res. Barnegat, N. J. Fred'k, b. ——. Lieut. in navy; died. Juliet, b. ——; m. Rev. Wm. L. Gaylord of Chicopee, Mass. Both dead; had 3 ch.

622. iii. FANNY, b. Oct. 26, 1765.

623. iv. FAITH, b. Nov. 17, 1773; m. Nathaniel Patten. Res. Troy, N. Y.

624. v. NANCY, b. Oct. 30, 1776.

625. vi. FLINT ROYAL, b. Feb. 4, 1772; m. Sally Hawlett.

626. vii. GEORGE FESTUS, b. Nov. 7, 1767; d. Mar. 2, 1772.

627. viii. FORMELLA, b. Dec. 23, 1769; d. Mar. 18, 1772.

265. ASA FOSTER (Nathan, Abraham, Abraham, Reginald), b. Stafford, Conn., July 15, 1746; m. Sept. 29, 1768, Huldah, Wheeler, who d. Aug. 5, 1774; m. 2d, May 30, 1776, Eliza Thompson. Res. Norwich, N. Y.

266. STANDISH FOSTER (Nathan, Abraham, Abraham, Reginald), b. Feb. 24, 1749, Conn;. m. at Canterbury, Conn., Mar. 23, 1774, Sarah Spaulding; d. Aug. 23, 1825. He removed from Canterbury, Conn., to Rowe. His will was made August 21, 1821, and proved Nov. 1, 1831, his son Festus Foster of Brimfield being executor.

Standish Foster Rowe, Festus Foster, son, executor of will, lived at that time in Brimfield, Mass. He gives legacies to his grandchildren, Mary W. Foster, Fisher Ames Foster, John Wells Foster, children of said Festus Foster; Sally Foster, a "daughter" and John Spaulding Foster grandson, son of Sally. [Greenfield Probate.] He d. Oct. 1, 1831. Res. Canterbury, Conn., and Rowe, Mass.

628. i. FESTUS, b. Canterbury, Conn., Sept. 30, 1776; m. Patience Wells and Mrs. Elizabeth ——.

629. ii. SALLY, b. Canterbury, Conn.; m. —— Foster and had a son John Spaulding Foster. [See probate records at Greenfield, Mass.]

267. REV. ISAAC FOSTER A. M. (Daniel, Abraham, Abraham, Reginald), b. Rowley, Mass., Feb. 19, 1725; m. 1747, Elizabeth Emerson of Topsfield. He received the degree of A. M. from Yale college in 1770. He preached in West Stafford, Conn., and while pastor, there was a division among the church members, he expounded a too liberal doctrine to please a few of the more conservative. He was far in advance of his time, especially in Calvinistic churches. The preaching of those days was that almost "every one ought to go to hell and thank God they were no worse used." He was a very learned man and his character was above reproach. His sermons in those days were about 50 years ahead of his colleagues. From a historic address delivered at Stafford, Conn., by Rev. C. C. Painter, July 9, 1876 it is gleaned that the church was organized in 1764 and its first pastor was Rev. Isaac Foster. It says a sketch of a remarkable family of which the present generation seems to be wholly ignorant—reference is to the Foster family. History says that Rev. Isaac departed from the doctrines he professed and became a Universalist. The seeds of Universalism sown by Mr. Foster produced abundant harvest. Charges were brought against him and he was deposed in 1779. He was pastor from 1764 to 1779. He was 40 when ordained. His two sons, Emerson and Daniel were graduated at Dartmouth. Emerson settled in Killingly and latter in New London, Conn., and later in Brooklyn, where he died. Daniel settled in New Braintree, Mass., and died there. Another son was Dan, a clergyman, but not a college graduate, settled in Windsor in 1771, removed to Vt., and died in Charlestown, N. H. in 1809.

Rev. Mr. Isaac Foster bought land in Stafford, Nov. 7, 1768, of Rev. Stephen Williams. That is the only mention I have found of that branch of the Foster family in Stafford records. He was born in Rowley. He was executor of his father's will and was given nearly all the parents' estate except a small bequest to the widow. No other child was given anything Isaac's son Dan was also given property by his grandfather Daniel at his death in 1752. He d. ——. Res. Harvard, Mass. and Stafford, Conn.

630. i. DAN, b. 1748; m. Rebecca Bogge.
631. ii. EMERSON, b. ——; m. —— ——.
632. iii. HANNAH, b. ——.
633. iv. DANIEL, b. 1751; m. Elizabeth Reed.
634. v. ELIZABETH, b. ——; m. Hezekiah Cady. Res. West Stafford, Conn.; ch: 1. Henry. 2. Isaac. 3. Jonas.
635. vi. ISAAC, b. ——; m. Rebecca Newcomb.
636. vii. NATHANIEL, b. ——. He was captured in the Revolutionary war.
637. viii. PRISCILLA, b. ——; m. Rev. Joel Foster.
638. ix. MARTHA, b.
639. x. JOHN, b. Dec. 4, 1760; m. Eunice ——.

269. DANIEL FOSTER (Daniel, Abraham, Abraham, Reginald), b. Rowley, Mass., Aug. 28, 1729; m. abt. 1750, —— ——. Res. Rowley, Mass.

640. i. ABRAHAM, b. ——; d. young.
641. ii. ISAAC, b. ——.
642. iii. DANIEL, b. ——.

272. JAMES FOSTER (Amos, Benjamin, Abraham, Reginald), b. Tewksbury, Mass Aug. 15, 1736; m. Dolly ——; m. 2d, Betty ——; m. 3d, Lydia ——. James, Tewksbury, letter date April 28, 1808, ex. April 27, 1809, wife Lydia, ch., Joseph. He d. 1809. Res. Tewksbury, Mass.

643. i. JAMES, b. Mar. 11, 1756.
644. ii. JOSEPH, b. Mar. 5, 1760; m. Sarah Frost.
645. iii. BENJAMIN, b. June 5, 1763; d. Feb. 22, 1822.
646. iv. BETTY, b. Mar. 5, 1766.
647. v. KEZIAH, b. Feb. 6, 1777; m. June 6, 1799, Samuel Slone.
648. vi. DOLLY, b. July 13, 1779.
649. vii. ABIGAIL, b. Jan. 18, 1781.
650. viii. JUDITH, b. Jan. 2, 1784.
651. ix. POLLY, b. Oct. 12, 1787.

273. JONATHAN FOSTER (Amos, Benjamin, Abraham, Reginald), b. Tewksbury, Mass. Aug. 23, 1732; m. there Lydia ——; she d. May 7, 1770; m. 2d, Oct. 18, 1770, Sarah Allen; she d. Sept. 16, 1775; m. 3d. in Chelmsford, Feb. 22, 1777, Mrs. Olive Harwood. Jonathan, Chelmsford letter date Nov. 13, 1782, ex. Jan. 25, 1784 incomplete. He d. in 1781. Res. Tewksbury and Chelmsford, Mass.

652. i. JONATHAN, b. Oct. 30, 1758; m. Rachel ——.
653. ii. MOSES, b. Oct 18, 1761; d. Jan. 1, 1783.
654. iii. LYDIA, b. July 10, 1764.
655. iv. AARON, b. Oct. 31, 1768; d. Nov. 14, 1768.
656. v. SAMUEL, b. Aug. 16, 1771. Samuel child of Jonathan, 1781, Tewksbury, minor under 14 years. Guardian paper July 31, 1781.
657. vi. SALLY, b.

274. CAPT. AMOS FOSTER (Amos, Benjamin, Abraham, Reginald), b. Tewksbury, Mass., Nov. 30, 1727; m. Hannah ——; m. 2d, Sarah ——. Amos of Tewksbury letter date April 11, 1798, ex. Nov. 3, 1799 wife Sarah. He d. Feb. 19, 1798. Res. Tewksbury, Mass.

658. i. AMOS, b. May 23, 1753; m. Beulah —— and Elizabeth Kitteridge.
659. ii. WILLIAM, b. Apr. 10, 1756; m. Olive Howard.
660. iii. HANNAH, b. Apr. 10, 1764.
661. iv. NATHAN, b. May 14, 1762; m. Miriam Hobbs and Sally Hobbs.
662. v. JESSE, b. Feb. 8, 1764. Middlesex probate says: Jesse, 1799, Tewksbury, non-compos mentis, guardian papers May 14, 1799; inventory recorded Sept. 21, 1802, incomplete.
663. vi. ELIZABETH, b. Feb. 19, 1766.
664. vii. SUSANNAH, b. Oct. 1, 1771.

665. viii. ALICE, b. Sept. 29, 1778; m. July 31, 1798, Amos Blanchard.
666. ix. ORPHA, b. 1785. Orpha, child of Amos of Tewksbury, minor over 14 years; guardian papers date April 11, 1799.
667. x. STEPHEN, b. abt. 1780. Stephen of Tewksbury non-compos, guardian paper date May 14, 1799.

279. GENERAL GIDEON FOSTER (Gideon, Benjamin, Abraham, Reginald), b. Danvers, Mass., Feb. 13, 1748; m. June 18, 1771, Mercy Jacobs, dau. of Daniel and Sarah (Dudley) of Boston; b. Nov. 6, 1750; d. Sept 7, 1825; m. 2d, Nov. 23, 1828, Mary Tapley.

"Gideon Foster was born in the house which formerly stood on the corner of Lowell and Foster streets. His father, Gideon Foster, was a native of Boxford; his mother Lydia Goldthwait, of this town. (Danvers.) His early opportunities of acquiring an education were few, but he diligently improved them. He wrote a handsome hand, and was a correct draughtsman and an accurate and skillful surveyor. For several short periods he was employed in school keeping, but the more pressing necessities of those days and the moderate means of the people afforded but little time for literary improvements. He was a man of more than common ingenuity as well as intelligence. As a mechanic he had much skill. The machinery of his mills was of his own planning and construction, and many practical mechanics and manufacturers have derived important advantages from his suggestions. "General Foster was honored and beloved and trusted by his fellow citizens, and in turn discharged all the important municipal offices of the town.

"For four years he was town clerk. He was long an active magistrate of the county, and for nine years a member of the state legislature.

"In the militia of the commonwealth he rendered good service, and he considered the volunteer military the safest and best means of our national defense.

"In 1792, Capt. Foster was promoted to the rank of colonel; in 1796, he was chosen-brigadier general; in 1801, he was elected major-general by the legislature in the house, receiving every vote, and in the senate there being but one dissenting voice.

"When our country was threatened with invasion during the last war, he was chosen commander of a company of exempts. The worthy veteran never lost his military ardor, but to the last the sound of the drum and trumpet was music to his ear. Indeed for almost a whole century there has been no day when the sword of the old soldier would not have been drawn and a vigorous blow struck for the defense of his country's rights. Nurtured in that school of patriotism which taught that opposition to tyrants is obedience to God, and which inculcated love of country next to love of heaven, his strong indignation was aroused by any wrong done her or danger threatened.

"Liberty and love of country were his early and abiding passions. His country's free institutions, good order, good laws and good rulers were the objects of his strongest affections. He not only loved them but he did what he was able, according to his judgment and understanding, to maintain and perpetuate them. No distance of place, no severity of the weather, no bodily infirmity, from the adoption of the constitution till the day of his death, more than sixty years, detained him from depositing his ballot for state officers.

"General Foster through his long life was a man of great energy, enterprise and industry. Two disastrous fires had robbed him of wealth, but on his little farm, with a Roman independence and more than Roman virtue, his own hands to the last ministered to his necessities. The threatenings of the enemy to destroy the military stores of the colony caused the Provincial Congress to order a draft of minute men—men ready at a minute's warning to take the field and face the enemy. of the companies drafted here, Gideon Foster was chosen commander. He was then twenty-six years of age.

"On the 19 of April, the day ever memorable for the Battle of Lexington, Capt. Foster marched with his company sixteen miles in four hours to West Cambridge, where they met the retreating Britons. His prowess, coolness and intrepidity on that day won for him high honors and imperishable fame.

"For more than eight months he commanded a company in Col. Mansfield's regiment in the army encamped about Boston.

"He was actively engaged on the 17th of June, the day of the battle of Bunker Hill, and ever while in the service, deserved and bore the character of a brave officer and a good soldier.

"General Foster's mind, always vigorous, retained much of its strength till within a few days of his decease. His confinement was short, and it was not until the fatal hour that immediate danger was apprehended. He died on Saturday, Nov. 1, 1845.

On all occasions his townsmen and neighbors manifested deep respect for his character and services. When it was learned that he was no more, the bells were tolled, business was suspended and a gloom pervaded the community; there was a voluntary and general mourning. The flag of our country was floating at half mast; a mournful token that one loved and honored had passed away. On one flag staff, wrapped among the stripes and the stars, was the pennon of the Foster Fire Company with the name of General Foster blazoned upon it. So are mingled with the fame of our country's revolutionary glory the name and exploits of the old soldier.

"The last commissioned officer of the Revolution, certainly of the early part of the Revolution, is dead. The veteran soldier, the last connecting link is broken, the comrade of Warren, Prescott and Stark, the man who held official intercourse with Ward, Putnam and Washington, has now gone to join the mighty host of the worthy dead.

The bugles wild and warlike blast
  Shall muster them no more;
An army now might thunder past
  And they not heed its roar.

The starry flag 'neath which they fought,
  In many a bloody day,
From their old graves shall rouse them not,
  For they have passed away."

The funeral procession was after the following order:

Escort consisting of the Salem Artillery, the Danvers Light Infantry, the Salem Light Infantry, and the Lynn Rifle Corps (the latter bearing a banner presented by the hands of General Foster to the company in 1836. This banner was shrouded in crape. The escort was a detachment from Gen. Sutton's brigade, and was under the immediate command of Col. Andrews). Hearse, flanked by a military guard, family of the deceased in carriages. Brig.-Gen. Sutton and staff and military officers in uniform, in carriages. Committee of arrangements officiating and other clergy, civil officers of the town, Danvers Mechanic Institute,

FIRE DEPARTMENT.

"Gen. Foster" Engine Company, No. 7 in dark dress with badges, "Volunteer" Engine Company, No. 8, with badges and in firemen's uniform, citizens of the neighboring towns, citizens of Danvers.

The muster rolls of the state give but four companies from Danvers, omitting the company of minute men commanded by Foster. Foster is set down as a lieutenant in Epps' company, but he himself informs us, that he was placed in command of a company a short time previous to the battle. Thus Danvers contributed five companies, commanded by Jeremiah Page, Samuel Flint, Samuel Eppes, Gideon Foster and Israel Hutchison, numbering in all above two hundred men from Danvers, besides those from Salem and Beverly. Thus they started for the scene of action. When the news of the intrusion of the British reached Danvers, Foster sent one of his lieutenants to Col. Pickering and obtained permission to start with his minute men, without waiting for the movements of the regiment. They arrived at West Cambridge, a distance of sixteen miles in four hours. There they met the retreating British, and poured in a most destructive fire. (G) Col. Pickering (H) with his regiment came on more slowly. Hon. D. P. King has thus described the scene:

"Our townsmen heard the roar of the artillery and the rattle of musketry and they panted to join in the deadly combat. A little west of meeting house is a hill around which the road wound in such manner as to conceal the British. Many of the men of Danvers went into a walled enclosure and piled bundles of shingles which were lying there to strengthen their breastwork; rumor had deceived them as to the force of the enemy. It was certainly their expectation here to have intercepted their retreat. Others selected trees on the side of hills from which they might assail the enemy. But they had little space for preparation. They soon saw the British in solid columns descending the hill on their right, and at the same moment discovered a large flank guard advancing on their left. The men in the enclosure made a gallant resistance but were overpowered by numbers. It was here that several of those whom we are proud to claim for our townsmen were slain. Some sought shelter in a neighboring house, and three or four, after they had surrendered themselves prisoners of war, were butchered with savage barbarity.

"Capt. Foster, with some of his men on the side of the hill, finding themselves nearly surrounded, made an effort to gain the pond. They passed along its margin and crossed the road directly in front of the British column. On the north side of the road they took position behind a ditch wall. From this casual redoubt they fired upon the enemy as long as any of them were within reach of their muskets. Some of them fired eleven times, with two bullets at each discharge, and it cannot be doubted that these winged messengers of death performed their destined work. The bodies of the slain were scattered along the road—the British were followed till they reached Charlestown Neck. Mortifying and severe to them were the defeats and losses of that day. Their killed, wounded and missing amounted to about 300—according to an account published at the time in the form of a hand bill, 42 Americans were killed and 22 wounded." Afterward ascertained to be 50 killed.

"Capt. Gideon Foster's company was stationed at Brighton, then called Little Cambridge. He was ordered by Gen. Ward to escort a load of ammunition to Charleston. Capt. Foster obeyed and met the Americans when on their retreat. Their powder was consumed and he supplied them with ammunition loose in casks, for one more grapple with death. Capt. Foster in his old age revived the reminiscences thus: "We took the ammunition in casks and conveyed it in wagons and delivered it freely with our hands and our dippers to their horns, their pockets, their hats and whatever else they had that would hold it. I well remember the blackened appearance of those busy in this work, not unlike those engaged in the delivery of coal on a hot summer day. At the same time we were thus occupied, the enemy's shot were constantly whistling by, but we had no time to examine their character or dimensions.

"I have often thought what might have been our condition had one of these hot shot unceremoniously come in contact with our wagons."

Capt. Foster's company belonged to Colonel Mansfield's regiment which was stationed on Prospect Hill. Gen. Putnam commanded there. An order was issued calling all the captains together. They were told that a captain was wanted to engage in a very arduous enterprise, and a volunteer was called for. When Foster found no one willing to offer services, he presented himself and was accepted. Several soldiers were drawn from each company and properly armed. They repaired to Gen. Putnam's quarters to receive instructions. After reviewing them, "Old Put" deprived them of their equipments and furnished them with axes, sent them into a swamp where they were engaged in cutting fascines (faggots) and in bringing them in on their backs.

The muster rolls present no proof that Gen. Foster was captain at Lexington. They showed but four companies, but he was present and acted in that capacity. The explanation of the matter lies in this: March 3, 1775, according to the Essex Gazette, it was voted in Danvers, that, agreeable to a vote of the Provincial Congress, a quarter of the soldiers in the town should be minute men. The minute men were given in part to Israel Hutchinson and in part to Gideon Foster. Foster's men are included in other companies; why they are not down in a separate list, under their commander cannot be told.

Had Col. Pickering been actuated by the same ardor that distinguished Gideon Foster, it is not probable that many would have remained of the British to have related the day's disaster. The retreat which was in a measure safely conducted would have been effectually intercepted, and death would have exulted over the number of his trophies.

Many years after his sanguinary day, Gen. Foster recalled the event thus: "I was then twenty-six years of age. About ten days before I had been chosen to command a company of minute men who were at all times to be in readiness at a minutes warning. They were so ready—they all assembled on the very spot where we are this day assembled—they all went and in about four hours from the time of meeting, they traveled on foot (full half the way upon the run) sixteen miles, and saluted the enemy. This they did most effectually, as the records of that day most clearly prove. I discharged my musket at the enemy a number of times (I think eleven) with two balls each time, and with well-directed aim. My comrade (Mr. Cleaves of Beverly) who was then standing by my side had his finger and ramrod cut away by a shot from the enemy. Whether my shot took effect, *I cannot say, but this I can say, if they did not it was not for the want of determined purpose in him who sent them."

In the second company of soldiers at Lexington, Gideon Foster is placed a second lieutenant in the muster rolls. He was appointed captain of a company of minute men but a few days before the battle, and John Endicott was elected lieutenant in his place. Before the battle Jeremiah Page's company elected Enoch Putnam, 1st lieutenant; William Towne, 2d lieutenant, and Joseph Porter, ensign. Flint's co. after

*These remarks were made at the laying of the corner stone of the Danver's monument.

the engagement, received Asa Prince as ensign in place of Israel Putnam. The town generously supported Geo. Southwich's family after his death. It is said that the Danvers' companies all followed the worthy example of Foster and went to Lexington without waiting for Pickering's regiment. The company to which Sylvester Osborne belonged (he was the youngest member) captured a wagon near Medford, which was carrying supplies to the British. He with others was detached to escort the prize to a place of safety, and they heard the report of the firearms immediately after leaving the main body.

When Foster's men threw themselves behind the enclosure from which they fired, Hutchinson, whose experience in the French wars gave him knowledge, warned them to beware of the flank guard. In their unacquaintance with military affairs they knew nothing of a flank guard, and firing on the main body as it passed, they rushed out to harass its rear, when, of course, they found themselves between two fires, where several fell. Job Wilson, on examining his pocket after the engagement, found his coat and a square foot of gingerbread perforated by a bullet. He d. Nov. 1, 1845. Res. Danvers, Mass.

668. i. GIDEON, b. Jan. 18, 1774; d. Nov. 18, 1775.
669. ii. LYDIA, b. Jan. 13, 1780.
670. iii. GIDEON, b. Apr. 22, 1782. A painter.
671. iv. JOHN, b. June 2, 1785.
672. v. MARCIA or MERCY, b. July 26, 1788.

279x. ASAHEL FOSTER (Gideon, Benjamin, Abraham, Reginald), b. Danvers, Mass., July 16, 1749; m. Joanna Symonds, b. Mar. 21, 1748. The Fosters are of English derivation and came to Massachusetts about 1640. They were intermarried with the Peabodys and Perleys previous to the coming of those families to America and while residents in Massachusetts; as well as since their settlement in Maine. Asael Foster came from Danvers in the year 1772, and first settled at a place in Bridgton, since known as "Hensborough," lot No. 4, range 19. He built the first frame house in Bridgton, and his wife was the first married woman that settled in that town. Mr. Foster died in Feb., 1820 "from the kick of a horse," aged 71 years, having had issue; eleven children.—[Hist. Harrison, Me.] He d. Feb., 1820. Res., Bridgton and Harrison, Me.

673-2. i. JOSEPH, b. Nov. 12, 1771.
674-2. ii. ASAEL, b. Oct. 4, 1773; m. Lucy Brackett and Lucy Crosby.
675-2. iii. BENJAMIN, b. Sept. 1, 1775; m. Nancy Veasey.
676-2. iv. FRANCIS, b. July 18, 1784; m. and res. So. Bridgton, Me.
677-2. v. MOODY, b. Mar. 4, 1787; m. and res. Vassalboro, Me.
678-2. vi. LUCY, b. Sept. 1, 1775.
679-2. vii. MARY, b. June 29, 1778.
680 2. viii. SARAH, b. July 28, 1782.
681-2. ix. JOANNA, b. June 2, 1780.
682-2. x. REBECCA, b. Jan. 31, 1789.
683-2. xi. MEHITABLE, b. July 29, 1791.

280. REV. BENJAMIN FOSTER, D. D., A. M. (Gideon, Benjamin, Abraham, Reginald), b. Danvers, Mass., June 12, 1750; m. Elizabeth Green Young, dau. of Dr. Thomas and Martha (Lynde) Greer, of Leicester, and gr.-dau. of Brig.-Gen. Timothy Ruggles; d. ——; m. 2d, in New York, —— ——.

Benjamin Foster, D. D., a brother of Gideon, was born at the same place June 12, 1750. He graduated at Yale college in 1775, and after completing his theological studies under the supervision of Dr. Stillman he commenced the work of the ministry, and was ordained in Leicester, Oct. 23, 1776. In January, 1784, he was settled as pastor of the First Baptist society. He remained but two years, however, when he removed to Newburyport, and soon after to New York, where, in the year 1798 he died a victim of the yellow fever, which then prevailed. He was devoted to his flock to the last, and fell a martyr to his faithfulness. He was a learned man, and a good minister. He published "The Divine Right of Immersion," in answer to a Mr. Fish, and defended "Primitive Baptism" in a letter to John Cleveland, and also published a treatise on the "Seventy Weeks of Daniel.'

At length a meeting house was completed at New Mills, in the year 1783, and in January of the year following, Rev. Benjamin Foster was invited to preach for the society six months, which invitation he accepted. In February the pews were sold at public vendue by Aaron Cheever. They brought about $2,000. In December of the same year Mr. Foster was engaged to supply the pulpit until May, 1785.

He remained but two years, and the society did not have constant preaching for nine years. In March, 1789, the committee was instructed to procure preaching once each month. In the following year the society listened to preaching one-third of the time, and in the year 1791 the services of Rev. Mr. Crossman were secured for one-fourth of the time. The next year a preacher was employed one-half of the time.—[Hist. of Danvers.]

Rev. Benjamin Foster, D. D., was settled over this Leicester society in 1772. He was born in Danvers in 1750, and was graduated at Yale college in 1771. He studied theology with the distinguished Dr. Stillman, of Boston; having become a convert, it is said, to the opinions which he afterward maintained, by having, while in the college, been appointed to defend infant baptism by sprinkling.

After remaining at Leicester about eight years the society being unable to provide him a suitable maintenance he was dismissed, and preached about two years in Danvers. He was a learned scholar and an eminent divine. He was honored with the degree of Doctor of Divinity from Brown university in 1792. While in Leicester he published a work on "Polemical Divinity," and subsequently a dissertation upon the "Seventy Weeks of Daniel." He was well acquainted with the Greek, Hebrew and Chaldaic languages, and had achieved a high reputation for learning and ability, when cut down in the midst of his usefulness and growing reputation. He married, for his first wife, Elizabeth Green, daughter of Dr. Thomas Green; and for his second, a lady of New York. Dr. Foster was succeeded by the Rev. Isaac Beals. From thence he removed to Newport, where he was settled over a society, and remained until 1788, when he removed to New York, where he became the minister of the First Baptist society in that city. Here he remained till his death, in 1798, in the forty-ninth year of his age. His death was as heroic as his life had been eminent for piety and usefulness. He was residing in the city when the yellow fever broke out in 1798. While others fled in consternation from the power of the destroyer he stood at his post undismayed; he shrank from no call of duty, and fell a martyr to devotion in his ministrations to the dying and the dead. He died Aug. 26, 1798.—History of Leicester. Res., Danvers and Leicester, Mass., and New York City.

291. DEA. PHILEMON FOSTER (Jonathan, Caleb, Abraham, Reginald), b. Ipswich, Mass., June 11, 1737; m. (pub.) Aug. 22, 1767, Ruth Perley, of Rowley, dau. of David and Elizabeth (Jewett) Perley, b. Sept. 2, 1747. He was in Capt. How's company in the Rev. war April 19, 1775. He d. May 10, 1818. Res., Ipswich, Mass.

673. i. DUDLEY, b. May 13, 1768.
674. ii. SARAH, bapt. July 30, 1770.
675. iii. PHILEMON, b. July 24, 1773; d. before 1780.
676. iv. PHILEMON, b. Feb. 5, 1779; m. Nabby Hobbs.
677. v. RUTH, b. Aug. 30, 1781.
678. vi. ELIZABETH, b. Mar. 26, 1785.

296. MOSES FOSTER (Jonathan, Caleb, Abraham, Reginald), b. Ipswich, Mass., Dec. 18, 1735; in the Line Brook Parish; m. April 30, 1789, in Topsfield, Mary Fuller, dau. of Timothy Fuller, of Middleton, Mass., whose second cousin, bearing the same name, was the grandfather of Margaret Fuller, Countess d'Ossoli. Moses Foster was scarcely of age at the opening of the war of Independence, but he entered the army and saw hard service. He was one of the Ipswich men who marched for Lexington, April 19, 1775; also in service in Rhode Island during the last five months of 1778. He was in the memorable expedition against Quebec in 1775 (Mass. Revolutionary Rolls, 12: 146, 14: 22, 41: 92, Coat Rolls 90). In 1787 he purchased 76 acres of land on the high ground, south of the Sougehan river, then in Amherst, N. H., but now included in the southern part of Milford, N. H., on most of which then stood an unbroken forest (Hillsborough Deeds, 21: 179). His first house was built on a site within a half a mile of the present residences of his grandsons, John Everett Foster, and Moses Freeman Foster. He d. Sept. 3, 1800, in Milford, N. H. His widow m. about 1801, Philip Butterfield.

679. i. MOSES, b. Dec. 25, 1790; m. Fanny Coggin and Dina Wallingford.
680. ii. ISAAC PLUMMER, b. Nov. 5, 1792; m. Harriet Brooks.
681. iii. TIMOTHY FULLER, b. Jan. 11, 1796; m. ——; d. Jan. 31, 1835.
682. iv. JOHN, b. Nov. 13, 1798; m. ——; d. Sept., 1833.

304. NATHAN FOSTER (Caleb, Caleb, Abraham, Reginald), b. Ipswich, Mass., ——; m. — —, Miriam ——. Res. "Pigeon Hill," Ipswich and Rockport, Mass.

683. i. ELINOR, bapt. Mar. 30, 1760, in Rockport, Mass.
684. ii. JEMIMA, bapt. Mar. 30, 1760.
685. iii. WILLIAM, bapt. Mar. 30, 1760; m. —— ——.
686. iv. NATHAN, bapt. Mar. 30, 1760.
687. v. EBENEZER, bapt. Mar. 30, 1760.
688. vi. JOHN, bapt. Mar. 30, 1760; m. Susannah Robinson.
689. vii. MIRIANN, bapt. Mar. 30, 1760.
690. viii. ZABUD, bapt. Mar. 21, 1762; m. Hannah Stone.

305. STEPHEN FOSTER (Stephen, Caleb, Abraham, Reginald), b. July 13, 1741, Ipswich, Mass.; m. Jan. 4, 1763, Abigail Boardman; m. 2d (pub.), Nov. 30, 1788, Sarah Dorman. He d. July 13, 1791. Res., Topsfield, Mass.

691. i. NATHANIEL, b. Oct. 31, 1763; m. Sept. 14, 1791, Salome Foster (Jonathan, Caleb, Abraham, Reginald), as stated elsewhere. Res., Topsfield.
692. ii. MATILDA (or "Martha"), b. Aug. 22, 1765; m. April, 1785, Samuel Bradstreet (Samuel, Samuel, John, Simon), to whom she was pub. Mar. 12, 1785.
693. iii. NABBY, b. ——; pub. Dec. 9, 1797, to Thomas Cummings.
694. iv. SARAH, b. ——; m. Lot Conant.

316. JACOB FOSTER (Jonathan, Isaac, Reginald, Reginald), b. Ipswich, Mass., July 15, 1746; m. ——, Sarah Wheeler. He was son of Jonathan Foster and Elizabeth Story, his wife. He was but eighteen years of age when his father moved from Ipswich, Mass., to Lincoln, Mass.; and Jacob moved to Lincoln, probably, at the same time. He subsequently resided at Lincoln until he moved to Hanover, N. H. He was residing at Lincoln when the war of the Revolution began, and in that war he served as a private in Capt. William Smith's company (from Lincoln), Col. Abijah Pierce's (Massachusetts) regiment, and took part in the fight at Concord Bridge, and in the running fight between Concord and Charlestown, April 19, 1775. In this fight his hat was pierced by a British bullet. He subsequently served in Capt. Farrar's company (from Lincoln), Col. Brooks' (Massachusetts) regiment; and also in Capt. John Hartwell's company (from Lincoln), Col. Eleazer Brooks' (Massachusetts) regiment; was at the fortifying of Dorchester Heights and bombardment of Boston. He was married at Lincoln, Mass., by Eleazer Brooks Esq., to Sarah Wheeler, of Lincoln. He moved from Lincoln, Mass., to Hanover, N. H., sometime between Feb. 7, 1788, and May 2, 1789; and died at Hanover, N. H., Nov. 8, 1791. His wife, Sarah Wheeler, died at Hanover, N. H., in 1799. Res., Hanover, N. H.

695¼. i. SALLY, b. April 16, 1781.
695½. ii. JACOB, b. Aug. 20, 1782; "was killed with thunder July 11, 1790."
695¾. iii. JONATHAN, b. Oct. 25, 1783; m. Betsey Eggleston (who d. at Mantua, O., Sept. 21, 1866); d. at Mantua, O., Sept. 28, 1866.
695-1. iv. ANNA, } b. Jan. 25, 1785.
695-2. v. BETSY, }
695-3. vi. WILLIAM, b. Oct. 25, 1786.
695-4. vii. PATTEY, b. Aug. 8, 1788.
695-5. viii. LUCY, b. June 15, 1790; m. Alpha Wright, of Tallmadge, O., Dec. 12, 1811; d. Sept. 30, 1875. After the death of her parents she was, at the age of nine years, received into the family of Mr. Martin Kent, of Hanover, N. H. (formerly of Suffield, Conn.), and was thereafter treated the same as if she had been his daughter. In the spring of 1807 Mr. Martin Kent left Hanover with his family, including Lucy Foster, and traveled with horses and wagons to the Connecticut Western Reserve in Ohio, where, in June or July, 1807, the family settled on six hundred acres of land, purchased by Mr. Kent, in what is now Suffield township, Portage county, O. Lucy Foster, in 1810, was called upon to teach the first school in Tallmadge township (now in Summit county, O.), and Dec. 12, 1811, she was married to Alpha Wright, of Tallmadge, by Rev. Joshua Beer, at the residence of Mr. Martin Kent, in Suffield, O.* She then moved to Tall-

*It appears that she was very thoroughly married, since the zealous divine kept the young couple standing before him while he delivered to them a homily more than an hour in length on the duties and responsibilities of the married state.

madge, O., the home of her husband, who, with his father, Capt. John Wright (a veteran of the war of the Revolution), had come from Winchester (Winsted), Litchfield county, Conn., to Ohio in 1802, and with his parents and three brothers had settled in Tallmadge, O., in 1809. In the war of 1812, Alpha Wright served as a sergeant in a company of riflemen, composed of his neighbors and friends. Before the war closed he was commissioned as ensign, but not while in the field.

It is well to consider the conditions under which Lucy Foster Wright passed these early years of her married life, especially since she and her husband were important factors in helping to mould this early frontier community; and so closely was her life inter-woven with that of the community that the character of that community in its early days shows us in strong light the kind of woman she was. The western line of Tallmadge township is only about two and a half miles east from what is known as the "Portage Path,"—the old Indian portage trail between the Cuyahoga and Tuscarawas rivers. This "Portage Path" formed a neutral highway of the Indians in their passage from Lake Erie, via the Cuyahoga, Tuscarawas and Muskingum rivers, to the Ohio river and the interior of the country. It was an old treaty boundary line, which, until after the War of 1812, was the extreme western limit of the white settlements on the Connecticut Western Reserve, except a mere line of scattered settlements along Lake Erie and a very few "clearings" of isolated settlers here and there in the interior. With these few exceptions the territory in Ohio west of this old boundary line was then a vast unbroken wilderness, inhabited only by Indians. The early settlers of Tallmadge township were animated with a very high degree of public spirit and patriotism. The township itself was named after its principal early proprietor, Col. Benjamin Tallmadge, of Litchfield, Conn., a brave and efficient officer of the Continental Army and a trusted friend of General Wasnington. The first white settler came to the township in 1807, and in 1810 a log school house was built and a school established, Lucy Foster being the first teacher. A township library was established Sept. 26, 1813, containing at first about seventy volumes of standard works; and soon after this a lyceum or debating society was formed. A building for an academic school was begun in 1814, and this school was opened in 1814 or 1815.

The company of riflemen with which Alpha Wright served in the war of 1812 was organized at a very early date, most of the men being residents of Tallmadge township. Alpha Wright, when twenty-one years of age, held a warrant as corporal in this rifle company, dated April 7, 1810. On the surrender of Gen. Hull, at Detroit, in August, 1812, the Indians generally being then allies of the British, the situation of the white settlers along this extreme frontier became most dangerous and critical. Their lives night and day were full of anxiety and dread. The men of the community, giving highest consideration to their country's need and the good of all, continued to maintain the company of riflemen; and this company was ordered into the service of the United States, August 22, 1812, and left their homes, taking the field for the defense of the northwestern frontier—an act of much greater self-denial and devotion to country than if the families of these men had been left in the greater security of homes remote from the frontier and its dangers. Among the women then left in this frontier settlement was Lucy Foster Wright, who had married Alpha Wright in the preceding December. Attack from the Indians was anticipated and dreaded, and the fear of this hung over the little settlement at all times. At night it was the custom for the women and children to be gathered together within the defensive walls of some log house, guarded by the very few men—principally old men—left in the settlement; or when an impending attack seemed more imminent, some (and Lucy Foster Wright was among these) were hidden over night in hollow trees or in the surrounding forest for greater safety. The log house of Alpha and Lucy Foster Wright was one of these temporary "forts," and it was under such circumstances as these that she lived during his absence with the army, and under these circumstances their first child was born, Oct. 2, 1812, during such absence of the father. After these eventful years of her early life Lucy Foster Wright lived to be the mother of a large family of sons and daughters, who have all occupied positions of honor and influence, and have continued the good work of their mother, in the communities in which they have lived. Strong and vigorous in mind and body until the last; through a long life always an earnest and active supporter of education, the church and all good works; honored, revered and beloved by all who ever knew her, this one of the early pioneers of a great State passed away at the age of eighty-five, having exercised no small influence upon the lives of many who have helped to make the State and nation what it is. She died at Tallmadge, O., Sept. 30, 1875. Alpha Wright, her husband, died at Tallmadge, O., March 1, 1856. Children, all born at Tallmadge, O.:

1. Philo, b. Oct. 2, 1812; m. at Hudson, O., June 29, 1837, Electa E. Coe, dau. of Rev. Harvey Coe, of Hudson, O., tutor in Western Reserve college; res., Hudson, O., and Detroit, Mich.; d. Dec. 3, 1844, at Detroit, Mich. Children all born at Hudson, O. 1. Edward Bingham, b. ——, 1838; Presbyterian minister; res., Austin, Tex.; was educated at Western Reserve college; served on U. S. Lake Survey under corps of engineers, U. S. Army; served as captain of artillery (Michigan volunteers) in civil war and was very severely wounded; received degree of D. D. from Western Reserve university; m. Evelyn Hunter Bell, of Austin, Tex. Ch: 1. Evelyn Bell, b. ——, 1879. 2. Charles Coe, b. ——, 1840; was educated at Western Reserve college; d. at New York City, N. Y., ——, 1863; unm. 3. Henry Martyn, b. ——, 1843; importer and jeweler; res., Detroit, Mich; was educated at Western Reserve college; served in Ohio volunteers in civil war; subsequently on U. S. Lake Survey under corps of engineers, U. S. army; m. Flora May Haight. Ch: 1. Edith Buell, b. ——, 1877.

2. William Wheeler, b. May 12, 1814; Congregational minister; res., Oberlin, O.; educated at Western Reserve college and Oberlin College; m. at Oberlin, O., Susan D. Allen, of Mansfield, Mass.; d. at Oberlin, O., Dec. 1, 1883. Children, all born at Oberlin, O.: 1. Ellen Elizabeth, b. ——, 1844; d. ——, 1859. 2. Albert Allen, b. ——, 1846; was educated at Oberlin college and Columbia college school of mines; served as lieutenant in Civil war; professor of geology Oberlin college; acting president of Oberlin college 1897 and 1898; res., Oberlin, O.; m. 1st, Mary Lyon Bedortha, of Saratoga, N. Y., who d. ——, 1877; m. 2d, Mary P. B. Hill. Ch. (by first wife): 1. Helen Bedortha, b. ——, 1876; (by second wife): 2. Norman Hill, b. ——, 1896. 3. Herbert Hornell, b. ——, 1848; professor of mathematics Fisk university; res., Nashville, Tenn.; educated at Oberlin college; m. Francis E. Bosworth. Ch: 1. Flora Fredrika, b. ——, 1875. 2. Ellen Elizabeth, b. ——, 1879. 4. Mary Martha, b. ——, 1857; educated at Oberlin college; m. Rev. Walter E. C. Wright; d. ——, 1888. 5. Stella Susan, b. ——, 1859; educated at Oberlin college; teacher, Peoria, Ill. 6. Fanny Foster, b. ——, 1862; educated at Oberlin college. Res., Cleveland, O.

3. Lucy Ann, b. Jan. 9, 1816; res., Tallmadge, O.; m. at Tallmadge, O., June 12, 1835, Rev. Luther Shaw, who d. Aug. 20, 1888, at Tallmadge, O., aged 88 years. She d. at Tallmadge, O., Feb. 2. 1899.

4. Clement, b. Jan. 2, 1818; d. Dec. 29, 1821.

5. Abigail, b. April 1, 1820; res., Holly, Mich.; m. at Tall-

madge, O., Rev. Loomis Chandler, who d. ——. Ch: 1. Edward Loomis, b. ——, 1847; architect; res., Los Angeles, Cal.; m. Rebecca Jergenson; d. ——, 1893. 2. Clement Long, b. ——, 1849; physician; res., Richmond, Mich.; m. Eugenia Davis; d. ——, 1892. 3. Hermann Francke, b. ——, 1852; publisher of music; res., Chicago, Ill.; m. Mrs. Lucy (Wetmore) Hinde. 4. Alice Amelia, b. ——, 1855; res., Holly, Mich.; m. Rev. Willis G. Clark. Ch: 1. Mary. 2. Malcom Willis. 3. —— ——. 5. Walter Henry, b. ——, 1859; salesman; res., Cincinnati, O. 6. Mary Edgerton, b. ——, 1863; res., Holly, Mich.

Clement, b. March 15, 1822; res., Tallmadge, O., where he has been a merchant for the last forty-eight years (1851-1899); township treasurer for more than forty years, and U. S. postmaster for more than twenty-five years; m. at Wadsworth, O., June 18, 1845, Lucy Ayer Whitney, dau. of Shubael Whitney and Sarah Mitchell, his wife, late of New York City and New Rochelle, N. Y. Lucy Ayer Whitney was b. in New London county, Conn., Nov. 16, 1822, and was a lineal descendant of the seventh generation from John and Elinor Whitney, who came from England and settled at Watertown, Mass., in June, 1635. [See Whitney Genealogy, by Fred C. Pierce.] She d. at Tallmadge, O., June 22, 1888. Children all born at Tallmadge, O.: 1. George Mitchell, b. Aug. 8, 1847; lawyer; res., Tallmadge and Akron, O.; was educated at public schools, Tallmadge academy and Western Reserve college, but left college early in the course; studied law and was admitted to the bar in Ohio, June 16, 1873; practiced law at Akron, O., for many years; devoted much time to study of sciences, and was appointed assistant geologist, U. S. Geological Survey; engaged in geological field work for the government for several years in Nevada, California, Yellowstone National Park, Idaho, Wyoming and Montana; stationed during winters at Salt Lake City, Utah; New York City, N. Y., and Washington, D. C.; in the Spanish-American war was commissioned second lieutenant and battalion adjutant Eighth Ohio Vol. Inf., and was detailed as acting ordnance officer; was subsequently appointed aide-de-camp and brigade ordnance officer on the staff of Brig.-Gen. George A. Garretson; served in Maj.-Gen. Nelson A. Miles' expedition to Cuba (Santiago campaign), and in expedition to Porto Rico, the first invasion and the following campaign; took part in fighting in Porto Rico, and was commended in official report; was also officially recommended for brevets for services in this campaign; is a member of the Philosophical Society of Washington, D. C.; an associate member of the Military Service Institution of the United States; a member of the society of the Sons of the American Revolution, of the society of the War of 1812, and of the military order of Foreign Wars of the United States; also a member of the Alpha Delta Phi college fraternity; m. at Akron, O., Oct. 18, 1876, Lucy Josephine Hale (b. at Akron, O., March 14, 1854), dau. of James Madison Hale and Sarah Allen, his wife, of Akron, O. Children, all born at Tallmadge, O.: 1. Clement Hale, b. July 4, 1882. 2. Allen Whitney, b. July 17, 1889. 3. George Maltby, b. June 24, 1892. 2. Charlotte Adella, b. Dec. 3, 1849; d. Sept. 20, 1851, at Tallmadge, O. 3. Clara Whitney, b. March 21, 1853; d. Aug. 31, 1854, at Tallmadge, O.

7. Amelia, b. Jan. 4, 1825; d. March 3, 1848, at Tallmadge, O.; unm.

8. Martha (twin), b. Jan. 21, 1827; res., Tallmadge, O.; m. at Tallmadge, O., Sept. 2, 1846, Homer Sackett Carter, for many years a merchant at Tallmadge; now retired from that business. Children, all born at Tallmadge, O.: 1. Homer Wright, b. Nov.

5, 1847; Congregational minister; res., Ripon, Wis.; state secretary of Home Missionary Society for Wisconsin; was educated at Oberlin college and Andover Theological seminary; received degree of D. D. from Oberlin college; m. at Brandon, Wis., June 3, 1885, Jennie McClelland, dau. of James and Barbara McClelland, of Brandon, Wis. Ch: 1. Homer McClelland, b. Feb. 21, 1887. 2. Martha May, b. Jan. 17, 1889. 3. James Treat, b. Aug. 4, 1891. 2. Mary Amelia, b. June 3, 1849; res., Tallmadge, O. 3. Ella Electa, b. Oct. 28, 1852; d. Aug. 17, 1854, at Tallmadge, O. 4. Howard Handel, b. June 9, 1855; professor of piano forte, Oberlin college; res., Oberlin, O.; educated at Oberlin and in Germany; m. at Tours, France, March 29, 1891, Harriet Newell Wright, dau. of Rev. James Lockwood Wright and Lucy Ann North, his wife, of Calumet, Mich. 5. Alpha Wright, b. May 26, 1858; d. Oct. 27, 1880; unm. 6. Starr Van Vleck, b. June 18, 1865; m. Ella Elizabeth Swift, dau. of Lieut. James A. Swift, Ninth cavalry, U. S. army; d. Dec. 30, 1892. Ch. 1. Margie Starr, b. Aug. 14, 1892. 7. Charles Edgerton, b. Nov. 24, 1869; medical student; res., New York City, N. Y.; educated at Oberlin college and Harvard university.

9. Mary (twin), b. Jan. 21, 1827; m. at Tallmadge, O., ——, 1849, Hon. Sidney Edgerton, lawyer, of Akron, O., who has served as prosecuting attorney of Summit county, O.; member of Congress from Ohio for two terms; Chief Justice of Idaho Territory, and the first governor of Montana Territory. His res. is Akron, O., where he is now (1899) practicing law. Mary Wright Edgerton d. at Akron, O., Aug. 3, 1884. Ch: 1. Martha Amelia, b. at Tallmadge, O., May 14, 1850; m. 1st, at Akron, O., Aug. 8, 1876, Herbert P. Rolfe, lawyer, of Great Falls, Mont., who d. ——; m. 2d., Norman Plassmann, of Great Falls, Mont., who d. about one year thereafter. Children, all by the first husband: 1. Mary Pauline, b. ——, 1877. 2. Harriet Louise, b. ——, 1879. 3. Helen Marsden, b. ——, 1882. 4. Lucia Ione, b. ——, 1884. 5. Martha Edith (twin), b. ——, 1886. 6. Herbert Edgerton (twin), b. ——, 1886. 7. Hester, b. ——, 1888. 2. Wright Prescott, b. at Tallmadge, O., Nov. 14, 1852; cadet U. S. military academy, West Point, July 1, 1870; commissioned second lieutenant, second artillery, U. S. army, June 17, 1874; first lieutenant, second artillery, U. S. A., March 23, 1881; associate professor of mathematics U. S. military academy, with rank of captain, July 1, 1893; served with army in the field during Spanish-America war of 1898; professor of mathematics U. S. military academy, with rank of lieutenant-colonel, Oct. 7, 1898; m. at New York City, N. Y., Fannie Ida Helmuth, dau. of Dr. William Tod Helmuth and Fannie Ida Pritchard, his wife, of New York City, N. Y. Ch: 1. Gladys, b. ——. 3. An infant; d. 4. Sidney Carter, b. June 6, 1856; d. 1895; unm. 5. Mary Paulina, b. July 11, 1858; librarian, Akron public library; res., Akron, O. 6. Francis L., b. ——, 1860; d. Oct. 2, 1861, "ae. 14 months." 7. Lucia Idaho, b. May 23, 1864; m. George E. Buckingham, of Akron, O.; res., Akron, O. Ch: 1. Dorothy Edgerton, b. ——, 1887. 2. Lucia Aurora, b. ——, 1891. 3. George Edward, b. ——, 1893. 4. Hesper Miriam, b. ——, 1895. 8. Lucy Ione, b. Sept. 10, 1867; res., Akron, O. 9. Nina, b. Oct. 4, 1869; m. at Akron, O., ——, Lieut. Walter M. Whitman, First cavalry U. S. army. Ch: 1. Sidney Edgerton, b. Feb. ——, 1898.

10. Benjamin Deming, b. June 30, 1829; res. Tallmadge, O.; m. at Tallmadge, O., Nov. 16, 1854, Nancy A. Treat, dau. of Calvin Treat and Jane Caruthers, his wife, of Tallmadge, O., b. Oct. 18, 1829; d. at Tallmadge, O, Jan. 31, 1894. Children, born at Tallmadge, O.: 1. Charles Handel, b. Aug. 17, 1855; educated at Western Reserve college and Amherst college; newspaper editor; general agent Mutual Life Insurance company of New-

ark, N. J.; res., Cleveland, O.; m. at Birmingham, Conn., Margaret Isabel Shelton, of Birmingham, Conn. Ch: 1. Marjorie Shelton, b. ——, 1886; d. ——, 1887. 2. Dorthea, b. ——, 1887. 3. Charles Shelton, b. ——, 1895. 2. Fanny Virginia, b. Oct. 26, 1858; d. at Tallmadge, O., Sept. 10, 1878; unm.

11. Handel Hayden, b. Feb. 13, 1832; d. July 18, 1854, at Akron, O.; unm.

12. Charles Storrs, b. Jan. 1, 1834; d. at Tallmadge, O., Oct. 6, 1854; killed by the accidental discharge of his gun; unm.

695-6. ix. JACOB, b. Feb. 29, 1792.

323. REV. JACOB FOSTER (Jacob, Isaac, Reginald, Reginald), b. Holliston, Mass., March 10, 1732; m. Oct. 13, 1756, Hepzibah Prentiss, dau. of Henry Prentiss, who was a cousin of Hon. John Prentiss, of Cambridge. She was bapt. Jan. 23, 1732; d. Nov. ——, 1811. He was graduated at Harvard college in 1754 in the class with Gov. John Hancock. He was ordained pastor of the church in Berwick, Me., in 1756. At his own request he was dismissed from his charge and entered the Continental army as chaplain of Col. James Scammon's regiment in 1777. Subsequently he was installed pastor of a church in Packersfield, N. H. (now Nelson), in 1781, where he ministered for ten years; when he took a dismission and died there in 1798. His wife was a relative of Hon. John Prentiss, of Keene, N. H., many years editor of the New Hampshire Sentinel. He d. Dec. 3, 1798. Res., Berwick Me., and Nelson, N. H.

696. i. HEPZIBAH, b. July 18, 1757; m. David Rainsford; res., Canterbury.

697. ii. JACOB, b. May 25, 1759; d. young.

698. iii. SOPHIA, b. May 19, 1760; m. Aug. 13, 1783, Samuel Griffin. Res. Nelson, N. H. He was b. 1756; d. Nelson, N. H., Feb. 2, 1811. She d. there March 6, 1846. Ch: 1. Samuel; no descendants. He was a strong, robust man, both in mind and body, and thoroughly enjoyed life; never had need to call a physician until his last illness, which was of short duration. Had a full set of double teeth all around, and never lost one, or suffered pain from them, although attaining the age of 86 years. He was fond of military life and made that a study. 2. Sophia; m. Josiah Parker. 3. Sally; m. Simeon Goodnow. They d. in Webster, N. Y. 4. Hepzibah; m. Nathaniel Abbott; res., Webster, N. Y. 5. Hannah; m. Simeon Wilson and Rufus Atwood. 6. Betsy; m. John Atwood; res., Webster, N. Y. 7. Priscilla; m. Otis Grow; no descendants. 8. Rebecca; m. Dexter Whitcomb; res., Boston. 9. Lois; m. Samuel Osgood, a son of Capt. Geo. W. Osgood, of Nelson, N. H. 10. Nathan, b. Nov. 25, 1785; m., Nelson, N. H., Sept. 11, 1808, Sally Wright, b. Dec. 24, 1786; d. Jan. 27, 1881. He d. April 15, 1872. Was a farmer, a successful teacher, and for many years was town clerk of Nelson. His health failed in early manhood; was a very promising young man. Was a man of sterling worth, and was much sought for as counselor and advisor. He loved his books, was a great Bible student, and the best commentary I was able to find, and one of the best teachers of those days. For 19 consecutive years he taught the school of his own town, and five of his seven children were his pupils. But he was not a strong man physically, and early broke down in health, so that his later years were spent quietly in his home, respected and beloved by all who knew him. Res., Nelson, N. H. Ch: 1. Samuel, b. Feb. 23, 1812; m. Nov. 30, 1836; d. Oct. 24, 1882; m. Pauline McCormick, of Ohio; a son is Alvaro N. Griffin; res., Kilburn, Wis. 2. Silence, b. Feb. 15, 1814; m. Dec. 7, 1837; d. March 14, 1866; m. Samuel L. Taggard; a son is Frank E.; res., 333 Union St., Lynn. 3. Mary, b. Feb. 16, 1816; m. June 6, 1850, Luther Smith; a son is Evander E.; res., Marlboro, N. H. 4. Gilman, b. Dec. 30, 1818; m. March 8, 1843; d. Oct. 6, 1862; m. Harriet Atwood; a dau. is Mrs. Geo. F. Winch; res., Marlboro, N. H. 5. Sophia, b. Aug. 15, 1821; m. Sept. 18, 1849; res., N.; m. Alfred Spaulding; res., Saxton's River, Vt. 6. Simon Goodell, b. Aug. 9, 1824; m., 1st, Sept. 10,

1850; 2d, Jan. 1, 1863, m. Sept. 10, 1850, Ursula Jane Harris; m. 2d, Jan. 1, 1863, Margaret Russell Lamson, b. Feb. 5, 1831; res., Keene, N. H. Gen. Simon G. Griffin was b. Aug. 9, 1824, in Nelson, N. H. For many years he was engaged in educational work; and for two years represented his town in the N. H. state legislature. In 1860 he was practicing law in Concord, N. H., and at the first call of President Lincoln for troops he volunteered as a private and was chosen captain of Company B, Second N. H. volunteer infantry. He commanded his company at the first battle of Bull Run; was promoted to lieutenant-colonel of the Sixth, N. H. Vols., and joined Burnside's expedition to North Carolina. He was rapidly promoted to colonel, brigadier-general and brevet major-general; seeing constant service at the front and being present in twenty-two great battles, besides numberless smaller fights. He commanded the second division Ninth army corps in the final assault on the lines in front of Petersburg, April 2, 1865, in which the heaviest fighting of the whole line fell to his lot; his division alone losing 725 men in killed and wounded—his charge being made by direction of General Grant, on the enemy's main line at the Jerusalem plank road, near the city. He also commanded his division at the surrender of Lee and in the grand review at Washington, May 23, 1865. After the war Gen. Griffin settled in Keene, N. H., and represented that town for three terms in the state legislature; two of which he served as speaker of the house. In 1887 and 1888 he was commander of the Massachusetts commandery of the military order of the Loyal Legion of the United States. He is now engaged in historical literary work. Ch: i. Charles Lamson Griffin, b. Aug. 15, 1864; m. April 4, 1894; res., 220 Broadway, N. Y. ii. William Lamson Griffin, b. Nov. 30, 1867; res., 220 Broadway, N. Y. 7. Sarah Augusta, b. Aug. 15, 1828; m. 1st, Feb. 11, 1857, Silas A. French, b. June 27, 1828; d. Nov. 21, 1857; m. 2d, June 2, 1874, Zenas H. Sherwin, b. Jan. 5, 1824; d. Mar. 4, 1897. She res., "The Albion," St. Paul, Minn. Ch: i. Silas Ervine French, b. July 6, 1852, in Nelson, N. H.; d. Sept. 8, 1854, in Nelson. ii. Leonard Webster French, b. Dec. 7, 1853; m. April 23, 1878. iii. Charles Milton French, b. Aug. 7, 1857; m. April 12, 1890, Nellie Rachel Troy, b. March 14, 1861, s. p. iv. Francis Adelbert French, adopted son, b. May 7, 1864; m. Sept. 22, 1886; P. O. address, St. Paul, Minn., for Leonard Webster French and for Francis Adelbert French. Charles Milton French, P. O. address, is Chicago, Ill., 6148 Kimbark Ave. He is Asst. Gen. Mgr. for Thiel's detective agency.

MRS. SARAH A. SHERWIN.

699. iv. NATHAN, b. Sept. 9, 1762; prob. lost at sea about 1790.
700. v. JACOB, b. June 23, 1764; m. Rebecca Vose.
701. vi. HENRY, b. Sept. 17, 1766; m. Susannah Hooper.
702. vii. ELIZABETH, b. Oct. 4, 1768; m. —— Beal.
703. viii. DAVID, b. Aug. 10, 1770; m. Mary White.
704. ix. CALEB, b. May 13, 1773; d. March 4, 1777.
705. x. REBECCA, b. Aug. 12, 1775; m. Salmon Hooper, and has left a large number of descendants. Among them is John Kilburn, Lowell, Mass., and Emiline Slade, of Fall River, Mass., the last, if alive, of that generation. I believe she has a son who is a lawyer in Fall River, Mass.

CHARLES M. FRENCH.

324. CAPT. WILLIAM FOSTER (Jacob, Isaac, Reginald, Reginald), b, Holliston, Mass., April 29, 1734; m. 1755, Hannah Durkee, dau. of Capt. William of Ipswich, b. 1735. She d. Feb. 21, 1823. 3. Captain William Durkee, b. Feb. 28, 1710; d. Jan. 15, 1795; m. Abigail Hovey, Feb. 8, 1732-3. She d. May 30, 1791. 2. William Durkee, b. abt. 1672 in New Hampshire; m. Rebeckah Gould of Ipswich (dau. Henry), Jan. 13, 1704. He d. March 2, 1732. 1. William Durkee, b. abt. 1630; m. Martha Cross of Ipswich. She d. Windham, Jan. 11, 1726-7. He was born in Holliston, Mass., and went to Hampton, Conn. in 1754; was a farmer and began farming in 1753 on a farm which was adjoining the town line of Hampton, Conn. He commanded the first company to take up arms against England from the town of Canterbury. When the news of the battle of Lexington reached Canterbury he marched at once with his company to Boston. During all the Revolutionary war he was recruiting officer for the state of Connecticut. In 1787 he moved with his family to Whitehall (then Skeensborough) New York, at the head of Lake Champlain. There he purchased 200 acres of land in the woods and began farming. During the latter part of his life he resided with his sons and died at his son Thomas' house. He d. May 16, 1825. Res. Holliston, Mass., Canterbury, Conn., and Whitehall, N. Y.

706. i. MARY, b. Nov. 17, 1758; m. July 9, 1778 in C., Capt. George Williamson Jr. He was b. 1754. He resided in Canterbury, Conn., and later in Amherst, Mass., and still later in Bangor, Me. He d. July 9, 1778. She d. Jan. 16, 1832. They had four sons and four daughters. 1. William D. 2. Asenath. 3. Robert. 4. George. 5. Mary. 6. Hannah. 7. Sarah; all dead. Only children of William D. living; viz.: Mrs. Caroline J. Chapman, Boston, Mass. Only children of George living: Mrs. E. W. Forsyth, Cambridge, Mass., Miss Helen Williamson, and Miss Mary Williamson, Southport, Me. No children of other brothers and sisters living. 1, George, a farmer in Pittston, Me.; Joseph, a lawyer in Belfast, Me., who was graduated at the Vermont university and was president of the senate in the Maine legislature. William D., the eldest son, attended Williams college in 1800 and finished his studies at Brown university where he was graduated in 1804. As his father was in modest circumstances and being the eldest of the family he was under the necessity of teaching school to defray his college expenses. He read law in Amherst until 1807 when he removed to Bangor, Me., and after further legal studies was

admitted to the bar in November of that year. Governor Sullivan commissioned him attorney for the county of Hancock, which office he held for eight years. In 1816 he was elected to the senate of Massachusetts, Maine being then a part of the old commonwealth, and was continuously elected until the separation in 1820. He was appointed president of the first senate of the state of Maine. Gov. King having been appointed Spanish commissioner, Mr. Williamson discharged the duties of the governor for about six months in the year. He was soon elected a member of Congress. Later he was judge of probate, justice of peace and president of the Bangor Bank. His first wife was a niece of Gen. Montague of Amherst and is second a daughter of Judge Phinehas White of Putney, Vt.; his third was the only surviving daughter of E. Emerson, Esq. of York, Me. He was particularly fond of literary pursuits, especially of an historical character. His great work was his History of Maine. He d. May 27, 1846.

The father, George, who m. a Foster, was a soldier in the Revolutionary army and a captain of artillery for some years after peace was declared. In 1793 he removed from Canterbury to Amherst, Mass., but d. in Bangor, Me., in 1822. Joseph, son of George, was b. in Canterbury, Conn., Aug. 5, 1789; m. Newburyport, Mass., June 14, 1824, Caroline Cross, b. March 5, 1798; d. June 22, 1852. He d. Sept. 30, 1854. Ch. 1. William Cross, b. Jan. 31, 1831; m. April 29, 1863; res., in Boston. 2. George Ralph, b. April 13, 1836; m. Oct. 16, 1884; res. in New York. 3. Caroline Cross, b. Dec. 18, 1841; m. Sept. 16, 1868; res. in Cambridge, Mass. Present name Caroline C. Willard. 4. Joseph, b. Oct. 5, 1828; m. Oct. 22, 1857, Ada Hortense Pierce, b. Aug. 20, 1834; d. March 19, 1872; res., Belfast, Me.; is a lawyer. Ch: i. Ada Caroline, b. Sept. 14, 1858; res. in Boston. ii. Frances, b. Oct. 6, 1860; m. Sept. 10, 1891. Present name, Frances A. Peirce; res., Frankfort, Me. iii. Joseph Jr., b. Feb. 14, 1869; m. Nov. 19, 1891; res. in Augusta, Me.

707. ii. HANNAH, b. Dec. 1, 1762; m. Ebenezer Williamson, of Middleboro, Mass., afterward of Canterbury and Brooklyn, Conn., and died at the latter place, Oct. 28, 1836, leaving no children.

708. iii. WM. DURKEE, b. Aug. 10, 1760; m. Hannah —— and Betsey Dorrence.

709. iv. BEULAH, b. Oct. 23, 1764; m. May 22, 1783, John Elderkin Waldo of Canterbury, Conn., and res. there. John Elderkin Waldo (Zachariah, Edward Jr., Lieutenant Edward, John, Deacon Cornelius) was son of Zachariah Waldo (a private in Captain John Douglas' Co. from July 18, 1775, to Dec. 16, 1775) and Elizabeth Wight (Joshua, Joshua, Thomas, Thomas), b. in Canterbury, Conn., Oct. 5, 1761; m. Beulah Foster May 22, 1783 who was b. in Canterbury Oct. 23, 1764. Ch: 1. Anna was b. March 16, 1784, in town of Hampton, Conn.; m. to David Hawley, July 31, 1806. (Rev. Sylvanius, Sylvanius, Joseph) b. Sharon, Conn., Jan. 27, 1786; d. Warsaw, N. Y., April 8, 1864. She d. Aug. 11, 1852. Ch: i. Huldah Lake, b. Whitehall, N. Y., July 9, 1812; living; m. Ensign Hiram Jordan. i½. Amelia Ann, b.——; m. George Ensign. ii. David Waldo, b. Warsaw, N. Y., Dec. 3, 1817; m. March 31, 1846, Julia Samantha Brown (dau. of John and Michael Sykes Brown), b. Gainesville, N. Y., Feb. 10, 1828. He d. Gainesville, Feb. 18, 1887. iii. Sarah Diantha, b. Warsaw, N. Y., May 24, 1820; d. Gainesville, May 24, 1885; m. at Warsaw, 1845, Samuel Benjamin Farr (son of Samuel Farr, b. Belfast, Mass., 1794; d. Greenville, Mich, ae. 61 years, and his wife Elizabeth Crawford), b. at West Sparta, N.Y.; d. Gainesville, May 26, 1885. iv. William Joseph, b. Warsaw, N Y., Oct. 3, 1822; d. Gainesville March 3, 1888; m. at Wethersfield, N. Y., Jan. 1, 1856, Almira Catharine Hewett (dau. of Rodolphus W. and Adelia M. Tainter Hewett), b. Wethersfield. Oct. 28, 1833; d. Gainesville, Aug. 23, 1892. v. Betsey Beulah, b. March 22, 1827, at Warsaw; unm.; living. vi. John Sylvanius, b. Warsaw, Oct. 5, 1830; d. Warsaw, Jan. 12, 1893;

m. Gainesville, Oct. 3, 1855, Sophia Melinda Luther (dau. Ellis Lawton Luther and Melinda Adams Lamb), b. Gainesville, Oct. 20, 1835; living.

Huldah Lake Hawley Jordan, daughter of Anna Waldo and David Hawley, b. July 9, 1812; m. Ensign Hiram Jordan, teacher and farmer, May 2, 1833. He was b. at Moriah, N. Y., Feb. 22, 1809; d. at Gainesville, July 12, 1889 (Rufus, John). Children born Gainesville, N. Y. i. Lucia, b. Aug. 19, 1835; d. Sept. 12, 1888; m. James Beadler. ii. Rufus, b. March 22, 1838; d. Aug. 26, 1862. iii. David Hawley, b. May 18, 1849; d. Nov. 2, 1849. iv. David Starr, b. Jan. 19, 1851. v. Mary, b. April 13, 1854. David Starr Jordan, president of Leland Stanford Jr. University, Cal., b. at Gainesville, N. Y., Jan. 19, 1851. Graduate Cornell university, 1872, M. D. 1875; Ph. D. 1878; LL. D. Cornell 1886. President University of Indiana 1885-91; assistant to the U. S. Fish Commission 1877-91; U. S. Commissioner in charge of Fur Seal Investigations, 1896-97; president Leland Stanford Jr. University since 1891. Author of various books and papers on zoology. Married March 10, 1875, Susan Bowen; d. Nov. 15, 1885, dau. of Sylvester S. and Monica (Frissell) Bowen of Peru, Mass. Married 2d, Aug. 10, 1887, Jessie L. H., b. Nov. 5, 1866, dau. of Charles S. and Cordelia (Cutter) Knight of Worcester, Mass., formerly of Ware, Mass. Ch: i. Edith Monica, b. at Irvington, Ind., Feb. 17, 1877. ii. Harold Bowen, b. Bloomington, Ind., July 23, 1882. iii. Knight Starr, b. Bloomington, Ind., Oct. 26, 1888. iv. Barbara, b. Palo Alto, California, Nov. 10, 1891. v. Mary Jordan Edwards, dau. of Hiram and Huldah Lake Hawley Jordan, b. April 13, 1854; m. Edward Junius Edwards (founder and first commander-general of society of American Wars), son of John and Nancy Stockton Edwards, Jan. 1, 1877. Res., Minneapolis, Minn. Ch: i. Arthur Jordan, b. at Galesburg, Ill., Nov. 30, 1877. ii. Flora Alice, b. at Galesburg, Ill., Oct 11, 1880. iii. John Paul, b. at Minneapolis, Minn. June 5, 1883. iv. Majorie, b. at Minneapolis, Minn., Sept. 10, 1885. v. Junius David, b. at Minneapolis, Minn., March 17, 1890. vi. Mary Stockton, b. at Chicago, Ill., Nov 12, 1893. 2. Mary; m. Warren Wheeler. 3. Zachariah, m. Laura Phelps. 4. William. 5. John Elderkin Jr. 6. Amelia; m. Cornelius Hawley, brother of David. 7. Rufus. 8. Hannah; d. young. 9. Seth Harden. 10. Enoch Wight. 11. Sarah Foster. John Elderkin Waldo was a farmer. He died Feb. 20, 1849. His wife's death following April 3, 1852.

DAVID STARR JORDAN, M.D., PH. D., LL. D.

710. v. SAMUEL SHEFFIELD, b. Nov. 20, 1766; m. Anna ——.

711. vi. DAN, b. Sept. 4, 1770; m. Mirriam Willson.

712. vii. ABEL, b. Nov. 12, 1772; m. Phebe —— and —— ——.

713. viii. SARAH, b. Jan. 7, 1775; m. Silas Mills.

714. ix. THOS. DURKEE, b. Sept. 29, 1777; m. Cynthia Wheadon; b. July 24, 1783; d. s. p. April 5, 1856. He d. May 29, 1855. Res., Aurelius and Mentz, N. Y.
715. x. JACOB, b. Mar. 24, 1872; m. Louisa Brooks.
716. xi. ABIGAIL, b. ——; m. Stephen Cooper Brooks. She was known as "Aunt Nabbie."
717. xii. SARAH, b. July 26, 1768; d. young.
718. xiii. ABIGAIL, b. Oct. 26, 1756; d. Nov. 9, 1756.
719. xiv. NANCY, b. ———; m. —— Hall.

328. ISAAC FOSTER (Jacob, Isaac, Reginald, Reginald), b. March 18, 1743, Holliston, Mass; m. Patience ——. He went from Mass. to Me. in 1765-70 and was accidently killed by a tree falling upon him.

Between 1760 and 1770 Isaac Foster settled in (New Boston) now Gray. He was the first Foster and ancestor of all of that name in that town at the present time. It is said of him that he was well educated, and came of good family. Some of the old people have told that he had two brothers come to see him and they were very nicely dressed and stopped at the hotel, claimed that he married beneath him. He d. ae. 45. Res. in Mass. and, Gray, Me.

720. i. JOHN, b. Oct. 1, 1768; m. —— ——.
721. ii. ISAAC, b. Jan 24, 1770.
722. iii. JACOB, b. Sept. 3, 1771; m. Mary Young.
723. iv. JOSEPH, b. March 23, 1773; m. June 26, 1796, Eunice Fogg. Res., Gray, Me.
724. v. SAMUEL, b. July 6, 1774; m. Martha Humphrey.
725. vi. RACHEL, b. April 28, 1776.
726. vii. WILLIAM, b. April 28, 1776; d. young.
727. viii. HEPSIBETH, b. July 21, 1777; d. s. p.
728. ix. MOSES TWICHELL, b. Dec. 23, 1778; m. April 27, 1802, Betsey Edwards. Res., Gray, Me.
729. x. WILLIAM, b. Oct. 7, 1783; m. Lucy Spencer and Sarah Jane Cheever.
730. xi. REBECCA, b. Feb. 24, 1784; m. —— Whitney; a des. is Enos Whitney. The following are names of Fosters and descendants of Fosters who reside in the vicinity of Gray and are supposed to be related to Isaac and Patience: Silas W. Foster, Gray, Me.; Samuel Foster, Gray, Me.; Samuel Howard Foster, Brunswick, Maine; George Foster, Mechanic Falls, Me.; Daniel Foster, Raymond; Marshal Morse, Gray, Me.; Jacob Foster, Gray, Me.; Leonard Foster, Poland, Me.; Samuel F. Dolley, Gorham, Me.

COL. JOSEPH FOSTER.

336. COL. JOSEPH FOSTER (Jeremiah, John, Reginald, Reginald), b. Ipswich, Mass., July 19, 1730; m. Oct. 18, 1756, Lydia Giddings, dau. of Daniel and Mary (Butler) b. 1732; d. July 27, 1784; m. 2d, 1790, Mrs. Hannah Somes; d. before 1810. Joseph Foster was born in Chebacco Parish, Ipswich, now the town of Essex, Essex County, Mass.; his father was Capt. Jeremiah Foster, of that place, born in 1691, in Ipswich, died March 25, 1769; his mother was Dorothy, daughter of Na-

thaniel and Joanna (Kinsman) Rust, of Ipswich; she was born July 14, 1700, and died May 14, 1745.

Joseph Foster was the seventh of a family of twelve children and a great-great-grandson of Reginald Foster. He was also a great-great-grandson of John Dane, of Ipswich, Mass., author of "A Declaration of Remarkable Providences in the Course of My Life. By John Dane, of Ipswich. 1682." Boston, 1854. Elizabeth, daughter of John Dane and wife of Reginald Foster, was his great-grandmother. Elizabeth Dane was a niece of Rev. Francis Dane, forty-eight years minister at Andover, Mass., who, boldly denouncing the witchcraft delusion of 1692, was prominently connected with the trials at Salem when almost every member of his family was under arrest or suspicion, and a daughter and granddaughter were tried and condemned to death.

Joseph Foster married Lydia Giddings, daughter of Lieut. Daniel Giddings, of Chebacco; she was the mother of all the children. He again married Hannah Somes, widow of Isaac Somes, with six children; they had no children. Isaac Somes was captain of the privateer ship Tempest, lost at sea in 1782. Hannah Somes was living in 1808, but died prior to May 9, 1810, when the administrator's account of her estate is dated.

In early life Colonel Foster made many voyages at sea, being in 1760, master of the schooner Wolfe, at Gibraltar, and in 1761 of the schooner Joseph, in the West Indies. In 1762, he returned and settled permanently in Gloucester, Mass. He was engaged in commerce, and from 1766 to 1771, and probably before and afterward, had vessels trading to Cadiz, Malaga, Gibraltar, St. Kitt's, Monte Cristo, St. John's, Guadaloupe, West Indies, also coasting and fishing. He was prominent at Gloucester during the Revolution, and was colonel of the forces there. In 1782, he was captured in command of the Rebel letter-of-marque ship The Polly, and was a prisoner of war on parole at Windsor, Nova Scotia, in July of that year. This parole paper is still preserved. He is said to have been drummed through Halifax, Nova Scotia, at that time, in retaliation for similar treatment inflicted by him on British prisoners at Gloucester. The following notices of Col. Joseph Foster are taken from the History of Gloucester, by John J. Babson, Gloucester, 1860, to which the family are indebted for much information. At a town meeting held in Gloucester, December 28, 1772, to protest against the "despotic measures adopted by the British Ministry" in opposition to the "rights and liberties of the people of the American colonies,"Joseph Foster was chosen one of the seven members of the "Gloucester Committee of Correspondence," then elected (p. 369), who, March 6, 1775, "were continued in office" (p. 374). In 1774 he was one of the five Selectmen of Gloucester (p. 583), and in 1775 he was the representative of the town in the General Court of Massachusetts (p. 594). In 1779 he was one of the five delegates to the convention to form the State Constitution (p. 595), and after the Revolutionary War he was again the representative to General Court, in the years 1784, 1785 and 1786, and one of the four representatives in 1788 (p. 594).

At a town meeting March, 1774, Joseph Foster was chosen one of the two "special constables" appointed, "in case the small-pox should come into town, they having had it" (p. 371).

In March, 1775, he gave £2-8s., being one of the largest contributors, towards £117 7s. 1d., raised in Gloucester, for the relief of the distress caused in Boston by the act of Parliament shutting up that port (p. 372).

"Tradition asserts that the merchants of the town" of Gloucester smuggled extensively during "the last years of our colonial existence," and "till their commerce was destroyed by the war. A story is told concerning one of those smuggling adventures, which is deserving of remembrance for a clever device of its chief actor. A schooner, belonging to Col. Joseph Foster, came in from a foreign port in the night; and, according to custom, the hatches were immediately opened, and the landing of the cargo was commenced, the owner himself assisting. A considerable part was landed and stored before daybreak; but more than half was still on board, and, early in the morning, a tidewaiter was expected from Salem. The fertile mind of Colonel Foster hit at once upon an expedient. On the Cut was a watch-house, where John M'Kean, a stout Irishman, had been employed, in a time of alarm about the small-pox, to stop all strangers entering the town, and subject them to a fumigating process. It is sufficient to say, that his majesty's officer of the customs was on that morning ushered into the watch-house by John M'Kean: that he was kept there all day, and released after dark, purified from all infectious disease, so far as a thorough smoking could do it" (p. 387).

In 1776, "five small armed vessels, commissioned by the State" of Massachusetts, "made Gloucester Harbor their rendezvous." "They cruised during the day in Boston and Ipswich Bays, generally returning to port at night." One of them, commanded by Captain Manly, captured a brig with a cargo of oats, bacon, porter and other articles. She was chased ashore by the frigate 'Milford,' on to the rocks at Brace's Cove, where the prize crew landed. Capt. Joseph Foster, with a company

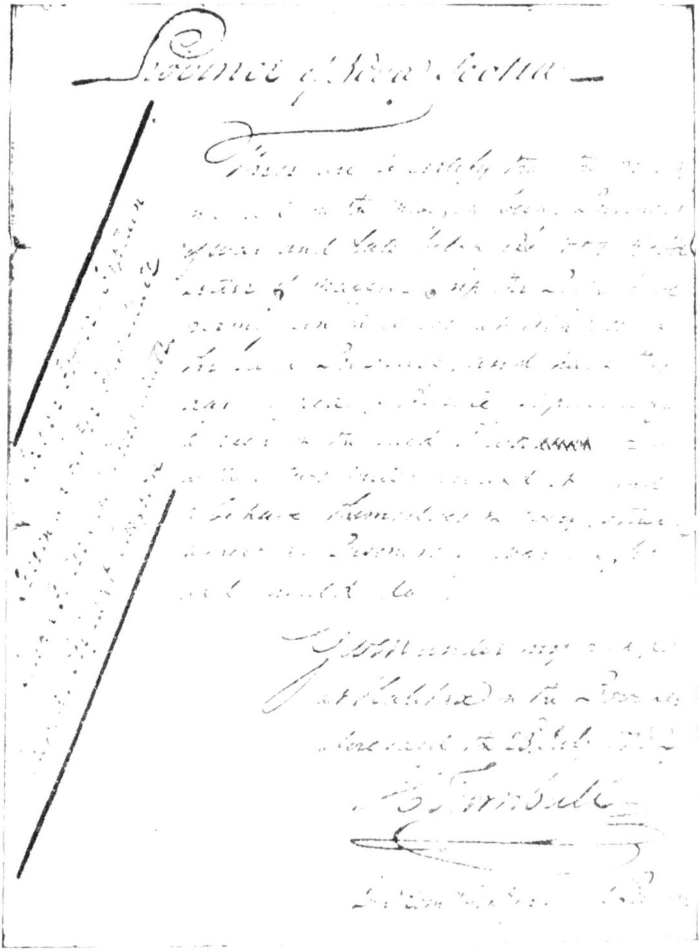

COL. FOSTER'S PAROLE.

of minute men, marched over from town to protect the vessel, in case the frigate should send a force to take possession of her. He got out some of the cargo; but, during the night, a boat's crew from the frigate boarded the brig, and set her on fire, by which she was destroyed" (p. 411).

It was in 1779, a "period of great poverty" in Gloucester, when paper money had depreciated to about one-seventieth of its nominal value," and "about one-sixth of the whole population were" "living chiefly upon charity," "that a large troop of women, in want of the necessaries of life, marched to Colonel Foster's store, and made known their determination to supply themselves with provisions and groceries from his stock, in spite of all resistance. Some of the number were prepared to take an exact account of the articles delivered to each person, with reference to payment, if they should ever be able to pay; but, pay or no pay, they would have them, and proceeded to help themselves accordingly. This merchant was one of the most ardent patriots of the town; and it is related of him that his conduct on this occasion proved him to be one of the most benevolent: for the tale of suffering and destitution that the women had to tell so touched his feelings, that he liberally supplied their wants, and dismissed them with words of the utmost kindness and sympathy" (p. 441).

In September, 1779, a convention of delegates to form a State Constitution assembled at Cambridge. Joseph Foster was one of the five delegates from Gloucester. "The convention completed their work in March, 1780; and submitted the Constitution they had agreed upon to the people of the State." At a town meeting held in Gloucester on the 22d of May, "the Constitution was accepted by a vote of forty-eight in its favor. No negative votes are recorded; nor is anything more known of the debate on the subject than that Captain Sargent and Colonel Foster said that they objected to it." The Constitution was adopted by the State (p. 442).

"In the year 1804, a prominent citizen of the town departed this life—Col. Joseph Foster; who died (December 10), aged seventy-four. Colonel Foster was a native of Ipswich. He was brought up in humble circumstances, and was indebted solely to his own energy and shrewdness for his advancement in life. He is supposed to have come to this town about 1760, and to have entered immediately upon those mercantile employments, in which, as a ship-master or merchant, he was afterward engaged to the end of his days. In the Revolutionary crisis, he was a patriot of the most ardent stamp; and was always ready to lend his personal exertions and his pecuniary means to help the town through the struggle. He was a man of rough manners; but he enjoyed the confidence and esteem of his townsmen, and was chosen frequently to various important public offices. He was several times elected representative (1775, 1784, 1785, 1786 and 1788), and was one of the delegates to the convention for forming the State Constitution (1779). He built and occupied a house near the easterly end of Front street (near the foot of Pleasant street), at the head of a lane leading to his wharf; but he had previously resided in a house, still standing (in 1860), at the head of Hancock street. His business had been pursued with such success, that he died possessed of a large estate."

On the space between Hancock street and Pleasant street, Gloucester, we still see three houses of the olden time, the first of which was the residence of one of the most distinguished patriots of that town, Col. Joseph Foster.

He left a son Joseph, who became a sea-captain, and was lost at sea about 1816; having never been heard from after leaving home on a voyage to the West Indies. He d. Dec. 10 1804. Res. Gloucester, Mass.

730. i. MARY, b. in 1757; m. July 17, 1777, Col. Nathaniel Wade; d. Oct. 26, 1826. Res. Ipswich, Mass. She d. Dec. 25, 1785 and he m. again. Ch.: Nathaniel, William Foster, Mary and Timothy. He sustained various trusts in the town; was long county treasurer, and representative from 1795, to 1817. He distinguished himself as a brave, patriotic and faithful officer in the Revolutionary War. He was at Bunker Hill—as captain of the Ipswich Minute Men—at Harlem and White Plains. Was colonel during the whole campaign in Rhode Island. While on duty there he sat president of the court martial in Providence, Dec. 23, 1777. In 1786 he commanded a regiment against the insurgents under Shay. For many years he was colonel of the Middle Essex regiment. When introduced to General LaFayette at Ipswich in 1824 the General immediately recognized him, and, grasping his hand, said, "My dear sir, I am rejoiced to see you; it is just such a starry night as we had when I met you in Rhode Island." Colonel Wade's benevolent manners and actions secured to him high and extensive esteem.

Colonel Nathaniel was son of Timothy and Ruth (Woodbury), b. Feb. 27, 1750. Ch.: 1. Nathaniel, b. May 3, 1778; m. Dec. 28, 1803, Hannah Hodgkins, b. 1780; d. Feb. 10, 1820. He d. Dec. 17, 1843. Res. Ipswich, Mass. 9 ch. 2. Wm. Foster, b. Jan. 3, 1780,; m. May 11, 1804, Mercy Lakeman, b. 1780; d. Dec. 1, 1843. He d. Sept. 23, 1851. Res. Ipswich. 10 ch. 3. Mary, b. Feb. 2, 1782;

d. unm. Jan. 8, 1861. 4. Timothy, b. Sept. 3, 1785; d. Nov. 26, 1785.

732. ii. JOSEPH, b. May 23, 1764; m. Rebecca Ingersoll.

733. iii. LYDIA, b. prob. 1760; m. March 5, 1780, John Osborne Sargent, of Gloucester. Both d. 1786. He was son of Epes, junior and gt. gr., son of William 2d. who was son of William and Mary, of Bristol, England. William, senior, went from Exeter, England, to Barbadoes, when young and was educated there. He returned to his native country, and there m. Mary 'Epes, who stole from her home in the habit of a milkmaid, to become his wife. Such is the family tradition. The son, who came to Gloucester, first appears there in 1678, when he had a grant of two acres of land, at Eastern Point, where he built a house. He was a mariner and owned a sloop, which he probably employed in coasting. The date of his death is not known; but it is certain that he d. before, June, 1707; perhaps at sea, as in the settlement of his estate no charges are made for sickness or funeral expenses. The inventory of his property amounted to £278. He m. June 21, 1678, Mary, daughter of Peter Duncan, who d. Feb. 28, 1725. They had fourteen children, but it is only by one son, Epes, b. in 1690, that the name has been perpetuated. Epes Sargent was a prominent citizen, and several of his descendants have been distinguished men. He m. April 1, 1720, Esther Maccarty, and again, Aug. 10, 1744, Mrs. Catharine Brown, of Salem; soon after this last date he removed to Salem, where he d. Dec. 6, 1762. His children by his first wife were: Epes, b. in 1721; Esther, 1722; Ignatius, 1724; James, 1726, d. in 1727; Winthrop, 1728; Sarah, 1729; Daniel, 1731; William, 1734; and Benjamin, 1736. By his second wife, he had Paul Dudley and John. His remains were brought to Gloucester, and placed in the family tomb. He acquired considerable property there as a merchant; was the principal acting magistrate in town for several years, and its representative in 1740. In Salem he took an active part in public affairs; was colonel in the militia, and long a justice of the General Sessions Court. An obituary notice in a newspaper of the day, gives him a high character as a merchant, magistrate and Christian. His son Epes, m. in 1745, Catharine, daughter of Hon. John Osborne, of Boston. She d. Feb. 7, 1788. An obituary notice contained in a Salem paper of the 19th of that month, describes her as a lady of eminent virtue. Early in life Mr. Sargent engaged in mercantile pursuits, in which he acquired a large property. A few years prior to the Revolutionary War, he owned 10 vessels, which were employed in the fishery and foreign commerce; and was carrying on at that time a very extensive trade; but the total suspension of his business, which the war occasioned, together with the embarrassing situation into which he was thrown by joining the unpopular side in the contest with the mother country, caused heavy pecuniary losses, by which his property became greatly reduced. He d. 1779, and left Epes and John. Ch. of Lydia: 1. Amelia Bernard, b. 1780; m. 1801, Daniel Rogers. She d., s. p., 1802. 2. Frances, b. 1782; m. April 8, 1805, John Baker. She d. Aug. 24, 1806, and left one ch. 3. Epes, b. March 7, 1784; m. Jan., 1806, Mary Pearson, d. 1807; m. second, Oct. 18, 1808, Hannah D. Coffin and Mary Otis Lincoln. His son John Osborne, b. Sept. 20, 1811, graduated at Harvard in 1830, studied law and after several years' practice in Boston and New York, finally settled in Washington. John Osborne Sargent was born in Gloucester, Mass., and passed his childhood there, and in the town of Hingham. He was sent to the Latin school in Boston, the prize annals of which, and the record of a Latin ode, and a translation from the Elegy of Tyrtæus of his composition, show his early proficiency in classical education. He passed to Harvard, and was graduated in 1830. While there he established the clever periodical of which we have already spoken in the notice of one of its contributors, Dr. O. W. Holmes, The Collegian. He was further assisted in it

by the late William H. Simmons, the accomplished elocutionist and essayist; Robert Habersham, Jr., of Boston, Frederick W. Brune, of Baltimore, and by his brother, Epes Sargent. On leaving college Mr. Sargent studied law in the office of the Hon. William Sullivan, of Boston, and commenced its practice in that city. This was at the period of political agitation attending the financial measures of President Jackson. Mr. Sargent became a political writer and speaker in the Whig cause, and was elected to the lower house of the Legislature of Massachusetts. For some three years he was almost a daily writer for the editorial columns of the Boston Atlas, and added largely by his articles to the reputation which the paper at that time enjoyed as an efficient, vigorous party journal. In 1838 Mr. Sargent removed to the city of New York, and was well known by his pen and oratory during the active political career which resulted in the election of General Harrison to the presidency. The Courier and Enquirer, for three or four years at this time, was enriched by leading political articles from his hand. At the close of the contest he reëngaged in the active pursuit of his profession. To this he devoted himself, with rigid seclusion from politics, for eight years, with success. He was drawn, however, again into politics in the canvass which resulted in the election of General Taylor, upon whose elevation to the presidency, he became associated with Mr. Alexander C. Bullitt, of Kentucky, in the establishment of the Republic newspaper at Washington. Its success was immediate and unprecedented. In about six months it numbered more than thirty thousand staunch Whigs on its subscription list. Its course, however, was not acceptable to the members of the Cabinet. A rupture was finally brought about, and he withdrew from the editorship of the paper. After Millard Fillmore was elected President, Mr. Sargent returned to the paper and edited it with great vigor, and was tendered the mission to China. His brother Epes, b. Sept. 27, 1813, was poet, journalist and author. During his childhood he lived in St. Petersburg; was educated at the Boston Latin School, and spent two or three years at Harvard. After leaving the college he passed an industrious literary life in New York and Boston. Beginning with school-boy effusions in The Literary Journal (conducted by himself and other students at the Boston Latin School) and The Collegian (a Harvard paper established by his brother, John Osborne Sargent), he was afterwards connected with the editorial staffs of the Token, Parley's Magazine, The New England Magazine, The Advertiser, of Boston (1837), The Mirror, of New York (1839-40), The New Monthly Magazine (New York, 1843), The Transcript, of Boston (1844-53), The School Monthly (Boston, 1858), and The New World, of New York. He was also a frequent contributor to The Knickerbocker Magazine, The Atlantic Monthly in its earlier days, and other periodicals. He also assisted Samuel G. Goodrich in preparing his "Geography" and several of the "Peter Parley" books. In 1836 Mr. Sargent wrote a play in five acts, "The Bride of Genoa," for Miss Josephine Clifton. This play was produced at the Tremont Theatre with great success, and was published in the New World under the title of "The Genoese." In the following year he wrote for Ellen Tree a tragedy, "Velasco," which was produced with success in Boston and frequently in England, where it was commended by Serjeant Talfourd and the elder Vandenhoff. Two other plays—"Change Makes Change," a comedy, and "The Priestess," a tragedy—complete his dramatic works. The first of these was produced at Niblo's Garden, in New York city, about 1839 or 1840, and afterward by Burton at Philadelphia. "The Priestess" was acted at the New Boston Theatre for thirteen nights in 1855, and twenty copies of the text was printed privately. Among the other works published by Mr. Sargent are the following: "Wealth and Worth" (1840), "What's to be Done?" (1841), "The Life and Services of Henry Clay" (1842), "Fleetwood," a novel (1845), "Songs of the

Sea" (1847), "The Mariner's Library," "American Adventures by Land and Sea" (1847), "Selections in Poetry" (1852), "The Critic Criticised," a reply to a review of Webster's Orthographical System in The Democratic Review for March, 1856, "Arctic Adventure by Sea and Land" (1857), "Poems," "Original Dialogues" (1861), "Six Charts for Use in Teaching Reading, Spelling, etc.," "Peculiar," a tale (1863), "Pianchette," an account of modern spiritualism (1869), "The Woman who Dared," a poem (1869), School Manual of English Etymology" (1873).

734. iv. SARAH, b. 1762; m. William Dolliver 3rd, of Gloucester, son of William and gr.-son of Peter and Abigail (Saunders). William was cousin of William, who m. her sister Elizabeth. Res. Gloucester, where she d. Nov. 1, 1836, s. p.

735. v. ELIZABETH, b. Jan. 22, 1766; m. Nov. 25, 1789, William Dolliver, of Gloucester, son of Peter and gr.-son of Peter and Abigail (Saunders). Res. Gloucester, Mass. He d. Oct. 10, 1841. She d. Jan. 22, 1854, in Boston. 7 ch.

736. vi. JUDITH, b. 1772; m. April 16, 1793, Thomas Bradbury Saunders; res. Gloucester and Dorchester. Being left a widow, she kept a fashionable young ladies' boarding school at Dorchester, with Miss Clemintina Beach, an English lady, from 1800 to 1820. She d. Oct. 22, 1841 in Dorchester, s. p.

737. vii. BENJAMIN, b. 1769; m. Mary Ingersoll.

738. viii. WILLIAM, b. Aug. 1, 1775; bapt. Oct. 1, 1775; n. f. k.; prob. d. young.

345. ZEBULON FOSTER (Moses, John, Reginald, Reginald), bap. Ipswich, Mass., Sept. 22, 1728; m. April, 7, 1750, Anna Knowlton, b. Sept. 22, 1728, dau. of Robert, of Manchester, Mass. Res. Ipswich, Mass.

346. MOSES FOSTER (Moses, John, Reginald, Reginald), b. abt. 1730, in Ipswich, Mass; m., Ashburnham Mary ——. He resided in the northeast part of the town, and, in company with Zimri Heywood, owned a mill. The site of the early mill is now in Ashby. In 1770 he removed to Shelburne. He d. res. Ashby and Shelburne, Mass.

739. i. MILICENT, b. May 1, 1758; d. Oct. 3, 1760.

740. ii. SARAH, b. April 14, 1760.

741. iii. KEZIAH, b. March 10, 1762.

742. iv. PHEBE, b. April 29, 1764; m. Nov. 21, 1782, Capt. David Merriam. He was in the Revolutionary War; resided in Ashburnham, Mass., and soon after his marriage moved to Brandon, Vt. She d. April 7, 1794; he m. 2d, and d. Feb. 15, 1849. Ch.: 1. Phebe, b. Dec. 26, 1783. 2. David, b. June 9, 1786. 3. Geo. W., b. Oct. 4, 1787. 4. Isaac Foster, b. July 27, 1790. 5. Cyrus, b. July 14, 1793. 6. Betsy, b. Sept. 13, 1796. 7. Alvin, b. March 26, 1802. 8. Angeline, b. July 18, 1808. 9. David; d. ——.

743. v. ESTHER, b. Jan. 19, 1767.

744. vi. BROOKS, b. March 14, 1769.

745. vii. MOSES, bap. Dec. 29, 1771.

347. CAPT. AARON FOSTER (Moses, John, Reginald, Reginald), b. Ipswich, Mass., ——, 1723; m. ——, Ruth Lowe, b. June, 1728; d. March 24, 1811. His will was probated Jan. 6, 1812. He was a soldier in the Colonial Wars, was at the taking of Louisburg, and later served in the Revolutionary War with his two sons, Moses and Thomas. In 1744-5 news of the war with France and Spain being received, preparations were made for the invasion of Nova Scotia. These were not completed until the following March, when troops sailed from Boston. The grand design was the capture of Louisburg, styled the "Dunkirk of America." Among the 3,000 troops called, Ipswich furnished her full quota. Tradition mentions "Aaron Foster," a young man of 23 years. Herein follows the young soldier's report; a bright, capable and vigorous "talk," showing the "stuff" of which such men are made. This expedition was one of the most remarkable events in the history of North America. When the news reached Boston the bells of the town rang merrily, and all the people were in transports of joy. The news spread rapidly through town, carrying gladness, and affecting Christian hearts with a sense of the interposition of God in behalf of the colonies! And well they might rejoice

and give thanks. It was a signal victory. Next year the French made great effort to retrieve their loss, but failed in each attempt.

The biography of Aaron Foster begins thus: "After the sermon by Dr. John Wise an infant is brought forward for baptism; its name is Aaron Foster. We look with deep interest upon this little face, for 'we' (as spirit of the later age) can tell, without the gift of prophecy, what manner of child this shall be. We follow him through childhood and youth, and see him rise to manhood. We see him a young soldier, age 23, in the combined army at the taking of Louisburg, and we behold him also traversing the ocean as captain of a vessel. We follow him into the Revolutionary army, fighting the battles of his country for liberty. We see him after the war at the head of a numerous family, and find him still living in the 19th century. After his departure from life we see, at his funeral, not only children, but a retinue of grandchildren, growing to respectability and usefulness. Among these we recognize 'Moses Foster,' of Wenham, 'Thomas Foster,' (father) and 'David Choate' and 'Rufus Choate,' of Boston. He d. Dec. 25, 1811. Res., Ipswich, Mass.

746. i. MOSES, b. Nov. 4, 1760; m. ——— ———.

747. ii. THOMAS, b. April 9, 1762; m. Sarah Storey.

748. iii. ZEBULON, b. Aug. 2, 1766; m. Polly Storey.

749. iv. MIRIAM, b. Nov. 28, 1771; m. Oct. 15, 1791, David Choate, b. Nov. 29, 1757. He d. March 28, 1808. She d. Jan. 14, 1853; res., Ipswich, Mass. She was his second wife, the first having d. s. p. in 1784. After his second marriage he established his home on Hog Island, where he continued to live until 1800, when he removed to the main land and died at the age of fifty. He was a man of uncommon intellectual endowments. He had a quick, accurate perception, full recollection and a judgment ever ready to decide, and never made more than one decision on the same subject. He lived the friend and supporter of virtue, order and steady habits. Ch. by Merriam: 1. Mary, b. Oct. 4, 1792; m. Nov. 28, 1813, Dr. Thomas Sewall. She d. March 29, 1855. They had one son and both d. in Rockville, Md. 2. Hannah, b. Aug. 12, 1794; m. Sept. 2, 1822, Rev. Robert Crowell. She d. Feb. 9, 1837. They had 6 ch.; res., Essex, Mass.; one is Prof. E. P. Crowell, Amherst, Mass. 3. David, b. Nov. 29, 1796; m. Jan. 14, 1828, Elizabeth Wade; res., Ipswich, Mass. Prominent citizen, teacher, magistrate, state senator. Ch.: a. David Choate, Jr., b. Nov 27, 1828; m. Jan 1, 1856, Susan E. Kimball; P. O. address, Salem, Mass. b. Helen Maria Choate, b. Sept. 16, 1831; d. Nov. 24, 1851. c. Rufus, b. March 24, 1834; m. Sept. 7, 1880, Sarah E. Burnham; P. O. address, Essex, Mass ; two ch. d. Hannah E. Choate, b. July 20, 1840; P. O. address, Salem, Mass. e. William C. Choate, b. Jan. 6, 1843; m., 1st, Lydia M. Gage, May 18, 1869; m., 2d, Elizabeth M. Norton, May 13, 1893. f. Washington, b. Jan. 17, 1846; m. Sept. 21, 1875, Grace R. Whitton; P. O. address, Greenwich, Conn. 4. Rufus, b. Oct. 1, 1799; m. March 29, 1825, Helen Olcott; 7 ch. Res., Boston. He d. in Halifax, N. S. It was every way desirable that one who had personal recollections of Rufus Choate should prepare a sketch of his life and character. All the more was this the case, inasmuch as the genius and the efforts of this man contributed so largely to the history of the family. There must yet be living many who can recall the charm of his personality and of his eloquence. Less than twenty years ago a writer remarked: "Boston swarms to-day with admirers of Choate." The present writer was never privileged to meet the great advocate. His eyes never watched those rapid and forceful gestures by which the soul sought to give expression to its passionate thoughts and feelings; his ears never drank in the music of that voice, which charmed as the fabled lyre of old. It can only be imagined, the reluctance with which he undertakes to write. There is but one reflection to lead him to take heart of grace in this attempt. If those who knew the man, who saw him daily in court and at his home, who listened to his impassioned pleadings and to his familiar table talk; if they despaired of being able to give us any adequate idea

of their conception of his learning, his power, his genius, his worth, it certainly will not be expected of one who never stepped upon the vantage ground of personal intercourse that he should be free from misgivings in regard to his ability to bring into near and distinct view the shining qualities of a mind so highly gifted, of a character so nobly grand. I cannot but regret for myself the unfulfilled desire of my youth, but no doubt those for whom I now write can draw from the ample sources to which I am compelled to resort, a better, a truer, a nobler idea of the man than I could have conveyed had I written under the most favorable circumstances. I recall that in the year of his death, one of his biographers, Mr. Edward G. Parker, said: "After all that those who knew and loved Mr. Choate can do, he will be forever unknown to those who never saw and heard him." Still, later on, Mr. Edwin P. Whipple wrote: "It is difficult for those who knew him to convey to a younger generation, which never passed "under the wand of the magician," the effect which he produced on their own minds and hearts. How, then, can a writer who comes to this work as I must come, when he reads these admissions on the part of those who wrote from within the circle of personal friendship—how can he have confidence in anything except in the benevolent indulgence of his readers? It must be a matter of profound satisfaction to us all that those who have written worthily of this member of our family, have done so with manifest affection and esteem. They have shown us, as Mr. Whipple has shown us, the effect which he produced on their own hearts and minds." I remember that Mr. Samuel Gilman Brown told me, when his "Life of Rufus Choate" was completed, in 1862, that the work had been one of interest and love. Mr. Joseph Neilson said of the many contributors to his volume of

HON. RUFUS CHOATE.

"Memories" "that a loving spirit moved them, and presided over their work." The part which Mr. Neilson himself took in the preparation of that work abundantly proves his own affectionate devotion to the memory of a brother in professional life.

Rufus Choate was born on Choate Island, Chebacco Parish, the second precinct of Ipswich, "Tuesday, Oct. 1, 1799, at 3 o'clock p. m.," as the event was carefully recorded by his father in the family Bible. This place of his birth remained one of his homes as long as he lived. One of his homes, we say, because when he was only about six months old his father purchased a house in the village of Chebacco, still retaining possession of the farm on the island. The summers of the lad were likely to be spent at the island home; the winters on the mainland. The situation of the farmhouse is well shown in a view of the island presented on an early print. According to the writer's recollection, the house stands facing about south by east, to speak in nautical language, which ought to be almost our mother tongue. The slope in front, somewhat steep, a thick-matted sward, always green, runs down fifteen or twenty rods, perhaps, to the broken bank of the creek. There is a fringe of bass-wood and other native trees along the shore. The near view is of marshes at low water, with a tidal stream winding and broadening down to the bay. At high water all that field is as a quiet lake. Its shelter from the sea is afforded by two bare arms of sand, the Loaf, or in the phrase of earlier times, Two-Penny Loaf, stretching up from the south toward Castle Neck, which is extended from the north. The whiteness of the sand, of which these barriers to the sea are formed, and the rounded heaps into which it is drifted by the winds, deceive unaccustomed eyes with the appearance of snow. Between the two points there is left an open space through which one looks out upon the limitless sea. The character of the scene is sculpturesque. Its beauty consists in clearness and grace of outline, in boldness of relief, and in its setting of untarnished blue. We dwell thus particularly upon the outlook from the home of the subject of this sketch, because a nature so sensitive as his must have received impressions from the surroundings in his earlier years that went with him through life. His ancestor, John Choate, settled in Massachusetts in 1667, and his grandfather of the same name was a member of the State Legislature from 1741 until 1761, and for five years a member of the Council. At an early age he was remarkable for his memory, and when he entered Dartmouth, in 1815, he was a good Greek and Latin scholar. He was graduated in 1819; studied law with Wm. Wirt, in Washington, at Ipswich and Salem; was admitted to the bar in 1823, and practiced in Danvers until 1828. In 1828 he removed to Salem, and in 1830 he was elected to Congress, where he distinguished himself in a speech on the tariff. He was re-elected the following term, but resigned in 1834, and removed to Boston, where he soon acquired fame as a lawyer, and occasionally delivered lectures on literary and historical subjects. In 1841 he was chosen to succeed Daniel Webster in the United States Senate, and delivered speeches on the McLeod case, the Bank bill, the confirmation of Mr. Everett as Minister to England, the Bankrupt law, on Mr. Clay's resolution for retrenchment and reform, the Naval Appropriation bill, the tariff, the bill to provide further remedial justice in the courts of the United States, on the ratification of the Webster-Ashburton treaty, the Oregon boundary, the Smithsonian Institution, and the annexation of Texas, which he opposed. He left the Senate in 1845, and resumed the practice of his profession, and from that time until his death there was no case involving great legal difficulties or pecuniary responsibility to which he was not summoned. In 1850 he traveled through Europe. He was a delegate to the national Whig convention, held in Baltimore in 1852, and he urged the nomination of Daniel Webster for the presidency. In 1853 he was a member of the convention for revising the Constitution of Massachusetts, and in the two years succeeding he took much interest in national politics, and supported Mr. Buchanan for President. He delivered an address at a Union meeting, in Faneuil hall, Boston, and one in Washington in February, 1851, and in July, 1853, read at Dartmouth college, a eulogy on Daniel Webster, which remains unsurpassed in that style of eloquence. His last public oration was given on July 4, 1853, on "American Nationality." Owing to impaired health, he planned a visit to Europe in 1859, but became so ill that he left his steamer at Halifax, where he died a few days after landing. Mr. Choate was an eloquent orator, who rarely indulged in invective, but excelled in quaint humor. He possessed great personal magnetism, a musical voice, wealth of learning and a sweet and gentle nature. He was frequently compared to Lord Erskine. His writings have been edited by S. G. Brown (2 Vols., Boston, 1862; see Recollections of Eminent Men, by Edwin P. Whipple, Boston, 1886). Mr. Choate married Miss Helen Olcott, of Hanover, N. H., in 1825, and their son Rufus, born in Salem, Mass., in 1834, died Jan. 15, 1866; was graduated at Amherst in 1855; was admitted to the bar in Boston in 1858, and served in the Civil War. He was promoted to the rank of captain, and resigned in 1862. 5. Washington, b. Jan. 17, 1803; d. Feb. 27, 1822, while in junior class at Dartmouth. 6. Job, b. Dec. 25, 1806; d. March 10, 1808.

750. v. RUTH, b. Oct. 19, 1754; d. Oct. 5, 1774.
751. vi. MARY, b. Aug. 16, 1756; m. 1812, Capt. Oliver Lakeman. She d. March 24, 1837,—a dau. is Mrs. E. A. Burnham, 498 Giddings ave., Cleveland, O.
752. vii. AARON, b. Oct. 7, 1758; d. June 7, 1762.
753. viii. AARON, b. Sept 10, 1764; d. April 13, 1798.
754. ix. JOANNA, b. Nov. 27, 1768. She d. Aug. 10, 1822.

364. CAPT. JONATHAN FOSTER (Jonathan, Jonathan, William, Reginald), b. Haverhill, Mass., Oct. 11, 1727; m. June 28, 1764, Rebecca Dorman, dau. of John and Rebecca (Smith), b. 1732; d. Oct. 16, 1794. He served in the French and Indian War, and was a lieutenant, and the family have his diary, which he kept in 1758. He was captain in the Revolutionary army. He d. July 28, 1813. Res., Boxford, Mass.

755. i. ISRAEL, b. March 16, 1765; m. Mehitabel Carleton.
756. ii. CHARLES, b. April 26, 1767; m. Lucy Austin and Mehitabel Chandler.
757. iii. BETSY, b. March 12, 1769; m. —— Spafford. Their son, Capt. Aaron, m. Betsy Foster (his cousin), a desc. is Israel Spafford, of Bradford, Mass.
758. iv. AMASA, b. May 8, 1771; m. Oct. 1, 1792, Betsey Poor.
759. v. JONATHAN, b. Feb. 3, 1774; m. Mary Kimball.
760. vi. PHINEAS, b. July 27, 1776; m. Frances Harrod.

366. RICHARD FOSTER (Jonathan, Jonathan, William, Reginald), b. Boxford, Mass., Feb. 20, 1732; m. Nov. 19, 1761, Elizabeth Kimball, of Andover. He d. ——. Res. Boxford, Mass.

761. i. JEDEDIAH, b. Nov. 25, 1762.
762. ii. PHINEAS, b. Aug. 1, 1764.
763. iii. ASA, b. April 29, 1776; m. Dolly Morrill.

371. ABNER FOSTER (Zebadiah, Jonathan, William, Reginald), b. Boxford, Mass., April 23, 1733; m. —— ——. Res., Newrey, Me.

764. i. ASA, b. ——; m. Anna Bartlett.
765. ii. ABNER, b. ——.
766. iii. DANIEL, b. ——.

378. WILLIAM FOSTER (John, William, William, Reginald), b. Andover, Mass., March 4, 1730; m. Jan. 9, 1755, Hannah Abbott, dau. of Capt. George and Mary (Phillips), sister of Rev. Samuel, b. Dec. 14, 1733, d. May 26, 1820. He was a yeoman. He d. Sept. 1, 1803. Res., Andover, Mass.

Wm. Foster and Anna Abbott, a granddaughter of old Samuel Phillips, the Salem goldsmith, started in with a fine old clock (still doing its time) in 1775. He lived over to 1803, having seen his only son in a unique business of boarding boys on a sort of school farm, perhaps better adapted for tender youth than the larger school on the hill. Miss Bailey has told us almost all that is known about this old home school. William expected to be married early, and built on the north wing of this delightful old haunt of the ancestral genii. But he put it off, perhaps, because his mother lived to 1820. There were the Rogers, nephews of Hannah, and the Browns of Sarah, over in Tewksbury, who of course, with the Kimball kin, would be pardoned for feeling a little hopeful pride in this childless Uncle William, who owned the center of the town and all the old paternal estate unbroken.—Miss Abbott.

767. i. HANNAH, b. June 20, 1756; m. Feb. 27, 1777, Lieut. Timothy Rogers, of Tewksbury; she d. Oct. 24, 1794.
768. ii. WILLIAM, b. June 1, 1758; m. Sarah Welch Kimball.
769. iii. MARY, b. July 21, 1763; m. Oct. 30, 1783, Timothy, son of Timothy and Sarah Ballard, b. July 28, 1757.
770. iv. SARAH, b. Sept. 9, 1765; m. June 8, 1794, Joseph Brown, of Tewksbury.

380. ENSIGN JOHN FOSTER (John, William, William, Reginald), b. Andover, Mass., Feb. 14, 1733; m. there, 1772, Hannah Ballard, b. ——, 1750; d. ——, 1811. She joined the church in 1786. Res., Andover, Mass.

771. i. JOHN, b. Feb. 10, 1773; m. Sarah Burt.
772. ii. WILLIAM P., b. Jan. 22, 1779.

382. ISAAC FOSTER (John, William, William, Reginald), b. Andover, Mass., April 28, 1737; m., prob. Jan. ——, 1761, Dorcas Jewett, of Tewksbury, b. ——, 1741; d. May 26, 1762; m., 2d, Ann ——; d. May 9, 1798. The following petitions present a vivid picture of the wanderings and adventures of an Andover soldier, who was taken captive by the Indians. These were the tales which our great-grandfathers used to tell to their children, gathered around the fire, of winter evenings, when the back-log blazed and the "mug of cider simmered slow," and, sipping it ever and anon, the hero of many fights waxed warm, and shouldering crutch, or seizing musket from over the chimney piece, showed how battles were fought in the "Old French War," kindling in young breasts the martial ardor that flamed up in Revolutionary fires. "The Petitions of Isaac Foster of Andover Humbly Sheweth: That, whereas he was an enlisted soldier, in the service of this Province, in Company 2 of Lieut.-Col. James Frye, in the year 1756 & in sd company proceeded to Fort William Henry,& on the 18th of Sept. following was by Detachment sent on a Scouting Party under the command of Capt. Hodges to the Westerly side of Lake George, and, on the 19th, the Party being surprised by a Large Body of the enemy & mostly killed or taken, he had the unhappy Fate to fall into the Hands of a Number of those barbarous Indians called Ottawas, inhabiting beyond Lake Superior; who, after having rifled his Pockets of $4, obliged him to proceed with them to a Lake called Almipagon, lying Northerly of Lake Superior 150 miles, and (as the French say) 1100 miles from Montreal. With the savages he was detained two years, during which time he suffered inconceivable hardships, and at the expiration of it, being permitted by his Indian owner to accompany him down the Lake to a French Place called Detroit, he there interceded with a Frenchman to ransom him, which he accordingly effected for three hundred Livres; which sum your Petitioner Discharged by Labour. And after being detained by the French at sd Detroit & Montreal near 14 months Longer he was brought to Crown Point at the time of the late exchange of Prisoners, and is since returned Home, having been absent (from the day he was taken) three years & two months. And whereas, he has received pay no longer than till the Day of his Captivity, he humbly begs your Excellency & Honors would take His case under your wise Consideration & and make him such further allowance for his time, &c., as in your great goodness & wisdom shall seem mete, which your humble petitioner, as in Duty bound, shall ever Pray.

"Andover, Jan. 7th, 1760. Isaac Foster."

This petition, drawn up so carefully, and written in every respect so correctly, bears evidence of being the composition of a man more accustomed to the use of the pen than the captive was, who had been three years campaigning. Who wrote it may be surmised from the fact that it was ordered to pay to Samuel Phillips, Esq., for the use of the petitioner in full remuneration for his services and sufferings within mentioned the sum of eight pounds. Three years before, the father of the petitioner, John Foster, had presented a petition for his son's pay, to be given to him.

He then supposed his son to be dead, not having heard from him for so long. Thus did the youth of Andover early mature in life's experience, and such were the suspense and anxiety of kindred "in regard to soldiers in the king's service:"—

"The Petition, of John Foster, of Andover, April 2, 1757. Humbly sheweth that Isaac Foster, a minor, the son of your petitioner, was a soldier in his Majesty's service in the expedition against Crown Point, in the year 1756, in the Company of Col. James Frye, and in the month of Sept. the said Isaac (as he was scouting on his duty) was either killed by the enemy or taken captive, by reason whereof his Gun was not Returned. Yet there is kept back, out of his wages, from your petitioner, for said Gun the sum of £4, so that, without the interposition of your Hon'r and Hon'rs your Petitioner might be a sufferer for omitting that which it was not his power to perform; your petitioner therefore humbly supplicates the consideration and favor of this Great and Wise Court, praying (with submission) that your Hon'r and Hon'rs would be pleased to allow him the said sum of £4, retained as aforesaid, or otherwise, as in your wisdom & Goodness you shall think fit and judge mete, and your Petitioner, as in duty bound, shall ever pray. John Foster."

"Ordered to be paid the full wages due to his son without any deduction."

What a day of happy surprise that must have been when the long-lost son returned to relate his manifold escapes and adventures!

Vol. 123, page 3, Reg. Deeds at Salem, Essex Co. Isaac of Tewksbury, in 1767, has an arrangment with David Trull and Charles Furbush for seven years—Nov 19, 1766: They pay him £4 a year all the part of the seven years he lives (which seems to indicate he is about through with farming) and rent a farm, "all I possess in Tewksbury in right of late wife Dorcas, dec., which lands are descended to me, in death of wife by courtesy of England: 100 acres in 3 parts; a homestead which he lives in and pays taxes on, with 1 cow, which they feed; reserving this dwelling house to Isaac & heirs & a piece of land, etc.; he to improve other lots named & parts about the barn & yard & pile wood—they to cut no timber save for fences—He to clear up the uncleaned land for his own use only, etc"—some arrangement, which is not clear to me; should like to know the relation of Charles Furbush and David Trull to this apparently old man with heirs. He may have held the property for baby Seth, but in seven years from 1766, Seth, born 1762, would be only 11 years of age, if alive. Johnson Brook and Sam Hazeltine (formerly of Bradford) are on his bonds. Ann may have been a Hazeltine and wife of his son Isaac. Res., Tewksbury, Mass.

773. i. SETH JEWETT, b. May 18, 1762.

774. ii. ABIAH, b. May 25, 1763; m. Sarah Whiting.

775. iii. MARY, b. Dec. 19, 1764.

776. iv. EZRA, b. March 20, 1767; m. Abigail ——. Hon. J. L. Davenport, of the Department of the Interior, writes as follows. "Ezra Foster made an application for pension on April 4, 1818, at which time he was 52 years of age, and residing at Lyman, N. H., and his pension was allowed for three years' actual service as a private in the Massachusetts troops, Revolutionary War. He enlisted at Tewksbury, Mass., and served under Captain Hudien and Colonel Tupper. His widow, Abigail, made application and received a pension for the service of her husband, as above set forth. He died Feb. 22, 1856. Their children's names were: Mary, Nancy, George, Isaac, Ezra, John, Lois and Joseph."

777. v. SOLOMON, b. May 6, 1769.

778. vi. ISAAC GRAY, b. June 22, 1771.

779. vii. JOHN, b. May 15, 1773; m. Betty Baldwin Stickney. John's age ——, who moved away with his Betty, from Andover, and died in Albany, Me., June 20, 1806. His widow took her letter from South church, and married, for her second, down there, Benjamin Clark, and I have written to a son, Daniel Clark, to hunt up the old gravestone.

"Isaac, of Tewksbury, sent his son John over here to marry Betty Baldwin Stickney, of the line of Blacksmith John, a resident of North Parish. They moved to Albany, Me., which John, shortly before his death, helped to survey. This family take a strong interest in old Andover."—Miss Abbott.

780. viii. JOEL, b. March 16, 1776.

781. ix. ANNA, b. Nov. 2, 1781; d. June 14, 1800.

383. GIDEON FOSTER (John, William, William, Reginald), b. Andover, Mass., Aug. 21, 1739; m. March 13, 1768, Elizabeth Russell, b. 1745; d. Sept. 15, 1820. "Gideon Foster and his wife, Elizabeth Russell, lived in the house that Dea. Ballard Lovejoy demolished to build his present residence. He had daughters only, was a veteran of the Revolution and the special care of his nephew, 'Master Billy,' to whose interest the father of the schoolmaster commends him when only a small boy, for had he not fought for his country when William, with the care of a large estate could not be spared in person? The old tannery, on his and the adjoining estate of his brother, John Ballard, was worked by him and the tenants of what must be now the Matthews place, then taxed as the estate of William, of Boston, and his brother John, at first a resident of Reading."—Miss Abbott. He d. Aug. 9, 1817. Res., Andover, Mass.

782. i. ELIZABETH, b. Feb. 23, 1769; d., of a fever, June 27, 1843; unm.

783. ii. ABIGAIL, b. Jan. 13, 1771; m. William Shattuck, of Hillsboro, N. H., Nov. 17, 1790.

784. iii. TAMISON, b. May 1, 1773; d. March 23, 1776.

785. iv. SARAH, b. June 14, 1775; m. May 19, 1803, Jonathan Gleason, of Andover.

786. v. PRISCILLA, b. April 5, 1778.

384. OBADIAH FOSTER (John, William William, Reginald), b. Andover, Mass., May 25, 1741; m. May 30, 1769, Hannah Ballard, dau. of Hezekiah and Lydia, b. Dec. 6, 1748; she m. (pub.), 2d, June 7, 1792, John Chandler; d. Dec. 22, 1838. "Obadiah Foster married Hanna Ballard, of Hezekiah's family, and they added lands and lent money and baptized the children regularly at the South Church; and Obadiah generously lends right and left his ready cash, in times when good silver was the currency, and died suddenly in 1780, with the new order of things to bother his widow. She thought there was a wide margin, but when the neighbors came to her help and balanced the books, her dower and the home lot was all that could be saved, and Obadiah's fair estate was severed far and wide. Joshua Chandler was ready to give her his first wife's charge, and, with her daughter Dorcas, she went over to the old Capt. John Chandler farm, still in the hands of Dorcas Foster's descendants. Space will not allow of the honorable mention of the descendants of Obadiah, who from Hudson and New Salem went west and south to build new commonwealths."—Miss Abbott. Administration on his estate was granted his widow Hannah, who gave bonds, with Hezekiah Ballard and Gideon Foster, Oct. 2, 1780. His real estate was valued at £1,253 9s. 8d.; personal estate £2,748. 16s. 1d. Yeoman. Hannah (Ballard) (Foster) Chandler gives a cow in her will to Lucy Foster, the negro girl, and names Sally Duncklee as her dau. He d. July 25, 1780. Res. Andover, Mass.

787. i. JOHN, b. March 3, 1770; m. Mary Danforth, Lucy Hastings and Mrs. Sally Morse Couch.

788. ii. OBADIAH, b. Nov. 28, 1771; m Dec. 25, 1800, Phœbe Doty, in New Salem, N. H. He d. in N. S., July 25, 1819. Was a blacksmith.

789. iii. HANNAH, b. Sept. 15, 1773; m. June 16, 1818, Abijah Cross, who d. Feb. 21, 1848. She d. June 15, 1832.

790. iv. FREDERICK, b. July 20, 1775; m. Nancy Finch of Newbury Dist., S. C. He d. in Eutaw, Ala., Aug. 5, 1836.

791. v. DORCAS, b. June 9, 1777; m. Oct. 18, 1798, Joshua Chandler, Jr. – son of Dorcas' step-father. She d. Dec. 21, 1830.

792. vi. GIDEON, b. May 23, 1779; m. Tabitha Robbins, Pamelia Winn and Mrs. Ruth Rose.

385. SOLOMON FOSTER (John, William, William, Reginald). b. Andover, Mass., April 14, 1743; m. Rebecca Brown, of Lincoln, b. 1751; d. June 26, 1815. Solomon, of Lincoln, letter date September 16, 1790, ex. October 8, 1790, wife Rebecca.
[Middlesex Probate.] He d. June 8, 1790. Res., Littleton and Lincoln, Mass.

793. i. SOLOMON, b. Oct. 20, 1774; m. Hannah Hodgman.

794. ii. MARY, b.——

795. iii. NATHAN BROWN, b. ——; a grandson is Nathan Huston, of Belfast, Me.

387. DEA. ASA FOSTER (Asa, William, William, Reginald), b. Sept. 11, 1733, Andover, Mass.; m. Boxford, Nov. 18, 1762, Hannah Symons, of Boxford, b. Nov. 5,

1733; she d. June 28, 1775; m., 2d., in 1776, Hannah Peters; d. Jan 11, 1815. He moved to Canterbury, N. H., from Andover. Was one of five brothers and two sisters who went to Canterbury, N. H., probably before 1772, as his father, Asa Foster, Gent., deeded to Asa Foster, Jr., of Canterbury, N. H., 240 acres of land in Canterbury that year. He was appointed deacon in 1773, and honorably sustained that office for more than forty years, until his death, Sept. 30, 1814. He was appointed civil magistrate May 16, 1791. He married, 1st, Hannah Symons, daughter of Joseph Symonds and Mary Peabody, and granddaughter of Wm. Peabody and Hannah Hale, and great-granddaughter of Mary (Reginald) Foster and Lieut. Francis Peabody. He d. Sept. 30, 1814. Res., Canterbury, N. H.

796. i. ASA, b. June 3, 1765; m. Sarah Morrill.

797. ii. MEHITABEL, b. Nov. 19, 1771; m. March 14, 1798, Benjamin Kimball, of Concord, N. H. He was born in Concord June 4, 1771, (John, Benjamin, Richard, Benjamin, Richard), d. Dec. 4. 1818. She d. Sept. 23, 1803, and he m., 2d, May 10, 1804, Rhoda Beaman. He had 3 ch. by each wife. By Mehitabel he had 1. Harriet, b. March 16, 1799; d. Oct. 21, 1881; m. William Green, March 19, 1828. She d. Dec. 21, 1881. He was b. Dec. 19, 1788, and d. Aug. 8, 1869. Their ch.: i. Harriet E. Green, b. Aug. 28, 1830, at Bristol, N. H. ii. Benjamin Kimball Green, b. Aug. 14, 1832; d. June 16, 1835. iii. Clarissa Harris Green, b. July 21, 1834; d. June 19, 1835. iv. Mary Green, b. May 3, 1836; m. Hon. J. C. A. Wingate, Oct. 19, 1860. She d. Nov. 3, 1876. v. Martha Green, b. June 7, 1838. vi. Annie Douglass Green, b. Jan. 12, 1842; m. Frank W. Robinson April 11, 1877. (She has written several books of poetry, Bristol, N. H.). vii. Clarissa Harris Green, b. Feb. 21, 1845; d. May 16, 1846. 2. Asa Foster, b. July 1, 1801; drowned Nov. 27, 1820. 3. Frederick P., b. Oct. 25, 1802; d. Sept. 28, 1803. A gr.-dau. is Harriet Green, residing in Bristol, N. H.

798. iii. SUSANNAH, b. Feb. 7, 1775; m. Nov. 24, 1793, Rev. Frederick Parker, b. in Shrewsbury, Mass., May 4, 1762; d. Apr. 20, 1802. Gr. Harvard in 1784; ordained in Canterbury in 1791. Res. Canterbury, N. H. Ch.: 1. Harriet, b. Aug. 21, 1794; d. Lowell, Mass., March, 1842. 2. Hollis, b. Aug. 15, 1796; d. Jan. 2, 1827. 3. Susanna, b. Jan. 23, 1799; d. Dec. 6, 1799. 4. Cyrus, b. Dec. 4, 1800; gr. Dartmouth, 1824; d. Edenton, Ga., Sept. 11, 1825. She d. Feb. 24, 1848, and left no descendants. Mrs. Parker survived her husband and children several years, and, becoming blind, spent her last days with her brother Asa at Canterbury, where she was tenderly cared for. (She was one of the sweetest, dearest women I ever knew.)

388. HON. ABIEL FOSTER (Asa, William, William, Reginald), b. Andover, Mass., Aug. 8, 1735; m. May 15, 1761, Hannah Badger, dau. of Gen. Joseph Badger, of Gilmanton, N. H. She d. Jan. 10, 1768, aet. 26; m, 2d, Oct. 11, 1769, Mary Rogers, b. Nov. 1, 1745. She d. in C. March 12, 1813. She was a daughter of Dr. Samuel and Hannah Wise Rogers, of Ipswich, Mass. Her father was a descendant of John Rogers, of Dedham, England, and Rev. Nathaniel, Rev. John and Rev. John, of Ipswich, Mass. Her mother was a daughter of Major Ammie Ruhamah Wise, who was a son of Rev. John Wise, of Ipswich, who was a son of Rev. Joseph Wise, of Roxbury, Mass. She died March 12, 1813. Among the household effects she brought to her new home was a fine Venetian mirror, which a great-great-grandfather, Rev. Nathaniel Rogers, brought with him to Ipswich, Mass., in 1636. This mirror is now in the possession of Mrs. Edward K. Warren, of Three Oaks, Mich., a daughter of Hon. Henry Chamberlain. He was born in Massachusetts, fitted for college and graduated at Harvard in 1756. Was ordained minister at Canterbury, N. H. He studied law, was admitted to the bar, after his removal to New Hampshire, where in 1784, he was one of the judges (chief justice) of the Court of Common Pleas for Rockingham county. Was representative in Congress from 1789 to 1791 and from 1795 to 1803. He was much employed in public business. Was one time president of the New Hampshire State Senate. His integrity, virtue and usefulness secured the esteem, confidence and favor of the people of New Hampshire and the respect of numerous friends. He was an intimate friend of Gen. Washington, whose miniature likeness on ivory, a gift from him, is in possession of one of Mr. Foster's descendants. A fair estimate of Mr. Foster's character and an interesting incident con-

HON. ABIEL FOSTER, M. C.

:d from a portion of the painting by Trumbull in the rotunda at Washington, of Gen. Washi
resigning his commission as Commander-in-Chief of the Army to Congress.

nected with some of his neighbors and constituency may be found in a letter written to a friend in New York in 1846 by Hon. Daniel Webster. "On a hot day (says Mr. Webster)—it must have been in one of the last years of Washington's administration—I was making hay with my father, just where I now see a remaining elm tree, about the middle of the afternoon. The Hon. Abiel Foster, M. C., who lived in Canterbury, six miles off, called at the house and came into the field to see my father. He was a worthy man, college learned, and had been a minister, but did not have any considerable natural powers. My father was his friend and supporter. He talked awhile in the field and went on his way. When he was gone, my father called to me, and we sat down beneath an elm on a haycock. He said, 'My son, that is a worthy man; he is a member of Congress; he goes to Philadelphia and gets six dollars a day, while I toil here. It is because he had an education, which I never had. If I had had an early education I should have been in Philadelphia in his place. I came near it as it was, but I missed it, and now I must work here.' 'My dear father,' said I, 'you shall not work; brother and I will work for you and wear our hands out and you shall rest.' And I remember to have cried, and I cry now at the recollection. 'My child,' said he. 'It is of no importance to me; I now live but for my children. I could not give your older brother the advantages of knowledge, but can do something for you. Exert youself; improve your opportunities. Learn—learn, and when I am gone, you will not need to go through the hardships which I have undergone, and which have made me an old man before my time.' The next May he took me to Exeter to the Phillips Academy, and placed me under the tuition of its excellent preceptor, Dr. Benjamin Abbott." Foster was present as a member of Congress in 1783, when General Washington resigned his commission as commander-in chief. The painting of this scene by Trumbull hangs in the rotunda of the Capitol at Washington. He sits in the foreground on the left of the picture as you look at it. General Washington presented him with his portrait in enamel. It is now in the possession of his great-grandson, Alfred Foster of Unionville Courthouse, South Carolina.. He d. Feb. 6, 1806. Res., Canterbury, N. H.

799. i. HANNAH, b. April 25, 1762; m. Jan. 13, 1781, —— Cogswell; m. June 14, 1785, Zebodah Sargent.

800. ii. WILLIAM, b. Dec. 24, 1763; m. Betsey Morrill.

801. iii. JAMES, b. Dec. 28, 1765; m. Mrs. Betsey Sanborn.

802. iv. SARAH, b. Dec. 30, 1767; m. —— Tilton.

803. v. MARTHA, b. Aug. 19, 1770; m. March 25, 1792, Col. Jeremiah Clough, Jr. Col. Jeremiah Clough, of Canterbury, N. H., was born Aug. 21, 1768. His father was Capt. Jeremiah Clough, of the Revolutionary army. Jeremiah Jr. was a soldier in the War of 1812, and died at Sackett's Harbor in 1814. Their children were: 1. Jeremiah Foster, b. Nov. 27, 1774, who m. Elenor Ham. Their children were (a) Mary, not m.; teacher in Mass. (b) Martha who m. Frederick Gerrey, of Sudbury, Mass., where he now lives—Noel C., Fred., Charles and Elenor. 2. Apphia, b. March 3, 1793, who m. Daniel Sawyer, of Canterbury, N. H. He died from an accident in 1826. She died at Lowell, Mass, 1836. Their children were (a) Mary, who m. Joseph W. Gale, of Pembroke, N. H. N. C. He died. She lives at 1014 Spring st., New Albany, Ind. (b). Sarah, who m. Hascall Combs, of Lowell, Mass. Had ch. He died. She lives with her sister, Mrs. Gale as above. (c) Nancy, m. Jonathan Kimball; 1 ch. She lives at 77 Tudor st., Chelsea, Mass. (d) Hannah, m. George Fox; 1 son, George, in the navy; 2 daughters; one m. Dr. C. S. Hazeltine of 3 John's Place, Grand Rapids, Mich; have ch. Dr. H. held a diplomatic station under President Cleveland. Caroline m. J. J. Brown, banker, etc., New Albany, Ind., where they now live; have ch. Henry Sawyer m. Mary Soule. Ch.: (1.) Arthur, Chicago, Ill. (2.) Helen M. Lombard, Boston, Mass.; has ch: (3.) Henry Sawyer, inventor of Sawyer's Bluing, lives at Chelsea, Mass. 3. Hannah, b. Aug. 11, 1796; m. Benjamin Sanborn, of Canterbury, N. H. Had ch: a Phebe, m. Frank Brown who lives at Concord, N. H. 4. Mary Rogers, b. June 16, 1798; d. Sept. 1, 1856; m., at Canterbury, N. H., Capt. John A. Chamberlain; b. 1794; d. 1853. Their ch. were: a. Martha Clough, who m. Thomas C. Bradley; he d. She now resides at Three Oaks, Mich. b. John, who m. ——; d. His son Judson now lives at Northfield, N. H.; c.

Mary, d.; d. Rebeca, d.; e. Elizabeth, who m. Cyrus C. Ryther and now lives at Dowagiac, Mich.; has ch. f. Jeremiah C. Chamberlain, who m. Grace Busby, has ch. and now lives at Chelsea, Mass. g. Caroline, who m. Hon. Wm. Chamberlain, now of Jackson, Mich. 5. Joseph, b. Sept 20, 1800; d. Sept. 25, 1825.

804. vi. ABIEL, b. Feb. 19, 1773; m. Susannah Moore.
805. vii. MARY, b. Oct. 1, 1774; m. June 7, 1795, Henry Gerrish, Jr., of Boscowen, N. H.
806. viii. ELIZABETH, b. March 9, 1777; m. March 25, 1800, Enoch Gerrish, of Boscowen, N. H.
807. ix. NANCY, b. May 25, 1782; m. Sept. 30, 1803, John Greenough. Res. C. Ch. Mary, b. July 1, 1804. 2. Frederic, b. April 1, 1806.

389. DANIEL FOSTER (Asa, William, William, Reginald), b. Andover, Mass., Sept 25, 1737; m. there Dec. 16, 1760, Hannah Kittredge. He d. Jan. 25, 1833. Res. Andover, Mass., and Canterbury, N. H.

808. i. DANIEL, b. at Andover, June 29, 1761.
809. ii. HANNAH, b. at Andover, Feb. 3, 1763.
810. iii. SIMEON, b. Jan. 22, 1765; m. Susanna Worthen.
811. iv. BETSEY, b. April 9, 1767.
812. v. JONATHAN, b. Aug. 15, 1769; d. Sept. 12, 1775.
813. vi. DORCAS, b. Nov. 24, 1770.
814. vii. ABIAH, b. Jan. 15, 1772; m. March 21, 1795, Elijah Sargent.
815. viii. ABIGAIL, b. April 3, 1776.
816. ix. RUTH, b. Sept. 14, 1779.
817. x. JEREMIAH C., b. April 6, 1784; m. Susanna Bradley.

391. DAVID FOSTER (Asa, William, William, Reginald), b. Dec. 24, 1741, Andover, Mass.; m., Nov. 24, 1768, Sarah Foster, b. 1750; d. abt. 1830. He d. abt. 1821. Res., Canterbury, N. H.

818. i. NATHANIEL, b. Nov. 19, 1769; d. April 11, 1773.
819. ii. SARAH, b. Aug. 21, 1771; m. S. Hall.
820. iii. NATHANIEL, b. Sept. 4, 1773.
821. iv. DAVID, b. April 1, 1776; m. Sarah Dearborn.
822. v. JOSEPH, b. Sept. 22, 1779.
823. vi. TIMOTHY, b. Aug. 21, 1782; m. Hannah Carter.
824. vii. ASA, b. Aug. 6, 1784; d. Jan. 10, 1785.

393. CAPT. JONATHAN FOSTER (Asa, William, William, Reginald), b. Andover, Mass., July 25, 1747; m. Ipswich, Nov , 1770, Lucy Rogers, dau. of Hon. Samuel, M. D., who was son of Rev. John, of Ipswich, and gr.-son of Rev. John, president of Harvard College. She was b. Oct. 19, 1748; d. abt. 1830. He d. 1815. Res. Canterbury, N. H.

825. i. SAMUEL H., b. Nov. 6, 1771; m. Elizabeth Symonds and Mercy Porter.
826. ii. JOHN, b. July 22, 1773; m. Sarah Kimball.
827. iii. LUCY, b. Sept. 1, 1777; m. Dec. 25, 1804., Thomas Ames. She d. in Canterbury, N. H., July 22, 1843. He d. there Nov. 19, 1840. They lived on the farm at the top of the hill west of the Free-will Baptist church. Was b. there Oct. 6, 1777. Ch.: 1. Maria, b. Sept. 25, 1805; m. Sept. 25, 1824, Jacob Gerrish, son of Henry, of Boscowen; moved to New Buffalo, Mich., in 1835. He d. Oct. 28, 1858; she m. 2d, April 16, 1864, Charles Moody, of Concord, N. H. He d. there April 6, 1869; she d. in Manchester, N. H., Oct. 1, 1879, s. p. 2. Frances Winkley, b. April 3, 1807; m. May 8, 1835, Rebecca Pearson Gerrish, dau. of Enoch, of Boscowen. Frances d. in New Buffalo, Mich., Aug. 30, 1838. Rebecca d. in Chester, N. H., 29, June, 1845, s. p. 3. Joseph Gerrish, b. April 30, 1808; m. Sept. 4, 1839, Elizabeth Gerrish, dau. of Henry; m. 2d, April, 18, 1844, Rebecca Van Dervanter. Joseph died in Three Oaks, Mich, Aug. 12, 1855. Elizabeth d. in Bertrand, Mich., Nov. 7, 1842. Rebecca m. 2d, Hon. Henry Chamberlain (see). He was supervisor of Wesaw and Bertrand townships, county commissioner in 1838, and represented Berrien county in the legislature in 1844. The ch. of Joseph G. and Rebecca Ames

were: 1. Elizabeth, b. Aug. 21, 1845; d. July 29, 1849. 2. Isaac, b. Feb. 11, 1847; d. Aug. 15, 1849. 3. Alice, June 8, 1850; d. Sept. 23, 1852. 4. Joseph Henry, b. July 18, 1853; m. Sept. 26, 1877, Mary M. Markham. He graduated at the school of Pharmacy in the University of Michigan, 1876. Was for some years a druggist at Niles, Mich., and afterwards was secretary of the Warren Featherbone Co., of Three Oaks, now in manufacturing business in Detroit, Mich. (Residence, 543 Lincoln Ave., Detroit, Mich.) The children of Joseph Henry and Mary M. (Markham) Ames are: Alice, b. Sept. 21, 1879; Laurence Joseph, July 7, 1881; Robert Herman; b. June 18, 1883; Warren Cheever, b. Jan. 3, 1886; Margery, b. ——4. Samuel Albert, b. June 1, 1810; m. Dec. 26, 1836, Maria Batchelder, of Canterbury, dau. of Eben. He d. Aug. 28, 1852; Maria d. in Omaha, Neb., Sept. 30, 1873. Ch.: i. Thos. P., b. April 26, 1838. ii. Francis W., b. April 22, 1842. iii. John A., b. March 25, 1845. They lived on the homestead of her father until 1848, when they moved to what is now the village of Penacook and afterwards to Concord. He was killed by being thrown from a carriage in Canterbury. 5. Phebe, b. Dec. 11, 1812; m. Nov. 10, 1836, Hon. Matthew Rowen, of White Pigeon, Mich. She d. there June 13, 1840. Ch.: i. Francis F., b. Feb. 24, 1838; m. Delia A. Byran. of Janesville, Iowa, 2 ch. She res. 228 W. 138th St., New York City. 6. Fisher, b. Oct. 18, 1814; m. Mary Plummer, dau. of Nathan., Feb. 15, 1844; d. Aug. 14, 1893. Mary d. 1895. He succeeded to the homestead of his father in Canterbury, and afterwards moved to Boscowen and later to Concord. Their ch. were: i. Sarah Plummer, b. in Boscowen, N. H., Jan. 10, 1845. ii. Henry Gerrish, b. in Boscowen, Sept. 16, 1848; m. Emily Robie, July 3, 1873. They reside in Penacook, N. H. Their child was Gracie Berson, b. Dec. 9, 1875; d. July 27, 1876. 7. Lucy Jane, b. Aug. 28, 1816; m. Hon. Matthew Rowen, of White Pigeon, Mich., Sept. 14, 1842, where six of their children were born; moved to Janesville, Iowa, where Matthew d. May 5, 1881. She now lives at Cedar Falls, Iowa. Ch.: i. Charles Augustus, b. June 19, 1843; d. Oct. 10, 1847. ii. Lucien G., b. Dec. 9, 1844; m. Mary A. Luke. iii. Florence M., b. Aug. 11, 1846. iv. Wm. Fremont, b. Dec 19, 1848; m. Harriet W. Triplet. v. Margaretta, b. Sept. 23, 1850. vi. Matthew A., b. Dec. 31, 1852; m. Mary J. Mahan. vii. Albert Ames, b. Nov. 19, 1856; m. Mary Elizabeth Coddington, of Janesville, Iowa, Sept. 14, 1880. Ch.: Howard Coddington, b. at Boulder City, Col., June 14, 1881. 8. Lucy Jane, b. June 22, 1860. 8. Caroline, b. Sept. 10, 1820; m. Abiel Moore Caverly, of London, March 25, 1845. Abiel, b. Nov. 28, 1817; d. in Pittsford, Vt., July 11, 1879. Caroline d. in Manchester, N. H., Feb. 2, 1851. 9 Martha Wheeler, b. Dec. 24, 1823; m. William Whittier Brown, M. D., of Manchester, May 12, 1846. William d. in Manchester, Jan. 6, 1874. She d. in Manchester, N. H., Nov. 27, 1895. Their ch. were: i. George Ames, b. in Manchester, April 29, 1848; d. April 13, 1849. ii. Frederick Whittier, b. in Boscowen, April 29, 1853; d. Feb. 20, 1855. iii. Grace Foster, b. in Manchester, Aug. 7, 1857; d. Oct. 15, 1862.

828. iv. HANNAH, b. April 26, 1784; m. Nov. 22, 1815, Joseph Moody. He was b. May 20, 1788; d. Penacook, N. H., March 2, 1879. Was a farmer. She d. Dec. 3, 1873. Ch.: i. Mary Jane, b. in Canterbury, Jan. 21, 1817; m. Capt. Nath'l Rolfe, of (Concord) Penacook, N. H., Jan. 1, 1839; d. there Aug. 8, 1876. They had six children. A son is Mr. Arthur Foster Rolfe, Penacook, N. H. ii. Nathaniel, b. in Canterbury, Jan. 25, 1818; m. Jane Lint, April 17, 1842. He d. at North Concord, Feb. 15, 1855. They had four children; one is Mrs. Enoch Jackman, Concord, N. H. iii. Lucy Ann, b. Oct. 19, 1823; m. Concord, N. H., May 11, 1850, Samuel Thomas Lancaster, b. July 12, 1825; d. Dec. 2, 1890. She res. 368 E. Merrimack St., Lowell, Mass. Ch.: a. Walter Moody (Lancaster), b. in Lowell, Mass., Nov. 6, 1857; m. Sarah Jenkins, dau. of J. Henry Hill Esq., of

Worcester, Mass., June 4, 1892. They reside in Worcester. Their children were (born in Worcester): 1. Southworth, b. Aug. 8, 1893. 2. Bruce, b. Aug. 22, 1896. iii. Mary Maude (Lancaster), b. Nov. 26, 1861, in Lowell. Addresses: Walter M. Lancaster, "Spy" office, Worcester, Mass. Miss M. Maude Lancaster, 368 East Merrimack St., Lowell, Mass.

829. v. ELIZABETH, b. May 15, 1775; m. —— Pickard.

409. DAVID FOSTER (David, Timothy, William, Reginald), b. Keene, N. H., May 9, 1755; m. 1786, Mary Dassance, dau. of Martin, a French refugee. In Revolutionary War. He. d. 1798. Res., Keene, N. H.

830. i. DAVID, b. Feb. 21, 1786; m. Mary Field.
831. ii. SAMUEL, b. Nov. 8, 1781; d. unm. Dec. 3, 1848.
832. iii. BETSEY, b. Oct. 28. 1783; d. unm. Nov. 7, 1810.
833. iv. POLLY, b. March 16, 1791; d. unm. April 26, 1848.
834. v. NANCY, b. Jan. 30, 1794; d. unm. Nov. 11, 1824.
835. vi. SALLY, b. 1796; d. 1798.

426. ISAAC FOSTER (Benjamin, Jacob, Isaac, Reginald). b. Ipswich, Mass., Feb. 18, 1728; m. Hampstead, N. H., Oct. 31, 1754, Mehitabel Worthing (or Worthen), dau. of Samuel, b. 1733; d. 1826. They were married by Rev. Henry True in Hampstead, N. H., and moved to Granville, N. S., in 1760, and resided there for nearly sixty years. His widow was unusually active for a woman of her years, and, to demonstrate to relatives and friends that this was so, participated in a dance when 92 years of age. Samuel Worthing's wife was Mehitabel Heath resided in 1732 in Timberlane; organized into a town in 1749, as Hampstead, N. H.. He d. Jan. 29, 1819. Res., Granville, N. S.

836. i. BENJAMIN, b. May 24, 1755 m. Elizabeth Richardson and Mary Robinson.
837. ii. JACOB, b. 1757; d. 1759.
838. iii. SARAH, b. Oct. 15, 1760; m. 1779, John Adams; had a son James, b. Aug. 4, 1780; m. Eleanor Chute, dau. of John, Jr.
839. iv. ISAAC, b. Aug. 4, 1763; m. Betsey Gilliott.
840. v. MEHITABEL, b. March 23, 1766; m. Thomas Phinney, son of Isaac and Anna (Thomas); res., Granville, N. S. He was b. 1765; d. Dec. 16, 1845. She d. April 1, 1858. Phinney had nine children: Isaac, b. 1787; m. Sarah Borden, 1819, and had seven children. She d. March 5, 1847, æt. 57. He d. April 14, 1867. 2. William, b. 1789; m. Rebecca (Goucher) Starratt. 3. Ann, b. 1791; d. 1794. 4. Cynthia, b. 1793; m. Thomas Horsefield, 1825; had three children; d. June 12, 1863. He (Horsefield) d. March 9, 1836. 5. Betsey, b. 1795; d. 1796. 6. Ann, b. 1797; m. William, son of Andrew Walker, 1816; had six children; d. Dec. 17, 1878. 7. Walter W., b. 1799; d. 1826. 8. Caroline, b. 1801; m. David Dill, and d. Dec. 13, 1863. He (Dill) d. 1849, æt. 59. 9. Elizabeth, b. 1803; m. David Felch Jr., March 12, 1833; had 6 children. He (Felch) d. 1868, æt. 67. 10. Phineas, b. 1805; m. Jerusha Foster (Isaac Jr.); had four children; d. July 14, 1873.
841. vi. ELIZABETH, b. Dec. 17, 1768; m. Dec. 24, 1789, Jordan Ricketson, son of Abednego Ricketson. They res. in Granville, N. S. She d. July 31, 1795; he then m. 2d, 1796, Hannah Parker. He was b. 1765; d. in 1832. Elizabeth had three or more ch.: 1. Henry, b. 1790; m. 1814, Charlotte Thomas. 2. Phebe, b. 1792; m. Theodore Hill. 3. Sarah, b. 1794; d. young.
842. vii. SAMUEL, b. Oct. 1, 1770; m. Betsey Wilson
843. viii. OLIVER, b. May 1, 1773; m. Cynthia Fellows and Betsey Saunders.
844. ix. ASA, b. Nov. 24, 1776; m. Roby Hicks.
845. x. JAMES, b. Jan. 24, 1780; m. Mrs. ——, in Mass.

427. EZEKIEL FOSTER (Benjamin, Jacob, Isaac, Reginald), b. ——, Mass., ——, 1730; m. at Hampstead, N. H., July 17, 1755, Mary Roberts, dau. of Daniel, b. ——, 1736; d. July 31, 1765; m. 2d, Sept. 30, 1770, Ruth Farnsworth, b. July 24, 1748. He was married by David Little, Esq., July 17, 1755, to Mary Roberts, at Hampstead, N. H.; went to Granville, N. S., with parents, his brother Isaac and three sisters in 1760. He d. ——. Res., Granville, N. S.

846. i. SARAH, b. ——, 1756; d. ——, 1760, in Hampstead, N. H.
847. ii. MARTHA, b. Aug. 13, 1757; m. 1777, Benjamin Chute, b. Sept. 27, 1754; d. Oct. 27, 1831. She d. Feb. 11, 1816. Res., Granville. Ch.: 1. James, b. April 29, 1778; m. Phebe Chute; res., Granville. 2. Mary, b. May 21, 1780; m. Aquilla Langley. 3. Seth, b. Sept. 15, 1782; m. Ann Fowler; res., Hampton, N. S. 4. Hannah, b. Dec. 19, 1784; m. Hanly Chute. 5. Benjamin, b. April 14, 1787; m. Hepzibah Fellows and Elizabeth Randall; res., Clarence, N. S. 6. Ezekiel, b. Jan. 6, 1790; m. Lydia A. Morse; res., Bridgetown, N. S. 7. Joseph, b. Dec. 9, 1792; m. Theresa Randall, and she m. 2d, Paoli Randall. 8. Eaton, b. Aug. 25, 1795; d. Sept. 22, 1796. 9. Martha, b. Aug. 17, 1799; m. Isaac Woodbury.
848. iii. JOHN, b. March 29, 1760; m. Elizabeth Ricketson.
849. iv. EZEKIEL, b. March 30, 1763; m. Elizabeth Dring.
850. v. JOSEPH, b. Oct. 18, 1771; m. Jane Ray.
851. vi. EZRA, F., b. Aug. 1, 1773; m. Luranna Troop.

430. JEREMIAH FOSTER (Benjamin, Jacob, Isaac, Reginald), b. ——, Mass., 1740; m. Jan. 5, 1768, Jemima Kent. He went to Nova Scotia about the time of the Revolution, but remained only a short time, and returned soon after, settling in Maine. Res., Nova Scotia and Maine.
852. i. JEREMIAH, b. Feb. 7, 1773; m. Sally Killam.
853. ii. [There were four sisters, one has descendants residing in Mass., another m. a Blaisdell, and resided in Chicago.]

431. ISAAC FOSTER (John, Jacob, Isaac, Reginald), b. Lebanon, Conn., in 1725; m. Deerfield, Mass., July 11, 1754, Irena Allen, b. ——, 1735; d. Dec. 13, 1762; m. 2d, ——, 1794, Edatha Miller; d. after 1796. Removed with father to Deerfield about 1741. Served in Old French and Indian War of 1746, also French War 1757, and in the Revolutionary War 1776 and 1777 at Ticonderoga and Bennington. Leading citizen of the town of Greenfield; member of the Committee of Safety; was selectman, assessor, sealer of leather, etc., for many years; married Irena, dau. of Edward and Mercy (Childs) Allen, of Deerfield. She died, and he married, 2d, Edatha Miller. He was a man much respected in Greenfield, and a man of considerable property; owned considerable land; had a large mansion house, which overlooked the whole town of Greenfield. From his porch he could see the smoke from every chimney in the town. He held the office of sealer of leather for forty consecutive years, and it is supposed he was a tanner by trade, on this account. As stated above, he was in the Revolutionary War, was a private in Capt. John Wells' Company, in Col. Timothy Robison's regiment of Hampshire County men. Saw service at Ticonderoga in 1777; also was in Capt. Timothy Childs' Company, Col. David Field's regiment; had active service at Bennington. He was buried in Greenfield. He d. March 19, 1796. Res., Deerfield and Greenfield, Mass. Children born at Greenfield:
854. i. DOROTHY, b. June 23, 1755; d. Sept. 8, 1768.
855. ii. WARHAM, b. May 12, 1757; d. Sept. 30, 1758.
856. iii. WARHAM, b. May 18, 1759; d. Sept. 18, 1777.
857. iv. ISAAC, b. April 3, 1761; m. Rebecca Hunt.

432. LIEUT. EZEKIEL FOSTER (John, Jacob, Isaac, Reginald), b. Lebanon, Conn., ——, 1727; m. May 23, 1751, Margaret Henry. Removed with his father to Deerfield 1741. Served in French and Indian Wars, 1747-48, under Lieut. Child; also as a lieutenant in Capt. Agrippa Wells' Company, Hampshire County troops in the Revolutionary War, 1775-77. Lieut. Ezekiel Foster m. 1751, Margaret Henry, at which date he was a resident of Deerfield. Served in Revolution, going out May 1, 1775, as second lieutenant in Capt. Agrippa Wells' Company, Col. Asa Whitcomb's Regiment. Travelled 112 miles; out 3 mos., 8 days; dis. Sept. 23, 1775; and in the discharge papers is spoken of as ensign. A Dr. Ezekiel Foster is given as being resident in District No. 4. Bernardston, in 1760. The date of his death coincides with that of Lieut. Ezekiel Foster, April 17, 1805, and I presume them to have been identical. An Ezekiel Foster was out on the western frontier for 20 days in 1756; had the title of corporal. He was in Capt. Israel Williams' Company, stationed at Colerain, Oct. 19, 1756, to Jan. 23, 1757, for which service he received 4 pounds, 12s. 5d.

"A legal meeting, held in 1773, of the Freeholders and other Inhabitants of Bernardston, held at the House of Elijah Sheldon in said town." when it was "voted that Messrs. Hezekiah Newcomb, Caleb Champion, Elijah Kingsley, Daniel Slate and Ezekiel Foster be a committee to plan ye pews in ye Meeting house according to Greenfield Meeting house; also to seet said house & order where people may erect pews, and the people that build pews shall hold them one year next ensuing, and no longer, unless the Town see cause, and the Committee are directed to observe this rule in seeting ye house, viz.: Age, Estate and Qualification." He d.——. Res., Bernardston, Mass.

858. i. EPHRAIM, b.——.
859. ii. EZEKIEL, JR., b. in 1752; m. Chloe Burnham.
859¼. iii. RUFUS, b. in 1761. At age of 19 was out in the Fourth and Fifth Cos., Fifth Regt., Hampshire Co., under Lieut.-Col. David Wells; mustered July 24, 1780. He m. and settled in Mich.
859½. iv. LURANY, m. —— Babcock; resided Caledonia, N. Y.
859¾. v. CHLOE, m. —— Gately; res., N. Y. State.

433. ENSIGN JOHN FOSTER (John, Jacob, Isaac, Reginald), b. Deerfield, Mass., ——, 1744; m. Deerfield, April 24, 1779, Mindwell Atherton, b. Nov. 4, 1766; d. abt. 1790; m. 2d, Hancock, N. H., Aug. 6, 1794, Lydia Foster, of Temple, N. H., b. Dec. 30, 1761; d. July 19, 1842. She was dau. of Joshua and Lydia (Peabody) Foster. (See Andover branch.) He served in the French and Indian Wars, from Greenfield, Mass., or Deerfield, and was also in the Revolutionary War. Was a farmer; moved to Bernardston, and in 1779 moved to Hancock, N. H. His first wife, Mindwell Atherton, was dau. of Oliver (5) and Mary (Severence, and gr.-dau. of Adonijah (4) and Anna (Barnard), who was son of Joseph (3) and Mary (Taylor), dau. of Capt. John Taylor, and gr.-son of Hope (2), who was son of Captain Humphrey, of Dorchester.

Sergt. John Foster's name appears on Maj. John Burke's enlistment roll, ending Nov. 30, 1758. Same name appears on another roll, enlisted as private. He was in Capt. Israel Williams' Company, stationed in Colerain, Oct. 19, 1756, to Jan. 23, 1757. In 1760 he is known to have resided on the Kingsley place, east of Bernardston village. Among town offices which he held were those of hog-reave, 1762-4-9; fence viewer, 1763-4; sealer of the market, 1764; surveyor of highways, 1764-66; tithing-man, 1765-68; sealer of leather, 1773-77-78-79-80. John Foster was of Deerfield, 1741; m. April 24, 1779-81, Mindwell Atherton, of Greenfield. He was a soldier in French and Indian Wars, 1746-57. Removed to Bernardston (Sheldon's Deerfield Hist.). In the Marriage-Intention Record at Bernardston he is given as John, Jr. (He may be the one whose death occurred at Burke Fort.) John Jr.'s name appears on Burke's roll, ending Nov. 30, 1758, beside that of John Foster. He d. July 10, 1810. Res., Hancock, N. H.

860. i. JOHN, b. Jan. 29, 1780; m. ——, ——.
861. ii. SARAH, b. ——; d. June 8, 1781.
862. iii. MERCY, b. March 30, 1786.
863. iv. ISAIAH, b. ——; m. Patty Hartwell.
864. v. JOSHUA, b. Feb. 12, 1796; m. Sally Hopkins, Mary Ann Fletcher and Mrs. Dorothy Little.
865. vi. REBECCA, b. Jan. 3, 1800.
866. vii. SILAS, b. ——; m. —— ——. A son is Marcus A., of Colorado Springs, Col.
867. viii. BETSEY, b. ——; d. Aug. 30, 1800.

435. CAPT. ELIJAH FOSTER (David, Jacob, Isaac, Reginald), b. Lebanon, Conn., Feb. 26, 1734; m. Sharon, Conn., Oct. 9, 1757, Deborah Holley. Capt. Elijah was born in Lebanon, Conn.; moved to Sharon with his parents, and was a highly-respected citizen there. He resided where Dr. Sears resided in 1842, and was an early favorite of the town. He was for many years the constable. He entered the Continental army as lieutenant in 1776, and was active in it until its close. He commanded one of the Connecticut companies during the war, and died of small-pox soon after one of his terms of service. His body is buried in the old graveyard at Sharon, and this is the epitaph on the gravestone:

Here lies the body of Lt. Elijah Foster,
Who died of small-pox, June 14, 1777,
In the forty-second year of his age,
On his return from the army.

Inspired with freedom and her virtuous cause,
To save his country from a tyrant's laws;
Resolved an end to the continued strife,
And, in the glorious conflict, lost his life.

He d. June 14, 1777. Res., Sharon, Conn.
868. i. OLIVE, b. Jan. 11, 1769.
869. ii. JOEL, b. Feb. 23, 1759.

438. COL. BENJAMIN FOSTER, JR. (Benjamin, Benjamin, Isaac, Reginald), b. Massachusetts, 1726; m. Scarboro, Me., March 26, 1747, Abigail Milliken, b. May 29, 1731, dau. of Edward, Esq.; d. ——; m. 2d, in Greenland, N. H., in 1765, Elizabeth Scott. He was colonel of the Sixth Lincoln County Regiment of Machias in Revolutionary War. He was born in the year 1726, and, while yet a child, went with his father to Scarboro, in Maine. There, when but eleven years of age he was left alone by his father to take care of a large stock of cattle during the winter, till the arrival of his father with the remainder of the family in the spring. He afterward joined the Provincial army, in the first French and Indian War, with Gen. Abercrombie, in his unsuccessful attack upon Fort Ticonderoga, the failure of which expedition he always attributed to lack of bravery and address in the English com-

MACHIAS, ME., HARBOR, HOLMES' BAY AND ROUND ISLAND.

mander. In such scenes as this of trial and danger he acquired a character for courage and fortitude well suited to the stern times in which he lived. No danger could daunt, no obstacles discouraged him, and, as he himself often said, "He never knew what fear was." He was one of the first settlers in East Machias, to which place he went in 1765, having then married his second wife, Elizabeth Scott, of a worthy family of two brothers and three sisters, who were also among the first settlers there. Being a man of the character above referred to and also of strict integrity and piety and deacon of the church, he was naturally a leading man, and was justly regarded as the father of the town. At the commencement of the Revolutionary War and after Boston had been taken by the British forces, the lumber trade, which was the only means of support of the little colony, was cut off, and the early settlers suffered for the necessities of life. Whole families subsisted for weeks on nothing but clams, and these most scantily dealt out. Day after day, for several weeks, Colonel Foster traveled a long distance to dig from the flats the only food which could be procured to save his large family from immediate starvation. Such was their suffering that assistance and provisions were at length sent to them from the Provincial government. It is related of the Colonel that, on the occasion of one of his visits to the clam flats, having filled his pockets with the savory bivalves, he became so exhausted that he sat down upon a rock and was making in his mind the choice of sitting there to be drowned by the flowing tide or taking up his bucket and trudging his weary way to his half-famished family, when he happened to raise his eyes, and discovered a long-expected vessel, laden with provisions for the starving pioneers. Immediately his feet and ankle-bones regained strength, and he hastened up to the town with the joyful news. In the year 1775, soon after the battle of Bunker Hill, Capt. Ichabod Jones, of Boston, a Tory in politics, obtained permission of the British admiral commanding at Boston to freight a small vessel with provisions to Machias, where some of his connections resided, on condition that he should bring back a cargo of wood and lumber for the use of the King's troops. In pursuance of this plan, a well-armed schooner, The Margaretta, Captain Moor, acted as convoy to Jones's vessel. The ships arrived at Machias, and the provisions were unloaded, and the loading of the vessel with lumber began. Foster, as well as a majority of the citizens, were zealously attached to the cause of liberty and looked with suspicion upon the arrival of the British vessel, and though as a matter of necessity they had consented to receive the provisions, yet they were highly exasperated at the idea of becoming agents to further the design of the enemy. On a pleasant Sunday morning the officer of the armed schooner went up to Machias to attend religious services; but the intrepid deacon and most of the leading men were not that day at their usual places for worship. At a spot in the woods, westerly from the village, and near a brook (see Foster's Rubicon), these daring heroes, isolated from all the rest of the world, were discussing the expediency of seizing and making prisoners of the British officers, and of taking the first naval prize ever taken from the mother country by her grown-up and restless daughter. To cut short the discussion and insure celerity of execution, Colonel Foster jumped across the brook and invited every man who was in favor of the plan to follow him. Every man soon followed him across the brook—the first instance, I presume, of ever "polling the house" in Machias parliamentary proceedings.

FOSTER'S RUBICON.

The British officers, for some cause, became suspicious, and, seeing the members of the council of war approaching, immediately took to their boats, and escaped just in time to prevent their seizure. Colonel Foster immediately consulted with Captain O'Brien, and it was speedily determined to give chase and capture the enemy. O'Brien took command of Jones's vessel, while Colonel Foster, with part of the company, took charge of another vessel, and with such weapons of defense and offense as they could hastily muster, these two vessels started in pursuit. I cannot learn that Foster's vessel had any part in the brave hand-to-hand contest which resulted in the capture of the "Margaretta," and the death of her brave commander, Captain Moor. The most reliable information which I can obtain is, that Foster's vessel accidentally got aground. The British vessel and Jones's vessel were afterward regularly adjudicated upon and condemned as lawful prizes, and the prize money distributed among the captors. About the same time an English tender arrived in the bay, and the captain came on shore to inquire for the "Margaretta." Capt. Stephen Smith, with a small party, near Buck's harbor, waylaid and took him prisoner, and O'Brien and Foster, with their two vessels, took both the tender and her crew. The crew were afterward sent as prisoners to Falmouth. The two brave commanders proceeded to the headquarters of the American army, then at Cambridge, to carry intelligence of the victory, and were there received with shouts of applause. Congress afterward voted them public thanks for their bravery and good conduct. In consideration of their gallant conduct, government proceeded to take some measures for the defence of this place, then so remote and exposed to the assaults of the enemy on account of their daring exploits. A fort was built at the Rim, near the "Avery House," and a garrison established under Colonel Allen.

EAST MACHIAS, ME.

In 1777, Sir George Collier, with a fleet of four vessels, arrived in the bay for the purpose of avenging upon the people of Machias the capture of the "Margaretta." Leaving the fleet below, he came up the river to reconnoitre or attack the town in boats. The inhabitants had prepared for defense. A breastwork had been thrown up at the Rim, just below the fort; an iron chain, suspended by a log boom, was stretched across the river and fastened to a rock on each side. Colonel Foster commanded at the breastwork on the Rim. After an engagement with the boats, with various accounts (some of them without doubt much exaggerated) of the loss of the British, but with none killed, and but one wounded of Colonel Foster's men, the boats retired. The next day the British advanced with an armed brig, and, under a heavy fire of cannon, landed a large body of men, who passed through the fort, broke the booms, and after burning and destroying two dwelling houses, and a building used as a guard-house, re-embarked on board, apparently satisfied with the glory of their exploit. An exaggerated account of this expedition was afterward published, stating that they had taken and destroyed two magazines full of leather, rice and other stores, which in fact was a shoemaker's shop, in which there might have been some hides. The brig sailed up the river under a continuous fire from each bank, Colonel Allen with the Indian allies on the right bank above Colonel Foster, and Captain Smith on the left bank. The crew of the brig were unable to land. Once they attempted it in a long boat, but Neptune, a noble Indian, under Colonel Allen, after having repeatedly requested the privilege of firing at the boat's crew, and being denied until they should come nearer, at last breaking over the authority of his commander, with a hasty expression of Indian eloquence, mingled with Yankee profanity, rushed into the river to his waist, and, raising his long gun with a deadly aim, fired; one officer fell in the boat. The boat returned to the brig and the brig returned down the river. The yells of the Indians and the shouts of the people nearly drowned the sound of the musketry, which followed their retreat with increased rapidity and effect.

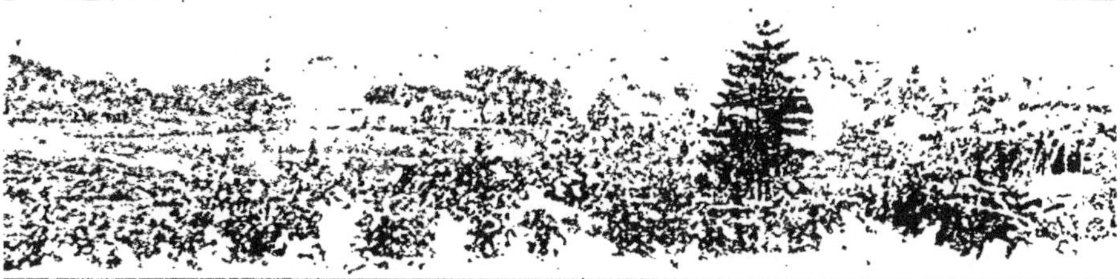

NEAR MACHIAS, ME.

On arriving near the fort the brig grounded on a point and swung off stern to the shore, when a deadly contest ensued, with considerable loss to the enemy. One incident connected with this engagement is worth relating. When the enemy surprised and took the fort and the inmates were hurrying out, Benjamin Gooch and Edgar Hathaway, two of the noted inhabitants of our town, stopped long enough to take up a plank in the floor, and drop through the swivel which they had to defend the fort; and they had just time to escape. When the brig was aground she was in fine position to be operated upon from Colonel Foster's entrenched position at the Rim. Gooch and Hathaway revealed the hiding place of the swivel; it was taken up and placed upon a rude stretcher, a blanket thrown over it, and, while those on board the brig were saying, "We have fixed one of them, they are bearing him off," the swivel was solemnly conveyed to the entrenched position, and there securely lashed to a pine stump, and its first discharge sent a messenger through a cabin window, which killed the steward and a dog on board the brig. The brig and the fleet afterwards retired, and the inhabitants were not again molested during the war. The loss on the part of the inhabitants was one killed and one wounded. Such was the issue of the Revolutionary battles fought in the town, and, while the spot where it happened is but a short distance from it, and the ruins of the fortifications may still be seen, yet few look upon them as the scene of as glorious a defence as the history of our country affords—and the man who conducted it is generally forgotten, and sleeps without any tombstone to mark the place of his last repose.

At the time of these stirring events, Colonel Foster was more than fifty years of age, and the father of a family of ten sons and two daughters. Most of them survived him and were respected and honored citizens of the town. Colonel Foster was a bold, energetic man, of strong feelings and generous impulses, of strict integrity and piety—a benefactor to the town, and one whose character has left its impress upon his succeeding generations, and whose virtues and suffering and noble deeds of daring should be kept in remembrance and fill a large space in the early history of that town. He d. July 4, 1818. Res., Scarboro and Machias, Me.

870. i. JACOB, b. ——; m. Anna Jones.
871. ii. DANIEL, b. ——; d. young.
872. iii. JOHN, b. ——; m. Phebe Burr.
873. iv. BENJAMIN, b. ——; m. Ruth Scott.
874. v. ABIJAH, b. ——; m. Apphia Talbott.
875. vi. ELIZABETH, b. ——; d. young.
876. vii. LEVI, b. ——; m. Sally Beal.
877. viii. BETSY, b. ——; m. Joshua Burr; removed to Trenton.
878. ix. ASA, b. ——.
879. x. SAMUEL, b. ——; m. Comfort Scott.
880. xi. DANIEL, b. ——, 1761; m. Hannah Gardner.
881. xii. GEORGE, b. ——; m. Cynthia Chase.

440. ISAIAH FOSTER (Benjamin, Benjamin, Isaac, Reginald), b. in New Hampshire, ——; m. ——, Lydia Fogg. In 1761 and 1762 western Maine was suffering from drought and forest fires. Isaiah Foster, of Scarboro, took a few companions and set out in a whale-boat eastward in search of marsh hay. Arrived at Machias, Foster was cheered with the sight of unscathed acres of grass, and also with what his trained eye saw was even more valuable—forests upon forests of timber close to an extraordinary water-power standing at the head of tide navigation. His report to stricken Scarboro led, in May, 1763, to the first permanent settlement at Machias. How Isaiah Foster stayed behind in Scarboro with his aged father, but let his younger brothers go to the new land, and how, at the elder Foster's death, so complete was this migration that there was no man left to help Isaiah in digging his father's grave, and how the former twice visited this colony of his planting, and the last time died on his way back at Cherryfield, are town traditions.

The severe drought had left the people there with not provisions enough for three weeks more. The little town consisted at this time of eighty families and a hundred single men. They kept only a few cows and some oxen for the log-hauling. Potatoes were almost the only vegetable, and of these there were not enough for their own consumption. Moose were abundant, but the art of hunting them was unknown to most of the earlier settlers. Long expeditions were exhausting to hungry men, who had sometimes found even the search for clams no easy task. They remembered well the "clam year" of 1767, when the vessel that was to bring them supplies had become ice-bound on her way, and for two months the people gleaned a scanty subsistence from potato sprouts and remnants of starching-flour and from the clam beds.

In justice to these men, who, it would seem, might have improved their lands more, it should be noted that Machias had at first supposed herself to be in the jurisdiction of Nova Scotia, and had applied to Nova Scotia for a township grant. When in 1770 the grant from Massachusetts was received, it was not to be valid until it had the King's signature. This uncertainty about ownership made the people the more intent on making the most out of what was theirs in hand—the unlimited lumber resources. There were no highways to connect them with the distant settlements, even feebler than themselves, and communication by water could easily be controlled by an invading foe. A little later they petitioned "The Honorable Congress of the Massachusetts Bay" "not for charity," but for supplies to be delivered to Smith and Stillman, who should "obligate themselves to pay the whole amount on demand in lumber." "We have no country behind us to lean upon," they said, "nor can we make an escape by flight; the wilderness is impervious, and vessels we have none." He d in Cherryfield, Me. Res., Scarboro and Machias, Me.

881½. i. BENEN, b. Nov. 14, 1760; m. Deborah Kinney.

882. ii. KEZIA, b. ——, 1769; m. Jan. 10, 1792, Bordman Johnson, b. Canterbury, N. H., Sept. 23, 1769; d. ——, 1858, at Jackson, Me. She d. Jan. 20, 1831. He was son of Benjamin, and gr.-son of Asa. Ch.: 1. Hannah, a child is Mrs. Bartlett Smith, 13 Buckingham St., Cambridge, Mass. 2. Portius, a child is Miss Harriet Johnson, Barre, Mass. 3. Charles, a child is Melville Johnson, Esq., Macwahoc, Me. 4. Cyrus, a child is Samuel A. Johnson, Joyland, Penn. 5. Benjamin, a child is Miss Laura Maria Johnson, Glencoe, Ill, Box 66. 6. Mary Ann; no children. 7. Laura Jane; no children. 8. Augusta, the widow of her one child, Perez Graves, lives in Orono, Me. 9. Samuel*, b. Sept. 23, 1815; m. Dec. 12, 1844, Ann Mary Upton, b. Aug. 31, 1822; d. Oct. 31, 1846. He was a teacher, and died Feb. 13, 1884, in Bangor, Cal. Ch.: i. Nancy Hattie, b. Oct. 29, 1845; m. March 4, 1875, John E. Hastings; res., 31 William St., Worcester, Mass. Ch.: a. Roland Johnson, b. Jan. 16, 1881.

883. iii. HANNAH, b. ——; m. Thomas Parsons. Res., Machias, Me. Ch.: 1. Ezekiel. 2. Wilmot; m. John Coxford. 3. Daniel. 4. Mary; m. John Hodsdon. 5. Dorothy; m. James Gould. 6.

---

*Samuel Johnson married three times. His first wife left but one child. His second wife was Abby Cates, of Thordike, Me.; married Dec. 25, 1851. She had one child, Arabella, who died Nov. 20, 1854, the mother dying soon after. He aftewards married Marilla Manson, Unity, Me., Nov. 20, 1862. Three children, Samuel Bordman, born Aug. 14, 1863, Jackson, Me.; Ezra Abbott, Dec. 6, 1865, Jackson, Me.; Abby Marilla, March —, 1870. The widow of Samuel Johnson and her three children live in Bangor, Butte County, Cal.

Sarah. 7. Keziah; m. ——. 8. Lydia. 9. Isaiah. 10. Benjamin.

884. iv. ROBERT, b. ——; m. Jane Patten.

441. WOODEN FOSTER (Benjamin, Benjamin, Isaac, Reginald), b. Maine, ——; m. ——, Frances Scott. He was a blacksmith by trade, and was residing in Scarboro, in 1763, where he was engaged by the Machias association to go with them there and assist in erecting a sawmill. He, however, ever after resided there. Res., Machias, Me.

885. i. JOHN WOODEN, b. ——; m. Lucy Chase and Mehitabel Meserve.

886. ii. SARAH, b. ——; m. Stephen Munson, son of Joseph and Sarah (Morse). Res., Machias. Ch: 1. Stephen. 2. Robert. 3. Moses. 4. Paul. 5. Foster. 6. Fanny; m. Elkanah Hanscom. 7. John. 8. Mark. 9. Eliza. 10. Sally.

887. iii. MOSES, b. ——; m. Drusilla West.

888. iv. JENNIE, b. ——.

889. v. PAUL, b. ——; m. Betsey Webber.

890. vi. JOEL, b. ——; m. Mary West.

891. vii. RUTH, b. ——; m. Nathan Hanscom, son of Aaron and Sally (Sevey). Res., Machias, Me. Ch.: 1. Susannah. 2. Fanny. 3. John. 4. Joel. 5. Rebecca, m. Joel Sevey. 6. Sarah, m. Hiram Nason. 7. William. 8. Ruth, m. Aaron Averill. 9. Phebe, m. Charles Cottell. 10. Nathan. 11. Hannah. 12. Josiah. 13. Samuel W.

892. viii. ELIAS, b. ——; m. Mary Gooch and Lucy Dorman.

893. ix. JAMES, b. ——, 1773; m. Lucy Gooch and Hannah Simpson.

442. EZEKIEL FOSTER (Benjamin, Benjamin, Isaac, Reginald), b. abt. 1734; in Mass., in that part later Maine; m. —— ——. He resided in Scarborough, but moved to Machias, Me., soon after his brother went there. He was one of the persons on board of the sloop, soon after the Revolutionary War broke out, who assisted in the capture of the "Margaretta," a sloop bound for Boston with lumber for the British. In the battle a number of persons were killed, and the crew of the Margaretta were taken to Machias as prisoners of war. Res., Scarborough.

894. i. EZEKIEL, b. ——.

895. ii. DANIEL, b. ——.

896. iii. BENJAMIN, b. May 1, 1777; m. Hannah Bartlett.

469. JEREMIAH FOSTER (Jeremiah, Abraham, Jacob, Reginald), b. at Ipswich, Mass., Jan. 6, 1740; m. Oct. 29, 1765, Sarah Fellows, dau. of Dea. Samuel. They resided in Ashburnham until 1773, when they moved to Shelburne. Res., Ashburnham and Shelburne, Mass.

897. i. SARAH, b. Aug. 10, 1766.

898. ii. AMOS, b. Oct 13, 1768.

899. iii. NATHAN, b. Nov. 27, 1771; m. Fanny Kirk and Hannah Baker.

470. DEA. SAMUEL FOSTER (Jeremiah, Abraham, Jacob, Reginald), b. at Ipswich, Mass., Jan. 8, 1741; m. July 6, 1769, Susanna Wood, dau. of Bennet, b. April 14, 1750; d. Oct. 31, 1839. He was a worthy and influential citizen. His name was found on the Ashburnham town records quite frequently. "Susanna Foster, guardian for Joel Foster, aged 13; Amos Foster, aged 11; Obed Foster, aged 6, and Susanna Foster, aged 3 years, minor children of Samuel Foster, late of Ashburnham, May 23, 1793. One of the witnesses is Nathaniel Foster, one of the bondsmen is Abraham Foster."—Worcester Probate.

Copy of the will of Samuel Foster, Sr., of Ashburnham, Mass., who was born in Ipswich, Mass., about 1741, and moved with his parents to Ashburnham, in 1757, where he died April 15, 1793.

In the name of God, Amen:

I, Samuel Foster, of Ashburnham, in the County of Worcester and Commonwealth of Massachusetts, yoeman, being sound in memory but weak in body, make and ordain this to be my last will and testament, revoking all former wills, and, first of all, I commend my soull to Almighty God, hoping for mercy and eternal salvation through Jesus Christ, the redeemer; and my body I assign to the earth from whence it was taken, believing I shall receive it again in the gracious morning of the resurrection. My personal charges I will to be paid, with all other debts, by my executor. As to the estate, real and personal, that I am possessed of, I give and bequeath in the following manner:

Imprimis: To Susanna, my dearly beloved wife, I give and bequeath all my household furniture, the west room in my house and the chamber over it and a free passage up the front stairs into it, a third part of the kitching chamber—viz.: the south-west end of the kitching—to use when she needs, and the use of the room back of the kitching, when she has occasion, without molestation, and the use of the cellar under the north-east front room, with the stairs that lead down to it. And further, for her comfortable subsistence, I will that my son Nathaniel, to be hereafter mentioned, or which son soever shall take my home place, shall annually, and from year to year, keep for her two good cows, summer and winter, and four sheep, and bring into the house and deliver to my beloved wife, eight bushels of Indian corn, six bushels of rye, and four bushels of wheat, two barrels of cider, one bushel of malt, fifteen pounds of flax, twelve pounds of sugar, one gallon of rum, one pound and half of tea. Further I will and ordain that she have the privilege of taking fruit out of the orchard in the season as she needs, and to have six bushels of winter apples; that she have fifteen cords of wood yearly, cut and fit for the fire, and the free use of the woodhouse. Likewise that she have a horse whenever she desires to ride to meeting or elsewhere, and also that the said son pay all the expenses accruing on account of her sickness, to physicians, nurses, etc., and provide annually one hundred pounds of merchantable beef, and 'tis my will and intentions that all of the above articles be merchantable.

Item. To Abraham, my first born, I give and bequeath the house in which he lives, together with the blacksmith shop, the land east of the house lying in a three square form and two acres round his barn, beginning at the road four rods west of the barn and running north far enough to take in two acres. Likewise, I give him what land I have lying south of the road, be the same more or less acres, with all the privileges therewith belonging on condition that he pay to his brother Jeremiah Bennet, when he comes of age, thirty pounds lawful money, and if he does not pay at the time to allow him interest until payment is made. Likewise, I give him my son Samuel, who is apprenticed to him, and not bound, till he is of lawful age, to do with him as if he was his own child; and further I give to my son Abraham my son Joel till he is of lawful age, to learn them both the blacksmith trade, and to furnish them with the tools proper to set up the trade with as they come of age. Such tools as he can make himself, he to find the iron and steel necessary to make them.

Item. To Nathaniel, my second son, I give and bequeath all my home place with the buildings, privileges, commodities, etc., keeping the part of the house reserved for the use of his mother, together with two other lots joining together—one of which I bought of Conn and Ames, and was laid to them to make up the Fourth Division Lot No. 22 equal to the other rights; The other I bought of John Cushing—together with my stock of cattle and husbandry tools, he to make provision bequeathed for his mother. I also give him my son Hosea till he comes of lawful age, to do with as his own and to give him then a pair of steers two years old the spring before. I also give him all my notes of hand and book debts, he at the same time to pay what debts I owe. I will further that he pay my sons Amos and Obediah twenty pounds lawful money each as they come of lawful age; to my daughter Susanna twenty pounds lawful money when she arrives at the age of eighteen, unless she should marry before that age, in that case to pay her the legacy upon her marriage. I also give him the use of the improvement on the lot I bought of Mr. Pope till my son Hosea comes of age, and likewise of the lot I have lying between Mr. Jones and Mr. Wetherbee, being on the road to Ringe, until my son Samuel comes of age, and that part of my house reserved for the use of his mother shall revert to him at her decease. In consideration of the privileges he has, I will and order him to pay all taxes on the lands I have willed to his brothers while they are minors.

Item. To Jeremiah Bennet, my third son, I bequeath thirty pounds lawful money, which I have ordered Abram to pay him when he is of age, and my share in the Ashburnham Library; and I have given him to John Cushing till he is of lawful age to deal with as his own.

Item. To my son Samuel I bequeath one half of my lot lying between Mr. Jones and Mr. Wetherbee as above mentioned or described.

Item. To my son Hosea I give and bequeath the lot I bought of Mr. Pope, No. 2 in the Fourth Division.

Item. To my son Joel one half of the lot in common with his brother Samuel, above mentioned.

Item. To my son Amos my lot which I bought of Mr. Haywood, which is No. 15, in the Fourth Division, and twenty pounds lawful money, to be paid by Nathaniel, when of lawful age.

Lastly. To my only daughter Susanna I give and bequeath the sum of twenty pounds lawful money, to be paid by Nathaniel as above mentioned. The lot I bought lately of my brother Jeremiah I would have him take back and give up my note, but if not I order my executor to sell it to discharge the debt. My wearing apparel I will to be divided equally between my sons Amos and Obediah.

My three pews in the meeting house I dispose of in the following manner: The pew behind the body seats adjoining to Mr. Jones I give and bequeath to my wife, the other two to my children to have equal rights in this property. Finally, I order my son Nathaniel to provide decent gravestones for me and his mother.

Thus have I disposed of my earthly possessions and do hereby constitute and appoint Susanna, my wife, and my son Nathaniel executors of this my last will and testament.

In witness whereof I have signed, sealed and declared this as my last will this twenty-eighth day of March, A. D., 1793.

(Signed) Samuel Foster.

In presence of
John Cushing — Attest, Theoph. Wheeler, Reg. of Probate.
Francis Lane
Elizabeth Dickenson.

A true copy: Examined.

He d. April 15, 1793. Res., Ashburnham, Mass.

900. i. ABRAHAM, b. April 8, 1770; m. Sarah Willard and Mary T. Davis.

901. ii. NATHANIEL, b. Dec. 26, 1771; m. Hepsibeth Cutting.

902. iii. JEREMIAH BENNET, b. Oct. 14, 1773; d. unm. May 3, 1846.

903. iv. SAMUEL, b. Feb. 9, 1776; m. Lydia Stearns.

904. v. HOSEA, b. Aug. 1, 1778; m. Polly Joslin.

905. vi. JOEL, b. Aug. 21, 1780; m. Dolly Wetherbee and Mrs. Ruth Fuller.

906. vii. AMOS, b. Nov. 16, 1782; d. unm. Sept. 1812.

907. viii. OBEDIAH, b. Oct. 25, 1786; m. (pub.) July 15, 1809, Deborah Willard, but d. unm. July 23, 1809.

908. ix. SUSANNAH, b. Sept. 25, 1789; m. Nov. 11, 1811, Capt. Francis Lane. She d. Mar. 15, 1867. He was a man of good judgment, and was successful in the conduct of the mill at Lane Village. He d. Oct. 11, 1856. Res., Ashburnham, Mass. Ch.: 1. Allen F., b. March 24, 1812; m. Laura P. Tyler; res., A.; 9 ch. 2. Hepsibeth C., b. June 14, 1813; m. Israel A. Packard; res., A.; 3. Amos F. b. Jan. 30, 1815; m. Martha Ward; res., A.; 10 ch. 4. Samuel, b. May 21, 1817; m. Nancy H. Eaton; res., A.; 5 ch. 5. Milton, b. Feb. 27, 1819; m. Mary Parkhurst and Mrs. Jane Pierce Flagg. 6 ch.; res., A. 6. Leonard, b. April 21, 1821; m. Lucy Pollard; res., A.; 1 ch. 7. Hosea, b. April 20, 1823; d. Aug. 7, 1828. 8. Susan W., b. Jan. 23, 1827; unm.; res., A. 9. Rebecca C., b. Jan. 29, 1827; m. Merrick Eaton; res., A. 10. Eleanor J., b. Jan. 27, 1829; m. Daniel W. Lane; res., A. 11. Hosea F., b. Feb. 7, 1831; m. Elizabeth E. Fairbanks, res., Tempelton. 12. Charles W., b. Aug. 15, 1833; m. Philena H. Packard; res., A.; 1 ch.

909. x. DOROTHY, b. Nov. 25, 1793; m. Feb. 16, 1815, Ezekiel Metcalf. She d. April 14, 1867. He was a farmer; resided on Foster Hill. Res., Ashburnham, Mass. He d. Feb. 26, 1852. Ch.: 1. Otis, b. Jan. 10, 1816; m. Sarah C. Davis; res., A; 3 ch. 2. Joel F., b. Jan. 6, 1819; m. Martha D. Davis; res., Leominster. 3. Mary Ann, b. April, 17, 1821; m. Orin Morton; res., A. 4. Sultina, b. Dec. 2, 1824; d. Sept. 29, 1840. 5. Lavina, b. Sept. 26, 1835; d. Sept. 14, 1848.

475. ABRAHAM FOSTER (Abraham, Abraham, Jacob, Reginald), bapt. Charlestown, Mass., Dec. 2, 1744; m. ——— ———. He was a cabinet maker. Res., in Ward 3 in 1780, Boston, Mass.

910. i. MARY, b. ———. Will of Mary Foster of Boston, single woman; brother Joseph Foster, two sisters, Sarah Foster and Rachel Foster; late

father Abraham Foster, deceased; nephews, Moses B. Foster and Joseph Foster and John Foster; niece, Sally Foster, and her brother, my nephew, John Foster, before named.

Dated Sept. 11, 1827, signed in presence of H. G. Foster, Nancy W. Foster and Susan H. Foster. Lib. 126, fol. 65-6.

; Petition. Joseph Foster and John Foster, of Boston, show that they are appointed exec's of will of Mary Foster, late of Boston, single woman, dec'd, who was of full age at time of making will. Jan. 21, 1828. Suff. Prob. Lib. 240, fol. 28.

911. ii. JOSEPH, b. ——; m. ——
912. iii. SARAH, b. ——.
913. iv. RACHEL, b. ——.

476. NATHANIEL FOSTER (Nathaniel, Abraham, Jacob, Reginald), bap. Nov. 7, 1742, First Church, Salem, Mass.; m. Nov. 22, 1764, Elizabeth Yell, dau. of Nathaniel and Elizabeth Yell, who was baptized Sept. 9, 1745. He d. April 29, 1773. Res., Salem, Mass.

914. i. ELIZABETH, b. in 1766; bapt. in First Church of Salem, Mass., May 1, 1768; d. in North Yarmouth, Me., April 1, 1826; m. Sept. 28, 1785, Nathan Safford, who was born in 1760, and d. in North Yarmouth, Me., Dec. 27, 1823. They had one child, and probably others. Nathaniel Safford, b. in Yarmouth, Me., June 13, 1786; removed to Salem, Mass., in 1806 and there d. Nov. 20, 1847, a merchant. He married, first, at Salem, Mass., Aug. 8, (Dec. 8, Town Records,) 1808, Sally Smith, adopted daughter of George K. (perhaps Kight) and Sally (Driver) Smith; she b. in Salem, Mass., July 11, 1791 and died there March 16, 1810. He married, 2d., Oct. 14, 1813, Hannah Woodbury (see Driver Family No. 50; also Appendix Ives Family, No. 62.)
915. ii. NATHANIEL, bap. July 31, 1768.
916. iii. SARAH, bapt. July 22, 1770.
917. iv. ABIGAIL, bapt. May 10, 1772.

502. JOSEPH FOSTER (Joseph, Joseph, Jacob, Reginald), b. Ipswich, Mass., Dec. 25, 1739; m. April 26, 1765, Elizabeth Hilton, of Manchester; b. 1748; d. July 19, 1834. Joseph Billerica, will date October 9, 1802, Prob. Jan. 18, 1803; wife, Elizabeth; ch.: Elizabeth Sumner, Dorcas, Hannah, Joseph, Samuel, John, Levi, and Benjamin Hilton ?]—Middlesex Probate. He d. Dec. 15, 1802. Res., Beverly and Billerica, Mass.

918. i. ELIZABETH, b. Feb. 5, 1766; m. James Sumner.
919. ii. JOSEPH, b. April, 1770,; m. Lucy Larkum.
920. iii. HANNAH, b. Mar., 1772; m. in Billerica, Benjamin Daland. He was born 1763; d. April 18, 1826. She d. June 1, 1834. Res., Billerica, Mass. Ch.: 1. Oliver Foster, bapt. Oct. 18, 1801. 2. Dau, b. Dec. 11, 1803. 3. Sally, bapt. Jan. 26, 1806. 4. Hannah, bapt. Dec. 20, 1806. 5. Eliza, bapt. Feb. 26, 1809. 6. Samuel, bapt. Aug. 11, 1811. 7. Fred'k Freeman, bapt. Sept. 25, 1814.
921. iv. SAMUEL, b. April 26, 1777; m. Anne Whitney.
922. v. DORCAS, b. Aug. 5, 1779; d. July 7, 1850.
923. vi. BENJAMIN, b. Sept. 1783; m. Martha Shed; b. March 23, 1790. Res., Lancaster, Mass.
924. vii. JOHN, b. Dec., 1785; d. Aug. 9, 1841.
925. viii. LEVI, b. July 1, 1788; m. Cile Davis.

506. DANIEL FOSTER (Joseph, Joseph, Jacob, Reginald), b. Feb. 14, 1745, Beverly, Mass.; m. there Aug. 2, 1774-5, Judith Woodbury; b. 1754; d. April 8, 1817. He d. Feb. 2, 1835. Res., Beverly, Mass.

926. i. DANIEL, b. Dec. 28, 1775; m. April 7, 1799, Lydia Whittridge; d. June 15, 1799, in Havana.
927. ii. EZRA TRASK, b. Oct. 4, 1777; d. Jan. 7, 1779.
928. iii. FANNY, b. March 25, 1779; m. Dec 13, 1798, Bartholomew Wallis.
929. iv. ISRAEL, b. Nov. 2, 1780; d. April 16, 1801; accidentally killed by gun.
930. v. JAMES, b. Aug. 20, 1782; m. Mary Vickery and Sarah Greeley.
931. vi. SETH, b. April 10, 1784; m. Nancy Goodridge.

932. vii. BETSEY, b. May 3, 1786; m. Dec. 4, 1806, John Buffington; d. March 5, 1858, in Boston.
933. viii. JOSEPH, b. May 17, 1789; m. Rebecca Batchelder.
934. ix. AUGUSTUS, b. Nov. 1, 1795; d. Aug. 4, 1796.

509. EZRA TRASK FOSTER (Joseph, Joseph, Jacob, Reginald), b. Sept. 29, 1752, Beverly, Mass.; m. Oct. 3, 1784, Sarah Stickney, dau. of William and Hannah Stickney, of Billerica; b. Nov., 1755; d. Jan. 23, 1849. Res., Beverly, Mass.
935. i. WILLIAM, b. July 31, 1786; m. Abigail D. Lovett.
936. ii. ———, b. ——; d. young.
937. iii. ———, b. ——; d. young.
938. iv. ABIGAIL, b. ——; m. Captain Ebenezer Meacom.
939. v. LYDIA, b. March 25, 1788; m. Nov. 13, 1817, James Stone.
940. vi. EZRA, b. Nov. 6, 1789.

520. JAMES FOSTER (Nathan, Joseph, Jacob, Reginald), b. Dec. 18, 1747, Ipswich, Mass.; m. —, Elizabeth Hiller. "To his integrity and benevolence there are many witnesses as he had acquaintance, and no person can be more sincerely lamented." She d. in 1806 or 1807. They had nine children, eight of whom survived their father. Elizabeth Foster, of Boston, widow, admitted administratrix on estate of James Foster, late of Boston, bookkeeper, decd. Nathaniel Foster, gent., of Boston, bound with her, Jan. 14, 1794.—Lib. 92, Fol. 621.

Abraham Foster, one of committee of appraisement.—Lib. 93, Fol. 60-1-2.

In adm. account, money paid to Susanna Foster, Rachel Foster, James H. Foster.—Lib. 93, Fol. 568-9.

Adm. acct. mentions Samuel Foster's note, James Joster, Jr.'s note, Nathaniel Foster, March 21, 1797.—Lib. 95, Fol. 113.

Decree on Settlement.—Eldest son James H. Foster; other heirs, William. John, Mary, Elizabeth, Margaret, Lydia, Abigail Foster, April 11, 1797.—Suff. Prob. Lib. 95, Fol. 140-1; Lib. 95, Fol. 137. He d. 1793. Res., Boston, Mass.
941. i. JAMES H., b. ——; unm. in 1863.

Will.—James H. Foster, of Boston. Widow Elizabeth G. Kellogg, estate she occupies in Gorham, Me.; Mary Ann Foster and Margaret H., her sister, wife of General Edward T. Smith, estate in Gorham adjoining estate which my brother, William H., lived in. Temperance H., wife of Thomas H. Shaw—sister Abigail Foster—Sarah Foster, Mary A. Foster and Joseph H. Foster; children of brother, John W. Foster, Caroline M. Barnard and her sister Adelaide Foster, daughter Elizabeth Anne Foster. Dated Oct. 29, 1860, Lib. 161, Fol. 34-5.; codicil May 16, 1862, 36; Prob. Jan. 19, 1863, Lib. 268, Fol. 440-1; Lib. 370, Fol. 191; Lib. 551, Fol. 371. Archibald Foster, one of appraisers of estate.—Suffolk Probate, Boston, Lib. 301, Fol. 213.
942. ii. MARY ANN, b. ——.
943. iii. ———, b. ——.
944. iv. ABIGAIL, b. ——.
945. v. ELIZABETH, b. ——; m. Amos Green; she d. in ——. He d. in 1812. They had one child, James Foster; b. in 1804; d. Sept. 19, 1821. She m. 2d. a Kellogg. Res., Gorham, Me.
946. vi. WILLIAM H., b. ——; resided in Gorham, Me.; d. in 1838.
947. vii. MARGARET H., b. —; m. General Edward T. Smith; d. in 1846, in Portsmouth, N. H.
948. viii. LYDIA, b. ——; d. in 1844, in Portsmouth, N. H.
949. ix. JOHN WELSH, b. June 16, 1789; m. Mary Appleton.

521. NATHANIEL FOSTER (Nathan, Joseph, Jacob, Reginald), b. Ipswich, Mass., Nov. 30, 1752; m. Susanna Hiller. He d. ——. Res., Boston, Mass.
950. i. HENRY GARDNER, b. Dec. 9, 1785; m. Anna A. Haven
951. ii. NANCY, b. ——.
952. iii. SUSAN, b. ——

523. ISAAC FOSTER (Isaac, Joseph, Jacob, Reginald), b. Billerica, Mass., March 8, 1745; m. Nov. 9, 1767, Lydia Bacon, dau. of Josiah; b. Aug. 23, 1747. Res., Billerica, Beverly, Newburyport and Marblehead, Mass.
953. i. ISAAC, b. March 9, 1768; m. Charlotte Whitman.
954. ii. JOSIAH, b. ——.

955. iii. WILLIAM, b. ——.
956. iv. IRA, b. ——.
957. v. SAMUEL, b. ——.
958. vi. DANIEL, b. about 1776; m. Philena Pettingill.

524. JACOB FOSTER (Isaac, Joseph, Jacob, Reginald), b. Billerica, Mass., Dec. 20, 1747; m. June 3, 1771, Hannah Frost, dau. of James; b. July 20, 1740. Res., Billerica, Mass., and ——.

959. i. JACOB, b. Feb. 20, 1772.
960. ii. JAMES, b. July 6, 1774.

526. DR. JOSEPH FOSTER (Isaac, Joseph, Jacob, Reginald), b. Billerica, Mass., March 21, 1750; m. Aug. 21, 1775, Sarah Baldwin, dau. of Benjamin; b. Aug. 1, 1751; m., 2d, Feb. 6, 1810, Mrs. Lucy (Fitch) Hill, dau. of Zachariah and wid. of Joseph; b. Billerica, b. March 2, 1783; d. Oct. 30, 1869. Joseph Billerica letter dated Aug 31, 1810, ex. Sept. 21, 1810; wife Lucy; [no children given.]—Middlesex Prob. He d. July 21, 1810. Res., Billerica, Mass.

961. i. SARAH, b. Nov. 18, 1776.
962. ii. SUSANNA, b. Dec. 3, 1778.
963. iii. JAMES, b. April 11, 1780.
964. iv. ANNA, b. Aug. 15, 1781.
965. v. ISAAC, b. May 27, 1785.

528. JOHN BRAINARD FOSTER (Isaac, Joseph, Jacob, Reginald), b. June 28, 1755; m. ——, Sarah Taylor who d. May 17, 1792; m., 2d, ——, Lydia Foster, who d. July 19, 1842. Res., Hancock, N. H.

966-1. i. JOHN, b. Jan. 29, 1780; m. —— Styles. He d. in Langdon, N. H. Ch.: 1. Rebecca, b. Jan. 3, 1800. 2. Betsey, d. Aug. 30, 1800.
966-2. ii. SARAH, b. June 28, 1782; m. Elisha Goodell, who d. in H. June 8, 1871.
966-3. iii. MERCY, b. March 30, 1786; m. Thatcher Bradford.
966-4. iv. ISAIAH, b. Oct. 28, 1789; m. Patty Phips Hartwell, who d. in 1879, in Hillsboro, N. H.
966-5. v. PERLEY, b. Sept. 20, 1792; m. Mary Gray.
966-6. vi. JOSHUA, b. Feb. 12, 1796; m. Sally Hopkins, Mary Ann Fletcher and Dorothy Little.
966-7. vii. SILAS, b. ——. He m. twice and d. in Colorado Springs, Col., Dec. 4, 1881. He had seven children in all; one was Marcus A., who m. Lizzie Harris.

529. DR. SAMUEL FOSTER (Isaac, Joseph, Jacob, Reginald), b. Billerica, Mass., Mar. 31, 1758; m. in Stratham, N. H., Feb. 19, 1789, Mary Colcord, of Brentwood; b. Dec. 14, 1765; d. Nashua, N. H., Dec. 3, 1860. History of Candia, N. H., has this concerning Dr. Samuel Foster: "Samuel Foster was born of English parents, in Billerica, Mass. He came to Candia in 1789, in which year he married Mary Colcord, of Brentwood. They had ten children. Dr. Foster served three years in the army during the war of Independence, and was in the battle of Monmouth. In 1812 he removed to Canterbury, N. H., and returned in 1815. He died in Brentwood in 1826." Dr. Foster must have been an interesting man, and a man of no small literary ability. He practiced medicine in his own and surrounding towns; got his pay when he could—fifty cents a visit, usually in barter, and was unable to collect much of it even at that—and reared a family of ten children. He used his influence with young people to induce them to get an education, and always helped them in any way he could. He d. in Brentwood, Jan. 15, 1826. Res., Candia, N. H.

967. i. MOSES, b. Nov. 3, 1793; m. Abigail F. Hunting.
968. ii. SAMUEL, b. Feb. 19, 1790; m. Dec. 12, 1817, Huldah Lund. He d., s. p. in Nashua, N. H., where he was a merchant, May 14, 1819.
969. iii. EBEN COLCORD, b. Dec. 5, 1791; m. Betsey Adams.
970. iv. POLLY, b. Nov. 27, 1795; d. Brentwood, Feb. 1, 1826.
971. v. FRANKLIN, b. Feb. 19, 1798; m. Marcy Hunting.
972. vi. HANNAH COLCORD, b. March 22, 1800; m. at Brentwood in Dec., 1827, Nathaniel Chase, of Brentwood. He was b. 1798; was a farmer and carriage manufacturer. She d. Nov., 1869. Had nine

children—six living, three dead. 1. Mary Foster, b. Feb. 16, 1828; m. in Kingston, N. H., in 1845, George Stevens Frost; b. June 1, 1825. He is a manufacturer of leather belting. Res., Spring Valley, Minn. Ch.: i. Addie M., b. 1845; m. 1863, James M. Poore. ii. Geo. J. S., b. 1849; d. in infancy. 2. Mrs. Nellie J. Emerson, "The Willard," San Diego, Cal.

973. vii. LYDIA BACON, b. May 22, 1803; res., Nashua, N. H.; d., unm., Aug. 22, 1884.

974. viii. LUCINDA SILSBEE, b. Sept. 9, 1805; m. Jan. 23, 1838, Samuel McQuesten; b. Litchfield, N. H., June 11, 1789; d. Aug. 5, 1861, in Manchester, N. H. She d. June 16, 1891. Ch.: 1. Samuel Foster McQuesten, b. in Manchester, N. H., May 4, 1839; d. June 13, 1863, in New Orleans, La. He was a soldier in the Sixteenth N. H. Vols. 2. David McQuesten, b. Jan. 2, 1846; d. Dec. 10, 1850. Samuel Foster and David were unm. 3. John Knox, b. May 27, 1842; m. in Bridgeport, Conn., Nov. 5, 1868, Lucia Cutler; b. May 4, 1839. He is a farmer; res., s. p., Manchester, N. H.

975. ix. SALLY STEVENS, b. June 7, 1809; m., June 6, 1832, Stephen French, of Bedford. He was b. in Bedford, Aug. 26, 1806; d. there July 16, 1866. She d. April 25, 1883. Res., Bedford, N. H. Ch.: 1. Benjamin Franklin, b. March 12, 1833; m. Sarah Park; and m., 2nd, in Portland, Ore., his present P. O. address. 2. Ellen Bacon, b. Jan. 13, 1835; m. Barney Hinckley, Jan. 4, 1886. P. O. address, Beach Bluff, Mass. 3. Celia Nott, b. Nov. 28, 1836; m. Rev. Alfred B. Dascomb, March 4, 1886. P. O. address, Westminster, Vt. 4. Sarah Emeline, b. Sept. 6, 1840; m. George O. Christian. P. O. address, 195 West Brookline St., Boston, Mass. 5. Mary Colcord, b. Oct. 30, 1838; d. March, 1841. 6. Robert Hall, b. Dec 2, 1842; d. Memphis, Tenn.; a member of Sixteenth Regt. N. H. Vols., Aug. 22, 1863. 7. James Edwards, b. Dec. 15, 1844; m., Oct. 22, 1885, Mrs. Ella L. (Nye) Huntoon, b. Jan. 19, 1849. Res., Bedford. Ch.: Harry Nye, b. May 4, 1889. 8. Harriett A., b. April 19, 1849; m. Charles E. Bursiel, Nov. 25, 1869; d. Nov. 8, 1888. 9. Alice Bird, b. Aug. 25, 1851; m. Prof. Henry Mills, April 13, 1880. Res., Binghamton, N. Y.

976. x. BETSEY, b. July ——, 1811; m. Feb. 16, 1836, Phinehas French, of Bedford. Ch.: 1. Horace, b. Feb. 16, 1837; m., April 4, 1865, Mary E. Gillette, b. Aug. 20, 1841. Captain. Res., W. Lebanon, N. H. Is postmaster. Ch.: i. Bessie Foster French, b. Jan. 8, 1866. ii. Nathan Gillette French, b. Sept. 8, 1867. iii. Martin Gillette French, b. Sept. 8, 1867. iv. Samuel Pingree French, b. May 6, 1871. v. Robert Horace French, b. June 20, 1873. vi. Frederick Reginald French, b. Sept. 25, 1873. vii. Ernest Eugene French, b. May 3, 1878. viii. John McQuesten French, b. April 21, 1879. 2. Charles, b. ——. He d. 1865. She d. May 14, 1839; and he m., 2d, Lydia G. Hardy and 3d, Anna Fisher.

535. TIMOTHY FOSTER (Jacob, Joseph, Jacob, Reginald), b. Billerica, Mass., Nov. 4, 1759; m., May 16, 1784, Sally Crosby, dau. of Seth; b. March 31, 1761. She d. Dec. 1, 1849. Timothy Billerica, letter date, Feb. 28, 1815. ex. May 23, 1815, wife Sarah, heir Clarissa.—Middlesex Prob. He d. Jan. 21, 1815. Res., Billerica, Mass.

977. i. CLARISSA, b. April 11, 1785; m., Oct. 13, 1816, Jeremiah Farmer, son of Oliver; b. April 10, 1771; d. March 2, 1836. She d. Feb. 20, 1873. Res., Billerica. Ch.: 1. Sarah Clarissa, b. Feb. 27, 1818; m. Dr. Henry Blanchard; b. Sept. 25, 1811; gr. Harvard coll., 1834. Physician in Neponset, Mass. 2. Timothy Foster, b. Aug. 10, 1824; m., 1862, Jane Leavitt. He d. May 27, 1871. Res., B.

538. JOSEPH FOSTER (Abraham, Joseph, Jacob, Reginald), b. Boston, Mass., —— ——; m., —— ——, Joseph Foster, of Boston, clerk, app. adm. of estate of Joseph Foster, silversmith, of Boston (who died May 16, 1839). May 25, 1840. Lib. 216, Fol. 220. Lib. 277, Fol. 187. Lib. 321, Fol. 105. Adm. of estate of Joseph

Foster granted to Spencer Beatley, of Chelsea, ship carver, guardian of Joseph Foster, the younger of that name, who before completing adm. of said estate became insane. Feb. 26, 1855. Suff. Prob. Lib. 225, Fol. 6. Lib. 185, Fol. 64. Lib. 326, Fol. 100. Lib. 292, Fol. 165. He d. May 16, 1839. Res., Boston, Mass.

978. i. JOSEPH, b. ——. He d. unm., July, 1855. Spencer Beatley of Chelsea, app. guardian of Joseph Foster of Boston, trader (an insane person), at request of his only brother, John Foster of Chelsea, Gent., Dec. 18, 1854. Lib. 407. Fol. 145. Lib. 409, Fol. 92. Lib. 410, Fol. 161. Lib. 292, Fol. 121. Lib. 153, Fol. 141. Spencer Beatley app. administrator on estate of Joseph Foster of Boston, Gent., dec'd., at request of the only heir at law, Aug. 13, 1855. Petition dated July 21, 1855. Bond, John Foster one of sureties. Lib. 225, Fol. 65. Lib. 185, Fol. 104. Lib. 292, Fol. 301. Lib. 326, Fol. 160. Administrators account, John Foster sole heir at law, March 17, 1856. Suff. Prob. Lib. 154, Fol. 156.

979. ii. JOHN, b. ——. Will, John Foster of Chelsea, Gent., Alice S. Beatley, wife of Spencer Beatley of Chelsea, trader dated Jan. 9, 1862. Lib. 164, Fol. 48-9. Probate Jan. 8, 1866. Lib. 269, Fol. 538. Lib. 371, Fol. 135. Lib. 303, Fol. 155. Exec. account, only person interested, Alice S. Beatley, April 20, 1868. Lib. 166, Fol. 259.

980. iii. SALLY b. ——; d. unm. Feb., 1855. Spencer Beatley of Chelsea, ship charver, app. adm. on estate of Sally Foster of Boston, Spinister, at request of her brother John Foster, Feb. 26, 1855. Lib. 225, Fol. 7. Lib. 185, Fol. 63. Lib. 326, Fol. 100. Lib. 292, Fol. 166. Lib. 153, Fol. 137-8.

543. HON. THEODORE FOSTER (Jedediah, Ephraim, Ephraim, Abraham, Reginald), b. Brookfield, Mass., April 29, 1752; m., Oct. 27, 1771, Lydia Fenner, dau. of Gov. Arthur Fenner of Rhode Island who gr. at Brown; b. March 1, 1748; d. June 1, 1801; m., 2d. June 18, 1803, Esther Bowen Millard of Foster, R. I.; b. June 15, 1785; d. Dec. 29, 1815. He entered Rhode Island college (now Brown university), in 1767, being graduated in the class of 1770, and in 1773, on receiving the degree of A. M., delivering an oration on "The Future Greatness of the American Colonies." He received the same degree from Dartmouth college in 1786. In 1794 he was chosen one of the trustees of Brown university, which position he held until 1822. After his graduation, he began the practice of the law in Providence. In 1772 he was appointed assistant clerk of the Superior Court. In 1773 he was made justice of the peace, and from 1775 to 1787 he held the position of town clerk. In 1777 he was made sheriff of Providence county. He served as deputy from Providence in the general assembly, in six sessions, the first being that of October, 1776. From 1776 to 1781 he served as secretary of the Rhode Island council of war. In 1781 occasion arose for dividing the town of Scituate, in the western part of the state. The newly created town was named Foster, in compliment to him. As early probably as 1789 he was acting as naval officer of Providence, resigning in 1790. On the adoption by Rhode Island in May, 1790, of the Constitution of the United States, he was one of the two senators chosen to represent the State in Congress. His term of service as senator was one of the longest on record, namely, thirteen years, 1790 to 1803, and has been surpassed by only three others from that State. During this public service his wife died at Providence, in June, 1801. The next twelve years of his life were passed chiefly on his estate at Foster. After the death of his second wife, Dec. 29, 1815, he returned to Providence making his home with his oldest daughter, Mrs. Stephen Tillinghast, whose husband was a grand-son of Governor Stephen Hopkins. At her house he died Jan. 13, 1828.

At two periods of his life, namely, from 1776 to 1785, and from 1803 to 1828, his time was largely devoted to the collection of historical materials. The papers left by him (many of which were placed in his hands by Governor Hopkins), amount to about one thousand and are preserved in sixteen bound volumes now in the possession of the Rhode Island Historical Society. He was one of the earliest members and first officers of that society, organized in 1822. In 1800 he was chosen a corresponding member of the Massachusetts Historical Society. A sketch of his "Life and Services" by William E. Foster, is printed, pages 11-134 of vol. vii. of the Collections of the Rhode Island Historical Society (1885), his "Materials for a History of Rhode Island" being printed pages 67-94 of the same volume. He was educated at the public school and by private instructors, fitted for college and was graduated at Brown university (then called R. I. college); m. Lydia Fenner of Providence, R. I., dau. of Arthur Fenner and sister of Governor James Fenner of R. I. He married for his 2d wife, Esther Brown Millard (dau. of Rev. Noah Millard of R. I., and Hannah Bowen). He was a lawyer at Providence. He was elected a justice of the peace for the town and county of Providence at the general State election in 1773, and was town clerk for twelve years (1775-87), and was in 1776 a member of the State Legislature. In 1787 he was elected a member of the Governor's council and was for thirteen years U. S. Senator (1709-1803). "He was a thoroughly unselfish man, and had literary tastes, personal friendships, and a love of nature which were far dearer to him than pecuniary gain." In personal appearance he was dignified and prepossessing and in stature above the average height. His face which was full and round, beamed with benignity and intelligence. He had a light complexion and blue eyes. His wife Esther Millard d. Dec. 29, 1815, æt. 30. Rev. Noah Millard, b. at Rehoboth, Mass., Oct. 10, 1758, was the son of Noah Willard and Jane Maxwell. He was a "Six Principle Baptist." He preached without ordination at Foster R. I. (a town incorporated in 1781 and named in honor of the Hon. Theodore Foster), for some 10 years (1795-1805). In April, 1805, he removed to Burrillville, R. I., where he was ordained, Oct. 15, 1806, and preached until his death, Oct. 25, 1834. He had 5 children: Hannah, Samuel, Esther Bowen, Theodore Foster and Arthur Lemuel.

Mr. Foster was a lover of the study of antiquities, particularly American and made considerable collections toward a history of Rhode Island, which he planned, but from habits of procrastination never executed. In the preface of his life of Roger Williams, Knowles used what he found advantageous to his purpose among Mr. Foster's papers. He died at the residence of his daughter, Mrs. Stephen Tillinghast. He d. Jan. 13, 1828. Res., Providence, R. I.

981. i. THEODOSIA, b Dec. 24, 1772; m, May 23, 1794, Stephen Tillinghast; b. Sept. 17, 1768; d. Sept. 24, 1839. He was son of Daniel Tillinghast* and Lydia Hopkins, dau. of Governor Hopkins, graduated at Brown university in 1778, a merchant at Providence, and president of an insurance company. He was highly respected for his upright and honorable character. He was established for several years in business in New York. She d. Sept. 24, 1839; he d. Feb. 6, 1841. Ch.: 1. George Hopkins Tillinghast, M. D., b. March 19, 1795, graduated at Brown university in 1814; was a physician and apothecary in Providence. When about entering upon medical practice, he was crippled for life by the falling of a piece of timber upon him in a tornado. He m., Oct. 16, 1825, Louise Lyman; b. at Newport, R. I., April 16, 1797, dau. of Chief Justice Daniel Lyman† of Providence and Mary Wanton. He d. Aug. 28, 1858, æt. 63. Ch.: a. Francis Theodosia Tillinghast, b. Oct. 13, 1826; d. Feb. 17, 1842. b. Charles Tillinghast, b. June 16, 1828; m. May 16, 1848, Lucy S. Leonard of Providence. He was a merchant in New York. He went into the late war for God and his native land and fell leading bravely on his company before the intrenchments at Newberne, N. C., when his fellow soldiers were just seizing upon victory, March 14, 1862, æt. 35. He had one child, Frances, who d. ae. 3. c. Julia Lyman Tillinghast, b. Nov. 2, 1830; m. John W Alom of Providence. d. Henry Lyman Tillinghast, b. Jan. 13, 1833; d. Feb. 25, 1862, from injuries received at the Battle of Bull Run. He was one of the first to enlist in the late rebellion in the First R I. regiment of union volunteers. e. Stephen Hopkins Tillinghast, b. May 9, 1835, is a resident of

---

*Daniel Tillinghast was descended from Pardon Tillinghast, the settler, who was born in 1622, at Seven Cliffs, near Beachy Head, Eng. He went first to Providence and thence in 1663 to Newport, R. I., but before 1677 returned to Providence again. He was in 1681 an elder of the old Baptist church. He built in 1700 at his own expense the first Baptist meeting house in that city, and gave a deed of it to the church, April 14, 1711. He m for a 2d. wife Lydia Taber of Tiverton, R. I. The name is said to be a corruption of the motto "Till in haste" which is found on the coat of arms, consisting of a crow, harrow and spade, indicating the life of a husbandman.

†Judge Daniel Lyman, b. in Durham, Conn., Jan. 27, 1756, left with his class, then junior at Yale, for Cambridge, Mass., after the news of the Battle of Lexington and was at once appointed Captain under Arnold, and the next year brigade-major under Gen. Fellows, and in 1778 adjutant general under Gen. Heath. He practiced law at Newport, R. I. for several years after the war. He was also Chief Justice of the State. He d. Oct. 16, 1830, aet. 74.

Providence. f. Julia Lyman Tillinghast, b. Nov. 2, 1830; m. Jan. 18, 1855, John W. Alom of Providence (son of John W. Alom and Celinda Barton), b. April 3, 1830. Ch.: i. Louise Lyman Alom, b. Jan. 12, 1856. ii. Annie Barton Alom, b. March 21, 1858. iii. Sophia Tillinghast Alom, b. March 19, 1860. 2. Ophelia Dwight Tillinghast, b. March, 19, 1769; d., aet. 14, Sept. 21, 1810.. 3. Hon. Charles Foster Tillinghast (son of Stephen Tillinghast and Theodosia Foster) b. June 18, 1797; m., May 15, 1822, Susan Richmond; b. May 27, 1800 (dau. of William Richmond, of Providence, and Clarissa Andrews). He was graduated at Brown university in 1814, and was a lawyer at Providence for nearly 50 years (1817-64). He was largely conversant with the details of the law of real estate and of conveyances and probate and especially with the whole system of private trusts, real and personal. He was a member in 1848 of the Constitutional Convention of R. I., and was at one time a member of the State Legislature. He d. Aug. 3, 1864. She d. Sept. 29, 1862. i. William Richmond Tillinghast, b. March 2; 1823, d. Dec. 1, 1847. He m. in, 1844, Frances Eliza Peckham, of Providence; b. Nov. 20, 1821. He resided in Providence when he d. Dec. 1, 1847. He had one child: g. Charles Foster Tillinghast, b. May 27, 1845, who resides in Pittsburg, Pa. h. Stephen Hopkins Tillinghast, b. June 15, 1826; d. Aug. 13, 1827. i. Sophia Foster Tillinghast, b. May 9, 1833, resides unm. in Providence. j. James Tillinghast, b. July 22, 1828; grad. at Brown university in 1849; a lawyer in Providence since 1851. He m., May 26, 1857, Sarah Benson Anthony (dau. of Henry Anthony, of Providence, and Charlotte Benson). Ch.: i. William Richmond Tillinghast, b. April 15, 1858. ii. Henry Anthony Tillinghast, b. Sept. 15, 1859. iii. Theodore Foster Tillinghast, b. Sept. 25, 1861. iv. Stephen Hopkins Tillinghast, b. April 17, 1863; d. March 7, 1865. v. Charles, b. Sept. 18, 1871. vi. Charlotte Lusanne, b. Nov. 16, 1872. 4. iv. Frances Theodosia Tillinghast, b. Oct. 15, 1798; d. March 9, 1818.

982. ii. AUGUSTA SOPHIA, b. April 7, 1773; d. Nov. 6, 1776.

983. iii. THEODORE DWIGHT, b. Sept. 10, 1780; grad. at Brown university in 1798, studied law and went to New Orleans, La., to practice his profession, but died soon after his arrival there, in the summer of 1802, of yellow fever, unm. By second wife:

984. iv. MAXWELL STEWART, b. Dec. 6, 1804; m. Mary Howard, Lydia —— and Maria Thompson.

985. v. SAMUEL WILLIS, b. in Foster, R. I., Nov. 30, 1806; m. Ruth Belden Seymour.

986. vi. DWIGHT CRANSTON, b. in Foster, R. I., Dec. 28, 1808; m. Alma Jeanette Seymour, and Cornelia Seymour.

987. vii. THEODORE, b. in Foster, April 3, 1812; m. Frances Delia Seymour and Betsey Morehouse.

988. viii. LUZELIA SARAH, b. in Foster, Oct. 4, 1815; m. Joseph Willard Seymour.; m. Jan. 3, 1834; b. March 1, 1811 (son of Ira Seymour, of Webster, Mich., and Betsey Morehouse), a miller in Scio, Mich., 1833-7 and afterward a merchant in Lima, Mich. (1837-9) and in Commerce, Mich. (1839-4), where he d. May 7, 1840. She m. for a 2d. husband Oct. 15, 1841, John Comstock; b. Dec. 19, 1813 (son of Rev. Elkanah Comstock, bapt., of Pontiac, Mich., and Sarah Green), a banker at Hudson, Wis., where they have resided since 1856. No children by this marriage. By her first husband she had one child.: 1. Theodosia Tillinghast Seymour, b. July 23, 1839; d. Aug. 15, 1839.

544. THEOPHILUS FOSTER (Jedediah, Ephraim, Ephraim, Abraham, Reginald), b. Brookfield, Mass., March 16, 1754; m., 1774, Susanna Packard; b. 1757; d. April 2, 1801; m., 2d., Hannah Crosby. He was a soldier in Revolutionary War in Captain Wright's Company, that marched to the alarm April, 1775. Hannah Crosby died without issue. He was a farmer at Brookfield, Mass., and afterward (1795-1833), at Wilmington, Vt., where he died; aet. 79. He had a light complexion and blue eyes. He d. Oct. 8, 1833. Res., Wilmington, Vt.

989. i. DOROTHY, b. March 22, 1776; m., Dec. 1, 1796, Edmund Livermore; d. June 2, 1842; aet. 66. He was born Aug. 16, 1769 (son of Daniel Livermore and Elizabeth Allen), a farmer at Wilmington, Vt., where he also kept public house for a time. He d. there June 30, 1834; aet. 65. She d. June 2, 1842; aet. 66. Ch.: 1. Semantha Livermore, b. May 28, 1798; d. Sept. 9, 1798. 2. Daniel Livermore, b. June 30, 1799; m., Jan. 21, 1828, Mary Ann Robinson. Res., Port Penn, Del. Ch: a. William Darrach Livermore, b. Dec. 20, 1828, an apothecary in Philadelphia, was drowned in the Delaware river, July 19, 1854. b. Origin Livermore, b. in Blairsville, Va., Sept. 16, 1830, an apothecary in Philadelphia; d. April 8, 1864. c. Mary E. T. Livermore, b. about 1832; d. soon. d. James Stuart Livermore, b. about 1834; d. soon. 3. Susan Livermore, b. March 27, 1801; m. Joel Nye, b. Apr. 18, 1824; of Toledo, Ohio, a farmer; b. in Brookfield, N. Y., Feb. 11, 1799, son of Jonathan Nye, of Hume, N. Y., and Betsey Alton, of Thompson, Conn. Ch.: i. Alonzo Randolph Nye, M. D., b. Feb. 20, 1825, a physician at New Orleans, La., where he d. July 31, 1853. ii. Daniel Henry Nye, b. May 31, 1828; was formerly a book seller at Toledo, Ohio. He enlisted in the late rebellion April 25, 1861, in the Fourteenth Ohio regt., Company A, for three month's service, and entered the Union army anew Aug. 13, 1861, for three years, as first lieutenant and quartermaster of the regt. In Dec., 1861, the Fourteenth Ohio, in which he was a soldier, the Fourth and Tenth Kentucky and Tenth Indiana regts. were formed into a brigade at Lebanon, Ky., and he was made A. C S., holding the office until his term of service was ended, Sept. 12, 1864. He took part in the battles of Wild Cat, Ky., Mill Spring, Ky., Corinth, Miss., Perryville, Ky., Chickamauga, Chattanooga and Mission Ridge, and was with General Sherman in his Atlanta campaign. He is a farmer now at Toledo, O. He m., Aug. 7, 1854, Emma Parker Swift, b. in Tiverton, R. I., June 19, 1835 (dau. of Albert Swift, of Toledo, and Catherine Estes). She d. Jan. 1, 1867. Ch.: a. Emma Swift Nye, b. Oct. 25, 1856; d. Oct. 2, 1858. b. Henry Case Nye, b. Feb. 1, 1858; d. Jan. 1, 1863. c. Emma Parker Nye, b. Dec. 31, 1866. iii. Edmund Dwight Nye, b. July 29, 1830; m., Aug. 3, 1853, Francis Lucinda Collins, b. —— 28, 1836, (dau. of Morgan Lewis Collins, of Toledo, and Lucinda Lewis); a lawyer engaged in commercial agency in New York but residing with his family in Brooklyn. Mrs. Lucinda Nye, d. Aug. 24, 1854, and he m., Nov. 7, 1855, Emma Caroline Jennison, b. Jan. 30, 1836. Ch. by first wife: d. Julia Francis Nye, b. March 7, 1854; d. Aug. 18, 1854. By second wife: e. Charles Edmund Nye, b. May 28, 1861; d. soon. f. Robert Hatfield Nye, b. June 30, 1863. g. William Nye, b. April 6, 1867. 4. Alonzo Livermore, b. Feb. 25, 1803; m., April 30, 1826, Elizabeth Brunner, b. Nov. 10, 1806 (dau. of Henry Brunner and Barbara Kern, of Jonestown, Pa.) He is a civil engineer and has been busy all his life on canals and railroads in New York, Pennsylvania and Kentucky. He was engaged in United States service in improving the Des Moines rapids in the Mississippi at Keokuk, Iowa, and also the Rock Island rapids. He resides at Mendota, Ill. His wife died March 10, 1861. Ch.: h. Pamelia Livermore, b. Feb. 15, 1827; d., ae. 22, May, 1849, in Kentucky. i. Fidelia Livermore, b. Jan. 17, 1829; m. Robert S. Howard. j. Maria Livermore, b. April 10, 1832; d. June 5, 1832. k. Horace Brunner Livermore, M. D., b. Aug. 23, 1833, a physician at Macomb, Ill. He m., April, 1856, a dau. of Rev. Mr. Hoffman, a Lutheran clergyman at Reading, Pa. He has one child: ix. John Alonzo Livermore, b. July, 1859. l. Alonzo Skiles Livermore, b. in Rumsey, Ky., Aug. 19, 1840; m., Jan. 9, 1865, Lelia Robinson, b. in New Iberia, La. He was at Union college, N. Y., in 1858. He resides in Memphis, Tenn., and was general superintendent of the Mississippi & Tennessee railroad. He has one child: ix. Lelia Livermore, b. Oct. 31, 1865. iix.

Fidelia Livermore, b. Jan. 17, 1829; m., June 2, 1851, Robert Smith Howard (son of Nathaniel Howard, of Kentucky), a corn merchant in New Orleans, La. Has had four children: ix. Eliza Maud Howard, b. in 1853. iix. Clara Amelia Howard, b. in 1855. iiix. Estelle Howard, b. in 1860. ivx. Robert Howard, b. Feb. 28, 1866. 5. Betsey Livermore, b. Aug. 20, 1805; m. Ira Adams; d. Oct. 25, 1852; m., Dec. 7, 1826, Adams was b. Feb. 3, 1803 (son of Nathaniel Adams, of Wilmington, Vt., and Abigail Miller), a farmer at Wilmington and in his later life a tinner. He d. Sept. 19, 1852, aet. 49. Ch.: 1. Susan Miranda Adams, b. Dec. 15, 1827; d. Aug. 7, 1831. 2. Susan Miranda Adams, b. Aug. 16, 1833; d. Dec. 1, 1852. 3. Harriet Pamelia Adams, b. Jan. 28, 1851; d. Oct. 18, 1851. 4. Cynthia Jeanette Adams, b. Nov. 3, 1835; m., Nov. 3, 1853, Daniel Cushman, a farmer in Wilmington, Vt., b. Jan. 3, 1832 (son of Silas Cushman and Cordelia Maria Haskins). She d. Sept. 22, 1860. Two children: i. Gilbert Leslie Cushman, b. Oct., 1856. ii. Florence Maria Cushman, b. Jan. 1, 1859. 6. Semantha Livermore, 2d., b. June 2, 1807; m., March 5, 1854, without issue, James Smith, of Wilmington, Vt., a farmer, b. Oct. 19, 1796 (son of Medad Smith, of Wilmington, and Elizabeth Hale). 7. Edmund Randolph Livermore, b. May 28, 1808; d. Nov. 11, 1831, while a member of Dartmouth college. 8. Pamelia Foster Livermore, b. March 21, 1811; m., May 14, 1850, Ruben Spencer, a farmer, near Mendota, Ill., b. Dec. 26, 1821 (son of Joseph and Huldah Spencer, of Wilmington). 9. Cynthia Livermore, b. March 23, 1813; d. Oct., 1830. 10. Jarius Livermore, b. Feb. 7, 1815; d. Dec. 9, 1862; m., Oct. 5, 1846, Abby Babb, b. Sept. 25, 1826, in Luzerne county, Pa., (dau. of John Babb and Susan Miller). He was a civil engineer in Kentucky, afterward a teacher in DesMoines county, Iowa, (1848-54), and at last a farmer in Onawa, Louisa county, Iowa, (1855-62), when he d. 1862. Ch.: a. Susan A. Livermore, b. June 15, 1848; m., March 7, 1864, Clark Moore, b. in West Virginia in 1844, a farmer in Inland, Cedar county, Iowa. They have a son, Oliver E. Moore. ii. Millard Fillmore Livermore, b. Aug. 27, 1850. iii. Cornelia Livermore, b. June 9, 1852; m., Oct. 17, 1868, William H. Brown, b. Aug. 2, 1846; a farmer in Ringgold county, Iowa. iv. Arthur Livermore, b. Aug 8, 1854. v. Mary L. Livermore, b. in Onawa Iowa, Aug. 4, 1856. vi. Pamelia B. Livermore, b. Aug. 15, 1858. vii. Stella A. Livermore, b. Jan. 4, 1862. 11. Harriett Newell Livermore, b. May 10, 1817; d. Aug. 31, 1838. 12. Henry Dwight Livermore, b. March 7, 1820; m., Feb. 8, 1855, Lydia Walker Corbett, b. July 25, 1821 (dau. of Philip Corbett, of Wilmington, and Eunice Hix), a farmer at Wilmington, Vt. He d. in 1827. His widow resides at Wilmington. They had one child: Cora Jane Livermore, b. Oct. 13, 1857.

990. ii. THEODORE ADELPHIDUS, b. March 22, 1778; m. Julia Green.

991. iii. JEDEDIAH, b. Aug. 5, 1780; m. Tamerson Gilbert.

992. iv. ABIGAIL, b. April 3, 1782; d. unm. May 25, 1803.

993. v. SARAH, b. June 27, 1784; m., in 1802, Daniel Biddecom, of Wilmington, Vt. He lived in Avon, N. Y., where he d. in 1813, leaving five daughters and one son.

994. vi. CLARRISA, b. June 26, 1786; d. April 20, 1848 aet. 62.

995. vii. LYDIA, b. Nov. 2, 1789; d. June, 1790.

996. viii. ELIJAH DWIGHT, b. April 12, 1791; m. Martha G. Lavalley, Mrs. Ruth C. Cody and Mrs. Fanny P. Eames.

997. ix. PEREGRINE PYNCHON, b. May 10, 1793; m. Rebecca Brown and Mrs. Catherine (Clark) Smith.

998. x. SUSAN, b. Sept. 22, 1795; m., Oct. 14, 1816, Jonathan Haskins, Jr., who d. Jan. 22, 1825, at Wilmington, and she m., Feb. 17, 1839, 2d. Dea. Freeman Haskins, of Wilmington. Children by the first marriage: 1. Achsah Ophelia Haskins, b. Dec. 5, 1817; m., in 1844, Chipman Swift Parmelee. 2. Marilla Elvira Haskins, b. March 16, 1620; m., June 16, 1842, Franklin Walker, of Perkins Grove, Ill. 3. William Freeman Haskins, b. May 6, 1822; m.,

Aug. 3, 1843. Lorene Miranda Cushman. 4. Hannah Foster Haskins, b. March 11, 1824; m., March 16, 1842, David Stannard, of Perkins Grove, Ill.

546. HON. DWIGHT FOSTER (Jedediah, Ephraim, Ephraim, Abraham, Reginald), b. Brookfield, Mass., Dec. 7, 1757; m., May 7, 1783, Rebecca Faulkner. She was the eldest daughter of Col. Francis Faulkner, of Acton, a leading citizen there and a good solider in the Revolution. He was descended from Francis, the son of Edmund, one of the first settlers in Andover, founder of the church in 1645. His wife was Dorothy Robinson. Rebecca's two brothers, Luther and William Emerson, graduated at Harvard college. Dwight was born on the old place, was graduated at college of Rhode Island (Brown university), in 1774 (M. A. ad eundem Harvard), taught school in several places, studied law partly with his brother, Theodore, in Providence, R. I., and partly with the celebrated Major Joseph Hawley, at Northampton; began the practice of his profession in Providence, but immediately on the death of his father, Oct. 17, 1779, he removed to Brookfield and was chosen to supply the vacancy from Brookfield in the convention for forming the Constitution of Massachusetts, created by his father's death. He was a lawyer of extensive practice and sustained many offices of trust and honor, having been high sheriff of the county, representative in Congress, senator in Congress from Massachusetts, elector of President, Chief Justice of Court of Common Pleas for the county of Worcester and member of the executive council of Massachusetts. He was a man of very considerable acquaintance, of great dignity and levity of manners and of unbending integrity. Before his death, for several years, he was laid aside from active usefulness by disease. In 1781 he was commissioned justice of the peace for the county of Worcester, Mass., and in 1788 also again, and at the same time one of the quorum. In 1792 he was made special justice of the court of common pleas, and in June, 1792, was appointed sheriff of the county. In November of the same year he was chosen one of the electors of the President and vice-president of the United States. He was afterward a member of Congress for three successive terms 1793-9, and United States Senator, 1800-3, when he resigned. In 1801 he was commissioned chief justice of the court of common pleas for Worcester county, and held the office for ten years. In 1818 he was made a member of the council of Massachusetts. He d. April 23, 1823, aet. 65. "He was a man of large intellectual acquirements, of unbending integrity and suavity of manners, and an influential member of the Congregational Church, in Brookfield. The last six or seven years of his life he spent chiefly in retirement. He had a light complexion and blue eyes." He d. April 23, 1823. Res., Brookfield, Mass.

999. i. PAMELA, b. March 4, 1784; d. unm. Sept. 16, 1807.

1000. ii. ALGERNON SIDNEY, b. Nov. 22, 1785; d. unm. July 25, 1823.

1001. iii. SOPHIA DWIGHT, b. July 30, 1787; m., Nov. 8, 1816, Samuel M. Burnside, of Worcester. Samuel M. Burnside was graduated at Dartmouth in 1805, the son of Thomas, who was born at Northumberland, Coos county, N. H. His early education was in the common schools of a new planted country, except nine months at an academy preparatory to admission to college. After being graduated he passed two years in superintending a female academy at Andover, Mass. In Oct., 1807, he began the study of law in the office of Hon. Artemas Ward, later Chief Justice of the Court of Common Pleas. No one was more able or willing to afford aid to his students. Familiar acquaintance with the principles of the common pleader, with uniform kindness and liberality, justified their affectionate reverence for the character of that able jurist and excellent man. His business was immense. He was, consequently, much from home at this period and his pupils were left to follow principally the dictates of their own judgment in regard to their course of reading. Mr. Burnside was admitted to practice in March, 1810, and was first sworn at the bar of the Supreme Judicial Court upon examination, being one of few persons who have been suffered to pass to that court without having previously been admitted at the lower tribunal. He began business in Westborough in the spring of 1810. In the autumn of that year he removed to Worcester and ever after resided there. Ch.: 1. Sophia Rebecca Burnside, b. about 1823; d. June 1836. 2. Harriet Pamela Burnside, b. in 1827; resides unm. at Worcester. 3. Elizabeth

Dwight Burnside, b. in 1829; resided num. at Worcester, and d. in Feb., 1899. A Worcester, Mass., paper, in referring to her death, said: "She had been ill of the grip for a week, but her friends had not realized the serious nature of her illness, and her death is a great shock to them. Miss Burnside, who was 70 years of age this month, was the younger of the two daughters of Samuel M. Burnside, who, in his day, was one of the foremost lawyers of this city. He married Sophia Dwight Foster, whose father was Dwight Foster, at one time Senator from Massachusetts, and whose mother was a sister of Alfred D. Foster. They had three children, one of whom died in infancy, while Elizabeth and Harriet have lived together until now the death of the younger breaks the companionship. The Misses Burnside have been throughout their lives among the most notable figures in the life of Worcester. Members of an old and distinguished family, possessing wealth and taste, they have had great advantages, of which they have made good use. They have been most unassuming in all that they have done, but those who have been privileged to come in intimate relationship with them know how bountiful has been their life in benefit and pleasure to others. Both have been devoted to books and music and flowers. Their library is one of the best in the city and Miss Elizabeth Burnside read and spoke several languages. They patronized all worthy musical entertainments and enjoyed at their home the performances of many musicians whose personal friends they became. Their gardens have always been among the finest in the city and their house has always been beautified with fragrant blossoms. Their hospitality has been proverbial and their home has always been open to friends. In their girlhood days there were no more brilliant belles in the city, and the elder men remember well what a privilege it once was to dance with Miss Lizzie or Miss Hattie Burnside. All these charming qualities the two sisters possessed in equal degree, but they are recalled with special clearness with relation to the one who has just passed away. Miss Burnside belonged to few organizations and took no prominent part in their management. Her charities were many, but they were bestowed privately, and only those who benefitted can fully realize the largeness of her heart and the extent of her generosity. She attended the First Unitarian church from earliest childhood and attended services whenever she was able. The only near relatives who survive Miss Burnside are her sister, Miss Harriet P. F. Burnside, two cousins living in this city, Mrs. Henry Clark and Mrs. R. P. Dunn, and the children of another cousin, Dwight Foster, of Boston. The property interests of the Misses Burnside were extensive, and these are now all vested in Miss Harriet Burnside. Beside the homestead, there is the Burnside block on Main street, the property at the corner of Main and Exchange streets, some property on Burnside court and more on Central street."

Thomas Burnside, the father, was a descendant of that colony of Scots, settling in the north of Ireland about 1650, many of whom emigrated to New England in 1719. Among them was Rev. James McGregorie, his maternal grandfather, ordained first minister of Londonderry, 1719, who d. March 5, 1720, leaving three sons, one of whom, Alexander, settled in Warwick, R. I. Susannah, only daughter of Alexander on the death of his father, was adopted and educated by her uncle James, himself childless; inherited with her brother his considerable estate and married Thomas Burnside. He was brought up in Londonderry, took an active part in the French wars and was in many bloody battles on the frontier and fought by the side of Wolfe on the plains of Abraham. He d. Nov. 3, 1798.

1002. iv. ALFRED DWIGHT, b. July 26, 1800; m. Lydia Stiles.

547. HON. PEREGRINE FOSTER (Jedediah, Ephraim, Ephraim, Abraham, Reginald), b. Brookfield, Mass., Dec. 28, 1759; m. there, July 10, 1770, Mrs. Polly (Parkman) Bradshaw. He was sergt. in Captain Asa Danforth's co. that marched from Brookfield Sept., 1777, and was in the battle of Saratoga, Oct. 7. He was a man of great energy. She was widow of Rev. Benjamin Bradshaw, a Pres. clergyman; b. at Westboro, Mass., May 18, 1756 (dau. of Ebenezer Parkman, afterward of Brookfield, Mass., and Elizabeth Harrington). He was a Revolutionary soldier and was present at the execution of Major Andre. His reverence for Washington was throughout life tender and strong. He removed May 7, 1782, to Providence, R. I., where he read and practiced law for a few years with his brother, Theodore. In 1786 he joined "The Ohio Company," formed in Massachusetts, under Gen. Rufus Putnam as its leader. The mechanics among them assembled at Danvers, Mass., Jan., 1788, and the surveyors at Hartford, Conn., and numbering 48 in all, set out as an advance party on their long and perilous journey. He was one of the 26 surveyors of the company. A great amount of snow had fallen all over the country during that winter, making their passage over the Alleghanies all the more tedious. But when once, with their teams, accoutrements and supplies, beyond these formidable barriers, they leaped with lion-like energy to their new work. The boat-builders and mechanics were ready with the aid of many other willing workers among the surveyors, by April 2d, to launch the craft which was to carry them all down the Ohio, with their teams and effects. This they called at first Adventure Galley, and afterward The Mayflower. The river was high, and they moved on rapidly to their new home in the wilderness, and about mid-day on April 7, 1788, they disembarked at the mouth of the Muskingum river. Having completed their surveys, and fixed the site of their proposed town, they called it Marietta, in honor of Marie Antoinette, who had recently shown distinguished regard to our new American minister at the Court of Versailles, then young Benjamin Franklin. He returned to his family at Providence, June 10, and finding a little daughter added to it in his absence, named it Betsey Marietta. He was not able to make arrangements to remove with his family at once, and while delaying for that purpose the Indian War broke out, and he did not go to his new western home until 1792. Hearing of many massacres by the Indians in the neighborhood of Marietta he went to Morgantown, W. Va., where he remained for four years, teaching school and engaging in whatever other business he could find. In 1796, when all was quiet on the border, he went with his family to Belpre, O. (beautiful meadow), where his part of the new purchase had been located, just opposite the mouth of the Kanawha river, and a little above the head of Blennerhasset Island. He writes thus about himself in his diary, June 9, 1794: "No acquisition of property knowledge or happiness. Knowledge, indeed I have gained of human nature, but find it worse and worse. Lord! when and where shall we find man virtuous!" Under date of July 10, following, he writes: "Fourteen years this day since I was married. We have probably been as happy, or more so, as couples in general. Take away the evils of life, or those that we call so, and little is left. Sum the hours of real happiness; they are few in number. There is little for which we should wish to live; and yet we are averse to death; more I think from the uncertainty of the future state than from an attachment to this life. At my setting out in life I labored under almost all the inconveniences which could attend a young man. Education I had not, at least a poor one; was too young to take upon me with apparent propriety the management of a family; my partner was, and ever since has remained, feeble, and unable to endure hardships; most of her time has been spent in confinement by sickness; she has brought me five children, who, by the goodness of God, have been as healthy as an equal number in families in general. At the commencement of matrimonial life, at twenty and a half years, all the property we had of any kind would not decently furnish a house. Nothing was apparently before us but extreme poverty; to work I was unable. But by the blessing of Divine Providence I was, and yet am, able with industry to maintain my family decently—enjoying all the blessings of life and many of its superfluities. For some years I lived at an expense of near $1,000 per annum. This, however, was previous to the paper money system in Rhode Island, to which I may attribute all of my misfortunes in a pecuniary point of view, and which ultimately drove me into the western wilderness; where the Lord only knows how it will fare with myself and family. I am in no business; important objections arise against my making application for admission to the practice of the law; to work I am unable (being at times a great sufferer from calculi in the bladder); property in this country I have but little of—nothing to enable me to join to any kind of business to advantage."

Under date of July 14, 1749, he writes: "In consequence of a commission from the governor of Virginia, appointing me a magistrate for the county of Monongalia. I have now three appointments from the governor and General Assembly, not one of which is worth a penny, and as little honor as pay. At the close of the day, at the house of W. M. Healey, the court and gentleman of the bar drank several bowls of toddy."

He resided at Belpre (1796-1804) until his death, Aug. 17, 1804; aet. 44. While in Virginia he was besides being chief magistrate in his county, associate judge also in the Court of Common Pleas, and a representative several times to the State Legislature. He was, when living in Ohio, a judge there also. He was distinguished for the uprightness and honorableness of his conduct at all times, for his great energy and perseverance, and for his fine personal appearance and affable manners. She m. in 1808, for a 3d husband, Major William Browning, a large farmer at Belpre, O., and at one time postmaster there. She was his 2d wife. By his first marriage he had three sons. He d. Sept., 1823, a few days before his wife, who d. Sept. 5, 1823. Res., Brookfield, Mass., and Marietta, O.

1003. i. POLLY PARKMAN, b. at Brookfield, Mass., March 19, 1781; m., May 2, 1802, Dea. William Dana; d. April 28, 1815, aet. 34. He was of Belpre, O., and afterward of Newport, O., where he was a merchant and farmer and large land owner, and in every way a very substantial man. He was b. Aug. 16, 1775, and was son of Capt. William Dana, of Amherst, Mass., and Mary Bancroft. She d. April 28, 1815, aet. 34. He d. June 24, 1851, aet. 75. Ch.: 1. Samuel Dana, b. July 3, 1803; m., Sept. 16, 1828, Louisa Thornly. 2. Elizabeth Harrington Dana, b. Nov. 19, 1804; m. Charles Haskell, and for a 2d husband, Dr. John McCracken. Haskell was a merchant at Newport, O.; b. 1801, son of Major Jonathan Haskell, of Belpre, O., and Phebe Green. He d. July 23, 1831, aet. 30; and she m., Nov. 4, 1834, John McCracken, M. D., b. Feb. 4, 1795; a physician of large practice in Pittsburg, Pa. (originally from county Down, Ireland); grad. at the University of Edinburg, Scotland. He d. March 21, 1859. Ch.: (a) Mary Ann Haskell, b. March 10, 1827; m. Rev. Thomas Johnson. (b) Pamelia Frances Haskell, b. Feb. 2, 1830; m. Dr. Robert T. Johnson. (c) Martha Jane McCracken, b. Aug. 13, 1835; a teacher in Pittsburgh, Pa. (d) William Dane McCracken, b. Sept. 5, 1842; an oil merchant in Cincinnati, O. He enlisted as a Union soldier in the civil war, in the Thirty-sixth Ohio Regt., in Sept., 1862, and was in the battles of Antietam, Md., and South Mountain, and was with General Rosecrans in his campaign in Tennessee. (e) Charles Haskell McCracken, b. Jan. 1, 1849; a clerk in Pittsburgh, Pa. (f) Mary Ann Haskell, b. March 10, 1827; m., July 6, 1848, Rev. Thomas Powell Johnston (Presb.), b. March 15, 1819, son of Thomas Johnston, of Wooster, O., and Abigal Powell; graduated at Jefferson college (Washington, Pa.) in 1845, and at the Western Theol. Sem. in Allegheny City, Pa., in 1848. He was pastor at Clarksville, Pa. (1848-58), at Lima, O. (1858-72), and was settled at Columbia, O., in 1872; but in May, 1873, returned to Lima, where he now resides and preaches a portion of the time at Ottawa, near by. Ch.: i. Mary Emma Johnston, b. Nov. 28, 1849. ii. Charles Haskell Johnston, b. Jan. 21, 1855. iii. Elizabeth Abby Johnston, b. Nov. 24, 1856. iv. Grace Dana Johnston, b. Feb. 27, 1868. (b) Pamelia Frances Haskell, b. Feb. 2, 1830; m., Oct. 24, 1850, Robert Thompson Johnston, M. D., b. Oct. 30, 1822 (son of Thomas Johnston, of Wooster, O., and Abigal Powell). He studied medicine at Willoughby Med. College, O. (1844-5), and since 1845 has been a physician at Bucyrus, O. Ch.: i. Belle Johnston, b. Nov. 10, 1853. ii. Frank Thompson Johnston, b. March 23, 1857. iii. Pamelia Dana Johnston, b. May 3, 1865. 3. Charles Dana, b. March 10, 1807; m., Sept. 1, 1831, Eunice Churchill, b. March 7, 1812 (dau. of Jacob Churchill, of Halifax, Mass., and Abigal Bosworth); a merchant at Newport, O. He d. Nov. 6, 1865. His widow resides still at Newport. Ch.: 1.

Charles Dana, b. June 22, 1832; d. June 23, 1834. 2. Charlotte Dana, b. April 3, 1835; d. Jan. 17, 1853. 3. Rev. Watson Dana, b. Nov. 12, 1837. He went from behind the counter into the pulpit, and took his theological course on horseback. He m., June 15, 1859, Sarah Mary Riley, b. Aug. 4, 1836, dau. of John Dye Riley and Elizabeth Leachman. He was settled at Metamora, O. Ch.: (a) Eva Dana (twin), b. May 2, 1860; d. May 3, 1860. (b) Charlotte Elizabeth Dana (twin), b. May 2, 1860; d. July 15, 1860. (c) John Charles Dana, b. Oct. 8, 1861. (d) Watson Dana, b. April 28, 1864. (e) Joseph McElhinney Dana, b. May 31, 1866. (f) Samuel Foster Dana, b. Aug. 19, 1868. (g) Caroline Bertha Dana, b. Nov. 30, 1870. 4. Amanda Newell Dana, b. Jan. 12, 1841; d. Oct. 29, 1845. 5. Lydia Abigal Dana, b. Jan. 4, 1844; d. Oct. 24, 1845. 6. Fanny Pamelia Dana, b. Oct. 25, 1848. 7. Maria Dana, b. March 8, 1851; m., Oct. 12, 1871, Calvin Thomas Riley, of Metamora, O. 8. William Dana, b. Sept. 14, 1855. 4. Francis Foster Dana, b. Dec. 6, 1809; m. Rev. Israel Archbold. He was b. Harrison county, Va., Nov. 24, 1807 (son of James Archbold, who came from Ireland in Nov., 1787, and m. Ann Kennedy, of Prince George county, Md.); grad. at Marietta college, O., in 1834 a Methodist clergyman, who preached successively in several places within the bounds of "The Pittsburgh Conference," 1834-59, and was an active and efficient minister in them all, at Barnesville, McConnellsville, Summerfield and Newport, O., and Pittsburgh. He d. at Hanover, O., May 18, 1859, aet. 52. His widow resided in Salem, O. Ch.: 1. William Dana Archbold, b. in McConnellsville, O., Aug. 30, 1835; m., June 28, 1857, Martha Hubbard Humason, b. in Twin, N. Y., Jan. 29, 1832 (dau. of Rev. Leonard H. Humarson and Mary Sykes); grad. at Allegheny Coll., Meadville, Pa., in 1856. He was for some time principal of Western Reserve Seminary. Later was a dry goods merchant at Fredonia, N. Y. (since 1866). Ch.: (a) William Edward Archbold, b. June 28, 1858, in Farmington, O.; d. there diphtheria July 18, 1862. (b) Mary Frances Archbold, b. Sept. 14, 1860, in Sharon, Pa.; d. of diphtheria, Aug. 16, 1862, in Farmington. (c) Charles Dana Archbold, b. in Titusville, Aug. 23, 1864. (d) James Humason Archbold, b. Fredonia, Sept. 10, 1866 (e) Julia Archbold, b. in Feb. in Fredonia, Sept. 5, 1868. 2. James Edward Archbold, b. Feb. 6, 1838; d. Feb. 9, 1843. 3. Phebe Maria Archbold, b. Aug. 5, 1840; m. Hon. Lorenzo B. Lockard, Oct. 25, 1859; b. Jan. 2, 1838 (son of William Lockard, of Hanover, O., and Sarah McBride); a merchant in Salem, O., and at one time (1868) mayor of the city. Ch.: (a) Vesta Lockard, b. Sept. 30, 1860. (b) William Lockard, b. Oct. 11, 1862; d. June 28, 1863. (c) Charles Archbold Lockard, b. July 5, 1864. (d) Francis Lockard, b. Aug. 1, 1868. 4. Charles Wesley Archbold, b. Jan. 18, 1843; m., June 20, 1865, Emma Owen Kibbe, b. Nov. 7, 1843 (dau. of Austin Durkee Kibbe, of W. Farmington, O., and Emily Parenthia Owen). He was a machinist at Corry, Pa. Ch.: (a) William Kibbe Archbold, b. at Farmington, June 5, 1866. (b) Emma Frances Archbold, b. at Corry, May 17, 1868. 5. Mary Elizabeth Archbold, b. April 11, 1843; a teacher in Salem, O. 6. John Dustin Archbold, b. July 26, 1848, has been engaged until of late in Titusville, Pa., in the oil business, but was later a petroleum merchant in New York, residing in Brooklyn. He m., Feb. 12, 1870, Anna Eliza Mills, b. Dec. 15, 1847 (dau. of Samuel Myers Mills, of Titusville, and Lavine Jenkins). One daughter: 1. Mary Lovina Archbold, b. Sept. 7, 1877.

1004. ii. SERAPH DWIGHT, b. at Providence, R. I., Nov. 2, 1782; m., June ——, 1805, John Breck, of Caswell, O.; d. July 31, 1806, aet. 23. He was of Boston, Mass.; b. March, 1779 (son of William Breck, b. in 1745; and d. Nov., 1819; a merchant in Boston, and Margaret Thomas, of Plymouth, b. in 1753 and d.

in 1820), a merchant at Caswell, O., in partnership with Frederic A. Foster, his uncle, and afterward, 1808-16, with Peregrine D. Foster, his cousin, son of Frederic A. Foster. She d. July 31, 1806; he d. March, 1816. They had one child: 1. William Foster Breck, b. May 14, 1806; m., Jan. 1, 1840, Elizabeth Cambell Smith, b. Oct. 31, 1820 (dau. of Dea. John Smith, of Worthington, O., and Olive Wilson, of Cooperstown, N. Y.); a merchant at Grove City, O., where he was suddenly killed by slipping off from a load of grain—the wheel running over his neck and breaking it instantly, Aug. 8, 1864, aet. 59. [Dea. John Smith was in early life a farmer, but in his, later years, after giving a large share of his property to the Am. Bible Society and to the A. B. C. F. M., went to Minnesota as a self-sustaining missionary to the Indians. After spending several years in such a way he returned to Worthington, O., to die, 1864, aet. 76. His consort died soon afterward, Aug. 26, 1864. Their son, Rev. Samuel Davis Smith, settled at Deleware, O., was Moderator of the O. S. General Assembly at St. Louis, Mo., in 1866.] Mrs. Breck resides at New Brighton, Pa. Ch.: 1. A child b. in 1840-1, that d. in a few hours. 2. John Breck (twin), b. Aug., 1842; d. in a few weeks. 3. Wm. Breck (twin), b. Aug., 1842; d. in a few weeks. 4. Seraph Wilson Breck, b. Dec. 24, 1844; m. Rev. Samuel A. Hughes. 5. George Foster Breck, b. Aug. 25, 1851. 6. Flora Estella Breck, b. Aug. 26, 1857. 7. Frank F. Breck, b. March 21, 1860. [Grove City, O., near Columbus, O., is a small village, built and improved by Mr. William F. Breck, and principally upon his wife's estate of 600 acres bequeathed to her by her father, upon which he erected a saw-mill in order to convert the large amount of black walnut timber growing upon it to a marketable use.] 4. Seraph Wilson Breck, b. Dec. 24, 1844; m. in 1864, Rev. Samuel Adams Hughes, b. at Freeport, Pa., March 4, 1835; grad. in 1861, at the Theol. Sem. in Allegheny City, Pa.; a Presb. minister in Grove City (1861-3); a chaplain in the United States army of volunteers (1863), and afterward settled at London, Pa., and then at Lawrenceburgh, Pa., 1874. Two children: (a) Ida Sloan Hughes, b. in 1865. (b) Elizabeth Louisa Hughes, b. in 1867.

1005. iii. PEREGRINE PITT, b. at Providence, Oct. 24, 1786; m. Elizabeth Cushing

1006. iv. BETSEY MARIETTA, b. at Providence, June 7, 1788; m., April 12, 1807, Stephen Dana; d. April 9, 1870, aet. 81. Dana b. at Amherst, Mass., Nov. 24, 1779 (son of Capt. William Dana and Mary Bancroft); a man like his brother, Dea. William Dana, of large means and solid worth, at Newport, O., having had 600 acres under high culture. He d. June 6, 1834. She d. April 9, 1870, aet. 81; for 36 years a widow and a faithful, happy and beloved member of the church of Christ. Ch.: 1. Seraph Dwight Dana, b July 29, 1808; m., Nov. 1, 1832, Colbert O'Neal, of Belpre, O., b. Jan. 15, 1805, in Culpepper county, Va. (son of John O'Neal and Judith Suttle; she d. Sept. 13, 1869, aet. 100. Her mental powers were bright to the end. She had been eminent for her piety from early life) He is a prosperous farmer at Belpre, O. Ch.: (a) Foster O'Neal, b. Aug. 5, 1833; m., April 29, 1867, Emily Barrick; large farmer in Belpre, O. (b) Amanda Ann Hazeltine O'Neal, b. in Belpre, Oct. 2, 1835; m., April 24, 1860, Thomas Rowland; farmer; res., Newport, O. (c) Edwin Russell O'Neal, b. Oct. 14, 1839; m., Sept. 17, 1863, Nancy Jane Scott; farmer; res., Belpre, O. 2. Mary Parkman Dana, b. May 23, 1810; m., Jan. 21, 1830, George Compton, b. in Winchester, Va., Aug. 29, 1801 (son of James Compton and Catharine Cunningham); a farmer at Bull Creek, Hood county, Va. Ch.: (a) Thomas Fredric Compton, b. Feb. 15, 1831; d. in Forest City, Col, April 2, 1855. (b) Stephen Dana Compton, b. Feb. 27, 1833; resides in California. (c) James Parkman Compton, b. July 17, 1835; d. Sept. 14, 1838. (d) Luther Barker

Compton, b. Oct. 4, 1837; d. Dec. 21, 1854. (e) William Henry Compton, b. Feb. 29, 1840. (f) Marietta Adela Compton, b. April 27, 1842; d. July 23, 1845. (g) Melissa Jane Compton, b. Aug. 7, 1844; d. Aug. 20, 1845. (h) Helen Mary Compton, b. Nov. 18, 1847; d. of consumption April 14, 1868. (i) Theodore Foster Compton, b. April 27, 1850; d. of consumption Aug. 26, 1872. 3. Amanda Frances Dana, b. Nov. 8, 1812; m., July 23, 1839, Seth B. Newell, and for second husband, Rev. Harvey S. Dale. Newell Jr., b. May 6, 1811 (son of Seth B. Newell, of Bethel, Me., and Betsey Kimball). He began to study for the ministry after having engaged in mercantile life for a short time in Boston, Mass., but was obliged, on account of weak eyes, to intermit his theological studies. In 1838 he established a school at McConnellsville, O., and afterward at Newport, O. He was a man of genial qualities, and of very agreeable address, and an earnest Christian and very useful. He d. at Newport, Jan. 29, 1841. She m., Sept. 12, 1842, Rev. Henry Smith Dale, b. Aug. 13, 1812 (son of Rev. Jeremiah Dale, of Danvers, Mass., b. in 1787, and Mehitabel Smith, of S. Hadley Mass.); grad. at Brown university in 1834, and at the Union Theol. Sem., New York, in 1841; tutor at Granville, Col., O. (1841-2); pastor of the Baptist church at Newport, O. (1842-51); at Lebanon O. (1852-6); and Prof. of Theology at the Farmount Theol. Sem., Cincinnati, O. (1856-7). He d. May 27, 1857, at Cincinnati. He was of a gentle and modest spirit, and earnestly devoted to the ministerial work. [Rev. Jeremiah Dale was the son of Ebenezer Dale Jr., of Davers, Mass., and Abigal Cutler. The parents of Ebenezer Dale Jr., b. Dec. 25, 1755, were Ebenezer Dale and Rebecca Preston, whom he m. Nov. 30, 1754. Ebenezer Dale Sr., b. March 7, 1739, was the son of John and Abigal Dale. Ch.: (a) Edward Richardson Dale, b. in Newport, O., May 31, 1844; m., Sept. 14, 1871, Sarah Vandever Ralston, b. Feb. 19, 1850 (dau. of William Lewis Ralston, of Marietta, O., b. Dec. 10, 1820, and Sarah Catharine Ward, b. March 18, 1819, whom he m. Aug. 31, 1847). He was cashier of the First National Bank at Marietta, O. He was quartermaster-sergeant in the civil war in the Seventy-seventh Ohio Regt. They have one child: i. Catharine Ralston Dale, b. June 27, 1872. (b) Theodore Dana Dale, b. in Newport, O., June 23, 1846. He was secretary and treasurer of the Marietta Iron Works Co., at Marietta. He was grad. at Marietta college in 1868. He m., May 15, 1873, Sophia Byington Dana, b. Jan. 28, 1853 (dau. of George Dana, of Belpre, O., and Lucy Minerva Byington, dau. of Rev. Cyrus Byington, missionary to the Choctaws. George Dana, son of Capt. William Dana and Mary Bancroft). He served in the civil war, in the army of the Potomac, in the One Hundred and Forty-eighth Ohio National Guards. (c) Harvey Ewart Dale, b. Oct. 9, 1848; d. Oct. 29, 1849. (d) Julia Theodosia Dale, b., May 6, 1851; m., Sept. 1812, David Dye Johnson, b. Aug. 18, 1843 (son of William Henry Johnson and Elizabeth Dye); grad. at Marietta Coll. in 1866; a lawyer at Parkersburgh, W. Va. (e) Frances Amanda Dale, b. Aug. 28, 1853. 4. Peregrine Foster Dana, b. June 27, 1815; a farmer since 1858 in Ottumwa, Iowa, and previously in Kirkville, Iowa, and Newport, O. He m., Feb. 9, 1837, Sarah Elizabeth Greene, b. July 24, 1818 (dau. of John Greene of Newport, O., and Mary Hill). She d. March 21, 1857 and he m., Sept. 15, 1857, for his 2d wife Catharine Plummer Tinkman, b. April 28, 1824 (dau. of Cornelius Tinkman, of Plymouth, Mass., and Harriet Plummer, of Marietta, O.). Ch.: 1. Mary Elizabeth Dana, b. March 21, 1838; d. June 10, 1852. 2. Sarah Melissa Dana, b. Feb. 6, 1840; d. April 7, 1857. 3. Capt. Newelle Bannister Dana, b. Feb. 10, 1842; d. April 16, 1870; enlisted in the civil war in company F, Fourth Iowa cavalry, Oct. 17, 1861. He was made corporal Jan. 1, 1862, and first sergeant March 1, 1863. He re-enlisted as a veteran soldier Dec. 12, 1863, at Vicksburg, Miss., and was made captain of his company April 29, 1864, and was mustered out of the service with his regiment at Atlanta, Ga., Aug. 8, 1865. He was in the Fourteen Mile Creek, Miss.; Jackson, Miss., in both May and July, 1863; the siege of Vicksburg, Miss., in June and July, 1863; Canton, Miss., July 17, 1863; of Guntown, Miss., June 10, 1864; of Tupelo, Miss., July 15, 1864; of Independence, Mo., Oct. 22, 1864; of the Big Blue, Mo., Oct. 23, 1864; of Osage, Kans., Oct. 25, 1864; of Ebenezer Ch., Ala., April 1, 1865; of Selma, Ala., April 2, 1865, and Columbus, Ga., April 16, 1865. He was at Macon, Ga., when the news of General Lee's defeat was received, and he participated in the pursuit of Jeff Davis. He traveled in the service over 14,000 miles. He m., Dec. 27, 1867, Mary Rudd, b. March 27, 1846 (dau. of Major Wilcox Rudd, of Wapello county, Iowa, and Rebecca ——). While a member of the Junior class of Iowa university, at Iowa City, he d. at Denver, Col., of consumption, April 16, 1870, aet. 28, being at the time on a tour for health and recreation. He was preparing himself for the ministry, and especially for missionary service in it. He excelled as a student in the languages and in metaphysics, and was also an active and devoted Christian. He had one child: 1. Albert Currier Dana, b. May 3, 1869; d. July 23, 1869. 4. Julia Battelle Dana, b. Feb. 23, 1844; m., Aug. 1, 1866, William Wallace Cole, of Nakaska county, Iowa; a farmer; b. Sept. 17, 1839 (son of William and Elizabeth Cole). One child: 1. Charles Cole, b. April 14, 1868. 5. Daniel Greene Dana, b. Dec. 7, 1845; m., Aug. 3, 1867, Mary Ann Hardesty, of Iowa (dau. of Thomas and Marie Hardesty). He enlisted in the civil war Feb. 13, 1864, in company F, Fourth Iowa cavalry. He has one child: 1. Thomas Peregrine Dana, b. Aug. 20, 1870. 6. John Greene Dana, b. June 2, 1848. 7. Nancy Ann Dana, b. Jan. 8, 1852; d. June 30, 1852. 8. Rufus Peregrine Dana, b. Oct. 18, 1853. 9. Augustus George Dana, b. Jan. 29, 1856; d. April 22, 1857. By second wife: 10. Cornelius William Dana, b. Aug. 31, 1858. 11. Lily Irene Dana, b. Oct. 25, 1859. 12. Corrie Dana, b. April 3, 1861. 13. Hetty Amanda Dana, b. Dec. 8, 1862. 5. William Pitt Dana, b. Aug. 1, 1817; m., April 28, 1841, Susan Edgerton Shipman, b. Dec. 14, 1821 (dau. of William Henry Shipman, b. at Marietta, O., April 14, 1793, and Mary Ann Edgerton, b. at Norwich, Conn., Dec. 15, 1798); a merchant at Marietta, O. She d. Dec 24, 1849, and he m. for his second wife, April 24, 1851, Ann Elizabeth Shipman, b. Sept. 8, 1826, sister to his previous wife. He d. of consumption July 18, 1853, aet. 36. He was a devoted Christian (Baptist). Children by first wife: 1. Mary Elizabeth Dana, b. at Carroll, O., Nov. 21, 1843; m., Nov. 6, 1865, Charles H. Newton; res., Marietta, O. 2 Charles Luther Dana, b. May 26, 1845, at Lancaster, O; m., Nov. 5, 1868, Mary Racer; res., Marietta, O. 3. Anna Maria Dana, b. at Marietta, O., April 19, 1847; m., May 4, 1870, Samuel Dorman Smith (son of Stephen Smith and Susan Racer). One child: 1. Maria Shipman Smith, b. Sept. 19, 1871. 4. Frances Gage Dana, b. May 27, 1848; d. July 3, 1848. 5. William Shipman Dana, b. Dec. 24, 1849; d. Feb. 18, 1850. By second wife: 6. Susan Shipman Dana, b. in Marietta, O., March 23, 1852. 6. Stephen Augustus Dana b. Aug. 27, 1819; m., Oct. 5, 1841, Jane N. Little; res., Newport, O.; b. in Newport, O., April 5, 1822 (dau. of Charles Little and Mary Allison Frazer); a large farmer, at Newport, O. Ch.: 1. Frederic Foster Dana, b. Nov. 30, 1843; a farmer and large land owner at Newport, O.; m., Nov. 19, 1872, Mary Ellen West, b. April 10, 1848, at Moundsville, W. Va. (dau. of Rev. John B West, of Newport, O., and Mary Alexander). He enlisted Aug. 31, 1862, in the Seventh Ohio cavalry, in the first brigade of the second division of the Mississippi, and served until the close of the war. He marched with Sherman to the sea, and was one of the cavalry companies sent to search for Jeff Davis, and was one of the guards appointed to conduct him to Atlanta. He saw much hard service, and was not once "off duty," or in the hospital during his three years' service in the rank and file. Of the 107 in his company that went to war but 31 returned to their homes. ii. Prescott Dana, b. Sept. 26, 1845; d. June 30, 1846. iii. Pamelia Little Dana, b. July 25, 1842; m., Nov. 14, 1865, Albert Wilbur Delancey Kraft, b. Sept. 27, 1838, at Wheeling, Va. (son of John Kraft and Caroline Klevies, b. both of them in Lanfeare, Hanover, Germany, who emigrated to America in 1834); an oil refiner and dealer, at Parkersburg, W. Va., and previously at Pittsburgh, Pa. He enlisted in the First Virginia Regt. of Union Vols. (Col. B. F. Kelly), under the first call for troops April, 1861, for three months, serving after two weeks' time as hospital steward. In Sept., 1861, he reenlisted for the war in the same regiment (Col. Thomas Thornburn), and Nov. 18, 1862, was commissioned assistant surgeon, and served in that capacity to the end of the war, having been educated as a chemist and druggist. Ch.: (a) Frederic Dana Kraft, b. at Newport, Sept., 13, 1866. (b) Homer Livingston Kraft, b. July 29, 1868. (c) Jane Estella Kraft, b. Dec. 14, 1869. 7. Theodore Sedgwick Dana, M. D., b. Oct. 27, 1821; grad. at Marietta coll. in 1843, and studied medicine in Cincinnati. He m. Jane Bartlett, without issue. He d. of consumption Jan. 22, 1850. He was a superior scholar, especially in mathematics and medicine and an earnest, thoughtful, devoted Christian. 8. Luther Dale Dana, b. April 17, 1826; m., Aug. 14, 1848, Nancy Ismond Baldwin, b. Jan. 6, 1826 (dau. of Jesse and Catharine Baldwin, of Gremsby, Upper Canada. She d. Dec. 18, 1851, and he m. for second wife, Jan. 13, 1853, Susan Rebecca Green, b. Oct. 28, 1825 (dau. of Richard Green, b. in Warwick, R. I., April 29, 1781—son of John and Mary Green—and Rebecca Lawton, b. in Portsmouth, R. I., 1791). He is a dealer in hats, caps, furs and furnishing goods, wholesale and retail, at Marietta. (a) Theodore Parkman Dana, b. June 5, 1849; d. Jan. 4, 1850. (b) Laura Marietta Dana, b. Jan. 21, 1851. (c) Ella Maria Dana, b. April 2, 1854; d. Aug. 24, 1854. (d) Harvey Dale Dana, b. July 6, 1857. (e) Luther Green Dana, b. Nov. 15, 1858. (f) Bessie Rebecca Dana, b. Aug. 9, 1860. (g) Arthur Dwight Dana, b. J y 23, 1861. (h) Caroline Melissa Dana, b. Jan. 16, 1863. (i) Mabel Foster Dana, b. Aug. 23, 1865; d. Oct. 22, 1865. 9. Melissa Barker Dana, b. Oct 23, 1829; d. Sept. 13, 1832.

1007. v. FREDERIC AUGUSTUS, b. at Providence, May 7, 1791; m. Sarah Arnold and Elizabeth Wilson.

1008. vi. THEODORE SEDGWICK, b. at Morgantown, Va., Feb. 19, 1795; d. Oct. 17, 1825, aet. 30. He m., in 1822, Jane Barkley, b. in 1791 (dau. of Thomas Barkley and Betsey Kilpatrick), without issue. He was a merchant at Belpre, O. She d. Feb. 10, 1831, aet. 40.

550. WILLIAM FOSTER (John, John, Ephraim, Abraham, Reginald), b. Andover, Mass., Oct. 3, 1743; m., Oct. 4, 1771, Mehitabel Fuller, of Middletown, b. 1743; d. 1830. He d. 1827. Res., Andover, Mass.

1009. i. WILLIAM, b. 1772; m., 1805, Phebe Holt, b. 1771; d. 1844. He d in Andover in 1833. Res., Londonderry, N. H.

1010. ii. JACOB, b. April 27, 1775; m. Ruth Kimball.

1011. iii. ISRAEL, b. ——; m., Oct. 10, 1802, Hannah Lee. Res., Manchester.

1012. iv. JOHN, b. Sept. 8, 1872; m. Lucy Hastings.*

1013. v. SALLY, b. ——.

556. JOHN FOSTER (John, John, Ephraim, Abraham, Reginald), b. Andover, Mass., Oct. 24, 1760; m., March 21, 1782, Dorcas Town, b. March 3, 1758; dau. of Joseph and Sarah; d. Feb. 27, 1838. He d. April 27, 1835. Res., Boxford, Mass.

*Or did John m., Jan., 1814, Mary Harris, and have 3 ch.

1014. i. JOSEPH, b. Aug. 5, 1783; d. at Boxford, unm., 1864.

1015. ii. JEMIMA, b. Dec. 27, 1785; m., Sept. 17, 1807, Emerson Hale, of Rindge, N. H., son of Moses, Jr. He d. June 18, 1852, aet. 68. She d. May 7, 1879. Res., Rindge, N. H. Ch.: 1. John Foster, b. Sept. 26, 1808; m., 1844, Rebecca Barley. He d. July 22, 1881, leaving one child. Martha Foster Hale, his wife, d. March, 1882. Martha F. m., Oct., 1873, George G. Rice. They reside in Rindge. One son, Harris. 2. Harris Hale, b. Aug. 10, 1813; m., July 6, 1869, Eliza Kimball. Resides in Rindge. No children. 3. Ruba, b. Dec. 7, 1815; m., May 9, 1839, Arad Adams, b. in Rindge, April 26, 1812, and d. at East Jaffrey, N. H., July 25, 1877. Their children are: Maria R. Adams, b. June 25, 1840, unm.; Mary E. Adams, b. May 8, 1843; d. Jan. 14, 1856. 4. Moody, b. April 17, 1820; m., June 6, 1844, Charlotte Keyes. She d. Feb. 2, 1847; m. 2d, Sarah E. Wright, of Enosburgh, Vt., who d. June 11, 1859. He d. April 28, 1860. No children. 5. Jemima, b. July 26, 1822; m., Nov., 1865, James Bancroft, who d. March, 1884. No children. She resides in Rindge.

1016. iii. DORCAS, b. July 21, 1791; m., May 29, 1817, Alfred Kimball, son of Daniel Kimball, of Andover, b. in 1791. He d. Sept. 23, 1828. She d. in Salem in 1878. Ch.: 1. Dorcas Foster, b. May 29, 1818. 2. Mary Elizabeth, b. July 30, 1823. 3. Sarah Fuller, b. March 17, 1826. 4. Alfred M., b. March 29, 1828.

1017. iv. JONAS, b. Nov. 15, 1793; m. Mary Apthorp and Lydia B. Messer.

1018. v. MOODY, b. April 29, 1797; m. Mary Symonds.

557. DAVID FOSTER (Stephen, John, Ephraim, Abraham, Reginald), b. Andover, Mass., March 5, 1745; m., Dec. 31, 1767, Ruth Peabody, of Boxford, dau. of John, Daniel, John, Mary (Foster) Peabody, Reginald Foster, b. 1745; d. 1818, He d. 1812. Res., Andover, Mass.

1019. i. DAVID, b.——.

1020. ii. SAMUEL, b.——.

1021. iii. HITTY, b. Aug. 28, 1776; m., 1802, Thomas Stickney, of Bradford. A gr.-son is George Tandy, city clerk, of Freeport, Ill., b. Groveland, Mass., June 23, 1843; unm.

1022. iv. MOSES, b. Aug. 6, 1780; m. Sarah Baldwin.

560. STEPHEN FOSTER (Stephen, John, Ephraim, Abraham, Reginald), b. Andover, Mass., July 3, 1751; m., Aug. 3, 1775, Rebecca Wood, in Bradford. Res., Boxford and Bradford, Mass.

1023. i. STEPHEN, b. ——.

1024. ii. JOHN, b. ——.

1025. iii. SAMUEL, b. ——.

1026. iv. JOSEPH, b. ——.

1027. v. EBENEZER, b. ——; m. Sarah Dane.

1028. vi. PHINEHAS, b. in 1781; m. Sarah Johnson.

564. JOHN FOSTER (Stephen, John, Ephraim, Abraham, Reginald), b. Andover, Mass., Dec. 10, 1759; m., Nov. 25, 1788, Sarah Ingalls, dau. of James and Mary (Frye) Ingalls, of Methuen, b. Oct. 5, 1761. He was in early life a founder, making silver shoe and knee buckles and sleigh bells; in after life a farmer. He d. Nov. 30, 1837. She d. July 23, 1849. Res., Andover.

1029. i. SALLY, b. Aug. 14, 1789; unm.; d. Dec. 4, 1870.

1030. ii. RUBY, b. Oct. 19, 1791; unm.; d. Aug. 5, 1812. The diary of Ruby Foster, published by her pastor, Rev. Dr. Eaton, of Boxford, gives the first record of the life of any woman teacher of the district schools. She writes (1810): "I have left our dear habitation and begun keeping school. Many were the tender emotions excited in my breast, and an undertaking so important and so new to me could not fail of engaging my solicitude and anxiety. God bless me in my school. Give my scholars hearts to obey and improve and myself redoubled activity, strength and wisdom."—Hist. Andover.

1031. iii. LUCY, b. Nov. 21, 1793; m., Oct. 30, 1827, Amos Kimball.

1032. iv. HANNAH, b. Dec. 22, 1795; unm.; d. March 4, 1863.
1033. v. STEPHEN, b. Feb. 15, 1798; m. Ann A. D. Davis.
1034. vi. ISAAC, b. July 7, 1806; m. Francis B. Lee.

565. NATHAN FOSTER (Stephen, John, Ephraim, Abraham, Reginald), b. No. Andover, Mass., Nov. 23, 1761; m., March 16, 1790, Susanna Barker, b. 1771; d. Feb. 10, 1842. He d. July 12, 1844. Res., Andover, Mass.

1035. i. SUSANNA, b. April 4, 1791; m., 1827, Amos Kimball, of Boxford; d. July 4, 1838.
1036. ii. SAMUEL, b. May 10, 1794; d. Jan. 14, 1812.
1037. iii. ABIGAIL, b. July 28, 1796; m., Nov. 11, 1819, Reuben Reed, of Salem.
1038. iv. NATHAN, b. Sept. 4, 1798; m. Harriet Berry.
1039. v. SALLY, b. Oct. 14, 1800; m., May 11, 1818, Silas Burnham, of Norwich, Conn.
1040. vi. REBECCA, b. Aug. 9, 1804; m., April 27, 1826, Jacob Farnham.
1041. vii. MARY BRIDGES, b. Aug. 19, 1807; m., Dec. 30, 1830, Enoch Frye, Jr., b. No. Andover, Mass., March 21, 1798; d. Sept. 26, 1883. She d. Sept. 13, 1867. He was a farmer. Res., No. Andover, Mass. Ch.: 1. Enoch Holten, b. Sept. 24, 1831; d. Oct. 12, 1834. 2. John Frye, b. May 4, 1833; d. July 18, 1853. 3. Susan Foster, b. March 16, 1835; m., Sept. 14, 1858, Rev. James M. Bell, Leominster, Mass. He was b. Feb. 25, 1833. Ch.: (a) John Frye, b. Oct. 4, 1859; d. Aug. 4, 1874. (b) Harry James, b. Aug. 19, 1861; m., Oct. 11, 1882. Res., Leominster, Mass. (c) Grace Lillian, b. Dec. 14, 1863; m., Sept. 22, 1886; d. Feb. 14, 1894. (d) Mary Gertrude, b. Nov. 30, 1869; m., Sept. 18, 1889; d. Aug. 6, 1890. (e) Hattie Florence, b. April 1, 1872; d. Dec. 11, 1876. (f) Enoch Frye, b. May 26, 1874. Res., Leominster, Mass. (g) Sidney Eugene, b. Feb. 13, 1879; Res., Leominster, Mass. Rev. James M. Bell graduated from New York university 1854; was in Andover theological seminary 1854-57; ordained and installed July 21, 1858. Pastorates: Ashby, Mass., '58-'64; Watertown, Mass., '65-'71; North Hadley, Mass., '72-'76; West Medway, Mass., '76-'86; Wayland, Mass., '86-'88; Lisbon, N. H., '88-'93; North Leominster, Mass., '93—. Was chosen principal of South grammar school, Watertown, Mass., 1872; invited to membership in faculty of Thayer college, Kidder county, Mo., 1876; trustee of Watertown free library, 1868 1869; author of public memorials of Captain Henry Bangs, 1861; Mrs. Caroline S. Wright, 1864; Mrs. M. F. Grant, 1867; John Frye Bell, 1874; Psi Upsilon class poet, 1854; former correspondent of Newbury Gazette, N. Y.; candidate for Massachusetts legislature, 1871; delegate to National Tri-ennial Council, St. Louis, 1880. Chairman of three different school boards. 4. Mary Elizabeth, b. Dec. 18, 1838; d. Oct. 11, 1840. 5. Harriet Abbie, b. Feb. 19, 1844; m. ——. Address, Mrs. Edward C. Fisher, Andover, Mass.
1042. viii. ELIZABETH BARKER, b. Dec. 10, 1792; m., Oct. 31, 1815, Francis W. Ingalls. Res., North Andover, and she d. Dec. 10, 1872. He was b. Aug. 18, 1793; d. Nov. 9, 1850. Was a farmer. Ch.: 1. George Francis, b. March 4, 1818; d. Feb. 24, 1879. 2. Charles Nathan, b. July 9, 1820; d. Aug. 9, 1886. 3 Hiram Augustus, b Aug. 10, 1822; d. Feb. 17, 1824 4. Sarah Foster, b. March 28, 1824; d. Aug. 1, 1857. 5. John Edward, b. April 29, 1826; d. ——. 6. Henry Franklin, b. April 19, 1830; d. Sept. 29, 1834. 7. Stephen William, b. Jan. 1, 1833; d. ——. (2) Charles N. was m. in Dec., 1845. Address of child Mrs. G. W. Fielding, No. 15 Putnam street, Somerville, Mass. (4) Sarah F., m. Oct., 1845. There were no children; her husband still lives. Address: Charles F. Johnston, North Andover, Mass. (5) John E., m. July, 1850, Mrs. O. N. Foster, North Andover. (7) Stephen W., m., Nov. 28, 1860, Sarah G. Gordhus, b. June 16, 1833. Res., North Andover, Mass. Ch: (a) Charles Johnson Ingalls, b. Oct. 19, 1862; d. Aug. 26, 1865. (b) Lizzie Frances Ingalls, b. Sept. 4, 1865; m. to William H. Lewis, June 27, 1896. Res., North

Andover. (c) Ida Bertha Ingalls, b. Aug. 11. 1867; m. to Oliver S. Hutchinson, June 27, 1838. Res., Burton avenue, Beverly, Mass. (d) Sarah Johnson Ingalls, b. May 23, 1871.] [Res., North Andover.

566. DANIEL FOSTER (Stephen, John, Ephraim, Abraham, Reginald), b. Andover, Mass., April 26, 1765; m. there Oct. 20, 1797, Hannah Swan; d. May 1, 1824. He d. Jan. 3, 1821. Res., Andover, Mass.

1043. i. DANIEL, b. June 26, 1800.
1044. ii. JOHN, b. Sept. 8, 1813.
1045. iii. HANNAH, b. Oct. 28, 1805.
1046. iv. ABIGAIL, b. ——, 1798.

572. FREDERICK FOSTER (Asa, Moses, Ephraim, Abraham, Reginald), b. Pembroke, N. H., Aug. 23, 1760; m., Sept. 6, 1785, Mary Eastman, b. Londonderry, N. H., March 6, 1765; d. Dec. 31, 1836, at Grand Menan, N. B. He d. Jan. 12, 1834. He resided in Pembroke, N. H.; was a soldier in the Revolutionary War; was a tavern keeper and mill owner and owned considerable real estate, but sold out and went to Grand Menan, New Brunswick, shortly after 1800. There he bought again, but subsequently lost all. Res., Pembroke, N. H., and Grand Menan, N. B.

1047. i. BETSEY GAINES, b. April 22, 1787; d. unm. at Rockport, Me.
1048. ii. SUSAN FREDERICK, b. Dec. 3, 1804; m., Aug. 21, 1834, Benjamin Varney Sumner. He was b. Dec. 17, 1804; d. Rockport, Me., Aug. 10, 1869. She d., Boston, May 16, 1893. Ch.: 1. Charlotte M., b. April 22, 1845; m., Oct. 30, 1870, Alfonso Crosby, b. Albion, Me., May 26, 1845. Ch.: (a) Charles Dane, b. April 3, 1873. (b) May Louise, b. Oct. 30, 1871. (c) Belle Martin, b. Nov. 12, 1876. (d) Henry Edwin, b. Jan. 29, 1880; all of 472 Quincy street, Dorchester.
1049. iii. ASA, b. Oct. 11. 1789; m. Mary Kent.
1050. iv. MARY EASTMAN, b. Sept. 15, 1791; d. unm. in Rockport, Me.
1051. v. RICHARD EASTMAN, b. Feb. 15, 1795; m. Nancy M. Luce.
1052. vi. LYDIA MERRILL, b. at Grand Manan, Jan. 27, 1802; m. Hugh McKay, of St. Stephens, N. B., d. at Calais, Me. Ch.: 1. Mary Elizabeth, m., Oct. 25, 1855, Melville Sumner. 2. John, m. Ann ———; lives at Camden, Me. Has dau., Mary.
1053. vii. SUSAN FREDERICKA, b. at St. Stephens, N. B., Dec. 3, 1804; d. at Boston, May 16, 1893; m. Benjamin Varney Sumner, at Calais, Me., Aug. 21, 1834. Children b. at Camden, Me.: 1. Melville, b. Nov. 9, 1835; m., at Rockport, Me., Oct. 25, 1855, Mary Elizabeth, dau. of Hugh McKay. 2. Aubine, b. Feb. 8, 1838. 3. Castlebrook, b. March 31, 1840; m. Harriet Gilkey, Oct. 12, 1862. 4. John Frederick, b. Aug. 3, 1842; m. at Damariscotta, Me., May 4, 1870, Mary Louise, dau. of Henry Wright. 5. Charlotte Marie, b. April 22. 1845; m. at Rockport, Me., Oct. 31, 1870, Alphonsa C. Pray, of Boston. Res., Dorchester, Mass. Benjamin Varney Sumner was b. at Boston Dec. 17, 1804, and was son of John Gabriel and Elizabeth (Moore) Sumner. Lived at Goldsboro, Me., and at Rockport, Me., where he died, Aug. 10, 1869.

578. CAPT. ENOCH FOSTER (Ephraim, Moses, Ephraim, Abraham, Reginald) b. April 27, 1770, Bow, N. H.; m. in Peacham, Oct., 1793, Polly Guy, b. May 10, 1776, of Peacham; d. Walden, Jan. 7, 1809; m., 2d March 10, 1810, Mrs. Susannah (Mudgett) Gould, wid. of Edward, b. Nov. 7, 1771; d. Dec. 15, 1832. He d. March 30, 1854. "Captain Enoch Foster, born at Bow, N. H., where he lived until thirteen years of age, at which time he removed with his parents to Peacham, Vt., where he lived until the year 1800, when he removed to Walden, Vt. Much of his early manhood was spent in the forest. He was often employed as a guide by the early settlers to conduct them to different parts of the country. Previous to 1854 Captain Foster and Indian Joe accompanied an official surveying party into northern Maine, acting as guides. Captain Foster was a man of stern integrity and possessed great energy, which, together, made him a friend of all. Many are the strangers who remember his generous hospitality. He was a member of the Congregational church for forty years, and died as he had lived, a zealous Christian."—Old Vermont Gazeteer. Res., Peacham and Walden, Vt.

1054 i. MERRILL, b. Feb. 10, 1795; m. Sally Gould.
1055. ii. PARLEY, b. Oct. 28, 1800; m. Nancy Bean.
1056. iii. MARTHA, b. Aug. 29, 1802; m., June 17, 1839, John Currier. She d. May 4, 1852. Ch.: 1. Ellen, b. ——; m. P. H. Hinckley, of Montpelier, Vt.
1057. iv. EPHRAIM, b. April 25, 1805; m. Emily Perkins and Maria S. Lowell.
1058. v. POLLY, b. April 27, 1808; she d. Nov. 1, 1843, s. p.
1059. vi. HANNAH, b. Oct. 13, 1811; m. S. Montgomery, b. Walden, Vt., Oct. 8, 1809; d. there Dec., 1888. She d. Oct. 17, 1839; m. 2d, Caroline Foster. He was a farmer. Ch.: 1. Giles F., b. ——; m., Sept., 1863, Emily R. Redington. They were missionaries in India. He d. in Adana, Turkey, Dec., 1863. She d. Beyrout, Syria, Feb. 19, 1898. Ch.: 1. Marshall F., b. ——. Res., Huron, So. Dak. 2. Marshall, b. March 26, 1839; m., Aug. 25, 1873, Flora Sibley, b. Nov. 28, 1839. He is a lawyer and was in the civil war for five years. Res., St. Johnsbury, Vt. Ch.: 1. Grace E., b. Dec. 19, 1879.

579. EPHRAIM FOSTER (Ephraim, Moses, Ephraim, Abraham, Reginald), b. in ———, 1767, m. Peacham, 1792, Jerusha Miner, b. April 16, 1771; d. March 23, 1813; m. 2d, Sarah Herrick. He d. Sept. 12, 1843. Res., Peacham, Vt.
1060. i. PRUDENCE, b. July 20, 1793; m. ——.
1061. ii. SYLVIA, b. Aug. 20, 1795; m., March 18, 1813, Henry Blake, of Pa. He was b. April 14, 1791, in Hopkinton, N. H.; d. June 4, 1871. She d. June 4, 1871. Was a farmer. Ch.: 1. Franklin, b. Feb. 6, 1815; m., 1897. 2. Sylvia A.; m. Edmund H. Dewey. Res., Canon City, Colo. He was b. Jan. 14, 1840; d. s. p, Aug. 5, 1885. Graduate Union College in 1858. Was a lawyer. 3. Henry, b. Feb. 3, 1817; m., Nov. 27, 1839, Rosanna P. Phillips, b. April 10, 1817. Res., East Hardwick, Vt. Ch.: (a) S. Florence Field, b. March 1, 1842, East Hardwick, Vt.; m. March 28, 1864. (b) Mary Joyse Blake, b. Aug. 24, 1848; unm. Res., East Hardwick, Vt.
1062. iii. FLORILLA, b. Feb. 6, 1798; m., May 15, 1823, Russell Clark, of P. He was b. Haverhill, N. H., April 10, 1795; d. in Peacham, Vt. in Aug., 1867. Was a farmer. She d. Jan. 7, 1832. Ch.: 1. Sarah Jerusha Clark, b. April 6, 1824, in Peacham; d. June 23, 1853; unm. 2. Elizabeth (Clark) Strobridge, Peacham, Vt., b. Feb. 1, 1826; m., May 4, 1848, LaFayette Strobridge. 3. Ephraim Wisson Clark, b. Feb. 9, 1828; m. Claripa Johnson, Jan. 22, 1857. She was b. Nov. 7, 1833. He is a farmer. Res., East Peacham, Vt. Ch.: (a) Dr. Edward Russell Clark, b. Dec. 3, 1851, Hastleton, Vt. (b) Jesse Merrill Clark, b. May 8, 1859, East Peacham, Vt. (c) Florella Foster Clark, b. Nov. 9, 1860, Plainfield, N. J. (d) Martha J. (Clark) Pedley, b. Sept. 11, 1862, Nugatu, Japan. (e) Mary C. (Clark) Gibson, b. Oct. 12, 1864, East Ryegate, Vt. (f) Charles Allen Clark, b. Oct. 6, 1866, Lynn, Mass. (g) Ephraim Wesson Clark, b. July 18, 1869, East Boston, Mass. (h) Elizabeth Clark, b. Feb. 27, 1872, East Peacham, Vt. (i) Joseph Leonard Clark, b. Oct. 9, 1873, Colorado Springs, Colo.
1063. iv. JOHN, b. Sept. 14, 1802; m. Luda Stuart.
1064. v. HIRAM, b. Dec. 9, 1805; m. Louisa A. Hale.
1065. vi. DANIEL, b. May 24, 1820; m. Mary Carpenter.
1066. vii. EPHRAIM, b. ——. He d. in St. Louis, Mo.
1067. viii. FRANKLIN, b. 1809; m. Eliza Blanchard and Jane Walker.

587. ABNER FOSTER (Elijah, Aaron, Ephraim, Abraham, Reginald), b. Bolton, Mass., Sept. 18, 1770; m. Judith Wetherby, b. 1771. She d. Dec. 23, 1818. He d. 1852. Res., Templeton and Phillipston, Mass.
1068. i. MARY, b. ——.
1069. ii. ELIZA, b. ——; m. Joshua French.
1070. iii. JOHN W., b. April 15, 1798; m. Dorinda Goddard.
1071. iv. SARAH, b. ——.
1072. v. LEVINA, b. ——.

1073. vi. ELIJAH CHESTER, b.——.
1074. vii. HEPZIBAH, b. ——.
1075. viii. ABNER N., b. ——.

588. ISRAEL FOSTER, (Elijah, Aaron, Ephraim, Abraham, Reginald), b. Bolton, Mass., Dec. 26, 1752; m. Susanna. Res., Bolton, Mass., and ——.

1076. i. TIMOTHY, b. Jan. 30, 1776.
1077. ii. LUCRETIA, b. March 9, 1777.

591. JEDEDIAH FOSTER (Elijah, Aaron, Ephraim, Abraham, Reginald). b. Bolton, Mass., April 30, 1772; m., June 8, 1807, Lydia Brigham, dau. of Alpheus and Lydia (Green),* b. Jaffrey, N. H., April 12, 17—. M. 2d, Linda Demary, b. Feb. 7, 1797; d. Aug. 24, 1869. He d. Troy, N. H., May 17, 1863; aet. 82. (?) Res., Jaffrey, N. H.

1078. vi. MARY JANE, b. May 29, 1830; m., Sept. 27, 1853, Charles Persons. He was b. Smithfield, R. I., March 5, 1825. Is a carpenter and builder. Res., Wakefield, Mass. Ch.: 1. Charles Frederick, b. Feb. 27, 1856, Boston, Mass.: d. May 23, 1862, Ohio, Herkimer county, N. Y. 2. Edward E. A., b. March 25, 1860; unm. Res., Wakefield, Mass. 3. Willard Ellsworth and (4) Willie Elmer (twins), b. June 17, 1862, town of Ohio, Herkimer county, N. Y. Willie Elmer d. Aug. 24, 1889; Willard Ellsworth d. Jan. 23, 1892. No marriages.
1079. viii. JONAS R., b. May 26, 1842. Res., 14 Victoria street, West Somerville, Mass.
1080. i. ALPHEUS, b. Dec. 13, 1809; d. Jan. 13, 1818.
1081. ii. ROXANNA, b. Aug. 8, 1810.
1082. iii. SOPHRONIA, b. July 11, 1816.
1083. iv LINDA SOPHIA, b. Feb. 18, 1826; d. 1897.
1084. v. HARRIET ELIZABETH, b. Apr. 27, 1828; d. Dec. 5, 1895.
1085. vii. EDWARD G., b. Oct. 22, 1833; m. Louisa A. Alexander.

601. ABIJAH FOSTER (Abraham, Abraham, Abraham, Abraham, Reginald), b. Topsfield, Mass., Sept. 12, 1762; m. in Keene, N. H., Feb. 16, 1797, Artemiria Blake, b. 1766; d. in 1837. He came from Salem, Mass., it is said and married a Miss Blake in Keene. He was b. Sept. 12, 1762, and was a merchant in Keene. He d. April 2, 1822. Res., Keene, N. H.

1086. i. ABIGAIL, b. Aug. 14, 1799; m. in Keene, Otis Bardwell, b. Deerfield, Mass., 1792; d. Walpole, N. H. She d. March 27, 1871 Ch.: 1. Mary Ann Foster Bardwell, m., 1847, E. Foster Cook; d. April 21, 1891, Rutland, Vt. 2. Sarah Bellows Bardwell, m. H. H. Eaton; d. Feb. 21, 1896, Decorah, Iowa. Ch.: (a) Mary Foster Cook. 3. Harriet O., b. Walpole, N. H., 1829; unm. Res., 26 Washington street, Rutland, Vt.
1087. ii. GEORGE A., b. Jan. 14, 1796.
1088. iii. MARY, b. Sept. 2, 1800.
1089. iv. ARTEMISIA, b. June 30, 1802; m., in Keene, N. H., John Leonard. Res., Orwell, Vt. She d. March 9, 1866. He d. in Orwell. He was a merchant, mill owner and farmer. Ch.: 1. John Wright Leonard, b. Nov. 2, 1826. 2. Charles Rich Leonard, b. Sept. 3, ——. 3. Lucius Artemisia Leonard, b. March 17, 1834. 4. Ernum Cullender Leonard, b. Dec. 3, 1841; m., March 7, 1867, Henry Rich, b. Sept. 23, 1838. He is a woolen manufacturer. Res., Baraboo, Wis. Ch.: (a) Robert Balfour Rich, Baraboo, Wis.; b. April 3, 1878. (b) Helen Teresa Rich, b. March 3, 1880; d. Dec. 2, 1880. Res., E. F. Hasty, 46 Sycamore street, Detroit, Mich.
1090. v. HARRIET, b. June 12, 1806; m., Milliken.——. Res., Clarendon, N. Y. A dau. is Mary Cook, of Canandaigua, N. Y.

---

*Alpheus Brigham, of Shrewsbury, and Lydia Green (b. Dec. 25, 1740), of Westboro, were m. in Jan., 1764. He was b. Shrewsbury April 30, 1746, and was son of Captain Asa, of Shrewsbury and gr. son of David, of Westboro, who was b. in Marlboro, April 12,1678, son of Thomas, Jr., and Mary (Rice). Thomas, Sr., came from London to America in the "Susan and Ellyn" in 1635.—[See Hists. Marlboro, Westboro and Shrewsbury.]

606. ALLEN FOSTER (Thomas, Abraham, Abraham, Abraham, Reginald), b. Ipswich, Mass., April 24, 1751; m. there Lucy Potter. He d. 1835. Res., Ipswich, Mass.

1091-2. i. SIMON, b. March 15, 1793; m. Mary Perkins and Eunice Perkins.
1092-2. ii. JOHN, b. ——.
1093-2. iii. MEHITABEL, b. ——; m. —— Noyes.

610. DANIEL FOSTER (Thomas, Abraham, Abraham, Abraham, Reginald), b. March 12, 1762, Ipswich, Mass.; m., Dec. 18, 1783, Dorothy Pingree, b. June 4, 1762; d. May 15, 1834, in Newburyport, Mass. Daniel fought in the Revolution; was in Lafayette's select batallion, and was presented by Lafayette with a sword as a mark of esteem. He held many offices in Newburyport; naval offices, etc., and seems to have been a cultured and respected gentleman. He d. Aug. 29, 1833. Res., Rowley and Newburyport, Mass.

1091. i. NATHANIEL, b. Feb. 28, 1797; m. Fanny B. Brockway.
1092. ii. DANIEL, b. ——; m. Charry Fuller.
1093. iii. SOLOMON, b. ——. Res., Pottsville, Pa
1094. iv. JESSE, b. ——; m. Ann E. Toppan.
1095. v. THOMAS, b. ——.
1096. vi. LOUISA, b. ——; d. unm.
1097. vii. MELICENT, b. ——; d. unm.

611. ASA FOSTER (Nathan, Nathan, Abraham, Abraham, Reginald), b. Warren, Mass., May 17, 1764; m. March 12, 1787, Elizabeth Thomas, b. April 15, 1769; d. Jan. 28, 1803. This part of Mr. Asa Foster's second will may be of interest. After providing for his four children. "I also give and bequeath unto my friends and neighbors, the inhabitants of the town of Rowe, from whom I have received many civilities, the sum of two hundred dollars, to be under the care of the selectmen of said town and to be kept upon interest forever for the particular benefit of schooling in said town. Said sum of two hundred dollars to be paid out of my personal property on obligations by my executors within one year after my decease. This gratuity is not a sudden emotion but has for a long time been contemplated, and all the returns and respect I wish for is the good advice which many may find leisure to give to my orphan children with a particular regard for their interests and happiness in this and a future world." He d. Aug. 19, 1803. Res., Rowe, Mass.

1098. i. ASA LANSFORD, b. Aug. 19, 1798; m., Louisa T. Chapman.
1099. ii. ELIZABETH, b. Feb. 8, 1796; m., Sept. 17, 1818, Major Samuel Horton Reed. She d. at R. Feb. 25, 1823. He was b. Petersham, Mass., Oct. 27 1794; d. Greenfield, Mass., July 14, 1874. Was High Sheriff of Franklin county for twenty years. 1. William, b. June 20, 1819; d. Nov. 16, 1874. 2. Elizabeth Foster, b. Aug. 2, 1821; d. Aug. 13, 1839. She was m. to Dr. Edward Marshall Wheeler. (a) Edward Reed Wheeler, b. at Paxton, Mass., Aug. 1, 1839. Received the degree of M. D. from the Bellevue Hospital Medical College in 1864; served three years as surgeon in the late Rebellion. Married, 1st, Anna E. M. Field (dau. of Walter and Mary Holton Field, June 24, 1865); she was born Aug. 2, 1838; d. Sept. 6, 1873. He m., 2d, Amelia R. Roeder (dau. of John Roeder, Nov. 24, 1874); she was b. July 16, 1840. Ch.: (b) Helen R., b. July 25, 1879; d. April 4, 1881. Children of Dr. Edward R. Wheeler and Anna Field Wheeler: (a) Walter Frisbie Wheeler, b. June 23, 1867; a graduate of the University of Pennsylvania; D. D. S. 1888. (b) Elizabeth Anna Wheeler, b. Jan. 20, 1873; m., June 30, 1896, Dr. Frank A. Hubbard, of Taunton, Mass. Ch.: (c) Eloise Barrett Hubbard, b. Dec. 29, 1897. Children of Dr. E. R. Wheeler and Amelia Roeder Wheeler: (d) Henry Hamilton Wheeler, b. Jan. 6, 1881. (e) Foster Reed Wheeler, b. May 5, 1882. William Reed, m. Elizabeth Kent Sayre, of Mauch Chunk, Pa., Sept. 17, 1846. She was b. Sept. 17, 1826; d. Jan. 15, 1853. Ch.: (a) William Reed, b. July, 1847; d. 1848. (b) Elizabeth Kent Reed, b. Jan. 7, 1849; (c) Samuel A. Reed, b. Aug. 1, 1850, unm. (d) Henry Lyman Reed, b. Sept. 5,

1851. Elizabeth Kent Reed, m. at Bethlehem, Pa., Harvey Sheldon Kitchel, Nov. 17, 1870. He was b. at Thomaston, Conn., Aug. 12, 1839. Resides at South Bethlehem, Pa. Ch.: (a) Robert Reed Kitchel, b. Sept. 9, 1871. (b) Anna Sheldon Kitchel, b. Aug. 23. 1873. (c) Harvey Dennison Kitchel, b. Oct. 10, 1877; d. April 2, 1878. (d) William Sayre Kitchell, b. March 4, 1879; d. May 26, 1896. (e) Harriet Tyrrell Kitchel, b. April 16, 1883. (f) Margaret Sheaffe Kitchel, b. Oct. 28, 1885. (g) Gladys Kitchel, b. Nov. 9, 1888; d. Jan. 28, 1890; resides South Bethlehem, Pa. Henry Lyman Reed, m. Lizzie S. McLean, Oct. 14, 1875; resides Montclair, N. J. One daughter: (a) Jennie Reed, b. Sept. 5, 1876; m. Louis Claude Evans, Oct. 23, 1895.

1100. iii. HANNAH, b. Jan. 15, 1801; m., May 3, 1825, Major Samuel Horton Reed. She d. Jan. 27, 1872. Ch.: 1. Samuel Reed, M. D., b. at Rowe, Mass., Jan. 31, 1826; d. Dec. 13, 1849, on his return from California. 2. Susan Willard Reed, b. at Rowe, Mass., May 28, 1828; d. Oct. 4, 1853, at Greenfield, Mass. 3 Henry Augustus Reed, b. at Rowe, Mass., June 9, 1832; d. Aug. 23, 1869, at Greenfield. 4. Hannah Flint Reed, b. at Rowe, Mass., June 7, 1838; d. Dec. 9, 1894. 5. Catharine Foster Reed, b. Jan. 22, 1841; resides at Greenfield, Mass.

1101. iv. JUSTUS, b. Feb. 10, 1794; d. March 16, 1795.

1102. v. THOMAS CONKEY, b. April 23, 1788; m., Nov., 1824, Charlotte Murdock, of Roxbury, Mass.; d. Aug. 12, 1830, s. p.

1103. vi. ASA, b. Aug. 4, 1791; d. Feb. 10, 1795.

612. REV. JOEL FOSTER (Nathan, Nathan, Abraham, Abraham, Reginald), b. April 8, 1755, Warren, Mass.; m., July 1, 1779, Priscilla Foster, dau. of Rev. Isaac, and sister of Rev. Emerson Foster, of Greenport, L. I., b. Aug. 23, 1756; d. Feb. 5, 1803; m., 2d, Sept. 26, 1803, Mrs. Mary Winship. She d. Nov. 1, 1833. He was b. in Western, now Warren, Mass.; fitted for college; entered Dartmouth, and was graduated in 1777. He was settled at New Salem, Mass., in 1779, and remained until 1802, when he was dismissed on account of the charges against his orthodoxy. In 1803 he was settled in East Sudbury (Wayland), and d. there. I have the following from "History of Churches and Ministers of Franklin County, Mass.," 1854 (at Antiquarian Library, Worcester, Mass.): "Rev. Joel Foster, second pastor of First Cong. Church, New Salem, Mass., settled June 9, 1779." I find among the Greenfield, Mass., deeds a Joel Foster, of New Salem, a clergyman bought land there of Daniel Giles, Oct. 27, 1794. Joel, of East Sudbury, will, date Sept. 18, 1812. Prob. Dec. 8, 1812; wife, Mary; ch.; son-in-law, Rev. Ezekiel L. Bascom, Sophia Huntington, Joel, Nathan L. [brother, Rev. John Foster, of Brighton]. He d. Sept. 24, 1812. Res., New Salem and East Sudbury, Mass.

1104. i. NATHAN LANSFORD, b. Dec. 8, 1787; m. Azubah L. Cone.

1105. ii. JOEL THEODORE, b. Dec. 9, 1785; m. ——; d. Dec. 13, 1813, in Burlington, Vt., and buried with military honors in Presbyterian church-yard.

1106. iii. SOPHIA AMANDA, b. Dec. 5, 1780; m., Oct. 21, 1798, John Huntington; res., Rowe, Mass. Had two daughters. She d. June 13, 1822. Ch.: 1. Fanny Caroline, b. Oct. 22, 1799; d. Oct. 1, 1801. 2. Alonzo Bascom, b. Nov. 3, 1801; m. ——; d. in Hartford. 3. John Edwin, b. April 4, 1805; d. May 12, 1805. 4. John Edwin, 2d, b. June 10, 1806; d. Dec. 16, 1813. 5. Joel Foster, b. Aug. 16, 1809; d. Aug. 16, 1809. 6. Sophia Caroline, b. Nov. 13, 1813; d. March 4, 1815. 7. Mary Foster, b. Feb. 13, 1816; d. Jan. 29, 1831. 8. Lucy Metcalf, b. July 27, 1819; d. Aug. 4, 1819. 9. Fanny Almeda, b. Sept. 4, 1820; d. July 31, 1837. John Huntington d. May 20, 1857, in Sunderland, Mass.

1107. iv. PRISCILLA ELVIRA, b. March 23, 1782; m., Sept. 24, 1800, Rev. Ezekiel L. Bascom. She d. April 6, 1801, at Northampton; buried at New Salem, Mass. The following are the notes I made in the New Salem cemetery:

"For other nymphs let vernal roses bloom,
Mine be the peaceful mansions of the tomb."

Priscilla Elvira Bascom, consort of Rev. Ezekiel L. Bascom,

of Gerry,* and daughter of Rev. Joel Foster, of New Salem, died at Northampton, April 6, 1801 (?), aet. 19.

"Peace to thy dust, dear friend, farewell,
Till sounds for me the village bell.
Oft as I tread this hallowed ground
My tears shall on thy grave be found."

1108. v. FANNY ALMEDA, b. Dec. 2, 1783; m., May 26, 1805, Samuel Elliott, Esq., of Brattleboro, Vt. She d. July 26, 1806, leaving Edwin Day, b. March 11, 1806; m. Jeanette ——; res., Providence, R.I. The father m. 2d, a dau. of Rutherford Hayes. He was b. Gloucester, Mass., Aug. 16, 1777; d. W. Brattleboro, Dec. 10, 1845. He was the first lawyer in B.; was postmaster for many years; was Judge of Probate, Representative in the Legislature. Several of his sons, by his second marriage, graduated at college.

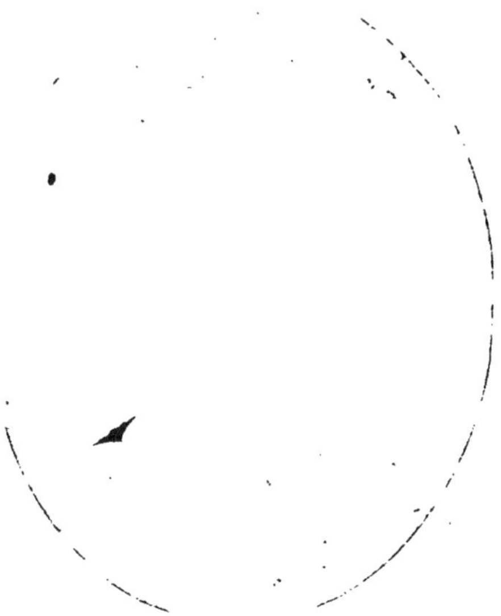

MRS. FANNY A. ELLIOTT.

613. REV. JOHN FOSTER, D.D., (Nathan, Nathan, Abraham, Abraham, Reginald), b. Warren, Mass., April 19, 1763; m. in Boston, April ——, 1785, Hannah Von Webster, b. ——, 1759; d. June, ——, 1840. She was aunt of Professor Webster.

He d. Sept. 15, 1829. Res., Brighton, Mass.

Rev. John Foster, of Brighton, delivered the Artillery election sermon of 1809. He was born in Western, now Warren, Mass., April 19, 1763, and graduated at Dartmouth college in 1783. He married in April, 1785, Hannah Webster, of Boston. Allibone, in his "Dictionary of Authors," mentions Mrs. Foster as having written "The Coquette; or, The History of Eliza Wharton," one of the earliest American novels. A church was organized Feb. 27, 1783, by the people living within the district now called Brighton. About thirty persons withdrew from the churches in Cambridge and Newton to form the First Church in Brighton. Rev. Mr. Foster was the first pastor of this newly-organized church, and was ordained to the christian ministry and installed as pastor November 1, 1784. He was one of the Board of Overseers of Harvard university; a member of various literary, benevolent and religious societies, and published between twenty and thirty of his sermons. Dr. Holmes, in the "Atlantic Monthly," when he portrays a few of the early ministers of the association with which his father was connected, and whom he met in his youth, says: "Following in the train, mild-eyed John Foster, D. D., of Brighton, with the lambent aurora of a smile about his pleasant mouth, which not even the Sabbath could subdue to the true Levitical aspect." Rev. Mr. Foster resigned Oct. 31, 1827, having completed the forty-third year of his ministry. He died at Brighton, Sept. 15, 1829, aged 66 years.

Hannah Foster, author, d. in Montreal, Canada. She was a daughter of Grant Webster, of Boston, and married John Foster, a minister, in Brighton, Mass., from 1784 till 1827. Mrs. Foster published "The Coquette; or, The History of Eliza Wharton," founded on fact (new ed., with a preface by Mrs. Jane E. Locke, 1855); "The Boarding-school" (1796), and "Lessons of a Preceptress" (1798).

*Now Phillipston, Mass.

1109. i. WAINWRIGHT, b. Feb. 4, 1786; d. ——.
1110. ii. JOHN, b. April 22, 1789. Res., Boston.
1111. iii. HANNAH WHITE, b. Dec. 22, 1790; m. —— Barrett; res., Montreal, Canada.
1112. iv. HENRY, b. May 31, 1793.
1113. v. ELIZABETH LANESFORD, b. Oct. 19, 1794; m. ——; res., Montreal, Canada.
1114. vi. HARRIET VAUGHN, b. Sept. 9, 1796; m. —— Cheney; res., Montreal, Canada.

614. DEA. NATHAN FOSTER (Nathan, Nathan, Abraham, Abraham, Reginald), b. Stafford, Conn., July 5, 1753; m., Oct. 21, 1773, Abigail Seeley, b. Oct. 2, 1756. He d. ——. Res., Preston and Warren, Mass.; moved to Rowe and to New York.

1115. i. TRYPHENA, b. ——; m. Ray ——, res., Norwich, N. Y.
1116. ii. REBECCA, b. ——, m Abner Chapin; res., Norwich.
1117. iii. ABIGAIL, b. ——; m. Dr. John Page; res., New Salem, Mass. John Page and Abigail Foster Page's children, as far as I found, were: 1. Joel F. Page, New Salem. 2. Priscilla Elvira Page Horton, New Salem. She had two boys, Wesley and Holly. Her husband died March, 1847. 3. Asabel Page. 4. Phebe Page Hastings (wife of Considu Hastings). Phebe had a daughter, Ophelia (wife of Colonel Andrews); New Salem. 5. Sophia Clarissa Page Hill, New Salem, Mass.
1118. iv. SOPHIA b. ——; m. Loveland Paddock; res.. Norwich N. Y. Some of the sons reside in Watertown. N. Y.
1119. v. ELIZA, b. ——; m. ——. Res., Norwich.
1120. vi. CLARISSA, b. ——; d. ——.
1121. vii. ANNA, b. ——; m. ——. Res., Norwich.
1122. viii. NATHAN, b. ——. Res., Watertown, N. Y
1123. ix. JUDE, b. ——.

615. CORP. JUDE FOSTER (Nathan, Nathan, Abraham, Abraham, Reginald), b. Warren, Mass., m. ——, Sarah Goodnough, of Princeton; and 2d after her death, Lydia M. ——. He served in the Revolutionary army; just when, the pension rolls don't say; was a corporal; granted a pension March 4, and died in 24 days. See Rev. Soldiers.

The Worcester County Probate records have this: "Joel Foster, of New Salem, was appointed administrator of Jude Foster, late of Paxton, in 1789. The children were: Sally, Polly, Betsey, Lydia and Judith. The widow was Lydia M. Joseph Dow was Judge." He d. March 28, 1789. Res., Rutland, Mass.

1124. i. POLLY, b.——; m. ——. She d. New York State.
1125. ii. BETSEY, b ——; m. —— Whitmore; res., Hartford, N. Y.
1126. iii. JUDITH, b.——. Res., N. Y.
1127. iv. SALLY, b. ——.
1128. v. LYDIA, b. ——.

620. HON. LAFAYETTE SABINE FOSTER (Daniel, Nathan, Abraham, Abraham, Reginald), b. Franklin, Conn., Nov. 22, 1806; m., Oct. 2, 1837, Joanna Boylston Lanman, dau. of Hon. James L., b. March 29, 1808; d. April 11, 1859. M. 2d, Oct. 4, 1860, Martha Prince Lyman. Lafayette Sabine Foster, born in Franklin, New London county, Conn., Nov. 22, 1806; married, Oct. 2, 1837, to Joanna Boylston Lanman, daughter of Hon. James Lanman, of Norwich, a judge of the Supreme Court of Connecticut and a senator of the United States; married October 4, 1860, for his second wife, Martha Prince Lyman, daughter of Hon. Jonathan Huntington Lyman, of Northampton, Mass. (see "Lyman Family," by Lyman Colman); died at Norwich, Conn., September 19, 1880. Children by first marriage, two daughters and a son, all of whom died in early childhood; by second marriage, no issue.

In a sketch of the life of one who has worthily attained high public distinction, particularly where that distinction is due to an unusual development of the noblest moral and intellectual faculties, it is but fitting that a few words should be said about his parents.

Capt. Daniel Foster, his father, was the son of Hannah Standish, a great-granddaughter of Capt. Myles Standish. He served under Gen. Gates in the War of the Revolution, and fought in the battles of White Plains, Saratoga and Stillwater. In

HON. LAFAYETTE SABINE FOSTER.

1802, at the age of forty-seven, he married, for his second wife, Welthea Ladd, of Franklin, where he made his home and where the subject of this sketch was born. He died January 28, 1824. His stirring patriotism and the stories of the war, which formed the earliest recollections of his son, probably had much to do in establishing indelibly that love of and pride in his native land which was so manifest in Mr. Foster's after-life.

Welthea Ladd, his mother, was connected by lineage with some of the principal colonial families of Eastern Connecticut. She was a woman of unusual energy, shrewdness, intellectual ability and conversational power; and it has been said by those who knew both mother and son, that there was a strong resemblance between them in intellectual traits. It is certain that he cherished the most tender, practical affection for her, and that, from his earliest years, when his earnings were but meager, to the day of her death, in 1851, his care for her and for his only sister was unceasing.

Mr. Foster's only inheritance from his parents was an honored name and an unstained character. He had to depend upon his own resources to gain an education, which in his childhood was begun in the common schools. At the age of sixteen he studied for nine months under Rev. Abel Flint, D. D., of Hartford, and during the two following winters taught school in his native town. In 1824 he completed his preparatory studies with Rev. Cornelius B. Everest, of Windham, and in February, 1825, entered Brown university, where he was graduated in September, 1828, with the highest honors of his class.

The following winter Mr. Foster taught as an assistant in the school of Mr. Roswell C. Smith, in Providence, and the next spring began the study of law at Norwich, Conn., in the office of Calvin Goddard, one of the leading lawyers of the State. In the autumn of 1829 he took charge of an academy at Centreville, Md; and during the year spent at that place was admitted to the Maryland bar. Then, returning to Norwich, he resumed his law studies under Judge Goddard. In 1831 he was admitted to the bar of New London county and immediately opened an office for practice in Norwich town—the old town some three miles north of Norwich proper. In 1833, at the solicitation of friends, he moved to Hampton, in Windham county, where he practiced for about a year, when he returned to the city of Norwich, which became his home for life and where he was active in his profession up to the time of his death.

Mr. Foster's deep interest in political questions led him to undertake, in 1835, the editorship of the "Norwich Republican," a Whig journal, but he was compelled to abandon that work after about a year by the rapid increase of his professional responsibilities. From the outset of his career he was very successful as a lawyer, rising with rapidity to a foremost position at the bar of his State, his mind being peculiarly analytical, his arguments clear, earnest and persuasive and his zeal untiring.

Despite his lucrative practice Mr. Foster was persuaded to enter politics, and, in the spring of 1839, was chosen a representative in the general assembly of Connecticut. This honor was repeated in 1840, 1846, 1847 1848, 1854, and again in 1870; after he had retired from the Senate of the United States and during the last four terms of his membership of the assembly he was Speaker of that body.

In 1850 and 1851 Mr. Foster was the candidate of the Whig party for governor of Connecticut. In both these years there was no choice by popular vote, a majority, not a plurality, being required by the State law, and the general assembly elected a democratic governor, although, in the latter year there was a small Whig majority in the assembly, and, there being a split in the party ranks, Mr. Foster's opponent, Hon. Thomas H. Seymour, was elected by the close vote of 122 to 121. Later in the same session an attempt was made to elect a United States senator, but again the Whigs could not unite on a candidate, and, although Mr. Foster, whose name was mentioned for that office as early as 1848, received within six ballots of the requisite number, no election was possible, and, the assembly adjourning without action, the next House, being Democratic, sent the Hon. Isaac Toucey to the senate.

The year 1851, however, was not without its successes. Mr. Foster was given the honorary degree of LL. D by Brown university, and chosen mayor of Norwich, to which office he was re-elected in 1852 by the absolutely unanimous vote of his fellow citizens—no ballot being cast against him, a well-merited and unusual compliment and especially gratifying, coming as it did from those who knew him best.

On the 19th of May, 1854, Mr. Foster was elected to the United States Senate, where he took his seat on the 4th of March, 1855, and served his State and country with honor and distinction for twelve years. His election for a third term was generally expected by the people of his State, but he did not receive the nomination of his party caucus. This was due to two causes, the first and real reason was a prejudice on the part of many people in the State against electing a United States senator to a third term; no one had ever been so elected and only six had been elected to a second term. The other cause was an erroneous impression industriously circulated that Mr. Foster was too friendly to Andrew Johnson, then President. That this impression was erroneous is very largely shown by the fact that although Mr. Foster's name was prominently mentioned in connection with the Austrian mission, then vacant, President Johnson did not nominate him for that post. The President may have thought that such a nomination would have been only too gratifying to the Senate, with which he was not on cordial or even friendly terms.

Mr. Foster's views regarding President Johnson were briefly stated to the writer of this article when he said that while he did not agree with him he did not think that he had been guilty of any act worthy of impeachment—or words to that effect. It is quite possible that Mr. Foster might have been elected to a third term in the United States Senate had he consented to run independently, as he was urged to do, but he refused absolutely to do so.

To enter into the details of Mr. Foster's senatorial career—1855 to 1867—would be almost like giving the political history of the causes that led up to the war of the Rebellion, and of the Rebellion itself, so closely was he identified with the legislation of those times. As early as 1854, in his inaugural address as speaker of the Connecticut legislature, he said "Our domestic policy on such a question as now agitates our country, is liberty—liberty and right, not slavery and might." In that he struck the key-note of his own being, for with him always, in all matters that came before him, the instant question for instant decision, was as to what was right, and his action, in following the right, was inflexible.

During the earlier portion of his senatorial career Mr. Foster was not a frequent participator in debate; but, on the 25th of June, 1856, he established for himself a high position as a debater, and a man of deep, calm, sound, dispassionate, judicial reasoning power. Matters pertinent to the Kansas and Nebraska bill were under discussion, and then, as also two years later, in connection with the Lecompton Constitution Bill, Mr. Foster most manfully opposed every measure tending to admit slavery north of 36° 30′ of latitude, as limited by the "Missouri Compromise."

As in this matter, so in all the acrimonious debates of ante-bellum days Mr. Foster maintained a firm and consistent position, ever opposing the aggressions of the pro-slavery element in the Senate, and upholding what he believed to be right in morals, politics and law.

The election of Mr. Lincoln having brought matters to a crisis, President Buchanan, in his message to Congress in December, 1860, referred to "the distracted condition of the country and the grievances between the slaveholding and the non-slaveholding States," and Mr. Powell, of Kentucky, introduced a resolution for the appointment of a committee of thirteen to consider this matter. Mr. Foster supported this resolution in the interest of harmony, although, as he said in one of his letters, "Disruption of the Union is, I believe, inevitable. . . . it will lead to war and bloodshed and I depricate it. Still, I am opposed to having slavery established or recognized by the constitution of the country beyond the limits assigned to it, be the consequences what they may," etc.

Probably no man in the Senate enjoyed more intimately the confidence of President Lincoln than did Mr. Foster. Often he was the spokesman of Mr. Lincoln's views.

On March 11, 1861, when Senator Wigfall, of Texas, declared in debate that he was "a foreigner and owed no allegiance to the government," Mr. Foster rose in his seat and moved Mr. Wigfall's expulsion, and his name was dropped from the rolls of the Senate.

In 1863 he advocated the compensated emancipation of slaves in Missouri.

In 1864 he advocated the repeal of the Fugitive Slave Act, but favored an amendment preserving the old act of 1793, by which the reclamation of the fugitive was hedged about with every publicity and form of law. This could only be applicable to fugitives from States not in rebellion, since all others had been emancipated on January 1, 1863 by Mr. Lincoln's proclamation, and was advocated as being but strict justice to the slaveholding States that remained in the Union, however at variance with the popular feeling at the North at that time.

In 1866 he opposed granting the right of franchise to negroes in the District of Columbia, simply because there was no educational qualification connected with it.

Mr. Foster aided in every manner possible the vigorous prosecution of the war. He advocated the increasing of the medical department of the volunteer service. He opposed the abandonment of the military academy at West Point. He was always most discriminating in his opinions, and some of his actions were therefore misconstrued in the excitement of the times though they had been upheld by the calmer judgment of later years.

He served on numerous committees, notably Indian Affair, Land Claims, and as chairman of those on Foreign Relations and Pensions.

On the 3d of March, 1865, he was made one of a special committee "to inquire into the present condition of the Indian tribes," etc., etc. He had frequently been called to the chair of the Senate, and on the 6th of March was chosen president pro tem. of the Senate. Upon the assassination of Mr. Lincoln, on the 14th of the following month, he became ex-officio vice-president of the United States, which position he held until he resigned it, on March 2, 1867, on account of the approaching expiration of his term as senator. There probably never was a better presiding officer in the Senate of the United States or in any other legislative body, as is shown by the very eulogistic resolution of thanks adopted upon his retirement. That he did not very seriously feel his defeat for a third term, is evidenced by his letter to a friend, in which he says: "The loss of my election did not seriously affect my digestion, or my sleep, and will not, I fancy, affect the crops."

The Special Indian Committee, of which he was a member, made an extended journey under a suitable military escort through Kansas, New Mexico and Colorado. Everywhere it was received with the greatest enthusiasm, and upon Mr. Foster, as acting vice-president of the United States, was bestowed the utmost respect and veneration by the thousands who flocked to see him and shake hands with him—the greatest "Father" they had ever beheld. He enjoyed the trip immensely and was unbounded in his enthusiasm at the beauty and magnificence of the country.

Upon Mr. Foster's retirement from the United States Senate in 1867 he at once returned to Norwich and resumed the practice of his profession, of which he was very fond, as is seen by his own words: "The position (United States senator) is a pleasant one, certainly quite the most so of any in our Government. Yet, for myself, I confess I prize professional honors—those of my own profession—more than any political distinction. Professional honors are not won without deserving them. Political preferment may be gained without merit and lost without crime."

While speaker of the assembly in 1870, Mr. Foster was chosen by that body associate justice of the Supreme court of the State, receiving every senatorial vote and 197 out of 202 votes in the House. He held this office with distinction until 1876, when, having reached the age of seventy, he was compelled to retire by statutory limitation.

In 1869 he had been urged to accept the Kent professorship of law at Yale, but had declined doing so. After his retirement from the bench, however, he consented to become a special lecturer there on "Parliamentary Law and Methods of Legislation," and in the anniversary exercises of 1879 delivered an exhaustive address on the duties of an advocate where he knows of the guilt of his client. He said: "It is the province and duty of an advocate to interpose all legal defenses for the benefit and protection of his client, and to see to it that no grounds are taken against him, but such as are warranted by law. This being done, whether the accused be acquitted or convicted, the duty of the advocate is done."

Mr. Foster's political experiences after his retirement from the United States Senate serve to show how entirely he was animated by the sense of duty. He did not believe in the wisdom of the "carpet-bag" form of government at the South, or in the financial policy of the administration, and, in 1872, supported Horace Greeley for President although he did not wholly represent his opinions. In 1875 he reluctantly accepted a democratic and liberal-republican nomination for Congress, although there was no hope for his election in his strong republican district.

Although Mr. Foster's life was so largely occupied with political and professional duties, he found time to serve on numerous boards and commissions. At one time he was a commissioner from Connecticut to settle the disputed boundary question with New York; at another to negotiate the purchase of Fisher's Island; at another to consider the feasibility of simplifying the system of legal procedure in the courts of the State. He was a member of the International Code Conference of America; of the Social Science Association; president of the New London County Historical

Society; honorary member of the Cobden Club of London, although a protectionist; Vice-President of the Congregational Union, and of the American Bible Society; a delegate of the Evangelical Alliance of the United States to Basle, Switzerland; president of the Conn. Congregational Club, etc.

Although Mr. Foster's public life was full of interest it was perhaps in his private life that he was seen at the best by his intimate associates. He was a man of the keenest, most sparkling wit of brilliant conversational power, of serious and yet playful mood, most courteous, polished and gentlemanly manner, always considerate of others, refined and never boisterous, abounding at times with supressed mirth and beaming over with light rippling laughter that was scarcely audible. He was always most differential to women, charitable to the poor, suitably familiar with all of whatever station in life, and interested in everything tending to the improvement of those about him.

Mr. Foster was married twice, and probably the greatest grief of his life was in the loss of his loved ones. The first Mrs. Foster was the daughter of a prominent Norwich family, and became the mother of three children all of whom died at an early age. The second Mrs. Foster, to whom he was married in 1860, shared with him the excitements and interests of the greater part of his public career, and has given to the world in a most interesting volume, a memorial of her husband, which, however, necessarily incomplete, has been largely used in compiling this sketch, and of which Phillips Brooks said: "It ought to be in every Young Men's Library in the land." With her he enjoyed such leisure as he was able to snatch from a life filled with political and professional obligations. Their chief pleasures were in the summers spent at their beautiful home in Norwich, where to this day, 1899, Mrs. Foster still resides, and in later years, in trips to the south in the winter. Despite his fondness for travel his visits to Europe were necessarily few and very short. He first crossed the ocean in 1846, before the days of steam, in the packet ship "Henry Clay," although he was able to stay away from home only a few weeks. His later trips were almost equally brief and did not occur until after he had retired from the United States Senate. From a financial point of view his public life was a detriment to him, as is usually the case with men of the highest integrity and closest application to duty. Whatever money he possessed was made in the practice of his profession, and very much the larger part of his fortune was acquired after he had retired from the Supreme bench at the age of seventy.

Besides the likeness published with this article, which is from a photograph taken from life, there is a fine marble bust of Mr. Foster, made by C. Calverley, in the Capitol at Washington, and an equally fine oil painting of him, by Mr. Lazarus of New York, in the Corcoran gallery at Washington.

Mr. Foster died on Sunday, September 19th, 1880, at his home in Norwich. On the Monday previous he was taken ill with a light malarial fever which gave those about him little anxiety until Friday afternoon when he was seized with a conjestive chill which was instantly followed by delirium and unconsciousness from which he never rallied. He lies buried at Norwich, in beautiful Yantic Cemetery, on the banks of the river of the same name.

The love which Mr. Foster bore for education and whatever tended to the betterment of mankind, found expression, not only during his life time but after his death, in munificent bequests to Yale college for the endowment of a professorship of common law, and to the Norwich Free Academy of which he had long been a trustee.

Rather than to enter further into a description of those traits which made Mr. Foster's life remarkable, it is well to quote briefly from what has been said of him by eminent men who knew him well:

"He obeyed the dictates of his conscience rather than the dictates of party or policy . . . . Because he did this, all men whose admiration is worth gaining shall bend in respectful, grateful homage to his memory."—"Norwich Star," Sept. 20, 1880.

"Mr. Foster had great breadth of mental vision. He was of a judicial cast of mind naturally. He never took partial or narrow views of things. This was true not only of his admirable service on the bench, but of his career as a senator and as an individual; and without doubt this trait had much to do with the reliance which Abraham Lincoln—noble, temperate, humane Lincoln—placed on him as a counsellor amid the perplexities and awful responsibilities of the war. Mr. Foster could not be partisan; neither could Mr. Lincoln."—"Norwich Bulletin," Sept. 24, 1880.

"Judge Foster is most remarkable for his verbal memory. It exceeds that of any one else I have ever known. He is always ready with the happiest of quotations from classical writers and poets, both in English and Latin."—Mr. John Hooker, Court reporter during Mr. Foster's judgeship.

"As a scholar, a lawyer and a statesman Mr. Foster ranked among the most distinguished members of the Senate; and the record that he made during the twelve years that he was a member of that body is one of which the State that honored him by placing him there may well be proud."—Col. John T. Wait.

"To his great learning, legal, scientific and literary, he added those accomplishments of mind and manner that fitted him to shine in private life, as well as at the bar, on the rostrum and in the halls of Congress. In his death he has bequeathed to all the living a notable, pure and Christian example, commanding universal respect, admiration and emulation."—Hon. John D. Park, Chief Justice of Conn.

"His style of speaking is classic and severe, distinguished by power of argument, appositeness of illustration, and close logical demonstration. Having a fine command of the purest English, and a knowledge of its weight and value seldom attained, he is enabled to make his argumentative efforts the more effective from the precision and perspicuity with which they are rendered. This makes him powerful in arguing intricate points of law before a court. When addressing a jury he manages to fix the attention of the jurors at the outset, before going into the merits of the case, and steadily retains it unbroken to the end."

"He possesses the highest power of wit, together with a keen sense of the ridiculous, and his retorts on occasions suitable for displaying those powers are unanswerable. No matter how trifling the amount or how uncertain the prospect of remunerat on for his services, he worked just as hard and with the same zeal as though the case involved large interests and abundant reward."—Sketches of Eminent Americans, 1852.

"So modest and unobtrusive was he in all his actions, so devoid was he of every thing in the nature of self-ostentation, that society in a measure failed, while he lived, to recognize as it should the daily beauty of his life."—Hon. David A. Wells.

"Few men of his age have kept so freshly the warm feelings of youth, or been so fully in sympathy with the changes of modern thought, and whatever belongs to genuine reform."—Prof. Simeon E. Baldwin.

"Among the men whom I have known in public and in private life, there is no one left for whom I had a higher regard or warmer respect."—Hon. Robert C. Winthrop.

"From my earliest recollection he has been a representative man, not only in Norwich, but in Connecticut, and before the entire nation; and throughout a long, unsullied political career he has been an example of enlightened, independent and patriotic statesmanship."—Pres. Daniel C. Gilman, of Johns Hopkins University.

"As a senator he was among the foremost when there were giants in that chamber. He was a trusted counsellor of Lincoln, and respected and beloved by his associates. As a judge, he was conscientious, dignified, learned, and impartial. As a lawyer, he was unsurpassed. He had every qualification needed to maintain a position in the front rank, whether as an advocate before the jury or the judges. In learning, eloquence, pathos, wit, argument, sarcasm, and tact—all brought to contribute toward the highest success in the noblest of professions—he was *facile princeps*."—Hon. Augustus Brandegee.

"When visitors from the Old World have come to see me, I have taken pride in pointing to the late acting Vice-President of the United States, taking his modest place and work on an equality with all the rest of us, as a noble and characteristic example of what is best in American republicanism."—Leonard Woolsey Bacon.

Considerable has been written in relation to the ancestry of Hon. Lafayette S. Foster, but until now I have not seen anything in print that has been authentic. I copy the following from his letters dated Norwich, Conn., Oct. 12, 1874: "Your father was the grandson of Nathan Foster, Nathan Foster was the eldest brother of Daniel Foster, my father. Their father's name was Nathan, and his wife, their mother, was Hannah Standish. She was the granddaughter or great-granddaughter of Myles Standish, I am not certain which. Her father, Josiah Standish, was living at Stafford, in this State, as early as 1720. His son-in-law, Nathan Foster, was also living there at the same time and he remained there till his death, which took place soon after 1750. They emigrated from Massachusetts, from Duxbury or Ipswich I believe, whether they came to Stafford together or not, I do not know. Nathan Foster, the elder, my grandfather, your great-great-grandfather, had eleven children, four sons and seven daughters. Nathan, the eldest son, was your great-grandfather; Daniel, one of the younger children, was my father. The other sons were Asa and Standish; the sisters were

Mary, Mehitabel, Sarah, Eunice, Lois, Hannah and Phebe. They were all married. Lois married a Palmer." Joanna Boylston Lanman was b. March 29, 1808, dau. of Hon. James Lanman of Norwich, Conn., and his wife Marion (Chandler). Joanna's father was graduated at Yale in 1778; was a lawyer; was member of the convention that formed the first constitution of Connecticut; was for two years a representative and for several years a senator in the Connecticut legislature; was for five years attorney for the State for New London county; was senator in Congress 1819-1825; was judge of the Supreme Court of Connecticut for three years, also mayor of Norwich for three years. Pet. to dispose of personal property, dated July 24, 1882. Frank Johnson app. by court at Norwich, Conn., Exec. of est. of Lafayette S. Foster, of Norwich, Conn. Suff. Co., Mass., Prob. Lib., 343, Fol. 532.. He d. Sept. 19, 1880. Res. Norwich, Conn.

1129. i. ALFRED STANDISH, b. 1840; d. Oct. 22, 1841; aet. 19 months.
1130. ii. JOANNA LANMAN, b. Oct., 1841; d. Nov. 24, 1844.
1131. iii. MARY CHANDLER, b. April, 1845; d. July 12, 1846, aet. 15 months.

625. FLINT ROYAL FOSTER (Daniel, Nathan, Abraham, Abraham, Reginald), b. Canterbury, Conn., Feb. 14, 1772; m., Norwich, Conn., Sally Howlett. She d. Morgan, Vt., aet. 61. He d. in 1813. Res., Morgan, Orleans county, Vt.

1132. i. DANIEL G., b. ——. He d. s. p.
1133. ii. PLINEY P., b. Oct. 10, 1801; m. Eliza Willard.
1134. iii. MARY, b. ——; m. —— Guilbert, son of Oram; res., Chicago.
1135. iv. NANCY, b. ——; m. —— Saunders, son of Oril; res., Rochester, N. H.

628. REV. FESTUS FOSTER (Standish, Nathan, Abraham, Abraham, Reginald), b. Canterbury, Conn., Sept. 30, 1776; m., Greenfield, Nov. 25, 1802, Patience Wells, b. ——, 1779; d. Brimfield, Mass., Nov. 20, 1819; m. 2d, Oct. 23, 1823, Mrs. Elizabeth, of Boston, who d. s. p.

Rev. Festus Foster, son of Standish Foster, sixth in lineal descent from Myles Standish, was born in Canterbury, Conn., Sept. 30, 1776. He remained on his father's farm till the age of eighteen years. His family about that time removing to Rowe, Mass. He was there prepared for college under the tuition of Rev. Preserved Smith, the minister of that town, and was graduated from Williams college in the year 1800. After leaving college he took charge of a Grammar school in Pittsfield, meanwhile entering on studies preparatory for the ministry, under the direction of Rev. Dr. Lathrop, of Springfield. He was ordained in Petersham, Mass., Jan. 13, 1802. In 1818 he removed to Brimfield, Mass., where he settled upon a farm, and spent his remaining days there. Mr. Foster represented the town two terms in the State Legislature, commanding attention on all occasions, and proved himself an influential and useful member of that body. He was a man of brilliant attainments. There was a quickness of wit, and a general freshness and raciness in his conversation, which made his talk peculiarly spirited and attractive. He left various published writings, chiefly sermons, and occasional addresses.—Extract from Hist. Brimfield, Mass.

He d. April 30, 1846. Res., Petersham and Brimfield, Mass.

1136. i. JOHN WELLS, b. March 4, 1815; m. Lydia L. Converse.
1137. ii. MARY WELLS, b. March 26, 1804; d. unm., Jan. 1, 1883.
1138. iii. DWIGHT, b. Aug. 14, 1806; d. unm.
1139. iv. CAROLINE, b. Feb. 1, 1809; d. unm.
1140. v. FISHER AMES, b. July 4, 1811; d. unm., March —, 1883.
1141. vi. FRANCIS FESTUS, b. March 24, 1818; d. unm.

630. REV. DAN. FOSTER, A. M. (Isaac, Daniel, Abraham, Abraham, Reginald), b. in 1748; m. ——, Rebecca Bogge. He received the degree of A. M. from Yale college and Dartmouth college, 1774. He did not graduate from any college. Had an excellent education; studied Divinity with his father; settled in Poquonock, Windsor, in 1771. He was dismissed because he preached Universalism—like his father. Removed to Vermont; later to N. H., and died in Charleston, N. H., 1809-10.

The forthcoming history of Congregational ministers of Vermont has this: "Rev. Dan. Foster was born in Stafford, Conn., about 1748. His father, Rev. Isaac Foster, was settled in West Stafford in 1764, and in later years became a Universalist. One of his brothers also had a similar career. He was not a college graduate, but received an honorary A. M. from both Yale and Dartmouth colleges in

1774. He was pastor at Poquonock, Conn., from 1771 to 1784, and at Weathersfield, Vt., from 1787 to 1799. Under his ministery this latter church became 'poisoned with errors, rent with divisions and disheartened by opposition,' and at its close was left with few members and in a low spiritual condition. He then removed to Charleston, N. H., where he taught a classical school, and acted as the supply of the Congregational church from 1804 till his death in 1809. Like his father and his brother, he at length avowed Universalism, and published a treatise in defence of that belief. He had one son and two daughters, and died at Charleston, aged 62 years." He d. in March, 1810. Res., Windsor, Conn., Weathersfield, Vt., and Charleston, N. H.

1142. i. REBECCA WAKELY, b. ——.

631. REV. EMERSON FOSTER (Isaac, Daniel, Abraham, Abraham, Reginald), b. Stafford, Conn., ——; m. —— ——. He was graduated at Dartmouth college in 1774. "The Rev. Emerson Foster, pastor of the church at Oyster Ponds, now Green Port, Long Island." He d. 1814, and is buried at Brooklyn Heights, N. Y. Res., Killingly, Conn.; Orange, Mass.; New London, Conn., and Green Port, L. I.

1143. i. HANNAH, b. ——.

1144. ii. MARGARET, b. ——; m. —— Moore. Ch.: 1. Amanda Elvira. 2. Lydia F.; m. Anson Green, May 14, 1836; she d. May 12, 1837. 3. ——. 4. Harriet. 5. Joel. 6. Justin F. 7 Whilley E. 8. Samuel. He had cousin, Isaac Foster, of Chatham, Conn., who had four children: Nelson, Margaret, Augusta, Hannah. Augusta Foster married Justin Foster Moore, a grandson of Rev. Emerson Foster.

633. REV. DANIEL FOSTER, A. M. (Isaac, Daniel, Abraham, Abraham, Reginald), b. Stafford, Conn., ——, 1751; m., Warren, Mass., Elizabeth Reed, of Warren, Mass., b. ——, 1753; d. Monson, Mass., Oct. 20, 1830. He was graduated at Dartmouth college in 1777. A. M. Harvard college 1785, and Brown university 1787. He married a Read of the same descent as Speaker Read, and preached in New Braintree, Mass. He d. ——, 1795. Res., New Braintree, Mass.

1145. i. SHERLOCK, b. ——; m. Tamma Reed and Abigail ——.

1146. ii. CHARLOTTE, b. ——. Joseph Dorr, Judge of Probate of Worcester county, appointed Reuben Reed guardian of Charlotte Foster, Luke Foster and Isalinda Foster, minor children of the late Rev. Daniel Foster, of New Braintree, April 24, 1798.

1147. iii. LUKE BALDWIN, b. ——, 1783; m. Eunice Knight.

1148. iv. ISALINDA, b. ——.

1149. v. ELIZABETH, b. ——. Betsey Foster, of New Braintree, was appointed guardian of Elizabeth Foster, daughter of the late Rev. Daniel Foster, of New Braintree, April 24, 1798. Benjamin Foster was appointed guardian of Fordyce Foster, son of Rev. Daniel Foster, late of New Braintree. Children, more than 14 years of age, electing their own guardian, 1798.

1150. vi. FORDYCE, b. ——, 1780; m. Elizabeth Wolcott.

1151. vii. DANIEL, b. ——.

635. REV. ISAAC FOSTER (Isaac, Daniel, Abraham, Abraham, Reginald), b. Stafford, Conn., ——; m. ——, Rebecca Newcomb, b. Dec. 29, 1758, dau. of James and Mrs. Submit (Downer) Davis. He was a Presbyterian, afterward an Episcopal clergyman.

Rev. Isaac Foster, of Hartford, Conn., "a young candidate, for settlement, arrived in Hallowell, April 13th, and the next Sunday preached in the meeting-house "by the desire of the committee," who, during the succeeding weeks, invited him to preach the three following Sundays. Having complied with this request, he officiated with so much satisfaction that a town meeting was called for the 8th of May, to see if the town would invite him to settle and provide for his "salary and settlement." Upon assembling a motion was submitted to invite him to settle in this town in the work of the ministry," which was taken by "polling the house," when fifty-seven were arrayed in favor of the motion and four against it.

A large committee was now raised (consisting of James Howard, Benjamin Pettingill, Samuel Cony, Noah Woodward, Jonathan Davenport, Jeremiah Ingraham, Samuel Badcock, Enoch Page, Simon Dearborn, Henry Sewall, Nathan Weston, Daniel Savage, James Page, Ezekiel Page and Daniel Cony), to report what stipulation should be made with Mr. Foster for "his support and maintenance." The committee, after the meeting had taken a half hour's recess, reported that the town should "pay £100 lawful money annually" as a salary, on condition that Mr. Foster "shall formally and regularly received ordination;" and that should be his salary as long as he "continues to be the town's minister and public teacher." To this they added "£50 settlement." The report was accepted, and £10 a year added to the settlement for the first five years.

A committee was appointed to inform Mr. Foster, who probably had returned to Hartford, of the result of the meeting. He arrived again at Hallowell, July 3d, and on the 5th answered the committee by letter, in which he says: "Taking under consideration the union which at present subsists, with the generosity that appears among you, I accept the call." He preached in the meeting-house Sunday, the 9th of July, also the 16th and the 23d. At the last date, Henry Sewall, in recording the fact, says he "preached poor doctrine." The next Sunday he exchanged with Rev. Thomas Moor, of Wiscasset. On the 6th of August he again preached, and as Sewall says, "Armenian doctrine." Two days after Sewall "had a conference with Mr. Foster," but "could not convince him of the impropriety of his doctrines." On the 12th he again conversed with him "respecting experience," and on the next day, which was Sunday, he records in his diary that "Mr. Foster preached rank Armenianism."

The following day, Monday, the 14th of August, a town meeting assembled to fix the time and make provisions for the ordination of Mr. Foster, at which Simon Dearborn, Joseph North and Wm. Howard were appointed a committee to confer with him in relation to the time, which was finally fixed for the second Wednesday in October. It was then determined to send to seven churches to assist on the occasion; three of which were to be nominated by the town, two by the church, and two by Mr. Foster. The town selected the churches at Bristol, Bath and Harpswell; and the church the churches of East Pownalborough and Falmouth, second Parish. The "letters missive" were drawn and signed by Daniel Cony, Joseph North and Brown Emerson in behalf of the town; two blanks left to be filled by Mr. Foster's nominations. A committee was appointed, consisting of Joseph North, Wm. Howard and Amos Pollard, to provide for the entertainment of the council.

Capt. Sewall, who had opposed the appointment of a day for the ordination, on the day succeeding the meeting "had a close, plain and solemn interview with Mr. Foster respecting his heretical doctrines." After this conference, and on the same day, Mr. Foster left for Connecticut, and returned October 2d with his family and his two brothers, John and Daniel, who were ministers and members by the candidates' nomination of the ordaining council.

Sewall, who doubtless was the embodiment of the opposition, on Wednesday, the 4th, "held a private fast at Esq. Pettingill's, respecting the approaching event of Mr. Foster's ordination," and "drew seven objections against his doctrines, to be laid before the council," a copy of which he presented to Mr. Foster on the 5th. Sunday, the 8th, the Rev. John Foster, the candidate's brother "preached flagrant Free-will doctrine," and Daniel Foster lectured at the meeting-house Monday; and according to Sewall he "preached poor doctrine."

At length, Wednesday, the 11th of October, the day appointed for the ordination, arrived. In the morning the council, composed of the two Fosters and Rev. Samuel Eaton of Harpswell, Rev. Alex. McLean of Bristol, and probably Rev. Thomas Moore of Pownalborough, assembled at Daniel Cony's house. Sewall was present and presented his "seven charges against the candidate's doctrines," and "endeavored to sustain them." The hearing upon these lasted until noon, when Sewall left the council to debate the matter. "The debate held till near sunset, when they proceeded to the meeting-house and laid hands on the candidate."

The opposition to Rev. Isaac Foster, which made its appearance at the time of his ordination, had increased and strengthened. Meetings were regularly held on the Sabbath at Benjamin Pettingill's, or Henry Sewall's house, which were occasionally attended by clergymen from a distance. The difficulty was aggravated and the opposition increased by the institution of legal proceedings, which grew out of the indiscretion of the parties. Captain Sewall had been provoked to the utterance of a charge "that Mr. Foster was a liar and he could prove it." Thomas Sewall was in some way connected with the charge. They were both summoned in January before Justice North, on a complaint to answer to the State. Captain Sewall records that he "did not pretend to deny" the charge, but offered evidence of its truth in justification. Whether the legal maxim of that day, "the more truth the greater libel," was invoked against him or his proof was insufficient, we are not informed. He was found guilty and fined 15 shillings and cost. From this judgment he appealed. But Thomas Sewall, who was fined 12 shillings, did not appeal.

The old matter of defamation between Mr. Foster and Henry and Thomas Sewall broke anew May 9th, when they were each sued by Mr. Foster in actions for damages, which were laid in the writs at £500. Paul Blake, an inhabitant of the town, was with great promptness dispatched by the Sewall's, the next day, after the service of the writs to Mendon, where Mr. Foster formerly preached, to procure evidence against him. He returned the 30th of the same month "with the depositions of two of the committee for procuring preaching" for that town. These related to "Mr. Foster's preaching there." However, previous to this, on the 24th of May, Thomas Sewall had agreed to submit his case to the determination of Thomas Rice, Jedediah Jewett and George Thatcher, but Captain Sewall, with more resolution, "concluded to stand on legal ground," and the action against him was entered at the June term of the court at Pownalborough, and continued by consent to the January term at Hallowell.—[Hist. of H.

He d. Jan. 1, 1801. Res., Augusta, Me., and Rehoboth, Somerset county, Md.

1152. i. ISAAC, b. Feb. 12, 1786; m. Nancy Planting and Mary Mather.

1153. ii. NATHANIEL, b. ——, 1788. He d. in Baltimore, Md., in 1807; a printer by trade.

1154. iii. REBECCA, b. ——; m. —— Pool; res., Baltimore, Md.

1155. iv. HIRAM, b. ——. After the death of his father, with his mother he went to South America after gold, and both are supposed to have died there. Nothing further ever heard from them.

639. REV. JOHN FOSTER (Isaac, Daniel, Abraham, Abraham, Reginald), b. Stafford, Conn.; m. ——, Eunice ——.

He was the son of Rev. Isaac Foster and was born in Stafford, Conn.; received an excellent education; graduated at college, and was ordained at Paxton, Mass., over the Congregational church, Sept. 8, 1785. This society had for some time been divided over trouble with their former pastor, Rev. Alexander Thayer, and was particularly divided over Mr. Foster's settlement, but after a long and warm contention among themselves, his friends carried their point, and the malcontents separated from the old society, and a new church was formed. Some idea may be obtained of the opposition made to the settlement of Mr. Foster from the following protest of several of his opponents:

"We, the subscribers, inhabitants of the town of Paxton, do hereby solemnly, sincerely and wholly protest and declare against the proceedings to be had and taken by the inhabitants of the said town of Paxton, now assembled in town meeting, the consequence of a warrant, signed by a major part of the selectmen of said town of Paxton, as illegal, unlawful and unconstitutional and unprecedented. And now the subscribers do further solemnly protest and declare that we will not, directly or indirectly, be out any cost, or charge, or pay any money that shall be assessed upon us, the subscribers, for settlement, or pledge, that the inhabitants of said town of Paxton shall agree to give Mr. John Foster, except it is taken from us by force, as it is our opinion that the constitution will not admit of any such precedent. And we request that this protest may be read in the said town meeting and recorded with the records in said town of Paxton. As witness ours, this thirteenth day of December, Anno Domini, 1784." Signed by twenty of the inhabitants

Mr. Foster remained pastor of the church for two years, and taking into consideration the wrangle among the church members was a remarkable record under the circumstances.

From Paxton he went to Taunton, and was installed May 16, 1792. He was born in Connecticut, and his father was a clergyman, as were his brothers. It is said of him at Taunton that no minister there was more admired, and that he owed a great deal of his prominence to his voice and solemn manner. His voice was unequaled for deep and solemn tones. He was very eccentric, and was dismissed from Taunton in 1799. From there he went to Stonington, Conn., where he preached and taught. Later he went to New York City, and taught there and preached occasionally. He afterward moved to Athens, N. Y. He d. ——, 184—. Res., Paxton and Taunton, Mass., and Jan., 1840, in Norwich, Conn., and Athens, N. Y.

1156. i. JAMES GARDINER, b. Paxton, Aug. 31, 1786; m. —— ——.

1157. ii. CICERO, b. Paxton, July 31, 1788.

1158. iii. NARCISSA, b. ——; m. —— Hull; res., New York.

644. JOSEPH FOSTER (James, Amos, Benjamin, Abraham, Reginald), b. Tewksbury, Mass., March 5, 1760; m. Aug. 30, 1790, Sarah Frost. He d. April 9, 1846. Res., Tewksbury, Mass.

1159. i. SALLY, b. April 30, 1791.
1160. ii. PATTY, b. Jan. 1, 1795.
1161. iii. BETTY KITTERIDGE, b. Dec. 3, 1798.
1162. iv. CLARISSA, b. March 13, 1802.
1163. v. JOSEPH, b. June 16, 1805.
1164. vi. MOSES, b. June 16, 1809; m., Dec. 29, 1834, Lucinda Chandler; res., Tewksbury.

652. JONATHAN FOSTER (Jonathan, Amos, Benjamin, Abraham, Reginald), b. Tewksbury, Mass., Oct. 30, 1758; m. ——, Rachel ——. Res., Tewksbury, Mass.

1165. i. RACHEL, b. July 22, 1785.
1166. ii. RHODA, b. Jan. 10, 1787.
1167. iii. LYDIA, b. Nov. 11, 1789.
1168. iv. JONATHAN, b. Jan. 7, 1793.
1169. v. NABBY, b. Oct. 25, 1795.

658. LIEUT. AMOS FOSTER (Amos, Amos, Benjamin, Abraham, Reginald), b. Tewksbury, Mass., May 23, 1753; m. ——, Beulah ——. She d. June 15, 1776; m. 2d, Elizabeth Kitteridge.

At the time of the dedication of the statue to Gen. Joseph Warren, at Charleston, in 1858, one of the speakers quoted the last works of the General on the authority of Amos Foster, a Revolutionary soldier, then residing in Tewksbury. The statement was questioned, and Mr. Foster wrote the following letter in relation to the matter:

"Sir,—I have read the piece in the Patriot, in which it is doubted whether the toast you gave on the 4th of July, as the words of Warren, are correct. They are strictly true, and stated exactly as I told you on the morning of the anniversary. I knew Dr. Warren before that day; had seen him among the troops at Cambridge, and am certain of the fact. His words made a lasting impression on my mind, and I have repeated them a thousand times. I was a private in Captain Walker's company, in Bridge's regiment, and was on the ground all the night before, building up the works. After the old engineer had fixed his stakes, Eliakim Walker, Jonathan Beard and myself (who are both living, I believe—Mr. Beard was at the celebration with me), though he had not got them quite straight, and we moved one of them to square it up.

The day of the battle I was near the redoubt; we did all we could; but were obliged to give up at last. The last time the British came up we were moving off all in a hurry into the rear of the redoubt, to stop them as they came up, and there it was that I saw General Warren; his clothes were bloody, when he cried out to us: 'I am a dead man, fight on, my brave fellows, for the salvation of your country.' We had no time to do much, but got off as quick as we could. I never saw Warren after that. The British fired upon us both small and large guns on the retreat, and more of us got off than could reasonably have been expected.

I knew General Putnam and Colonel Prescott well. I saw Putnam riding around, very active. I saw him ten times at least, I should think. Putnam went off with David Baily and a number of others, and they took tools with them to intrench on Bunker Hill, but a number of them came back again. I was close by Asa Pollard when he was killed. The ball struck the ground and hopped along before it struck him. Mr. Benjamin Baldwin rolled him up in a blanket, and they carried him off and buried him. I do not know anything more of a very great importance. I saw a good deal, and remember a great deal, but it is not worth writing, that I know of. I am willing to tell all I know. It appears to me that the blood was running down his (Warren's) arm, or side, when he spoke the words, but we were all in such a hurry, I won't be certain about that. I shall send an order for my money under the resolve. I am, sir,

Your most obedient servant

Amos Foster.

General William H. Sumner."

Amos, of Tewksbury; will, date Oct. 7, 1835; Prob. Nov. 10, 1835; Ch., Elizabeth Blanchard, Hannah Griffin, Enoch, Amos, Zephaniah Foster. He d. in 1835. Res., Tewksbury, Mass.

1170. i. BEULAH, b. May 31, 1776; m. Amos Blanchard, of Wilton, N. H. Beulah, of Tewksbury; child of Amos, Jr.; minor, under 14 years; guardian paper date March 10, 1790.

1171. ii. ELIZABETH, b. Aug. 4. 1783; m., Dec. 5, 1809, Isaac Blanchard. He was b. Wilton, N. H., May 25, 1785; d. Oct. 29, 1857. She d. Nov. 2, 1874. Was a manufacturer of furniture. Ch.: 1. Isaac, b. Jan. 6, 1811; m., Jan. 10, 1838; d. March 13, 1885. 2. Eliza, b. Dec. 24, 1812; m., Nov. 20, 1834; d. April 14, 1856. 3. Hannah, b. Jan. 18, 1815; m. July 20, 1858. 4. Amos Foster, b. May 2, 1817; m. Sept. 15, 1860; d. Nov. 14, 1895. 5. Sarah Griffin, b. April 23, 1819; d. March 25, 1829. 6. Clara, b. Nov. 23, 1821; m., Aug. 27, 1846, John F. Kimball, b. Sept. 23, 1824. Is a banker. Res., s. p., Wilton, N. H. P. O. box 293. 7. Gardner, b. Aug. 30, 1829; m. March 21, 1860. Isaac's son, Charles F. Blanchard, Lowell, Mass. Amos Foster's son, Arthur Foster Blanchard, St. Louis Park, Minn.

1172. iii. AMOS, b. May 30, 1785; m. Rhoda Foster.

1173. iv. HANNAH, b. Sept. 3, 1789; m., Oct. 5, 1810, Moses Griffin, of Pepperell, Mass. He was b. Tewksbury, Mass., Sept. 29, 1787; d. Jan. 18, 1875. She d. Aug. 4, 1854. Ch.: 1. Moses E. Griffin, b. Jan. 28 1812; m. Feb. 22, 1859; d. July 5, 1897. Mr. George Griffin, East Pepperell, Mass. 2. Hannah Griffin, b. Sept. 12, 1814; d. unm. Aug. 14, 1866. 3. Enoch Griffin, b. Dec. 4, 1818; d. unm. Aug. 24, 1871. 4. Rebecca Griffin, b. March 4, 1821; m. Darius B. Sibley, July 22, 1857. P. O. address, Mrs. D. B. Sibley, Pepperell, Mass. 5. John H., b. Sept. 29, 1824; unm. Is a farmer. Res., Pepperell, Mass., box 18.

1174. v. ZEPHANIAH KITTERIDGE, b. Sept. 22, 1791; m. Mercy T. Trull.

1175. vi. ENOCH, b. Jan. 13. 1794; m. —— Tenney. He d. Feb. 1, 1856, s. p.

659. WILLIAM FOSTER (Amos, Amos, Benjamin, Abraham, Reginald), b. Tewksbury, Mass., April 10. 1756; m., May 14, 1784, Olive Howard. She d. Aug. 31, 1847. Olive of Tewksbury, widow, quar. bond, April 27, 1847. Res. Tewksbury, Mass.

1176. i. OLIVE, b. April 7, 1786.

1177. ii. WILLIAM, b. Feb. 9, 1789; m. Anna ——.

1178. iii. LUCY, b. June 26, 1791.

661. NATHAN FOSTER (Amos, Amos, Benjamin, Abraham, Reginald), b. Tewksbury, Mass., May 14, 1762; m. Norway, Me. (the first marriage in that town), May 17, 1791, Miriam Hobbs, b. July 17, 1772; d. Dec. 24, 1804; m. 2d., Sally Hobbs, sister of his first wife, b. Jan. 8, 1782, dau. of Jeremiah, of Hopkinton, Mass., and Norway, Me. Nathan Foster was born in Massachusetts and before reaching his majority went to Maine. He located at what was later incorporated as Norway. Was always a farmer. He took a prominent part in all of the town's affairs. His death was very sudden. He went to the barn to attend to his stock and was found dead in the yard, where he had fallen, as was supposed, in a fit of apoplexy. He d. Feb. 5, 1836. Res. Norway, Me.

1178-2. i. NATHAN, b. April 9, 1794; m. Mrs. Sarah (Gilson) Wheelock.

1179-2. ii. MIRIAM, b. May 18, 1791.

1180-2. iii. HANNAH, b. Oct. 14, 1792; d. June 22, 1811.

1181-2. iv. AMOS, b. March 31, 1796; d. April 20, 1827. He was a soldier in the War of 1812 in Capt. Amos Town's company.

1182-2. v. JEREMIAH, b. Sept. 23, 1797. He was corporal in Capt. Amos Noyes' Company in the "Aroostook War" in 1839, in Maine. m. —— ——.

1183-2. vi WILLIAM, b. April 5, 1799; m. Calista Wood.

1184-2. vii. SAMUEL, b. Feb. 15, 1804; d. July 6, 1806.

1185-2. viii. SALLY, b. Aug. 31, 1805; d. July 10, 1806.

1186-2. ix. SALLY, b. April 17, 1807; m., April 11, 1842, Hon. David Frost. He was b. Dec. 12, 1809. She d. Sept. 3, 1844. Res. Norway, Me. Was a school-teacher; justice of the peace, 28 ye rs; selectman, 4 years and representative in the legislature. Ch.: 1. Irving, b. May 23, 1843; m., Nov. 10, 1872, Jennie A. Richardson. Res. Norway, Me. Ch.: i. Minnie Wadsworth, b. Aug. 31, 1891. 2. Serena L., b. Aug. 13, 1844; m., Oct. 10, 1872, Alvin R. Frost. Res. Norway, Me.

1187-2. x. SAMUEL, b. Jan. 27, 1809; m. Sarah —— and Caroline Cross. Res. Norway, Me.

1188-2. xi. SERENA, b. Dec. 11, 1810; m., Nov. 13, 1838, Simeon Frost. He was b. Nov. 28, 1811. She d. Dec., 1842; m. for his third wife, Hannah Foster; she res. in Lawrence, Mass. He d. Sept. 12, 1882. Ch.: 1. David Francis, b. Aug. 18, 1839. 2. William Edwin, b. Dec. 6, 1842.

1189-2. xii. HANNAH, b. June 22, 1813; m. Simeon Frost. He was b. Nov. 28, 1811. Frost d. Dec. 1842; m. for his third wife Hannah Foster. She res. in Lawrence, Mass. He d. Sept. 12, 1882. Ch.: 1. David Francis, b. Aug. 18, 1839. 2. William Edwin, b. Dec. 6, 1842.

1190-2. xiii. LUTHER F., b. March 3, 1815; m. Eunice B. Millett.

1191-2. xiv. DAVID, b. May, 1818; m. Hannah——. The widow res. Lawrence, Mass., with m. dau.

1192-2. xv. HARRIET, b. Oct. 5, 1820; d. June 1, 1828.

1193-2. xvi. LYDIA, b. Jan. 17, 1823; m., 1842, Wm. Frost, Jr. He was b. Jan. 9, 1812. By Lydia he had two children; m. 2d. and d. March 18, 1882.

1194-2. xvii. CLARISSA, b. Jan. 27, 1826; m. Fred Knight. She d. leaving two or three sons who res. in So. Dak.

674-2. ASAEL FOSTER (Asael, Gideon, Benjamin, Abraham, Reginald), b. Bridgton, Me., Oct. 4, 1773; m. Amherst, Me., Lucy Bracket, b. Gorham, Me., March 18, 1774; d. Aug. 28, 1819; dau. of Capt. John of Harrison; m. 2d., Lucy Crosby, b. Amherst, N. H., Feb. 9, 1793; d. March 30, 1861. He d. March 14, 1851. Res. Bridgton and Harrison, Me.

1179. i. SALLY F., b. June 30, 1797; m., March 22, 1815, Ansel T. Archer. She d. Oct. 29, 1865.

1180. ii. STEPHEN B., b. Sept. 11, 1800; m., Dec. 21, 1828, Olive Goodwin. He d. March 15, 1842.

1181. iii. JOHN B., b. March 4, 1803; m., June 2, 1829, Hannah Silsby. He d. March 31, 1848.

1182. iv. GEO. F., b. Sept. 4, 1805; m., Aug. 8, 1831, Eunice Brewer. He d. Sept. 27, 1853.

1183. v. MEHITABEL S., b. Nov. 26, 1808; m., June 10, 1832, Jonathan Smith. She d. 1849.

1184. vi. MARY ANN, b. May 7, 1812; m., Dec. 1, 1831, Richard Goodwin. She d. May, 1870.

1185. vii. JOANNA S., b. Sept. 30, 1815; m., Sept. 30, 1835, William Stanwood; m. 2d., Emerson Orcutt; she d. 1895.

1186. viii. MOODY A., b. July 19, 1823; m., Nov. 5, 1851, Martha Bunker.

1187. ix. LUCY A., b. May 27, 1825; m., April 27, 1842, Daniel Jordan. She res.——

1188. x. AVILDIA G., b. July 31, 1828; m., Sept. 29, 1850, Thos. Foster.

1189. xi. FRANCIS B., b. Dec. 15, 1831; m. Jan. 1, 1856, Martha Orcutt.

1190. xii. EMELINE, b. Dec. 5, 183—.

675-2. CAPT. BENJAMIN FOSTER (Asael, Gideon, Benjamin, Abraham, Reginald), b. Bridgton, Me,, 1770; m. Nancy Veasey of Denmark, Me.; b. 1769; d. 1859. Benjamin Foster purchased the land of Thomas Perley, then in Bridgton, now in Harrison, bordering on Crooked river and near the land of Major Emerson. Here he had a rude camp and worked clearing land several years previous to his marriage. He afterward erected a frame house and married Nancy Veasey of Denmark. He planted 12 acres of corn on burnt land the first year of his residence in Harrison. Some years after his marriage and when the population of his town had increased, Mr. Foster built a small "grocery" which was continued many years. The store was the place where many curious scenes were enacted. Being near the course of the river, the drivers resorted thither, where they could wet the inside to correspond with the outside. At one time one of the lumber drivers feigned sick and one Old Doctor Black was called to Mr. Foster's to prescribe for him. While there the doctor was invited to take some of the ardent, which to refuse in those days would have been considered a transgression of the rules of propriety; consequently he shared in the "flow of the bowl" and was soon as merry as the merriest. Now the doctor had a white faced horse and Capt. Foster had a white faced steer, and when the doctor had become so intoxicated as not to discriminate, the drivers changed the saddle and bridle from the horse to the steer, and placed the doctor upon his back. The poor frightened creature was not acquainted with such a harness and, raising his tail high in the air, bellowed and dashed down the yard, precipitating the medicine man headlong into the mud. Capt. Foster was once camping in Bridgton when an old horse, belonging to a neighbor, kept eating from his hay stack. The owner was requested to take care of the horse again and again, but took no heed. Coming in from the wood one evening the old horse was found eating from the captain's hay. Without any delay, Foster commanded one of the men to hold the horse, when going into camp for a brand of fire, he made it fast to the horse's tail and giving him a smart cut with a stick sent him dashing down the road. The running of the horse through the wind caused the fire to burn more brightly, frightening him more and more and he never ceased running until he reached his owner's barn and stood trembling before the door. It may be unnecessary to say that the horse never returned to trouble Capt. Foster's hay.

I have now to relate the most curious and sad affair (perhaps) in the experience of Mr. Foster, and one which occurred in his early years.* He had been on an evening visit to his intended and was returning when he stumbled upon a huge bear. The bear made for him at once, and to escape, Foster made haste to climb a small tree, one which he supposed too small for the bear to hug. But he soon saw his bearship coming up after him. He climbed as far as he dared to, lest his weight should break the tree. The bear took his heel in her teeth, tearing away the slipper and flesh, and, losing her hold, fell to the ground. Foster then supposed his danger past, but he was again disappointed. She had no sooner recovered her feet than she climbed the tree again, this time tearing the flesh away from his heels, clean to the bones and both man and bear fell to the ground, the tree breaking. Mr. Foster was top of the heap when they struck the ground, and ran with all his might toward his home—the bear did not follow—and was so wild with fear that he did not feel the pain of his feet until going through a field of rye stubble which pricking the mangled flesh, caused him severe distress. He was made a cripple for life, and probably considered his bride a costly prize. Captain Foster died in Harrison at the advanced age of 84 years, having issue, eight children.

Many years after, this story got into the papers, and some believed and some did not believe it. Captain Foster at one time went to New York State, and stopping at a hotel, he heard the story told by strangers to him and some said they would not believe it, then Foster, not known to the company said, "I suppose I can show you the heel if you will not believe it without," and suiting the act to the word, unclothed his feet and showed the heel crippled. The writter has often seen the heels and heard the story by the old fireside in Grandfather Foster's home in South Harrison, Me., when but a mere boy of ten years, so that there would be much fear of bears when returning home a short distance of a few rods in the evening, after a short visit at grandpa's.

Surely if the young Foster was a reader of the Bible he must have believed the words of Hosea, 13, 8 verse: "I will meet them as a bear that is bereaved of her whelps, etc."

Captain Foster died in Harrison at the age of 84 years, having eight children, some of whom died very young. He was what was called a successful man in the things of this world, being able in his old age to give each son living a good and fertile farm. He was often elected to fill some important office in town affairs, as selectman, etc.

Those settlers were skilled in lumbering, and acquainted with hardships and the use of the musket. They knew how to endure the deprivations of the early settlers. They were men well adapted to the work of the pioneer, and they did that work nobly and fearlessly.

We must remember that they had to evade the torch and scalping knife of the redmen, and sufferings from cold, exposure and hunger.

*This adventure did not occur after his removal to the east side of Long Pond. Mr. Foster was reared near the line between Bridgton and Denmark, consequently had not far to go. I give the tradition as related by his own family.

Tneir camps were at first built of logs and chinked with moss in winter. The floors, if any, were hewn logs, fireplace of stones. From such rude homes many noble men and women were reared, who have gone out to make this land what it is to-day. He d. 1854. Res. Harrison, Me.

1191. i. AMOS P., b. Oct. 11, 1804; m. Annie Knight.
1192. ii. BENJAMIN S., b. June 25, 1806; m. Esther T. Cushman.
1193. iii. ABIGAIL L., b. May 25, 1808; d. young.
1194. iv. THOMAS V., b. Dec. 17, 1810; m. Mary Ann Phinney and Alvilda G. Foster.
1195. vi. VALENTINE LOWELL, b. Aug. 7, 1815; m. Julia Scribner, Ellen Blake and Susan Newcomb.
1196. vii. GEORGE, b. 1817; m Ann Osgood.
1196½ viii. JOSEPH, brother of George as above, d. when a young man at home.
1197. ix. NANCY, b. Aug. 25, 1813; d. young.

675. PHILEMON FOSTER (Philemon, Jonathan, Caleb, Abraham, Reginald), b. Ipswich, Mass., Feb. 5, 1779; m. (pub.) Jan. 16, 1800, Nabby Hobbs. Res. Ipswich, Mass.

1198. i. SARAH, b. Feb. 24, 1807; m., in Ipswich, Daniel Proctor Pingree. Both are dead. Ch.: 1. A dau. Melinda; m., 1848, Alvin T. Conant. He enlisted in the Civil War in Co. K., 40th Regt., Mass. Vol. Mustered in, Sept. 3, 1862; d s. p. on Folly Island, S. C., Oct. 16, 1863 2. Mary Abigail; m., April, 1859, Gilbert Rogers Conant, b. Aug. 19, 1832. Ch: Rogers Gilbert, b. Jan. 7, 1860; d. young. He d. Linbrook Parish, Ipswich, Oct. 19, 1859. She m. 2d., 1865, Allen Perley of Rowley. Res., Rowley.
1199. ii. DAVID b. Aug. 23, 1809; m. Angelina W. Pingree.
1200. iii. LUCY HOBBS, b. Dec. 4, 1811; m., Oct. 16, 1832, Joseph Conant. Res. Rowley. Both d., s. p.
1201. iv. LYDIA BURPEE, b. June 25, 1815; m. Curtis Taylor. Both d. Lydia Taylor had one son and one daughter. The whereabouts of son Cyrus Edwin is unknown to me. She has a daughter, Mrs. Sarah Conant living in Topsfield.
202. v. GORHAM PARSONS, b. March 15, 1818; m., Oct. 27, 1843, Mary Foster, dau. of Simon; no ch. living. He d. Nov. 5, 1851. (See)
1203. vi. ALMIRA PARSONS, b. Jan. 8, 1821; unm. Res. Ipswich.
1204. vii. CYRUS, b. July 27, 1823. Res. Linbrook Parish, Ipswich; m. Martha Potter.
1205. viii. PHILEMON CUMMINGS, b. March 23, 1805; m. Eliza Felton and Hannah Pickard.
1206. ix. NABBY, b. Nov. 26, 1802; m. Albert Brown. Both deceased. She d. July 17, 1878; he d. July, 1889. 1. Lavinia Foster Brown, East Boxford, Mass. 2. Eliza Cleaveland Brown, deceased. 3. Ruth Emily Brown, b. April 9, 1833; m. in Ipswich, Andrew Dodge. Res., Peabody, Mass. Ch.: i. Jennie M. Dodge, b. Sept. 11, 1852; m. ii. Luke Dodge, b. Sept. 28, 1853; deceased. iii. Cornelia Dodge, b. July 17, 1855; deceased. iv. Loretta Storie Dodge, b. Feb. 28. v. Abbie Lavinia Dodge, b. Nov. 8, 1860 vi. Samuel Dane Dodge, b. Feb. 17, 1876; 22 years old. 4. Sophia Dodge Brown; deceased. 5. Luther Chaplin Brown, deceased child Forest Elsworth. 6. Hannah Almira Brown; deceased.

679. MOSES FOSTER (Moses, Jonathan, Caleb, Abraham, Reginald), b. Dec. 25, 1790, in the second house built by his father upon his Milford estate; m. first, May 8, 1817, Fanny Coggin, daughter of Joseph Coggin, of Mount Vernon, N. H.; b. April 27, 1799; d. May 9, 1842; and 2d., Sept. 27, 1842, Diana Wallingford, daughter of Benjamin Wallingford, of Milford. He greatly enlarged the house left him by his father, living in it until 1847, when he relinquished it to his son, John Everett Foster, in whose possession it still is. From 1847 to his death, April 4, 1873, he resided in a house built by him in the former year in the village of Milford. Res., Milford, N H.

1207. i. JOSEPH COGGIN, b. April 11, 1818; m. Abigail Ann Eaton and Julia Ann Gould.

1208. ii. REUBEN FULLER, b. Jan. 19, 1821; m. Elizabeth Ames.
1209. iii. JOHN EVERETT, b. May 17, 1824; m. Sophia P. Farley.
1210. iv. MOSES FREEMAN, b. Jan. 6, 1832; m. Adelaide L. Doane.
1211. v. DIANA, b. Sep. 5, 1845; d. Sept. 5, 1845.
1212. vi. BENJAMIN F. b. Oct. 8, 1846; m. Celia F. Peabody.
1213. vii. GEORGE WALLINGFORD, b. June 20, 1848; d. July 7, 1848.
1214. viii. DIANA WALLINGFORD, b. July 3, 1849; d. July 12, 1849.

680. ISAAC PLUMMER FOSTER (Moses, Jonathan, Caleb, Abraham, Reginald), b. March 5, 1792, in Milford; m., Nov. 16, 1816, Harriet Brooks, of Salem. In 1810 he removed to Salem, almost at once connecting himself in business with the late Thomas Brooks, whose daughter he married, and succeeding to the business in 1816. After fifty-seven years of active business life, he retired in 1873, and was succeeded by his son Isaac Plummer Foster, who carries on the business on the same spot at the head of Derby wharf, where it has now been conducted for seventy-three years past. She d. May 2, 1880. He d. May 22, 1881.

1215. i. HARRIET, b. Sept. 13, 1817; m., Aug. 12, 1856, Rev. Luther G. Bingham, who d. Jan. 22, 1878, in Middlebrook, N. J.
1216. ii. SAMUEL BROOKS, b. July 19, 1819; m. Mary H. Worcester.
1217. iii. MARY, b. May 23, 1823; m., Dec. 15, 1853, Roland J. Edwards, who d. Sept. 19, 1877, in Salem. She d. June 22, 1879.
1218. iv. ISAAC PLUMMER, b. Sept. 4, 1827; m., March 14, 1852, Harriet Leavitt, dau. of Oliver R. Leavitt, of Salem, Mass.
1219. v. ADELINE BROOKS, b. Jan. 6, 1832; d. June 23, 1868.
1220. vi. MARIA, b. March 6, 1833, in Salem; m., Sept. 22, 1858, Aaron Augustus Smith, son of Aaron Smith of Salem, for many years of the firm of G. M. Whipple & A. A. Smith, booksellers and publishers, and later inspector of the Salem Water Department. Ch.: 1. Stephen Augustus, b. June 10, 1859. 2. Edward Pingree, b. July 15, 1863; d. July 16, 1863. 3. Arthur Foster, b. Sept. 20, 1866.

685. SERGT. WILLIAM FOSTER (Nathan, Caleb, Caleb, Abraham, Reginald), bapt. Rockport, Mass., May 30, 1760; m. ——— ——. He served in the Revolutionary War for many years and resided in Bristol, Me. Was sergeant in the Massachusetts State troops. Was granted a pension July 22, 1834 while, residing in Lincoln county, Me. He was in the battle of Bunker Hill. He d. — -. Res. Bristol, Me.

1221. i. THOMAS D., b. 1782; m. Joanna Carter.
1222. ii. EBENEZER, b. 1780; m. Margaret Bates.

688. JOHN FOSTER (Nathan, Caleb, Caleb, Abraham, Reginald), b. bapt. Rockport, Mass., March 30, 1760; m. Susannah Robinson, of Plymouth, Mass. She was granddaughter of Rev. John Robinson, the Pilgrim pastor who came over in the Mayflower. She d. in 1842. He served in the Revolutionary War and was said to have been at the Battle of Bunker Hill. He was granted a pension but it was afterward suspended by the Government as it was said "the name was not on the rolls. No such corps as he alleges was maintained in 1779 and he did not serve six months." He moved from Rockport to John's Island, Bristol Bay, coast of Maine. He d. aet. 75, in 1837. Res. Bristol, Me.

1223. i. SARAH, b. 1781; m., 1804, Rev. John Thurston. He was son of Captain John of Rockport, Mass; was b., 1781 and d. Nov. 9, 1835. She d. Nov. 26, 1847. He was a farmer, mariner and school teacher in So. Bristol, Me. Was a preacher and a man of great strength and agility. It is said of him that he was one of nature's noblemen. Ch.: 1. Susan S. b. 1805; d. 1831. 2. Nancy, b. April 21, 1808; m., 1828, Capt. Robert Russell. 3. Sarah, b. 1809; d. Aug. 20, 1848. 4. Eliza, b. March 13, 1812; m. Capt. Loring Pierce; res. Southport, Me. 5. Almina, b. 1813; d. 1831. 6. John, b. 1815; m. Mrs. Almina Given; wrecked on Rye Beach, N. H. Nov. 1850. 7. Mahala, b. 1817; m. Capt. Daniel Cameron, 2d. 8. Thomas Foster, b. Sept. 21, 1822; m. Alice Vose Albee. 9. Ambrose, b. 1824; d. 1826. 10. Harvey b. 1826; d. 1830. 11. Arville Lyons, b. June 27, 1827; m. Capt. Daniel Cameron, 2d, selectman, town treasurer of Southport, Me.

* See New Eng. [illegible]

1224. ii. THOMAS, b. July 16, 1789; m. Jane Sproul.
1225. iii. NANCY, b. Feb. 12, 1783; m., Dec. 24, 1800, Capt. William Thurston, b. Aug. 27, 1778; son of Capt. John; d. June 11, 1852. He was a pilot in Castine and Pemaquid. Res. Deer Isle, Me. 1. William, b. Nov. 9, 1802; m. Margaret McKay. 2. Solomon, b. Feb. 16, 1804; m. Margaret McKay. 3. Matilda, b. May 15, 1808. 4. Geo. Washington, b. March 13, 1810; m. Sarah McKay and Mrs. Mary Sproul. 5. Nancy, b. May 18, 1812; m. John Blaisdel of Bristol. 6. Susan Foster, b. April 3, 1822; m. Eben Trask and Capt. Charles D. Ferrin of Brunswick, Me., who died near Aspinwall, Dec. 22, 1856.
1226. iv. ABBY, b. ——; m. John Stinnson of Deer Island, Me.
1227. v. ALEXANDER ROBINSON, b. ——; m. Betsey Thurston.
1228. vi. JOHN, b. ——; m. Mary Mann.
1229. vii. SUSAN, b. ——; m. Capt. James Sproul of Bristol, Me. They had 6 children.

690. ZEBARD FOSTER (Nathan, Caleb, Caleb, Abraham, Reginald), bapt. Rockport, Mass., March 21, 1762; m., Bristol, Me., Hannah Stone, b. 1770; d. Dec. 17, 1859. He was in the Revolutionary War from Mass. He d. Nov. 12, 1831. Res., Knox and Montville, Me.

1230. i. ZEBARD, b. Oct. 7, 1802; m. Mary Thompson.
1231. ii. JOB, b. —.
1232. iii. SALLY, b. — .
1233. iv. HANNAH, b. —.
1234. v. BETSEY, b. —
1235. vi. WILLIAM, b. —.
1236. vii. MARTHA, b —
1237. viii. MIRIAM, b. —.
1238. ix. THOMAS STONE, b. Aug. 7, 1811; m. Caroline A. Sproul.

700. JACOB FOSTER (Jacob, Jacob, Isaac, Reginald, Reginald), b. Berwick, Me., June 23, 1764; m., Oct. 3, 1786, Rebecca Vose. She d. Aug. 30, 1841. He served his time as an apprentice in Watertown, Mass. He afterward resided at Charlestown, Mass., at the corner of Main and Union streets, where he pursued his calling of a cabinet maker, and originated the business which was afterward successfully carried on by his son Charles and others, under the style of Foster, Lawrence & Co. Many stories are told of his eccentricities. He was married by the Rev. Mr. Robbins of Milton, to Rebecca, dau. of David and Sarah Vose, of Milton. Jacob, Charlestown, letter date, May 21, 1839, ex. Aug. 20, 1839, wife Rebecca. Ch. Jacob, next of kin, Charles, Henry, Edwin F. Adams, Rebecca Damon, Sarah V. Waldo. [Middlesex Prob.] He d. Sept. 1, 1838. Res. Charlestown, Mass.

1239. i. SUSAN, b. March 31, 1787; m. Henry Adams, son of the Rev. Zabdiel and Elizabeth Boylston Adams, Jan. 1, 1807. Their children b. at Charlestown were: 1. Henry Augustus Adams, b. July 13, 1807; d. Jan. 31, 1823 at sea. 2. Edwin Foster Adams, b. Oct. 7, 1809. He is a merchant of Boston, formerly a member of the firm of Henry Foster & Co., of Pernambuco, Brazil, where he resided many years. He has held various offices of public trust in Charlestown, where he resided, at No. 32 Cordis street. He married Caroline Matilda, daughter of Nathan and Sarah (Leah) Webb, Aug. 18, 1835. Their children born at Charlestown: 1. Caroline Matilda Adams, b. May 20, 1836; d. Oct. 17, 1853, at Charlestown. 2. Henry Clarence Adams, b. Sept. 22, 1847; member of the firm of Gill & Lootz, commission merchants, 9 Center Wharf, Boston. Resides with his father. 3. Alice Foster Adams, b. March 29, 1851; d. Aug. 10, 1852, at Lynn. 3. George Billows Adams, b. July 24, 1812; d. aet. 15 years, 10 months, 17 days. Mrs. Adams died at Lexington, Jan. 12, 1834. Mr. Adams married twice subsequently. He was b. May 13, 1779, at Lunenburg, graduated at Harvard university in 1802, studied law with his brother Z. B. Adams in Charlestown, where he afterward practiced. He resided at Richmond, Va., Ashburnham, Lexington, and Somerville, Mass., at which latter place he died Nov. 13, 1862.

1241. iii. REBECCA, b. May 23, 1792; m. Joseph Damon, son of Isaac and Persis Damon of East Sudbury, now Wayland, Mass., Aug. 1817. They had issue: 1. Albert Foster Damon, b. June 21, 1818, at Wayland. He is a merchant residing in Philadelphia. He was formerly partner in the house of Henry Foster & Co., of Pernambuco, Brazil, where he married Charlota, daughter of John and Fillipa Mathues of that place Nov. 19, 1846. Their children were born as follows: i. Joseph Augusta Damon, b. Nov. 8, 1847 at Pernambuco. Res. in Philadelphia with his father. ii. Eliza Henrietta Damon, b. Nov. 23, 1848, at Clinton, Mass; d. at Pernambuco, Feb. 28, 1853. iii. John Mathues Damon, b. July 17, 1850, at Pernambuco. Resides at Philadelphia. iv. Albert Forster Damon, b. Sept. 16, 1853, at Pernambuco. Resides at Philadelphia. v. Carlota Louisa Damon, b. Oct. 21, 1855, at Pernambuco; d. at sea Dec. 12, 1859. vi. Ellen Constance Damon, b. Nov. 23, 1857, at Philadelphia. vii. Caroline Matilda Damon, b. Nov. 8, 1860, at Philadelphia. viii. William Prentice Damon, b. March 11, at Philadelphia. 2. Ellen Augusta Damon, b. April 21, 1820, at Milton. She married Rev. Charles Maning, son of Charles and Elizabeth Bowers of Boston, Oct. 26, 1841. They reside in Clinton, Mass., where Mr. Bowers was settled as pastor of the Baptist church. He represented that town in the State legislature during 1864-5-6. i. Charles Albert Bowers, b. Dec. 2, 1842, at Lexington. Graduated at Harvard university, 1864. Studied theology, and while a student at the Newton Theological Seminary, died at Clinton, Oct. 29, 1865 of phthisis. ii. Helen Adelaide Bowers, b. April 28, 1846, at Concord; d. Sept. 20, 1849 at Clinton. iii. Cornelia Vose Bowers, b. April 23, 1848 at Clinton; is now principal of the South Worcester Grammar School. iv. Arthur Foster Bowers, b. Aug. 4, 1850, at Clinton; was a member of the class of '71 at Brown university. v. George Cummings Bowers, b. Nov. 19, 1852, at Clinton; was a clerk with Sargent Bros. & Co., 106, Devonshire street, Boston. vi. Walter Prentice Bowers, b. May 19, 1855, at Clinton. vii. Clarence Henry Bowers, b. Sept. 14, 1851, at Clinton. viii. Edwin Foster Adams Bowers, b. Feb. 2, 1864, at Clinton. The last three attended school at Clinton. Mr. Damon was born Dec. 10, 1790; d. Dec. 27, 1820, at Wayland of typhus fever. Mrs. Damon resided with her son in Philadelphia.

1242. iv. SARAH VOSE, b. Sept. 3, 1795; m. Charles Frederick Waldo, son of Jonathan and Militiah (Messenger) Waldo of Salem. Mr. Waldo was sailing master on board the United States frigate Constitution and lost a leg in the engagement between that vessel and the British frigate Java. Their children were: 1. Charles Foster Waldo, b. April 18, 1818. He now resides in London, England, where he has done business for many years. He married Sophia Briggs, dau. of Captain Robert Ball and Sarah (Barker) Edes of Charlestown, June 24, 1844. She was born at C. May 2, 1820. They have had: i. Sarah Ellen Waldo, b. Aug. 29, 1845, at Boston, now in England. ii. Sophia Briggs Waldo, b. — at Newton; d. ——, England. iii. Mary Edes Waldo, b. —. Brooklyn, N. Y.; d. Nov. 1, 1859, Manchester, England. 2. Sarah Emily Waldo, b. Nov. 30, 1819. She was for several years a missionary at Corfu, when she married John York of Zante, April 18, 1848. Their children were: 1. George Waldo York, b. Aug. 14, 1849, at Zante; d. Oct. 20, 1850, at Dresden. ii. Emily Catharine York, b. Jan. 5, 1851, at Charlestown; d. there Sept. 22, 1851. Mrs. York d. at Charlestown Jan. 9, 1851. A life of Mrs. York has been written containing an account of her missionary labor. Mr. York has since married again and now resides at Washington, D. C. 3. Mary Jane Waldo, b. Jan. 2, 1822. Married Augustus Joseph, son of Samuel and Deborah Archer of Salem, Mass., May 11, 1841. Mr. Archer resides and does business in Salem. They have had issue all born in Salem. i. Caroline Emily Archer, b. March 7, 1842. ii. Emily Waldo Archer, b. April 6, 1844. iii. Agnes Deborah Archer,

b. July 1, 1846; d. Nov. 30, 1852. iv. Mary Waldo Archer, b. Sept. 18, 1848; m. in Salem, June 1, 1870, by the Rev. Mr. Briggs to Charles Henry, son of Joseph Merrill and Laura (Page) Doe, of Cambridgeport. They reside at Worcester, where Mr. Doe, is senior proprietor of the Worcester Evening Gazette. v. Charles Frederick Archer, b. Nov. 1, 1859. 4. Susan Adams Waldo, b. April 17, 1826. 5. Charlotte Louise Waldo, b. Dec. 18, 1828. vi. Phebe Messenger Waldo, b. Feb. 4. 1831. (The last three at 27 High street, Charlestown.) Mr. Waldo was born at Salem Dec. 20, 1783; d. at Charlestown, Aug. 30, 1838. Mrs. Waldo d. at Charlestown June 8, 1851.

1243. v. CHARLES, b. June 13, 1789; m. Lydia Webb, and Susannah Catharine Rogers.

1244. vi. HENRY, b. Dec. 8, 1801; m. Mary Taber Swift.

1245. vii. JACOB, b. June 7, 1803; m. Louise Webb.

701. HENRY FOSTER (Jacob, Jacob, Isaac, Reginald, Reginald), b. Berwick, Me., Sept. 17, 1766; m., May 24, 1792, Susannah Hooper, b. ——, 1772; d. April 17, 1847. He attended the Academy at Exeter, N. H., for a season, after which he came from Nelson to Walpole, about 1790, to engage in teaching school. Susannah, daughter of Capt. Levi Hooper, was one of his pupils, of whom he became enamored, and afterward married. His marriage induced him to buy a farm in the neighborhood of his father-in-law, where he remained during life. He taught school several winters after his marriage. Although bred in the severe orthodoxy of his day, in his mature years he took a wide departure from the teachings of his father, and nothing delighted him more than a discussion on religious topics with his townsmen, he always taking the most extreme opposite views from the religious conventionalities of the day. He preferred Blackstone to theology, and acquired a better knowledge of the law than many of his contemporary practitioners. He was also a diligent student in science, and, being far in advance of his neighbors in knowledge, and of decided opinions of his own, he was not so popular as he might otherwise have been with many of his townsmen; still his weight of character had a potent sway, and everybody feared his criticisms. He held the office of deputy sheriff many years; was selectman one year, and for some time justice of the peace. He d. Sept. 6, 1852. • Res., Walpole, N. H.

1246. i. SALLY, b. June 1, 1793; m. Dr. Ebenezer Crain, of Springfield, Vt., and had thirteen children. She d. Aug. 19, 1839. Ch.: 1. Henry Foster, a physician; m. Helen, dau. of Judge Porter, of Springfield, Vt., and had eight ch., six of whom are living; one is Richard, a physician. 2. Joshua. 3. Susan. 4. Mary Ann; m. Joseph Merrick, of Pennsylvania; they have two ch. living. 5. Louisa Maria. 6. Pauline. 7. Frank Eleazer. 8. Noble; m. Kate Suyder, of Pennsylvania, niece of Governor Snyder; they have two ch. living. 9. Frederick; m. Martha Williams, of Springfield, Vt., and had six ch. 10. Sarah. 11. Francis. 12. Franklin E.; m. Fanny Whitney, of Cambridge, Mass.; they have five ch., and reside in Chicago, Ill. 13. Charles S.; m. Laura Mattisson, of New York City; they had one ch.; he m. 2d, Laura B. Merriam, of Greenfield, Mass., and had four ch. He has been a successful wholesale merchant in Boston, Mass.

1247. ii. SUSAN, b Aug. 24, 1794; m. Levi Hall, and had six ch. She d. Nov 27, 1838.

1248. iii. HENRY PRENTICE, b. Oct. 10, 1796; m. Philena Russell and Eliza Marsh.

1249. iv. LEVI HOOPER, b. Feb. 1, 1799; m. Fanny Fitch, Mrs. Harriet Temple and Mrs. Mary S. Crossett.

1250. v. SOPHIA, b. Feb. 28, 1803; m., June 25, 1826, Dexter Anderson, b. Deerfield, Mass., May 28, 1798; d. Sept. 30, 1877. She d. Sept. 6, 1878. Res., Keene, N. H. Ch.: 1. Helen Sophia Anderson, b. Aug. 2, 1827; m. Sept. 30, 1850; d. Sept. 3, 1876. Son, Frank Smith, Bedford Ave., Brooklyn. 2. Chas. D. Anderson, b. Sept. 18, 1829; twice m.; 1st, May 31, 1858; 2d, Helen H. Holmes, Sept. 1, 1864; d. Aug. 4, 1868; no children. 3. Lucy Nermile Anderson, b. Dec. 3. 1831; m. to E. S. Blanchard, May

28, 1855. Address, 31 Madison St., Rutland, Vt. 4. Henry F. Anderson, b. July 8, 1834; m. Jan. 21, 1865; d. April, 1888. 5. Caroline L. Anderson, b. Jan. 16, 1837; m. Dec. 13, 1865. P. O. address, 646 Third Ave., Detroit, Mich. Mrs. R. S. Southgate. 6. Lizzie V. Anderson, b. Aug. 16, 1847; m. to E. M. Southgate, Nov. 30, 1870. P. O. address, Auburndale, Mass. 7. Isabella A., b. Nov. 8, 1839; m., Oct. 26, 1865, Dr. Herman J. Smith, b. Nov. 15, 1836. Res., 805 Merrimack St., Lowell, Mass. Ch.: (a) Tanole H. Smith, b. May 5, 1870. (b) Foster Hanson Smith, b. Jan. 11, 1877. (c) Reginald Foster Smith, b. Sept. 16, 1878.

703. DAVID FOSTER (Jacob, Jacob, Isaac, Reginald, Reginald), b. Berwick, Me., Aug. 10, 1770; m. ——, Mary White, dau. of John, of Westmoreland, N. H., b. ——, 1776; d. Newark, Vt., Dec. 29, 1861. He went to N. H. with his father and family, and moved to Lyndon, Vt., from Walpole in 1805; was a farmer. He d. May 14, 1814. Res., Lyndon, Vt.

1251. i. DAVID, b. ——; d. Irasburg, Vt., 1841.

1252. ii. JOHN, b. ——; d. Athens, East Tenn., 1893.

1253. iii. MARY, b. Aug. 9, 1801; m., Sept. 16, 1828, Obed Johnson, b. Salem, Mass. March 17, 1787, was a farmer; d. June 12, 1858. She d. Sept. 6, 1888. Ch.: 1. David Foster, b. Aug. 17, 1829; m., Aug. 26, 1854, Mary C. Kinney, b. Aug. 26, 1829; d. May 6, 1870. Res., Newark, Vt. Ch.: (a) Fritz Lavinus Johnson, b. Sept. 28, 185—; m. Nov. 23, 1887; lives at Charlestown, Mass. (b) Avuline Elisabeth Johnson, b. Nov. 14, 1857; is a school-teacher in public schools in San Francisco, Cal. (c) Frank Henry Johnson, b. May 27, 1860; m. Sept. 14, 1892. P. O. San Francisco, Cal. 2. Louisa T., b. Nov. 15, 1831; m., March 30, 1847, George E. Powers, b. Feb. 4, 1824. Res., West Burke, Vt. Ch.: (a) Hattie L. Powers, b. March 9, 1849; m. Jan. 28, 1868; d. Feb. 9, 1882. 3. Ruth F., b. — ; m. Johnson; res., Steele Ways Mills, P. O.

1254. iv. REBECCA, b. ——; d. 1838, Surrey, N. H.

1255. v. GEORGE T., b. June 4, 1810: m. Ann Eliza Baxter.

1256. vi. ELIZA, b. —— ; d. 1887, Alabama.

1257. vii. JACOB PRENTISS, b. ——; m. Jane Leitch and Matilda Cahoon.

708. WILLIAM DURKEE FOSTER (William, Jacob, Isaac, Reginald, Reginald), b. Canterbury, Conn., Aug. 10, 1760; m. Hannah ——; m., 2d, ——, Betsey Dorrence. William was taken prisoner by the Algerian pirates and was confined in the Barbary States for a long time. His friends gave up all hope of ever seeing him alive, but he was finally restored to them. He d. ——. Res., Canterbury, Conn., and —— ——.

1258. i. ABIGAIL, b. Jan. 15, 1780.

1259. ii. JACOB, b. March 24, 1782.

1260. iii. He had four or five other ch.

710. CAPT. SAMUEL SHEFFIELD FOSTER (William, Jacob, Isaac, Reginald, Reginald), b. Nov. 20, 1766, Canterbury, Conn.; m. ——, Anna ——. He was captain of one of the river steamboats on the Hudson river. He d. ——. Res., Batavia, N. Y.

1261. i. ALEXANDER H., b. ——; m. ——.

1262. ii. HANNAH, b. ——; m. Peter Jensen, and had one son and three daus. She d. in Batavia.

1263. iii. MATTHEW O., b. ——; m.; had five ch., and d. west.

1264. iv. GEO. WASHINGTON, b. ——; d. March, 1855.

1265. v. WM. CONLEY, b. ——; went South n. f. k.

1266. vi. GERTRUDE, b. ——; m. Beverly Davenport; res., Mich.; d. 189—.

711. CAPT. DAN FOSTER (William, Jacob, Isaac, Reginald, Reginald), b. Sept. 4, 1770, Canterbury, Conn.; m. ——, Merriam Willson, b. Jan. 1770; d. Sept. 20, 1853. He was captain in the War of 1812. In an early rhyme he is alluded to:

"Captain Dan is the man
That calls the Silver Greys together.
He swears they shall
Their task fulfill
In spite of wind or weather.
Mr. Jones, with his good old bones,
Thinks he has a hard station
Because he has
To stand on guard
Besides to weigh the rations."

He d. June 21, 1853. Res., Pawlet, Vt.; Whitehall, Mentz and Schroon, N. Y.
1267. i. AMANDER, b. ——. Res., Boston.
1268. ii. JAMES T., b. ——. Res., Aurora, N. Y.; Prof. college there.

712. CAPT. ABEL FOSTER (William, Jacob, Isaac, Reginald, Reginald), b. Canterbury, Conn., Nov. 17, 1772; m. ——, Phebe ——; m. 2d —— ——. He was captain of a military company in the War of 1812. He d. March 5, 1813. Res., Whitehall, N. Y.
1269. i. WILLIAM ABEL, b. ——; m. Clarissa Hays.
1270. ii. There were five other ch.

715. CAPT. JACOB FOSTER (William, Jacob, Isaac, Reginald, Reginald), b. March 24, 1782, Westminster Society, in Canterbury, Conn.; m., May 15, 1806, Louisa Brooks, b. Jan. 4, 1786; d. May 20, 1864.

He moved with his parents when five years of age to New York State, and located in the woods. When but five years of age was most forward scholar in school. At an early date, when at school, was elected captain of a military company. Worked on a farm many years, and at sixteen taught school; later worked for his brother on his farm, and still later taught school. Then bought a farm and joined the children. Was first lieutenant of an artillery company, and after the death of his brother Abel he was made captain of the company and tendered their services to Secretary of War Eustis. Moved to Pennsylvania, but returned to New York State. In April, 1827, was elected commissioner of highways at Mentz, N. Y., and also held other town offices. Moved to Port Washington, Wis., in 1846, and died there. He d. June 15, 1865. Res., Mentz, N. Y., and Port Washington, Wis.
1271. i. MASON DURKEE, b. Feb. 6, 1807; m. Romina Bird.
1272. ii. ANN ELIZA, b. Feb. 24, 1809; m., Nov. 24, 1831, William Ogden Thomas. Res., Port Byron, N. Y. Ch.: 1. William Henry, b. ——. Res., Wolcott, Wayne Co., N. Y.
1273. iii. JOHN CHAMBERLAIN, b. Sept. 28, 1812; m. Julia A. Haseltine.
1274. iv. JOEL BARLOW, b. Sept. 25, 1814; d. unm. at Port Washington, Wis., July, 1861.
1275. v. GEORGE WARREN, b. Sept. 13, 1817; m. Mary E. Coe.
1276. vi. MARY LOUISA, b. Aug. 17, 1819; m., Nov., 1842, Nathaniel M. Graham. Res., 418 Marshall St., Milwaukee, Wis. He was b. April 8, 1817; d. Aug. 17, 1887; was a merchant. Ch.: 1. Warren Merrick, b. Sept. 18, 1842; d. Aug. 26, 1861. Died from wounds received at Battle of Falling Waters, Va. 2. Amander Foster, b. July 1, 1844; d. June 21, 1849. 3. Albert Foster, b. March 18, 1846. Address, Eau Claire, Wis. 4. Frances Antoinnette, b. July 2, 1848. Address, Mrs. William A. Ehlman, 132 Nineteenth St., Milwaukee, Wis. 5. Mary Eliza, b. Aug 21, 1850. Address, Mrs. W. P. Bishop, 128 Seventeenth St., Milwaukee, Wis. 6. Harriet Elizabeth, b. Oct. 25, 1854. Address, 418 Marshall St., Milwaukee, Wis. 7. Adelaide Lillian, b. Jan. 27, 1857. Address, Mrs. J. R. Williams, 2834 Cedar, Milwaukee, Wis.
1277. vii. HOWEL COOK, b. March 18, 1822; d. Sept. 2, 1824.
1278. viii. JACOB THOMAS, b. June 23, 1827; m. Sarah Maria Pidge, Anna Barber and Georgia Huston.

720. JOHN FOSTER (Isaac, Jacob, Isaac, Reginald, Reginald), b. ——, Mass., Oct. 1, 1768; m. —— ——. Res., Bridgewater, Danbury and Moretown, Vt.
1279. i. ANNA, b. July 22, 1789; d. June 12, 1804.
1280. ii. LYDIA, b. April 24, 1791.
1281. iii. JOHN, b. Jan. 26, 1793.
1282. iv. OLIVER, b. March 19, 1795; d. Oct. 11, 1811.

1283. v. POLLY, b. Nov. 29, 1796; m., May 21, 1822, Oliver Clark.
1284. vi. MINDWELL, b. June 18, 1799.
1285. vii. HIRAM, b. June 6, 1801.
1286. viii. HARRIET, b. Feb. 25, 1803; d. Jan. 20, 1821.
1287. ix. ANNA, b. Dec. 6, 1804.

722. JACOB FOSTER (Isaac, Jacob, Isaac, Reginald, Reginald), b. Gray, Me., Sept. 22, 1771; m. there July 28, 1796, Mary Young; b. Feb. 28, 1771; d. W. Gray, June 24, 1842. He d. June 23, 1854. Res., Gray, Me.

1288. i. DORCAS, b. April 5, 1801; m., Feb. 4, 1847, Samuel Harmon, of Windham. She d. in Wautoma, Wis.
1289. ii. MARY, b. Nov. 19, 1796; m., Feb. 19, 1832, John Hunnewill. Res., Windham, Me.
1290. iii. JOB Y., b. Dec. 28, 1803; m. Statira Leighton.
1291. iv. BETSEY L., b. Aug. 3, 1806; m. Jan., 1835, Shadrach Humphrey, b. Gray, Me., Jan. 17, 1802; d. April 17, 1890. She d. Feb. 6, 1885. Res., Gray. Was a farmer and teacher. Ch.: 1. Cynthia J., b. Jan., 1835; d. Dec. 17, 1896; son, Willard J. Mayberry, Mechanic Falls, Me. 2. Adeline F., b. Sept. 17, 1836; m. W. S. Noryles. Address, Newhall, Me. 3. John W., b. March 20, 1838; d. Sept., 1895; son, John W. Humphrey, North Gray, Me. 4. Elizabeth, b. Oct. 14, 1840; d. May, 1896, without issue. 5. Delphina N., b. Nov. 13, 1842; m. Jacob N. Merrill, of Windham. Address, Windham Center, Me. 6. Shadrach Granville Humphrey, b. April 8, 1845; m., March, 1872, Almeda Frank, b. Sept., 1851; d. July 4, 1872; m. 2d, Aug. 28, 1874, Abbie L. Frank, b. Oct. 30, 1847. Res., N. Gray, Me. Is a farmer and teacher. Ch.: (a) Almeda, b. July 4, 1872; d. Sept., 1873. First child of second family, Effie B., b. March 2, 1874; m. Eugene Ray, 1891; P. O., Dry Mills, Me. (b) Nellie J., b. Sept. 6, 1875. P. O., North Gray, Me. (c) George G., b. Oct. 9, 1877. P. O., North Gray, Me. (d) James B., b. Feb. 20, 1880. P. O., North Gray, Me.
1292. v. SHEPHEL, b. Feb. 12, 1809; m. Rosana Dolloff.
1293. vi. JOHN, b. Aug. 17, 1811; m., March 4, 1832, Priscilla Benson and Ann Hodgkins. Res., Gray, Me.
1294. vii. MOSES, b. Dec. 17, 1798; d. Oct. 2, 1801.
1295. viii. HANNAH, b. ——; d. ——.
1296. ix. SUSAN, b. ——; d. ——.

724. SAMUEL FOSTER (Isaac, Jacob, Isaac, Reginald, Reginald), b. Gray, Me., July 18, 1774; m., July 21, 1799, Martha Humphrey, b. Nov. 20, 1784; d. July 25, 1850. He d. March 11, 1857. Res., Gray, Me.

1297. i. JAMES H., b. ——. Daniel, of Raymond, and Leonard, of W. Poland, Me., are sons.
1298. ii. SOLOMON BERRY, b. Nov. 4, 1810; m. Eunice Ricker.
1299. iii. MARTHA, b. ——; m. in Gray, Jan. 31, 1829, George Dolley. Res., Gorham, Me. She d. 1848. Ch.: 1. Geo. C.; res., East Waterloo, Me. 2. Orrin; res., Cumberland Mills, Me. 3. William; res., Windham, Me. 4. Mrs. Lucinda Robinson; res., Raymond, Me. 5. Mrs. Elizabeth Strout; res., Raymond, Me. 6. Samuel Foster, b. April 12, 1839; m., Jan. 23, 1863, Eliza H. Cummings, b. March 7, 1840; res., Gorham, Me.; is a contractor. Ch.: (a) Walter Dolley, b. Jan. 27, 1878. (b) Irvin Samuel Dolley, b. May 8, 1876. (c) Grace Leah Dolley, b. Nov. 17, 1873.
1300. iv. SAMUEL J., b. June 14, 1808; m. Annie Emerson.
1301. v. MAHALA WINTER, b. July 30, 1819; m. June 14, 1846, Azariah Humphrey. b. Dec. 3, 1807; d. North Gray, July 19, 1884. She d. April 28, 1886; was a farmer; res., North Gray. Ch.: 1. James Clement, b. May 22, 1857; m. May, 1870; res., North Gray. 2. Charlotte Frances, b. Oct. 3, 1846; m., Dec. 1, 1877, Alvin Scott Doughty. b. June 29, 1849. Is a millman; res., North Gray. Ch.: (a) Annis Jeanette, b. Nov. 17, 1870; d. Feb. 6, 1888. (b) Clara Hall, b. Aug. 17, 1873; m., July 31, 1896, Oscar C. Stinchfield. Res., North Gray.

1302. vi. CHARLOTTE, b. — —; m. Noah Ricker; res., Cumberland Mills, Me. She d. one year after m., leaving son. Samuel Ricker went west and d. 1897. A child is Martha Knight; res., C. M.

1303. vii. MIRIAM S., b. ——; m. —— Fogg; res., Gray, Me. A son is Scammon Fogg; res., Gray, Me.

729. WILLIAM FOSTER (Isaac, Jacob, Isaac, Reginald, Reginald), b. Gray, Me., Oct. 7, 1781; m. abt. 1804, Lucy Spencer; d. Aug. 1, 1826; m. 2d, Sarah Jane Chever, b. 1792; d. Feb. 25, 1861. He was a farmer and lumberman. He d. Sept. 2, 1857. Res., Argyle, Me.

1304. i. PHILIP, b. in 1806; m. Fannie Cummings.

1305. ii. ISAAC, b. March 21, 1807; m. Rachel Jane Chever and Sarah Jane Howard.

1306. iii. MARTHA, b. May 13, 1811; m., Bangor, Me., 1831, Charles Hellenbrand; res., Salem, Oregon. He was b. Nancy, France, in 1809; d. Salem, Oregon, Oct. 2, 1872. She d. March 23, 1895. Ch.: 1. Charles W., b. Bangor, Me., Dec. 13, 1845; m., Jan. 29, 1871, Alvina Short, b. Dec. 14, 1858. He is a confectioner and restauranter; res., Salem, Oregon. Ch.: (a) C. N. (b) Lottie J.

1307. iv. JANE, b. ——; m. —— Kimbell; res., Bangor, Me., and d. there.

1308. v. NANCY, b. ——; m. —— Libby. She d. Mattawamkeag, Me., May 8, 1897. A son is W. F.; res., Mattawamkeag, Me.

1309. vi. LUCY R., b. April 15, 1821; m., Jan. 12, 1837, Thomas Finson Rowe; res., Eddington, Me. He was b. Brewer, Me., Sept. 8, 1813; d. Feb. 19, 1882. She d. Dec. 31, 1887. Res., Eddington, Me. Ch.: 1. Thomas Foster, b. Feb. 18, 1838; m. abt. 1870. Res., Whitesboro, Mendocino Co., Cal. 2. Ann Mariah, b. Nov. 19, 1839; d. Nov. 22, 1842. 3. Lucy Maryett, b. Dec. 2, 1841; d. June 5, 1842. 4. Charles Albert, b. April 10, 1843; m. spring of 1865. Res., Brewer, Me. 5. Lucy Mariah, b. Aug. 23, 1844; d. Oct. 16, 1844. 6. Ella Frances, b. Dec. 11, 1845; m., Aug. 29, 1865, Zenas Rogers Farrington. Res., 33 Smith St., Portland, Me. He was b. March 31, 1833; d. Sept. 8, 1896. Was a manufacturer. Ch.: (a) Albert Rogers Farrington, b. July 12, 1866. Res., 33 Smith St., Portland, Me. (b) John Cuyler Farrington, b. Jan. 14, 1868. Res., Melville, Mont. (c) Abbie Louis Farrington, b. Nov. 14, 1869. Res., 33 Smith St., Portland, Maine. (d) William Rowe Farrington, b. July 15, 1871; m. Sept. 4, 1896. Res., 4 Mt. Vernon St., Boston, Mass. (e) Florence Marsh Farrington, b. Sept. 3, 1873; d. Aug. 10, 1882. (f) Ella Marion Farrington, b. Nov. 17, 1876. Res., 33 Smith St., Portland, Me. (g) Herbert Oscar Farrington, b. March

H. H. ROWE.

14, 1880. Res., 33 Smith St., Portland, Me. 7. Llewellyn Osborn, b. May 16, 1847; m. abt. 1875. Res., Big Rapids, Michigan. 8. Eva Jane, b. May 16, 1848; m. Nov., 1868. Res., Bethel, Maine. 9. Florence, b. June 20, 1851; d. Oct. 27, 1851. 10. Lucy Farr, b. Dec. 1, 1853; d. Feb. 4, 1862. 11. Henry Herbert, b. May 2, 1855; m. abt. 1880. Res., Salt Lake City, Utah. 12. Ernest, b. Sept. 30, 1856; m. abt. April, 1881. Res., Salt Lake City, Utah. 13. Addie Marilla (twin), b. Jan. 22, 1859; m. Nov. 13, 1878; d. Nov. 14, 1879. 14. Fannie Louisa (twin), b. Jan. 22, 1859; m. May, 1879. Res., Cumberland, Me. 15. Mary Althea, b. Aug. 19, 1862; m. June, 1881; d. Feb. 14, 1887. Her child, Leon Edgar Morse, resides at Eddington, Me. 16. Carrie Elma, b. Feb. 16, 1867; m. July 4, 1883; d. Jan. 21, 1888. Her child, Bernice Elinor Day, resides at Salt Lake City, Utah, care Henry H. Rowe.

1310. vii. WILLIAM CHARLES, b. Sept. 8, 1823; m. Rosanna Grant.

1311. viii JOSEPH W., b. Oct. 24, 1815; m. Harriet L. Scammon.

1312. ix. HERMAN N., b. July 5, 1826; m. Eliza Moore.

732. CAPT. JOSEPH FOSTER (Joseph, Jeremiah, John, Reginald, Reginald), b. Gloucester, Mass., May 23, 1764; m., Nov. 3, 1782, Rebecca Ingersoll, dau. of Medifer and Dorothy (Low), b. Aug. 26, 1759; d. April 27, 1820. He was third mate of the Rebel Letter of Marque ship "The Polly," of which his father was captain; captured in 1782 by the English, and was a prisoner of war on parole at Windsor, Nova Scotia, in July of that year. (For copy of parole of Capt. Joseph Foster, see page 185 of this book.) He m. at the house of his father, who then resided at the "Farms" in Gloucester, Rebecca Ingersoll, daughter of Medifer (David, Samuel, George, Richard), and Dorothy (Low) Ingersoll, of Gloucester; b. Aug. 26, 1759, in Gloucester. He resided in Gloucester and was one of the selectmen in 1798, 1804, 1805, 1806 and 1807, being a republican in politics. He attended the Independent Christian church. He was the administrator of the estate of his father. He was a sea captain and was lost at sea in 1816, having never been heard from after sailing from Gloucester, Aug. 3, 1816, in the sloop "William," belonging to William Pierce & Sons, bound to the Island of Guadalupe, West Indies. He is supposed to have been lost in a hurricane, about the middle of September, near that island. His wife d. April 27, 1820. He d., was lost at sea, Sept. 1816. Res. Gloucester, Mass.

1313. ii. JOSEPH, b. Aug. 2, 1784; m. Adelaide C. Spalding.

1314. i. JOSEPH, b. Aug. 10, 1783; d. July 5, 1784.

1315. iii. LYDIA, b. Dec. 26, 1785; d. Oct. 5, 1786.

1316. iv. LYDIA, b Feb. 4, 1787; m., Sept. 24, 1817, Senter Merrill of Gloucester., b. April 12, 1788. Res. Gloucester and Boston. He d. Dec. 9, 1856 She d. Feb. 12, 1863. Ch.: 1. Josephine Augusta, b. 1818; d. Nov. 21, 1822. 2. Josephine Augusta, b. July 1, 1822; d. unm. Jan. 19, 1892. 3. Octavia Maria, b. Aug., 1820; unm. Res. Gloucester. 4. Octavius Augustus, b. Aug. 1, 1820; m. Mary Eliza Wonson. Res. Gloucester. He d. Dec. 25, 1893. 1 ch., Grace Lovis, b. June 19, 1852.

1317. v. BENJAMIN, b. April 12, 1788; m. Ruby Frye.

1318. vi. REBECCA, b. Feb. 21, 1792; d. June 1, 1792.

1319. vii. REBECCA, b. Nov. 2, 1793; m. in Gloucester, David Elwell, of Gloucester, born May 6, 1788, son of Isaac Elwell, born July 12, 1743, in Gloucester; died Jan. 22, 1832, and Martha (Brown), his wife, born Aug. 16, 1747, in Gloucester, died Dec. 21, 1788; Isaac Elwell's second wife was Mrs. Tamma Davis, born July 26, 1741, died March 15, 1833. Residence, Gloucester. She died Dec. 23, 1828, in Gloucester. David Elwell again married Aug. 8, 1830, in Gloucester, Mary Ellery Calder, of Gloucester; res. Boston and vicinity; they had 4 ch. She d. Jan. 27, 1892, at Arlington, Mass., in her ninetieth year. The first merchant vessel to carry the Stars and Stripes through the Straits of Magellan, was the Endeavor, of Salem, Captain, David Elwell, in 1824. (Prbele's History U. S. Flag, p. 362.) He d. April 27, 1870, in Fernandina, Florida, while on a visit to his descendants there. Children born in Gloucester: 1. Nancy Davison, b. in May 24, 1817; m. Sept. 24, 1840, in Boston, Francis H. Flagg, of Boston; b. Feb. 23, 1811; res. Tallahassee, Florida; she d. June 25, 1843, at Bel Air, near Tallahassee. Francis H. Flagg m. 2d., Mary Elizabeth Maxwell, only child of William McWhir Maxwell, of Tallahassee, by his first wife; his second wife was Rebecca Foster Elwell; and had children. He died Dec. 12, 1872, in Tallahassee. Child: 1. Isaac, b. in 1841; d. Oct. 16, 1841. 2. Rebecca Foster, b. April 3, 1819; m., June 7, 1842, in Tallahassee, Florida, William McWhir Maxwell, of Tallahassee (his second wife), b. Dec. 27, 1807, in Bryan County, Ga, Res. Bel Air, near Tallahassee.

1320. viii. JEREMIAH, b. Oct. 25, 1794; d. 1795.

1321. ix. JEREMIAH, b. Dec. 1, 1797; m. Caroline Stevens and Charlotte Babson.

1322. x. MARY ELIZA, b. Dec. 1, 1797; d. Dec. 1, 1797.

1323. xi. THOS. JEFFERSON, b. Jan. 20, 1801; m. Julia Ann Babson and Rebecca Elwell.

1324. xii. MARY FRANCES, b. Jan. 30, 1802; m., Sept. 1824, Eben Hough Redding of Gloucester. He was born in Gloucester, Mass., Sept. 24, 1780 and died in New York aet. 93. He was a tinsmith in early life, joined the Gloucester artillery company, June 17, 1817, became fireman in 1830 and member of the Independent Parish Committee in 1835. In 1840 or thereabouts he moved to Boston, thence to New York; in both places he was weigher and gauger. He passed his last days with his grandchildren. Res. Spring Valley, N. Y. She d. May, 25, 1886. He d. ——. Ch.: 1. Frances Winship, b. Oct. 1, 1825; m., Nov. 16, 1872, Dr. Daniel D. Smith, M. D. She d. March 11, 1885. Res. 22 E. 11th street, New York, N. Y. 2. William Foster, b. June 16, 1829; m., Nov. 9, 1859, Emilie K. Hurxthal, b. Jan. 22, 1837. Was captain 24th Mass. Regt. in civil war. He d. March 7, 1876. Res. Spring Valley, N. Y. 5 ch. 3. Annie Hough, b. April, 1835; m., Jan, 1859, Wm. Fettyplace Endicott of Salem, b. June 29, 1835. Res. Spring Valley, N. Y., s. p.

1325. xiii. ARRIA, b. Oct. 23, 1804; m. in 1832, James Ellery. She d. 1850. Res. Gloucester, Mass. James Ellery was a descendant of William Ellery, an early settler of Gloucester, where he married, Oct. 8, 1663, Hannah, daughter of William Vinson. She died Dec. 24, 1675, and he again married, June 13, 1676, Mary Coit. He had thirteen children, and died Dec. 9, 1696. His son, Nathaniel, born March 31, 1683, married, Jan. 1, 1711, Abigail Norwood, who died three months later, and he again married, Feb. 16, 1721, Ann Sargent, born 1692, daughter of William Sargent, 2d, and granddaughter of William and Mary (Epes) Sargent. A fine portrait of this lady, in her advanced years, by Copley, is in possession of a descendant. She died Oct. 8, 1782. Mr. Ellery died May 30, 1761. William Ellery, signer of the Declaration of Independence, and the distinguished theologian and divine, William Ellery Channing, D. D., were both descendants of William Ellery of Gloucester. Notices of William Ellery and his descendants, from which the above information is taken, will be found in Babson's History of Gloucester, pages, 84-87, and 157, and in notes and Additions, Part 1st, pages 18-21. Children born in Gloucester: 1. Edward Epes, b. March 30, 1833; m., Aug. 1, 1854, Mrs. Mary J. Bates, of Baltimore, Md. He was in 1864 the Union or Republican candidate for Congress in the fifth district, consisting of wards 7, 10, 13 and 14 of New York City; he received 3921 votes, Wm. B. Maclay (Mozart), 4286, and Nelson Taylor (Tammany), who was elected, 9272. She d. Aug. 12, 1864, in New York. He d. Dec. 22, 1864, in New York. Children born in New York: i. James Henry Friend, b. May 8, 1855; m., Sept. 18, 1877, Anna Maria Lloyd; five children. ii. Joseph Edgar, b. May 15, 1857. Both engaged in 1885 in the printing business, at 27 Beekman street, New York. iii. Theodore Nelson, b. after 1857; d. young. iv. Edward Epes, b. after 1857; d. young. 2. Joseph Foster, b. Dec. 25, 1834; m. Mrs. Phoebe Brewster. Res. in 1885,

522 Lafayette Avenue, Brooklyn, N. Y. No children. 3. Eben Hough Redding, b. July 10, 1837; m., Jan. 10, 1860, Charlotte E. Surguy, of Cincinnati, Ohio. Res. in 1885, with his brother James Odell Ellery, at 544 Lafayette Avenue, Brooklyn, N. Y., but traveling south much of the time. He d. June 18, 1886, in Memphis, Tenn. 2 ch.—4. James Odell, b. June 11, 1839; m., Dec. 25, 1866, Julia Mahlar. He was Customs officer, Barger office, New York, N. Y. 4 ch. 5. Geo. Henry, b. Oct. 8, 1844; m., Nov. 1, 1870, Mary Abrams. Res. New York, N. Y. 1 ch.

737. BENJAMIN FOSTER (Joseph, Jeremiah, John Reginald, Reginald), b. Gloucester, 1769; m., Jan. 11, 1789, Mary (Polly) Ingersoll, dau. of David. In Aug., 1791, he was master of the brigantine "Polly" of Gloucester, from Martinique, and he was also master of the same vessel in May, 1792 and in March, 1793. April 4, 1794, the brigantine "Polly," Benjamin Foster, master, was captured at Point à Pitre, Guadaloupe, by the "Siren" or "Sirius," an English frigate, George Engleton, commander one of Admiral Jarvis' fleet. The "Polly" was ladened with molasses, coffee, sugar, etc., and with cargo was valued at £ 6.571. 10. 0. "Polly" was the name of his wife. He is last mentioned in Colonel Foster's books in June, 1795. She is last mentioned in Feb. 1796. He d. between 1799 and 1800. His widow m., Dec. 1800, Joseph Locke, a merchant of Boston, whose first wife was her sister Martha Ingersoll and who d. s. p. Mary became the mother of Mrs. Frances Sargent Osgood, the poetess, of Mrs. E. D. Harrington, the author of various graceful compositions, and of Mr. A. A. Locke, a brilliant and elegant writer in prose and verse, for many years connected with the public journals. Mr. Joseph Locke d. April 17, 1838. His wife d. July 22, 1849. Frances Sargent Locke, b. June 18, 1811, in Boston; m., in 1835, Samuel S. Osgood, the artist, and d. May 12, 1850, in New York. Notices of her life will be found in the American Encyclopædia, Johnson's Universal Cyclopædia, and Allibone's Dictionary of Authors; and notices, with portraits and selections from her poems, in Duyckinck's Cyclopædia of American Literature, and in Griswold's, May's, and Read's Female Poets of America, from the last of which the following is taken: "Frances Sargent Osgood, the subject of this notice, was the daughter of the late Joseph Locke, and was a native of Boston, in which city she resided until her marriage with Samuel S. Osgood, an artist of distinction. A noted writer says of her, in a critique: 'Her personal not less than her literary character and existence, are one perpetual poem. Not to write poetry—not to think it—act it —dream it, and be it—is entirely out of her power.' Her first volume, The Wreath of Wild Flowers, was published in England during a visit to that country, immediately after her marriage. In the words of the critic already quoted, 'there was that about the volume—that inexpressible grace of thought and manner, which never fails to find a ready echo in the heart.' The next collection of her poems was published in New York, about three years since (1846), and was most favorably received by the public and the press throughout the country. A charming naiveté, an exquisite simplicity, an inimitable grace, with at times a thrilling and impassioned earnestness, are Mrs. Osgood's chief characteristics as a writer. We close our remarks with a just and beautiful tribute to our fair authoress, from the pen of a sister poetess: 'With her beautiful Italian soul, with her impulse, and wild imagery, and exuberant fancy, and glowing passionateness, and with the wonderful facility with which, like an almond tree casting off its blossoms, she flings around her heart tinted and love-perfumed lays, she has, I must believe, more of the improvisatrice than has yet been revealed by any of our gifted countrywomen.' Mrs. Osgood died in May, 1850." 2 children. He d. —. Res. Gloucester, Mass.

1326. i. ANN MARIA, b. 1795. Her father died during her infancy, and her mother m., Dec. 1800, Joseph Locke, of Boston. She was educated in Boston, and married, in 1821, Thomas Wells, of Boston, an officer of the United States Revenue Service, and the author of some prize poems printed in Kettell's Specimens of American Poetry. He was son of Capt. Thomas Wells and a grand-son of Samuel Adams, the father of the Revolution. She began to write verses when very young, but published little until her marriage. In 1831 she published Poems and Juvenile Sketches, and afterward occasionally contributed to periodicals, her chief attention having been given to a young ladies' school. Notices of her life will be found in Allibone's Dictionary of Authors, and Duyckinck's Cyclopædia of American Literature, page 456, vol. 2; and notices with selections from her poems, in Kettell's Specimens of American Poetry, and in Griswold's, Read's and May's Female Poets of America, from the last of which the following is taken: "Miss Foster, now Mrs. Wells, was born about the year 1794, in Gloucester, Mass., but was educated in Boston, and has lived there ever since. She is a highly accomplished woman, possesses a well-furnished mind, and as admirable a talent for drawing and music as for poetry. She was also, when young, no less distinguished for her exquisite beauty, than from her genius and accomplishments. Her poems were published in a volume, in 1831, but are not so generally known as they deserve to be. The specimens we subjoin are delightful for their touching simplicity, purity of thought, and fervor of feeling. Mrs. Wells is a sister of Mrs. Frances S. (Locke) Osgood, who when a child, was her loved and loving pupil, as we gather from a verse of pleasant but half mournful memory." 1. Thomas Foster, b. July 22, 1822, in Boston; m., Oct. 7, 1849, Sarah Morrill of Roxbury, Mass; b. June 11, 1829. Res. Winchester, Mass. Four children. 2. Samuel Adams, b. April 2, 1824, in Boston; m. 1st, Angeline P. Bates, of Springfield, Mass; 2d, June 20, 1861, Lavina Howard Oldfield. He d. August 30, 1864, in Virginia City, Nevada. Three children. 3. William Vincent, b. Jan. 31, 1826, in Boston. He m., Jan. 19, 1854, in San Francisco, Laura Ann (Wheelock) Jones. He was the author of the Life and Public Services of Samuel Adams (his great-grandfather) Boston, 1865, 3 vols. 8vo. He served as an aide-de-camp to Maximilian in Mexico and was with him "to the last." No ch. iv. Anna Maria, b. Sept. 2, 1828; m., Jan. 3, 1849, James D. Whelpley, M. D. She d. July 9, 1860, and Dr. Whelpley m. 2d. Mary Louise Breed; after his death his second wife m. Jacob Storer, son of Rear Admiral G. W. Storer, U. S. Navy, of Portsmouth, N. H. Ch.: Anna Vincent, b. Oct. 18, 1853, an accomplished singer and artist; m., Feb. 9, 1871, Dr. Edward Renouf, of Boston, Mass., and soon after marriage went to Europe with him. 2 ch. The following lines are copied from an old song in possession of the family; they are among the best Mrs. Wells ever wrote, and the music, which is particularly well adapted to the lines, made the song a great favorite. It will tenderly recall their old homes to the wanderers of the family.

NEW ENGLAND.

ANNA MARIA WELLS

New England, New England, my home o'er the sea,
  My heart, as I wander, turns fondly to thee,
For bright rests the sun on thy clear winding streams,
  And soft o'er thy meadows the moon pours her beams.
New England, New England, my home o'er the sea,
  The wanderer's heart turns in fondness to thee.

Thy breezes are healthful, and clear are thy rills,
  And the harvest waves proudly and rich on thy hills,
Thy maidens are fair and thy yeomen are strong,
  And thy rivers run blithely thy valleys among.
New England, New England, my home o'er the sea,
  The wanderer's heart turns in fondness to thee.

There's home in New England where dear ones of mine
  Are thinking of me and the days of "lang syne"
And blest be the hour, when my pilgrimage o'er,
  I shall sit by that hearth-stone and leave it no more.
New England, New England, my home o'er the sea,
  My heart as I wander turns fondly to thee.

746. MOSES FOSTER (Aaron, Moses, John, Reginald, Reginald), b. Nov. 4, 1760, Ipswich, Mass.; m. ———. Was in the Revolutionary War. He married and lived in the town of Wenham, a much respected citizen and an honored man. He had a family of sons and daughters, whom he lived to see in their own homes. He d. Nov. 20, 1812. Res. Wenham, Mass.

1328. i. WILLIAM, b ——; m. Mariah Andrews.
1329. ii. WARREN, b. ——; m. Judith Burnham.

*747. THOMAS FOSTER (Aaron, Moses, John, Reginald, Reginald), b. Ipswich, Mass., April 9, 1762; m., Nov. 29, 1787, Susan Storey, b. Mar. 14, 1766; d. Hamilton, Mass., June 15, 1848. He was in the Revolutionary War. He was an upright honest man, caring for his home and family till his country's call "to arms." He enlisted promptly with his father and went to join Washington at Cambridge. He was mustered out, with honor, with others who survived, but his health was gone. Susanna Story was one of the most remarkable women of her time. It is to such women as she that the races are largely indebted for the wonderful powers of mem-

* See additional notes in: "Foster, ~~Z. L.~~ - Ancestry of Zeon L. Foster, N.Y., 1920. ~~Type~~ written sheets.

ory and of appreciation, of all facts, circumstances and conditions which make up the average life, whether of poverty or of riches, of intelligence or its opposite in the human species. Compelled by hard conditions to rear her children as she could (for her husband had served through the War of the Revolution and came home disabled, broken in health, etc.), she never faltered in duty. Whatever her hand found to do she did, and taught her children to be self-supporting and to aid each other while her hands were busy. She "taught" these children the rudiments of knowledge, but it was not alone the "knowledge" which she gained from authors (for that was exceedingly limited) but it was the common sense application to everything which belonged to her life. She could find a sermon in every circumstance, a lesson for daily practice in each event, and in her own whole conduct there was an unfailing lesson for every child. Every one loved her for her pure morality, her high standard of right and her sweetness of manner and gentle courtesy to all neighbors and friends alike. He d. Nov. 10, 1809. Res., Essex, Mass.

1330. i. THOMAS, b. Dec. 30, 1790; m. Sarah Lakeman.

1331. ii. DAVID CHOATE, b. Nov. 5, 1806; m. Martha Lamson and Nancy Lamson.

1332. iii. RUTH L., b. July 31, 1804; m. in Hamilton, Mass, George Woodbury. She d. Sept. 7, 1881. They had: 1. Fred'k. 2. Martha L. 3. Charles E , all deceased.

1333. iv. SALLY, b. Oct. 1, 1788; m. Moses Marshall. Sally Foster m. —— Marshall. Ch. of —— and Sally Marshall: Sallie, Susan, Foster. Know nothing of these: M. M. Lufkin, Essex, Mass., or Latham Morris Whiteside, Chicago, Ill.

1334. v. AARON, b. Dec. 25, 1789; d. unm. in 1807. He followed the sea.

1335. vi. SUSAN, b. Sept. 15, 1794; d. Nov. 1811.

1336. vii. JULIA A., b. Oct. 1, 1796; m. Capt. Humphrey Lakeman of Ipswich. She d. aet. 91 and he aet. 70. Res., Ipswich, Mass. Ch.: 1. Martha J. 2. Caroline S. Her dau. is Miss Carrie L. Lakeman, of Ipswich, Mass. 3. James Henry, b. Nov. 22, 1833; m., June 6, 1864, Louise A. Stone, b. Sept. 14, 1844. He d. April 15, 1894. Res., Ipswich. Ch.: a. Harvey S. Lakeman, b. March 9, 1865; d. Aug. 23, 1866. b. Howard Lakeman, b. June 27, 1866; m. March 10, 1891. Address, Ipswich, Mass. c. J. Walter Lakeman, b. March 25, 1868; d. Aug. 16, 1869. d. Annie Louise Lakeman, b. Dec. 12, 1869; d. Aug. 13, 1870. e. Curtis E. Lakeman, b. Oct. 10, 1881. Res., Ipswich.

1337. viii. CLARISSA, b. Dec. 26, 1798; m. Eli Sheldon of Beverly. She d. Nov. 8, 1853. Ch.: 1. Laura. 2. Clarissa. 3. Edward. 4. Everett 5. Julia Ann.

1338. ix. CHARLES WM., b. Aug. 23, 1801; d. at sea, 1843.

1339. x. EDWARD, b. June 8, 1809; d. April 9, 1811.

748. ZEBULON FOSTER (Aaron, Moses, John, Reginald, Reginald), b. Chebacco, now Essex, Aug. 2, 1766; m., Nov. 30, 1794, Polly Story, dau. of William of Essex, b. Aug. 3, 1770; d. Aug. 3, 1851. Mr. Story was a captain in the Revolution and his commission is now in the possession of Capt. Jeremiah Foster of Henniker. Mr. Foster went to that town in March, 1814, and settled upon the hill so long known as "Foster Hill." He resided here the remainder of his days. He d. Dec. 16, 1849. Res., Henniker, N. H.

1340. i. LYDIA, b. Nov. 2, 1795; m., Nov. 24, 1814, Alexander Whitney and removed to New London in 1825-6. d. April 27, 1875; eleven children.

1341. ii. ZEBULON, Jr , b. Sept. 6, 1797; m. Abigail Wheeler, Lois Whitney and Eliza A. Folsom.

1342. iii. ELIZA F., b. June 30, 1799; m., Feb. 17, 1825, John Peters. He was a cabinet maker by trade, res. in West Henniker, N. H. She, d. June 18, 1855. He was b. Sept. 29, 1796. Son of Jacob and Sarah W. (Eager); m a second wife and d., April 4, 1876. Ch.: 1. John F. b Feb. 14, 1826; m. Hattie J. Heath. Res., Concord, N. H. 2. Eliza M., b. Aug. 14, 1827; m. Levi. C. Newton. 3. Walter H., b. March 2, 1831; d. April 13, 1846.

1343. iv. WILLIAM S. b. March 19, 1801; m. Harriet Page and Mary Cooledge.

1344. v. POLLY, b. April 23, 1803; m., April 17, 1827, Ira Colby. He was b. Henniker, N. H., Dec. 31, 1803; was a farmer; d. July 7, 1873, in Claremont. Ch.: 1. Zebulon F. Colby, b. Oct. 22, 1828; d. March, 1833. 2. Ira Colby, Jr., b. Jan. 11, 1831; m., June 20, 1867, Louisa M. Way, b. Oct. 13, 1843. Res. Claremont, N. H. Ch.: Ira Gordon Colby, b. Jan. 11, 1872. ii. Bertha Maria Colby, b. July 11, 1878; d. Aug. 10, 1879. Polly Foster Colby who died in Claremont, N. H., May 15, 1896, aet. 93 years and 22 days, was born in Essex, Mass. Her son, Hon. Ira Colby, was a prominent lawyer and her daughter, Mariette, was long a principal teacher in Africa and now resides in Claremont, N. H. Hon. Ira Colby, Jr., was a representative in the legislature of New Hampshire in 1864 and 1865. Was a member of the Senate in 1869 and 1870, representative to the republican national convention in 1876, representative in the legislature in 1881 and 1883 and in 1887. For more than twenty years he was appointed and elected State's attorney for the county of Sullivan. Has been in the practice of law since 1860 at Claremont. His son, Ira Gordon Colby, who is a graduate of Dartmouth college and Boston University Law School, is now associated in business with him. 3. Adeline R. Colby, b. Nov. 22, 1833, now Adeline R. Gibson (widow), Waterloo, Wis. 4. George F. Colby, b. July 5, 1836, now of Elgin, Neb. 5. Caroline Colby, b. Sept., 1837; d. March, 1838. 6. Mary Etta Colby, b. April 19, 1839, now in Chicago, 114 So. Wood St. 7. Helen Maria Colby, b. March 12, 1842, now lives in North Carolina; is Helen M. Vose. 8. Anna Eliza Colby, b. Jan 7, 1844; d. Sept. 24, 1871; was Anna E. Vose.

HON. IRA COLBY.

1345. vi. JEREMIAH, b. June 22, 1805; m. Adeline Rice and Martha B. Huntoon.

1346. vii. MICAJAH, b. Aug. 27, 1807; m. Betsey Tucker.

1347. viii. MIRIAM, b. Sept. 19, 1810; m., April 3, 1834, Moody Tucker. He was a life-long resident of Henniker, N. H., a selectman and worthy citizen, b. Dec. 25, 1806, son of Thomas and Charlotte (Green). Ch.: 1. Thomas F., b. Oct. 12, 1836; m., Dec. 23, 1859, Mary J. Sanborn. Res., Lawrence, Mass. 2. Emily M., b. Oct. 10, 1834; d. June 10, 1838.

755. ISRAEL FOSTER (Mathew, Jonathan, Jonathan, William, Reginald), b. Boxford, Mass., March 16, 1765; m., April 17, 1794, Mehitabel Carleton, b. Feb., 1765; d. Nov. 17, 1853. He d. April 2, 1855. Res., Boxford, Mass.

1348. i. REBECCA, b. ——; d. young.

1349. ii. RICHARD, b. ——; m. ——.

1350. iii. PHINEHAS, b. ——.

1351. iv. FRANCIS, b. ——.
1352. v. ELIZA, b. ——.
1353. vi. JONATHAN, b. ——
1354. vii. BETSEY, b. Dec. 1, 1796; m., Nov. 7, 1822, Capt. Aaron Spofford. Capt. Aaron Spofford was a veteran of the War of 1812. Daniel W. Spofford was a member of Company A, Nineteenth regt. M. V. M., in War of Rebellion; Aaron b. Feb. 1, 1795; d. May 28, 1879. She d. June 2, 1879. Res., West Boxford, Mass. Ch.: 1. Rebecca F., b. Feb. 4, 1824; m., Nov. 26, 1851, Samuel Killam. Res., 56 Forrester St., Salem, Mass 2. Phinehas, b. Dec. 13, 1825. Res., Topsfield, Mass. Phinehas Foster Spofford was captain of Company ——, in South Carolina Eighth regiment in War of the Rebellion, and after Lee's surrender was sheriff of Chesterfield county, S. C., for eighteen years, resigning his position on account of ill health. 3. Eliza J., b. Feb. 2, 1828; m. Lorenzo D. Wheeler. 4. Sarah A., b., Dec. 1, 1829; d. in infancy. 5. Julia M., b. Jan. 18, 1831; m., Nov. 3, 1848, Joseph B. Perkins. Res., 15 French St., Lynn, Mass. 6. Mehitabel, b. Feb. 24, 1832; m., Aug. 13, 1854, John Hale. Res., Georgetown, Mass. 7. Aaron, b. April 20, 1833; d. Aug. 30, 1862. Killed in the battle of Grovetown; was in Company E, Twelfth regiment, Mass. Vols. 8. Harriet, b. Oct. 1, 1836; d. Jan. 9, 1874. 9. Israel, b. May 8, 1839; m., May 25, 1871, Rebecca P. Stocker, b. Jan. 11, 1849. Res., Bradford, Mass. Was a carpenter. Ch.: (a) Carrie Emma, b Sept. 28, 1872; d. March 26, 1898. (b) Allen Pierce, b. Dec. 3. 1874 (c) Bertram Horner, b. July 24, 1876. (d) Hattie Rebecca, b. July 16, 1877. (e) Jennie Foster, b. April 17, 1879. (f) Grace Winifred, b. Feb. 18, 1887. Address of Bertram H. Spofford, Atkinson Depot, N. H.

756. DEA. CHARLES FOSTER (Jonathan, Jonathan, Jonathan, William, Reginald), b. Boxford, Mass., April 26, 1767; m., March, 1796, Lucy Austin, of Andover, b. 1770; d. March 28, 1805; m., 2d, Nov. 19, 1807, Mehitabel Chandler, dau. of Ephraim and Mehitabel (Barker), b. 1783; d. Aug. 11, 1826. He d. July 10, 1851. Res., Andover and North Andover, Mass.

1355. i. BETSEY, b. March 12, 1809.
1356. ii. JOHN PLUMMER, b. Oct. 28, 1817; m. Sarah A. Peabody.
1357. iii. MEHITABEL G, b. April 7, 1813; m. —— Robinson. Res., Boyne, Mich.
1358. iv. LUCY, b. Nov. 17, 1800.
1359. v. JOANNA CHANDLER, b. Sept. 9, 1808.
1360. vi. REBECCA, b. June 12, 1797; m., Nov., 1828, Benjamin Robinson. She d. Oct. 24, 1864. He was b. Nov. 21, 1797, in Beverly, Mass.; d. Boxford, Sept. 29, 1855. Was a farmer. Ch.: 1. Eliza Ann Robinson, b. Oct. 8, 1829. Res., Boyne, Mich. 2. Rebecca J. Robinson, b. June 14, 1832; m. Samuel G. Cooper. Res., 18 Hanover St., Worcester, Mass. 3. John V. Robinson, b. May 2, 1835; m. Helen M. Dakin. Res., Peabody, Mass., 81 Endicott St. 4. Charlotte P. Robinson. b. Aug. 10, 1837; m. Samuel Williams. Res., 493 Washington St., Dorchester, Mass. 5. Enoch K. Robinson, b. Nov. 16, 1841; m. Annie Hudson. Res., Boyne Falls, Mich.
1361. vii. CHARLES WILLIAM, b. June 9, 1815; m. and had two sons, Fred and Nathaniel.
1362. viii. ELIZABETH, b. Feb. 28, 1803.

759. JONATHAN FOSTER (Jonathan, Jonathan, Jonathan, William, Reginald), b. Boxford, Mass., Feb. 3, 1774; m., Dec. 24, 1800, Mary Kimball, b. 1777; d. June 7, 1854. He d. Nov. 17, 1856. Res., Boxford, Mass.

1363. i. MARY, b. Oct. 12, 1801; Dec. 24, 1833, Christopher Howe. He was b. March 31, 1791; d. July 13, 1876. She d. Methuen, Mass., Aug. 31, 1886. Ch.: 1. Mary Jane, b. Nov. 23, 1835; d. April 13, 1893. 2. Albianne Henrietta, b. Jan. 30, 1842. Res., Methuen, Mass. 3. Albion Henry, b. Jan. 30, 1842. Res., N.

Braintree, Mass. 4. Caroline Augusta, b. Aug. 13, 1837; m., June 2, 1870, William M. Rogers, b. Sept. 14, 1833. Res., Methuen, Mass. Ch.: i. Christopher Howe Rogers, b. May 6, 1871. Amherst college, B. A.; Boston University, LL. B.; attorney at law, Gloucester, Mass. ii. Annie Tenney Rogers, b. Aug. 19, 1876; d. March 17, 1877.

1364. ii. ELEANOR, b. Feb. 26, 1804; m. in West Boxford, Joseph Hyde Huntington, of Norwich, Conn. She d. ——, 1866. He was b. June 11, 1811; d. 1865. Was a furniture dealer. Ch.: 1. Sarah Williams Huntington, b. Brunswick, O., June 27, 1837. Present address, Washington, D. C. 2. George Frederic, b. Feb. 27, 1839, in Brunswick, O.; d. April 30, 1855, Norwich, Conn. 3. Charles Lyman Foster, b. Aug. 3, 1841; m., Oct. 7, 1869, Ella Shaffer, b. Dec. 18, 1848. Res., Cincinnati, O. Is in the china and glassware business. Ch.: (a) Hyde Shaffer, b. July 16, 1870; d. Feb. 20, 1871. (b) Ruth, b. Oct. 8, 1873. (c) Eleanor, b. March 19, 1883. P. O. of both, Hamilton, O.

1366. iv. JONATHAN EDWARDS, b. May 9, 1815; m. Susan R. Peabody.

1367. v. GEORGE NOYES, b. March 31, 1817; m. Martha Jane Symonds.

1368. vi. ASA KIMBALL, b. Feb. 20, 1807; d. Nov. 13, 1835; unm.

760. PHINEHAS FOSTER (Jonathan, Jonathan, Jonathan, William, Reginald), b. Boxford, Mass., July 27, 1776; m. Aug. 25, 1805, in Haverhill, Mass., Frances Harrod, b. ——, 1783; d. Boston, March 23, 1872.

Will—Phinehas Foster, late of Boston. Ch.: John H. Foster, William H. Foster, George Foster, Francis Foster, Edward Foster, Frances H. Foster. Dated June 26, 1835; prob. Sept. 21, 1835; Lib. 133[2], Fol. 218.

Petition for trusteeship mentions Frances Foster, widow of the late Phinehas Foster. Lib. 329, Fol. 91. Lib. 338, Fol. 19. Nov. 13, 1837.

Trustees account mentions Charles P. Foster, George Foster, Edwin Lemist, guardian for Robert M. Foster and Elizabeth A. Foster, Francis Foster, Frances H. Downes, Edward Foster. April 13, 1868. Lib. 166, Fol. 245-6. Lib. 333, Fol. 9-10. Lib. 275, Fol. 225-6. Lib. 168, Fol. 441. Lib. 458, Fol. 557-8. Lib. 241, Fol. 67. Lib. 242, Fol. 163. Lib. 253, Fol. 8. Lib. 249, Fol. 133. Lib. 319, Fol. 62. Lib. 134[2], Fol. 245. Lib. 139[2], Fol. 41. Lib. 449, Fol. 162-182. Suff. prop.

Frances Foster, of Boston, widow, appointed guardian for Francis Foster, a minor above 14 years; Edward Foster, a minor under 14 years; Frances H. Foster, a minor under 14 years; children of Phineas Foster of Boston; merchant; dec'd. Oct. 10, 1836. Lib. 378, Fol. 10. Lib. 404, Fol. 42. Lib. 408, Fol. 43.

Minor petition for sale of real estate mentions Francis Foster, Edward Foster, Frances H. Foster, minors, John H. Foster, William H. Foster, George Foster, tenants of land and house in Haverhill; land deeded from Anna Harrod et al. to Phinehas Foster, Jan. 13, 1830. Oct. 10, 1836. Lib. 357, Fol. 124. Lib. 358, Fol. 140. Lib. 359, Fol. 152. Lib. 360, Fol. 80. Lib. 362, Fol. 45. Lib. 135, Fol. 37. Lib. 139[2], Fol. 287.

Petition dated Nov. 15, 1841. Frances Foster, guardian of above Frances H. Foster and Edward Foster. Lib. 362, Fol. 147-240.

Final account of Frances Foster, guardian, mentions Edwin Lemist, guardian for Robert M. Foster and Elizabeth A. Foster, Edward Foster, Frances H. Foster, now Frances H. Downes, widow. April 13, 1868. Lib. 166, Fol. 251.

He d. Sept. —, 1835. Res., Boston, Mass.

1369. i. WILLIAM HENRY, b. Jan. 9, 1810; m. Hannah G. Locke.

1370. ii. CHARLES P., b. Oct. 14, 1806; d. unm.

Will—Charles P. Foster, of Boston. Sister, Mrs. F. H. Downes; Mary Foster, daughter of my brother William Foster; Mrs. Downes, three daughters; E. A. Foster, daughter of brother Frank Foster; cousin, Susan, wife of William Boyd, of Portland, Me. Dated Oct. 26, 1872. Prob. Sept. 8, 1879. Lib. 515, Fol. 62.

Petition for probate. Charles P. Foster died Aug. 13, 1879. Heirs at law, Frances H. Downes, of Boston, sister; William H. Foster, Brookline, brother; George Foster, New Orleans, brother; Edward Foster, Boston, brother; Elizabeth A. Foster, niece and minor. Aug. 19, 1879. Lib. 514, Fol. 145. Lib. 517, Fol. 323.

1371. iii. JOHN HARROD, b. May 2, 1808; d. unm.
1372. iv. GEORGE, b. Feb. 10, 1815; m. Adele Ruston, ——— —— and —— ——.
1373. v. FRANCIS, b. Aug. 4, 1819; m. Sarah E. Lemist.
1374. vi. EDWARD, b. Sept. 27, 1813; d. Jan. 12, 1814.
1375. vii. FRANCES HARROD, b. June 25, 1827; m. John Downes. She d. Nov. 25, 1896. John Downes was son of Commodore Downes, U. S. N. Ch.: 1. Lieut. John Downes, U. S. N. Address, Naval Hospital, Quincy, Mass. 2. Francis Foster Downes. Res., Eliot St., Jamaica Plains, Mass. 3. Philip Verplanck Hoffman Downes. 4. Frances Harrod Downes; m. Lieut. Arthur P. Nazro, U. S. N.; d. Nov. 1, 1893. 5. Adele Rushton Downes. 6. Mary Campbell Downes.
1376. viii. EDWARD, b. June 12, 1824; d. unm. Dec., 1882. Lemuel Shaw, of Boston appointed administrator of estate of Edward Foster, of Boston, d. Dec. —, 1882; leaving no widow; next of kin being William H. Foster, of Brookline, brother; George Foster, residence unknown, brother; Frances H. Downes, of Boston, widow, sister; and Elizabeth A. Foster, of Boston, niece. Jan. 15, 1883; Lib. 547, Fol. 339. Lib. 545, Fol. 140. Lib. 568, Fol. 8. Suff. Prob.

763. ASA FOSTER (Richard, Jonathan, Jonathan, William, Reginald), b. Boxford, Mass., April 29, 1776; m., Jan. 20, 1802, Dolly Morrill, of Salisbury. He d. Dec. —, 1831. Res., Boxford, Mass.

1377. i. ARCHELAUS MORRILL, b. March 10, 1803; d. March 24, 1827.
1378. ii. ASA, b. Nov 10, 1806; d. April 22, 1835, n. c. m.
1379. iii. RICHARD KIMBALL, b. Aug. 21, 1809; m. Elizabeth Webb.

764. ASA FOSTER (Abner, Zebediah, Jonathan, William, Reginald), b. Newry, Me., ——; m. ——, Anna Bartlett, dau. of Enoch. He d., ae. 85. Res., Newry, Me.

1380. i. NATHAN, b. ——; m. Patty Stearns.
1381. ii. REUBEN B., b. ——; m. Sarah Bartlett.
1382. iii. ENOCH, b. Jan. 1, 1799; m. Persis Swan and Mrs. Amaziah Nutting.
1383. iv. ELI, b. ——; m. Dorcas Bartlett.
1384. v. BENJAMIN, b. ——; m. Louisa Coburn.
1385. vi. ASA, b. ——.
1386. vii. JOEL, b. ——.
1387. viii. SILAS, b. ——.
1388. ix. BETSEY, b. ——.
1389. x. ANNIE, b. ——.
1390. xi. SUBMIT, b. ——.
1391. xii. LYDIA, b. ——.
1392. xiii. POLLY, b. ——.
1393. xiv. ELHANAN BARTLETT, b. Feb. 13, 1823; m. Mehitabel Chapman. He was a farmer. Res., No. Waterford, Me.

768. WILLIAM FOSTER (William, John, William, William, Reginald), b. Andover, Mass., June 1, 1758; m., Aug. 27, 1826, Sarah Welch Kimball, b. Dec. 20, 1786; d. March 16, 1850. His mother was a sister of the John Abbot, who helped found the Andover Theo. Seminary. They resided together. "Master Billy," or "Master William," as he was called, kept a family school for boys for several years, and after his mother's death, married Miss Kimball, of Plaistow, N. H.

The private boarding school of Master William Foster was opened some years after Phillips' Academy, and was chiefly intended for boys who did not wish to take a classical course. Mr. Foster lived on his father's estate, the home of his boyhood. He made additions to the house to adapt it to the wants of his large household, which numbered sometimes more than twenty-five. The ancient house, as he remodeled it, still stands—a long rambling building, nestled under the hill, a little off Central street, a half mile west from the South Church. Near the street was a school-house, now removed.

The old family manse has names of boys carved on its walls, and many nicks of their penknives in its wainscotings. A large part of the furniture and books of

Master Foster are stored in the garret, queer chests of drawers, strong desks, and toilet sets, at which, no doubt, reluctant lads made themselves presentable at early morning hours. Some aged persons now remember having seen the boys at table, seated on long benches, and each with a bowl of milk or chocolate, and the fresh loaf, baked on the great brick oven's bottom, nicely swept clean of the live coals. The boys had ovens in the sand-hill, near the house, where at night, when they were supposed to be safe in bed, they roasted unlucky chickens, which disappeared mysteriously from the roost. Mrs. Foster's mother presided over the household—a gentle, placid lady of the old school; a sister of Samuel Abbott, Esq., the founder of the Theological Seminary. She d. in 1820, aged eighty-seven. The school was continued until within a few years of her death. Mr. Foster married, late in life, Miss Sally Kimball, of Plaistow, N. H. He had one son, the late Mr. William P. Foster.—Hist. Andover.

He d. Aug. 30, 1843. Res., Andover, Mass.

1394. i. WILLIAM PHILLIPS, b. Jan. 21, 1830; m. Jane C. Kimball and Anna M. Barrows.

771. JOHN FOSTER (John, John, Jonn. William, William, Reginald), b. Andover, Mass., Feb. 10, 1773; m., April 25, 1797, Sarah Burt, of Reading, b. Nov. 13, 1774; d. July 21, 1828. He d. in 1855. Res., Andover, Mass., and Loudon, N. H.

1395 i HANNAH BALLARD, b. Nov. 25, 1797; m., Dec. 2, 1821, James Howarth, b. Nov. 30, 1793, in Rochdale, England; d. Penacook, N. H., March, 1872. She d. Aug., 1864. Was a manufacturer. Ch.: 1. Joseph Howarth, b. Dec. 11, 1821; d. Aug. 2, 1823. 2. Sarah Ann Fielding Howarth, b. Oct. 1, 1823; m. Jonathan Walsh, b. July 9, 1817; d. June, 1897. Was a manufacturer. Ch.: (a) Hannah F., b. Sept. 25, 1847. (b) James Newton, b. April 28, 1850; d. Aug., 1855; res., Penacook, N. H. 3. Hannah Almira Howarth, b. Oct. 15, 1825. Address, Hannah Almira Page, West Hampstead, N. H. 4. Joseph Newton Howarth, b. Jan. 2, 1829; d. Oct. 15, 1830. 5. James William Howarth, b. Aug. 17, 1831. Address, Clara F. Sargent, 53 Pillsbury St., Concord, N. H.

1396. ii. SARAH, b. Aug. 19, 1799; m. in Andover in 1834, John F. Howarth. He was b. Lancashire, England, Nov. 30, 1795; d. Loudon, N. H., Dec. 10, 1843. Was a woolen manufacturer. She d. Oct. 24, 1887. Ch.: 1. Martha Jane Howarth, b. March 10, 1835; d. April 17, 1849. 2. Mary Ann Howarth, b. Sept. 3, 1837; m. Henry A. Harris, Nov. 27, 1867. Res., Lawrence, Mass. Ch.: (a) Carrie Goldsmith Harris. (b) George Alfred Harris. 3. William H. Howarth, b. Jan. 21, 1840; d. Feb. 2, 1860. 4. Sarah F. Howarth, b. April 7, 1842; d. Dec. 18, 1868.

1397. iii. JOHN, b. July 23, 1802; m. Sarah Harding.

1398. iv. WILLIAM, b. Jan. 12, 1806; d. young.

1399. v. MARY OSGOOD, b. Sept. 29, 1812; m. Jonathan Blood, s. p.

1400. vi. WILLIAM PITTS, b. Dec., 1810; m. Lucinda Randall.

774. ABIAL FOSTER (Isaac, John, William, William, Reginald), b. Tewksbury, Mass., May 25, 1763; m., Nov. 23, 1788, Sarah Whiting, dau. of Samuel. He was in Rev. War for three years. Res., Billerica, Mass.

1401. i. SARAH, b. May 14, 1793; m. William Denton, of Braintree. Ch.: 1. William Pitt; m. and had one child.

1402. ii. MIRIAM, b. March 2, 1797; m. April 15, 1832, in Boston, Luke Brooks. She d. Jan. 26 1876. Ch.: 1. Sylvanus Foster, b. Jan. 15, 1834; d. unm. Oct. 13, 1884. 2. Eugene Denton, b. Feb. 20, 1835; m., Feb. 12, 1874, Sarah Whitney, of Henniker, N. H. Res., Cambridge, Mass., 21 Lee St. Ch.: (a) Marion R. Brooks, b. March 26, 1875; m. Gorham H. Davis. Res., Arlington, Mass. (b) Lyman W. Brooks, b. Nov. 9, 1876. Res., 21 Lee St., Cambridge, Mass. (c) Edith D. Brooks, b. Sept. 19, 1878. Res., 21 Lee St., Cambridge, Mass. (d) Philip W. Brooks, b. May 15, 1883. Res., 21 Lee St., Cambridge, Mass. (e) Shirley Foster, b. July 3, 1885. Res., 21 Lee St., Cambridge, Mass. (f) Eugene Childs, b. March 11, 1887. Res., 21 Lee St., Cambridge, Mass. (g) Robert Larkin, b. Jan. 2,

1890. Res., 21 Lee St., Cambridge, Mass. (h) Marguerite, b. March 24, 1892. Res., 21 Lee St., Cambridge, Mass. (i) Horace Howard, b. June 17, 1894. Res., 21 Lee Street, Cambridge, Mass. 3. Rebecca King, d. unm. 4. Lyman G., d., aet. 15 mos.

EUGENE DENTON BROOKS

787. JOHN FOSTER (Obadiah, John, William, William, Reginald), b. March 3, 1770, in Andover, Mass.; m., in 1799, Mary Danforth, dau. of Samuel and Mary (Toothaker), b. March 1, 1780, in Billerica; d. Nov. 27, 1802; m. 2d, June 14, 1803, Lucy Hastings, dau. of Benjamin and Experience (Ball), of Bolton, b. Feb. 26, 1783; d. Sept. 10, 1842; m. 3d, Jan. 25, 1843, Mrs. Sally Morse Couch, of Boscawen, N. H.; d. Jan. 24, 1866. He lived in Andover and Tewksbury until 1810, when he removed to Nottingham, West N. H., afterward called Hudson, and was there engaged in mercantile pursuits until 1830; thence he removed to Warner, N. H., where he resided until his decease, April 13, 1846. Mr. Foster possessed a quick and sound judgment, great energy of character and rare virtues. He was mild, frank, manly and determined in action, urbane and conciliatory in manners, exemplary in habits, and "scrupulously faithful and conscientious in the discharge of all the duties of life." While he had no fondness for, and would rarely accept public office, his kindliness of heart and good judgment drew many to him for suggestions and advice. His influence was widely felt in every community in which he resided. He had eight children: two by his first wife, and six by the second. He d. April 13, 1846. Res., Andover, and Tewksbury, Mass., and Hudson and Warner, N. H.

1403. i. HERMAN, b. Oct. 31, 1800, in Andover; m. Harriet Mary Ann Whittemore, of West Cambridge, Mass., now Arlington.

1404. ii. SABRA, b. May 31, 1802, in Andover; m., Dec. 25, 1822, Dr. Isaac Tewsbury, of Hampstead, N. H.; d. Nov. 25, 1858.

1405. iii. CHARLES, b. May 11, 1804, in Tewksbury, Mass.; m. Ann Evans, of Charlestown, Mass. He d. Jan. 19, 1850. She d. Nov. 9, 1851. Ch.: 1. Martha Ann, b. Nov. 20, 1825; d. Aug. 14, 1870. 2. Benjamin Hastings, b. Nov., 1828; d. April 26, 1870.

1406. iv. EMILY, b. Aug. 25, 1813, in Hudson, N. H.; m., March 8, 1838, Ebenezer Sargent Badger, of Warner, N. H.

1407. v. JOHN, b. Dec. 30, 1817; m. Harriet Sanford.

1408. vi. GEORGE, b. Sept. 23, 1821; m. Salome F. Little.

1409. vii. JOHN H., b. Dec. 7, 1811; d. April 26, 1818.

1410. viii. MARY JANE, b. Nov. 17, 1808; d. Nov. 1, 1809.

792. GIDEON FOSTER (Obadiah, John William, William, Reginald), b. May 23, 1779, Andover, Mass; m., Oct. 14, 1804, Tabitha Robbins, b. 1782; d. Mar. 29, 1812; m. 2d., March 28, 1814, Pamelia Winn, b. 1778; d. Feb. 29, 1842; m. 3d, April 13, 1843, Mrs. Ruth Rose, b. April, 1788; d. Oct. 24, 1868. He was keeper of the alms-house. He purchased in Charlestown, of O. Holden, lot on New street and other property of John Smith. In 1818 he made other purchases of Sarah Herricks. He was adm. of the estate of W. Bisphenn in 1815. He d. April 24, 1865. Res. Charlestown, Mass.

1411. i. JAMES FREDERICK, b. March 17, 1806; m. Caroline D. Bedney.

1412. ii. WILLIAM, b. Feb. 14, 1808; m. Elizabeth Wheeler.

1413. iii. MARY ROBBINS, b. Dec. 26, 1809; m. Dexter Bowman; a descendant is Mrs. Charles Foster of Bangor, Me.
1414. iv. THOMAS ROBBINS, b. Dec. 23, 1811; m. Caroline Alley.
1415. v. GIDEON, b. Sept. 22, 1816. Went west.
1416. vi. JOSEPH WINN, b. July 24, 1818; m. Sarah Alley.
1417. vii. FRANCIS, b. Jan. 1820; d. Sept. 2, 1820.
1418. viii. FRANCIS. b. Sept. 13, 1822; m. Lucy M. Robinson.
1419. ix. MARIA JACKSON, b. Oct. 2, 1825; m. Rev. Henry Fred'k Bond of West Newton, Mass.: had 3 ch.: 1. d. Francis Henry, b. July 27, 1847, Charles Edward, b. May 18, 1849. He was b. May 12, 1820, was grad. at Harvard, 1840 and theological department, 1845; ordained at Barre, Mass., Jan. 7, 1846. Is now at Newton.

793. SOLOMON FOSTER (Solomon, John, William, William, Reginald), b. Littleton, Mass., Oct. 26, 1774; m. in Mason, N. H., March 29, 1802, Hannah Hodgeman, b. April 7, 1784; d. Nov. 28. 1852. He was a farmer. Solomon, Lincoln, will date December 7. 1847, probate Aug. 14, 1866, no widow; ch: William, Rebecca Brooks of Lincoln, widow. [Midsex Prob.] He d. June 29, 1866. Res. Lincoln, Mass.

1420. i. REBECCA, b. Sept. 15, 1803; m., Dec. 5, 1822, Asa Brooks, b. 1800; d. s. p., 1858. She d. March 20, 1882.
1421. ii. WILLIAM, b. July 28, 1815; m. Alice Clark.

796. COL. ASA FOSTER (Asa, Asa, William, William, Reginald), b. June 3, 1765, Canterbury, N. H.; m. there Nov. 10, 1794, Sarah Morrill, dau. of Dea. David, b. May 17, 1772; d. in Canterbury, N. H., March 28, 1868. He was a farmer and prominent citizen. At the age of fifteen enlisted in Capt. Ebenezer Webster's company, Col. Moses Nichol's regiment of New Hampshire militia, which was sent in 1780 to West Point then under the command of Benedict Arnold. Here he was for a short time one of that traitor's body guard. It was not long after he was relieved from that service that Arnold's treachery was discovered. He was a witness of Arnold's daring escape when he rode down the steep cliff to the boat which took him down the river to the British ship Vulture. He retained his interest in military affairs after the close of the war and served for many years as colonel of the militia, but he finally resigned, having become convinced that war was an unchristian and uncivilized mode of settling disputes. He m. Sarah dau. of Dea. David and Abigail (Emerson) Morrill. He passed most of his life in Canterbury, raised a family of twelve children; was noted for his rugged honesty and devotion to what he believed right; was prominent in the early days of anti-slavery agitation in advocacy of freedom for the slave, and in general was an ardent friend of all reform. He died at the age of 95, Aug. 21, 1861. Res. Canterbury, N. H.

1422. i. ASA EMERSON, b. Sept. 20, 1795; m. Maria Chickering.
1423. ii. LUCY WILSON, b. Jan. 20, 1797, m. Caleb Morse Woodman of Newbury, Mass. Jan. 15, 1823, at Canterbury, N. H. He was b. June 19, 1785; d. June 12, 1862 at Middletown, Conn. She d. Feb. 8, 1888, at Middletown, Conn. Their ch.: 1. Mary Woodman, b. March 28, 1824; d. in infancy. 2. Henry C. Woodman, b. Aug. 26, 1825; m. Harriet J. Wright, Aug. 26, 1855. He d. Jan. 25, 1898. She was b. Feb. 11, 1839, at Rocky Hill, Conn. No children. 3. Hannah Foster Woodman, b. Dec. 31, 1827; m. Arthur Benjamin Calef of Northfield, N. H., March 21, 1853, at Canterbury, N.H. She d. Jan. 14, 1892, at Middletown, Conn. He was b. June 30, 1825, graduated at Wesleyan University, 1851, admitted to bar 1852. He is now a lawyer at Middletown, Conn. Ch: i. Jeremiah Francis Calef, b. Oct. 14, 1855, graduated at Wesleyan Uni. 1877 and Yale Medical College, 1880; m. Laura D. Hutchinson of Cromwell, Conn., April 10, 1883. She was born June 23, 1851. He is now an M. D. at Middletown, Conn. Their ch. are: a. Lucy Foster Calef, b. April 9, 1884; d. in infancy. b. Edith Dart Calef, b. Dec. 1, 1885. c. Irene Hutchison Calef, b. April 9, 1891. d. Arthur Benjamin Calef, 3d, b. July 28, 1892. ii. Arthur Benjamin Calef, Jr., b. Feb, 20, 1859, admitted to the bar 1885; m. Minerva C. Harkum, Dec. 29, 1881, at Baltimore, Md. She was b. Oct. 22, 1861. He is now a lawyer at Middletown, Conn. Their children are: a. Jere-

miah Francis Calef, b. March 30, 1885. b. Robert Calef, b. May 1, 1893. iii. Edward Baker Calef, b. Jan. 25, 1862; m. Helen Walton, Oct. 20, 1883. She was b. July 4, 1868, at Sheffield, Eng. Their ch. are: a. Charles Harold Calef, b. Nov. 28, 1885. b. Ethel M. Calef, b. Nov. 15, 1887 c. Helen Calef, b. Jan. 22, 1894 and d. Sept. 27, 1896. 4. Asa Foster Woodman, b. Jan. 29, 1831; d. at Worcester, Mass., May 15, 1857. He was superintendent of American Telegraph Co.'s line between Boston and Calais until failing health compelled him to resign, and he died soon after a the age of 26. He was the inventor of a telegraphic repeater 5 Susan Caroline Parker Woodman, b. Oct. 30, 1834. A teacher at Middletown, Conn. 6. Helen Amanda Woodman, b. April 2, 1837; d. in infancy. 7. Horace Charles Woodman, b. Jan. 30, 1839; d. in infancy.

1424. iii. HANNAH, b. April 2, 1798; d. unm. June 13, 1826.

1425. iv. ADAMS, b. Feb. 22, 1800; m. Sarah Bradley Eastman.

1426. v. HARRISON, b. Sept. 30, 1801; m Caroline Chadwick, and d. s. p., Nov. 30, 1841, in Salem, Ohio.

1427. vi. MEHITABEL, b. Oct. 31, 1803; m., Jan. 1, 1833, Eliphalet Kilburn, Jr., of Boscawen, N. H.; b. Mar. 16, 1804; d. Aug. 14, 1863. She resides at Fontanelle, Iowa. Ch.: Galen Kilburn, b. May 7, 1834; m. 1st, Jennie Mather, Jan. 5, 1860, at Fontanelle, Iowa. She d. Sept. 6, 1875; he m. 2d, Emily Baker, Nov. 15, 1876. He died at Creston, Iowa, where he was practicing law, April 28, 1883. Ch. of Galen and Jennie Kilburn: 1. Lucien Mather Kilburn, b. March 18, 1861. 2. Ella Anna Kilburn, b. July 17, 1863. 3. Edmund LeClair Kilburn, b. Dec. 16, 1866. 4. Fannie Louise Kilburn, b. June 10, 1870. 5. Winnie Aimie Kilburn, b. Nov. 24, 1874. Children of Galen and Emily Kilburn: 1. Clarence Eugene Kilburn, b. Sept. 4, 1877; d March 18, 1880. 2. Norman Whipple Kilburn, b. July 1, 1882. 2. Sarah Jane Kilburn, b. April 5, 1836; d. Nov. 3, 1855. 3. Ann Eliza Kilburn, b. May 5, 1839; d. in infancy. 4. Lucien Morrill Kilburn, b. Jan. 20, 1842; m. Lizzie H. Peet, Oct. 19, 1870, at Fontanelle, Iowa. He is a member for his second term, of Iowa State Senate, from xvi district. She was b. Jan. 1, 1847, in Maine. Their ch. are: a. Charles Wheelock Kilburn, b. July 3, 1872, graduated at Highland Park Normal College, 1893; post-graduate Pen. Art, 1894; d. April 22, 1897, while teaching at Memphis, Mo. b. Geo. G. Kilburn, b. Jan. 6, 1874, graduated at Highland Park Normal

HON. LUCIEN M. KILBURN.

College, 1893. c. Mary Louise Kilburn, b. Nov. 30, 1880. 5. Charles Kilburn, b. Dec. 14, 1847; d. Sept. 8, 1869. They lived in Boscawen, N.H. Eliphalet Kilburn was a prominent citizen of Boscawen, being identified with all the interests of his community. He was strongly interested and actively engaged in propagating anti-slavery ideas, and in building up a right sentiment in regard to general morality. Of their children, only two, Galen F. and Lucien M., lived to active manhood. Hon. Galen F. emigrated to Iowa and settled in Adair county in 1858. He studied law with C. C. Cole of Des Moines and practiced in Fontanelle for years. Was a member of the Iowa house of representatives in the 12th general assembly. Afterward moved to Creston and died in 1887. Hon. Lucien M. served in the 16th N. H. Vols., in the War of the Rebellion, as captain of Co. E. The regiment was assigned to the 19th army corps and served in the department of the gulf. After his return to New Hampshire he served two years as superintendent of schools in Webster county. He went to Iowa in 1868 and settled in Adair county, where he has since resided. He was elected to the State Senate in 1893 to fill a vacancy caused by the election of the incumbent to Congress, and was reelected to a full term in 1895. He is an earnest advocate of reform in the administration of public affairs and an active worker along any line which benefits the public and his fellow citizens.

1428. vii. SARAH, b. Dec. 7, 1805; d. unm. May 31, 1890, a teacher in Cleveland, Ohio.

1429. viii. GALEN, b. Oct. 10, 1807; d. s. p., March 9, 1895. He was born in Canterbury, N. H., was fitted for college at Gilmanton Academy in the same State. He studied law with Hon. Henry Shippen at Meadville, Pa., and afterward with Hon. T. H. Sill in Erie, Pa. This was after he had graduated at Amherst college in 1831. He was admitted to the bar in Erie and practiced his profession in that city until 1863. He continued in business there several years longer, but in 1869 returned to his native town where he resided until his death from pneumonia. He never married.

1430. ix. STEPHEN SYMONDS, b. Nov. 17, 1809; m. Abby Kelly.

1431. x. DAVID MORRILL, b. Oct. 11, 1811; m. Sarah B. Robertson.

1432. xi. NEWEL ABBOT, b. Feb. 7, 1814; m. Eliza Jane Allison and Ellen French.

1433. xii. CAROLINE, b. Jan. 13, 1816; res. unm. 29 Kenyon st., Hartford, Conn. "At the age of eighty-two her interest in the questions of the day is as vivid, and her sympathies are as warm as if half a century of active life lay before her. She is loved and admired by all who are fortunate enough to come within the circle of her influence."

800. WILLIAM FOSTER (Abiel, Asa, William, William, Reginald), b. Canterbury, N. H., Dec. 24, 1763; m., June 10, 1792, Betsey Morrill, b. May 30, 1770. He d. July 10, 1825. Res. Canterbury, N. H.

1434. i. PATTY, b. March 24, 1793; m., Aug. 2, 1834, Enoch Gerrish.

1435. ii. CHARLES, b. Oct. 4, 1794; m., Ruth Tilton.

1436. iii. CHARLOTTE, b. Oct. 11, 1796; m., June 28, 1827, Samuel Moor of Loudon, N. H. She d. Dec. 17, 1885. Ch.: Kate, b. 1830; m. Ira G. Rowe. Ch: 1. Samuel, d. May 9, 1877. 2. Annie M., Res., 40 Jefferson av., Rochester, N. Y.

1437. iv. PEARSON MORRILL, b. July 28, 1798; d. unm., March 12, 1870.

1438. v. HYRAM, b. April 2, 1800; m. Cordelia Hogle.

1439. vi. RUTH CHICKERING, b. Nov. 23, 1802; d. Aug. 17, 1821.

1440. vii. LUCINDA, b. May 7, 1804. unm. d. Rochester, N. Y. in 1892.

1441. viii. WILLIAM HENRY H., b, Aug. 21, 1806; m. Rowena Wheelock.

1442. ix. ABIGAIL, b. Aug. 6, 1808; m. Amaziah Wood. She d. Dec. 7, 1873 in Rochester, N. Y.

1443. x. MARY, b. June 10, 1810; d. April 3, 1813.

1444. xi. ARTHUR MASTEN, b. Feb. 19. 1812; m. Jane Sheldon.

1445. xii. MIRIAM, b. Oct. 19, 1816; m. Ira G. Rowe. She d. June 8, 1859, leaving. 1. Martha, b. Oct. 11, 1850, unm. 2. Arthur, b. Jan. 21, 1854, unm. 3. Foster, b. May 1, 1856, unm.

801. JAMES FOSTER (Abiel, Asa, William, William, Reginald), b. Canterbury, N. H., Dec. 28, 1765; m., Jan. 19, 1790, Mrs. Betsey Sanborn, b. Aug. 18, 1764. Res., Canterbury, N. H.

1446. i. HANNAH, b. March 1, 1791.
1447. ii. JAMES GILMAN, b. Feb. 22, 1793; d. Oct. 15, 1794.
1448. iii. THOMAS, b. Jan. 29, 1795; d. March 11, 1795.
1449. iv. CLARISSA, b. June 11, 1796.
1450. v. JEREMIAH, b. Aug. 4, 1798.
1451. vi. JOHN TAYLOR GILMAN, b. July 19, 1800.
1452. vii. PETER, b. April 27, 1803.

804. ABIEL FOSTER (Abiel, Asa, William, William, Reginald), b. Canterbury, N. H. Feb. 19, 1773; m., Feb. 25. 1796, Susannah Moore, b. April 9, 1775; d. Solon, Ohio, June 22, 1853. She was the daughter of Captain Samuel and Susanna (Webster) Moore of Canterbury, N. H. Abiel died Feb. 24, 1846. Both died and buried at Solon, Ohio. Abiel Foster, Esq., son of Rev. Abiel and Mary Rogers Foster, was a tall, fully six feet, well-proportioned man, weighing about 220 pounds. His hair was of a light color and he had a fair complexion, florid when young. He was educated in part at the famous Phillips Academy, Exeter, N. H. He had a good academic education, and was noted for the beauty and regularity of his penmanship. He was at the national capital one or more times when his father was in Congress. He read law and was well versed in its general principles. For more than thirty years he held a commission as a justice of the peace, and at one time most of the civil business of Canterbury and vicinity was before him. He was in 1816 clerk of the New Hampshire Senate. It is presumed that he intended to enter public life, but the change in political parties prevented it. He was a Federalist. He lived on the homestead but never took great interest in agriculture, nor did he perform much labor on the farm. He was at one time in trade at Canterbury. He sent his eldest son to Dartmouth college, and all his children obtained fair to good educations. In 1836, he emigrated to Columbus, Ohio, his daughters Augusta, Sarah and Catharine going with him. His son Abiel was at that time principal of a high-school at Columbus. His daughters Eliza and Martha Jane were matrons or teachers in State institutions. In 1843, he and his wife went to Solon, Ohio, where they lived with his daughters Susan Stephens and Nancy Hannaford until the time of his death. He d. in Solon O., Feb. 24, 1846. Res., Canterbury, N. H.

1453. i. POLLY, b. Jan. 1, 1797; m., June 18, 1817, Moses Chamberlain. Moses Chamberlain, son of Major Moses and Rebecca (Abbott) Chamberlain was born in Loudon, N. H., Feb. 7, 1792. Till about twenty-one his time was spent in the common schools, about his father's farm and mills, and as clerk for Hon. Stephen Ambrose, merchant of East Concord, N. H. About 1815 he went to Pembroke, N. H., and engaged in trade, remaining there until 1835, when leaving his family in Pembroke, he spent nearly a year in Ohio and Michigan, purchasing in the latter State a large tract of unimproved lands. Returning he was in trade in Concord, N. H., till the fall of 1843, when with most of his family he moved to Michigan to improve his estate, now in Three Oaks, where the rest of his life was spent. He was deeply interested in religion, schools, and reforms; like all traders of his time sold liquors, till convinced of its wrong, and in 1829 gave it up, the first one in New Hampshire to do so, it is said, from principle. With others organized a Congregational church at Three Oaks, which is now the oldest, largest and strongest of that denomination in southwestern Michigan. He died Feb. 12, 1866, at Three Oaks, Mich. He married Mary (Polly) Foster, born Jan. 1, 1797, daughter of Abiel Foster, Esq., of Canterbury, N. H., June 18, 1817. She d. June 18, 1870, at Three Oaks, Mich. He was b. Feb. 7, 1792. in Loudon, N. H.; d. Three Oaks, Mich., Feb. 12, 1866; was a merchant and farmer. She d. June 18, 1870. Ch.: 1. Mary Foster, b. Nov. 3, 1818; m., at Concord, N. H., Nov. 1, 1838, Hale Esterbrook Crosby of Concord, N. H. He was born at Ashburnham, Mass., Oct. 18, 1816, and was a printer at Concord, N. H., and merchant at Ashby, Mass., and merchant and farmer at New Buffalo, Mich. He was representative in the Michigan legislature in 1856 and has held many township offices, now lives at Three Oaks, Mich. She died at Three Oaks, Mich., Jan. 7, 1890. 2. Mellen, b. June 4, 1821; m., June 6, 1846, Martha Ann, dau. of Col. Jesse Putnam of Danvers, Mass. Res., Chelsea, Mass. No children. She died April 25, 1887. 3. Henry, b. March 17, 1824; m. 1st, Sarah Jane Nash, Jan. 16, 1851. She was born Sept. 11, 1830; d. June 1, 1852. 2d, Mrs. Rebecca Vandevanter (Ames), Nov. 19, 1856. She was born Aug. 7, 1825; d. Aug. 27, 1896. 4. Elizabeth, b. Oct. 18, 1826; m., Oct. 18, 1849, John Gardiner Mason. She d. March 27, 1850. He was b. April 13, 1819, at Symbronius, N. Y.; d. at Howell, Mich., 188—. 5. William, b. Feb. 7, 1834; m., March, 20, 1857, Caroline S. Chamberlain, at Canterbury, N. H. She was born Oct. 29, 1834.

Ch. of Hale E. Crosby and Mary Foster Chamberlain: a. Josiah Birney, b. June 2, 1842, in Boscawen, N. H.; m., Sept. 28, 1869, Cornelia Frances Hammond of Three Oaks, Mich. Former residence, New Buffalo, Mich. b. William Hale, b. July 23, 1844, at New Buffalo, Mich.; d. July 27, 1844. c. Charles Hale, b. June 27, 1849; d. July 12, 1850. d. Henry Chamberlain, b. Nov. 22, 1852; m., June 18, 1884, Stella Geenemeyer of Princeton, Ill.; farmer, res., New Buffalo, Mich. e. John Abbot, b. Dec. 10, 1854, graduated at Olivet (Mich.), and Harvard Medical Colleges, studied in Paris and Berlin hospitals, now practicing physician at Minneapolis, Minn.; m., June 25, 1884, Adelaide Randall Upton.

MRS. MARY FOSTER CHAMBERLAIN.

Children of Henry Chamberlain and Sarah Jane Nash: 1. Henry Nash, b. Nov. 21, 1851. Children of Henry Chamberlain and Rebecca Vandevanter Ames. 2. Mary Louise, b. May 17, 1858; m., Feb. 18, 1880, Edward Kirk Warren. Res., Three Oaks, Mich. He is the inventor and patentee of "Featherbone" and is the president of the Warren Featherbone Co., of Three Oaks, Mich. He was born in Ludlow, Vt., April 7, 1847, the son of Rev. Waters and Caroline C. (Parsons) Warren. The father was born in Ludlow in 1800 and the mother in Sandisfield, Mass., in 1813. They were married in 1833 and had four sons. His father, who was a Congregational minister, removed to Michigan in 1858 and was settled at Three Oaks as home missionary pastor. It has been the home of the family since that time. Edward entered the employ of Henry Chamberlain as clerk in a dry goods and general store in 1864, five years later entered the partnership of McKie & Warren, dry goods, ten years later succeeded Henry Chamberlain in the dry goods business there, in the fall

HON. HENRY CHAMBERLAIN.

of 1882 invented what is now known as featherbone. Since that time he has been exclusively engaged in developing that industry. He now employs three hundred people there and about seventy-five at their branch factory at Porter, Ind. 3. Rebecca Belle, b. Oct. 13, 1859; m., June 16, 1884, Lee Chamberlain at Three Oaks, Mich., iron merchant of Columbus, Ohio, now of Los Angeles, Cal. He was born Sept. 7, 1856. 4. Paul Mellen, b. Feb. 28, 1865. His preliminary education was obtained in the village school of Three Oaks, Cushing academy, Ashburnham. Mass., Olivet college, the mechanical department of the Michigan Agricultural college and Sibley college of Cornell university. A constructive faculty early developed decided him to follow mechanical engineering. The degree of B. S. was conferred on him by the Michigan Agricultural college in 1888 and the degree of M. E. by Cornell university in 1890. At the university his name was on the honor list for a "tnesis of distinguished excellence," the subject being "Losses of Heat in the Steam Cylinder and Their Amelioration." The results of his experiments excited the attention of engineers in this country and in Europe and are now accepted as correct. On leaving he took a position as assistant engineer with Frick Co., engineers of Waynesboro, Pa., whose principal business was building machin-

PAUL MELLEN CHAMBERLAIN, B. S., M. E.

ery for and equipping power plants and refrigerating and ice-making plants. In this position the variety of work given him ranged through the various operations of calculating and designing machinery and plants, erecting them and testing when completed. The winter previous to the World's Fair he went with the Hercules Iron Works of Aurora, Ill., as mechanical engineer and for them designed special machines for their Columbian exhibit which ended in a disastrous fire. Owing to the stagnation of business and engineering enterprises at this time he accepted the position of assistant professor of mechanical engineering at the Michigan Agricultural college. Here he brought to bear on his work his practical knowledge of engineering with very satisfactory results and found the field so inviting that he has remained in it, keeping in close touch, however, with active practice by occasionally engineering consultation work. In 1896 at the opening of Lewis Institute he took the position of assistant professor of drawing and machine design, in charge of the department and has since been promoted to associate professor of mechanical engineering, which position he now holds. He is a staunch believer in the advantages of technical education and thinks that when its teachers have approximated an ideal standard the mutual training given the student will excel that formerly attained through what is usually classed as culture studies. In societies he is a member of the college fraternity of Delta Tau Delta, Tau Beta P, The Technical Honor Fraternity corresponding to Phi Beta Kappa of the classics, The American Society of Mechanical Engineers and the Technical Club of Chicago. He m., April 23, 1891, Olivia Langdon Woodward, at Chicago, Ill., their acquaintance beginning at Cornell. Their ch. are: 1. Rebecca Vandevanter, b. Mar. 6, 1892. 2. Wheelock, b. Oct. 14, 1894. 3. Olivia, b. Nov. 22, 1897. Olivia L. W. was born July 8, 1869, at Fulton, Ill.

Children of William and Caroline S. Chamberlain: a. Alice, b. Oct. 14. 1858; m., April 14, 1881, James H. Hatfield, res., Kalamazoo, Mich. b. Grace Amanda, b. Mar. 1, 1861; m., Feb. 16, 1897, Daniel Tellier, Jr.; res., Jackson, Mich. c. Moses Abbot, b. July 25, 1863; d. Oct. 20, 1875. d. Lucy Florence, b. June 29, 1866; m., Feb. 27, 1889, Frederick A. Parsons, res., Bridgeport, Conn. e. Carrie Elizabeth, b. June 20, 1869; m., Aug. 17, 1893, Dr. E. L. McCann, res., Chicago, Ill. f. William Oliver, b. July 27, 1872; m., Sept. 1, 1897, Josephine Supple of Jackson, Mich., res., Kalamazoo, Mich. g. Benjamin Ralph, b. July 24, 1882.—Mellen Chamberlain, LL. D., son of Moses and Mary Foster Chamberlain, was born in Pembroke, N. H., June 4, 1821. His early life was spent on the farm, in his father's store, and teaching district schools. He fitted for college at Pembroke academy and the Literary Institute; graduated at Dartmouth college, 1844; was principal of the Brattleborough (Vt.) high school, 1844-7; member of the Dane law school, Cambridge, Mass., and librarian, 1847-8; lawyer, Boston, Mass., Jan., 1849-66; judge of the municipal court, Boston, and several years chief justice, 1866-78, and librarian of the Boston Public Library, 1878-90. He represented the thirteenth Suffolk district in the legislature, 1857-8, serving on the special committee for the revision of the statutes; State senator, 1863-4, the last year chairman of the judiciary committee. He had previously served on the school committee, as alderman, and city solicitor. He is a member of the Massachusetts Historical Society, corresponding member of the Royal Society of Northern Antiquarie, Copenhagen, Denmark, and other historical societies, and Fellow of the American Academy of Arts and Sciences. He has now in preparation a history of Chelsea, Mass., of which he has been a resident since

HON. MELLEN CHAMBERLAIN, LL. D.

1849; LL. D. from Dartmouth college, 1885. He has written many papers for publication, and delivered many addresses which were of great historical value. He has made one of the largest private collections of historical documents, manuscripts, autographs, portraits and engravings which he has by testamentary bequest left to the Boston Public Library, and which has been transferred and placed in a room in the library fitted up for that special purpose. He married Martha Ann, daughter of Col. Jesse Putnam, of Danvers, Mass., June 6, 1849.—Henry Chamberlain, son of Moses and Mary (Foster) Chamberlain was born in Pembroke, N. H., March 17, 1824. He was a student in the Pembroke "Gymnasium" in 1841; clerk in his father's store, Concord, most of the time, August, 1836-43, save at Ashby, Mass., awhile 1840-1; went with his father's family to Michigan, 1843, and worked on his father's farm till 1850. He then went to Three Oaks, Mich., where he has since resided. There he cleared a large farm, dealt in merchandise and real estate, laid out and named village and township of Three Oaks; has taken great interest in opening highways, building school-houses and churches, and the material improvement of the country; has held most offices in the school district, village and township; many years a member ofthe board of control of county affairs; member of the legislature, 1849, and member of the State board of agriculture, having control of the Michigan Agricultural college, 1883-6. He was grand-master of Masons in Michigan in 1872 and member of the Michigan semi-centennial commission, 1885. A democrat in political affiliations, he has received the votes of his party for State senator, member of the constitutional convention, three times for Congress, three times for United States senator and once for governor. He married 1st, Sarah Jane Nash, Jan. 16, 1851. She was b. Sept. 11, 1830, and d. June 1, 1857. 2d, Mrs. Rebecca Vandevanter Ames, at Marion, Ind., Nov. 19, 1856. She was b. Aug. 7, 1825, and d. Aug. 27, 1896.

William Chamberlain, son of Moses and Mary (Foster) Chamberlain, was born in Pembroke, N. H., Feb. 7, 1834. He went to Michigan with his father's family, and cultivated the homestead farm till 1864, when he moved to the village of Three Oaks, Mich., and engaged in mercantile business till 1892, but still carrying on his farm. He has been an active worker in church and Sabbath school, and deacon of the Congregational church for many years; has acceptably filled many local offices; was many years one of the county superintendents of the poor, and later one of the board of inspectors of Michigan State prison; president of the Michigan State Agricultural Society in 1888, and many years one of the executive committee; member of House of Representatives, 1871-3, and Senate 1879-8; member of the commission for revision of the State laws of taxation, 1883; and since April, 1893, warden of the Michigan State prison, at Jackson, which position he has filled with much ability. His financial management has been as successful as his discipline. He married Caroline S. Chamberlain at Canterbury, N. H., March 20, 1857. She is a granddaughter of Martha Foster Clough, who was a daughter of Hon. Abiel Foster.

1454. ii. ABIEL, b. June 19, 1798; m. Pamelia Judd.

1455. iii. CHILD, b. April 23, 1800; d. in one hour.

1456. iv. SUSANNA, b. June 12, 1801; m., Jan. 18, 1825, Asa Stevens. She d. Jan. 27, 1858 at Solon, Ohio. 1. Alfred, b. in New Hampshire Dec. 25, 1825; married. 2. Abiel Foster, b. in New Hampshire, Aug. 27, 1827; married. 3. Martha Amanda, b. in New Hampshire, March 2, 1833; m. —— Little, lives at Granville, Ohio. 4. Susan Augusta, b. in Solon, Ohio, Nov. 2, 1837. 5. Emma E. b. in Solon, Ohio, Sept. 19, 1840.

1457. v. NANCY, b. Feb. 9, 1803; m., July 8, 1828, Reuben M. Hannaford. He was born in Canterbury, N. H., May 1, 1800; d. Nov. 1884. She d. March 8, 1858, at Solon, Ohio. 1. Eliza, b. in New Hampshire, July 1, 1829; married. 2. Martha Jane, b. in New Hampshire, Nov. 17, 1830; m. N. C. Bosworth; lives in Cleveland, Ohio. 4. Susan Minerva, b. Solon, Ohio, July 15, 1832; m. —— Smith. 5. Katharine Foster, b. Solon, Ohio, May 12, 1834; m. Henry B. Chase; lives in Rockford, Ill. 6. Charles A., b. in Solon, Ohio, Feb. 26, 1836; lives, Solon, Leelanaw Co., Mich. 7. William, b. Solon, Ohio, Feb 25, 1838; m., Dec. 30, 1858, Julia M. Barnard, b. Feb. 17, 1838. He is a farmer and carpenter. Res., Benzonia, Mich. Ch.: a. Wm. Henry Hannaford, b. Feb. 25, 1866—May 4, 1887. b. Ellen J. Hannaford Beuford, b. Jan., 1863; m., May 1, 1884. c. Hope L. Hannaford Kreamer, b. Aug. 4, 1869; m. Aug. 18, 1896.

1458. vi. JOSEPH, b. Nov. 7, 1804; m., Minerva M. Means.

1459. vii. ELIZABETH, b. Feb. 28, 1806; m., Oct 27, 1834, Isaac Dalton; d. s. p. Nov. 26, 1841; had a dau. Susan Elizabeth, b. Oct. 28, 1841; d. young.

1460. viii. AUGUSTA CAROLINE, b. Oct. 14, 1807; m., Aug. 17, 1843, Rufus Hubbard; d. s. p. 1882, Moline, Ill.

1461. ix. MARTHA JANE, b. April 26, 1810; m., Sept. 20, 1839, John Roy. Res., Morrison, Ill. She d. 1881. Had two sons and one dau. John E., b. —, is a resident D. D., of Chicago.

1462. x. SARAH, b. May 25, 1811; d. unm. Solon, Ohio, 1883.

1463. xi. CATHARINE, b. Sept. 16, 1812; d. of a spotted fever, March 29, 1813.

1464. xii. CATHARINE, b. July 31, 1816; m., Jan. 2, 1844, D. C. Judd; d. s. p Spartanburg, S. C., Nov. 4, 1858.

1465. xiii. A still-born child, June 1, 1817.

810. SIMEON FOSTER (Daniel, Asa, William, William, Reginald), b. Canterbury, N. H., Jan. 22, 1765; m., Oct. 29, 1801, Susanna Worthen, b. Chester, Feb. 22, 1777; d. Jan. 16, 1830. He d. April 25, 1825. Res., Canterbury, N. H.

1466. i. EDMUND GREENLEAF, b. Nov. 2, 1802.

1467. ii. MARY, b. Sept. 23, 1806; m. —— Pickard. Ch.: 1. Greenleaf Augustus Pickard. Res., Ipswich, Mass.

1468. iii. JOHN HUBBARD, b. March 4, 1808.

1469. iv. JOSEPH MOODY, b. Jan. 5, 1811; m. Elizabeth Fellows.

1470. v. BENJAMIN OSGOOD, b. Aug. 1, 1813.

817. JEREMIAH C. FOSTER (Daniel, Asa, William, William, Reginald), b. Canterbury, N. H., April 6, 1784; m. there March 4, 1813, Susannah Bradley, b. July, 1784; d. Sept. 5, 1824. He d. May 14, 1839. Res., Canterbury, N. H.

1471. i. CHARLES HENRY, b. Dec. 15, 1813; m. in Berrien county, Mich., Louisa Aldrich. He is a house and sign painter. Had several children, but they are all dead—unm. Res., Larrabee, Iowa.

1472. ii. JONATHAN B., b. Sept. 10, 1816; m. Mary H. Fellows.

1473. iii. ELIZABETH, b. Jan. 10, 1824; unm. Oct. 10, 1841.

1474. iv. SUSANNA, b. March 6, 1822; d. unm. Dec. 23, 1877.

821. DAVID FOSTER (David. Asa, William, William, Reginald), b. Canterbury, N. H., April 1, 1776; m. in Loudon, Sarah Dearborn, of Loudon, N. H. She d. in LaSalle, Ill., Oct. 1, 1855. He was a farmer. He d. in Buda, Ill., Sept. 10, 1843. Res., Canterbury, N. H.

1475. i. FRANKLIN, b. April 29, 1806; m. Harriet Kendall.

1476. ii. MARY FRANCES, b. Dec. 7, 1804; m., May 24, 1841, William T. Randall. She d. s. p. Nov. 19, 1863.

1477. iii. SARAH, b. Aug. 1, 1808; m. Dixwell Lathrop. She d. s. p. July 7, 1878.

1478. iv. GEORGE W., b. June 2, 1816; m. Clara Dole; d. 1871.

1479. v. JOSEPH, b. July 8, 1810; m. Elizabeth B. Vaughn and Elizabeth Childs.

1480. vi. HENRY BRADLEY, b. Dec. 11, 1820; m. Harriet S. Dole.

1481. vii. LUCY, b. July 11, 1812; m. Frederick Tucker. She d. ——.

1482. viii. EMMA, b. Aug. 12, 1824; m. in Concord, N. H., Nov. 22, 1842, Charles E. Flinn, b. Feb. 8, 1817; d. Jan. 13, 1878. Res., De

Kalb, Ill. Was a druggist. Ch.: 1. Mary R., b. Feb. 26, 1853; d. Sept. 25, 1864. 2. Adelaide, b. Oct. 8, 1858; d. Oct. 9, 1864. 3. Wilkie, b. May 31, 1863; d. Sept. 7, 1864. 4. Edward Roy, b. April 3, 1866.

823. TIMOTHY FOSTER (David, Asa, William, William, Reginald), b. Canterbury, N. H., Aug. 21, 1782; m. Dec. 25, 1804, Hannah Carter. He d. Aug. 10, 1851. Res., Canterbury, N. H.

1483. i. STEPHEN BARTLETT, b. Aug. 23, 1816; m. Nancy Bean Sibley.
1484. ii. JOHN CARTER, b. Jan. 18, 1807; m. Ruth M. Pingry.
1485. iii. HANNAH ELIZA, b. Aug., 1809. She d. July, 1834.
1486. iv. MARTHA KITTREDGE, b. Feb. 10, 1819; She d. Jan. 1872, at St. Paul, Minn.

825. SAMUEL H. FOSTER (Jonathan, Asa, William, William, Reginald), b. Canterbury, N. H., Nov. 6, 1771; m., July, 1797, Elizabeth Symonds. She d. June 25, 1801; m., 2d, May 16, 1802, Mercy Porter, of Danvers, Mass., who d. in New York City in 1847. She was dau. of Thomas (Nathaniel, Joseph, John), and great-great-granddaughter of John Porter, of "Porter's Plains," Danvers (also called "Porter of Salem") Freeman, 1633, who was disarmed in 1636 for being a supporter of Ann Hutchinson, and was warned to leave Boston in 1637, went to Hingham; was representative to General Court in 1644, and selectman of that town. He m. Mary Gardiner. He d. in 1846. Res., Newburyport, Mass., and New York City, N. Y.

1487. i. SAMUEL ROGERS, b. Sept. 19, 1798, in Newburyport, Mass.; d. ——, 1803.
1488. ii. CAROLINE, b. Aug. 30, 1800; m. Sept. 30, 1821, Mark Healey, of Boston. She d ——, 1871. Ch.: 1. Caroline W., b. 1822; 1822; m. Rev. C. H. Dall. 2. Ellen, b. 1825. 3. Marion, b. 1827. 4. Frances, b. 1829. 5. Ann, b. 1832. 6. George, b. 1834. 7. Charles, b. 1836. 8. Emily, b. 1838.
1489. iii. SAMUEL HENRY, b. Jan. 24, 1804; m. Eliza ~~Wheaton~~, of Portland, Me.
1490. iv. CHARLES WILLIAM, b. Aug. 20, 1805.
1491. v. MARIA ELIZA, b. April 8, 1807.
1492. vi. EDWARD AUGUSTUS, b. Nov. 9, 1808.
1493. vii. GEORGE JAMES, b. July 27, 1810.

826. CAPT. JOHN FOSTER (Jonathan, Asa, William, William, Reginald), b. Canterbury, N. H., July 22, 1773; m. ——, Sarah Kimball. She d. Newark, N. J., aet. 69. He d. in New York City in 1834 Res., Canterbury, N. H.

1494. i. JOHN SAMUEL, b. Feb. 17, 1802.
1495. ii. ABEL KIMBALL, b. June 13, 1803.
1496. iii. AMMI RUHAMA, b. July 1, 1805; m. Mrs. Lancaster.
1497. iv. GEORGE WILLIAM, b. July 22, 1807.
1498. v. MOSES BROWN, b. April 11 1810.
1499. vi. EDWARD HORATIO, b. April 9, 1814.
1500. vii. FINETTE, b. April 12, 1815; m. —— Lancaster.

830. DAVID FOSTER (David, David, Timothy, William, Reginald), b. Keene, N. H., Feb. 21, 1786; m. May 11, 1812, Mary Field, dau. of Thomas, of Keene, N. H.; d. March 1, 1841. He d. Nov., 1863. Res., Whitestown, N. Y.

1501. i. THOMAS, b. Sept. 2, 1820; m. Eliza P. Skaats.
1502. ii. MARY, b. Oct. 6, 1813; m. William Montgomery; d. without children, Oct. 27, 1850.
1503. iii. DAVID, b. Nov. 11. 1815; d. unm. 1850.
1504. iv. CHARLES, b. Jan. 1, 1818; m. Clara Henry; had children, Clara and Henry, both of whom d. unm.; Charles d. Aug. 4, 1854.
1505. v. HENRY, b. ——; m. ——; d. Aug. 7, 1854; left no children.
1506. vi. ELIZABETH, b. Oct. 18, 1822; d. unm. Aug., 1837.

836. BENJAMIN FOSTER (Isaac, Benjamin, Jacob, Isaac, Reginald), b. Hampstead, N. H., May 24, 1755; m. there Jan. 23, 1776, Elizabeth Richardson, of Granville, dau. of Col. Philip, b. 1758; d. Nov. 28, 1828; m. 2d, Nov. 3, 1831, Mrs. Mary Robinson Peck, dau. of Edward. She d. 1854. She was wid. of Job Peck. Benjamin Foster, son of Isaac and Mehitabel (Worthen) Foster, was born in Hamp-

stead, N. H., May 24, 1755, and came with his parents, his grandparents (Foster), one uncle and two aunts, to Granville, N. S., about 1759 or 1760, soon after the evacuation of the French. They received from the British government a grant of a large area of land opposite Port Royal, on the other side of the Annapolis river, and some of their descendants are still living on this land. He married, first, Elizabeth, daughter of Col. Philip Richardson. He married, second, Mary Pamelia, widow of Job Peck. He d. Nov. 13, 1842. Res., Granville, N. S.

1507. i. BENJAMIN, b. Aug. 2, 1782; m. Mary Randall.

1508. ii MEHITABEL, b. May 6, 1778; m., Jan. 6, 1798, Abraham Chute, b. Feb. 18, 1775; d. July 20, 1847. Res., Berwick, N. S. She d. Jan. 20, 1864. Ch.: 1. Elizabeth, b. April 20, 1799; m. Nelson Van Buskirk. 2. Benjamin Foster, b. Jan. 31, 1801; m. Hannah Calkins. Res., Cornwallis, N. S. 3. John Nelson, b. Dec. 3, 1804; m. Sarah Parker. Res., Berwick, N. S. 4. William Henry, b. Dec. 21, 1806; m. Lovina Skinner. Res., Cornwallis. 5. Susanna, b. April 3, 1809; m. Richard Woodworth. 6. Mary, b. April 20, 1811; m. John Taylor, son of James, Jr., and Elizabeth (Foster). 7. Philip Richardson, b. Dec. 9, 1813; d. March 2, 1826. 8. Samuel Burton, b. March 19, 1816; m. Harriet Chute. Res., Joe Davies, Minn. 9. Thomas Ansley, b. May 11, 1819; m. Margaret Skinner and Mary Hendry. Res., Berwick.

1509. iii. ELIZABETH, b. Sept. 1, 1780; m., March 10, 1801, James Taylor. Res., Annapolis, and Digby, N. S. She lived to the remarkable age of 107 years, and died March 9, 1888. Ch.: 1. Ambrose, b. Jan. 11, 1802; m. Mary Rice. 2. Eliza, b. Sept. 28, 1803; m. Abba Ash; had fourteen children. She d. 1844, aet. 44. He m. 2d, Matilda Bishop; had nine children; d. 1884. 3. Mehitabel, b. Nov. 2, 1805; m. John Bayne, Digby, N. S. 4. John, b. Oct. 4, 1807; m. Mary Chute. 5. James, b. Feb. 15, 1809; m. Lucy (Foster) Sampson, a widow. 6. William H., b. July 3, 1811; m. Matilda, dau. of Artemas Odell. 7. Abner, b. Oct. 22, 1813; m. Eliza Chandler. 8. Stephen, b. Sept. 9, 1815; m. Eliza Chatner. 9. Fred W., b. Feb. 3, 1819; m. Abba, dau. of Joshua Beals; d. 1891; had six children. 10. Benjamin F., b. Oct. 22, 1822; m. Elsie Armstrong; had two children. 11. Henry H., b. Nov. 10, 1823; drowned about 1840. 12. Abba L., b, Jan. 19, 1829; d. 1830.

1510. iv SAMUEL, b. Sept. 9, 1784; m. Lydia Chute and Catherine Crisp.

1511. v SUSANNA, b. Aug. 31, 1786; m. ——, 1801, Francis Tupper. Had six children. He was b. 1781; d. Nov. 17, 1842. She d. Dec. 15, 1882.

1512 vi. MARY, b. Dec. 29, 1788; m. ——, Samuel Tupper. He d. April 23, 1817. She m. 2d, March 25, 1818, Augustus Tupper. He d. April 11, 1850. She d. Oct. 20, 1849.

1513. vii. ISAAC, b. April 9, 1791; m. Elizabeth Patterson.

1514 viii. ABNER, b. May 9, 1793; m. Sarah Wheelock and Hattie Elliott.

1515 ix. SOLOMON, b. Aug. 3, 1797; m., Aug., 1821, Susan Phinney. She d. Sept. 6, 1894. He d. Jan. 29, 1862. Res., Granville, N. S.

1516. x. PHILIP R., b. July 3, 1799; m. Susan Frail, dau. of William. He had a son William who m. Rebecca A. Fuller. No children.

1517. xi. HELEN F., b. Aug. 3, 1801; d. Dec. 10, 1833.

1518. xii. CATHERINE, b. Nov. 28, 1804; m., March 21, 1822, Enoch Dodge, son of Gardiner. They res. at Bridgton, N. S. Had four children: Manford, Maria, Mary and Enoch, who is now postmaster at Bridgton.

839. ISAAC FOSTER (Isaac, Benjamin, Jacob, Isaac, Reginald), b. Granville, N. S., Aug. 24, 1763; m. there 1790, Betsey Gilliott, dau. of William. He moved to Wilmont, N. S., in 1802. He d. June 3, 1852. Res., Wilmont, N. S.

1519. i. CHARLES, b. ——, 1795; m. Mary Banks and Mary A. Green.

1520. ii. MARY, b. ——, 1797; m. Charles Dunn, son of John. She d. 1840. He was b. 1795; d. 1873. Ch.: 1. Susan; m. Ambrose Corbit, son of Ichabod. 2. Elizabeth; m. Stephen T. Foster, son of Samuel. 3. Isaac F., b. Oct. 9, 1824; m. Eliza J. Spinney, dau. of David. They had three children, who reside in Clifton, Mass. 4. Charles H.; m. Eunice Bowlby, dau. of Solomon.

1521. iii. BETSEY M., b. ——, 1799; ——, Daniel Vaughn.
1522. iv. HANNAH, b. ——, 1801; m. Edward Foster, son of Samuel.
1523. v. ANN, b. Aug. 20, 1803; d. in Clarence, N. S., Sept. 15, 1889.
1524. vi. ARCHIE G., b. ——, 1805; killed in 1811.
1525. vii. JERUSHA, b. April 7, 1807; m., March 15, 1832, Phinehas Phinney, son of Thomas.
1526. viii. WILLIAM, b. Dec. 27, 1813; m. Hannah Huntington.

842. SAMUEL FOSTER (Isaac, Benjamin, Jacob, Isaac, Reginald), b. Granville, N. S., Oct. 1. 1770; m. ——, Betsey Wilson. Res., Annapolis, N. S.
1527. i. EDWARD W., b. ——; m., 1826, Hannah Foster, dau. of Isaac, Jr.
1528. ii. MARGARET, b. ——; m. Ariel Corbet.
1529. iii. CLARK, b. ——.
1530. iv. MARY, b. ——; m. Edward Bruce.
1531. v. ZIPPORAH, b. ——; m. Edward Gilliott.
1532. vi. MATILDA, b. ——; m. John Millner.
1533. vii. JOHN, b. ——; drowned.
1534. viii. CORBIT, b. ——; m. ——.

843. OLIVER FOSTER (Isaac, Benjamin, Jacob, Isaac, Reginald), b. Granville, N. S., May 1, 1773; m., Nov. 13, 1796, Cynthia Fellows, dau. of Israel; d. Nov. 8, 1813; m. 2d., Jan. 1, 1817, Betsey Saunders, dau. of Daniel, b. 1789; d. May 5, 1871. He was a farmer. He d. June 5, 1827. Res., Bridgton, N. S.
1535. i. DAVID, b. June 19, 1797; m. Mary Clark and Azubah Wheelock.
1536. ii. CYNTHIA, b. March 24, 1799; m. Job Randall, b. 1788. She d. leaving one son, Oliver. Job m. 2d, Mary Parker.
1537. iii. ARCHIBALD MARSDEN, b. April 14, 1801; m. Eliza Bent.
1538. iv. ANN, b. July 1, 1803; m. William Fitch, b. 1794, son of Fred Fitch. Res., Horton and Cornwallis, N. S.
1539. v. MARIA, b. Aug. 23, 1807; d. April 25, 1822.
1540. vi. JERUSHA, b. May 19, 1809; m., July 19, 1829, Henry Ruppee, son of William. Had three children.
1541. vii. ROBERT H., b. March 5, 1812; m. Elizabeth Hall.
1542. viii. SUSAN, b. Nov. 8, 1813; m. ——, Israel L. Bent, son of Joseph. He was a farmer. Res., Bridgton, N. S. Ch.: 1. Israel, b. Oct. 2, 1849; m., Dec. 4, 1872, Isabelle Coldwell, at Berwick, N. S. Res., South Lincoln, Mass. Ch.: (a) Nellie Ray Bent, b. April 21, 1874. Res., Oracle, Ariz. (b) Hyland Fairbanks Bent, b. Nov. 17, 1875. Res., South Lincoln, Mass. (c) Edwin Stearns Bent, b. June 17, 1877. Res., 21 Worcester St., Boston. (d) Jennie Beatrice Bent, b. Dec. 1, 1878. Res., 21 Worcester St., Boston. (e) Lalia Estella Bent, b. Sept. 18, 1881. Res., 21 Worcester St., Boston. (f) Ralph Waldo Bent, b. May 29, 1883. Res., South Lincoln, Mass. (g) Bertha Woodworth Bent, b. April 27, 1885. Res., South Lincoln, Mass. (h) Ethel Foster Bent, b. Jan. 12, 1893. Res., South Lincoln, Mass.
1543. ix. OLIVER, b. Oct. 17, 1817; m. Helen Woodbury.
1544. x. ISRAEL, b. April 22, 1819; m. Mrs. Minetta (Foster) Morse and Mrs. Ann (Manning) Brown.
1545. xi. MARY ANN, b. ——, 1821; m. William Morse and J. M. Brown. Had four children. Res., Lauranceton, Annapolis county, N. S.
1546. xii. DANIEL, b. ——, 1824; m. ——.
1547. xiii. CHARLES WILLIAM, b. ——, 1826; m. and resides in California.

844. ASA FOSTER (Isaac, Benjamin, Jacob, Isaac, Reginald), b. Granville, N. S., Nov. 24, 1776; m. July 26, 1798, Ruby Hicks, dau. of Thomas and Sarah (Chute), b. 1782; d. July 1, 1863. He was a miller. He d. Sept. 20, 1854. Res., Bridgton, N. S.
1548. i. HARRIET, b. April 26, 1799; m. Nathan, son of Amos and Susan (Chute) Randall, Jan. 21, 1819; d. Aug. 21, 1889. He d. 1864, aet. 73, without issue.
1549. ii. IRENE, b. March 17, 1802; m. Charles, son of Maurice Peters, Jan. 11, 1826; had six children; d. Oct. 9, 1865.
1550. iii. AVISA, b. Oct. 12, 1804; m. Capt. James Peters, 1821; d. 1880. He d. 1855. Sea captain and lived at Bridgton and West Port.

1551. iv. WILLIAM W., b. Aug. 15, 1806; m. Harriet Calvert, of St. John, N. B., 1837. She d. 1840. He m. 2d, Hannah Wheelock, 1843; d. July 20, 1873. She d. Dec. 24, 1890; left no children.
1552. v. SUSAN ANN, b. Sept. 16, 1808; m. Jacob, son of Benjamin Foster, Jr., of Cornwallis, Feb. 13, 1833. She d. ——. He d. March, 1892, aet. 82, without issue.
1553. vi. LOUISE JANE, b. May 4, 1811; m. Binca Chute; lived at Bear River; then moved to Ontario; had a large family.
1554. vii. MINETTA, b. Feb. 7, 1813; m. Obadiah Morse, Jr., Sept. 17, 1834. Had one son by Morse, who married a daughter of Robert Foster, son of Oliver; m. 2d, Israel Foster; had by Foster several children; d. ——.
1555. viii. OLIVER G., b. Dec. 11, 1816; m. Eliphal A. Chute, Dec. 8, 1843; d. in Bayham, Ont., where he moved and lived, April 8, 1894; had several children.
1556. ix. S. MATILDA, b. Dec. 16, 1818; m. J. Chute, of Bear River, N. S.; moved to Boston, and d. there. They had several children.
1557. x. LEAH, b. Jan. 27, 1820; m. J. M. Chute, of Bear River; moved and settled in Ontario.
1558. xi. ELIZA, b. March 5, 1823; had six children by Charles Hill, whom she m. Jan. 30, 1850. They live in Lynn, Mass.

848. REV. JOHN FOSTER (Ezekiel, Benjamin, Jacob, Isaac, Reginald), b. Hampstead, N. H., March 29, 1760; m., Dec. 26, 1781, Elizabeth Ricketson, dau. of Abednego. She d. April 7, 1852. He was a local preacher in the M. E. church. Went to Nova Scotia with his parents. He d. Sept. 29, 1827. Res., Aylesford, N. S.

1559. i. PHEBE, b. May 28, 1783; d. June 6, 1783.
1560. ii. JOHN, b. April 11, 1784; m. Sarah Brown.
1561. iii. RUTH, b. Aug. 12, 1787; m., May 21, 1807, Walter Wilkins. Had eleven children. She d. Nov. 24, 1865.
1562. iv. PHEBE, b. Jan. 28, 1790; m., 1823, James Roach. Had four children.
1563. v. FREDERICK, b. May 13, 1792; m. Rachel Benedict.
1564. vi. WILLIS, b. Nov. 15, 1794; m. Susanna Pierce and Nancy Foster.
1565. vii. ELIZABETH, b. Dec. 23, 1796; m. Oct. 10, 1817, James Pierce, son of William and brother of Susanna. She d. Dec. 30, 1825. Three children.
1566. viii. HENRY, b. May 29, 1799; m., March 15, 1827, Jane Trusdell. He d. Nov. 5, 1870. Res., N. S.
1567. ix. EZEKIEL, b. July 26, 1801; m. Eliza Dugan.
1568. x. MARY ANN b. Jan. 10, 1804; m., Jan. 1, 1829, Zebulon Neily. She d. Jan. 9, 1871. Had four children.
1569. xi. BAYARD, b. July 8, 1808; m. Mary Ann Foster, dau. of Ezra F. She d. Oct. 5, 1879. He d. Aug. 12, 1885. Res., N. S.

849. EZEKIEL FOSTER (Ezekiel, Benjamin, Jacob, Isaac, Reginald), b. Granville, N. S., March 30, 1763; m., May, 1803. Elizabeth. Dring, dau. of Joseph. She m. 2d, Jan. 17, 1854, Benjamin Rhoades. He d. Aug. 26, 1829. Res., Granville, N. S.

1570. i. THOMAS, b. ——, 1804; m. Mary Wheelock.
1571. ii. EZRA, b. ——, 1807; m., Nov. 8, 1831, Hannah Bohaker, dau. of Michael. He d. April, 1880. Res., G.; six children.
1572. iii. ELIZABETH ANN, b. ——, 1809; m. Abel Wheelock; a son, Joseph Israel, b. Jan. 1, 1828, m. Elizabeth Foster, dau. of Thomas Foster; and m. 2d, Ruth Bent.
1573. iv. MARY F., b. 1811; m. William Banks; d. Jan. 1, 1877.
1574. v. TAMER, b. 1814; m. Benjamin Randall; had four children.
1575. vi. ATHALINDA, b. 1816; d. May 9, 1846.
1576. vii. ADOLPHUS W., b. 1818; m. Caroline, dau. of Jonathan Woodbury; had four children.
1576½. viii. ISRAEL, b. 1821; d. 1822.
1577. ix. MARTHA, b. 1824; m. Rev. Isaac, son of Lewis McAnn. He was a Methodist preacher; lives in Vermont.

850. JOSEPH FOSTER (Ezekiel, Benjamin, Jacob, Isaac, Reginald), b. Oct. 18, 1771, Granville, N. S.; m., Nov. 25, 1795, Jane Ray, dau. of James and Mary. Res., Nictaux, Annapolis county, N. S.

1578. i. RUTH, b. 1796; killed by the falling of a tree March, 1814.
1579. ii. EZEKIEL, b. 1799; m., June 21, 1821, Mary A. Waters.
1580. iii. HANNAH, b. 1802; m. Newcomb Bent; had 3 daus; one d. young. Harriet A., m. Augustus Bryden, they had 4 children, 2 girls and 2 boys; Naraway Bryden m. Miss Franklin; res., Somerset, King county, N. S.; the other son, John, resides in the U. S. One of the girls m. Isaac Merton; res. Somerset; and the other girl is married and resides in Shelburne county, N. S.
1581. iv. JANE, b. 1801; m. Abel Wheelock and had 8 ch.
1582. v. JOSEPH, b. 1805; m. Zilpah Martin, dau. of Michael.
1583. vi. JOHN M., b. 1807; m. Lucilla Woodbury, dau. of Fairfield, who was son of Dr. Jonathan Woodbury. Res., Nictaux, N. S., and Halifax, where John M. d. He had one son, Fletcher, who died unm.
1584. vii. SOPHIA ANN, b. 1807; m. Edward Martin, son of Michael.
1585. viii. EZRA, b. Sept., 1814; m. Mary Ann Burkitt and Mercy Ann Van Buskirk

851. CAPTAIN EZRA FARNSWORTH FOSTER (Ezekiel, Benjamin, Jacob, Isaac, Reginald), b. Granville, N. S., Aug. 1, 1773; m., Jan. 24, 1798, Susanna Troop, dau. of John and Eunice (Fellows) of Aylesford, N. S., b. 1780; d. 1875. He was born in Granville, N. S., and married Susanna, dau. of John Troop, of the same place. He was commissioned lieutenant in 1812, and is said to have served in the active militia during the war and retired with the rank of captain. He removed to Bridgton before 1824, and later to Aylesford, in the same province, where he died in 1864. Res. Bridgton, N. S.

1586. i. NANCY, b. Jan. 25, 1799; m., Jan. 20, 1833, Willis Foster, son of John; res. Aylesford, N. S.; son of his father's half brother. She was his second wife, and the mother of his third son, William Rufus Leggett Foster (above mentioned), captain of militia, now living at North Kingston, N. S.
1587. ii. GILBERT, b. Sept. 16, 1800; d. unm. in 1865.
1588. iii. RUFUS, b. June. 3, 1802; m. Christiana Lough.
1589. iv. MARY ANN, b. April 22, 1804; m. Bayard Foster. Res., Aylesford; brother of Willis, s. p.
1590. v. WM. YOUNG, b. May 22, 1806; m., 1835, Minetta Leonard, dau. of Seth, Esq.; was county treasurer of Annapolis county. Res. B. He, Wm.Y., d. 1898; had children: a son, Leonard, who died young; and three daughters, Charlotte, Jane and Clara. Charlotte left Bridgton with her husband, whose name was Forsyth, lived for a time at some other places in North America, and finally settled in Belfast, Ireland, where she died, leaving children; Jane died unm.; Clara is the wife of Ambrose Bent, a man of some means who lives a few miles above Bridgton. The widow, Minetta, dau. of George Leonard, is living at Bridgton, or with her dau. Clara. William Y. Foster was a member of the political party which favored the confederation of the provinces, and was a defeated candidate at the first election for members of the house of commons of Canada. He held offices of trust in town and county affairs, and, though over ninety years of age, was deputy prothonotary at the time of his death. (Further information might be had by writing to Mrs. Ambrose Bent, Paradise, N. S.)
1591. vi. GEORGE, b. Aug. 18, 1808; d. 1870.
1592. vii. LUCY, b. Aug. 21, 1810; m. William Lough. She d. s. p.
1593. viii EUNICE, b. Oct. 25, 1812; m. Frederick Ludwig Boehm Vroom; had 5 children; m. June 15, 1836; lives or lived in St. Stephen, N. B. Frederick Ludwig Boehm Vroom (William's brother, of Loyalist descent, son of George Vroom, J. P., of Clements, N. S., and a descendant of Cornelis, son of Peter Vroom, one of the early dutch settlers of New Amsterdam, now New York.) Ch.: William E. Vroom, of the firm of Vroom & Arnold, ship brokers, St. John, N. B., who has children and grand-children; Georgiana, now of Boston, Mass.; Frances Frederica, died in infancy; Mary,

wife of Dr. Thomas Bingay, Westport, N. S., has children and grand-children; Caroline, died in infancy; Jessie, wife of George Graves, Aylesford, N. S., has children, and a son who died in infancy.

1594. ix. ISRAEL, b. May 8, 1815; d. Dec. 18, 1817.

1595. x. F. ELIZA, b. July 6, 1817; m. William Vroom, brother of Frederick; had 3 children: Frances Eliza, now living in St. Stephen, N. B.; widow of William Vroom, of St. Stephen. Children: 1. James, town clerk of St. Stephen. 2. William Frederick, a graduate of Teacher's college, New York, now teaching in New York City. 3. Edwin Gilbert, furniture dealer in St. Stephen; two children. 4. Charley Napier, U. S. vice-consul at St. Stephen; two children. 5. The Rev. Fenwick Williams Vroom, B. D., professor of divinity in King's college, Windsor, N. S.; one child, Victoria. 6. Beatrice, living with their mother in St. Stephen. 1. James' American ancestors of the name of Vroom were Cornelis (Pieterse) or Cors (Pieterssen) Vroom, in Nieuwe Amsterdam, about 1643; Hendrick (Corsz or Corssen) Vroom, b. 1653; Hendrick Vroom of the Raritan, b. 1683; Hendrick Vroom, b. probably at Piscataway on the Raritan, sometime after 1711; John Vroom, U. E.; George Vroom, J. P., b. 1783, who came with his father, John (or Jan) from New Jersey to Nova Scotia after the close of the Revolutionary War; William Vroom, b. 1812.

1596. xi. SUSAN, b. July 1, 1822, still living with Capt. W. R. L. Foster, No. Kingston, N. S.

852. DEA. JEREMIAH FOSTER (Jeremiah, Benjamin, Jacob, Isaac, Reginald), b. New Hampshire, Feb. 7, 1773; m. Sally Killam, b. Hamlet, Mass., Nov. 26, 1770; d. Aug. 28, 1855. This branch of the Foster family trace their ancestry to pre-Revolutionary stock. At the breaking out of the war for independence, there were three brothers named Foster living in the colony of Massachusetts. Two of those, being Royalists, went to one of the British provinces, but the third, whose name was Jeremiah, enlisted in the continental army and served until the close of the war, when he settled in New Hampshire. This third brother was the father of Jere Foster, or as he was commonly known Dea. Jere Foster, who was born in New Hampshire, on the seventh day of Feb., 1773. He had four sisters but no brothers. Dea. Jere married Sally Killum, who was born at Hamlet, Mass. They had a family of three children. Two years after the birth of Solomon, Jere Foster moved to Maine, which was at that time a district belonging to the State of Massachusetts, and settled at Weld, a place remarkable for its beautiful and picturesque scenery of lakes and mountains, but at that time little better than a wilderness. Here he engaged in farming and there the third child, Hiram, was born. Jere Foster passed the remainder of his days in Weld and died at the advanced age of 95 years. His daughter Sally married Daniel Dolley. He d. aet. 94, Oct. 24, 1867. Res., Weld, Me.

1597. i. SOLOMON K., b. March 27, 1803; m. Adeline Billington.

1598. ii. HIRAM, b.——; m. Eliza Howard.

1599. iii. SALLY POTTER, b. Goffstown, N. H.; m., July 17, 1798.

857. ISAAC FOSTER (Isaac, John, Jacob, Isaac, Reginald), b. Greenfield, Mass., April 3, 1761; m., Oct. 28, 1789, Rebecca Hunt. Served in the Revolutionary War 1777; m. Rebecca, dau. of John and Rebecca (Paine) Hunt of Belchertown. Was one of the proprietors of Amherst. Built the first house in the East Parish, also erected a hotel and other buildings. In 1799 he went from Hartford to New York on a southern trading expedition. Was caught in a storm, driven to sea and shipwrecked. Was rescued and taken to Savannah, Ga. He decided to locate in the south but on account of financial disturbances in the north changed his mind. Afterward when en route for his home via Montreal was attacked by the smallpox and died at Whitehall, N. Y., in 1800. His widow removed with family to Western N. Y., where she married Abijah Scovil of W. Bloomfield, N. Y., a Revolutionary soldier. She survived her second husband several years and died at Aurora, Ohio, Jan. 23, 1854. Scovil d. 1827. He d. 1800. Res., Belchertown and Amherst, Mass.

1600. i. ISAAC, b. 1771; d. young.

1601. ii. WILLIAM, b. March 24, 1793; d. unm., Aug. 7, 1847; buried at Aurora, O. He was b. in Greenfield, Mass., became a cripple in infancy from the effects of a fever and lost the use of his limbs. He went to Coshocton, N. Y., with his mother after the death of his father, but soon returned east and located at Shrewsbury, Mass. With a younger brother they began the manufacture of combs. He also learned the printer's trade. Having disposed of this factory the family located in Harpersfield, Ohio, and later moved to Murray, N. Y. Late in life he supplied various pulpits and preached many interesting sermons.

1602. iii. ISAAC, b. Nov., 1794; m. Sarah Eggleston.

1603. iv. DOROTHY, b. Sept., 1796; m. Ransom Rowley of Syracuse, N. Y.; d. Dec., 1853, Aurora, O. No children.

1604. v. MARCUS, b. Dec. 4, 1798; m., Eliza Sleeper.

1605. vi. SAMUEL, b. May 8, 1800; m. Mary W. Walker.

859. CAPT. EZEKIEL FOSTER (Ezekiel, John, Jacob, Isaac, Reginald), b. Bernardston, Mass., in 1752; m. there Chloe Burnham, b. 1757; she d. July 9, 1849. He was in the Revolutionary War and was captain. Captain Foster was captain in the Revolutionary War, and was said to have been one of Washington's body-guards, but whether this last statement is true I do not know, but have always been told so. He also did work in breaking up a fanatical and immoral sect known as the "Dorrellites" which flourished for a time in Leyden and adjoining towns, among the most ignorant and emotional portion of the people. He confronted the leader at one of his meetings and making him confess in the presence of his followers that he was a fraud, his religion a delusion, and his promising he would abandon it, and go to work and get an honest living, and this Dorrell did, and lived there till he was somewhere upward of 90 years old, and the sect of course perished. All this you will find in brief in any history of Massachusetts. I last saw it in a book called the "History of the Connecticut River Valley in Massachusetts." He d. aet. 72, in Leyden, Mass., and was buried June 17, 1824, in old Beaver Meadow yard. Res., Bernardston, Mass.

1606. i. EZRA, b. Sept. 21, 1779; m. Nancy Smith.

1607. ii. ELIAKIM, May 29, 1786; m. Wealthy A D. Phelps.

1608. iii. HORACE, b.——; m.——. Res. near Hamilton, Ontario.

1609. iv. JOSIAH, b. in 1784; m. ——. Annie Eustis.

1610. v. RUFUS, b. ——; m. ——. Res. near Hamilton, Ontario. A relative is Dr. Ralph Malcolm, Scotland, Ontario.

1611. vi. EZEKIEL, b.——; m., d. s. p. Ezekiel Jr., was a deer reave in Bernardston, Mass., in 1779. Served with his father in military affairs, being discharged Sept. 23, 1775; was also in the army in 1778. He removed to Canada where he married and died s. p., and his property was divided between the Canadian government and his heirs at Leyden.

1612. vii. ELECTA, b. June 12, 1796; m., Aug. 29, 1815, Major Samuel Eason; b. July 24, 1783 He was a tanner, currier and shoemaker. She d. July 20, 1860. He d. July 26, 1860. Ch.: 1. Mary Eason, b. Nov. 23, 1816; d. Mar. 31, 1840. 2. Samuel Eason, b. Feb. 9, 1818; d. Jan. 11, 1896. 3. Sarah Eason, b. Oct. 15, 1820; address Mrs. Charles Potter, Gulford Centre, Vt. 4. Chloe Eason, b. Mar. 31, 1825; d. Aug. 25, 1850. 5. Silvia Eason, b. Feb. 14, 1828; d. Sept. 26, 1876. 6. Caroline Eason, b. July 6, 1833; dead. 7. Eli W. Eason, b. Aug. 20, 1830; d. Mar. 17, 1896. 8. Ellen C. Eason, b. May 26, 1836; d. July 31, 1854. 9. Timothy W. Eason, b. Aug. 2, 1840; m. at Vernon, Vt., Dec. 9, 1868, Emma L. Eddy, b. Sept. 13, 1845. Res., Brattleboro, Vt. Ch.: Lucy Myrtelle Eason, b. Nov. 23, 1869; Warren Verne Eason, b. Apr. 9, 1874; Myrtelle Eason, Brattleboro, Vt.; W. Verne Eason, 160 Main St., Fitchburg, Massachusetts. 10. George L. Eason, b. May 15, 1543. Res., Des Moines, Iowa. 11. Warren E. Eason, b. Feb. 16, 1823. Res., Brattleboro, Vt.

860. JOHN FOSTER (John, John, Jacob, Isaac, Reginald), b. Deerfield, Mass., June 29, 1780; m. ————. Res., Vermont.

1612-2. i. JOHN, b. ——; m. Ruth Rich.

863. ISAIAH FOSTER (John, John, Jacob, Isaac, Reginald), b. New Hampshire, ——; m. ——. Patty Hartwell. Res., Hillsboro, N. H.

1613. i. CHARLES H., b. ——, 1819; m. Martha A. Sargent.

864. JOSHUA FOSTER (John, John, Jacob, Isaac, Reginald), b. Deerfield, Mass., Feb. 12, 1796; m., Oct. 8, 1816, Sally Hopkins, of Antrim, N. H., b. May 14, 1795; d. March 11, 1824; m. 2d, March 22, 1825, Mary Ann Fletcher, of Peterboro, N. H.; d. May 28, 1851; m. 3d, in Peterboro, N. H., Oct. 16, 1851, Mrs. Dorothy Little, of Peterboro, b. Jan. 30, 1814. He was a tanner. He d. March 16, 1867. Res., Hancock, N. H.

1614. i. ELIZABETH M., b. March 3, 1820; m., Dec. 28, 1838, Zebedee Bagerly. Res., Seneca, Mich. She d. Feb. 4, 1897; a son John resides Canandaigua, Mich.
1615. ii. CALISTA, b. ——; d. ——.
1616. iii. OTIS, b. ——; d. ——.
1617. iv. LYDIA, b. ——; d. ——.
1618. v. CHARLES O., b. Feb. 15, 1826; m. Mary Ann Gray.
1619. vi. SARAH L., b. ——; d. Aug. 1, 1849.
1620. vii. ADOLPHUS G., b. Feb. 19, 1835; m. Ellen H. Lakin.
1621. viii. ELWIN C., b. Oct. 23, 1852; m. Ann M. B. Shaw.

870. JACOB FOSTER (Benjamin, Benjamin, Benjamin, Isaac, Reginald), b. Maine, ——; m. ——, Anna Jones. She d. Trenton, Me. He d. Trenton, Me. Res., Machias, Me.

1622. i. HOWARD, b. ——.
1623. ii. NAHUM, b. ——.
1624. iii. HARRIET, b. ——.
1625. iv. LOUISA, b. ——; m. William Chaloner, Jr., son of Dr. William.
1626. v. DANIEL, b. March 10, 1792; m. Maria Somes.
1627. vi. SALLY J., b. ——; m. —— Somes.
1628. vii. BETSEY, b. ——; m. —— Burr.
1629. viii. ANN, b. ——; m. —— Townsend.
1630. ix. CHARLES, b. ——.

872. JOHN FOSTER (Benjamin, Benjamin, Benjamin, Isaac, Reginald), b. Maine, ——; m. ——, Phebe Burr. Res., Machias, Me.

1631. i. SUSAN, b. ——; m., ——, Moses Hovey.
1632. ii. WILLIAM, b ——.
1633. iii. MARY, b.——; m. John Coffin Talbot, son of Peter and Lucy (Hammond) of Stoughton, Mass. Res., Machias, Me. Ch.: Stephen P., William H., John C., George F., Emma C. F., b. ——; m. Josiah P. Keller; Thomas H., Susan H., Mary E.
1634. iv. HENRY, b. ——.
1635. v. EMMA C., b. ——.

873. BENJAMIN FOSTER (Benjamin, Benjamin, Benjamin, Isaac, Reginald), b. Maine,—— m. ——. Ruth Scott. Res., Machias, Me.

1636. i. SIMEON b.——; m. Katherine Farnsworth.
1637. ii. THANKFUL, b. ——; m. Tristram Moore.
1638. iii. ASA, b. ——.
1639. iv. LETTICE, b. ——; m. Lawrence Williams.
1640. v. JEREMIAH, b. ——.
1641. vi. SUSAN, b. ——; m. Samuel Burnham.
1642. vii. SALLY, b. ——; m. Wade.

874. ABIJAH FOSTER (Benjamin, Benjamin, Benjamin, Isaac, Reginald), b. ——, Maine; m. Apphia Talbot, dau. of Peter and Lucy (Hammond); res., Machias, Me.

1643. i. ABIGAIL, b. ——.
1644. ii. LUCY, b. ——.
1645. iii. ELIZA, b. ——; m. Jeremiah Foster.
1646. iv. HARRIET, b.——.
1647. v. APPHIA, b. ——.
1648. vi. CHARLOTTE, b. ——.
1649. vii. MARY, b. ——; m. Phinehas Foster.
1650. viii. FREDERICK, b. ——.
1651. ix. STEPHEN T, b. ——.

876. LEVI FOSTER (Benjamin, Benjamin, Benjamin, Isaac, Reginald), b. ——, East Machias, Me.; m. Sally Beal. He d. aet. 95. Res., Machias, Me.

1652. i. EDWARD, b. June 30, 1793; m. Fanny Cilley.
1653. ii. SUSAN, b ——.
1654. iii. BETSEY, b. ——; m. George H. Avery, son of James and Rebecca (Edes) of Boston. Res., Machias, Me. Ch.: James E., Samuel T., Sally E., m. Joseph Libby; Susan F., m. James Stuart; Betsey, m. Atkins Gardner; George H., Rebecca, Mary H.; m. Joseph Miles, Julia, Caroline, Levi F.
1655. iv. PHEBE, b. ——; m. Luther Hall.
1656. v. WARREN, b. ——.
1657. vi. GEORGE, b. Nov. 10, 1804; m. Sarah Libbey and Caroline De Wolfe.

879. SAMUEL FOSTER (Benjamin, Benjamin, Benjamin, Isaac, Reginald), b. ——, Maine; m. Comfort Scott. Res., Machias, Me.

1658. i. BENJAMIN, b. —— 1793; m. Joanna Foster.
1659. ii. ALFRED, b. ——.
1660. iii. MEHITABEL, b. ——; m. W. W. Foster
1661. iv. CLARISSA, b ——; m. S. C. Foster.
1662. v. SUSAN, b. ——; m. William Marsh.
1663. vi. HORATIO, b. ——.
1664. vii. ELIZABETH, b. ——; m. Elijah Wilder.
1665. viii. S. FREEMAN, b. ——.
1666. ix. J. ANDREW, b. ——.
1667. x. GEORGE H., b. ——.
1668. xi. JACOB, b. ——.

880. DANIEL FOSTER (Benjamin, Benjamin, Benjamin, Isaac, Reginald), b. Scarboro, Me., in 1761; m. Hannah Gardner. She d. in Vermont.

Daniel Foster was born in Scarboro, Maine, in 1761, enlisted in the 7th Mass. regiment to serve six months during the War of the Revolution; married Hannah Gould of Portland, Maine; removed to Antwerp, N. Y., in 1819, and died there. He d. July 16, 1841. Res., Portland, Me., and Antwerp, N. Y.

1669. i. JOHN WOODIN, b. Nov. 3, 1801; m. Harriet E. Gould.
1670. ii. There were fifteen children in all; n. f. k.

881. GEORGE FOSTER (Benjamin, Benjamin, Benjamin, Isaac, Reginald), b. East Machias, Me.; m. Cynthia Chase, dau. of Capt. Wm. She d. in New York City in 1856 while visiting her son Daniel and is buried in Greenwood.

He was the youngest son of Col. Benjamin Foster of Machias, Me., and who was one of the first settlers of that place and came from Mass. George, his son, married Cynthia Chase, and made their permanent home on Lower Side in the Parish of St. Davids, N. B. They were the early settlers of that place and had to clear their farms and build their roads. He came with three others; one Robert Towers, one Scott and another, whose name I do not remember. They were all stalwart men, and well qualified to do the hard things of a first settler's life. He was a tall, well-formed, handsome man, with blue eyes and a fine tenor voice, and he loved music. He was of a mechanical turn and had a work shop on his farm where he made wagons, plows, sleds, yokes and all such farm implements. He also made cooper ware. He was called a good workman and never made a sham thing, and always finished his work. He had a clean farm and always a neat garden, where he liked to be. He led a quiet life and was a great reader, and in his latest years had in store a fund of knowledge of the world's history. He lived to be past eighty years. When past labor he went to Presque Isle and lived in his daughter Cynthia's family till his death. He d. 1855. Res., Machias, Me.

1671. i. VASHTI, b. ——; m. Samuel Scott; a des. is Miss Eliza Hitchings, of Blaine, Me.
1672. ii. J. HARRIS, b. ——; m. ——. A des. is Mrs. Myra Godding of Maple Grove, Me.
1673. iii. DANIEL, b. ——; m. and resides in New York City. Was a stair builder. No issue living.
1674. iv. CYNTHIA, b. Dec. 11, 1806; m., Nov. 2, 1826, Benjamin Whidden. He was a son of George Whidden and Mary Runnels. She was the daughter of Benjamin Runnels, who lived at Skowhegan,

Maine. Benjamin Whidden was born in Clinton, Kennebec county, Me., in 1796. For a part of his boyhood days, his family lived in Canaan, Me. When he was seven years of age his father died. He had two brothers, David and Samuel, and three sisters, Olive, Sally and Nancy. At the age of sixteen he enlisted in Co. B., 21st, U. S. Regular army, U. S., for three years or during the War of 1812. His enlistment was at Augusta, Me. In comparison with the movements of an army to-day it may be stated, that from that place to Sacket's Harbor, N. Y., he marched on foot, carrying his musket and equipments. He arrived with his regiment by a forced march on the morning of the day of the battle of Sacket's Harbor. The timely arrival of the regiment decided the battle. His story of the battle is this: "The place was defended by N. Y. militia under General Jacob Brown. The regulars had been for several days hastening their march through a forest country and arrived at night, the day before the battle within about twenty miles, when dispatch came to come on, immediately, if possible. A call for volunteers was made for a night march. He volunteered, when within four miles of the harbor at the residence of General Brown, where they rested, but only for a short time, for the guns of the British ships had begun to bombard the town. They 'fell in,' and at quick-march arrived in view just at daylight. From an ascent, and within a mile of the place he saw the flashes of the guns and the landed line of red coats, who had entered the town. The militia were yielding, but stubbornly. The regulars were halted only to form and load musket and fix bayonet. As they came up, he heard the officers of the militia say to their men, 'Stand your ground a few minutes; the regulars are with us.' One volley was fired; a charge was quickly made. The militia cheering and filling up the charging line. The British were cleared from the shore, leaving quite a number of dead and wounded. Among these was a general, Riale. He says this hard march, the scene of the dead and wounded lying around in the streets and yards, made him homesick and tired of war. He was then only a boy, and who wonders? He was at the battles of the Fort Erie, at Chippewa, Williamsburg, and at Lundy's Lane; was one of Col. Miller's charging party, who took the heights with thirteen cannons. He heard the words of Gen. Scott, "Col. Miller, will you lead them?" and the answer, "I will try, sir." In this charge within a few yards of the British guns, he fell severely wounded. After being in hospital awhile, he returned to his command. When the news of peace came, the army of the North was about to disband, when it was discovered that an attack on New Orleans was threatened, and his regiment, with others, were put en route for that point, and when they got as for as Pittsburg, Pa., the news of Jackson's victory caused them to return to Buffalo, where the father was discharged. He came directly to his home in Maine. About that time there was an attraction to the forests of New Brunswick, where lumbering and shipbuilding was a rising business. Thither, with many others from this State, he went. There he bought a wild farm, married and made a home. He followed farming and lumbering, making a good living with but moderate gain of property till 1840, when he sold out and moved to Presque Isle, Aroostook county, Maine. Here he cleared a good farm and helped make the town what it was. In June, 1863, he died. He had been a democrat till Winfield Scott, his old colonel and afterward, general, was nominated by the Whigs for the presidency—he voted for him. After that, he was a republican, voting for Fremont and Lincoln. He was in favor of the prohibition of the liquor traffic and an abstainer for many of his last years. He was a Universalist in faith and went out from this life with the same cheerfulness and hope and courage he had always shown to be his inspiration. He was

b. Clinton, Me., Oct. 13, 1796; d. May 27, 1863. She d. May 2, 1888. Res., St. Davids, N. B. Ch.: 1. George F., b. July 18, 1826; m., April 2, 1846, Hannah C. Oliver, b. March 19, 1833. He res. So. Presque Isle, Me. Ch.: (a) Jessie Freemont, Nov. 6, 1846. Married June 5, 1881; d. May 6, 1895 at Presque Isle, Me. (b) George Benjamin, b. Oct. 19, 1858; m. Feb. 19, 1882; P. O., So. Presque Isle. (c) Cassius Clay, b. April 9, 1860; m. May 4, 1891; P. O., Orono, Me. (d) Hope May, b. Oct. 29, 1875; P. O., So. Presque Isle, Me. (e) Annie Moulton, b. Aug. 8, 1863; d. Sept. 18, 1864. 2. Mary, b. March 29, 1830 (Mary Rackliffe P. O., Maple Lake, Minnesota. 3. Vashti Harriet, b. Nov. 13, 1832 (Mrs. V. H. Downes, P. O., Houlton, Me.) 4. Sarah Jeanette, b. Jan. 31, 1838 (Mrs. Jenny Dunn, P. O. Houlton, Me.) 5. Daniel, b. Dec. 29, 1834; d. Aug., 1834; d. at ten years. 6. Emma Lavina, b. Aug. 7, 1839; d. Nov. 18, 1857; d. at seventeen years. 7. Effie, b. Sept. 8, 1848. Mrs. Effie Eastman, Ft. Fairfield, Me: child of Effie. P. O. and address, Daisy Eastman, Houlton, Me; child of Sarah J.; Elouise Ludwig, Houlton, Me; child of Mary, Ambrose Rackliffe, Monticello. Minnesota. 1. Geo. F. born in the Parish of St. Davids in the Province of New Brunswick in a new log house built by his father on his then almost wild-woods farm. In Sept., 1840, his father went with his family and all his possessions to Presque Isle, in Aroostook county, Me. He was one of the first settlers in that town. At twenty-one he went to Bangor, Me., and worked at carpentering there and at Winterport, Hamden, Maine, and one winter at Salisbury, Mass. For two years he was away from home when he came back, and worked at the same as his principal occupation ever since. In 1854 he went to New York and was with his uncle, Daniel Foster, a stair builder in that city for six months. While there he attended and took lessons at the Cooper Institute in mechanical and architectural drawing; Prof. David Payton was his teacher. In the spring of 1854 he returned to Presque Isle and followed his trade, taking an active part in the affairs in the town or plantation as it was then. He held the office of the first treasurer of the town, and has been placed in some place of trust in town nearly every year since 1853. Married Miss Hannah O. Oliver, of Houlton, Maine. Established a home in Presque Isle. About that time he was commissioned as deputy sheriff, and served four years; by this means he became much better acquainted with the people of the county, and others of the State. In 1863, received a commission of Governor Washburn as a provost marshal of Northern Aroostook. After the Peninsular campaign by Gen. McClellan, quite a large number of soldiers had come home on furlough; surgeon's furlough, "or sick leave" as it was called, and were absent over the limited time. His duty was to examine all such, their papers, and report them by copy, to look into their physical condition or ability to return to their respective commands and use his best judgment in ordering them to the front; seeing to their transportation. In case that he was not obeyed, he was to arrest them, ordering all such as wore the army uniforms to assist. He was also furnished with a list of all absentees from the army; deserters as well. These he was commanded to arrest and place in the county jail and report. He carried a command to all post masters and revenue officers to assist in carrying out these orders. He immediately attended to these duties, traveling over a large territory in out-of-the-way places finding some deserters; some hundreds of others. He had no trouble and rather enjoyed the work. In October, 1864, he was drafted into the service. He was then a deputy sheriff and one of the selectmen of the town. He would long before have volunteered, but it seemed more his duty to stay with his little family so dependent on him and attend to other duties. He was enrolled in the 16th Maine volunteers, but upon request was transferred to the 3d Maine Battery, which was then in front of Petersburg, Virginia, where he went. One of his tent mates, a relative, Theodore B. Foster, of Ashland, was of the direct line of Col. Ben Foster; was a congenial camp fellow and true soldier, and a worthy descendant of his grand-sires. He might say this was flattery, but his associates will say it is but just compliment. President Lincoln was with them a little while on the day of the surrender of Petersburg, where he mingled with the men and took a lesson on Whidden's gun, having the privates show him how to handle and aim it, asking the name of the parts. They gave him hearty cheers when he left, which he acknowledged by a tip of his tall hat. On the 17th of June, 1865, at Augusta, Me, he was mustered out because the war had ended and our flag waved over an undissevered Union. In February, 1866, he bought, in company with John H. Sprague, a saw and shingle mill at So. Presque Isle, which he has to now, 1890, occupied, and operated in part and for the last fifteen years as a carpenter's machine shop, making doors, sashes, blinds, furniture, house finish and general job woodwork. In 1867, on a bolt in the republican party, he was elected to the legislature of the State, and served the term. It was not of his asking, because he never aspired to official place. Since 1882, he has accepted the nomination of senator twice and sheriff once. As it now seems to him, he will enjoy his independence during the remainder of his life.

1675. v. HANNAH, b. ——. 1804; m., St. Davids, N. B., James Cloudman. He was b. ——., Wakefield, N. H., 1806; d. Portland, Maine, Oct., 1892. She d. Presque Isle, Me., 1887. Ch.: 1. Lydia Emeline, b. 1833; m., 1859, Charles Dunn, b. Dec. 4, 1813. Res., Houlton, Me. Ch.: Charles Dunn, Jr., born June 9, 1861; m. Nov. 21, 1888,—living at Woodfords, Cumberland county, Me.; m. Grace E. Walton; b. Nov. 2, 1862. Is a farmer, proprietor of Elm Ridge Farm, dairyman and breeder of Jersey cattle; ch.: a. Esther Cloudman; b. May 6, 1891.

1676. vi. LYDIA, b. ——; d. ——; m. —— Cameron; ch.: 1. George F., who is city treasurer, Bangor, Maine.

1677. vii. JOHN, b.——; married, but no issue living.

881½. BENEN FOSTER (Isaiah, Benjamin, Benjamin, Isaac, Reginald) b. Scarboro, Me., Nov. 14, 1760; m., in 1782, Deborah Kinney, b. Jan. 30, 1763; d. Apr. 13, 1850.

Hon. John L. Davenport, First Deputy Commissioner of the Bureau of Pensions, writes as follows:

"Benan Foster made an application on Dec. 4, 1832, at which time he was 72 years of age and residing at Wakefield, York county, Maine, and his pension was allowed for two years and nine-months, actual service as a private in the Massachusetts Troops, Revolutionary War. He enlisted at Machias, Me., and served under Capt. Moore and Col. Allen. His widow, Deborah, made application and received pension for the service of her husband as above set forth. He was born in Scarboro, Maine, and died Oct. 24, 1843.(?) Their children's names were: Loas, Lydia, Mary, James, Benan, Susannah, Israel, Gideon, Elizabeth, Jepthah and Moses."

A descendant writes: "Family tradition says that he (Benen) was born in Salem, Mass., and Perley Derby, of Salem, to whom I wrote inquiring, said he was probably descended from John, of Salem. Benen Foster was born in the United States, I am sure, for he is always spoken of among the older members of the family as being a 'Yankee' 'born in the States.' I have hoped to find him, or of him, in Machias, Me., because he enlisted as private in Capt. Jabez White's regiment July 15, 1776; dis. Dec. 13, 1776; raised for defense of Machias against Nova Scotia. Also in Capt. Dyer and West's regiments, May, 1777. He received bounty from Lincoln county, Me., and was in artillery company off and on from 1777 to 1778. This I learned at Archives, Boston State House." Another descendant sends the following: "Benjamin Foster, b. Scarborough, Mass. (later Maine), Nov. 14, 1760, d. Oct. 16, 1839; m., 1782, Deborah Kinney (in Sunbury county) b. Jan. 30, 1763, at

Burton, New Brunswick; d. Apr. 13, 1850. Benjamin and Deborah had children as follows: Loas, Lydia, Mary, James, Benjamin, Susannah, Israel, Gideon, Elizabeht, Jepthah, John Moses, Aaron. I think this proof that Benan was a contraction of Benjamin." He d. in N. B., Oct. 16, 1839. Res., Oromucto, N. B., and Wakefield, Maine.

1677- 1. i. LOAS, b. Apr. 21, 1783; d. 1811.
1678- 2. ii. LYDIA, b. July 15, 1785; d. 1880.
1679- 3. iii. MARY, b. Oct. 17, 1787; d. 1868
1680- 4. iv. JAMES, b. Nov. 3, 1789; d. 1869.
1681- 5. v. BENEN, b. Sept. 30, 1792; d. 1850.
1682- 6. vi. SUSANNAH, b. Sept 20, 1794; d. 1882.
1683- 7. vii. ISRAEL, b. Aug. 14, 1796; d. 1840, Boston.
1684- 8. viii. GIDEON, b. Aug. 20, 1798; d. 1845.
1685- 9. ix. ELIZABETH, b. Sept. 19, 1800; d. 1860.
1686-10. x. JEPTHAH, b. Jan. 22, 1803; d. 1870.
1687-11. xi. JOHN MOSES, b. May 7, 1805; m. Sarah S. Wheeler.
1688-12. xii. AARON, b. Dec. 15, 1809; d. 1809.

884. ROBERT FOSTER (Isaiah, Benjamin, Benjamin, Isaac, Reginald), b. Maine; m. there Jane Patten. She d. Bangor, Me., aet. 99. He d. Cherryfield, Me., aet. 80. Res., Columbia, Maine.

1678. i. AZRO, b. Jan. 18, 1812; m. Attazera D. Shattuck.
1679. ii. GILBERT, b.——.
1680. iii. ANN, b. ——.
1681. iv. ABIEL, b. ——.
1682. v. JOHN, b. ——.
1683. vi. ROBERT, b. ——.
1684. vii. SUSAN, b. ——.
1685. viii. LOUISA, b. ——; m. James A. Wakefield. Res., Chicago.
1686. ix. GEORGE, b. ——.
1687. x. FRANK, b. ——.
1688. xi. FRED, b. ——.

885. JOHN WOODEN FOSTER (Wooden, Benjamin, Benjamin, Isaac, Reginald), b. ——; m. Lucy Chase; m. 2d., Mehitabel Meserve. Res., Machias, Maine.

1689. i. JENNIE, b. ——; m. Nathaniel Babb.
1690. ii. SALLY, b. ——; m. Joseph Larabee.
1691. iii. FANNY, b. ——; m. John White; m. 2d. —— McGlauflin.
1692. iv. JOHN WOODEN, b. ——, 1810; m. Caroline Rackliff and Mrs. Maria Simonton.
1693. v. THANKFUL, b. ——; m. Amos Ackley.
1694. vi. CHARLES, b. ——.
1695. vii. ISAIAH, b. ——.
1696. viii. RUTH, b. ——; m. Levi Chase, son of Ephraim and Lydia (Hathaway). Res., Machias, Me. Ch.: Cyrus, Charles, Cynthia, m. Parker Dennison; Lucilla, Mary E., m. John Parsons; Esther L., m. Gilbert Dennison and Ezra Dennison; Isaiah, Eveline, m. ——McGuire; Amanda, m. Wm. Hautley; Deborah, m. Stephen Pigeon.
1697. ix. MERCY, b. ——; m. Pearl Howe.
1698. x. LUCY, b. ——; m. Moses Elsemore.
1699. xi. SALLY, b. ——; m. Jacob Crosby.
1700. xii. POLLY, b. ——; m. —— Butler.
1701. xiii. SUSAN, b. ——.
1702. xiv. SOLOMON M., b. ——.

887. MOSES FOSTER (Wooden, Benjamin, Benjamin, Isaac, Reginald), b. ——; m. Drusilla West. Res., Machias, Maine.

1703. i. WILMOT, b. ——; m. Wm. Foster.
1704. ii. LYDIA, b. ——.
1705. iii. JABEZ W., b. ——.
1706. iv. AARON MOSES, b. ——.
1707. v. CYRUS W., b. ——.
1708. vi. JOANNA, b. ——; m. Benjamin Foster.

1709. vii. PHINEHAS, b. Mar. 17, 1795; m. Ruth Rich and Mary Coffin Foster.
1710. viii. EZRA, b. ——.
1711. ix. DRUSILLA, b. ——; m. John F. Harris.
1712. x. CYNTHIA, b. ——; m. Stephen T. Harris.
1713. xi. JEREMIAH, b. ——.

889. PAUL FOSTER (Wooden, Benjamin, Benjamin, Isaac, Reginald), b. ——; m. Betsey Webber. Res., Machias, Maine.
1714. i. MARTHA, b. ——; m. T. P. Folsom and Henry S. Chase, son of Wm. and Lucy (Smith).
1715. ii. JAMES, b.——.
1716. iii. NATHAN W., b. ——.
1717. iv. ELIZA, b. ——; m. Luther Carey.
1718. v. JOEL,b. ——.
1719. vi. HIRAM, b. ——.

890. JOEL FOSTER (Wooden, Benjamin, Benjamin, Isaac, Reginald), b. ——; m. Mary West. Res., Machias, Maine
1720. i. STEPHEN, b. ——.
1721. ii. JOEL, b. ——.
1722. iii. EZEKIEL, b. ——.
1723. iv. STEPHEN C., b. ——.
1724. v. REBECCA, b. ——; m. Alfred Foster.

892. ELIAS FOSTER (Wooden, Benjamin, Benjamin, Isaac, Reginald), b. ——; m. Mary Gooch, dau. of Benj. and Molly (Nash); m. 2d., Lucy Dorman. Res., Machias, Maine.
1725. i. REBECCA, b. ——.
1726. ii. SARAH, b. ——; m. R. Pagan Buckman.
1727. iii. WOODEN, b. ——.
1728. iv. MARY, b. ——.
1729. v. JANE, b. ——; m. Geo. W. Blake.
1730. vi. EZRA, b. ——.
1731. vii. LEWIS, b. ——.
1732. viii. MARY, b. ——; m. Jacob Day.
1733. ix. GILBERT D., b. ——.
1734. x. LEONARD, b. ——; d. ——.
1735. xi. LEONARD C., b. ——.
1736. xii. WILLARD W., b. ——.
1737. xiii. E. BURTON, b. ——.
1738. xiv. S. HARRIS, b. ——.
1739. xv. ALMIRA, b. ——; m. Albion P. Wellington.
1740. xvi. A. LORING, b.——.

893. JAMES FOSTER (Wooden, Benjamin, Benjamin, Isaac, Reginald), b. Machias, Me., in 1773; m. Lucy Gooch, dau. of Benj. and Molly (Nash); d. Oct., 1829; m. 2d, Hannah Simpson. He d. Feb. 21, 1848. Res., E. Machias, Maine.
1741. i. CHARLES, b. Oct. 10, 1803; m. Lavinia P. Chase.
1742. ii. LOUISA, b. ——.
1743. iii. ELIZABETH, G., b. ——.
1744. iv. LOUISA, b. ——; m. Simeon Chase.
1745. v. ANN, b. ——; m. Josiah P. Kellar.
1746. vi. OLIVE, b. ——.
1747. vii. FRANCES U., b. ——; m. David Brown.

896. BENJAMIN FOSTER (Ezekiel, Benjamin, Benjamin, Isaac, Reginald), b. Limerick, Me., May 1, 1777; m., Limerick, Me., Oct., 1797, Hannah Bartlett. She d. Dover, Me., aet. 79. He was a farmer. He d. Nov., 1867. Res., Dover, Maine.
1748. i. ERASTUS, b. Oct 25, 1801; m. Betsey Clough.
1749. ii. ISAIAH B., b. May 30, 1803. A dau. is Mrs. Albina Emery, Sherman Mills, Maine.
1750. iii. SUSAN, b. Apr. 14, 1805. A son is B. B. Smith, Dover, Maine.
1751. iv. MARY, b. Aug. 9, 1806; d. s. p.

1752. v. JOSEPH, b. Mar. 24, 1808. A dau. is Caroline B. Kempton, Phillips, Maine.
1753. vi. LEIGHTON, b. April 19, 1810; m. Clarissa Ricker.
1754. vii. LYDIA, b. April 10, 1812.
1755. viii. JANE, b. Jan. 30, 1814.
1756. ix. B. C. B., b. Oct. 30, 1815.
1757. x. KEZIAH, b. ——. A dau. is Mrs. Cynthia J. Ingalls, Sherman Mills, Maine.

899. NATHAN FOSTER (Jeremiah, Jeremiah, Abraham, Jacob, Reginald), b. Nov. 27, 1771, Ashburnham, Mass.; m. Shelburne, Franklin county, Mass., Fanny Kirk. She d. Colerain, Mass. M. 2d., Hannah Baker. He d. Friendship, N. Y., Feb. 8, 1856. Res., Shelburne, Mass. and Wirt, New York.

1758. i. JOHN, b. Nov. 11, 1795; m. Bernice Harris.
1759. ii. SALLY, b. ——.
1760. iii. NATHAN, b. ——.
1761. iv. LEONARD, b. ——.
1762. v. AUSTIN B., b. Nov. 11, 1807; m. Sarah W. Stout.
1763. vi. HANNAH, b. ——.
1764. vii. LEWIS, b.
1765. viii AUNTICE, b. ——.
1766. ix. AMOS b.———.
1767. x. PHEBE b. ——.
1768. xi. ELECTA b. ——.

900. ABRAHAM FOSTER (Samuel, Jeremiah, Abraham, Jacob, Reginald), b. Ashburnham, Mass., Apr. 8, 1770; m., Jan. 26, 1792, Sarah Willard, dau. of Dea. John; d. July 24, 1831; m. 2d., Jan. 1, 1827, Mary T. Davis, dau. of Ebenezer B. Davis. She d. Apr. 29, 1853. He was a blacksmith and farmer and resided on the farm where Coughlin now resides. Sarah Willard was great-great-granddaughter of Simon Willard of Concord, Mass. He d. Dec. 12, 1837. Res., Ashburnham, Mass.

1769. i. JOHN W., b. May 12, 1794.
1770. ii. SALLY, b. Oct. 17, 1792; she d. s. p.
1771. iii. MARY J., b. June 20, 1810; m. —— Watts; went west.
1772. iv. ELIJAH WILLARD, b. Oct. 8, 1807; m. Tryphene Lovewell.
1773. v. ABIGAIL, b. July 6, 1796. She d. s. p.
1774. vi. LUCINDA WILLARD, b. June 9, 1798; m. John Bowman. She d. s. p. (Samuel, John of Lexington). Res., Berkshire county, Mass. He d. 1830, aet. 37; she d. 1862. Ch.: 1. Jane. 2. Harriet. 3. Hannah. 4. Isaac. 5. Stillman Winthrop. 6. Foster. 7. John, b. April 16, 1822; m., Aug. 10, 1848, Eliza Powell Giddens; b. Oct. 25, 1823. He d. in Boston, Aug. 4, 1882. Ch.: 1. Samuel Stillman Bowman, b. Apr. 29, 1849; m. Janet Patterson, of Baltimore, Md.; their only child, John Alexander Bowman, b. Apr. 3, 1886, Washington, D. C. 2. George Foster Bowman, b. Jan 25, 1851; d. Nov. 26, 1890, Portland, Oregon. 3. Sarah, b. Nov. 4, 1858; m., Oct. 4, 1892, Joseph VanNess; b. Dec. 13, 1849. Res., s. p., Lexington, Mass. 4. Ida Corrinne Bowman, d. 1860. 5 John Thomas Bowman, d. 1860, Tallahassee, Fla.
1775. vii. SOPHIA, b. Sept. 21, 1800.
1776. viii. HARRIET WILLARD, b. June 16, 1805; d. s. p.
1777. ix. ABRAHAM, b. July 14, 1802; d. s. p.

901. NATHANIEL FOSTER (Samuel, Jeremiah, Abraham, Jacob, Reginald), b. Ashburnham, Mass., Dec. 26, 1771; m., Jan. 11, 1795, Hepsibeth Cutting, dau. of Samuel. He was a farmer in the northwest part of town and conducted a sawmill. Until the death of another person by the same name he was styled Jr. He d. Sept. 30, 1836. Res., Ashburnham, Mass.

1778. i. RHODA, b. Dec. 15, 1795; m., Nov. 23, 1820, Asa Smith, of Gardner. She d. Oct. 30, 1821, leaving Asa F., b. Oct. 20, 1821; m. Fidelia Jackson.
1779. ii. SAMUEL, b. July 28, 1799; m. Emeline Kibling.
1780. iii. EMMA, b. Dec. 29, 1803; m. Thomas Bennett, of Gardner. She moved to Ashburnham about 1824, and remained a number of

years. He was interested in a sawmill. He was b. Gardner, Jan. 14, 1798. His oldest ch. was b. in G. and the others in Ashburnham, Mass. He finally removed to Athol and d. there in 1884. Ch.: 1. Mary Ann, b. Oct. 24, 1823. 2. Nancy Maria, b. Nov. 28, 1825. 3. Albert Thomas, b. Oct. 3, 1827. 4. Helen Augusta, b. Sept. 10, 1829. 5. Samuel Foster, b. Aug. 25, 1831. 6. Geo. Anson, b. June 30, 1833.

1781. iv. EUNICE, b. ——; m. Henry Carter, of Leominster; 4 ch.

1782. v. NANCY, b. ——; m. Metaphor Kendall, of Leominster. She d. 1843. and left 5 ch.

1783. vi. MARY, b. ——, 1807; m., April 14, 1832, Stillman D. Benjamin, of Shirley, Mass. Ch.: 1. Sidney W., b. May 25, 1833; m., 1873, Mary Harris, of Ashburnham; res., Shirley. 2. Viola D., b. Aug. 4, 1836; m. Stephen H. Kimball. Res., Everett, Mass. 3. Mary Jane, b. Mar. 24, 1841; m., 1865, L. L. Brown. Res., Harvard. 4. Frances Ann, b. Oct. 24, 1845. Res., Shirley. Mary, d. Dec. 25, 1882.

1784. vii. ADELINE, b. Sept. 30, 1809; m., Sept. 11, 1832, Albert Lamb, of Leominster.

1785. viii. ELVIRA F., b. ——; m. Stephen Dodge, of Leominster.

1786. ix. LEONARD, b. Apr. 14, 1814; m. Malvina Lawrence, Clarissa Cole, and Sarah Howard.

1787. x. EMMA, b. Sept. 3, 1801; d. young.

1788. xi. HEPSIBETH, b. Oct. 13, 1797; d. Dec. 14, 1809.

903. SAMUEL FOSTER (Samuel, Jeremiah, Abraham, Jacob, Reginald), b. Ashburnham, Mass., Feb. 9, 1776; m., Feb. 5, 1799, Lydia Stearns; b. Mar. 24, 1780. She was dau. of William Stearns and Lydia Davis and gr.-dau. of Hon. Isaac Stearns, of Billerica. He was a soldier in the French and Indian War; Was a representative and senator in the State legislature and highly respected as a soldier, civil magistrate and a Christian. He was son of John, and gr.-son of John, whose father was Isaac, the emigrant ancestor who came to America in 1630 with Sir Richard Saltonstall, and located in Watertown. He was a selectman and highly respected; came probably from Parish of Wayland in Suffolk in England. He d. April 24, 1868. Res., Stoddard, N. H.

1789. i. STEARNS, b. Dec. 26, 1799; m. Cynthia Wilson and Mary Fuller.

1790. ii. LYDIA, b. Aug. 22, 1801; m., Nov. 24, 1824, Dea. Luke Joslin; b. Dec. 22, 1797. Res., Stoddard, N. H. Ch.: 1. Gilman, b. Dec. 25, 1825; m., Feb. 20, 1851, Susan A. Williams. 2. Albert, b. Oct. 27, 1828; d. July 13, 1850. 3. Elsie, b. July 21, 1832; m. Dr. Ira F. Prouty; b. Nov. 9, 1812. She d. Jan. 17, 1882. He was grad. of Dartmouth in 1837, and Medical University, city of New York, 1882. Res., Keene, N. H.

1791. iii. MARIA, b. Apr. 29, 1804; m., Nov. 4, 1823, Stephen Wood; b. Jan. 11, 1800; d. Apr. 30, 1874. He was deacon of the Congregational church in Hancock, N. H., for forty-eight years. Ch.: 1. Franklin Salmon, b. Jan. 8, 1825; m. Margaret Jane Coe. Res., Albion, N. Y. 2. Sabrina, b. Feb. 9, 1830; m., Sept. 21, 1869, Dea. Alfred Hardy. Res., Greenfield, N. H. 3. Orren Stearns, b. Oct. 13, 1837; d. Mar. 30, 1839. 4. Alden Samuel, b. Jan. 30, 1840. He was in the Civil War. Res., Hancock, N. H., on old homestead.

1792. iv. HOSEA, b. Apr. 13, 1806; m. Mary G. Rice.

1793. v. SELINA, b. July 5, 1809; m., Feb. 16, 1830. Mark Bowers. Res., Hancock, N. H. Ch.: 1. George, b. Oct. 10, 1831; m., Dec. 28, 1858, Urina E. Brackett. He was a dentist. Res., Nashua, N. H. 2. Almira, b. Oct. 14, 1832; m. Reuben M. Sawyer. Res., Nashua. 3. Caroline, b. April 30, 1835; m., Adams A. Roberts. Res., Kansas. 4. Albert, b. Apr. 11, 1837; m. Melvina E. Hart; he grad. Dart. Coll. 1863 and Andover Theo. Sem., 1868. Settled in Macon, Mo., as pastor of Cong. church. Later res., Huntington W. Va. and Ruggles, Ohio. 5. Cynthia, b. May 17, 1839; m. Asa D. Wood; res., Hancock, N. H. 6. Horace S., b. July 17, 1841; was in Mass. Regt. in Civil War and d. Feb. 28, 1862. 7. Samuel O., b. Dec. 13, 1843; m. Susan Sharp. He is a dentist. Res., Hillsboro, N. H.

1794. vi. EMILY, b. Dec. 19, 1811; m., Oct. 10, 1833, Dea. Edward Haywood; b. Apr. 26, 1810. Res., until 1869, Hancock, N. H. He d. Nov. 6, 1883, Hyde Park, Mass. Ch.: 1. Sarah M., b. July 27, 1835; m. J. Ellery Piper of Boston. 2. Sylvia A., b. July 4, 1837; d. Apr. 3, 1838. 3. Cynthia F., b. Sept. 10, 1839; m. Luke P. Wil-

MRS. MARIA FOSTER WOOD.

DEACON STEPHEN WOOD.

lard of Boston. 4. Edward S., b. June 30, 1841; m. Emma Washburn. 5. Milan A. (twin), b. June 7, 1843; d. June 25, 1843. 6. Mary A. (twin), b. June 7, 1843; d. July 14, 1843. 7. Lydia Alice, b. Oct. 24, 1847; d. Sept. 13, 1853. 8. Fred A., b. Jan. 31, 1856; d. June 14, 1860.

1795. vii. SAMUEL, b. Nov. 29, 1815; m. Mary S. Palmer.

1796. viii. ELECTA, b. Nov. 10, 1817; d. Dec. 25, 1818.

1797. ix. ELECTA, b. June 10, 1825; m., June 15, 1850, James Downing; b. April 8, 1815. Son of Thomas. She d. May 18, 1858, and he m. again. He d. Feb. 29, 1876. Ch.: 1. Martha Foster, b. May 12, 1842. 2. Mary Monroe, b. Nov. 23, 1843. 3. Thomas, b. Aug. 3, 1845. 4. Amasa Albert, b. Apr. 29, 1847. 5. George Henry, b. Jan. 22, 1849. 6. Warren, b. March 23, 1850. 7. John, b. Oct. 20, 1851. 8. Walter, b. Aug. 6, 1853

904. HOSEA FOSTER (Samuel, Jeremiah, Abraham, Jacob, Reginald), b. Ashburnham, Mass., Aug. 1, 1778; m. there Dec. 8, 1803, Polly Joslin; b. 1781; d. Aug. 9, 1838. He d. Feb. 23, 1855. Res., Verona, New York.

1798. i. POLLY, b. ——; m. Justus Brewster, of V.; had ch.: Amos F., Mary, Susan F., and Polly J., who m. a Williams. Res., Verona, New York.

1799. ii. SUSAN, b. Sept. 16, 1806; m., Jan. 25, 1832, Ed. Smith Latham, of Seneca Falls, N. Y. He was b. Manchester, N. Y., Oct. 7, 1808; d. Seneca Falls, N. Y., Mar. 5, 1867 She d. Apr. 2, 1892. Ch.: 1. Caroline Eugenia Latham, b. Sept. 16, 1836; d. Mar. 27, 1837. 2. Hosea Foster Latham, gr. Hobert College; b. June 1, 1838; d. July 30, 1882; unm. 3. Susan Imogene Latham, b Mar. 26, 1840; d. Aug. 5, 1842. 4. Susan Imogene Latham, b. Dec. 8, 1842; m., Dec. 16, 1863, John Marshall Guion, b. Mar. 9, 1832; d. July 26, 1891. Res., Seneca Falls, N. Y., 41 W. Bayard St. Ch.:

1. Edward Latham Marshall Guion, b. Aug. 25, 1866, Seneca Falls, N. Y. 2. John Marshall Guion, b. Aug. 14, 1871, Seneca Falls, N. Y.

1800. iii. CAROLINE, b. Oct. 10, 1810; m., Feb. 21, 1833, Oscar Granger. He was b. Vernon, N. Y., May 1, 1793; d. Sept. 20, 1874. He was a glass manufacturer and res. in Saratoga Springs, N. Y. She d. Dec. 18, 1871. Ch.: 1. Lyman F., b. Dec. 13, 1840; d. Troy in Aug., 1872. 2. Antoinette S., b. July 13, 1834; m., June 20, 1854, John T. Carr; b. Sept. 28, 1822; d. Aug. 25, 1889. He was a lawyer. Ch.: 1. Clarence G. Carr, b. Jan. 30, 1856; m., Oct. 20, 1880, Sara H. Sutherland; P. O. address, 3232 Tenth Ave., south, Minneapolis, Minn. 2. Carrie Carr, address, 204 Caroline St., Sar. Springs. 3. Foster Granger, b. in Vernon, Oneida Co., May 1, 1846, is dead. He had two ch.: 1. Imogene Granger, b. in Greenfield, Saratoga Co., N. Y., May 8,1870. 2. Carrie Granger, b. in Greenfield, Saratoga Co., N. Y, June 1, 1875. Foster m. Alice Scott in May, 1868. Both res.in Ballston, N. Y.

1801. iv. HOSEA, b. May 1,1819; m. Cornelia Scaden.

905. JOEL FOSTER (Samuel, Jeremiah, Abraham, Jacob, Reginald), b. Ashburnham, Mass., Aug. 21, 1780; m. there in 1805, Dolly Wetherbee, of Ashby, Mass.; b. Feb. 21, 1774,; d. May 23, 1838; m. 2d, Apr. 23, 1839, Mrs. Ruth Fuller, wid of Benj.; b. 1774; d. Apr. 3, 1850. He was a valuable citizen, was in town office several years and ably and faithfully discharged every trust. He d. Sept. 6, 1859. Res., Ashburnham, Mass.

1802. i. HARRIET, b. Sept. 10, 1806; m., Apr. 1, 1830, James Hayward, of Ashby. She d. Apr. 10, 1839. He m. 2d, Melinda Corey.

1803. ii. JOEL, b. July 15, 1808; d. Mar. 31, 1814.

1804. iii. JEROME W., b. Dec. 15, 1810; m. Mary Colson.

1805. iv. DOROTHY, b. Sept. 6, 1813; m., June, 1833, Lewis G. Houghton, of Ashby. She d. Dec. 31, 1863. He was born Apr. 12, 1804, son of Elijah and Sarah.

911. JOSEPH FOSTER (Abraham, Abraham, Abraham, Jacob, Reginald), b. Boston, Mass., ——; m. Res., Boston, Mass.

1806. i. MOSES B., b. ——.

1807. ii. JOSEPH, b. ——.

1808. iii. JOHN, b. ——.

1809. iv. SALLY, b. ——.

919. JOSEPH FOSTER (Joseph, Joseph, Joseph, Jacob, Reginald), b. Billerica, Mass., Apr., 1770; m. Lucy Larkum. She m. 2d, Sept. 23, 1816, Jesse Webster. Joseph Billerica letter date Dec. 7, 1815, ex. Sept. 11, 1816, wife Lucy; ch.: Elvira C. Lucy. [Mid. Prob.] He d. Nov. 21, 1815. Res., Billerica, Mass.

1810. i. JOSEPH, b. ——, 1794; d. Dec. 18, 1815.

1811. ii. LUCY, bapt. Oct. 13, 1799; d. young.

1812. iii. LUCY, bapt. June 19, 1803.

1813. iv. ELVIRA CATHERINE, b. ——.

921. SAMUEL FOSTER (Joseph, Joseph, Joseph, Jacob, Reginald). b. Billerica, Mass., Apr. 26, 1877; m., Jan. 14, 1802, Anne Whitney, dau. of Daniel and Sarah; d. Apr. 13, 1857. Samuel.Billerica will dated Mar. 26, 1850, Prob. Sept. 1, 1857, wife Anna ["heirs presumptive and all parties interested?"] James Damon, Sally F. Damon, Elizabeth A. Foster, Joseph Foster, Sumner Foster, Dudley Foster, guar. for Anna L. Foster, Edward M. Foster and Francis H. Foster. [Midsex Prob.] He d. Aug. 1, 1857, Billerica, Mass.

1814. i. THOMAS, b. Dec. 4, 1803; d. Dec. 29, 1804.

1815. ii. SALLY, b. Nov. 9, 1805; m., Jan. 23, 1827, James Damon, of Reading, a son of E. H. Damon. Res., Ipswich.

1816. iii. ELMIRA, b. Sept. 7, 1807; d. Feb. 18, 1809.

1817. iv. DUDLEY, b. Nov. 15, 1809; m. Louisa Pollard and Mary A. ——.

1818. v. EDWIN, b. Feb. 1, 1812; m. Ann L. Callender. A son, Frank Homer is with R. H. Stearns & Co., Boston, Mass.

1819. vi. DANIEL WHITNEY, b. Mar. 23, 1814; d. June 6, 1815.

1820. vii. ELIZABETH ANN, b. Mar. 22, 1816,; d. June 27, 1816.

1821. viii. ELIZABETH ANN, b. July 2, 1817; unm.

1822. ix. MARY, b. July 13, 1819; m., Feb. 23, 1843, Edward Mansfield. She d. Oct. 14, 1846, s. p.
1823. x. JOSEPH, b. July 20, 1821; m. Lydia A. Dutton.
1824. xi. JONATHAN, b. Jan. 1, 1823.
1825. xii. SUMNER, b. Jan. 28, 1829; m. Elizabeth Putnam and Mary F. ——. A son, James E.; res., Danvers, Mass., and dau., Mrs. Geo. E. Sawyer; res., Belmont, N. H. Sumner d. Feb., 1895. Sumner North Reading, letter date Jan. 22, 1895, ex Mar. 8, 1895, wife Mary F. Ch.: Mary, Eunice Sawyer, wife of George E. Sawyer, of Belmont, N. H. James E. Foster, of Danvers, Mass. Midsex Prob.]

925. LEVI FOSTER (Joseph, Joseph, Joseph, Jacob, Reginald), b. Billerica, Mass., July, 1788. m., Aug. 27, 1815, Cile Davis, dau. of Timothy; b July 20, 1792. He resided in that part of Chelmsford, now Lowell, Mass., later near Fox Hill, at Holden Place He d. June 15, 1863. Res., Charlesford, Mass.

1826. i. LAURA, b. ——; m. Henry Blanchard, of Wilmington, Mass.
1827. ii. CELIA, b. ——; m. Amosa Holden; b. Oct. 12, 1813. Res., South Marlow, N. H. Ch.; 1. Albert S., b. June 22, 1851. 2. George E., b. Sept. 11, 1854. 3. Herbert J., b. July 12, 1858. 4. Ellen C., b. Oct. 24, 1865.
1828. iii. LEVI THOMAS, b. ——; m. Mariah E. Richardson.
1829. iv. JOHN, b. 1828; d. Dec. 14, 1851.

930. JAMES FOSTER (Daniel, Joseph, Joseph, Jacob, Reginald), b. Beverly, Mass., Aug. 20, 1782; m., Jan. 14, 1807, Mary Vickery, dau. of Knott Vickery, b. Dec. 27, 1786; d. Aug. 1, 1840; m. 2d, Oct. 18, 1844, Sarah Greeley, b. Marblehead, 1787; d. Sept. 22, 1872, dau. of Nicholas and Mary. Was a cordwainer. He d. Sept. 27, 1854. Res., Beverly, Mass.

1830. i. DANIEL, b. Oct. 10, 1807; m. Elizabeth Woodbury and Elizabeth A. Sisson.
1831. ii. JAMES, b. Mar. 25, 1809; m. Mary Rogers.
1832. iii. MARY ANN, b. Feb. 22, 1811; pub. May 6, 1838; Ebenezer S. Webber.
1833. iv. CAROLINE, b. Dec. 5, 1813; m., Dec. 30, 1849, Philip Lee, Jr.; d. Mar. 17, 1884.
1834. v. ALFRED, b. Nov. 29, 1819; m. Augusta Lovett.
1835. vi. ADDISON W., b. Nov. 26, 1822; m. Lucy A. Hogerseil.
1836. vii ABBIE, b. Jan. 7, 1816; m., Sept. 19, 1844, James J. Kimball, of Charleston, Mass.
1837. viii ELIZA A., b. ——; m., Dec. 5, 1856, John E. Wallis, b. 1819; son of Josiah and Ruth.

931. SETH FOSTER (Daniel, Joseph, Joseph, Jacob, Reginald), b. Beverly, Mass., Apr. 1, 1784; m., Jan. 2, 1814, Nancy Goodridge; b. Jan. 2, 1784; d. June 6, 1843. He d. Aug. 8, 1843. Res., Beverly, Mass.

1838. i. WILLIAM AUGUSTUS, b. Oct. 24, 1814; m. Mary Raymond and Julia F. Trow.
1839. ii. SETH, b. June 12, 1826.
1840. iii. DANIEL, b. Dec. 23, 1821; m. Louisa Dodge.
1841. iv. SAMUEL GOODRIDGE, b. May 24, 1827; m. Caroline Emmons.
1842. v. CHARLOTTE, b. Dec. 23, 1819; m. She d. June 26, 1892. Ch.: 1. ——, b. ——; m. Arthur Stockman. Res., Portland, Me.
1843. vi. JAMES, b. Mar. 4, 1830; d. Mar. 8, 1830.
1844. vii. JAMES, b. May 27, 1831; d. at sea. Date of death unknown.
1845 viii ELLEN, b. Jan. 5, 1824; d. Dec. 20, 1875.
1846. ix. ELLEN, b. Jan. 2, 1818; d. Apr. 2, 1820.
1847. x. NANCY, b. Mar. 24. 1816, d. ——.

933. JOSEPH FOSTER (Daniel, Joseph, Joseph, Jacob, Reginald), b. Beverly, Mass., May 17, 1789; m., April 7, 1816, Rebecca Batchelder,* dau. of Asa and

*CAPT. ASA BATCHELDER (Jonathan, Jonathan, John, John), b. Beverly, Mass., April 17, 1761; m., Sept. 8, 1785, Rebecca Beckford, b. 1761; d. Feb. 12, 1824. He was in the Revolutionary War, in Capt. Billy Porter's company, in Col. Ebenezer Francis' regiment; pay abstract for forty days' rations from date of enlistment, Feb. 13, 1777, to time of arrival at Bennington; marched March 12, 1777; also private in Captain Porter's company in Col. Benjamin Tupper's regiment. Continental army pay accounts for service from Jan. 1 to Feb. 13, 1780. He d. Washington, N. C. Oct. 9, 1810. Res., Beverly, Mass. Ch.: 1. Betsey, b. July 12, 1786; m. Nathaniel Batchelder, 2d; d. Aug. 28, 1844. 2 Asa, b. Aug. 14, 1788; d. at sea Sept. 10, 1810. 3. Rebecca, b. July 19, 1791; m. Joseph Foster.

Rebecca, b. July 19, 1791; d. Oct. 4. 1826. He d. Aug. 24, 1871. Res., Beverly, Mass.

1848. i. BETSEY BATCHELDER, b. ——, 1817; d. Nov. 1, 1821.

1849. ii. BETSEY BATCHELDER, b. May 2, 1819; m. 1st, Jan. 22, 1846, John W. English. He was b. 1820, son of Philip and Rebecca. M. 2d, April 23, 1857, Elisha P. Rich; d. June 14, 1882.

1850. iii. SALLY STANDLEY, b. Jan. 3, 1822; m., June 10, 1856, Philip Lee, Jr., widower, aet. 42, son of Philip and Abigail; d. May 26, 1865.

1851. iv. REBECCA BECKFORD, b. Aug. 8, 1826; d. Aug. 12, 1826.

935. CAPT. WILLIAM FOSTER (Ezra T., Joseph, Joseph, Jacob, Reginald), b. Beverly, Mass., July 31, 1786; m. ——, Abigail Dike Lovett, dau. of William Herrick and Abigail (Dike) Lovett, b. April 6, 1802; d. June 9, 1859. Was a master mariner. He d. Mar. 6, 1868. Res., Beverly, Mass.

1852. i. ABIGAIL STEPHENS, b. Oct. 29, 1822; m., June 23, 1846, Capt. Edward Meacom; d. Jan. 5, 1892, at Salem.

1853. ii. SARAH ELIZABETH, b. July 7, 1829; d. May 5, 1833.

1854. iii. WILLIAM LOVETT, b. Nov. 4, 1837; mariner; d. unm. June 13, 1858; consumption.

1855. iv. JOHN ELLINWOOD, d. of cholera infantum, 1841-2.

949. JOHN WELSH FOSTER (James, Nathan, Joseph, Jacob, Reginald), b. June 6, 1789; m. Aug. 31, 1824, in Portsmouth, N. H., Mary Appleton, b. in 1789, in Boston, dau. of Dr. Nathaniel Walker Appleton (Nathaniel, Nathaniel, John, John, Samuel) and Sarah, dau. of William Greenleaf, of Boston (as stated in the Genealogy of the Appleton Family; W. S. Appleton, Boston, 1874, p. 22).

Mrs. Foster's great-grandfather was Rev. Dr. Nathaniel Appleton, of Cambridge, in honor of whom the Appleton Chapel, at Harvard university was named, and Dr. Appleton's grandfather was President John Rogers, of Harvard. A grandson of her cousin, Nathaniel Appleton, of Haverhill, is Frederic W. Putnam, curator of the Peabody museum, of American Archaeology, of Harvard university.

John Welsh Foster, after his father's death, in 1793, lived for nine years with his uncle, Joseph Hiller, then collector of the port of Salem. He settled in Portsmouth, N. H., in 1812, and in 1819 was chosen deacon of the Unitarian church; he held that position and was one of the superintendents of the Sunday school as long as he lived.

A memorial of John W. Foster, edited by Andrew P. Peabody, D. D., pastor of the church, was published in Portsmouth, in 1852. He d. Jan. 10, 1852, in Portsmouth. She d. ——, 18—.

Administration of estate of John Welsh Foster, of Portsmouth, N. H., granted to next of kin in Massachusetts, James H. Foster, of Boston, merchant, March 15, 1852. Bond: James H. Foster, Charles S. Foster. Lib. 223, Fol. 195. Lib. 289, Fol. 89. Lib. 325, Fol. 31. Adm. acct. mentions Mary A. Foster and Joseph Hiller Foster, execs. of will of John W. Foster, S. H. Foster, M. A. Foster, heirs of J. W. Foster. Lib. 150, Fol. 156. Suff. prob.

1856. i. JOSEPH HILLER, b. Aug., 1825; m. Adelaide Morgan.

1857. ii. SARAH H., b. ——; unm. Res., Portsmouth, N. H.

1858. iii. MARY A., b. ——; unm. Res., Portsmouth, N. H.

950. HENRY GARDNER FOSTER (Nathaniel, Nathan, Joseph, Jacob, Reginald), b. Boston, Mass., Dec. 9, 1785; m. Framingham, Mass., March 3, 1824, Anna Angier Haven, of Framingham, Mass, dau. of Dea. Moses Pike, b. March 14, 1795 (Gideon, Moses, Nathaniel, Richard, the emigrant). She d. Nov. 26, 1853. He was a man of scholary tastes and much family pride, and the family genealogy was carefully preserved. He was a prominent citizen of Boston; was of the firm of Walley & Foster, East India merchants, who owned their ships in the palmy days of old Boston's India trade. He was one of the founders and supporters of the Swedenborgian church in Boston.

Reginald Foster, of Boston, commission merchant (eldest son), appointed administrator of estate of Henry G. Foster, gentleman, of Boston (who died March 21, 1861), at request of the only other person interested in the estate. April 1, 1861. Lib. 229, Fol. 210. Lib. 370, Fol. 381. Inventory mentions money due from H. Haven Foster. Lib. 298, Fol. 97. Adm. acct., Henry H. Foster and Reginald

Foster, each one half of estate. June 3, 1861. Lib. 159[1], Fol. 444-5. He d. March 21, 1861. Res., Cambridge, Mass.

1859. i. EMILY, b. May, 1825; d. Sept., 1832.
1860. ii. HENRY HAVEN, b. Jan. 2, 1827; d. unm. Aug., 1862.
1861. iii. REGINALD, b. June 25, 1828; m. Anna Maria Wentworth.
1862. iv. OLIVIA, b. April 22, 1830; d. Sept., 1832.

953. ISAAC FOSTER (Isaac, Isaac, Joseph, Jacob, Reginald), b. Marblehead, Mass., March 9, 1768; m. in Andover, N. H., 1795, Charlotte Whitman, b. Abington, Mass., March 9, 1771; d. March 25, 1840. She was dau. of John of Weymouth, b. Oct. 9, 1740; m. (pub. Jan. 15, 1763) Betty, probably daughter of Samuel and Sarah (Gurney) Tyrell, b. Oct. 17, 1745; settled for a time at Abington. In the record of his father's will is mentioned as a "laborer, resident of Abington;" in 1782 there was a John Whitman taxed at Bedford, and there is a lot in that town still known as the Whitman lot; it is probably this John, as his brother Levi was already a resident of Bedford; he later resided at Acworth, N. H.; according to tradition in the family of the eldest daughter there were seven children. Mrs. Foster removed with her parents to Andover, N. H., being then about 18; after her marriage resided for a few years at Acworth, N. H.; then removed to Moretown, where she d. He d. Sept. 8, 1851. Res., Moretown, Vt.

1863. i. SARAH, b. June 28, 1796; m., Oct. 29, 1820, Lyman, son of Ephraim and Sally (Perkins) Cobb, b. Feb. 28, 1797; d. Aug. 8, 1869; a tailor. Res., Moretown. She resided with her adopted son at Somerville, Mass., and d. Feb. 2, 1890. Two ch.: 1. William Cobb, b. May 19; d. May 20, 1822. 2. Charlotte Cobb, b. Oct. 2; d. Oct. 10, 1825. 3. Rev. William Cobb High, b. March 30, 1822, son of LaRue and Sally (Carpenter) High; was adopted by Mrs. Cobb; he m., March 30, 1843, Dianthe J., daughter of Calvin and Sophia Campbell Clark, b. Jan. 15, 1822; a minister of the M. E. church; now settled at Somerville. Three ch.: (a) N. Jennie High, b. Jan. 2, 1844; d. April 25, 1865. (b) Ella C. High, b. May 21, 1849; d. Sept. 19, 1864. (c) Belle High, b. April 28, 1857; m., Nov. 28, 1878, Thomas R., son of John Thomas and Rebecca (Grinnell) Willston, b. Aug. 20, 1853. Res., 39 Columbus Ave., Somerville. Two ch.: i. William High Willston, b. Oct. 10, 1881. ii. Jennie Alfreda Willston, b. May 20, 1883.
1864. ii. WILLIAM BACON, b. Nov. 26, 1798; m. Eliza W. Washburn and Mrs. Lidde (Bowman) Nobles.
1865. iii. ELON, b. April 6, 1801; d. March 2, 1814.
1866. iv. CALVIN REY, b. Oct. 15, 1803; m. Susan Spooner.
1867. v. LEONARD ROBERTSON, b. April 9, 1807; m. Jane Boyington Johnson and Liva Ann Evans.
1868. vi. ISAAC GILLMAN, b. March 25, 1812; m. Elizabeth Mayo, Lucretia Hathaway, Malinda M. Perkins and Mrs. Elizabeth Loviza (Faunce) Brigham.
1869. vii. JOHN WHITMAN, b. July 12, 1813; m. Louisa A. Davis.

958. DANIEL FOSTER (Isaac, Isaac, Joseph, Jacob, Reginald), b. Newburyport, Mass., about 1776; m. ——, Philena Pettingill, b. 1769; d. Augusta, Oct. 4, 1824. He was an inspector of brick and mortar in Augusta (see North's History) and he married the daughter of Benjamin Pettingill, a prominent citizen of that place, whose services are quite fully recorded in North's History of Augusta, and in Chaffin's History of Easton, Mass. He enlisted in the army and was in the battle of Tippecanoe, in Indiana, which was fought on the banks of the river of that name, Nov. 5, 1811. The Indians, under Tecumseh's brother, the Prophet, were defeated by the United States troops, under Gen. Wm. H. Harrison. Mr. Foster was said to have been in that battle, and was never heard of afterward.

His wife was a daughter of Benjamin Pettingill and Mrs. Judith (Castle) Atherton. Benjamin, who went to Augusta from Easton, Mass., at the time of the first settlement in Hallowell in 1779, was then 59 years of age. He was a magistrate, selectman and moderator at town meetings. He d., prob., in 1811. Res., Augusta, Me.

1870. i. DANIEL, b. July 5, 1799; m. Rebecca Eaton.
1871. ii. CONY, b. April 16, 1801; m. Caroline Brown.
1872. iii. MARY, b. ——; d. when a child.

966-5. MAJOR PERLEY FOSTER (John, Brainard, Isaac, Joseph, Jacob, Reginald), b. Greenfield, N. H., Sept. 20, 1792; m. ——, Mary Gray. He was ship's carpenter on Commodore Perry's flag ship on Lake Erie. He d. Nashua, N. H., Dec. 22, 1843. Res., Whitefield and Hancock, N. H.

1872¼. i. JONH GRAY, b. May 27, 1823; m. Mary Mole and Anna Johnson.
1872⅓. ii. NEWMAN S., b. Nov. 20, 1816; m., June 2, 1842, Mary E. Jones; d. Dec. 23, 1862.
1872½. iii. MARY JANE, b. Aug. 5, 1818; d. March 14, 1848.
1872⅔. iv. MOSES GRAY, b. March 30, 1830; d. July 14, 1853.
1872¾. v. PERLEY, b. Sept. 1, 1833; d. Dubuque, Iowa, Aug. 19, 1856.
1872⅞. vi. GEORGE, b. Oct. 12, 1835; d. May 31, 1859.
1872-2½. vii. EDWIN, b. ——, 1819; m. Sarah Fox Bullard.

966-6. JOSHUA FOSTER (John, Isaac, Joseph, Jacob, Reginald), b. Hancock, N. H., Feb. 12, 1796; m., Oct. 8, 1816, Sally Hopkins; m. 2d, March 22, 1825, Mary Ann Fletcher; m. 3d, Oct. 16, 1851, Dorothy Little. He d. April 16, 1867. Res., Hancock, N. H.

1872-2. i. ELIZABETH, b. ——; m. Zebedee Bagerly. Res., Seneca, Mich. Ch.: 1. John. 2. George. 3. Abbey Ann.
1872-3. ii. CHARLES O., b. Feb. 26, 1826; m. Mary Ann Gray and had one child, Ada.
1872-4. iii. SARAH L., b. Feb., 1829; m., Oct. 28, 1847, Lewis G. Ney. She d. Aug. 1, 1849.
1872-5. iv. ADOLPHUS G., b. Feb. 19, 1835; m., Oct. 28, 1858, Ellen Lakin.
1872-6. v. ELWIN C., b. ——, 1852; m. Annie Shaw.

967. MOSES FOSTER (Samuel, Isaac, Joseph, Jacob, Reginald), b. Candia, N. H., Nov. 3, 1793; m. Chelmsford, Mass., June 20, 1822, Abigail Fuller Hunting, b. Jan. 15, 1798, Chelmsford; d. Worcester, Jan. 18, 1877. He was a carpenter. He d. Mar. 28, 1861. Res., (Dunstable) Nashua, N. H., and Clinton, Mass.

1873. i. MARY ELIZABETH, b. Feb. 21, 1824; d. June 22, 1825.
1874. ii. SAMUEL, b. Feb. 9, 1826; d. Bedford, N. H., Nov. 4, 1833.
1875. iii. GEORGE HUNTING, b. March 7, 1828; m. Martha A. Bidwell.
1876. iv. ABIGAIL BARBER, b. Jan. 30, 1830; m. Elisha Tolman; d. Jan., 1876; m. 2d, in Harrison, Me., Aug. 5, 1879, Walter Powers Harmon. She res. 25 Abbott St., Worcester, Mass. He was b. Oct. 20, 1807; d. s. p. Sept. 14, 1882.
1877. v. ELIZABETH HUNTING, b. Nov. 7, 1832; d. Jan. 26, 1836.
1878. vi. JANE FRANCES, b. Nov. 18, 1835; m., Aug. 7, 1855, Wm. R. Chamberlin. She d. Feb. 22, 1882. He was b. July 17, 1827, Norwich, Vt.; d. North Dana, Mass., Aug. 11, 1880. Ch.: 1. Edward Foster, b. Aug. 5, 1874; m. June 30, 1897. Address, 8 Commercial St., Boston, Mass. 2. Alice J. C., b. June 11, 1868; m., April 30, 1891, Everett Kimball, b. Oct. 26, 1864. Res., Littleton Common, Mass. Ch.: (a) Gladys Lucinda Kimball, b. June 5, 1892. (b) Catharine Kimball, b. March 6, 1895. (c) Evelyn Dorice Kimball, b. April 22, 1896. (d) Mary Frances Kimball, b. June 18, 1897
1879. vii. LUCINDA, b. Aug. 25, 1840; unm. She d. June 11, 1885. Ithaman W. Beard, of Dover, N. H., appointed administrator of estate of Lucinda Foster, of Boston, single-woman; d. June 11, 1885, leaving next of kin George H. Foster, of Worcester, Mass., brother; Abby B. Harmon, of Worcester, sister; Alice J. Chamberlin, Littleton Common, Mass., minor child and niece; Edward F. Chamberlin, of Yarmouthville, Me., minor nephew. Sept. 14, 1885. Lib. 574, Fol. 465. Lib. 574, Fol. 133. Lib. 575, Fol. 232. Suff., Mass., probate.

969. EBEN COLCORD FOSTER (Samuel, Isaac, Joseph, Jacob, Reginald), b. Dec. 5, 1791, Candia, N. H.; m., Sept. 8, 1818, Betsey Adams, b. Pembroke, N. H., Oct. 22, 1794; d. Oct. 10, 1871. He d. Feb. 18, 1865. Res., Manchester, N. H.

1880. i. JOHN ADAMS, b. Sept. 10, 1819; m. Laura Lund.
1881. ii. HARLAN PAGE, b. June 30, 1836; d. Jan. 17, 1837.
1882. iii. SARAH ADAMS, b. Jan. 9, 1823; d. April 4, 1895.
1883. iv. CHARLES TUFTS, b. Jan. 8, 1821; d. Feb. 17, 1823.

1884. v. SAMUEL MOULTON, b. Mar. 18, 1833; d. Feb. 28, 1836.
1885. vi. EBEN EDWARDS, b. Feb. 15, 1827; m. ——— ———.
1886. vii. LUCY PAYSON, b. June 2, 1831; m., April 3, 1851, James O. Adams. She d. Feb. 11, 1852.
1887. viii SAMUEL T., b. Oct. 3, 1838; m. Elizabeth Pinkerton.

971. FRANKLIN FOSTER (Samuel, Isaac, Joseph, Jacob, Reginald), b. Billerica, Mass., Feb. 19, 1798; m., Jan. 12, 1826, Mary Hunting, b. Feb. 28, 1800; d. Sept. 7, 1875. Franklin Foster, fourth son of Samuel, was educated mostly by his father, who was accurate and careful, as the traditions of the family show, and secured thoroughness as far as the means of the family allowed. Three of the sons and three of the daughters showed the result of his endeavors in their mental clearness and comprehension. Franklin followed his eldest brother to the town then called Dunstable, now Nashua, on the Merrimac. There he followed his trade of wheelwright, which he abandoned later to engage, early in the forties, in lumbering for the then new enterprise of railroad building. He lived in the one house for nearly forty years, where he cared for his mother until the ripe old age of ninety-four. He was an ardent temperance advocate and freesoiler; a man modest in his opinion of himself and reverent and devout toward his God. He d. Sept. 15, 1865. Res., Nashua, N. H.

1888. i. MERCY, b. Sept. 5, 1838; m., Dec. 1, 1869, Rev. Ithamar Warren Beard, b. Feb. 23, 1840. Rev. Ithamar Warren Beard, b. at Pittsfield, N. H., Feb. 23, 1840; brought up from the age of three years in Lowell, Mass.; was educated there and in Cambridge public schools, Groton academy and Harvard college, class of 1864. Admitted to the Middlesex Bar in 1864. Ordained to the ministry in the Protestant Episcopal church in 1873, from Cambridge Theological school. Has served in two parishes—South Groveland, Mass., for three years; Dover, N. H., for twenty-two years. Ch.: 1. Theodora, b. March 3, 1871. 2. Ithamar Mansur, b. Nov. 28, 1872. Res., Dover, N. H. Ithamar Mansur Beard, b. in Lowell, Mass., in 1872; educated in Dover public schools, Holderness (N. H.) School for Boys, Phillips Academy, Andover, Mass., and Harvard college, class of 1895. Has taught one year in the New Hampshire college, Durham, and as tutor two years in Rumford Falls, Me. 3. Eliza Warren, b. Oct. 28, 1874. 4. Mary, b. Nov. 14, 1876. 5. Allison, b. Aug. 29, 1879. 6. Margaret, b. Dec. 31, 1881; d. Aug., 1889.
1889. ii. FRANKLIN, b. Oct. 31, 1841; m. Lydia Hale and Annie Melissa Wheeler. Both wives d. s. p. He resides Nashua, N. H.
1890. iii. ELIZABETH, b. Feb. 3, 1827; d. Jan. 22, 1836.
1891. iv. BENJAMIN FRANKLIN, b. Sept. 17, 1829; d. Feb. 12, 1830.
1892. v. MARY, b. June 18, 1830; d. Nov. 24, 1831.
1893. vi. NATHAN HUNTING, b. Nov. 17, 1832; d. unm., Nov. 20, 1880.
1894. vii. CHARLES, b. May 28, 1834; d. Dec., 1836.
1895. viii. ELIZA AMES, b. Oct. 3, 1836; m. John Quincy Lund. Res., 13 Centre St., East Somerville, Mass.

984. MAXWELL STEWART FOSTER (Theodore, Jedediah, Ephraim, Ephraim, Abraham, Reginald), b. Providence, R. I., Dec. 6, 1804; m., Aug. 27, 1823, Mary Howard; b. Nov. 12, 1795 (dau. of Silas Howard of Burrillville, R. I., and Mary Bowen). She d. May 24, 1835; and he m. a 2d wife Lydia ——, who d. soon, and afterward m. a 3d wife, Maria Thompson. He was a farmer at Burrillville. He d. there May 9, 1849, aet. 44. He resided for a short time at Syracuse, N. Y. Res., Burrillville, Rhode Island.

1896. i. ESTHER, b. May 30, 1824; d. Dec. 9, 1831, aet. 7.
1897. ii. EMELINE, b. Apr. 4, 1825; m. Lewis Chamberlain, Mar. 8, 1847; b. Nov. 1, 1825 (son of Alpheus Chamberlain and Lydia Brown); a farmer at North Coventry, Conn. He enlisted Aug. 5, 1861, at Harrisville, R. I., as a private in the Fourth R. I. Regt., Co. D, and was in the Burnside expedition in Virginia, Maryland, North Carolina, etc. After a year and a quarter of service he was compelled by long sickness to leave the army. Ch.: a. Mary Elizabeth Chamberlain, b. June 9, 1849; m., Sept. 20, 1866, John Hervey Talcott; b. Sept. 7, 1846 (son of Dea. Joseph Talcott of Coventry

and Abigail Turner); a farmer in Coventry. One ch., Mary Abigail Talcott, b. Oct. 9, 1867. b. Martha Malinda Chamberlain; b. Feb. 26, 1853; m. Nov. 11, 1869, John E. Wright, and has 2 ch.: 1. Lulu May Wright; b. Sept. 25, 1871. 2. Lillian Wright; b. July 25, 1873. c. Sarah Louise Chamberlain; b. Feb. 16, 1855; m., Mar. 4, 1874, Elias F. Wilcox (son of Stephen E. Wilcox of Norwich, Conn., and Eliza S. Bushnell), b. in Sprague, Conn., Oct. 6, 1853. d. Fredric Leroy Chamberlain, b. July 21, 1860. e. Dwight Merrick Chamberlain, b. Feb. 18, 1865; d. Mar. 21, 1865.

1898. iii. GEORGE, b. about 1838, resides in Syracuse, New York.

1899. iv. RUBY, b. about 1841.

985. SAMUEL WILLIS FOSTER (Theodore, Jedediah, Ephraim, Ephraim, Abraham, Reginald), b. Foster, R. I., Nov. 30, 1806; m., Feb. 23, 1829, Ruth Belden Seymour; b. Nov. 6, 1808 (dau. of Ira Seymour, of Webster, Mich., and Betsey Morehouse). He removed in May, 1828, to Dexter, Mich., then all out a wilderness, and in 1830 to Scio, Mich., where he followed milling (flour and lumber) for many years. He was very zealous in advocating anti-slavery and temperance principles of private and public action at a time and in a section where such ideas were especially unpopular. In the rage for emigration to California in 1850, he went there also, for purposes of mining, and shortly after his arrival d. in San Francisco, Oct. 11, 1850. He was a man of positive convictions, generous sympathies and great energy of character. His widow resided at Hudson, Wis., and d. March 25, 1870. Res., Dexter and Scio, Mich.

1900. i. OSCAR, b. Aug. 15, 1830; d. Sept. 16, 1830.

1901. ii. ANDREW DWIGHT, b. Aug. 5, 1832; m. ——.

1902. iii. ESTHER, b. Sept. 17, 1834; m., June 5, 1857, Theodore S. Seymour. Res., Milford, Iowa, and Duluth, Minn. He was b. July 1, 1828, s. p.

1903. iv. BETSEY SEYMOUR, b. Nov. 22, 1837, d. Sept. 13, 1838.

1904. v. JOSEPH SEYMOUR, b. Feb. 21, 1842; d. Oct. 4, 1842.

1905. vi. IRA SEYMOUR, b. April 1, 1846; m. Grace Louise Selleck.

986. DWIGHT CRANSTON FOSTER (Theodore, Jedediah, Ephraim, Ephraim, Abraham, Reginald), b. Foster, R. I., Dec. 28, 1808; m., June 8, 1832, Alma Jeanette Seymour, b. March 19, 1816, dau. of Ira Seymour, of Webster, Mich., and Betsey Morehouse. She d. in Scio, Mich., Jan. 11, 1843. He m. 2d, Nov. 1, 1843, Cornelia Seymour, her sister; b. April 17, 1806. In 1836 he removed to Scio, Mich., and engaged in milling with his brother Samuel (1836-43). In 1843 he removed to Commerce, Mich., where he was miller (both flour and lumber) until his death Aug. 16, 1852, aet. 43. He was a zealous advocate of the rights and interests of the neglected and abused classes of society. His widow resided at Detroit, Mich., in 1874. Res., Scio and Commerce, Mich.

1906. i. EDWARD DWIGHT, b. at Scio, May 12, 1838, a leather merchant in Detroit (Mumford, Foster & Co.); m. Marian Langley.

1907. ii. LYDIA, b. at Scio, July 23, 1840; d. July 26, 1843.

By second wife:

1908. iii. LYDIA, 2d, b. at Commerce, Mich., May 30, 1845; m. Sept., 1870, David Wilson, of Crawfords Quarry, Mich. Res., Stanton, Wis. He was b. July 4, 1840. Is a farmer. She d. Jan. 16, 1899. Ch.: 1. Lydia May Wilson, b. Aug. 29, 1871; d. Aug. 13, 1872. 2. Charles Albert Wilson, b. April 8, 1874; m., March 9, 1898, Miss Alice Lincoln. P. O. address, Stanton, Wis. 3. Edward Day Wilson, b. Sept. 24, 1875. P. O. address, Hagensville, Mich. 4. Rillah L. Wilson, b. Jan. 12, 1877; m., July 5, 1897, R. H. Simons. P. O. address, Cheboygan, Mich.

1909. iv. MARY, b. Feb. 12, 1848, at Commerce; has been an invalid and bed-ridden for many years.

987. THEODORE FOSTER (Theodore, Jedediah, Ephraim, Ephraim, Abraham, Reginald), b Foster, R. I., April 3, 1812. In 1827, when 14 years of age, he shipped as a sailor boy on a vessel bound for the East Indies. Having received ill treatment, he deserted the ship at New Orleans and actually came back on foot from that distant point to his home in Rhode Island. Finding that his father had died in his absence, he went to Dexter, Mich., in 1829, where his brother, Samuel, then

lived. On the formation of the Abolition party he became one of its most active members. He edited "The Signal of Liberty" at Ann Arbor, 1841-7, which in 1847, was merged in "The National Era," published at Washington, D. C. He advocated, earnestly, the election of James G. Birney to the presidency. He was considered by leading anti-slavery men a very able and clear-headed writer on our national duties, interests and dangers. He edited also for some time after 1847 "The Free Democrat" of Detroit. In 1855, he was appointed by Governor Bingham one of the Building Commissioners for The Reform School at Lansing, Mich., and before its completion, in 1856, was made its superintendent and held the office for 4 years (1856-60), being afterward also on the Board of Control. He was clerk of the city of Lansing, Mich. (1861-2), deputy-collector (1863-4) and editor (1864) of the Lansing State Republican, a position which poor health compelled him to resign soon. He d. of consumption Dec. 27, 1865, aet. 53. He was equally modest and earnest constitutionally conservative; he was from deep moral conviction thoroughly radical. Naturally very sensitive to misappreciation and opposition and obloquy, he yet delighted in defending and promoting everywhere, as opportunity offered, whatever seemed to him to be truest and best, no matter what were the odds against him. He was a man of quick perceptions, strong memory and philosophic habits of thought, with fine logical powers of reasoning. He was also a close student, and much addicted to literary occupations. He had dark hair and eyes and a florid complexion. He m., July 15, 1832, Francis Delia Seymour; b. June 9, 1804 (dau. of Ira Seymour, of Victor, N. Y., and Betsey Morehouse, afterward of Webster, Mich.)

1910. i. CHARLES TILLINGHAST, b. at Scio, Mich., Jan. 16, 1834, enlisted May 11, 1861, in the Third Mich. Regt., and joined the army of the Potomac under General McClellan. The regimental color-bearer having been killed at the battle of Williamsburgh, the colonel asked the regiment, "Who will take the colors?" No one else offering to take such a risk, he slipped forth from the ranks, after a brief delay, and said: "I will take them; they shall not go a begging." He bore them into the next battle at Fair Oaks, May 31, 1862, knowing that he was marching to certain death, and was shot in the left side of the neck. He held fast to the dear flag after he had fallen, and said with his last breath: "Let some one take the colors."

1911. ii. FRANCES (Fanny), b. at Ann Arbor, Dec. 19, 1842; m., April 18, 1864, Albert Eugene Cowles; b. May 14, 1838, at Chardon, O. (son of Joseph Phelp Cowles and Fanny Howe). He was grad. at the law department of the University of Michigan in 1862, and since May, 1864, practiced law at Lansing, Mich. They have an adopted daughter, Grace Cowles; b. June 2, 1870.

1912. iii. SEYMOUR, b. at Ann Arbor, July 1, 1845; enlisted Dec. 20, 1863, among the U. S. Sharpshooters, 3d brigade, 3d division, 2d army corps, and served until the end of the war. He was in all the battles of the Wilderness at Todd's Tavern, Po River, Spottsylvania, North Ann River, Cold Harbor, Petersburg, Va., Weldon R. Road, Deep Bottom, Boydton Plank Road, etc., in all forty-six skirmishes and battles, and was not once wounded. He was mustered out at Detroit, July 17, 1865. He resides now at Lansing. Postmaster State Constitutional Convention, 1869; city clerk of Lansing, 1874-5-6; city treasurer, 1877-8-9; clerk of State House of Representatives, 1885-7-9; appointed postmaster of Lansing, 1889, by President Harrison—resigned March 4, 1893; member of State House of Representatives, 1895; receiver of the People's Saving Bank, 1896; appointed postmaster of Lansing by President McKinley, 1897. He m., May 25, 1871, Mary L. Woodworth; b. Jan. 4, 1847. Ch.: 1. Charles Woodworth, b. March 28, 1873. Lawyer. Res., L. B. L.—University of Michigan, 1895; LL. B.—University of Michigan, 1896; circuit court commissioner Ingham county, Michigan, 1898; practicing law at Lansing, Mich. 2. Walter Seymour, b. Sept. 23, 1877. He is now (1898) junior in the literary department at the University of Michigan. 3. Gertrude, b. Oct. 27, 1879. 4. Theodore George, b. Feb. 23, 1888.

990. JUDGE THEODORE ADELPHIDUS FOSTER (Theophilus, Jedediah, Ephraim, Ephraim, Abraham, Reginald), b. March 22, 1778; m., 1803, Julia Green (dau. of Judge Jacob Green, who was brother to Gen. Nathaniel Green of Revolutionary memory). He was graduated at Brown university in 1800, studied law with Gen. Ives at Gr. Barrington, practiced the profession at Providence and was made judge (of what court not known to the writer). He d. in 1825, aet. 47. He had two daughters and three sons. His daughters were Ann and Harriet. Res., Providence, R. I.

1913. i. ANN, b. about 1804; m. a Mr. Post, who lived at Niagara Falls, N. Y., and afterward at Wheeling W. Va. They were lost with their four children on board of a schooner in a gale while on their way from Cleveland to Buffalo.

1914. ii. HARRIET, b. about 1806; m. a Mr. Cramer of Parkman, Geauga Co., O.

The names of the sons of Judge Theodore A. Foster and their history the author was not able to ascertain, although striving earnestly to do so.

991. JEDEDIAH FOSTER (Theophilus, Jedediah, Ephraim, Ephraim, Abraham, Reginald), b. Rhode Island, Aug. 5, 1780; m., Nov. 12, 1804, Mrs. Tamason (Gilbert) Billings, of Hardwick, Mass.; b. in Brookfield, Mass., Jan. 3, 1776, dau. of Jedediah Gilbert and Prudence Fairbanks; a farmer of Paw Paw Grove, Ill., since 1846. She d. Feb. 7, 1857. Res., Wilmington, Vt., and Paw Paw, Ill.

1915. i. MARY, b. Sept. 25, 1807; m., 1838, Sylvester B. Hosmer. He d. 1859. She resided, in 1874, in Parkman, O.

1916. ii. DWIGHT, b. March 25, 1809; m. Betsey Brownell.

1917. iii. SUSANNA PACKARD, b. at Wilmington, Vt., March 15, 1812; m., April, 1843, at Eaton, O., David Detamore; b. Aug. 17, 1814, in Virginia; a carpenter at Paw Paw Grove. He d. Aug. 19, 1859. She has a dau., a Mary Ellen Detamore; b. March, 1852; m. ——, Dr. T. D. Palmer. Res., 691 Washington Boulevard, Chicago.

996. ELIJAH DWIGHT FOSTER (Theophilus, Jedediah, Ephraim, Ephraim, Abraham, Reginald), b. Brookfield, Mass., April 12, 1791; m., Oct. 10, 1814, Martha Green Lavalley; b. at Harwick, R. I., Sept. 1, 1780. She d. at Greenbush, N. Y., July 16, 1823, and he m., Oct. 5, 1823 at Greenbush, for 2d wife, widow Ruth Cornelia Cady nee Nichols; b. at Springfield, Mass., April 12, 1794, widow of Joseph Cady, dau. of Joshua Nichols originally of Brookfield, Mass., and Abiah Mather. She d. at West Creek, Ind., Nov. 29, 1850, aet. 56, and he m., Aug. 5, 1851, for 3d wife, widow Fanny P. Eames, nee Parmelee; b. at Wilmington, Vt., Sept. 11, 1795 (dau. of Dea James Parmelee and Caroline Webster). He is a farmer. Res., West Creek, Ind.

1918. i. ELIZA DWIGHT, b. at Wilmington, Vt., Jan. 12, 1816; m. Harvey Coleman, at Euclid, O., May 10, 1837. Coleman was b. at Euclid, March 4, 1811 (son of Jacob Coleman; b. Aug. 6, 1791, and d. at Morgantown, Ind., March 8, 1861, and Elizabeth Thomas; b. June 17, 1789), a merchant and manufacturer, Morgantown, Ind. he d. at Hinsley, Ind., May 9, 1843, aet. 27. Ch.: 1. Alonzo Coleman, b. at Euclid, June 14, 1838; d. at Hinsley, Ind., Dec. 6, 1841. 2. Elizabeth Mary Coleman, b. at Hinsley, Aug. 14, 1840; m., Oct. 20, 1856, Israel Egbert; b. July 12, 1831 (son of James and Sarah Egbert, a merchant at Morgantown, Ind.). a. Mary Eliza Egbert, b. Sept. 14, 1857. b. Emily Ann Egbert, b. Nov. 23, 1859. c. James Harvey Egbert, b. Aug. 15, 1861. d. Horatio Seymour Egbert, b. July 22, 1864. e. Rachel Adelia Egbert, b. Dec. 14, 1866.

1919. ii. ALFRED DWIGHT, b. at Athens, Pa., Jan. 22, 1818; m. Sarah Emeline Hathaway.

1920. iii. GEORGE LYMAN, b. at Athens, April 20, 1820; m. Temperance Hathaway and Lucy Jane Hathaway.

1921. iv. SUSANNA PACKARD, b. at Athens, March 29, 1822; d. at Greenbush, N. Y., May 31, 1833.

1922. v. MARTHA CORNELIA, b. at Troy, Pa., Sept. 12, 1824; m. Melvin A. Halsted, May 14, 1842; b. March 19, 1821 (son of William Halsted, of Lowell, Ind.; b. Aug. 23, 1795, and d. July 22, 1834, and Patty Haskins; b. Nov. 8, 1799, and d. Nov. 30, 1850, whom he m. March 22, 1820), a miller at Lowell, Ind., of which village, recently incorporated, he was the founder. He lived at Pittstown, N. Y. Ch.: 1. William Nichols Halsted, b. Dec. 13, 1843; m., Feb. 8, 1866, Louisa Vandecar (dau. of Peter Vandecar, of West Creek, and Wealthy Clark); a carpenter at Lowell, Ind. 2. Mary Theresa Halsted, b. Nov. 15, 1849; d. July 24, 1857. 3. Theron Haskin Halsted, b. April 4, 1853. 4. An infant daughter, b. and d. Aug. 16, 1865.

1923. vi. MARIA NICHOLS, b. at Troy, Pa., Jan. 11, 1827, m. Joseph Martelle, a farmer in California, who d. without issue.

1924. vii. ALMON NEWTON, b. at Athens, Pa., July 10, 1828.

1925. viii. THEOPHILUS RANDOLPH, b. at Burlington, Pa., April 28, 1830; m. Margaret Foley.

1926. ix. ELEANOR, b. at Burlington, March 25, 1832; m. James Brennon, May 17, 1851. Brennon was b. at Boston, O., July 31, 1819; son of William and Lucina Brennon; lives at West Creek, Ind. Ch.: 1. Cornelia Lucina Brennon, b. June 23, 1852. 2. Julia Ann Brennon, b. Nov. 27, 1854. 3. William Perry Brennon, b. March 22, 1859. 4. George Dwight Brennon, b. Jan. 31, 1861. 5. Melvin Amos Brennon, b. Sept 11, 1865.

1927 x. LEWIS, b. at Troy, Pa., March 28, 1834; m. Roxana A. Knapp.

1928. xi. VOLNEY ORLAND, b. at Mayfield, O., Feb. 23, 1837; d. March 26, 1837.

1929. xii. SUSANNA DIANA, b. at Euclid, O., Feb. 23, 1838; m. Alexander McElrath Stewart; moved to Missouri and d. there.

1930. xiii. HARRIET, b. at Hinsley, Ind., March 23, 1841; m., Feb. 20, 1866, Ezra Brownell; b. March 25, 1838 (son of Dr. Alvah Brownell); a farmer at Eagle Creek, Ind. Two children: a. Frank Alvah Brownell, b. Nov. 14, 1866. b. Fredrick Dwight Brownell, b. June 25, 1868.

997. REV. PEREGRINE PYNCHON FOSTER (Theophilus, Jedediah, Ephraim, Ephraim, Abraham, Reginald), b. Wilmington, Vt., May 10, 1793; m. at Coventry, R. I., Nov. 21, 1812, Rebecca Brown, who d. about 1824, and he m. for 2d wife, May 20, 1827, at Granville, Pa., widow Catharine Smith, nee Clark (widow of Amos Smith, of Candor, N. Y., and dau. of Nathaniel and Huldah Clark of Granville, Pa.); b. at Granville, Mass., June 24, 1798. She has resided of late, at Elmira, N. Y., having been a widow for the second time since 1834. He was a Free-Will Baptist. He preached for a time at Granville, Pa., and in 1830, removed to Ohio, and preached to the Baptist churches at Farmington and Southington, O. He worked during week-time on his farm, like the early ministers of New England. He d. of pneumonia at Farmington, O., Feb. 17, 1834, aet. 40. He lived a useful life, and d. a happy death.

1931. i. MARY ANN, b. at Warren, R. I., Nov. 3, 1813; m., Aug. 14, 1833, Horatio N. Converse, a merchant at Parkham, O., and afterward at Cleveland, O. He was subsequently agent at Madeleine Island, Lake Superior, for the Upper Lake's Fur Trading Company, and afterward a forwarder at Sault St. Marie. She d. at Lithopolis, O., Feb. , 1853. He m. again.

1932. ii. SUSAN PACKARD, b. at Coventry, R. I., April 12, 1815; m., April 18 1842, Lewis Knapp; b. Dec. 26, 1812 (son Daniel and Christina Knapp, of Pompey, N. Y.); a merchant tailor at Kenosha, Wis. He has also a malt house, and prepares barley for manufacture into beer and ale. No issue.

1933. iii. ALFRED, b. Sept. 29, 1816; m. Catherine Van Wagner.

1934. iv. CHARLES, b. at Coventry, R. I., April 7, 1818; m. (whom not ascertained) and had three children; his widow m. afterward a Mr. Ackerman, of Brighton, Macoupin county, Ill.

1935. v. ELIZA, b. June 19, 1819; m. Sherman Carlton, of Mantua, O., who lived in Franklin, O. He d. in 1851, and she m. for 2d husband, a Mr. Holden, of Franklin. He d. soon. She resides in Osceola, Wis. Children by first marriage: 1. Charles Carlton, b. about 1839, was a Union soldier in the civil war, and lost a leg in the battle on the Big Sandy River. 2. Robert Carlton, b. about 1841, was a Union soldier in the civil war; lives in Pittsburg and is married. 3. Nelson Carlton, b. about 1843, was a Union soldier in the civil war and d. of a fever. 4. Francis Carlton (twin), b. about 1845; resides in Mantua, O. 5. Forest Carlton, (twin), b. about 1845; resides in Mantua, O. By second marriage she had two children.

1936. vi. HORACE, b. at Columbia, Pa., March 21, 1821, was accidentally shot when a young man while out hunting with a friend.

1937. vii. PHILANDER PACKARD, b. at Troy, Pa., Nov. 20, 1823; m. twice; was a Union soldier in the civil war, and d. at Raleigh, N. C., in 1864. By second wife:

1938. viii. LUTHER CLARK, b. at Granville, Pa., May 24, 1828; m., Mary E. Witherspoon and Charlotte Lindsay.

1939. ix. HARRIET AMELIA, b. in Farmington, O., June 5, 1831; m., Nov. 13, 1856, as his 2d wife. Aaron Canfield Chapman; b. April 29, 1818, at Berkshire, N. Y. (son of Jedediah Chapman and Constant Canfield), a farmer in Newark Valley, Tioga County, N. Y. No issue.

1002. HON. ALFRED DWIGHT FOSTER (Dwight, Jedediah, Ephraim, Ephraim, Abraham, Reginald), b. Brookfield, Mass., July 26, 1800; m., Feb. 14, 1828, Lydia Stiles; b. Templeton, Mass., Jan. 27, 1806; she died Aug. 2, 1887.

He was born on the old homestead in Brookfield; received his preparatory education by private instruction and at Leicester academy; was graduated at Harvard college in 1819; studied law with his uncle, Samual M. Burnside, Esq., in Worcester, Mass,; was admitted to the bar in 1822, and resided in Brookfield until 1824, when he moved to Worcester; was professional partner of Mr. Burnside until 1827, when he retired from practice. He was representative in the general court in 1831-2-3 and selectman in 1832; was a member of the governor's council. He was a trustee of Leicester academy and of Amherst college; trustee and treasurer of the State Lunatic Asylum for many years. To know Mr. Foster was to love and respect him; to the manners of a real gentleman, were added that kindness and benevolence of character so universally admired by all capable of appreciating such qualities. He was chairman of the two commissions appointed concerning the State Reform school in Westborough, Mass.,— one to procure the site, plans and estimates for the buildings, and frame needful laws for the right management of the institution when established; and the other, to erect the buildings themselves. He was also for several years a trustee of Amherst college and a corporate member of the A. B. C. T. M. He was for many years (1832-52) an active member of the Congregational church, which, when he joined it, was under the care of Rev. J. S. C. Abbot. His personal presence was dignified and commanding. An extract from a letter written playfully by himself, Jan. 19, 1842, to his cousin, Fredric A. Foster, Esq., of Lancaster, Ohio, where he lived, and who kindly put it into the authors' hands, will place him clearly before the reader's eye. "Now if you wish to know me," he says, "imagine a man about five feet, ten and one-half or eleven inches high, with broad shoulders; a little round, oblong, fat face; large abdomen, bald head, except as it is covered with a wig; hazel eyes, and weighing from 275 and 300 pounds, and you have me. Then for character, say generally, professedly religious, a member of an orthodox church, and though far from meeting his own views of duty, maintaining such a walk as not, so far as he knows, to bring reproach upon his brethren; cautious but not shrewd in the management of his business; a whig, though not a rabid bank-whig in politics; social in his feelings and yet living very much retired, and going into very little company; teetotaler in temperance and a moderate eater, and yet having the gout occasionally, as he supposes by inheritance; having very few friends, but those few rather warmly attached, and he may say as few enemies that he knows of. Excuse this egotism; if it amuse you I shall be glad. It is honest." His personal presence is said by many to have been manly and noble. He is described as a man of naturally quick perceptions, a tenacious memory, strong powers of reasoning and careful habits of observation, and as having broad and generous views of things and being a many-sided man, and eminently genial in his disposition, and public spirited. In his religious character he is represented as having been entirely unassuming, but at the same time earnest, resolved, reliable, courageous and catholic, and altogether free from everything like ostentation or pretense in word or deed. Mr. and Mrs. Foster were distantly related, both being descendants of Reginald Foster, the emigrant, through his grand-son, Ephraim

Foster, of Ipswich, Mass. Lydia, b. Jan. 27, 1806 (dau. of John William Stiles; b. in Keene, N. H., Feb. 22, 1777, and d. in Worcester, Mass., Sept. 14, 1836, and Mary McCarthy, b. in Fitchburg, Mass., Aug. 8, 1775, and d. in Worcester, Aug. 1, 1838. She was dau. of Thaddeus McCarthy, M. D., son of Rev. Thaddeus McCarthy, D. D., pastor for nearly forty years of the Old South Church at Worcester. Her mother's name was Cowden of Scotch-Irish descent, like her husband.) He d. Aug. 3, 1853. Res., Worcester, Mass.

1940. i. DWIGHT, b. Dec. 13, 1828; m. Harriet P. Baldwin.

1941. ii. MARY STILES, b. May 23, 1830; m. as his second wife, Jan. 25, 1855, Rev. Robinson Potter Dunn, b. in Newport, R. I., May 31, 1825. Eldest son of Theophilus Calhoun Dunn, M. D.; b. in New York, July 8, 1800, of parents from Devonshire, Eng., a physician in Newport, and Elizabeth Potter; b. Jan. 23, 1806.; graduated at Brown university in 1843, and remained there until 1845 as assistant librarian and instructor in French. He resigned and graduated at Princeton Theological Seminary in 1849. He was for a short time settled over the first Presbyterian church in Camden, near Philadelphia, but was soon called to the professorship of rhetoric and English literature in Brown university, which office he held for sixteen years, until his death, 1851-67. He was a man of high literary ideals and attainments and of varied and finished scholarship, being familiar with French and German classics, as well as with the Latin, Greek and Hebrew. He was twice invited to Princeton, once as instructor in Hebrew, while settled at Camden, and again while at Providence as professor of English literature. He was a frequent contributor to the Princeton Review, and to the Bibliotheca Sacra, and was busy at the time of his death in editing one of the volumes of Langes' Commentary on the Old and New Testaments. He d. of erysipelas, after a short illness in Newport, R. I., Aug. 28, 1867. His first wife was Maria Stillé, dau. of John Stillé, of Philadelphia, whom he m. Sept., 1848, and who d. the following year. His widow resided at Worcester, Mass. They had one child: i. Dwight Foster Dunn, b. Dec. 11, 1865, at Providence.

1942. iii. REBECCA FAULKNER, b. April 1, 1832; m., May 16, 1854, Dr. Henry Clark, b. Oct. 3, 1824, in Marlboro, Mass. (son of Benjamin Clarke and Lucy Howe), a physician at Worcester. He was grad. at Harvard Med. school in 1850 and pursued his professional studies afterward in France and Germany. He d. in Worcester, April 17, 1880. Ch.: 1. Alfred Dwight Foster Clarke, b. July 12, 1855; d. Sept. 20, 1866. 2. Louisa Hoar Clarke, b. Aug. 1, 1859. 3. Harriet Elizabeth Clarke, b. Oct. 31, 1860.

1005. PEREGRINE PITT FOSTER (Peregrine, Jedediah, Ephraim, Ephraim, Abraham, Reginald), b. Oct. 24, 1786, Providence, R. I.; m. Oct. 7, 1806, Elizabeth Cushing, b. Nov., 1777 (dau. of Col. Nathaniel Cushing, of Belpre, O., originally of Boston, Mass., and Elizabeth Heath, of Pembroke, Mass.). He was a merchant at Gallipolis, O. He d. Feb. 28, 1815, aet. 28. She d. without issue June 29, 1864, aet. 87; a widow for 49 years. She was a practical, earnest, superior Christian lady. [Colonel Cushing was conspicuous in the Revolutionary War. He went with the Ohio company to Marietta in 1788, and for three years encountered with them the terrors of Indian border warfare.]

1007. FREDERIC AUGUSTUS FOSTER (Peregrine, Jedediah, Ephraim, Ephraim, Abraham, Reginald), b. Providence, R. I., May 7, 1791; m., Nov. 13, 1817, Sarah Arnold, b. Oct. 2, 1800 (dau. of Henry Arnold, a merchant at Lancaster, O., and Mary Bowman, dau. of Simeon Bowman and Mary M. Easter. They were both born at Hagerstown, Md.; he, Sept. 30, 1776, and she, Oct., 1782, and were m. in 1798. He d. Sept. 8, 1857; she d. Sept. 29, 1834). She d. Aug. 21, 1842, aet. 42, and he m., for 2d wife, Oct. 8, 1844, Elizabeth Wilson, b. Dec. 30, 1813 (dau. of Col. Robert Wilson, of Lancaster, O., and Jane Donivan. He was b. in Harrisburgh, Pa., in 1777, and settled in 1798, in Fairfield county, O., and m. her in 1809, and d. in 1844, aet. 67. She was from Shippensburgh, Pa., and was b. in 1784, and d. in 1844, aet. 60. He was, in 1812, in the army of the Northwest, and was colonel of cavalry under Gen. William Henry Harrison). He was for nearly 25 years an active and successful merchant at Lancaster, O. (1810-32), and a deacon, afterward ruling elder in the Presbyterian church. He has been a life-long teetotaler, and active in matters of temperance, benevolence and social progress, and was (1874) living and full of energy in a ripe and fresh old age. He has held at various times a number of important civil trusts: as director for settling up the affairs of the Lancaster bank at the expiration of its charter; receiver and paymaster for the construction of "The Lateral Canal," from Lancaster to Carroll. He has had much to do in managing estates left to his care as administrator, executor and trustee of the same. For 20 years (1832-52) he was much employed in erecting stores and homes upon his lands at Lancaster and Carroll, and especially at Carroll, which he did very much in connection with his nephew, W. Foster Breck, to develop and establish as a young and thriving town.

1943. i. PEREGRINE DWIGHT, b. Feb. 18, 1819; m. Margaret Mary Deuble and Martha Buckingham.
1944. ii. HENRY BOWMAN, b. Dec. 28, 1820; d. Sept. 18, 1831, aet. 10.
1945. iii. MARIE LOUISE, b. March 25, 1825; m. James E. Cheney.
1946. iv. FREDRIC AUGUSTUS, b. Jan. 4, 1833; d. July 2, 1856, aet. 23.
1947. v. SARAH JANE, b. Dec. 19, 1834; m., June 12, 1856, John Franklin Holmes, b. at Black Rock, N. Y., Dec. 31, 1833 (son of William Franklin Holmes, of Rochester, N. Y., b. at Amherst, N. H., Jan. 28, 1807, and of Jane Antoinette Pierce, b. Oct. 9, 1811) He was at first book-keeper of the Eagle Bank, of Rochester, N. Y., and afterward cashier of the First National Bank, of Hartford, Conn. He was later cashier of the Mechanics' and Farmers' Bank, at Rochester. She d. May 22, 1858, of consumption at Rochester without issue.
1948. vi. MARTHA ELLEN, b. Feb. 21, 1837; d. April 24, 1837.
1949. vii. WILLIAM BRECK, b. Nov. 11, 1838; d. Jan. 28, 1862, aet. 23, of camp fever at Somerset, Ky., after three months' brief service as a Union soldier, in the Seventeenth O. Regt. He went to war full of eager enthusiasm to serve his country to the utmost of his ability in the hour of its greatest trial.
1950. viii. WILLIAM PARKMAN, b. Sept. 15, 1845; Supt. of the telegraph office at St. Louis, Mo
1951. ix. THEODORE NEWTON, b. Aug. 28, 1847; m.——.

1017. CAPT. JONAS FOSTER (John, John, John, Ephraim, Abraham, Reginald), b. North Andover, Mass., Nov. 15, 1793; m., 1st, Nov. 4, 1817, Mary Apthrop, of Chatham, Mass., b. July 25, 1794; d. Nov. 1, 1828; m., 2d, Dec. 2, 1829, Lydia Richardson Messer, of Methuen. She was b. Nov. 19, 1808; d. April 24, 1889, in Georgetown, Mass. He removed to Salem before 1817; kept wood and lumber wharf near North bridge, and d. ——, in Salem.

1952. i. MARY O, b. April 20, 1825; m. William Sawyer, July 17, 1845. Res., Georgetown, Mass. He was b. Oct. 28, 1813; is a box manufacturer. Ch.: 1. William Foster Sawyer, b March 20, 1847; m. June 5, 1873. Postoffice, Cliftondale, Mass. 2. Mary Elizabeth Sawyer, b. Sept. 6, 1850; m. Oct. 15, 1873; d. Nov. 30, 1881.
1953. ii. ALMIRA, b. ——; m. Frank Adams. Res.. Georgetown.
1954. iii. CHARLES IRA, b. Jan. 18, 1837; m. Martha Farms Cressy.
1955. iv. LYDIA AUGUSTA, b. ——; m. George S. Hutchings, organ manufacturer, Boston. Their dau. is Mrs. Alice Holden, of Cambridgeport, Mass.
1956. v. SUSAN, b. ——.
1957. vi. JONAS A., b. in 1832; d. Aug. 11, 1833.
1958. vii. MOODY, b. Nov., 1834; d. April 6, 1835.

1018. MOODY FOSTER (John, John, John, Ephraim, Abraham, Reginald), b. Boxford, Mass., April 29, 1797; m. Feb. 1, 1825, Mary Symonds, dau. of John and Elizabeth (Pickering) Symonds, b. Feb. 1, 1801. He came to Salem after his brother Jonas, and was partner with him. He d. April 15, 1834, in Salem. His widow was living in Salem in 1873.

1959. i. JOHN M., b. Dec. 2, 1825.
1960. ii. MARY E., b. Aug. 24, 1827.
1961. iii. CAROLINE R., b. Oct. 24, 1828.
1962. iv. JOSEPH S., b. Aug. 29, 1830.

1022. LIEUT. MOSES FOSTER (David, Stephen, John, Ephraim, Abraham, Reginald), b. Aug. 6, 1780, Andover, Mass.; m. Billerica, 1810, Sarah Baldwin, of Billerica, b. June 3, 1788; d. Jan. 29, 1850.

Moses Foster was a native of North Andover, Mass. David Smith Foster, being the youngest of ten children, remembers some of the sayings of his father's earlier exploits and business methods. That when a young man, he carried upon his back, in a common sack, a kit of tools for mending and repairing shoes, calling upon the village and country people soliciting work. That after accumulating a small sum of money in this manner he embarked in a small way in a general country store, keeping such goods as were called for in the line of dry goods, groceries, etc. Opening his place of business in the village of North Andover, Mass. That he frequently made trips to Boston on horseback, with saddlebags attached to the saddle. Said bags to contain the smaller articles of his purchase. A baggage-wagon freight business was conducted by one of the enterprising citizens of North Andover, and orders for West India goods and the heavier articles of merchandise were given exclusively to this "freighter." The baggage-wagon in those days, with its four horses attached, was one of the sights, and when the driver mounted his seat, with reins in hand, ready to start for Boston, a crowd of village lookers-on gathered and gave the driver "a merry cheer and good luck to you," repeating this exercise on every start and return of the baggage-wagon to and from Boston. He accumulated by strict attention to his business a competency, carefully investing the same; and in the purchase of small parcels of woodland, which latter purchases proved quite remunerative. He retired from active business when David was quite a young lad. He was fond of figuring out problems in algebra, and would spend many hours in this pastime in his later years. His investments in wood and timber land proved so satisfactory to him that in his will (of which David now has a copy), made on the 29th day of October, 1850, a clause was inserted whereby he decrees that a certain piece or parcel of woodland, situated in North Andover, Mass., shall not be sold and conveyed during the lifetime of his said children; or either of them, to the end that said woodlands may produce another growth of wood before they are so conveyed. Suffice it to say that $3.500 worth of wood was cut and sold from this piece or parcel of land, and the proceeds divided as provided by the terms of his will. David assumed the carrying out of this clause of his father's will, and still holds possession of the land, but the growth of wood upon said land has not proved so prolific up to date as to warrant his following such a procedure in making my last will and testament of this particular piece of woodland. David now has in his possession the original deed of the same property, conveyed to his father by Frederick Frye, recorded in register of deeds, Essex county, Salem, Mass., July 19, 1817. His father was of robust build, fond of home and his children, and it was his delight to have them all together there on a Thanksgiving Day. He passed on in the year 1865 at the ripe old age of 85 years, respected by his neighbors and beloved by his children, only two of whom out of the ten remain; namely: David and his sister, Mrs. John F. Kimball, of Andover, Mass. He d. Jan. 23, 1865. Res., Andover, Mass.

1963. i. SARAH, b. May 12, 1811; d. an infant.

1964. ii. SAMUEL, b. March 29, 1812; d. Oct. 18, 1815.

1965. iii. MARY PEABODY, b. Jan. 16, 1814; m. Charles Barnes, Nov. 17, 1841, of Leicester; d. May 7, 1882. Mary Peabody (Foster) Barnes left two children, a son, Charles Henry, that has since died, and a daughter, Sarah Foster, that is still living. Her address is 13 Lynde St., Salem, Mass.

1966. iv. MOSES, b. Oct. 8, 1815; d. Feb. 17, 1817.

1967. v. SARAH WILSON, b. Dec. 25, 1817; d. March 27, 1847, unm.

1967½. vi. SUSAN, b Nov. 18, 1819; d May 19, 1850, unm.

1968. vii. MOSES, b Aug. 29 1821; d June 27, 1895; m. Oct. 28, 1851, Clara M. Hyde; m., 2d, Dec. 8, 1858 Caroline Hall.

1969. viii. CLARISSA, b. April 8, 1823; m. Hiram Berry, July 29, 1847; d. Aug 27, 1897. Clarissa (Foster) Berry had two sons, both dead, Alfred d. young, and Clarence Herford d. in 1881. He left two children, one d. young, the other, Herford Berry, is still living. Mr John F. Kimball is his guardian.

1970. ix. ELIZABETH, b. July 15, 1824; m. John F. Kimball, Dec. 25, 1867. No children.

1971. x. DAVID SMITH, b. May 26, 1826; m. Agnes F. Byers, March 7, 1854.

1027. EBENEZER FOSTER (Stephen, Stephen, John, Ephraim, Abraham, Reginald), b. Mass., ——; m. ——, Sarah Dane. Res., Andover, Mass.

1972. i. PAULINA, b. June 6, 1820; d. Jan. 28, 1821.
1973. ii. PAULINA, b. Feb. 20, 1822.
1974. iii. MARY JANE, b. Dec. 2, 1826; pub. June 27, 1845, Theodore Goodrich.
1975. iv. HARRIET MARIA, b. April 23, 1830.
1976. v. SARAH, b. June 3, 1812; m., Feb. 5, 1838, Israel Foster.
1977. vi. DANE, b. Jan. 19, 1814; m. Mary S. Carlton.
1978. vii. AUGUSTA, b. Nov. 2, 1815; m., Nov. 12, 1840, James C. Adams, b. Oct. 15, 1816. Res., Hammonton, N. J.
1979. viii. MARTHA, b. Aug. 7, 1817; m., Oct. 13, 1839, Aaron Dunn.
1980. ix. HENRY, b. April 22, 1819.
1981. x. GEORGE OTIS, b. Feb. 21, 1833.

1028. PHINEHAS FOSTER (Stephen, Stephen, John, Ephraim, Abraham, Reginald), b. Bradford, Mass., in 1781; m., June 27, 1805, Sarah Johnson. He d. Sept. 5, 1854. Res., Andover, Mass.

1982. i. EBENEZER, b. Sept. 5, 1805; m., May 9, 1833, Ellen H. Purvis. Res., A.
1983. ii. AARON, b. Dec. 27, 1808.
1984. iii. JOHN J., b. April 27, 1811.
1985. iv. SAMUEL. b. March 9, 1813.
1986. v. SARAH DANE, b. Oct. 17, 1815; d. Dec. 2, 1835.
1987. vi. PHINEHAS, b. Jan. 31, 1820.
1988. vii. DAU., b. ——, 1827; d March 26, 1833.
1989. viii. SIMEON. b. ——.

1033. REV. STEPHEN FOSTER, M. A. (John, Stephen, John, Ephraim, Abraham, Reginald), b. Andover, Mass., Feb. 15, 1798; m. ——, Ann A. D. Davis. He graduated at Dartmouth college in 1821, and at Andover Theological Seminary in 1824; was ordained in 1824; he was a home missionary in Texas, and first professor of Latin and Greek, and afterward president of East Tennessee college, Knoxville; he d. Jan. 11 1835, in Knoxville, Tenn.

1990. i. SARAH J., b. ——; m. Samuel A. Rhea. She was a missionary to Persia.

1034. REV. ISAAC FOSTER (John, Stephen, John, Ephraim, Abraham, Reginald), b. Andover, Mass., July 7, 1806; m., July 2, 1834, Frances B. Lee, dau. of Ebenezer and Lydia Lee, of Hanover, N. H. He graduated at Dartmouth college in 1828 and from 1830 to 1839 was a teacher in Portland, Me.; Exeter, N. H., and Kingston, R. I. Res., in 1873, North Andover. He lived in the old Foster house, built in 1715, where his great-great-grandfather, Ephraim Foster, or the latter's son, Ephraim Foster, settled.

1991. i. CHARLES LEE, b. March 2, 1836; graduated at Dartmouth college in 1860; served in the Union army in the war of the Rebellion; d. Aug. 8, 1863, in New Orleans, La.
1992. ii. ELLEN FRANCES, b. Nov. 14, 1842; m., Sept. 26, 1865, Harrison G. Chandler, of Chandlerville, Ills.
1993. iii. CLOEA AUGUSTA. b. October 24, 1843; m., Sept. 19, 1864, Samuel W. Knapp, of Salem.

1038. NATHAN FOSTER (Nathan, Stephen, John, Ephraim, Abraham, Reginald), b. North Andover, Mass., Sept. 4, 1798; m. there Dec. 25, 1832, Harriet Berry, b. Dec. 31, 1806; d. March 10, 1878. He was a farmer. He d. Nov. 24, 1877. Res., Andover, Mass.

1994. i. CHARLES SAMUEL, b. Dec. 13, 1833; m. Sarah E. Bixby and Ellen E. Rea.
1995. ii. HARRIET, b. Dec. 3, 1837; m., June 29, 1858, Dr. Harlan H. Pillsbury. Res., Palo Alto, Cal.
1996. iii. ORRIN NATHAN, b. April 5, 1843; m. Emma W. Ingalls.

1049. ASA FOSTER (Frederick, Asa, Moses, Ephraim, Abraham, Reginald), b. Pembroke, N. H., Oct. 11, 1789; m., Grand Menan, N. B., Nov. 10, 1814, Mary Kent, dau. of John and Susanna. He always resided at Grand Menan, where he was a farmer. Res., Grand Menan, N. B.

1997. i. MATILDA, b. ——; m. Wm. Flagg, and d. in 1845, in Medford, Mass.
1998. ii. EZRA, b. ——.
1999. iii. ASA EASTMAN, b. ——.
2000. iv. JOHN KENT, b. ——.
2001. v. RICHARD E., b. ——.
2002. vi. ELIZABETH, b. ——; m. —— Wall.
2003. vii. LEONARD, b. ——. Res., San Diego, Cal.
2004. viii. WILLIAM, b. ——; d. in California.
2005. ix. NANCY CHENEY, b. ——; m. —— Merrill.
2006. x. MOSES GERRISH, b. ——; m. Susan Cheney, of Grand Menan. Res., Oakland, Cal.

1051. RICHARD EASTMAN FOSTER (Frederick, Asa, Moses, Ephraim, Abraham, Reginald), b. Pembroke, N. H., Feb. 15, 1795; m., Nov. 21, 1849, at Long Island, Nancy Maria Luce, who was b. June 30, 1813. Lived and d. at Eureka, Cal.
2007. i. LYDIA, b. Nov. 19, 1853; d. July 12, 1854.
2008. ii. LEWIS, b. April 5, 1855; d. Sept. 6, 1859.

1054. MERRILL FOSTER (Enoch, Ephraim, Moses, Ephraim, Abraham, Reginald), b. Peacham, Vt., Feb. 10, 1795; m., Dec. 1, 1816, Sally Gould, b. Gilmantown, N. H., July 5, 1795; d. June 3, 1865. He was a farmer. He d. May 27, 1855. Res., South Walden, Vt.
2009. i. EDWARD GOULD, b. April 10, 1821; m. Jeannette W. Vance and Elizabeth T. Howe.
2010. ii. HARVEY A., b. March 22, 1828; m. Mary F. Montgomery.
2011. iii. CAROLINE, b. July 20, 1817; d. Feb. 2, 1868; m. Sereno Montgomery, b. 1809; was a lawyer; d. Walden, Vt., Dec. 11, 1888. Ch.: 1. Marshall, b. ——. Res., St. Johnsbury, Vt. 2. Merrill E., b. Jan. 27, 1848; m., Oct. 10, 1871, Mary A. Hogan, b. May 20, 1856. Is a commercial traveler. Res. s. p., Burlington, Vt.
2012. iv. JANE GUY, b. Dec. 3, 1818; d. s. p., April 10, 1864.
2012½. v. PHILENA M., b. May 9, 1826; m., Jan. 4, 1855, Oliver M. Clifford, b. July 6, 1825; was a trader and d. May 16, 1883. Res., South Danville, Vt. Ch.: 1. Gertrude Clifford, b. Sept. 6, 1856; m. May 21, 1878. Mrs. Gertrude Greenbank, South Danville, Vt.
2013. vi. SALLY G., b. March 17, 1830; d. s. p., July 12, 1855.
2014. vii. CHARLES M., b. Oct. 3, 1835. Res., Baker City, Oregon.
2015. viii. SUSAN F., b. April 13, 1838; m., June 10, 1858, Capt. Williams Davis, b. Jan. 18, 1821; d. Dec. 11, 1886. He was a sea captain and merchant. They reside at Danville, Vt. Ch.: 1. Agnes Foster Davis, b. April 14, 1863; d. April 2, 1864. 2. Sydney Foster Davis, b. June 17, 1871. Postoffice, Cabot, Washington county, Vt.
2016. ix. EMILY PERKINS, b. Aug. 21, 1833; d. s. p., Dec. 19, 1863, m. —— Vincent.

1055. PARLEY FOSTER (Enoch, Ephraim, Moses, Ephraim, Abraham, Reginald), b. Oct. 28, 1800; m., March 31, 1823, Nancy Bean. He d. April 14, 1844. Res., ——.
2017. i. MARY, b. ——; m. in Berlin, Vt., Nov. 25, 1844, James Bidwell Scoville. He was a farmer. Res., Berlin, Vt., and d. Nov. 25, 1883. She d. April, 1894. Ch.: 1. Isabell F. Scoville, b. Aug. 20, 1849. 2. Mary Elizabeth Scoville, b. Oct. 19, 1851 (wife of John R. King). 3. Harriet (widow of Porter Randell), b. June 21, 1854. Ridgeland Ave., Oak Park, Ill. 4. Julia Scoville, b May 8, 1857, Ridgeland Ave., Oak Park, Ill. 5. James Pearly Scoville, b. June 1, 1860. 6. Chas. O. Scoville, b. Dec. 1, 1862; m. at New Haven, Conn., June 1, 1892, Lena May Isbell, b. Nov. 13, 1867. He is an Episcopal clergyman. Res., 90 Lake Place, New Haven, Conn. Ch.: 1. Helen May, b. Aug. 16, 1893 7. Alice Foster Scoville, April 2, 1866, Salt Lake City, Utah. 8. Harry Douglas, Scoville, Nov. 4, 1870. Res., Oak Park.
2018. ii. DOUGLASS, b. ——; d. unm.

1057. EPHRAIM FOSTER (Enoch, Ephraim, Moses, Ephraim, Abraham, Reginald), b. Peacham, Vt., April 25, 1805; m. in Wheelock, Vt., Oct. 11, 1832, Emily Perkins, b. Dec., 1811; d. July 2, 1858; m., 2d, April 14, 1860, Maria S. Lowell, b. April 15, 1811. He was a farmer. He d. Oct. 2, 1873. Res., Walden, Vt.

2019. i. GEORGE P., b. Oct. 3, 1835; m. Sarah S. Hubbell.
2020. ii. CARLOS BAXTER, b. in 1846; d. unm. in 1865.
2021. iii. MARY C., b. in 1834; d. in 1849.
2022. iv. MARGARET M., b. March 7, 1843; m., Dec. 4, 1860, John A. Farrington, b. Dec. 31, 1832. Is a merchant. Res., Cabot, Vt. Ch.: Julia A. and Edward Foster.
2023. v. CURTIS E., b. May 19, 1853; d. unm., Nov. 10, 1885. He was in the wholesale boot and shoe trade in Lynn.
2024. vi. JULIA EMILY, b. ——, 1850; d. ——, 1867.

1063. JOHN FOSTER (Ephraim, Ephraim, Moses, Ephraim, Abraham, Reginald), b. Peacham, Vt., Sept. 14, 1802; m. there June 19, 1832, Luda Stuart. He was a farmer. He d. Barton, Vt., Aug., 1863. Res., Peacham, Vt.

2025. i. ETHAN E., b. Peacham, Vt., m. Dec. 31, 1864, Josephine D. Merriam, b. Aug. 12, 1844. He is a farmer. Res. s. p. Barton, Vt.

1064. HIRAM FOSTER (Ephraim, Ephraim, Moses, Ephraim, Abraham, Reginald), b. Peacham, Vt., Dec. 9, 1805; m., Troy, Vt., 1835, Louisa Agnes Hall, b. July 29, 1817; d. Nov. 29, 1893.

Hiram Foster was born in the town of Peacham, Vt., in 1835. He married Louisa Agnes Hall. To them were born eleven children, William W., Franklin, Harriet, Betsey P., infant daughter, Edward E., Charles M., Freeland H., Julia E., Alice M., and Mary E. In 1848 he moved to Barton, Vt., and the next year to Irasburg, where he lived to the age of 72. His wife was 12 years younger, and lived to the age of 75. Nine of the children are living. Forty-one grandchildren have been born at this date (1898), twenty-nine of which are living. There are fourteen great-grandchildren at this writing. In religion he was a Congregationalist; in politics, a Republican; in business, a farmer. He d. ——, 1877. Res., Peacham, Vt.

2026. i. WILLIAM W., b. July 14, 1836; m. Jennie M. Dame.
2027. ii. FRANKLIN, b. May 16, 1838; d., 1874.
2028. iii. HARRIET, b. Jan. 5, 1840; m. Horatio P. Allard. He d. 1863, leaving (1) Walter L., (2) Eugene and (3) Frank Ellsworth, b. May 12, 1861. Mrs. Allard m., 2d, Joseph F. Preston, b. 1820. Res., Hanover, N. H. Ch.: 1. Jos. Franklin, b. Feb. 17, 1868. Is a journalist. Res., unm., 39 Hancock St., Boston, Mass. 2. Harriet, m., Dec. 25, 1893, F. Herbert Bacheller. Res., Appleton St., Manchester, N. H.

Following the death of his father, Frank Ellsworth went to live with his maternal grandparents, at Irasburgh, where he made it his home until he was seventeen years of age, receiving his early education in the district schools of that town. In 1878 he went to Hanover, N. H., to attend the High School, where he fitted for college, residing with his mother, Mrs. Joseph F. Preston; entered Dartmouth in 1881 and was graduated in the Class of 1885. Throughout this college course he was entirely dependent upon his own resources, meeting his expenses by teaching school winters, and during the summer vacations availed himself of whatever employment he was able to secure. In August, 1885, he was elected principal of the Boston Farm School. May 15, 1888, he married Ada E. Booth, youngest daughter of Samuel S. Booth, of Norwich, Vt. Resigning his position as principal of the Boston Farm School in September, 1889, he entered the Boston University School of Medicine, taking the full course, and graduated with the Class of '92. While pursuing his studies at the University, he was appointed principal of the Malden Evening School, which position he held until 1897. From April, 1891-2 he was House Surgeon at the Boston Homeopathic Medical Dispensary. In June, 1892, he opened an office at 39 Hancock St., Boston, Mass., where he has since been engaged in active general practice. He was elected in 1894 Instructor of Physiology at the Boston University School of Medicine, which position he retains. Is a member of the American Institute of Homeopathy, Massachusetts Homeopathic Medical Society, Secretary of the Boston Homeopathic Medical Society, and Medical Director of the Boston Mutual Life Insurance company. He has one child, Beatrice, b. Dec. 10, 1893.

2029. iv. DAUGHTER, b. Dec. 26, 1843; d. Dec. 27, 1843.

2030. v. BETSEY P., b. Oct. 26, 1841; m. —— Hawse. Res., Hanover, N. H.

2031. vi. EDWARD E., b. April 15, 1845; m., and Res. Caney, Kans.

2032. vii. CHARLES M., b. Jan. 11, 1846; m. Theresa Schwartz.

2033. viii. FREELAND H., b. Dec. 4, 1849; m. Ida L. Gilles.

2034. ix. JULIA E., b. July 24, 1852; m., June 25, 1873, Leon D. Hard. Res., Manchester, N. H., 584 Beech St. He was b. Aug. 25, 1850. Ch.: 1. Gertrude, b. Feb. 20, 1875.

2035. x. ALICE, b. Sept. 29, 1854; m., Dec. 25, 1873, Charles S. Gibb. Res., Barton Landing, Vt. He is a shoemaker. Was b. March 5, 1851. Ch.: 1. Hugh Wallace Gibb, b. Oct. 17, 1878; d. Feb. 1, 1879. 2. Harry Gibb, b. Sept. 13, 1880; d. Oct. 4, 1881. 3. Arthur Charles Gibb, b. March 19, 1882. 4. Oscar Edward Gibb, b. Aug. 27, 1884. 5. Karl Alton Gibb, b. March 3, 1887; d. Sept. 13, 1893. 6. Iva Belle Gibb, b. Aug. 1, 1892; d. Nov. 24, 1893.

2036. xi. MARY E., b. Nov. 9, 1859; m., Dec. 25, 1880, George Nye. Res., Barton, Vt. He is a manufacturer of woodwork. Was b. May 17, 1854. Ch.: 1. Erwin Leslie Nye, b. April 5, 1882; d. Aug. 23, 1883. 2. William Foster Nye, b. July 11, 1885. 3. Ina Julia Nye, b. March 8, 1887. 4. Helen Ruby Nye, b. July 25, 1889. 5. Ruth Elva Nye, b. Aug. 8, 1892. 6. Sylvia June Nye, b. June 30, 1898.

1065. DANIEL FOSTER (Ephraim, Ephraim, Moses, Ephraim, Abraham, Reginald), b. Peacham, Vt., May 24, 1820; m., Marshfield, Vt., March 14, 1849, Mary Carpenter, b. Dec. 3, 1831. He is a retired farmer. He emigrated from Vermont to Iowa in 1861. Res., West Liberty, Iowa.

2037. i. IDA E., b. June 22, 1855.

2038. ii. EVA E., b. June 30, 1856.

2039. iii. MATTIE, b. April 6, 1864.

1067. FRANKLIN FOSTER (Ephraim, Ephraim, Moses, Ephraim, Abraham, Reginald), b. Peacham, Vt., in 1809; m., March 9, 1837, Eliza Blanchard; b. 1813; d. 1848; m., 2d, Dec. 4, 1849, Jane Walker; dau. of Jabez and Betsey; d. March 3, 1868. Res., Peacham, Vt.

2040. i. MARTHA S., b. ——; m., Dec. 4, 1860, Levi S. Sewell, of St. Johnsbury, Vt. He was b. March 7, 1834. She d. Nov., 1862. Ch.: 1. Martha Foster, b. April 30, 1862; m., Oct. 15, 1885, Fred L. Davis. Res., Gloucester, Mass. He is a grocer. Ch.: (a) G. Bradford Davis, b. Sept. 14, 1886; d. April, 1896. (b) Blanche Davis, b. Feb. 24, 1890. (c) Margaret L. Davis, b. May 23, 1895. (d) Fred Leland Davis, b. Dec. 6, 1897; d. Dec. 9, 1897.

2041. ii. SARAH BLANCHARD, b. Aug. 29, 1837; m., May 20, 1863, William Harrison Shaw; b. May 20, 1836. She d. July 17, 1872. Res., St. Johnsbury, Vt. Ch.: 1. Lizzie Shaw, b. in St. Johnsbury, Vt., July 13, 1867; d. at Peacham, Vt., Oct. 8, 1867. 2. Bertie W. Shaw, b. in St. Johnsbury, Vt., July 7, 1869; d. at St. Johnsbury, Vt., Sept. 1, 1870. 3. Helen Foster, b. Nov. 11, 1865, is an artist; unm. Res., St. Johnsbury, Vt.

2042. iii. EDNAH, b.——; m. William Robinson. Res., South Peacham, Vt.

1070. JOHN WETHERBY FOSTER (Abner, Elijah, Aaron, Ephraim, Abraham, Reginald), b. Templeton, Mass., April 15, 1798; m., in Athol, April 18, 1826, Dorinda Goddard; b. Athol, July 27, 1805; d. May 30, 1874. He was a carpenter and millwright. John W. Foster, who was born in Templeton, Mass., in 1798, was of the sturdy New England nature, and spent his life for the betterment of mankind by following the pursuits of thought and work for which he was best fitted. He was mechanically inclined, and was endowed with more of that which men call genius than is the ordinary mechanic. This line of work came very natural to him as his father, Abner Foster, was a mechanic of no ordinary ability—he was the patentee of the first mortising machine used in the making of sash and blinds. His patent was signed by Andrew Jackson as president of the United States, and Martin Van Buren, as secretary of state. John W. followed his father's footsteps. He was the inventor of the first rolling machine used by shoemakers in place of the lap stone. He also put together the first power loom ever brought to this part of the country. He afterward duplicated this loom and made many of them for one of the pioneer woolen manufactories, the late Rufus Bullock, of Royalston. He d. leaving five sons and three daughters, Sept. 8, 1849. Res., Phillipston and Athol, Mass.

2043. i. LUCY AUGUSTA, b. March 8, 1827; m., June 10, 1849, Freeborn R. Fay. Res., Athol, Mass. He was b. Jan. 16, 1827; d. April 27, 1865. Ch.: 1. Leona M., b. July 31, 1852; m., April 28, 1873; present name Gates. 2. Flora A., b. Aug. 21, 1854; d. Feb. 16, 1855. 3. Waldo E., b. Dec. 10, 1860; m., May 29, 1889. 4. Helen A., b. Sept. 5, 1863.

2044. ii. SARAH JUDITH, b. Dec. 18, 1828; d. May 10, 1832.

2045. iii. CHARLES AUGUSTUS, b. Nov. 28, 1830; m., Apr. 12, 1854, Sarah Robbins, of Warwick. He d. March 10, 1855, in Athol, Mass.

2046. iv. HENRY CLAY, b. June 3, 1832; m. Louise O. Fisher, Margaret M. Foster and Fannie E. Conwell.

2047. v. DANIEL WEBSTER, b. Aug. 17, 1833; m., Jan. 29, 1857, Olive Smith and m., 2d, May 13, 1861, Hannah Smith. He was in the Civil war in Thirty-sixth Mass. Regt., d. s. p., Newport News, Va., Feb. 14, 1863.

2048. vi. ELECTA G., b. March 10, 1835. Res., Athol Center, Mass.

2049. vii. SARAH LEVINA, b. Sept. 17, 1839; m., Jan. 1, 1877, George W. Drury. Res., A. C.

2050. viii. ELMER GODDARD, b. July 26, 1841; d. Feb. 24, 1869. He served in the Civil war in a batallion in Fort Warren, Boston Harbor.

2051. ix. ABNER LEROY, b. July 17, 1846; d. Aug. 19, 1849.

2052. x. WILLIAM HALE, b. Sept. 5, 1836; m. S. Maria Clark.

1085. EDWARD S. FOSTER (Jedediah, Elijah, Aaron, Ephraim, Abraham, Reginald), b. Jaffrey, N. H., Oct. 22, 1833; m. Boylston, Mass., Nov. 13, 1863, Louisa A. Alexander; b. 1825; d. May 13, 1894. He is a farmer. Res., Troy, N. H.

2053. i. FRANK E., b. Feb. 13, 1866; d. Sept. 12, 1872.

2054. ii. LEON W., b. Sept. 3, 1871. Res., Keene, N. H.

1091. HON. NATHANIEL FOSTER (Daniel, Thomas, Abraham, Abraham, Abraham, Reginald), b. Rowley, Mass., Feb. 28, 1797; m., Newburyport, Oct. 15, 1823. Fanny Bird Brockway; b. Feb. 7, 1800; d. April 18, 1876. He was born in Rowley, but before his majority, moved to Newburyport, where he married. He was always interested in military matters; was captain of the Newburyport military company, and was one of the reception committee from that city to receive General Lafayette. He was a staunch churchman, and for over fifty years was warden in St. Paul's church in that city. He held many offices in the town and for a time was representative in the legislature. He d. Oct. 21, 1893. Res., Newburyport, Mass.

2055. i. NATHANIEL, b. Aug. 8, 1830; m. Catherine L. Woods.

2056. ii. FRANCES LOUISE, b. March 24, 1835; unm. Res., 22 Prospect St., Newburyport, Mass.

1091-2. SIMON FOSTER (Allen, Thomas, Abraham, Abraham, Abraham, Reginald), b. Ipswich, Mass., March 15, 1793; m. there, Oct. 16, 1814, Mary Perkins; d. July 4, 1826; m., 2d, Eunice Perkins; b. Oct. 25, 1807; d. March 11, 1881. Was a carpenter and farmer. He d. Feb. 23, 1897. Res., Ipswich, Mass.

2056-2. i. EDMUND K., b. Dec. 28, 1815.

2057-2. ii. PERKINS, b. July 25, 1818; m. Martha Mears.

2058-2. iii. SIMON, b. June 19, 1822; d. March 5, 1847.

2059-2. iv. NATHANIEL, b. Dec. 6, 1825. Res., Ipswich, Mass.

2060-2. v. MARY, b. Dec. 25, 1827; m., Nov. 22, 1843, Gorham P. Foster (see); d. Nov. 5, 1851; m., 2d, Asa Lord; d. Feb. 27, 1844; m., 3d, Edward Plouff. Res., Ipswich, Mass. Ch.: 1. Mary J. Foster, b. Oct. 14, 1845; d. Nov. 28, 1847. 2. Lewis T. Foster, b. June 17, 1848; d. March 16, 1866. 3. Gorham Foster, b. March 28, 1851; d. March 25, 1880.

2061-2. vi. EPHRAIM, b. April 6, 1832. Res., Salem, Mass.
2062-2. vii. DOLLY A., b. Oct. 11, 1836; d. April 14, 1858.
2063-2. viii. FANNY W., b. Oct. 8, 1841; d. May 7, 1876; m. —— Towle. Children of the above: George E. Foster, Evanston, Ill. Howard M. Towle, Kensington, N. H.

1092. DANIEL FOSTER JR. (Daniel, Thomas, Abraham, Abraham, Abraham, Reginald), b. Newburyport, Mass., ——; m., May 16, 1811, in Tiverton, R. I., Charry Fuller, dau. of Rev. Martin and Mary Fuller, of Royalston, Vt. Res., Tiverton, R. I.

1094. JESSE FOSTER (Daniel, Thomas, Abraham, Abraham, Abraham, Reginald), b. Newburyport, Mass.; m. there ——, Ann E. Toppan. He d. ab. 93. Res., Pottsville, Pa.
2057. i. CLEMENT STORER, b. Aug. 18, 1823; m. Rebecca McCamant.
2058. ii. THOMAS, b. July 20, 1819; m. Amanda M. Ruch.
2059. iii. FREDERICK L., b. ——. Hon. Res., Philadelphia, Pa. Address, 423 Market St. Has the sword Lafayette presented to his grandfather.
2060. iv. ANN ELIZA, b. Nov. 1, 1821; m., Sept. 7, 1842, Oliver Dobson. Res., Pottsville, Pa., Mahantango St. He was b. July 15, 1810; d. Feb. 22, 1874. Was a hatter and furrier. Ch.: 1. Emma Louisa Dobson, b. Pottsville, Sept. 1, 1843. 2. Mary Eliza Dobson, b. Pottsville, July 17, 1846. 3. Caroline Briggs Dobson, b. Pottsville, April 6, 1849; m. John E. Waters, May 17, 1871. One son, Oliver, and daughter, Grace, lives at Bridgeport, O. 4. Oliver Dobson, Jr., b. Pottsville, June 9, 1851; d. Feb. 22, 1877. 5. Hannah Dobson, b. Pottsville, Oct. 7, 1853; d. July 26, 1854.

1098. ASA LANESFORD FOSTER (Asa, Nathan, Nathan, Abraham, Abraham, Reginald), b. Rowe, Mass., Aug. 19, 1798; m., Wilkesbarre, Pa., Aug. 24, 1822, Louise Trott Chapman; b. Northampton, Mass., July 15, 1801; d. Eckley, Pa., March 4, 1861. His parents died when he was quite young, but he was reared among his relatives, who gave him a good common school education. In 1818, he emigrated to Pennsylvania and was engaged in mercantile business at Berwick and at Bloomsburg and, in 1826, in Philadelphia. In 1827 he accepted an offer and took charge of the extensive store of the Lehigh Coal and Navigation Company at Mauch Chunk, Pa. He soon became identified with the progress and development of the Lehigh region, and, with the permission of his employers in 1829, he purchased a press and office material of a printing establishment and the apprenticeship of a Mr. Listy, and they published the first newspaper in Mauch Chunk, which became very popular as a news messenger from the first coal and lumber region of the Lehigh, and Mr. Foster devoted all his spare time in writing and collecting matter for "The Lehigh Pioneer," and soon became one of the leading men of the region. He devoted much of his time to the study of geology of the coal formations, in which science he became expert. His services were much in demand and greatly appreciated by companies and individuals contemplating the purchase of coal lands and opening mines. He was extensively engaged in the coal business at one time as stockholder and superintendent of a company formed in 1838, but lost heavily by the great freshet of 1841. Later, he became one of a firm who for twenty years successfully and profitably conducted the mining operations of the "Council Ridge Colliery." He lived a consistent and Christian life, measuring all his social and business relations with his fellow-men by the Golden Rule. He was a communicant of the Protestant Episcopal church, active, liberal and influential in all church and charitable work. In politics, he was a Federalist, a Whig and a Republican. He d. Jan. 9, 1868. Res., Wilkesbarre, Pa.
2061. i. THOMAS LANESFORD, b. Aug. 30, 1823; m. Henrietta Pratt.
2062. ii. CHARLES EDWARD, b. Feb. 15, 1826; m. Mary A. Jeffery.
2063. iii. MARY CHAPMAN, b. June 4, 1829; m., June 2, 1855, Col. Ely Taylor Connor. He was killed in battle at Malvern Hill. Was colonel of the Eighty-first Pa. Regt. Vols. She d. Dec. 5. 1861. Ch.: 1. William Foster, b. April 16, 1857; d. Dec. 5, 1861. 2. Rachel Louise, b. May 1, 1859; m., ——, Edward Loomis. Res., Aspen Park, Elmira, N. Y.
2064. iv. ELIZABETH REED, b. Sept. 9, 1832; m., Dec. 9, 1857, Eaton N. Frisbie. She d. June, 1878, s. p. Res., Elmira, N. Y.

1104. NATHAN LANESFORD FOSTER (Joel, Nathan, Nathan, Abraham, Abraham, Reginald), b. New Salem, Mass., Dec. 8, 1787; m., May 30, 1811, in East Haddam, Conn., Azubah Louisa Cone; b. Jan. 14, 1788; d. Philadelphia, Pa., Dec. 9, 1859. He was born in the old hill town of New Salem, Mass., where he lived until 1803. The following two years he resided in Sudbury, Mass. He went to Brattleboro, Vt., to study or read law with his brother-in-law, Samuel Elliott Esq., and remained there until after his sister's death in July, 1806. Then he taught school at Sudbury, finally drifted down the Connecticut valley to the town of East Haddam, where he taught a select school, after a few years of practice at law, having been admitted to the bar. He taught a select school in Hartford, Conn., a term of years, then he returned to East Haddam, and settled at a locality which he gave the classic name of "Mount Parnassus," which still bears that name. He taught a select school at that place for fifteen years, then his health failing he sought a warmer clime, and moved his family to Philadelphia in October, 1840. Was the projector of the Branch Peare Society in East Haddam; was town clerk and treasurer of East Haddam covering a period of more than twenty years; was a highly respected citizen; a man of marked individuality who had scores of acquaintances and whose influence in his walks of life left an abiding impression. He married Azubah Louisa Cone, second daughter of William Cone, Esq., of East Haddam, one of the first families of the town. (William Cone was captain of a company of volunteers from East Haddam, 1776.) He was author of a book entitled "The Last of This Family." The following was written by Nathan Lanesford Foster in relation to his ancestors:

NATHAN LANESFORD FOSTER.

"In the cold bosom of our kindred earth,
Our common Alma Mater, in the soil
Of three New England States, repose the manes
Of my progenitors—the progeny
Of Standish, Pilgrim Father, Puritan,
Foremost among the hundred pious ones,
Who 'mid December's icy blasts, debarked
On Plymouth's bleak, inhospitable shore,
Where, dashed on rocks, the broken billows roar!
There, too, my kindred, in collateral line,
All, All repose! for Death not one has spared—
Death, sateless tyrant! and the grave insatiate,
Found want of room in all New England's soil!
For this magnanimous, imperial state (N. Y.)
Folds, in her wide domain, my kindred dust;
Near Brooklyn's heights, unhonored with a stone
To point affection to his lowly bed,
Repose the ashes of God's minister,
The Reverend Emerson.
But thee, lorn fair one!
The tender branch of that beloved stock,
By chance I found surviving; and I come
To greet thee, loved one! on this distant shore."

Another poem of his began as follows:

'Perhaps, who chance to read the poet's strain
May claim an outline of his history.
Know, then, though sorrow is the lot of man,
That 'sorrow, like my sorrow,' few have known—
The last survivor of my father's house—
Not much unlike the 'scathed pine,' I stand
A beacon to the world, a living proof
That sorrow, anguish, care, bereavement, death,
Are foreordained man's cheerless heritage!

2065. i. ELIZABETH LOUISA, b. Jan. 7, 1815; m. June 18, 1837, Eleaza Watrous Mather. She d. Feb. 5, 1882; he was b. March 28, 1812; d. March 20, 1887. Was a farmer. Ch.: 1. Nathan Augustus Mather, b. March 22, 1843; m. May 25, 1892, Mrs. Kate Urquhart Edwards Holmes, b. Nov. 7, 1854. Res., Hadlyme, Conn. He is a music dealer. 1. Ch.: William Rawson Isham, b. Jan. 11, 1879. 2. Kate Louise Warner, b. Nov. 20. 1852; m. Nov. 25, 1880, Erastus S. Warner; s. p. 3. Fanny Foster Dickinson, b. Oct. 28, 1854; m. Oct. 28, 1881. P. O. address, Essex, Conn., Thomas Newton Dickinson, Jr., b. Jan. 28, 1852. He owns the witch hazel distillery. Ch.: (a) Elizabeth Foster, b. May 28, 1883. (b) Fanny Marguerite, b. Sept. 6, 1885; d. Feb. 21, 1893. (c) Harriet Salome, b. Jan. 23, 1888. (d) Dorothy Mather, b. Jan. 26, 1890. (e) Mary Catherine, b. June 21, 1892. (f) Thomas Leon, b. Oct. 19, 1893. (g) Everett Newton, b. July 10, 1896. (h) Priscilla Lansford, b. Feb. 18, 1899. 7, Mary Helen, b. Nov. 18, 1838; m. Feb. 27, 1860; Roswell Doan Spencer, b. March 26, 1837. Res., Thompsonville, Conn. Ch.: (a) Agnes Isabel, b. Feb. 17, 1861. (b) Robert Emmett, b. Nov. 4, 1864; m. Oct. 14, 1891, to Annie Hope Bisland (Scotch); four children. (c) Herbert Doane, b. Oct. 2, 1868; drowned June 23, 1885. (d) Roswell Donald, b. Feb. 8, 1871; m. Oct. 18, 1893, Martha Agnes Craig (Scotch); two children. (e) Helen Mather, b. Nov. 12, 1882. Roswell Donald's P. O. add., Hartford, Conn. All the others, Thompsonville, Conn. Mrs. E. Louisa Mather has written essays, stories and poems for the Ladies' Repository, from 1847 to 1874; for the Trumpet, Ambassador, Golden Rule, Odd Fellows' Offering, etc., on religious subjects, capital punishment, woman's suffrage, etc. I will transcribe a few verses from her poem:—

MRS. ELIZABETH L. F. MATHER.

MEAR.

I heard the words of the preacher
As he read that hymn so dear,
Which mother sang at our cradle
To the ancient tune of Mear.

I longed for the land of summer,
Life's river, with waters clear,
And the calm, sweet eyes of mother,
Who sang the old tune of Mear.

Oh! tale of the shepherd's watching,
Over their flocks in the night;
Of the dear Lord sending angels
Enshrouded in glory bright!

O, story told in the Orient,
To each wondering shepherd's ear,
That story sung by my mother
To the hallowed tune of Mear.

O, pure white babe of the manger!
Thy story shall ever run,
'Til redemption's work is finished,
All souls to God's kingdom won!

Ah me! the father has rested
Many and many a year;
The mother who sang by our cradle,
Has gone to a higher sphere.

Brothers and sisters have parted;
Some live in the better land,
And some, awaiting their summons,
Sojourn on the earth's bleak strand.

I feel when we meet up yonder,
Where cometh no sigh nor tear,
Our mother will softly sing us
The grand, sweet old tune of Mear!

2066. ii. EDGAR THEODORE, b. April 7, 1823; m. Anna Lippincott.

2067. iii. JOEL WILLIAM LANESFORD, b. May 28, 1813. Joel William Lanesford Foster [mariner], died at Genoa, Italy, some time the latter part of the year 1848; having sailed from Boston, June, 1848, for Genoa, and on return of the vessel in which he sailed, to the port of Boston early in the year 1849, news was brought of his death, in Genoa, after two days' illness of a fever. Anno Etatis 36th. He was unmarried.

MY BROTHER'S GRAVE.

[Joel W. L. Foster.]

By Mrs. E. L. Mather.

Genoa's marble palaces and halls
Are bathed in the sweet moonlight, and the sea
Reflects the glorious stars, whose soft light falls,
Like words of balm to set the captive free.

And on thy grave, my brother, those blest rays
Fall fondly where no tear of love was shed,
When thou, in the fresh vigor of thy days,
Upon a foreign shore laid'st down thy head,

And died with stranger-voices in thine ear,
Without thy mother's glance, thy sister's kiss,
Without a word to breathe that hope so dear,
The hope of meeting in a world of bliss.

Farewell on earth, dear brother! oh, no more
Thy home shall be on ocean's heaving wave;
Its billows all are passed, its dangers o'er,
Thou sleepest sweetly in thy lonely grave.

* * * * * * * *

Then fare thee well! Upon Genoa's shore
Thy body mingles with the flowery sod!
Yet look we up, where pleasures evermore
Surround thee, with thy Father and thy God.

* * * * * * *

Ah! then, dear brother! in the "better land,"
I trust to meet thee, where no parting tone
Will reach our re-united household band,
All met, in joy, to worship round the Throne!

2068. iv. WILLIAM CONE, b. May 8, 1817; d. Oct. 11, 1817.

2069. v. MARIE ANTOINETTE, b. Nov. 29, 1818; m. April 26, 1840, John Holmes. She m., 2d, Sept. 17, 1866, Drury Holmes. Res., East Haddam, Conn. She d. Aug. 30, 1873. Ch.: 1. John, b. Oct. 14, 1841; m. Leora Luther. Res., Hadlyme, Conn. 2. Henry, b. Dec. 3, 1842; d. Jan. 5, 1885. 3. Reginald Heber, b. Nov. 19, 1845; d. May 31, 1862. 4. William Cone, b. Jan. 22, 1848; m., Nov. 30, 1870, Ella Williams. He d. Dec. 8, 1888. Ch.: (a) Antoinette Foster, b. March 13, 1872. (b) Reginald Charles, b. Oct. 4, 1873. 5. Mary Louise, b. Oct. 20, 1851; d. April 4, 1854. 6. Charles Atwood, b. April 7, 1855; d. April 11, 1871.

2070. vi. JOHN WEBSTER, b. Feb. 19, 1821; m. Elizabeth Cahoone and Nancy Cutler.

2071. vii. MARY SOPHIA, b. July 27, 1825; m. July 27, 1845, George Henry Chadwick. Res., 1757 Lambert street, Philadelphia, Pa. Ch.: 1. George Lanesford, b. July 10, 1846. 2. William Foster, b. Aug. 20, 1848. 3. Mary Louise. 4. Lemuel. 5. Charles.

2072. viii. CATHERINE LUNAN TONNELE, b. Feb. 8, 1828; m. March 8, 1849, William King. He was b. Aug. 5, 1823. Is a retired oil merchant. Res., 1523 Poplar street, Philadelphia, Pa. Catherine L. T. Foster was born in East Haddam, Connecticut, daughter of Nathan Lanesford and A. Louisa Foster. Removed with her parents to Philadelphia, where she was educated and subsequently married. Mr. King, though at first in the drug trade, turned his attention to the refining of oil, and for forty years was in the business for himself, on Arch street, above Front. About ten years ago he retired, leaving two of his sons, William R. and R. H. King, in control. Mr. King is a prominent Mason, and member of the Knights Templar, Order of Odd Fellows, and other fraternal organizations. As vice-president of the Northern Home for Friendless Children, treasurer of the Albion society, director of the Medico-Chirurgical Hospital, and member of the Union League, Mr. King has a large acquaintance among business and professional men. He is a trustee of the Society of the Sons of St. George, having been born in Gloucestershire, England, seventy-six years ago, and a director both of the Guarantee Trust and Safe Deposit Company and the Eighth National Bank. Mrs. King is likewise prominent in charitable work, is president of the Seaside Home, Cape May Point, and is an active worker in the Women's Christian Temperance Union. Ch.: 1. Henri Chapman, b. Sept. 25, 1852; m., April 8, 1874. Res., 4706 Windsor avenue, Philadelphia, Pa. 2. William Ritterson, b. Jan. 30, 1855; unm. Res., 1523 Poplar street, Philadelphia, Pa. 3. Fannie Foster (Mrs. Robert P. DeSilver), b. Aug. 24, 1857. Res., 1628 Wallace street, Philadelphia, Pa. 4. Reginald Heber, b. Nov. 25, 1864; m., Nov. 17, 1892. Res., 1825 Green street, Philadelphia, Pa. 5. Frank Era, b. Aug. 9, 1868; m. Oct. 20, 1892. Res., 1523 Poplar street, Philadelphia, Pa.

MRS. CATHERINE L. T. KING.

2073. ix. REGINALD HEBER, b. Sept. 10, 1831; m. Joanna Dilkes.

2074. x. HENRI LYSANDER, b. Sept. 17, 1833; m. Angelica Constantia Wenzell.

1133. PLINY P. FOSTER (Flint R., Daniel, Nathan, Abraham, Abraham, Reginald), b. Norwich, Conn., Oct. 10, 1801; m. in Vermont, Eliza Willard. She d. Dec. 27, 1841. Was a farmer. He d. Nov. 26, 1875. Res., Morgan, Vt.

2075. i. IRA, b. April 21, 1824; d. Feb., 1894. Res, Mass.
2076. ii. WESLEY W., b. Jan. 2, 1828. Res., Manchester, N. H.
2077. iii. ERWIN W., b. Dec. 5, 1836; m., Sept. 5, 1893, Arabella Marshall, b. April 3, 1847. Is a dealer in country produce. Res., s. p., Manchester, N. H.
2078. iv. EDWIN D., b. Dec. 5, 1836; m. Carrie M. Jenness.
2079. v. LEMUEL R., b. March 4, 1841. Res., W. Charlestown, Vt.
2080. vi. CHARLES H., b. April 19, 1850; m. Jennie M. Shedd.
2081. vii. FLINT R., b. July 4, 18—. Res., East Bolton, Canada.
2082. viii. MARTHA H., b. Oct. 5, 1834. Res., Auburn, N. H.

1136. DR. JOHN WELLS FOSTER (Festus, Standish, Nathan, Abraham, Abraham, Reginald), b. Petersham, Mass., March 4, 1815; m., Brimfield, Oct. 24, 1839, Lydia Lyon Converse, b. March 4, 1815; d. March 30, 1895.

John Wells Foster, L.L. D., was a lineal descendant of Myles Standish. He was born in Petersham, Mass., March 4, 1815, where his father, Festus Foster, a graduate of Williams College, and a man of vigorous intellect and brilliant attainments, was minister for a long term of years. His mother was Patience Wells, a member of the celebrated Wells family of Massachusetts, and from whom he received his baptismal name. After he had acquired the rudiments of learning, as taught in the public schools of the town, he went to Wilbraham Academy, from there entering the Wesleyan University, at Middletown, Conn., in 1831. After graduating with high honors, he began the study of law, remaining in New England one year, when he removed to Zanesville, O., continuing his law studies in the office of Goddard & Convers, and was admitted to the bar. After practicing law awhile, he finally chose civil and mining engineering as his pursuit in life. His education, which was broad and liberal, was the foundation on which he built enduring fame. He soon became a recognized authority in geology and metallurgy, and was employed by Eastern capitalists to examine the mining regions and report results. In the geological survey of the State of Ohio, he was selected by Professor Mather as one of his assistants, and made a valuable report on the Ohio coal fields. He was employed by several mining companies to visit the Lake Superior copper mining regions. In 1847 the government instituted a geological survey of that country, under direction of Dr. Jackson. Mr. Foster was appointed one of the assistants, the labor giving him wide scope for the exercise of his mind in the department of science in which he subsequently became famous. Professor J. D. Whitney was his chosen companion and associate. Two years later the completion of the work was entirely confided to them. The result of their labor was a volume entitled, "Foster & Whitney's Report on the Lake Superior Region," which was published by direction of Congress. This work now remains the authority on the subject of which it treats, and was one of the most valuable reports ever made to Congress. At the meeting of the American Association for the Advancement of Science, which met in Cincinnati in 1851, Agassiz rose at the close of the communication, and declared it to be one of the grandest generalizations ever made in American geology. In 1854 Mr. Foster was prominent in Massachusetts politics. To him more than to any one man did Governor Gardner owe his election. He was elected by the Legislature one of the Governor's Executive Council, and was recognized as the power behind the throne. Had his tastes inclined toward a political life, he would have attained high public position, but he forsook politics for more congenial pursuits, and gave himself unreservedly to science and literature. In 1858 he made Chicago his home, where for a time he was Commissioner of the Land Department of the Illinois Central Railroad, and held a similar position on the Chicago & Alton, but the pursuit of knowledge was the ambition of his life, and he soon gave up all else and once more turned his undivided attention to science, where his heart had always led him.

He served as professor of Natural History in the University of Chicago, which honored itself by honoring him with the degree of Doctor of Laws.

In 1869 Mr. Foster was chosen president of the American Association for the Advancement of Science, in recognition of his distinguished services in the cause of science. He was also an honorary member of many learned societies at home and abroad. Perhaps it was in Europe that the scientific labors of Mr. Foster were most highly prized. His fame had crossed the ocean, and the scientific men of Europe, such as Tyndall, Huxley, Lisle and Lubbock, were his intimate friends and corres-

DR. JOHN WELLS FOSTER, L.L. D.

pondents. His place among the scientific men of this continent, and of this age, is in the front rank, and his name stands in history side by side with Agassiz and Maury. In 1869 Mr. Foster published a comprehensive and interesting book, "The Mississippi Valley; its Physical Geography," including sketches of the topography, botany, climate, geology, etc. Unfortunately the plates were destroyed in the great fire, but the work took at once high rank as a scientific authority on the subjects of which it treats. Just prior to his death he published a most valuable work in the department of archæology, which he had made his specialty. It is entitled, "Pre-Historic Man," and gives the results of his investigation of the mounds found in various places in the Western States.

He was editor of the Lakeside Monthly, and at all times contributed important papers to various scientific societies, Silliman's Journal, American Naturalist, and other scientific periodicals.

He was one of the founders of the Chicago Academy of Science and its president, which office he held at the time of his death. So interested was he in its success that long after he had become a victim to his hereditary enemy—the gout—he would attend the meetings when every step was painful, forgetting his suffering in the companionship of the congenial souls he found there, all interested in the subjects that lay so close to his heart. Among his many accomplishments, he possessed the gift of being very clever with his pen. He had books filled with pen and ink drawings, many being sketches of the Lake Superior regions, showing him to be an excellent artist. He also finished from his easel several landscapes, which have been pronounced admirable by art connoisseurs.

In the spring of 1873, his health becoming very precarious, he removed from Chicago to Hyde Park, where he could enjoy the open fields and fresh country air. The change seemed to benefit him, and he was looking forward to the writing of another book, for which he had abundant material prepared. But it was not to be. After enjoying his country home for one short month, on Sunday, June 29th, with the setting of the sun, the summons came, and he departed without a blemish on his character, as a man or author, leaving nothing but "sweet memories in each mourner's heart." Personally, Mr. Foster was a noble specimen of manhood, of commanding height, strong, finely built, portly, and of handsome features. His head bore the stamp of intellect. In manner he was courtly and courteous, genial and kind to all. Notwithstanding his genius and great learning, he had the simplicity of a little child, and all those virtues that shine so brightly in every-day life. His varied experience, his wide and accurate knowledge of facts, his intellectual comprehensiveness and discriminativeness, made him the peer of the foremost scholars of his time, while his personal and social qualities made him respected and loved by all who came within the radius of his winning personality. It has been said by many who knew him well, that he had not an enemy on earth.

He d. June 29, 1873. Res., Hyde Park, Chicago, Ill.

2083. i. MARQUIS CONVERSE, b. June 1, 1841; d., 1841.

2084. ii. SOPHIA ELIZABETH, b. Aug. 20, 1844; m. in Chicago, July 13, 1875, Judge George Gifford Symes, b. April 28, 1840; d. Nov. 3, 1893. Res., Denver, Col. Ch.: 1. Katharine Foster Symes, b. Aug. 17, 1876. 2. John Foster Symes, b. Feb. 10, 1877. 3. Mary Gifford Symes, b. Nov. 18, 1879; d. July 8, 1895. 4. George Gifford Symes, b. Aug. 9, 1884.

2085. iii. MARY WELLS, b. July 27, 1845; d., 1847.

2086. iv. HARRIET LYON, b. Oct., 1847; d., 1848.

2087. v. ALICE EUDOCIA, b. Dec. 16, 1851; m., in Chicago, June 28, 1871, James McKibben Sanger, b. March 16, 1844; d., Sept. 19, 1877; m., 2d, Nov. 2, 1885, Walter Scott Cheesman, b. June 27, 1837; Res., 1540 Lincoln Avenue, Denver, Colorado. Ch.: 1. Madeline Standish Sanger (twin), b. March 11, 1872; d. Aug. 5, 1872. 2. George Pullman Sanger (twin), b. March 11, 1872. 3. John Foster Sanger, b. Dec. 7, 1873. 4. Gladys Cheesman, b. July 9, 1887.

2088. vi. KATE CONVERSE, b. May 8, 1856; d. 1879.

1145. SHERLOCK FOSTER (Daniel, Isaac, Daniel, Abraham, Abraham, Reginald), b. Warren, Mass., ——, 1786; m. there 1815, Tamma Reed, b. 1793; d. Warren, 1817; m., 2d, ——, Abigail ——. He was a farmer. His widow, Abigail, was appointed guardian of their children, Tamma, Joseph B., Abigail, Isabella F., and Daniel O., of Sherlock Foster, late of Warren, 1837. He d. Feb. 25, 1836. Res., Warren, Mass.

2089. i. LOUIS READ, b. April 12, 1815; m. Charlotte Fay and Julia Gay.

2090. ii. ELIZA ANN, b. April 5, 1813; m., Jan., 1834, Luke Tucker Draper. He was b. 1814; d. Nov., 1867; m., 2d, William Fosket. Ch.: 1. Delia Tucker Draper, b. Mar. 4, 1838; d. May 18, 1897. 2. Elizabeth Foster Draper, b. April 25, 1836. Mrs. Elizabeth Church, Meriden, Conn.

2091. iii. TAMMA, b. ——; m. ——, —— Moody.

2092. iv. JOSEPH BRADFORD, b. ——. A son, William B., res., Rockville, Conn.

2093. v. ABIGAIL, b. ——.

2094. vi. ISABELLA F., b. ——; m. —— Jones.

2095. vii. DANIEL O., b. ——.

MRS. ELIZABETH F. DRAPER.

1147. REV. LUKE BALDWIN FOSTER (Daniel, Isaac, Daniel, Daniel, Abraham, Abraham, Reginald), b., New Braintree, Mass., ——, 1783; m., May 27, 1813, Eunice Knight, of Warren. She d. there in 1822. He was a member of the first class graduated from the Academy in Monson. He entered Burlington College where he studied for the ministry, graduating in 1811; he was ordained as pastor of the church at Rutland, Mass., Feb. 24, 1813. His life work was soon accomplished, for the Lord called him home after a pastorate of four years; he was strongly attached to his church by whom he was greatly beloved. He died, aged 28 years; his wife died in 1822. In Rutland he purchased the farm formerly owned by Rev. Mr. Buckminster.

From History of Rutland, Mass.: "Mr. Foster's ordination, Feb. 8, 1813. At a church meeting, duly convened at the meeting-house, twelve o'clock, at noon—voted, that, whereas, the town has concurred with the church in the invitation of Mr. Luke Baldwin Foster, to take the pastoral charge of the church and congregation in this town, and the said Mr. Foster having given his answer in the affirmative, they will now proceed to invite the following churches, viz.: The church in Shrewsbury, Holden, Paxton, Oakham, Barre, Hubbardston, Princeton, Hardwick, Monson and the Second Church in Wilbraham, to convene with their pastors and delegates to form an Ecclesiastical Council, for the purpose of separating the said Mr. Foster to the work of the Gospel ministry in Rutland. Voted that Dea. Jonas How, Dea. Lilly Flint and Mr. Jonas Reed be a committee to wait on the venerable council with a copy of the proceedings of the church. The ordination was on Feb. 24, 1813, when the Rev. Mr. Luke Baldwin Foster was separated as minister of the church and society in Rutland."

Mrs. Eunice Foster, widow, adm. of the estate of Rev. Luke Baldwin Foster, late of Rutland. June, 1817. Judge Nathaniel Paine.—Worcester Probate.

He d. May 23, 1817. Res., Rutland, Mass.

2096. i. FANNY FIDELIA, b. in 1814; d., 1817.

2097. ii. SAMUEL KNIGHT, b. Sept. 25, 1816; m. Sarah B. Stebbins.

1150. FORDYCE FOSTER (Daniel, Isaac, Daniel, Abraham, Abraham, Reginald), b. New Braintree, Mass , ——, 1780; m., Bangor, Me., Nov. 26, 1807, Elizabeth Wolcott, b. Charlton, Mass., Oct. 15, 1783; d. ——, 1868.

He fitted for college, but did not enter on account of ill health. He read fluently in Greek and Hebrew, and on account of his health went to sea. He made the trip to Calcutta, and was absent nearly a year. This was in 1800 He stopped at Canton, China. While there, in company with one of the sailors, he took one of the ship's boats and visited the city. While there two men took him and the sailor by the arm, and without saying a word, marched them back to their boat. He was a farmer and jeweler and died in Quechee, Vt. He d. Aug. 3, 1827. Res., Southbridge, Mass., and Quechee, Vt.

2098. i. ELIZABETH READ, b. April 26, 1809; d. Aug. 7, 1810.
2099. ii. ELIZA BRADFORD, b. Aug. 4, 1810; d. Oct. 15, 1811.
2100. iii. JANE FRANCES, b. Nov. 7, 1811; m. in 1831, Judge John Porter.

The death of Hon. John Porter, of Hartford, Vt., which recently occurred at his home, in that town, removes an honored and venerable citizen and a prominent public man. The deceased was a veteran county officer and a pioneer Republican. For over thirty-five years he held the office of Probate Judge in Windsor county, being in continuous active service up to the week of his death. He was a faithful and competent official. Judge Porter was a leading Republican and served as a member of the first Republican State Committee. He was also a Fremont Presidential Elector in 1856. He was one of the commissioners having charge of the rebuilding of the State House in 1857. From 1860 to 1872 Judge Porter was a director of the Vermont and Canada railroad, at one time being vice-president. For thirty years he was a director in the Woodstock bank. He was a member of the State Senate from 1836 to 1845. He was a delegate to the Republican National Convention, and was a delegate to the Republican State convention in 1884, when his son, Hon. C. W. Porter, of Montpelier, was nominated for Secretary of State. Judge Porter was born in Hartford in 1798, and lived in his native town for eighty-eight years. He was universally esteemed. He was b. 1798; d., 1886. She resides in Quechee, Vt. Ch.: 1. John Foster Porter, b. May 11, 1832; grad. from Dart. Col. in 1855, and was a prominent lawyer in Troy, N. Y., and d. in 1885. 2. Jane Frances, b. April 6, 1834. Res., Brookline, Mass. 3. Louise Adelaide, b. Sept. 21, 1836. Lives in New Bedford, Mass. 4. Henry Wolcott, b. Aug. 5, 1841; d., 1842. 5. Mary Elizabeth, b. Aug. 21, 1843; d., 1847. 6. Charles Wolcott, b. July 1, 1849; d., 1891. He graduated at Andover, Mass., and was a lawyer in Montpelier, the capital of the State, and was Secretary of State for six years, and died at 42 years.

JUDGE JOHN PORTER.

2101. iv. JAMES WOLCOTT, b. Nov. 16, 1813; m. Harriet Richards.
2102. v. FORDYCE, b. Dec. 10, 1815; m. Adeline J. Tower.
2103. vi. JULIA ELIZA, b. Nov. 9, 1820; m. Capt. Nathan Simmons; a sea captain. Both dead. She d. 1895.
2104. vii. ELIZA WOLCOTT, b. March 12, 1826; m. ——, Asa C. Nichols. Res., ——, Cal. He was a hardware merchant there and died.

1152. ISAAC FOSTER (Isaac, Isaac, Daniel, Abraham, Abraham, Reginald), b. Stafford, Conn., Feb. 12, 1786; m. ——, 1809, Nancy Planting, his own cousin, b. 1786; d. Oct., 1823, in Marsfield, Conn.; m., 2d, Jan. 3, 1824, Mary Mather, of Ogden, N. Y.; d. Dec. 29, 1851. Res., Spencerport, N. Y.

1156. JAMES GARDNER FOSTER (John, Isaac, Daniel, Abraham, Abraham, Reginald), b. Paxton, Mass., Aug. 31, 1786; m. —— ——. He resided in Athens in 1842. Res., Athens, N. Y.

2105. i. NINA, b. ——.
2106. ii. LOUISA, b. ——.
2107. iii. MARY, b. ——.

1172. AMOS FOSTER (Amos, Amos, Amos, Benjamin, Abraham, Reginald), b. Tewksbury, Mass., May 30, 1785; m. Nov. 23, 1813, Rhoda Foster, b. 1787. She d. June 3, 1846. He d. Sept. 20, 1863. Res., Tewksbury, Mass.

2108. i. ELIZABETH, b. Feb. 10, 1816; d. Feb. 13, 1816.
2109. ii. OLIVER, b. July 2, 1818; m. Abbie Hill.
2110. iii. RHODA, b. Aug. 30, 1819; m., April 26, 1840, George W. Maynard. She d. Feb. 26, 1884. A son, Charles H., resides in Chicago, Ill.
2111. iv. HANNAH, b. Dec. 1, 1820; m. —— Frost. Res., Lawrence, Mass., 48 Washington St.

1174. ZEPHANIAH KITTERIDGE FOSTER (Amos, Amos, Amos, Benjamin, Abraham, Reginald), b. Tewksbury, Mass., Sept. 22, 1791; m. ——, 1822, Mercy T. Trull, b. ——, 1793; d. ——, 1885. He was a farmer.

Zephaniah, Tewksbury; letter, date Nov. 21, 1837; ex. same; wife, Mercy. Ch.: Elizabeth O., Enoch, Joel, John T., Mary Ann, Zephaniah P.; all minors.

Mercy, Tewksbury; will date April 18, 1867. Prob. Sept. 20, 1881. Ch.: Mary Ann Fanner, wife of Joseph Fanner, of Tewksbury; Zephaniah P. Foster and John T. Foster, of Tewksbury; Joel Foster, of Methuen; Enoch Foster, of Tewksbury; Elizabeth O., wife of Nathaniel P. Cole, of San Francisco, Cal.

He d. Sept. 11, 1837. Res., Tewksbury, Mass.

2112. i. ENOCH, b. April 22, 1831; m. Mary J. Frost.
2113. ii. MARY ANN, b. March 9, 1823; m. Aug. 26, 1843, Joseph S. Farmer. Res., T.
2114. iii. ZEPHANIAH P., b. Dec. 26, 1824; m. Emily B. Carleton.
2115. iv. JOHN T., b. May 20, 1827; m. Susan H. Chandler.
2116. v. JOEL, b. March 3, 1829; m. Sarah M. Gray.
2117. vi. ELIZABETH O., b. July 30, 1833; m., April 20, 1855, Nathaniel P. Cole. Res., San Francisco, Cal.

1177. WILLIAM FOSTER (William, Amos, Amos, Benjamin, Abraham, Reginald), b. Tewksbury, Mass., Feb. 9, 1789; m. ——, Anna ——. Res., Tewksbury, Mass.

2118. i. MARY ANN, b. Oct. 17, 1809.
2119. ii. CHARLES, b. Feb. 23, 1813.
2120. iii. LUCY SAUNDERS, b. Aug. 5, 1815.

1178-2. NATHAN FOSTER (Nathan, Amos, Amos, Benjamin, Abraham, Reginald), b. Norway, Me., April 9, 1794; m. in Tewksbury, Mass., Mrs. Sarah (Gibson) Wheelock, b., Dunstable, Mass., Dec. 30, 1791; d., Nashua, N. H., July 13, 1882. He was born on the old place in Norway, Me., where he resided until a young man, when he went to Tewksbury, Mass., and was there married. His wife had two little sons, by a former husband. They had six children. The four oldest were born in Tewksbury, and the other two in Norway, to which place he afterward moved, and ever after resided. Was a soldier in the War of 1812, in the Company of Capt. Amos Town. Was a farmer, often selectman, a Methodist, Whig, and a very intelligent man. He died of a fever, Jan. 9, 1837. Res., Norway, Me.

Correction for the Foster Family
1899. p. 330

Josephine Augusta Foster
B. Oct. 19 1821
D. Nov. 4 1894
M. Oct. 23 1845
Stephen Romer Roe
B. Oct. 15 1808
D. Dec. 22 1885
Charles Francis Roe
B. May 1 1848
M. July 29 1874
Katherine Bissell Bogert
B. Sept 16 1852
James Gardiner Foster
Paxton, Ct.
B. Aug. 31 1786
D. Oct. 29 1864
M. May 10 1810
Ann E. Colsen -Athens, N.Y.
B. Jan 19 1789
D. Feb. 3 1867
Josephine Auguta Foster)
Stephen Romer Roe)

Made by Mrs. C. F. Roe,
35 E. 37th. St. City.

2121. i. WALTER BAILEY, b. Norway, Me., Jan. 17, 1817; d. St. Louis, Mo., March 31, 1871, unm.
2122. ii. HANNAH AUSTIN, b. Sept. 15, 1824; m. Jonathan Morse, at Lowell, May 1, 1851. She d., Boston, July 8, 1864.
2123. iii. CALVIN BRADLEY, b. 1825; d. July 4, 1837, at Norway, Me. He was drowned accidentally while in bathing with other boys, getting beyond his depth.
2124. iv. AMOS, b. Oct. 10, 1827; m. Annie Olivia Seavey.
2125. v. LEONA EMILY, b. Aug. 13, 1831, Norway, Me.; m., July 13, 1859, Alfred M. Norton, of Nashua, N. H.
2126. vi. ELLEN FRANCES, b. April 2, 1833; m., Sept. 29, 1852, Charles S. Whitehouse, of Genio, N. H. Those deceased did not leave any children.

1182-2. CAPT. JEREMIAH FOSTER (Nathan, Amos, Amos, Benjamin, Abraham, Reginald), b. Norway, Me., Sept. 23, 1797; m. — — ——. He was captain of the North Norway military company. Jeremiah Foster, Jr., served as private in Company E, First Maine Regt. Vols. for three months. He enlisted in Co. E, Fourteenth Maine Regt. in 1861 and was discharged for disability; was mustered in with Co. G, Twenty-ninth Maine Regt. in 1863 and was discharged for disability in 1864. Res., Norway, Me.

2127. i. JEREMIAH, b. ——.
2128. ii. WILLIAM HENRY, b. ——; d.; 2 ch. and widow res. Hyde Park, Mass.

1183-2. WILLIAM FOSTER (Nathan, Amos, Amos, Benjamin, Abraham, Reginald), b. Norway, Me., April 5, 1799; m. there May 26, 1830, Calista Wood, b. July 16, 1809; d. Oct. 19, 1881. William, son of Nathan Foster, the early settler, was born on the farm at Norway Center, April 5, 1799, where he died, January 26, 1884. Mr. Foster came of a family which had many of those characteristics that distinguished the early settlers of this town. While a boy, he started out for himself by apprenticing himself to Daniel Town, the veteran blacksmith, where he soon became proficient in the art. Having served his time, he started on foot for Massachusetts, and on his arrival there he found employment in doing the iron work in a shipyard. He afterward received an invitation from Mr. Town to return to Norway and go into partnership with him, which he accepted. About the year 1829 he built a shop at Frost's Corner, got married and commenced life in earnest. His industry and thrift resulted in the acquisition of a competence which served to render comfortable his later years. In 1844 he gave up the shop and went to farming on the land where he spent the remainder of his life, save a few years at South Paris, where he moved, that his children might enjoy better educational advantages, and where he served as postmaster. He returned to Norway in 1860. He joined Oxford lodge of Masons in 1824, and ever had a strong attachment to the order. By his wife, Calista Wood, of Waterford, he had seven children, four of whom survived him. He died January 26, 1884. Res., Norway, Me.

2129. i. WILLIAM FRANKLIN, b. Jan. 14, 1833; m. Almira H. Smith.
2130. ii. NATHAN ALBERT, b. Oct. 4, 1835; m. Harriet N. Grover.
2131. iii. OLIVE S., b. Dec. 7, 1830; m. Jan., 1850, Theodore Lyman Lasselle, b. Oct. 26, 1826. She d. March 24, 1867; a son is George, in Norway; William F. Lasselle, Leominster, Mass.
2132. iv. MIRIAM HOBBS, b. July 23, 1839; m. April 24, 1862, Leon M. Peirce, 247 Union street, Springfield, Mass. L. M. Peirce was born in West Boylston, Mass., June 21, 1833, and graduated at Colby University. He was a successful high school teacher for ten years, since which time he has been in the music business in Springfield, Mass., which has grown extensively under his management. Ch.: 1. Leona May, b. Aug. 4, 1863. Res., 247 Union street. 2. William Foster, b. Feb. 3, 1868.

[Mount Vernon, Ohio, Republic, April 1, 1896.]

President-elect of Kenyon. A biographical sketch of the Rev. William Foster Peirce, the new head of Gambier's educational interests. His election everywhere well received, and his acceptance hoped for and expected—Interested in all Gambier institutions. The election of Professor Peirce to the presidency of Kenyon has been received with great satisfaction, not only in Gambier and Mount Vernon, but by all friends of Kenyon. His name was not presented to the trustees by the nominating committee, but his election was unanimous; and one of the trustees has described their deliberations as pervaded by a solemnity which seemed directly due to the guiding presence of a Higher Power.

REV. WILLIAM FOSTER PEIRCE.

If this be so, then all friends of Gambier can rest assured that no mistake has been made, and that in due time a better and a greater work than ever before will be inaugurated upon the hill.

Professor Peirce was waited upon at Gambier last Friday evening by the executive committee of the trustees, Hon. C. Delano and Rev. G. F. Smythe, of this city, and Chas. E. Burr and T. P. Linn, of Columbus, and formally notified of his election. While he will probably not return them a formal answer for a couple of weeks, the Republican feels warranted by all the circumstances in stating that it is practically certain that he will accept the trust.

If he accepts the office, William Foster Peirce will probably be the youngest college president in the United States. He is only twenty-eight years old, having been born at Chicopee Falls, Mass., February 3, 1868.

The son of Mr. L. M. Peirce, of Springfield, Mass., a large dealer in pianos and organs, he traces his lineage back to John "Peers," who came from England to Massachusetts in 1636. The name since then has been variously spelled. For 250 years the family has been of the traditional orthodox New England faith, known as Congregational. Professor Peirce is, so far as he knows, the only churchman in his large family, on either his father's or mother's side.

At the Springfield High School he was prepared for college, entering Amherst at the early age of sixteen. Although he took the classical course he was greatly interested in natural science, and, until his senior year he expected to become a practical chemist. For two summers during his course he attended the Amherst Summer School, doing laboratory work in science. But in his senior year he elected the study of philosophy with Prof. Garman, who is an inspiration to every Amherst student, and he discovered a decided taste for philosophy, and determined to make the teaching of philosophy his profession. At Amherst he had the honor to be elected to the Senior Scientific Society and to the Phi Beta Kappa Society, and these elections well indicate his all-around scholarship.

Being graduated in 1888, he spent a year in business with his father, in which he gained a practical knowledge of book-keeping and much valuable experience. In 1889 he entered for a year the Graduate school of Cornell University, for the study of philosophy and economics. His thesis for the degree of M. A. was presented to his alma mater instead of to Cornell. It was a masterly production on the "Methods of Inducing Introspective Power: one Aspect of the Pedagogics of Psychology." It has since been published as a monograph by the Ohio University.

After the course at Cornell, Professor Peirce taught in a boys' boarding school in Northern Massachusetts. In June, 1891, he was married to Miss Louise Fagan, of Hackettstown, N. J., the happy event being the outcome of an acquaintance and attachment formed in the Graduate school at Cornell. At the age of eighteen Miss Fagan was graduated from Vassar College. After a year of graduate work at Vassar in philosophy and English she went to Cornell at the same time as Professor Peirce, for further work on these lines.

In January, 1892, Professor Peirce came to the Ohio University at Athens as substitute for the professor of psychology and pedagogy. His work there was so acceptable that the chair of philosophy and ethics was created for him, and he was elected to it. But at the same time he was considering the chair of history and economics in the University of Colorado, and the Spencer and Wolfe professorship of mental and moral philosophy at Kenyon. Although, of the three positions the one at Kenyon was much the least attractive financially, the high reputation of Kenyon in the East and the fact that it was the college of his church, determined him to come to Gambier.

He has steadily grown in the esteem of his colleagues and acquaintances. With unusual mental strength and attainments he unites unusual loveliness of character and grace of manner. A profound scholar, he is a man of the times, awake to present day interests. His interest in Kenyon is deep and strong. In the spring of 1893 he wrote for the University Magazine, of New York, some elaborate articles on the college, which were published with handsome illustrations. His ideals for the college are high, and his interest in all the departments of the institution is intense. It is safe to say that if his ideals can be realized, new life will be infused into all of them. He appreciates the academy as a high-class preparatory school, and has the cordial respect and regard of the regent and masters. He appreciates the purpose and opportunity of Bexley Hall, having himself been ordained to the diaconate in June, 1894, and expecting soon to be advanced to the priesthood. He will have the cordial co-operation of the Bexley professors. Professor Peirce is a member of the County Teachers' Association and also of the State Teachers' Association. In the Ohio College Association at Sandusky last summer he opened the debate on Corrections for Cramming. Of the learned society for Psychological and pedagogical inquiry, the membership of which is limited to twenty-five specialists, Professor Peirce is a member and is also its secretary and treasurer.

With a high place already among profound and accurate scholars Professor Peirce nevertheless takes a very active interest in all forms of athletic exercises, and is the star tennis player of Gambier. He can umpire a game of football or baseball acceptably, and his genuine interest in such things brings him very close to the hearts of the students.

For three months last summer in the absence of the rector, Professor Peirce conducted the services at St. Paul's church, this city, and made many warm friends among our citizens, who will wish him all success and every blessing in the great work before him.

2133. v. HANNAH MARIA, b. Jan. 17, 1845; d. July 4, 1870.
2134. vi. CHARLES C., b. Dec. 7, 1846; m. Dora E. Wheeler.
2135. vii. GEORGE W., b. July 10, 1849; m. Elizabeth P. Witt.

1190-2. LUTHER FARRER FOSTER (Nathan, Amos, Amos, Benjamin, Abraham, Reginald), b. Norway, Me., March 3, 1815; m. there April 9, 1839, Eunice B. Millet, b. April 15, 1817; d. Dec. 2, 1865. He was a blacksmith. He d. May 14, 1853. Res., Norway, Me.

2136. i. WALLACE VALENTINE, b. Jan. 13, 1840; m. Abbie Thomas.
2137. ii. HELEN AUGUSTA, b. Jan. 1, 1842; m. L. L. Andrews. Res., Cumberland Mills, Me. 1 ch., Dora E. m., Charles Elwell. Res., Westbrook, Me.
2138. iii. EUNICE E., b. Feb. 1, 1847; m. Nov., 1869, J. W. Bacon. 1 ch., Mary J.; unm.
2139. iv. LIZZIE E., b. June 5, 1849; d. unm.
2140. v. SARAH H., b. Jan. 29, 1853; m. June 1, 1872, G. A. Morse. Ch.: 1. Etta A. 2. Luther G. 3. Harold A.
2141. vi. MARTHA JANE, b. March 24, 1845; m. Dec. 29, 1868, Jason F. Rowe, b. Aug. 10, 1841. He is a cordwainer. Res., Norway, Me. Ch.: 1. Bessie M. Rowe, b. May 31, 1871; m. Feb. 20, 1896, Eugene L. Hutchins. Res., Rochester, N. H.

1191. AMOS P. FOSTER (Benjamin, Asael, Gideon, Benjamin, Abraham, Reginald), b. Brighton, Me., Oct. 11, 1804; m. Mrs. Annie Knight, of Otisfield. She d. ——, 1869. He settled in Harrison. He was a farmer by occupation, living where Samuel Pitts now lives on the Pond road. Mr. Foster removed to Otisfield some years since, where his wife died in 1869. Res., Harrison, Me.

2142. i. BENJAMIN, b. ——; m. Susan E. Clark.
2143. ii. ABIGAIL, b. ——; d. young.
2144. iii. ANN, b. ——; unm. Res., Massachusetts.
2145. iv. KATE, b. ——; m. Dexter Andrews, of Otisfield. Res., Norway, Me.

1192. BENJAMIN S. FOSTER (Benjamin, Asael, Gideon, Benjamin, Abraham Reginald), b. June 25, 1806, Harrison, Me.; m. Jan. 15, 1832, Esther T. Cushman, b. May 11, 1803; d. May 22, 1885. He resided on the homestead of his father. He d. April 14, 1867. Res., Harrison, Me.

2146. i. CYRUS K., b. Jan. 12, 1833; m. Mary E. Morrow.
2147. ii. EZRA T., b. May 11, 1834; m., 1861, Marrilla Morrow. Res., Harrison, in the same house with his brother Cyrus.
2148. iii. CHARLES W., b. Feb. 3, 1836; m. Frances A. Libbey.
2149. iv. NELLIE C., b. ——; m. Fuller. Res., Cotuit, Mass.

1194. THOMAS VEASEY FOSTER (Benjamin, Asael, Gideon, Benjamin, Abraham, Reginald), b. Dec. 17, 1810; m., June 8, 1828, Mary Ann Phinney; m. 2d, Nov. 29, 1850, Alvilda G. Foster (his cousin), dau. of Asael. Mr. Foster settled in Stoneham after a short residence in Harrison, and has speculated in land and horses. Has had issue; five children. Res., Stoneham, Mass.

2150. i. STEPHEN, who m. Emma Robinson; now dead.
2151. ii. EMELINE, m. —— Purington, of Lynn, Mass.; now dead.
2152. iii. ABIGAIL, m. to Eben Leach, of Portland.
2153. iv. ADALINE, m. to Augustus Baker.
2154. v. NANCY, b. Aug. 25, 1813.

1195. VALENTINE LOWELL FOSTER (Benjamin, Asael, Gideon, Benjamin, Abraham, Reginald), b. Aug. 7, 1815; m. Julia Scribner; m. 2d., ——, Ellen Blake; m. 3d, ——, Susan Newcomb. He also lived in South Harrison, and a farmer by occupation, although a lumber dealer to some extent. He had issue; six children. Res., Harrison, Me.

2155. i. JOSEPH, b. March 1, 1843; m. Hannah Edson, of Harrison, and resides in that town.
2156. ii. ALBERT, b. July 9, 1845; d. Jan. 11, 1847.
2157. iii. MARY, b. Dec. 12, 1847; m. —— Hamblin.
2158. iv. FRANK.
2159. v. ELLEN, and one other.

1196. GEORGE FOSTER (Benjamin, Asael, Gideon, Benjamin, Abraham, Reginald), b. ——, 1817; m. Ann Osgood, of Bridgton, Me. (own cousin). George was first a trader in a small store at Harrison village; also a land speculator for several years in Harrison, then moved to Portland, Me. He finally became quite wealthy. He kept a large wholesale flour store in Portland, and dealt largely in lumber out West and up in New Hampshire. He has issue; four children. She was a very estimable lady of many friends wherever she lived and was beloved by all who knew her. Res., Portland, Me.

2160. i. CLINTON, b. ——; d. ——.
2161. ii. ARTHUR, b. ——; d. ——.
2162. iii. ROSE, b. ——; d. ——.
2163. iv. EMMA, b. ——.

1199. DAVID FOSTER (Philemon, Philemon, Jonathan, Caleb, Abraham, Reginald), b. Ipswich, Mass., Aug. 23, 1809; m. there July 19, 1831, Angelina Webster Pingree, b. Feb. 21, 1812; d. Jan. 12, 1879. He d. Sept. 4, 1892. Res., Ipswich, Mass.

2164. i. ELIZABETH B., b. Sept. 15, 1832; m. Jan. 31, 1854, —— Wiley. She d. June 6, 1876. A son is Elmer H. Res., Ipswich, Mass. P. O. box 221.
2165. ii. ANGELINA A., b. May 6, 1834 Res., 35 Bow street, Beverly, Mass.
2166. iii. SOLOMON L., b Sept. 27, 1836; m. Mary A. Langley.
2167. iv. OLIVE J., b. April 11, 1839; m. April 28, 1852, —— Knowlton. Res., 14 St. Peter street, Salem, Mass.
2168. v. DAVID C., b. March 28, 1846; d. Sept. 13, 1848
2169. vi. ELEANOR A., b May 6, 1850. Res., 35 Bow street, Beverly, Mass.
2170 vii. CYNTHIA P., b. March 13, 1854; m. June 30, 1874, Dennison Moore. Res., Boxford, Mass.

1204. CYRUS FOSTER (Philemon, Philemon, Jonathan, Caleb, Abraham Reginald), b. Ipswich, Mass., July 27, 1823; m. ——, Martha Potter. He d. March 7, 1898. Res., Ipswich, Mass.

2171. i. CYRUS E., b. ——. Res., Roslindale, Mass.

1205. PHILEMON CUMMINGS FOSTER (Philemon, Philemon, Jonathan, Caleb, Abraham, Reginald), b. Ipswich, Mass., March 23, 1805; m. Eliza Felton; m. 2d., Ipswich, Hannah Pickard, b. Dec. 21, 1820. Res., Georgetown. Philemon Cummings Foster was the second child of Philemon Foster, Jr., and Naby Hobbs, His occupations were shoemaker and farmer. He lived the most of his life in Ipswich, Rowley and Georgetown, and died in Georgetown, and was buried in Ipswich, Mass. He d. Sept. 1, 1876. Res., Georgetown, Mass.

2172. i. ELIZA MARY, b. ——; m. Benjamin Fuller. Res., Boxford, Mass.
2173. ii. WALTER CUMMINGS, b. ——; d. ——.
2174. iii. RICHARD R., b. Nov. 11, 1842; m. Harriet E. Towle.
2175. iv. HANNAH ANGELIA, b. Oct. 1, 1845; m. Daniel Woodbridge Dresser. Res., Rowley.
2176. v. BENJAMIN FRANKLIN, b. Feb. 12, 1849; m. Jemima Alfretta Dexter.
2177. vi. DAVID PHILEMON, b. Nov. 21, 1853; unm. Res., Rowley, Mass.

1207. REV. JOSEPH COGGIN FOSTER, D. D., A. M. (Moses, Moses, Jonathan, Caleb, Abraham, Reginald), b. Milford, N. H., April 11, 1818, in the second house built by his grandfather, Moses Foster, of Ipswich; m. 1st., April 14, 1843, Abigail Ann Eaton, dau. of Dea. Washington and Hannah (Low) Eaton, of East Weare, N. H., who d. Sept. 11, 1864, and 2d. May 1, 1866, Julia Ann Gould, dau. of Dea. John Gould, of Dover, N. H., b. 1819.

Rev. Joseph Coggin Foster, D. D., was born in Milford, N. H., April 11, 1818. On his father's side he was in the sixth generation from the emigrant, Reginald Foster of 1638, through Abraham, Caleb, Jonathan, Moses, Moses. Grandmother, Mary Fuller. Mother, Fanny Coggin. When about sixteen years old, he became an apprentice in the printing-office of the Farmers' Cabinet, Amherst, N. H., where he derived great advantages from the exchange list of periodicals and from a bookstore connected with the office. From there he went to the Literary and Theological Institution, now Colgate University, Hamilton, N. Y. In August, 1841, he graduated at the New Hampton Theological Institution, New Hampshire, having devoted about five years to studies preparatory to the gospel ministry. His first pastorate was in Brattleboro, Vt., where he was ordained pastor of the Baptist church, January 19, 1843. In this position he remained till July, 1856—more than thirteen and a half years. From this place he went directly to Beverly,

Mass., where he was installed as pastor of the First Baptist church, August 7, 1856. This pastorate continued until January, 1873—about sixteen and a half years. From this place he removed to Randolph, Mass., where he was installed pastor of the Baptist church January 23, 1873. This pastorate continued till January, 1882—nine years. He then became associate editor of the Watchman, Boston, the Baptist paper of New England. He still remains connected with that paper, March 9, 1898, having been engaged in this service more than sixteen years. During the nearly forty years of his work as pastor of these churches he baptized 331 candidates, and served on town school committees twenty-nine successive years. He received the honorary degree of A. M. from Brown University, Providence, R. I., in 1857, and the honorary degree of D. D. from the Central University, of Iowa, at Pella, Ia., in 1883. He saw much development of the churches to which he ministered, as shown by various kinds of efficiency, including benevolent contributions and extensive improvement of church property. In two instances superior houses of worship were built under his administration. He was actively engaged in educational and denominational work, holding responsible positions on various boards, and performing much official, secretarial and financial services. Some of his publications have had extensive circulation. He has written much for the periodical press aside from his editorial work. He is now, March 9, 1898, within about one month of eighty years of age.

The Boston Transcript, in a lengthy obituary notice, says: "From the beginning he was actively engaged in educational and denominational work. He served on town school committees nearly thirty successive years, and for a considerable number of years he was chairman of the school committee in Beverly, up to the time of his removal from the town. When he left the town, he had just been re-elected for three years. In Randolph he was one of the trustees of the public library from its opening in 1884, as long as he remained in the town, being vice-president most of the many years. He held various responsible positions on boards of benevolent societies, especially in sectarial and financial service. He was recording secretary of the Northern Baptist Educational Society fourteen years, from 1868 to 1882, and treasurer of the conference of Baptist ministers in Massachusetts thirty-one years, from 1865 to 1896, in which time he had charge of about $100,000 for the benefit of indigent, aged and disabled Baptist ministers. He served three years as a member of the board of the American Baptist Missionary Union, from 1852 to 1855. For twenty-two successive years he never attended the association to which his church belonged without being either clerk or moderator. Some of his publications have had extensive circulation, one of which, a tract on "Baptism and Communion," has been in great demand, several hundred thousand copies having been printed. An eight-page tract on "Responsibilities for Intemperance," was published by the National Temperance Society in New York and placed among their standard works. From an early period of his life he wrote for newspapers, and he continued to do so through his years as a student and a pastor. For three years he wrote a weekly Boston letter for the Watch Tower, a Baptist paper in New York. In December, 1881, he became assistant editor of the Watchman, and remained upon the editorial staff for more than fourteen years, till December, 1896. The honorary degree of A. M. was conferred upon him by Brown University in 1857, and of D. D. by Central University at Pella, Ia., in 1883."

The will of Rev. Joseph C. Foster, late of Randolph, contains the following public bequests: One thousand dollars each to the American Home Baptist Mission Society of New York and the American Baptist Missionary Union of Boston, said bequests to be paid on the death of the testator's wife, and $300 to the conference of Baptist ministers in Massachusetts. On the death of his wife a trust fund, of which she has the income during life, is to be divided share and share alike, among the following societies: The Baptist Education Society of New York, for the benefit of the Hamilton Theological Seminary; Conference of Baptist Ministers in Massachusetts; the Massachusetts Baptist Convention and the Northern Baptist Education Society. The testator names as executors of his will his wife, Julia G. Foster, his son, William E. Foster, and Francis I. Hazelwood, D. D., the district secretary of the Baptist Home Missionary Society. The will was drawn January 18, 1893. He died in Augusta, Ga., March 16, 1899. Residence, Randolph, Mass.

2178. i. WILLIAM EATON, b. June 2, 1851; m. Julia Appleton.

1208. REUBEN FULLER FOSTER (Moses, Moses, Jonathan, Caleb, Abraham, Reginald), b. Jan. 19, 1821, in Milford, N. H.; m., Nov. 9, 1843, Sarah Elizabeth Ames, dau. of William Ames, of Hollis, N. H. He early removed to Concord,

N. H., where he engaged in the hardware business, and later, largely in real estate. He d. May 25, 1856, in Concord. She m., 2d, Oct. 4, 1864, Deacon Ireneus Hamilton, of Lyme, N. H., who d. Aug. 19, 1876.

2179. i. HARRIET BROOKS, b. Sept. 19, 1847; d. Aug. 4, 1849.
2180. ii. HENRY FULLER, b. July 17, 1849; d. Aug. 21, 1850.
2181. iii. CHARLES BROOKS, b. May 16, 1851; m., Sept. 16, 1875, Grace Ellen Hunt, dau. of Albon Hunt, of Concord, N. H.

1209. DEA. JOHN EVERETT FOSTER (Moses, Moses, Jonathan, Caleb, Abraham, Reginald), b. May 17, 1824, in Milford in the house in which his grandfather, his father, he himself, and his son, have successively lived; m., Feb. 15, 1848, Sophia Phelps Farley, dau. of Jesse Farley, of Hollis, N. H.

DEACON JOHN E. FOSTER.

Deacon and Mrs. John E. Foster celebrated their golden wedding Tuesday afternoon and evening, Feb. 15, 1898, at Milford, N. H., a very large company of friends and relatives being present. The reception was at their residence, on Federal hill, and among those present were Mr. and Mrs. Jefferson Farley, of Hollis, who, fifty years ago, stood as groomsman and bridesmaid when Mr. and Mrs. Foster were united in marriage, and who aided in the reception of the guests. Letters of regret were received from Governor Ramsdell, Prof. A. E. Dolbear of Tufts College, the Rev. C. H. Thornton, field secretary of the Congregational Building society of Chicago; W. E. Foster, librarian of the Providence public library; Mrs. Humphrey Moore, of Milford, and Mrs. W. E. Hidden. The presents were very numerous, over $100 in gold being received, $50 of which was from the Congregational church. Three original poems were read by Mrs. B. F. Foster, one of which was written by Jesse Webster Foster, a grandson, and was pronounced very meritorious. Deacon John E. Foster was born where he now resides, and was the son of Moses and Fanny (Coggin) Foster, who, in early life, came here from Massachusetts and bought the farm which ever since has remained in the family. The family history in this country dates back to 1630, when Reginald Foster came over from England and settled in Massachusetts. Of the children of Moses Foster four are still living—the Rev. Joseph C. Foster of Randolph, Mass., Moses F. and Benjamin F. Foster and Deacon J. E. Foster, who are residents of Milford. Mr. Foster acquired his education in the public schools of this town and the Literary and Scientific Institute of Hancock. In early life he taught school in Amherst and in Illinois, and later was engaged, for a time, in probate business in Hillsborough. A large portion of his life, however, has been devoted to agricultural pursuits, and at 74 years of age is still a prosperous and successful farmer. For twenty-five years a deacon of the Congregational church, he has always been an earnest worker for the religious and educational development of his town and has been an active agent in the collection of data for the forthcoming history of the town. Politically, he has been a life-long Republican. Fanny (Coggin) Foster, who, for fifty years, has shared the joys and sorrows of the good deacon's home life, and contributed very largely to its comfort and happiness, was one of ten children born to Jesse and Mary (Phelps) Farley, of Hollis, her great-grandfather Farley moving from Bedford to Hollis and establishing his home there in the primeval wilderness. Of the ten children three, besides Mrs. Foster, are still living, namely: John, Alfred and Jefferson Farley, all residents of Hollis at the present time. Mr. and Mrs. Foster have two children, George E. Foster, managing editor of the Ithaca, N. Y., Democrat, and Flora S., wife of George N. Woodward, of this town. Res., Milford, N. H.

2182. i. GEORGE EVERETT, b. Aug. 27, 1849; m. Mary Burrit.
2183. ii. FLORA SOPHIA, b. April 18, 1866; m., Oct. 27, 1886, George N. Woodward, of Nashua, N. H., son of Aaron B. Woodward, of Amherst, N. H.

1210. MOSES FREEMAN FOSTER (Moses, Moses, Jonathan, Caleb, Abraham, Reginald), b. Jan. 6, 1832, in Milford, N. H.; m., Sept. 13, 1860. Adelaide Lutheria Doane, dau. of Zenas Doane, of Lawrence, Mass. From 1850 to 1858 he was connected with various manufacturing establishments in Massachusetts, and since 1858 has resided chiefly in the South, being engaged in the business of cotton manufacturing. He was from 1870 to 1876 superintendent of the Langley Manufacturing Co., Langley, S. C., but is now living in Milford, N. H.

2184. i. FANNY DOANE, b. April 16, 1862; m., Jan. 6, 1897, Ralph C. Bartlett.

1212. BENJAMIN FRANKLIN FOSTER (Moses, Moses, Jonathan, Caleb, Abraham, Reginald), b. Oct. 8, 1846, in Milford, N. H.; m., May 25, 1869, Celia Frances Peabody, daughter of Ezra Brown Peabody, of Milford, a descendant of Reginald Foster, through his daughter Mary Foster, who m. Lieut. Francis Peabody, of Topsfield, as stated elsewhere.

2185. i. HATTIE MARIA, b. Aug. 3, 1873.

1216. MAJOR SAMUEL BROOKS FOSTER (Isaac P., Moses, Jonathan, Caleb, Abraham, Reginald), b. July 19, 1819, in Salem; m., Feb. 21, 1842, Mary Haraden Worcester, dau. of Rev. Samuel Worcester, D. D., of Salem. He was engaged in business in Salem, and afterward in Boston from 1862 till his death in 1872. He held a commission as Major in the Salem Cadets, and was an active member of the Ancient and Honorable Artillery company, of Boston, from 1853. He d. March 13, 1872, in Boston. She d. Nov. 4, 1872.

2186. i. SAMUEL WORCESTER, b. July 16, 1844.
2187. ii. MARY LOUISA, b. July 24, 1846; d. in 1847.
2188. iii. HARRIET, b. Dec. 4, 1849; d. April 3, 1867.
2189. iv. ANNA JANE, b. June 24, 1853; d. Oct. 26, 1872.

1221. THOMAS D. FOSTER (William, Nathan, Caleb, Caleb, Abraham, Reginald), b. Bristol, Me., ——, 1782; m. Montville, Dec. 12, 1812, Joanna Carter, b. ——, 1793; d. Unity, Me., Dec. 14, 1885. He d. July 30, 1835. Res., Montville, Me.

2191. i. THOMAS ALBERT, b. Feb. 20, 1827; m. Eliza McManus, Adelaide Woodman and Mary Woodman.
2191. ii. ESTHER CARTER, b. Sept. 13, 1815; m. in Unity, Me., in 1843, John Perley, b. Mar. 15, 1812; d. May 20, 1895. She d. Oct. 30, 1890, leaving Eliza Jane Perley, a teacher; Res., Ontario, Cal.; Roscoe John Perley; Res., Unity, Me., and Mrs. Helen Perley Clark, who had three children, Amy G., Gretchen and Effie.
2192. iii. ANN C., b. ——; m. —— Bean; s. p.
2193. iv. ELIZA J., b. ——; m. —— Carter. She d., leaving three children —one is Mrs. Esther Ann Carter. Res., Belfast, Me.
2194. v. EBENEZER, b. ——; m. ——.

1222. EBENEZER FOSTER (William, Nathan, Caleb, Caleb, Abraham, Reginald), b. Bristol, Me., ——, 1780; m., Dec. 21, 1801, Margaret Bates, b. ——, 1780; d. Knox, Me., 1876. He d. Feb. 1, 1811. Res., Montville, Me.

2195. i. DANIEL, b. Dec. 5, 1802; m. Sarah Hussey.
2196. ii. ELIZABETH, b. ——; m. —— Watts.
2197. iii. SUSAN, b. ——; m. —— Watts. Ch.: 1. John J. Watts, Freedom, Me. 2. Mrs. Mary Emery, Lowell, Mass.

1224. THOMAS FOSTER (John, Nathan, Caleb, Caleb, Abraham, Reginald), b. Bristol, Me., July 16, 1789; m. there June 10, 1813, Jane Sproul, b. Dec. 30, 1793; d. July 20, 1868. Was an inholder. Thomas was one of the men who helped to garrison the fort at Bristol during the war of 1812. Being at that time a young married man, his wife, with her infant in her arms, sat on the hills all day Sunday watching the fight. The English officer often coming to their farm house for pork, eggs, etc., that they wanted, and returning to their ships in boats. At the age of 87 he walked from Castine, Me., to Ellsworth, Me., not because he was obliged to, but for a whim. This was printed in all the leading Maine papers. He was for many years the proprietor of the Old Ellsworth House, and after him his son Joseph kept it until his health failed. He had twelve children. He d. April 18, 1887. Res., Bristol and Ellsworth, Me.

2198. i. EMELINE N., b. Feb. 16, 1823; m., March 12, 1863, Willard Deveraux. Res., s. p., Castine, Me.

2199. ii. CAROLINE, b. Jan. 22, 1814; m. in Bristol, Me., Capt. William McFarland. Res., South Bristol, Me., b. 1808; d. Pensacola, Fla., June 26, 1848. Ch.: 1. Bambridge; Res., South Bristol. 2. Leander; Res., South Bristol. 3. William Adison, b. Oct. 18, 1840; Res., South Bristol. 4. Abby Jane; m. Mr. Thorp; Res., South Bristol.
2200. iii. ZABUD, b. July 16, 1816; m. Nancy B. Miller.
2201. iv. MARY JANE, b. April 11, 1818; m., Jan. 31, 1843, Samuel Kelsey, of Bristol, Me. He was b. June 15, 1812; d. Jan. 2, 1880. Was a ship builder. She d. July 30, 1892. Ch.: 1. William T., b. Oct. 25, 1847; m. Sarah E. Hodgdon. Res., South Bristol, Me. Five children. 2. Frances M.; a dau. is Mabel B. Barlow, East Boothbay, Me. 3. Edward J.; d., s. p.
2202. v. ELIZA P., b. May 13, 1824; m. John Noyes, of Boston. She d. s. p. He was a soldier in the Civil War.
2203. vi. ABBIE, b. Jan. 4, 1820; m. —— Hunnewell and Capt. Horatio Hodgdon. Res., Castine; s. p.
2204. vii. STETSON, b. Aug. 26, 1828; m. Margaret Nichol.
2205. viii. JOSEPH H., b. ——, 1838; m. Annie Black.
2206. ix. THOMAS A., b. Sept. 7, 1830; m. Matilda S. Thompson.
2207. x. ARNOLD B., b. Nov. 25, 1826; d. unm.
2208. xi. FRANCIS L., b. Aug. 14, 1832; d. young unm.
2209. xii. JOSEPH H., b. ——; d. ——.

1227. ALEXANDER ROBINSON FOSTER (John, Nathan, Caleb, Caleb, Abraham, Reginald), b. Bristol, Me. ——; m. ——, Betsey Thurston, dau. of Ambrose and Polly (Gamage). She d. Sept. 6, 1870. He d. ——, 1869. Res., Bristol, Me.

2210. i. AMBROSE, b. ——.
2211. ii. ALEXANDER, b. ——.
2212. iii. FREDERICK, b. ——.
2213. iv. ELIJAH, b. ——.
2214. v. JOHN JACKSON, b. ——.
2215. vi. THOMAS, b ——. Res., Rockland, Me.
2216. vii. CHARLOTTE TRUMBALL, b. ——; m. ——, William Cunningham, of New Castle, Me.
2217. viii. BELINDA, b. ——.
2218. ix. NANCY THURSTON, b. ——.
2219. x. DEBORAH TARR, b ——.
2220. xi. HARRIET THORP, b. ——.

1228. JOHN FOSTER (John, Nathan, Caleb, Caleb, Abraham, Reginald), b. Bristol, Me., ——; m. ——, Mary Mann. He d. ——. Res., ——.

2221. i. ANNIE, b. ——; m. ——, Hawes Garish, of Boston.
2222. ii. JOHN, b. ——. An artist. Res., Boston.
2223. iii. THOMAS, b. ——. A painter. Res., Boston.
2224. iv. EMILY, b. ——; m. ——. Went to California.

1230. ZABUD FOSTER (Zabud, Nathan, Caleb, Caleb, Abraham, Reginald), b. Bristol, Me., Oct. 7, 1802; m., Freedom, April 14, 1823, Mary Thompson, b. 1805; d. Montville, Me., March 6, 1894. He d. March 6, 1894. Res., Montville, Me.

2225. i. EDWARD VOSE, b. July 30, 1831; m. Sarah Jane Smith and Martha Longley Allis Smith.
2226. ii. JOHN WESLEY, b. ——. Res., Washington, D. C.
2227. iii. LAURA, b. ——; m. —— Madison. Res., Port Jefferson, L. I.

1238. THOMAS STONE FOSTER (Zabud, Nathan, Caleb, Caleb, Abraham, Reginald), b. Montville, Me., Aug. 7, 1811; m. there Dec. 6, 1840, Caroline A. Sprowl, b. Nov. 18, 1821. He was a farmer. He d. Aug. 6, 1887. Res., Montville, Me.

2228. i. MARY A., b. March 27, 1846; m. —— Thompson. Res., Montville.
2229. ii. THOMAS LORIN, b. May 5, 1848; m. ——.
2230. iii. CARO V., b. Dec. 17, 1850; m. and d. March 26, 1881.
2231. iv. JOHN S., b. Jan. 15, 1852; m. Hattie J. Higgins.

2232. v. ANNETTE A., b. Nov. 1, 1854; d. Sept., 1855.
2233. vi. AMOS C., b. Nov. 28, 1856; d., April 7, 1877.
2234. vii. CHARLES A., b. Dec. 9, 1858; d. June —, 1889.
2235. viii. BURTON F., b. Nov. 23, 1844; m. Mary Ellen Briggs.

1243. CHARLES FOSTER (Jacob, Jacob, Jacob, Isaac, Reginald, Reginald), b. Charlestown, Mass., June 13, 1789; m., Nov. 17, 1823, Lydia Webb, dau. of Nathan and Sarah Leach, b. Boston, April 2, 1801; d. Sept. 21, 1827; m., 2d, Nov. 10, 1828, Susannah C. Rodgers, dau. of Jonathan and Ann, of Boston, b. Sept. 1, 1800; d. Oct. 25, 1865. He was senior partner of the firm of Foster, Lawrence & Co. Resided for several years at Winter Hill, Somerville; but during the latter years of his life at Cordis street, Charlestown. He was remarkable for his benevolence and charity. He d. Sept. 1, 1866. Res., Charlestown, Mass.

2236. i. MARY LOUISA, b. Charlestown. She married George Francis, son of Edward and Ruth (Torrey) Cutter, of Boston, June 29, 1847. Mr. Cutter was born Aug. 30, 1819. Is a paymaster in the United States navy, and has been over twenty-five years in the service. They now reside at No. 43 Chestnut St., Charlestown. Mr. Cutter being at present stationed at this navy yard.
2237. ii. CHARLES, b. Oct. 27, 1826; m. Charlotte M. Bowman.
2238. iii. LYDIA WEBB, b. Dec. 8, 1830. Resides at Brooklyn, L. I.
2239. iv. ANN ROGERS, b. Jan. 10, 1832; m. Daniel Alford, son of David Ambrose and Hannah (Stone) Sanborn, Oct. 6, 1853. Mr. Sanborn is engaged in business in New York, residing in Brooklyn. Ch.: 1. Mary Louise Sanborn, b. May 20, 1858, at Boston; m. —— Buchanan, of Brooklyn. 2. Charles Foster Sanborn, b. Aug. 5, 1859, at Somerville; d. Sept. 30, 1881. 3. William Adams Sanborn, b. Sept. 4, 1864, at Charlestown; m., Oct. 30, 1884, Nellie A. Quimby. Res., s. p. Hartford, Conn.
2240. v. SUSAN ADAMS, b. Jan. 30, 1835. She m. Rev. Stephen Henry, son of James and Huldah (Maffet) Camp, of Hartford, Conn., July 26, 1865. They reside in Brooklyn, where Mr. Camp is settled as pastor of Unity church. They have adopted Willie Warren, b. in Scotland, May 29, 1862.
2241. vi. SARAH CATHARINE, b. Dec. 13, 1836. She m. Frederick, son of Isaac and August (Shaw) Hobbs, Oct. 13, 1858. They have had born at Charlestown: 1. Annie Hobbs, b. May 31, 1860. 2. Frank Edward Hobbs, b. April 18, 1862; d. Aug. 31, 1864. 3. Frank Foster Hobbs, b. April 5, 1867.

1244. HENRY FOSTER (Jacob, Jacob, Jacob, Isaac, Reginald, Reginald), b. Charlestown, Mass., Dec. 8, 1801; m., Aug. 14, 1837, Mary Taber Swift, dau. of Josiah and Elizabeth Hathaway. He was a merchant of Boston, doing business with Pernambuco, South America, at which place he resided many years, and founded the house of Henry Foster & Co. Mrs. Foster resided at No. 21 Monument Square, Charlestown. He d. June 12, 1855. Res., Charlestown, Mass.

2242. i. GEORGE HENRY, b. June 20, 1838; m. Constance Atherton.
2243. ii. ARTHUR VOSE, b. Nov. 26, 1839; d. Jan. 2, 1840.
2244. iii. WILLIAM ROSS SWIFT, b. April 10, 1841; d. Dec. 24, 1850.
2245. iv. MARY SWIFT, b. May 29, 1846.
2246. v. FREDERICK PRENTISS, b. Aug. 17, 1851; graduated at Harvard College, Class of '75.
2247. vi. HORACE WALDO, b. Aug. 15, 1853, at Needham. Attended school at Charlestown.

1245. JACOB FORSTER (Jacob, Jacob, Jacob, Isaac, Reginald, Reginald), b. Charlestown, Mass., June 7, 1803; m., June 22, 1830, Louisa Webb, of Boston. He was a commission merchant in Boston, for many years having his office at No. 26 Long Wharf. He was married by the Rev. Warren Fay, to Louisa, dau. of Nathan and Sarah (Leach) Webb, of Boston. Jacob, Charlestown; will date Dec. 15, 1856; prob. Aug. 11, 1857; wife, Louisa; chil., Edward J. Edward J., child of Jacob (of Charlestown) and Louisa; Forster guard.; bond Aug. 11, 1857. He d. July 7, 1857. Res., Charlestown, Mass.

2248. i. LOUISA, b. July 2, 1831.
2249. ii. CHARLES HENRY, b. Oct. 22, 1836.
2250. iii. EDWARD JACOB, b. July 9, 1846; m. Anita D. ——.

1248. HENRY PRENTICE FOSTER (Henry, Jacob, Jacob, Isaac, Reginald, Reginald), b. Walpole, N. H., Oct. 10, 1796; m., Walpole, 1823, Philena Russell, b. April 23, 1803, dau. of Thomas; d. April 27, 1839; m., 2d, Nov. 11, 1840, Eliza Marsh, dau. of Daniel, b. Nov , 1801; d. Nov., 1885.

Henry Prentice Foster was the eldest son of Henry and Susanna (Hooper) Foster, and was born in Walpole, N. H., in 1796, and died in the same town in 1861. He served as a private in the War of 1812; his service consisting of a few months of garrison duty at Portsmouth, N. H., just before the close of the war. A few years after he purchased a farm in Walpole, where he went to reside with his young bride, Miss Philena Russell, of Walpole family, also which has always taken a front rank in local affairs, and from whom came as a direct lineal descendant John Edward Russell, P. H. D., a professor at Williams College, and at one time a popular lecturer at the Harvard Divinity School, supplying for Prof. C. C. Everett, the able dean of that school, who was absent in Europe for few years.

By this marriage there were born two sons and a daughter, Caleb Foster, now a venerable, respected and well-to-do farmer, of Walpole; Henry Thomas, who died in Walpole, in 1879, and Elizabeth Philena, who afterward married Dr. A. J. Huntoon, who went to Topeka, Kans., to reside as one of the first settlers in 1857, where she died in 1893. Philena, his first wife, died in Walpole in 1839. The subject of this sketch married for a second wife Eliza Marsh, and from this union were born Charles Marsh, now practicing law in Topeka, and Katie J., who married Benjamin Adams, of East Derry, N. H., where she now resides. Henry P. Foster was a man of more than ordinary ability. His advice and counsel was much sought and prized by his fellow-townsmen, and he was often urged to accept local municipal offices, both town and county, but he uniformally refused. He had but a common school education, but was an extensive reader. His extreme modesty was a source of regret to his friends and neighbors, and probably prevented him from holding many positions of trust. His first wife was a zealous worker in the Washingtonian Temperance movement, and through her influence he became a total abstainer, and to this is largely due the fact that all his male descendants, now numbering twelve, have always strictly followed his example in this respect.

His sterling honesty and uprightness was in keeping with his Puritan ancestry and their traditions which always surrounded him. His frugality and excellent judgment brought him in middle life independent circumstances for the times and surroundings in which he lived, and when in later years he retired from business, to lead a quiet life in the beautiful village of Walpole, he became a fair type of the country gentleman, peculiar in those days to rural New England. He inherited from his father a direct, frank and positive manner of speech, and an abhorrence of duplicity or any appearance of the same, which has remained a universal family trait among all his descendants. He d. Aug. 18, 1861. Res., Walpole, N. H.

2251. i. CALEB, b. March 22, 1825; m. Isabel Eliza Marsh.

2252. ii. HENRY THOMAS, b. Oct. 15, 1826; m. Hannah M. Fuller.

2253. iii. ELIZABETH PHILENA, b. Nov. 1, 1828; m., Nov. 29, 1854, Dr. Andrew J. Huntoon, of Langdon, N. H., b. Feb. 29, 1832. They had four children—one living, Julia P., b. Oct. 28, 1868; m. Thomas E. Pounds, Oct., 1890. Res., Topeka, Kans. E. P. d. April 1, 1891.

2254. iv. CHARLES MARSH, b. Oct. 17, 1841; unm. Res., Topeka, Kans. Charles Marsh Foster was born in Walpole, N. H., on a farm. His father, Henry Prentiss Foster, a farmer, married for a second wife Eliza Marsh, and to them was born the subject of this sketch. He attended the District School and High School of his native town and spent a short time in Kimbal Union Academy, at Meriden, N. H., where he was graduated about 1860. He at once entered Harvard College and took a degree of A. B. in 1864; studied law with the Hon. F. A. Vose in his native town, then practiced law for a short time in Alstead, N. H., and in 1868 moved to Topeka, Kans. His precocity as a scholar, from the beginning of his school life, was the comment of the town, and the recollections of it have been prominently interwoven with the traditions of his historic birthplace.

The above is from relatives of his family, and what follows is from a mere acquaintance without kinship to him.

He has lived in the city of Topeka nearly thirty years, and during all his stay here has never made an enemy or deserved one. His whole life here has been a literary abstraction. He has been the constant source of supply for nearly every lawyer in the State, and especially in times of their extremity has he been a common fount upon which attorneys of this State have constantly drawn and never exhausted; it has become proverbial concerning his knowledge of law generally, as found in *nisi prius* decisions, unpublished decisions, out of print reports. that wherever there has been a decision rendered by some means he has obtained and carries it in his head. The person who writes this sketch never, in his life, saw or heard of a man who was such a wilderness, such a mass of knowledge or information, and in whatever direction knowledge or information ramifies. By his most intimate friends he has never yet been discovered devouring a book for any length of time, and he always has known its contents. The finances of this country, the local politics of this country, and any sort of information concernng the people, that would seem to have been local, and with but little extended notoriety, were equally familiar to him. A learner of languages, simply attracted by coming upon a stray book of the languages. A professor of thorough bass and harmony for a period in an Academy of music here, after a casual study of some treatise on that subject which he accidentally picked up. Whatever the writer may say in relation to him, of good or bad, it will not at all molest the serenity of this gentleman, unless there is an error in the fact. He has lived for thirty years in an entirely literary atmosphere; has taken no note of things temporal as concerned himself personally. He has been the kind friend of Judges from the Supreme Justice down. He has been the assistant counsel, unpaid at that, in any number of cases where he has rendered great services to the lawyers engaged, and had he had the commercial element in his make-up and could have understood life, other than its literary abstractions, he would have been one of the most famous men in the Foster tribe.

The people of Topeka are his friends; they must be, because he has done everything in the world that he could do for everyone that ever called upon him for a favor.—Joseph G. Waters.

2255. v. KATIE JANE, b. Feb. 22, 1845; m., Dec. 13, 1885, Benjamin Adams. Res., Derry, N. H. Ch.: 1. Benjamin Foster, b. Sept. 9, 1888.

1249. LEVI HOOPER FOSTER (Henry, Jacob, Jacob, Isaac, Reginald, Reginald), b. Walpole, N. H., Feb. 1, 1799; m. May 8, 1822, Fanny Fitch, dau. of Henry and Fanny (Gage), b. Feb. 18, 1803. She d. June 2, 1868; m. 2d., Jan. 18, 1872, Mrs. Harriet Temple. She d. Aug. 12, 1876; m. 3d., Dec. 5, 1876, Mrs. Mary S. Crossett. He was a farmer. He d. Feb. 11, 1882. Res., Walpole, N. H.

2256. i. GEORGE H., b. April 2, 1825; m. Lydia Ham.

2257. ii. HELEN MARIA, b. June 17, 1830; m. Dec. 16, 1857, Edward F. Hooper. 1 ch., d. infancy. Res., Putney, Vt.

2258. iii. FANNY SOPHIA, b. Dec. 25, 1834; m. April 1, 1858, Edward Kenwood Reynolds, of Maryland. Had 2 daus. Res., Washington, D. C.

2259. iv. ISABELLA H., b. Aug. 24, 1840; m. May 18, 1863, Henry M. Elwell, of Langdon, N. H. Had 3 ch. She d. Oct. 26, 1869.

2260. v. SOPHIA b. June 25, 1800; d. Aug. 9, 1802.

2261. vi. SOPHIA, b. Feb. 28, 1803; m. June 25, 1826, Dexter Anderson. Ch.: 1. Helen S., m. Dr. Orrin H. Smith, Sept. 10, 1850; Res. in Brooklyn, N. Y.; has 3 ch. 2. Charles Dexter, m. Ada A., only dau. of Dr. Thomas Powers, of Woodstock, Vt.; m. 2d., Helen H. Holmes, 1864. 3. Lucy Merrill, m. Dr. Blanchard and has 1 ch. 4. Henry Foster, graduated at Dartmouth, studied law and is now in practice in New York. He m. Bell Fitz Randolph, of New York. Res., Rockaway, N. J. 5. Caroline L., m. Robert S. Southgate, 1865. Issue, 3 ch. 6. Belle S., m. Dr. Herman J. Smith, 1865; Res. in Lowell, Mass. Issue, 3 ch. 7. Lizzie T., m. Rev. Mr. Southgate in 1865, pastor of the Congregational church in Dedham, Mass. Mr. Anderson's children were all born between 1827 and 1847. The two oldest are not living.

2262. vii. CALEB, b. ——, 1803; d. ——, 1820.

2263. viii. JACOB, b. ——, 1807; d. ——, 1809.

1255. DR. GEORGE TIFFANY FOSTER (David, Jacob, Jacob, Isaac, Reginald, Reginald), b. Lyndon, Vt., June 4, 1810; m. Pittsfield, Mass., Jan. 30, 1847, Ann Eliza Baxter, b. July 26, 1816; d., May 5, 1897. George Tiffany Foster was born at Lyndon, Vt. Prepared himself for college and took partial courses at Middlebury College, Vermont, and at Wesleyan College, Middletown, Conn. Supported himself by teaching in the intervals of his attendance at the college. About 1840 he was the principal of the City academy, Hudson, N. Y., where he was very popular, until he left to pursue his studies. He attended lectures at the Berkshire medical college, Pittsfield, Mass., and then at the Albany medical college, Albany, N. Y., where he graduated with the degree of M. D., January 26, 1847. Four days later, January 30, 1847, he married Anna Eliza Baxter, at Pittsfield, Mass., and shortly afterward settled in Windsor, Mass., where a daughter, Adeline Augusta Foster, was born April 15, 1848. In 1850 he moved to Chatham Four Corners, N. Y., where he practiced medicine for ten years. Here two children were born, Isabella Jones Foster, June 15, 1852, and Mathias Lanckton Foster, June 17, 1859. During this time he was an ardent abolitionist and entered with zeal into the controversies of the day to the great detriment of his practice. During the three years 1857-1860 he kept a private school. Finally, his health gave away, he left Chatham and moved to Pittsfield, Mass., where he lived quietly in a semi-invalid condition until his death from dysentery, October 22, 1890. While he lived in Pittsfield, the Prohibitionist party was organized, and he was one of the fifteen voters who supported that ticket the first year in that town. He died October 22, 1890. Residence, Pittsfield, Mass.

2264. i. ADELINE AUGUSTA KNIGHT, b. April 15, 1848. Add., Westfield, Mass. Has a son, Joseph Hyde Knight, b. May 30, 1872.

2265. ii. ISABELLA JONES, b. June 15, 1852; d. May 21, 1857.

2266. iii. MATHIAS LANCKTON, b. June 17, 1859; m. Constance Hunter Savage.

1257. JACOB PRENTISS FOSTER (David, Jacob, Jacob, Isaac, Reginald, Reginald), b. Lyndon, Vt.; m. —— Jane Leitch; m. 2d., Matilda Cahoon. Res., Passumpsic, Vt.

2267. i. JACOB P., JR., b. Aug., 1845. Res., Brookhaven, Miss.

2268. ii. MARY F., b. ——; m. —— Bowman. Res., Brookhaven, Miss.

2269 iii. DAVID JOHNSON, b. July 27, 1857; m. Mabel M. Albee.

2270. iv. JOHN CAHOON, b. ——. Res., Passumpsic, Vt.

2271. v. REBECCA, b. ——; m. —— Somers. Res., Passumpsic, Vt.

2272. vi. LENORA, b. ——; m. —— Sanborn. Res., Passumpsic, Vt.

2273. vii. BESSIE, b. Nov. 29, 1847; m. March 13, 1868, in Barnet, Vt., Jerome H. Eastman, b. Nov. 20, 1844. He is a farmer. Res., Quechee, Vt. Ch.: 1. Walter Ray, b. April 15, 1875.

1261. ALEXANDER HAMILTON FOSTER (Samuel S., William, Jacob, Isaac Reginald, Reginald), b. Batavia, N. Y., ——; m. ——, ——. He d. May 24, 1884. Was killed by the cars. Res., Batavia, N. Y.

1269. WILLIAM ABEL FOSTER (Abel, William, Jacob, Isaac, Reginald, Reginald), b. Batavia, N. Y., ——; m. ——, Clarissa Hayes. Res., New York, N. Y.

2274. i. LOUISA, b. ——, m. —— Ash. Res., Spirit Lake, Iowa.

2275. ii. JAMES, b. ——; m. Louisa Thomas.

1271. DR. MASON DURKEE FOSTER (Jacob, William, Jacob, Isaac, Reginald, Reginald), b. Feb. 26, 1807; m. ——, Romina Bird. After his death she m. again. He was a physican and surgeon at Port Gibson, Manchester, Ontario county, N. Y. Was a successful practitioner and is buried in Auburn, N. Y., s. p.

1273. JOHN CHAMBERLAIN FOSTER (Jacob, William, Jacob, Isaac, Reginald, Reginald), b. Sept. 28, 1812, Whitehall, N. Y.; m. Jan. 26, 1837, Julia A. Haseltine, b. Aug. 16, 1818; d. ——. He d. June 17, 1872. Res., Port Byron, N. Y.

2276. i. DAVID H., b. Hamilton, N. Y., Aug. 8, 1843.

2277. ii. JOHN JACOB, b. Sept. 23, 1852; m. Minerva Hill.

2278. iii. FRANCES T., b. March 4, 1849; d. ——.
2279. iv. MARY E., b. May 16, 1840.
2280. v. AUGUSTINA C., b. March 4, 1838.

1275. CAPT. GEORGE WARREN FOSTER (Jacob, William, Jacob, Isaac, Reginald, Reginald), b. Sept. 13, 1817, Whitehall, N. Y.; m. Oct. 18, 1848, Mary Elizabeth Coe, b. Oct. 23, 1830. At the age of five years he moved with his parents to the town of Mentz, Cayuga county, in the same state. Here he attended the district schools and also worked on his father's farm. At the age of fifteen he taught the district school in a neighboring district and also again in his seventeenth year. The next year was occupied in home study and reciting at the academy in Auburn, which was five miles distant and to which he walked twice a week. In 1837 he entered the law office of Hon. William H. Seward, where he remained until 1841 and during which time he served as clerk of the Court of Civil and Criminal Jurisdiction. He was also deputy clerk of the United States district court for the Northern district of New York. In the fall of 1842 he entered Yale law school, and remained one year and finished all the studies in the course. After his return from law school he practiced law at Port Byron for two years. In the fall of 1845 he came West, arriving at Milwaukee September 21, 1845, and opened a law office there. That winter, not finding the law business lucrative, he taught school at Port Washington. In the fall of 1846 he commenced surveying and also did conveyancing for the new settlers, who were then pouring in; his law business also began to grow. In 1879 he moved to Appleton, Wis., where, on account of his heavy professional labors, his nervous system broke down completely and he was compelled to give up his profession entirely and remove to Port Washington, where he again resumed his practice in 1884 and continued in active practice until his death. He was one of the leading members of the Wisconsin bar. During the war he was appointed judge-advocate by the governor of Wisconsin with the rank of captain, and was also appointed specil district attorney to prosecute those engaged in the draft riots at Port Washington. He was one of the leading citizens and the original mover toward the building of a harbor at Port Washington—went to Washington and appeared before the committee on rivers and harbors, and his labors procured the first appropriation for the harbor improvement. He was an excellent German scholar and proficient in Greek, Latin and French. He was a profound scholar, and in all his researches he worked back to the fundamental principle of the subject under discussion. He was in all his professional labors a profound lawyer in all the meaning of that word. He was a staunch Republican in politics and before the organization of that party was a Whig. He died February 6, 1895. Res., Port Washington, Wis.

2281. i. SOPHIA LOUISE, b. Feb. 29, 1852; d. Sept. 13, 1864; unm.
2282. ii. ADDIE COE, b. Dec. 25 1861; d. Sept. 20, 1864; unm.
2283. iii. WILLIAM MASON, b. July 1, 1859; unm. Received a common school education and attended Lawrence University, at Appleton, Wis., for one year; admitted to the bar in 1884, and practiced law at Milwaukee, Wis, since 1888. Politics, Republican.
2284. iv. GEORGE CHAMPLIN, b. Oct. 30, 1856; unm. Res., Hurley, Wis. Profession, lawyer. Admitted to the bar Jan. 30, 1877, at Port Washington, Wis. County judge of Florence county, Wis., in the years 1883, 1884 and 1885. District attorney of Iron county, Wis, for the years 1895, 1896, 1897 and 1898. Politics, Republican.
2285. v. CHARLES LINNEUS, b. March 21, 1865; d. Jan. 23, 1887; unm.
2286. vi. ANNIE STEWART, b. Aug. 29, 1866; unm.
2287. vii. FREDERICK ALBERT, b. June 20, 1871; unm. Res., Milwaukee, Wis. At the age of eight years he moved, with the rest of his father's family, to Appleton, Wis., where they lived for a few years, when, on account of his father's ill health, they returned to Port Washington. He there attended the public and high schools and was graduated from the latter at the age of fifteen. He then attended the high school at Niles, Mich., for a short time. In his seventeenth year he entered a law office in Milwaukee, Wis., where he remained until the winter of 1891, when he entered the University of Wisconsin, taking two years of academic work and then entering the law department of the university, from which he was graduated with the class of 1895. Before entering law school, he took and passed the state bar

examination and was admitted to the bar. While in the law department of the university, he was private secretary to Justices Cassaday and Orton, of the Wisconsin Supreme Court. He is a member of the Chi Psi fraternity. After finishing his law course he entered the legal department of the Santa Fé railroad company at Chicago. In 1896 he removed to Milwaukee, where he is practicing his profession. In politics he has followed in the footsteps of his father. Addresses: William M. Foster, 101 New Ins. Bldg., Milwaukee, Wis.; Annie S. Foster, res., Milwaukee, Wis.

1278. COL. JACOB THOMAS FOSTER (Jacob, William, Jacob, Isaac, Reginald, Reginald), b. Mentz, N. Y., June 23, 1827; m. Port Washington, Wis., Nov. 26, 1849, Sarah Mariah Page, b. May 5, 1833; d. Dec. 8, 1866, accidentally killed in a mill at Hokah, Minn., by her dress catching in machinery; m. 2d, Jan. 3, 1869, Anna Barber, b., 1826; d. Feb. 2, 1893; m. 3d, Nov. 29, 1893, in Chicago, Georgia Huston, b., 1867. Res., Chicago, Ill., 231 Forty-second street.

2288. i. JACOB FRANK, b. March 28, 1851; m. Clara Walton.
2289. ii. GENEVIEVE SARAH, b. Sept. 25, 1853; m., April 15, 1869, Lewis Cass Foote. Res., Waterloo, Iowa; 2 ch.
2290. iii. CLARK HARROLD, b. Dec. 11, 1859; m. Hattie Kellogg.

1290. JOB YOUNG FOSTER (Jacob, Isaac, Jacob, Isaac, Reginald, Reginald), b. Gray, Me., Dec. 28, 1803; m. there April 8, 1827, Stateria Leighton, of Falmouth. Res., Gray, Me.

2291. i. JULIA ANN C., b. ——; m., Oct. 29, 1848, Job A. Spencer. Res., Dry Mills, Me.

1292. SHEPHEL FOSTER (Jacob, Isaac, Jacob, Isaac, Reginald, Reginald), b. Gray, Me., Feb. 12, 1809; m. Jan. 17, 1836, Rosana Dolloff, of Paris, b. Oct. 25, 1814; d. March 23, 1890. He was a farmer. He d. Oct. 22, 1891. Res., Gray, Me.

2292. i. DORCAS C., b. Feb. 17, 1837.
2293. ii. MARSHALL, b. Sept. 14, 1838; m. Feb. 12, 1883, Margaret Eleanor Young Rude, b. Prince Edward's Island, July 12, 1847. He is a farmer. Res., s. p., Gray Corner, Me.
2294. iii. JACOB, b. Aug. 4, 1841; m. Mary Allen.
2295. iv. ANNE M., b. Dec. 19, 1846.
2296. v. DANIEL A., b. May 7, 1851.
2297. vi. EDWARD P., b. Aug. 1, 1853.
2298. vii. MARY H., b. Nov. 3, 1855.
2299. viii. SHEPHEL GRANVILLE, b. April 11, 1856; m. Carrie J. Davis.

1298. SOLOMON BERRY FOSTER (Samuel, Isaac, Jacob, Isaac, Reginald, Reginald), b. Gray, Me., Nov. 4, 1810; m. Nov. 4, 1835, Eunice Ricker, of Poland, b. March 4, 1817; d. Jan. 16, 1869. He was a carpenter and farmer. He d. Jan. 27, 1883. Res., Gray, Me.

2300. i. THOMAS J., b. Oct. 17, 1836; m. Mary R. Devine.
2301. ii. RUTH JORDAN, b. April 18, 1839; m. Dec. 2, 1865, Samuel P. Cummings, b. Aug. 19, 1837. Res., North Gray, Me. Ch.: 1. Eliza J. Cummings, b. July 17, 1866; d. July 28, 1866. 2. Eugene I. Cummings, b. Aug. 29, 1867; m March, 1892. Add., Cumberland Mills, Me. 3 Lewis W. Cummings, b. Oct 29, 1868; m. Oct. 15, 1891. Add., Millville. Mass. 4. Lena A. Cummings, b. July 17, 1871; d. Sept. 14, 1872. 5. Ethel I. Cummings, b. June 27, 1873. Add., Lewiston, Me. 6. Adelbert B. Cummings, b. June 17, 1875. Add., North Gray, Me. 7. Bessie W. Cummings, b. Oct 27, 1878. Add., North Gray, Me.
2302. iii. LAVINA C., b. Jan 23, 1842; w. f. k., Aug., 1877.
2303. iv. HENRY M., b. April 22, 1844; d. Aug. 27, 1858.
2304. v. HORACE C., b. Sept. 7, 1847; m. Annie M. Frank.
2305. vi. CHARLES J., b. Dec. 16, 1849; m. Ella C. Spiller.
2306. vii. JOHN R., b. Dec. 16, 1851; m. — ——.
2307. viii. EARNEST, b. March 14, 1853; d March, 1854.
2308. ix. ANNIE L., b. Aug. 6, 1855; d. Jan. 3, 1878.
2309. x. HENRY W., b. Dec. 11, 1857; m. Jennie E. Colley.

1300. SAMUEL J. FOSTER (Samuel, Isaac, Jacob, Isaac, Reginald, Reginald), b. Gray Me., Jan. 14, 1808; m., at Poland, 1828, Annie Emerson, of Poland. He d. May 21, 1877. Res., Gray, Me.

2310. i. MARTHA A., b. ——; m., Oct. 1, 1848, Charles E. Libby.
2311. ii. HANNAH C., b ——; m., Sept. 16, 1849, Marshall Morse.
2312. iii. JONATHAN O., b. Nov. 29, 1833; m. Jan. 2, 1897.
2313. iv. JANE, b. ——; m. Joel S. Bailey.
2314. v. GEORGE, b. Jan. 19, 1839. Res. in California.
2315. vi. SAMUEL J., b. in 1844; m. and Res. North Gray, Me.
2316. vii. SILAS W., b. Dec. 22, 1835; m. Sarah J. Bailey and Angie A. Briggs.

1304. PHILIP FOSTER (William, Isaac, Jacob, Isaac, Reginald, Reginald), b. Argyle, Me., ——, 1806; m. there about 1827, Fannie Cummings, d. July, 1829; m. 2d., ——, 1834.—Was a farmer and stock raiser. Philip Foster was born in Maine and married Miss Fannie Cummings. He was employed by a company to go to California to build some mills. A ship was loaded with machinery, and he was put in charge, but on the passage the ship went to Honolulu, Sandwich Islands, and was there about six months, and Mr. Foster proceeded to Portland, Ore. He finally settled at Oregon City and entered the mercantile business, but later he engaged in the building of the toll road across the Cascade mountains, having his headquarters on the west side. Here he established a trading post to furnish supplies to the immigrants. Mr. Foster was one of the earliest settlers of Oregon, coming about 1843. He died in 1887, at the age of eighty years. His wife died one year after marriage. He d. Clackamas, E. Ore., 1887. Res., Argyle, Me.

2317. i. GEORGE, b. ——. Res., Vancouver, Ore.
2318. ii. LUCY A., b. ——; m. —— Burnett. She d. Dec. 26, 18—. A des. is Burnice Howell, of Portland, Ore.
2319. iii. FRANK W., b. ——; m. ——.
2320. iv. JAMES W., b. May 22, 1829; m. Louisa M. Rockhill.
2321. v. MARY, b ——.
2322. vi. MARTHA, b. ——.
2323. vii. ISAAC, b. ——.
2324. viii. EGBERT, b. ——. Res., Eagle Creek, Ore.

1305. ISAAC FOSTER (William, Isaac, Jacob, Isaac, Reginald, Reginald), b. Argyle, Me., March 21, 1807; m. Rachel Jane Cheever, b., 1816; d., Oct. 7, 1838; m. 2d. Sarah Jane Howard, b. Aug. 3, 1821; d. Sept. 23, 1895. Was a farmer and lumberman. He d. Oct. 29, 1886. Res., Argyle, Me.

2325. i. HARVEY, b. ——.
2326. ii. WILLIAM STINSON, b. Aug. 18, 1845; m. Sarah A. Bussell and Nancy B. Jones. Relatives are Mrs. John B. Bussell, Old Town, Me.; Mrs. Sarah A. Foster, Old Town, Me.; Andrew H. Tibbetts, Old Town, Me.; Harvey Foster, 5 Sherwin street, Waterville, Me.

1310. WILLIAM CHARLES FOSTER (William, Isaac, Jacob, Isaac, Reginald, Reginald), b. Argyle, Me., Sept. 8, 1823; m. Nov. 27, 1856, Rosanna Grant, b. Oct. 31, 1838. He is a farmer and lumberman. Res., Argyle, Me.

2327. i. LUCY R., b. March 12, 1864; m. —— Littlefield. Res., Greenbush, Me.
2328. ii. ESTHER, b. Feb. 15, 1866; d. Dec. 24, 1884.
2329. iii. MARY E., b. March 28, 1868; m. —— Ballard. Res., Old Town, Me.
2330. iv. ALBERT F., b. Sept. 27, 1870.
2331. v. STEPHEN A., b. Dec. 2, 1872; m. and Res. Argyle, Me.

1311. JOSEPH WELLINGTON FOSTER (William, Isaac, Jacob, Isaac, Reginald, Reginald), b. Maine, Oct. 24, 1815; m. in Franklin Dec. 9, 1837, Harriet L. Scammon, b. Sept. 29, 1807; d. July 14, 1868, at Franklin, Me. Joseph W. Foster was born at Oldtown, Penobscot county, Me.; educated in common schools and seminary. At the age of twenty-one years went to Washington county in charge of lumbering operations at Cherryfield, on the Narraguagus river, where he built mills and operated for some years. Was married to Miss Harriet Scammon, of Franklin, while in business in Cherryfield. Some years after moved to Franklin, Hancock county, and continued in the lumbering business till an old man. He was a man of good habits; strictly temperate, a devout member of the church; a trusted public officer all his life; never allowed the needy to go from his home empty-handed. The last year of his life was spent in Big Rapids, Mich., where he died at the age of about sixty years, June 19, 1869. Res., Franklin, Me.

2332. i. STEPHEN W., b. Feb. 22, 1839; m. Louisa F. Fickett.
2333. ii. BETSEY J., b Aug. 21, 1840. She d. 1862.
2334 iii. JOHN H., b. Feb. 11, 1842; m. Georgiana Dykins.
2335. iv. OPHELIA MARIA, b. Sept. 23, 1843; m. Nov. 21, 1861, Orin S. Donnell, b. Jan. 8, 1838. Res., Franklin, Me. Ch.: 1. Hattie Louise, b. Sept. 13, 1862. 2. Caddie Marie, b. Nov. 14, 1863. 3. Harlal L., b. Oct. 2, 1870. 4. Mabel C., b. Aug. 8, 1877. Hattie L. Graves, North East Harbor, Me.; Caddie M. Blaisdell, Franklin, Me.
2336. v. MARTHA ANN, b. April 24, 1845.
2337. vi. JAMES F. b. Sept. 4, 1847.
2338. vii. DUDLEY W., b. Nov. 1, 1848; m. Clara M. Wakefield.

1312. HEMAN NICKERSON FOSTER (William, Isaac, Jacob, Isaac, Reginald, Reginald), b. Argyle, Me., July 5, 1826; m. March 13, 1849, at Greenbush, Me., Eliza Moore, b. May 3, 1832. He is a farmer and lumberman. Res., Argyle, Me.

2339. i. HARRITTA, b. Feb. 8, 1850; Mrs. Isaac Terrill, Oldtown, Me.
2340. ii. LUCY J., b. Dec. 23, 1851; d. Aug. 24, 1858.
2341. iii. SARAH E., b. Oct. 14, 1854; d Feb 2, 1895.
2342. iv. NANCY E., b. Jan. 18, 1857; d. Sept. 1, 1858.
2343. v. RUEL H., b. Jan. 20, 1859; m. April 15, 1883. Add., Argyle, Me.
2344. vi. ADONIRAM, b. April 20, 1861; d. April 21, 1861.
2345. vii. ANDREW W., b. Nov. 27, 1863; m. June, 1886 Ad., Augusta, Me.
2346 viii. ADELBERT E., b. Feb. 11, 1866; m., November, 1894. Add., Argyle, Me.
2347. ix. ARTHUR M., b. Aug 25, 1868; d. Sept. 5, 1879.
2348. x. NORA M., b. July 8, 1871; d. March 16, 1879.

1313. CAPT. JOSEPH FOSTER (Joseph, Joseph, Jeremiah, John, Reginald, Reginald), b. Gloucester, Mass., Aug. 2, 1784; m., Sept. 2, 1838, Adelaide Coues Spalding, dau. of Dr. Lyman and Elizabeth (Coues), b. Dec. 3, 1805. She d., Portsmouth, N. H., Sept. 24, 1898. He was a sea captain. After attending school in Boston he decided to go to sea at once, and made his first voyage in the Massachusetts, William Vinson Hutchings, of Gloucester, master, a large ship belonging to Boston. While at Batavia the ship was engaged to go to Japan, and proceeded under Dutch colors to Nagasaki, where the Dutch were allowed to send one vessel every year, this being the only trade allowed with foreigners. The Massachusetts was at Nagasaki during the winter of 1799-1800, and is believed to have been the second American vessel which visited that country. A Japanese picture, brought home on that voyage, marked "Joseph Foster, Jr., Ship Massachusetts, William Hutchings, master, Japan, 1799," and "Japan, April, 1800," is still preserved. He was captain of the private-armed schooner-of-war Sword Fish in 1812. He married, May 17, 1806, Lucy Elwell, of Gloucester, born February 16, 1784; died September 7, 1837. He again married, September 2, 1838, in Portsmouth, N. H., Adelaide Coues Spalding, born December 3, 1805, in Portsmouth, daughter of Lyman Spalding, M. D., and Elizabeth (Coues) Spalding of that place. Notices of Dr. Spalding will be found in the Spalding Memorial, page 130, the Rambles About Portsmouth, Allibone's Dictionary of Authors, the American Cyclopædia, and Johnson's Universal Cyclopædia, from the last of which the following is taken: Lyman Spalding, M. D., was born June 5, 1775, at Cornish, N. H., graduated at Dartmouth college in 1798; studied medicine and aided in the establishment of the medical school of Dartmouth, where he delivered the first course of lectures on chemistry; began the practice of his profession at Portsmouth, in 1799; in 1812 became president of the College of Physicians and Surgeons, in Western New York; removed to New York City in 1813; planned the United States Pharmacopœia, and in 1820 was one of the committee for its publication; was a skillful anatomist, and member of many learned societies in Europe and America. Died October 30, 1821, in Portsmouth, N. H. Captain Foster died December 19, 1843, on board brig Ventrosa, of Boston, at Holmes' Hole, Mass. The Gloucester Telegraph, noticing his death, said: "It is with the deepest pain and sorrow that we announce the death of Captain Foster. His loss is most keenly felt in this whole community. Captain Foster was a man much esteemed and respected by all who were acquainted with him for his honesty, integrity and kindness of heart. He had been for many years a shipmaster of the first respectability and standing from this port and Boston." Mrs. Foster died in Portsmouth, N. H., Sept. 24, 1898. "Died.—Foster. In this city, September 24th, at the residence of her son, Pay Inspector Joseph Foster, United States Navy, Mrs. Adelaide Coues Foster, aged ninety-two years, nine months and twenty-one days, daughter of Lyman Spalding, M. D., of Portsmouth, and widow of Capt. Joseph

CAPT. JOSEPH FOSTER.

Foster, of Gloucester, Mass. Funeral this Monday afternoon at half past two o'clock."—[Portsmouth, N. H., Chronicle, Sept. 26, 1898.] "Adelaide Coues Foster. —Mrs. Adelaide Coues Foster, the aged and esteemed widow of Joseph Foster, and mother of Pay Inspector Joseph Foster, United States Navy, died at the residence of her son in this city, early on Saturday after a long illness. Her age was ninety-two years, nine months and twenty-one days. She is survived by two sons."—[Portsmouth, N. H., Chronicle, Sept. 26, 1898.] He died at sea Dec. 19, 1843. Res., Gloucester, Mass., and Portsmouth, N. H.

2349. x. JOSEPH, b. June 17, 1841; m. Helen Dickey.
2350. i. JOSEPH, b. Feb. 2, 1807; d. Feb. 2, 1807.
2351. ii. LUCY ELWELL, b. Aug. 12, 1808; m. Sept. 11, 1832, Solomon Stanwood. She d. Aug. 7, 1892, in Gloucester. Solomon Stanwood, son of Richard I. Stanwood, of Gloucester; b. in 1808, in Gloucester. Residence, Gloucester and Boston. She d. Aug. 7, 1892, in Boston. He d. October 16, 1881, in Boston. The following notice was printed in a Boston paper at that time: "Solomon Stanwood, an old and respected citizen of Boston, died on October 16 last, at the age of seventy-three years. His father and brothers were noted shipmasters in their day, and he was himself a survivor, probably the only one, of the crew of the Augusta, a ship of less than 200 tons, which, under the command of his father, Capt. Richard [Goss] Stanwood, made a trading tour "'round the world" some sixty years ago, touching at Valparaiso and other points on the Pacific, the Sandwich Islands and Manila. From the latter port a cargo of hemp and sugar was brought to Boston. The voyage was considered a remarkable one. Mr. Stanwood lived in Boston many years and had a large circle of friends." Children born in Gloucester. 1. Amelia Foster, b. July 28, 1833; d. March 13, 1834, in Gloucester. 2. Amelia Foster, b. Jan. 20, 1835; d. June 5, 1852, in Boston.
2352. iii. AMELIA, b. Dec. 8, 1810; d. unm. Oct. 22, 1872. Will.—Amelia Foster, of Boston, single woman. Sister, Lucy E. Stanwood, of Boston; late father, Capt. Joseph Foster, of Gloucester; only brother, William Foster, of Boston. Dated, April 26, 1866. Lib. 459; Fol. 115. Prob., December 2, 1872. Lib. 459; Fol. 115. Petition for administrator mentions Amelia Foster, died October 22, 1872. Her heirs at law, William Foster, of Severance, Kas.; Lucy E. Stanwood, of Boston, wife of Solomon Stanwood; Joseph Foster, of Portsmouth, N. H.; Lyman S. Foster, of New York, brothers and sisters of the deceased. November 12, 1872. Suff. Co., Mass., Probate, Lib. 459; Fol. 204. Lib. 460; Fol. 446-634-653.
2353. iv. CAROLINA, b. Sept. 7, 1812; d. unm. Sept. 14, 1812.
2354. v. JOSEPH, b. March 2, 1815; d. unm. July 10, 1837, of yellow fever on board barque Burlington, Captain Evans, at Havana, Cuba, of which vessel he was chief mate.
2355. vi. JOSEPH, b. Oct. 21, 1813; d. May 1, 1814.
2356. vii. EDWARD, b. Aug. 9, 1817; d. Aug. 7, 1817.
2357. viii. WILLIAM, b. Dec. 12, 1819; m. Caroline M. Harvey.
2358. ix. ADELAIDE COUES, b. Sept. 3, 1839; d. Sept. 14, 1840.
2359. xi. LYMAN SPALDING, b. Nov. 25, 1843; m. Elmira S. Hallet.

1317. CAPT. BENJAMIN FOSTER (Joseph, Joseph, Jeremiah, John, Reginald, Reginald), b. in Gloucester, April 12, 1788; m., April 19, 1821, Ruby Frye, dau. of John and Betsy (Noyes) Frye; b. April 4, 1802, in Andover, and d. Dec. 28, 1838, in Gloucester. He d. in Surinam, South America, Sept. 23, 1842. Res., Gloucester, Mass.

2360. i. BENJAMIN FRANKLIN, b. June 25, 1822; d. March 15, 1853.
2361. ii. DAVID ELWELL, b. May 5, 1824.
2362. iii. JOHN FRYE, b. Sept. 30, 1826. Res., Gloucester; m. Mary Ann Norris.
2363. iv. GRANVILLE, b. March 30, 1829; a mariner; unm.; accidentally drowned, Aug. 25, 1859, in the Mississippi river, at New Orleans.
2364. v REBECCA, b. Dec. 22, 1832; m., Oct. 20, 1861, in Gloucester, Francis White Homans, of Beverly, Mass., son of William and Sarah (Downing) Homans, of Beverly, b. Dec. 19, 1832, in Beverly. Res., Gloucester. No children.

1321. CAPT. JEREMIAH FOSTER (Joseph, Joseph, Jeremiah, John, Reginald, Reginald), b. Gloucester, Mass., Dec. 1, 1797; m., May 10, 1821, in Gloucester, Caroline Stevens, dau. of Cyrus Stevens, of Gloucester; b. Dec. 26, 1797, in Gloucester; d. March 30, 1830, in Gloucester. He again married Nov. 6, 1834, in Gloucester, Charlotte Babson, dau. of Joseph and Mary (Babson) Babson, of Gloucester;

b. July 15, 1808, in Gloucester; d. July 1, 1864, in Gloucester. He was a sea captain, and d. April 15, 1869, in Somerville, Mass.

2365. i. SIDNEY MASON, b. June 29, 1822; m. Elizabeth Ann Dean.

2366. ii. CAROLINE FRANCES, b. Aug. 19, 1824; d. Feb. 21, 1825.

2367. iii. CAROLINE STEVENS, b. Aug. 20, 1826; m., Oct. 14, 1847, in Gloucester, Joseph Lowe Stevens, son of Joseph L. and Dorothy, b. Oct. 31, 1822; d. Jan. 3, 1885. She d. Nov. 23, 1886. Ch.: 1. Caroline, b. Jan. 23, 1850; m., Sept. 13, 1881, John Francis Locke, of Castine, Me. One son. 2. Helen, b. April 25, 1852. 3. Joseph Buckminster, b. Oct. 24, 1859; d. Aug. 6, 1861. 4. Mary Lowe, b. Dec. 13, 1862. 5. George Blanchard, b. April 25, 1865; grad. Harvard 1886.

2368. iv. GEORGIANA, b. May 25, 1828; d. Feb. 18, 1829.

2369. v. JEREMIAH, b. June 18, 1829; d. Aug. 12, 1830.

2370. vi. JEREMIAH, b. Oct. 21, 1841; m. Elizabeth K. Clark and Harriet N. Burnham.

1323. CAPT. THOMAS JEFFERSON FOSTER (Joseph, Joseph, Jeremiah, John, Reginald, Reginald), b. Gloucester, Mass., Jan. 20, 1801; m., Feb. 26, 1826, there Julia Ann Babson, dau. of Joseph and Mary (Babson), b. April 29, 1806; d. April 6, 1834; m., 2d, Nov. 3, 1835, Elizabeth Elwell, dau. of Robert and Betsey (Webber), b. Feb. 10, 1814; d. June 18, 1889.

The following extracts are taken from a notice printed in the Gloucester Telegraph, of Gloucester, Nov. 7, 1865: "Capt. Thomas J. Foster, one of our most worthy citizens, died quite suddenly at his residence yesterday morning. In early life Captain Foster was engaged in the trade between this port and Surinam, then the leading business of our merchants. Having obtained a sufficient competency, he retired from business, and of late years he has followed no particular occupation. He was for many years elected Overseer of the Poor, which office he filled with much advantage to the town. He was a man of strict honesty and integrity, whose word was as good as his bond, and in the circle of his family and friends his sudden departure creates a void that can never be filled. He was a kind and sympathizing neighbor, and in times of sickness and distress was ever ready with a willing heart and helping hand." He d. Nov. 3, 1865. Res., Gloucester, Mass.

2371. i. JULIA ANN, b. Jan. 3, 1828; m., Nov. 10, 1849, in Gloucester, Joseph Story Hooper, of Manchester, Mass., son of Joseph Hooper, of Manchester. Res., Dubuque, Iowa. He d. Jan. 17, 1877. Ch.: 1. Fannie Foster, b. Dec. 24, 1852, in Manchester; d. Oct. 24, 1860, in Manchester. 2. Mary Elvia, b. Feb. 2, 1860, in Dubuque. 3. Joseph Crafts (twin), b. Aug. 7, 1861, in Dubuque. 4. Thomas Foster (twin), b. Aug. 7, 1861, in Dubuque; d. Nov. 20, 1871, in Dubuque. 5. Henry Story, b. Aug. 10, 1863, in Dubuque. 6. Charles Nelson, b. March 19, 1865, in Dubuque.

2372. ii. REBECCA INGERSOLL, b. Aug. 21, 1829; m., Aug. 6, 1853, in Gloucester, Capt. Charles Nelson, of Frederickshaven, Denmark, whose original name of Christian Neilsen was so changed by the Legislature of Massachusetts. He was a sea captain and was lost at sea in the winter of 1863, with wife and only surviving child, in the ship "Romance of the Seas," bound from Hong Kong, China, to San Francisco, Cal. Ch.: 1. Charles Ericson, b. June 13, 1857, in Shanghai, China; lost at sea with his parents in 1863. 2. Albert, b. July, 1859, in Oakland, Cal.; d. June 28, 1860, in Oakland, Cal.

2372½. iii. MARY ELIZA, b. Nov. 24, 1830; unm. Res., Dubuque, Iowa.

2373. iv. THOMAS JEFFERSON, b. Sept. 26, 1833; m. Ella Amanda Winant.

2374. v. ELIZABETH, b. Jan. 22, 1837; unm.; d. Feb. 13, 1888, in Gloucester; res., Gloucester.

2375. vi. FLORENCE, b. Feb.; 1839; unm.; d. Aug. 10, 1892, in Somerville, Mass.; res., Gloucester.

1329. WARREN FOSTER (Moses, Aaron, Moses, John, Reginald, Reginald), b. ——; m. ——, Judith Burnham.

Will—Warren Foster, of Boston; wife, Judith B. Foster; daughter, Sophia B.

Foster; children, Nancy K. Lowe, Elmira Sweet, Mary E. Stinson, Judith M. Goodwin, Sylvester Goodwin, of Brooklyn, N. Y. Dated July 13, 1871. Lib. 572, Fol. 6. Prob. Sept. 7, 1885. Lib. 578, Fol. 305. Petition for administrator. Warren Foster died Nov. 30, 1883, leaving a widow, Judith B. Foster; next of kin being Judith M. Goodwin; Elmira Sweet, of Melrose; Mary E. Stinson, Sophia B. Foster, both of Boston; all daughters of deceased, and Ruth A. Sampson and Frances F. Lowe, grand-daughters. Suff. Prob. Lib. 578, Fol. 305. Lib. 573, Fol. 228. Lib. 574, Fol. 148.

He d. Nov. 30, 1883. Res., Essex and Boston, Mass.

2376. i. JOHN, b. ——; prob. d. young.

2377. ii. ELIZABETH, b. ——; m. ——, Ebenezer Low. Res., 1 New St., E. Boston. They had three daughters and one son (two daughters only survive, one of whom keeps house for her father at No. 1 New St., E. Boston—Miss Frances Low—an excellent young woman).

2378. iii. ELMIRA, b. ——; m. —— Sweet.

2379. iv. SOPHIA B., b. ——; d. umn.

2380. v. NANCY K., b. ——; m. —— Lowe.

2381. vi. MARY E., b. ——; m. —— Stinson.

2382. vii. JUDITH M., b. ——; m. Sylvester Goodwin, of Brooklyn, N. Y.

1330. THOMAS FOSTER (Thomas, Aaron, Moses, John, Reginald, Reginald), b. Essex, Mass., Dec. 30, 1790; m., Nov. 12, 1814, Sarah Lakeman. b. Nov., 1796; d. July 3, 1843.

There was nothing particular in the life of Mr. Foster different from the average New Englander of his time. He was a most devoted husband and father, in its broadest, truest sense. He shared all study with his children, and no children ever had more patient and tender rearing , or more thorough training. He was also a student of history, and, in the varied ways, an indefatigable reader—always posted in matters political, social or religious. He believed in "equality of rights between the sexes," being equally jealous for the daughters as the sons. No man ever had more pride in his daughters than had he. The habit of the time was to put the sons in the advance column—always. Not so with him,—his daughters were his pride, though he dearly loved his boys. He d. March 4, 1873. Res., Beverly, Mass.

2383. i. CAROLINE FRANCES, b. Nov. 10, 1826; m., Dec. 19, 1849, in Boston, George C. Taft; d. Feb. 17, 1854; m., 2d, in Boston, Aug. 27, 1862, J. B. Cunningham; d. Aug. 27, 1882. She resides Indianapolis, Ind., Enterprise Hotel. Ch.: 1. Mellen Parker Taft, b. at Scituate, Mass., Dec. 30, 1849; d. at Roxbury, Sept. 4, 1850. 2. Ida Taft, b. Dec. 6, 1852; res., Banning, Cal; m., ——, James F. Bird, assistant auditor of the Pullman Palace Car Co.; offices, Pullman Bldg., room 305, Chicago, Ill. 3. Fred Arms Cunningham, b Nov. 10, 1865; d. on the Chicago & Erie railroad, Aug. 27, 1891.

George C. Taft was a native of Uxbridge, Mass., a son of Mellen and Maria T. Taft. He was of delicate constitution, of the nervous sort; a brilliant pupil in his early life, energetic and ambitious to gain knowledge for its own sake as well as "the better opportunity." In his native town he passed all school examinations satisfactorily, and was some time under tuition of Rev. A. L. Stine, of Boston, with a view of teaching. From that he went to some college in New Jersey. Later, he returned to Massachusetts on account of ill-health. While he was yet a boy his father died, and his mother desired him to remain near home, and, with alternate teaching and mercantile employment, the following years he lived at Roxbury, Mass., and then went to the old home place, where he entered the office of the Whitin Bros., cotton and flannel manufacturers, at Whitinsville, Mass.

James B. Cunningham was a civil engineer of much ability and practical knowledge in his profession. This, then, comprised all the departments that are now reduced to specialties. Mr. Cunningham had been well reared and carefully educated, though possessing an enthusiastic temperament, which inclines one to be erratic in plans, and their operations. He was generous and loyal with friends, but not always just to himself. His professional labor was remunerative, but his health failed in late years, and he died in Boston. One son was born to his home—Fred Arms Cunningham—who lost his life in 1891 in railway service, at 25 ye rs. He married Elizabeth Young, of Oak Point, Banarentine county, Quebec. One son was born, and yet lives—Samuel Adams Cunningham—now 7 years of age. He was an intense reader of history; a real student, loving the work. He attended Chauncey Hall School, in Boston, for a time, and was markedly prominent in declamations and their selection, which he was allowed to choose. As an arithmetician he was beyond the average boy of his years, and fairly equal in other departments. Very early he had read Scott's works, and could repeat many poems with telling power. Was exceedingly modest in all efforts, and few beside immediate friends knew his ability. His opportunities were cut short by the death of his father, and his work changed.

2384. ii. ALDEN BRADFORD, b. March 29, 1834; m. Fannie Murch and Celeste H. Morse.

2385. iii. THOMAS A., b. Sept. 7, 1823; m. Judith Judkins.

2386. iv. SUSAN, b. ——; m. ——, Gilman M. Burnham. She d. s. p.

2387. v. SARAH L., b. Feb. 21, 1819; m., Dec. 25, 1846, Enoch Small Hamilton. He was b. Sept. 12, 1824; d. May 10, 1891. She d., East Boston, Aug. 30, 1886. Ch.: 1. Sarah Frances, b. and d. in 1849. 2. Gilman M. B., b. Sept. 14, 1850; d. Dec. 25, 1881. 3. Charles E. F., b. Jan., 1852; d. Aug., 1852. 4. Elizabeth Davis, b. Oct. 28, 1847; m., Dec. 28, 1870, Warren Emerson Belcher, b. May 24, 1847; d. Nov. 2, 1888. Was in the postal service. She resides Winthrop, Mass. Ch.: 1. Warren Hamilton, b. Aug. 16, 1871; m., Oct. 1, 1891, Ella May Kinnear, of E. Boston. Ch.: (a) William Warren, b. Dec. 8, 1891. (b) Lester Hamilton, b. March 13, 1893. (c) Dorothy May, b. Nov. 6, 1894. (d) Eldridge Foster, b. March 1, 1898. 2. Charles Davis, b. Nov. 11, 1873; m., April 14, 1897, Katharine O. Borden, of E. Saugus. Ch.: (a) Laura E., b. Oct. 15, 1897. 3. Salina Eva, b. Nov. 1. 1875; d. Sept. 8, 1878. 4. Ethel Lincoln, b. May 13, 1878. 5. Arnold Lakeman, b. Aug. 22, 1880. 6. Salina Gertrude, b. Feb. 13, 1884. 7. Joseph, b. Aug. 9, 1887.

2388. vi. ELIZABETH H., b. Dec. 20, 1818; m., Dec. 28, 1843, Charles N. Turner, b. June 12, 1818; d. May 14, 1853. Was a contractor and builder. She resides 124 Princeton St., East Boston, Mass. Ch.: 1. Elizabeth A. Turner, b. Sept. 27, 1844. Res., 124 Princeton St., E. Boston, Mass. 2. Frances H. Turner, b. July 31. 1846. Res., 124 Princeton St., E. Boston, Mass. The two daughters have been public school teachers for many years. They are "past grand" in length of service and ability also. They are, with their mother, active workers in behalf of suffrage for their sex.

2389. vii. CHARLES EDWARD, b. March —. 1830; d. unm., in California. While crossing a rapid stream his boat overturned in the current—this, on his way, from San Francisco, to his saw-mill, at Redwoods. His was an uncommonly bright and cheerful temperament; active and ambitious. He very early manifested business qualifications, and with his genial manner he became successful before he was of age. The mother died in 1847, and to him, of all the children, this was a bitter loss. He was the dearly loved brother; always kind, generous and careful of his home life. He left, with his elder brother-in-law, Gilman M. Burnham, for the gold regions of California in May, 1849.

2390. viii. AUGUSTA CLARA, b. ——; d.; aet. 15.

2391. ix. MARILINE, b. ——; m. ——, Albert M. Palmer; s. p.

2392. x. CHARLOTTE ANNA, b. ——; m. ——, David A. Stone.

2393. xi. LUCRETIA BROWN, b. March 6, 1836; m., Feb. 28, 1859, Capt. Charles Whitney Lamson. Res., 498 Winthrop Ave., New Haven, Conn. He was b. May 18, 1820. Was master of a merchant ship for many years. The home was at Beverly, Mass. (the old time home of the Whitney family, of whom his mother was one.) Captain L. died at home Nov. 30, 1889. A very worthy man, devoted to home and family, and true in all relations. He left a widow and three children, one son and two daughters: 1. Charles Alden, b. Oct. 16, 1861; m. Ida M. Bradstreet, May 2, 1893. 2. Clara Whitney, b. Dec. 12, 1865, in Beverly; m. F. S. Andrew, Dec. 3. 1891. Res., Beverly. 3. Alice Palmer, b. Jan. 1, 1869; m. William P. Walker, Sept. 1, 1892. Res., Beverly.

1331. DAVID CHOATE FOSTER (Thomas, Aaron, Moses, John, Reginald, Reginald), b. Nov. 5, 1806, Essex, Mass., m., in Beverly, Martha Lamson. She d. Jan. 21, 1829; m., 2d, in Beverly, Nov., 1830, Nancy Lamson, b. March 5, 1810; d. Nov. 1, 1895. He was a cabinet maker. He d. July 15, 1872. Res., Boston, Mass.

2394. i. MARTHA ANN, b. Aug. 24, 1832; unm. Res., No. 2 Kearsage Terrace, Roxbury.

2395. ii. EMILY SUTTON, b. Oct. 7, 1835; m., March 20, 1862, Capt. John W. Beckford. Res., 14 Washington St., Beverly, Mass. He was b. Nov. 15, 1834; d. Nov. 17, 1873. He was a master mariner. Ch.: 1. Emmeline Ober Beckford, b. Nov. 15, 1865; m. George V. Brown, Oct. 27, 1892. 2. Ruth Smith Beckford, b. Jan. 25, 1869. 3. Francis Sutton Beckford, b. Oct. 5, 1873.

2396. iii. CHARLES WILLIAM, b. May 15, 1842. Res., Melbourne, Australia. Married Marian ——. Ch.: 1. Charles Robert, b. Feb. 29, 1867; d. Nov., 1869. 2. William Francis, b. Dec. 25, 1869. 3. Charles Ernest, b. Sept. 11, 1872. 4. Emily Daisy, b. Nov. 20, 1874; d. Feb. 11, 1888. 5. George Herbert, b. Feb. 2, 1877. 6. Horace Lamson, b. June 26, 1879.

2397. iv. SUSAN STORY, b. July 26, 1849. Res., 2 Kearsage Terrace, Roxbury.

2398. v. GEORGE MARSHALL, b. Aug. 15, 1851. Res., Roxbury, Devon St. Married, at Boston, March —, 1881, Emma I. Sawyer. Ch.: 1. Ruth Lamson, b. Jan. 8, 1883; d. Dec. 2, 1887. 2. Miriam Choate, b. Sept. 20, 1887. 3. Josephine Elizabeth, b. ——.

2399. vi. DAVID FRANCIS, b. Jan. 19 1829; m., Nov. 24, 1853, in Beverly, Sarah Devereux Wells, b. Dec. 27, 1831; d. May 15, 1876. He is an engineer. Ch.: 1. Sarah Elizabeth, b. March 6, 1856; unm. Res., 339 Blue Hill Ave., Roxbury. 2. Amelia Frances, b. in Roxbury, Nov. 8, 1859; m., in Boston, May 31, 1882, Franklin H. Newell. Ch.: (a) Edith Devereux, b. in Boston, Feb. 23, 1884. (b) Bertha Frances, b. in Boston, Sept. —, 1887 (?). 3. Francis Lamson, b. in Roxbury, April 19, 1861; d. Aug. 31, 1861. David Francis Foster m., 2d, May 4, 1880, Mary A. C. Warren, at Burlington, Vt. She d. March 13, 1896. No children.

1341. HON. ZEBULON FOSTER (Zebulon, Aaron, Moses, John, Reginald, Reginald), b. Sept. 6, 1797; m., Aug. 26, 1823, Abigail Wheeler, who d. April 16, 1831; m., 2d, Lois Whitney, March 15, 1832, who d. Aug. 24, 1852; m., 3d, Eliza A. Folsom, Aug. 23, 1853. s. p. by his third wife. He was one of the representatives of the town in 1845-46; selectman in 1832-38-41-42-49-57; was captain of the Rifles. Res., Henniker, N. H.

2400. i. SUSAN W., b. Sept. 28, 1823; m. Harrison A. Rice.

2401. ii. WARREN S., b. Sept. 12, 1830; m., Jan. 28, 1858, Caroline Smith, dau. of Parker and Martha (Smith). He was several years connected with the railroads in Illinois as conductor. Ch.: 1. Mary W., b. Jan. 14, 1859. 2. Orah C., b. July 18, 1861. 3. Jessie W., b. Oct. 26, 1869. Ch. by 2d wife:

2402. iii. CAROLINE F., b. Nov. 6, 1835; m. William O. Folsom, Nov. 6, 1861. She d. 1866, and he m., 2d, Julia Whitney, dau. of Frederic and Fidelia. Is a merchant, Justice of the Peace and quorum; has been selectman and town treasurer.

1343. HON. WILLIAM S. FOSTER (Zebulon, Aaron, Moses, John, Reginald, Reginald), b. March 19, 1801; m., Dec. 27, 1827, Harriet Page, of Antrim; m., 2d,

Nov. 28, 1850, Mary Cooledge. William S. Foster was a carpenter by trade, and came to Antrim in the spring of 1826 to help build the Center church. He boarded with Stephen Paige and thus became acquainted with his daughter Harriet, whom he married December 27, 1827, after which he continued to reside in this town. In 1829 he moved on to the William McDole place, where he lived forty-six years. He married, second, Mary Cooledge, November 28, 1850. Mr. Foster was representative of the town; was chairman of the selectmen during the war, and was called to fill many positions of trust and honor. In old age he made profession of his faith in Christ. After a long and painful sickness, he passed away in Christian confidence and peace. He died July 10, 1875. Residence, Antrim, N. H.

2403. i. STEPHEN P., b. in 1828. He left Antrim in early manhood, and was last heard of in London in 1851.
2404. ii. WILLIAM S., b. in 1830; m. Margaret Shaw, of Massachusetts. Res., Mobile, Ala.
2405. iii. AARON W., b. in 1832, and went South. He entered the Rebel army, lost an arm at Malvern Hill, and d. from effects thereof in 1872.
2406. iv. JENNETTE A., b. in 1834; d. April 6, 1858.
2407. v. JOHN W., b. in 1837; m. Hannah E. Hunt.
2408. vi. HENRY H., b. in 1841. He entered the Union army, the Seventh N. H. regt., and d. in the service, in Florida, in 1862.
2409. vii. LEONARD M., b. in 1846; d. in 1853.
2410. viii. HARRIET A., twin sister of Leonard M.; d. in 1849.

1345. CAPT. JEREMIAH FOSTER (Zebulon, Aaron, Moses, John, Reginald, Reginald), b. June 22, 1805; m., Jan., 1833, in Henniker, Adeline, dau. of Jacob Lovisa Rice, of that town, who d. Sept. 7, 1863; m. 2d., April 23, 1864, Martha B. Huntoon, of that town; resided on the homestead until recently; representative in 1857-8; often one of the selectmen of the town; filled many positions of trust with fidelity; very efficient as a commander of the Rifles and Grenadiers; was a civil engineer. Res., Henniker, N. H.

2411. i. JACOB R., b. Feb. 4, 1834; m. Georgia Nash and Mary Nash.
2412. ii. CHARLES S., b. Jan. 26, 1838; m.; Aug. 11, 1862, Julia, dau. of Luther and Sally Goss, of this town; d. Jan. 22, 1864.
2413. iii. SUSAN MARIA, b. July 30, 1840; m. Hon. W. E. Cogswell. William Elbridge was b. Feb. 27, 1835; m., Dec. 4, 1862. He d. Sept. 27, 1875, leaving six children. He was town clerk and treasurer for many years and representative for two years. Res., Henniker, N. H. Ch.: 1. Addie Frances, b. Aug. 25, 1864. 2. Charles Elbridge, b. Jan 1, 1866. 3. Anna Mabel, b. Sept. 3, 1869. 4. Frank Selwyn, b. Sept. 17, 1871; d. April 18, 1878. 5. Albert Foster, b. Oct. 2, 1873. 6. Martha Haskell, b. April 24, 1875.
2414. iv. WILLIAM H., b. July 13, 1842; m., Jan., 1867, Emma Clement, of Hillsborough; d. June 5, 1879.
2415. v. EDWIN SCOTT, b. March 22, 1845; m., Sept., 1868, Elvira Tabor, of Bristol, druggist; res. in Haverhill, Mass. Widely known as a musician.

1346. MICAJAH FOSTER (Zebulon, Aaron, Moses, John, Reginald, Reginald), b. Henniker, N. H., Aug. 27, 1807; m., April 5, 1838, Betsy Tucker. Lived in this town until April, 1855, when he removed to Iowa, where he still resides. Ch. b. here. Res., Henniker, N. H., and ——, Iowa.

2416. i. HOMER T., b. Dec. 22, 1839.
2417. ii. MARY M., b. Dec. 28, 1842.
2418. iii. EVALINE, b. Aug. 27, 1844.
2418½. iv. EDEN S., b. Feb. 18, 1847.
2419. v. ZELDA J., b. April 5, 1849.

1356. JOHN PLUMMER FOSTER (Charles, Jonathan, Jonathan, Jonathan, William, Reginald), b. North Andover, Mass., Oct. 28, 1817; m., West Boxford, Dec. 9, 1845, Sarah A. Peabody, b. Feb. 16, 1818; d. March 13, 1896. He was a farmer. John P. Foster was born at North Andover, in the same house in which he died, was educated in the public schools and always following the life of farming and raising of fruit trees and large quantities of fruit. He d. June 4, 1891. Res., North Andover, Mass.

2420. i. JOHN FRANK, b. Nov. 21, 1846; d. unm. at North Andover.
2421. ii. ANNIE F., b. Sept 28, 1848; was a school teacher; d. Dec. 6, 1880; unm.
2422. iii. LEWIS PLUMMER, b. Oct. 1, 1850; d. Dec. 19, 1856.
2423. iv. SARAH PEABODY, b. Dec. 25, 1852; unm.; Res., North Andover, Mass.
2424. v. HORACE K., b. Dec. 5, 1854; m. Florence K. Holman.
2425. vi. CHARLES CHANDLER, b. Nov. 19, 1856; drowned July 25, 1863.
2426. vii. GEORGE BYRON, b. Dec. 1, 1858; m., Nov. 5, 1896, Margaret Vinal Brooks; Res., s. p., Trinity Court, Boston, Mass.; she was b. April 10, 1863. He graduated from Phillips Academy, Andover, Mass., 1879; Amherst College, 1883. With Massachusetts National Bank, Boston.

1366. JONATHAN EDWARDS FOSTER (Jonathan, Jonathan, Jonathan, Jonathan, William, Reginald), b. Boxford, Mass., May 9, 1815; m., Jan. 10, 1843, Susan R., dau. of Benjamin and Rachel (Hunting) Peabody, of Boxford. He d. of small pox Jan. 28, 1867. She was b. Feb. 1, 1816. Res., Boxford, Mass.

2427. i. THOMAS PEABODY, b. Oct. 30, 1843; d. unm., Feb. 15, 1891.
2428. ii. REGINALD DANA, b. Feb. 18, 1848; unm. Res., West Boxford, Mass.
2429. iii. ELIZA EDWARDS, b. Nov. 23, 1850; d. April 20, 1872. Res., West Boxford, Mass.
2430. iv. FANNIE FLORENCE, b. Sept. 3, 1855; d. of consumption Aug. 23, 1878.

1367. GEORGE NOYES FOSTER (Jonathan, Jonathan, Jonathan, Jonathan, William, Reginald), b. West Boxford, Mass., March 31, 1817; m., at North Andover, Dec. 17, 1846, Martha Jane Symonds, b. Aug. 12, 1823; d. Jan. 24, 1865; m. 2d, 1870, Mrs. Mahala B. Sanborn. She d. s. p., Sept., 1891. George Noyes Foster, born March 31, 1817, at West Boxford, Mass. "He attended District No. 5 school, the same one I did; how long I do not know. I believe he worked for his father, who owned a large farm, and was considered to be well-off. He also 'worked out' on farms, as most young men did in those days. Was a lieutenant in the local militia. Married when he was twenty-nine years old, and lived for a short time in Bradford. His father bought and gave him the farm on which he lived, in Georgetown, Mass., till the spring of 1866, when he sold it at auction to one Weston, who owned a saw mill near by. Soon after selling his farm he moved to Groveland, near the old ferry, where he resided till he died, respected by all who knew him." His occupation in Groveland was mostly carpenter work. He d. Jan. 10, 1880. Res., Groveland, Mass.

2431. i. WILLIAM COLE, b. July 21, 1849; d. unm. Oct. 20, 1870.
2432. ii. MARY KIMBALL, b. March 22, 1853; m., Sept. 6, 1886, Perry Matson, b. Nov. 11, 1853; is a shoe agent. Res., Whitman, Mass. Ch.: 1. Eleanor Howe, b. Jan. 21, 1890.
2433. iii. ELEANOR AUGUSTA, b. Oct. 4, 1857. Res., 31 Upton street, Boston, Mass.
2434. iv. JONATHAN MYRON, b. Sept. 18, 1847; m. Eulalie V. B. Lapeaele.

1369. WILLIAM HENRY FOSTER (Phineas, Jonathan, Jonathan, Jonathan, William, Reginald), b. Boston, Mass., Jan. 9, 1810; m., in Lowell, May 26, 1846, Hannah Goodwin Locke, of Lowell, b. Dec. 24, 1815; d. March 25, 1893. Joseph L. Foster, of Newton, appointed administrator of estate of Hannah Goodwin Foster, of Boston, died March 25, 1893, leaving husband, William H. Foster; next of kin, John H. Foster, Medford, son; Mary H. Foster, Boston, daughter; Charles Foster, Calcutta, E. I., son; Williiam Foster, Boston, son; Joseph L. Foster, Newton, son. June 1, 1893. Lib. 674; Fol. 420. He d. Oct. 30, 1894. Res., Dorchester, Mass.

2435. i. JOHN HARROD, b. April 27, 1847, m. Mary Gardner Churchill.
2436. ii. MARY HAVEN, b. Dec. 19, 1848; unm. Res., Perrin Road, Brookline, Mass.
2437. iii. CHARLES, b. March 6, 1850; m. Elizabeth Yonge Andros.
2438. iv. WILLIAM, b. Nov. 12, 1851; m., Jan., 1882, ——. Res., Hotel Belleview, Boston, Mass.
2439. v. JOSEPH LOCKE, b. Nov. 14, 1853; m. Elizabeth L. Harlow.

1372. GEORGE FOSTER (Phineas, Jonathan, Jonathan, Jonathan, William, Reginald), b. Boston, Mass., Feb. 10, 1815; m., ——, Adele Rushton; d. New Orleans, March 28, 1857; m. 2d., —— ——. He d. in New Orleans. Res., New Orleans, La.

2440. i. RUSHTON, b. ——. Res., New Orleans, La.
2441. ii. DAUGHTER, b. ——; in a convent.

1373. FRANCIS FOSTER (Phineas, Jonathan, Jonathan, Jonathan, William, Reginald), b. Boston, Mass., Aug. 4, 1819; m. in Calcutta, East Indies, Aug. 1, 1860, Sarah Elizabeth Lemist, b. July 14, 1836. Was a merchant. He d. Aug. 14, 1867. Res., Boston and New York City.

2442. i. FRANCIS, b. May 11, 1861; d. Sept. 28, 1867.
2443. ii. ROBERT MONTGOMERY, b. Aug. 23, 1862; d. March 1, 1870.
2444. iii. ELIZABETH ADAMS, b. May 29, 1865; unm. Res., 22 Kenilworth avenue, Roxbury, Mass. Lemuel Shaw, of Boston, appointed guardian of Elizabeth Adams Foster, born May 29, 1865, child of Francis Foster, late of Boston, deceased, and Sarah Elizabeth Foster, his widow. May 27, 1872. Lib. 457; Fol. 481.
Inventory mentions personal estate of Elizabeth A. Foster; cash of J. H. and W. H. Foster, trustees. Lib. 468; Fol. 486.
Sarah E. Woodman, formerly Sarah E. Foster, appointed guardian of child, Elizabeth A. Foster. February 18, 1878. Lib. 503; Fol. 375-520.
Inventory mentions Horatio Woodman, one of appraisers. Lib. 502; Fol. 122.

1379. RICHARD KIMBALL FOSTER (Asa, Richard, Jonathan, Jonathan, William, Reginald), b. Boxford, Mass., Aug. 21, 1809; m., ——, Elizabeth Webb. Res., Boxford, Mass.

2445. i. RICHARD ALLEN, b. Nov. 15, 1843.
2446. ii. ELIZABETH A., b. March 19, 1846; m. L. H. Cheney.
2447. iii. WILLIAM WEBB, b. Oct. 24, 1848; d. May 1, 1849.

1380. NATHAN FOSTER (Asa, Abner, Zebediah, Jonathan, William, Reginald), b. Newry, Me., ——; m., ——, Paty Stearns. He d. ——. Res., Bethel, Me.

2448. i. ASA, b. Oct. 16, 1816; d. Dec. 20, 1816.
2449. ii. NATHAN F., b. and d. Aug., 1817.
2450. iii. THOMAS JEFFERSON, b. May 1, 1820; d. March 29, 1823.
2451 iv. LOIS, b. June 11, 1822.
2452. v. THOMAS JEFFERSON, b. June 8, 1824; m. Nan C. Bennett.
2453. vi. REUBEN BALL, b. July 25, 1826; m. Salome G. Eames..

1381. HON. REUBEN B. FOSTER (Asa, Abner, Zebediah, Jonathan, William, Reginald), b. Newry, Me., ——; m., ——, Sarah Bartlett, dau. of Stephen. Reuben B. Foster, son of Asa and Anna (Bartlett) Foster, of Newry, was born in that town and fitted for college, but did not enter. He was by trade a carpenter, an ingenious workman, and taught school winters during his early manhood. He finally decided on farming as his life business, and purchased the farm consisting of intervale and upland which Gideon and Silas Powers had previously occupied. He commenced at once to bring his land into a higher state of cultivation, in which he succeeded. He was a man of superior judgment and intelligence; and of a scientific cast of mind. He studied out methods for changing coarse material to dressing, and had practiced it for years before Bomer patented his process, which was identical with that of Mr. Foster's. He was a great reader and well acquainted with history, both ancient and modern. He employed a large number of men to carry on his farm, and in the various branches of farming, including stock raising, he did a larger business than any one in his section of the State. He raised large crops of grain and grass, and delighted in a large yield of yellow corn. He attended personally to all the details of his business, rarely leaving the farm, unless called away on urgent business. He was on the board of selectmen in Hanover and served one or more terms in the Legislature. He married Sarah, daughter of Stephen Bartlett, a most amiable woman, and a model farmer's wife. He survived his wife several years, and was gathered to his fathers several years ago. He died ——. Res., Bethel, Me.

2454. iv. REUBEN B., b. Feb. 8, 1833; m. Dorcas Howe.
2455. i. AGNES, b. Jan. 27, 1837; m. Lawson C. Smith, of Newry. She d., and he m., 2d., Ruby Mason.
2456. ii. FRANCES, b. Feb. 7, 1829; d. Oct., 1831.
2457. iii. SARAH B., b. May 21, 1831; m. Asa R. Howe. She d. Oct. 13, 1862.
2458. v. FRANCES, b. Dec. 23, 1834; d. Nov. 12, 1854.
2459. vi. JOAN AMANDA, b. Dec. 2, 1836; m. Edwin L. Hoyt.
2460. vii. JULIA B., b. Aug. 9, 1838; m. Charles R. Abbott; m., 2d., Oscar D. Rolfe, of Rumford.
2461. viii. HELEN, b. Nov. 11, 1840; m. Galen Howe. She d. May 29, 1875.
2462. ix. NELSON B., b. July 2, 1842; d. Sept., 1844.
2463. x. LUCIEN L., b. Dec. 27, 1844; d. May 3, 1864.
2464. xi. L. LETITIA, b. Jan. 16, 1848; m. Henry S. Hastings. She d. Aug. 24, 1866.

1382. ENOCH FOSTER (Asa, Abner, Zebediah, Jonathan, William, Reginald), b. Jan. 1, 1799, Sundy River, Newry, Me.; m. there, July, 1824, Persis Swan, b.——, 1806; d. April 9, 1859; m. 2d, April 16, 1861, Mrs. Louisa Cutting, widow of Amaziah. He was a farmer and resided in Newry. He d. Dec. 26, 1881. Res., Bethel, Me.

2465. i. BETSEY, b. March 25, 1825; m. David Emery; m., 2d., Joseph A. Knapp. She d. Oct. 14, 1879.
2466. ii. ORRIN, b. March 27, 1827; m. Mary O. Styles.
2467. iii. BEULAH BARTLETT, b. July 1, 1829; m. Albert D. Styles. She d. 1880.
2468. iv. ENOCH, b. May 10, 1839; m. Adaline O. Lowe and Sarah W. Chapman.

1383. DEACON ELI FOSTER (Asa, Abner, Zebediah, Jonathan, William, Reginald), b. Newry, Me., ——; m.,——, Dorcas Bartlett, dau. of Stephen. She d. April 29, 1887. Deacon Eli Foster was the son of Asa and Anna (Bartlett) Foster, of Newry, and was born in that town. When he became of age he married Dorcas, daughter of Stephen Bartlett, of Bethel, and settled on wild land situated on the road between Locke's Mills and the Androscoggin river, though at the time he erected his house the road had not been built. His land consisted of lowland and upland, and when he selected his building lot he exercised that judgment and foresight with regard to future wants, not often shown by the early settlers. The spot selected was where the lowlands joined the upland, near a beautiful brook which comes from the hills at this point and meanders through the level ground to Otter brook. He left the forest on the high ground in the vicinity of his buildings, which consisted largely of the sugar maple, standing, and they are standing to this day and constitute one of the finest sugar orchards in the town. On the hill east of this maple grove he cleared land for pasturage, and the level ground was cleared up for meadow and crops. The broad area of high interval, almost a dead level, and stretching away across Otter brook and to the hills beyond attracts the attention and elicits the admiration of all passersby. Mr. Foster's education was somewhat limited, but he had natural abilities of a high order. He was a model farmer and a first-class business man. His thrift, which was the result of prudence and economy, sometimes excited the envy of his less fortunate neighbors, and even of those who were often glad to have the benefit of his better circumstances. He was kind hearted and accommodating, social in his tastes and habits and rendered needed assistance to the poor by giving them employment at seasons when they could find it nowhere else. His wife was a helpmeet indeed. She was skilled in all the domestic arts for which the settlers' wives were distinguished—carding, spinning and weaving both flax and wool. She furnished clothing for the household, beginning with the raw material and ending with the made-up and finished garments. In the evening, after the household duties had been carefully attended to, she would sit with knitting work in hand, and it was marvelous to witness the numerous pairs of hose, linen for summer and woolen for winter wear, and mittens, she would produce in a single year. Mr. Foster was chosen deacon of the Baptist church and was filling the position at the time of his death. He was a man of decided views, a strong temperance man, and a few years before his death gave up the use of tobacco, of which he had long made use. His wife survived him many years, dividing her time between the old homestead, occupied by her only son, and the home of her eldest daughter, Mrs. Ira Cushman, of South Bethel. He d. Jan. 6, 1873 Res., Bethel, Maine.

2469. i. VIRTUE WILLIS, b. Aug. 1, 1826; m. April 11, 1848, Ira Cushman, b. Jan. 25, 1821, son of Deacon John; resided on the old place of his father, and then exchanged farms with John Chase for the Needham farm, near Walker's Mills. Res., Bethel, Me. Ch.: 1. Eli Foster, b. May 30, 1849; m. Ellen F. Swan. 2. Isaac Allerton, b. Jan. 7, 1854; m. Lillie E. Swan 3. Dorcas Sophia, b. Feb. 4, 1860. 4. Virtue Gertrude, b. April 9, 1870.

2470. ii. SOPHIA BARTLETT, b. Sept. 13, 1828; m., Dec. 18, 1848, Rev. Dr. Hiram C. Estes. Rev. Hiram Cushman Estes, D. D., son of John and Sarah (Andrews) Estes, was born in Bethel July 27, 1823. He was brought up on a farm, but early developed a love of learning and a passion for books. Like many other New England youths, he was obliged to depend mainly upon his own efforts for the means necessary to a course of study; and in his case, as in many others, the fact was demonstrated that a determined will is quite sure to open a way. After leaving the town school he attended Bethel Academy; the Turner High School, which was then in charge of John M. Adams, of Rumford, now of Deering; and at North Yarmouth Academy, working upon the farm portions of each year and teaching in winter to meet his expenses. He entered Waterville College, now Colby University, in 1843, and graduated with honor in 1847. He studied theology at the Cambridge (Mass.) Divinity School and was ordained to the work of the ministry at Auburn, in this State, May 16, 1850. For three years, from 1842 to 1845, he was agent for the American Baptist Missionary Union in the State of Maine. Settled over the church in East Trenton from 1845 to 1860; at Leicester, Mass., from 1860 to 1862; at Jericho, Vt., from 1862 to 1872; over the Baptist church in Paris from January 1, 1873, to July 1, 1883. and from September 1, 1883 to September, 1885, at Winchenden, Mass. While at Trenton he was elected to the Legislature, in 1858, and served as chairman of the Committee on Education on the part of the House, to which position he was admirably adapted. The degree of D. D. was conferred upon him by his alma mater in 1872, and never has this important degree been more fitly bestowed by that institution. March 1, 1886, he was again called to the Baptist church in Leicester and his connection with that church still continues. Dr. Estes is a profound scholar, a forcible and interesting writer, and whatever he undertakes to do he does well. He has written and delivered several lectures, which have been highly spoken of by those best qualified to judge. His only published volume is an essay entitled, "The Christian Doctrine of the Soul," which appeared in 1873 from the press of Noyes, Holmes & Co., of Boston. It is a duodecimo of 163 pages, and a model of concise and logical writing. It was well received by all denominations of Christians. Several of his occasional sermons have been printed and widely read. He has also prepared and published a history of the Baptist church in Leicester, a work requiring much patient research and admirably done. Dr. Estes was married December 18, 1848, to Sophia Bartlett, daughter of Deacon Eli Foster, of Bethel, and the following are their children: 1. David Foster, b. Oct. 18, 1851. He was graduated from University of Vermont, 1871, and from the Newton Theological Institution, 1874; pursued special studies in theology at the University of Goettingen, 1878-79; ordained at Manchester, Vt., Aug. 19, 1874; pastor of the Baptist church, Manchester, 1874-76; Belfast, Me., 1876-78; Vergennes, Vt., 1880-83; professor and acting-president Atlanta Baptist Seminary, Atlanta, Ga., 1883-86; pastor at Holden, Mass., since 1886. He married, May 12, 1880, Effigene Lydia, daughter of Truman Chittenden Galusha, of Jericho, Vt., b. Sept. 14, 1858; has one child: (a) Walter Dalton Estes, b. at Vergennes, Vt., July 22, 1881. 2. Walter Dalton, b. July

20, 1855. He was a young man of great promise, and while a student of law at Richford, Vt., he drank water from a poisoned well and thereby lost his life. He d. Feb. 22, 1878. 3. Alice Maud, b. Feb. 13, 1874. She was graduated from Leicester Academy in the class of '91.

2471. iii. DAVID T., b. Sept. 5, 1831; m. Harriet B. Crockett.

1384. REV. BENJAMIN FOSTER (Asa, Abner, Zebediah, Jonathan, William, Reginald), b.———; m., Oct. 20, 1827, Louisa Coburn, dau. of Moses and Esther (Spalding), b. Aug. 5, 1810. He was a well-known Methodist preacher and was settled in various parts of Maine. He d. April 14, 1891. Res., Bethel, Me.

2472. i. MOSES COBURN, b. July 29, 1827; m. Francina Smith.
2473. ii. MARCIA, b. Sept. 22 1831; d. July 22, 1833.
2474. iii. LEONA ROBERTS, b. Dec. 30, 1835; d. Jan. 1, 1886.
2475. iv. NELLIE MARCIA, b. Jan. 4, 1849.

1393. ELHANAN BARTLETT FOSTER (Asa, Abner, Zebediah, Jonathan, William, Reginald), b. Newry, Me., Feb. 13, 1823; m., ——, Mehitabel Chapman. He was a farmer. Res., North Waterford, Me.

2476. i. LAFAYETTE S., b. May 15, 1855; m. Mary Etta Glovar.

1394. WILLIAM PHILLIPS FOSTER (William, William, John, William, William, Reginald), b. Andover, Mass., Jan. 21, 1830; m. there Dec. 1, 1853, Jane C. Kimball, b. Oct. 14, 1830; d. May 20, 1859; m., 2d., Jan. 22, 1862, Anna M. Barrows. She res. Southern Pines, N. C. William Phillips was born in 1830, when his father was seventy years old; it was his only marriage. His life was short; he was always a delicate child and for years before he died fought lung consumption. He devoted himself to caring for the old homestead which his son, Francis Homer, now owns, and spent most of his life there. He d. Feb. 28, 1871. Res., Andover, Mass.

2477. i. ANNA JANE, b. Dec. 11, 1854; d. Sept. 29, 1861.
2478. ii. WILLIAM PHILLIPS, b. July 11, 1856. Res., California.
2479. iii. JOHN CHARLES, b. Feb. 7, 1859; m. Katherine Virginia Van Doren.
2480. iv. SARAH ANNA, b. Aug. 24, 1865; m. Rev. Fred D. Greene, June 25, 1890. They went to Turkey as missionaries of the A. B. C. F. M. for four years. Mr. Greene is now employed as financial agent of the American Bible Society, New York. Their children are: 1. Phillip Foster Greene, b. May 29, 1892. 2. Joseph Kingsbury Greene, b. Dec. 30, 1894. 3. Edward Barrows Greene, b. Sept. 25, 1896.
2481. v. FRANCIS HOMER, b. April 7, 1867; m. Mary J. Sweet.

1397. JOHN FOSTER (John, John, John, William, William, Reginald), b. Andover, Mass., ——, 1802; m., Haverhill, April 28, 1829, Sarah Harding, b., ——, 1804; d. Roxbury, Jan. 25, 1866. He d. Sept. 3, 1849. Res., Andover, Mass.

2482. i. JOHN W., b. March 11, 1840; m. Mercy F. Gilman.
2483. ii. CHILD, b. May 28, 1832; d. same day.
2484. iii. CHILD, b. Feb. 11, 1833; d. same day.
2485. iv. NEWELL H., b. April 13, 1834; d. May 13, 1840.
2486. v. ELLEN I., b. Nov. 12, 1838; m. —— Whittaker. Ch.: 1. Harrie T., b. ——. Res., 27 Greenville street, Roxbury, Mass.
2487. vi. FRANK E., b, ——. Res., "The Orleans," 4301 Oakenwald avenue, Chicago, Ill.
2488. vii. SARAH H., b. Nov. 10, 1845; m. —— Goldie. Res., 3 St. 'James court, Roxbury, Mass.

1400. WILLIAM PITTS FOSTER (John, John, John, William, William, Reginald), b. Andover, Mass., Dec. —, 1810; m., Haverhill, Oct. 23, 1842, Lucinda Randall; d. Feb. 4, 1885. He was a harness manufacturer. He d. May 18, 1882. Res., New Durham, N. H., and Methuen, Mass.

2489. i. HORACE DANIEL, b. April 6, 1844; d. Nov. 8, 1889.
2490. ii. MARY OSGOOD, b. Dec. 5, 1849; m., ——, 1872, —— Mack. Ch.: 1. Ida. Res., 71 Broadway, Methuen, Mass.
2491. iii. HELEN LUCINDA, b. June 24, 1852; d. Dec. 29, 1887.
2492. iv. JOHN WILLIAM, b. Aug. 25, 1854; m. Marguerite Hussey.
2493. v. FRED, b. July 15, 1859; m. —— ——.

1403. HON. HERMAN FOSTER (John, Obadiah, John, William, William, Reginald), b. Andover, Mass., Oct. 31, 1800; m., Nov. 8, 1826, Harriet Mary Ann Whittemore, of Arlington, Mass, b. Aug. 13, 1806. Herman Foster, in early life fitted for college, but a disease of the eyes compelled him to abandon his cherished intention. He acquired his education at the common schools and at the Atkinson Academy. Dartmouth College, however, in view of his distinguished abilities and position, in 1861, conferred upon him the honorary degree of A. M. For several years he was engaged in teaching school. He then established himself in a mercantile business in Boston. This pursuit he followed for some years, and then, abandoning it, went to Warner, N. H., where his father then lived, and began the study of law in the office of the Hon. Henry B. Chase, of that town, and was admitted to the bar in 1839. He married Harriet Mary Ann Whittemore, of West Cambridge, now Arlington, Mass., who still survives, and by whom he had two children, who died in infancy. In November, 1840, Mr. Foster went to Manchester, N. H., and began the practice of his profession. Growing in influence with the growth of the city, he has, for a generation, maintained a high position as a citizen, a financier, a legislator, as well as an attorney and counsellor. To him by the citizens of Manchester, before and since its organization as a city, have been committed many offices of honor and responsibility. He was one of its prominent men and impressed his character on many of the institutions of the city, while in the process of formation, and in a manner to merit a cherished remembrance. He was treasurer of the town of Manchester in 1842 and 1843. He was sent to represent the city in the House of Representatives in New Hampshire in 1845 and 1846 and again in 1868 and 1869. He was State Senator in 1860 and 1861, being President of the Senate in 1861. He was solicitor of the city in 1857. In August, 1862, he was appointed by President Lincoln assessor of internal revenue for the Second District of New Hampshire, resigning in February of the next year. As a financier, the good judgment and ability of Mr. Foster were evidenced in his connection as a trustee and one of the investing committee of the Manchester Savings Bank—said to be one of the best-managed institutions of its kind in the country—from its organization, in 1846, to his death; as treasurer and clerk of the Manchester Gas-light Company since its organization, in 1850; as a director of the old Amoskeag Bank for many years; for the last three or four years a director of the Amoskeag National Bank, and as one of the first directors and clerk of the Manchester & Lawrence Railroad. In all these trusts he was diligent, thoughtful and honest. From articles communicated to the Manchester papers by Judge Daniel Clark, of the Circuit Court of New Hampshire, and Judge Clough, of Manchester, the friends and co-laborers of Mr. Foster, to which I am indebted in preparing this notice, I had the following summary of his character: "Mr. Foster was, in many respects, a remarkable man. He had characteristics which stamped him as an individual much more deeply and distinctly than most men. While belonging to and making one of the great mass of individuals of which mankind is composed he was, so to speak, more clearly and sharply individualized than most others. There was a steady firmness about him, coupled with a singular diffidence and gentleness, to such a degree as placed these qualities sometimes in striking contrast. His perceptions were distinct and accurate; his intelligence wide and clear; his purpose firm; his thoughts and actions independent; his decision manifest, and his will tenacious. All his qualities were strong and conspicuous. Such was the power of his memory that dates, places, persons, facts, occurrences, what was said, who said it, when and where, though many years ago, were engraven upon it as it were upon a plate of steel. He could quote from the speeches of Burke, Erskine, Phillips and Webster, from the poetry and plays of Virgil, Byron and Shakespeare. In business he was careful, painstaking and methodical, attending to the minutest details, sometimes seeming slow and over-cautious, yet so prompt and decided in action as to shut out every idea of hesitancy or vacillation. Deliberation in him was coupled with strength. In his profession as an attorney he was active and vigilant, qualities which, in the law-practice that existed prior to the coming in of the bankrupt act, were among the most useful and successful. No business entrusted to him was ever neglected. Money collected for his clients was always ready for them. As a counsellor he formed his opinions upon careful study and examination, and they were generally correct and reliable. In the preparation of a case he was thorough. He was seldom caught unprepared. Towards his brethren in his profession he was courteous, affable, true and polite, and he commanded the respect of all who knew him. As a politician he was not a partisan in any sense. He had none of the business unfairness or intolerance of a partisan; but he was a strict party man, liberal and frank, consistent and reliable.

He believed in independence of thought and action; he hated servility. As a man he was honest and upright. He loved truth, hated dissimulation and never misled by misrepresentation or deceitful acts or appearances. As a citizen, he was always the friend of good order; willing to bear a just share of the burdens of society, ready to respond to its requirements and always benevolent and kind. As a friend, he was sincere and true. In religion he was a Unitarian, and was one of the founders and most liberal supporters of that Church in Manchester. His theory and practice were founded on the Gospels He was benevolent, charitable and tolerant." To this summary of character I add, as a suitable conclusion to this paper, the testimony of one who has known and loved him as a brother. In a note, in answer to some inquiries, he says: "Of the first half of my brother's life I know but little, as, during that period, I was young, and he lived most of the time in Massachusetts. That he may have made some mistakes is not unlikely; few have lived who have not done so. But for nearly forty years of his life I can speak from personal knowledge; and during that period he has been entirely correct; upward and onward in goodness; hightoned, straightforward, square and upright, gentle and kind as a loving mother, ever ready to join in a helping hand in liberal measure to our less fortunate brothers and sisters, and in other directions when duty called. In his life there is so much of good, beautiful, consoling memories that I cannot think of him in sadness. He died February 17, 1875. Res., Manchester, N. H.

1405. CHARLES FOSTER (John, Obadiah, John, William, William, Reginald), b. Tewksbury, Mass., May 11, 1804; m. ——, Ann Evans, of Charlestown, Mass.; d. Nov 9, 1851. He d. Jan. 19, 1850. Res., Charlestown, Mass.

2494. i. MARTHA ANN, b. Nov. 20, 1825; d. Aug. 14, 1870.

2495. ii. BENJAMIN HASTINGS, b. Nov., 1828; d. April 26, 1870.

1407. JOHN FOSTER (John, Obadiah, John, William, William, Reginald), b. Hudson, N. H., Dec. 30, 1817; m., July 4, 1843, Harriet Sanford, of Boston. Removed from Warner, N. H., where his parents resided, to Boston, Mass., Sept. 1, 1836, and in 1839 he, with Horace B. Taylor, commenced business under the style of Foster & Taylor. The firm is still continued as originally formed.

Will.—John Foster, of Boston, merchant; daughter, Fanny Foster; children of sister, Emily, F. Badger; brother in-law, Ebenezer S. Badger; husband of said Emily F. Badger; children of brother, George Foster; children of sister, Sabra F. Tewksbury; Susan Sanford, sister of my late wife; Thomas W. Sanford, Samuel S. Payne, nephew of my late wife; late wife's niece and namesake, Harriet S. Preble. Dated Nov. 21, 1896. Lib. 727. Fol. 86-94. Prob. May 13, 1897. Lib. 730, Fol. 379. Petition for administrator. John Foster died April 9, 1897; next of kin, Fanny Foster, daughter, B st n. Lib. 730, Fol. 379. He d. in 1897. Res., Boston, Mass.

2496 i. GEORGE SANFORD, b. April 26, 1844; d. July 24, 1851.

2497. ii. HARRIET LUCY, b. Jan. 9, 1849; d. March 8, 1851.

2498. iii. FANNY, b. June 15, 1852; unm. Res., 25 Marlborough St., Boston, Mass., P. O. box 1589.

1408. HON. GEORGE FOSTER (John, Obadiah, John, William, William, Reginald), b. Hudson, N. H., Sept. 23, 1821; m., Feb. 7, 1847, Salome T. Little, of Boscawen, N H.; b. Aug. 9, 1825; d Dec. 12, 1897.

Another prominent name is added to the too rapidly increasing list of our city's honored dead. The Hon. George Foster, who has generally been regarded of later years as a resident of Manchester, died at his home, in Bedford, Monday afternoon, at eighteen minutes past five o'clock, of rheumatism; aged fifty-nine years.

Mr. Foster was the son of John Foster, of Hudson. He was the youngest of a family of six children, two of whom, John Foster, Esq., a retired merchant, of Boston, and Emily, wife of E. S Badger, of Warner, are living. The deceased members are Herman, of this city; Sabra, wife of Dr. Tewksbury, of Lawrence, and the mother of Mrs. Joseph White, of Boston, Mass.; Charles, who died many years ago, and George, whose death it is our sad duty to chronicle to-day. The early life of the deceased was passed in Hudson until eight years of age, when he removed to Warner, where he resided until December, 1859. He then took up his residence in Warner, in which town he lived until Nov 20, 1868, the date of his moving to Bedford, and taking possession of the Chandler place, on which he has since lived.

About 1850 he disposed of his business and became a partner in the lumber trade with H. D. Robertson, an occupation that he successfully followed up to the time of his death, a period of thirty-one years. By the death of Mr. Robertson the partnership was dissolved, and a new partnership was formed with Moses A. Hodgdon, of Weare. This continued till the year 1867, when Mr. Foster went West with the view of permanent settlement. Being dissatisfied with the chances for business success, he returned home, and became a member of the lumber dealing firm of Clough & Foster, his partner being Gilman Clough, Esq. Under this name a large and lucrative business has since been carried on. Mr. Foster was an enthusiastic and successful farmer, and his homestead in Bedford was one of the largest, best tilled and most productive in this section of the State. He delighted in fine stock, immense crops and a large dairy, and they were always to be found on his premises.

HON. GEORGE FOSTER.

Mr. Foster had held during his lifetime several important offices of honor and responsibility. He held a number of town offices in Warner, and during the war filled the position of Assistant Assessor of the Second Collection District, and several other offices under the government. In the year 1872 Mr. Foster was the Republican candidate from his district for State Senator, and was elected. The following year he was re-elected to the same office.

Through life Mr. Foster had been a tireless and indefatigable worker. He saw in every formidable obstacle only something to be overcome. Thrown entirely upon his resources in early boyhood, he carved out for himself both honor and fortune by the sheer force of a strong manly nature.

Mr. Foster was a man of great resources. He had a strong body and an active well-balanced mind. He had courage, sagacity and endurance. He never rested and never turned from a task because it was difficult. These qualities enabled him to succeed when most other men would have failed, and he did succeed in whatever he undertook. He was widely known and generally respected, and his death will cause deep regret far beyond the family of which he was the loved and loving head.

He was generous and open-handed, and his kindly and genial nature found in giving only one of the many ways of manifestation, and made him friends wherever he went.—Newspaper obituary.

He d. March 21, 1881. Res. Bedford, N. H.

2499. i. LUCY ALMA, b. Feb. 6, 1848; d. May 30, 1855.

2500. ii. SARAH MULE, b. April 25, 1850; m., Oct. 9, 1877, Edmund B. Hull. He was b. May 11, 1850. Res., Manchester, N. H. Ch.: 1. Harry Foster Hull, b. July 24, 1878, Bedford, N. H. 2. Grace E. Hull, b. Oct. 14, 1880, Bedford, N. H. P. O. address, Manchester, N. H.

2501. iii. JOHN, b. March 5, 1852; m. M. Lizzie McCrillis.

2502. iv. A SON, b. April 27, 1855; d. April 28, 1855.

2503. v. GEORGE SANFORD, b. July 8, 1857; m. Etta F. Moulton.

2504. vi. CHARLES ELIPHALET, b June 12, 1860; m. Bertha J. Cheney.

2505. vii. HERMAN, b. Aug. 3, 1863; m. Nancy E. Barr.

2506. viii. LUCY MARY, b. April 30, 1865; m. ——, —— Stewart. Res., Marlboro, Mass.

1411. JAMES FREDERICK FOSTER (Gideon, Obadiah, John, William, William, Reginald), b. Charlestown Mass., March 17, 1806; m. there April 3, 1828, Caroline Dothwait Bedney, b. Sept. 1, 1807; d. Aug. 1, 1888. He was a truss maker.

Petition of Gideon Foster, gentleman of Woburn, friend of James F. Foster, of Boston, truss maker, that said James F. is an invalid person, and requests that guardian be appointed. Jan. 15, 1844. Lib. 407, Fol. 54. Bond mentions Gideon Foster, of Woburn, gentleman, and Thomas R. Foster, of Boston, gentleman. Jan. 29, 1844. Lib 410, Fol. 55. Lib. 408, Fol. 282. Lib. 281 Fol. 100. Petition for appointment of guardian for James F. Foster, by Henry J. Foster, of New York; Caroline P. Foster, of Boston, and Mina P. Mansfield of Roxbury. Dec. 9, 1861. Suff. Prob. Lib. 418, Fol. 588.

He d. Dec. 1, 1882. Res., Boston and Roxbury, Mass.

2507. i. WILLIAM FREDERICK, b. Dec. 12, 1829; d. Feb. 5, 1830.

2508. ii. ALMIRA PENDER, b. March 7, 1831; m., April 7, 1853, Gideon I. Mansfield. Res., 87 Bloomfield St., Dorchester, Mass. He was b. March 12, 1829; d. Dec. 2, 1890. Was a dry-goods' merchant. Ch.: 1. Gideon M. Mansfield, b. 1853, in Dorchester. 2. Frederick H. Mansfield, b. 1855, in Dorchester. 3. Adaline Story Mansfield Austin, b. 1853, in Dor. 4. Amelia Milton Mansfield Bumpus, b. 1859, in Meriden, Conn. 5. Caroline L. Mansfield, b. 1861, in Dorchester. 6. Alice M. Mansfield (Lewis), b. 1863, in Bethlehem, N. H. 7. William C. Mansfield, b. 1867, in Dorchester. 8. Anna Foster Mansfield, d. July 13, 1869. 9. Marion F. Mansfield Fogg, b. 1870, in Dorchester.

2509. iii. FREDERICK, b. Dec. 15, 1833; m. Margaret R. Todd.

2510. iv. HENRY JACKSON, b. Feb. 29, 1836; m. Susan Augusta Plummer.

2511. v. CAROLINE PAMELIA, b. March 7, 1838; m., March 9, 1864, Brig.-Gen. Charles A. White. Res., Greeley, Col. Charles A. White, b. Sept. 19, 1836, in West Deering, N. H.; private Co. A, Third Mass. Vol. militia in War of Rebellion, from April 16th to July 22, 1861; captain Third New Hampshire Vol.; brevet lieutenant colonel United States volunteers, Aug. 12, 1861, to Aug. 2, 1865; severely wounded at battle of Deep Bottom, Va., Aug. 16, 1864; chief engrossing clerk Colorado Senate in 1883; brigadier-general Colorado militia, 1878-79; postmaster Greeley, Col., under Pres. Arthur and Cleveland, 1884-87; mayor of Greeley, Col., 1888-89. Ch.: 1. Almira Caroline, b. Oct. 13, 1867. 2. Emily Foster, b. Sept. 30, 1871; m., Jan. 2, 1893, Augustus M. Plumb, in Greeley, Col. 3. Augusta Woodbury, b. Sept. 30, 1871; m., May 2, 1897, Harry DeVotse. 4. Dorman Eaton, b. Oct. 19, 1875; was in the Cuban war as private Co. D, First Col. Vols., and was near Manila, Philippine Islands in August, 1898.

2512. vi. LYDIA EMILY, b. May 31, 1840; unm. Res., 89 Waltham St., Boston, Mass. Is a nurse.

2513. vii. GIDEON, b. Sept. 15, 1842; d. March 12, 1846.

2514. viii. ANNA MARIA, b. June 22, 1845; unm. Res., 89 Waltham St., Boston, Mass. Is a teacher.

2515. ix. JOSEPH B., b. April 5, 1848. Res., Parkman St., Dorchester, Mass.

1414. THOMAS ROBBINS FOSTER (Gideon, Obadiah, John, William, William, Reginald), b. Dec. 23, 1811, Charlestown, Mass.; m., ——, Caroline Alley. Res., Mass.

2516. i. DAUGHTER, b. ——; m. Dorman B. Eaton. Res., E. 27th St., New York City, N. Y.

1418. FRANCIS FOSTER (Gideon, Obadiah, John, William, William, Reginald), b. Charlestown, Mass., Sept. 13, 1822; m., Sept. 10, 1846, Lucy M. Robinson, b. Jan. 4, 1826; d. April 15, 1863. He d. in Memphis, Tenn., Sept. 23, 1872. Res., Lynn, Mass.

2517. i. HENRY FRANCIS, b. July 5, 1847, in Dedham, Mass.; d. July 12, 1847.

2518. ii. THEODORE DEXTER, b. May 4, 1852, in Lynn, Mass.; m. Mary Ella Littlefield.

2519. iii. HENRY FRANK, b. May 24, 1855, in Lynn, Mass.; d. Sept. 29, 1856, in Chicago, Ill.

2520. iv. FRANCES GERTRUDE, b. Sept. 20, 1859, in Hudson, Wis.; m. William Laurence Clark, July 3, 1884, at Boston. Ch.: 1. Lester Searing Clark, b. June 12, 1886, at Woburn; d. Dec. 27, 1891. 2. William Foster Clark, b. July 16, 1887, at Brooklyn, N. Y. 3. Genevieve Laurence Clark, b. May 23, 1893, at Jamaica Plains, Mass. Address, Mrs. W. L. Clark, Fowler St., Dorchester, Mass.

2521. v. CHARLES THOMAS, b. Jan. 20, 1862, at Memphis, Tenn.; m. Fanny Sprague.

1421. WILLIAM FOSTER (Solomon, Solomon, John, William, William, Reginald), b. Lincoln, Mass., July 28, 1815; m., Waltham, June 23, 1842. Alice Clark, b. March 5, 1817; d. May 2, 1890. He is a farmer. Res., Waltham, Mass., 68 Lyman St.

2522. i. EMMA REBECCA, b. Aug. 17, 1843; unm. Res., at home.
2523. ii. EDWARD CLARK, b. April 7, 1852; m. Helen Pierce.
2524. iii. WILLIAM LOWELL, b. June 24, 1860; d. Sept. 11, 1877.

1422. ASA EMERSON FOSTER (Asa, Asa, Asa, William, William, Reginald), b. Canterbury, N. H., Sept. 2, 1795; m., Amherst, N. H., Sept. 8, 1830, Maria Chickering, b. Dec. 1, 1803; d. June 24, 1859.

Asa E. Foster, the eldest son of Asa Foster and Sarah Morrill, was born in Canterbury, N. H., Sept. 2, 1795. He remained with his parents till he was twenty-one, then, receiving an injury on his ankle, which incapacitated from hard labor, he gave his attention to acquiring an education, and was graduated from Dartmouth College in 1822, where he was considered the best mathematician in his class. He taught school awhile in Gilmanton, N. H. Nov. 12, 1827, he became principal of tne Erie Academy, at Erie, Pa., where he taught more than eight years, and then opened the Erie Institute, a private school, in which he remained thirteen years. He was very thorough and conscientious in all his work; so that his influence was felt and acknowledged by the many hundreds who were under his instruction, and have since become honored in the many various professions and occupations in which they have engaged. He was married, Sept. 8, 1830, at Amherst, N. H., to Maria Chickering. On Feb. 23, 1833, a daughter was born to them, named Sarah Maria. His wife died June 24, 1859, leaving him sad and lonely. The remainder of his life was spent sometimes at his home in Erie, at other times either with his friends, in New England, or with his daughter, where he was always welcomed, not only by her family, but also by the community in which was their home—first at Portland, N. Y., then at Salem, Ind., where he died Oct. 9, 1875. Res., Erie, Pa., and Salem, Ind.

2525. i. SARAH, b. Feb. 23, 1833; m., Oct. 6, 1859, Rev. Irving Ira St. John. Res., Salem, Ind. Ch.: Julia (9) Maria St. John, b. Nov. 11, 1860; m. Clarence Steuben Palmer, July 28, 1886. He was born Jan. 27, 1858; graduated at Hamilton College, N. Y., 1879. Now a lawyer at Kansas City, Mo. Ch.: (10) Clarence Foster Palmer, b. Aug. 26, 1888. (10) Edward Pringle Palmer, b. Jan. 20 1891. (10) Herbert St. John Palmer, b. Feb. 26, 1893; d. July 24, 1894. (9) Herman Foster St. John, b. Feb. 22, 1864; d. May 1, 1885. (9) Mary Ella St. John, b. April 6, 1866; m. William L. Roberts, Sept. 16, 1891. She d. Oct. 13, 1896. Ch.: (10) Margaret St. John Roberts, b. June 5, 1892. (10) Caroline Lloyd Roberts, b. Oct. 28, 1893. (10) William Irving Roberts, b. July 28, 1895. (9) Edward Emerson St. John, b. May 26, 1868. (9) Carrie Eliza St. John, b. July 24, 1871. (9) Merle Irvin St. John, b. Dec. 11, 1873.

Rev. Irving Ira St. John was born in Eden, N. Y., May 10, 1832. Prepared for college at Grand River Institute, Austinsburgh, and Kingsville Academy, Ohio; attended Genesee College, N.Y., and Hartford Theological Seminary, Conn. (then known as Theological Institute of Connecticut); licensed by the Presbytery of Erie, and ordained by the Presbytery of Buffalo; married Miss Sarah Maria Foster, only child of Mr. and Mrs. A. E. Foster, at Erie, Pa., Oct. 6, 1859; pastor of the Portland and Panama churches, New York, and of the Salem and several other churches in Indiana. He is now pastor of the New Philadelphia and Walnut Ridge churches in the Presbytery of New Albany.

1425. ADAMS FOSTER (Asa, Asa, Asa, William, William, Reginald), b. Canterbury, N. H., Feb. 22, 1800; m., Nov. 21, 1832, Sarah Bradley Eastman, gr.-dau. of Sarah Foster and Timothy Bradley, b. Aug. 6, 1805, Concord, N. H.; d. Worcester, Mass., Oct. 1, 1893. His will is on Probate Court records at Worcester. He d. in 1873. Res., Worcester and Holden, Mass.

2526. i. CYRUS PARKER, b. Aug. 26, 1833; d. Sept. 23, 1838.

2527. ii. ANN MARIA, b. Aug. 3, 1836; m., May 30, 1858, Frank J. Kinney. She d. June 13, 1890. Ch.: 1. Herbert R. Kinney, b. June 23, 1860; m. Lillian M. Robbins, Nov. 20, 1884. She was b. April 20, 1860. Ch.: (10) George H. Kinney, b. May 28, 1886. (10) Alfred R. Kinney, b. March 20, 1889. 2. Lorenzo Foster Kinney, b. Oct. 8, 1861; graduated at Amherst Agricultural College, 1888; m Helen M. Wells, July 9, 1891. She was b. Nov. 3, 1861. Ch.: (10) Foster Wells Kinney, b. Aug. 17, 1892. (10) Lorenzo Foster Kinney, b. Dec. 11, 1893. (10) Esther Lee Kinney, b. March 6, 1896. (10) Helen Wells Kinney, b. July 7, 1897. 3. Henry Eastman Kinney, b. March 14, 1866. 4. Emma Flora Kinney, b. Sept. 13, 1868. 5. Asa Stephen Kinney, b. Aug. 23, 1873; graduated Amherst Agricultural College 1896. 6. Clarence Walter Kinney, b. Aug. 30, 1875. 7. Sarah Clarissa Kinney, b. Sept. 27, 1877.

2528. iii. EMMA ELIZA, b. Aug. 27, 1839; d. Aug. 17, 1858.

2529. iv. ASA EASTMAN, b. May 31, 1841; m. Sophia Steele.

2530. v. CHARLES TYLER, b. Oct. 9, 1843. Res. Worcester; unm.

1430. STEPHEN SYMONDS FOSTER (Asa, Asa, Asa, William, William, Reginald), b. Canterbury, N. H., Nov. 17, 1809; m., in Penn., Dec. 21, 1845, Abby Kelley, b. Jan. 15, 1811; d. Jan. 14, 1887

Stephen S. Foster, Abolitionist, born in Canterbury, N. H; died near Worcester, Mass. He learned the carpenter's trade, then studied with the intention of becoming a minister; was graduated at Dartmouth in 1838, and studied theology in the Union Theological Seminary, New York; but, because he was precluded from advocating Abolition in the pulpit, he deserted that profession in order to engage in the anti-slavery contest. He was an earnest orator, a master of denunciation and invective, and was frequently the victim of mob violence. He is described in one of Lowell's anti-slavery poems as

"A kind of maddened John the Baptist
To whom the hardest word comes aptest,
Who, struck by stone or brick, ill-starred,
Hurls back an epithet as hard,
Which, deadlier than stone or brick,
Has a propensity to stick."

While in the theological seminary he induced some of his classmates to join with him in a meeting to protest against the warlike preparations then going on, arising from the dispute with Great Britain over the northwestern boundary. The refusal of the faculty to allow the chapel to be used for such a meeting made him dissatisfied with the churches, because they countenanced war; and when he became an anti-slavery agitator of the moral-force school, instead of a Congregational minister, he directed his attacks chiefly against the church and the clergy, because they upheld slavery. Since the people of the New England towns could not be induced to attend anti-slavery lectures, he was accustomed to attend church meetings and claim there a hearing for the enslaved, and was often expelled by force, and several times imprisoned for disturbing public worship. Other Abolitionists adopted the same plan of agitation, which was very effective. He lived for many years on a farm in the suburbs of Worcester. He published articles in periodicals on the slavery question, and in 1843 a pamphlet, entitled, "The Brotherhood of Thieves: a True Picture of the American Church and Clergy;" in the form of a letter to Nathaniel Barney, a reprint of which was issued by Parker Pillsbury (Concord, 1886). His wife, Abby Kelley, reformer, was born in Pelham, Mass., and died in Worcester, Mass. Her parents, who were descendants of Irish Quakers, removed to Worcester while she was an infant. Her education was finished at the Friends' School, in Providence, R. I., after, which she taught for several years in Worcester and Millbury, and in a Friends' School in Lynn, Mass. She resigned her post about 1837, and began lecturing as an anti-slavery advocate, being the first woman to address mixed audiences in favor of Abolition.

Though sincere in her conviction and womanly in her delivery, she suffered many indignities in Connecticut during her lectures. While speaking in Pennsylvania, she met Stephen S. Foster, whom she married in New Brighton, Pa. The two continued their public addresses, and on one tour in Ohio, Mrs. Foster spoke every day for six weeks. They settled on a farm near Worcester, which was their home up to the time of Mr. Foster's death.

About 1850 Mrs. Foster began to be actively interested in the cause of woman suffrage, making many speeches in its advocacy and that of prohibition. She took an extreme view of these questions, and in argument was pronounced and aggressive. Alike in their belief, regarding woman suffrage and their protests against taxation without representation, both Mr. and Mrs. Foster refused to pay taxes on their home estate, because the wife was not permitted to vote, and this resolution was followed by the sale of the home for two consecutive years, but it was bought in by their friends, and finally redeemed by Mr. Foster. Mrs. Foster's last public work was an effort made to raise funds to defray the expenses of securing the adoption of the Fifteenth amendment in the doubtful States. In June, 1886, she attended an anti-slavery reception in Boston. The day preceding her fatal illness she finished a sketch of her husband for this work. Personally, Mrs. Foster was amiable and unassuming, but never lacked the courage to proclaim and defend her advanced opinions. James Russell Lowell pays this tribute to Mrs. Foster:

"A Judith, there, turned Quakeress,
Sits Abby, in her modest dress.
No nobler gift of heart or brain,
No life more white from spot or stain,
Was e'er on Freedom's altar laid,
Than hers—the simple Quaker maid."

He d. Sept. 8, 1881. Res., Worcester, Mass.

2531. i. ALLA WRIGHT, b. May 19, 1847; unm. Res., Roxbury, Mass. Is a teacher. She was graduated at Vassar in 1872. Post-graduate Cornell in 1874.

1431. HON. DAVID MORRILL FOSTER (Asa, Asa, Asa, William, William, Reginald), b. Canterbury, N. H., Oct. 30, 1811; m., St. Albans, Me., Nov. 18, 1837, Sarah Bradley Robertson, b. Sept. 8, 1813; d. July 19, 1885; gr.-dau. of Sarah Foster and Timothy Bradley. Was a farmer. He was for a number of years a leading member of the New Hampshire House of Representatives. He d. Nov. 24, 1884. Res., Canterbury, N. H.

2532. i. EDWARD HORATIO, b. Oct. 13, 1839; d. 1897; m. Ella M. Merrill and Blanche Smith.

2533. ii. HARRY EARL, b. Sept. 8, 1841; d. Oct. 12, 1858.

2534. iii. CAROLINE ELIZABETH, b. Oct. 16, 1844; m., Feb. 28, 1883, Charles W. Emery. He was a graduate at Dartmouth College. Res., Oakland, Cal. Ch.: 1. Nathan Emery, b. Dec., 1883; d. ——.

2535. iv. NEWELL K., b. April 10, 1849; m. Jennie Smiley and Maude A. W. Camp.

1432. HON. NEWELL ABBOTT FOSTER (Asa, Asa, Asa, William, William, Reginald), b. Canterbury, N. H., Feb. 7, 1814; m., Portland, Me., ——, Eliza Jane Allison, b. July 24, 1816; d. June 18, 1854; m., 2d, in 1861, Ellen French. He was chief owner of the Portland (Me.) Daily Press, and a very prominent Republican, having been for some years a member of the State Legislature. He was the leading spiritualist in Portland. He was a printer by trade. Entered the army a few months before the close of the Civil War; he was in no battles. He d. Nov. 20, 1868. Res., Portland, Me.

2536. i. LEROY ALLISON, b. March 13, 1843; m. Emma Eastman.

2537. ii. ADELAIDE ELIZA, b Jan. —, 1853; m., Oct. 23, 1886, Austin Brainard, of Haddam, Conn. Res., 29, Kenyon St., Hartford; graduated at Vassar, 1875. He was b. Sept. 6, 1862. He graduated at Cornell, 1883; admitted to bar 1886; a lawyer at Hartford, Conn. Ch.: 1. Helen Allison Brainard, b. Dec. 5, 1889. 2. Lawrence Brainard, b. Jan. 20, 1895; d. April 14, 1895.

1435. CHARLES FOSTER (William, Abiel, Asa, William, William, Reginald), b. Oct. 4, 1794, Canterbury, N. H.; m. ——, Ruth Tilton. He d. July 4, 1869. Res., ——.

2538. i. FRANK, b. ——; m. —— Coe.

2539. ii. MARTHA, b. ——, m. —— Roberts. Ch.: Arthur and Newton.
2540. iii. CHARLES, b. ——; unm.

1438. HYRAM FOSTER (William, Abiel, Asa, William, William, Reginald), b. Canterbury, N. H., April 2, 1800; m. ——, Cordelia Hogle. He d. Aug. 11, 1849. Res., Rochester, N. Y.

2541. i. WILLIAM, b. ——; m. Mary Sawyer. Had a son, Elmer.
2542. ii. SARAH, b. ——; m. Truman Palmer. Res., Eldred, Pa.
2543 iii. CHARLES, b. ——; m. Emily ——. Had Charles, Emma, Albert, Grace, Frank and Mabel. The father d. in 1896. Frank resides Eldred, Pa.
2544. iv. ELLEN, b. ——; m. Edmund Palmer. Had Abbie, Charles Emma, Edward, Effie and Lulu. Res., Caneadea, N. Y.
2545. v. CORDELIA, b. ——; m. Thomas Wainman. Had, Mary, m. E. G. Piper; Ella, m. Elmer Miller; Ida; Fannie, m. Webster Cronk, d. Aug. 30, 1877; Carrie, m. Emory Burgess; Floyd, Edith. A des. is Mrs. J. H. Stoody, Hamburg, N. Y.
2546. vi. HORATIO, b. ——; m. Mary —— and had Hiram, Harry, Horatio and Cora.
2547. vii. HIRAM, b. Nov. 24, 1840; m., Nov. 13, 1866, Martha J. Shepherd, b. June 8, 1844. He d. Richmond, Va., Feb. 6, 1896. Ch.: 1. Helen, b. 1876, who resides, 761 W. 16th St., Los Angeles, Cal. 2. Fred S., b. Oct. 22, 1867; m., and resides Stillwater, Minn. 3. Hiram Lewis, b. April 15, 1879; d. April 24, 1880. 4. Eva, b. June 25, 1869; m. Rev. Edward Borncamp, June 26, 1895, and resides 124 Huntington Ave., Boston, Mass. He is assistant minister at Trinity church, Boston. Ch.: i. Frederick Foster, b. April 19, 1896. ii. Robert Parker, b. Sept. 17, 1898. The father, Hiram Foster, was a wholesale dealer in carriages and agricultural implements at St. Paul and Stillwater, Minn., and Richmond, Va.

1441. WILLIAM HENRY H. FOSTER (William, Abiel, Asa, William, William, Reginald), b. Canterbury, N. H., Aug. 21, 1806; m. ——, Rowena Wheelock. He d. July 29, 1861. Res., Rochester, N. Y.

2548. i. HENRY, b. June 10, 1842; unm.
2549. ii. ADDIE, b. May 9, 1847; m. George Vernon.
2550. iii. ELLA, b. Nov. 29, 1850; m. Jacob Wendling and had Mabel, William and George.
2551. iv. ALFRED, b. June 27, 1849; d. Feb. 10, 1873.
2552. v. LILLIE, b. Aug. 3, 185—; m., March 22, 1883, G. Spencer Shimmin. Res., 218 W. 15th St., Los Angeles, Cal.

MRS. G. SPENCER SHIMMIN.

1444. ARTHUR MASTEN FOSTER (William, Abiel, Asa, William, William, Reginald), b. Canterbury, N. H., Feb. 19, 1812; m. ——, Jane Sheldon. He d. Dec. 31, 1848. Res., Rochester, N. Y.

2553. i. CARRIE, b. ——; d. aet. 3.
2554. ii. ELLEN, b. ——; m. Charles Sheffield. Ch.: 1. Carrie, b. Oct. 13, 1864. 2. Florence, b. May 11, 1866; d. Feb. 2, 1883. 3. Arthur, b. Aug. 17, 1868. 4. Charles, b. Nov. 3, 1879.

1454. ABIEL FOSTER (Abiel, Abiel, Asa, William, William, Reginald), b. Canterbury, N. H., June 19, 1798; m., March 19, 1835, Pamelia Judd. He d. ——, 1874. Res., Columbus, Ohio, and Greenville, S. C.

2555. i. ABIEL ABBOTT, b. Sept. 30, 1836; m. Julia Worthington and Mrs. Ella F. McCouts.

2556. ii. SUSAN AMELIA, b. Sept. 5, 1838; m., in Greenville, S. C., Simms F. Clary, of Greenville county, S. C. Ch.: 1. Helen Elizabeth, m. Frank C. Greene, of Greenwood, S. C. Ch.: (a) Helen Elizabeth Greene. (b) William Francis Greene. (c) Marguerite Greene. (d) Ruth Clary Greene. (e) Lois Clary Greene. (f) Annie Judd Greene. (g) Arthur Maxwell Greene. (h) Harriet Caroline Greene. 2. Frances Amelia; m. Arthur Middleton, of Charleston, S. C. No children. 3. Harriet Catharine; m. Franz Engels, of Germany, in Europe. Ch.: (a) Antoinette Amelia. (c) Jennie Guerard. Res., Enoree, S. C. 4. James Edward; unm. Res., Greenwood, S. C. 5. Caroline Augusta; m. Charles Blake Alexander, of Greensboro, N. C. Ch.: (a) James Clary.

2557. iii. HELEN MARIA, b. Nov. 5, 1840; unm. A teacher. Res., Spartanburg, S. C.

2558. iv. SARAH ELIZABETH, b. Jan. 3, 1845, in Limestone Springs, S. C.; m.; had one dau., deceased. Sarah d. in 1868.

1458. ELDER JOSEPH FOSTER (Abiel, Abiel, Asa, William, William, Reginald), b. Canterbury, N. H., Nov. 7, 1804; m., in Union county, South Carolina, Dec. 27, 1831, Minerva M. Means, of Meansville, S. C., b. Oct. 20, 1808; d. Nov. 26, 1896.

JOSEPH FOSTER.

Joseph Foster, grandson of the Rev. Abiel Foster, pastor of the Congregational church of Canterbury, N. H., and for fourteen years their representative in Congress, and son of Abiel Foster and Susannah Moore, was born in Canterbury, N. H. He was educated and lived there until 1826. He then came to South Carolina; assisted his brother Abiel in his school at Greenville, S. C., for a year or more, after which he went to Meansville, Union county, and taught school until he married Minerva M. Means, Dec. 27, 1831. They then moved to their own home, three miles distant, near Fair Forest Presbyterian church. They were regular attendants at this church, of which he was an elder. Their five children, three daughters and two sons, were baptized there. He was engaged in teaching and farming until August, 1847. He moved to Spartanburg, S. C., so as to secure better educational advantages for his children, and to enter into mercantile business, which he did in partnership with David C. Judd, which was not dissolved until his death, Jan. 30, 1877. He continued farming in Union county, the greater part of the time over-looked by his negro men. After their freedom they remained on his place and conducted the farm, much to his satisfaction.

He was an active, industrious man, cheerful in disposition; had many friends among both old and young; took a lively interest in school and church work; was always a temperance man: was anxious that his children should be useful men and women.

His death was sudden. After breakfast with his family he went, as usual, to his business house, and before an hour died with paralysis of the brain. His wife, four children and two grandsons survived him. His eldest daughter, Susan E. Foster married Samuel C. Means. Alfred H. Foster, eldest son, married Henrietta V. Brandon. They have three daughters, Isabel, Mary Emma and Louise. They reside in Union, S. C. Isabella J. Foster, second daughter, married Robert Hett Chapman, of Ashville, N. C. They died early in life leaving two sons, James A. Chapman, of Middlesboro, Ky. He married Rachel McMaster, of Winsboro, S. C. They have three children, Laura Foster, James Alfred and Robert Hett. Robert Hett Foster Chapman married Hattie L. Craton, of Rutherfordton, N. C. They had one child, a daughter, Margery, and live in Spartanburg, S. C. S. Laura Foster married E. C. McLaughlin, who died in 1890. Joseph Adolphus Foster, second son and youngest child, married Sallie G. Farrar, of Union, S. C. He died Nov. 15, 1886.

He d. Jan. 31, 1876. Res., Union, S. C., and Spartanburg, S. C.

2559. i. SARAH LAURA, b. Feb. 10, 1842; m., July 5, 1876, E. C. McLaughlin. He is a bank cashier; d. Dec. 8, 1890. She res. s p., Spartanburg, S. C., 80 Main St.

2560. ii. ALFRED H., b. Dec. 7, 1835; m. Hettie V. Brandon.

2561. iii. SUSAN E., b. March 29, 1834; m., Dec. 6, 1881, Samuel C. Means, b. Jan. 9, 1830. He is a planter. Res., s. p., Spartanburg, S. C.

2562. iv. ISABEL J., b. Oct. 6, 1838; m., Oct. 20, 1858, Robert H. Chapman. She d. Oct. 10, 1866. He d. March, 1865. Ch.: 1. Robert H., b. Oct., 1859; d. July, 1862. 2. Clara Bell, b. July, 1861; d. July, 1862. 3. James Alfred b. at Spartanburg, S. C., Feb. 7, 1863; m. Rachel McMasters, of Winnsboro, S. C. Ch.: 1. Robert H. Foster, b. at Spartanburg, S. C., Aug. 4, 1865; m. Hattie Craton, of Rutherfordton, N. C., June 20, 1888. 2. Margery.

2563. v. JOSEPH ADOLPHUS, b. March 19, 1846; m., February 23, 1881, Sally G. Farrar, of Pinckney, S. C. He d. Spartanburg, S. C., Nov. 15, 1886, s. p.

JOSEPH ADOLPHUS FOSTER.

Joseph Adolphus Foster, second son of Joseph Foster, was born March 19, 1846, in Union county, S. C. His father moved to Spartanburg, S. C., when he was about sixteen months old. He attended the town and St. John's schools until prepared for Wofford College; graduated there in 1867. Dr. Carlisle, the president, in speaking of him said: "Dolph Foster's college course brings nothing up in the recollection of his professors which they wish to forgive or forget. He entered the Freshman class an untried modest boy, and finished the senior year a tried modest man." The subject of his graduating speech was, "Prepare thyself for the wall, and thou wilt not be left in the way." This was the principle of his life. Whatever he undertook he did well. He was of medium size, handsome, well-formed, brown hair, blue eyes, manners and morals of an elegant gentleman. He taught school in Tennessee for one year; after that he went into business in the city of New York, in which he continued as long as he lived. He married Miss Sallie G. Farrar, of Union county, S. C., Feb. 23, 1881. His health failed in the spring of 1886. He lived until Nov. 15, 1886. Nothing was left undone for his recovery; but he passed away at his home in Spartanburg, S. C., much regretted by all who loved him and knew him. He was a member of the Presbyterian church, of which he was a liberal supporter, always taking a lively interest in its welfare.

1469. JOSEPH MOODY FOSTER (Simeon, Daniel, Asa, William, William, Reginald), b. Canterbury, N. H., Jan. 5, 1811; m., Oct. 16, 1837, Elizabeth Fellows, b. Nov. 14, 1814; d. Aug. 26, 1881. He was a carpenter by trade. He d. Aug. 12, 1896. Res., Canterbury, N. H.

2564. i. FRANCES ELIZABETH, b. July 9, 1842; m., July 7, 1859, Benjamin Franklin Hileman and m., 2d, May 27, 1884, Nathan French. Res., Canterbury.

2565. ii. SUSAN AUGUSTA, b. March 4, 1847; m., Jan. 19, 1871, at Concord, Henry Hiram Houser, b. April 25, 1845. Res., Canterbury. Ch.: 1. Elizabeth Foster Houser, b. Nov. 3, 1871; unm. Res., Canterbury, N. H. 2. Joseph Moody Houser, b. Sept. 18, 1873; m. in 1894. Res., Canterbury, N. H. 3. Harry Hiram Houser, b. July 25, 1879; unm.

1472. JONATHAN B. FOSTER (Jeremiah, David, Asa, William, William, Reginald), b. Canterbury, N. H., Sept. 10, 1816; m., Dec. 5, 1838, Mary H. Fellows, b. Sept. 1, 1818. He was a farmer. He d. April 18, 1896. Res., Canterbury, N. H.

2566. i. MOSES AUGUSTUS, b. Oct. 23, 1843; m. Ruth A. Richardson.

2567. ii. SUSAN ELIZABETH, b. Jan. 23, 1842; m., Feb. 26, 1868, Dr. Henry R. Brown, b. March 11, 1841. Res. Leominster, Mass. Ch.: 1. Karl L., b. Feb. 7, 1870, Leominster, Mass. 2. Louis H., b. Aug. 16, 1872, Worcester, Mass. 3. Arthur, b. May 8, 1872; d. Aug. 16, 1872. 4. Anson W., b. Oct. 9, 1874, Hanover, N. H. All unm. He attended the public schools in his native town, Loudon, N. H., until the age of fourteen; then studied a few terms in an Academy. When not in school, he worked with his father at his trade—that of carpenter, and occasionally in the winter months taught a district school. In September, 1862, he enlisted in the Fifteenth New Hampshire Volunteers—a nine months' regiment. They were sent to Louisiana, and took part in the siege and capture of Port Hudson. At the expiration of term of service they were sent to New Hampshire, and discharged, Aug. 13, 1863. He commenced the study of medicine and graduated at New York, March, 1867. He at once went into practice in Waterbury, Conn. July, 1864, he went to Leominster, Mass., where with the exception of about three years that he was in New Hampshire, he has resided, and built up an elegant practice. He is highly esteemed and respected by the entire community.

2568. iii. JEREMIAH C., b. Oct. 19, 1840; m. Nellie M. Bennett and Henrietta Brown.

2569. iv. AUGUSTA O., b. Oct. 23, 1845; m., April 15, 1868, John J. Bailey. Res., Leominster, Mass. She d. Nov. 14, 1871. A child is Mary A.

2570. v. MARY H., b. July 7, 1851; m., Nov. 19, 1872, John J. Bailey. Res., L.

2571 vi. MARTHA J., b. July 7, 1851; m., Jan. 1, 1884, John W. Douglass, of Wallingford, Conn. She d. March 30, 1886. Ch.: 1. George F., b. March 30, 1886; d. March 28, 1887.

1475. FRANKLIN FOSTER (David, David, Asa, William, William, Reginald), b. Canterbury, N. H., April 29, 1806; m., Oct. 8, 1832, Harriet Kendall, b. ——, 1810; d. Aug. 18, 1857. Was a farmer. He d. May 22, 1880. Res., Boston, Mass., and Buda, Ill.

2572. i. HARRIET, b. ——, 1834; m. ——, 1858. She d. ——, 1879.

2573. ii. HENRY L., b. Sept. 26, 1836; m. Sarai C. Weston.
2574. iii. EDWARD, b. ——, 1838.
2575. iv. SARAH, b. ——; m. —— Clark. Res., 269 South Grant Ave., Denver, Col.
2575½. v. SIDNEY, b. ——: d. ——.
2576. vi. ADDIE, b. ——; d. ——.
2577. vii. LUCY, b. ——; m. —— Burnett. Res.. Galva. Ill.
2578. viii. ELLA, b. ——; m. —— Dyer. Res., Redfield, Iowa.

1478. REV. GEORGE WASHINGTON FOSTER (David, David, Asa, William, William, Reginald), b. Canterbury, N. H., June 2, 1816; m. ——, Clara M. Dole. He d. ——, 1871. Res., Buda, Ill.
2579. i. WILLIAM F., b. ——. Res., Warsaw, Ill.
2580. ii. ANNA AUGUSTA, b. ——; m. —— Ely. Res., Victoria, Ill.
2581. iii. CHARLES HENRY, b. ——; m. and d., leaving Lillie and Clara. Res., Normal, Ill.
2582. iv. EDWARD, b. Feb. 10, 1862; unm. Res., Denver, Col. He is circulator of the Republican.

1479. JOSEPH FOSTER (David, David, Asa, William, William, Reginald), b. Canterbury, N. H., July 8, 1810; m. 1834 in Princeton, Ill., Elizabeth Boyer Vaughan, b. 1817; d. 1865; m., 2d, 1869, Elizabeth Childs; d. 1892.

Joseph Foster was born near Concord, N. H.; received common school education; was apprenticed to carpenter at age of sixteen; worked at trade until twenty-one years of age; emigrated to Bureau county, Illinois, about 1833; married Elizabeth B. Vaughan; settled on prairie, near French Grove, in Concord township; kept country hotel on public road for about sixteen years, until C. B. & Q. railroad was built; was father of four sons and two daughters; three sons now survive him. He moved to Marquette, Mich., on Lake Superior, in 1864, for benefit of health of family. His wife died at Marquette, Mich., in 1865. He moved back to Illinois in 1869, and married Elizabeth Childs; resided there until 1875; then settled in the city of Creston, Iowa. His second wife died in 1892. At the age of eighty-four years he made a successful trip alone to Seattle, Wash., to visit his youngest son. He died at Creston, Iowa, and was buried at Buda, Ill.

He d. Oct., 1894. Res., Buda, Ill., and Creston, Iowa.
2583. i. WILLIAM H., d. about 1854.
2584. ii. JOHN MARSHALL, d. about 1869.
2585. iii. FLORA A., d. about 1862.
2586. iv. MARY J., d. about 1862.
2587. v. ALPHONSO, d. about 1862.
2588. vi. HORATIO O., Creston, Iowa.
2589. vii. JAMES ELMER, Olney, Wash.
2590. viii. JOSEPH A., b. Feb. 10, 1847; m. Cora E. Whiting.

1480. HENRY BRADLEY FOSTER (David, David, Asa, William, William, Reginald), b. Canterbury, N. H., Dec. 11, 1820; m. in Boston, Mass., Oct. 24, 1844, Harriet Salome Dole, b. May 24, 1823; d. April 7, 1894. Res., Concord, N. H. A druggist.
2591. i. EDWARD HENRY, b. April 9, 1848; unm.; d. Nov. 5, 1869.
2592. ii. HELEN FRANCES, b. Feb. 19, 1846; m., Oct. 17, 1871, G. A. W. Dodge. Res., New Haven, Conn.
2593. iii. HATTIE JANE, b. Dec. 11, 1851; m., Sept. 30, 1875; d. Sept. 23, 1895.
2594. iv. MAITLAND P., b. Oct. 28, 1862; m. Res., Wakefield, Mass.

1483. STEPHEN BARTLETT FOSTER (Timothy, David, Asa, William, William, Reginald), b. Canterbury, N. H., Aug. 23, 1816; m. Manchester, Dec. 26, 1855, Nancy Bean Sibley, b. Jan. 16, 1826. Jeweler and watchmaker. He d. June 29, 1875. Res., Boston, Mass.
2595. i. STEPHEN BARTLETT, b. Jan. 1, 1856; unm. Res., 134 Charles St.
2596. ii. JOHN ROY, b. Sept. 9, 1863; unm. Res., 134 Charles St.
2597. iii. LILLIETTE, b. May 19, 1867; m., Dec. 25, 1892, Samuel G. Cook. Res., Boston. Has one son, Handel Gibson Cook.

1484. JOHN CARTER FOSTER (Timothy, David, Asa, William, William, Reginald), b. Canterbury, N. H., Jan. 18, 1807; m., Salisbury, N. H., Aug. 5, 1828, Ruth M. Pingry, b. Jan. 31, 1810. She m. 2d, a —— Dunlop. Res., West Salisbury, N. H. He was a jeweler. He d. Pittsburg, Pa., April 12, 1835. Res., Salisbury, N. H.

2598. i. JOHN PINGRY, b. July 23, 1829; d. Juncton, Va., July 11, 1851.
2599. ii. MARY PINGRY, b. July 11, 1831; m. ——. She d. Salisbury, N. H., March 11, 1871.
2600. iii. WILLIAM PINGRY, b. Sept. 26, 1833; d. Sept. 16, 1834.

1496. AMMI RUHAMA FOSTER (John, Jonathan, Asa, William, William, Reginald), b. Canterbury, N. H., July 1, 1805; m., June, 1839, Finette Foster Lancaster, b. April 12, 1815; d. March 24, 1885. He was a farmer and carpenter. He d. ——. Res., Newark, N. J.

2601. i. JAMES CALEB, b. May 6, 1847; m. Sophia Smith.
2602. ii. SARAH ALMENA, b. March 26, 1843; m., June 27, 1869, Charles Albert Martin. He was b. July 31, 1838; d. June 16, 1890. Ch.: 1. Grace Augusta Martin, b. April 13. 1875; m. Leonard Moores Merrill Nov. 15, 1892. Res., Ayers Village, Mass.
2603. iii. EDWARD HORATIO, b. Dec. 4, 1848; m. Addie F. Jenkins.
2604. iv. ORIETTA AUGUSTA, b. July 5, 1854; m., Jan. 1, 1878, Alfred Usher Prescott. Res., 18 Elm street, Charlestown, Mass. He is a provision dealer. Was b. Jan. 30, 1841. Ch.: 1. Edward Alfred Prescott, b. Oct. 27, 1848; d. Feb. 13, 1879. 2. Franklin Newell Prescott, b. June 10, 1880. 3. Willard Lincoln Prescott, b. Feb. 12, 1884. 4. Frances Annette Prescott, b. Sept. 9, 1888. All Res. 18 Elm street, Charlestown, Mass.
2605. v. CLARA ELIZABETH, b. April 2, 1859; m., June 20, 1881, George L. Webster. Res., 17 West street, Haverhill, Mass. Ch.: 1. George F., b. Feb. 2, 1883.

1501. THOMAS FOSTER (David, David, David, Timothy, William, Reginald), b. Whitestown, N. Y., Sept. 20, 1820; m., in 1848, Eliza P. Skaats, dau. of David Skaats and des. of Rev. Gideon Skaats, Dutch clergyman in Albany in 1652. She was b. Dec. 26, 1828. He had a common school education in Whitestown; was a merchant in Utica from 1840 to 1893; was a man of great information, acquired by diligent reading. Possessed the largest and best-selected library in the vicinity; was a man of wealth and taste; had a fine collection of paintings and art treasures collected in Europe, where he resided for considerable periods. Mr. Foster was prominent in railroad building and was vice-president of the Utica City National Bank. He d. Feb. 23, 1893. Res., Utica, N. Y.

THOMAS FOSTER.

2606. i. DAVID SKAATS, b. Jan. 23, 1852; m. Mary Williams.
2607. ii. ABBOTT, b. Jan. 25, 1850; m., June 13, 1872, Sarah B. White, dau. of Nelson L., of Danbury, Conn. s.p. Res., New York City and Litchfield, Connecticut. He was born at Utica, N. Y., January 25, 1850; was in business there from 1871 to 1889, when he retired.

Since that time, when not traveling, he has lived in the city of New York, which is his present residence.

2608. iii. THOMAS L., b. March 17, 1853; m., 1878, Kate Sharp, dau. of John, of Louisville, Ky., Ch.: 1. Thomas, b. 1881. 2. Sharp, b. 1883.

1507. BENJAMIN FOSTER (Benjamin, Isaac, Benjamin, Jacob, Isaac, Reginald), b. Granville, N. S., Aug. 2, 1782; m. there Oct. 31, 1804, Mary Randall, dau. of Samuel and Sarah (Prince). She was of the fifth generation from Elder John Prince, of Hull, Mass., b. 1786; d. March 18, 1871. She was the daughter of Samuel and Sarah (Prince) Randall. Sarah (Prince) Randall was the daughter of Col. Christopher Prince, who came from Boston, Mass., to Annapolis, 1770. Col. Christopher Prince married Mollie Foster, daughter of Hopestill Foster, who lived on Newburn street, now Washington street, Boston, and owned what is called Foster's wharf, and was a large ship owner. Benjamin Foster, son of Benjamin and Elizabeth (Richardson) Foster, was born in Granville, N. S., August 2, 1782; married Mary, daughter of Samuel and Sarah (Prince) Randall, grand-daughter of Col. Benjamin Prince, in 1804, and settled near Bridgetown, N. S., where he was very prosperous as a farmer. In 1846 he, with his son Edward, removed to Berwick, N. S. She died March, 1871. They had six sons, and Mr. Foster, living to be 100 years old, had a centennial dinner August 2, 1882, at which all of his sons were present. He died three days after, August 5, 1882. He d., ae. 100 years and 3 days, Aug. 5, 1882. Res., Granville and Berwick, N. S.

2609. i. ABRAHAM, b. Aug. 23, 1805; m. Rachel Morton.

2610. ii. ISAAC, b. Oct. 27, 1806; m. Rebecca Taylor.

2611. iii. JACOB, b. April 27, 1810; m., Dec. 23, 1835, Susan Ann Foster. S. p. He d. June 10, 1892. Res., Bridgeton, N. S.

2612. iv. WILLIAM WORTHING, b. Aug. 2, 1812; m. Sarah Marshall. S. p. Res., Granville and Berwick, N. S., and Portland, Me. He d. in latter place in 1891.

2613. v. ROBERT, b. Dec. 13, 1813; m. Martha Norton and Elizabeth Taylor.

2614. vi. EDWARD CLARK, b. May 27, 1817; m. Harriet L. Tupper.

1510. SAMUEL FOSTER (Benjamin, Isaac, Benjamin, Jacob, Isaac, Reginald), b. Granville, N. S., Sept. 9, 1784; m., March 17, 1805, Lydia Chute, b., ——, 1784; d. Dec. 20, 1833; m. 2d, Dec. 4, 1835, Catherine Crisp, dau. of Thomas, of New Brunswick, d. April 10, 1881. He d. July 29, 1879. Res., Granville, N. S.

2615. i. THOMAS, b. ——, 1807; d., ——, 1818.

2616. ii. SAMUEL, b. April 22, 1809; m., 1835, Mary Marshall.

2617. iii. JOHN VAN BURIN, b. Feb. 17, 1811; m., 1835, Elizabeth Marshall.

2618. iv. LUCY, b. Sept. 30, 1813; m., ——, 1835, John Sampson; m. 2d, 1845, James Taylor.

2619. v. HARRIS, b. June 28, 1815; m. Martha Chute, Lavina Cogswell and Mrs. Mary A. (Brown) Chute. He is postmaster at Hampton, N. S.

2620. vi. RUBY ANN, b. April 12, 1817; m., April 23, 1840, William H. Maccavoy. Had 6 ch. Res., Granville, N. S.

2621. vii. ABIGAIL, b. Feb. 1, 1819; m., ——, 1838, Abraham Brooks Smith. Res., New Brunswick.

2622. viii. STEPHEN T., b. Oct. 20, 1821; m. Elizabeth Dunn, dau. of Charles. He d. July 11, 1857.

2623. ix. ABNER, b. March 3, 1823; m., ——, 1846, Louisa Dodge, dau. of Josiah.

2624. x. SUSAN, b. May 9, 1826; unm.

2625. xi. JACOB, b. Feb. 9, 1828; m. Ann McCabe and Theresa Eagleson.

2626. xii. LYDIA, b. April 6, 1836; m., ——, James Snow, son of Sylvanus.

2627. xiii. THOMAS H., b. July 20, 1837; m. Elizabeth Ann Foster.

2628. xiv. JOSEPH J., b. Feb. 28, 1839; drowned June 30, 1860.

2629. xv. MELISSA, b. Dec. 6, 1841; m. Ingram Snow, bro. of James.

2630. xvi. HENRIETTA, b. Aug. 16, 1842; m. John Viditoe, son of Parker.

2631. xvii. DAVID M., b. June 24, 1844; m. Henrietta Dunn and Adelia Foster.

2632. xviii. ALONZO, b. March 10, 1846; m., April 16, 1871, Fidetia Glass. 8 ch.

2633. xix. ELLEN, b. Feb. 16, 1848; m. Gilbert Viditoe.
2634. xx. ADONIRAM JUDSON, b. Dec. 7, 1851; m. Susan Wilson.

1513. ISAAC FOSTER (Benjamin, Isaac, Benjamin, Jacob, Isaac, Reginald), b. April 9, 1791, Granville, N. S.; m., Oct. 6, 1814, Elizabeth Patterson. She d. April 8, 1868. He d. Nov. 19, 1867. Res., Hampton, N. S.

2635. i. JAMES P., b. July 7, 1815; m. Mary T. Graves.
2636. ii. BENJAMIN, b. June 21, 1816; m. Elizabeth M. Chute. Res., Hampton, N. S.
2637. iii. ELIZABETH, b. Nov. 22, 1817; m. Benjamin Rumsey. Res., Port Lorne, N. S.
2638. iv. AUGUSTUS, b. Nov. 23, 1819; d. about 1850.
2639. v. AMBROSE, b. April 16, 1821; m. Martha Knowles, of Liverpool, N. S., and Ellen Holland, of Lawrence, Mass.
2640. vi. WILLIAM, b. April 26, 1824; m. Hannah Bogert.; d. 1890.
2641. vii. PHILIP R., b. May 16, 1826; m. Martha Hogan; 6 ch.
2642. viii. JOHN, b. June 1, 1828; m. Diadama Spurr and Harriet Marshall.
2643. ix. MARY J., b. June 1, 1830; m. Fred Benedict, 1851; m. 2d, Thomas Roland.
2643¼. x. LOUISA C., b. May 22, 1834; d. in Lynn, April 6, 1894; m. Jacob Farnsworth.
2643½. xi. MARIA, b. Dec. 23, 1837; m. Peter White; m. 2d, Napoleon Wood. Lived in Lynn, Mass.

1514. ABNER FOSTER (Benjamin, Isaac, Benjamin, Jacob, Isaac, Reginald), b. May 9, 1793, Granville, N. S.; m., Oct. 29, 1818, Sarah Wheelock, dau. of Benjamin, d. Feb. 3, 1838; m. 2d., ——, Hattie Elliott. She d. June 20, 1880. He d. Aug. 12, 1875. Res., Granville, N. S.

2644. i. AMBROSE, b 1820; d. 1821.
2645. ii. MARY ELIZABETH, b. Nov. 3, 1821; m. Elijah Phinney.
2646. iii. ABEL, b. Aug. 28, 1823; m. Evaline Young.
2647. iv. HELEN, b. Nov. 28, 1828; m. John Newcomb. Had one son, now in Arcadia University, a Baptist minister.
2648. v. CATHERINE, b. Aug. 11, 1830; d. Jan., 1894.

1519. CHARLES FOSTER (Isaac, Isaac, Benjamin, Jacob, Isaac, Reginald), b. Wilmont, N. S., ——, 1795; m., ——, 1820, Mary Banks; m. 2d., ——, Mary A. Greene, whose father was a Quaker preacher. Res., Wilmont, N. S.

2649. i. ELNORA, b. ——; m. David Edgeley.
2650. ii. ELIZA, b. ——; m. Isaac Banks, son of George.
2651. iii. MARIA, b. ——; m. Joshua Ray, son of John.
2652. iv. ABBA, b. ——; m. David Morrison.
2653. v. MARY, b ——; m. Henry Jackson.
2654. vi. LOUISE, b. ——; m. Isaac Moore.
2655. vii. BECCA, b. ——; m. William Neely.
2656. viii. EMMA, b. ——; m., ——, Arthur Rumsey, son of Benjamin.
2657. ix. NORMAN, b. ——; m. Agnes Burbridge, dau. of George.
2658. x. ——, b. ——; m., ——, Henry Morris. Res., Harbourville, Kings county, N. S.

1526. WILLIAM FOSTER (Isaac, Isaac, Benjamin, Jacob, Isaac, Reginald), b. Dec. 27, 1813, Wilmont, N. S.; m., ——, Hannah Huntington. Res., Nova Scotia.

2659. i. ELIZABETH, b. ——; m. William Rumsey.
2660. ii. B. WATSON, b. ——; m. Melintha Douglas.
2661. iii. EMMA C., b. ——; m. Major Messinger, son of Daniel; m. 2d, ——, John W. Jenness. Res., Lynn, Mass.
2662. iv. LEWIS J., b. ——. Res., Cincinnati, Ohio.
2663. v. WILLIAM B., b. ——; m. Alice Zoar.
2664. vi. DELACY E., b. ——; m. Sophia Vroom, dau. of John A. and Mary J. (Chute).
2665. vii. ANNIE L., b. ——; m. Burton Bowlby. Res., Lawrence, Mass.

1535. DAVID FOSTER (Oliver, Isaac, Benjamin, Jacob, Isaac, Reginald), b. June 19, 1797; m., ——, 1827, Mary Clark, b. ——, 1803; d. Feb. 23, 1840; m. 2d., ——, Azubah Wheelock. He d. Dec. 27, 1862. They had 7 ch. Res., Nova Scotia.

1541. ROBERT H. FOSTER (Oliver, Isaac, Benjamin, Jacob, Isaac, Reginald) b. March 5, 1812; m., ——, Elizabeth Hall. He d., ——, 1849. Res., Nova Scotia.
2666. i. DAUGHTER, b. ——; m. Nathan Moore.

1543. OLIVER FOSTER (Oliver, Isaac, Benjamin, Jacob, Isaac, Reginald), b. Bridgeton, N. S., Oct. 17, 1817; m. there Jan. 24, 1843, Helen Woodbury, d. Dec. 20, 1897. He was a farmer. He d. April 18, 1889. Res., Bridgeton, N. S.
2667-2. i. SIDNEY M., b. Aug. 8, 1846; m. Della E. Bishop.
2668-2. ii. ROBERT H., b. Aug. 19, 1848; m., Feb. 11, 1878, Caddie Bruce, b. Dec. 14, 1847; d. Jan. 28, 1893; m. 2d, Oct. 11, 1893, Mrs. Effie Fullerton, b. Aug. 18, 1862. Is a farmer. Res., s. p., Wolfville, N. S.
2669-2. iii. RUPERT D., b. July 15, 1853.
2670-2. iv. JAMES T., b. Dec. 5, 1854. Res., Britle, Manitoba.
2671-2. v. ELIZABETH IDA, b. Sept. 13, 1856; d. Aug. 5, 1861.

1544. ISRAEL FOSTER (Oliver, Isaac, Benjamin, Joseph, Isaac, Reginald), b. Bridgeton, N. S., April 22, 1819; m., Oct. 6, 1849, Mrs. Minnetta (Foster) Morse, dau. of Asa Foster and widow of Obediah Morse, Jr., b. Feb. 7, 1813; d. Jan. 2, 1890; m. 2d, Mrs. Ann (Manning) Brown, widow of Ansley Brown. He d. Sept. 16, 1892. Res., Bridgeton, N. S.
2667. i. EDWARD CHIPMAN, b. Dec. 22, 1853; m. Alma S. Balcom.
2668. ii. HENRY RUPPEE, b. Jan. 14, 1855; d. May 14, 1867.
2669. iii. CHARLES A., b. March 16, 1851; m. Annie Lee.

1560. JOHN FOSTER (John, Ezekiel, Benjamin, Jacob, Isaac, Reginald), b. Aylesford, N. S., April 11, 1784; m., July 14, 1813, Sarah Brown. He d. Feb. 21, 1857. Res., Aylesford, N. S.
2670. i. WILLIS, b. in 1814; m. Charlotte Baker. They had 9 ch.
2671. ii. EZRA, b. in 1816; m. Elizabeth Spinney.
2672. iii. MARSDEN, b. in 1818; m. Mary Foster, dau. of Fred and Mrs. Eleanor (Middlemas) Gates, widow of Martin.
2673. iv. ELIZABETH, b. in 1820; m. Edward Orpin, son of George.
2674. v. MARY A., b. in 1822; m. John Earl.
2675. vi. JOHN W., b. in 1824; m. Mary A. Clark, dau. of Matthew. Had 6 ch.
2676. vii. PHEBE, b. ——; m., ——, William Selfridge, Jr.

1563. FREDERICK FOSTER (John, Ezekiel, Benjamin, Jacob, Isaac, Reginald), b. Aylesford, N. S., May 13, 1792; m., ——, 1814, Rachel Benedict, dau. of Jabez. She d., Tremont, N. S.; ae. 90. Was a farmer. He d. April 16, 1825. Res., Morden, N. S.
2677. i. ELIZABETH, b. ——, 1815; m., ——, John Warwick.
2678. ii. WILLIAM, b. ——, 1817; m. Mary Jane Roach. A son, Frank. Res., Greenwood, N. S.
2679. iii. CHARLES, b. July 26, 1818; m. Mary Jane Woodbury.
2680. iv. MARY b. ——, 1821; m. Marsden Foster.
2681. v. JAMES, b. ——, 1823; m. Charlotte Patterson, dau. of William. Res., Cornwallis, N. S.

1564. WILLIS FOSTER (John, Ezekiel, Benjamin, Jacob, Isaac, Reginald), b. Nov. 15, 1794; m., ——, 1826, Susanna Pierce, dau. of William, d. July 12, 1834; m. 2d, June 20, 1835, Nancy Foster, dau. of Ezra, of Bridgeton, N. S.; d. ——, 1897. He d. Jan. 29, 1875. Res., Nova Scotia.
2682. i. GEORGE, b. in 1827; m. Adelaide Foster, dau. of Ezra, of Bridgeton, N. S.
2683. ii. JOHN, b. ——, 1830; m. Susan Neily.
2684. iii. SUSANNA, b. in 1834; d. Oct. 9, 1834.
2685. iv. WILLIAM R. L., b. Nov. 15, 1835; unm. Res., Aylesford, N. S.

1567. EZEKIEL FOSTER (John, Ezekiel, Benjamin, Jacob, Isaac, Reginald), b. July 26, 1801, Aylesford, N. S.; m., Sept. 5, 1822, Eliza Dugan, dau. of John and Margera (Barss), b. Jan. 11, 1806; d. April 20, 1878. He was a farmer. He d. in North Kingston, N. S., April 21, 1889. Res., Aylesford, N. S.
2686. i. MARY ANN, b. Sept. 11, 1824; m., July 19, 1845, Ingersoll Patterson. He was b. Aylesford, N. S., March 8, 1822; d.

there July 16, 1880. She d. Feb. 14, 1873. Ch.: 1. Edgar R. Patterson; d., Nov. 11, 1872. 2. George E. Patterson, living in Massachusetts. 3. I. Willett Patterson, d. Feb. 10, 1875. 4. Albert D. Patterson, res., 115 Fifth Street, Providence, R. I. 5. Elizabeth Patterson, d. June 14, 1858. 6. Annie Bell Patterson, b. July 23, 1859; m., Feb. 13, 1878, Dana B. Smith. Res., Kingston, N. S. He is a farmer and lumber merchant, and was b. June 27, 1850. Ch.: (a) Albert M. Smith, b Nov. 4, 1878. (b) R. Heber, b. Nov. 27, 1879. (c) Ethel M., Smith, b. Oct. 19, 1883. (d) Percy A. Smith, b. May 27, 1891. 7. Ida M. Patterson, b. June 15, 1861; living in Massachusetts. 8. Bessie L. Patterson, d. June 26, 1872. 9. Susan Patterson, b. Aug. 14, 1865; lives in Lynn, Mass.

2687. ii. ALBERT D., b. Dec. 6, 1828; m. Martha Larkin; m. 2d, Elizabeth Parsons; m. 3d, Margaret Reed; m. 4th, Agnes Neily.

2688. iii. SUSAN, b. March 6, 1831; m. Willett Chute.

2689. iv. ELIZABETH, b. 1838; m., ——; ——.

2690. v. LUCY, b. 1842; m. Charles Proctor.

2691. vi. LYDIA, b. Nov. 18, 1849; m., March 20, 1869, Edward M. Doyle, b. Sept. 15, 1840. Lives in Lynnfield, Mass.; s. p.

1570. THOMAS FOSTER (Ezekiel, Ezekiel, Benjamin, Jacob, Isaac, Reginald), b. Granville, N. S., in 1804; m., Feb. 12, 1827, Mary Wheelock, sister of his sister Elizabeth Ann's husband, Thomas Wheelock. She d. Aug. 16, 1859. Res., Southbridge, Mass.

2692. i. ELIZABETH, b. ——.

2693. ii. SARAH ANN, b. ——.

2694. iii. LOUISA, b. ——.

2695. iv. EZEKIEL, b. ——.

1588. RUFUS FOSTER (Ezra F., Ezekiel, Benjamin, Jacob, Isaac, Reginald), b. June 3, 1802; m., Aug. 4, 1838, Christiana Lough. He was a builder. He d. in Dartmouth, N. S. Res., Aylesford, N. S.

2696. i. JAMES GILBERT, b. June 13, 1839; m. —— ——.

2697. ii. WILLIAM R., b. Nov. 5, 1843; m. Frances M. Weeks.

2697¼. iii. EDWARD, b. ——.

2697⅓. iv. HENRY C., b. ——. Removed to Texas.

2697½. v. SUSAN, b. ——; m. Thomas M. Cutter. Res., Dartmouth, N. S.

2697¾. vi. BESSIE E., b ——; m. John Hollis, who d. about 1880. Ch.: 1. Rose. Res., Dartmouth, N. S.

1597. HON. SOLOMON KILLAM FOSTER (Jeremiah, Jeremiah, Benjamin, Jacob, Isaac, Reginald), b. Deering, N. H., March 27, 1803; m., Dec. 24, 1829, Adaline Billington, b. Oct. 4, 1807; d. May 1, 1884. Solomon Killam Foster in his youth taught school, but later in his life he engaged in farming, owning considerable land and also a lumber mill at Weld. He lived at Weld throughout his life and held town offices continually from the time of his majority until his death, which occurred at Weld, February 4, 1857. He was town treasurer for thirty years, and in 1847 he was a member of the Maine legislature. He usually had charge of all legal business for the town, and, according to an old New England custom, was known as Squire Foster. He was married, Dec. 24, 1829, to Adaline Billington, who was born at Wayne, Me., October 4, 1807, and died at Weld, May 1, 1884. They had six children, all born at Weld, who lived to attain their majority. He d. Feb. 4, 1857. Res., Weld, Me.

2698. i. EZEKIEL P. E., b. April 25, 1839; m. Rebecca S. Baker.

2699. ii. HIRAM W., b. Nov. 18, 1830; m. Adaline Colby.

2700. iii. SARAH NANCY, b. Nov. 26, 1831; m., Nov. 26, 1856, Dr. Charles A. Cooledge. Res., Canton, Me. He was b. Dec. 29, 1830. They have two ch.: Henry E. Cooledge, A. M., a graduate of Bates College and Charles M. Cooledge, M. D., a graduate of Dartmouth Medical School. Ch.: 1. Martin E., d. in infancy; b. April 1, 1859. 2. Henry E., Lisbon Falls, Me.; b. Dec. 23, 1860. 3. Charles M., North Waterford, Me.; b. Sept. 25, 1864. Henry married, April 26, 1882; Charles, Feb. 22, 1885.

2701. iv. DANIEL B., b. Sept. 14, 1833; m. Mrs. Wealthy Everett.

2702. v. NATHAN N., b. Nov. 12, 1835; m. Mary Philbrick.
2703. vi. EPHRAIM R., b. May 6, 1837; m. —— ——.

1598. HIRAM FOSTER (Jeremiah, Jeremiah, Benjamin, Jacob, Isaac, Reginald), b. in New Hampshire, — —; m., Dec. 15, 1835, Eliza Howard. He was a farmer and mill owner. He d. Aug. 15, 1850. Res., Weld, Me.

2704. i. SOLOMON, b. ——; d. ——.
2705. ii. ROSINA, b. ——; d. ——.
2706. iii. JAMES, b. ——; d. ——.
2707. iv. SOLOMON GEORGE, b. June 16, 1841; m. Addie Welch. Was a clergyman. He d. s. p.
2708. v. ELIAB JONES, b. June 19, 1844; m. Susan Smith.
2709. vi. CRISINDA, b. June 7, 1846; m., April 1, 1876, Albert M. Childs. Res., Weld, Me.
2710. vii. HIRAM O., b. Nov. 30, 1850; m. Mary J. Phinney.

1602. ISAAC FOSTER (Isaac, Isaac, John, Jacob, Isaac, Reginald), b. Greenfield, Mass., Nov., 1794; m., ——, 1818, Sarah Eggleston. Removed with his mother to the State of New York, Orleans county; married Sarah Eggleston, dau. of Frank, at Carlton, N. Y. He afterward lived at Murray. In 1829 he started for Pittsburg, Pa., intending to go down the Mississippi and Ohio rivers on a trading trip to New Orleans. It is supposed he was murdered, as he had considerable money with him. He died about 1830. Res., Murray, N. Y.

2711. i. ISAAC, b. in Murray, N. Y., Sept. 10, 1819; m. Catherine W. Jeffreys.
2712. ii. REBECCA, b. 1821, in Murray, N. Y.; m., 1844, John Bidwell. Removed to Plainfield, Ill.; d. s. p.
2713. iii. CHAUNCY, b. in 1821. Became a sailor and was shipwrecked on the Laura Baven off coast of Louisiana in 1856.
2714. iv. SON, b. 1825; d. in infancy.

1604. MARCUS FOSTER (Isaac, Isaac, John, Jacob, Isaac, Reginald), b. Greenfield, Mass., Dec. 4, 1798; m., Oct. 7, 1821, Eliza Sleeper, of Murray, N. Y. Removed with the rest of his family to Western New York. His widow married again and removed to Oakland county, Mich. His children were born at Murray, N. Y. He d. April 16, 1831. Res., Murray, N. Y.

2715. i. JOHN W., b. Jan. 20, 1823; d. Sept. 12, 1824.
2716. ii. WILLIAM ROWLEY, b. June 4, 1825; m. Amanda M. Kellogg and Clarissa M. Welfare.
2717. iii. JANE M., b. Jan. 6, 1827; m. Fayette B. Shaw. Lived at Joliet, Ill.; d. about 1860. He was a boot and shoe dealer. Had 1 ch.: 1. Ella, b. 1849; m. and moved to Helena, Mont.
2718. iv. BENJAMIN FRANKLIN, b. Dec. 13, 1828; d. Nov. 6, 1829.

1605. SAMUEL FOSTER (Isaac, Isaac, John, Jacob, Isaac, Reginald), b. Greenfield, Mass., May 28, 1800; m., Nov. 30, 1832, Mary Worthington Walker; b. 1809; d. Dec. 3, 1897. Was about ten years old when his family removed to western New York; lived at Rochester, N. Y. Returned to Massachusetts in 1830. Married Mary W., dau. of Josiah and Rhoda (Root) Walker, of Belchertown, Mass. Lived at Belchertown until 1846; removed to Sheboygan Falls, Wis. In 1848 removed to Russell, Ohio. In 1855 to Oswego, Ill. Died at Bloomington, Ill. His widow died at Chicago, Ill. Mrs. Mary W. Foster had been a resident of Illinois for forty-two years and died at the residence of Mrs. H. D. Chapin, her daughter, 855 Jackson Boulevard. The remains were taken to Bloomington for interment. Mrs. Foster was born in Belchertown, Massachusetts. She was a daughter of Josiah Walker, and a descendant of Richard Walker, who settled at Lynn, Mass., in 1635. Besides her daughter she was the mother of four sons, now living—Samuel W. Foster, of Chanute, Kan.; E. W. Foster, of Chicago; A. G. Foster, of Tacoma, Wash., and W. M. Foster, of Basehor, Kan. While residing in East Bloomfield, N. Y., he worked summers on his farm and winters traded with the Indians in Canada. He had some exciting adventures with the Indians and half-breeds. In 1828 he purchased 120 acres of land on the east side of the Genesee river just below the falls. This farm is now covered by the city of Rochester, N. Y. He paid $6 an acre for the land and sold in two years for $20 an acre. Returning to Massachusetts he located in Belchertown, married, and engaged in mercantile business. He purchased large quantities of goods in the West and made a purchasing tour of this kind every year. In April, 1846, he located near Plymouth, Sheboygan county, Wis. The following year he moved to Russell, Ohio, and engaged in manufacturing at Chagrin Falls. In 1861 he moved to Williamstown, Ill., and in 1863 to Atlanta, Ill., where he died, July 7, 1872. Res., Bloomington, Ill. Children b. at Belchertown, Mass.

2719. i. SAMUEL WALKER, b. Sept. 12, 1833; m. Mary F. Gill.

2720. ii. EVERETT WORTHINGTON, b. March 17, 1835; m. Laura J. Beall.

2721. iii. ADDISON GARDNER, b. Jan. 28, 1837; m. Martha A. Wetherby.

2722. iv. ARTHUR MIDDLETON, b. Feb. 12, 1839; d. April 12, 1839.

2723. v. WILLIAM HENRY, b. Aug. 17, 1840; m. Mary Maher.

2724. vi. SARAH REBECCA, b. Sheboygan Falls, Wis., Nov. 6, 1846; d. Sept. 3, 1848.

2725. vii. MARY ELIZABETH, b. Russell, Ohio, April 29, 1850; m. H. D. Chapin, of Chicago, Ill., March 3, 1875, at Bloomington, Ill. He was b. Bangor, Me., Jan. 8, 1846. Is a book dealer and is quite well known in literary circles His place of business is on Van Buren Street. Ch.: 1. May Laura, b. Aug. 3, 1877. 2. Harry Foster, b. June 25, 1879. 3. Martha Lucy, b. Oct. 8, 1887.

1606. CAPT. EZRA FOSTER (Ezekiel, Ezekiel, John, Jacob, Isaac, Reginald), b. Bernardstown, Mass., Sept. 21, 1779; m., Nancy Smith, b. Chesterfield, N. H., Oct. 25, 1781; d. Feb. 21, 1875. He was a farmer. He was captain of the State militia, also selectman and overseer of the poor; m. Nancy, dau. of Moses Smith, of Chesterfield, N. H. He d. March 1, 1864. Res., Leyden, Mass.

2726. i. NANCY, b. May 6, 1808; m., March 6, 1829, Charles A. Hebeard; d. July 14, 1849. Ch.: 1. Dr. Ezra Armstrong Hebard, b. March 2, 1830, of Grand Rapids, Mich.; m., Dec. 3, 1854, Martha I. Thornington, b. June 20, 1832; d. Jan. 12, 1891. Is a physician and surgeon. Ch.: (a) Charles E., b. Feb. 28, 1858. Res, Grand Rapids, Mich. 2. Sylvia Maria Cusick, of Otsego, Mich., b. March 1, 1834. 3. Franklin Foster Hebard, b. July 14, 1845; d. s. p. Dec. 1, 1876. 4. Mary Ann, b. July 31, 1831; m., July 4, 1849, Jeremiah Ball Haney, b. April 30, 1831. He d. Feb. 5, 1882, at Grand Rapids, Mich. He was a book-keeper and teacher. Ch.: (a) Nancy Louisa, b. July 3, 1850. P. O. address, Dr. N. Louisa Andrus, 222 Jefferson Street, Grand Rapids, Mich. (b) Ezra, b. Sept. 6, 1851, d. 1851. (c) Hannah Estelle, b. Jan. 12, 1853; m., 1876, to L S. Provin. Res., Grand Rapids, Mich. (d) Ellen Eliza, b. Dec. 17, 1854; m, 1878, to Albert G. Ellis. Res., Plainfield avenue, Grand Rapids, Mich. (e) Mary Abigail, b March 15, 1856; d. Aug., 1858. 5. Florence, b. Sept., 1852. 6. Celia Collettee, b. Jan. 12, 1859; d. Aug 17, 1863. 7 Clara Chamberlin, b. Oct. 15, 1860; d. Oct. 21, 1879. 8. Ida Evelyn, b. July 7, 1862; m., 1883, to George Weaver. Res., 185 West Division street, Grand Rapids, Mich. No ch. 9. Frank Ellis, b. Nov. 20, 1864; m., 1883, to Louella Pickett. Res., Ionia, Kent county, Mich. 10. Lulu May, b. May, 1867; d. 1867. 11. Charles Ernest, b. March 30, 1869; m., 18—, to Lulu M. Waite. Res, 180 W. Division street, Grand Rapids, Mich. 12. Myrta A., b. Aug. 14, 1870; m., 1888, to Abraham Sanford. Res., 180 W. Division street, Grand Rapids, Mich. 13. Herbert Elwood, b July 10, 18—; m., 18 –, to Martha Bush. Res., Ouray, Col. 14. Leroy Winfred, b. 1875; d. 1876.

2727. ii. POLLY, b. Oct. 30, 1809; d. Nov. 12, 1809.

2728. iii. SYLVIA, b. Feb. 12, 1811; d. Feb. 25, 1857.

2729. iv. MARY, b. March 2, 1813; d. July 8, 1852.

2730. v. EZRA, b. Feb. 2, 1815; m. Sarah A. Wilbur and Susan A. Mowrey.

2731. vi. JOSEPH SMITH, b. Dec. 18, 1816; m. Olive Newton.

2732. vii. SARA MARIA, b. April 2, 1819; m. Nelson J. Warner, Oct. 14, 1844. She d., 1896. Had 4 ch.; all dead.

2733. viii. LOUISA SOPHIA, b. May 4, 1824; d. Feb. 5, 1848.

2734. ix. RANSOM STUART, b. Feb. 9, 1826; m. Climena Frizzell.

1607. ELIKIAM FOSTER (Ezekiel, Ezekiel, John, Jacob, Isaac, Reginald), b. Leyden, Mass., May 29, 1786; m., in Pownal, Vt., Dec. 27, 1815, Wealthy Ann

Dickinson Phelps, b. Aug. 22, 1791; d. Jan. 15, 1861. His life was uneventful except in one unimportant particular, to-wit: Being a partial cripple and unfitted to some extent to run a farm. He taught school for a winter or two and then learned the saddler's trade, and traveled on horseback over nearly all the Northern States. Spent one winter in the city of Boston, one in Hartford, Conn., and considerable time in Canada with his three brothers there. Was in Rochester, N. Y., when the city consisted of one log house and one log barn. He did not marry and settle down until he was about twenty-seven or twenty-nine years old, though he left home when about seventeen. There was education in this sort of life, but on the whole it was probably a damage to him, in making him restless, and no doubt it shortened his life. He was respected and esteemed for his intelligence, honesty, sound judgment, and kindness of heart, and at his death he had not an enemy in the world. He died February 4, 1859. Res., Leyden, Mass., and Mantua, Ohio.

2735. i. MARIA LOUISA, b. Dec. 21, 1816; m. Richard Longhead. Ch.: 1. Mary Ann; 2. Byron Burritt; 3. Horace Mann; 4. Elizabeth. Byron B. is a physician; res., Ravenna, Ohio.

2736. ii. MARY ANN, b. in 1818; m. Sylvester Bissell. She d. July 19, 1841, leaving a child, b. 1841, which d. ae. 4.

2737. iii. CAROLNE, b. June 12, 1820; m. Norman Wilcox. She d. July 5, 1890 Her ch. d. before her: Wallace, Edson and Ellen, unm.

2738. iv. HARRIET, b. Feb. 20. 1825; d. unm., Feb. 10, 1862.

2739. v. WEALTHY PHELPS, b. Sept. 18, 1822; m., in Ohio, Calvin Brewster. She d. July 17, 1896. He was a farmer and d. in March, 1867, in Auburn, Ohio. Ch.: 1. Edna, b. 1841. 2. Calvin Henry, b. May 21, 1844. 3. Betsy Lumbard, b. 1846. 4. Alta, b. 1848. 5. William Dwight, b. 1851. 6. Milton Foster, b. Jan. 11, 1854; m., Oct. 31, 1878, at Chagrin Falls, Ohio, Mary Lanspach, b. March 11, 1854. He is an undertaker and furniture dealer in Chagrin Falls. Ch.: (a) Cave M. Brewster, b. May 19, 1881. (b) Minnie Brewster, b. March 5, 1884, Chagrin Falls, Ohio. 7. Harriet, b. 1857.

2740. vi. HORACE BURNHAM, b. April 26, 1828; m. Abbie Neal and Mary Wood.

2741. vii. LUCIUS COOLEY, b. April 26, 1831; m. Edna L. Brewster.

1609. JOSIAH FOSTER (Ezekiel, Ezekiel, John, Jacob, Isaac, Reginald), b. Bernardstown. Mass., 1784; m, ——, Annie Eustis, b. 1792; d. Aug. 26, 1846. He d. Oct. 20, 1826. Res., Bernardstown, Mass.

2742. i. THOMAS JEFFERSON, b. Dec. 6, 1822; m. Miss Potter, Mrs. Susan W. (Robbins) Foster, and —— ——.

2742-2. ii. JOSIAH, b. ——; m. Mary M——, who d. in Albany, N. Y., April 22, 1851, ae. 42.

2742-3. iii. WASHINGTON, m. and d. New Haven, Conn., Aug. 24, 1836.

2742-4. iv. DAUGHTER, m. —— Gilbert.

2742-5. v. GEORGE, b. ——.

2742-6. vi. WILLIAM WINCHESTER, b. Aug. 23, 1820; m. Susan M. Robbins.

1612-2. JOHN FOSTER (John, John, John, Jacob, Isaac, Reginald), b. ——, Vermont; m. there Ruth Rich. He d. in Vermont. Res., Moretown, Vt.

2742-2. i. JOHN RICH, b. Nov. 7, 1834; m. Delia Wells.

2743-2. ii. CHARLES A., b. March 2, 1822; m. Hulda Ann Spooner.

2744-2. iii. RUEL S., b. ——; m.; has a son, Rufus. Res., East Burke, Vt.

2745-2.-iv. HARRIET, b. ——; m. N. K. Herrick. Res., Middlesex, Vt.

1613. CHARLES H. FOSTER (Isaiah, John, John, Jacob, Isaac, Reginald), b. Hillsboro, N. H., —— 1819; m., ——, Martha A. Sargent. He went to Antrim, N. H., in 1855, into a house moved from Stoddard for that purpose and put opposite the old Burns mill on Stoddard road. He went there to run the mill but moved away in two years. He had two sons, Charles N., and Leona W., the latter of whom was born in that town. Res., Antrim, N. H., and —— ——.

2743. i. CHARLES N., b. ——.

2744. ii. LEONA W., b. ——.

1618. CHARLES O. FOSTER (Joshua, John, John, Jacob, Isaac, Reginald), b. Hancock, N. H., Feb. 15, 1826; m., Nashua, N. H., Oct. 25, 1853, Mary A. Gray, b. Oct. 2, 1828. Res., Russell, Kan.

2745. i. ADA, b. Dec. 25, 1854.

1620. HON. ADOLPHUS G. FOSTER (Joshua, John, John, Jacob, Isaac, Reginald), b. Feb. 19, 1835, Hancock, N. H.; m., Oct. 28, 1858, Ellen H. Lakin, b. Jan. 13, 1838. He was born in Hancock and has always resided there. Was representative in the general court of New Hampshire at Concord in 1879-80; was selectman of Hancock for six years and chairman of the board for three. Res., s. p. Hancock, N. H.

1621. ELWIN CARTER FOSTER (Joshua, John, John, Jacob, Isaac, Reginald), b. Hancock, N. H., Oct. 23, 1852; m., Boston, Jan. 2, 1876, Anna M. B. Shaw, b. July 10, 1857. He is general manager of the Lynn & Boston railroad company. Office, 333 Union street. Res., Lynn, Mass.

1626. CAPT. DANIEL FOSTER (Jacob, Benjamin, Benjamin, Benjamin, Isaac, Reginald), b. Trenton, Me., March 10, 1792; m., Nov. 14, 1824, Maria Somes. Was a farmer. Capt. Daniel Foster, the son of Jacob Foster, was born at Trenton, Me. His entire life, from early manhood, was spent on his farm in that town, although at times he engaged in other interests. Although his early opportunities for education were limited, owing to the sparsely settled condition of Eastern Maine, broad and careful reading all his life gave him a fund of general information excelled by few. He was married, November 14, 1824, to Maria Somes, of Mount Desert, Me., with whom he lived most happily till his death, April 16, 1864. Under the old militia laws he was for many years captain of the Trenton militia company. In politics he was a Whig and a follower of Henry Clay until the formation of the Republican party which he then joined, and always an earnest opponent of human slavery. He died April 16, 1864. Res., Trenton, Me.

2746. i. AUGUSTUS E., b. June 2, 1826; was in Thirty-eighth Mass. Regt.; killed Port Hudson, June 14, 1863.

2747. ii. LEWIS S., b. July 2, 1827; d. June —, 1858.

2748. iii. CLARISSA S., b. Aug. 30, 1829; d. Aug. 27, 1854.

2749. iv. DANIEL S., b. May 22, 1831. Res., 44 Alder street, Waltham, Mass.

2750. v. EDWARD S., b. Aug. 20, 1833; d. of wounds received at Petersburg, June, 1864; m. Mrs. Clara Moore, Lawrence, Mass. Edward was in First Maine Regt., heavy artillery, in civil war.

2751. vi. CHARLES H., b. Nov. 13, 1836; d. Dec. 30, 1836.

2752. vii. JOHN P., b. May 27, 1839. Res., Winthrop, Mass.

2753. viii. NAHUM, b. July 31, 1842; d. April 29, 1843.

2754. ix. FREDERICK W., b. Feb. 5, 1845; m. Mary E. Webster.

2755. x. CLARISSA S., b. ——; m., June 23, 1849, Cornelius W. Milliken, of Trenton. No living ch.

1636. SIMEON FOSTER (Benjamin, Benjamin, Benjamin, Benjamin, Isaac, Reginald), b. Machias, Me.; m., ——, Katherine Farnsworth. He d., ——, Cooper, Me. Res., St. Davids, N. B.

2756. i. ALBERT G., b. in 1804; m. Nancy Cameron.

2757. ii. FRANKLIN, b. ——.

2758. iii. THEODORE, b. ——.

2759. iv. JAMES, b. —.

2760. v. HENRY, b. ——.

2761. vi. EDWIN, b. ——.

1652. EDWARD FOSTER (Levi, Benjamin, Benjamin, Benjamin, Isaac, Reginald), b. East Machias, Me., June 30, 1793. m., ——, Fanny Cilley, b. Oct. 10, 1795; d. —1851. He d. ae. 60. Res., Milltown, Me.

2762. i. EDWARD AUGUSTUS, b. Aug. 10, 1830; m. Laura H. Foster.

2763. ii. SARAH ELIZABETH, b. May 22, 1821; m., Aug. 8, 1842, Joshua Allen. Res., Ludington, Mich. He was b. Dec. 28, 1809. Is a lumber dealer. Ch.: 1. Eugene Clarence Allen. 2. Fannie Foster Allen. 3. Mrs. Frank Newton Latimer. The latter's husband is a physician and a druggist. Res. of each, Ludington, Mich.

2764. iii. MARIA L., b. April 8, 1824; m., Aug 3, 1844, John Roger Stanchfield. She d. June 22, 1880. He was b. Greene, Me., June 20, 1814; d. Winthrop, Me., Aug., 1860. Was a lumberman. Ch.: 1. Emma, b. May 26, 1845. Res., Ludington, Mich. M., March 6, 1878, Judge James B. McMahon, b. April 17, 1847. He is a circuit judge. Ch.: (a) Donald J. McMahon, b. March 6, 1880. Res., Ludington. (b) Joseph Stoddart McMahon, b. Jan. 22, 1883; d. Nov. 22, 1890. 2. Edward Foster, b. Nov. 21, 1847; m. Ellen F. Woodward, Augusta, Me., July 7, 1873; d. in Ludington, Mich. No ch. now living. 3. Fanny Foster, b. Calais, Me., in 1849; d. in infancy.

2765. iv. GEORGE WARREN, b. June 20, 1825; he d. s. p. May 31, 1850.

2766. v. LUTHER HALL, b. May 31, 1827; m. Lucy A. Schram.

2767. vi. WILLIAM L., b. March 19, 1835. He d. s. p. in the civil war.

1657. GEORGE FOSTER (Levi, Benjamin, Benjamin, Benjamin, Isaac, Reginald), b. East Machias, Me., Nov. 10, 1804; m., ——, Sarah Libby; m. 2d, ——, Caroline De Wolf, b. April 9, 1822. He d. Sept., 1882. Res., Calais, Me.

2768. i. ALBERT H., b. Aug. 27, 1855; m. Laura J. Potter.

2769. ii. LOUISE, b. ——; d. ae. 11 years.

2770. iii. LAURA ELLEN, b. ——; m. ——. She d. ——.

2771. iv. JAMES WARREN, b. ——; d. in infancy.

2772. v. MARIA, b. ——; d .in infancy.

2773. vi. MINNIE ELIZA, b. Feb. 14, 1859; m. —— Dudley. Res., Merrill, Wis.

2774. vii. CARRIE DE WOLFE, b. March 20, 1863; m., Oct. 21, 1889, Frank Barnard Deming, b. April 4, 1864. Res., s. p. Calais, Me. Ticket agent for C. P. R. R.

2775. viii. CHARLES AUDUBON, b. ——; d. young.

1658. BENJAMIN FOSTER (Samuel, Benjamin, Benjamin, Benjamin, Isaac, Reginald), b. ——, 1793; m., ——, Joanna Foster, his second cousin, grand-dau. of Colonel Benjamin's brother. Benjamin Foster went to Dennysville, Me,. in 1824; was the son of Samuel and grandson of Col. Benjamin Foster, of Machias, distinguished as a leader in the military exploits of the Revolution, which made that settlement famous. Benjamin m. Joanna, grand-dau. of Col. Benjamin Foster's brother. Res., Dennysville, Me.

2776. i. EMMA, m. Edward Wiswell; m. 2d, John Allan.

2777. ii. LYDIA W., m. John Wiswell.

2778. iii. JULIA, m. Charles H. Kilby.

2779. iv. JOANNA E., b. 1825; d. ——.

2780. v. DRUSILLA, b. 1829; m. Charles H. Hobart.

2781. vi. BENJAMIN A., b. 1829; d. ——

1669. COL. JOHN WOODIN FOSTER (Daniel, Benjamin, Benjamin, Benjamin, Isaac, Reginald), b. Portland, Me., Nov. 3, 1801; m., Antwerp, N. Y., 1827, Harriet Elizabeth Gould, b. 1801; d. March 12, 1856. Was a farmer. Woodin Foster, the youngest son of Daniel and Hannah Foster, who was born at Limerick, Me., in 1801, married Harriet Elizabeth Gould, formerly of Chester, Vt., in 1827, was commissioned lieutenant-colonel of the One Hundred and Eighty-fourth N. Y. infantry, in 1830; removed to Williamstown, Jefierson county, Kan., between 1850 and 1860, and died there. He d. 1885. Res., Antwerp, N. Y., and Williamstown, Kan.

2782. i. PUBLIUS DARWIN, b. Dec. 13, 1829; m. Amanda E. Warren.

2783. ii. LAURETTE ELIZABETH, b. ——, 1831; m. —— Bates. Res., Williamstown, Kan.

2784. iii. ANNA SOPHIA, b. ——, 1835. Res., Williamstown, Kan.

2785. iv. JENNIE MARIA, b. Oct. 22, 1842; m., Williamstown, Kan., Nov. 7, 1861, Moulton Guy Farnham, b. Aug. 30, 1829. He is in the insurance business and res. 289 Virginia street, Buffalo, N. Y. Ch.: 1. Moulton Gould Farnham, b. Sept. 19, 1862. 2. Charles Foster Farnham, b. Nov. 6, 1872. 3. Minnie Adelaide Farnham, b. May 1, 1870. All the above reside at 289 Virginia street, Buffalo, N. Y. 4. Fred Everette Farnham, b. July 22, 1864; d. Jan. 23, 1870.

1678. AZRO FOSTER (Robert, Isaiah, Benjamin, Benjamin, Isaac, Reginald), b. Columbia, Washington county, Me., Jan. 18, 1812; m., Boston, April 2, 1837, Attezra Dearborn Shattuck, b. April 21, 1816; d. Dec. 2, 1890. He d. Sept. 26, 1878. Res., Andover, Mass., and Pekin, Ill.

2786. i. GEORGE B., b. April 7, 1838; m. Sarah E. Tackaberry.
2787. ii. HENRY A., b. June 9, 1840; m. Marguerett Beaugrand.
2788. iii. HELEN FRANCES, b. July 26, 1842; m., Jan. 25, 1866, Leander King. Res., Peoria, Ill. He was b. March 3, 1838; d. April 10, 1897. Ch.: 1. Harry Foster King, b. Nov. 22, 1866; d. Dec. 16, 1875. 2. Edward Foster King, b. Oct. 4, 1868; d. May 24, 1882. 3. May Foster King, b. Sept. 1, 1872; m., June 25, 1895, to Dr. R. L. Baker. Res., 613 Fayette street, Peoria, Ill. 4. Alta Foster King, b. Sept. 22, 1884; living. Res., 613 Fayette street, Peoria, Ill.
2789. iv. MARY LOUISA, b. June 23, 1846; m. Thomas S. King. Res., 805 Amsterdam avenue, New York, N. Y.
2790. v. EDWARD IRVING, b. ——, 1852. Res., Cedar Rapids, Iowa.

1687-11. JOHN MOSES FOSTER (Benen, Isaiah, Benjamin, Benjamin, Isaac, Reginald), b. Oromucto, N. B., May 7, 1805; m., in 1827, Sarah Smith Wheeler, b. April 14, 1810; d. April 11, 1866. Was a cooper. John Moses Foster was born and married in Burton, Sanbury county, N. B., moving when married to Wakefield, N. B., where he was a farmer for a few years, when he moved to Woodstock, N. B., where he followed the occupation of employing cooper and tradesman. A liberal in politics. From early youth throughout his long life a devoted Christian man. Amiable in disposition to the extent of never making an enemy and beloved by all who knew him. Very fond of fishing, trapping and the gun. He d. April 5, 1888. Res., Woodstock, N. B.

2790-1. i. ISABEL, b. Sept. 23, 1828. Present address, 11 Walnut avenue, North Cambridge, Mass.
2791-2. ii. SAMUEL NUTT, b. March 2, 1830; m. Francis A. Foster and Mrs. Melissa J. Doty.
2792-3. iii. ODBER MOSES, b. Sept. 11, 1832; m. Harriet E. Smith and Elizabeth Campbell.
2792-4. iv. CECELIA, b. Feb. 18, 1834. Res., 269 Brookline street, Cambridgeport, Mass.
2793-5. v. ALMIRA, b. Sept. 3, 1836; d. April 7, 1892.
2794-6. vi. AUGUSTA, b. Jan. 27, 1841.
2795-7. vii. ELIZABETH ANNE, b. March 29, 1845; d. Jan. 20, 1889.
2796-8. viii. PARKER HUMPHREY, b. May 13, 1846; m. Mary A. Sprague.

1692. JOHN WOODIN FOSTER (John W., Woodin, Benjamin, Benjamin, Isaac, Reginald), b. about 1810 in Machias, Me.; m., July 12, 1840, Caroline Rockliffe; m. 2d, Nov. 7, 1847, Mrs. Maria Simonton. He is a merchant. Res., Rockland, Me.

2791. i. EMILY, b. Dec. 2, 1840.
2792. ii. ISAAC I., b. in 1849.
2793. iii. FREEMAN F., b. in 1851.

1709. HON. PHINEAS FOSTER (Moses, Woodin, Benjamin, Benjamin, Isaac, Reginald), b. East Machias, Me., March 17, 1795; m. Ruth Rich. She d. soon; m., East Machias, Me., 1829, Mary Coffin Foster, b., 1806; d., 1890. Phineas Foster was born in what is now East Machias, Washington county, Me., about 1796. Married first Ruth Rich, whose children were Ezra Warren and James Rich; both are now dead. Married for second wife, Mary Coffin Foster, who had a large family of children; those now living are: Phineas, Mary Coffin, Harriet Josephine, Abbie Melvina and Susan Wilmot. He was a farmer and lumberman. He resided in East Machias till 1844 when he moved to Marion in the same county, where he was engaged in farming and lumbering, until his death in the early seventies. He was a member of the House of Representatives in 1848 or 1849. He also held various town offices, such as selectman, etc. He d. in 1871, in Marion, Me., ae. 75. Res., Denneysville, Me.

2794. i. PHINEAS, b. June 8, 1831; m. Ellen Jane Bolton.
2795. ii. MARY C., b. ——; m. Keezer. Res., San Francisco, Cal.
2796. iii. SUSAN W., b. ——; unm. Res., Lowell, Mass.

2797. iv. ABBIE M., b. ——; unm. Res., Lowell, Mass.
2798. v. HARRIET J., b. ——; unm. Res., Lowell, Mass.
2799. vi. EZRA WARREN, b. ——; d. ——.
2800. vii. JAMES RICH, b. ——; d. ——.

1741. CHARLES FOSTER (James, Worden, Benjamin, Benjamin, Isaac, Reginald), b. East Machias, Me., Oct. 10, 1803; m., Aug. 19, 1827, Lavinia Pickett Chase, b. June 30, 1807. He d. Dec. 26 1870. Res., East Machias, Me.
2801. i. JAMES W., b. July 5, 1831; d. unm. July 15, 1856.
2802. ii. LAURA F., b. Sept. 6, 1837; m. Sept. 9, 1869.
2803. iii. CHARLES WARNER, b. Aug. 8, 1833; d. unm. Dec. 8, 1859.
2804. iv. LUCY E., b. Aug. 12, 1840; d. unm. Dec. 4, 1859.
2805. v. J. KELLER, b. April 17, 1843.
2806. vi. FREDERICK A., b. Oct. 22, 1846; m. Abbie M. Weston and S. Elizabeth Loring.

1748. ERASTUS FOSTER (Benjamin, Ezekiel, Benjamin, Benjamin, Isaac, Reginald), b. Oct. 25, 1801, Limerick, Me.; m., Phillips, Me., Jan. 5, 1823, Betsey Clough, b. March 11, 1800; d. March 11, 1877. Was a farmer. He d. Garland, Me., Feb. 11, 1887. Res., Dover, Me.
2807. i. HARRIET N., b. Jan. 7, 1826; m., May 22, 1851, Dr. David Evans, b. July 28, 1821; d. May 25, 1875., Res., Dover, Me. Ch.: 1. Liston P. Evans, b Aug 2, 1852; m., Nov. 23, 1874. Res., Dover, Me. 2. Hattie F. Evans, b. Oct. 4, 1856. Res., Dover, Me.
2808. ii. ELEANOR, b. Nov. 28, 1823, m., July, 1851, d. Sept. 10, 1885. Address a child, Ellsworth Hall, Litchfield, Minn.
2809. iii. BENJAMIN J., b. Oct. 5, 1827; d. Dec. 9, 1852.
2810. iv. ELIZABETH C., b. April 20, 1831. Address, Mrs. E. C. Freeman, 353 Sixth Ave., Brooklyn, N. Y.
2811. v. RELIEF S., b. April 2, 1834; d. Sept. 13, 1856.
2812. vi. JOHN C., b. May 18, 1836. Address, Skowhegan, Me.
2813. vii. GEORGE W., b. July 8, 1839; d. April 8, 1865.

1753. LEIGHTON FOSTER (Benjamin, Ezekiel, Benjamin, Benjamin, Isaac, Reginald), b. Limerick, Me., April 19, 1810; m. New Portland, Clarissa Ricker, b. April 6, 1811; d. Waverly, Iowa, Oct. 14, 1889. Is a farmer. Res, Waverly, Iowa.
2814. i. RUTH F., b. March 2, 1834; m. in Belvidere, Ill., Oct. 15, 1860, —— Allen.
2815. ii. JOHN R., b. in New Portland, Me., Feb. 13, 1836; d. in Waverly, Iowa, May 25, 1891. He was in the army three years.
2816. iii. SETH L., b. in Dover, Me., June 20, 1842. Address, Waverly, Iowa.

1758. JOHN FOSTER (Nathan, Jeremiah, Jeremiah, Abraham, Jacob, Reginald), b. Colerain, Mass., Nov. 11, 1795; m., Virgil, N. Y., 1818, Bernice Harris. He d. ——, 1837. Res., Virgil, N. Y., and Zanesville, N. Y.
2817. i. FANNY, b. Aug. 22, 1819; m. Homer, Mich., 1841, Edward Henderson. He was b. 1807; d. April 23, 1898. Was a druggist. Res., Homer, Mich. Was postmaster there for sixteen years—served during President Lincoln's administration. Ch.: 1. W. E. Henderson, b. Oct. 1, 1845. Res., 360 West Sixty-fifth St., Chicago, Ill. 2. Sarah Peppet, b. April 26, 1850. Res., 409 W. Mason St., Jackson, Mich.
2818. ii. PERCELLA, b. Nov. —, 1825.
2819. iii. SALLIE, b. Oct. 28, 1829; m. —— Arthur; sons Peter and Arthur. Res., Toledo, O.

1762. AUSTIN BAKER FOSTER (Nathan, Jeremiah, Jeremiah, Abraham, Jacob, Reginald), b. Shelburne, Mass., Nov. 11, 1807; m. Groton, N. Y., Dec. 20, 1827, Sarah W. Stout, b. Sept. 23, 1810; d. Friendship, N. Y., Nov. 17, 1858. He was a farmer.

Austin Baker Foster was born in Franklin county, Mass. His father's name was Nathan Foster, whose wife was Sally Baker. About 1815 Austin's father moved to Virgil, Cortland county, N Y. Later Austin married Sarah W. Stout, at Groton, Tompkins county, N. Y., and about 1830 moved to Friendship, Alleghany county, N. Y. Mr. Foster was a devoted Christian man, a member of the Baptist church, and after the death of his wife, in November, 1859, gave much of his time to church building and Sunday-school work. He was a speaker of a good deal of force and ruggedness. He was a man of great physical strength as well as positive moral character. His ancestors were of those who came from England, so the family legend runs, and landed near Plymouth in 1636. Mr. Foster died in Michigan, at Cooper, Kalamazoo county, Sept. 5, 1892. Res., Virgil, N. Y., and Cooper, Mich.

2820. i. ANDREW S., Aug. 5, 1836; d. Sept. 24, 1847.
2821. ii. SARAH A., b. Sept. 12, 1833; m. ——, Ammon Gordon. She d. ——, 1881. A son is Will Gordon, of Friendship, Wis.
2822 iii. GEORGE PARKER, b. Feb. 10, 1839; m. —— ——.
2823. iv. MARIAN A., b. Aug. 29, 1846; m., Dec. 25, 1865, Alfred J. Coon. Res., Friendship, N. Y., b. Aug 15, 1846. Is a sexton. Ch.: 1. Maria Coon Moses, b. Sept. 3, 1869; m., Nov. 26, 1889. Res., Cuba, N. Y. 2. Grace Coon, b. April 4, 1877. 3. Mae Coon, b. March 3, 1883. 4 Edna Coon. b. Feb. 13, 1885. 5. Minnie Coon, b. Sept. 3, 1869; d. March 22, 1870.
2824. v. SIDNEY A., b. May 17, 1849; m. Ella J. Dyer and Clara P. Hill.
2825. vi. CORNELIA W., b. March 25, 1831; m., Oct. 21, 1852, Amos M. Hart, b. March 7, 1828; d. July 26, 1877; m., 2d, —— Huntley. Res., Cooper, Mich. Ch.: 1. Andrew S. Hart, b. March 14, 1854, in Cussawayo, Pa.; m. Mary Kimball, Aug. 19, 1874. Res., 566 Twenty-seventh St., Chicago, Ill. 2. George A. Hart, b. Nov. 4, 1862, in Friendship, N. Y.; m. Hannah Sheehan, 1888. Res., 5727 Union Ave., Chicago, Ill. 3. Mrs. Mary Hart Allen, b. Sept. 7, 1865, in Friendship, N. Y.; m. Frank Allen, October, 1886. Res., 527 Thirty-eighth St., Chicago, Ill. 4. Sarah R. Hart, b. Aug. 26, 1869; d. Jan. 5, 1871, Plainwell, Mich.

1772. ELIJAH WILLARD FOSTER (Abraham, Samuel, Jeremiah, Abraham, Jacob, Reginald), b. Ashburnham, Mass., Oct. 8, 1807; m. in Hubbardston, Tryphena Lovewell, b. Jan., 1807; d. Nov. 20, 1873. He was a farmer. He. d. April, 1882. Res., Gardner, Mass.

2826. i. ABIGAIL, b. June 17, 1835; d. Dec. 12, 1840.
2827. ii. ALVARA, b. Feb. 15, 1838; m, Mrs. Lois Irene (Goodwin) Puffer.
2828. iii. ADDISON, b. Feb. 22, 1840.
2829. iv. WILLARD, b. Oct. 1, 1842; m., April 31, 1866, Emma Putney. He d. May 17, 1878, s. p.
2830. v. HENRY, b. Aug. 7, 1845; m. Lynetta Goodwin.
2831. vi. MARY L., b. April 15, 1848; d. June 7, 1861.
2832. vii. JANE, b. Dec. 29, 1830; d. April 15, 1832.
2833. viii. SEWALL, b. April 29, 1833; m. Sarah Ann Smith.

1779. SAMUEL FOSTER (Nathaniel, Samuel, Jeremiah, Abraham, Jacob, Reginald), b. Ashburnham, Mass., July 28, 1799; Dec. 15, 1825. Emeline Kibling, dau. of John. Will of Samuel Foster, of Fitchburg; wife, Emeline; daughter, Louise E. Merritt; 1878. He d. ——, 1878. Res., Ashburnham and Fitchburg, Mass.

2834. i. SARAH A., b. March 27, 1827.
2835. ii. CHARLES S., b. June 6, 1828.
2836. iii. LEONARD G., b. Aug. 26, 1837.
2837. iv. ELLEN, b. ——.
2838. v. EDWIN. b. ——.
2839. vi. GEORGE, b. ——.
2840. vii. LOUISA E., b. ——; m. —— Merritt. Res., Fitchburg.

1786. LEONARD FOSTER (Nathaniel, Samuel, Jeremiah, Abraham, Jacob, Reginald), b. Ashburnham, Mass., April 14, 1814; m., April 18, 1838, Malvina Lawrence, of Ashburnham, dau. of Capt. Moses. She d. Aug. 28, 1848; m., 2d, ——, 1850, Clarissa Cole; m., 3d, ——, 1862, Sarah Howard. He resided in the northwest part of the town. For many years he was actively engaged in the manufacture of lumber, and was frequently chosen to positions in town affairs. Res., Ashburnham, Mass.

2841. i. WALDO A., b. Oct. 6, 1841; m. H. Elizabeth Chandler.

2842. ii. JENNIE A., b. Sept. 6, 1839; m. Webster Maynard, of Winchendon. She d. July 16, 1861.
2843. iii. EMMA L., b. Oct. 7, 1847; drowned June 14, 1850.

1789. STEARNS FOSTER (Samuel, Samuel, Jeremiah, Abraham, Jacob, Reginald), b. Stoddard, N. H., Dec. 26, 1799; m., Feb. 3, 1825, Cynthia Wilson, b. Sept. 8, 1804; d. July 9, 1844; m., 2d, Dec. 3, 1845, Mary Fuller, b. June 13, 1813. He d. Aug. 23, 1882. Res., Stoddard and Keene, N. H.
2844. i. HENRY, b. March 2, 1826; d. March 3, 1826.
2845. ii. EDWIN, b. Nov. 18, 1828; d. Feb. 8, 1832.
2846. iii. GEORGE, b. June 10, 1830; m., Feb. 25, 1857, Dollie E. Whicher, b. March 15, 1837.
2847. iv. AMELIA, b. June 3, 1838; d. Nov. 9, 1838.
2848 v. EMMA L., b. Sept. 16, 1843; d. Sept. 17, 1844.
2849. vi. MARY A., b. June 25, 1849.
2850. vii. WILLIAM S., b. Sept. 1, 1851.

1792. HOSEA FOSTER (Samuel, Samuel, Jeremiah, Abraham, Jacob, Reginald), b. Stoddard, N. H., April 13, 1806; m. there Nov. 7, 1833, Mary G. Rice, b. Worcester, Mass., March 14, 1816 [see Rice Genealogy]; d. July 27, 1895.

Hosea Foster was born in Stoddard, N. H., in 1806, on the farm in the west part of the town, near the hill known as the "Pinnacle," where his father, Samuel, had settled in 1799, when he came to Stoddard from Ashburnham, Mass. Here he lived continuously until 1868, when he moved to Keene and bought a farm west of the city, still occupied by his son Charles. He was a man of steady, industrious habits, and sound and conservative judgment, and always held the respect and confidence of his neighbors and townspeople. He and his father before him carried on in connection with their farm a blacksmith shop. In those days almost all the hardware used in house building in the country towns was the direct product of the smith's handicraft, as were also the generality of household implements and farm tools. The old Foster house was built with hand-hammered nails, hinges, door-latches, etc. Mr. Foster was killed in Keene in the winter of 1872 by a load of wood, which he was drawing from a wood-lot, on West Hill, being overturned upon him.

He d. by accident Feb. 7, 1872. Res., Stoddard and Keene, N. H.
2851. i. ALVIN RICE, b. Oct. 14, 1834; m. Mary J. Sargent and Mrs. Eliza A. Scott.
2852. ii. SARAH MOORE, b. April 9, 1837; d. Nov. 23, 1858.
2853. iii. EDWIN STEARNS, b. Dec. 21, 1840; m. Ella S. Houghton and Clara Fay.
2854. iv. CHARLES MERRICK, b. Nov. 16, 1843; m., Oct. 15, 1885, Josephine L. Paige, b. July 12, 1847. He is a farmer. Res., s. p., 597 West St., Keene, N. H.
2855. v. HORACE ELMORE, b. Aug. 22, 1846; d. Jan. 9, 1853.
2856. vi. ELLA FRANCELIA, b. Feb. 20, 1856; m., Nov. 12, 1889, Ellery E. Rugg. Res., 24 Park Ave., Keene, N. H. He is a carpenter, b. June 7, 1841, s. p.

1795. SAMUEL FOSTER (Samuel, Samuel, Jeremiah, Abraham, Jacob, Reginald), b. Stoddard, N. H., Nov. 29, 1815; m., Nov. 5, 1845, Mary S. Palmer, b. Aug. 23, 1823; d. Sept. 25, 1846. He was a merchant; was buried with his family in Mt. Auburn.

Will—Samuel Foster, Jr., of Boston, merchant; sisters, Mariah Foster Wood, Emily Foster Hayward and Selina Foster Bowers, of Hancock, N. H., Lydia Foster Joslin, of Stoddard, N. H., and Electa Foster Downing, of South Marlow, N. H.; brothers, Stearns Foster and Hosea Foster, of Stoddard, N. H.; niece, Elsey Joslin, daughter of Luke and Lydia F. Joslin; nephew, George Foster, son of Stearns Foster; father, Samuel Foster. Dated July 17, 1850. Prob. Aug. 26, 1850. Lib. 148^2, Fol. 64-65-66. Lib. 150^1, Fol. 9. Lib. 450, Fol. 172. Lib. 288, Fol. 326. Lib. 151^2, Fol. 27. Lib. 324, Fol. 174. Lib. 264, Fol. 208. Lib. 243, Fol. 286.

He d. Aug. 5, 1850. Res., Boston, Mass.
2857. i. MARY ALICE, b. Sept. 20, 1846; d. in infancy.

1801. HOSEA FOSTER (Hosea, Samuel, Jeremiah, Abraham, Jacob, Reginald), b. in Verona, N. Y., May 1, 1819; m. in Durhamville, N. Y., Feb. 4, 1841,

Cornelia C. Seaden, b. Oct. 8, 1822; d. March 31, 1888. He was a farmer. He d. Aug. 22, 1883. Res., Lenox, N. Y.

2858. i. CATHERINE, b. March 3, 1842; d. March 3, 1849.
2859. ii. JOHN WESLEY, b. March 17, 1848; m., Dec. 16, 1874, Frances Wilcox. Res., Clockville, N. Y. Had a dau., Grace Irvine, b. Jan. 25, 1881.
2860. iii. EMMA C., b. May 10, 1851. Res., Alene, Madison county, N. Y.
2861. iv. N. JENNIE, b. Jan. 11, 1846; unm. Is a milliner. Res., Little Falls, N. Y.
2862. v. VELTON A., b. March 26, 1856; m., Nov. 9, 1895, Georgia Bell Wilcox. Res., 607 Seventh Ave. s., Minneapolis, Minn.
2863. vi. EDWARD L., b. April 26, 1859. Res., Canastota, N. Y.
2864. vii. L. IMOGENE, b. April 26, 1865; m., March 4, 1892, Edwin J. New. Res., Alene, Madison county, N. Y.
2864½. viii. GEORGE W., b. March 6, 1844; d. March 19, 1844.

1804. JEROME W. FOSTER (Joel, Samuel, Jeremiah, Abraham, Jacob, Reginald), b. Ashburnham, Mass., Dec. 15, 1810; m., April 24, 1834, Mary Calson; d. March 24, 1887.

He inherited in an eminent degree a firmness of character and soundness of judgment which distinguished his ancestors. Mr. Foster was a man of varied employments, and many trusts were safely confided to his efficient management. He was a civil engineer, a Justice of the Peace, for many years superintendent of the postoffice, and was frequently employed in the conduct of town affairs. He was a trustee of Cushing Academy and a member of the committee of construction, and to his prudent and sagacious counsels the Academy is much indebted. For eighteen years he was town clerk. The records by him transcribed are expressed with precision and orderly arrangement. In every labor of an industrious life Mr. Foster has left his impress of mature judgment and integrity of character. If he never sought the applause of his fellowmen and never suggested his own advancement, he did not fail to receive the spontaneous confidence and unqualified respect of all who knew him. Mr. Foster was reserved in manner and associative in his habits of thought, yet he never failed in the discharge of important trusts, nor in courage to maintain his convictions of right and duty. He was prominent in all measures pertaining to the welfare of the town, and on questions of moment his advice was frequently sought, and in his loyal service the best interests of the community were encouraged and advanced. He d. March 23, 1871. Res., Ashburnham, Mass.

2865. i. GEORGE C., b. Jan. 21, 1835; m. Sarah E. Bemis.
2866. ii. MARY C., b. March 12, 1838; m. in A, Feb. 9, 1858, Josiah Payson Sawtelle. Res., New York City, N. Y. Ch.: 1. Nettie A., b. Sept. 25, 1868; d. May 25, 1871. 2. Annie C., b. Sept. 4, 1872; d. April 6, 1876. She resides Hardeeville, Fla.
2867. iii. JEROME W., b. Nov. 5, 1839; d. April 5, 1841.
2868. iv. HARRIET N., b. July 28, 1843; m., July 1, 1875, Goldsbury H. Pond, of Franklin, Mass. Res., 56 W. Twelfth St., New York City, N. Y.
2869. v. SUSAN R., b. Nov. 12, 1844; d. Aug. 14, 1866.
2870. vi. C. LUCRETIA, b. June 1, 1846; unm.; d. Jan. 12, 1890. Res., A.
2871. vii. ELLA JANE, b. Nov. 11, 1847; d. May 28, 1861.
2872. viii. D. JOSEPHINE, b. Dec. 26, 1849; d. Nov. 18, 1869.
2873. ix. EMMA DELPHIA, b. Feb. 6, 1852; d. Sept. 14, 1852.
2874. x. EMMA, b. June 15, 1853; d. Sept. 7, 1861.
2875. xi. JEROME, b. June 5, 1856; d. Oct. 29, 1856.

1817. DUDLEY FOSTER (Samuel, Joseph, Joseph, Joseph, Jacob, Reginald), b. Billerica, Mass., Nov. 15, 1809; m., May 21, 1835, Louisa Pollard, dau. of William, b. May 23, 1810; d. Feb. 28, 1882; m., 2d, Mary A. ——. He resided near the Howe school, of which he was trustee from the first and was treasurer; was town clerk and treasurer for twenty-five years. He assisted in publishing History of Billerica. Dudley, Billerica, letter date Feb. 5, 1895; ex. March 25, 1895; wife Mary A.; children, Frank D. Foster, of North Andover, Mass., John H. Foster, of Billerica. He d. Jan. 3, 1895. Res., Billerica, Mass.

2876. i. FRANCIS DUDLEY, b. Aug. 30, 1836; unm. Res., North Andover Depot, Mass. Is a manufacturer. Has been organist of Congregational church for thirty-two years.

2877. ii. JOHN HOWARD, b. March 9, 1844; m., Sept. 2, 1874, in Billerica, Ellen Bryant Mathews, b. March 6, 1846. He is in the insurance business. Res., s. p., Billerica, Mass.

1823. JOSEPH FOSTER (Samuel, Joseph, Joseph, Joseph, Jacob, Reginald), b. Billerica, Mass., July 20, 1821; m. there Lydia A. ——. She m., 2d, Daniel L. Giles, and resides Lincoln, Mass.

Joseph, Billerica, letter date April 5, 1859; ex. same; wife, Lydia Ann; children, Damon, Whitney and Annie.

Damon, Whitney and Annie Whiting Foster, of Lincoln, minors, children of Joseph and Lydia Ann Foster, late of Billerica; guardian bond Feb. 1, 1866.

He d. ——, 1859 Res., Billerica, Mass.

2878. i. ANNIE WHITING, b. ——.

2879. ii. WHITNEY, b. ——.

2880. iii. DAMON, b. ——; d. unm., 1872. Damon Foster, of Concord, letter date July 15, 1872; ex. Oct. 8, 1872; no widow; next of kin, Lydia A. Giles, wife of Daniel L. Giles, Lincoln, mother; Whitney Foster, brother; Annie W. Foster, sister; Harriet L. Giles, half sister, all of Lincoln.

1828. LEVI THOMAS FOSTER (Levi, Joseph, Joseph, Joseph, Jacob, Reginald), b. Billerica, Mass., ——, 1824; m., May 24, 1849, Mariah Elizabeth Richardson, dau. of John b. April 12, 1828. She m., 2d, Sept. 19, 1855, Elbridge Teel, of Medford. Levi T., of Billerica, letter date Oct. 11, 1853; ex. Nov. 8, 1853; wife, Mariah E.; children, John P. and Laura M. He d. Sept. 30, 1853. Res., Billerica, Mass.

2881. i. LAURA MARIA, b. Aug. 27, 1850, in Lawrence, Mass.

2882. ii. JOHN R., b. April 8, 1853; d. July 5, 1877.

1830. DANIEL FOSTER (James, Daniel, Joseph, Joseph, Jacob, Reginald), b. Beverly, Mass., Oct. 10, 1807; m., July 28, 1831, Elizabeth Woodbury, b. Aug. 20, 1809; d. Jan. 2, 1871; m., 2d, Aug. 6, 1871, Elizabeth R. Sisson, b. 1833, at Boston. Was a merchant, and in 1846 he was inspector of customs. He d. Sept. 14, 1891. Res., Beverly, Mass.

2883. i. ELIZABETH W., b. April 16, 1832; d. Feb. 26, 1892.

2884. ii. CHARLES CARROLL, b. Feb. 22, 1834; m. Sarah E. Burke.

2885. iii. LOUISA W., b. Aug. 3, 1837; m. Elbridge Fisk, Nov. 21, 1860; d. Jan. 1, 1892, diabetes.

2886. iv. CLARISSA L., b. Dec. 15, 1846; d. Feb. 1, 1847.

2887. v. FRANCIS AUGUSTUS, b. May 14, 1849; mariner; m., March 10, 1875, Martha L. Grant.

2888. vi. HENRY AUSTIN, b. Oct. 4, 1851; m. Anna L. Morgan.

1831. JAMES FOSTER (James, Daniel, Joseph, Joseph, Jacob, Reginald), b. Beverly, Mass., March 25, 1809; m., Oct. 24, 1830, Mary Rogers, b. ——, 1808; d. Dec. 2, 1879, dau. of Benjamin and Martha. He d. ——. Res., Beverly, Mass.

2889. i. MARY AUGUSTA, b. May 18, 1846.

1834. ALFRED FOSTER (James, Daniel, Joseph, Joseph, Jacob, Reginald), b. Beverly, Mass., Nov. 29, 1819; m., March 9, 1848, Augusta M. Lovett, b. 1825, dau. of Stephen and Rebecca. Res., Beverly, Mass.

2890. i. JULIETTE AUGUSTA, b. May 10, 1849; d. Jan. 22, 1865.

1835. ADDISON W. FOSTER (James, Daniel, Joseph, Joseph, Jacob, Reginald), b. Beverly, Mass., Nov. 26, 1822; m. ——, Lucy Ann Hogerzeil. Was a cordwainer. He d. March 28, 1894. Res., Beverly, Mass.

2891. i. SIMEON H., b. April 31, 1862; drowned Sept. 6, 1865.

2892. ii. ADDISON, b. Jan. 10, 1864.

2893. iii. AARON, b. ——; d. Aug. 3, 1864.

2894. iv. GEORGE ADDISON, b. Jan. 29, 1861.

2895. v. ARTHUR W., b. March 28, 1856.

2896. vi. JAMES ADDISON, b. April 3, 1855; d. Aug. 17, 1855.

2897. vii. ADDISON, b. Aug. 20, 1858; d. Aug. 31, 1858.

2898. viii. CARRIE, b. June 4, 1865.
2899. ix. JAMES E., b. Aug. 13, 1859.
2900. x. ANNA D., b. March 1, 1867.
2901. xi. LUCY ANN, b. July 2, 1869.
2902. xii. MARY ALICE, b. May 23, 1857; m., Jan. —, 1882, Charles Sumner Goodridge, b. 1857.

1838. WILLIAM AUGUSTUS FOSTER (Seth, Daniel, Joseph, Joseph, Jacob, Reginald), b. Beverly, Mass., Oct. 24, 1814; m., June 20, 1832, Mary Raymond, b. 1813; d. s. p. Feb. 7, 1871; dau. of Thomas and Elizabeth; m., 2d Nov. 18, 1872, Julia Frances Trow, b. June 18, 1845, dau. of Daniel and Martha P. (Trask); d. Feb. 22, 1897. He was a shoe manufacturer. He d. July 24, 1898. Res., Beverly, Mass.

2903. i. WILLIAM AUGUSTUS, b. Dec. 12, 1873; unm.; is a land surveyor. Res., 37 Railroad Ave., Beverly, Mass.
2904. ii. ARTHUR TROW, b. May 12, 1879; unm. Res., Beverly.
2905. iii. MARION RAYMOND, b. Sept. 15, 1872; d. April 29, 1890.

1840. DANIEL FOSTER, 2d (Seth, Daniel, Joseph, Joseph, Jacob, Reginald), b. Beverly, Mass., ——, 1823; m., May 28, 1845, Louise Dodge, b. 1825, dau. of Thomas and Mary. Was a shoe manufacturer. He d. June 6, 1892. Res., Beverly, Mass.

2906. i. MARY ALICE, b. Feb. 23, 1863; m., July 16, 1886, James G. Baker, of Boston, b. 1865 in E. Orleans, Mass., son of Benoni and Sarah.
2907. ii. LOUISA, b. June 8, 1864; d. Sept. 2, 1864.
2908. iii. WILLIAM AUGUSTUS, b. April 22, 1860; m. —— —— and Emma F. Clough.
2909. iv. MARY LOUISA, b. Feb. 23, 1843; d. Sept. 22, 1846.
2910. v. DANIEL PAGE, b. Dec. 7, 1858.
2911. vi. JESSE, b. May 29, 1866.
2912. vii. ELLEN, b. Dec. 17, 1856.
2913. viii. SETH, b. Oct. 4, 1847; m. Mary J. McLean.
2914. ix. DANIEL, b. Oct. 16, 1848; d. Oct. 27, 1848.
2915. x. DANIEL PAGE, b. Sept. 28, 1850; d. Oct. 2, 1853.
2916. xi. DANIEL PAGE, b. Aug. —, 1854; d. Sept. 12, 1854.
2917. xii. MARY LOUISA, b. Oct. 27, 1853; d. Feb. 15, 1858.

1841. SAMUEL GOODRIDGE FOSTER (Seth, Daniel, Joseph, Joseph, Jacob, Reginald), b. Marblehead, Mass., May 24, 1827; m., Sacramento county, Cal., Sept. 23, 1860, Caroline Emmons, b. April 24, 1824; d. May 25, 1891. He has been justice of the peace for twenty-five years and notary public. In 1850 was a Whig. Arrived in California June 12, 1850; became a charter member of the first Republican club ever organized on the Pacific coast, in 1856. Hon. Cornelius Cole, E. B. Crocker and C. P. Huntington were also charter members of the same club; voted the Republican ticket ever since. Res., Perkins, Cal.

2918. i. WILLIAM AUGUSTUS, b. Nov. 22, 1865. Res., Perkins, Cal.

1856. JOSEPH HILLER FOSTER (John W., James, Nathan, Joseph, Jacob, Reginald), b. Aug., 1825; m., ——, Adelaide Morgan. "The death of no member of our community could cause deeper or more extended sorrow than that of Joseph Hiller Foster. He was born at Portsmouth in August, 1825, and on the 1st of December, 1847, became a member of the firm of John W. Foster & Son, booksellers, then doing business at No. 5 Market street, in this city. After the death of his universally beloved father, on the 10th of June, 1852, Mr. Foster carried on the book and stationery business on Market and Congress streets until his election to the important office of treasurer of the Portsmouth Savings Bank in 1877, which position he held at the time of his death, on Monday last. Though of a retiring and modest disposition and disinclined to hold public office, he served faithfully and well as a member of the school committee in 1856, as a member of the Common Council in 1864, and as an alderman in 1865 and 1866, and in the latter position served as chairman of several important committees. No man enjoyed the confidence of the public and stood higher in public estimation than did Mr. Foster. He was an earnest worker in all charitable and benevolent enterprises, contributing everything in his power to alleviate the distress of mankind. He was for some years a director of the Portsmouth Howard Benevolent Society, secretary of the

City Missionary Society and clerk of the Chase Home for Children. He enjoyed the society of agreeable companions, and was for more than thirty years clerk of the Federal Fire Society, and secretary of the Portsmouth Chess Club almost as long. He was interested in the improvement of our city, and took an important part in the securing of Langdon Park, and served as treasurer of the park association. He was a man of fine literary tastes, an extensive reader, a good critic of literary productions and especially fond of good poetry. He served for many years as a director in the Portsmouth Athenæum. In his death the South Parish has lost one of its most steadfast and conscientious members. It will be difficult to fill his place elsewhere, but especially in the church where he worshiped. His whole life was an example of an unostentatious Christian—pure, earnest, genial, benevolent, true to himself and the faith which he professed. The words spoken of his lamented father are equally applicable to him: 'A truly good man has departed,' yet he has bequeathed to his friends a rich legacy in the example and Christian influence which he has left behind. He was a man of inflexible honesty. Entrusted with millions of dollars, he accounted for every penny. The numerous positions of treasurer which he held attest his well-deserved reputation for honesty among his neighbors. Those who knew only the public and outward life of Mr. Foster were not aware of the strongest and finest trait in his character. He was happiest in his home life and in his family relations. We sympathize deeply with his afflicted family in their great loss; for the blow is more severe to them on account of his love for home. He was an earnest worker in whatever he undertook, and, up to last November, he managed the large monetary interests entrusted to his care with skill and fidelity. The death of his son, William Russell Foster, two years ago, was a severe shock to him, and although he bravely tried to conceal his sorrow, in order to prevent suffering to others, yet his hidden grief, together with his business cares, evidently sapped his strength. In November last, by direction of his physician, he gave up his business and went to Bermuda to obtain renewed strength, if possible, from change of scene and climate, but he soon returned, and has since been confined to his room. He possessed a sound and well-balanced mind, refined tastes, a genial manner, a kind heart, an even temper, joined with inflexible uprightness and steadfastness of purpose. His memory is most precious to those who knew him best."—Portsmouth Journal, March 28, 1885. He died March 23, 1885. Res., Portsmouth, N. H.

2919. i. JOHN WELCH, b. ——; d. young.
2920. ii. WILLIAM RUSSELL, b. April 11, 1855; was graduated at Harvard College 1875; city solicitor of Portsmouth; d., unm., March 10, 1883.
2921. iii. MARGARET, b. ——, 1860.
2922. iv. ELIZABETH HILLER, b. ——, 1872.

1861. REGINALD FOSTER (Henry G., Nathaniel, Nathan, Joseph, Jacob, Reginald), b. Cambridge, Mass., June 25, 1828; m., Boston, Mass., Oct. 27, 1857, Annie Maria Wentworth, b. March 31, 1833, dau. of James and Abigail (Dunbar), of Boston. Reginald, of Framingham, letter date, November 6, 1895; ex. November 29, 1895; wife, Annie M.; ch., Annie R. Foster, of Framingham.—Middlesex Prob. He d. Oct. 16, 1895. Res., Framingham, Mass.

2923. i. ANNIE REGINA, b. Jan. 13, 1862; unm. Res., Framingham, Mass. She has her great-grandparent's Nathaniel's and Susannah's miniature portraits and their children's, Henry, Nancy and Susan, as well as their fine old snuff-boxes and silverware and his pension claim for services during the Revolution. He was one of the officials of the Massachusetts Bank, Boston. She has, since her father's death, found her pen a necessary aid in the problem of living and is now on the editorial staff of the Saturday Evening Gazette, Boston.

1864. WILLIAM BACON FOSTER (Isaac, Isaac, Isaac, Joseph, Jacob, Reginald), b. Acworth, N. H., Nov. 26, 1799; m., May 29, 1825, Eliza West, dau. of Elisha and Mrs. Ruth (Goodale) Tryror Washburn, b. June 27, 1802; d. Dec. 19, 1846; m., 2d., Feb. 27, 1848, Lidde (Bowman) Nobles, b. April, 1800; d. Jan. 31, 1880. He d. Oct. 30, 1885. Was a farmer. Res., Moretown, Vt.

2924. i. CALVIN WASHBURN, b. July 1, 1826; m., June 1, 1849, Mindia, dau. of Henry and Mary (Turner) McClure, b. June 10, 1830; d. Aug. 1, 1870; m. 2d., Jan. 1, 1871, Louisa M., (Chatham) (Duncan) Smith, d. June 29, 1872; m., 3., 1877, Mouisa J., dau. of John

A. Milliard. Was a farmer. Res., Moretown, Vt. Ch.: 1. Henry William Foster, b. Sept. 22, 1859; unm. at home in Moretown.

2925. ii. CHARLOTTE WHITMAN, b. July 7, 1828; m., Dec. 19, 1847, Charles C. Lee, b. Dec. 27, 1827; a farmer. Res., Newark, Vt. She d. July 8, 1853. Ch.: 1. Sarah Lee, b. April 22, 1849; m., Dec. 27, 1869, Charles Bean, b. Feb. 22, 1849; a farmer. Res., Newark, Vt. Ch.: (a) Arthur Lome Bean, b. May 4, 1871. (b) William H. Bean, b. July 7, 1873. (c) Fred C. Bean, b. June 29, 1875. (d) Gertie E. Bean, b. Oct. 1. 1876. (e) Annie M. Bean, b. Dec. 1878; d. Jan. 29, 1879. (f) Elgie M. Bean, b. Jan. 2, 1880. (g) Harry C. Bean, b. March 8, 1882. (h) Grace Bean, b. Dec. 29, 1885. 2. Leonard B. Lee, b. July 22, 1851; d. Jan., 1859.

2926. iii. GILMAN WILLIAM, b. Oct. 2, 1838; d. June 28, 1839.

2927. iv. SARAH ELIZA, b. Aug. 1 1840; m., March 1, 1859, Nahum G. Aldrich, b. Dec. 3, 1831; a farmer. Res., Moretown, Vt., where she d. Aug. 18, 1873; he m., 2d, Nov. 6, 1879, Mary E. Townsend, b. March 29, 1834. Ch.: 1. William Alonzo Aldrich, b. Oct. 2, 1860; m, May 24, 1887, Ida Lee, b. April, 1869. 2. Jennie Eliza Aldrich, b. Jan. 12, 1867; m., Sept. 12, 1885, Fred Fitch, of Stowe, Vt. 3. Harriet Abigail Aldrich, b. Oct. 30, 1869.

1866. CALVIN REG FOSTER (Isaac, Isaac, Isaac, Joseph, Jacob, Reginald), b. Moretown, Vt., Oct. 15, 1803; m., Oct. 25, 1825, Susan, dau. of Thomas and Susanna Combs Spooner, b. Jan. 26, 1800; d. July 4, 1874; a carriage maker. He d., Moretown, Vt., July 16, 1885, aet. 82. Res., Moretown, Vt.

2928. i. THEY HAD one ch. that d. in infancy; adopted son, Albert Lovejoy, of Moretown.

1867. HON. LEONARD ROBERTSON FOSTER (Isaac, Isaac, Isaac, Joseph, Jacob, Reginald), b. Moretown, Vt., April 9, 1807; m., Oct. 10, 1832, Jane Boynton, dau. of Ebenezer and Jane (Osgood) Johnson, b. June 1, 1812; d. Feb. 4, 1859; m., 2d., April 10, 1862, Liva Ann, dau. of Ezra and Lucy (Bacon) Evans, b. Nov. 7, 1831; a merchant. He d. Jan. 5. 1897. Res., Waterbury Center, Vt. Mr. Foster was of Puritan ancestry, the four generations preceding him being born in Beverly, Mass. His father, Isaac Foster, Jr., and his mother, Charlotte Whitman, of Weymouth, Mass., were married one hundred years ago, and soon after made their way over bad roads and blazed paths to establish a home in the wilderness of Central Vermont. They carried their religion with them, and into this pious home the son was born. In after years he said: "I have loved the Lord and prayed to Him ever since I can remember." In his seventeenth year he professed religion and joined the Methodist Episcopal Church, of which he was a faithful member until his death. He held its offices, gave for its charities, and labored to promote its success. Two of his sons were in the war, and one of them, who bore his father's name, was killed in the battle of Cedar Creek. In politics he was an Abolitionist, and represented that party in the Legislature of Vermont in 1852. In 1832 he married Jane Boynton Johnson, a devout woman and a true helpmeet, who died in 1859. It is related that at their marriage they knelt in prayer with the minister. In his home, for sixty five years, the family altar was a place of blessing and a throne of power. He was married in 1862 to Ann L. Evans, who survives him. He was the father of eleven children, six of whom are living—Rev. Elon Foster, D. D., of the New York Conference; Mrs. Eliza J. Clapp and Luther O. Foster, of Roberts, Wis.; Ebenezer J. Foster, M. D., of Boston, Mass.; L. Whitman Foster and Arthur M. Foster, of LaCrosse, Wis. He knew the Bible almost by heart. He had great power in prayer. He kept up the practice of singing at the family altar till the last. Well may the children of such a father call him blessed. Such lives as this have built up the church.

2929. i. ELON, b. June 22, 1833; m. Sarah Palmer.

2930. ii. ELIZA JANE, b. Feb. 15, 1837; m., Feb. 27, 1856, William L., son of Rufus and Wealthy P. Spaulding Clapp, b. Dec. 10, 1824; a farmer. Res., Warren, Wis.; P. O. add., Roberts, Wis. Ch.: 1. Otis Foster Clapp, b. March 31, 1857; m., Jan. 5, 1883, Constance, dau. of Angus and Eveline (Caldwell) Sutherland, b. Oct. 25, 1864; a farmer. Res., Warren, Wis. Ch.: (a) William

Angus Clapp, b. Dec. 7, 1884. (b) Eveline Foster Clapp, b. Aug. 31, 1868; d. March 31, 1887. 2. Wealthy J. Clapp, b. April 28, 1862; m., March 8, 1884, Charles Edward, son of Thomas William and Catharine (Cooke) Glasspoole, b. March, 1861. Res., Duluth Minn. Ch.: (a) Leonard Charles Glasspoole, b. Oct. 19, 1885; d. Dec. 27, 1886. (b) (A daughter) Glasspoole, b. June 17, 1887; d. June 18, 1887. 3. Bessie S. Clapp, b. April 24, 1870.

2931. iii. LUCRETIA, b. Feb. 15, 1837; d. Sept. 18, 1886 (twin).

2932. iv. LUTHER OSGOOD, b. March 27, 1841; m., Jan. 3, 1864, Lucy B., dau. of Wright and Christina Spaulding Haskins, b. April 24, 1843; the proprietor of the Green Mountain farm and dealer in blooded stock. Res., Warren, Wis.; P. O. add., Roberts, Wis. Ch.: 1 Elon Foster, b. July 5, 1875.

2933. v. ELVIRA ELIZABETH, b. March 6, 1843; m., July 3, 1864, Elias, son of Henry and Ursula (Chapman) Haskins, b. Nov. 10, 1837; a mechanic. Res., Warren, Wis.; P. O. add., Roberts, Wis. Ch.: 1. Leonard N. Haskins, b. May 10, 1865. 2. William C. Haskins, b. June 10, 1872.

2934. vi. LEONARD ROBINSON, JR., b. Nov. 3, 1844; was killed at the battle of Cedar Creek Oct. 19, 1864.

2935. vii. DR EBENEZER JOHNSON FOSTER, b. Jan. 15, 1847; graduated at Hahnemann Medical College, Philadelphia, Pa., 1869; same year received a diploma from Keene School of Anatomy, of Philadelphia; is settled in the practice of his profession at Waterbury, Vt.; has devoted a great deal of time to music, and has both taught and composed; has also exhibited some of his paintings, for which he has received prizes at the county fairs; unm. Add., Roberts, Wis.

DR. E. J. FOSTER-EDDY.

2936. viii. LUKE WHITMAN, b. Jan. 13, 1850; m. Alice Fuller.

2937. ix. ARTHUR M., b. April 24, 1863; m. Ella M. Fuller.

2938. x. EMMA L., b. April 17, 1865; d. Aug. 14, 1882.

2939. xi. LEONARD ROBINSON, JR., b. Dec. 19, 1873; d. Feb. 28, 1877.

1868. ISAAC GILLMAN FOSTER (Isaac, Isaac, Isaac, Joseph, Jacob, Reginald), b. Moretown, Vt., March 25, 1810; m., 1st, Dec. 6, 1832, Elizabeth Mayo; m. 2d, Feb. 2, 1838, Lucretia, dau. of Asa and Polly Peck Hathaway, b. April 3, 1815; d. Jan. 2, 1839; m. 3d, 1844, Melinda Maria, dau. of Joel Perkins; b. Canada, 1816; d. March 29, 1853; m. 4th, Nov. 24, 1853, Mrs. Elizabeth Loviza Brigham, dau. of Joseph and Sarah (Springer) Faunce and wid. of Elisha Warren Brigham, b. June 1, 1813; a carpenter. He d. Northfield, Vt., Oct. 1, 1875; served in Co. E, 8th Vermont Vols. She res. 539 Main street, Springfield, Mass. Res., Northfield, Vt.

2940. i. MARGARET, d. aet. 14 months.

2941. ii. MARIA MATILDA, b. Oct. 28, 1844; m., Nov. 29, 1862, Henry Kirk, son of Gillman Taylor and Lucy Stiles (Hawks) Eaton, b. Moretown, Vt., Aug. 25, 1837; she d. 1896. Res., Northfield, Vt. Ch.: 1. Alice Lucretia Eaton, b. March 30, 1865. 2. Gertrude Emma Eaton, b. Feb. 16, 1868; m., Feb. 16, 1885, Charles H. Cady.

2942. iii. LUCRETIA CLARA, b. Sept. 4, 1848; m., Nov. 23, 1867, James Wilbur, son of William and Louisa (Hunt) Atherton, b. March 25, 1839; cabinet maker. He is dead; she resides at 678 Congress street, East Detroit, Mich. Ch.: 1. Louise J. Atherton, b. June 24, 1869. 2. Mary V. Atherton, b. May 6, 1871; d. Aug. 9, 1872. 3. Clara M. Atherton, b. Nov. 7, 1872. 4. Maud M. Atherton, b. Oct. 18, 1874; d. May 7, 1876. 5. George W. Atherton, b. Oct. 27, 1876.

2943. iv. MARTHA ANN, b. Nov. 20, 1854; m., March 25, 1879, William Sheridan, son of Beriah and Melvina (Murray) Sherman, b. Feb. 17, 1850. Res., Merrick, Mass. Ch.: 1. Alice Louise Sherman, b. March 25, 1881. 2. Lilla Melvina Sherman, b. Aug 20, 1882.

1860. JOHN WHITMAN FOSTER (Isaac, Isaac, Isaac, Joseph, Jacob, Reginald), b. Moretown, Vt., July 12, 1812; m., Oct. 30, 1838, Lucia A., dau. of John B. and Nancy (Atkins) Davis, b. Oct. 24, 1820; a farmer. He d. in Moretown, Vt., May 12, 1875. Res., Moretown, Vt.

2944. i. GILLMAN G., b. Nov. 15, 1842; m. Elvira Harlow.

2945. ii. ELLEN L., b. Oct. 28, 1848; m., Dec. 9, 1866, Orlando, son of Joseph and Louise (Cameron) Foster; served during war in Vermont regt. as lieutenant; no issue. Res., Stowe, Vt.

2946. iii. EDWIN A., b. Sept. 12, 1850; m. Mary E. Chaffee.

2947. iv. NETTIE L., b. Feb. 21, 1853; m., Dec. 31, 1871, William, son of Thomas and Amanda (Luce) Russell, b. April 23, 1849; a farmer. Res., Moretown, Vt. Ch.: 1. Olin E. Russell, b. Oct. 31, 1872. 2. Ellen Russell, b. April 12, 1878.

2947½. v. ADA C., b. July 17, 1857; m., Aug. 9, 1879, Hilman Hezekiah, son of Hezekiah and Clarisa (Ferry) Johnson, b. Aug. 31, 1857. Res., Waterbury Center, Vt. Ch.: 1. Leon Clifton Johnson, b. May 18, 1882. 2. Nettie Evelyn Johnson, b. March 20, 1884.

1770. DANIEL FOSTER (Daniel, Isaac, Isaac, Joseph, Jacob, Reginald), b. Augusta, Me., July 5, 1799; m. there Jan. 7, 1822, Rebecca Eaton, b. Nov. 30, 1798, at Binghamton, N. Y.; d. Nov. 11, 1856, in Augusta; m., 2d, Dec. 5, 1857, Cynthia Maria E. Coleman, b. Vassalboro, Me., Aug. 8, 1830. He was a farmer. She was of Bingham. They were among the original seventeen members of the First Baptist Church in Augusta. He d. March 7, 1881. Res., Augusta, Me.

2948. i. IRA H., b. Jan. 8, 1823; m. Amanda M. Crandall.

2949. ii. TIMOTHY DANFORTH, b. March 10, 1825; m. Ann S. Clark.

2950. iii. DANIEL WINTHROP, b. April 27, 1829; m. Dorcas L. Marshall.

2951. iv. LYDIA, b. March 12, 1831; m., March 1, 1848, Levi Ward. Ch.: 1. Daniel W., b. Dec. 8, 1848; m. Mary Gardner. 2. Charles E., b. Nov. 22, 1857; m. Carrie Wright and Annie B. Caswell; five ch.

2952. v. GEORGE BOARDMAN, b. June 14, 1834; d., s. p., July 4, 1894.

2953. vi. JOHN AVERY, b. Nov. 8, 1839; m. Clara Ann Tucker.

2954. vii. ALBERT L., b. April 20, 1845; m., Dec. 24, 1866, Francena A. Knowlton, b. 1850. Res., s. p., Riverside, Me.

2954½ viii. LUCINDA, b. Sept. 29, 1827; d. same day.

1771. CONY FOSTER (Daniel, Isaac, Isaac, Joseph, Jacob, Reginald), b. Augusta, Me., April 16, 1801; m. Vassalboro, Me., May 11, 1829, Caroline Brown, b. Sept. 14, 1807; d. Riverside, Me., Oct. 4, 1888. She was dau. of Benjamin and Polly (——) Brown. Was a farmer and merchant.

Cony Foster, the youngest child of Daniel Foster and Phillena Pettingell, was born in Augusta, Me., April 16, 1801. His father enlisted in the United States service when Cony was two years old. His mother was left with three children to struggle along in the world. She was a pious woman, and though poor, she had the consolation of religion to support her. She availed herself of every opportunity to send her children to school. The two older children were put out to live where they could earn their living. Cony, being the youngest, was kept at home, and no means within the power of his mother was spared to give him a good school education. His mother supported herself and son by taking in weaving and going out nursing. Cony, when out of school, spent much of his time working for his mother, picking up wood, etc. What little work he could do for the neighbors he was glad to get, and when he was seven years old would often work for two cents a day.

When he was ten years old a gentleman let him a piece of land to plant, and he raised thirty-eight bushels of corn. This was a great help to his mother. From this time for a number of years he took land to plant on shares, and raised corn and potatoes sufficient to support the family. When he was twelve years old he began to study arithmetic. With some money that he had saved, he walked five miles to a bookstore, and bought himself a slate and arithmetic. These he kept until he went through the book, and for many years afterward. He also made a manuscript and set down every sum in Kinnie's Arithmetic. He also commenced the study of English Grammar, and gave his whole attention to it. In three weeks from the commencement he could parse well in the first class in school, in which paper essay was used. From this time until he was seventeen years old he continued to go to school, which was only kept about three months in the year, and that in the winter time. He had to walk three miles to the school.

CONY FOSTER.

From 1813 to 1819 his older brother, Daniel, was at home, and the two boys had each a steer calf. They made a little yoke and sled and hauled up their wood with them, and kept them until they became oxen. About 1816 the boys bought a possession of fifty acres of land, where they cut hay, etc. In a year or two they built a small house and a forty-foot barn. Here they lived, with their mother, in peace and happiness a number of years. In the year 1819 Daniel took unto himself a wife. In the winter of 1819, Cony, who was eighteen years old, took a town school to teach in Readfield, Me., and, although he was young and the school had the reputation of being a very bad and unruly one, yet he managed to give such general satisfaction that he was asked to keep the school the next winter, which he did with like good success. After this he kept a school in his own neighborhood. In the winter of 1821 he kept another school in Augusta and boarded with the School Agent. Here he slept in the chamber of a log cabin so low that he could not stand up straight to dress himself, and although schoolmasters were at that time looked up to as an exalted order of beings, still Master Foster was not so "starched up" but that he could put up with almost any inconvenience. In fact, his main desire was to please those with whom he labored—"to rear the tender thought and teach the young idea how to shoot." In the years, 1822-3-4, he taught three different schools in the town of Vassalboro, Me., giving good satisfaction in all. In the fall of 1824 he attended China Academy one quarter, where he studied navigation, surveying, rhetoric and algebra. His mother died in the fall of 1824, while he was at China Academy. This was a severe affliction to him.

In the spring of 1825 Cony sold out his interest in the home they had built to his brother Daniel, and Daniel lived there until his death and raised a family of children. In the summer of 1825 Cony went into the employ of Eveleth & Hartwell, merchants, of Augusta, as a clerk. In this situation he remained about two years, and kept the books of the firm.

An eventful period in Mr. Foster's life occurred in 1827. He became acquainted with Miss Caroline Brown, a blooming girl of twenty, daughter of Benjamin Brown, of Vassalboro, a prominent citizen and business man of Maine. About this time a proposition was made to Mr. Foster by Mr. Brown to go to the Penobscot river to engage in lumbering and mercantile business. A copartnership was accordingly entered into, which continued seven years, when the partnership was mutually dissolved. An attachment was formed between Mr. Foster and Miss Caroline Brown from their first acquaintance, which at length was consummated by their marriage, in May, 1829. In that year Mr. Foster built him a fine residence in Orono, Me., in which he lived until his death, Feb. 22, 1875, and raised a large family of children. After the partnership between Mr. Foster and Mr. Brown was dissolved Mr. Foster continued the business for some twenty years, and prospered. In 1834 Mr. Foster was chosen Treasurer of the town of Orono, which office he held for three successive years. In 1840, upon the division of the town, he was elected one of the Selectmen, and for three years after the first he was Chairman of the Board of Selectmen, Assessors and Overseers of the Poor of Orono, viz., 1841-2-3. In 1845 he was chosen Collector of Taxes, which office he held for four successive years. In 1846 he was again chosen Chairman of the Board of Selectmen, Assessors and Overseers of the Poor. He held the office of Justice of the Peace from 1840 to the time of his death (1875). In 1855 he was again elected one of the Selectmen, and also again in 1863 and 1864. In 1860 he was chosen Collector of Taxes and held the office six years in succession, having in both terms been Collector of Taxes ten years, and collected between $200,000 and $300,000.

Mr. Foster had passed through a variety of circumstances. He had known what it was to be poor, and he had known what it was to enjoy a competence, but through it all he never did a dishonorable act, and when he died left a name in the town in which he had lived so long, as an honest, upright man, whose word was as good as his bond.

He d. Feb. 22, 1875. Res., Orono, Me.

2955. i. BENJAMIN B., b. Nov. 23, 1831; m. Sarah Gibson Howell.
2956. ii. CHARLES HENRY, b. Feb. 18, 1830; m. Sue Agnes Carter.
2957. iii. WILLIAM WIRT, b. Nov. 23, 1831; m. ——, Sarah ——. He d. Boston, Mass., s. p., Dec. 8, 1888.
2958. iv. CAROLINE ELIZABETH, b. Jan. 16, 1837; d. March 22, 1856.
2959. v. LYMAN BEECHER, b. March 10, 1841; m. Mary C. Etheridge and Susan Alice Spencer.
2960. vi. EVELYN LINCOLN, b. April 3, 1843; d. Aug. 6, 1847.
2961. vii. EDWARD FRANKLIN, b. Oct. 23, 1845; d. Dec. 2, 1845.
2962. viii. GEORGE BURGESS, b. Oct. 19, 1850; m. Christine Hanson.

1872¼. GEN. JOHN GRAY FOSTER (Perley, John, Isaac, Joseph, Jacob, Reginald), b. Whitefield, N. H., May 27, 1823; m., ——, Mary Mole; m., 2d, ——, Anna Johnson.

John Gray Foster was born in Whitefield, N. H., May 27, 1823; died in Nashua, N. H., Sept. 2, 1874. He was graduated at the United States Military Academy in 1846; assigned to the engineer corps, and served in the Mexican war under General Scott, being engaged at Vera Cruz, Cerro Gordo, Contreras, Churubusco and Molino del Rey, where he was severely wounded. He received the brevets of First Lieutenant and Captain for gallantry. He was assistant engineer in Maryland in 1848-52, and on coast survey duty in Washington, D. C., in 1852-4, and after promotion to First Lieutenant acted as assistant professor of engineering at West Point in 1855-7. At the beginning of the civil war he was stationed at Charleston, S. C., and safely removed the garrison of Fort Moultrie to Fort Sumter during the night of Dec. 26 and 27, 1860. He was breveted Major for the distinguished part he took in this transfer, and was one of the defenders of the fort during its subsequent bombardment. He was made Brigadier-General of Volunteers Oct. 23, 1861; commanded a brigade in Burnside's North Carolina expedition and received the brevet of Lieutenant-Colonel for his services at Roanoke Island. While in command of the Department of North Carolina, with the rank of Major-General of Volunteers, in 1862-3, he conducted several important expeditions. He had charge of the combined Departments of Virginia and North Carolina, from July until November, 1863, and afterward of the Army and Department of the Ohio, which he relinquished in December, 1864, on account of severe injuries from the fall of his horse. After the termination of his sick leave he commanded the Depart-

GEN. JOHN G. FOSTER.

ment of the South, co-operating efficiently with General Sherman and preparing to assist in the reduction of Charleston under Sherman's orders, when suffering caused by his old wound obliged him to transfer the command to Gen. Quincy A. Gilmore. In 1865 he was breveted Brigadier-General in the regular army for gallant services in the capture of Savannah, Ga., and Major-General for services in the field during the rebellion. He was in command of the department of Florida in 1865-6, and on temporary duty in the engineer bureau of Washington in 1867. He afterward served as superintending engineer of various river and harbor improvements. His submarine engineering operations in Boston and Portsmouth harbors were conducted with great ability, and were eminently successful. He contributed articles to periodical literature on engineering topics and published "Submarine Blasting in Boston Harbor" (New York, 1869).

The United States Register, official, at West Point, has the following: "John G. Foster, b. ——, N. H.; was appointed in New Hampshire ——. Military History: Cadet at the United States Military Academy from July 1, 1842, to July 1, 1846, when he was graduated and promoted in the army to brevet second lieutenant, corps of engineers, July 1, 1846; served as assistant engineer in the engineer bureau at Washington, D. C., 1846; in the war with Mexico, 1847-8; attached to the company of sappers, miners and pontooniers, being engaged in the siege of Vera Cruz, March 9-29, 1847; battle of Cerro Gordo, April 17-18, 1847; battle of Contreras, Aug. 19-20 (brevet first lieutenant Aug. 20, 1847, for gallant and meritorious conduct in the battles of Contreras and Churubusco, Mexico), 1847; battle of Churubusco, Aug. 20, 1847; battle of Molino del Rey, Mexico; (brevet captain Sept. 8, 1847, for gallant and meritorious conduct in the battle of Molino del Rey, Mexico), Sept. 8, 1847, where he was severely wounded; on sick leave of absence, disabled by wounds, 1847-8; as assistant engineer in building Fort Carroll, Patapsco (second lieutenant, corps of engineers, May 24, 1848) river, Maryland, 1848-52; at coast survey office, Washington, D. C., March 20, 1852, to April 26, 1854; as assistant engineer in building Fort Carroll, Maryland, 1854; at the (first lieutenant corps of engineers, April 1, 1854) Military Academy; as principal assistant professor of engineering, Jan. 11, 1855, to June 27, 1857, and as superintending engineer of the survey of the site of fort at Willets' Point, Long Island, N. Y., 1857; of preliminary operations for building fort at Sandy Hook, N. J., 1857-8; of building Fort Sumter, and repairs of Fort Moultrie, Charleston Harbor, S. C., 1858-61; in charge of Forts Macon and Caswell, North Carolina, 1858-61, and of construction of Fort Carroll (captain of corps of engineers, July 1, 1860; for fourteen years continuous service) Maryland, 1859-60.

"Served during the rebellion of the seceding states, 1861-66, as chief engineer of the fortifications of Charleston harbor, S. C., being engaged in strengthening the works in anticipation of attack upon them; transporting the garrison of Fort Moultrie to Fort Sumter, Dec. 26, 1860; and in defence of (brevet major, Dec. 26, 1860, for the distinguished part taken by him in the transfer of the garrison of Fort Moultrie to Fort Sumter, South Carolina) Fort Sumter, Dec. 27, 1860, to April 14, 1861, including its bombardment, April 12-14, 1861, when it was surrendered and evacuated; as assistant engineer in the engineer bureau at Washington, D. C., April 22 to May 5, 1861; as superintending (major Eleventh Infantry, May 14, 1861—declined) engineer of the construction of Sandy Hook fort, New Jersey, May 11 to Nov. 22, 1861; in command of troops at Annapolis, Md., Nov. 25 to Dec. 20 (brigadier general United States Volunteers, Oct. 23, 1861); on General Burnside's North Carolina expedition, commanding brigade, Dec. 20, 1861, to July 1, 1862, being engaged in the capture of Roanoke Island (brevet lieutenant-colonel, Feb. 8, 1862, for gallant and meritorious services in the capture of Roanoke Island, North Carolina) with its garrison and armament, Feb. 8, 1862; capture of Newbern (brevet colonel, March 12, 1862, for gallant and meritorious services in the capture of Newbern, N. C.) March 14, 1862, and bombardment of Fort Macon, which capitulated April 26, 1862; in command of the Department of North Carolina, July 1, 1862, to (major-general United States Volunteers July 18, 1862,) July 13, 1863 (his force constituting the Eighteenth Army Corps, Dec. 24, 1862), during which time he successfully conducted the expedition to burn the Goldsboro railroad bridge, December, 1862; being engaged in the action of Southwest Creek, Dec. 14, 1862; combat of Kinston, Dec. 15, 1862; action of Whitehall, Dec. 17, 1862; action of Goldsboro bridge, Dec. 18, 1862; repulse of (major corps of engineers, March 3, 1863,) the rebel attack on Newbern, March 14, 1863, and defence of Washington, N. C., March 29 to April 16, 1863, when the siege was raised; in command of the Department of Virginia and North Carolina, July 15 to Nov. 13, 1863; and of Army and Department of the Ohio, Dec. 12, 1863, to Feb. 9, 1864, which he was obliged to relinquish in consequence of severe injuries from the fall of his horse, Dec. 23, 1864; on sick leave, awaiting orders, at Baltimore, Md., Feb. 9 to May 5, 1864; in command of the Department of the South, May 26, 1864 (brevet brigadier-general United States army, March 13, 1865, for gallant and meritorious services in the field during the rebellion) to Feb. 11, 1865, and of the Department of Florida, Aug. 7, 1865, to (mustered out of volunteer service Sept. 1, 1866,) Dec. 5, 1866; and on temporary duty in the engineer bureau, Washington, D. C., January, 1867, to May 10, 1867; lieutenant-colonel, corps of engineers, March 7, 1867."

Will—John G. Foster, an officer in the corps of engineers, United States army; house in Nashua, N. H., to my mother, wife, Anna Johnson Foster, and my daughter, Annie Mole Seton, my late wife, Mary Mole Foster. Dated, Nashua, July 22, 1874. Pro. Oct. 5, 1874. Lib. 472; fol. 67. Petition for executor, John Gray Foster; died Sept. 2, 1874. Lib. 472; fol. 147, 104, 105. Lib. 482; fol. 416. Suffolk, Mass., Prob.

He d. Sept. 2, 1874. Res., Nashua, N. H.

2962¼. i. ANNIE MOLE, b. ——; m. ——, Capt. Henry Seaton, of the United States Army, at Fort Sheridan, Chicago.

1872-2. COL. EDWIN FOSTER (Perley, John, Brainard, Isaac, Joseph, Jacob, Reginald), b. Greenfield, N. H., in 1819; m. in Hancock, N. H., Sarah Fox Bullard. He was a stage owner. He d. in N. H., in 1859. Res., Bennington, N. H.

2962½. i. CHARLES E., b. March 16, 1844; m., Manchester, Nov. 5, 1889, Emma M. Meldrum, b. 1854. s. p. Res., Manchester, N. H. Address., 852 Elm St., R. 23. He was in the civil war from April, 1861, to December, 1865.

1875. GEORGE HUNTING FOSTER (Moses, Samuel, Isaac, Joseph, Jacob, Reginald), b. Nashua, N. H., March 7, 1828; m., Clinton, Mass., March 7, 1854, Martha Ann Bidwell, b. June 12, 1828. The compiler is indebted to Mr. Foster for the copy of the Foster coat-of-arms, found elsewhere. Res., Worcester, Mass., 25 Abbott street.

2963. i. MARY HAMILTON, b. Nov. 15, 1856; d. Jan. 31, 1860.
2964. ii. WILLARD MALLALIEU, b. Oct. 12, 1858; m. Emeline E. Sherwood.
2965. iii. ALLEN HUNTING, b. Sept. 25, 1862; unm. Res., at home.
2966. iv. EDWIN CHASE, b. Jan. 14, 1866; d. April 17, 1873.
2967. v. CLARA BIDWELL, b. July 7, 1868; d. April 22, 1873.

1880. JOHN ADAMS FOSTER (Eben C., Samuel, Isaac, Joseph, Jacob, Reginald), b. Sept. 10, 1819, Manchester, N. H.; m. ——, Laura Lund. Res., Salena, Cal.

2968. i. JANE, b. ——.
2969. ii. ——, b. ——.
2970. iii. ——, b. ——.
2971. iv. JOHN ADAMS, JR., b. ——.

1885. EBEN EDWARDS FOSTER (Eben C., Samuel, Isaac, Joseph, Jacob, Reginald), b. Feb. 15, 1827, Manchester, N. H.; m. —— ——. Res., Lawrence, Mass.

2972. i. LUCY, b. ——; m. —— Adams.
2973. ii. LIZZIE, b. ——.
2974. iii. MINNIE, b. ——. Res., Lawrence, Mass.

1887. SAMUEL TUFTS FOSTER (Eben C., Samuel, Isaac, Joseph, Jacob, Reginald), b. Oct. 3, 1838; m., July 25, 1864, Elizabeth Aiken Pinkerton, b. March 22, 1840. He d. May 25, 1876. Res., Manchester, N. H.

2975. i. PAUL PINKERTON, b. ——. With "The Youth's Companion," Perry, Mason & Co., Boston, Mass.
2976. ii. ELIZABETH ADAMS, b. ——.

1901. ANDREW DWIGHT FOSTER (Samuel W., Theodore, Jedediah, Ephraim, Ephraim, Abraham, Reginald), b. Scio, Mich., Aug. 5, 1832; m. —— ——. He d. Farmington, Wash., Aug. 1, 1883. Was a miller and wheelwright. Res., River Falls, Wis.

2977. i. SAMUEL WILLIS, b. Dec. 21, 1863; m. Laura Buckley.
2978. ii. ELLA, b. ——, 1866; d. 1872.
2979. iii. MORT WEST, b. April 31, 1873. Res., Medford, Oregon.
2980. iv. CHARLOTTE GRACE, b. June 10, 1877. Res., Medford, Oregon.

1905. IRA SEYMOUR FOSTER (Samuel W., Theodore, Jedediah, Ephraim, Ephraim, Abraham, Reginald), b. Flint, Mich., April 1, 1846; m., Hudson, Wis., Oct. 5, 1871, Grace Louise Selleck, b. June 23, 1855. She resides Cuthbert, Ga.

He was born in Michigan, and spent most of his life at Hudson, Wis., removing from that point to Dickinson county, Iowa. As a mere boy he abandoned a lucrative position to enter the army, enlisting in Company A, Forty-fourth Wisconsin Infantry, being mustered out at the close of the war. He went to Milford in 1868. In 1871 Miss Grace L. Selleck, of Hudson, Wis., became his wife. During all his long residence in Iowa Mr. Foster was held in warm esteem. He was an important factor in local development. For years he held proprietary connection with the Milford Water Power Improvement Company, which erected at Milford the best mill in that region in pioneer days. He was a general dealer at Milford for a considerable period, and was postmaster during the Arthur administration. He was for two terms a member of the Board of Supervisors, and most of this period its Chairman and most active spirit. In all these relations he made a good record, steadily growing in public and private esteem. Ever public-spirited, he did his full share in the development of his section, and witnessed with sincere satisfaction the growth of the county and the prosperity of the people. Few men in the county ever had so wide a circle of personal friends. His friendship was warm and biding and ever to be prized. He was loyal ever, and thoughtful and helpful. He failed not in appreciation of favors received, and it was ever a pleasure to do him kindly service. He was a member of Wallar Post, G. A. R.

Mrs. Foster has this copy in her possession: "Hon. Jedediah Foster was born in Andover, Mass., Oct. 10, 1726; descended from Sir Reginald Foster, who was made a peer by Queen Elizabeth, July 21, 1661. His descendant, Sir Reginald, came to this country because of troubles during the reign of Charles I."

He d. Austin, Tex., Feb. 21, 1891. Res., Milford, Iowa.

2981. i. STURGES BURTON, b. January, 1875, d. October, 1875.
2982. ii. DENA LOUISE, b. Aug. 6, 1889. Res., Cuthbert, Ga., Randolph Hotel.

EDWARD D. FOSTER.

1906. EDWARD DWIGHT FOSTER (Dwight C., Theodore, Jedediah, Ephraim, Ephraim, Abraham, Reginald), b. Scio, Mich., May 12, 1838; m., Detroit, Mich., March 23, 1871, Marian Langley, b. Feb. 15, 1845.

During his childhood his health was such that he could not apply himself to study, and in 1852, when he was fourteen, his father died, in Commerce, Mich., leaving the mother and his two young sisters entirely dependent udon him. since which time his life has been one of close application to business. He came to Detroit in June, 1854, and engaged as hardware clerk. In 1858 he entered a leather store. In February, 1863, established in the leather and finding business, and the manufacture of lasts, etc; firm name Mumford, Foster & Co., which continued until 1888; then continued alone, as E. D. Foster & Co., until 1897, when he closed out the business. From a strong belief in the economic advantage to society of life insurance, he has for twenty years taken an active interest in fraternal beneficiary orders, as a means for the mechanic and middle classes, who, with small monthly payments, could protect their families when they would be unable to carry old-line protection. Has been more especially interested as an officer in the Ancient Order of United Workmen and National Union. He is now second Vice-President of the Standard Savings and Loan Association. Res., Detroit, Mich.

2983. i. FRANCES ALMA, b. May 21, 1872. Is a teacher in Detroit High School.
2984. ii. CHARLES LANGLEY, b. Sept. 19, 1873; unm. Res., Ypsilanti.
2985. iii. ALBERT DOUGLAS, b. Feb. 13, 1875. Medical student in University of Michigan, class '99.
2986. iv. CLARA AGNES, b. May 20, 1879.
2987. v. EDWARD DWIGHT, b. Sept. 8, 1881.
2988. vi. WILLIAM HENRY, b. Dec. 2, 1883.

1910. DWIGHT FOSTER (Jedediah, Theophilus, Jedediah, Ephraim, Ephraim, Abraham, Reginald), b. Wilmington, Vt., March 25, 1809; m. ——, 1833, Betsey Brownell, b. May 5, 1811 (dau. of Thomas Brownell, of Pownall, Vt., and Betsey Parker), a farmer in Paw Paw Grove, Ill. He was in early life a hotel-keeper and stage proprietor in Pownall, Vt., for several years. His wife died there October, 1855. Res., Paw Paw, Ill.

2989. i. BLACKMAN N., b. Sept. 25, 1834; m. Harriet Downs.

1919. ALFRED DWIGHT FOSTER (Elijah D., Theophilus, Jedediah, Ephraim, Ephraim, Abraham, Reginald), b. Jan. 22, 1818, Athens, Pa.; m., April 4, 1840, Sarah Emeline Hathaway, b. in Poultney, N. Y., May 31, 1817 (dau. of Peter Dickenson Hathaway, afterwards of West Creek, Ind., and Rebecca Hayward); a merchant at Crown Point, Ind., where he died Oct. 20, 1860, aet. 42. His widow resides at Crown Point.

2990. i. GEORGE DWIGHT, b. June 11, 1843; m. Burdette E. Thomas and Jane A. McPherson.
2991. ii. MAHLON BETHUEL, b. Feb. 25, 1846; d. Sept. 1, 1846.
2992. iii. PERRY ALFORD, b. July 23, 1848; is a farmer at Morgantown, Ind.
2993. iv. CHARLES HATHAWAY, b. Sept. 12, 1851; d. July 14, 1865.
2994. v. HARRIET ELIZABETH, b. Jan. 11, 1858.

1920. GEORGE LYMAN FOSTER (Elijah D., Theophilus, Jedediah, Ephraim, Ephraim, Abraham, Reginald), b. April 20, 1820; m., Jan. —, 1842, Temperance Hathaway, b. Sept. 19, 1819 (dau. of Peter Dickenson Hathaway, of West Creek, Ind., and Rebecca Hayward). She d. Nov. 19, 1843, aet. 24, and he m., 2d, March 22, 1845, Lucy Jane Hathaway, b. April 19, 1828 (dau. of Paul Hathaway, of Sherburne, Ill., and Melissa Langdon), a large farmer (700 acres) at West Creek, Ind., formerly, but since 1869 has resided at Parker, Montgomery county, Kans. Ch. by second wife:

2995. i. CHARLES, b. Jan. 9, 1847; d. March 20, 1847.
2996. ii. EDWIN, b. Sept. 7, 1849.
2997. iii. VOLNEY ORLANDO, b. Oct. 10, 1851.
2998. iv. EDSON, b. May 23, 1854.
2999. v. ALBERT, b. Dec. 25, 1857.
3000. vi. ELIZA, b. April 29, 1859.
3001. vii. EMILINE, b. Nov. 10, 1861.
3002. viii. MARTHA, b. Nov. 16, 1864.
3003. ix. MARILLA, b. June 5, 1868.

1925. THEOPHILUS RANDOLPH FOSTER (Elijah Dwight, Theophilus, Jedediah, Ephraim, Ephraim, Abraham, Reginald), b. April 28, 1830, Burlington, Pa.; m., Dec. 6, 1851, Margaret Foley, b. May 20, 1832 (dau. of John Foley, of Adel, Iowa, and Sarah Hayworth); a farmer. Res. at Adel, Iowa.

3004. i. FRANCES, b. Sept. 29, 1852.
3005. ii. SUSAN, b. Dec. 14, 1854; d. Aug. 22, 1856.
3006. iii. LUCY ANN, b. Jan. 6, 1857.
3007. iv. MARTHA HARRIET, b. March 12, 1859.
3008. v. FANNY ALMEDA, b. Feb. 6, 1861.
3009. vi. DANIEL, b. May 27, 1863.
3010. vii. GEORGE LYMAN, b. July 30, 1865.

1927. LEWIS FOSTER (Elijah D., Theophilus, Jedediah, Ephraim, Ephraim, Abraham, Reginald), b. Troy, Pa., March 28, 1834; m., Nov. 19, 1855, Roxanna Augusta Knapp, b. at Florence, O., March 20, 1836 (dau. of Charles and Amanda Knapp, of Coldwater, Mich.); a farmer. Res., at Pottowattamie, Kans. (since 1858.)

3011. i. MARY ELVIRA, b. at West Creek, Ind., Aug. 5, 1856.
3012. ii. CHARLES LYMAN, b. at Pottowattamie, Sept. 9, 1858.
3013. iii. WILLIAM ORLANDO, b. Sept. 19, 1860.
3014. iv. CORNELIA AMANDA, b. Feb. 15, 1866.

1933. ALFRED FOSTER (Peregrine P., Theophilus, Jedediah, Ephraim, Ephraim, Abraham, Reginald), b. Coventry, R. I., Sept. 29, 1816; m. in 1838, at Mantua, O., Catharine VanWagner; a farmer at Millington, Mich.; was for some years a tanner in Ohio

3015. i. THEY had three children.

1938. LUTHER CLARK FOSTER (Peregrine P., Theophilus, Jedediah, Ephraim, Ephraim, Abraham, Reginald), b. in Pennsylvania, May 24, 1828. He was a teacher for a few years in Tennessee (1848-51). In 1853 he removed to Elmira, N. Y., and since 1855 has been principal of Grammar School No. 1 in that city. He m., Jan. 29, 1851, Mary Elizabeth Witherspoon, b. May 27, 1833 (dau. of Wesley and Sarah Witherspoon, of Maury county, Tennessee). She d. April 7, 1852, and he m., 2d, April 18, 1854, Charlotte Lindsey, b. Feb. 2, 1827.

Luther Clark Foster, Superintendent of Ithaca schools from 1875 to the time of his death, Feb. 13, 1894, was born at Canton, Bradford county, Pa. While he was a child his parents moved to Farmington, O., where he lived until he became a young man. The father was a Baptist minister; but when he moved to what was then considered the West, he took up a new farm, and began to hew out a place for himself. He built a log house and moved into it before there were any doors, putting up blankets at the openings. He preached part of the time, and winters he taught school, boarding around. At one of the places where he was boarding he was put, as usual, in the best room, cold and uncomfortable, where he took a severe cold, and, returning home, died at the age of forty-one. After the father's death the family went through many privations. The mother eked out a scanty living, after selling the place and moving near the seminary at Farmington, by taking boarders, keeping a cow, and working with her own hands. The lad attended school and did what he could to help. He received, practically, all his school education at this place. At the age of sixteen he began teaching school, boarding around, as his father had done. He continued this for four years, and then went to Maury county, Tennessee, where he remained another four years, conducting a school, which was supported by the rich planters of that section. He saw much of slavery, and understood the sentiment of the South, preceding the war, fully. He foresaw the coming of the war, and knew that the condition of things then existing could not possibly last. His experience then had, in after years, a great effect on his opinions regarding Southern questions, and he entertained a high opinion of Southern character. In 1852 he returned to the North and came to Elmira. He did not at that time, nor indeed for many years later, expect to remain permanently in the profession of teaching, and took up the first occupation that came to hand. He worked in a hardware store, and took considerable interest in public events. Somehow he became a nominee of the Know-Nothing party for the office of Supervisor, and was elected, serving one term. He ever afterward looked back to this as an odd episode in his life. He became an ardent Republican when that party was formed, with full knowledge of what the curse of slavery was to both North and South. In recent years he took a rather independent view in politics, never manifesting any extremes, not even letting his own family know how he voted, but without question voting for Republican principles always, while cutting the names of men who were, in his judgment, unfit to be the office bearers of his country.

In Elmira he married Charlotte Lindsey. In 1855 he became teacher of the public school on William street, known as School No. 1. This school was in bad condition. Private schools flourished in the city. Very soon, however, the private schools began to disappear, as the public school became efficient. For twenty years he was identified with the public school system of Elmira, doing more than anyone else to build up the graded school system there. About 1870 a new structure for his school was erected on Sullivan street. The internal arrangement of this building was planned by him, and has been the model for other buildings erected later in Elmira. Indeed the High School building in Ithaca follows the same plan. When our High School was built, he spent many weeks considering what would be the best plan, and in visiting other places, but at last could find no plan which met the purpose so well as the old plan he had used in Elmira. He made there a reputation as an extraordinarily good teacher and thorough educator.

In 1875 he was called to Ithaca. It was a very great trial for him to give up his home in Elmira, to which he had become attached, and it was with considerable hesitation and doubt that he took up the work here, foreseeing, as he did, the difficulties which would be in the way. An entirely new system of the schools was to be inaugurated, and he felt that failure for him would be disastrous, but he recognized the opportunity which it gave him of a larger field of usefulness, and he bravely attempted the task. The papers of Elmira spoke of him in the very highest terms and prophesied that Ithaca people would find in him just the man they were looking for, and that he would more than fulfill their highest expectations.

He labored unceasingly and spared himself not at all in his efforts to make the public school system of the city of Ithaca as good as it possibly might be. A remarkable fact in connection with his work is that the city felt no burden nor increase of taxes while erecting elegant buildings and increasing the school facilities to their present state.

He would have done well in many other callings. He was very skillful with his hands, and was always felt competent to go ahead with any sort of work. He had all the qualifications for a good business man, in that he was methodical, accurate, of good judgment and conservative. He would not have succeeded, however, in many kinds of business, because of his conscientious desire to give every man with whom he dealt, "good measure, pressed down, shaken together, and running over."

He was conscientious to the last degree. He considered every man's rights, every child's rights, and he would sacrifice himself, always, rather than to in anywise contravene the rights of another, or, in the least, seem to do so. He was approachable by every person, would listen to every complaint and judge with absolute justice, and always with sympathy. It was his pleasure always to help those young men and women who were trying to make a way for themselves, securing their own education. In financial and other ways he has been the greatest friend of many a young man and woman. Those who have been employed under his supervision will all say with one voice that they had no better helper in carrying on the work with which they were entrusted. He was a friend indeed. He was faithful and always to be counted upon. During the nineteen and one-half years of his service in Ithaca he missed but one meeting of the board, and that was the last before his death. He was a progressive man. He was never satisfied with what had been done, but believed that, with greater effort and with more time, better things would come after. If he had any motto at all, it was "Excelsior." He kept this motto before the pupils, having printed, year after year, on the merit card, the picture of a boy climbing up the mountain with a flag, in illustration of Longfellow's poem. It was always with him, higher, higher. And yet he was conservative. He never adopted a plan carelessly, but always thought it out in his own mind to its last results before putting it into operation. He never followed other people's views blindly.

From his youth he was always pure-minded and modest. He never asserted himself, but took great pride in doing his work thoroughly well and letting that speak for him. In his last days he took immense satisfaction in and was touched by the appreciation which the citizens of Ithaca manifested for him and his work. He persevered to the end. He wanted to die in the harness; and so he did.

He was early identified with the State Council of School Superintendents, and was considered among its members as one of the first educators in the State. His advice was sought from all quarters. Some years ago he read before the Council a paper on Truants and Incorrigibles, advocating the establishment by the State of New York of an industrial school, to which this class of children might be sent. The proposed measure was vigorously pushed, a bill was passed appropriating $50,000 to establish such a school, but was prevented from becoming a law by the veto of Governor Cornell. The matter was pressed again, from year to year, until the present Compulsory Education Law was passed and put into successful operation. This is mentioned simply to show how his influence extended beyond Ithaca, and that his ability was recognized elsewhere; but it would be a task in itself to catalogue all the good work he has done.

He died at his home, in Ithaca, nearly sixty-seven years of age. He had been failing, was becoming gradually paralyzed for the preceding eighteen months. During all this time he had borne up bravely, and strove to accomplish all his work, which, at last, he was not able to do without assistance. But, to the end, he never lost his full mental grasp of affairs, and directed as well as ever, what he could no longer do himself.

The public school system of Ithaca, and especially the Ithaca High School, which crowns it all, whose high standing is due to his wise direction from the beginning, may well stand as his monument.

He d. Feb. 13, 1895. Res., Elmira and Ithaca, N. Y.

3016. i. A child, unnamed, b. April 7, 1852, that d. July 3, 1852.

By his second wife:

3017. ii. CHARLES EBENEZER, b. Jan. 31, 1855; m. Julia Carpenter.

3018. iii. HENRY WARD BEECHER, b. Sept. 21, 1856; m. Lydia R. Peck.

3019. iv. LUTHER CLARK, b. Jan. 12, 1858; m. Alice Allen.

3020. v. CARRIE DELPHINE, b. June 12, 1859; m., in 1895, Aaron C. Weaver. Res., 226 Fifteenth St., Buffalo, N. Y. Carrie D. was graduated at Ithaca High School in 1880; taught for a number of years here; studied stenography; clerk of the Northern Pacific Railway at St. Paul, s. p.

3021. vi. CHARLOTTE AMELIA, b. Nov. 26, 1864; graduated at Cornell, Ph. B., 1888; began teaching at once in Elmira, N. Y.; called to Ithaca High School in 1892; remained here since, in charge of Latin department.

3022. vii. ROBERT OSMON, b. Oct. 23, 1867; m. Fiosina Dilger.

1940. HON. DWIGHT FOSTER (Alfred D., Dwight, Jedediah, Ephraim, Ephraim, Abraham, Reginald), b. Worcester, Mass., Dec. 13, 1828; m., Aug. 20, 1850, Harriet Perkins Baldwin, b. April 3, 1830 (dau. of Hon. Roger S., of New Haven, and Emily Perkins). His mother was dau. of Roger Sherman, one of the signers of the Declaration of Independence. Roger Sherman Baldwin was State and United States Senator and Governor of Connecticut.

He was educated in the public schools at Worcester, fitted for college, entered Yale and was graduated in 1848. He studied law with Barton & Bacon, at Worcester; Samuel C. Perkins, in Philadelphia, and at the Harvard Law School; was admitted to the bar in 1849. He at once began the practice of his profession in Worcester, and was associated at different times with Peter C. Bacon, Benjamin F. Thomas, James E. Esterbrook and George W. Baldwin. In 1854 he was colonel and aid-de-camp on Hon. Emory Washburn's staff; was judge of the Probate Court, and in 1860 was elected Attorney-General of the State. In 1864 removed to Boston, where he resided. He was for three years Attorney-General of Massachusetts (1863-6); has been one of the Supreme Judges of the Supreme Court of the State. He also served, in 1877, as agent of the United States in the Halifax Fishery Commission; and was from 1856 to 1863 and from 1880 to 1884 a member of the Executive Council of the American Antiquarian Society.

"Dwight Foster was fitted for college at Newport, R. I., by Rev. Dr. Thayer; entering Yale University in September, 1844, and graduating August, 1848. In 1851 he entered the Harvard Law School. In 1858 went into the office of Hon. Peter Bacon, at Worcester; was admitted to the bar in 1859, and for many years enjoyed a large and lucrative practice in the county. He was elected Attorney-General of Massachusetts in 1861. After serving four years he resumed his general practice. During his incumbency of the above office he greatly distinguished himself in the management of the government's case in the trial of Geo. C. Hersey, at Dedham, in April, 1861, for the murder of Betsey Frances Tirrell. Aug. 31, 1866, Mr. Foster was appointed by Governor Bullock, Associate Justice of the Supreme Judicial Court, which position he resigned Jan. 12, 1869, to again resume practice, and became counsel of the New England Mutual Life Insurance Company."—(Boston paper.)

Judge Foster died at his residence, 18 Chestnut street, Boston, Mass., April 18, 1884, of valvular disease of the heart.

From "Tributes of the Bench and Bar" we copy a few extracts:

"By this event the Commonwealth has lost a distinguished citizen, the bar an accomplished leader and associate, and the community an adviser of eminent learning and ability. Called to the Supreme Bench at an early age, he exhibited the highest qualities as a jurist. He gave clear expression to the doctrines of the law, with a terseness and facility which showed his perfect comprehension of the principles of the science, especially in the great department of equity and commercial law; his thorough knowledge of men and affairs, gained by extensive practice; his sound legal instinct and strong sense of justice, enabled him to give direction to the course of jurisprudence and to form the law in those branches in which it is the most susceptible of growth, and therein to do the highest work and best service of a good judge. By his early retirement from the bench this court lost a most valuable associate and distinguished ornament. In personal character he was remarkable for independence and courage. He was above the reach of prejudice, and his opinions, broadly formed and strongly held, were forcibly and fearlessly expressed. His originality of view and independence of the social or provincial bias by which we are surrounded, made his conversation always instructing and interesting. He lived almost entierly in his family, and I need not say how much he was idolized there, or how much he deserved it."– Resolutions and remarks of Mr. Robert D. Smith.

Attorney-General Sherman closed his remarks by saying: "Judge Foster had no struggles with poverty while climbing the rugged path of learning, but in home, ancestry, wealth and social position he had all that heart could desire, and he appreciated and improved these advantages, graduating with the highest honors of his class. He was thoroughly equipped and qualified for the duties of his chosen profession. He has left an example worthy of imitation, and we may be consoled by his peaceful death. At night he closed his eyes and went quietly to sleep. 'And then the dark-browed mother, Death, bent down her face to his, and he was borne to Him.'"

Mr. George Shattuck said: "Judge Foster brought to Boston a splendid moral courage and self-reliance. He maintained a sturdy independence, and formed and expressed his opinions without regard to those around him."

Chief Justice Morton said, in conclusion: "It is not necessary that we should multiply words of praise. The achievements of his life are his highest praise; the record which he left is his highest monument. He died in the full maturity of his powers, before age had dimmed his mental faculties, transmitting to his children, with added lustre, a name which has been held in high honor since the birth of our Commonwealth. The death of such a man, upright, able, learned, independent, fearless, hospitable and generous, is a public calamity."

Will, Dwight Foster, of Boston—wife, Henrietta P. Foster; son, Alfred Dwight Foster—dated July 2, 1876. Lib. 556, fol. 125-151. Prob. May 12, 1884. Lib. 558, fol. 345. Petition for administrator—Dwight Foster, died April 18, 1884, leaving a widow, Henrietta P. Foster; next of kin: Alfred D. Foster, of Boston, son; Emily B. Thacher, of New Haven, Conn., daughter; Roger Foster, of New York, son; Mary R. Foster, of Boston, daughter; Burnside Foster, of Boston, son; Reginald Foster, of Boston, son; Elizabeth S. Foster, of Boston, minor daughter. Suff. Prob., Lib. 558, fol. 345.

He d. April 18, 1884. Res., Worcester, Mass.

3023. i. ALFRED DWIGHT, b. April 27, 1852; m. Evelyn Margaret Palmer-Samborne.

3024. ii. EMILY BALDWIN, b. Feb. 17, 1854; m. ——, Dr. James K. Hache. Res., New Haven, Conn.

3025. iii. ROGER SHERMAN BALDWIN, b. April 21, 1857; unm. Res., New York, N. Y. Address, Mills Bldg., 35 Wall St.

Roger Foster was born at Worcester, Mass.: educated for college at the Boston Latin School and Marburg University, Germany; was graduated at Yale in 1878; at the Columbia College Law School in 1880; admitted to New York bar in 1880, and has since practiced law in New York City. His office is in the Mills Building, 35 Wall street. He has written several law books and pamphlets. His most important publications are: "A Treatise on Federal Practice," now in its second edition, and "Commentaries on the Constitution of the United States, Historical and Juridical," of which one volume only has been published. He was appointed by Governor Flower a member of the Tenement House Commission of 1894, and drafted the laws enacted in 1895 at the recommendation of that committee. He is unmarried. His residence is at 69 West Fifty-fifth street, New York.

3026. iv. MARY REBECCA, b. May 6, 1859; m., Sept. 14, 1886, Rev. Bradley Gilman. Res., Springfield, Mass. He was b. Jan. 22, 1857, in Boston; was graduated from Harvard College in 1880 and from Harvard Divinity School in 1884. He was settled over the Unitarian Church, in Belmont, Mass., for two years; then seven years in Concord, N. H., and was settled over the Church of the Unity, in Springfield, Mass., in 1892. He is an author and has written for Scribner's, Harper's and Christian Register, and published "The Musical Journey of Dorothy and Delia," "The Kingdom of Coins." Ch.: 1. Dorthy Foster, b. Feb. 3, 1891, in Concord.

3027. v. BURNSIDE, b. May 7, 1861; m. Sophie V. Hammond.

3028. vi. REIGINALD, b. Jan. 2, 1863; m. Harriet Story Lawrence.

3029. vii. HENRIETTA BALDWIN, b. Aug. 8, 1865; d. Jan. 23, 1867.

3030. viii. ELIZABETH SKINNER, b. Jan. 10, 1868; unm. Res., 447 Fairfield St., Boston.

Burnside Foster, of Boston, appointed guardian of his sister, Elizabeth Skinner Foster, of Boston, b. Jan. 10, 1868, child of Dwight Foster, of Boston, deceased, and Henrietta P. Foster, his widow, April 28, 1884.

Bond—Alfred D. Foster, surety. Suff. Prob., Lib. 561, fol. 406.

1943. PEREGRINE DWIGHT FOSTER (Frederic A., Peregrine, Jedediah, Ephraim, Ephraim, Abraham, Reginald), b. Feb. 8, 1819; m., Sept. 10, 1846, Margaret Mary Duble, b. Sept. 9, 1827 (dau. of Henry Duble, of Lancaster, Ohio, and Susanna McDill). She d. Aug. 27, 1850, and he m., 2d, March 19, 1857, Martha Buckingham, of Newark, Ohio, b. Feb. 6, 1825 (dau. of Rev. Bradford Buckingham, of Newark, Ohio, and Maria Darlington, whom he m., Aug. 15, 1809. She was b. in Winchester, Va., Jan. 5, 1790, and d. March 23, 1831. He was b. in Fairfield, Conn., June 9, 1785, and d. Feb. 7, 1850). He was graduated at Miami University, Ohio, in 1837, and began a course of legal study, which weak eyes caused him to abandon. He was a merchant at Keokuk, Iowa (1846-69), and since September, 1869, has been such in Glenwood, Mills county, Iowa. [Henry Duble, b. in 1797; d. May 28, 1844, aet. 47. His wife, Susanna, b. in 1789; d. Oct. 14, 1834, aet. 45.]

3031. i. CHARLES FREDRIC, b. June 9, 1847; m. Mary Ann Haley.

3032. ii. HENRY ARNOLD, b. July 21, 1849; d. Aug. 28, 1850.

3032½. iii. MARIE LOUISE (dau. of Fredric Augustus Foster, of Lancaster, Ohio, and Sarah Arnold), b. March 25, 1825; m., July 15, 1846, James Edwin Cheney, b. April 10, 1821, (son of Col. William Cheney, of Newport, N. H., and one of its founders, b. in Alstead, N. H., in 1776, and Tryphena Hatch, widow previously of Deacon Joseph Farnsworth, of Newport, N. H., b. in Alstead, N. H., Feb. 29, 1784. He was a merchant and a public-spirited citizen, and an active devoted Christian (Baptist). She was full of faith and of good deeds. One of her last sayings to a friend, in parting from him here, was too good to be forgotten. "Brother," she said, "the children of God never see one another for the last time.") He has been at different times a manufacturer and merchant for many years, at Rochester, of stoves, tinware and ironware, for household uses, and of Kedzie's Patent Filters. Ch.: 1. James Edwin Cheney, b. July 21, 1847; graduated at Rochester University, in 1867, read law with Hon. Henry R. Sheldon, of Rochester, and was admitted to the bar in December, 1868; is a practicing lawyer at Rochester (Goddard & Cheney). 2. Foster Hallet Cheney, b. Feb. 6, 1849; is a clerk in the store of Peregrine D. Foster & Co., at Glenwood, Iowa (since 1871). He m., Oct. 2, 1873, Martha Rosanna Blackburn, b. Dec. 31, 1851 (dau. of Thomas Blackburn, of Beaver City, Neb., and Sarah Counts).

1951. THEODORE NEWTON FOSTER (Fredric A., Peregrine, Jedediah, Ephraim, Ephraim, Abraham, Reginald), b. Aug. 28, 1847; m. —— ——. He was engaged in telegraph office for some years at Lexington, Ky., but of late in Cincinnati, Ohio. He m., and has one child.

3033. i. CLARA BELLE, b. Aug. 1, 1871.

1954. CAPT. CHARLES IRA FOSTER (Jonas, John, John, John, Ephraim, Abraham, Reginald), b. Salem, Mass., Jan. 18, 1837; m., at Beverly, July 1, 1860, Martha Farnis Cressy, b. May 25, 1833. Seaman sixteen and one-half years, later provision dealer. Charles Ira, Cambridge; letter dated April 13, 1880; ex. April 15, 1880; wife, Martha F.; children, Charles A., Helen A., Annie F. and Mary B., minors.—Middlesex Pro. He d. April 2, 1880. Res., North Cambridge, Mass.

3034. i. CHARLES AUGUSTUS, b. March 28, 1861; m. Cora E. Tower.
3035. ii. HELEN ADAMS, b. Sept. 21, 1869. Res., 99 Russell St., Waltham, Mass.
3036. iii. ANNIE FIELDER, b. Feb. 5, 1871. Res., 99 Russell St., Waltham, Mass.
3037. iv. MABEL LOUISE, b. Nov. 23, 1872; d. Aug. 27, 1875.
3038. v. MAY BUTMAN, b. Feb. 21, 1874. Res., 99 Russell St., Waltham, Mass.

1068. HON. MOSES FOSTER (Moses, David, Stephen, John, Ephraim, Abraham, Reginald), b. North Andover, Mass., Aug. 29, 1821; m., Guilford, Vt., Oct. 28, 1851, Clara M. Hyde; d. Jan. 6, 1856; m., 2d, Dec. 8, 1858, Caroline Hall, at Chesterfield, N. H., b. May 26, 1834.

He was born in Andover, in what is now North Andover. Attended Franklin Academy and Dartmouth College, graduating from the latter institution in 1841; studied law under M. W. Hazen, in Andover; taught school, spending also a year at the Dean Law School of Harvard University. About 1848 he began the practice of law for himself, and in 1855 was married. In the meantime he had served a year in the Massachusetts Legislature. In 1856 his wife died, and in 1858 he married Caroline Hall, of Wolfboro, N. H. He had accepted, in 1857, the cashiership of the Andover National Bank, which office he retained until his death. For thirty-nine years he served as clerk of the parish for Christ Church (Episcopal) of Andover. He was at various times treasurer of the Prenchard Free (High) School, and president of the Andover Savings Bank. He died of apoplexy, after an illness of five days, June 27, 1895. Res., Andover, Mass.

3039. i. ANNA DWIGHT, b. June 7, 1860. Res., Andover, Mass., Box 326.
3040. ii. EDWARD REGINALD, b. Nov. 30, 1861. Res., Andover, Mass., Box 326. Is assistant cashier Andover National Bank. He attended grammar schools of Andover; entered Phillips Academy, and graduated from the English department of said institution in 1880. He then took a course in Bryant & Stratton's Commercial College, and in the fall of 1882 entered the service of the Andover National Bank as book-keeper. He subsequently became teller, and on the death of his father, in 1895, was elected cashier. He is still in the employ of the bank.
3041. iii. ARTHUR HALLAM, b. Aug. 31, 1863; m., Oct. 15, 1895, Lehel L. Peters. Res., Haverhill, Mass., s. p. He attended grammar schools of Andover and Bryant & Stratton's Commercial School. About 1880 he entered the service of the American Waltham Watch Co., at Waltham, Mass., but in 1885 left to take an extended trip through the West. He has since worked for Boston jewelers, studied engraving in Chicago, and lived in Livingston, Mont. In 1891 he became assistant to a Mr. Darling, jeweler, of Stoughton, Mass., and remained with him until July, 1897. At present he is not employed, and is living in Haverhill.
3042. iv. HERBERT BALDWIN, b. Nov. 12, 1874. Address, Johns Hopkins University, Baltimore, Md. He is a graduate of Harvard. He attended private school, grammar and high schools in Andover, and fitted for college at Phillips Andover Academy; entered Harvard College in the fall of 1892, and graduated in June, 1895; taught school in 1896-97, and is at present studying in the graduate department of Johns Hopkins University. His specialty is Classical Philology. He spent last summer at the American School of Archæology, Athens, Greece.

1071. HON. DAVID SMITH FOSTER (Moses, David, Stephen, John, Ephraim, Abraham, Reginald), b. North Andover, Mass., May 26, 1826; m., March 7, 1854, Agnes Furguson Byers, b. Brechin, Scotland, Jan. 17, 1836.

Mr. David S. Foster, the popular and efficient gentleman, who at present presides at the head of our city government, says the Beloit (Wis.) Free-Press, has on two previous terms served the people of this city in the same capacity, discharging the important duties of this responsible office most creditably to himself and satisfactorily to his constituents.

Mr. Foster is a native of Andover, Mass., where he graduated from the celebrated Phillips Academy. In 1843 he located in Boston, remaining there until 1856, when he concluded to make the city of Beloit his future home, arriving here on the 18th of March of that year. From that time until 1869 Mr. Foster was actively engaged in mercantile business in this city; during the latter year, however, he retired from active business, and did not again enter upon an active mercantile life until 1880, when he purchased the book and stationery business of H. F. Hobart, East Bridge street, which had been conducted for several years by that gentleman. Mr. Foster continued this business until 1885, when he disposed of it to his sons, which enterprising gentlemen immediately added the fine drug store adjoining, both of which they are now successfully conducting.

HON. DAVID S. FOSTER.

Mr. Foster was first elected to the mayorality of this city at the 1870 and 1871 term. During this administration Mr. Foster's tact, experience and managerial ability were brought to bear on the city affairs generally in so efficient a manner, that, in 1874, he was again elected as mayor. The able manner in which he conducted the city government during that term but served to strengthen the confidence of our people in his ability and wisdom, and this spring, although desirous of leading a more retired life, Mr. Foster was importuned so persistently to permit his name to again be used in nomination, that he finally yielded, receiving the nomination by both Democrats and Republicans, and was elected without any practical opposition. Although sixty-three years of age, Mr. Foster still retains all the vigor and managerial ability of his earlier years, which, as usual, he is earnestly devoting to the interests of the people who were so determined that he should represent them in the head of the city government.

Mrs. Foster, to whom he was married before coming West, and who is a most amiable and estimable lady, is also still enjoying the best of health, as well as the honors of her husband. Socially, Mr. Foster is a genial, cultured gentleman, and is held in the highest esteem by all classes. His present administration bids fair to outrival all his previous efforts to benefit our city, and is meeting with universal approval by all our citizens. Res., Beloit, Wis.

3043. i. JOHN A., b. Feb. 1, 1855; unm. Res., Beloit. John Alfred Foster was born in Boston, and with his parents went to Beloit, Wis., when a little over one year old, reaching the above place March 17, 1856. Received a common school education, but on account of feeble health was obliged to give up his school, and when quite a lad, occupied his time, in a small way, making, by hand, paper boxes, for the use of a small confectionery store in this city, and from this beginning has grown a large and properous business in the same line, requiring various machines adapted to the business of manufacturing paper boxes, in all varieties and styles now in use by confectioners, and very largely in use by shoe manufacturers; supplying the boot and shoe plant of the celebrated firm of John Foster & Co., of this city, with their boxes, numbering hundreds of thousands, which reach every portion of the United States. This business requires a large force of assistance, mostly girls and young ladies, superintended by one or more gentlemen. Orders from all sections of the country are daily received, and the product of this box manufactory, under the firm name of John A. Foster, Beloit, Wis., thus reaches out far and near.

3044. ii. FRANK SMITH, b. June 9, 1861; m. Elizabeth Kerr.
3045. iii. JOSEPH BYERS, b. Dec. 23, 1862; m. Olive J. Flynn.
3046. iv. DAVID HUMPHREY, b. Aug. 19, 1873; m. Fannie E. Schutt.

1977. DANE FOSTER (Ebenezer, Stephen, Stephen, John, Ephraim, Abraham, Reginald), b. Andover, Mass., June 19, 1814; m., May 14, 1840, Mary S. Carlton. Res., Andover, Mass.

3047. i. CHARLES E., b. Oct. 7, 1841.

1994. CHARLES SAMUEL FOSTER (Nathan, Nathan, Stephen, John, Ephraim, Abraham, Reginald), b. North Andover, Mass., Dec, 13, 1833; m., Jan. 6, 1857, Sarah E. Bixby, dau. of Deacon Samuel, b. March, 1830; d. Jan. 16, 1860; m., 2d, Oct. 13, 1863, Ellen E. Rea, b. March 5, 1844. She resides North Andover. He was a farmer. He was educated at the public schools and spent a few years in Franklin Academy in his native town. He was quite an active member of the Congregational church. Was a Democrat in politics and very zealous for the welfare of his party. He d. Oct. 7, 1883. Res., North Andover, Mass.

3048. i. NATHAN, b. Feb. 18, 1858; m. Grace P. Webster.
3049. ii. WALLACE REA, b. Aug. 2, 1864; m. Fannie F. Parrish.
3050. iii. HARLAN ELMER, b. April 3, 1866; m. Carrie B. Burgess.
3051. iv. HERBERT LORING, b. Nov. 8, 1870; m. Nellie May Long.
3052. v. LAURA GREENBANK, b. May 13, 1873; m., Sept. 6, 1892, George D. Ward. Res., Andover, Mass.. She united with the Congregational Church when only fourteen years of age; graduated from High School in the class of '91. Was married to George D. Ward (b. Aug. 12, 1863, in Lawrence, Mass.), at North Andover, by the Rev. H. H. Leavitt, pastor of the Congregational church. His second wife's father was William Rea, a descendant of Daniel Rea, that came to Plymouth about 1650, afterward settled in Danvers, Mass. Her mother was Harriet Bradstreet, a descendant of Governor Simon Bradstreet, of Massachusetts. Ch.: 1. Edna May, b. May 13, 1894.

1996. ORRIN NATHAN FOSTER (Nathan, Nathan, Stephen, John, Ephraim, Abraham, Reginald), b. North Andover, Mass., April 5, 1843; m., Dec., 25, 1868, Emma W. Ingalls, b. Nov. 21, 1852. He is a farmer. Res., North Andover, Mass.

3053. i. MINNIE EMMA, b. Oct. 17, 1869; m., June 29, 1893. Address, Mrs. William C. Goodwin, 463 Washington St., Haverhill, Mass.
3054. ii. ARCHER ORRIN, b. March 29, 1873; m., Oct. 27. 1897, Miss Kittie Agnes Lacy. Address, North Andover, Mass.
3055. iii. HARRY CLIFFORD, b. Sept. 3, 1880. Address, North Andover, Mass.

2009. EDWARD GOULD FOSTER (Merrill, Enoch, Ephraim, Moses, Ephraim, Abraham, Reginald), b. South Walden, Vt., April 10, 1821; m., Sept. 18, 1849, Jeannette Webster Vance, b. July 2, 1825; d. Dec. 8, 1864; m., 2d, Dec. 10, 1865, Elizabeth Tolman Howe, b. Nov. 1, 1823. She resides 242 Adams St., Dorcester, Mass. He was a machinist. He d. Oct. 7, 1881. Res., Dorcester, Mass.

3056. i. CHARLES EDWARD VANCE, b. Aug. 27, 1860; d. unm. An artist.
3057. ii. ALICE, b. Nov. 11, 1851; m., Sept. 6, 1876, Adelbert A. Buffum, b. Aug. 16, 1845; d. Sept. 4. 1884. He is a merchant. Res., 236 Adams St., Boston, Mass. Ch.: 1. Lillian Foster, b. Oct. 11, 1878; d. Oct. 2, 1881.

2010. HARVEY A. FOSTER (Merrill, Enoch, Ephraim, Moses, Ephraim, Abraham, Reginald), b. March 22, 1828, South Walden, Vt.; m., Oct. 27, 1859, Mary F. Montgomery, b. May 28, 1831. He was a farmer and painter. He d. July 8, 1890. Res., South Walden, Vt.

3058. i. EDWARD H., b. Jan. 11, 1870; m., May 14, 1892, Avinona M. Farr, b. June 7, 1869. He is a farmer. Res., s. p., South Walden, Vt.

2019. BRIG.-GEN. GEORGE PERKINS FOSTER (Ephraim, Enoch, Ephraim, Moses, Ephraim, Abraham, Reginald), b. Walden, Vt., Oct. 3, 1835; m.. Wolcott, Vt., July 5, 1864, Sarah Salome Hubbell, b. May 29, 1840; d. Oct. 28, 1891.

GEN. GEO. P. FOSTER.

Gen. George P. Foster was born in Walden, Vt., in 1835. He had an academic education, going to Morisville Academy. In September, 1861, he enlisted in the Fourth Vermont Regiment, and was elected captain of Company G; was commissioned as such Sept. 11, 1861, and was mustered into the United States service on Sept. 21, 1861, at Brattleboro, and left at once for the seat of war. In July, 1862, he was promoted to major of the regiment. On Nov. 5, 1862, he was appointed lieutenant-colonel, and Feb. 3, 1864, he was promoted to colonel of the regiment, and commanded it thenceforth until it was mustered out of the service, July 13, 1865, at the close of the war. Colonel Foster shared the arduous service and the glory of the old First Vermont brigade, of which he was one of the bravest and best officers, and in which his regiment had a name second to no other as a fighting regiment. On May 5, during the fearful fighting in the Wilderness, in which the Vermont brigade was kept so constantly at the front and lost 1,400 officers and men, killed and wounded, Colonel Foster was severely wounded in the thigh. Gen. L. A. Grant, later Secretary of War, in his official report, alluding to Colonel Foster's wound, speaks of him as "an officer whom we may well delight to honor."

Colonel Foster returned to the command of his regiment as soon as his wound permitted; went with the brigade to the Shenandoah Valley and distinguished himself at the battle of Cedar Creek, Oct. 19, 1864. At the opening of that memorable battle he was corps officer of the day for the Sixth Corps, and had charge of the picket line upon the right. At a later stage he commanded the brigade and the left of the line at the last stand made before Sheridan arrived, when, as was said in one of the accounts of the battle, "That unyielding centre, held like a wall of adamant by the Vermont Brigade, saved the army." "For gallant and meritorious services before Richmond and in the Shenandoah Valley" Colonel Foster was breveted as Brigadier-General from Aug. 1, 1864. In 1870 General Foster was appointed United States Marshal of Vermont, and held the office at the time of his death, having been twice reappointed. He was a capable and efficient marshal, and distinguished himself especially during the Fenian invasion of Canada from our northern border, in 1867, when he arrested General O'Neill, commanding the Fenian forces, in the midst of his army, and took him from the field in a carriage. The only city office he held was that of Chief Engineer of the Fire Department, which he accepted and held for a single year, in 1876, in order to straighten out what threatened to be a troublesome muddle in the department. He d. March 19, 1879. Res., Burlington, Vt.

3059. i. CARL HUBBELL, b. May 15, 1866; m. Gertrude H. Kyes.
3060. ii. COLIE EMILY, b. July 27, 1871. Res., unm., Burlington, Vt.

2026. LIEUT. WILLIAM WIRT FOSTER (Hiram, Ephraim, Ephraim, Moses, Ephraim, Abraham, Reginald), b. North Troy, Vt., July 4, 1836; m., Newport, Vt., Feb. 12, 1867, Jennie M. Dame, b. Jan. 26, 183—.

William Wirt Foster was the oldest child of his parents, and was born in Troy, Vt. Received a common school and academic education; a farmer by trade; a member of the M. E. Church; in politics a Republican. On Sept. 19, 1861, he enlisted in Company I of the First Vermont Cavalry Volunteers, and served four years in the War of the Rebellion. Our history, "Vermont in the Civil War," gives a list of seventy-five battles it was engaged in, fifty-two of which stand to his credit. He came out as First Lieutenant, much broken down in health, but since his father's death has owned and carried on the old Foster Hill farm. In 1867, while living at Newport, Vt., he married Jennie M. Dame. They have had four children, none living. In 1868 he went to New York City, living there eight years, in the sewing machine business, returning to Vermont and the old farm in 1876. Has been superintendent of the Barton Landing M. E. Sunday School about twenty years. The old farm, though much run down at the time of his return, in 1876, has responded grandly to hard work. It is a haven of rest to the Fosters, as evidenced by the gathering the 30th of June, 1898, to the Foster reunion. They were all Sons and Daughters of the Revolution, for his great-grandfather, Ephraim Foster, Sr., was a captain, and had a land grant from Congress, and his sister was the wife of one Colonel Elkins. On Grandfather Hall's side were staunch patriots. His mother was a Sherman, Sarah Sherman, a relative of the Shermans who figured so prominently in the late Civil War and Grandma Hall was the daughter of John and Rebecca Martin. He served three years in the War of the Revolution. Res., Barton Landing, Vt.

3061. i. EDWIN DAME, b. Aug. 9, 1869; d. Feb. 2, 1873.
3062. ii. KATIE, b. Nov. 5, 1873; d. Nov. 6, 1873.
3063. iii. JESSIE MAY, b. June 10, 1878; d. July 21, 1881.
3064. iv. WILLIE NEWCOMB, b. Oct. 26, 1886; d. Oct. 26, 1886.

2032. CHARLES MELVILLE FOSTER (Hiram, Ephraim, Ephraim, Moses, Ephraim, Abraham, Reginald), b. Irasburg, Vt., Jan. 11, 1846; m., Feb. 10, 1883, Theresa Schwartz, b. June 16, 1866. He is a dealer in produce and foreign and domestic fruits, in Spreckel's Market. Res., San Francisco, Cal., 729 Market St.

3065. i. LOTTIE, b. Jan. 18, 1884. Res., at home, 710 Taylor St., San Francisco.

2033. HON. FREELAND H. FOSTER (Hiram, Ephraim, Ephraim, Moses, Ephraim, Abraham, Reginald), b. Barton, Vt., Dec. 4, 1849; m., Dec. 4, 1887, Ida L. Gilles, b. Sept. 12, 1855. Is a farmer; owns Lakeside farm and Foster's Grove. Has been Representative in the Vermont Legislature. Res., Barton, Vt.

3066. i. HOWARD E., b. Oct. 9, 1879.
3067. ii. MAYNARD E., b. April 12, 1894.

2046. HENRY CLAY FOSTER (John W., Abner, Elijah, Aaron, Ephraim, Abraham, Reginald), b. Phillipston, Mass., June 3, 1832; m. in Athol, Mass., in 1852, Louise O. Fisher; m., 2d, in Texas, in 1869, Margaret M. Foster, of Tennessee; m., 3d, in Texas, in 1874, Fannie E. Conwell. Res., s. p., Aurora, Wise Co., Texas.

2052. WILLIAM HALE FOSTER (John W., Abner, Elijah, Aaron, Ephraim, Abraham, Reginald), b. Pillipston, Mass., Sept. 5, 1836; m., Winchester, N. H., April 9, 1859, Sarah Maria Clark, b. July 17, 1838, dau. of Endor and Mary Ann (Fasset). He is a machinist. He enlisted in the civil war in Co. A, Twelfth regt., Vermont Vols. He returned home and took up his trade as a machinist, for which he was so well fitted. By his industry and thrift he raised a family of four sons and two daughters, and, feeling that his whole duty was not done, when the opportunity presented itself, he took two orphan nieces, all of which he did with credit to himself and to the town of Orange, where the larger portion of his life has been spent. He is an active member of the Universalist church, a member of the Masonic order and of the Grand Army of the Republic. Res., Orange, Mass.; P. O. Box 884.

3068. i. FRANK A., b. April 10, 1860; m. Bertha F. Miner.
3069. ii. ALBERT CLARK, b. July 5, 1862; m., Jan. 1, 1887, Idella F. Rice. Res., South Athol, Mass.
3070. iii. HENRY WILLIAM, b. Nov. 2, 1863; m. Lulu M. Hadley and, 2d, Frances Monty.
3071. iv. CLARA ELECTA, b. June 11, 1867; m., July 13, 1886, John Wood, b. July 6, 1859. Res., Orange, Mass. Ch.: 1. Florence Mar-

tha, b. Oct. 30, 1888. 2. Mildred Electa, b. April 23, 1896. 3. Alice Eldora, b. May 7, 1887; d. Aug. 8, 1887.

3071½.v. ALICE MARIA. b. July 5, 1869; m., Oct. 31, 1894, Earnest Parsons. She d. Feb. 17, 1898. Ch.: 1. Francis, b. Feb. 3, 1898.

3072. vi. WALTER RICHARD, b. Nov. 30, 1877. Res., Orange, Mass.

3072½.vii. GRACIE, b. Nov. 4, 1881; d. Nov. 8, 1881.

2055. NATHANIEL FOSTER (Nathaniel, Daniel, Thomas, Abraham, Abraham, Abraham, Reginald), b. Newburyport, Mass., Aug. 8, 1830; m., April 15, 1857, in Boston, Catherine Louise Woods, b. Nov. 30, 1833. He is in the insurance business. Res., 447 Beacon street, Boston, Mass.

3073. i. EMELINE LOUISE, b. Aug. 21, 1858; unm. Res., 447 Beacon street, Boston, Mass.

2057. CLEMENT STORER FOSTER (Jesse, Daniel, Thomas, Abraham, Abraham, Abraham, Reginald) b. Portsmouth, N. H., Aug. 18, 1823; m., in Pottsville, Pa., 1847 Rebecca McCamant, b. May 22, 1829; d. June 23, 1889. Clement Storer Foster was born at Portsmouth, N. H. He was the son of Jesse and Anne Eliza (Tappan) Foster, of Newburyport, Mass., who were temporarily in Portsmouth at the time of his birth. In 1831 he removed with his parents from Newburyport, Mass., to Pottsville, Pa., where his father engaged in mercantile business. He was educated in the public schools and in private schools at Pottsville, until he reached young manhood. In compliance with his father's idea, that every boy should learn a trade or profession, he learned his trade as a machinist in Snyder & Haywood's shops, in Pottsville. Upon the completion of his apprenticeship his father sent him to Philadelphia, to gain a broader experience in the larger shops of that city. From Philadelphia he went to Harper's Ferry, where he worked some months in the United States Government arsenal. From there he returned to Pottsville and engaged in mercantile business. In 1846 he married Rebecca McCamant, daughter of Dr. John McCamant, of Pottsville, Pa. He continued in the mercantile business in Pottsville, Tamaqua, Minersville and Ashland, Pa., until the year 1890, except for a time in Minersville, during the "fifties," when he superintended the construction of the Minersville water works. He took an active local interest in politics, and, up to within a few years of his death, he was a strong believer in the principles of the Democratic party. He was the father of eleven children, seven of whom survive, viz.: Frank A. Foster, Orwigsburgh, Pa ; Rufus J. Foster, Scranton, Pa.; Elizabeth T. (Mrs. James Reed), Fennville, Mich.; Clement S., Utica, N. Y.; Margaret G., Brooklyn, N. Y.; Norman W., Buffalo, N. Y.; and Helen V., New York City. He died at Harrisburg, Pa., Feb. 12, 1892. He was a member of the Masonic fraternity, and a Presbyterian in his religious belief. Res., Harrisburg, Pa.

3074. i. RUFUS JAMES, b. Oct. 10, 1856; m. Jennie B. Taylor.

3075. ii. FRANK A., b. ——. Res., Orwigsburgh, Pa.

3075-2. iii. ELIZABETH T., b. ——; m., ——, James Reed. Res., Fennville, Mich.

3075-3. iv. CLEMENT S., b. Dec. 10, 1860; m. Florence J. Seman.

3075-4. v. MARGARET G., b. ——. Res., Brooklyn, N. Y.

3075-5. vi. NORMAN W., b. Nov. 25, 1865; m. Helen E. McDermott.

3075-6. vii. HELEN V., b. ——; unm. Res., New York City.

2056-2. EDMUND KIMBALL FOSTER (Simon, Allen, Thomas, Abraham, Abraham, Abraham, Reginald), b. Ipswich, Mass., Dec. 28, 1815; m., Nashua, N. H., March 8, 1843, Mary Jane Alley, b. June 5, 1818. He d. Aug. 5, 1867. Res., Boxford, Mass.

3075-6⅛. i. INFANT SON, b. Jan. 3, 1844; d. Jan. 17, 1844.

3075-6¼. ii. JAMES HENRY, b. April 15, 1845; d. Aug. 15, 1845.

3075-6½. iii. GEORGE EDMUND, b. April 21, 1848. He is a clerk in the Chicago & Northwestern Railway office in Chicago. Res., 1135 Hinman avenue, Evanston, Ill.

3075-6⅝. iv. H. JENNIE, b. June 4, 1858. Res., 1135 Hinman avenue, Evanston, Ill.

3075-6¾. v. CHARLES F., b. March 20, 1861; d. Sept. 11, 1863.

2057-2. PERKINS FOSTER (Simon, Allen, Thomas, Abraham, Abraham, Abraham, Reginald), b. Ipswich, Mass., July 25, 1818; m., Nov. 14, 1844, Martha Mears, b. Essex, Mass. Was a shoemaker. He d. Worcester, Mass., July 9, 1877. Res., Beverly, Mass.

3076-2. i. SIMON, b. April 3, 1851; d. Sept. 2, 1854.
3077-2. ii. MARTHA ANN, b. Dec. 15, 1852; d. Sept. 6, 1854.
3078-2. iii. CHARLES SIMON, b. July 29, 1855.
3078-2. iv. WARREN B, b. July 30, 1845; m. Hannah I. Legrov.

2058. THOMAS FOSTER (Jesse, Daniel, Thomas, Abraham, Abraham, Abraham, Reginald), b. Portsmouth, N. H., July 20, 1819; m, in Pottsville, Pa., March 15, 1842, Amanda M. Ruch, b. Sunbury, Pa., Aug. 25, 1822. He d. Dec. 13, 1886. Res., Pottsville, Pa.

3076. i. THOMAS J., b. Dec. 31, 1842.
3077. ii. SOLOMON, b. Dec. 25, 1844; attorney.
3078. iii. MARY AGNES, b. Feb. 21, 1847; m. W. H. Daniels. Res., Pottsville, Pa.
3079. iv HENRY A., b. Oct. 9, 1849.
3080. v. WILLIAM WETHERELL, b. June 5, 1855.
3081. vi. JOHN RUCH, b Sept. 27, 1857.
3082. vii. JACOB S., b. Oct. 18, 1862; m. Cecilia A. Schilling.

2061. THOMAS LANESFORD FOSTER (Asa L., Asa, Nathan, Nathan, Abraham, Abraham, Reginald), b. Bloomsburg, Pa., Aug. 30, 1823; m., Beaver Meadow, Pa., Nov. 10, 1847, Henrietta Pratt, b. Oct. 12, 1828. He studied law and was admitted to the bar at the age of twenty-one years, and located at Mauch Chunk, Pa. There he practiced his profession for twenty years, during which time he held and satisfactorily administered several offices of trust in the municipal government of the town and county. He was for several years the secretary and treasurer of the Middle Coalfield poor district, and for six years was county superintendent of public schools. Upon the organization of the Second National Bank, of Mauch Chunk, in 1864, he was elected cashier and soon became president, which position he now holds, having been connected with the bank for thirty-five years. Residence, Mauch Chunk, Pa.

3083. i. CHARLES WILLIAM, b. Oct. 27, 1848; m. Florida H. Thompson.
3084. ii. EMILY PRATT, b. June 17, 1851; m., Oct. 26, 1882, Thomas W. Brown. Res., 9 Northampton street, Wilkesbarre, Pa.
3085. iii. LOUISA CHAPMAN, b. Feb. 10, 1868. Res., Mauch Chunk, Pa.
3086. iv. HARRY WORTHINGTON, b. Feb. 10, 1871. Res., Mauch Chunk, Pa.
3087. v. ASA LANESFORD, b. Jan. 9, 1859; m. Mary MacCalla.
3088. vi. THOMAS LANESFORD, b. Sept 3, 1873; d. Nov. 1, 1887.

2062. CAPT. CHARLES EDWARD FOSTER (Asa L., Asa, Nathan, Nathan, Abraham, Abraham, Reginald), b. Bloomsburg, Pa., Feb. 15, 1826; m., San Francisco, Cal., May 13, 1854, Mary A. Jeffrey, b. Nov. 5, 1824. His wife was Mary Anne Jeffrey, daughter of John and Ann (Williams) Jeffrey, of Auckland, New Zealand. As a young man he learned the printer's trade, and for a few years worked at it, during which time he was associate editor and publisher of the only newspaper then published in Carbon county, Pa. In February, 1849, he joined a company of colonists and went to California on a sailing vessel around Cape Horn, the voyage occupying seven months. After some experience in gold-mining, he located at San Francisco, then for the most part a canvas city of tents among the sand hills, where he received the appointment of an officer in the United States revenue department in the custom house. Returning to Pennysylvania in 1857, he located at Eckley, Pa., and was employed in the mercantile department of the Council Ridge Coal Co. until the commencement of the war, in 1861, when he recruited a full company of soldiers and joined the Eighty-first regt., Pennsylvania Vols., as captain. Since the close of the war he has resided at Mauch Chunk and East Mauch Chunk, Pa., variously engaged in business and as magistrate and chief burgess. Res., s. p., East Mauch Chunk, Pa.

2066. EDGAR THEODORE FOSTER (Nathan L., Joel, Nathan, Nathan, Abraham, Abraham, Reginald), b. Hartford, Conn., April 7, 1823; m., Mauch Chunk, Pa., May 18, 184-, Anna Lippincott, b. Feb. 15. 1829; d. Nov. 18, 1881. Res., Mauch Chunk, Pa., and 1483 E street, New Whatcom, Wash.

3089. i. MARY LIPPINCOTT, b. May 17, 1852; m., Camden, N. J., Jan. 2, 1882, George L. Parker, b. Sept. 4, 1845. He is a book-keeper and salesman. Res., 334 Broad street, Meriden, Conn. Ch.: 1. George Lippincott, b. April 23, 1891; d. July 20, 1891.

3090. ii. ELEANOR LIPPINCOTT, b. July 10, 1849; m., ——, 1875, Theodore Blake. Res., Haddonfield, N. J. Ch.: Frederick, May, Edgar, Charles, Harry, Eleanor.

3091. iii. LOUISA, b. April 28, 1853; d. Nov. 13, 1853.

3092. iv. JOSEPH LIPPINCOTT, b. Oct. 22, 1855. Res., 113 North Fifth street, Philadelphia, Pa.

3093. v. ELIZABETH, b. Oct. 10, 1857; m., ——, 1877, C. H. Clift. Res., New Whatcom, Wash. Ch.: 1. Comty H., b. June 18, 1882. 2. Agnes, b. Dec. 22, 1879; m. S. S. Shea, Dec. 22, 1897. 3. Frank, b. Sept. 8, 1884. 4. Edith, b. July 8, 1887. 5. Bessie, b. March 3, 1894.

3094. vi. EDGAR T., b. Sept. 30, 1859; d. March 4, 1894. Res., Collingdalle, Pa.

3095. vii. ANNIE L., b. March 28, 1862; unm. Res., Haddonfield, N. J.

3096. viii. CATHERINE, b. May 7, 1864; d. Aug. 14, 1864.

3097. ix. EMILY, b. Oct. 3, 1865; m., Dec. 10, 1880, Robert Clark. Ch.: 1. S. Girard. Res., Stanwick, N. J.

3098. x. HENRY LANESFORD, b. Oct. 30, 1870. Res., Philadelphia, Pa.

2070. JOHN WEBSTER FOSTER (Nathan L., Joel, Nathan, Nathan, Abraham, Abraham, Reginald), b. Philadelphia, Pa., Feb. 19, 1821; m., 1841, Elizabeth Cahoone; she d. Dec., 1842; m., 2d, 1843, Nancy Cutler. He d. March 20, 1863. Res., Paterson, N. J.

TO MY BROTHER, JOHN WEBSTER FOSTER.

[By Mrs. E. Louisa Mather.]

Brother, as I read thy letters, while the sun sets o'er the lea,
How the mists of time all gather, rolling back to Memory's sea!
And the rainbow tints of child-land span the past's own sad abyss,
While I think of our last parting, of the tearful silent kiss.

And our father! weary pilgrim on this barren earthly shore,
He has dropped his mortal vestments for the immortal evermore;
In the summer-land of angels, meeting all his loved again;
How his tender heart rejoices, free from every throb of pain!

And our brother, he who battled with the angry storms of life;
He, whose sun set in its morning, when the blackened clouds were rife—
He has passed from strife to calmness, to celestial peace above,
Where the sunlight e'er is shining on the rivers of God's love.

Oh, my brother! thou hast met them, the beloved of other years,
From the infant in its cradle to the aged full of years,
Do they, in their home of beauty—dost thou—ever think of me,
As I sail along life's river to death's yet unsounded sea?

Yea, I know I am remembered, by each thrill that doth arise
In my bosom, true and faithful to the dwellers in the skies;
By each tear, delicious, falling, do I feel your presence near,
By the chain of love, e'er drawing my own spirit to your sphere.

3099. i. ELIZABETH C., b. Feb., 1847; m. —— Wheaton. Res., Paterson, N. J.

3100. ii EDGAR THEODORE, b. Nov. 6, 1844; d. April 25, 1846.

2073. REGINALD HEBER FOSTER (Nathan L., Joel, Nathan, Nathan, Abraham, Abraham, Reginald), b. Sept. 10, 1831; m., Jan. 12, 1860, Joanna Dilkes He died in the war, 1864. Res., New Jersey.

3101. i. MARY, b. ——.

2074. HENRI LYSANDER FOSTER (Nathan L., Joel, Nathan, Nathan, Abraham, Abraham, Reginald), b. Sept. 17, 1833, East Haddam, Conn.; m., May 15, 1855, Angelica Constantia Wenzell, b. Dec. 23, 1838. He was born in Connecticut and resided there until ten years of age, when he went to Philadelphia, Pa., and resided there until 1871. While there was a broker in petroleum. Was educated in the public schools of the Quaker City. From 1871 to 1876 was a resident of New York City, in the oil business. From 1876 to 1892 resided in Oil City, Pa., in the same business. While residing there was for ten years president of the Oil City Oil Exchange. There he was a member of the Episcopal church; was senior warden and lay reader. For fourteen years he has been treasurer of the Board of Missions of the diocese of Pittsburg. He came to Chicago in 1894, and has been a commission merchant since then. Res., Chicago, Ill.; P. O. Box 182, or 102 Rialto Building.

3102. i. FRANKLIN BACON, b. July 31, 1856; m. Victoria McCready.
3103. ii. LAURA LOUISE, b. March 30, 1859; m., May 15, 1880, Theodore C. Ives. He is a civil engineer; has two ch., Elsie and Victoria, and res. Rockford, Ill.
3104. iii. EDGAR THEODORE, b. Sept. 26. 1866; unm. Res., Haworth, Bergen county, N. J.
3105. iv. MABEL CONSTANCE, b. April 5. 1875; unm. Res., "The Newbury," Dearborn avenue, Chicago, Ill.

2078. EDWIN D. FOSTER (Pliny P., Flint R., Daniel, Nathan, Abraham, Abraham, Reginald), b. Morgan, Vt., Dec. 5, 1836; m., Dec. 27, 1858, Carrie Matilda Jenness, b. March 8, 1841. Was a soldier during the civil war; is a farmer. Res., Smithland, Iowa; P. O. Box 66.
3106. i. HERBERT I., b. Nov. 11, 1859; m. —— ——.

2080. CHARLES H. FOSTER (Pliny P., Flint R, Daniel, Nathan, Abraham, Abraham, Reginald), b. Morgan, Vt., April 19, 1850; m. in Salem, Vt., Sept. 7, 1872, Jennie M. Shedd, b. Dec. 23, 1854. Res., West Charlestown, Vt.
3107. i. WATIE M., b. Nov. 26, 1873 (Mrs. E. D. Bullard).
3108. ii. RITIE J., b. Aug. 22, 1875 (Mrs. J. H. Merrill).
3109. iii. JOHN E., b. Nov. 15, 1877.
3110. iv. LINNIE E., b. Nov. 11, 1879 (Mrs. G. F. Shannon).
3111. v. NELLIE V., b. May 1, 1881.
3112. vi. GLADYS V., b. March 19, 1884.
3113. vii. RAYMOND S., b. Sept. 27, 1888.
3114. viii. KATHLEEN V., b. Dec. 21, 1890. Res., West Charleston, Vt.

2089. LOUIS REED FOSTER (Sherlock, Daniel, Isaac, Daniel, Abraham, Abraham, Reginald), b. Warren, Mass., April 12, 1815; m. Charlotte Fay, b. 1815, d. Nov., 1844; m. 2d, Ware, Nov. 10, 1846, Julia Gay Foster, b. June 30, 1825 (see elsewhere). She res. West Brookfield, Mass. He was a farmer. He d. Sept. 13, 1874. Res., Ware, Mass.
3115. i. JULIA MARIA, b. Nov. 20, 1848.
3116. ii. ANNIE ELIZABETH, b. Nov. 4, 1849; m. in Worcester, Mass., Dec. 31, 1870, John Gardner. She d. Oct., 1883, in West Brookfield, Mass.
3117. iii. ELISHA FREEMAN, b. Sept. 14, 1850; m., Nov., 1872, Julia B. Rand. Res., Belmont, Mass.
3118. iv. MARY PUFFER, b. Jan. 2, 1852; unm.; a teacher. Res., West Brookfield, Mass.
3119. v. TAMMIE FIDELIA, b. Nov. 4, 1853.
3120. vi. GEORGE WASHINGTON, b. March 19, 1856.
3121. vii. EMMA JULIA, b. March 11, 1858; m., Nov., 1879, George T. Rand, of Boston. Res., 336 Highland avenue, West Somerville, Mass.
3122. viii. ABBIE JANE, b. April 1, 1860; m., June 26, 1885, Frank W. Combs. Res., 16 Arlington street, Chicopee Falls, Mass.
3123. ix. MYRTIE BELLE, b. Aug. 24, 1862; unm. Res., East Northfield, Mass. She is matron of the Northfield Seminary.
3124. x. LOUIS EDWARD, b. Feb. 13, 1838; m., Nov., 1866, Frances Bartlett, of South Boston; d. June 24, 1896. Was in First Massachusetts Cavalry, civil war. His wife is dead. He left one son, in Boston.
3125. xi. ELGIN REED, b. June 28, 1839; m. Percena E. Fay.
3126. xii. JOSEPH MILTON, b. Aug. 24, 1840; m., April 19, 1869. Was in civil war, in Thirty-seventh Massachusetts regt. Res., South Braintree, Mass.
3127. xiii. CHARLOTTE ANN, b. Dec. 20, 1842; m. —— Conkey; m., 2d, — Paige. Res., Hardwick, Mass.
3128. xiv. INFANT, b. ——, 1846; d. young.
3129. xv. NELLIE ETTA, b. Dec. 16, 1864.
3130. xvi. CARRIE FRANCES, b. Jan. 19, 1866; m., Sept. 19, 1887, Hovey W. Davis. Res., West Brookfield, Mass.
3131. xvii. WILLIAM DANIEL, b. Nov. 3, 1869.

2097. DEA. SAMUEL KNIGHT FOSTER (Luke B., Daniel, Isaac, Daniel, Abraham, Abraham, Reginald), b. New Braintree, Mass., ——, 1815; m., in Springfield, Mass., April 24, 1839, Sarah B. Stebbins, of Springfield. He was of Monson. Samuel was left an orphan at the age of six years and went to live with his uncles, first in Warren and later in Brimfield. He attended school at both Dudley and

Samuel K. Foster.

Wilbraham academies. At the age of fifteen he went to Monson to earn his own living and obtained a position in the woolen mills of Holmes & Reynolds, where he remained, working up through the different departments until he became superintendent. In 1869 he removed to Springfield, and was employed by the Boston & Albany Railroad for ten years, when he gave up this work, and for several years was a professional nurse—a vocation for which he had great aptitude; he was afterward employed at the United States armory, until 1893, when he gave up active business. Soon after coming to Springfield he became a member of the North Congregational church, and in 1874 was elected deacon, an office which he retained through life; he was a member, and for several years served as chaplain, of Hampden Lodge of Masons. Mr. Foster was married to Sarah Bliss Stebbins, daughter of Deborah and Ithamar Stebbins, of Springfield, Mass. Mr. Stebbins built the first house upon the street which afterward took his name, and here the young couple were married by Dr. Osgood, pastor of the First Congregational church. Three children were born to them: Sophia Fidelia, William Wilberforce and Harriet Bartlett, two of whom with the widow, survive him; the youngest, wife of T. L. Avery, having died in 1888. On April 24, 1889, Mr. and Mrs. Foster celebrated the golden anniversary of their marriage, when children, grandchildren and friends gathered to congratulate them upon the ending of fifty happy years of wedded life. A pretty feature of the occasion was the christening of Charles Samuel, an infant son of William W. Foster, by Rev. L. H. Cone, pastor of Olivet church. Mr. Foster was a godly man, whose whole life was filled with kind deeds. He passed peacefully to mansions prepared for him, without a moment of pain. While partaking of the evening meal, surrounded by loved ones, like one of old, he "was not," for God had taken him home. He d. Dec. 17, 1896. Res., Monson and Springfield, Mass.

3132. i. SOPHIE FIDELIA, b. April 10, 1841; m., Feb. 22, 1871, Charles H. Churchill, b. Sept. 21, 1846. He was a son of Joseph and Caroline. Charles Henry Churchill, husband of Sophia Foster Churchill, was born in Chicopee, Mass., Sept. 21, 1845. He attended the high school at that place, and was afterward employed in the postoffice in Springfield until he entered the banking business there. He is now cashier of the Second National Bank. Ch.: 1. Harriet Foster Churchill, b. Dec. 10, 1879, Springfield, Mass. 2. Arthur Henry Churchill, b. June 28, 1881; d. Dec. 28, 1881. 3. Winfred Howard Churchill, b. Dec. 31, 1870; d. July 12, 1888. (Adopted, Oct. 8, 1876) 4. Mabel Anna Churchill, b. March 2 1873, Springfield, Mass.; m., Sept. 19, 1894, Paul G. Norton, Springfield, Mass. (Adopted, Oct. 8, 1876.)

3133. ii. HATTIE BARTLET, b. Feb. 22, 1852; m., Aug. 14, 1884, Theodore L. Avery, b. ——, 1839, son of Sidney S. and Julia. Res., Springfield. Ch.: 1. Emma Harriet, b. ——. Res., 103 Thompson street, Springfield, Mass.

3134. iii. WILLIAM WILBERFORCE, b. Sept. 18, 1845; m. Julia N. Arms.

2101. DR. JAMES WOLCOTT FOSTER (Fordyce, Daniel, Isaac, Daniel, Abraham, Abraham, Reginald), b. Southbridge, Mass., Nov. 16, 1813; m. in Attleboro, June 27, 1839, Harriet Draper Richards, of Attleboro, b. Nov. 5, 1814; d. Aug. 13, 1873. He d. Sept. 17, 1885. Res., Attleboro, Mass.

3131-2. i. JANE FRANCIS, b. Jan. 22, 1841; m., Jan. 10, 1871, Edward E. Barrows. She d., s. p., March 10, 1892.

3132-2. ii. JAMES RICHARDS, b. May 2, 1844; m. Eva Phillips.

3133-2. iii. HENRY WOLCOTT, b. May 27, 1847; d. July 17, 1848.

3134-2. iv. HENRIETTA, b. July 14, 1849; m., Nov. 17, 1874, Walter G. Clark. Ch.: 1. Edward Foster, b. June 6, 1879. Res., North Attleboro, Mass.

2102. DR. FORDYCE FOSTER (Fordyce, Daniel, Isaac, Daniel, Abraham, Abraham, Reginald), b. Southbridge, Mass., Dec. 10, 1815; m., Cohasset, Mass., March 20, 1847, Adeline Jane Tower, b. Feb. 9, 1820. Dr. Foster studied medicine and afterward attended medical lectures at Woodstock, Vt. He went to Cohasset, Mass., in the fall of 1844 to begin the practice of medicine, and became a member of the Massachusetts Medical Association. Continued to practice in that town until August, 1867, when he removed to Sandy Hill, N. Y., practicing his profession there until a few years before his death—his health causing him to relinquish it. He was United States medical and surgical examiner for several years. The following is the obituary notice which appeared in one of the local papers: "Dr. Fordyce Foster, a resident of this town for the last twenty-two years, died at his home, March 19, 1890, after an illness of several months, aged seventy-four years. He came here with his family from Cohasset, Mass., in August, 1867. He was a son of Fordyce Foster and Elizabeth Wolcott and a lineal descendant of Gov. William Bradford, of Plymouth, Mass., in the seventh generation. He is survived by four children: Julia P., Elizabeth W., Nichols T. and Mrs. C. Bloomingdale. Dr. Foster was a kindly gentleman and a physician of much experience. He did much good in this community, and will be remembered, by the poor particularly, for his many acts of benevolence. He had few familiars, but with those who knew him well he held free converse and exhibited reading and information that would surprise many with whom he was not thoroughly acquainted. He died March 19, 1890. Res., Cohasset, Mass., and Sandy Hill, N. Y.

3135. i. ELLA FRANCIS, b. June 23, 1848; m., March, 1870, at Sandy Hill, N. Y., to William H. H. Miller, who died at an hospital at Albany a few years since. She died in November, 1875, leaving one child, a son, Samuel, who was born Sept. 17, 1873. After her death he was taken care of by Mr. and Mrs. Scott, of Baltimore, and, I think, has been adopted by them since, as he has taken the name of Samuel Miller Scott, and was married, Nov. 17, 1897, to Mamie L. Hartzell, of Baltimore, where they reside at the present time.

3136. ii. JULIA SIMMONS, b. Jan. 27, 1852.

3137. iii. ELIZABETH WALCOTT, b. June 9, 1854.

3138. iv. NICHOLS TOWER, b Sept. 2, 1856.

3139. v. ADDIE JANE, b. Oct. 7, 1860.

3140. vi. HARRIET RICHARDS, b. Nov. 17, 1863; m. Cornelius Bloomingdale, Oct. 12, 1887, at Sandy Hill, N. Y. They res., s. p., Glens Falls, N. Y.

2109. OLIVER FOSTER (Amos, Amos, Amos, Amos, Benjamin, Abraham, Reginald), b. Tewksbury, Mass., July 2, 1818; m., Oct. 27, 1842, Abbie Hill., b. Aug. 10, 1821; d. June 26, 1879. He was a farmer. He d. Feb. 29, 1882. Res., Tewksbury, Mass.

3141. i. MARTHA A., b. Feb. 15, 1846; m., June 4, 1872, Jacob Lewis Burtt, b. Sept. 15, 1842. Is a farmer and wood and lumber dealer. Res., s. p., Tewksbury, Mass.

3142. ii. GEORGE OLIVER, b. June 4, 1848; d. Jan. 1, 1880.

3143. iii. CHARLES AMOS, b. Jan. 31, 1852; m. Hannah Jane Fletcher.

3144. iv. FRANK MACE, b. Oct. 17, 1857; m. Annie M. Harnden.

2112. HON. ENOCH FOSTER (Zephaniah K., Amos, Amos, Amos, Benjamin, Abraham, Reginald), b. Tewksbury, Mass., April 22, 1831; m., in Reading, Oct. 4, 1852, Mary J. Frost, b. Aug. 27, 1833. Enoch Foster, son of Zephaniah K. and Mercy T. (Trull) Foster, was born in Tewksbury, Middlesex county, Mass., April 22, 1831. He attended the common schools, where he received his early educational training. He began business life as a manufacturer of furniture with his brother and Nathaniel P. Cole, under the firm name of J. E. Foster & Co., in April, 1851. In a few years the firm name was changed to Foster & Cole. In 1856 Foster & Cole sold out to Wood Brothers and bought out the furniture wareroom of C. G. Weaver & Co., in Lowell, and soon after admitted Francis Kingman, of Reading. The parties who bought out the manufacturing business, being unable to carry out their contract, Foster & Cole were to resume control of their business, and, therefore, sold their Lowell interests to Adams & North. They were afterwards interested in several furniture manufacturing and wholesale and retail establishments in Massachusetts and California. In 1886 Mr. Foster closed out nearly all of his interests in the wholesale, retail and manufacturing business and turned his attention to farming, his present occupation. Mr. Foster was married, in Reading, to Mary J., daughter of Aaron and Mary A (Jaques) Frost. They have no children. Mr. Foster has been called to serve his municipality as town clerk, selectman, town treasurer, justice of the peace, etc. He has been representative to the general court two sessions. His church connections are with the Congregational church and society, of which he is deacon and treasurer. Res., s. p., Tewksbury, Mass.

2114. ZEPHANIAH P. FOSTER (Zephaniah K., Amos, Amos, Amos, Benjamin, Abraham, Reginald), b. Tewksbury, Mass., Dec. 26, 1824; m., March 15, 1855, Emily B. Carleton. Res., Tewksbury, Mass.

3145. i. ENOCH W., b. Dec. 9, 1855; m. Lillian Shedd.
3146. ii. HATTIE, b. Nov. 15, 1856; d. Jan. 16. 1857.
3147. iii. ALBERT LEWIS, b. Nov. 23, 1857; m., June 23, 1886, Susie M. Gardner. Res., Tewksbury, Mass.

2115. JOHN T. FOSTER (Zephaniah K., Amos, Amos, Amos, Benjamin, Abraham, Reginald) b. Tewksbury, Mass., May 20, 1827; m., March 1, 1852, Susan H. Chandler. John T., of Tewksbury.—Letter date, Dec. 6, 1881; ex, March 1, 1883; wife, Susan R.; ch., Anna C. Foster, Carrie F. Foster, John E., Howard W., Arthur L., all of Tewksbury. He d. in 1883. Res., Tewksbury, Mass.
3148. i. ANNA C., b. May 3, 1855; m., Sept. 22, 1883, Fred J. Boynton.
3149. ii. CARRIE FRANCES, b. Feb. 10, 1857; m., Oct. 5, 1885, Ralph M. Cole.
3150. iii. JOHN EDWARD, b. Jan. 16, 1860. Res., Tewksbury, Mass.; P. O., Lowell, Mass.
3151. iv. HOWARD WYMAN, b. March 2, 1862; m. Nellie E. Boutwell.
3152. v. ARTHUR LANG, b. Nov. 2, 1865.

2116. JOEL FOSTER (Zephaniah K., Amos, Amos, Amos, Benjamin, Abraham, Reginald), b. Tewksbury, Mass., March 3, 1829; m. there Sept. 25, 1860, Sarah M. Gray. Res., Tewksbury and Methuen, Mass.
3153. i. ALICE GREY, b. Oct. 7, 1861.
3154. ii. FREDERICK W., b. Nov. 21, 1863. Res., Methuen, Mass.
3155. iii. LEONA ELIZABETH, b. May 5, 1865.
3156. iv. HELEN GERTRUDE, b. July 27, 1876.

2124. AMOS FOSTER (Nathan, Nathan, Amos, Amos, Benjamin, Abraham, Reginald), b. Tewksbury, Mass., Oct. 10, 1827; m., Portland, Me., April 30, 1860, Annie Olivia Seavey, b. Aug. 16, 1832; merchant. When quite a young man he went to Norway, Me., to live, and, after the death of his father to Lowell, Mass., where he lived until a young man; then went to Boston and engaged in the clothing business with the largest clothing establishment in Boston at that time. Afterward formed a partnership known as Hatch, Johnson & Foster in wholesale men's furnishing goods, doing the largest business in that line in the city, with a branch in New York. After twelve years the partnership was dissolved, each going into a separate business, Mr. Foster taking a retail men's furnishing goods store. He is a member of the Boston light infantry company and Columbian Lodge of Free Masons. He died March 31, 1899. Res., 5 Howland street, Roxbury, Mass.
3157. i. LEONA ADELAIDE, b. ——. Res., 5 Howland street, Roxbury, Mass.
3158. ii. GERTRUDE WELLINGTON, b. ——. Res., 5 Howland street, Roxbury, Mass.
3159. iii. CHARLES HORACE, b. ——. Res., 585 Congress street, Portland, Me.

2129. WILLIAM FRANKLIN FOSTER (William, Nathan, Amos, Amos, Benjamin, Abraham, Reginald), b. Norway, Me., Jan. 14, 1833; m. there Feb 25, 1867, Almira H. Smith, dau. of Mark Poole Smith, b. Aug. 6, 1838. He d. Nov. 11, 1883. Res., Norway, Me.
3160. i. EFFIE J., b. Aug. 10, 1869; d. Dec., 1869.
3161. ii. WINNIE, b. Sept. 6, 1870.
3162. iii. HENRY B., b. Aug. 30, 1872. Res., Norway, Me.
3163. iv. FANNY, b. June 26. 1879; d. April 5, 1880.

2130. NATHAN ABBOTT FOSTER (William, Nathan, Amos, Amos, Benjamin, Abraham, Reginald), b. Norway, Me., Oct. 4, 1835; m. there May 22, 1859, Hattie N. Grover, b. Dec. 20, 1845. He d. April 15, 1891. Res., Norway, Me.
3164. i. FRED A., b. June 23, 1865. Res., Norway, Me.

2134. CHARLES CLINTON FOSTER (William, Nathan, Amos, Amos, Benjamin, Abraham, Reginald), b. Norway, Me., Dec. 7, 1846; m., Leominster, Mass., Dec. 7, 1877, Dora E. Wheeler, b. June 12, 1851. He was born in Maine, and while a young man went to Leominster, Mass. He engaged in the retail boot and shoe business with his brother, under the firm name of Foster Bros. He erected a handsome business block on the corner of Main and West streets. He soon disposed of this business and engaged in the manufacture of shirts with the Leominster Shirt Co. This business is one of the most extensive in Leominster, and of its kind in the East. Res., 58 Grove avenue, Leominster, Mass.

3165 i HENRY P., b. Sept. 12, 1878, at Springfield, Mass Res., 3 Webster street, Worcester, Mass.

3166. ii. CHARLES W., b., Chicopee, Mass., Nov. 13, 1879. Res., 58 Grove avenue, Leominster, Mass.

3167. iii. GEORGE M., b. April 24, 1881, at Chicopee, Mass. Res., Mount Hermon, Mass.

3168. iv. RALPH W., b. Sept. 25, 1882, at Chicopee, Mass. Res., 58 Grove avenue, Leominster, Mass.

3169. v. FRANK N., b. Aug. 23, 1888, at Leominster, Mass.

3170. vi. HELEN L., b. June 1, 1892, at Leominster, Mass.; d. Jan. 28, 1893.

2135. GEORGE WASHINGTON FOSTER (William, Nathan, Amos, Amos, Benjamin, Abraham, Reginald), b. Norway, Me., July 10, 1849; m. there in 1874, Elizabeth Porter Witt, b. April 26, 1850, dau. of Thomas and Rachael (Porter). Mr. Foster was born in Maine, and when twenty years of age located in Leominster, Mass, where he ever after made his home. At first he was clerk in a store and later in company with his brother engaged in the retail boot and shoe business. He soon erected a handsome business block and engaged in the retail grocery business. This was soon abandoned. In 1886 he united with the F. A. Whitney Carriage Co., and at his death was one of the directors of the company. He was held in the highest esteem by his business associates and his townpseople. He was a member of the orthodox church. He died Jan. 5, 1891. Res., Leominster, Mass.

3171 i. ALICE M., b. ——. Res., 23 Grove street, Leominster, Mass.

2136. WALLACE VALENTINE FOSTER (Luther F., Nathan, Amos, Amos, Benjamin, Abraham, Reginald), b. Norway, Me., Jan. 13, 1840; m. there July 20, 1879, Abbie Thomas, of Harrison, Me. He was a private in Co. G, First Maine Regiment during the Civil War and later in the Maine Coast Guards, in 1865. Res., Norway, Me.

2142. BENJAMIN FOSTER (Amos P., Benjamin, Asael, Gideon, Benjamin, Abraham, Reginald), b., Harrison, Me.; m., ——, Susan E. Clark. He settled on his father's homestead and had two ch. Res., Harrison and Otisfield, Me.

3172. i. ROSE, b. ——.

3173. ii. CLARA, b. ——.

2146. CYRUS K. FOSTER (Benjamin S., Benjamin, Asael, Gideon, Benjamin, Abraham, Reginald), b. Jan. 12, 1833; m., Nov. 12, 1860, Mary E. Morrow, b. Dec., 1837. Was a farmer and farmed land given him by his father. Res., Harrison, Me.

3174. i. CORA E., b. July 17, 1861; d. ——.

3175. ii. GEORGE F., b. Jan. 14, 1864; d. ——.

3176. iii. NELLIE W., b Aug. 28, 1865; d. ——.

3177. iv. INFANT, died.

2148. REV. CHARLES W. FOSTER (Benjamin S., Benjamin, Asael, Gideon, Benjamin, Abraham, Reginald), b. February 3, 1836, Harrison, Maine; m., Feb. 8, 1859, Frances A. Libbey, b. Bridgeton, Maine, 1844. Charles W. Foster married Frances A. Libbey at the residence of Rev. J. T. Hawes, then pastor of the Congregational church at Bridgeton; settled on the old homestead of his father until 1872, when he moved to Bridgeton. At the time of the civil war he volunteered in September, 1864, for one year; acted as clerk in the adjutant-general's office at Camp Berry, Portland, Me.; then went to the First Maine Battery, for which he enli ted in Winchester, Va., and was mustered out of the service July 15, 1865, in Portland, Me. When he enlisted for the war it was said by one of the disloyal neighbors "that he hoped he would be placed in the front ranks, and be the first man to be shot." All because of his sympathy for the colored race in bondage in the South under their tyrannical task-masters. He lived to see the colored race in America set free. He came home to wife and friends in South Harrison, and in 1870 in the month of March, a series of meetings were held in the old Methodist meeting house, South Harrison (said meeting house since destroyed by fire), held by Rev. Leonard Green and Rev. G. T. Ridlon. A very extensive interest prevailed for several months, people coming a long distance over hills and dales through snow and mud, with lanterns in hand, to the great revival meetings in South Harrison. It was in said meetings that Charles W. Foster was converted to God, and not to man or the church, on March 30, 1870. It was soon after his baptism that he felt the call from God to enter the ministry and preach the Gospel to others that were lost. For three years the struggle over this duty went on in his own breast, until he moved to Bridgeton, Me., in 1873, when he attempted to take up the cross that had kept him back so long. His first sermon was attempted in the Ground Hill school house, in York, Me, and from the words of Scripture recorded in Matt. 22:42, "What think ye of Christ." In about four years afterward he had occasion to preach in the same school house, and was told that his first sermon was not yet forgotten by many persons in the community; said they: "We remember your text and sermon very distinctly." He came home and commenced preaching in the Kansas school house, in Bridgeton, where a great revival broke out, and for many weeks there was no cessation of interest by day or by night. He was afterward pastor of the Free Baptist church in Bridgeton for nearly nine years, where many were converted and joined the church. At the Kansas school house about fifty were reclaimed and converted. Rev. N. T. Ridlon, of Saco, Me., came at his request and baptized for him, as he was not then ordained to the ministry. He was ordained and set apart to the work of the Gospel ministry October 19, 1875, in Central Hall, Bridgeton, Me., by Revs. Hezekiah Short, Nathaniel T. Ridlon, John H. Mugridge executive board to ordain in Christian conference. The hall owned by Hon. N. S. Littlefield, and son F. J. Littlefield, although a large one, was filled, and the music for the occasion was furnished by the choir of the Universalist church in that village. In Bridgeton he was chosen by the town to act as treasurer for three years, and at the close of his last term as treasurer he received a call from the Free Baptist church of Phillips, Franklin county, Me., which he accepted, and served as its pastor for six years from the day he accepted it, when he resigned, to accept a call from the Free Baptist church at Presque Isle, Aroostook county, Me., which pastorate in Aroostook he held over five years. At Phillips, Me., he was visited by a great affliction in the death of his oldest child, a daughter, Susie S. Foster, eighteen years and nine months of age. She was a beautiful singer. In about a year afterward his aged mother, Esther T., came from Waltham, Mass., to his home in Phillips, as she said, "to die." And on May 22, 1885, she did die after a lingering sickness, aged 82 years, and was buried by the side of her husband, in South Harrison, Me. From the Free Baptist church at Presque Isle and Caribou a great work was done, in the repairs of the church at Presque Isle. The audience room had never been completed, while the house was built nine years before. But at this time it was thoroughly completed into a very handsome auddience room. The exterior of the church was most thoroughly painted in colors, spire and all, and was a very splendid edifice inside and out. The dedication took place July 17, 1889, the pastor being invited to preach the dedicatory sermon from Psalm 122d, 1st verse, "I was glad when they said unto me, 'Let us go into the house of the Lord.'" In May, 1893, he received a call from the Union church in Cotuit, Mass. He visited the church and accepted the call, and commenced his labors July 2, following. In 1894 he broke down with nervous prostration. The several physicians he employed called it general nervous prostration of all the vital forces, but they stoutly affirm that he will yet be able to take up his work again. Residence, Bridgeton, Me., and 35 Taylor street, Neponset, Mass.

3178. i. SUSIE S., b. June 25, 1865; d. April 14, 1884.
3179. ii. CHARLIE F. b. Oct. 10, 1866; m. Jennie Parkinson.
3180. iii. HELEN L., b. July 20, 1869; m., Aug. 16, 1888, Charles H. Fuller, b. March 11, 1865. He is a painter. Res., s. p. Cotuit, Mass.
3181. iv. WALTER R., b. June 12, 1879.

2166. SOLOMON LOWE FOSTER (David, Philemon, Philemon, Jonathan, Caleb, Abraham, Reginald), b. Ipswich, Mass., Sept. 27, 1836; m. there Sept. 7, 1875, Mary Abbie Langley, b. Nov. 21, 1845. He is a railroad employe. Res., Ipswich, Mass.; address, P. O. Box 243.

3182. i. GERTRUDE MABEL, b. Sept. 7, 1881. Res., Ipswich, Mass.

2174. SERGT. RICHARD R. FOSTER (Philemon C., Philemon, Philemon, Jonathan, Caleb, Abraham, Reginald), b. Ipswich, Mass., Nov. 11, 1842; m., Aug. 1, 1875, Harriet Elma Towle, of Medford, b. March 4, 1846. He was born in the parish of Limebrook, more commonly called "Firetown," town of Ipswich, county of Essex, State of Massachusetts, on the Boston & Newburyport turnpike, which, in those days, was a toll-road; his father kept one of the toll-gates. The nearest house toward Boston was nearly a half-mile away and the nearest one Newburyport way a little over one-half mile. Their's was the last house going north before reaching the Rowley line, the next neighbor being in the town of Rowley, in a small settlement of fifteen houses called "Sodom." The home was situated about two miles from the school house. Consequently, at the age of fifteen years, he moved to the town of Rowley, locating on a farm near the villages of Sodom and Rooty Plains (the latter is now known as Millwood). He worked on the farm in summer, and, attending school, about one and a half miles away, in Rooty Plains, in the winter time, received all the schooling he ever had in these two country schools, "Fire town" and "Rooty Plains." In 1859 he moved to Georgetown. Here he worked at pegging shoes (brogans, such as were sold in the South for the use of slaves). In the spring of 1860 he moved to Rowley, and in 1861, at the breaking out of the War of the Rebellion, he was living with an uncle, Samuel Pickard. There was a company of militia in the town, designated as Company C, First Battalion Rifles, Mass. Volunteer Militia. This battalion was commanded by Maj. Ben Perley Poor, a noted journalist, and was located as follows: Company A, at West Newbury, the home of the Major; Company B, in Byfield, a borough situated partly in Georgetown and Rowley, the larger part being in Newbury; Company C, in Rowley. He enlisted in this company (C) and went into camp with it in Rowley on the 26th of June, 1861, later on going into camp at Lynnfield, Mass., where this battalion became the nucleus of the Nineteenth Regiment, Massachusetts Infantry, each company retaining its original letter in the regiment. On the 26th day of July, 1861, he was mustered into the United States service with the rest of the company. August 28, 1861, he left the State for the front. During the summer they were encamped about one mile from Edwards' Ferry, in Maryland, where they became a part of Lauder's Brigade. A part of the time Companies B and C were on detached service in support of a section of Vaughn's Rhode Island Battery, near the Potomac river. On the 21st and 22d of October the regiment took part in the Ball's Bluff affair, one company crossing at Edwards' Ferry, and the rest of the regiment being stationed on Harrison's Island. It was while here that he first heard the whistle of Rebel bullets. He did picket duty with his company and worked on block houses during the winter of 1861-62 along the Potomac river. In March, 1862, marched from Muddy Branch to Edwards' Ferry, Maryland, thence by canal boat to Harper's Ferry; from Harper's Ferry marched to Berryville, back to the Ferry, and from thence to Washington city via the Baltimore & Ohio Railroad, where they became a part of the Army of the Potomac, as Dana's Brigade, Sedgwick's Division, of Sumner's Corps, afterward known as the Third Brigade, Second Division, Second Corps. He took part with his company in the Peninsula campaign, coming under fire first at Yorktown, in many skirmishes, then at West Point, Fair Oaks, Peach Orchard, Savage's Station, Glendale and Malvern Hill; was in camp at Harrison's Landing through July, leaving there on the 16th of August and going to Washington, marching to Newport News by way of Yorktown, and being transported from Newport News to Alexandria by the transport Atlantic. Took part in covering Pope's retreat at the Second Bull Run, thence to Antietam, in which the Nineteenth Massachusetts took a prominent part, losing many men in killed and wounded. Without enumerating the marches and incidents of his army life, which he has contributed for publication in the Georgetown (Mass.) Advocate, he took part in the battles of Fredericksburg, December 11 and 13, 1862, and again on March 3, 1863; Gettysburg, July 2 and 3, 1863, after which he was sick three months, most of the time being in the Camden Street Hospital, Baltimore, Md. Rejoined the regiment at Warrenton, Va., and took part in the Mine Run campaign, from November 24 to December 1, 1863, and the battles of the Wilderness and Spotsylvania. Was captured May 15, 1864; was in prison at Andersonville, Milan and Savannah, Ga., and Florence, S. C., and was paroled at Goldsborough, N. C., about the 1st of March, 1865, returning to the regiment after a month's sick furlough at home. In November, 1862, was appointed corporal, and in April, 1864, sergeant. Re-enlisted with his company December 21, 1863, and was at home with it on a 30-day veteran furlough, from February 10 to March 10, 1864. After returning to the company, the 17th of May, 1865, he was detailed as sergeant of mounted pioneers at corps headquarters, where he remained until the regiment was discharged, on the 30th day of June, 1865. He was never wounded in any of the many encounters he took part in, but did, on the 13th of December, 1862, at Fredericksburg, get a minie ball through his haversack. He took part with his company in the grand review in Washington at the close of the war. Peace proclaimed, he again took up shoemaking, working with varying success for several years; but, finally, on account of poor health—a legacy from his service in the war—he was obliged to look for different employment. He worked nearly three years in Amsterdam, N. Y., in a shoe factory, returning to Massachusetts on account of ill health. In February, 1890, he received the appointment of adjutant of the Soldier's Home in Massachusetts, and came on duty, as such, on the 17th of the month, and is now in the same position. On the 4th of May, 1876, he was appointed a justice of the peace for the State of Massachusetts by Gov. John D. Robinson, and reappointed by Gov. William E. Russell, on the 4th day of May, 1893. Justices of the peace in Massachusetts are not appointed for counties now, but for the State. Res., s. p., Soldier's Home, Chelsea, Mass., of which he is Adjutant.

2178. WILLIAM EATON FOSTER (Joseph C., Moses, Moses, Jonathan, Caleb, Abraham, Reginald). b. June 2, 1851, in Brattleboro, Vt.; m., March 2, 1886, Julia Appleton, dau. of Elisha Williams Appleton (John White, Samuel, Isaac, Isaac, Samuel, Samuel), librarian of the Providence public library since 1877; graduated at Brown University in 1873. He has published "Libraries and Readers," 1883; "Stephen Hopkins, a Rhode Island Statesman," 1884; "Early Attempts at Rhode Island History" (in "Collections of Rhode Island Historical Society, vol. vii"), 1885; "Town Governments in Rhode Island," 1886, besides various biographical publications. Res., Providence, R. I.

2182. GEORGE EVERETT FOSTER (John E., Moses, Moses, Jonathan, Caleb, Abraham, Reginald), b. Aug. 27, 1849, Milford, N. H., m., July 14, 1874, Mary Lord Burrit, dau. of Rev. Charles D. Burrit, and gr.-dau. of a sister of Noah Webster, b. Sept. 7 1848. He was educated at the Milford High School, New London Literary and Scientific Institution and took three years special course in literature, history and journalism at Cornell University, Ithaca, N. Y. His life has been devoted to journalism and literary pursuits. Editorial work: Reporter of Binghamton (N. Y.) Times, 1872-3; founder and editor of Milford (N. H.) Enterprise, 1874-87, and Wilton (N. H.) Journal, 1875-87; editorial staff of Daily Journal, Ithaca, N. Y., 1887-88; city and news editor of Democrat, Ithaca, N. Y., 1889-92; news writer for Ithacan, 1892-3; editor of Ithaca Democrat, 1893 to June, 1894; editor and business manager of Democrat from June, 1894, to ——; special correspondent Boston (Mass.) Daily Herald, 1875-77; Boston Daily Globe, 1885-87; New York Tribune, 1888-90; New York Times, 1890-91—; Chicago Times, 1891 —, Chicago Mail, 1891 —. A serial story in Ithaca Democrat, "Ned, the Farmer Boy," 1889. Twice visited the Indian Territory. Works published: "Se-quo-yah, the American Cadmus and Modern Moses," illustrated, 12 mo.; pp. 262; Philadelphia, 1885. "Literature of the Cherokees: also Bibliography and Story of their Genesis," 12mo., cloth; pp. 110, Ithaca, N Y. "Story of the Cherokee Bible," 12mo., Ithaca, N. Y, 1897. "Story of an Indian Tribe," 1897. In preparation, 1897: "History of Indian Territory." "John Ridge; a Cherokee Romance." Among the newspaper and magazine contributions to Indian literature may be mentioned: In Boston Transcript, "Education Among the Cherokees," 1888, "Education Among the Arapahoes," 1888; "A Story of the Cherokees," July 23 and 25, 1889. In Frank Leslie's Illustrated Weekly, "A Contrast," illustrated, 1887; "Indian Progress"; "A Zigzag Journey through the Indian Territory," illustrated with original lead pencil sketches, August 11, 1888. In Magazine of American History, "Journalism Among the Cherokees," July, 1887. In Frank Leslie's Popular Monthly, "Among the Cherokees," illustrated, February, 1887; "A Fishing Party in the Creek Nation," May, 1889; "Pottawatomie Traditions of Gen. W. H. Harrison," illustrated, May, 1890. In Woman's Magazine, "Origin of the First Cherokee Hymn," 1885; "Our Cherokee Sister," 1886; "Elizabeth Moody," 1887; "Through the Cherokee Nation," 1888. In Green Bag Magazine, "A Legal Episode in the Cherokee Nation," 1892. In the Century Magazine, "The Cherokee Emancipation Proclamation," open letter, 1888. Among the other miscellany and romance which has been received with favor may be mentioned: In Comfort Magazine, "A Cherokee High Tea." In Souvenir of Journalism, "Infelicities of Rural Journalism," illustrated, 1886. In Woman's Magazine, "A Rose of Long Ago," 1885. A poem on the above story was written by a Texan poet, which was published in the same magazine. "About Women, by a Man," October, 1886; "About Women, by a Man," November, 1886. "Robert B. Thomas and His Almanac," 1888. In Home and Country Magazine, "Mrs. Dobson's Ghost," 1896. The Cherokee Senate passed a resolution of thanks in 1885, thanking the author for his efforts in their behalf, which was forwarded under the seal of the Cherokee Nation. He taught school in Brookline, N. H., and in Spencer, N. Y. Was for two terms tutor in English at Cornell university. Also special lecturer on philology for two terms at Francestown (N. H.,) Academy. Residence, Ithaca, N. Y.

3183. i. JESSE WEBSTER, b. Feb. 11, 1880. Early in life he showed poetical and artistic tendencies. His first poetical articles appeared in papers in 1892, at the age of twelve. He received the N. Y. Press second prize for story, in 1893, at the age of thirteen. His Christmas gift to friends in 1892 was a souvenir brochure of his own poetry. In 1893 he published his second souvenir, setting considerable of the type himself. His collected poems, printed in 1894, at the age of fourteen years, made about one hundred pages. His first printed cartoon was published Aug. 5, 1896, at the age of sixteen years. His first metal engraving was printed April, 1897. He took the Conservatory art course at Ithaca, 1896. Entered Ithaca High School, 1897.

2190. DR. THOMAS ALBERT FOSTER (Thomas D., William, Nathan, Caleb, Caleb, Abraham, Reginald), b. Montville, Me., Feb. 20, 1827; m., in Unity, Me., Eliza McManus; m. 2d, South Montville, Me., 1857, Adelaide Woodman, b. 1832; d. 1865; m. 3d, in Augusta, 1868, Mary Woodman, b. 1836. He d. Nov. 27, 1896. Res., Portland, Me.

3184. i. BRAZILLAI BEAN, b. ——, 1848; m. —— ——.

3185. ii. CHARLES W., b. April 29, 1850; m. Etta B. Parker.

3186. iii. ARIETTA, b. ——, 1860; m., ——, 1886, —— Jones. Res., Bowrey Beach, Me.

3187. iv. ELLMA WOODMAN, b. ——, 1870; unm. Res., Portland, Me.

3188. v. JOANNA CARTER, b. Oct. 15, 1864; m., Sept. 2, 1891, J. J. Hunt, b. Dec. 27, 1853. He is a merchant, s. p. Res., Jonesboro, Tenn.

3189. vi. HENRY, b. ——; d. aet. 2 years.

3190. vii. SERENA, b. ——; d. aet. 2 years.

3191. viii. TWO OTHER CHILDREN d. in infancy.

2194. EBENEZER FOSTER (Thomas D., William, Nathan, Caleb, Caleb, Abraham, Reginald), b. Bristol, Me., ——; m. there ——. He d. —— ——. Res., Monticello, Me.

3192. i. ZELISCO, b. ——. Res., Montville, Me.

3193. ii. OLIVE, b. ——; m. —— Kirkpatrick. Res., Fort Fairfield, Me.

3194. iii. ARTHUR, b. ——. Res., Colorado.

2195. DANIEL FOSTER (Ebenezer, William, Nathan, Caleb, Caleb, Abraham, Reginald), b. Montville, Me., Dec. 5, 1802; m., May 10, 1827, Sarah Hussey, b. May 23, 1803; d. April 16, 1877. He was a farmer and lumberman. He d. April 17, 1880. Res., Montville and Fort Fairfield, Me.

3195. i. JAMES E., b. April 2, 1828; d. May 5, 1828.

3196. ii. BETHIAH H., b. Feb. 13, 1830; m., Aug. 26, 1852, —— Chase.

3197. iii. BENJAMIN B., b. July 5, 1832; m. Feb. 9, 1857, and died Jan. 13, 1863.

3198. iv. H. LINCOLN, b. July 3, 1834; m. Zipra Bishop.

3199. v. LIZZIE, b. Oct., 3, 1835; m., March 16, 1863, —— Robbins.

3200. vi. MARY C., b. Dec. 11, 1839; d. April 15, 1846.

3201. vii. ADDELIA F., b. March 17, 1842; m., March 1, 1876, —— Richardson.

3202. viii. NELLIE RANDALL, b. July 15, 1844.

3203. ix. GEORGE, b. Sept. 15, 1847; m., Feb. 17, 1869, —— ——.

2200. ZABUD FOSTER (Thomas, John, Nathan, Caleb, Caleb, Abraham, Reginald), b. Bristol, Me., July 16, 1816; m., Oct. 7, 1844, Nancy Blunt Miller, b. May 13, 1822; d. June 16, 1888. He was a carpenter by trade, but had other occupations during his life. He does nothing now, because of old age. His politics of later years has been Democratic. He attended the Congregationalist church, but is now a member of the Methodist. Res., Bar Harbor and Ellsworth, Me.

3204. i. ALUILDA M., b. May 1, 1845; m. Mrs. Irving Osgood. Res., Ellsworth, Me.
3205. ii. JAMES E., b. Dec. 15, 1846; m. Ella M. Marshall.
3206. iii. MILLER N., b. Oct. 22, 1848. Res., Wakefield, Mass.
3207. iv. STETSON THOMAS, b. July 25, 1850; m. Alice L. Whiton.
3208. v. SARAH C., b. Sept. 6, 1852; m. Gaten S. Osgood, of Bluehill, Me.
3209. vi. FRANK L., b. Nov. 1, 1854. Res., Bar Harbor, Me.
3210. vii. AUSTIN M., b. May 24, 1857. Res., Ellsworth, Me.
3211. viii. JOHN B., b. Oct. 19, 1859. Res., Deer Island, Me.
3212. ix. CURTIS R., b. July 25, 1861; m. Minnie M. Goodwin.
3213. x. ALBERT E., b. June 7, 1864. Res., Ellsworth, Me.

2204. CAPT. STETSON FOSTER (Thomas, John, Nathan, Caleb, Caleb, Abraham, Reginald), b. Bristol, Me., Aug. 26, 1828; m., ——, Margaret Nichol; was a sea captain. Res., Thomaston, Me.
3214. i. AFTON LINCOLN, b. ——; d. ——.
3215. ii. MAUD, b. ——; d. ——.

2205. JOSEPH HENRY FOSTER (Thomas, John, Nathan, Caleb, Caleb, Abraham, Reginald), b. Bristol, Me., in 1838; m., in Boston, Mass., Nov., 1858, Annie Black, of Ellsworth, Me., b. Dec. 26, 1843. She m., 2d, E. E. Morgan, of Auburndale, Mass. He was an inn-keeper, kept the old Ellsworth House. Annie Black was the daughter of John Black, granddaughter of Col. John Black and Mary Cobb, whose brother, David, was a surgeon in the Revolutionary War and served under Washington. A liquor case used by him in that service is now in Mrs. Joseph Foster's possession. Samuel C. Cobb, ex-mayor of Boston, and George F. Root, musical composer, are cousins of Annie Black. He d. Feb. 12, 1864. Res., Ellsworth, Me.
3216. i. FANNIE COBB, b. Dec. 27, 1862; m., June 27, 1883, Seth I. Johnson, b. Jan. 20, 1862. Is a police officer. Res., 418 Chestnut street, West Newton, Mass. Ch.: 1. Henry Ellsworth Johnson, b. July 13, 1884. 2. Eleanor Irving Johnson, b. Aug. 9, 1887. 3. Albert Darwin Johnson, b. March 11, 1890. 4. Emilie Story Johnson, b. Sept. 17, 1892; d. same day. 5 Harold Foster Johnson, b. Jan. 20, 1894. 6. Fannie Hazel Johnson, b. May 25, 1896.

2206. THOMAS A. FOSTER (Thomas, John, Nathan, Caleb, Caleb, Abraham, Reginald) b. Bristol, Me., Sept. 7, 1830; m., July 9, 1856, Matilda S. Thompson, of Bristol, Me., b. Sept. 6, 1834. He is a farmer. Res., South Bristol, Me.
3217. i. LOUIS F., b. Dec. 12, 1863. Res., South Bristol, Me.
3218. ii. NANCY, b. May 12, 1857; d. Jan. 11, 1873.
3219. iii. ANNIE J., b. ——; m. —— Thompson.
3220. iv. GUSSIE G., b. June 7, 1869.
3221. v. FRED M., b. Jan. 24, 1876.

2225. EDWARD VOSE FOSTER (Zebud, Zebud, Nathan, Caleb, Caleb, Abraham, Reginald), b. Montville, Me., July 30, 1831; m., Northampton, Mass., May 25, 1857 Sarah Jane Smith, b. July 30, 1837; d. May 9, 1858; m., 2d, June 18, 1860, Martha Longley Allis Smith, b. Nov. 23, 1843. Edward Vose Foster left home at an early date, and had little educational advantages. Worked in Massachusetts and Connecticut as mechanic up to 1851, when he went to California, crossing the isthmus by the Nicaragua route. Was in the mines for a year, then started home, was shipwrecked off Lower California and rescued by a ship returning to San Francisco. Stayed in California for two years more, then returned to Massachusetts, where he became connected with large works making guns and bayonets for the Government. Was not permitted to enter the civil war owing to a severe accident in the works early in the period, in which his skull was badly crushed. In 1869 entered mercantile life in Northampton, Mass., and left it through the financial crisis in 1875. Afterward was engaged in hotel-keeping at Turner's Falls, Mass., leaving there for New York City in 1891, where he has been since. Residence, New York, N. Y.
3222. i. HORATIO A., b. Jan. 12, 1858; m. Florence Louise Root.
3223. ii. EVA GERTRUDE, b. Feb. 26, 1862. Res., 533 East 120th street, New York City.

3224. iii. IDA MAUD, b. March 27, 1867. Res., 140 East 48th street, New York City.

2231. JOHN SPROUL FOSTER (Thomas S., Zabud, Nathan, Caleb, Caleb, Abraham, Reginald), b. Montville, Me., Jan. 15, 1852; m. there Nov. 13, 1880, Hattie J. Higgins. He lived at home with his parents until he was seven years of age, then went to live with his grandfather on his mother's side, John Sproul, of Montville, for whom he was named. Lived there some three years and attended the common district school. His duties while there was to care for a large stock of cattle and sheep and to aid his aged grandparents in such work as appertained to the farm. His grandparents were very dear to him, and he delighted to do such things as pleased them. When the civil war closed his uncle came home from the army, and he returned to his own home and began to attend the academy at Freedom village, which was about one and one-half miles from his home, boarding at home and ringing the bell to pay his tuition. This he did most of the time while attending the academy. Hon. N. A. Luce was the principal at this time. After completing his study at the academy he took a short course at Castine normal school, and taught several schools in his and adjoining towns. In 1870, 1871 and 1872 he traveled extensively in the New England States visiting almost every town. He read law in Belfast, Waldo county, Me., and was admitted to the Waldo bar in November, 1877, and taught school three months the following winter, and then opened a law office in the town of Thorndike in March, 1878, where he practiced for two years, during which time he held the office of collector and town clerk. In May, 1880, he moved to Rockport and continued the practice of his profession. He married Miss Hattie J. Higgins, of Thorndike, and has since resided in Rockport, Me. He has held the office of collector of the town of Camden, now Rockport, one year, and treasurer of said town two years, director of schools for three years, one of the school committee for three years and superintendent for four years, and is still holding that office at this writing. He is of English, Scotch and Irish descent. He has been successful in his chosen profession. Res., s. p., Rockport, Me.

2235. BARTON F. FOSTER (Thomas S., Zabud, Nathan, Caleb, Caleb, Abraham, Reginald), b. Montville, Me., Nov. 23, 1844; m., Lawrence, Mass., 1873, Mary Ellen Briggs, b. March 26, 1850. He is a lawyer. Res., Hulldale, Me.

3225. i. FRED A., b. March 30, 1874. Res., 38 Branch street, Lowell, Mass.
3226. ii. FLORA MAY, b. Sept. 30 1880.
3227. iii. JOHN SPROUL, b. May 2, 1884.
3228. iv. FLORA MAY, b. — —; d. Sept. 30, 1880.

2237. CHARLES FOSTER (Charles, Jacob, Jacob, Jacob, Isaac, Reginald, Reginald), b. Oct. 27, 1826, Charlestown, Mass., m., Oct. 10, 1861, Charlotte Messer Bowman, dau. of Dexter and Nancy Robbins (Foster), b. July 18, 1835. He is largely engaged in the manufacture of tooth-picks at Cambridge, Mass., in which place he now resides. He previously spent several years of his life at Pernambuco, Brazil. Res., Charlestown, Mass.

3229. i. CHARLOTTE BOWMAN, b. Dec. 13, 1863.
3230. ii. ANNIE EATON, b. Nov. 26, 1864.

2242. HON. GEORGE HENRY FOSTER (Henry, Jacob, Jacob, Jacob, Isaac, Reginald, Reginald), b. June 20, 1838, at Charlestown, Mass.; m., Oct. 16, 1867, Constance Atherton, dau. of Henry Lee and Almira Steward Woodworth Atherton, of New York. Graduated at Harvard university 1857. Studied law and was admitted to the bar of New York May 16, 1861, and is now a member of the law firm of Weeks & Foster, 58 Wall street, New York. At his death he was president of the Board of Aldermen of New York City. He d. in 1888. Res., New York, N. Y.

3231. i. HENRY ATHERTON, b. Sept. 26, 1868.

2250. DR. EDWARD JACOB FORSTER (Jacob, Jacob, Jacob, Jacob, Isaac, Reginald, Reginald). b. Charlestown, Mass., July 9, 1846; m., Sept. 5, 1871, Anita D. Lyon. Dr. Edward Jacob Forster was born in Charlestown, Mass., graduated M. D. from Harvard college in 1868. Soon after went to Europe, studying his profession in Paris and Dublin; at the latter place, he became a Licentiate in Midwifery of the King and Queens College of Physicians in Ireland. He was, in

1870, practicing in Charlestown. Mass. At his death he was on Gov. Greenhalge's staff. Was a member of the Massachusetts Medical society; visiting physician Boston City hospital; member of the Boston Society for Medical Improvement; of Society of Medical Observation; life member of the Massachusetts Horticultural society; author of "Manual for Medical Officers of the Militia of the United States." His wife, whom he married September 5, 1871, was a daughter of Dr. Henry Lyon and grand-daughter of Dr. Abraham Rand Thompson, both residents of Charlestown, Mass., and graduates of Harvard college. Dr. Forster was the author of "A Genealogy of the Fo(r)ster Family," a pamphlet of 22 pages, reprinted from the Genealogical Register of 1876. He was a member of the New England Historical-Genealogical society and of the Wisconsin Historical society.—American Ancestry.

Will.—Edward J. Forster, of Boston, physician.—Wife, Anita D. Forster. Thomas G Frothingham and Henry W. Bragg. Witness, Joseph W. Foster. Dated June 27. 1891.—Lib. 714; Fol. 107. Prob. June 11, 1896.—Lib. 717; Fol. 409. Petition for administrator.—Edward J Forster, died, Boston, May 15, 1896; next of kin, Anita D. Forster, widow; Teresa L. Forster, Boston, daughter; Elizabeth T. Forster, Boston, daughter; Ruth Forster, Boston, daughter, aged 18 years.—Lib. 717; Fol. 409. He d. May 15, 1896. Res., Charlestown and Boston, Mass.

3231¼. i. TERESA L., b. ——.

3231½. ii. ELIZABETH T., b. ——.

3231¾. iii. RUTH, b. ——, 1878. Many friends witnessed the marriage of Miss Ruth Forster, daughter of the late Dr. Edward J. Forster, of this city, and Mr. George Hunt Ingraham, of Milton, at the Unitarian church in that town. The bridegroom is the son of Mr. and Mrs. Andrew Ingraham, of New Bedford. The ceremony was performed by Rev. Roderick Stebbins, of Milton. Miss Elizabeth T. Field of Boston was maid of honor, and Mr. Joseph Everett Chandler served in the capacity of best man. Messrs. Horace Cecil Fisher of Brookline, Frederick E. Forster, Arthur Ingraham and Edward Ingraham of New Bedford, Louis W. Pulsifer of New York, and James H. Batchelder of Boston, were the ushers. Mr. Lewis E. Tilden played the organ selections, including the processional and recessional bridal marches. Following the ceremony, a reception was given at the home of Mr. Ernest W. Bowditch, of Milton, by whom the bride was given in marriage. Mrs. Bowditch is a cousin of the bride.—Boston Transcript, June, 1899.

2251. CALEB FOSTER (Henry P., Henry, Jacob, Jacob, Isaac, Reginald, Reginald), b. Walpole, N. H., March 22, 1825; m., Nov. 11, 1851, Isabel Eliza Marsh, dau. of Edmund E., b. Sept. 11, 1826; d. May 14, 1893. He is a farmer. Res, Walpole, N. H.

3232. i. EDWARD PRENTISS, b. Sept. 21, 1852; m. —— ——.

3233. ii. WESLEY CALEB, b. Aug. 13, 1856; m, June 10, 1885. Res., Walpole, N. H.

3234. iii. ALFRED MILAN, b. Feb. 10, 1858; m. Jan. 30, 1884. Res., Los Angeles, Cal.

3235. iv. HIRAM HERMER, b. Dec. 4, 1862; m. Jan. 13, 1897. Res., Walpole, N. H.

2252. HENRY THOMAS FOSTER (Henry P., Henry, Jacob, Jacob, Isaac, Reginald, Reginald), b. Walpole, N. H., Oct. 15, 1826; m., April 29, 1855, Hannah Morrill Fuller, of Westmoreland, N. H., b. Sept., 1833; d. July 27, 1897. He was a farmer. He d. April 17, 1879. Res., Walpole, N. H.

3236. i. WILLIS CHRISTOPHER, b. Oct. 6, 1858; m. Katie Callahan.

3237. ii. VELMA ELSIE, b. Nov. 7, 1859; unm. Res., Keene, N. H.

3238. iii. FLORENCE JOSEPHINE, b. July 20, 1870; is a teacher. Res., Baltimore, Md.

3239. iv. FRANK HENRY, b. Jan. 6, 1857; m. Harriet B. Franks.

3240. v. ANNIE REYNOLDS, b. Aug. 10, 1871; m., June 6, 1894, Daniel C. Cahalane, b. Feb. 25, 1868. Res., Keene, N. H. Ch.: 1. Reginald Foster, b. Jan. 16, 1897.

3241. vi. ADINE PHILENA, b. Sept., 1861; unm. Res., Keene, N. H.

2256. GEORGE HENRY FOSTER (Levi H., Henry, Jacob, Jacob, Isaac, Reginald, Reginald), b. Walpole, N. H., April 2, 1825; m., Feb. 27, 1850, Lydia Ham, b. Feb. 19, 1833. He is an ice dealer. George H. Framingham.—Letter date, October 11, 1898; ex, November 4, 1898; wife, Lydia C.; children, George W., Charles L., both of Framingham.—Middlesex Prob. He d. Nov., 1898. Res., Walpole, N. H., and South Framingham, Mass.

3242. i. CHARLES LEVI, b. Dec. 24, 1851; m. Aug. 8, 1875. Res., South Framingham, Mass.

3243. ii. GEORGE W., b. May 26, 1856; m. Aug. 6, 1880 and June 27, 1887. Res., South Framingham, Mass.

3244. iii. ANNIE MAY, b. May 23, 1854; d. April 7, 1861.

3245. iv. ABBIE FRANCES, b. Nov. 24, 1858; d. April 7, 1861.

2266. DR. MATTHIAS LANCKTON FOSTER (George T., David, Jacob, Jacob, Isaac, Reginald, Reginald), b. Chatham, N. Y., June 17, 1859; m., Summit, N. J., Nov. 14, 1894, Constance Hunter Savage, b. Jan. 10, 1867. Matthias Lanckton Foster was born at Chatham Four Corners, N. Y.; moved to Pittsfield, Mass., at one year of age; prepared for college in high school, Pittsfield, Mass; entered Williams College, Williamstown, Mass., in 1877; graduated there in the class of 1881, and delivered a dissertation at commencement. Graduated at the College of Phyiscians and Surgeons, New York City, in 1885, and received the second Hassen prize. Immediately thereafter secured an appointment on the house staff of St. Luke's hospital, New York City, and served the full course on the surgical side. Left the hospital December, 1886, and commenced private practice. Was appointed on the surgical staff of the Manhattan Eye and Ear Hospital in May, 1887, and still holds the position of assistant-surgeon in that institution. Was appointed attending surgeon to the Out-Door department of Bellevue hospital in February, 1887, and resigned at the expiration of a year. Was appointed instructor in otology at the New York Polyclinic in 1888, and resigned the position in 1892. Appointed instructor in ophthalmology in the New York Polyclinic in 1889 and resigned in 1892. Is a member of the Medical Society of the County of New York and served as delegate to the Medical Society of the State of New York in 1896, 1897 and 1898. Is a member of the Society of the Alumni of St. Luke's Hospital and of the Williams College Alumni Association, of New York. Became an F. & A. M. in 1891 and was master of Concord Lodge, No. 50, during 1895. Gave up the general practice of medicine and became a specialist in diseases of the eye and ear in 1891, and since that time has devoted himself mainly to private practice in those branches. He is the author of a number of articles, principally on matters relating to diseases of the eye; was a collaborator in the preparation of Foster's Encyclopaedic Medical Dictionary, and also of Foster's "Practical Therapeutics," both published by D. Appleton & Co. Res., 22 East Forty-first street, New York, N. Y.

3245-2. i. HAMILTON KNIGHT, b. Sept. 10, 1895.

2269. HON. DAVID JOHNSON FOSTER (Jacob P., David, Jacob, Jacob, Isaac, Reginald, Reginald), b. Barnet, Vt., July 27, 1857; m., Oct. 4, 1883, Mabel M. Albee, b. Oct. 13, 1864. He is a lawyer. Res., Burlington, Vt.

3246. i. MABEL, b. July 28, 1885.

3247. ii. MATILDA, b. Oct. 12, 1886.

3248. iii. MILDRED, b. Feb. 13, 1895.

2277. JOHN JACOB FOSTER (John C., Jacob, William, Jacob, Isaac, Reginald, Reginald), b. Port Byron, N. Y., Sept. 23, 1852; m., Oct. 9, 1871, Minerva Hill, b. Dec. 18, 1854. Res., Greenville, Mich.

3249. i. KATHERINE M., b. April 15, 1874.

3250. ii. JOHN JACOB, b Jan. 16, 1896.

2288. JACOB FRANK FOSTER (Jacob T., Jacob, William, Jacob, Isaac, Reginald, Reginald), b. March 28, 1851; m., June 20, 1878, Clara Walton. He is general superintendent of the South (Washington) Park. Res., 5200 Grand Boulevard, Chicago, Ill.

2290. CLARK HARROLD FOSTER, (Jacob T., Jacob, William, Jacob, Isaac, Reginald, Reginald), b. Dec. 11, 1859; m., Dec., 1884, Hattie Kellogg. Res., 5800 Dearborn street, Englewood, Chicago, Ill.

2294. JACOB FOSTER (Shephel, Jacob, Isaac, Jacob, Isaac, Reginald, Reginald), b. Gray, Me., Aug. 4, 1841; m., June 5, 1877, Mary Allen, b. ——. He d. July, 1886. Res., West Gray, Me.

3251. i. AGNES MARY, b. March 19, 1878. Res., West Gray, Me.

2299. SHEPHEL GRANVILLE FOSTER (Shephel, Jacob, Isaac, Jacob, Isaac, Reginald, Reginald), b. Gray, Me., April 11, 1856; m., Nov. 27, 1884, Carrie J. Davis, b. May 7, 1857. He is a farmer. Res., Gray, Me.

3252. i. IRENE A., b. Dec. 1, 1887.
3253. ii. BENNIE SHEPHEL, b. April 8, 1890; d. Sept. 21, 1890.
3254. iii. ELWOOD GRANVILL, b. April 24, 1896; d. Aug. 29, 1897.

2300. THOMAS JEFFERSON FOSTER (Solomon B., Samuel, Isaac, Jacob, Isaac, Reginald, Reginald), b. Gray, Me., Oct. 17, 1836; m., Dec. 31, 1861, Mary Rolf Devine, b. April 13, 1840. He is a machinist. Res., Cumberland Mills, Me.

3255. i. HELEN MARY, b. Sept. 26, 1862; m., Oct. 17, 1893, Arthur P. Tenny, b. Jan. 9, 1859. Is a bank teller. Res., s. p., Haverhill, Mass.
3256. ii. ALICE HART, b. Feb. 16, 1866; m., July 30, 1891, Rev. George A. Sisson. Res., North Dighton. Three children.
3257. iii. LAURA EUNICE, b. Sept. 15, 1868.
3258. iv. GEORGE JENKINS, b. March 2, 1873.
3259. v. EDWARD EMERY, b. May 4, 1871.

2304. HORACE C. FOSTER (Solomon B., Samuel, Isaac, Jacob, Isaac, Reginald, Reginald), b. Gray, Me., Sept. 7, 1847; m. there Sept. 7, 1871, Annie M. Frank, b. April 2, 1852. He is a lumber dealer and owner of plaining mills. Res., Rumford Falls, Me.

3260. i. GRACE EDITH, b. July 10, 1872.
3261. ii. CLARENCE MILFORD, b. Aug. 8, 1874; d. Feb. 3, 1897.
3262. iii. THOMAS H., b. Nov. 3, 1875.
3263. iv. EUNICE R., b. March 19, 1877; d. June 27, 1894.
3264. v. PERLEY W., b. April 10 1879.
3265. vi. LENA M., b. June 19, 1882; d. March 25, 1894.
3266. vii. MILDRED L., b. Aug. 7, 1888.
3266½. viii. WILMA F., b. July 21, 1890.

2305. CHARLES J FOSTER (Solomon B., Samuel, Isaac, Jacob, Isaac, Reginald, Reginal). b Gray, Me., Dec. 16, 1849; m. in 1876, Ella C. Spiller. Res., North Gray, Me.

3267. i. ADDIE G., b. Oct. 1, 1877; m., July, 1897, Harry Kneal. Res., North G
3268 ii. WILLIS H , b. July 2, 1879.
3269. iii. ANNIE G., b. Sept. 1, 1884.

2306. JOHN R FOSTER (Solomon B., Samuel, Isaac, Jacob, Isaac, Reginald, Reginald), b. Gray, Me., Dec. 16 1851; m. in 1873, ——. He d. July 27, 1897. Res., Maine.

3270. i. STEPHEN, b. ——. Res., Greenwood, Me.

2309. HENRY W. FOSTER (Solomon B., Samuel, Isaac, Jacob, Isaac, Reginald, Reginald), b. Gray, Me., Dec. 11, 1857; m., Dec. 27, 1882, Jennie E. Colley, b. Dec. 27, 1858. He is a civil engineer. Res., Cumberland Mills, Me.

3271. i. ETHEL MAY, b. Nov. 7, 1883.
3272. ii. MABEL WINNEFRED, b. Nov. 11, 1885.

2316. SILAS WAYMOUTH FOSTER (Samuel J., Samuel, Isaac, Jacob, Isaac, Reginald, Reginald), b. Gray, Me., Dec. 22, 1835; m. there June 17, 1860, Sarah Jane B[illegible]ley, b. Jan. 28 1836; d. Oct. 29, 1879; m., 2d, Sept. 27, 1881, Angie A. Briggs, b Aug 6, 1850. He is a mason and building contractor. Res., Dry Mills, Me.

3273. i EUGENE, b. Sept 21, 1861; d ——.
3274 ii JUSTILL, b Jan 28, 1864; d. ——.
3275 iii. STEPHEN M , b. ——.
3276 iv SAMUEL S., b ——.
3277 v EUGENE, b April 28, 1885.
3278 i. MABEL, b. March 14, 1887.

2320. JAMES W. FOSTER (Philip, William, Isaac, Jacob, Isaac, Reginald, Reginald), b. Argyle, Me., May 22, 1829; m. Eagle Creek, Oregon, Jan. 28, 1867, Louisa M. Rockhill, b. Dec. 25, 1848. He is a farmer, stock, fruit and grain dealer.

SILAS W. FOSTER.

James W. Foster, one of the pioneers of the State of Washington, was born in the State of Maine; was there reared and sent to the common school. Our subject was of such a tender age that he does not have any memory of the mother who passed away so soon, but he was kindly reared by his grandparents. In 1852 he had earned enough to enable him to pay his passage to San Francisco, to which city he sailed, around Cape Horn, reaching there that same fall, and then going by a steamer to Portland, and to the home of his father. He took up a donation claim of 160 acres, improved the land, and lived there until 1859, when he came to Walla Walla, Wash., taking a claim here six miles southeast of the town, toward Cottonwood, and on Springbranch, at the foot-hills. Here he now resides, having improved his farm and put it into a good condition. For several years he was engaged in breeding and selling fine blooded horses, by which enterprise he made considerable money. Some of these horses brought from $500 to $3,000; but of late years he has devoted his attention to farming. Horticulture has deeply interested Mr. Foster, and he was the first man in Walla Walla county to set out an orchard, and he now has an area of eighty acres set out in all kinds of fruits. He transported his original trees over the Cascade mountains, from Portland, Oregon, by means of pack-horses, and at night would bury the trees to keep them from freezing. Owing to his inability to afford himself equal protection, he had his feet frozen on the journey. The climate of this State favors the growing of fine fruit, and from this source he has a good income. Mr. Foster has made it one rule of his life never to have anything that he could not pay for, and never to buy anything merely because it was cheap. One source of honest pride is, that he has never had a mortgage on his place, and was never asked to give security when borrowing money at the bank. He has one of the finest vineyards in the county, and his farm and orchard always supply all that is choicest in the products of the land. When he first settled here he had no neighbors, and had to get his supplies from pack-trains. Many times has he seen the day when the larder contained nothing but beans. On one occasion he went four days with-

JAMES W. FOSTER, SR.

out food of any sort. He took part in the Indian wars, enduring many hardships at that time, but has lived through all, and is now able to enjoy the fat of the land.

Our subject has worked indefatigably during his residence on the coast, and all that he owns he has gained by his own industry and management. He belongs to the People's Party, and his first presidential vote was for Weaver, in 1892. The reason he never before voted for president was because he happened to be on the frontier or in a Territory at the time of the election.

In 1867 our subject married Miss Louisa M. Rockhill, a native of Iowa. Her parents, Anthony and Rosetta Rockhill, came to Washington in 1864; were natives of Ohio, and are now living near Dayton. Mr. and Mrs. Foster are the parents of nine children. Res., Walla Walla, Wash.

3279. i. JAMES W. Jr., b. Dec. 2, 1867; m., December, 1894. Res., Walla Walla, Wash.
3280. ii. FANNIE R. McFARLANE, b. Oct. 15, 1869; m., Dec. 31, 1891. Res., Walla Walla, Wash.
3281. iii. CHESTER U., b. Dec. 30, 1871; m., April 19, 1898, — — ——. Res., Walla Walla, Wash.
3282. iv. JESSIE MAY, b. March 15, 1875; m. —— Ferguson, April 20, 1895. Res., Walla Walla, Wash.
3283. v. CECIL NELSON, b. Dec. 11, 1877. Res., Walla Walla, Wash.
3284. vi. LOUISA MARY. b. Feb. 20, 1880; d. Feb. 26, 1880.
3285. vii. IVA CLARA, b. June 24, 1882.
3286. viii. LOIE L., b. Feb. 20, 1886.
3287. ix. MILDRED L., b. June 13, 1888.
3288. x. ETHEL C., b. Nov. 24, 1891.

2326. WILLIAM STINSON FOSTER (Isaac, William, Isaac, Jacob, Isaac, Reginald. Reginald), b. Argyle, Me., Aug. 18, 1845; m., Sept. 6, 1866, Sarah A. Bussell; d. May 30, 1878; m., 2d, June 22, 1880, Nancy B. Jones, b. Dec. 14, 1846. He was a farmer and lumberman. Res., Argyle, Me.

3289. i. WILLIE PERCIVAL, b. Oct. 6, 1882; d. April 26, 1883.

2332. STEPHEN W. FOSTER (Joseph W., William, Isaac, Jacob, Isaac, Reginald, Reginald), b. Cherryfield, Me., Feb. 22, 1839; m. there April 20, 1865, Louisa F. Frickett, b. June 2, 1841. Is a lumberman and farmer. Res., Big Rapids, Mich.

3290. i. WILL A., b. June 12, 1868; m., June 28, 1895. Res., Tomahawk, Wis.
3291. ii. C. RAE, b. Sept. 27, 1877.

2334. JOHN H. FOSTER (Joseph W., William, Isaac, Jacob, Isaac, Reginald, Reginald), b. Franklin, Me., Feb. 11, 1842; m. Haverstraw, N. Y., Aug. 1, 1868, Georgiana Dykins, b. July 29, 1850. He is a contractor and builder. Res., Ashland, Wis.

3292. i. JOHN W., b. May 6, 1869; m., Feb. 8, 1896.
3293. ii. BERTHA L., b. Oct. 18, 1870; d. Sept. 27, 1873.
3294. iii. PERCY J., b. Aug. 12, 1872; m., Dec. 31, 1895.
3295. iv. HOWARD D., b. April 10, ——.
3296. v. CHARLES I., b. June 11, 1878.
3297. vi. HARRY L., b. Sept. 2, 1886.

2338. CAPT. DUDLEY W. FOSTER (Joseph W., William, Isaac, Jacob, Isaac, Reginald, Reginald), b. Franklin, Me., Nov. 1, 1848; m., Nov. 19, 1870, Clara Miriam Wakefield. b. Dec. 5, 1848. His early life was spent upon the ocean, in which business he engaged at the early age of fourteen; went up the various stages of the trade to master at the age of twenty-one years; continued in this business until 1873, in which time was master of four ships. In 1873 left the ocean and came to Michigan and engaged in the lumbering business, and is still so engaged. Res., Big Rapids, Mich.

3298. i. LEWIS W., b. June 20, 1872. Res., Big Rapids, Mich.
3299. ii. EDWARD S., b. Feb. 16, 1875: m., Jan. 1, 1898. Res., 304 West One Hundred and Fifty-fourth St., New York City.
3300. iii. MATTIE LOUISE, b. April 1, 1878. Res., Big Rapids, Mich.
3301. iv. SUSIE MABEL, b. Feb. 1, 1880; d. Aug. 23, 1883.
3302. v. HATTIE GAIL, b. Feb. 23, 1882; d. April 1, 1891.
3303. vi. GROVER C., b. March 29, 1889.

MAJOR JOSEPH FOSTER.

PAYMASTER U. S. N.

2359. MAJOR JOSEPH FOSTER (Joseph, Joseph, Joseph, Jeremiah, John, Reginald, Reginald), b. Gloucester, Mass., June 17, 1841; m., Oct. 7, 1875, Helen Dickey, dau. of David and Lois Leverett (Nelson), of Lowell, Mass. Removed to Portsmouth, N. H., in November, 1850; educated in the public and private schools of Portsmouth; clerk with Edward F. Sise & Co., 75 Market street, Portsmouth, dealers in coal, salt and crockery, from March 9, 1857, to October, 1862. Entered the United States navy October 3, 1862; commissioned as Paymaster United States Navy Feb. 23, 1877. Res., Portsmouth, N. H.

Paymaster Foster is a member of the Grand Army of the Republic, and served as delegate-at large from New Hampshire to the Twenty-sixth National Encampment, G. A. R., held at Washington, D. C., in September, 1892. He is a member of the New England Historic Genealogical Society, and has taken much interest in genealogy and local history. He is also a member of the Massachusetts Society Sons of the American Revolution, in the right of his grandfather, Captain Joseph Foster[6], of his great-grandfather, Colonel Joseph Foster[5], and of his mother's paternal grandfather, Colonel Dyer Spalding, of Cornish, N. H.; and of the Society of Colonial Wars in the State of New Hampshire in the right of his grandfather's grandfathers, Captain Jeremiah Foster[4], and Lieutenant Daniel Giddings, both of Chebacco (now Essex), Ipswich, Mass., and both of the Sixth Company, Fifth Massachusetts Regiment, Colonel Robert Hale, in the successful Louisburg Expedition of 1745.

He married in Lowell, Mass., Helen Dickey, daughter of David and Lois Leverett (Nelson) Dickey, of Lowell; born Jan. 13, 1853, in Haverhill, N. H. Mrs. Foster is a member of the New Hampshire Society of the Colonial Dames of America in the right of her ancestor, John Leverett, Governor of Massachusetts (1673-79), who, born in Boston, England, returned from Boston, New England, in 1645, and served as captain in the Parliamentary Army, when he became a friend of Oliver Cromwell, during whose protectorate he afterward resided in London as agent of the Colony of Massachusetts Bay. She is also a descendant of Thomas Dudley, second Governor of the Colony of Massachusetts Bay (1634, 1640, 1645, 1650). The following record of Paymaster Foster's navy services is taken from "Hamersly's Records of Living Officers of the Navy," Philadelphia, 1890. A few sentences have been added to complete it to 1898.

"He was born in Gloucester, Mass., June 17, 1841. Res., Portsmouth, N. H. Appointed from New Hampshire. Entered the service as Captain's Clerk Oct. 3, 1862; attached to the Steamer Augusta, Commander E. G Parrott, South Atlantic Blockading Squadron (1862-3); was present at the attack of the Rebel iron-clads on the blockading Squadron at Charleston, S. C., Jan. 31, 1863, and at Admiral Dupont's first attack on Charleston, April 7, 1863. Appointed acting assistant paymaster Oct. 19, 1863; attached to the Steamer Acacia, South Atlantic Blockading Squadron (1863-5), which was stationed most of the time off Charleston, S. C.; was ashore under fire of Battery Marshall, Sullivan's Island, Sept. 14, 1864, and captured the British blockade running Steamer Julia, Dec. 23, 1864; was present at the fall of Charleston, Feb. 10, 1865, and at the re-raising of the United States flag on Fort Sumter, April 14, 1865; attached to the Steamer Commodore McDonough, South Atlantic Blockading Squadron (1865), and the Steamer Tallapoosa, Gulf Squadron (1865-6). While attached to the Steamer Commodore McDonough he saved his official books and papers from the wreck of that vessel, which foundered at sea, Aug. 23, 1865, on the passage from Port Royal, S. C., to New York, nothing else being saved on the ship; transferred to the regular navy and commissioned as assistant paymaster, July 23, 1866. Promoted to passed assistant paymaster, May 10, 1867; attached to the Steamer Aroostook, Asiatic Station (1866-9); Steamer Shawmut, North Atlantic Station (1871-5); Torpedo Station, Newport, R. I. (1876-9); commissioned as Paymaster, Feb. 23, 1877; attached to the Steamer Monocacy, Asiatic Station (1879-82); acting as fleet paymaster for ten months of that time, when he negotiated a large amount of exchange in a satisfactory manner, for which he was specially mentioned in the annual report of the Fourth Auditor of the Treasury for the year 1882; attached to the Naval Asylum, Philadelphia (1883-6); special duty Navy Yard, Portsmouth, N. H. (1887); attached to the Steamer Pensacola, North Atlantic Station (1888); General Store-keeper Navy Yard, Norfolk, Va. (1889); waiting orders (1890)."—Hamersly's Records of Living Officers of the United States Navy, Philadelphia, 1890, page 303.

His later naval record is as follows: Paymaster of the Navy Yard and Purchasing Pay Officer, Portsmouth, N. H. (1890-3); attached to the Cruiser San Francisco, North Atlantic, South Atlantic and European Stations (1893-6), during which time the San Francisco bore the flags of Rear Admirals A. E. K. Benham, Oscar F. Stanton, William A. Kirkland and Thomas O. Selfridge; was present at Rio Janeiro, Brazil, Jan. 29, 1894, when Admiral Benham cleared his fleet for action in defense of American interests endangered by the Brazilian ships-of-war in revolt against the government of that Republic; Fleet Paymaster of the European Station (1895-6); Paymaster of the Navy Yard and Purchasing Pay Officer, Portsmouth, N. H. (1896-8); Paymaster United States Naval Station, Key West, Fla. (naval base for the Spanish war), May and June, 1898; promoted to Pay Inspector June 15, 1898; Paymaster of Navy Yard and Purchasing Pay Officer, Portsmouth, N. H., July, 1898.

JOSEPH FOSTER, JR.

3304. i. JOSEPH, b. Oct. 31, 1880, at Shanghai, China. He is a student at Harvard University, class of 1902.

3305. ii. BEATRICE, b. July 30, 1882, at Chefoo, China.

3306. iii. DOROTHY, b. July 21, 1886, at Philadelphia, Pa.

3307. iv. ISABEL, b. Dec. 26, 1892, at Portsmouth, N. H.

2357. WILLIAM FOSTER (Joseph, Joseph, Joseph, Jeremiah, John, Reginald, Reginald), b. Dec. 12, 1819; m., Nov. 29, 1843, in Boston, Caroline Matilda Harvey, dau. of Capt. James T. and Hannah (Smithers) Harvey, of Salem, Mass.; b. July, 1818, in Salem. Res., South Danvers and Boston, Mass., and Severance, Doniphan county, Kans. He d. Nov. 23, 1881, in Severance. She d. about Nov. 30, 1881, in Severance. Res.. Boston, Mass.

3308. i. WILLIAM ELWELL, b. July 31, 1849; m., Aug. 19, 1868, in Severance, Mary Magdeline Pry, b. Oct. 16, 1853, in Clark county, Ohio. He d. Sept. 6, 1880, in St. Jose, Mo. Children born in Severance, Kans.: 1. Harvey Stanwood, b. Feb. 10, 1871. 2. Charles Pearl, b. Oct. 18, 1873. 3. Caroline Matilda, b. Nov. 22, 1875; d. March 1, 1877. 4. William Nash, b. Sept. 11, 1877; d. Dec. 5, 1877. 5. William Frank, b. July 12, 1879.

2359. LYMAN SPALDING FOSTER (Joseph, Joseph, Joseph, Jeremiah, John, Reginald, Reginald), b. Nov. 25, 1843; m., Sept. 3, 1872, Elmira Stephanie Hallet, dau. of Stephen and Eliza Baldwin (Coningham) Hallet, b. Buenos Ayres, South America and gr.-dau. of Stephen H. Hallet, architect of the original capitol at Washington, D. C. He removed to Portsmouth, N. H., in November, 1850, and to New York City in October, 1864. Stationer and printer at 33 Pine St.; Recording Secretary Linnæan Society of New York, and member of American Ornithologists Union; Superintended Division of Spanish America. Mr. Foster's deep interest in and consequent profound study of birds and bird life is well known to all his friends, and make him a high authority on everything pertaining to ornithology. He is a member of the American Ornithologists Union, Council of the Scientific Alliance of New York, New York Academy of Sciences, Linnæan Society of New York, New York Zoological Society, and the West Side Natural History Society of New York, of which latter he is Vice-President. He is publisher of The Auk, a quarterly journal of ornithology, and the author of the following books, viz.: "The Published Writings of George N. Lawrence," by L. S. Foster; "Bulletin No. 40, United States National Museum," Washington, 1892; "A Consideration of Some

Ornithological Literature, with Extracts from Current Criticism, Part 1, 1876-1883," by L. S. Foster; "Abstract of Proceedings of Linnæan Society of New York, No. 6, New York, 1894." Res., New York, N. Y., 33 Pine St.

3309. i. ELMIA ADELAIDE, b. Aug. 29, 1874.

2362. JOHN FRYE FOSTER (Benjamin, Joseph, Joseph, Jeremiah, John, Reginald, Reginald), b. Sept. 30, 1826; m., Dec. 27, 1847, in Gloucester, Mary Ann Norris, dau. of George and Mary (Jones) Norris, b. March 11, 1827, in Gloucester.

John Frye Foster followed the sea for twenty-one years, going around the world seven times as mate of ships; his last voyage was as sailing master, reaching home in May, 1862. He served during the war of the Rebellion in the Union army, having, as shown by the official records, enlisted Aug. 11, 1862, in Company F, Thirty-fifth Regiment, Massachusetts Volunteer Infantry; was mustered into the service of the United States Aug. 19, 1862, for three years, and discharged March 12, 1863. He was promoted to Corporal in the Color Guard December 11, and lost his right arm at Fredericksburg, Va., Dec. 13, 1862. He wrote, some years before his death, the following account of his army experience: "My service in the army was short and sweet, four months in the field and three months in the hospital; put right into battle without any drill. I enlisted Aug. 2 [11], 1862, mustered in Augnst 11th [19], and went in Company F, Thirty-fifth Massachusetts Infantry; left Boston August 20th, and went into battle at South Mountain, Maryland, September 15th, and Antietam September 17th; then started, October 24th, south through Virginia; November 18th our brigade went into camp on the north side of the Rappahannock river, opposite Fredericksburg, under General Burnside, remained there until December 12th, and then crossed the river. On Dec. 13, 1862, at 1 p. m., went into battle on the right, under General Sumner. I was wounded soon after by a piece of shell. So I lost my whole arm, amputation at the shoulder joint. If I had not fallen in good hands, I should not have lived. John A. Hosack, Surgeon of Fifty-first Pennsylvania Regiment, and Colonel Hartruff, fixed it up for me, and it was such a fine job that Surgeon General Barnes wanted to know who did it; but I did not find out until October, 1883, when I went to Gettysburg with the boys, and coming back, stopped in Philadelphia, one day, and went into Post 2, Grand Army of the Republic, and there I found out." He d. Oct. 11, 1887, in Gloucester.

3310. i. MARY ELLA, b. July 15, 1849; d. Dec. 3, 1851.

3311. ii. BENJAMIN HOWARD, b. Aug. 15, 1852; m., Dec. 14, 1876, Lizzie Florence Bass. He d. Jan. 4, 1886. Ch.: 1. Howard Benton, b. Dec. 19, 1877. 2. Marion Ella, b. April 25, 1879. 3. Frederick Reginald, b March 11, 1883.

3312. iii. WILLIAM BENTON, b. May 13, 1856.

3313. iv. JOHN F. ANKLIN, b. March 7, 1858; d. Aug. 25, 1859.

3314. v. JOHN EVERETT, b. Sept. 4, 1860.

3315. vi. GEORGE NORRIS, b. Dec. 8, 1863.

3316. vii. FREDERICK CHICKERING (twin), b. Oct. 7, 1866.

3317. viii. FRANCIS HOMANS (twin), b. Oct. 7, 1866.

2365. SIDNEY MASON FOSTER (Jeremiah, Joseph, Joseph, Jeremiah, John, Reginald, Reginald), b. June 29, 1822; m., July 14, 1849, in Boston, Elizabeth Ann Dean, dau. of Jarvis and Eliza (Tuttle) Dean, of Boston, b. Aug. 18, 1824, in Norton, Mass. Res., Boston. He d. Oct. 12, 1889, in Boston. Children born in Roxbury, now Boston:

3318. i. ELIZABETH GERTRUDE, b. April 12, 1850; m., April 28, 1885, Clarence Lovejoy Marston. Ch.: 1. Gertrude Clare, b. Aug. 29, 1886.

3319. ii. HENRY STEVENS, b. June 16, 1853; d. May 4, 1875.

3320. iii. MARY ELIZA JACKSON, b. March 15, 1856; d. March 15, 1856.

3321. iv. EDWIN Le BETTER, b. June 15, 1861.

3322. v. CHARLOTTE WHITE, b. Aug. 31, 1864; m., Oct. 16, 1890, William G. Cousens.

2370. JEREMIAH FOSTER (Jeremiah, Joseph, Joseph, Jeremiah, John, Reginald, Reginald), b. Oct. 21, 1841; m., July 18, 1871, in Gloucester, Elizabeth K. Clark, dau. of George and Elizabeth K. (Tucker), b. March 8, 1847; d. May 31, 1883; m., 2d, Dec. 29, 1884, Harriet N. Burnham. Jeremiah Foster served during the war of the Rebellion in the Union army, having, as shown by the official records, enlisted Sept. 15, 1862, in Company G, Eighth Regiment, Massachusetts Volunteer Infantry; was mustered into the service of the United States on the same day, for nine months, and discharged as Corporal Aug. 7, 1863, on expiration of service. Res., Gloucester, Mass.

3323. i. GERTRUDE, b. July 16, 1872; d. July 16, 1872.
3324. ii. GEORGE CLARK, b. Aug. 25, 1873.
3325. iii. JOSEPH, b. Nov. 30, 1874; d. April, 1893.
3326. iv. JEREMIAH, b. Sept. 6, 1878.

2373. THOMAS JEFFERSON FOSTER (Thomas J., Joseph, Joseph, Jeremiah, John, Reginald, Reginald), b. Sept. 26, 1833; m., Dec. 25, 1867, in San Francisco, Cal., Ella Amanda Winant, b. Sept. 21, 1844, in Rossville, Staten Island, N. Y. She d. June 21, 1886. Res., San Francisco, Cal.; Yaquina, Yaquina Bay, Oregon; and in 1887, Alameda, Cal.

3327. i. MABEL FLORENCE, b. Sept. 24, 1868, in San Francisco, Cal.
3328. ii. THOMAS JEFFERSON, b. Dec. 31, 1870, in Oakland, Cal.
3329. iii. KATE PATRICK, b. Oct. 16, 1872, in Oakland, Cal.
3330. iv. FREDERICK BENEDICT, b. April 13, 1875, in Oakland, Cal.

2384. ALDEN BRADFORD FOSTER (Thomas, Thomas, Aaron, Moses, John, Reginald, Reginald), b. Essex, Mass., March 29, 1834; m., 1st, Mary Frances Murch; m., 2d, E. Boston, Nov. 2, 1867, Celeste Helena Morse, b. Nov. 21, 1847.

Alden Bradford Foster was of a delicate constitution, though he lived the average length of years. He was a painstaking student, a careful business man, exemplary in habit and in life. He married early in life Miss Mary Frances Murch, and a little later they migrated to California, where after giving birth to two children his wife died of consumption. The shock of his loss so unmanned him that he returned to his old home, E. Boston, taking with him the young son, a boy of six or seven years. The second child, an infant daughter, was left with an aunt, who resided then with her husband. Returning to E. Boston he became clerk in his elder brother's employ, and there remained till his death. Meanwhile he took for a second wife Miss Celeste Morse. By this marriage he had two sons, both bright, intelligent young men. One is named Fred, the other William Foster. His death occurred from a very severe cold, which terminated in la grippe, when he passed away very suddenly. He d. Jan. 26, 1890. Res., California and East Boston, Mass.

3331. i. FREDERICK ALDEN, b. Dec. 18, 1869; m. Jennie McLaren.
3332. ii. CHARLES EDWARD, b. Aug. 11. 1858; m. Mary Lynch.
3333. iii. LUCRETIA, b. ——. On the death of her mother she was adopted by a Mr. Gilman M. Burnham. Res., San Francisco.
3334. iv. WILLIAM EMERY, b. May 26, 1874; m., June 24, 1896, in Maryland, Nancy Eugenie Sparklin, b. Sept. 20, 1876. He is a clerk in the First Ward National Bank. Res., 223 Trenton St., E. B.

2385. THOMAS AUGUSTUS FOSTER (Thomas, Thomas, Aaron, Moses, John, Reginald, Reginald), b. Charlestown, Mass., September, 1823; m. —— Judith Judkins, of Franklin, N. H. She resides with her one child, Mrs. C.

Thomas Augustus Foster was born in Charlestown. He died through an accident on a steam tug, in Boston Harbor, June 1, 1872. He was a builder, contractor of ships, etc., with large works at E. Boston, under firm name of Foster & Leighton. A man highly respected in business, etc., intelligent and upright in character; a prominent Mason; a true husband and father, son and brother.

Mary M. Foster, of Boston, appointed administratrix of estate of Thomas A. Foster, of Boston, died June 1, 1872, leaving a widow, Judith R. Foster, next of kin being Mary M. Foster, daughter, and Florence F. Crosby, of Boston, granddaughter, a minor. June 10, 1872. Lib. 457, fol. 412. Inventory, Alden B. Foster, one of appraisors. Lib. 457, fol. 688. Lib. 459, fol 665. Lib. 471, fol. 604. He d. June 1, 1872. Res., Boston, Mass.

3335. i. FLORENCE F., b. ——; m. William A. Crosby, of Wilmington, Del. She d., leaving Florence F.
3336. ii. MARY M., b. ——, m. William A. Crosby.
3337. iii. ——, b. ——; d. in infancy.

2407. JOHN W. FOSTER (William S., Zebulon, Aaron, Moses, John, Reginald, Reginald), b. Antrim, N. H., 1837; m., in 1862, Hannah E. Hunt, of Newton, N. J.; settled in Clinton Villiage where he was engaged in the manufacture of bedsteads. He was a young man of excellent character and unusual promise. He d. in the prime of life and deeply mourned. He d. April 13, 1868. Res., Clinton Village, N. J.

3338. i. HARRIETT A., b. Feb. 27, 1863.
3339. ii. EMMA J., b. Aug. 2, 1866.
3340. iii. WILLIAM S., b. March 20, 1868.

2411. JACOB RICE FOSTER (Jeremiah, Zebulon, Aaron, Moses, John, Reginald, Reginald), b. Henniker, N. H., Feb. 4, 1834; m., April 30, 1867, Georgie Nash, of Great Falls, who died, and he married second wife October, 1874, Mary Nash. Resides now in Fryeburg, Me.; machinist and manufacturer of shoe pegs; an excellent musician; several years an artist of much merit in photographic pictures. Res., Henniker, N. H., and Fryeburg, Me.
3341. i. EDWIN J., b. March 19, 1868.
3342. ii. GEORGE R., b. May 11, 1869.
3343. iii. HELEN MAY, b. in Concord, Dec. 7, 1871.
3344. iv. ADALINE R., b. in Andover, April 15, 1875.

2424. DR. HORACE KENDALL FOSTER (John P., Charles, Jonathan, Jonathan, Jonathan, William, Reginald), b. North Andover, Mass., Dec. 5, 1854; m., Dec. 19, 1889, Florence K. Holman, b. April 13, 1856. He is the fifth child of John P. and Sarah A. Foster; was educated in the Common Schools of North Andover; graduated from the High School of the same town in 1871; worked on the farm a year; fitted for College at Phillip Academy, Andover, and entered Dartmouth College in 1875, and graduated in 1879; studied medicine in Dartmouth Medical College, and graduated in 1882; took post graduate courses in New York for one year, and then located in the general practice of medicine in Peabody, Mass., in 1883, and has been there since that time. Since his stay there has served four years upon the school board; is Medical Examiner of the Eight Massachusetts District, and has just been elected President of the Essex District of Massachusetts Medical Society, and is a member of Massachusetts Medico Legal Society. Res., Peabody, Mass.
3345. i. KENDALL PEABODY, b. Jan. 10, 1891.
3346. ii. CHANDLER HUNTING, b. April 4, 1893.
3347. iii. RACHEL, b Dec. 26, 1895.

2434. JONATHAN MYRON FOSTER (George N., Jonathan, Jonathan, Jonathan, Jonathan, William, Reginald), b. Bradford, Mass., Sept. 18, 1847; m., Lawrence, May 6, 1869, Eulalie Victoria Benlier Lapeaele, b. Jan. 27, 1849.

Jonathan Myron Foster, b. Bradford, Mass., Sept. 18, 1847; soon after moved to Georgetown, Mass., on farm, when six years of age; 1853 attended school in West Boxford, Mass., his grandfather's district, No. 5—called Sodam District at his death; 1856 sent to Georgetown school, Spofford's Hill District; went there six years; then, 1863, one term to High School in village; then learned shoemaker's trade and worked at that and farming until February, 1865; then enlisted (Georgetown quota); assigned to Company A, First Battalion Heavy Artillery Massachusetts Volunteers; stationed at Fort Warren, Boston Harbor, Massachusetts; discharged Oct. 20, 1865—expiration of war; following winter (1866) attended Comeis Commercial College, Boston; then spring at home; summer in store in Boston; then fall shoemaking in Lynn; then winter (1867) in grocery store in Lynn; then one year with Davis & Fruber machine shop, North Andover Depot, Mass.; then (1868) with Atlantic Cotton Mills, Lawrence, Mass., five years (1868 to 1873), as bobbin boy, loom fixer and second hand; then six years (1873 to 1879) with Pacific Mills, Lawrence, as loom fixer; then six and a half years (1879 to 1885) with Peabody Mills, Newburyport, Mass., as overseer of weaving; then about two years (1885 to 1887) with Jos. Bancroft & Sons, of Rockford, near Wilmington, Del., as manager of their cotton mill; then four years (1887 to 1891) again with the Pacific Mills, Lawrence, Mass., as overseer of weaving; then with the Boston Manufacturing Company, of Waltham, Mass., six years and two months, from June, 1891 to September, 1897, as overseer of all their weaving. Now, from last fall overseer of cloth room of Hamilton Manufacturing Company, Lowell, Mass. May 9th expect to go to New Orleans, La., as overseer of weaving for the Maginnis Cotton Mills of that city. While in Newburyport owned yacht and belonged to American Yacht Club of that city, also member of Grand Army of the Republic, and a member of Isaac Parker Lodge of Free Masons, in Waltham, Mass. Res., Lowell, Mass., 201 Middlesex St.
3348. i. GUY WILLIAM, b. May 9, 1872; d. Sept. 9, 1897.

2435. JOHN HARROD FOSTER (William H., Phinehas, Jonathan, Jonathan, Jonathan, William, Reginald), b. April 27, 1847, Dorchester, Mass., m., Dec. 12, 1872, Mary Gardner Churchill, b. April 4, 1847. He is the manager for the State of

Maryland for the Sun Life Insurance Company, of Canada. Res., Baltimore, Md., 46 Bank of Baltimore Building.

3349. i. JOHN HARROD, JR., b. Sept. 20, 1875.
3350. ii. REGINALD, b. July 15, 1881.
3351. iii. HELEN MASON, b. Jan. 11, 1880; d. May 2, 1884.

2437. CHARLES FOSTER (William H., Phinehas, Jonathan, Jonathan, Jonathan, William, Reginald), b. March 6, 1850, Dorchester, Mass.; m., in Taunton, Dec. 10, 1884, Elizabeth Yonge Andros, b. June 12, 1852. Res., East Norton, Mass.

3352. i. ELIZABETH ANDROS, b. in Taunton, Mass., Sept. 20, 1885.
3353. ii. RICHARD ANDROS, b. in Taunton, Mass., Nov. 18, 1887.
3354. iii. GOODWIN LEBARON, b. in Calcutta, E. I., June 4, 1891.
3355. iv. SYBIL, b. in Calcutta, E. I., Nov. 30, 1892.

2439. JOSEPH LOCKE FOSTER (William H., Phinehas, Jonathan, Jonathan, Jonathan, William, Reginald), b. Dorchester, Mass., Nov. 14, 1853; m. at Hingham, Oct. 8, 1878, Elizabeth Luther Harlow, of H., b. Oct. 26, 1855. Cashier Atlas National Bank. Res., Newton Centre, Mass., 147 Lake Ave.

3356. i. MARGARET HARLOW, b. Aug. 9, 1881.

2452. THOMAS JEFFERSON FOSTER (Nathan, Asa, Abner, Zebediah, Jonathan, William, Reginald), b. Bethel, Me., Oct. 8, 1824; m., Gorham, N. H., Feb. 8, 1855, Nan C. Bennett, b. Aug. 28, 1829. He is a farmer. Res., Bethel, Me.

3357. i. ANDREW J., b. July 14, 1858; d. ——.
3358. ii. HATTIE L., b. Dec. 12, 1861.

2453. REUBEN BALL FOSTER (Nathan, Asa, Abner, Zebediah, Jonathan, William, Reginald), b. Bethel, Me., July 25, 1826; m., in 1850, Salome G. Eames, b. Oct. 13, 1830. She resides 768 Main St., Waltham, Mass. Wholesale merchant. He d. July 29, 1892. Res , Boston, Mass.

3359. i. FRANCELLA AMANDA, b. May 7, 1851; d. August, 1855.
3360. ii. LILLIAN AUGUSTA, b. Jan. 3, 1858; d. July, 1860.
3361. iii. GRACE MAY, b. Sept. 1, 1865; m., Feb. 11, 1885, Frank Bigelow Reynolds. Res., 76 Adelaide Ave., Providence, R. I.
3362. iv. CAROLYN SALOME, b. July 17, 1867; m., Jan. 14, 1892, Joseph Stickney. Res., 42 W. Fifty-seventh St., New York, N. Y.

2454. HON. REUBEN B. FOSTER (Reuben B., Asa, Abner, Zebediah, Jonathan, William, Reginald), b. Feb. 8, 1833; m., ——, Dorcas Howe, of Hanover. Res., Waterville, Me.

2466. ORRIN FOSTER (Enoch, Asa, Abner, Zebediah, Jonathan, William, Reginald), b. Bethel, Me., May 27, 1827; m., Sept. 16, 1849, Mary O. Styles, b. May 21, 18—.

Bears have sometimes been very troublesome to the farmers of Bethel, by killing their sheep, robbing the bee-hives and raiding the corn-fields, but rarely has human life been endangered by them. A young man in the adjoining town of Newry had a thrilling adventure, an account of which is well worth preserving. It was in the year 1846, on the 16th day of September, that Orrin, son of Enoch Foster, a boy of about sixteen years of age, was sent by his father to look up some cattle which had strayed away from the mountain pasture into the woods. His route took him up the side of Puzzle Mountain, through pasture and forest, and when about two miles from home, he came across a path, which led to a brook. Thinking he had found the trail of the lost cattle, he pressed on, and soon heard the sound of some animal in the bushes near by, and going toward the point from which the sound seemed to proceed, he was surprised and alarmed at the appearance of a huge bear, which, with eyes flashing fire and gnashing teeth, sprang toward him from a thicket not three rods away. Foster tried to encourage a small dog, which accompanied him, to attack the monster, but he cowardly shrunk away and hid himself in the bushes. Foster then turned and went about two rods to a sapling beech, which was the only tree in the vicinity, and which was about seven inches in diameter at the ground. The body of the tree was smooth, and the lower limbs were about eight feet from the ground. The bear, with jaws distended, and eyes glowing like fire, was close upon him, and his only chance was in being able to climb the tree. He sprang with all his strength, and tried to grasp the lower limbs, but failed, but he seized the trunk of the tree with both his hands and drew his fee up. The bear, comprehending his intentions, sprang after him, but happily falling a little short of his aim, he struck at the root of the tree. Foster succeeded in reaching the limbs, and as the bear recovered, he again sprang and raked Foster's foot as he was drawing himself into the branches. He came very near drawing Foster down, but with all his strength he broke away and ascended the tree, with the bear in close pursuit. He went up nearly thirty feet from the ground, where the tree was so small that he could easily clasp it in his hands, and the bear, foaming with rage and disappointment, was about four feet below him. The tree began to bend under the great weight, and Foster tried to balance it, but the bear kept slowly advancing. In this moment of extreme peril it occurred to Foster to try and shake his pursuer from the tree. Securing his hold with a vice-like clutch, and with all his strength, quickened and increased by the fear of a horrible death, he shook the tree, and the bear being unable to sustain his weight on the under side, fell to the ground. His fall of twenty-five feet momentarily stunned him, but he soon sprang up and made several unsuccessful efforts to re-climb the tree, but each time fell back. While bruin was trying to climb up a second time, Foster was not idle. Taking out his jack-knife, he descended the tree a short distance, and cut off a large limb, about five feet long, which he whittled to a point at one end, intending to make an attempt at the bear's eyes, should he succeed in re-climbing the tree. Being foiled in his attempts at climbing, he watched Foster's motions for a few moments, and then went for the dog. But the dog was not pleased with bruin's attentions and kept himself at a safe distance from his bearship, and finally left for home. The bear then returned to the foot of the tree and vented his anger in dismal howls and in gnashing his teeth. He would then follow the cattle path for twenty rods or more, and then return to the tree, thinking, probably, that Foster had availed himself of his absence and had descended from the tree. He tried this ruse again and again, but at last he became discouraged at the prospect of an evening meal in this direction, and about sunset, with a howl that seemed to shake the mountain and reverberate through its dark ravines and caverns, he slowly retired. When Foster rushed against the beech, he bruised his stomach, and after the immediate danger from the bear had passed, his chest began to pain him severely, and he found it was badly swollen. He was without coat, and exposed on the north side of a mountain to the chilly blasts of an autumn night. He also began to suffer from hunger and thirst, having neither ate nor drank since morning. His hands and feet were badly swollen by holding on to the tree, and the blood rushed to his head and throat, so as to almost produce delirium. He had called for assistance until his voice had failed him, and after the bear left him he did not dare to leave the tree, fearing the monster might still be lurking near, ready to pounce upon him. This occurred on Sunday, and his parents had attended religious services at some distance from home and had stopped with a friend to take tea. Returning at night, they found the dog had returned without his master, and from his uneasiness they felt certain that Orrin had met with some accident and was detained on the mountains.

The news quickly spread through the neighborhood, and some twenty persons assembled with lanterns and tin trumpets, and with lighted torches. Dividing into small squads, they ascended the mountain, blowing their trumpets and building bonfires, to much of which young Foster, from his elevated perch in the tree-top, was a silent spectator. But he was so debilitated that he could neither go down from the tree nor make himself heard. It was eleven o'clock when three persons approached the tree, and among them he recognized the voice of his father. The hour of deliverance had come, and he was soon in the midst of his friends. After having his limbs chafed for awhile, he was able, with the assistance which he received, to descend the mountain and reach his home, but it was more than a year before he was able to perform much labor. To him his deliverance was like a renewal of life. While the hungry bear was exerting all his strength to reach him, he expected to be torn in pieces, and when the monster left him, death still seemed to hover near him in the fearful forms of cold, hunger and exhaustion. While in the tree, when hope had nearly abandoned him, Foster started the blood from his arm with the point of his knife, and with a pointed stick as a pen, and the blood as writing fluid, he inscribed upon his pocket handkerchief the words, "Killed by a bear," and then tied the handkerchief to the tree, that should he never return, his friends might learn of his terrible fate. Res., Bethel, Me.

3363. i. LUELLA LARON, b. July 8, 1850; m., Dec. 24, 1868, Edward F. Philbrook. She d. in Chicago, May 17, 1876.

3364. ii. CLIFTON O., b. June 21, 1857; d. Aug. 10, 1862.

3365. iii. EGLINA F., b. Jan. 29, 1859; m., Feb. 8, 1877, Everett Hammas. Res., Anoka, Minn.
3366. iv. PERSIS, b. April 14, 1860.
3367. v. MAY INEZ, b. Nov. 30, 1861; m., Sept. 14, 1881, William Williamson. Res., 2359 Calumet Ave., Chicago, Ill.
3368. vi. CLIFTON O., b. Nov. 26, 1864; m., Dec. 25, 1889.
3369. vii. WALTER ALMONT, b. Oct. 4, 1870; m., Sept. 10, 1892, Alma G. Walker.

2468. HON. ENOCH FOSTER (Enoch, Asa, Abner, Zebediah, Jonathan, William, Reginald), b. Newry, Me., May 10, 1839; m., Waterville, Me., June 9, 1864, Adaline Owen Lowe, of W., dau. of Ivory and Jane (Walker). She b. Nov. 10, 1842; d. June 13, 1872; m., 2d, June 3, 1873, Sarah Walker Chapman, dau. of Robert A. and Frances (Carter), b. Feb. 1, 1844.

Hon. Enoch Foster, son of Enoch and Persis (Swan) Foster, was born in Newry, Me., May 10, 1839. He spent his boyhood days upon his father's farm; attended the town schools, subsequently attended Gould's Academy, and at the Maine State Seminary. He pursued a partial course at Bowdoin College; studied law in the office of Hon. Reuben Foster, at Watervi le; graduated from the Law School at Albany, N. Y., and having been admitted to the Oxford bar, he commenced practice at Bethel, in 1865. After the breaking out of the war of the Rebellion he enlisted and was mustered into the United States service as Second Lieutenant of Company H, Thirteenth Maine Regiment, Dec. 13, 1861. He was subsequently promoted to First Lieutenant; served as Provost Marshal under General Banks, and resigned that position to take part in the Red River campaign. He was discharged from the service March 11, 1865, his term of enlistment having expired.

In the practice of law Mr. Foster was successful from the start, and soon held an enviable position at the Oxford County bar. A close student, a fluent and eloquent advocate, and added to this, a love of his profession, could not fail of bringing him prominently before the public in a short time. He was elected attorney for the State for the county of Oxford, and served two full terms of three years each, ending Jan. 1, 1874. The same year he was elected member of the State Senate, and re-elected the following year. March 24, 1884, he was appointed by Governor Robie an Associate Justice of the Supreme Judicial Court of the State of Maine, and reappointed by Governor Burleigh in 1891. As a member of the highest judicial tribunal of the State, he has taken high rank, and his decisions in law in nisi prius have rarely been overruled by the full court. His opinions from that court are clearly and succinctly drawn, are good examples of condensed, yet comprehensive composition. Res., Bethel, Me.

3370. i. JOHN DORR, b. Aug. 15, 1866; d. April 2, 1872.
3371. ii. ROBERT CHAPMAN, b. April 19, 1880.

2471. DAVID TRICKEY FOSTER (Eli, Asa, Abner, Zebediah, Jonathan, William, Reginald), b. Bethel, Me., Sept. 5, 1831; m., April 2, 1852, Harriet B. Crockett, dau. of Daniel H. and Rebecca (Bacon). He lives on the homestead of his father. Is a good farmer, an honest and upright man and highly esteemed by the people of his town. The fine mansion erected by his father was destroyed by fire in July, 1891, with nearly all its contents. Res., Bethel, Me.

3372. i. STEPHEN H., b. Dec. 27, 1858; m., Sept. 21, 1890, Ella J. Bartlett. Res., B.
3373. ii. M. ETTA, b. Jan. 11, 1861; d. same month.
3374. iii. SUSIE HELEN, b. Nov. 24, 1864; m. ——, Azel B. Bryant.
3375. iv. DANIEL C., b. July 24, 1867.
3376. v. DAVID FOSTER, b. Dec. 28, 1872.
3377. vi. HATTIE MAY, b. May 9, 1877.

2476. LAFAYETTE STEPHEN FOSTER (Elhanam B., Asa, Abner, Zebediah, Jonathan, William, Reginald), b. Newry, Me., May 15, 1855; m., in Newry, Mary Etta Glovar. He is a provision dealer. Res., Presque Isle, Me.

3378. i. EVA F., b. Nov. 18, 1883.
3379. ii. EARL LAFAYETTE, b. March 18, 1887.

2479. JOHN CHARLES FOSTER (William P., William, William, John, William, William, Reginald), b. Feb. 7, 1859; m., September, 1889, Katherine Virginia Van Doren, of Virginia, b. Sept. 25, 1860. Res., Oakland, Cal., 1122 Magnolia St., s. p.

2481. FRANCIS HOMER FOSTER (William P., William, William, John, William, William, Reginald), b. Andover, Mass., April 7, 1867; m., Haverhill, Oct. 16, 1895, Mary Jackson Sweet, b. June 13, 1870. Civil engineer. Res., Andover, Mass.

3380. i. WILLIAM PHILLIPS, b. Oct. 1, 1897.

2482. JOHN W. FOSTER (John, John, John, John, William, William, Reginald), b. Andover, Mass., March 11, 1840; m., Lawrence, Jan. 1, 1864, Mercy F. Gilman, b. May 20, 1842. Was an upholsterer. He d. March 1, 1886. Res., Lawrence, Mass.

3381. i. NEWELL H., b. Sept. 22, 1868.
3382. ii. ERNEST G., b. Sept. 25, 1873; d. July 5, 1875.
3383. iii. GRACIE L., b. Dec. 4, 1877; d. Feb. 15, 1878.
3384. iv. HARRIE Y., b. Dec. 4, 1877.
3385. v. HERBERT W., b. June 17, 1866; m., June 17, 1896, Nellie F. Norris, b. March 28, 1866. Is a painter and decorator. Res., s. p., Washington Ave., Andover, Mass.

2492. JOHN WILLIAM FOSTER (William P., John, John, John, William, William, Reginald), b. New Durham, N. H., Aug. 25, 1854; m., Exeter N. H., May 16, 1880 Marguerette Hussey, b. Aug. 7, 1858. He is a mechanic. Res.,71 Broadway, Methuen, Mass.

3386 i. MABEL FRANCES, b. March 11, 1881. Res., 488 Columbus Ave., Boston.
3387. ii. FRED EDGAR, b. Aug. 27, 1884. Res., Columbus Ave., Boston, Mass.

2493. FRED FOSTER (William P., John, John, John, William, William, Reginald), b. July 15, 1859; m. —— ——. He d. Aug. 26, 1893. Res., Methuen, Mass.

3388. i. WILLIAM FRANCIS, b. ——. Res., M.

2501. JOHN FOSTER (George, John, Obadiah, John, William, William, Reginald), b. March 5, 1852, Warner, N. H.; m., Manchester, Feb. 18, 1881; M. Lizzie McCrillis, b. June 5, 1856. Lawyer. Res., s. p., Manchester, N. H.

2503. GEORGE SANFORD FOSTER (George, John, Obadiah, John, William, William, Reginald), b. Warner, N. H., July 8, 1857; m., Sept. 23, 1879, Etta Frances Moulton, b. Salmon Falls, N. H. Lumber dealer. He d. Aug. 13, 1882. Res., Bedford, N. H.

3389. i. GEORGE SANFORD, b. April 20, 1882.
3390. ii. ETHEL DEANE, b. Feb. 10, 1881; m. —— Ellis. Res., Magog, Quebec.

2504. CHARLES ELIPHALET FOSTER (George, John, Obadiah, John, William, William, Reginald), b. N. Weare, N. H., June 12, 1860; m., Manchester. Aug. 24, 1892, Bertha June Cheney, b. June 10, 1861. Farmer. Res., Manchester, N. H., 2004 Elm St.

3391. i. ELECTA LITTLE, b. May 20, 1896.
3392. ii. CHARLES R., b. Oct. 17, 1897.

2505. HERMAN FOSTER (George, John, Obadiah, John, William, William, Reginald), b. Aug. 3, 1863; m., Feb. 9, 1888, Nancy Emma Barr, b. Dec. 21, 1862; d. Dec. 21, 1892; m., 2d, Aug. 3, 1898, Mary Almeda Woolsey, b. July 31, 1871.

Herman Foster, fifth son and seventh child of Salome F. Little and George Foster, was born in Weare, N. H. Five years later his father moved to Bedford, three miles from the city of Manchester. Here in a little red school-house the younger children received their early education. Later on he entered the Manchester schools, pursuing a classical course with the intention of entering college. These hopes, however, were not to be realized, for by the death of his father, in 1881, the care of the homestead was thrown upon the three younger children. In connection with this Mr. Foster carried on an extensive milk business and a small wood and lumber business. He married Nancy Emma Barr, second daughter and fourth child of Lucy Whitford and David Barr, of Bedford. He, with his brother Charles and sister Mary, remained on the homestead, caring for their mother, whose health was in a gradual decline. On the 14th of December following, a son,

George Reginald, was born. Mrs. Foster unfortunately inherited a predisposition to consumption, and her health began to fail rapidly. In August, 1892, Mr. Foster sold out his business and hurriedly left for Denver, Col., with his wife and children. The change in climate seemed at first beneficial, but she soon again began to fail rapidly, her death occurring on her thirtieth birthday anniversary.

HERMAN FOSTER.

Returning to Bedford her death was followed by the death of Lucy Salome. Undismayed by these disappointments and trials, he struck out against the advice of friends for a wider field. He entered Emerson College of Oratory, Boston, Mass., from which he was graduated with honor in 1896. In the following October he entered the Law School of Boston University, where he is continuing his study of law in connection with a real estate business recently opened.

On Aug. 3, 1898, he was married to Miss Mary A. Woolsey, eldest daughter of Minerva Wilson and John D. Woolsey, of Livingston Manor, N. Y., and related to the late President Theodore Dwight Woolsey, of Yale College. Miss Woolsey was a classmate of Mr. Foster at Emerson College and a teacher of ability and experience.

Possessed of some means, Mr. Foster shows some excellent business qualities. Slow to reach conclusions, his judgment when formed is sound and accurate. He is broad and liberal in his views, active and aggressive in his policy. His impartial and unbiased actions show an appreciation of what is right and noble, while his sense of honor and justice deprecates and despises that which is debasing and wrong. He has a wide circle of friends, both in the commercial and social world, who wish him the success which he assuredly merits. Mr. and Mrs. Foster's residence is in an attractive and pleasant part of Boston, which will be their future home. Res., Everett, Mass., and 140 St. Botolph St., Boston.

GEORGE REGINALD FOSTER.

3393. i. GEORGE REGINALD, b. Dec. 14, 1888.

3394. ii. LUCY SALOME b Sept. 21, 1890; d. April 26, 1893.

2509 FREDERICK FOSTER (James F., Gideon, Obadiah, John William, William, Reginald), b. Boston, Mass., Dec. 15, 1833; m., Oct. 13, 1863, Margaret R. Todd, b. Oct. 13, 1842. Retired. Res., Elizabeth, N. J. [illegible]

3395. i. WILLIAM HENRY, b. July 23, 1864; m., Dec. 17, 1888, Katharine W. Davis. Res., Elizabeth, N. J.
3396. ii. FREDERIC LAWRENCE, b. March 9, 1868. Res., Elizabeth, N. J.
3397. iii. LOUISE HARTMAN, b. Feb. 4, 1870. Res., Kingston, N. Y.
3398. iv. CAROLINE TODD, b. June 21, 1874. Res., Elizabeth, N. J.
3399. v. HERBERT HASTINGS, b. Feb. 12, 1877. Res., Elizabeth, N. J.
3400. vi. JESSIE HALL, b. Dec. 25, 1880. Res., Elizabeth, N. J.
3401. vii. MARGARET, b. March 3, 1881, Elizabeth, N. J.; d. Jan. 15, 1883.

2510. HENRY JACKSON FOSTER (James F., Gideon, Obadiah, John, William, William, Reginald), b. Feb. 29, 1836, Boston, Mass.; m., Brooklyn, N. Y., Dec. 13, 1866, Susan Augusta Plummer. She is now in Elko, Nev.

Henry Jackson Foster, son of James Frederick and Caroline Dorthwait Foster, was born in Boston, Mass. In his early manhood he removed to New York and was in the employ of the Metropolitan Bank till the breaking out of the war of the Rebellion; when a member of the Seventh Regiment New York State National Guards, he left for Washington, D. C., with that command; in April, 1861, having served that term of enlistment as Adjutant of the One Hundred and Thirty-third New York State Volunteers; he served for three years, mostly in the Department of the Gulf. During this period he was for nine months Provost Marshal of the Province of La Fouche, La. I think he was also on the staff of General Banks, and again of General Bowen.

Mrs. Foster's first maternal ancestor in this country was William White, born in Norfolk county, England, 1610; landed at Ipswich, Mass., 1635. It will be interesting to know that "he married, second, Sept. 21, 1682, Sarah Foster, the widow and second wife of Reginald Foster, who settled in Ipswich, Mass., about 1638. [See Gen. William White.] Her first paternal ancestor was Francis Plummer, who was one of the first settlers of Newbury, Mass., about 1633. He was one of the first settlers and was one of the grantees of the Indian deed of Haverhill, dated Nov. 15, 1642, which instrument was, it is said, both written and witnessed by him." Res., New York, N. Y., Carlton House.

3402. i. PHILIP PLUMMER, b. Oct. 3, 1871, in Brooklyn, N. Y.; unm. Res., Spokane, Wash. He was born in Brooklyn, N. Y., at the home of his grandfather, John Lincoln Plummer. His early years were spent in North Adams, Mass., and later he attended Phillips Academy, Andover, Mass. After a short business experience in New York he began in 1891 his business life in the then new settlement of Everett, on Puget Sound, Wash. In 1896 he removed to Spokane, Wash., where he is now engaged in business.

3403. ii. ELIZABETH PLUMMER, b. Dec. 30, 1868; m., April 30, 1895, George Samson Brown. Res., Elko, Nev., son of Rev. Thomas Edwin Brown, D. D. Ch.: 1. Philip Foster, b. Dec. 7, 1896.

George Samson Brown, son of the late Rev. Thomas Edwin Brown, D. D., a Baptist clergyman, and Elizabeth Campbell Samson, was born November 26, 1865, in Brooklyn, N. Y.; was graduated at Brown university, class of 1888; studied law at Columbia law school and was admitted to the New York State bar May 15, 1890. In the same year he went to the State of Washington, where he practiced his profession at Everett and Tacoma. In the spring of 1897 he accepted the legal charge of some mining companies, operating in the vicinity of Elko, Nev., where he now resides.

2518. THEODORE DEXTER FOSTER (Francis, Gideon, Obadiah, John, William, William, Reginald), b. Lynn, Mass., May 4, 1852; m., Cambridge, Mass., June 15, 1881, Mary Ella Littlefield, b. April 6, 1855; stationer, at 168 Devonshire street. Res., Cambridge, Mass.

3404. i. HARRY LITTLEFIELD, b. March 6, 1883.
3405. ii. FRANCIS LEON, b. Aug. 11, 1887.

2521. CHARLES THOMAS FOSTER (Francis, Gideon, Obadiah, John, William, William, Reginald), b. Memphis, Tenn., Jan. 20, 1862; m., Nov. 15, 1887, Fanny Sprague. Res., South Weymouth, Mass.

3406. i. PAULINE, b. May 1, 1892.

2523. EDWARD CLARK FOSTER (William, Solomon, Solomon, John, William, William, Reginald), b. April 7, 1852, Lincoln, Mass.; m., April 19, 1886, Helen Pierce, b. Dec. 30, 1849. Edward C., of Lincoln, letter date, March 12, 1895; ex. April 13, 1895; wife, Helen P.; children, Percival H., minor.—Middlesex Probate. He d. Feb. 25, 1895. Res., Lincoln, Mass.

3407. i. PERCIVAL HOAR, b. Jan. 24, 1889.

2529. ASA EASTMAN FOSTER (Adams, Asa, Asa, Asa, William, William, Reginald), b. May 31, 1841; m., May 30, 1873, at Reno, Nev., Sophia Steele. He d. Jan. 28, 1887. Res., Reno, Nev.

3408. i. SARAH E., b. Feb. 23, 1874; m., Dec. 10, 1893, O. M. Harshbarger. Res., Reno, Nev. Ch.: Asa Foster, b. Sept. 23, 1894.

3409. ii. LUCY, b. April 30, 1876.

2532. DR. EDWARD HORATIO FOSTER (David M., Asa, Asa, Asa, William, William, Reginald), b. Canterbury, N. H., Oct. 13, 1839; m., July 12, 1872, Ella M. Merrill, d. 1876; m. 2d, Oct., 1879, Blanche Smith. He was graduated at medical college and was a practicing physician. He d. in 1897. Res., Concord, N. H.

3410. i. EDWARD LORD, b. May 21, 1873.

3411. ii. REGINALD SMITH, b. ——, 1880.

3412. iii. CLARA, b. ——.

2535. DR. NEWELL KELLEY FOSTER (David M., Asa, Asa, Asa William, William, Reginald), b. Canterbury, N. H., April 10, 1849; m., Dryden, N. Y., Feb. 3, 1875, Jennie Smiley, b. Sept. 13, 1851; d. July 23, 1893; m. 2d, Oakland, Cal., Jan. 15, 1895, Maude A. W. Camp, b. Dec. 8, 1870. He was graduated at Cornell in 1873 and at Long Island Hospital in 1878. Res., Oakland, Cal.

3413. i. HENRY EMERSON, b. Aug. 18, 1881.

3414. ii. RUTH MAUDE, b. July 26, 1896.

2536. LEROY ALLISON FOSTER (Newell A., Asa, Asa, Asa, William, William, Reginald), b. Portland, Maine, March 13, 1843; m., Worcester, Massachusetts, August 25, 1874, Emma Eastman, b. March 15, 1850. He began his college life at Wesleyan College, Middletown, Conn. Later he was at Ann Arbor, Mich., whence he was recalled by his father's death.—In 1870 he entered Cornell university in its first class and graduated there in 1872. He then became business manager of the Portland Press, having inherited one-third interest in that paper. He remained in this position till about a year before his death; he then sold out, and his health being poor, went to Colorado, thinking to go into cattle raising, and died there. He d. Denver, Col., March 29, 1882. Res., Portland, Me., and 65 Mason street, Worcester, Mass.

3415. i. CLIFFORD HALL, b. Aug. 29, 1877; unm. Res., Worcester, Mass.

3416. ii. CORNELIA CHASE, b. May 5, 1879.

2555. ABIEL ABBOTT FOSTER (Abiel, Abiel, Abiel, Asa, William, William, Reginald), b. Columbus, Ohio, Sept. 30, 1836; m., Greenville, S. C., Nov., 1868 Julia Amelia Worthington, b. March, 1836; d. Feb. 30, 1873; m. 2d, May, 1875, Mrs. Ella Eliza (Fuller) McCouts, b. Dec., 1848. He is a merchant. Res., Spartanburg, S. C.

3417. i. KATE WORTHINGTON, b. Oct. 18, 1869.

3418. ii. LEWIS WORTHINGTON, b. Feb. 22, 1873.

3419. iii. JULIA AMELIA, b. Feb. 22, 1873.

3420. iv. ALFRED FULLER, b. April 7, 1876.

3421. v. HELEN ELIZABETH, b. July 15, 1880.

3422. vi. MARY ROGERS, b. Feb. 1, 1887.

3423. vii. EDITH ROSALIE, b. June 11, 1893.

3424. viii. MABEL FLORA, b. Feb. 27, 1878; d. Nov. 2, 1880.

3425. ix. DAVID JUDD, b. Jan. 14, 1884; d. Dec. 21, 1884.

2560. CAPT. ALFRED H. FOSTER (Joseph, Abiel, Abiel, Asa, William, William, Reginald), b. Union county, S. C., Dec. 7, 1835; m., in Union, Aug. 31, 1876, Hettie V. Brandon, b. March 4, 1850. Alfred H. Foster was born in Union county, S. C.; received his education in Spartanburg Male Academy; went into the store of Foster & Judd when quite a boy; remained there until the beginning of the civil war; volunteered in the Fifth South Carolina regt. April 13, 1861, transferred to Confederate service in June, 1861, when he was elected captain of his company. He served through the war as captain, the first year in the Fifth South Carolina regt. and the last three years as captain of Co. D, Palmetto sharpshooters, was in the first battle of Bull Run and in all the other important battles of the Army of Northern Virginia, excepting Chancellorsville and Gettysburg; went with Longstreet's command to Tennessee, returning to Virginia in time for the Wilderness campaign. He was in command of his regiment during the retreat from Petersburg to Appomattox. After the war he returned to South Carolina; remained in Spartanburg until the latter part of 1867; went to New York City, remained there in business one year when he came to Union, S. C., which has since been his home. He has been engaged for thirty years, lacking a few months, in the mercantile business, being the head of the firm of Foster & Wilkins, Foster, Wilkins & Co., and A. H. Foster & Co. He married Hettie V. Brandon. They have three daughters. Res., Union, S. C.

CAPT. ALFRED H. FOSTER.

3426. i. ISABEL, b. Aug. 9, 1877.
3427. ii. MARY EMMA, b. June 21, 1880.
3428. iii. H. LOUISE, b. Nov. 16, 1884.

2566. MOSES AUGUSTUS FOSTER (Jonathan B., Jeremiah, Daniel, Asa, William, William, Reginald), b. Canterbury, N. H., Oct. 23, 1843; m. there Oct. 21, 1868, Ruth A. Richardson, b. Aug. 24, 1848. He is a farmer and breeder of blooded stock. Res., Canterbury, N. H.

3429. i. CHARLES THOMAS, b. July 22, 1869; m. Eva Gertrude Hill.
3430. ii. JONATHAN BRADLEY, b. Sept. 6, 1871; m. Fannie W. Osborne.
3431. iii. GEORGE RICHARDSON, b. April 18, 1874; m. Maude M. Perry.
3432. iv. LAURA M., b. Sept. 29, 1875; m., Sept. 6, 1897, —— Federhen; he is a lawyer. Res., 240 Washington street, Quincy, Mass.

2568. DR. JEREMIAH CLOUGH FOSTER (Jonathan B., Jeremiah, Daniel, Asa, William, William, Reginald), b. Canterbury, N. H., Oct. 19, 1840; m., Dec. 25, 1864, Nellie M. Bennett, of Newport, N. H.; d. Dec. 26, 1873; m. 2d, Shrewsbury, Mass., Feb. 26, 1875, Henrietta Brown, b. Worcester, Mass., Aug. 16, 1851. Dr. Jeremiah C. Foster was born in Canterbury, N. H. He graduated from Bowdoin College, Me., as a physician in the year 1866. At the breaking out of the Civil war, in 1861, being two years in college, he enlisted in the Second United States Berdan's sharpshooters and served nearly four years. He was severely wounded in the second battle of Bull Run, being shot through the thigh, which wound always troubled him more or less during his life. He also contracted chronic diarrhoea, which was, after many years of suffering, primarily the cause of his death, ending in consumption of the bowels. After he came home from the war, he returned to college and finished his course and graduated. In referring to his death, the Barre, Mass., paper says: "Dr. J. C. Foster, of Barre, died, aged forty years, and was buried at Shrewsbury, Mass. He was a resident of Shrewsbury several years and then removed to Barre. He was skillful and successful in his profession. During the Rebellion he was an assistant-surgeon in the army. His funeral was held in the M. E. Church, September 26. Six of the G. A. R. post acted as pallbearers, and all of the members were present and acted as escort. A large concourse of people was in attendance. The floral offerings were numerous and beautiful. His death brought sorrow to many homes, where he was loved, both as a physician and a friend. Rarely have we met with a man of so good impulses or of such an unselfish disposition. While in the army, he contracted a disease, from which he has been an almost constant sufferer. By faithfulness and perseverance he had acquired an excellent practice. Every one who knew him well loved him. We have lost a good citizen, a faithful physician and a true friend." He died Barre, Mass., September 24, 1881. Res., Brunswick, Me., and Shrewsbury, Mass.

3433. i. NELLIE CORA, b. March 23, 1866; m., in Newport, N. H., W. E. Whipple. Res., 433 Congress street, Portland, Me.

2573. HENRY L. FOSTER (Franklin, David, David, Asa, William, William, Reginald), b. Boston, Mass., Sept. 26, 1836; m., in Buda, Ill., Oct. 14, 1866, Sarai C. Weston, b. March 6, 1843; d. June 27, 1897; is a farmer. Res., Buda, Ill.

3434. i. HARRIET W., b. Buda, Ill., Aug. 27, 1868.
3435. ii. ARTHUR K., b. Buda, Ill., Aug. 20, 1872; m., Dec. 16, 1897. Res., Buda, Ill.
3436. iii. ALBERT W., b. Buda, Ill., June 25, 1874.

2590. JOSEPH A. FOSTER (Joseph, David, David, Asa, William, William, Reginald), b., Buda, Ill., Feb. 10, 1847; m., July 18, 1870, Cora E. Whiting, b. July 16, 1854. Born near Buda, Bureau County, Ill. He received a common school education; raised on a farm; enlisted at age of 17 in United States volunteer service, and not accepted; went with parents to Marquette, Mich., in fall of 1864; clerked there in drug store until 1869, then went in drug business at Princeton, Ill. Married Cora E. Whiting, of Marquette, Mich.; moved to Marquette, Kan., in 1873, where he has since resided; have four sons and four daughters living; has been engaged in mercantile and drug business; was postmaster for twelve years. Res., Marquette, Kan.

3437. i. FRED M., b. Sept. 22, 1874.
3438. ii. MAUD E., b. Feb. 28, 1876.
3439. iii. MABEL C., b. Oct. 5, 1877.
3440. iv. INEZ L., b. Oct. 20, 1879.
3441. v. LEO A., b. Jan. 4, 1882.
3442. vi. EDDY M., b. May 25, 1887.
3443. vii. JOSEPH H., b. Aug. 7, 1890.
3444. viii. RUTH, b. July 1, 1893.

2601. JAMES CALEB FOSTER (Ammi R., John, Jonathan, Asa, William, William, Reginald), b. New York, N. Y., May 6, 1847; m., in Lincoln, Neb., July 26, 1875, Sophia Smith, b. July 26, 1858. He is a mining expert. Res., Durango, Colorado.

3445. i. GEORGE LANCASTER, b. May 16, 1876.
3446. ii. EDWARD HORATIO, b. Nov. 10, 1877.
3447. iii. CLARA AMELIA, b. Sept. 17, 1879.
3448. iv. FINETTE AUGUSTA, b. Jan. 27, 1881.
3449. v. CLARENCE LEROY, b. Dec. 18, 1882.
3450. vi. ALBERT, b. Oct. 29, 1888.
3451. vii. FRANK, b. Sept. 6, 1891.
3452. viii. HENRY, b. Sept. 28, 1884; d. June 18, 1885.
3453. ix. JACOB, b. Aug. 10, 1890; d. Aug. 17, 1890.

2603. EDWARD HORATIO FOSTER (Ammi R., John, Jonathan, Asa, William, William, Reginald), b. Newark, N. J., Dec. 4, 1848; m., Mount Vernon, N. H., Nov. 26, 1874, Addie Frances Jenkins, b. July 10, 1853; d. Sept. 26, 1897; he is a farmer. Res., Groveland, Mass.

3454. i. ILDAGERTE MAY, b. February 4, 1876.
3455. ii. HENRY JAMES, b. Feb. 3, 1878.
3456. iii. BESSIE ALICE, b. Jan. 28, 1880.
3457. iv. NELLIE AUGUSTA, b. March 9, 1883. Res., 1746 Mississippi avenue, St. Louis, Mo.
3458. v. MABELLE ELLA, b. July 23, 1886.
3459. vi. FLORENCE ETHEL, b. Dec. 28, 1890.

2606. DAVID SKAATS FOSTER (Thomas, David, David, David, Timothy, William, Reginald), b., Utica, N. Y., Jan. 23, 1852; m., March 26, 1874, Mary C. Williams, dau. of William A., of Little Falls, N. Y. She d. Aug. 10, 1895. David

Skaats Foster is a coal and iron merchant of Utica, N. Y. He was educated in Germany and speaks five languages; is the author of several books in prose and poetry, to-wit: "Rebecca the Witch," published by Putnam in 1888; "Elinor Fenton," published by Lippincott in 1892; "Spanish Castles by the Rhine," published by Holt & Co. in 1897; "Prince Timothy," published by J. Brisben Walker, of the Cosmopolitan, 1898. It is a curious fact that Thomas Foster, his three sons, Abbott, David and Thomas, and grandsons, David and Reginald, are the only living descendants of the David Foster who was born in Boxford, Mass., in 1704; and as Amos the brother of this David, died childless, and as the descendants of Jeremiah, his other brother, died out in two or three generations, it is safe to presume that these six Fosters are the only descendants of Timothy Foster, the son of William, the son of Reginald. Residence, Utica, N. Y.

DAVID SKAATS FOSTER.

3460. i. GERARD S., b. Jan. 27, 1880.
3461. ii. BERNARD D., b. Jan. 27, 1880.

2609. ABRAHAM FOSTER (Benjamin, Benjamin, Isaac, Benjamin, Jacob, Isaac, Reginald), b. Granville, Nova Scotia, Aug. 23, 1805; m., in 1825, Rachel Morton, of Wilmont, Annapolis county, Nova Scotia. He d. ——. Res., Portland, Me.

3462. i. MARY ANN, b. ——; m. Benjamin Burnham. Res., Rochester, N. H.
3463. ii. HARRIET, b. ——; m. —— Libbie. Res., San Francisco, Cal.
3464. iii. DAUGHTER, b.——; m. a naval officer. Res., New York City.
3465. iv. SARAH M., b. ——; m. —— Thomas. Res., Portland, Me.
3466. v. FREDERICK, b. ——. Res., Portland, Me.
3467. vi. EDWARD, b. ——. Res., Portland, Me.

2610. ISAAC FOSTER (Benjamin, Benjamin, Isaac, Benjamin, Jacob, Isaac, Reginald), b. Granville, Nova Scotia, Oct. 27, 1806; m., Wilmont, Nova Scotia, 1829, Rebecca Taylor, dau. of Deacon Stephen, b. Dec. 6, 1809; d. Feb. 25, 1895. He was a carpenter. He d. Aug. 31, 1882. Res., Aylesford, Nova Scotia.

3468. i. PAOLI R., b. May 8, 1836; m. Adelaide L. Crocker.
3469. ii. MARY OLEVIA, b. July 16, 1830; m., June, 1864, John L. Sanford. Res., Medford, Cornwallis, county of Kings, Nova Scotia. They had two sons, who res. on the homestead. Ch.: 1. Levetta Lawson, b. July 26, 1865; m., April 20, 1892, Cora M. Patterson. Res., Aylesford, Nova Scotia; 3 ch. 2. Marion O., b. Oct. 16, 1867; unm. Res., Medford, Nova Scotia.
3470. iii. ROBERT, b. Dec., 1834; d. young.
3471. iv. JOSEPH MORTON T., b. May 18, 1832; m. Elizabeth Johnson and Jane Baker.
3472. v. STEPHEN TAYLOR, b. Sept., 1849. Went to California; unm.
3473. vi. CARR, b. April, 1841; d. Feb., 1842.
3474. vii. JACOB, b. April 16, 1840; m. Henrietta McPherson.
3475. viii. ESTHER, b. July 7, 1845; m. Anthony Stephens. Res. in Auburn, Nova Scotia. Has one son, Seward.
3476. ix. BENJAMIN, b. June 3, 1847; d. in 1849.
3477. x. BENJAMIN PRINCE, b. June 4, 1850; m. Ellen Hanna.
3478. xi. SYKES, b. Dec. 7, 1852; d. April, 1859.
3479. xii. MARTHA ELLA, b. Oct. 4, 1855; m., March 10, 1879, George E.

EDWARD C. FOSTER.

Randall. Res., Harmony, Nova Scotia. He is a farmer; was born April 22, 1853. Ch.: 1. Addie L., b. Dec. 30, 1879. 2. Alice, b. Feb. 8, 1881. 3. Ella May, b. Sept. 3, 1882. 4. Ennas Omar, b. Feb. 17, 1887. 5. Waldo E., b. April 5, 1888. 6. Lela, b. May 16, 1889. 7. Rupert, b. July 6, 1895.

2613. ROBERT FOSTER (Benjamin, Benjamin, Isaac, Benjamin, Jacob, Isaac, Reginald), b. Granville, Nova Scotia, Dec 13, 1813; m., ——, Martha Morton, of Digby, Nova Scotia; m. 2d, Elizabeth Taylor. He d. in Nova Scotia. Res., Nova Scotia.

3480. i. MARTHA, b. ——; m., ——, Daniel Frank. Res., Meriden street, East Boston.
3481. ii. TERRESSA, b. ——; m., ——, John Acre. Res., East Boston.
3482. iii. ALVENIA, b. ——; m. —— Hat. Res., East Boston, Mass.

2614. EDWARD CLARK FOSTER (Benjamin, Benjamin, Isaac, Benjamin, Jacob, Isaac, Reginald), b. Granville, Nova Scotia, May 27, 1817; m. there Oct. 12, 1847, Harriet Lovica Tupper (John, Miner, Elias, Eliakim, Thomas, Capt. Thomas was from Sandwich, England, to Sandwich, Mass., 1635), b. March 8, 1826.

Edward Clark Foster, son of Benjamin and Mary (Randal) Foster, was born near Bridgeton, Nova Scotia, May 27, 1817. He was educated there and by private teachers; taught school from 1837 to 1846. In 1846 he and his father moved to Berwick, Nova Scotia, where they purchased a large farm. Married, October 12, 1847, Harriet L. Tupper in Tupperville. He was a large country merchant and did a successful business, retiring in 1874. Living in the heart of the apple-producing belt of Nova Scotia, he was a large operator in apples, shipping to the United States and Europe. He was appointed postmaster in 1877, retiring in 1897. Mr. and Mrs. Foster, who are still living, celebrated their golden wedding October 12, 1897, which was attended by three of their sons with their wives and several of their grandchildren. Mr. Foster has always been an ardent member of the Methodist church and has been a delegate quite frequently in the conferences of the District Province and Dominion. He has been a life-long conservative, but was only once a candidate for office, which was at the first election after the confederation, when he was induced to become a candidate for Parliament from Kings county, but was unsuccessful. He was the first in his line of the family to enter into commercial pursuits, as all of his ancestors, from Reginald to his father, were tillers of the soil. Mr. and Mrs. Foster are living comfortably in their home in Berwick, enjoying a ripe old age.

Another correspondent sends me the following: First a farmer and crown land surveyor; second, a merchant; in 1866 was chosen to contest the county in the first general election after the confederation of the British provinces in North America in behalf of the government, as the measure of confederation was unpopular, especially among the common people and lower classes, he was beaten by a majority of seventeen—only two government men taking their seats in Nova Scotia. In 1877 was appointed postmaster for the town of Berwick, held the office for twenty years and retired September 30, 1897, at the age of eighty years. Residence, Berwick, Nova Scotia.

3483. i. JOHN RUPERT, b. July 30, 1848; m. Isabel McDonald, Victoria A. Dunlap and Minnie L. Ross.
3484. ii. MINER TUPPER, b. July 6, 1850; m. Sarah Rudolph.
3485. iii. MARY ELIZABETH, b. May 18, 1852; m., Halifax, Nova Scotia, Oct. 2, 1876, Lorenzo F. Darling, b. June 29, 1836. He was a wholesale jeweler in Halifax, Nova Scotia, now retired from business. Res., s. p., Riverside, Cal. Mrs. Darling writes: "My Grandmother Foster was Mary Randall, the grand-daughter of Mary Foster, of Boston, who was the wife of Col. Christopher Prince. They went to Annapolis, Nova Scotia, in 1770, and they took with them two slaves and splendid silver plate. Foster's wharf, in Boston, was a point associated with her family. Our immediate family have few, if any, relics. My brother Miner and myself destroyed a portrait of Col. Christopher Prince when we were children and yet I remember it distinctly. It was on a heavy piece of white paper, about six inches by nine inches, yellowed with age. The figure sat on a chair smoking a long-stemmed pipe. He was dressed in a frock coat with full skirts

and lappets, knee breeches and low shoes with buckles. He had blue eyes and rosy cheeks. How many times I have regretted this destruction! I have heard my grandfather speak of the metal-seal commissions of the king, in the use they afforded him and his brothers as sinkers in their river trouting. I have, however, two pieces of worsted work, executed by Mary Foster (Mrs. Christopher Prince), my great-great-grandmother, of Boston."

3486. iv. GEORGE EDWARD, b. Jan. 21, 1861; m. Lora M. Underhill.
3487. v. THOMAS HARRIS, b. June 4. 1855; d. Feb. 4, 1856.
3488. vi. DOUGLASS B., b. March 30, 1864; m. Addie F. Cole.

2627. THOMAS H. FOSTER (Samuel, Benjamin, Isaac, Benjamin, Jacob, Isaac, Reginald), b. July 20, 1837; m., May 12, 1861, Elizabeth Ann Foster, dau. of Benjamin and Eliza (Chute). Res., Nova Scotia.
3489 i. DUDLEY, b. ——; at maturity he was only twenty-seven inches in height.

2635. JAMES P. FOSTER (Isaac, Benjamin, Isaac, Benjamin, Jacob, Isaac, Reginald), b. July 7, 1815; m., in 1853, Mary T. Graves, dau. of Phinehas. He was a ship owner, a merchant and postmaster. Res., Port Lorne, Nova Scotia.
3490. i. THEY HAD two children.

2642. JOHN FOSTER (Isaac, Benjamin, Isaac, Benjamin, Jacob, Isaac, Reginald), b. June 1, 1828; m., ——, Diadama Spurr, dau. of Josiah; m. 2d, ——, Harriet Marshall. Res., Nova Scotia.
3491-2. i. ZEBUDA, b. ——.
3492-2. ii. DAWSON, b. ——.

2667. EDWARD CHIPMAN FOSTER (Israel, Oliver, Isaac, Benjamin, Joseph, Isaac, Reginald), b. Bridgeton, Nova Scotia, Dec. 22, 1853; m., June 28, 1872, Alma S. Balcom, b. Dec. 2, 1855. Res., Lawrencetown, Nova Scotia.
3491. i. HENRY RUGGLES, b. Nov. 29. 1873.
3492. ii. FRANK OTTO, b. Nov. 20, 1875; m. Marion A. Kelley. Res., Lawrencetown, Nova Scotia.
3493. iii. MAGGIE MAUD, b. March 9, 1878.

2667-2. SIDNEY M. FOSTER (Oliver, Oliver, Isaac, Benjamin, Jacob, Isaac, Reginald), b. Bridgetown, Nova Scotia, Aug. 8, 1846; m., Bear River, Nova Scotia, Dec. 27, 1882, Della E. Bishop, b. March 6, 1858; he is a farmer. Res., Bridgeton, Nova Scotia.
3494-2. i. ALBERT ERNEST, b Jan. 24, 1883; d. Feb. 14, 1883.
3495-2. ii. HELEN BEATRICE, b. Dec. 25, 1884; d. Dec. 29, 1884.
3496-2. iii. ERNEST McL., b. July 24, 1885.
3497-2. iv. FLORENCE VIVIAN, b. Aug. 17, 1887.
3498-2. v. RALPH OLIVER, b. May 23, 1890.
3499-2. vi. PERCIVAL STARR, b. June 17, 1893.
3500-2. vii. GLADYS MAY, b. Feb. 28, 1896.

2669. CHARLES A. FOSTER (Israel, Oliver, Isaac, Benjamin, Joseph, Isaac, Reginald), b. Bridgetown, Nova Scotia, Nov. 16, 1851; m., Amherst, Nova Scotia, Aug. 14, 1872. Annie Lee, b. Dec. 10, 1848. He is a stove molder. Res., 101 Central avenue, Chelsea, Mass.
3494. i. CARRIE MINETTA, b. Aug. 31, 1876.
3495. ii. CHARLES LOUIS, b. Oct. 28, 1878.

2679. CHARLES FOSTER (Frederick, John, Ezekiel, Benjamin, Jacob, Isaac, Reginald), b. Aylesford, Nova Scotia, July 26, 1818; m., at Kingston, Feb. 26, 1845, Mary Jane Woodbury, b. March 14, 1823; d. April 25, 1896; he was a farmer; he d. Nov. 5, 1896. Res., Tremont, Nova Scotia.
3496. i. RACHEL ELISABETH, b. June 26, 1846; m. James Brown, June 1, 1869. Res., Torbrook, Annapolis county, Nova Scotia.
3497. ii. ISAAC WOODBURY, b. June 13, 1848; m. Ada B. Tufts and Lucilla V. Howe.
3498. iii. EDITH SOPHIA, b. Oct. 13, 1850; m. George Woodbury, Feb. 12, 1879. Res., 68 Warrenton street, Boston, Mass.

3499. iv. ELMER ELLSWORTH, b. March 27, 1862; m. Annie Smith, Jan. 16, 1895. Res., Tremont, Nova Scotia.

2653. JOHN FOSTER (Willis, John, Ezekiel. Benjamin, Jacob, Isaac, Reginald), b. in 1830; m., ——, Susan Neily, dau. of Zebulon Neily. Res., Nova Scotia.

3500. i. ARCH, b. ——; m. —— Taylor, dau. of Rev. James Taylor, an M. E. clergyman; and 2d, —— Ryan, dau. of Rev. Mr. Ryan, an M. E. clergyman.

3501. ii. DAUGHTER, b. ——; m. Rev. Mr. Duncan.

2666. HON. JAMES GILBERT FOSTER (Rufus, Ezra F., Ezekiel, Benjamin, Jacob, Isaac, Reginald), b. Aylesford, Kings county, Nova Scotia, June 13, 1839.

HON. JAMES G. FOSTER.

His father, Rufus Foster, was descended from a family of the United Empire loyalists, who took refuge in Nova Scotia at the time of the American revolution; and his mother, Christina Foster, was of Scotch descent, having come when about seven years of age with her parents from Scotland, and the family settled in the same province. James Foster received a common school education and studied law with the Hon. Alexander James. On the 10th of May, 1864, Mr. Foster was admitted an attorney-at-law and barrister of Her Majesty's Supreme Court of Judicature, and on the 20th of May, 1865, he became a partner with Mr. James in his legal business, and this partnership continued until Mr. James was elevated, in January, 1877, to the Supreme Court of Nova Scotia as judge in equity, when a dissolution took place. Mr. Foster then took his brother, William R. Foster, into partnership with him, and now the old business is carried on by the new firm. On February 23, 1867, he was appointed a notary public, and on the 9th of October, 1878, he was made a Queen's counsel by the Nova Scotia government. In September, 1863, Mr. Foster was appointed first lieutenant in the Sixth regiment, Halifax county militia, and on June 19, 1865, was promoted to the captaincy of the Fifth company of the same corps. He attended the military school of instruction at Halifax and passed an examination, taking a second-class certificate for candidates for commissions in the active militia November 12, 1869. In August, 1883, he was appointed major in the reserve militia of the Nova Scotia regimental division of the county of Halifax from No. 7 company division. From May, 1879, to May, 1882, he held the office of recorder and stipendiary magistrate of Dartmouth, and on May 29, 1879, was appointed justice of the peace for the county of Halifax. On the 6th of July, 1874, he was made a commissioner for arranging and preparing for the press and indexing the Fifth series of the Revised Statutes of Nova Scotia, and in August, 1886, was appointed registrar of the Court of Probate for the county of Halifax. From June, 1877, to March, 1886, Mr. Foster held the position of vice consul for the Netherlands at Halifax. During the years 1880 and 1881 he negotiated with several railway syndicates for the purpose of carrying out the scheme for amalgamation and completion of the Nova Scotia railways, proposed by the local government of the time; and in 1881 he was authorized by Cyrus W. Field and associates, who were large owners of the Pictou coal mines, to negotiate proposals for that purpose with the local government and the late Sir Hugh Allan, then owner of the Eastern Extension railway in Nova Scotia, one of the railways in question. The government, however, was pledged to what is known as the Plunkett syndicate, which finally fell through, and the government was defeated in the general elections of the following year, 1882. The policy of the succeeding government being averse to the scheme for railway amalgamation, and railway interests becoming, in the meantime, much depressed, Mr. Field and his friends did not care to renew the proposals. Mr. Foster was brought up in and has always been a member of, the Church of England. He has represented the parish of Dartmouth as a lay delegate in the synod of the diocese of Nova Scotia and Prince Edward's Island, since April 13, 1874; and on the 23d of April, 1879, was made one of the executive committee of the synod. During the years 1877, 1883 and 1886, he represented the same diocese as one of its delegates in the provincial synod of Canada. Mr. Foster is a Liberal in politics, and, at the general election in 1882 was a candidate for the House of Assembly of Nova Scotia, but failed to secure his election, having been defeated by a trifling majority. Residence, Halifax, Nova Scotia, and 16 East Eighty-seventh street, New York City.

2697. HON. WILLIAM R. FOSTER (Rufus, Ezra F., Ezekiel, Benjamin, Jacob, Isaac, Reginald), b. Aylesworth, Kings county, Nova Scotia, Nov. 5, 1843; m., Sept. 11, 1873, Frances Morris Weeks, b. Dec. 6, 1845; barrister in Halifax, Nova Scotia; Foster & Foster, 3 Prince street. Res., Dartmouth, Nova Scotia.

3501½. i. FRANCES MARIA, b. June 22, 1878.

3501¾. ii. WILLIAM GOVE, b. Feb. 5, 1881.

2698. EZEKIEL PORTER EASTMAN FOSTER (Solomon K., Jeremiah, Jeremiah, Benjamin, Jacob, Isaac, Reginald), b. Weld, Me., April 25, 1839; m. there May 29, 1860, Rebecca Soule Buker, b. July 16, 1834. Ezekiel Porter Eastman is the youngest son of Solomon K. Foster. His occupation is farming. He was married to Rebecca S. Buker, who was born at Avon, Me., July 16, 1834. They have two children. Res., Weld, Me.

3502. i. HAYNES BUKER, b. Dec. 24, 1861; m. Jan. 3, 1891, ——. Res., Weld, Maine. Ch:. 1. Leslie Maynard, b. Dec. 28, 1891. Was a millwright.

3503. ii. NATHAN GRANT, b. March 31, 1865. He graduated from Colby University in 1893 and is a teacher. He is a Free Mason and belongs to the Alpha Tau Omega fraternity; is an A. M.

NATHAN G. FOSTER, A. M.

2699. HIRAM WESTERN FOSTER (Solomon K., Jeremiah, Jeremiah, Benjamin, Jacob, Isaac, Reginald), b. Weld, Me., Nov. 18, 1830; m., Feb., 1854, Adaline Augusta Colby, b. June 14, 1836. She d., Weld, Me., Oct. 22, 1894. He is a carpenter by trade and has been engaged in the manufacture of box and spade handles at different periods of his life. He is a Free Mason and has two children. Res., Weld, Me.

3504. i. WILLIAM PRESCOTT, b. Aug. 19, 1856; m. Ruby Hinckley.

3505. ii. CHARLES SUMNER, b. Dec. 20, 1859; m. Hattie Robertson.

2701. DANIEL BILLINGTON FOSTER (Solomon K., Jeremiah, Jeremiah, Benjamin, Jacob, Isaac, Reginald), b. Weld, Me, Sept. 14, 1833; m., ——, Mrs. Wealthy Everett. Daniel Billington Foster was the third child of Solomon K. Foster. Like his father, he engaged in teaching, but while yet a young man he emigrated to Kansas, where he took part in the fierce struggle then going on there between the Free Soil party and the pro-Slavery party. He was a member of Jim Lane's free soil army, and at the breaking out of the civil war enlisted in the First Kansas cavalry and served during the war, being once wounded in the arm. He married Mrs. Wealthy Everett, and at his death left one son, Walter, who is married and still lives in Kansas. He died ——. Res., Carbondale, Kan.

3506. i. WALTER, b. ——.

2702. NATHAN NORRIS FOSTER (Solomon K., Jeremiah, Jeremiah, Benjamin, Jacob, Isaac, Reginald), b. Weld, Me., Nov. 12, 1835; m., ——, Mary Philbrick, of Phillips, Me. He is a farmer and lived for some years in the town of Weld, Me., but finally moved to Kansas. He married Mary Philbrick, of Phillips, Me., and has three children; the eldest, Frank Herbert, lives at Carbondale, Kan., and is a dealer in live stock. He is a Free Mason and a Knight of Pythias. Res., Weld, Me., and Carbondale, Kan.

3507. i. FRANK, b. ——. Res., Carbondale, Kan.
3508. ii. HATTIE MAY, b. ——.
3509. iii. ———, b ——.

2703. EPHRAIM ROLLIN FOSTER (Solomon K., Jeremiah, Jeremiah, Benjamin, Jacob, Isaac, Reginald), b. Weld, Me., May 6, 1837; m. —— ——. Ephraim Rollin Foster was the fifth child of Solomon K. He went to sea when about eighteen years of age, serving first on a whaler, then on merchantmen and finally in the United States navy. At the breaking out of the civil war he was on the old frigate Constilation, which was off the coast of Africa watching for slavers. He was an officer on Farragut's flagship, the Hartford, when the forts Jackson and St. Philip were passed and New Orleans taken, and he commanded a gunboat at the taking of Mobile. After the war he settled in Florida and engaged in raising oranges, where he was killed by lightning. He was a Free Mason and left a wife and one daughter. He d. ——. Res., Florida.

3510. i. DAUGHTER, b. ——.

2708. ELIAB JONES FOSTER (Hiram, Jeremiah, Jeremiah, Benjamin, Jacob, Isaac, Reginald), b. June 19, 1844; m., June 19, 1868, Susan Smith. He d. June 5, 1892. Res., ——.

3511. i. ELIZABETH., b. ——; m. —— Dyer. Res., Brunswick, Me.

2710. HIRAM ORLANDO FOSTER (Hiram, Jeremiah, Jeremiah, Benjamin, Jacob, Isaac, Reginald), b. Weld, Me., Nov. 30, 1850; m. there May 4, 1874, Mary J. Phinney, b. Nov. 15, 1857; he was a farmer. He d. Jan. 13, 1898. Res., Weld, Me.

3512. i. CHARLES SHERBROOK, b. June 6, 1875; m. Berdina Whittemore (b. Nov. 13, 1881), March 26, 1898. Res., Phillips, Me.
3513. ii. LILLIAN MAY, b. Nov. 12, 1877.
3514. iii. GRACE ELIZA, b. Nov. 15, 1882.
3515. iv. WILLIAM ORLANDO, b. Feb. 9, 1884.
3516. v. ARTHUR HARRY, b. Aug. 28, 1885.
3517. vi. HAROLD H., b. May 2, 1887.
3518. vii. PHILOH DOW, b. July 14, 1894.

2711. ISAAC FOSTER (Isaac, Isaac, Isaac, John, Jacob, Isaac, Reginald), b. Murray, N. Y., Sept. 10, 1819; m., Sept. 5, 1856, Catherine Wilks Jeffreys, b. Scotland. She res. Auburn, N. Y. His wife was a native of Scotland and came to this country in 1854. For some years he resided with his grandmother. He d. in 1878. Res., Murray, N. Y.

3519. i. CHAUNCEY, b. Nov. 25, 1855
3520. ii. WILLIAM, b. May 24, 1857; m. ——.
3521. iii. ISAAC, b. July 2, 1859; d. June 16, 1860.
3522. iv. FRANKLIN F., b. ——, 1861; m. ——.

2716. WILLIAM ROWLEY FOSTER (Marcus, Isaac, Isaac, John, Jacob, Isaac, Reginald), b. Murray, N. Y., June 4, 1825; m., July 1, 1853, Amanda M. Kellogg, dau. of John C. and Hannah (Sweet), d. April 29, 1855; m. 2d, Sept. 30, 1856, Clarissa M. Welfare, dau. of James and Elizabeth (Osborne), d. Dec. 17, 1893. Born in New York State he moved to Michigan with his mother in 1832. Resided at Russell, Ohio, Sheboygan, Wis., and Walled Lake, Mich. In 1849 he went to Panama and spent four years in South America. Returned to Michigan and resided at Milford, and moved to Pontiac. Res., Pontiac, Mich.

3523. i. AMELIA, b. Oct. 13, 1854; m., July 2, 1876, Abel G. Smith.
3524. ii. JAMES W., b. Sept. 18, 1857; d. Dec. 10, 1857.
3525. iii. ELIZA E., b. Dec. 21, 1858; m., Aug. 6, 1877, James Galligan. Res., Clarkson Station, Mich. Ch.: 1. Rosa M., b. April 19, 1879 2. Eliza A., b. Feb. 21, 1881. 3. William R. F., b. June 19, 1883; d. Dec. 21, 1883. 4. Margaret M., b. Oct. 7, 1884. 5. Clarissa, b. April 17, 1886.
3526. iv. GEORGE B., b. March 20, 1862; m. Emma Concle.
3527. v. MARCUS, b. June 8, 1868.

2719. SAMUEL W. FOSTER (Samuel, Isaac, Isaac, John, Jacob, Isaac, Reginald) b. Belchertown, Mass., Sept. 2, 1833; m., April 24, 1867, Mary Frances Gill. He emigrated to Sheboygan county, Wis., in 1846; moved to Geauga, Ohio, and to Genesee county, N. Y., in 1849; was clerk in a dry goods store in Cleveland and later worked in Chicago. Engaged in mercantile business in Oswego, Ill., and later at Plano, Ill. In 1856 he went to Topeka, Kan., and after residing there a short time, moved to Wabasha, Minn., and later to Middletown, Ill. He was sutler of the Third Minnesota infantry until 1865. The following year he went to Neosho county, Kan., and soon moved to Atlanta, Ill. After his marriage he engaged in business in Wabasha, Minn., but soon moved to Kansas, and was one of the original settlers in Chanute, where he now resides. Res., Chanute, Kan.
3528. i. RICHARD EVERETT, b. Oct. 12, 1868; m. Lulu Wissett.
3529. ii. LILLIE FRANCES, b. Feb. 14, 1871; d. Aug., 1876.
3530. iii. REGINALD R., b. Oct. 3, 1874. Res., Fairplay, Mo., and Chanute, Kan.
3531. iv. FRANCES ALICE, b. Oct. 22, 1877. Res. at home.

2720. COL. EVERETT WORTHINGTON FOSTER (Samuel, Isaac, Isaac, John, Jacob, Isaac, Reginald), b. Belchertown, Mass., Nov. 17, 1835; m., Aug. 31, 1864, Laura Josephine Beall, dau. of Hamilton and Eliza (Sherred), d. Nov. 8, 1878; m. 2d, Oct. 3, 1883, Mrs. Rhoda L. (Walker) Skinner, d. March 31, 1893. He emigrated to Sheboygan, Wis., with his father, and later lived in Geauga county, Ohio. Attended school at Chester Academy, Ohio, in 1849 and 1850, and the following two years at Western Reserve Institute at Hiram, Ohio. Moved to Kendall county, Ill., and taught school. Attended Knox College at Galesburg, and moved to Wabasha county, Minn.; was county surveyor and first county auditor of that county. Enlisted April 26, 1861, in Company I, First Minnesota, three months' service, was mustered out in June to make room for 3-year men. Enlisted again as captain in Company G, in October, 1861, and served through the war in that regiment, and was mustered out as lieutenant-colonel in 1865, having resigned. After his marriage he resided on a cotton plantation near Little Rock, Ark.; was commissioned surveyor-general of Louisiana and resided in New Orleans from 1870 to 1874. Removed to Bloomington, Illinois, and remained until 1877. Returned to New Orleans in the fall of 1877 and left the next year for the north, on account of yellow fever. Resided in Chicago in 1879 and emigrated and settled in Spink county, Dakota, in 1880. Lived at Greenwood as agent for the Yankton Indians from 1890 to 1894 and at Armour, South Dakota. Both wives are buried in

COL. EVERETT W. FOSTER.

Bloomington, Ill. He is at present a resident of Chicago and is the land commissioner for the Wisconsin Central railway. He is a member of the Minnesota Historical Society, Minnesota Commandery of the Loyal Legion and the South Dakota Sons of the American Revolution. Res., 322 Jackson Boulevard, Chicago, Ill., and now at 2527 Second Ave. s., Minneapolis Minn.

3532. i. LAURA WORTHINGTON, b. June 26, 1865; m., April 14, 1892, Frank L. Selleck. Res., Owatonna, Minn., s. p.

3533 ii. NELLIE VIRGINIA, b. Jan. 19, 1868; m., July 8, 1891, Arden F. Hammond. Res., Chicago, Ill. Ch.: 1. Esther Nyle, b. June 19, 1892. 2. Nellie Arden, b. June 16, 1895.

3534. iii. ARTHUR BEALL, b. Feb. 1, 1870. Res., Tacoma, Wash. Attended college at Brookings, Dakota, and is now employed by the St. Paul & Tacoma Lumber Co.

3535. iv. KIRK EVERETT, b. Nov. 8, 1873; d., Chicago, Nov., 1879.

3536. v. EDWARD WALKER, b. Jan. 24, 1876. Graduated at Pillsbury Academy, Owatonna, Minn., in 1895. Is employed by the St. Paul & Tacoma Lumber Co., at Tacoma, Wash.

2721. HON. ADDISON GARDNER FOSTER (Samuel, Isaac, Isaac, John, Jacob, Isaac, Reginald), b. Belchertown, Mass., Jan. 28, 1837; m., Nov. 19, 1863, Martha A. Wetherby.

Addison G. Foster was born January 28, 1837, at Belchertown, Mass., and is a descendant of Reginald Foster, who landed at Ipswich, Mass., in 1638. His father, Samuel Foster, was a thrifty village merchant, and his mother was a descendant from the Gardner family, who came over from England shortly after the landing of the Mayflower. When thirteen years of age, Mr. Foster accompanied his parents to Sheboygan Falls, Wis., where his father, in 1850, secured land and began to clear it for a farm. That was where Mr. Foster got his first experience in logging. Afterward he and his brother started for Pike's Peak, but they turned back, and he taught school in Missouri and afterward returned home and went to Wabasha, Minn. In 1863 he married Martha Ann Wetherby, of Pennsylvania, who was then visiting Wabasha. He held the offices of county surveyor and county auditor. Afterward he was engaged in forwarding and commission business in Lake City and Red Wing, Minn. In 1877 he formed a partnership with Col. C. W. Griggs in the fuel and contracting business, which partnership has continued to this day.

In 1879 they formed the Beaver Dam Lumber Company and in 1884 incorporated the Lehigh Coal & Iron Company. He is still a leading officer in those companies and vice-president of the St. Paul & Tacoma Lumber Company, organized in 1888, since which time he has made his home in Tacoma. His wife and two sons are living. Harry Gardner Foster is engaged in the lumber and shingle business in Tacoma and Addison Foster is now at Yale College.

Mr. Foster takes an active part in the management of the company affairs, and often puts on his hob-nail boots and spends days at a time in examining and sizing up logs the company wishes to buy.

For ten years Mr. Foster has been engaged in business in Tacoma, and there is no more enthusiastic advocate of or believer in the future of Washington and the Puget Sound country.

Besides his extensive lumber and milling interests, Mr. Foster is largely interested in the Wilkeson Coal & Coke Company and in Villa Park real estate.

When a resident of St. Paul, Mr. Foster was a neighbor of and ward worker with Senator C. K. Davis. It was then he received his first training in the game of politics, and he is no novice at the game. He managed the successful Congressional campaign of S. P. Snyder in the Fourth Minnesota district, was instrumental in the election of Hon. L. F. Hubbard as governor of Minnesota, brought out and elected Dar S. Hall to Congress and was the leading supporter of Senator McMillan, of Minnesota, in all his campaigns.

Mr. Foster was sustained in his contest by the ambitious of Mrs. Foster, who, although a home lover, and who is known as a domestic woman, is helpful and hopeful for the success of whatever her husband undertakes.

"In training my sons for a business career," says Mr. Foster, "I try to impress upon them the necessity of a good education for a foundation. Then I tell them if they are to engage in merchandising, it is best to deal in commodities, something the people must have, like coal, wood and lumber. The cheaper you can make and sell commodities, the more the people will use them. I believe in the magnitude of a business more than in high profits on a small business."

After Mr. Foster had been elected to the high office of United States Senator in 1899 by both branches of the Washington legislature in joint session, he was called upon and said:

"Gentlemen of the Legislature of Washington: Heartily and honestly my thanks are tendered you for the great honor you have bestowed upon me. I thank you all—from my ever-loyal and true home guard to the whole State at large.

HON. ADDISON G. FOSTER.

We have had three weeks of a sharp Senatorial contest, but for my part the end has been reached without any feeling of animosity, or, indeed, anything but the very best of good-will to all.

"In fulfilling the duties of my office I shall know no county and in business no party. In political affairs it shall be my aim to upbuild the Republican party, disregarding factional strife if any has existed in the past.

"We now have a united country—North, South, East and West—all striving to outdo the other in patriotic progress. Under the leadership of our noble president our nation is forging ahead as never before. We have a bright and brilliant future, and our ambition, as a State, should be to lead the procession.

"A most commendable move in this direction, during the past fiscal year, is found in the fact that the merchant marine of Washington gained the enviable distinction of attaining a greater per cent. of increase than any other State in the Union, and yet this is but a feeble beginning compared with what we can, and actually are destined to accomplish.

"It is our duty to build up the State, open the rivers and improve harbors, establish new commercial enterprises both by land and by sea, and so conduct our affairs, including the acts of this legislature, that new people and new capital will be attracted to us. We should be fired with the spirit of progressiveness of the aggressive quality and by our industry, integrity and enterprise make Washington as illustrious among the States as is the name of the father of our country among men.

"Sound money and expansion, the building up of our merchant marine and a tariff protection for several of the chief products of this State involve great issues, which can only be upheld by sustaining the policies of the Republican party. It is plainly our duty to encourage the maintenance of party organization and to accord generous recognition to the manly and self-sacrificing efforts of our citizens who, working along recognized and approved lines of Republican party organization, best serve what, at the polls, constitute their masters—the great body of thrifty, patriotic and justice-loving people. Gentlemen, again I thank you most heartily and sincerely."

On Senator Foster's return to his home in Tacoma he was met with such a reception as could not, under any circumstances, fail to impress him with the regard in which the people of Tacoma hold him.

From the time he first arrived at the Northern Pacific depot until he alighted from his carriage at the residence of Col. Griggs, at the corner of North Fourth street and Tacoma avenue, his progress along the streets was one continued ovation.

The Northern Pacific train bearing Senator-Elect Foster back to his home in Tacoma arrived at the station on time. For an hour previous to the arrival of the train, admirers of Mr. Foster gathered at the depot in anticipation of his arrival. By 4:20 o'clock several thousand people were congregated in the vicinity. Some swarmed the platform, others the waiting rooms and the remainder on the street outside. Flags, roosters of the golden hued variety, and bunting were very much in evidence. Finally, the train pulled in, and he was given a most enthusiastic ovation, which was followed by an address.

Just after Mr. Foster was elected United States Senator, from Washington to Washington, his partner, Colonel Griggs, said:

"The good people of Tacoma and of the State are to be congratulated upon the selection of such an able man to represent them in the Senate of the United States. Undoubtedly, he will have as much influence in that body as any other man who could be sent from the Northwest.

"Mr. Foster has been a firm believer in the great future of this State. He has reiterated again and again his belief that the State of Washington has no superior in the Union, and with its coal and timber and other resources, it is truly the Pennsylvania of the West.

"He is not only an able and efficient man, but trustworthy in every respect, and can always be relied upon to stand by the interests of the people, not only of his own locality, but of every other portion of the State.

"He is a man exceedingly broad in his views, and can be strictly depended upon to do what is right, not only to his friends, but to those who may have been opposed to him politically, and entirely independent of any political bias.

"He is a man in the prime of life, in good, robust health, and with ample physical power to stand the demand made upon a Senator in the great capital of our nation.

"Our personal relations have always been very intimate; no brothers could be more so We have never had a word, and therefore I can speak with the fullest confidence of his ability and integrity. I feel there is no question about the good results he will be able to secure for the State of Washington. We have been partners for over twenty-five years. We were engaged together in the warehouse and wholesale provision business at Duluth. About two years after that the firm of Griggs & Foster embarked in the fuel and contracting business. We operated extensively in lands, purchasing 110,000 acres of wheat lands in Dakota in 1880 of the Northern Pacific. The counties of Griggs and Foster were organized there. We have also been in the lumber business at Cumberland, Wis., for about fifteen years under the title of the Beaver Dam Lumber Company.

"We came to the State of Washington for the purpose of looking over the situation about twelve years ago with our families. After visiting Seattle, Tacoma and other sections of the State we made up our minds this was the State we desired to make our future home. We purchased a large tract of land in connection with Mr. Hewitt, Mr. Jones and others, which was finally accepted in May, 1888. Then we formed the St. Paul & Tacoma Lumber Company. I was elected president and Mr. Foster vice-president, which positions have been steadily held having been re-elected at the recent meeting of the company on the 25th of January."

Congratulations were pouring in upon Col. Griggs after the result of the caucus was announced last night.

Col. Everett W. Foster, a brother of Addison G. Foster, served in the war for the Union in the Third Minnesota volunteer infantry, of which Colonel Griggs had command. "He was the same stripe of man as the Senatorial nominee," said Colonel Griggs, "a cordial, able man, making friends not only with the military, but with civilians and everyone with whom he came in contact. He is now residing in the city of St. Paul. Two of Colonel Foster's sons are with us in Tacoma—Arthur Beal Foster and Everett Walker Foster—and they are our most trusted employes.

The Tacoma paper, in referring to Mr. Foster's election to the United States Senate, said editorially:

The election of Hon. Addison G. Foster by the legislature to-day is assured by the action of the Republican caucus last night, in which fifty-eight Republican members pledged themselves to vote for that gentleman. This is a result of the brief and dignified contest for the senatorship, which is a matter for congratulation to every citizen of this State.

Mr. Foster is a man of unquestioned ability and integrity, whose long and active business life has been devoted to affairs of large magnitude. He is fully competent to represent this State in the Senate, and will be the peer of any Senator who has yet been sent from Washington in looking after the interests and growing needs of the State.

Mr. Foster has been a life-long, active Republican, always taking a practical working part in the interests of his party, but he cannot be called a politician. Politics has been an incident rather than an occupation, in his busy business life.

While the other large cities of the State have been continuously represented in the United States Senate, Tacoma has never enjoyed that honor, and this and the fact that eastern Washington is the home of both of the United States Senators from this State, gave Mr. Foster's candidacy logical and geographical strength in other parts of the State.

While Mr. Foster is a loyal and patriotic citizen of Tacoma, he is just as loyal and patriotic a citizen of the State of Washington, and as earnest in aiding and in the development and growth of the State as of his native city. He will be a Senator for the whole State, knowing no particular locality, and possesses a broad, fair-mindedness which will give equal consideration to all sections.

Mr. Foster will not be one of the talkers of the Senate, but he will be found among the constructive statesmen whose judgment is relied upon; a Senator like Philetus Sawyer, who accomplishes more practical good for Wisconsin than did the more brilliant Carpenters and Doolittles.

Mr. Foster is fully abreast, if not ahead, of the times, upon the great questions of vital interest to this young and growing State, and will take an active, prominent part in the constructive work of the Senate, and make his influence felt both in national legislation and that which affects his State.

The nomination of Mr. Foster was a good day's work for the people of this State and for the Republican party of Washington, and to no one should higher praise be given than to Senator John L. Wilson, whose magnanimous and patriotic action has not only prevented a long and bitter contest, but has made him many new friends and kindled anew the affection of his thousands of former admirers.

Residence, Tacoma, Wash.

3537. i. HARRISON GARDNER, b. March 8, 1866; m. Elizabeth D. Gibson.

3538. ii. FRANK WALKER, b. May 19, 1870; d. June 10, 1872.

3539. iii. MARTHA ROWENA, b. Oct. 8, 1873; d. June 23, 1885.

3540. iv. CHARLES ADDISON, b. March 14, 1879. He is at college at Andover, Mass.

2723. WILLIAM HENRY FOSTER (Samuel, Isaac, Isaac, John, Jacob, Isaac, Reginald), b. Belchertown, Mass., Aug. 17, 1840; m., Feb. 3, 1867, Mary Maher, of Chicago, d. Nov., 1892. He moved with his family to Illinois in 1854 and two years after went to Chicago as clerk in Barnum Bros.' store; enlisted in Battery M, First Missouri artillery, discharged in 1864. Went to Neosho county, Kan., in 1866, with his brother, S. W.; later went to Chicago and was married there. Went to Arkansas in 1867, to Kansas in 1868, to New Orleans in 1871, to Eau Claire, Wis., in 1875. Later resided in Dakota, South Dakota and finally Kansas. Res., Basehor, Kan.

3541. i. MARY, b. April, 1868; d. young.
3442. ii. EVERETT, b. April 26, 1869; is in the newspaper business. Res., Hankinson, No. Dak.
3543. iii. GRACE, b. June 26, 1871. Res., Minneapolis, Minn.
3544. iv. WILLIAM F., b. April 23, 1874. Res., Minneapolis, Minn.
3545. v. MARY, b. June 26, 1876; m., April 20, 1896, R. B. Williard. Res., Sisseton, So. Dak.

2730. EZRA FOSTER (Ezra, Ezekiel, Ezekiel, John, Jacob, Isaac, Reginald), b. Feb. 2, 1815, Leyden, Mass.; m. there May 6, 1846, Sarah A. Wilbur, b. 1818; d. June 14, 1862; m. 2d, May 17, 1863, Susan A. Mowrey, b. Sept. 15, 1840; he was a farmer. Ezra Foster and his brother Ransom were both very intelligent, highly-respected gentlemen, much interested in all that pertained to their family, especially Ezra. He had been for many years a school-teacher, not being a robust man and unequal to the hard life of a farmer, although he owned, and with the help of others, successfully carried on a farm. The two brothers were among the substantial men of Leyden. He d. Sept. 7, 1897. Res., Leyden, Mass.

3546. i. FRANK W., b. Sept. 9, 1848; m., Dec. 10, 1873, Martha D. Pond, b. Jan. 6, 1849; is a traveling salesman. Res., s. p., Greenfield, Mass.
3547. ii. EDGAR SMITH, b. May 5, 1851; d. Sept. 27, 1869.
3548. iii. CHARLES LEE, b. April 5, 1853; d. Sept. 26, 1869.

2731. JOSEPH SMITH FOSTER (Ezra, Ezekiel, Ezekiel, John, Jacob, Isaac, Reginald), b. Dec. 18, 1816, Leyden, Mass.; m., July 11, 1843, Olive Newton, b. Dec. 26, 1811; d. Sept. 21, 1895; he was a farmer. He d. April 29, 1893. Res., Leyden, Mass.

3549. i. ASAHEL N., b. July 12, 1857; m. Mary Perkins.
3550. ii. JOSEPH LEROY, b. June 13, 1846; m. Effie Wilder.

2734. RANSOM STUART FOSTER (Ezra, Ezekiel, Ezekiel, John, Jacob, Isaac, Reginald), b. Leyden, Mass., Feb. 9, 1826; m. there Feb. 18, 1852, Climena Frizzell, b. April 19, 1827; d. June 16, 1897; she was a dau. of Rufus and Sabra. He is a farmer and resides on the farm which has been in the family for nearly one hundred and fifty years; is a substantial and respected citizen. Res., Leyden, Mass.

3551. i. MARY CLIMENA, b. April 13, 1853; m., June 25, 1873, Henry C. Potter Leyden. She d. Sept. 10, 1880; he d. Jan. 29, 1880, s. p.
3552. ii. CHARLOTTE LOUISA, b. Sept. 24, 1854; m., May 1, 1878, Frank J. Allen. Res., Greenfield, Mass.
3553. iii. LEONORA HARRIET, b. Oct. 17, 1856; m., Oct. 30, 1878, to Fred A. Cowan, of Natural Bridge, N. Y. Lived there seventeen years; present add., Greenfield, Mass.
3554. iv. NANCY SOPHIA, b. Oct. 14, 1858; m., Oct. 4, 1881, Dr. Daniel Griffin. Res., 96 Bay View avenue, Lynn, Mass. He was b. Oct. 14, 1858; is a dentist by profession; is a graduate of the Boston Dental College and ex-member of the common council of Lynn.
3555. v. SARA SABRA, b. Oct. 25, 1861; d. July 4, 1883.
3556. vi. FRANK RANSOM, b. Feb. 4, 1867. Res., Leyden, Mass.
3557. vii. LILIA ELSIE, b. Aug. 28, 1870. Res., Leyden, Mass.

2740. HORACE BURNHAM FOSTER (Elikiam, Ezekiel, Ezekiel, John, Jacob, Isaac, Reginald), b. Leyden, Mass., April 26, 1828; m., Aug. 19, 1855, Abbie Neal, b. May 1, 1824; d. Jan. 16, 1880; m. 2d, Nov. 9, 1881, at Clinton, Conn., Mary Wood, b. May 2, 1843. When one year old moved to Arlington, Vt.; in his fourth year moved to North Bennington, Vt. Remained there until May 29, 1837, and then removed with all the family to Mantua, Portage county, Ohio, and there his father and mother remained until the former died and then the family broke up; he had gone long before. When he was eighteen years old, he commenced preparing for college and taught school winters; one winter in Mantua and one in Twinsburg. In the fall of 1848 he entered Western Reserve College at this place, then a very famous college, but now removed to Cleveland and is part of Western Reserve University. In a class of twenty-eight young men [no girls] stood at the head of his class, and took the valedictory, which is the only honor he ever received, and graduated in 1852. The next year, 1852-3, was at the head of the preparatory department of Western Reserve College; had seventy pupils, all boys. The next two years was tutor in college. In 1855-6 was superintendent of the public schools of Akron. In the fall of 1856 up to January 1, 1857, was tutor in place of professor (tutor pro professore) in Western Reserve College again. Then quit teaching wholly and continued his legal studies, which he had pursued while teaching, and in March, 1857, was admitted to practice law in all of the courts of the State of Ohio. He opened an office in Hudson, and having partners a portion of the time in Akron, practiced in Summit, Portage and Cuyahoga counties, mostly in Summit, always had all he could do, generally more, and wore himself out in the business. Of course he has made some money, but the game is hardly worth the ammunition expended. He never sought office; he thought it did not pay and thinks so now. He held some local offices from a sense of duty only. Res., Hudson, Ohio.

3558. i. JESSIE E., b. Jan. 24, 1859; m., Oct. 30, 1889, William B. Parmelee. Res., Hudson, Ohio. He was born in Twinsburgh, Summit county, O., May 1, 1859, and is in the ninth generation from John Parmelee, who landed at Guilford, Conn., in 1639. He is the common ancestor of all the Parmelees in the United States. Ch.: 1. Joel Royce, b. Oct. 22, 1890; d. Oct. 23, 1890. 2. Howard Foster, b. Jan. 8, 1893; d. Feb. 5, 1897. 3. Abbie Neal, b. Dec. 8, 1894.

3559. ii. HORACE WOOD, b. July 28, 1882.

3560. iii. MARIE JOSEPHINE, b. Oct. 20, 1885.

2741. LUCIUS COOLEY FOSTER (Elikiam, Ezekiel, Ezekiel, John, Jacob, Isaac, Reginald), b. April 26, 1831, Arlington, Vt.; m., March 1, 1860, Edna L. Brewster, b. Oct. 12, 1840; a descendant of Elder Brewster, who came over in the Mayflower. She d. 1886. He removed when a babe to North Bennington, Vt., and from there, when six years old, to Mantua, Portage county, Ohio. He, as the youngest child of his parents, remained at home tilling the few acres his father owned, and also at times helping the neighboring farmers, until about 1860 or 1861, when he married, rented a farm, and began his life work as a farmer. He soon accumulated enough to buy a farm of his own, in Auburn, Geauga county, Ohio, where he resided until his death. He left surviving him his widow, who died about one year after him, and one child. He was a model farmer, an admirable man, kind-hearted, honest, pure, clear-headed and sound in judgment, and had the friendship and confidence of all who knew him. As an example, one township election he failed to attend, and in a few days after found that he had been nominated by his party (Republican), and had been elected by the unanimous vote of both parties justice of the peace, without his solicitation and knowledge. His life illustrates the familiar lines:

> "Only the actions of the Just,
> Smell sweet and blossom in the dust."

He d. Dec. 29, 1885.

3561. i. LUCY BREWSTER, b. May 13, 1868; m., Jan. 1, 1889, William H. Shackson. Res., Chagrin Falls, O. Ch.: 1. Edna L., b. May 29, 1895. He is a farmer; was b. May 20, 1864.

2742. THOMAS JEFFERSON FOSTER (Josiah, Ezekiel, Ezekiel, John, Jacob, Isaac, Reginald), b. Bernardston, Mass., Dec. 6, 1822; m. —— Potter, of Leyden; she d. and he m. 2d, Deerfield, Mass., Mrs. Susan W. (Robbins) Foster, b. June 6, 1821; d. April 29, 1886; m. 3d, ——— in Ohio. He was a miller and a farmer. He d. June 26, 1896. Res., Bernardston, Mass.

3562. i. ELLEN N., b. Aug. 2, 1858; m., April 16, 1889, Edward Jennes Jones, b. Aug. 6, 1852. Res., Greenfield, Mass. Is a school-teacher and farmer. Ch.: 1. Amasa Foster, b. May 11, 1890.
3563. ii. JENNIE AMANDA, b. Aug. 13, 1861; d. April 25, 1886.

2742-0. WILLIAM WINCHESTER FOSTER (Josiah, Ezekiel, Ezekiel, John, Jacob, Isaac, Reginald), b. Bernardston, Mass., Aug. 23, 1820; m., April 6, 1842, Susan W. Robbins, dau of Nathan, of Deerfield. She m. 2d, his brother, Thomas Jefferson Foster. He d. May 22, 1855. Res., Bernardston, Mass.
3563 2. i. FREDERICK W., b. July 22, 1843; d. July 9, 1846.
3563-3. ii. LUETTE LOUISE, d. Aug. 21, 1850, aet. five years.
3563-4. iii. NATHAN W., d. Sept. 15, 1850, aet. five years.

2742-2. JOHN RICH FOSTER (John, John, John, John, Jacob, Isaac Reginald), b. Moretown, Vt., Nov. 7, 1834; m., Waterbury, Vt., April 25, 1859, Delia Wells, b. July 10, 1836; d. Aug. 20, 1887. He d. April 20, 1897. Res., Clinton, Mass.
3564. i. RICHARD WELLS, b. Oct. 27, 1878; is now, 1898, a student at Harvard College. Add., 61 Brattle street, Cambridge, Mass.
3565. ii. THREE OTHER ch.; d. young.

2743-2. CHARLES A. FOSTER (John, John, John, John, Jacob, Isaac, Reginald), b. March 2, 1822, in Vermont; m., May 22, 1847, Hulda Ann Spooner, b. Sept. 24, 1824. He is a farmer; has been justice of the peace. Res., Middlesex, Vt.
3566. i. ELLA H., b. March 23, 1848; m., Nov. 1, 1870, E. W. Crown, of Milton, Vt.
3567. ii. JOHN E., b. Nov. 15, 1851; m. and had two sons, Edward and John.
3568. iii. JULIA E., b. Sept. 27, 1854.
3569. iv. CHARLES F., b. June 1, 1856.
3570. v. ARTHUR L., b. Jan. 19, 1858. Res., Hartford, Conn.
3571. vi. JESSE J., b. March 6, 1864.
3572. vii. CARRIE R., b. Feb. 28, 1866.
3573. viii. ERNST H., b. July 25, 1867.

2754. FREDERICK W. FOSTER (Daniel, Jacob, Benjamin, Benjamin, Benjamin, Isaac, Reginald), b. Trenton, Me., Feb. 5, 1845; m., Castine, Me., June 25, 1877, Mary Elizabeth Webster, b. Oct. 10, 1851. Frederick Williston Foster, son of Daniel Foster, and youngest of a family of nine children, was born at Trenton, Me. Spent the first twenty-one years of his life on his father's farm, and since then, with but little variation, has been engaged in the work of teaching. In 1872 he graduated from the State Normal School at Castine, Me. Taught Lamoine High School during two years and finished a course of study at the Classical Institute, Waterville, Me. From 1876 until 1889 he taught in the State Normal School at Castine, since which time he has worked under the American Missionary Association, of New York; for two years, 1889-1891, was principal of Chandler Normal School at Lexington, Ky., and from 1891 to the present time, 1898, principal of Dorchester Academy, McIntosh, Ga. He married Mary E. Webster, of Castine; united with the Congregational church at Castine in 1872, and in 1890, with his wife and oldest child, Helen, joined the Second Presbyterian church at Lexington, Ky. Residence, Castine, Me.
3574. i. HELEN JEANNETTE, b. July 9, 1879.
3575. ii. EDITH MARIA, b. March 22, 1884.

2756. ALBERT G. FOSTER (Simeon, Benjamin, Benjamin, Benjamin, Benjamin, Isaac, Reginald), b. St. David's, New Brunswick, in 1804; m., in Charlotte county, New Brunswick, Sept. 12, 1825, Nancy Cameron, b. 1800; d. April 29, 1880; he was a farmer and blacksmith. He d. in Ashland, Me., Jan. 21, 1848.
3576. i. CATHERINE M., b Sept. 27, 1826; m., July 27, 1845, —— ——. Res., Pine City, Minn.
3577. ii. ELIZA C., b. June 5, 1830; m., June 15, 1853, —— ——. Res., Ashland, Me.
3578. iii. FRANCIS, b Dec., 1827; d. ——.
3579. iv. DEBORAH F., b. March 28, 1832; m., ——, 1859, —— ——. Res., Readfield Depot, Me.

3580. v. ELLEN C., b. March 28, 1832; m., Feb. 7, 1856, ——— ———. Res., Ashland, Me.

3581. vi. THEODORE B., b. April 9, 1841; m., Nov. 7, 1867, Ann E. McKay, b. April 17, 1837; is a farmer. Res., s. p., Ashland, Me.

2762. EDWARD AUGUSTUS FOSTER (Edward, Levi, Benjamin, Benjamin, Benjamin, Isaac, Reginald), b. Machias, Me., Aug. 10, 1830; m., Fon du Lac, Wis., April 20, 1856, Laura Helen Foster, b. Aug. 8, 1834; d. March 26, 1896. Res., Wausau, Wis.

3582. i. HARVEY H., b. March 15, 1857: m. Elisabeth Wallin.

3583. ii. MAY C., b. Oct. 9, 1858; m., June, 1884, Lucius K. Baker. She d. in 1889. Ch.: 1. Helen. Res., Ashland, Wis.

3584. iii. ALICE, b. Dec. 25, 1864. Res., Wausau, Wis.

3585. iv. GEORGE E., b. May 13, 1866. Res., Wausau, Wis.

3586. v. FANNY, b. Sept. 25, 1868. Res., Wausau, Wis.

3587. vi. ANNIE LAURIE, b. Nov. 14, 1879. Res., Wausau, Wis.

2765. LUTHER HALL FOSTER (Edward, Levi, Benjamin, Benjamin, Benjamin, Isaac, Reginald), b. East Machias, Me., May 31, 1827; m., May 24, 1855, Lucy Amelia Schram, b. Aug. 27, 1832; murdered by a burglar. He d. June 29, 1896. Res., Ludington, Mich.

3588. i. FRANK A., b. March 24, 1856; m. Charlotte P. Wood.

3589. ii. EDWARD CLARENCE, b. Nov. 11, 1859; m. ——— ———.

2768. ALBERT H. FOSTER (George, Levi, Benjamin, Benjamin, Benjamin, Isaac, Reginald), b. Calais, Me., Aug. 27, 1855; m., Boston, Oct. 3, 1883, Laura J. Potter, b. July 4, 1857; he is a furniture dealer. Res., Dalton, Mass.

3590. i. HARRY P., b. April 10 1885.

3591. ii. STEVE P., b. July 18, 1888.

3592. iii. GEORGE P., b. July 20, 1892.

2782. PUBLIUS DARWIN FOSTER (John W., Daniel, Benjamin, Benjamin, Benjamin, Isaac, Reginald), b. Antwerp, N. Y., Dec. 13, 1829; m., Killingly, Conn., Sept. 28, 1857, Amanda Elizabeth Warren, b. July 18, 1831. The subject of this sketch was educated in the public and select schools of Antwerp. He studied law in the office of Judge Daniel Kellogg, of Saxton's River, Vt., and was admitted to the bar in 1852. He settled at Antwerp, having been admitted to practice before the courts of Jefferson county, N. Y., in 1853. In 1855 he was largely instrumental in establishing Antwerp Academy of which he was a trustee and secretary of the board of trustees until he removed from the town. On September 28, 1857, he married Amanda Elizabeth Warren, daughter of Dyer and Minerva (Durfee) Warren, of Killingly, Conn., and a graduate of Mount Holyoke Seminary. While living in Antwerp two children were born to them, Warren Worden, on August 10, 1858, and Harriet Minerva, on January 6, 1861. After aiding to recruit Company D., First New York light artillery, and Company C, Tenth New York heavy artillery, he received an appointment in the war department at Washington, D. C., in 1863. There he served as secretary of the relief committee of the New York Soldiers' Aid Association. In Washington, D. C., Elizabeth Hearty, on June 22, 1868, and Irving Lysander, on July 6, 1870, came to bless their union. He was admitted to the bar of the United States Supreme Court in 1870, and practiced his profession at the capital, until he removed to Killingly, Conn., where he died on September 2, 1897. In politics he was first a Free Soiler and later a Republican. He had been a representative to the Grand Lodge of the I. O O. F. in both New York and Connecticut. He was a member of the Grand Division of the Sons of Temperance, of the Independent Order of Good Templars, of the Temple of Honor, and the Killingly Grange. His voice, his vote and his influence were always opposed to the saloon and his life was a consistent example of temperance. He united with the Presbyterian church when fourteen years of age, and for almost sixty years was connected with various Sabbath schools as scholar, teacher or superintendent. His last words were the Lord's prayer, and he passed on sustained by an unfaltering trust in Jesus with the confident belief in immortality. He d. Sept. 2, 1897. Res., Antwerp, N. Y., and Killingly, Conn.

3593. i. WARREN WORDEN, b. Aug. 10, 1858; unm. Res., Washington, D C. His parents went to Washington, D. C., when he was about five years old and his early education was obtained in the private and public schools there. He graduated from the

Preparatory School of Columbian University, and when the family removed to Connecticut, was a student in the University. He received the degree of M. D. from the medical school of Harvard University in June, 1882. The practice of his profession was pursued several months in company with Dr. F. S. Burgess, of Moosup, Conn., and then for over five years in Putnam, Windham county, Conn. Since 1887 he has been living in Washington, D. C., connected with the United States Bureau of Pensions, of which he is one of the medical examiners. He is a member of the First Congregational church of that city, various medical societies, several Masonic bodies, the A. O. U. W., etc.

3594. ii. HARRIET MINERVA, b. Jan. 6, 1861; m., Oct. 14, 1891, John Gillespie Moore. Res., 238 Seventy-fourth street, Windsor Park, Chicago, Ill. He was b. Jan. 6, 1860; is a grocer. Ch.: 1. Mildred Moore, b. Jan. 2, 1893. 2. Warren Gillespie, b. Feb. 23, 1897.

3595. iii. ELIZABETH HEARTY, b. June 22, 1868; d. Sept. 24, 1869.

3596. iv. IRVING LYSANDER, b. July 6, 1870; m., June 9, 1898, Nellie O. Patterson. Res., State College, Center county, Pa.

2786. HON. GEORGE B. FOSTER (Azro, Robert, Isaiah, Benjamin, Benjamin, Isaac, Reginald), b. Boston, Mass., April 7, 1838; m., May 16, 1861, Sarah E. Tackaberry, b. Oct. 10, 1838; d. Feb. 13, 1879; he is a lawyer. Res., Peoria, Ill.

3597. i. MIDDLETON T., b. April 22, 1862; d. Nov. 10, 1866.

3598. ii. ARTHUR B., b. Nov. 12, 1863; m. Lily M. Armour.

3599. iii. FLORENCE O., b. Oct. 13, 1866; m., Sept. 17, 1878, W. A. Fleming. Res., Brainerd, Minn.

3600. iv. EUGENE B., b. ——; d. in infancy.

3601. v. WALTER H., b. June 26, 1870. Res., Peoria, Ill.

3602. vi. GILBERT E., b. June 10, 1874; d. in infancy.

2787. HENRY ALLINE FOSTER (Azro, Robert, Isaiah, Benjamin, Benjamin, Isaac, Reginald), b. Andover, Mass., June 9, 1840; m., Milwaukee, Wis., March 6, 1880, Marguerite Beaugrand, b. Sept. 28, 1848; is a coal operator. Res., s. p., Des Moines, Iowa.

2794. CAPT. PHINEHAS FOSTER (Phinehas, Moses, Worden, Benjamin, Benjamin, Isaac, Reginald), b. Dennysville, Me., June 8, 1831; m., Hallowell, Me., Oct. 17, 1859, Ellen Jane Bolton, b. Nov. 21, 1839. He was born in Dennysville, Me.; resided in East Machias, attending the public schools and Washington Academy until he was thirteen years old, when he moved to Marion with his father, where he was bred on the farm and was lumbering until he was twenty-one. Then went to East Machias and engaged in the lumber business until 1859. Was messenger to the governor and council in 1859 and 1860; was married to Ellen Jane Bolton at Augusta, Me.; enlisted in Company D, First Maine cavalry, in September, 1861; was made sergeant when the regiment was mustered into United States service in October. During the spring and summer of 1863 was at headquarters Second division, Cavalry corps, when commanded by Brig.-Gen. D. M. Gregg; was in command of his escort and orderlies; was promoted to first-lieutenant of Company D, in February, 1864; was in command of Company D from the latter part of June till November, 1864, when he returned to Augusta, Me., where the regiment was mustered out of the service. He was with the regiment in the field all the time, and participated in most of the engagements and skirmishes in which the regiment was engaged in. He had two horses shot under him, one at Deep Bottom, the other at Trevilian Station, in Virginia. His regiment was with the Army of the Potomac. In February, 1865, he emigrated to what was then Washington Territory, arriving at Fort Gamble in April, where he resided till 1878, when he went to Tacoma, where he now resides. He has been engaged in lumbering since he went to that coast; is a member of the G. A. R., also of the military order of the Loyal Legion; is a past-commander of Custer Post, the second largest post in this department; is treasurer of the Washington commandery of the Loyal Legion. Residence, 220 North Tacoma avenue, Tacoma, Wash.

3603. i. WALTER BOLTON, b. June 24, 1866; d. June 11, 1869.

3604. ii. MARION W., b. June 29, 1871; d. Aug. 16, 1876.

3605. iii. DAISY DEAN, b. March 28, 1875. Res., 220 North Tacoma avenue, Tacoma, Wash.

3606. iv. ANNIE BOLTON, b. Oct. 28, 1860; unm.; teacher of music. Res., 220 North Tacoma avenue, Tacoma, Wash.

2791-2. SAMUEL NUTT FOSTER (John M., Benen, Isaiah, Benjamin, Benjamin, Isaac, Reginald), b. March 2, 1830; m., July 30, 1853, Frances A. Foster, b. Feb. 24, 1834; d. March 11, 1878; m. 2d, Oct. 6, 1878, Mrs. Melissa J. Doty, b. Jan. 21, 1834. Res., Mullock, Assa., N. W. T.

3605-1. i. ALMA E., b. May 29, 1856; m., Oct. 18, 1874, De Lancy A. Foster. Ch.: 1. Allen L. Foster, b. Aug. 6, 1875; d. April 1, 1895. 2. Frank F. Foster, b. June 14, 1877. 3. Della M. Foster, b. Feb. 12, 1879; m. Oct., 1898, Randolph A. Tompkins, and lives at Mt. Pleasant, Carleton Co., N. B. 4. Byron D. Foster, b. July 5, 1881. 5. Ethel H., b. Oct. 26, 1883. 6. Mabel Wynn, b. Dec. 13, 1885. 7. J. Talmage, b. April 5, 1888. 8. Phyllis F., b. Feb. 8, 1891. 9. Hazel A., b. Feb. 7, 1894. 10. Bertha L., b. June 2, 1897. Res., Lansdowne, Carleton county, New Brunswick. De Lancy Allen Foster, b. Oct. 14, 1845, at Frederickton, N. B.; B.; he was son of Joseph W. Foster, b. April 5, 1819, at Merimichi, N. B.; Joseph W. Foster, the son of Joseph Foster, and his (Joseph's) father came to the province of New Brunswick in 1783, settling in Merimichi until the great fire there, when he moved to Frederickton, N. B. De Lancy Allen Foster's mother's maiden name was Charlotte M. Tompkins, b. March 29, 1824; m. Nov. 28, 1844: her parents came from New York State. De Lancy Allen Foster's brothers and sisters names are Charles E. Foster, b. Dec. 19, 1847; Almeda L. Foster, b. July 6, 1850; John B. Foster, b. Dec. 21, 1852; Henrietta E. Foster, b. Nov. 28, 1855, and Lorenzo R. Foster, b. Sept. 10, 1858.

3605-2. ii. ARMINA, b. March 29, 1858; m., July 16, 1881, David Brown. Res., Carleton county, N. B. (probably Lansdowne).

3605-3. iii. SAMUEL N., JR., b. May 19, 1860; m., Sept. 6, 1891, Elsie Eleanor Moore, dau. of George Houghton Moore and Moriah Eleanor Moore. The Moores were all born in Henderson county, N. C. Ch.: 1. Alma Eleanor, b. Dec. 2, 1892. 3. Ada Blanche, b. July 15, 1894. 3. Charles Alvin, b. Dec. 24, 1897. Res., for nine years, Brevard, Transylvania county, N. C.

3605-4. iv. EVA FRANCES, b. April 21, 1880.

2792-3. ODBER MOSES FOSTER (John M., Benen, Isaiah, Benjamin, Benjamin, Isaac, Reginald), b. Sept. 11, 1832 in Wakefield, N. B.; m., Sept. 4, 1854, Harriet E. Smith, b. 1839; d. Jan. 1, 1877; m. 2d, in 1885, Elizabeth Campbell, by whom he has no issue. Res, Houlton, Me.

3605-5. i. CLEMENTINA, b. June 25, 1855; m. Oliver Bryant, s. p.

3605-6. ii. ELLEN CORILLA, b. April 20, 1857; m., June 27, 1883, James Duncan MacDonald, s. p.

3605-7. iii. FRANK CLAYTON, b. Dec. 5, 1863; m., Aug. 16, 1885, Alma Churchill, b. June 30, 1866. Res., Woodstock, N. B. Ch.: 1. Clayton Graves Foster, b. April 22, 1886. 2. Gladys Harriet Foster, b. Oct. 25, 1889. 3. Nellie Levina Foster, b. April 14, 1891. 4. Jessie Corilla Foster, b. Dec. 29, 1892.

3605-8. iv. CAROLINE, b. Dec. 27, 1867; m. George Smith. Res., Hermon Pond, Me., s. p.

3605-8¼. v. JUDITH CARRIE, b. Oct. 23, 1859; d. April 23, 1861.

3605-8½. vi. WILLIAM, b. Jan. 16, 1874; d. July 25, 1875.

2796-8. PARKER HUMPHREY FOSTER (John M., Benen, Isaiah, Benjamin, Benjamin, Isaac, Reginald), b. Woodstock, N. B., May 13, 1846; m., in Boston, Mass., Aug. 20, 1878, Mary Azzie Sprague, b. Nov. 16, 1858; he is a commercial printer. Parker Humphrey Foster came to Boston in 1863 and completed his trade; started in business for himself in 1872 in the printing and publishing business, which he now, 1899, carries on; an independent in politics; fond of all athletic sports, particularly his gun and dog. Married in 1878; moved to Arlington to reside in 1881; an Orthodox in religion. Res., 796 Massachusetts avenue, Arlington, Mass.

3606-1. i. MARION (girl), b. corner Bartlett avenue and Massachusetts avenue, Arlington, Mass., Oct. 29, 1882.

3607-2. ii. GEORGE PARKER, b. at 9 Avon Place, Sept. 5, 1884, Arlington, Mass. Both living with parents (Feb. '98) at 796 Massachusetts avenue, Arlington, Mass.

PARKER H. FOSTER.

2806. FREDERICK AUGUSTUS FOSTER (Charles, James, Worden, Benjamin, Benjamin, Isaac, Reginald), b. E. Machias, Me., Oct. 22, 1846; m., Sept. 10, 1868, Abbie M. Weston; m., 2d, Sept. 4, 1889, S. Elizabeth Loring. Silk manufacturer. Res., Newton Centre, Mass. 70 Grey Cliff Road.

3607. i. MABEL A., b. Jan. 26, 1876.

3608. ii. PAUL W., b. Nov. 5, 1880.

2822. GEORGE P. FOSTER (Austin B., Nathan, Jeremiah, Jeremiah, Abraham, Jacob, Reginald), b. Wirt, N. Y., Feb. 10, 1839; m. ——, 1865, —— ——. Was in Civil war. He d. Nov. 7, 1877. Res., Plainwell, Mich.

3609. i. ELMER C., b. ——. Res., P.

2824. SIDNEY ALGERNON FOSTER (Austin B., Nathan, Jeremiah, Jeremiah, Abraham, Jacob, Reginald), b. Wirt, N. Y., May 17, 1849; m., Jan. 5, 1869, Ella Jane Dyer, b. Aug. 22, 1850; d. 1875; m., 2d, June 17, 1877, Clara P. Hill, b. Aug. 5, 1850.

Sidney Algernon Foster, youngest of the family of Austin Baker Foster, was born in the township of Wirt, Allegany county, N. Y. He acquired such an education as his circumstances would permit, and in 1865 came through to Adams county, Wisconsin, with a team. There he worked at various occupations. Drove stage, worked on a farm, served an apprenticeship in the printing business, worked as a section hand on the C., M. & St. Paul Railway, "run" the river and settled to his trade and continued in the newspaper field as foreman and proprietor until 1884. He was Chief Clerk of the House of Representatives of Iowa. Has always been an active Republican in politics and has participated in the speaking campaigns of the party in Iowa and in other States for more than twenty years.

In 1897 his name was quite prominently mentioned in connection with the nomination for Governor of Iowa, but Mr. Foster declined to enter among the list of candidates. In 1884 he began the organization of the Royal Union Mutual Life Insurance Company, was made the Secretary, and still holds the position. He is the author of the sentiment, "In all that is good, Iowa affords the best." In 1886 he declined a Congressional nomination by his party, preferring to continue in business rather than embark in a political life. Res., Des Moines, Iowa, 911 Third street.

3610 i. ALBERT S., b. Durand, Wis., Oct. 24, 1869; m., Spring Valley, Wis., Feb. 2, 1898, Ida May Kirk, b. Feb. 20, 1874. He is a farmer. Res., Durand, Wis., s. p.

3611. ii. DON H., b. July 17, 1879. Res., Des Moines, Iowa.

3612. iii. GLADYS H., b. June 27, 1887. Res., Des Moines, Iowa.

3613. iv. WILLARD H., b. Nov. 19, 1891. Res., Des Moines, Iowa.

2827. ALVARA FOSTER (Elijah W., Abraham, Samuel, Jeremiah, Abraham, Jacob, Reginald), b. Gardner, Mass., Feb. 19, 1837; m., in Ashburnham, May 31, 1865, Mrs. Lois Irene (Goodwin) Puffer, b. Aug. 7, 1838. He is a farmer. Res., Ashburnham, Mass.

3614. i. ABBIE L., b. June 25, 1860; m. in 1889, Alfred Heywood. Res., Hubbardston. He was son of William and Annie. Had three children, Nathaniel, Ralph and Marion Lois.

3615. ii. EDWARD WILLARD, b. March 11, 1870; m. Grace Coleman.

2830. HENRY FOSTER (Elijah W., Abraham, Samuel, Jeremiah, Abraham, Jacob, Reginald), b. Aug. 7, 1845; m., Dec. 20, 1872, Lynetta Goodwin. Res., West Gardner, Mass.

3616. i. GEORGE EDWIN, b. in 1875.

SIDNEY A.FOSTER.

2833. SEWALL FOSTER (Elijah W., Abraham, Samuel, Jeremiah, Abraham, Jacob, Reginald), b. Hubbardston, Mass., April 29, 1833; m., Dedham, Mass., Oct. 4, 1865, Sarah Ann Smith, b. July 4, 1837. Res., Fitchburg, Mass., 63 South Street.

3617. i. MARY ALICE, b. Aug. 31, 1874; unm. Res., at home.

2841. WALDO A. FOSTER (Leonard, Nathaniel, Samuel, Jeremiah, Abraham, Jacob, Reginald), b. Ashburnham, Mass., Oct. 6, 1841; m., Dec. 31, 1870, H. Elizabeth Chandler. Was in employ of Fitchburg railroad for years. Res., Fitchburg, Mass.

2851. ALVIN R. FOSTER (Hosea, Samuel, Samuel, Jeremiah, Abraham, Jacob, Reginald), b. Oct. 14, 1834, Stoddard, N. H.; m., Feb. 2, 1866, Mary J. Sargent; d. June 15, 1877; m., 2d, June 13, 1880, Mrs. Eliza A. Scott. He was a carpenter. Res. Keene, N. H.

3618. i. HERBERT A., b. March 27, 1867; m. Annis Burke.

3619. ii. NELLIE M., b. Sept. 17, 1872; unm. Res., Keene, N. H.

2853. EDWIN STEARNS FOSTER (Hosea, Samuel, Samuel, Jeremiah, Abraham, Jacob, Reginald), b. Dec 21, 1840, Stoddard, N. H.: m., Brattleboro, Nov. 26, 1868, Ella S. Houghton, b. Dec. 18, 1846; d. May 12, 1889; m., 2d, at Keene, N. H., Feb. 12, 1890, Clara Fay, of Marlow.

Edwin Stearns Foster was born in Stoddard, N. H., on the farm on which his father and grandfather had lived since the removal of the latter from Ashburnham, Mass., in 1799. At the age of twenty he left home and went to Keene, where he worked for a short time at the carpenter trade, going from there to Ashburnham, Mass. In 1863 he went to Springfield Mass., where he was employed in the United States Arsenal until July 9, 1864, when he enlisted in Company A, Eighth Massachusetts Volunteer Militia, to serve one hundred days, or during the war. Was discharged Nov. 10, 1864, by reason of expiration of term of service. His company was not engaged in any action during the time of his service, serving most of the time at guard duty in Baltimore. In the year 1865 he was employed in Chicago, from which place he went to Brattleboro, Vt., and with fourteen others formed a company and built the Brattleboro Melodeon factory. In 1868 he sold his interest in that company and went to Keene, N. H., where for some years with his brother Alvin, and afterward by himself, he carried on the business of contracting and building, until 1890, when he removed to Manchester, N. H., and became associated as superintendent with an architect. Mr. Foster has always been actively interested in public affairs. While in Keene he was for many years a member of the Board of Sewer and Water Commissioners. Res., Manchester, N. H.

3620. i. FRANK H., b. Sept. 10, 1869; m. Inez E. Fairbanks.
3621. ii. HARRY S., b. May 17, 1871; m. Amy Otis.
3622. iii. GEORGE EDWIN, b. Aug. 13, 1872. Is a watchmaker. Res., Brattleboro, Vt.
3623. iv. LOUISA BELLE, b. Aug. 13, 1876. Res., Manchester.
3624. v. CARL HOSEA, b Jan. 3, 1883. Res., Manchester.
3625. vi. GRACE ADELINE, b. Feb. 23, 1884. Res., Manchester.
3626. vii. MARY HOOPER, b. Aug. 18, 1891. Res., Manchester.

2865. GEORGE COLSON FOSTER (Jerome W., Joel, Samuel, Jeremiah, Abraham, Jacob, Reginald), b. Ashburnham, Mass., Jan. 21, 1835; m., Aug. 10, 1856, Sarah E. Bemis, dau. of William, b. Oct. 20, 1837. He is proprietor of a livery stable and a farmer and a useful and active citizen. Is now an undertaker. Res., Ashburnham, Mass.

3627. i. CHARLES WILLIAM, b. May 16, 1858. Res., 201 Eighth Ave., New York City.
3628. ii. GEORGE ORLANDO, b. June 17, 1862; d. Feb. 12, 1883.

2884. CAPT. CHARLES CARROLL FOSTER (Daniel, James, Daniel, Joseph, Joseph, Jacob, Reginald), b. Beverly, Mass., Feb. 22, 1834; m., June 19, 1859, Sarah E. Burke, b. 1839, dau. of Edward and Martha. He was a master mariner. Res., Beverly, Mass.

3629. i. ALICE LOUISE, b. Aug. 10, 1860; d. April 15, 1862.
3630. ii. CARL WALLIS, b. Aug. 9, 1878.
3631. iii. MARTHA H., b. Oct. 27, 1870; d. Jan. 31, 1889.
3631½. iv. NELLIE CARROLL, b. Nov. 6, 1863.

2887. FRANCIS AUGUSTUS FOSTER (Daniel, James, Daniel, Joseph, Joseph, Jacob, Reginald), b. Beverly, Mass., May 14, 1849; m., March 10, 1875, Martha L. Grant. He was a mariner. Res., Beverly, Mass.

3632. i. BESSIE GRANT, b. Sept. 23, 1876; d. Aug. 19, 1877.
3633. ii. ——, b. July 24, 1878.
3634. iii. LIZZIE HALE, b. May 16, 1879.
3635. iv. ROBERT GRANT, b. June 11, 1881.

2888. HENRY AUSTIN FOSTER (Daniel, James, Daniel, Joseph, Joseph, Jacob, Reginald), b. Beverly, Mass., Oct. 4, 1851; m., Jan. 21, 1875, Anna L. Morgan, b. in 1854, dau. of William and Eliza (Kennison). Res., Beverly, Mass.

2908. WILLIAM AUGUSTUS FOSTER (Daniel, Seth, Daniel, Joseph, Joseph, Jacob, Reginald), b. Beverly, Mass., April 22, 1860; m., Nov. 18, 18—, —— ——; m., 2d, April 15, 1884, Emma Frances Clough, b. 1864, dau. of George A. and Nancy. He is a shoemaker. Res., Beverly, Mass.

3636. i. GRACE LOUISE, b. June 23, 1884.
3637. ii. HELEN PAGE, b. Dec. 11, 1889.

2913. SETH FOSTER (Daniel, Seth, Daniel, Joseph, Joseph, Jacob, Reginald), b. Beverly, Mass., Oct. 4, 1847; m., Nov. 2, 1885, Mary J. McLean, b. 1864, in N. S., dau. of Donald. Res., Beverly, Mass.

3638. i. EMMA FRANCES, b. Jan. 7, 1890.
3639. ii. HARRY IRVING, b. Nov. 30, 1888.
3640. iii. ELSIE, b. Aug. 18, 1887.

2929. REV. ELON FOSTER, D. D. (Leonard R., Isaac, Isaac, Isaac, Joseph, Jacob, Reginald), b. June 22, 1833; m., April 27, 1857, Sarah, dau. of Walter Clark and Phebe (Worrall) Palmer, b. Aug. 6, 1834. His early life was that of many another farmer son; days full of toil, with intervals of study at the district school. He made use of his opportunities, however, and later attended Newberry Seminary, Vermont. From there he went to the General Theological Institute (now Boston Theological Seminary), where he was graduated with the degree of B. D., in 1855. Joining the Conference of the Methodist lEpiscopal Church; he immediately entered upon the work of a pastor in East Hebron, N. Y., and the following year he was stationed at Troy, N. Y.; in 1857-58 in Williston, Vt. In 1859 he was transferred to the New York Conference and stationed (1859-60) in Salisbury, Conn.;

1861 City Mission, New York; 1862-3 Brewster's Station, N. Y.; 1864 New Castle, N. Y. In all of these appointments his labors were effective, resulting in enlarged membership and increased spiritual devotion in the church. His chosen work, however, he was compelled to relinquish by an accident on the Harlem Railroad in 1864, in which he was so injured internally as to render further pastorial work impossible. From 1864 to 1867 he was engaged in editing and publishing the "Guide to Holiness." In the latter year he began the preparation of "Foster's Cyclopedia of Illustration," the first volume of which was issued in 1870. It attained great popularity. No less than 10,000 were sold the first year. Another volume of illustrations, covering poetical literature, followed in 1872; another of prose, like the first, was issued in 1877, and still another of poetical illustrations in 1880. Sixty-five thousand volumes have been sold, and through them Dr. Foster (for he received the degree of Doctor of Divinity from the Upper Iowa University in 1879) feels that he has preached to a larger congregation than he had conceived when he entered the ministry. Only recently he received a note from a grateful preacher from which the following is taken: "Your name will be known in the world so long as preachers preach and books are known, and they are books, too, that mightily preach and teach." Dr. Foster has traveled in every state and in most of the territories of the Union. Seriously impaired health compelled him in April, 1896, to take the "superanuate" relation to the New York Conference. Thus retired from active service he still continues the studious habits of his earlier years, finding his happiness therein. Res., 147 Hewes St., Brooklyn, N. Y. He d. Nov. 15, 1898.

REV. ELON FOSTER, D. D.

3641. i. PHOEBE PALMER, b. June 18, 1858; unm. Res., 147 Hewes St., Brooklyn, N. Y.
3642. ii. CHARLES LEONARD, b. Sept. 11, 1859; m. Evelina M. Smith; graduated at Wesleyan University, Middletown, Conn., 1881; receiving degree of A. M., in 1884; studied law at Cambridge College Law School, graduating in 1883; is engaged in the practice of law at 18 Wall St., New York City.
3643. iii. JENNIE LANKFORD, b. July 11, 1862; d. Nov. 22, 1881.

2936. LUKE WHITMAN FOSTER (Leonard R., Isaac, Isaac, Isaac, Joseph, Jacob, Reginald), b. Moretown, Vt., Jan. 13, 1850; m., June 7, 1876, Alice, dau. of Isaac and Sarah (Shafer), Fuller, b. July 11, 1852; a merchant. Res., Lone Rock, Wis., and LaCrosse, Wis., 403 Main St.
3644. i. GERTIE MAY, b. Dec. 3, 1877.
3645. ii. ALFRED LEONARD, b. Jan. 22, 1881.

2937. ARTHUR M. FOSTER (Leonard R., Isaac, Isaac, Isaac, Joseph, Jacob, Reginald), b. April 24, 1863; m., April 2, 1883, Ella M. Fuller, b. May 19. 1856; sister of Alice; a manufacturer; did reside at Lone Rock. Res., La Crosse, Wis., 403 Main St.
3646. i. HARRY CLYDE, b. Aug. 13, 1884.
3647. ii. LYNN EMMONS, b. Aug. 8, 1886.

2944. GILMAN G. FOSTER (John W., Isaac, Isaac, Isaac, Joseph, Jacob, Reginald), b. Nov. 15, 1842; m., Oct. 4, 1875, Elvira J., dau. of Lewis and Sarah (Haws) Harlow, b. Dec. 6, 1844; a tub manufacturer. Res., Stowe, Vt.

3648. i. A SON, b. May 23; d. July 4, 1881.
3649. ii. ETHEL EDNA, b. Sept. 14, 1883.

2946. EDWIN A. FOSTER (John W., Isaac, Isaac, Isaac, Joseph, Jacob, Reginald), b. Sept. 12, 1850; m., May 13, 1878, Mary E., dau. of Hiram and Clarrisa (Martin) Cnaffee, b. July 21, 1860; a farmer. Res., Moretown, Vt.
3650. i. GERALD (twin), b. April 6, 1880.
3651. ii. ELMER (twin), b. April 6, 1880.

2948. IRA H. FOSTER (Daniel, Daniel, Isaac, Isaac, Joseph, Jacob, Reginald), b. Augusta, Me., Jan. 8, 1823; m., Scranton, Pa., Sept. 15, 1864, Amanda M. Crandall, b. Brooklyn, Pa., May 16, 1836. He d. Aug. 23, 1888. Res., Scranton, Pa., and Binghamton, N. Y.
3652. i. JENNIE C., b. June 17, 1865.
3653. ii. EMERETTE, b. Dec. 2, 1866.
3654. iii. D. WINTHROP, b. July 6, 1870.
3655. iv. IRA H., JR., b. Aug. 16, 1873.
3656. v. HELEN, b. May 19, 1877.

2949. TIMOTHY DANFORTH FOSTER (Daniel, Daniel, Isaac, Isaac, Joseph, Jacob, Reginald), b. Augusta, Me., March 10, 1825; m., Dec. 15, 1858, Ann Sims Clark, b. Dec. 29, 1832. She m., 2d, —— Spaulding. Res., Augusta. He was a farmer. He d. Dec. 21, 1871. Res., Augusta, Me.
3657. i. CARRIE ELLA, b. May 28, 1862; d. May 30, 1877.
3658. ii. DANIEL EATON, b. Nov. 29, 1866; unm.; is a farmer and dairyman. Res., Augusta.

2950. DANIEL WINTHROP FOSTER (Daniel, Daniel, Isaac, Isaac, Joseph, Jacob, Reginald), b. Augusta, Me., April 27, 1829; m., Boston, Mass., Sept. 2, 1852, Dorcas L. Marshall, b. Detroit, Mich., Sept. 22, 1830. Merchant. Res., Melrose, Mass. Address, Boston, Mass., 97½ Portland St.
3659. i. ANNIE LAKEMAN, b. Jan. 25, 1855; m., Eugene H. Moore, Nov. 24, 1874. Res., Melrose, Mass. Ch.: 1. Gertrude Foster, b. Aug. 14, 1879. 2. Irma Agnes, b. June 22, 1883. 3. Winthrop Watson, b Sept. 25, 1886.
3660. ii. ALICE LOUISE, b. Feb. 3, 1856; m. George A. Aldrich, May 12, 1880. Res., Dorchester, Mass. He was b. Aug. 31, 1858; is a wholesale grocer. Ch.: 1. Gladys Viola, b. Sept. 24, 1888.
3661. iii. GERTRUDE, b. Jan. 21, 1859; m. Frank A. Messenger, Jr., Jan. 4, 1883. Res., Melrose, Mass.
3662. iv. HELEN AGNES, b. Nov. 3, 1861; m. George E. Wheeler, Oct. 2, 1882. Res., South Sioux Falls, S. D.

2953. JOHN AVERY FOSTER (Daniel, Daniel, Isaac, Isaac, Joseph, Jacob, Reginald), b. Augusta, Me., Nov. 8, 1839; m., Jan. 1, 1870, Clara Ann Tucker, b. April 16, 1849; d. Jan. 13, 1893. Res., Augusta, Me.
3663. i. IRA HADLEY, b. Feb. 10, 1872; m. Hattie M. Stone.
3664. ii. BURTON LEE, b. March 19, 1878. Res., 97½ Portland St., Boston, Mass.

2955. COL. BENJAMIN BROWN FOSTER (Cony, Daniel, Isaac, Isaac, Joseph, Jacob, Reginald), b. Orono, Me., Nov. 23, 1831; m. at Canandaigua, N. Y., Dec. 24, 1863, Sarah Gibson Howell, b. June 20, 1842; d. Feb. 16, 1897, dau. of Thomas Morris and Louisa (Young) Howell.

Benjamin Brown Foster graduated at Bowdoin College in 1855 with "first honors." Was a clerk in the War and Postoffice Departments at Washington; entered the army from which he afterward resigned, receiving from the President, in 1868, brevet commissions of Lieutenant-Colonel, and Colonel. He practiced his profession of law in Norfolk, Va.; was appointed Judge of the Court of the corporation of the city of Norfolk and Judge of the Hustings Court of Portsmouth, and was elected Commonwealths Attorney for the county of Norfolk. In November, 1873, he removed to Brooklyn, N. Y., with his family, practicing law in New York City, at 60 Wall street. He is a member of the military order of the Loyal Legion. Res., Canandaigua, N. Y., and Norfolk, Va., and Lincoln Club, Putnam Ave., Brooklyn, N. Y.
3665. i. HOWELL, b. Canandaigua, N. Y., Nov. 17, 1864; unm. Res., New York, N. Y. Address, 170 William St. He is with Schief-

felin & Co., in New York City; is a member of the military order of Loyal Legion and of the society of Colonial Wars.

3666. ii. WINTHROP, b. Canandaigua, June 14, 1867; unm.

3667. iii. LOUISE, b. Norfolk, Va., Jan. 21, 1869; m. Dr. Ira Ayer, Aug. 18, 1892. Ch. 1. Phillis, b. May 5, 1893. 2. Margaret, b. June 29, 1894. Address, 214 Greene Ave., Brooklyn, N. Y.

3668. iv. GIBSON and Greig (twins), b. Norfolk, July 21, 1871. Greig died July 12, 1872. Gibson unm.

3669. vi. RAYMOND, b. Norfolk, June 19, 1875; m. at Poughkeepsie, N. Y., June 8, 1898, Alice Adriance, dau. of Edgar C.

3670. vii. COLEMAN, b. Jan. 29, 1878; d. July 19, 1878.

2956. COL. CHARLES HENRY FOSTER (Cony, Daniel, Isaac, Isaac, Joseph, Jacob, Reginald), b. Orono, Me., Feb. 18, 1830; m. May 1, 1860, Sue Agnes Carter, dau. of Perry and Priscilla Carter, of Murfreesboro, N. C.

Charles Henry Foster was born in Orono, Me. He came of sturdy New England stock. His father was a prominent merchant and distinguished citizen of Orono, and his maternal grandfather was Benjamin Brown, founder of the Insane Asylum at Augusta, Me., and one of the wealthiest citizens of the Pine Tree State, whose portrait now hangs in the State House at Augusta, as one of the three men most distinguished in Maine for benevolence and public spirit. The subject of this sketch was noted for his manly characteristics and his studious habits as a boy. When he entered Bowdoin College, he had already secured a fair collegiate education, mainly by his own exertion, and he graduated with first honors in 1855. During his college life he found opportunity for much metaphysical research, and he wrote with so much force and originality on this and kindred subjects that the productions of his pen were in demand among the leading magazines of the day.

This inclination to magazine writing he never lost, contributing frequently to Blackwood's, Harper's and the North American Review. His latest magazine article was a sketch of the Gatling gun, and its inventor, published in Potter's Monthly. Having determined to devote himself to the law, Mr. Foster, after leaving college, at once entered upon a course of study in the office of ex-Governor Israel Washburn, and speedily attracted the close attention of that eminent jurist. Ultimately Mr. Washburn offered him a partnership in the business, but young Foster determined to cast his lot in the South, and in 1858 he located at Norfolk, Va., as editor of the Day Book. After remaining in Norfolk a year he removed to Murfreesborough, N. C., where he took editorial charge of the Citizen, a Democratic paper, and also began the practice of law. He was very successful in both callings, and the outbreak of the war found him pleasantly situated and prospering in every way. When North Carolina seceded, Mr. Foster remained true to the Union. The bitterness of sectional feeling then prevailing was such that his outspoken views not only ruined his business but nearly cost him his life. He had before this married Miss Sue Agnes Carter, a daughter of one of the richest and most prominent men of Murfreesboro. This alliance at first somewhat modified popular feeling toward him, but when under special direction of President Lincoln, he recruited a regiment of loyal North Carolinians for service in the eastern part of the state the outburst of public indignation and resentment was intensified by reason of it. Colonel Foster was actuated by principle in this matter, and the fact that his wife was held as a hostage and a price put upon his own head did not cause him to swerve a hair's breadth from what he felt to be his duty. He strengthened the Federal arm mightily in North Carolina, but his men—three companies of the First and the whole of the Second (his own) regiment were hanged without mercy whenever captured. Colonel Foster was himself surprised at a cabin where he was resting for the night, and taken prisoner. But one of his guard, whose gratitude for favors done was stronger than his love for the Confederacy, contrived to let the captive get away. Colonel Foster had many narrow escapes, and was identified with all the stirring scenes of the war enacted between Norfolk and Beaufort. The warfare he made was as high-toned and honorable as anything the records of chivalry can show. Under fire he was as cool as when on parade. He knew no fear except to do a mean act, and his tender care of his men caused him to be almost idolized by them. It was the belief of the North Carolina Confederates that Colonel Foster would wage a war of reprisal; but when it was found that he spared the defenseless, respected property rights and used his independent command simply in the interest of earnest, steadfast loyalty to the Union, and without a thought of personal ends or of private revenge, his name became a prized household word with thousands who, in 1862, wished to take his life. Colonel Foster came through the war with a reputation so high for every social and soldiery quality that the people of Murfreesboro (where he still made his home) were anxious to honor him. He was chosen a professor in the Chapel Hill Seminary, and was elected to the Thirty-ninth Congress to represent what was then called the Chapel Hill district, but reconstruction not having been accomplished, he was not admitted to the seat, and although he afterward took an active part in the politics of reconstruction and won fame as a stump-speaker, he steadily refused office of any kind. He again returned to the practice of law, making collections of claims a specialty. He raised subscriptions and had all the families of his soldiers made comfortable, and he freely gave legal advice and assistance to such of his men as survived. At this period he was a correspondent of the New York Herald, doing much exceptionally valuable political and general work for that paper. In 1878 he came to Philadelphia, because of the ill-health of his wife, and in the interest of several Southern papers. He was promptly admitted to the bar of this city, but without attempting to build up a practice, became confirmed in his devotion to journalism, making a connection with the Philadelphia Record, which continued until his death. He read Greek and Latin as fluently as he did English, and his critical knowledge of those languages was surprising. When one of the encyclical letters of Pope Leo XIII was published in this country a few years ago, Mr. Foster pointed out gross errors in the official translation, and received the thanks of gentlemen high in the Catholic Church for the service rendered. He was an omnivorous but discriminating reader, and classical authors were almost as familiar to him as his Bible.

For more than three years Mr. Foster has been editor-in-chief of the Record. It is no praise to him nor dispraise of others to say that there is not a writer for the press in Philadelphia so well equipped that he could fill the chair of our dead friend. He was a thoroughly educated man, not only in the lore of the schools but in the experience of active life. The loss of such a man is a deprivation to thousands who have never seen or known him. There is nothing that can give a keener pang to grief than to see so much that is good and true and noble in the world utterly perish out of it at the fell stroke of death.

One of Mr. Foster's brothers, Benjamin B. Foster, was Corporation Judge of the Courts of Norfolk and Portsmouth, Va., for several years after the war, and also United States Commissioner and Register in Bankruptcy there. Later he was Assistant United States District Attorney in New York, and is now a prominent lawyer in that city.

He d. March 14, 1882. Res., Murfreesboro, N. C., and Philadelphia, Pa.

3671. i. CAROLYN AGNES, b. Feb. 15, 1861; m., June 2, 1890, Dr. Edgar M. Marbourg; m. at Denver, Col. Res., Pueblo, Col. Ch.: 1. Edgar Foster, b. April 22, 1897.

3672. ii. ELLEN CARTER, b. Aug. 3, 1864; m., Dec. 23, 1887, Charles M. Stone. Res., Ardmore, Pa. Ch.: 1. Charles Allison, b. Aug. 12, 1889.

3673. iii. CHARLES CONY, b. July 29, 1866; d. in infancy.

3674. iv. CHARLES JOSEPH, b. Sept. 18, 1868; d. in infancy.

3675. v. SUE BROWN, b. Sept. 18, 1868; m., Oct. 30, 1889, Thomas M. Browning, of Philadelphia.

3676. vi. BENJAMIN BROWN, b. Aug. 11, 1870; m. Pearl C. Lewis. Res., Pueblo, Col. She was b. 1880.

2059. LYMAN BEECHER FOSTER (Cony, Daniel, Isaac, Isaac, Joseph, Jacob, Reginald), b. Orono, Me., March 10, 1841; m., June 27, 1867, Mary Cheny Etheridge, dau. of Joseph H. and Mary Eliza; d. Dec. 13, 1868; m., 2d, Oct. 5, 1874, Susan Alice Spencer, dau. of George W. and Angelica. He d. May 29, 1894. Res., Portsmouth, Va.

3677. i. MARY CHENY, b. Nov. 28, 1868; m., April 18, 1885, William F. Durfey. She d. Aug. 10, 1887.

3678. ii. BENJAMIN HARTSOOK, b. Nov. 18, 1875.

3679. iii. UPSHUR, b. July 28, 1877; d. April 28, 1878.

3680. iv. CAROLINE, b. Nov. 20, 1879.

3681. v. CHRISTINE, b. Oct. 6, 1881.

3682. vi. CHARLES ALBERT, b. Feb. 27, 1885.

3683. vii. ROGER WILLARD, b. Jan. 5, 1888; d. Feb. 12, 1889.

2962. GEORGE BURGESS FOSTER (Cony, Daniel, Isaac, Isaac, Joseph, Jacob, Reginald), b. Orono, Me., Oct. 19, 1850; m. in Boston, Oct. 2, 1877, Christine Marie Hanson, b. Feb. 24, 1858.

George Burgess Foster, youngest child of Cony Foster and Caroline Brown Foster, was born in Orono, Me. He attended the public schools in the town until he was fourteen years old, when he entered the store of Robert Cromby, of Orono, as clerk. He remained there one year, and then worked for Joseph B. Chase in the same town as clerk. The following winter he attended the Bryant & Stratton Commercial College, in Bangor, Me., and then went into the employ of Weed & Fifield, wholesale and retail clothiers, of Bangor, as salesman. He remained with this concern some two years, but wishing to see more of the world he went to Boston in 1868, when he was eighteen years old, and entered the employ of William Wolff, hat and cap manufacturer, as traveling salesman. He continued with Wolff two years, and then took a better position with Gould, Davenport & Spaulding, wholesale hatters, on the road as traveling salesman. He continued with them until forced to give up on account of sickness.

After regaining his health Mr. Foster learned the confectionery business, and in 1878 went to Salem, Mass., and opened a store for the manufacture of the finer lines of confectionery. Mr. Foster did a prosperous business in Salem, and after remaining there eight years, during which he was married, sold his business out to a good advantage, and went to Florida with his family to spend the winter. He remained in Florida nearly a year, and on returning to Boston made an engagement with the D. S. McDonald Co., manufacturers of fine confectionery, as traveling salesman. He remained with the McDonald Co. for a number of years, and until they sold the factory to Aldrich & Smith, and then took the position as manager for the new concern.

In 1891 Mr. Foster located himself and family in Malden, Mass., and in 1895 erected a fine residence at 39 Starbird street in that city, where he still lives.

3684. i. MANON, b. Jan. 10, 1879; d. Oct. 5, 1879.
3685. ii. GEORGE B., JR., b. at Salem, Mass., July 27, 1884.
3686. iii. MARJORIE LOUISE, b. Bucksport, Me., March 24, 1890.
3687. iv. CHRISTINE, b. at Malden, Mass., April 17, 1893.

2964. WILLARD MALLALIEU FOSTER (George H., Moses, Samuel, Isaac, Joseph. Jacob, Reginald), b. Oct. 12, 1858, Clinton, Mass.; m. in Lowell, Oct. 15, 1879, Emeline Elizabeth Sherwood, b. March 22, 1857. He is a civil engineer. Res., Lowell, Mass., 64 Grove St.

3688. i. ALICE LUCINDA, b. Nov. 2, 1880; d. Sept. 26, 1881.
3689. ii. WILLARD M., JR., b. June 20, 1888; d. June 23, 1888.

2977. SAMUEL WILLIS FOSTER (Andrew D., Samuel W., Theodore, Jedediah, Ephraim, Ephraim, Abraham, Reginald), b. River Falls, Wis., Dec. 21, 1863; m., Coeur d'Alene, Idaho, July 6, 1866, Laura Buckley. He is a contractor. Res., Spokane, Wash., 525 Blaine Ave.

3690. i. EDITH DELLE, b. April 7, 1894.

2989. HON. BLACKMAN NEWELL FOSTER (Dwight, Jedediah, Theophilus, Jedediah, Ephraim, Ephraim, Abraham, Reginald), b. Pownal, Vt., Sept. 25, 1834; m. there Harriet Downs, of Pownal. He was a farmer. Was in 1867 a member of the Vermont Legislature. Moved to Chicago in 1873, and has been a commission merchant since 1876. His office is in the "Brother Jonathan" building, opposite the Board of Trade. Res., s. p., Pownal, Vt., Chicago, Ill., Board of Trade.

2990. GEORGE DWIGHT FOSTER (Alfred D., Elijah D., Theophilus, Jedediah, Ephraim, Ephraim, Abraham, Reginald), b. June 11, 1843; m., Nov. 17, 1864, Burdette E. Thomas, b. Nov. 12, 1841, at Potter, N. Y., dau. of Ambrose Spencer Thomas, b. there in 1804, and d. October, 1870, and 2d, Jane A. McPherson, b. in Seneca, N. Y., in 1810, and d. in Potter, December, 1866. He is a merchant at Crown Point, Ind.

3691. i. MARY, b. Jan. 30, 1866.
3692. ii. ALFRED DWIGHT, b. Nov. 11, 1869.

3017. CHARLES EBENEZER FOSTER (Luther C., Peregrine P., Theophilus, Jedediah, Ephraim, Ephraim, Abraham, Reginald), b. Jan. 29, 1855, Elmira, N. Y.; m. Ithaca, Sept. 17, 1879, Julia Wisner Carpenter, b. Aug. 9, 1855.

Charles E. Foster took a partial course in Cornell University; rowed on the Freshman crew which defeated Harvard in 1888; entered the drug business as clerk at Youngstown, O.; married Julia Carpenter, of Ithaca; was for some years confidential clerk with Strong, Cobb & Co., of Cleveland, wholesale druggists; later at Detroit, Mich., with Parke, Davis & Co., chemical manufacturers; now at Cleveland, O., conducting a drugstore under the firm name of The Foster Co., druggists. Res., Cleveland, O., Hough Ave., cor. Crawford.

3693. i. FRANKLIN LUTHER, b. Nov. 29, 1882.
3694. ii. EDNA MAY, b. April 22, 1886.

3018. HENRY WARD BEECHER FOSTER (Luther C., Peregrine P., Theophilus, Jedediah, Ephraim, Ephraim, Abraham, Reginald), b. Elmira, N. Y., Sept. 21, 1856; m., Nov. 17, 1880, Lyra Rosalind Peck, b. Nov. 1, 1854.

Henry W. was graduated from Cornell University with degree of A. B., 1877; taught two years; studied law in meantime, and admitted to bar at Ithaca, 1880; went to Allegan, Mich., same year; admitted to bar at once; began practice alone; later was with W. B. Williams, ex-Congressman, and then Commissioner of Railroads in Michigan; firm Williams & Foster; later with Padgham & Padgham; J. H. Padgham being Judge of Probate, Philip Padgham later becoming Circuit Judge; later he took hold of a hardware concern, in which relatives were interested, and which had failed (located still at Allegan), and closed up the assignment, taking the business in firm name of Foster & Turner; continued in that three years; called to Geneva, N. Y., in 1886, to take interest in nursery business, which he conducted up to 1894 under firm name of H. W. Foster & Co., in connection with W. L. McKay, his old college chum; called to Ithaca in 1894 to assist his father; chosen his successor in 1895, continuing here to date. Res., Ithaca, N. Y.

3695. i. CARLOTTA SNOW, b. Nov. 27, 1881; d. June 9, 1890.
3696. i. DWIGHT ELLIOTT, b. Feb. 15, 1884.
3697. iii. MARION EDITH, b. Feb. 22, 1887; d. February, 1890.
3698. iv. GERTRUDE ELAINE, b. Oct. 1, 1889.
3699. v. HENRY ALDEN, b. Sept. 20, 1891.

3019. LUTHER CLARK FOSTER (Luther C., Peregrine P., Theophilus, Jedediah, Ephraim, Ephraim, Abraham, Reginald), b. Jan. 12, 1858; m. ——, Alice Allen. He worked in iron mills at Youngstown, O., for several years; about 1880 married Alice Allen; began railroading; elected one of the chief officers, Organizer of the Brotherhood of Railroad Breakmen; continued in that eight years; after retirement returned to Ithaca; now in coal business under name of L. C. Foster. Res., Ithaca, N. Y.

3700. i. ROBERT, b. ——.
3701. ii. EDWARD, b. ——.

3022. ROBERT OSMUN FOSTER (Luther C., Peregrine P., Theophilus, Jedediah, Ephraim, Ephraim Abraham, Reginald), b. Oct. 23, 1867; m. ——, 1893, Fiorina Dilger. He is in the book business; is the proprietor of Foster's bookstore. Res., Ithaca, N. Y.

3702. i. ENOLA B, b ——.
3703. ii. OSMOND F., b. ——.

3023. ALFRED DWIGHT FOSTER (Dwight, Alfred D., Dwight, Jedediah, Ephraim, Ephraim, Abraham, Reginald), b. Worcester, Mass., April 27, 1852; m. in England, Nov. 17, 1892, Evelyn Margaret Palmer-Samborne, b. June 27, 1862.

Alfred D. Foster, vice-president of the New England Mutual Life Insurance Company, was born at Worcester, Mass. He received his preliminary education at the Boston Latin School and at the famous University in Cambridge; then he took a course in law. From Harvard he obtained the degree of B. A.; from the Boston University that of LL.B. He was admitted to the Massachusetts bar in 1876, and practiced law in Boston from 1876 until 1893. From 1884 to 1893 he acted as counsel of the New England Mutual Life Insurance Company. In 1887 he was chosen as a director of the company, and he remained on the board ever since. On the death of Joseph M. Gibbens, in January, 1893, he was elected vice-president. The duties of vice-president vary, and some life insurance companies possess three or four. The New England Mutual has only one, and Mr. Foster is consequently kept busy. His training and energy make him a particularly useful member of the official staff, and eminently fit him for company management, in conjunction with Secretary

Trull, during the occasional absences of the New England's universally respected president, Benjamin F. Stevens. Res., 87 Milk St., Boston, Mass.

3704. i. MARGARET, b. Sept. 3, 1893.
3705. ii. DWIGHT, b. Jan. 7, 1895.
3706. iii. FRANCIS B., b. Dec. 4, 1895.
3707. iv. HILDA SAMBORNE, b. March 23, 1897.

3027. DR. BURNSIDE FOSTER (Dwight, Alfred D., Dwight, Jedediah, Ephraim, Ephraim, Abraham, Reginald), b. Worcester, Mass., May 7, 1861; m., Jan. 1, 1894, Sophie Vernon Hammond, dau. of Gen. John H. Hammond. Graduated at Yale University in 1882; received degree of M. D. from Harvard University in 1885; Home Surgeon at Massachusetts General Hospital, Boston, until 1887; studied in Europe for a year and then moved to Minneapolis, Minn.; after practicing there for five years moved to St. Paul, where he now resides. Is professor of Dermatology and lecturer on the History of Medicine in University of Minnesota. Res., St. Paul, Minn.; address, Lowry Building.

3708. i. DAUGHTER, b. ——.

3028. REGINALD FOSTER (Dwight, Alfred D., Dwight, Jedediah, Ephraim, Ephraim, Abraham, Reginald), b. Worcester, Mass., Jan. 2, 1863; m. in Boston, March 8, 1893, Harriette Story Lawrence, b. June 10, 1867. He graduated at Yale College in 1884; admitted to the bar in Boston in 1887. Since then engaged in the practice of his profession in Boston. Res., Boston, Mass., 48 Hotel Fenway; address, 87 Milk St.

3709. i. RUTH, b. Jan. 3, 1894.
3710. ii. DOROTHY DWIGHT, b. Sept. 30, 1895; d. March 23, 1898.

3031. CHARLES FREDERIC FOSTER (Peregrine D., Frederic A., Peregrine, Jedediah, Ephraim, Ephraim, Abraham, Reginald), b. June 9, 1847; a merchant of Glenwood, Iowa; m., April 28, 1872, Mary Ann Haley, b. Sept. 27, 1853, dau. of John Haley and Sarah Haley, being of the same name before marriage. He enlisted in 1864 as a Union soldier in Company C, of the Forty-fifth Iowa regiment.

3711. i. FREDERIC DWIGHT, b. Feb. 2, 1873.

3034. CHARLES AUGUSTUS FOSTER (Charles I., Jonas, John, John, John, Ephraim, Abraham, Reginald), b. Beverly, Mass., March 28, 1861; m., in Waltham, June 3, 1889, Cora Eveylin Tower, b. April 10, 1864. He is a watchmaker. Res., Waltham, Mass., 92 Russell St.

3712. i. WARREN ELLSWORTH, b. March 9, 1890; d. March 24, 1895.
3713. ii. BRYANT CRESSY, b. May 29, 1891.

3044. FRANK SMITH FOSTER (David S., Moses, David, Stephen, John, Ephraim, Abraham, Reginald), b. June 9, 1861, Beloit, Wis.; m., Monmouth, Ill., Jan. 17, 1887, Elizabeth Kerr.

Frank Smith Foster received a high school education and graduated in high standing from the Beloit High School under the tutorship of Professor Beach in the year 1879. After graduating, was offered, accepted and held the position of drug clerk for Dr. H. P. Strong, of this city, for two years, giving up this position to take a course of pharmacy at the Chicago College of Pharmacy, graduating in the year 1883. During his college vacation took charge of a drugstore at Cedar Lake, Wis. After graduating he was offered a position as head drug clerk of the firm of Smith & Dunbar, of Monmouth, Ill., which position he filled most acceptably for one year, when he was induced to return to his native city, Beloit, Wis., where he opened and successfully carried on the drug business under the firm name of Foster Brothers, in connection with the book and stationery business. A dissolution of the firm took place and Frank Smith continued the drug business until the spring of 1896, when he closed out his business. Was elected alderman from the First Ward of this city, and served in this capacity from 1887 to 1890. While on a recent visit to the parents of his wife, Mr. and Mrs. Kerr, of Monmouth, Ill, he was urgently requested by his old employer, Mr. Dunbar, to make Monmouth his future home and take his old position as head clerk, which position he at once accepted, removing his family to Monmouth, Ill., in the spring of 1897. No children from this union. Res., Monmouth, Ill, s. p.

3045. JOSEPH BYERS FOSTER (David S., Moses, David, Stephen, John, Ephraim, Abraham, Reginald), b. Beloit, Wis., Dec. 23, 1862; m. there Jan. 19, 1887, Olive J. Flynn.

The subject of this sketch received a high school education and graduated in high standing from the Beloit High School under the tutorship of Professor Beech in the year 1881. Engaged in the book and stationery business, succeeding his father in the year 1884, and in connection with his brother, Frank Smith Foster, engaged in the drug, stationery and book business, under the firm name of Foster Brothers, for a few years, when the firm dissolved. Frank Smith continuing the drug business and Joseph Byers the book and stationery business, each successively carrying on the business until a sale of their respective lines of business was made. Later on, Joseph Byers was offered a position by his older brother, John Alfred, as superintendent of his box factory, in this city, where he still holds the position as superintendent, giving satisfactory results of his qualification. During the session of the Wisconsin Legislature, in the winter of 1897, he was appointed Document Clerk under Sergeant-at-Arms Hambright, of Racine, Wis. He is an ardent Republican, taking an active part in city, county and State politics. Two children from this marriage union. Res., Beloit, Wis.

3714. i. ESTHER SMITH, b. April 29, 1888.
3715. ii. MARY AGNES, b. April 25, 1891.

3046. DAVID HUMPHREY FOSTER (David S., Moses, David, Stephen, John, Ephraim, Abraham, Reginald), b. Aug. 19, 1873, Beloit, Wis.; m., Milwaukee, Aug. 21, 1895, Fannie Elizabeth Schutt. Received his schooling at the Beloit High School and Beloit College Academy, succeeding his father in the book and stationery business in the year 1895, and is still engaged successfully in this line of business. Res., Beloit, Wis.

3716. i. DAVID SMITH, b. Feb. 10, 1897.

3048. NATHAN FOSTER (Charles S., Nathan, Nathan, Stephen, John, Ephraim, Abraham, Reginald), b. North Andover, Mass., Feb. 18, 1858; m., June 22, 1882, Grace P. Webster. He spent his early school days at the Kimball District School, afterward spending a year at the Johnson High School, North Andover. He was married to Grace Pearl Webster, b. January, 1861. He is an energetic farmer, and lives on the ancient homestead of Ephraim Foster, grandson of Reginald Foster, and noted for the large and beautiful elm tree, still vigorous, and said to be the largest tree in the county. Res., North Andover, Mass.

3717. i. REATA PEARL, b. Aug. 13, 1883.
3718. ii. CHARLES HENRY, b. Dec. 1, 1884.
3719. iii. ERNEST WEBSTER, b. July 7, 1886.
3720. iv. FRANK NATHAN, b. April 14, 1888; d. Sept. 10, 1888.
3721. v. RUTH BIXBY, b. Aug. 30, 1889.
3722. vi. MARY CLIFFORD, b. April 19, 1891.
3723. vii. GUY ELSMERE, b. Dec. 5, 1892.
3724. viii. SARAH CAROLINE, b. Feb. 18, 1894; d. Feb. 18, 1896.
3725. ix. GRACE HELEN, b. June 28, 1896; d. Aug. 14, 1896.
3726. x. RALPH SARGENT, b. Sept. 24, 1897.

3049. WALLACE REA FOSTER (Charles S., Nathan, Nathan, Stephen, John, Ephraim, Abraham, Reginald), b. North Andover, Mass., Aug. 2, 1864; m., April 11, 1893, Fannie F. Parrish, b. Sept. 6, 1867. He spent his early days in Kimball School; entered the Johnson High School and graduated in the class of 1881; spent fourteen months in Montana with his uncle, Loring B. Rea, on the cattle ranches; returned in October, 1885. He spent a few years at home on the farm, afterward going to State of Washington, and settling at Wilbur, Wash. Here he became acquainted with the youngest sister of senior partner of the firm of J. M. Parrish & Co. They were married at Hillsboro, Oregon. Res., Creston, Wash.

3727. i. MAY ELLEN, b. Oct. 10, 1894.
3728. ii. WALLACE PARRISH, b. Jan. 10, 1898.

3050. HARLAN ELMER FOSTER (Charles S., Nathan, Nathan, Stephen, John, Ephraim, Abraham, Reginald), b. North Andover, Mass., April 3, 1866; m., June 22, 1892, Carrie B. Burgess. Educated at the public schools in his native town; learned the carpenter's trade. Res., Somerville, Mass.

3729. i. ESTHER FRANCES, b. Dec. 26, 1893.
3730. ii. MARION LOUISE, b. Oct. 17, 1895.
3731. iii. LILLIAN ELMA, b. Oct. 28, 1896; d. Jan. 22, 1897.
3732. iv. ELLA MAY, b. Dec. 24, 1897.

3051. HERBERT LORING FOSTER (Charles S., Nathan, Nathan, Stephen, John, Ephraim, Abraham, Reginald), b. North Andover, Mass., Nov. 8, 1870; m., Nov. 9, 1897, Nellie May Long, b. Jan. 7, 1876. He is a farmer. He spent his early school days in Kimball School; was one year at Johnson High School, afterward taking a commercial course. He resides on the old homestead, s. p. Res. North Andover, Mass.

3059. CARL HUBBELL FOSTER (George P., Ephraim, Enoch, Ephraim, Ephraim, Moses, Ephraim, Abraham, Reginald), b. May 15, 1860, in Burlington, Vt.; m., Dec. 27, 1888, Gertrude Harding Kyes. He is an undertaker. Res., Peterboro, N. H.

3733. i. GEORGE CURTIS, b. April 2, 1893.
3734. ii. WINSLOW KYES, b. Jan. 19, 1895; d. Oct. 6, 1895.

3068. FRANK AUGUSTUS FOSTER (William H., John W., Abner, Elijah, Aaron, Ephraim, Abraham, Reginald), b. Templeton, Mass., April 10, 1860; m., Providence, R. I., Dec. 19, 1889, Bertha Frances Miner, b. Oct. 17, 1866, dau. of James and Sarah (Colwel). When quite young, he showed an inclination to follow in the footsteps of his father, and become a machinist. (As far as he can learn, the Fosters have been of a mechanical turn of mind for many generations.) He was therefore apprenticed to learn the machinist's trade. He also attended the Orange High School, from which he was graduated. He also attended the Polytechnic Institute, of Worcester, Mass., from which he was graduated B. S. from the Department of Mechanical Engineering in 1882. He has since followed his profession in several cities of New England. For the last four years he has resided in Montreal (of which Westmount is a suburb), where he has been Assistant Superintendent and Mechanical Engineer for the Canadian branch of a large manufacturing concern of New York. Res., Montreal, Canada, 4455 St. Catherine Street, Westmount.

3735. i. CONSTANCE HELLEN, b. Jan. 19, 1895.

3070. HENRY WILLIAM FOSTER (William H., John W., Abner, Elijah, Aaron, Ephraim, Abraham, Reginald), b. Athol, Mass., Nov. 2, 1863; m., Orange, June 3, 1886, Lulu M. Hadley, b. March 19, 1864; m., 2d, Dec. 1, 1892, Frances Monty, in Chicago. He is a traveling salesman. Res., W. Medford, Mass.

3735-2. i. CLAUD HADLEY, b. Jan. 6, 1888; d. Sept. 29, 1888.

3074. RUFUS JAMES FOSTER (Clement S., Jesse, Daniel, Thomas, Abraham, Abraham, Abraham, Reginald), b. Minersville, Pa., Oct. 10, 1856; m. there Sept. 9, 1884, Jennie Bennett Taylor, b. Jan. 8, 1859.

Rufus James Foster, son of Clement Storer and Rebecca McCamant Foster, was born at Minersville, Pa. In 1861 he removed with his parents to Ashland, Pa., where he was educated in the public and private schools, graduating from the Ashland High School in 1874. In the fall of the same year he secured a position in the mining engineering department of the Philadelphia & Reading Coal & Iron Co. He remained at this occupation, filling various positions until Sept. 1, 1887, when he resigned to accept the position of editor of The Colliery Engineer, a technical mining paper at that time published at Shenandoah, Pa. In the fall of 1888 he acquired an interest in the business, and the publication was moved to Scranton, Pa., the largest city in the anthracite coal regions. The scope, influence and circulation of The Colliery Engineer rapidly increased, and in 1890 The Colliery Engineer was incorporated. Mr. Foster was chosen one of the directors of the company, and was elected President of the board, a position which he has continuously filled since then. In connection with the original publication The Colliery Engineer Co. owns and conducts The International Correspondence Schools, which furnish technical education by an original correspondence system, which has proven very successful. The company also owns and conducts several other monthlies of a technical educational character. The correspondence schools were conceived and developed by Mr. Thomas J. Foster, the original owner of The Colliery Engineer, who at present is general manager and treasurer of the company. In his work on this line he was constantly aided by the subject of this sketch, who besides being a business associate is a cousin.

The subject of this sketch was married to Jennie Bennett Taylor, youngest daughter of the late Jos. F. Taylor, of Minersville, Pa. One son, now a boy thirteen years, was the fruit of this union.

Mr. Foster is a member of the various Masonic bodies, up to and including the Knights Templar, of St. Luke's Protestant Episcopal Church of Scranton, Pa., of the New England Society of Northeastern Pennsylvania, of the Pennsylvania Society Sons of the Revolution, of the Engineers' Club of Scranton, Pa., the Scranton Club, and the Board of Trade of Scranton. Res., Scranton, Pa.

3736. i. JOSEPH TAYLOR, b. June 1, 1885.

3075-3. CLEMENT STORER FOSTER (Clement S., Jesse, Daniel, Thomas, Abraham, Abraham, Abraham, Reginald), b. Minersville, Pa., Dec. 10, 1860; m., March 7, 1887, Florence J. Seman, b. July 4, 1858. Printer, telegrapher and editor on "The Press." Res., Utica, N. Y.

3736¼. i. MARGUERITE ELIZA, b. March 17, 1890.

3075-5. NORMAN WALLACE FOSTER (Clement S., Jesse, Daniel, Thomas, Abraham, Abraham, Abraham, Reginald), b. Ashland, Pa., Nov. 25, 1865; m., Freehold, N. J., May 16, 1888, Helen Estelle McDermott, b. March 23, 1869.

Norman Wallace Foster was born at Ashland, Pa., youngest son of Clement S. Foster and Rebecca H. McCamant Foster; educated in public and private schools; at the age of eighteen years entered railroad service and filled various positions in same for thirteen years. In 1897 entered service of The Colliery Engineer Company, and was appointed Superintendent shortly afterward, with headquarters at 426 and 428 Ellicott Square, Buffalo, N. Y. Res., Buffalo, N. Y., 426 Ellicott Square.

3736-1¼. i. DONALD McDERMOTT FOSTER, b. Feb. 24, 1889.

3736-1⅓. ii. RUFUS JAMES FOSTER, JR., b. Dec. 9, 1896.

3736-1½. iii. LYDIA McDERMOTT FOSTER, b. Dec. 8, 1898. All 535 Auburn Ave., Buffalo, N. Y. (temporarily).

3078-2. WARREN B. FOSTER (Perkins, Simon, Allen, Thomas, Abraham, Abraham, Abraham, Reginald), b. Danvers, Mass., July 30, 1845; m., Middletown, Aug. 16, 1866, Hannah I. Legrov. He is a manufacturer of infants' shoes. Res., Danvers, Mass.

3736-2. i. EDMOND P., b. Feb. 7, 1867. P. O., Ipswich, Mass.

3736-3. ii. WILLIAM M., b. March 20, 1869. P. O., North Danvers, Mass.

3753-4. iii. SARAH M., b. March 29, 1873.

3736-5. iv. CHARLES E., b. Sept. 3, 1875. P. O., Danvers, Mass.

3736-6. v. BERTIE F., b. Dec. 29, 1877. P. O., Danvers, Mass.

3736-7. vi. WARREN E., b. Jan. 6, 1888; d. Sept. 18, 1888.

3082. JACOB SEITZINGER FOSTER (Thomas, Jesse, Daniel, Thomas, Abraham, Abraham, Abraham, Reginald), b. Pottsville, Pa., Oct. 18, 1862; m., New Philadelphia, Pa., Oct. 19, 1884, Cecelia A. Schilling, b. Pottsville, Pa., Sept. 13, 1864. He is an editor. Res., Pottsville, Pa.

3737. i. CATHERINE CECILA, b. Jan. 4, 1886.

3738. ii. CECIL ADAM, b. Sept. 13, 1887.

3083. CHARLES WILLIAM FOSTER (Thomas L., Asa L., Asa, Nathan, Nathan, Abraham, Abraham, Reginald), b. Mauch Chunk, Pa., Oct. 27, 1848; m., Dec. 10, 1874, Florida Hale Thompson, b. Feb. 7, 1852; d. Dec. 28, 1884. He was an editor. He d. Feb. 23, 1895. Res., Redbank, N. J.

3739. i. FRANK WORTHINGTON, b. Aug. 20, 1879. Res., Westfield, N. J.

3740. ii. VIRGINIA MAY, b. July 6, 1881. Res., 121 Hicks St., Brooklyn, N. Y.

3741. iii. ASA LANESFORD, b. Sept. 20, 1877; d. December, 1878.

3742. iv. LANESFORD, b. Feb. 13, 1883. Res., 9 Northampton street, Wilkesbarre, Pa.

3743. v. FLORIDA HALE, b. Oct. 4, 1875. Res., 121 Hicks street, Brooklyn, N. Y.

3087. ASA LANESFORD FOSTER (Thomas L., Asa L., Asa, Nathan, Nathan, Abraham, Abraham, Reginald), b. Mauch Chunk, Pa., Jan. 9, 1859; m., Wallingford, Pa., April 30, 1889, Mary MacCalla, b. May 31, 1865. He is agent for a railway company. Res., 228 South Third street, Philadelphia, Pa.

3744. i. HELEN ARRISON, b. April 4, 1893.

3745. ii. THOMAS LANESFORD, b. Aug. 18, 1894.

3102. FRANKLIN BACON FOSTER (Henri L., Nathan L., Joel, Nathan, Nathan, Abraham, Abraham, Reginald), b. Philadelphia, Pa., July 31, 1856; m., in

1886, Victoria McCready. He is a commission merchant on Van Buren street. Res., 318 Hampden Court, Chicago, Ill.

3746. i. DOUGLAS, b. ——.
3747. ii. DONALD, b. ——.
3748. iii. EARL, b. ——.
3749. iv. FRANCIS, b. ——.

3106. HERBERT I. FOSTER (Edwin D., Pliney P., Flint R., Daniel, Nathan, Abraham, Abraham, Reginald), b. Smithland, Iowa, Nov. 11, 1859; m. —— ——. Res., Smithland, Iowa.

3750. i. HERBERT BLAINE, b. ——.
3751. ii. MAUDIE P., b. ——.

3125. ELGIN REED FOSTER (Louis R., Sherlock, Daniel, Isaac), b. Hardwick, Mass., June 28, 1839; m., Ware, Nov. 27, 1862, Percena E. Fay, b. March 17, 1842. He is superintendent of the cemetery. Res., Ware, Mass.

3752. i. BERTIE E., b. 1865; d. 1866.
3753. ii. HARRY, b. 1873; d. 1875.
3754. iii. ALICE H., b. 1876.

3134. WILLIAM WILBERFORCE FOSTER (Samuel K., Luke B., Daniel, Isaac, Daniel, Abraham, Abraham, Reginald), b. Springfield, Mass., Sept. 18, 1845; m., June 5, 1872, Julia M. Arms. Res., Springfield, Mass.

3755. i. CHARLES SAMUEL, b. Oct. 22, 1888.

3132-2. DR. JAMES RICHARDS FOSTER (James W., Fordyce, Daniel, Isaac, Daniel, Abraham, Abraham, Reginald), b. North Attleboro, Mass., May 2, 1844, m., June 19, 1879, Eva Phillips, of Boston, Mass. Res., North Attleboro, Mass.

3756. i. BLANCHE, b. June 17, 1880; d. Dec. 16, 1880.
3757. ii. HARRIET EVA, b. June 14, 1881; d. May 14, 1890.

3143. CHARLES AMOS FOSTER (Oliver, Amos, Amos, Amos, Amos, Benjamin, Abraham, Reginald), b. Tewksbury, Mass., Jan. 31, 1852; m., Nov. 12, 1879, Hannah Jane Fletcher, b. Aug. 28, 1852. He is a farmer. Res., East Billerica, Mass.

3758. i. BERTHA MAUD, b. Jan. 11, 1886.
3759. ii. HERBERT LEWIS, b. Dec. 20, 1889.

3144. FRANK MACE FOSTER (Oliver, Amos, Amos, Amos, Amos, Benjamin, Abraham, Reginald), b. Tewksbury, Mass., Oct. 17, 1857; m., North Wilmington, Mass., Dec. 23, 1880, Annie M. Harnden, b. Oct. 17, 1859. Mrs. Foster has rendered the compiler valuable assistance. He was born in the old home, which, at one time, was the property of Amos Foster, the Revolutionary hero. It was a large, square, white house with green blinds, shaded by lovely great elms, a typical New England home, with its brick oven and open fire-places; although, after stoves became common, most of the fire-places were closed by sheet iron. The old home descended from father to son, until the summer of 1893, when the great barn was struck by lightning, and, being connected with the house by sheds and carriage house, everything was burned to the ground. The place was very attractive, always being kept in good repair, both outside and in—a thrifty farmer's home. In the fire was lost the flint-lock gun that his great-grandsire carried in the Revolutionary war. Having, in the course of nature, inherited his share of the farm, it naturally followed that he should be a farmer, and he followed that calling until he disposed of his part of the estate and moved to Andover, where he learned the carpenter's trade. Res., Andover, Mass.

3760. i. WILLIAM HARNDEN, b. July 22, 1886.
3761. ii. KENNETH CLEMONS, b. Feb. 8, 1895.

3145. ENOCH W. FOSTER (Zephaniah P., Zephaniah K., Amos, Amos, Amos, Benjamin, Abraham, Reginald), b. Tewksbury, Mass., Dec. 9, 1855; m., Dec. 16, 1876, Lillian Shedd. Res., Tewksbury, Mass.; P. O., Wilmington, Mass.

3762. i. GEORGE ENOCH, b. May 10, 1877.
3763. ii. ERNEST ALBERT, b. July 18, 1880.
3764. iii. ETHEL, b. March 18, 1882.

3151. HOWARD WYMAN FOSTER (John T., Zephaniah K., Amos, Amos, Amos, Benjamin, Abraham, Reginald), b. Tewksbury, Mass., March 2, 1862; m. there Dec. 11, 1889, Nellie E. Boutwell. Res., Tewksbury, Mass.; P. O., Lowell, Mass.

3765. i. MARION SWAN, b. May 16, 1891.
3766. ii. HOWARD H., b. March 7, 1893.
3767. iii. BOUTWELL, b. Dec. 15, 1894.

3179. CHARLES F. FOSTER (Charles W., Benjamin S., Benjamin, Asael, Gideon, Benjamin, Abraham, Reginald), b. Oct. 10, 1866; m., in Stamford, Conn., Jan., 1891, Jennie Parkinson. Charles F. Foster was killed almost instantly by falling from the platform of the Boston & Albany road train from Boston, while returning to his home, in Newtown, Mass. He had issue two children, Annie and Harold, now living in Levarton, Lincoln, England. She was of English birth, and, after Charlie's death, she returned to her parental home. He d. Feb. 26, 1895. Res., Newton, Mass.

3768. i. ANNIE, b. ——. Res., Levarton, Lincoln, England.
3769. ii. HAROLD, b. ——. Res., Levarton, Lincoln, England.

3184. DR. BRAZILLAI BEAN FOSTER (Thomas A., Thomas D., William, Nathan, Caleb, Caleb, Abraham, Reginald) b. Portland, Me., ——, 1848; m. —— ——, 1870. Res., Portland, Me.

3185. DR. CHARLES W. FOSTER (Thomas A., Thomas D., William, Nathan, Caleb, Caleb, Abraham, Reginald), b. Unity, Me., April 29, 1850; m., Wayne, Me., July 6, 1876, Esther Bennett Parker, b. Aug. 23, 1848. Res., Woodfords, Me.

3770. i. RACHEL JONES, b. July 14, 1877.
3771. ii. ESTHER PERLEY, b. Jan. 17, 1881.

3198. H. LINCOLN FOSTER (Daniel, Ebenezer, William, Nathan, Caleb, Caleb, Abraham, Reginald), b. Montville, Me., July 3, 1834; m., Fort Fairfield, June 31, 1861, Zipra Bishop. He is a farmer. Res., Fort Fairfield, Me.

3772. i. ARTHUR C., b. May 13, 1862; d. May 21, 1862.
3773. ii. DANIEL A., b. Aug. 21, 1863.
3774. iii. MARIA (Reed), b. Sept. 21, 1869.
3775. iv. DELIA HACKENBRED, b. May 23, 1871.
3776. v. JOHN C., b. Nov. 11, 1874.
3777. vi. ETTIE, b. May 1, 1879.

3205. JAMES E. FOSTER (Zabud, Thomas, John, Nathan, Caleb, Caleb, Abraham, Reginald), b. Bristol, Me., Dec. 15, 1846; m., Ellsworth, Me., Aug. 1, 1864, Ella M. Marshall, b. June 5, 1852. He is a carpenter by trade and owns a livery stable. Res., Bar Harbor, Me.

3778. i. NANCY E., b. Feb. 8, 1874.

3207. STETSON THOMAS FOSTER (Zabud, Thomas, John, Nathan, Caleb, Caleb, Abraham, Reginald), b. Bristol, Me., July 25, 1850; m., Hingham, April, 1878, Alice Lincoln Whiton, b. Oct. 1, 1854. He was born in Bristol, Me., going to Boston when twenty-one years of age, having, in Ellsworth, Me., previously, learned the cabinet-maker's trade. After five years in one of the leading decorative houses in Boston, he started in his present business, furniture, draperies and wall papers, 30 Franklin street, for himself in 1878 and has continued it to the present time. He has always taken an active part in all the details of his most complicated business. He has succeeded, socially he has done his part in the church and the community where he located and married twenty years ago in Hingham, Mass. He has held many prominent offices in town affairs, banks, church, Masonic, clubs, etc., and he has the respect of a large business and social acquaintance. He has never aspired for political office, although asked to accept nominations many times. It can be all summed up in these words: A man who has tried to do his part in the world as God has given him power to see it, to God, his neighbor, and himself. He is now one of the parish committee of the oldest church in the United States, built in 1681, at Hingham, Mass.; now Unitarian. Res., Hingham, Mass. Boston address, 30 Franklin street.

3779. i. FRANCIS RICHMOND, b. July 22, 1882, at Mount Holyoke Seminary.

3780. ii. HANNAH WHITON, b. Aug., 1884; d. May, 1886.
3781. iii. LEWIS WHITON, b. Sept., 1887.
3782. iv. MARJORIE LINCOLN, b. Aug., 1889.
3783. v. HELEN MILLER, b. Sept., 1894.

3212. CURTIS R. FOSTER (Zabud, Thomas, John, Nathan, Caleb, Caleb, Abraham, Reginald) b. Ellsworth, Me., July 25, 1861; m., Dec. 24, 1882, Minnie M. Goodwin, b. Dec. 25, 1861. He is an undertaker. Res., Ellsworth, Me.
3784. i. PAULENE M., b. Aug. 3, 1884.

3222. HORATIO ALVAH FOSTER (Edward Vose, Zabud, Zabud, Nathan, Caleb, Caleb, Abraham, Reginald), b. Philadelphia, Pa., Jan. 12, 1858; m., Chicago, Dec. 22, 1893, Florence Louise Root, b. Oct. 9, 1865.

HORATIO A. FOSTER.

Horatio Alvah Foster, born of New England parents, in Philadelphia, during a short sojourn in that city; spent early life, until 1883, in Northampton; attended the common schools and high school of that place until 1876, then commencing work in a factory office; at nineteen was appointed superintendent of the mill, a small cotton factory, and filled the position for five years, the last two being as treasurer. He left to take a position as paymaster and clerk for a railroad contractor for a year or more, and, in 1884, entered the employ of the Daft Electric Co., in Jersey City. In 1885 installed one of the earliest electric street railways, that in Baltimore, running from near the city line to Woodbury. In 1886 he became connected with the Thomson-Houston Electric Co., of Boston, and from then until July, 1891, acted as expert engineer for that company in various places, but principally in Philadelphia and New York. In July, 1891, was appointed expert for the electrical division of the United States Census Bureau and collected all financial and technical statistics for all kinds of electrical plants in St. Louis, Mo., and New York State, afterward compiling the same in the census office, Washington, D. C. On May 1, 1893, became editor of "Electrical Industries," a technical journal published in Chicago, and as such wrote up many of the electrical and mechanical exhibits at the World's Fair. Leaving there in September, became assistant to Prof. George Forbes, F. R. S., electrical engineer for the Niagara Falls Power Co., and, when Professor Forbes' duties were completed, in December, 1894, was detailed by the Cataract Construction Co. to make tests for the determination of the cost of steam power in Buffalo and other cities. He is now consulting electrical and mechanical engineer in Buffalo, N. Y., for general work, and especially for the Cataract Construction Co. and its allied interests, the Niagara Falls Power Co. and the Cataract Power and Conduit Co. He is the author of "Central Station Book-Keeping," "Central Station Management and Finance," "Electrical Engineer's Pocket-Book" (in press, Van Nostrand). He is a member of the American Institute of Electrical Engineers. the American Society of Mechanical Engineers, the New York Electric Society and Franklin Institute. Res., 71 Highland avenue, Buffalo, N. Y.
3785. i. MARTHA, b. and d. Dec. 29, 1894.
3786. ii. RICHARD ROOT, b. April 11, 1898.

3236. WILLIS CHRISTOPHER FOSTER (Henry T., Henry P., Henry, Jacob, Jacob, Isaac, Reginald, Reginald), b. Walpole, N. H., Oct. 6, 1858; m.,

March 25, 1884, Katie Callahan, b. April 18, 1860. He is a farmer. Res., Walpole, N. H.

3787. i. MADALENE KATIE, b. Oct. 11, 1895.

3230. FRANK HENRY FOSTER (Henry T., Henry P., Henry, Jacob, Jacob, Isaac, Reginald, Reginald), b. Walpole, N. H., Jan. 6, 1857; m., Topeka, Kan., June 3, 1884, Harriet Botsford Franks, b. March 16, 1861.

Frank Henry Foster, eldest born of Henry Thomas Foster and Hannah Morrill Foster (née Fuller), was born on a farm in the town of Walpole, N. H., on the sixth day of January, 1857. This farm, which was purchased by his grandfather in 1824, is still in the possession of the family, being now owned by the younger brother of Frank Henry, Willis C. Foster. There are four girls and two boys in the family, all of whom are living. In the order of their ages, they are Willis Christopher, Velma Elsie, Adine Philena, Florence Josephine and Annie Reynolds. The subject of this sketch knows the value of an education and the supreme advantage of relying upon one's own resources, for he obtained his education at the district school in Walpole and at the High school in Walpole village, walking three and one-half miles to and from his school. At the age of sixteen years he taught a district school in Dublin, N. H., in order to secure the means to further educate himself, and was graduated from the Kimball Union Academy, Meriden, N. H., June 19, 1877, having entered that institution in December, 1874. Owing to the severe and long-continued illness of his father, the young man was constituted head of the family, farming in the summer time and teaching school in the winter to make both ends meet. In 1879, he entered the law office of Davenport & Eddy, Brattleboro, Vt., as a student, and in October, 1881, he matriculated in the junior class of the law department, Michigan University, at Ann Arbor, Mich. In the spring of 1882, three weeks before graduation, he was transferred to the senior class and was graduated with that class, in March of the same year. The following month he removed to Topeka, Kan., and began the practice of law, where he has ever since remained. June 3, 1884, he was married to Miss Harriet B. Franks, of Topeka, a talented musician and cultured lady. From the beginning he took an active interest in the cause of temperance, which is in the prohibition phase in the State of Kansas, and has been one of the most zealous and indefatigable workers in behalf of that and of other reforms that tend to the upbuilding of the home and State. January 1, 1896, without any solicitation on his part, he was named as chairman of the metropolitan police board of the city of Topeka, and while he remained a member of that board he reduced lawbreaking and crime to a minimum. He is a charter member of the Saturday Night Literary Club, one of the oldest and most noted, as well as most unique, clubs in the State of Kansas. He is, and has been for years, one of the sources of inspiration and a pillar of strength of the Unitarian Society of Topeka. He is a prominent member of his profession, a leader in church and civic affairs, and has, already, although still a young man, accomplished much for good government and good order in the community in which he lives. He is a man of rare moral courage, of unceasing industry, resolute in purpose, faithful to his convictions and loyal to his friends. Res., s. p., Topeka, Kan.

3331. FREDERICK ALDEN FOSTER (Alden B., Thomas, Thomas, Aaron, Moses, John, Reginald, Reginald), b. East Boston, Mass., Dec. 18, 1869; m. there June 12, 1896, Jennie McLaren, b. Dec. 14, 1873. He is a clothing cutter. Res., 223 Trenton street, East Boston, Mass.

3788. i. MILDRED McLAREN, b. Jan. 13, 1897.

3332. CHARLES EDWARD FOSTER (Alden B., Thomas, Thomas, Aaron, Moses, John, Reginald, Reginald), b. Boston, Mass., Aug. 11, 1858; m., Jan. 15, 1885, Mary Lynch, b. Jan. 29, 1865. He is a wood dealer. Res., 9 Colton Place, San Francisco, Cal.

3789. i. JESSIE, b. Dec. 14, 1886.
3790. ii. ALDEN E., b. Sept. 6, 1888.
3791. iii. HAROLD, b. Aug. 6, 1890.
3792. iv. DANIEL, b. Dec. 6, 1892; d. April 27, 1893.
3793. v. RUTH, b. Feb. 18, 1895.

3429. CHARLES THOMAS FOSTER (Moses A., Jonathan B., Jeremiah, Daniel, Asa, William, William, Reginald), b. Canterbury, N. H., July 22, 1869; m. in Tilton, Oct. 25, 1893, Eva Gertrude Hill, b. Aug. 8, 1869. He is a real estate dealer. Res., Leominster, Mass.

3794. i. MALCOLM HILL, b. July 28, 1894.
3795. ii. GORDON CHASE, b. Feb. 21, 1897.

3430. JONATHAN BRADLEY FOSTER (Moses A., Jonathan B., Jeremiah, Daniel, Asa, William, William, Reginald), b. Canterbury, N. H., Sept. 6, 1871; m., June 14, 1893, at Quincy, Mass., Fannie Warren Osborne, b. Aug. 22, 1869. He is a farmer. Res., Canterbury, N. H.

3796. i. KENNETH RICHARDSON, b. Feb. 5, 1896.
3797. ii. WARREN BRADLEY, b. Feb. 5, 1896.

3431. GEORGE RICHARDSON FOSTER (Moses A., Jonathan B., Jeremiah, Daniel, Asa, William, William, Reginald), b. Canterbury, N. H., April 18, 1874; m., June 12, 1895, Maude Marion Perry, b. Oct. 17, 1871. He is a book-keeper in the employ of Gen. William F. Draper. Res., s. p., Milford, Mass.

3468. REV. PAOLI RANDALL FOSTER (Isaac, Benjamin, Benjamin, Isaac, Benjamin, Jacob, Isaac, Reginald), b. Aylesford, Nova Scotia, May 8, 1836; m., Brookfield, Nova Scotia, Adelaide L. Crooker, dau. of Dr. Crooker, of Lunenburg county, Nova Scotia, b. Jan. 22, 1845. He was born at Aylesford, Kings county, Nova Scotia. When but nine years of age he went to live with his paternal grandparents, and continued with them for a number of years. At the age of thirteen he professed religion, and was baptized by the late Rev. William Chipman, at Berwick, on May 20, 1849. After a few years he returned to his parental home at Aylesford, where after a long and testing struggle he became convinced that it was his duty to devote his life to the work of the Christian ministry. Having reached this conclusion he entered on a course of study with this object in view. He was licensed to preach in the year 1860, and for a number of years engaged in evangelistic work, assisting pastors and helping needy churches. During these years revival followed revival, and hundreds professed faith in Christ. On September 9, 1860, he was ordained at Kempt, Queens county, Nova Scotia, and entered on regular pastoral work, in which he has continued in Nova Scotia and Ontario. Res., s. p., Arcadia, Yarmouth county, N. S.

3471. JOSEPH MORTON T. FOSTER (Isaac, Benjamin, Benjamin, Isaac, Benjamin, Jacob, Isaac, Reginald), b. May 18, 1832; m., Elizabeth Johnson, of Digby; m., 2d,——Jane Baker. He d. May 13, 1892. Res., Aylesford, N. S.

3798. i. INFANT; d. young.
3799. ii. NORMAN, b. ——.
3800. iii. ISAIAH, b. ——.
3801. iv. GEORGE, b. ——.
3802. v. LILLA, b. ——.
3803. vi. BESSA, b. ——.
3804. vii. HENRY L., b. ——.
3805. viii. EDWARD, b. ——.
3806. ix. ELLA, b. ——; d. May 25, 1892.
3807. x. EMMA, b. ——; m. W. J. Barrow. Res., Watertown, Mass.
3808. xi. ISAAC HOWARD, b. ——; d.——1893.
3809. xii. BERTON, b. ——.
3810. xiii. INGRAM, b. ——.
3811. xiv. SEWARD, b. ——.
3812. xv. MABEL, b. ——.
3813. xvi. CHARLES, b. ——.
3814. xvii. JANE, b. ——.

3474. JACOB FOSTER (Isaac, Benjamin, Benjamin, Isaac, Benjamin, Jacob, Isaac, Reginald), b. April 16, 1840; m., Jan. 1, 1866, Henrietta McPherson, dau. of Donald and Lettie (Parker), of Brookfield, N. S., b. Jan. 11, 1840. He was a blacksmith; went from Aylesford, N. S., to Methuen, Mass., in October, 1889, and in 1890 to Watertown, Mass. Res., Cold Brook, Kings county, N. S., and Watertown, Mass.

3815. i. EUDORA LETTIE, b. Aug. 18, 1868.
3816. ii. MAGGIE AGATHE, b. Sept. 18, 1870.
3817. iii. MAY LAVINIA, b. Jan. 1, 1876.
3818. iv. COLBERT LEATON, b. Oct. 3, 1872; d. Oct. 11, 1878.
3819. v. HALLET RAY, b. Nov. 19, 1874.
3820. vi. LEWIE, b. Sept. 30, 1879; d. Sept. 30, 1879.
3821. vii. LOTTIE, b. Sept. 30, 1879.

3477. BENJAMIN PRINCE FOSTER (Isaac, Benjamin, Benjamin, Isaac, Benjamin, Jacob, Isaac, Reginald), b. London, England, June 4, 1840; m., Montreal, Canada, Ellen Hanna, b. Aug. 12, 1841. He is a carpenter. Res., s. p., Fall River, Kan.

3483. JOHN RUPERT FOSTER (Edward C., Benjamin, Benjamin, Isaac, Benjamin, Jacob, Isaac, Reginald), b. July 30, 1848, Berwick, N. S.; m. at Halifax, N. S., Sept. 29, 1875, Isabel Maud McDonald, b. May 2, 1855; d. Dec. 7, 1876; m., 2d, at Moncton, N. B., in August, 1884, Victoria A. Dunlap; m., 3d, March 31, 1898, Minnie L. Ross, dau. of Dr. Ross. He was a merchant in Halifax, N. S.; then Moncton, N. B.; then Victoria, B. C.; now with Ceylon Tea Co. Of late years he has been engaged as follows: In 1889 went to Vancover, B. C.; imported teas from China and Japan; shipped to above places thoroughbred Holstein and Jersey cattle, from large ranch of his on Fraser river; also dealt in real estate; went from there to World's Fair, Chicago, 1893, for Ceylon, India; from there to Mid-Winter Fair, San Francisco, as Commissioner for Ceylon; at present time is tea broker and manufacturer's agent. Res., Sacramento, Cal., P. O. Box 512.

JOHN R. FOSTER.

3822. i. LORENZO JAMES STEWART, b. Sept. 15, 1876; unm. Res., Windsor, N. S.; now, 1898, student in Arts University of Kings College, Windsor.
3823. ii. CUBA, b. in 1886. Res., Moncton.

3484. MINER TUPPER FOSTER (Edward C., Benjamin, Benjamin, Isaac, Benjamin, Jacob Isaac, Reginald), b. July 6, 1850, Berwick, N. S.; m., Feb. 9, 1875, Sarah Rudolph, dau. of Capt. Rudolph, of Halifax. He is a wholesale merchant in the tea business, and has a large interest in the gold mining business of the Province. Was one of the city fathers (alderman) for nine years, and resigned in 1897 to contest for a seat in the Dominion Parliament to represent the city and county of Halifax in behalf of the Conservative party in the Government. With the others of his party lost his election by a majority of seventy-four, but was about four hundred ahead of any one of his party in the county, and polled the largest vote of any of his party in the province. Had eight children. Res., Halifax, N. S.

3824. i. EDWARD RUDOLF, b. March 18, 1876; d. March 8, 1880.
3825. ii. FRANK TUPPER, b. Jan. 21, 1878.
3826. iii. BRENTON BEEBE, b. April 21, 1881.
3827. iv. MINNIE KNIGHT, b. April 7, 1883.
3828. v. HATTIE BELL, b. Jan. 22, 1886.
3829. vi. GLADYS MURRAY, b. June 29, 1889.
3830. vii. MARGUERITA RUDOLF, b. Sept. 13, 1892.
3831. viii. DOROTHY, b. July 6, 1896.

3486. GEORGE EDWARD FOSTER (Edward C., Benjamin, Benjamin, Isaac, Benjamin, Jacob, Isaac, Reginald), b. Jan. 21, 1861, Berwick, N. S.; m., Oct. 14, 1890, Winchester, Mass., Lora Mary Underhill, b. Aug. 5, 1867. Is a member of the Mosler Safe Co., on Sudbury St. Res., s. p., Cambridge, Mass. Boston office, 53 Sudbury St.

3488. DOUGLASS BENJAMIN FOSTER (Edward C., Benjamin, Benjamin, Isaac, Benjamin, Jacob, Isaac, Reginald), b. Berwick, N. S., March 30, 1864; m. in Somerville, Mass., Feb. 6, 1889, Addie Florence Cole, dau. of Barna S. and Sarah A. (Hopkins) des. of Stephen Hopkins of the Mayflower, b. April 27, 1868.

Douglass Benjamin Foster, son of Edward C. and Harriet (Tupper) Foster, was born in Berwick, N. S., March 30, 1864; was educated in the schools of that town and in 1881 came to Boston and entered the employ of Henry Callender & Co., wholesale grocers, with whom he remained until 1890, when he associated himself with Osgood C. Caswell, under the firm name of Caswell & Foster, to carry on the wholesale tea and coffee business, in which they are now engaged, at 38 and 39 India street, Boston. He married Addie F., daughter of Barna S. and Sarah (Hopkins) Cole, in Somerville, Mass., Feb. 6, 1889, in which city they now reside. Mr. Foster swung into the Democratic column in 1884 with many more of the young men of his state at that time. He has been a candidate of his party for several offices in his city and state, but the district in which he lives has always been too overwhelmingly Republican to permit of a Democrat being elected. He is a member of the Young Men's Democratic Club, of Massachusetts, and at present belongs to the gold wing of the party. He served two years as president of the Somerville Cycle Club, and is a prominent member of the Central Club, the leading social club of his city. Res., Somerville, Mass. Boston office, 38 and 39 India St.

3832. i. MARION FENWICK, b. Dec. 22, 1889.

3497. ISAAC WOODBURY FOSTER (Charles, Frederick, John, Ezekiel, Benjamin, Jacob, Isaac, Reginald), b. Margaretville, N. S., June 13, 1848; m., in Kingston, N. S., June 5, 1877, Ada Belle Tufts; d. March 22, 1878; m., 2d, Jan. 1, 1881, in Marlboro, Mass., Lucilla Viola Howe, b. June 17, 1850. He is a lumberman. Res., Framingham, Mass.

3832-1. i. FRANK ELSWORTH, b. June 4, 1881.
3833-1. ii. ADA BELLE, b. Oct. 20, 1882.
3834-1. iii. BEATRICE HOWE, b. April 15, 1885.
3835-1. iv. MYRTLE JANE, b. Aug 20, 1888; d. May 13, 1889.
3836-1. v. MILTON DAY, b. Sept. 1, 1890; d. Aug. 26, 1891.

3504. WILLIAM PRESCOTT FOSTER, A. M. (Hiram W., Solomon K., Jeremiah, Jeremiah, Benjamin, Jacob, Isaac, Reginald), b. Weld, Me., Aug. 20, 1856; m., June 16, 1886, Ruby Hinkley, b. Aug. 3, 1865.

William Prescott Foster, A. M., was born at Weld, Aug. 19, 1856. He graduated from Bates College in 1881, and later was principal of Ellsworth Academy. He was admitted to the bar and began the practice of law at Bar Harbor, but later moved to Massachusetts, and is now practicing his profession in Boston. He is interested in literature and his poems are published in the leading magazines of this country. He was married to Ruby Hinkley, the beautiful and accomplished daughter of Thomas Hinkley, of Ellsworth, a man well known in Maine political circles. Res., Bar Harbor, Me., and Boston, Mass., 23 Court St.

3833. i. SHILA, b. Dec. 2, 1887.
3834. ii. NEWTON HINKLEY, b. May 30, 1889.

3505. CHARLES SUMNER FOSTER (Hiram W., Solomon K., Jeremiah, Jeremiah, Benjamin, Jacob, Isaac, Reginald), b. Weld, Me., Dec. 20, 1859; m., Dec. 25, 1890, Hattie Robertson. Charles Sumner, the second son of Hiram Western Foster, was born at Livermore, Me., Dec. 20, 1859. By occupation he is a farmer. Res., Weld, Me.

3526. GEORGE B. FOSTER (William R., Marcus, Isaac, Isaac, John, Jacob, Isaac, Reginald), b. Commerce, Mich., March 20, 1862; m., Feb. 25, 1882, Emma Concle. Res., Pontiac, Mich.

3835. i. ETTIE MAY, b. May 22, 1883.
3836. ii. FREDERICK, b. Dec. 27, 1885.

3528. RICHARD EVERETT FOSTER (Samuel W., Samuel, Isaac, Isaac, John, Jacob, Isaac, Reginald), b. Wabasha, Minn., Oct. 12, 1868; m., March 12, 1893, Lulu Wissett. He is in mercantile business in Fairplay. Res., Fairplay, Mo., and Ogema, Wis., s. p.

3537. HARRISON GARDNER FOSTER (Addison G., Samuel, Isaac, Isaac, John, Jacob, Isaac, Reginald), b. Wabasha, Minn., March 8, 1866; m., at Lexington, Ky., June 6, 1889, Elizabeth Dunster Gibson, dau. of Col. Hart Gibson. Attended Yale College; is in the shingle business. Res., Tacoma, Wash.

3837. i. HART GIBSON, b. Sept. 2, 1890.
3838. ii. ADDISON GARDNER, b. March 21, 1894.

3549. ASAHEL NEWTON FOSTER (Joseph S., Ezra, Ezekiel, Ezekiel, John, Jacob, Isaac, Reginald), b. Leyden, Mass., July 12, 1857; m., Jan. 15, 1885, Mary Perkins, b. Aug. 12, 1866. He was a farmer. Res., Leyden, Mass.

3839. i. GEORGE H., b. Feb. 4, 1887.
3840. ii. CHARLES N., b. Dec. 7, 1888.
3841. iii. EMILY T., b. Aug. 17, 1890.
3842. iv. SARAH A., b. Sept. 14, 1892.
3843. v. MARY E., b. Feb. 6, 1894.
3844. vi. BERNICE C. H., b. March 21, 1897; d. March 21, 1898.

3550. JOSEPH LEROY FOSTER (Joseph S., Ezra, Ezekiel, Ezekiel, John, Jacob, Isaac, Reginald), b. Lyden, Mass., June 13, 1846; m., Wardsboro, Vt., June 1, 1881, Effie Wilder, b. Dec. 17, 1859. He is a farmer. Res., Wardsboro, Vt.

3845. i. HERBERT, b. ——; d. Aug. 20, 1883.
3846. ii. MINNIE O., b. Sept. 21, 1884.

3582. HARRY HOWARD FOSTER (Edward A., Edward, Levi, Benjamin, Benjamin, Benjamin, Isaac, Reginald), b. Oshkosh, Wis., March 15, 1857; m., Grand Rapids, Mich., June 15, 1886, Elizabeth Wallin, b. Aug. 23, 1858. Res., Merrill, Wis.

3847. i. MARION, b. April 3, 1888.
3848. ii WALLIN, b. Aug. 10, 1889.
3849. iii. MAY, b. Nov. 20, 1891.

3588. FRANK A. FOSTER (Luther H., Edward, Levi, Benjamin, Benjamin, Benjamin, Isaac, Reginald), b. Oshkosh, Wis., March 24, 1856; m., June 11, 1884, Charlotte Patterson Wood, b. Dec. 13, 1858.

Frank A. Foster was born at Oshkosh, Wis., March 24, 1856, removing to Styles (or Stiles), Wis., in 1857; to DeWitt, Clinton county, Iowa, in 1860, and to Muskegon, Mich., in 1862. In November, 1866, moved to Pere Marquette, Mason county, Mich. (now city of Ludington), where he has resided ever since. He has attended school as follows: 1866-70 Ludington Public School; 1870-71 Lake Forest Academy, at Lake Forest, Ill.; 1871-72 Ellsworth, Me., High School; 1873-76 Olivet College, Michigan; 1876-77 Ann Arbor, Mich., High School; 1877-78 University of Michigan, class of '81. In 1872-73 run a grocery store at Ludington. In 1878 was called home to attend to his father's estate. During 1879-80 was engaged in the insurance business. In 1881-82 assisted in the management of a planing mill and sash, door and blind factory. In 1883 entered the railway mail service on the run between Ludington, Mich., and Toledo, O., serving six years. In the fall of 1888, being discharged from the railway mail service by the Democratic administration for "offensive partisanship," was elected county treasurer of Mason county, serving four years—the limit in Michigan; since which time has been engaged in the insurance business and secretary of the local Building and Loan Association.

In 1880 joined the Freemasons, and ever since has been an enthusiastic member of the Blue Lodge, Chapter, Council, Commandery and Consistory, having served as presiding officer of the Chapter, Council and Commandery.. In politics has been a Republican, and besides serving four years as county treasurer has been supervisor of his ward five years, and in such capacity has been chairman of the County Finance Committee four years. Has also served as secretary of the Republican County Campaign Committee.

His wife, Charlotte Patterson Wood, was the daughter of Col. Alfred Benning Wood, of East Saginaw, Mich. Res., Ludington, Mich.

3850. i. LUTHER BENNING, b. Oct. 16, 1886.
3851. ii. EDWARD WOOD, b. July 22, 1892.

3597. FIRST LIEUT. ARTHUR B. FOSTER (George B., Azro, Robert, Isaiah, Benjamin, Benjamin, Isaac, Reginald), b. Pekin, Ill., Nov. 12, 1863; m., June 18, 1889, Lily M. Armour, b. July 21, 1870. He is quartermaster Nineteenth Infantry, United States army, at Ponce, Porto Rico. Res., Ft. Brady, Mich., and Tampa, Fla.

3851½. i. ARTHUR EDWARD, b. June 1, 1896; d. Oct. 16, 1898.

3615. EDWARD WILLARD FOSTER (Alvara, Elijah W., Abraham, Samuel, Jeremiah, Abraham, Jacob, Reginald), b. March 11, 1870; m., Nov. 24, 1892, Grace Coleman, b., Gardner, Aug. 16, 1873. Res., Leominster, Mass.

3852. i. GUY, b. ——, 1893; d. 1893.

3853. ii. CARL, b. ——, 1894.

3618. HERBERT A. FOSTER (Alvin R., Hosea, Samuel, Samuel, Jeremiah, Abraham, Jacob, Reginald), b. Stoddard, N. H., March 27, 1867; m., W. Swanzy, N. H., June 6, 1888, Annis Burke, b. Feb. 20, 1868. He is an architect and carpenter. Res., Rutland, Mass.

3854. i. PAUL R., b. at Keene N. H., Oct. 1, 1889.

3855. ii. LAURENCE B., b. at Keene, N. H., July 26, 1891; d. May 4, 1892.

3856. iii. CLIFFORD H., b. at Keene, N. H., July 26, 1893.

3620. FRANK HOUGHTON FOSTER (Edwin S., Hosea, Samuel, Samuel, Jeremiah, Abraham, Jacob, Reginald), b. Sept. 10, 1869, Keene, N. H.; m., Concord, N. H., Jan. 10, 1895, Inez Emma Fairbanks, b. Feb. 9, 1871.

Frank Houghton Foster was born in Keene, N. H., Sept. 10, 1869, where he resided with his parents until 1887. In 1886 he left school, after partially completing his high school course, and entered the office of his father, a contractor and builder. In 1887 he left home to accept a position as teller in the National Bank of Lebanon, of Lebanon, N. H., where he remained for about ten years, being promoted to position of assistant cashier in 1895. He was married in January, 1895, in Concord, N. H., to Miss Inez Fairbanks, daughter of Charles Fairbanks. In February, 1897, Mr. Foster removed to Claremont, N. H., to accept the cashiership of the Claremont National Bank, which position he now holds. Res., Claremont, N. H.

3857. i. ELEANOR STEWART, b. June 1, 1897.

FRANK H. FOSTER.

3621. HARRY STEWART FOSTER (Edwin S., Hosea, Samuel, Samuel, Jeremiah, Abraham, Jacob, Reginald), b. May 17, 1871, Keene, N. H.; m., June 28, 1893, Amy Otis, of Hillsboro Bridge, N. H.

Harry Stewart Foster was born in Keene in 1871. He was educated in the public schools and learned the carpenter's trade, which he still follows. He removed to Manchester, N. H., about 1890. Res., s. p., Manchester, N. H.

3642. CHARLES LEONARD FOSTER (Elon, Leonard R., Isaac, Isaac, Isaac, Joseph, Jacob, Reginald), b. Lakeville, Conn., Sept. 11, 1859; m., Bridgeport, Conn., Feb. 6, 1890, Evelene M. Smith, dau. of Horace Smith, of Bridgeport, Conn. A lawyer at 18 Wall St., New York.

Charles Leonard Foster was born Sept. 11, 1859, in Lakeville, town of Salisbury, Litchfield county, Conn., where his father, Rev. Dr. Elon Foster, was then pastor of the Methodist Episcopal Church. His boyhood was passed in New York and Brooklyn in attendance upon the University Grammar School and Adelphi Academy. He completed his preparatory college course in 1877, at the Centenary Collegiate Institute, Hackettstown, N. J. He passed examinations for both the University of the City of New York and Wesleyan University, Middletown, Conn. Deciding upon the latter College, he took its regular classical course, receiving the degree of B. A. in 1881, and M. A. three years later. After graduation he took up the study of law, entering the office of Olin, Rives & Montgomery, and also matriculated at Columbia University Law School, from which he received the degree of L. L. B. in 1883. In the spring of the same year he was admitted to practice at the bar of the State of New York. In the fall of 1883 he entered the office of Arnoux, Ritch & Woodford, which afterward became Ritch, Woodford, Bovee & Wallace, his success being identified with that of said firm. In politics he is a Republican. In religion a Methodist. Res., Brooklyn, N. Y., 270 Hewes St.

3858. i. ELON, b. Sept. 14, 1892.

3859. ii. EVELENE SMITH, b. Jan. 5, 1897.

3663. IRA HADLEY FOSTER (John A., Daniel, Daniel, Isaac, Isaac, Joseph, Jacob, Reginald), b. Augusta, Me., Feb. 10, 1872; m., Feb. 21, 1893, there, Hattie M. Stone, b. July 25, 1872. He is a carpenter and joiner. Res., s. p., Augusta, Me.

THE DORCHESTER BRANCH.

3860. REV. THOMAS FOSTER, b. England; m. there Abigail Wimes, dau. of Mathew, of Ipswich, England.

In the name of God Amen the xxijth day of September in the xiiijth yeare of the raigne of our Sovereign lord Charles by the grace of God of England Scotland France & Ireland King defender of the faith de Annoque dni 1638. I Thomas Forster of Ipswich in the countie of Suffolk Clarke being sicke in body but of good & p'rfect remembrance God be thanked therefore doe ordain & make this my last will & testament in manner & form following First and most principally I doe most humblie comend my soul to God and most stedfastly believing In and through the only death merits and passion of Jesus Christ my alone Saviour & all sufficient Redeemer to have free pardon and remission of all my sins & to be an inheritor with him in his everlasting Kingdom prepared for his elect before the beginning of the world And my body to the earth from whence it came And as for that small estate which God of his goodness hath lent me in this life I doe by his divine permission dispose thereof as followeth that is to say I will and bequeath my messuage or tenement wherein I do now inhabit and dwell situate in the parish of St Matthew and the parish of St Mary at the tower in Ipswich or in either of them to my executors hereafter named and to their heirs and assigns to the use intent and purpose that they do within one year next after my decease make sale thereof for the best price that can be obtained And the monies for which the same shall be sold I will shall be devided in form following, viz.: to my son Richard Foster £20. To my son Thomas Foster £20 to my son William Foster £20 the remainder of the monies shall be equally devided between and among my three daughters Sarae Smith the wife of John Smith Elizabeth the wife of William Ferris and Jane Ladbrooke widow I will and bequeath to the said Jane Ladbrooke my great chest in the hall the bedstead feather bed and all the furniture thereonto belonging except the red blanskett standing in my hall chamber Item I give and bequeath unto the said Elizabeth Ferris my daughter the black trunk standing in the said hall chamber and the bedstead and bedding and all the furniture thereunto belonging standing in the butterie chamber with the said red blanskett And I further give and bequeath unto my said two daughters Elizabeth and Jane all such firing of wood brome and coals as I shall have at the time of my decease Item I give unto the said Richard my son my great backed leather chair standing in the parlour Item I give unto Robert Ladbrooke my grandchild my great joined chair in the parlour and also the handle bedstead and bed with all the furniture standing in the butterie chamber All my other household stuff linen brass and pewter and movables whatsoever I give and bequeath unto my said three daughters Sarrae Elizabeth and Jane to be equally devided amongst them And I will and my mind is that all my apparel and all my books shall be sold and the monies thereof arising to be equally devided amongst my said two daughters Elizabeth and Jane And all other my monies debts and goods whatsoever not by me herein before given (my debts probate of this my last will and funeral expenses discharged) I will shall be and remain to my said two daughters Elizabeth and Jane to be equallie devided And of this my last Will and Testament I do ordain and make the said Richard my son and Jane my daughter my executors And thus giving all honour praise and glory to God Almightie I conclude this my last will and testament—His testibus, John Lambe, John Hawys—Executed by mark.

Proved December 5, 1638.

(Commissary and Archdeaconry
Court of Suffolk—Filed Will, s. a.)

He d. in England in 1638. Res., Biddenden and Ipswich, England.

3861. i. RICHARD, b. in England, abt. 1595; m. Patience Bigg.

3862. ii. THOMAS, b. in England, abt. 1600; m. Elizabeth ——.

3863. iii. WILLIAM, b. in England, in 1618; m. Susanna ——, and Anne Brackenberry.

3864. iv. SARAH, m. John Smith.
3864¼.v. ELIZABETH, m. William Ferris.
3864½.vi. JANE, m. —— Ledbrooke. Had a son Robert.

3861. RICHARD FOSTER (Thomas), b. England, prob. at Biddenden, abt. 1595; m. there Patience Bigg, a sister of John Bigg and of the husband of Rachel Bigg. She was b. 1595.

17 Aprilis, 1635 This p'ties hereonder expressed are to be transported to New England imbarqued in ye Elizabeth Wm. Stagg Mr. Cert. from the Minister and Justices of the Peace of their conformitie to the Church of England, they have taken the oaths of Allegeance and Supremacie. Such is the heading in the entry in the Rolls office Chancery Lane, London, signed by Patience ffoster, aged 40, and son Hopestill ffoster, aged 14.

In 1635 there arrived in Massachusetts many ships with passengers from England, and the plantation at Dorchester attracted its full share of them. This year there arrived among the passengers in the "Elizabeth" Patience Foster and her son Hopestill.

In 3 Mass. Hist. Coll. viii, 261, is extract from the record of London custom house, where these names, with that of Rachel Bigg, 6, are given. Of the accuracy of this part of the copy a genuine doubt being felt. By kindness of the official keeper of that record at Westminster, a fac-simile was obtained, for a few lines, and thus its exactness proved. That another numeral, perhaps on the left, perhaps on the right, of the figure 6, denoting the years of Rachel Bigg was omitted by the clerk, in 1635, must be evident to all, for in her will, Nov. 17, 1646, she calls husband aged, and names her nephew, Hopestill F., probably the fellow passenger, to whom she makes bequest. See 3 Mass. Hist. Coll. x, 131.—Savage.

"All of these facts point to certain conclusions, viz.: That prior to 1639 Patience Foster was a widow, and as there is no mention of her husband's death here, nor of his being alive here, it seems indisputable that he never came here; but that her son, Hopestill, was made a freeman, church member and a husband in 1639. As I have said, if he were only fourteen in 1635 this would be marvelous; but if the custom house entry of age was wrong, as it was in regard to his grandmother, Rachel Bigg, there is no inconsistency. In fact I incline to think the age given him was seventeen instead of fourteen, and then he would be twenty-one when he took up these responsibilities in 1639. Mr. Savage, in his transcript of these list of emigrants, has pointed out numerous instances of evident mistakes in the ages given, all recognized in other ways as children of Capt. Hopestill Foster and his wife, Mary, daughter of James Bates, and of course the same three named by their grandmother, Rachel Biggs, in her above will of November, 1646. Now Captain Hopestill was presumably married in 1639, the same year that the freeman was admitted, and that he was made a church member also. In Dorchester Town Records, as printed, p. 25, in the division of lands, widow Foster had an acre next to Mr. Bates, at the Neck, in January, 1637-8; in March, 1637-8, she has two acres and thirty rods. In 1641 (p. 45) persons putting horses on the Neck were to report to Hopestill Foster; in 1644 Hopestill Foster was one of three to settle with John Glover. From that date we trace Captain Hopestill, of Cranbrook, deceased. I omit many other interesting references. Now, the widow, Rachel Bigg, in 1646 mentions her nephew, Hopestill Foster, and his children, Thankful, Hopestill and Patience. In regard to the word "nephew" I made a surprising blunder, treating it as equivalent to son-in-law, and meaning by it the husband of Patience Foster, who came over with Mrs. Bigg, in fact the word "nephew" in English wills of that date means very often, if not invariably, "grandson" See on this point the standard dictionaries. This makes everything harmonious. (1) Mrs. Patience Foster, the emigrant of 1635, was doubtless a widow, and the christian name of her husband was Richard. Her son (2), Hopestill Foster, born 1620, or 1621, was the first of these names in Dorcester; was the nephew, i. e., grandson of Rachel Bigg, and in 1653 he and his cousins, the Stowes, divided the lands of their "deceased uncles, Smallhope Bigg and John Bigg," both of Kent. Against this is only the tradition, or idea, that Patience Foster's husband was named Hopestill, and that he came to Dorcester, substantiated by the fact that a Hopestill Foster was a freeman May 22, 1639. Art. Co., 1642, and selectmen 1645. (I do not find a selectman then, it being an error for 1655.) These offices seem beyond the reach of a boy born in 1620. But look at the other side. In the Dorchester Church Record, we find admitted prior to November, 1639, Rachel Bigg, Patience and Hopestill Foster. In the same record, Thankful Foster, bapt. Dec.

27, 1640, "married to Mr. Baker, of Boston." Later note on the church record: Hopestill Foster, March 10, 1644. Patience Foster, July 16, 1646.

"Though considerable has been written about Capt. Hopestill Foster, much was incorrect, and I must confess to have been one of the blunderers. This is especially in regard to the idea that his father came to New England. The true record begins with the fact that on April 17, 1635, he embarked on the 'Elizabeth,' of which William Stagg was master. I agree with Mr. Savage that the age of Rachel Bigg was a clerical error, and that she was the Rachel Bigg whose will of Nov. 17, 1646, is in our Suffolk wills, and which is annotated by me in the Register, vol. 29. p. 253. In the same notes will be found the will of John Bigg, of Maidstone county, Kent, England, dated March 27, 1641-2, proved Feb. 7, 1642-3. He mentions his mother, his sister Foster and his brother Stowe, all three in New England; cousin James Bates, of New England, his brother Smallhope Bigg."—Whitmore.

"Savage says that Hopestill Foster came to Dorchester in 1634, or a little earlier, and had his wife Patience, etc. This is probably an error. It is quite probable that the husband of Patience Foster never came to this country, and that his name was not Hopestill, but Richard. Patience Foster, who came to this country in 1635 with her son Hopestill, aged fourteen, and her mother, Rachel Bigg, aged six [probably an original clerical error for sixty], was called widow Foster at the assignment of Neck lands, in Dorchester, in 1637. Smallhope Bigg, of England, mentions in his will his mother, Rachel Bigg, and his sister, Patience Foster, and Elizabeth Stowe, living in New England. He leaves to Hopestill Foster, 'son of my sister,' three hundred pounds. Again, he mentions Patience Bigg, alias Foster, wife of Richard Foster, and Elizabeth Bigg, alias Stowe, wife of Richard Stowe. This last is a clerical error, for he has already spoken of 'my brother John Stowe.' Vol. 38, p. 60. John Bigg, brother and chief heir of Stanhope Bigg, in his will, dated March, 1641, mentions his mother Rachel, his sister Foster, and his brother Stowe [whose wife is probably now deceased], living in New England. A certain portion is to be given eventually to Hopestill Foster and the sons and daughters of Stowe. To these he is evidently uncle. Vol. 29. pp. 253-240. In Rachel Bigg's will, Nov. 17, 1640, Suffolk Wills, I-89, she mentions her son-in-law John Stow and her nephew [grandson] Hopestill Foster; Thankful, his daughter; Hopestill, his son; and Patience, his daughter. This is probably the order of their ages [the sisters]. The first mention of Hopestill Foster in Dorchester records is 1 of 1 mo., 1641, when he was made fence viewer. This was at the March election. As he must have been at least twenty-one at this time he must have been born as early as March, 1620. In 1635 his age was given as fourteen. (Will, July 19, 1676.) He died Oct. 14, 1676, aged fifty-six. [Sewall.] [Hopestill, Jr., mentioned on p. 145 of Dorchester, is son of this one.] He was made freeman in 1643. He married Mary Bate, daughter of James Bate, who was called 'cousin' by John Bigg, and who with all his family came over in the same ship with Hopestill Foster and his mother. She died Jan. 4, 1702-3, aged eighty-four years. [The ages of the Bate family as given in the ship list are as follows: James Bate, fifty-three; Alice Bate, fifty-two; Lydia, twenty; Marie, seventeen; Margaret, twelve; James, five.] She was probably older than her husband."—Miss Mary Pierce, of Weston.

Sept. 14, 1653, Hopestill Foster signs an agreement in relation to land of deceased, uncles Smallhope Bigg and John Bigg, of the county of Kent, in Old England. The lands were in Crambrooke, Withersham and Lidd.—See Boston Probate records.

Vol. 51, p. 194, Archæology Cantiana (Vol. 20, London, 1893), prints an abstract of Kentish administrations, 1604-1649, extracted from the Act Books of the Prerogative Court of Canterbury, from which the following is taken:

"Fol. 166; name of deceased, Foster Richard (relict Patience renounses), Parish Biddenden; to whom granted, John Bigg, maternal uncle of Mary, Hopestill and John Foster, children, minors; date, 1630, 3 May."

Albert C. Bates, Hartford, Conn.

202 High St., Hartford, Conn., Aug. 16, '98.

Dear Sir: Absence from the city must excuse delay in acknowledging yours of the 6th. I have no special interest in, or special material concerning, the Foster family. My only interest was an effort to establish a connection between the Bigg and Bate families in England. Yours truly

Albert C. Bates.

Mr. F. C. Pierce.

These parties, April 17, 1635, hereunto expressed are to be transported to New England, imbarqued in Elizabeth. Certificates from Ministers and Justices of the

Peace of their conformite to Church of England. They have taken the oaths of allegeance and supremacie. James Bate, husbandman, fifty-three; Alice, fifty-two; Lydia, twenty; Maria, seventeen; Margaret, twelve; James, nine; Hopestill Foster, fourteen.

He d. in Biddenden, Kent, England, abt. 1639.

3865. i. HOPESTILL, b. Biddenden, England, 1621; m. Mary Bate.
3866. ii. JOHN, b. ——, Biddenden, England.
3867. iii. MARY, b. ——, Biddenden, England.

3862. SERGT. THOMAS FOSTER (Thomas), b. England, abt. 1600; m. prob. abt. 1635, Elizabeth ——. She d. Jan. 29. 1694 5.

Thomas Foster came to America in the ship Hercules, with his brother William in 1634. He was the gunner at the castle. In 1639, at a meeting in Boston, of Mr. Thomas Oliver, Thomas Leaverett, Mr. William Colburn, Mr. Robert Keavne, Capt. Edward Gibon and Jacob Elyott, there was granted to Thomas Foster, the gunner at the castle, a great lot at the Mount (Mt. Wollaston, Braintree) for six heads, upon condition expressed for "Mount Wollystone lands." This property he conveyed in 1647 to Thomas Beamont, of London, mariner. Mt. Wollaston was incorporated as Braintree in 1640.

In 1640 he was residing in Weymouth and there his first child was born. He owned land in Weymouth in 1642: "Three acres on the east field, first granted to John Allin, bounded on the east with Jeffeny Staples' land, on the west with the land of Edward Bates." He disposed of his remaining land in Boston limits in 1647 to William Brown, of Salem. While residing in Boston, in 1642, he was admitted a freeman, and on his removal to Billerica, was admitted there in 1647. The following year he moved to Braintree, and before 1659 was residing in Billerica.

He went from Braintree to Billerica. In June, 1659, he received a grant of an eight-acre lot. His home lot was fifty acres, his house lot being part of it, lying on the east end of Bare Hill, bounded by Shawshine road, on the west ninety and four pole, by William Hamlet on the north one hundred and two poles; by ye common, east, ninety poles; by a highway on the southwest eighty-six poles.

Farmer Savage and Paige are our authorities for considering Thomas Foster, of Weymouth, Braintree and Billerica, one and the same person. From Pattee's History of Braintree, p. 470, part of the testimony of Henry Leonard, concerning some coal at the forge, reads:

"Sworn Oct. 27, 1655. Mr. Gifford gave me orders that if Goodman Foster, or some others of Braintree, could make any use of them (the coals) I should dispose of them. Whereupon Goodman Foster had about two half loads, and some of the rest of the neighbors thereabout fetched some of them. but they were so bad they would fetch no more, and Goodman Foster took as much paynes about them as they were worth, and although they would serve his turn, they would not serve us at the Forge."

From Hazen's History of Billerica: Thomas Foster lived east of Bare Hill, the hill south of the village. "The first list of town officers, 1659-60, names Thomas Foster as one of the selectmen. He held the same office for 1660-61-63-65-67-69. In 1660 Thomas Foster was chosen 'eldest corporal of the Trayne Band.'

"5: 5 mo: 1675. In pursuance of an order from Hon. Concil, sent unto them by warrant from ye worshipful Simeon Willard, Esq., Sergeant Major in reference to the gathering the inhabitants of ye town into several garrisons according to their best policy.

"For ye south end of ye town, Sergeant Foster's house is appointed and so to take his son Joseph Foster, James Frost, Joseph French, Joseph Walker, Daniel Rogers, John Kitteridge, Thomas Richardson and 2 soldiers in all, 10 soldiers and 6 houses.

"11: 9 mo: 1670. Thomas Richardson being convicted of taking two loads of cedar from our swamp and transporting ye same out of town, contrary to our towne orders, is fined 30s, which Thomas Foster paid for him, he agreeing to build 22 poles of four raile fence for Foster." The tax list for 1679 shows that Sergeant Foster was rated for 5s, one poll. The highest rating on the list is for 13s.

We now quote from Dr. Paige: (Gen. Reg. xxvi, 394.) "Thomas Foster was a blacksmith, and the progenitor of a long line of blacksmiths. According to the fashion which then prevailed, the scrivener was careful to describe him as sergeant in a deed dated November, 1679, wherein Thomas and wife Elizabeth convey land to Moses Haggett for £8."

In his old age he was repeatedly called before the Middlesex County Court and punished for worshiping the God of his fathers after the way his judges called heresy. To the first accusation he offered satisfactory defense, but afterward he was condemned. Thus it is recorded: "Oct. 4, 1671: Thomas Foster appearing before the Court, to answer the presentment of the grand jury for absenting himself from the public ordinances of Christ on the Lord's day, pleaded that the reason of his absence was the providence of God necessitating him thereto was discharged, paying costs June 18, 1672; George Farley, Thomas Foster and William Hamlet being presented for breach of the Ecclesiastical laws, they all confessed the presentment, were admonished and ordered to pay costs, 4s, 6d, a piece."

"June 15, 1675. Thomas Foster, appearing before the court to answer the presentment of the grand jury for not attending the public worship of God on Sabbath days and days of humiliation aud thanksgiving, and by his own confession, in open court, being convicted of constant and ordinary frequenting the meeting of the Anabaptists on Lord's day, is sentenced to pay a fine of £5 and costs, amounting to 8s, 6d." "If Mr. Foster was heretic," says Dr. Paige, "his posterity made ample amends by service to the Orthodox church in the office of deacon."

No record is found of his marriage, but in March, 1648, and in November, 1679, he had a wife Elizabeth; probably the same who is provided for by his will. She was no doubt the mother of his children. Mrs. Elizabeth Foster died Jan. 29, 1694-5. She had namesakes in her daughter, Mrs. Frost, and four of grandchildren.

Thomas Foster died in Billerica, April 20, 1682. The following is his will, recorded in the Middlesex Probate Records:

I Thomas Foster being very weak in body, yet of perfect memory, and of a disposing mind do make my last will and testament as followeth. And in the first place I Committ my soule to God that gave it, and my body to the earth to a decent buriall and as for that small portion of ye good things of this life which God hath graciously continued to mee, I do thus dispose of them and first I do will that all my just debts be discharged, with ye charge of my funerall, nextly I do will that my dear wife may have a comfortable and honorable maintenance out of ye remainder during ye time of her natural life. Also I do give to my son-in-law James Frost a good Cow, or four pound in case it be to be had out of my estate after ye decease of my wife; lastly I do nominate and impower my son Joseph Foster to be my sole executor, and I do put my wholl estate both personal and real in his hands, after my decease, for ye accomplishment of the premises, as witness my hand and seal this eighteen day of April in ye year of our Lord, God, one thousand six hundred eighty and two. Thomas Foster.

Signed and sealed in presence of us.

Jonathan Danforth sen]
Jonathan Danforth jun]

June 20 82 Jonathan Danforth sen & jun appearing under oath in court as witnesses to ye above will

Jonathan R. Cdmingbon?]
Cunningham?]

The inventory of the estate was taken June 17, 1682, by Jonathan Danforth, senior and Joseph Thompson; it amounted to £98, 17, 0.

Thus, in a few pages, is set down all that is known of Sergeant Thomas Foster, whose numerous descendants are now scattered throughout our country.

Though but a humble citizen, content in times of peace to labor at his anvil, yet the alarming cry of war found him ready to buckle on the sword; and conscience, too, in the wordy conflicts of his day, proved him the bold defender of his convictions.

His bones are dust
His good sword rust
His soul is with the saints we trust.

"I found the transfer by John Curtis, in old Boston Court Records alludes to his estate as formerly Thomas Foster, of Braintree, and 1669 it was. Then the next year Thomas, of Roxbury, is named as on the border line of an estate. The last probably Dr. Foster, who gave it up before he died, in Cambridge, in 1680. Thomas, of Billerica, only, owned the estate then in halves, so I think in his old age he bought this farm with young Joseph, and probably promised him the whole when he died. All the other sons were well helped out."—Miss Abbott.

Rev. B. Beadham, of Newton, North Wales, England, writes: "Thomas Foster, Boston, 1641, who came in the Hercules, 1634, and was a gunner at the Castle, is also mentioned in that valuable, but ludicrously mis (or rather non-) edited book,

32

'Thomas Lechford's Note-Book,' p. 135, and also p. 377, of the printed edition. We learn from Lechford that the son in New England was Thomas."

He d. April 20, 1682. Res., Boston, Weymouth, Woburn, Braintree and Billerica, Mass.

3868. i. THOMAS, b. Aug. 18, 1640; m., Oct. 15, 1662, Sarah Parker, of Cambridge.

3869. ii. JOHN, b. Oct. 7, 1642; m. Mary Chillingsworth.

3870. iii. INCREASE, b. abt. 1644; mentioned by Savage, but nothing further.

3871. iv. ELIZABETH, b. abt. 1646; m. Deacon James Frost, of Billerica, Jan. 22, 1666. He was son of Deacon Edmund Frost. Res., Billerica, where he d. 1711. She d. 1726. Ch.: 1. Thomas, b. 1667. 2. John, b. 1668. 3. Samuel, b 1670. 4. Elizabeth, b. 1672; m. Peter Cornell. 5. Edmund, b. 1675. 6. Mary, b. 1676; m. John Walker. 7. Sarah, b. 1678; m. —— Howard; he d. bef. 1711. 8 Hannah, b. 1680. 9. Joseph, b. 1682. 10. Abigail, b. 1685; m. Ephraim Kidder. 11. Benjamin, b. 1687. 12. James, b. ——.

3872. v. HOPESTILL, b. March 26, 1648; m., Oct. 15, 1670, Elizabeth, widow of Thomas Whittemore.

3873. vi. JOSEPH, b. March 28, 1650; m. Dec. 11, 1672, Alice Gordon, of Roxbury; m., 2d, Margaret Brown; m., 3d, Mrs. Rebecca Danforth.

3863. CAPT. WILLIAM FOSTER (Thomas), b. in England abt. 1618; m. —— Susanna. She d. and he m., 2d, Anne Brackenbury, b. 1628; d. Sept. 22, 1714.

William was admitted to the church of Charlestown 15(6) 1652. Savage says he was of Boston, 1644, with wife Susanna. He was evidently the passenger of his name in the Hercules from Southampton, in 1634. William Foster, of Charlestown was aged about eighty at his death, while this identification would make him eighty-three, which is hardly inconsistent, and it may be noticed that his grandson, Richard, is called eighty-two on his tombstone, when he was really but little over eighty. This, however, is mere conjecture. We know that William Foster had for his wife Anne, daughter of William Brackenbury, of Charlestown and Malden, and that she was admitted to the church, 23(7), 1652. He was a sea captain, and in 1669 master of the Dolphin. Mather, in his Magnalia, iii, 183, has this mention of him. It is found in the "Life of the Rev. John Eliot."

"There was a Godly Gentleman of Charlestown, one Mr. Foster, who, with his son, was taken captive by Turkish Enemies. Much Prayer was employed, both privately and publicly by the good people here, for the Redemption of that Gentleman; but we were at last informed that the Bloody Prince, in whose dominions he was now a Slave, was resolved that in his Life time no Prisoner should be released; and so the Distressed Friends of this prisoner now concluded our Hope is lost! Will upon this Mr. Eliot in some of his next Prayers before a verry solemn Congregation verry broadly beg'd Heavenly Father, work for the Redemption of thy poor Servant Foster; and if the Prince detains him will not, as they say, dismiss him long himself lives Lord, we pray thee to kill that Prince; kill him, and glorify thyself upon him. And now behold the answer. The poor Captiv'd Gentleman quickly returns to us that had been mourning for him as lost Man, and brings us News that the Prince which hitherto held him, was come to an Untimely Death, by which means he was now set at Liberty."

The date of this captivity is fixed by John Hull, who wrote in his diary, 1671, "8 ber, 21. We received intelligence that William Foster, master of a small ship, was taken by the Turks as he was going to Bilboa with fish." (He was redeemed and came home 9 ber, 1673.) His good social position is shown by the fact that his son Isaac stood first in rank in a class of eleven at Harvard College. He died at Charlestown, May 8, 1698, and his widow Sept. 22, 1714, in her eighty-sixth year. In his will he mentions his kinswoman, Elenor Davis, in England, and her daughter, Mary Davis. The town records thus mention his death: "William Foster, Navegator, aged about 80 years, dyed May 8, 1698."

Will—In the name of God Amen I William Foster of Charlestown in ye County of Middlesex in New England being weak and ill in body but of good and perfect memory blessed be God for it. And knowing the uncertainty of this life, and desirous to settle things in order do make constitute and appoint this to be my last will and Testament. Implims?] I committ my Soul to Almighty God my Creator assuredly believing I shall receive pardon of my sinns in and through Jesus Christ my Dear Redeemer and my body to the earth from whence it was taken to be decently buried at ye discreshion of my Executors hereafter named. And as touching such worldly Estate as ye Lord hath graciously Lent me, my will is it be disposed and Imployed as hereafter mentioned. First hereby revoking and making void all and every other will or wills by me heretofore made by word or writing. Do constitute and appoint this to be my last will and testament and no other.

Item I will that all my just debts or duties I ow in right or Conscience to any person whatsoever, my funerall Charges as also all those legacies hereafter named shall be well and truly paid in convenient time after my Decease by my Executors.

Item I do give ye improvement of my Dwelling house, Orchard and ground thereto belonging and adjoining as also my two pieces of wharfe and Creek and my wood Lott in ye first Division of Lotts, and movables to my beloved wife Ann Foster for her comfortable Subsistence, till and so long as she continueth my widow Fully impowering her with my other executors hereafter named to sell either or both the said pieces of Wharfe and wood Lott in ye First Division or movables for ye better inabling of them to pay my Said Debts and Legacies.

Item I do give and bequeath as follows viz.: To my daughter Mary Phillips I do give ye fifteen pounds to me due from her husband in part of payment for ye mill, it proving a hard bargaine to him, as also my Second Division of my wood Lott lying next or near Redding the same to be her and her heires forever.

Item I do give to my Grand Daughter Ann Foster five pounds to be paid by my Executors when she marrieth provided she marrieth with ye consent of her Father and Mother and her Unckle and Aunt Stanley, otherwise she shall have no more than any other of my Grandchildren, and ye remainder of ye Five pounds to be equally divided amongst my Grandchildren then Surviving.

Item I give to all ye rest of my grandchildren five shillings apiece to be paid by my Executors, to say, those ye are ten years of age within a twelve month after my Decease, and to ye rest as they shall arrive at Ten years of age.

Item I do give to my Kinswoman Elenor Davis in England and her Daughter Mary Davis Twenty Shillings apiece to be within a twelvemonth after my Decease. And as my Dwelling house Orchard and Lane adjoining as aforesaid at my wife's Decease I do give ye same to my two Sonnes Richard Foster and John Foster to be equally divided betwixt them by two indifferent men; and my son Richard after such division shall have his first choice And ye same to be to them and to their heirs forever. Further my will is that if my said wife shall see cause to marry againe she shall then have but her third as ye law provides and that what remains at her decease to be divided amongst my Children (to say) the thirds of ye housing and lands to my said Sonns Richard and John and the movable to my other children then surviving: Further my will is that if any of my Children shall murmer and be dissatisfied with my disposall of my Estate by this my last Will and Testament, that he or they so doing shall lose the benefit of their legacie or legacies and ye same shall be equally divided to and amongst those other of my children that shall rest satisfied herewith this my will.

Item I constitute and appoint my bloved wife Ann Foster and my sonnes Richard Foster and John Foster joint Executors of this my last will and testament. In testimony whereof I have hereunto set my Hand and affixed my Seal May the 7th 1696.

Annog R R is Gulielmi zty Anglice &c octavo

his
William X Foster
mark.

Signed published and declared by s'd Wm Foster to be his last will and Testament in presence of us

Sam'l Phipps
Thomas Walker
Michael Brigden

Prob. July 7 1698.

He d. May 8, 1698. Res., Charlestown, Mass.

3874. i. ISAAC, b. about 1652; m. Mrs. Mehitable Wyllis Russell.

3875. ii. JOHN, b. July 15, 1656; d. Dec. 19, 1659.

3876. iii. ANNE, bapt. Sept. 5, 1658; m. Capt. Eleazer Phillips, of Charlestown. She d. Dec. 1, 1695. He was son of Henry, of Dedham; was a victualer; was admitted to the church Nov. 25, 1705. She owned the covenant Oct. 12, 1684, and died in Charlestown. Ch.:

1. Henry, b. Dec. 28, 1680; d. Jan. 11, 1680. 2. Eleazer, b. April 23, 1682: m. Lydia Waite and Elizabeth Langton. Res., C. 3. Ann, b. Aug. 26, 1684; m. Thomas Ruck, of C. Res., to Salem. 4. William, b. March 31, 1687; d. April 13, 1687. 5. Nathaniel, b. May 24, 1688; d. Aug. 16, 1688. 6. Isaac, b. July 3, 1689; d. Dec. 27, 1689. 7. Joseph, b. July 17, 1690; town clerk; m. Elizabeth Gibson. Res., C. 8. Elizabeth, b. Nov. 23, 1692; m. Joseph Lemmon. 9. Jonathan, b. Nov. 19, 1695; saddler; m. Sarah Lynde. Res., C.

3877. iv. MARY, bapt. May 6, 1660; m., Aug. 8, 1676, James Smith; he d. Sept. 18, 1678, and she m. April 18, 1681, Capt. Timothy Phillips, and he d. April 30, 1755. He was a shipwright; one of the impressed men in 1675. Res., Charlestown. Phillips was a victualer, constable 1687. Mary owned the covenant Oct. 12, 1684, and was admitted to the church, Nov. 21, 1714. Ch.: 1. Henry, b. June 16, 1682. 2. Mary, b. Aug. 3, 1684; m. John Kidder, of C. 3. Timothy, b. Dec. 24, 1686; d. Jan. 17, 1712. 4. Ann, b. March 24, 1688; m. Joseph Newell. 5. Sarah, b. Aug. 30, 1691; m. Thomas Jackson. 6. John, b. July 14, 1694; m. Frances Garland and Alice Phillips. Res., C.

3878. v. RICHARD, b. Aug. 10, 1663; m. Parnell Winslow.

3879. vi. ELIZABETH, b. April 5, 1665; m., July 5, 1692, Isaac Goose, or Vergoose, of Boston, as his second wife. He d. Nov. 29, 1710, ae. 73.

Mother Goose, or Grandmother Goose, as she is sometimes called, was not a fictitious, but a real individual. Her maiden name was Elizabeth Foster, and she was born in 1665. She married Isaac Goose in 1693, and a few years after became a member of the Old South Church, in Boston, and died in 1758. The first edition of her songs, which were originally sung to her grandchildren, was published in Boston in 1716 by her son-in-law, Thomas Fleet. It is said that Fleet, out of respect for her, collected the little songs that she sang to her grandchildren into book form and published them for the use of mothers in America. The original editions of Mother Goose's Melodies are now very rare and valuable, but so many subsequent issues have been made that the book is one of the best known in the English language. The song of the little girl and her little curl does not appear in some of the early editions, and was probably added to the collection by some editor subsequent to Fleet.—Globe Democrat.

3880. vii. JOHN, b. Aug. 10, 1666; m. Sarah Richardson and Esther Lathrop.

3881. viii. DEBORAH, b. Feb. 28, 1668; d. April 22, 1668.

3865. CAPT. HOPESTILL FOSTER (Richard Thomas), b. England in 1621; m., in Dorchester, Mary Bate, dau. of James, b. England 1618; d. Jan. 4, 1702. His father was James Bates or Bate, and with his children came over from England in 1635 in the same ship with Widow Foster and her son. He had the title of Mr. prefixed to his name. His wife was Alice and in the list of passengers he was styled husbandman. He was born in 1582, joined the church in 1636, was selectman in 1637, 1638 and 1651 and represented Hingham in 1641. He may have come from Sid Town, Kent, England, for his son Richard resided there. James was probably brother of Edward, of Weymouth, and of Clement, of Hingham. Foster came from London in the ship Elizabeth, Captain Stagg, in 1635, with his mother, he then being fourteen years of age and she was forty. The son's name appears in the town records of Dorchester in 1636. The mother had a share in the Neck lands in 1637. Hopestill signed the covenant in 1638, joined the artillery company in 1642, and was ensign in the Dorchester train band under Capt. Humphrey Atherton in 1644; was selectman in 1646 and for thirty years after with occasional intervals; was a deputy to the court in 1652 and afterward a justice or commissioner of trials. He resided near the present southwest corner of Adams and Centre streets. His will is dated July 19, 1676. He gave £5 toward the Free Schools to be added to "Brother Gibson's legacy." He was a brewer, and very active in town affairs.

These parties, April 17, 1635, hereunto expressed, are to be transported to New England imbarqued in Elizabeth. Certified from ministers and justices of the peace of their conformite to Church of England. They have taken the oaths of allegiance and supremacie. James Bate, husbandman, fifty-three; Alice, fifty-two; Lydia, twenty; Maria, seventeen; Margaret, twelve; James, nine; Hopestill Foster, fourteen.

Captain Hopestill Foster was evidently a very active man, and his name for years is on nearly every page of the Dorchester records. In 1654 he is called "ensign," and so on for eight years; in 1662 he is called "lieutenant," under Captain Clapp; and in 1666 he became "captain," by which title he was known till his death. He held many town offices, as treasurer, etc.; was selectman in 1655 and many subsequent years, and was deputy to the General Court annually from 1659 to 1676, excepting 1671, when he was commissioner for small causes, eventually dying in office. This must be an unusual tenure of office.

I shall not attempt to trace Captain Foster's purchases of land, except as they may be evidence of pedigree. Hopestill Foster married Mary, daughter of James Bate, of Dorchester, who was a cousin to John Bigg. She came in the ship with the Fosters, and was reported as aged seventeen; a slight evidence that Hopestill's age is incorrectly given. Their children's births were copied from Dorchester town records, and the baptisms from Dorchester church records. Mrs. David W. Foster has the unrecorded original of an indenture between Edmond Brown, of Boston, shopkeeper, and Elizabeth, his wife (heretofore the wife of Hopestill Foster, of Dorchester, soap boiler, deceased); Hopestill Foster, of Boston, gunmaker; Samuel Foster, of Boston, goldsmith (sons of said Hopestill Foster); Timothy Nash, of Boston, merchant, and Mary, his wife; one of the daughters of Hopestill Foster and Elizabeth Foster, of Boston, spinster, another daughter of Hopestill Foster, of the one part, and James Foster, of Dorchester, yeoman, of the other part, selling to J.F. for £40 a parcel of upland in Dorchester, about twelve acres, part of estate of Sd Hopestill Foster, bounded northerly by the highway leading toward Castle Island, easterly by land of James White, westerly by land of Isaac Jones, southerly by saltmarsh of Capt. Samuel Clapp and saltmarsh of Samuel Lopley Note.—Livery of Seizen given by E. Brown and Hopestill Foster 12 m., April 10, 1694. March 31, 1698. H. F. and Samuel F. acknowledged before Sam Sewall.

Again it appears by Suffolk deeds, Vol. XXI., Fol. 524, that on April 23, 1696, James Foster, of Dorchester, and wife Anna; Standfast Foster, of Dorchester, and wife Abigail; Thankful Baker, widow; Patience, wife of Thomas Brown, of Sudbury, gentleman, and Mary, wife of Samuel Ward, of Boston, cooper; all children of Capt. Hopestill Foster, and also Hopestill Foster, of Boston, gunsmith; one of the grandsons of Captain Hopestill, sold land to Matthias Puffer, of Dorchester.

By a deed, dated Dec. 31, 1703, recorded in 1715, Suffolk deeds 29, Fol. 223, it seems that Standfast Foster bought land of Thomas Brown, of Sudbury, who married Patience, one of the daughters of Capt. Hopestill Foster; James Foster, son of Captain H.; Mary Ward, widow, a daughter of H. F.; Hopestill Foster, gunsmith; and Silence Eliot, widow; two of the grandchildren of Captain H. F. It mentions that Hopestill, Elisha and Comfort, three sons of Captain H. F., were then deceased. All of these relations are plain except Silence Eliot. It is pointed out in Sewall's Diary, Vol. iii, p. 333, that she was the daughter of a daughter of Captain Hopestill. James Foster had a daughter Silence Foster, as we shall see, born in 1677; but Silence Eliot, who was the wife of Joseph Eliot, of Boston (son of Jacob Eliot), died June 8, 1744, aged seventy-eight, as her tombstone in the Granary yard testifies. She was born in 1666. Now it is certain that Captain Hopestill's eldest daughter married Jan. 8, 1663-4, John Baker, of Boston, and had John, born at Boston, Feb. 26, 1664-5, and Silence, born at Dorchester (see records) May 28, 1666, "daughter of John Baker, of Boston, deceased." John Baker's will, dated March 26, 1666, proved July 5th, following, is in Suffolk Wills I, 471. In it he mentions wife Thankful, son Thomas, daughter Elizabeth, a child unborn, and makes his father, Hopestill Foster, his uncle Richard Baker, and his cousins William Ireland, overseers. He mentions his sister, Catherine Johnson; his wife's uncle, Bates, and gives his son, Thomas, the land that was his grandfather Swift's, at Dorchester Neck.

Savage was entirely wrong about John Baker. This will shows still more error in Savage. (Vol. I, p. 97 and Vol. IV, p. 241.) Savage says that John Baker, of Boston, blacksmith, married Nov. 5, 1657, Joan, daughter of Thomas Swift, of Dorchester, by whom she had five sons and one daughter, of whom only Thomas and Elizabeth survived. Then he denounces the record of the marriage and the first four births as falsely made on the Boston records, because the marriage record of 1657 says, "married by John Winthrop, governor," though he died in 1649 (see Boston Records, printed edition, p. 62). Now the explanation is ludicrously simple.

It was a clerical error, for John Endicott, governor, whose name is added to the next entry, and so for twenty more marriages on the same page. It is only a proof that eight years after his death, a clerk would mechanically write Gov. John Winthrop's name.

Boston records say that Joanna, wife of John Baker, died July 21, 1663, and this makes everything clear. By his first wife (Swift) Baker had only Thomas and Elizabeth, and by his second wife (Foster) he had the child unborn in March, who was named Silence. Later, undoubtedly, John, the first child of this marriage, had died, not being named in the will, and Silence was thus the only heir of her mother, Thankful (Foster) Baker, and therefore she joined in the deed we cited.—Whitemore.

Another heir James Foster and wife Anna, Standfast and Abigail, both of Dorchester; Thankful Bates, widow; Thomas Brown, of Sudbury, and wife Patience; Sam Ward, cooper, of Boston, and wife Mary; all children of Capt. Hopestill Foster, and grandson Hopestill, first son of the oldest third Hopestill (called gunmaker), sell land to M. Puff, 1696.

Hopestill Foster and three others in 1653, all nephews of Smallhope and John Bigg, of Kent, England, sign an agreement.

In 1664, with others, he signed a petition to the Governor and General Court as "Hopestill Foster, Jr."

There had been during the lifetime of Josias Chickatabut a disagreement between him and King Philip, of Mount Hope, about the boundary lines of their jurisdictions. The following letter was written by Squamaug to Captain Foster in relation to the matter:

Capt. ffoster: My respects to yourself and the rest of your selectmen. Sir, these are to intreat you by this bearer whom I send to you on purpose, send mee the five pounds that you engaged to my deceased brother should be payed in the beginning of this winter past; I have at pr sent many ocations, but intend shortly to come over and treat further with you. I know noe reason that the mount hope Sachem's pretended title to some of the lands mentioned in your deed should frustrate the agreement; if possibly that Sachem had any land within your bounds it is but very little aboue the pattent line, and the Colloney of plymouth have purchased it of him before the pattent lines were run. If you will give him for your securaty your maye, but I am well assuered that plymoth men have deeds for it already; and you have enough of us for your mony whoe are the knowne proprietors; thus hoping wee shall have noe controversy, I take leaue and remayne, sir, your ffrend and servant

DANIELL (alias) SQUAMUCK, Sachem

Mattakeeset, Mar 19, 1669-70

CAPT. FOSTER TO KING PHILIP OF MOUNT HOPE.

To Philip, Sachem of Mount Hope, Capt. Foster of Dorchester sendeth greeting. You may by this understand I re'd your letter dated June the 15th 1670, wherein you desire a meeting about land at pole plaine and within our township. It seems there is some difference about the land whose it is, wee say tis ours already both by grant from our Court and also by agreement with Indians, who say that it is theirs, and engaged to cleare any clayme that philip or any others should make to it, and therefore think it not needful to trouble ourselves any further, yet because you have desired a meeting once before and now againe, we shall some of us be together with some of the bay Indians give you a meeting if the lord permits at Captain Hudson's farme at Wading river upon the 12th of July next; then and there may be heard any difference as to the land within our township to Plymouth & the bay patent line; not else at present, but remain your friend

H. Foster with the
Consent of the townsmen*

Dor. this 22nd, June 1670

KING PHILIP'S' REPLY TO THE ABOVE MEETING.

Philip Sachem of mount hope To Capt. Hopestill Foster of Dorchester Sendeth Greeting

Sir, you may please to remember that when I last saw you att Wading river you promised mee six pounds in goods; now my request is that you send me (by?) this Indian five yards of White light collored serge to make me a coat and a good holland shirt redy made, and a pair of good Indian breeches all of which I have present need of therefore I pray him faile not to send them by my Indian and with

* These letters are copied from the originals now among the ancient documents of Dorchester.

them the several prices of them; and silk & buttens & 7 yards Gallonnes for trimmings: not else at present to trouble you with only the subscription of

KING PHILIP his Majesty P. P.

Mount hope the 15th of May 1672

The History of the Ancient and Honorable Artillery company has this of him: "Hopestill Foster (1642) and his mother, Patience, are recorded as being in the second emigration to Dorchester Plantation, which was in 1635. Hopestill was then fourteen years of age. He married Mary, daughter of James Bates. She died in 1703, aged eighty-three years. He joined the Dorchester church in 1638; became a freeman in 1639; was ensign of the Dorchester train band under Humfrey Atherton (1638) in 1644, and subsequently its captain. He served as a selectman from 1645 to 1674 inclusive, except 1646-9, 1657, 1653 and 1667. In 1675 he was elected but declined. He was a deputy to the court in 1652, and afterward a commissioner of trials. By his will, witnessed July 19, 1676, he gave five pounds toward the free school. He resided near the northwest corner of Adams and Centre streets. He was a brewer, active in all town affairs, a man of judgment and deserved popularity. He died Oct. 15, 1676. He was fourth sergeant of the Artillery Company in 1647. His son, Hopestill Foster (H. C., 1667), became a member of the same in 1673, and his grandson, Hopestill, in 1694."

"The tomb stone which marks the spot where he was buried is nearly as fresh in appearance now (1859) as when first erected. Captain Foster was one of the leading men of the place, and his death was 'a great loss to the town.' "

Will—Capt. Hopestill Foster—Dorchester. Wife, Mary, executrix, mentions two youngest sons, Comfort and Standfast; son, Hopestill; young Hopestill, my grandson; son John; son James; son Elisha; daughter Thankfull Baker; daughter Patience Browne; daughter Mary. Will dated July 19, 1676. Witnesses made oath before county court in Boston, Nov. 2, 1676, Lib. 6; Fol. 136-138.

He d. Oct. 15, 1676. Res., Dorchester, Mass.

3882. i. HOPESTILL, b. March 10. 1645; m. Elizabeth Payson.

3883. ii. JOHN, bapt. Dec. 10, 1648; m. (?) Mrs. Abigail Hawkins Moore Kelland.

3884. iii. JAMES, b. April 13, 1651; m. Capen and Anna Lane.

3885. iv. ELISHA, bapt. Aug. 23, 1653; m. Sarah Payson.

3886. v. THANKFUL, bapt. Dec. 27, 1640; m., Jan. 8, 1663, John Baker, of Boston. She d. Jan. 27, 1697. Their dau. Silence m. Joseph Eliot.

3887. vi. COMFORT, b. July 28, 1658, "died in the King's service," Jan. 5, 1688.

Administrator to estate of Comfort Foster, sometime of Dorchester, husbandman, died some years since; died intestate, in his Majesty's service; granted to Standfast Foster, of Dorchester; Malster, his brother. Dated, Nov. 14, 1700.—Suff. Prob. Lib. 14; Fol. 244.

Some of my correspondents state that Comfort m. Ellenor ——, who d. Jan. 3, 1735. I don't think so.

3888. vii. STANDFAST, b. Sept. 13, 1660; m. Abigail Holman and Sarah ——.

3889. viii. PATIENCE, bapt. Aug. 16, 1646; mentioned in Rachel Bigg's will, Nov. 17, 1646; m. Major Thomas Brown, of Sudbury. Major Brown was a prominent resident of Sudbury; was son of Capt. William and Mary Besbeech; also deacon and representative. The major was born May 22, 1645; was captain in the Indian wars. Patience d. Aug. 15, 1703; and he m., 2d, March 1, 1704, Mrs. Mary (Danforth) Phipps, dau. of Gov. Thomas Danforth, and widow of Solomon. Ch.: 1. Mary, m., June 27, 1693, Jonathan Willard, who d. 1706. 2. Thankful, m. Joseph Hubbard. 3. Patience, m., Dec. 1, 1704, Daniel Stone, and Nathaniel Rice. 4. Elizabeth, m., Nov. 7, 1708, Hopestill Bent. 5. Silence, m. —— Herds. 6. Hannah. 7. Eunice, b. and d. May 9, 1709.

3890. ix. MARY, bapt. Feb. 10, 1655; m. about 1680, Ephraim Sale, his second wife; m., 2d, Dec. 10, 1691, Samuel Ward.

3891. x. RICHARD, b. March 29, 1663; d. Oct. 6, 1663.

3868. DR. THOMAS FOSTER (Thomas, Thomas), b. Weymouth, Mass., Aug. 18, 1640; m., Oct. 15, 1662, Sarah Parker, of Cambridge, dau. of Robert Parker,

b. April, 1640. She m., 2d, March 30, 1687, Peter Brackett, of Billerica, bapt. 1637. She d. April 18, 1718. He d. before Sarah.

Thomas Foster (1668), of Roxbury, son of Thomas Foster, of Weymouth and Braintree, and a nephew of Hopestill (1642), was born at Weymouth. He moved to Roxbury about 1662, and removed to Cambridge about 1672. He married Sarah Parker. On the court files of 1678 he is styled "physician." He died Sept. 16, 1679, according to the town records, or Oct. 28, 1679, as inscribed on his headstone, aged thirty-nine years.

She was daughter of Robert Parker and wife Judith. He was a butcher in Boston and Roxbury. He was in Roxbury Oct. 15, 1662, and bequeathed property to his daughter, Sarah Foster, in 1684. Foster is styled a physician in the court files.

His epitaph is as follows:

Memento te esse mortalem.
Fugit Hora.
Here lies the body of Thomas
Foster Aged 39 yrs Died
Oct 28, 1679

The Middlesex Probate records say: Thomas, 1680, Cambridge, inventory; date October 4, 1680; Sarah Foster, administratrix; very incomplete.

He d. Oct. 28, 1679. Res., Roxbury and Cambridge, Mass.

3892. i. THOMAS, b. Aug. 1, 1663; d. Aug. 14, 1663.
3893. i½. THOMAS, b. June 4, 1665; m. Experience Parker.
3894. ii. SARAH, b. June 3, 1667; m. Sept. 22, 1686, Thomas Williams, of Stow.
3895. iii. HANNAH, b. July 23, 1669.
3896. iv. JONATHAN, b. Sept. 21, 1671; m. Abigail ——.
3897. v. ELIZABETH, b. Sept. 26, 1677.

3869. DEACON JOHN FOSTER (Thomas, Thomas), b. Oct. 7, 1642, in Weymouth, Mass., m. abt. 1663, Mary, dau. of Thomas Chillingsworth, of Marshfield, who d. Sept. 25, 1702. He m., 2d, Sarah Thomas, Dec. 30, 1702. Was a blacksmith; selectman in 1690; was elected deacon April 6, 1700, and ordained July 20, 1701. His death is recorded in Marshfield thus: "Deacon John Foster deceased June the 13 day 1732 in the 91 year of his age and left 7 living children, 45 grandchildren and 83 G. Grandchildren and had 26 G. children die before himself." Sarah died May 26, 1731.

Mary was the daughter of Thomas Chillingsworth who was first known as an inhabitant of Lynn, Mass., in 1637. He lived a short time in Lynn, removed to Sandwich and thence to Marshfield, where he settled. Was representative to General Court from Marshfield in 1648 and 1652. He died early in 1653. Administration of his estate was granted March, 1653, to his widow, Joanna ——, who m., 2d, May 17, 1654, Thomas Doggett, and was buried in Marshfield, Sept. 4, 1684. His children were: 1. Elizabeth, b. ——; d. unm. Sept. 28, 1665. 2. Mehitable, b. ——; m. Justus Earns, of Marshfield, May 2, 1661. 3. Mary, b. ——; Deacon John Foster. 4. Sarah, b. ——; m. Samuel Sprague, the last secretary of Plymouth Colony.

His gravestone, as well as that of his second wife, and his daughter Deborah, is still to be seen in the old graveyard at Marshfield. It is said he resided near South river, on lands inherited from Thomas Chillingsworth.

Will—In the name of God amen I Sarah Foster wife to John Foster of Marshfield in ye County of Plymouth in ye Province of ye Massachusetts Bay in New England ye 20th day of May anno-Domini 1731 Being very sick and weak in body but of sound mind and memory and being desirous to settle what Estate I have Do make and ordain this my last will and Testament in manner and form following that is to say I Commend my soul to God my Creator and my body to ye Earth from whence it was taken to be buried in Decent Christian burial and as To such worldly goods and Estate and money and all whatsoever sort of Estate that shall anywise appear to be mine my mind & will is that ye same shall be imployed & disposed as followeth:

That is to say I give and bequeath unto my Cousin John Balston my Cobirons. Item I give and bequeath unto Nehemiah Herrindon ye Lad which liveth with us that black heifer that is Called mine.

Item. I give and bequeath all ye Remainder of my Estate whatsoever it is or of what sort forever it may be that appeareth to be mine unto my Cousin John Balston my Cousin mary Stetson and to my son in law Thomas Foster and to my daughter in law Deborah Foster to be Equally divided between ye sd John Balston Mary

Stetson Thomas Foster Deborah Foster and Lastly I do hereby Constitute & appoint my son in law Thomas Foster to be sole Executor of this my last will & testament. in witness whereof I have hereunto set my hand & seal ye day and year above written

Signed sealed and declare by ye sd Sarah Foster to be her last will & testament in ye presence of

Robert Howland
William Howland
Arthur Howland

her
Sarah X Foster } Seal
mark

June the 23: 1731 The within named Robert Howland William Howland and Arthur Howland made oath that they saw the Within Named Sarah Foster Late of Marshfield in the County of Plymouth deceased signe seal and heard her declare the within Written to be her last will and Testament and that they at the same time in the presence of the Testator set to their hands as Witnesses: and that according to the best of their observation she then was of a sound and disposing mind and memory.

Before Isaac Winslow Judge of Probate

Children born Marshfield:

3898. i. ELIZABETH, b. Sept. 24, 1664; m. William Carver, of Marshfield, Jan. 18, 1682-3. He was the centenarian. She d. June, 1715.

3899. ii. JOHN, b. Oct. 12, 1666; m., 1692, Hannah Stetson, of Scituate.

3900. iii. JOSIAH, b. June 7, 1669; m. Sarah, dau. of Samuel Sherman, of Marshfield.

3901. iv. MARY, b. Sept. 13, 1671; m. John Hatch, of Marshfield, Dec. 30, 1696. She died April 3, 1750.

3902. v. JOSEPH, b. abt. 1674; m., Sept. 8, 1696, Rachel Bassett, of Sandwich.

3903. vi. SARAH, b. abt. 1677; d. April 7, 1702; m. Nathan Thomas; m., 2d, Jedediah Bourne. Res., Plymouth, Mass.

3904. vii. CHILLINGSWORTH, b. July 11, 1680; m. Mercy Freeman.

3905. viii. JAMES, b. May 22, 1683; d. July 21, 1683.

3906. ix. THOMAS, b. in 1686; m. Faith (Oakman), widow of Benjamin White.

3907. x. DEBORAH, b. abt. 1691; d unm., Nov. 4, 1732.

Will—The 10th day of July 1732. In ye name of God amen I Deborah Foster of Marshfield in the County of Plymouth in ye Province of ye Massachusetts in New England Being very weak & infirm of body but of perfect sound mind & memory & Calling to mind the uncertainty of this Life & being desirous to settle things in order do make & ordain this my Last will & Testament in manner & form following viz: principally I Commend my soul to God my Creator & my body to ye Earth from whence it was taken to be buried in such decent manner as to my Executors hereafter named shall be thought most meet and Convenient and as to such worldly goods & Estate as ye Lord in mercy hath lent me my mind & will is that ye same shall be employed & disposed of as in this my will is Expressed. that is to say—I give & bequeath unto my brother Thomas Foster my best feather bed one Coverled a blanket & apair of sheets & my goldneck lace and my still & one half of all my silver money.

Item I give and bequeath unto my sister Mary Hatch my best suit of Clothes & my best lace Cap my new bedticking my silk scarf and my new silk gloves & my new silk hood and ye other half of all my silver money.

Item I give and bequeath unto my Cousin Mary Mackfarland my oldest feather bed a coverled & blanket and a pair of sheets Item I give unto my Cousin Sarah Tailer Thirty shillings in money or good Bills of Credit on sd Province. Item I give unto my Cousin Millicent Carver my Gold locket Item I give unto my sister Mary Hatch my Cousin Mary Standish my Cousin Mary Mackfarland and my Cousin Elizabeth Tailer all ye Remainder of my wairing apparrel that is not above disposed of to be equally divided amongst them four. Item I give all ye Remainder of my moveable Estate and all ye money which is due to me by bonds or bills that shall be

Remaining after all my Just debts and funeral Charges are well and truly paid by my Executor hereafter named—ye one half to my brother Thomas & my sister Mary Hatch Equally between them two and the other half unto my brother John Foster my brother Josiah Foster & my brother Joseph Foster & brother Chillingsworth Foster the other half Equally between them four.

And Lastly I do hereby Constitute and appoint my brother Thomas Foster sole Executor of this my last will and Testament In witness whereof I have hereunto set my hand & seal ye day and year above written

Testament In witness whereof I have hereunto set my hand & seal ye day and year above written

signed sealed published and declared by the said Deborah Foster ye Testatrix to be her Last will and Testament in ye presence of

her
Deborah X Foster (Seal)
mark

Arthur Howland
Abigail Howland
Sarah Peter son

December the 13: 1732: The within named Arthur Howland Abigail Howland and Sarah Peterson made oath that they saw the within named Deborah Foster sign seal and heard her declare the within written Instrument to be her last Will and Testament and that they at the same time in the presence of the sd Testator set to their hands as Witnesses; and that according to the best of their observation she then was of a sound and disposing mind and memory.

Before Isaac Winslow Judge of Probate.

3872. HOPESTILL FOSTER (Thomas, Thomas), b. Weymouth, Nov. 26, 1648; m. Oct. 15, 1670, Mrs. Elizabeth (Pierce) Whittemore, wid. of the second Thomas Whittemore, of Woburn, whom she m. Nov. 9, 1666, and had one son Joseph. She was dau. of Sergt. Thomas Pierce, of Woburn, b. Dec. 25, 1646. After Foster's death she m., 3rd, March 23, 1680, Nathaniel Peirce, b. Dec 4, 1655; d. 1692, son of Robert Peirce, and had three children. He was a blacksmith. He became a resident of Woburn about the time of his marriage. He seems to have sympathized and suffered with his father for conscience' sake. Thus it is recorded, Dec. 19, 1675, Hopestill Foster and John Peirce, of Oburne, appearing before the court to answer the presentment of the grand jury for turning their backs on the holy ordinance of baptism, confessed the presentment, and, being the first time, the court sentenced them to be admonished, which was accordingly performed in open court, and, paying fees of court, were discharged. Like his brother, Thomas, he died before his father. From his inventory it is learned that he died in 1679, when he was but thirty-one years of age. The amount of his inventory was £47-2-6. It was taken by James Converse, Jr., and Gersham Flag. In the list was a Smith's shop, anvil and tongs. The administrator of his estate was granted his widow Elizabeth. The settlement shows an inventory of Thomas Whittmore's estate which Hopestill Foster took into his hands when he married. He d. May 26, 1679. Res., Woburn, Mass.

3908. i. THOMAS, b. April 17, 1672; d. May 1, 1672.

3909. ii. ABIGAIL, b. March 12, 1673; m. Timothy Farley, of Billerica, b. July 29, 1680. Their dau., Abigail, b. Sept. 8, 1705; d. Stoughton, April 29, 1750; m. Benjamin Easte, and had Benjamin, Jr., b. Sept. 21, 1743, killed at Bunker Hill, June 17, 1775; by wife Mary Wales had Caleb, b. Oct. 3, 1774; d. March 29, 1820; a dau. was Sophia Bigelow Easte (see Dorchester line).

3910. iii. JOHN, b. Feb. 14, 1676.

3911. iv. MERCY, b. Feb. 26, 1678.

3873. DEACON JOSEPH FOSTER (Thomas, Thomas), b. Weymouth, Mass., March 25, 1650; m. Dec. 11, 1672, Alice Gorton, of Roxbury, dau. of John, bapt. March 5, 1652; d. May 17, 1712; m., 2d, Margaret Brown, of Sudbury; d. March 22, 1717; m., 3d, Mrs. Rebecca (Parker) Danforth, wid. of Jonathan and dau. of Jacob, of Chelmsford, b. 1661. She d. March 25, 1754. He was a blacksmith and resided in Billerica. If he was not a farmer, he owned considerable property. He was one of the proprietors of Rutland and sold his share, one thirty-second part, consisting of 2,700 acres to Jonathan Waldo, of Boston, for £25. This was Jan. 12, 1715. He was deacon of the first church of Billerica, and for many years his associate in office was his brother-in-law, Deacon James Frost. In his will, July 26, 1721, he names his wife Rabackah, son Thomas, daughter Elizabeth Wilson and her children. The will mentions a marriage contract with his wife dated June 26, 1718. The inventory of his estate amounted to £777.

Joseph Foster's will—1st In the nam and feer of God Amen: the sixth of May on thousand seven hundred and twenty on I Joseph Foster of Billerica in the County of Middlesex in his Majestys Provence of the Massachusetts bay in New England being weak in body but of perfect?] mind and memory, blased?] be God for it. Tharfor?] being of a dissposing?] mind I do ordain this instrument to be my last will and testament the which let no man altar or change and I do hereby make void all former wills by me made and in the first place I do humbly give my soul into the hands of God Father son and holy spirit three glorious parsons?] but one Infinite and eternal escence hoping for salvation in and throu?] the merits of Jesus Christ aloan?]: and do firmly believe that allthou this body of mine shall moulder in the dust yet at the great day when all shall appeer before God that then I shall with these eyes see God and dwell in his prasence?] to all etarnity.

2nd I give my body to the arth to a dasent buriall at the discration of my executors and overseers in hops?] of a glorious Rasuraction]: and as to that estat which God hath blest me with what is left after my debts and funarall charges are defraied?] I do give and dispose?] of the same in the form and manner following and first: I give unto my loving and beloved wife Rabackah Foster forty pounds currant money to be paid to her in a year after my deseace and I do further give her the liberty to take whatever she brought with her to my hous boath within doors and without acording? to my pramice?] that I made with her and I do further give her a mo[u?]rning sute throu?]out and I do further give her the liberty of any room in my house for a year after my deseace or longer tim?] if shee does desier it that so shee may have the liberty of spending that pravision that shee has helpt labor for, boath of meat and drink and 10 pounds mor?] if shee lives with me five years and I do further give her my brindled?] heifer.

secondly I do give unto my son Thomas Foster my homestead my hous and barn and my shop and tools in the shop and the ground that the shop stands upon: and I give to him my lot on the east side of the country road which I call my homestead. This I give unto him and his hairs?] forever but not to dispose of in his life tim and he may give it to his children at his death.

thirdly I give to my daughter Elizabeth Willson the homestead that I had of Doctor John Kittrige whar Thomas Foster now lives and I do further give unto her my Nuttings meadow with all the land that I have upon Beare hill all on the wast side of the country road this I give unto her and to her hairs forever.

Fourthly I give unto my grandson Joseph Willson twanty pounds which he shall have as followeth, that is my young hors at ten pounds, and my gun that he trains with at forty shillings and my lot at the great swampe at eight pounds which doo make it twanty pounds also I give him an ax and a syth and sickle and a cow the bast that is left and I give him my new bridle and my old sadle if he sees good to accept of it this I give to him and to his hairs forever.

Fifthly I give unto my granddaughter Johannah Willson twanty pounds to be paid to her by my executors in a cow and a bed and the rast in money. I also give her a platter and a grat bason and a little bason and two spoons and my bias skillet and the chest that she lays her clothes in and a lining?] wheel and six wooden plates and a chaire. These I give to her and her haus forever. This money that is to be paid to Johannah above what her bed and cow comes to shall be paid out of ye movables or else they may be sold for money to make it: and all the rest of my movables both within doors and without both cattle and all other things both wood and iron without doors and bras and pewter within doors and all other movables except that I have given to Joseph Willson and Johannah Willson they shall be equally divided between my son Thomas Foster and my daughter Elizabeth Willson and in cas?] they cannot agree in thar devission I do appoint my trusty friends Bengemen Thompson and John Blanchord to make thar divission for them and if they cannot agree I appoint Mr. Joseph Stevens to joyn with them and to make a finall ishew?]

And as for my ought?] lands which I rasarve they shall be to pay my debts and my wive's dowry and my funarail charges my wive's dowry will be about aight and forty pounds in all besides her liberty in the hous as I have given her in my will and if she shall live with me five years from our first marriage than shee shall have ten pounds mor And thar is forty pounds dew to Mr. Jonathan Waldo at Boston: and about three pounds ten shillings dew to the Captain Thomas Pattin. This is all that I owe that I ramamber now to pay thes debts and dowry.

I leave three divissions?] of land the one lys on the wast side of Concord River between Cpt John Hills and said river about three score and sixteen laces? [acres] which I esteem to be worth about fifty five or sixty pounds. the other lot lys in othe Swamp near seventeen acres?] which I esteem about fifty five pounds. the other lot lys on the north side of rubish meadow befor Willyam Colbys door about sixteen acers which I value at thirty five pounds: these lots of land to be soald to pay lagoisons?] [legacies?] And I do order and give full power unto my Executors to make sale of said parcle?] of land according to thar best judgement and discration and to make payment to the full unto all thos that I am obliged unto that are her?] sat down in my will and whan every one is paid and charges defraid my will is that my grandchildren all axcept Joseph and Johannah Willson shall have an equal shear of what is left.

And if my grandson Joseph Willson doos not lick?] what I have given him as to the colt and the lot at the grat swamp than he shall have twanty pounds in money in lew of it and five pounds in money for what work he has dun for me this last yer and if what is left to pay debts and logasions?] fall short than I order my son and daughter equally to make up and what is over thar children equally to shar in it: my will is that what I give to my Daughter Willson shall be wholly at her disspos during her life and shee shall have the liberty of dissposing of it for the cumfort of her life.

And I do constitute and appoint and fully impower my trusty friends John Blanchord and Bengemin Thompson to be my lawful executors of this my last will and testament and that they may execute it honestly to the full in every part of it and I do ratifie and confirm this and no other to be my last will and testament in witness wharof I have herunto seat my hand and seale the 26 of July, 1721

Signed sealled published pronounced and declared by the said Joseph Foster to be his last will and testament in the prasence of the subscribers

In the seventh yer?] of the Reign of our sovereign Lord George by the grace of God of England Scotland France and Ierland?] King

Joseph Foster

Joseph Stevens
Benjamin Frost
Prob. December 18, 1721

He d. Dec. 4, 1721. Res., Billerica, Mass.

3912. i. ELIZABETH, b. Oct. 7, 1673; m. Oct. 27, 1694, John Wilson, Jr., b. Jan. 3, 1672-3; ch.: 1. Joseph and 2. Joanna.
3913. ii. JOSEPH, b. July 15, 1678; d. in infancy.
3914. iii. THOMAS, b. Feb. 11, 1681; m. Hepsibah ——.
3915. iv. SARAH, b. Aug. 23, 1683; d. Sept. 5, 1683.
3916. v. JOHN, b. May 12, 1685; d. Nov. 12, 1685.

3874. REV. ISAAC FOSTER (William, Thomas), b. Charlestown, Mass., about 1652; m., 1680, Mrs. Mehitable* (Wyllis) Russell, wid. of Rev. Daniel Russell, of Charlestown and dau. of Samuel Wyllis, of Hartford, Conn. She m., 3d, Rev. Timothy Woodbridge, successor of her second husband in the Hartford church. He graduated at Harvard College in 1671; was probably the son taken prisoner with his father; was admitted to the church of Charlestown Oct. 28, 1677; made Freeman of the Colony Oct. 2, 1765; and Fellow of Harvard College May 22, of the same year; as a candidate for settlement was sought by several churches, and, in 1680, he became minister of the church at Hartford. He d. Aug. 20, 1682, and Rev. Simon Bradstreet, of New London, thus notices the event in his journal. "Mr. Isaac Forster pastor of ye old chh at Hartford dyed. He was aged about 30, a man of good Abilities. His death has made such a breach yt will not easily bee made up. His widow married thirdly, Rev. Timothy Woodbridge, his successor in the church of Hartford "

When a committee of the town of Charlestown was about selecting a successor to the Rev. Thomas Shepard in 1678 the opinions of Rev. John Sherman Mather and Rev. President Oakes were requested as to the "fittest" person for their minister and these gentlemen recommended Mr. Foster as the "fittest and suitablest person" for that place.

*Sometimes in Hartford Conn., Records, Mabell.

Mrs. Russell had one child by Rev. Russell, Mehitable O., m. Rev. John Hubbard, of Jamaica, L. I., June 12, 1701. He d., and Mehitable m., 2d, Dec. 9, 1707, Rev. Samuel Woodbridge.

Vol. iii, p. —, Hartford Law Records. Whereas Samuel Wyllys Esq., late of Hartford . . . My ever Honored Father Deceased did in his lifetime make conveyance of Several Parcels of Land lying in the township of Hartford, afsd. particularly one tract of land lying on the East Side of Connecticut River to Mr. Daniel Russell, also one home Lott adjoyning to and being part of the Home Lott. lately belonging to the said Samuel Wyllys, to his daughter Mabell Foster, and did receive full satisfaction or payment for the same, and also a tract of Land lying at a place commonly known by the name of Rocky Hill, in Hartford aforesd. Conveyed to John Blackledge, late of Hartfd Deceased as by the respective deeds on record will now more fully appear And Whereas I Hezekiah Wyllys, of Hartford, aforesd, Son and heir to said Samuel Wyllys, Esq. Deceased by Virtue and Right of the Last Will of George Wyllys, Esq. My Ever Honrd grandfather setling by Entail Speciall all his Lands in Hartford aforsd. On me I have now just right and Claim to all or part of the aforementioned Lands which are now in possession of Timothy Woodbridge, of Hartford aforesaid or sold by him—Wherefore, Know all men by those presents that I, the said Hezekiah Wyllys, upon the Consideration of what hath been formerly paid for the above mentioned Lands by the Said Daniel Russell, and Mable Foster, and further for the Consideration of the Same of five shillings lawful money of Connecticut to me in hand paid before the Insealing and delivery of these presents, Give, grant, Remise, Release, and Quit Claim, for myself and my heirs forever unto the said Timothy Woodbridge, his heirs, and assigns, all my right title and Claim whatsoever unto the aforementioned tract of Land lying on the East Side of the Connecticut River in Hartford aforesaid now Sold by Timothy Woodbridge to Hezekiah Sorter, of Hartford Containing four (4) miles in Length and about Eighty two rods in breadth be the same more or less abutting North on Land late belonging to the Said Samuel Wyllys; East on the Common Lands West on Connecticut River 444 etc Hezekiah Wyllys. 11 March, 1714-5 (the other properties included in this Quit Claim)

Note—Mr. George Wyllys was an Original Proprietor in Hartford.

Vol. 4; p. 86, Hartford Probate Records.—An Inventory of Estate of Rev. Isaac Foster, was Exhibited in Court proved and ordered to be recorded as the Court Grant Administration upon the Estate to Mrs. Mehetable Foster, 6 March, 1684.

Page 123—The Court being moved to come to a Distribution of the Estate of the late Reverend Mr. Isaac Foster, deceased Considered the Same and what hath been preserved (?) before them by those concerned & finding by a writing made by the sayd Mr. Foster, a Mrs. Mehetable Russell, before marriage bearing date 27th January 1679 recorded wherein it is agreed that in case the sayd Mr. Foster, should decease before the sayd Mrs. Mehetable & leave issue behind him of her the sayd Mrs. Mehetable the Estate should descend to her the said Mrs. Mehetable & their heirs which agreement though it seems to be Contradicted by another writing made by them and recorded made after their marriage yet it doth not alter the force and Virtue of the former & therefore, this Court doth Judge the former writing to give the rule for Dividing the Estate & their being one third part of the Estate of Mrs. Mehetable Russell, that She received by Mr. Daniel Russell, Last Will at her dispose & so no more belonging to Mr. Foster.

We therefore Distribute his Estate as followeth

Two Hundred pounds to Miss Ann Foster, to be paid her at the age of Eighteen years or day of Marriage which shall first & the remainder of the Estate to be Mrs. Mehetable Woodbridge & her heirs forever. Miss Ann Foster, to be paid in good and current pay of the country.

At a Special Court Held at Hartford, 27 December, 1686.

Vol. 4, p. 181-2; An Inventory of the Estate of Mr. Isaac Foster, taken the 12 of February, 1683, by us whose names are Under written.

Amount	£1507—15—04
Smalll articles of Household use	
A Negro	£ 22—30—00
A Farm at Hoccasseell	£200—00—00
The Home Lot	£200—00—00
50 acres of Land at Rocky Hill	£ 40—00—00
Due the Estate in Money	£170—50—00
half the farm at Cambridge	£500—00—00

Land at Middletown	£ 74—00—00
Land at Winter Harbor, Sundries, Etc	£131
Total	£1507—15—04
Debts due from the Estate to Mrs. Mehetable Russell by her Father	£573—16—00
Mr. Wyllys on House Lot	£ 30—00—00
Sundries	£ 30—00—00
Legacy	£ 20—00—00
Other Legacies	£ 36—18—00
Due at Charleston	£ 10—00—00
	£618—14—00

the Sundries are not counted in the Sums I give the principal Items for the hints therein Contained.

1716, April 11. On the land records of Hartford, vol. 3, p. 11, is a quit claim by Mabel Foster, showing her the daughter of Mr. Samuel Wyllys, of Hartford; the quit claim was to —— Woodbridge. It may safely be assumed that Mabel was Mrs. Mehetable, contracted to Mabel; that the daughter of Samuel Wyllys first married Daniel Russell. She as his widow married Rev. Isaac Foster and as his widow married —— Woodbridge. Possibly I may be wrong.

Epitaphs from old (1st-Church) Cemetery Hartford:

The old Brownstone table in this cemetery in the rear of the 1st Church premises has upon its upturned face deeply cut, and very plain to read the following inscriptions:

Here lies Intered the
Body of the Revd Mr.
Timothy Woodbridge
Who Departed this Life
April 30 1732
In the 51 year of his
Ministry
also of the
Rev. Isaac Foster
Pastor of the First Church
Who was ordained in 1679
and died in January 1683
Mabel Wyllys
Wife of ye Revd Timothy Woodbridge
and formerly Wife of ye Revd
Isaac Foster died Dec.br 21st A D, 1698
Aged 40 years

He died Jan. 20, 1683. Res., Hartford, Conn.

3917. i. ANN, b. ——; m., Nov. 29, 1699, Rev. Thomas Buckingham, of Hartford.

3878. CAPT. RICHARD FOSTER (William, Thomas), b. Charlestown, Mass., Aug. 10, 1663; m., May 4, 1686, Parnel Winslow, only child and dau. of Isaac and Mary, b. Nov. 14, 1667; d. April 24, 1751. He was admitted to the church Feb. 16, 1700; was a mariner; was captain of the pink, "Mary and Elizabeth" in 1687; arrived home from Saltintootha, May 24, 1693; was captain of a pink sailing vessel from Boston to Nevis, May 30, 1713. His wife owned the covenant and was admitted to the church May 17, 1702.

Richard Foster's Will—In the Name of God Amen I Richard Foster of Charlestown in the County of Middlesex in His Majesty's Province of the Massachusetts Bay in New Engld. Esqr. being weak in Body yet of perfect Memory Thanks be to God therefor Calling to mind the mortality of my Body and knowing that it is appointed for all men once to Dy, Do make and Ordain this my last Will and Testament. Principally I Recommend my Soul into the hands of God that gave it hoping for Mercy thro the Merits of my Dear Redeemer, and my Body I commit to the Dust to be buried with a Decent and Christian Burial (at the Discretion of my Executors hereafter named) Firmly believing that at the General Resurection I shall receive the Same again by the Mighty power of God, and as Touching such worldly goods and Estate as God hath pleased in his Providence to bless me with all I demise give and dispose of in the following manner:

Impris. My Will is that all my Just Debts and Funeral Charges be paid and discharged by my Executors hereafter named.

Item I give and Bequeath unto my Beloved wife Parnel (after my Just Debts and Funeral Charges are paid) all my Estate both Real and Personal during her natural life for her maintenance with liberty to sell or dispose of what part of my personal Estate she shall think fit, and also full power to sell part of my Real Estate as she think necessary for the use of aforementioned, what of my Estate shall remain after my wife Decease, her Debts and funeral Charges paid, and after its being apprised as near as may be by men upon Oath to the true value thereof, I Give and Dispose of the same in the following manner.

Item I Give and Bequeath unto my son Richard Foster the sum of Four hundred pounds.

Item I Give and Bequeath unto my son Isaac the sum of Four hundred pounds

Item I Give and Bequeath unto my Daughter Parnel Codman the sum of Forty five pounds.

Item I Give and Bequeath unto my Daughter Ann Perkins the sum of Thirty nine pounds.

Item I Give and Bequeath unto my Daughter Sarah Calef the sum of thirty-two pounds

Item I Give and Bequeath unto my Daughter Elizabeth McDaniel the sum of Thirty pounds.

Item I Give and Bequeath unto my Grandsons Samuel and Richard Carey the sum of Thirteen pounds to be equally divided betwixt them, and what remains of my Estate beside the severall Sums before given and Bequeathed and paid according to the apprisment shall be Divided into Seven Equal parts. To each child one seventh part and to my two Grandchildren aforementioned one Seventh part Equally between them, But if my Estate should fall Short of paying what I now give, Then each child and Grandchild shall abate in proportion to what I now give and also to what my Daughters have had of me at and after marriage as money then went, an account thereof is Entered on my book and at the foot signed by me.

Item I Give and Bequeath unto my sons Richard and Isaac Equally the Property of my Pew in the meeting house reserving to my Daughters the liberty and priviledge of sitting therein during their lives.

Furthermore my will and meaning is that my two sons viz. Richard and Isaac have the remaining part of all my Real Estate after my wifes Decease as it is apprised as aforesaid they paying my other children and Grandchildren their proportionable part as aforementioned and I do hereby appoint my Beloved wife Parnel and my two sons Richard and Isaac to be Executors of this my last Will and Testament and I do hereby disallow revoke and disanull all and every other former Will or Testament Legacies or Bequeasts by me heretofore made or requested to be made, Ratifying and confirming this and no other to be my last Will and Testament, In Witness whereof I have hereunto Set my hand and seal this Twenty second Day of January Anno Domini 1735-6?] In the Ninth year of His Majestys Reign.

Richd. Foster

Signed Sealed Published Pronounced and Declared by the said Richard Foster to be his Last Will and Testament in the presence of us who Subscribed our names in presence of said Foster

Matthew Johnson
Joseph Austin Jr.
Joseph Phillips.
Prob. January 14, 1745

He d. 1745. Res., Charlestown, Mass.

3918. i. PARNELL, b. Feb. 23, 1687; d. Nov. 14, 1687.

3919. ii. RICHARD, b. Nov. 28, 1689; d. Feb. 11, 1694.

3920. iii. MARY, b. Feb. 16, 1692; m., Dec. 9, 1712, Capt. Samuel Carey. She d. Dec. 23, 1718. He was son of Jonathan, and a ship chandler; admitted to the Charlestown church Jan. 5, 1717. His wife owned the covenant Dec. 9, 1712, and was admitted to the church June 30, 1717. After her death he m. again. Ch. by Mary: 1. Samuel, b. Nov. 29, 1713 (captain); m. Margaret Greaves. 2. Richard, b. Feb. 17, 1716; m. Anna ——; was a distiller in Medford. 3. Jonathan, bapt. Nov. 30, 1718; d. Jan. 3, 1718. Eight ch. by second wife.

3921. iv. RICHARD, b. March 23, 1694; m. Sarah Emerson and Mary Foye.

3922. v. PARNELL, b. Aug. 25, 1696; m. John Codman. He was son of Stephen (Robert of Salem); was a sea captain, b. Sept. 29, 1696. She was admitted to the church Dec. 20, 1719, and d. Sept. 15, 1752. He was poisoned by slaves in his household in 1755. Res., Charlestown. Ch.: 1. John, b. Feb. 14, 1719; m. Abigail Asbury. Res., Haverhill. His son was Hon. John, of Boston. 2. Stephen, b. Feb. 23, 1721. 3. Parnel, b. May 18, 1723; m. Enoch Bartlett. 4. Elizabeth, b. Dec. 23, 1724; m. William Davies. 5. Mary, b. Dec. 10, 1726; m. Joshua Moody. 6. Richard, b. June 23, 1729. 7. Benjamin, b. March 14, 1731. 8. Ann, b. Nov. 19, 1732; m. John Butler. 9. Benjamin, b. June 22, 1735. 10. Isaac, bapt. Aug. 21, 1737 (soldier); m. Abigail Foster. 11. Katharine, b. April 22, 1739; m. Elnathan Jones.

3923. vi. ANN, b. Nov. 8, 1699; m., Nov. 6, 1721, Rev. Daniel Perkins, of Bridgewater.

3924. vii. SARAH, b. Nov. 16, 1701; m., July 19, 1723, Dr. Peter Calef, of Charlestown; he d. Oct. 11, 1735, and she within a year. He was a physician. She owned the covenant 1723; was admitted a member in 1727. Res., Charlestown. Ch.: 1. Joseph, bapt. May 3, 1724; m. Frances Thompson. 2. Sarah, bapt. Jan. 8, 1726. 3. Mary, b. June 28, 1728; d. young. 4. Peter, b. October, 1729. 5. Mary, b. April, 1732; m., 1758, Stephen White. 6. Parnel, b. July 7, 1733; d. young. 7. Parnel, b. 1734; m. Edward Coffin.

3925. viii. ISAAC, b. Jan. 30, 1704; m. Eleanor Wyer.

3926. ix. ELIZABETH, b. Aug. 21, 1706; m. Timothy McDaniel, of Boston, afterward of Charlestown.

3927. x. KATHARINE, b. April 6, 1713; d. Feb. 11, 1716.

3780. CAPT. JOHN FOSTER (William, Thomas), b. Charlestown, Mass., Aug. 10, 1666; m., May 31, 1692, Sarah Richardson, of Newbury, dau. of Mr. John, b. Sept. 9, 1674; m., 2d, Sept. 12, 1718, Esther Lathrop. She m., 2d, Sept. 12, 1726, Francis Norwood, of Gloucester. He was a master mariner; was captain of a ship for Barbadoes in 1696. His first wife owned the covenent June 30, 1693, and was "bapt. at Newbury," and admitted to the church April 21, 1699.

The Middlesex Probate records say: "John, capt., Charlestown, letter date Aug. 16, 1723; ex. Sept. 9, 1726; wife, Esther; chil., Elizabeth, minor; guardian papers Sept. 21, 1726.

He d. June 14, 1723. Res., Charlestown, Mass.

3928. i. ABIGAL, b. April 20, 1693; m., 1st, May 11, 1710, Jabez Salter; m., 2d, Dec. 15, 1715, Edward Cruft. She m. her first husband in Boston and resided there. She d. in 1742, and left an estate to her heirs.

3929. ii. SARAH, b. Aug. 31, 1696; d. March 15, 1698.

3930. iii. MARY, b. Aug. 15, 1698; m., June 25, 1717, Robert Nowell; m., 2d, Jan. 15, 1732, Samuel White. White d. before 1742.

3931. iv. ELIZABETH, b. 1712; m., Nov. 13, 1735, John Smart, in Boston, and 2d, Feb. 14, 1740, Sendall Williams, of Boston, who was a wire-cooper. He joined deed with Foster heirs in 1742.

3872. ENSIGN HOPESTILL FOSTER (Hopestill, Richard, Thomas), b. Dorchester, Mass., March 10, 1645; m. there Feb. 15, 1667, Elizabeth Payson, of Roxbury, dau. of Giles Payson.* His widow in 1694 was wife of Edmund Brown.

"Hopestill Foster (1673), of Boston, soapboiler, son of Captain Hopestill (1642) and Mary (Bates) Foster, of Dorchester, and father of Capt. Hopestill Foster (1694), of Boston, was born in Dorchester, where he was baptized. He was admitted a freeman in 1673, and became a member of Mather's Second church. He married Elizabeth Payson, of Roxbury. He was first sergeant of the Artillery Company in 1675, and became a captain in colonial militia. He served the town as constable in 1674-5, and Dec. 28, 1676, was appointed one of a committee, as suggested by the 'Honored Council,' to guard the town against a conflagration. He died in Boston in 1678. His widow married Edmund Brown (1692)."—Hist. Ancient and Honorable Artillery Co.

Hopestill died about 1677, and his widow married Edmund Brown, of Boston,

* I state her name was Payson on authority of Mary F. Pierce, of Weston.

before 1694. He was a constable in Boston, 1675; on a committee for the town in 1676. By Suffolk Deeds (Vol. 37, Fol. 233) it seems that Aug. 7, 1700, there was a settlement of the estate of Hopestill F., soapboiler. This deed was acknowledged Nov. 14, 1715, by Elizabeth Brown, the widow, and Hopestill F., gunmaker, the eldest son, but was not recorded until May 18, 1724, after the latter's death. Suffolk Deeds (Vol. 38, Fol. 27), Elizabeth Brown assigned her rights under date of July 10, 1724, to her daughter Elizabeth Foster, widow and shop-keeper.

Administrator of estate of Ensign Hopestill Foster, late of Boston, deceased, intes., granted to Elizabeth Foster, widow; relict of said Hopestill, in right of self and children; granted Jan. 28, 1678. Lib. 12, Fol. 270-271. Inventory mentions money due from Father Payson.

He d. Oct. 15, 1676. Res., Dorchester and Boston Mass.

3932. i. HOPESTILL, b. abt. 1670; m. Elizabeth Phipps.
3933. ii. SAMUEL, b. Dec. 27, 1676; m. Rebecca Brisco.
3934. iii. MARY, b. July 22, 1671; m., April 2, 1694, Timothy Nash.
3935. iv. ELIZA, b. July 26, 1669; m., May 28, 1694, Christopher Killiowe.

3883. JOHN FOSTER, ESQ. (Hopestill, Richard, Thomas), bapt. Dorchester, Dec. 10, 1648; did he m. in Dorchester, Nov. 28, 16—, Mrs. Abigail Hawkins (Moore) Kellend? wid. of Thomas Kellend, former wid. of Samuel Moore, whom she m. May 13, 1660, and dau. of Thomas Hawkins, a freeman, 1639, from London, not a ship carpenter, but a navigator.

MASSACHUSETTS COAT OF ARMS.
[Designed by John Foster.]

Captain Hawkins was a large land owner in Dorchester, later moved to Boston, where he built a very large ship. She sailed for Malaga in 1645, in company with another ship, and both were lost on the coast of Spain. He was wrecked the next year on the same spot when in company with some persons from London. In 1646 he arrived in Boston, commanding a London ship. In November, 1648, Winthrop writes his son that news is received from England by Captain Hawkins' ship (God being pleased to send him, Hawkins, to Heaven by the way).

Foster began teaching school in Dorchester in October, 1669, at £25 per year. In article fourth, of his agreement, it was "granted as a liberty to ye Master, if he see it meete for to go once in a fortnight to a lecture." His salary in 1670 was £30. On Dec. 23, 1672, it was agreed that Mr. Foster "shall teach such lattin schollars as shall come to his fathers hous one wholl yeer next ensueing from the first of January next, and to instruct and give out Coppies to such as come to him to learne to writte—" "for his paines to have £10." There is a fac-simile of his signature to this agreement. In 1674 his "recompence" for teaching grammar scholars in English, Latin and writing, "at ye schole-house" was £30.

The same year the General Court granted permission to establish a printing press in Boston. One was set up by Mr. Foster in 1675. This was the first printing house in Boston. He also compiled an almanac in 1675-80, and was author and printer for the years 1676-78-79-81, the latter being the year of his decease. Among other works he printed Increase Mather's Exhortation to the Inhabitants of New England ("Are to be sold over against the Dove") 4 to 1676; Hubbard's Election Sermon, delivered May 3, 1676, 4 to 1676; I. Mather's Brief History of the Warre with the Indians, etc., 4 to : a relation of the Troubles with the Indians, and other works by Mather; Rev. John Eliot, Samuel Willard, etc.

The elegies upon his death are printed entire in Simond's History of South Boston.

In 1681 it is said the town of Dorchester lost one of its jewels in the person of John Foster, Esq. He was graduated at Harvard College in 1667. Shaw, in his description of Boston, says he opened the first printing house in Boston, which was about 1675. The first book he published was printed in 1676, and the last in 1680. He was a great mathematician, and made, calculated and published almanacs. In an almanac for 1681 "he annexed an ingenious dissertation on comets, seen in Boston, in November and December, 1680." It is not so much to be wondered at that the people were astonished and affrighted at the comet of that time if the account of the late writer be true, which says its trail reached from near the horizon to the

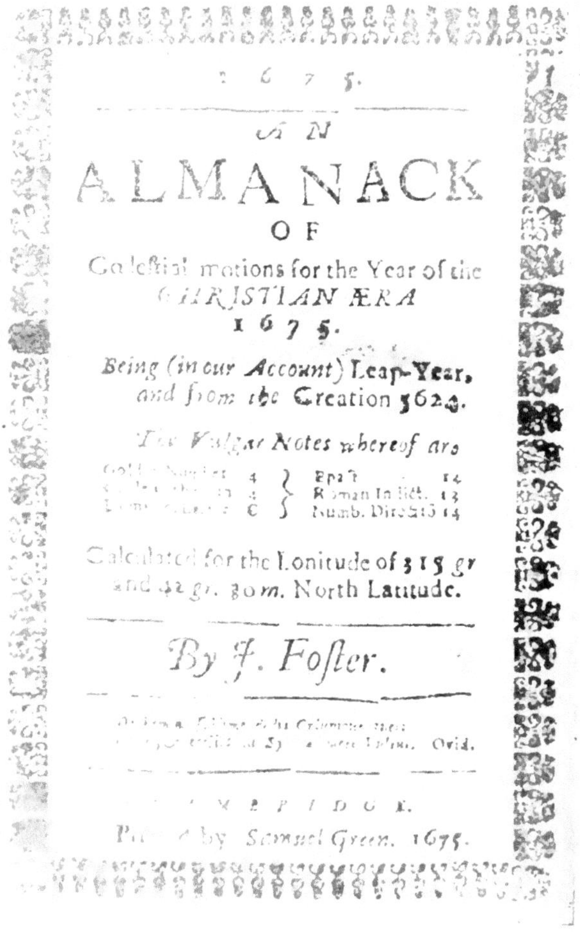
1675.

AN

ALMANACK

OF

Cœlestial motions for the Year of the

CHRISTIAN ÆRA

1675.

Being (in our Account) Leap-Year, *and from the* Creation 5624.

The Vulgar Notes whereof are

	4	Epact	14
	4	Roman Indict.	13
	C	Numb. Direct.	14

Calculated for the Lonitude of 315 *gr* and 42 *gr.* 30 *m.* North Latitude.

By J. Foster.

Ovid.

Printed by Samuel Green. 1675.

FAC-SIMILE OF COVER OF JOHN FOSTER'S ALMANACK, 1675.

cinith. There was a printing press in Cambridge, near the vicinity of the College in 1638, conducted by a Mr. Green, and it was there he undoubtedly learned to handle the types.

Mr. Foster, in his will, desired to have a handsome gravestone. There is a curious device upon it, to represent his skill in astronomy, etc., and also upon it the following inscription:

"The Ingenious
mathematician and Printer Mr. John Foster
aged 33 yrs died Sept. 9, 1681.
April 1682.

"Astra Corlis Vivens, Moriens super Aettera Foster,
Sconde precor: Caelurn Metiri disce supremum;
Metior atque meum est Emit mihi divis Jesus—
Nec teneor Quicquam nisi Gratis solvere."

Upon the foot stone is the following:

Ars illi sua Census Erat. Ovid "Skill was his cash."

In Thomas' History of Printing, this is translated as follows:

"Thou, O Foster, who on earth didst study the heavenly bodies, now ascend above the firmament and survey the highest heavens. I do survey and inhabit this Divine region. To its possession I am admitted through the grace of Jesus; and to pay the debt of gratitude I hold the most sacred obligation."

Mr. Joseph Capen, the minister of Topsfield, who was the friend and townsman of Mr. Foster, wrote the following poem upon his death:

"Thy body, which no activeness didst lack,
Now's laid aside like an old Almanack;
But for the present only's out of date,
'Twill have at length a far more active state.
Yea, tho' with dust thy body soiled be,
Yet at the resurrection we shall see
A fair EDITION, and of matchless worth,
Free from ERRATAS, new in Heaven set forth.
'Tis but a word from God to Great Creator
It shall be done when he saith Imprimatur."

On the last page of William Brattle's Ephemeris for 1682 appeared the following notice: "Advertisement of Suitable Verses Dedicated to the Memory of the Ingenious Mathematician and Printer, Mr. John Foster." Synchronous with the almanacs printed by Samuel Green and Marmaduke Johnson at Cambridge, 1675-1681, appeared the famous Boston Almanacks, compiled and printed by John Foster. May 26, 1674, the General Court "granted that there may be a printing press elsewhere than at Cambridge." In accordance with this privilege, in 1675, John Foster, of Dorchester, began his services as printer at "The Sign of a Dove;" and the same year he issued a sermon by Increase Mather, though his Almanac for 1675 was printed at Cambridge by Samuel Green. On his foot-stone is the laconic motto, "Skill was his Cash." Very typical of colonial elegiac verse is the eulogy on Foster by Joseph Capen, 1687. The closing lines suggest Franklin's epitaph for himself.

Later issues bear Foster's name in large letters at the top of the title-page, while he sometimes inscribes himself "Astrophil." The almanac for 1678 contains thirty-two pages, and records Courts, Commencements, Dog-Dayes and like varied events. A careful explanation of the nine columns on each month's calendar elucidates the astronomical and nautical data. Among the elementary directions is this: "The time of (Sun's) setting may be found by subtracting the time of rising from twelve, what remains is the time of the sun's setting." John Foster, as printer, was succeeded by Samuel Sewall."—N. E. Magazine.

Will.—John Foster, lately of Boston, now of Dorchester, mentions natural brethren, Thankfull, Patience, James, Elisha, Mary, Comfort, Standfast and Hopestill; sister Baker, sister Thankfull Baker, sister Mary Sale; cousins Silence Baker and Thankfull Browne; mother executrix. Will dated July 18, 1681. Probated Oct. 6, 1681. Lib. 6; Fol. 419. Inventory mentions John Foster, deceased Sept. 9, 1681. Mary Foster executrix. Lib. 9; Fol. 105.

He d. Sept. 9, 1681. Res., s. p., Boston, Mass.

3884. CAPT. JAMES FOSTER (Hopestill, Richard, Thomas), b., Dorchester, Mass., April 13, 1651; m. there, Sept. 22, 1674, Mary Capen, dau. of John. She d. Feb. 8, 1678; m., 2d, Oct. 7, 1680, Anna Lane, dau. of Capt. Job. She d. Sept. 29, 1732, ae 68. James Foster was elected selectman in 1690-94-95-96-97-99; was constable in 1680. Capt. Foster was elected one of the committee in 1705 to see that the wharf be built at Wales creek. James Foster and Anna Lane, dau. of Job Lane, who, with the Fishers, Averys, Metcalfs, of Dedham and Dorchester, where old James then was—a Bullard, a Dwight, all heirs of Job Lane, of Marlboro estate, sell land to a tenant, Thomas Wait, in Malden, where the Lanes used to live, along with Hopestill Foster; Thomas, of Weymouth, son James and Anne, had to wait till daughter Anna was of age and Patience, two of them girls, who sign in behalf of the minor brother and sisters—John, Jemima, Mary, Elizabeth, James and Hopestill. Anna, wife of James, died Sept. 29, 1732, in the sixty-eighth year, and he died Oct. 4, 1732, in his eighty-second year. His children's marriages are shown by the following deed. Suffolk Deeds (Vol. 48, fol. 76), John Foster and wife Mary, of Boston; blacksmith James Foster, Jr., and wife Priscilla, of Dorchester, yeoman; Hopestill Foster, Jr., and wife Sarah, of Boston, housewright; Silence, wife of John Clap, of Sudbury; Anna, wife of Robert Field, of Dorchester; Patience, wife of Samuel Saville, of Braintree; Jemima, wife of Robert Spur, of Dorchester;

FOSTER COAT OF ARMS AND GRAVE STONE OF CAPT. JAMES FOSTER.

Elizabeth, wife of Ebenezer Bernard, of Woodstock; Thankful Foster, Spinster. All children of James Foster. James Foster's tombstone is in the old Dorchester yard, and bears the coat-of-arms. It records the death of James and his wife, both in 1732, and under the rules of the Heraldic Journal this coat must be considered as strong presumptive evidence of the right of the family to use arms. James was the son of an immigrant, and the inscription is earlier than the period of the assumption of arms here.

Will.—James Foster, of Dorchester, yeoman, considering my advanced age, Anna, wife, son James, son Hopestill, eldest son John, daughters Silence, Anna, Patience, Jemima, Elizabeth and Thankful—daughters, grandfather Lane, father Hopestill, James exec. Dated June 25, 1728.

Prob. Oct. 16, 1732. Lib. 31, Fol. 137.

He d. Oct. 4, 1732. Res., Dorchester, Mass.

3936. ii. THANKFUL, b. March 30, 1683; d. March 1, 1700.

3937. i. SILENCE, b. April 4, 1677; m., May 26, 1698, John Clap, of Sudbury.

3938. iii. ANNA, b. Jan. 27, 1684; m., June 1, 1710, Robert Field, of Dorchester. Annie Foster and Robert Field married June 1, 1710. 1. Anna Field, dau., b. Aug. 5, 1713, and Humphrey Atherton m. Oct. 1, 1730. 2. Anna, dau., b. June 30, 1731; m. to Samuel Bird by Rev. Jonathan Bowman. He is called of Stoughton, she of Dorcnester; ch: (a) Samuel, 1749; (b) John, 1750; (c) Enoch, 1751; (d) Elijah, 1753; (e) Ann, 1754; (f) Elizabeth, 1756; (g) Mary, 1758; d. 1764; (h) Ebenezer, 1761; (i) Olive, 1763; (j) Mary, 1765; (k)Sarah, 1767; (l) Hannah, 1769. 3. John, b. April 4, 1750; m. Joanna Esty, dau. of Deacon Benjamin Esty, of Sharon, Mass. John Bird died March 10, 1777, while a soldier in the Revolutionary War. Three ch: (a) Abner, b. March 18, 1771; d. Oct 24, 1837. (b) Betsey, b. April 17, 1773; d. May 13, 1848. (c) Calvin, b. March 10, 1775 Abner. 4. Bird, m. Polly Gay, dau. of Lieutenant Lemuel and Abigail Davenport Gay, March 12, 1793.

3939. iv. PATIENCE, b. Feb. 12, 1686; m., Feb. 7, 1716, Samuel Savel, of Braintree.

3940. v. JOHN, b. Feb. 9, 1688; m. Mary——.

3941. vi. JEMIMA, b. Dec. 9, 1690. m., Dec. 22, 1720, Robert Spur, of Dorchester.

3942. vii. MARY, b. Oct. 13, 1692; d. unm.

3943. viii. ELIZABETH, b. Feb. 6, 1694; m., Sept. 29, 1715, Ebenezer Barnard, of Woodstock.

3944. ix. JAMES, b. Dec. 8, 1698; m. Priscilla ——.

3945. x. REBECCA, b. Sept. 14, 1700; d. Sept. 28, 1700.

3946. xi. HOPESTILL, bapt. Feb. 15, 1701; m. Sarah Allen.

3947. xii. THANKFUL, b. July 15, 1704; m., May 29, 1728, John Shaw, of Pomfret, Conn.

3948. xiii. MARY, b. June 17, 1675; d. Oct 29, 1675.

3885. ELISHA FOSTER (Hopestill, Richard, Thomas), b. Dorchester, Mass., Aug. 23, 1653; m. April 10, 1678, there, Sarah Payson, of Roxbury. She m. 2d, March 26, 1685. Ebenezer Wiswall. She d. June 21, 1714. Wiswall was b. Dorchester, 1646; d., Newton, June 21, 1691, son of Elder Thomas. He d. s. p. Oct. 16 1682. Res., Dorchester, Mass.

In 1775 there were nine dwelling houses on the neck, now South Boston, the location of each of which may be seen by consulting a map now in the possession of the Massachusetts Historical Society, drawn by order of the British general then in Boston; also the road and principal trees. Mrs. Foster's house was one of the best in the neighborhood and it was difficult to convince the continentalers that it did not belong to a tory, as some of the rooms were even papered, which was considered very luxurious in those days. This house was the most westerly on the neck and was burned by the British, who then had possession of Boston.

In 1747 the preaching of Rev. Mr. Whitfield caused considerable trouble among the churches in Massachusetts, on account of the members leaving and refusing to return in their former parishes. There was trouble in the Dorchester church and among those who separated from the old society was Edward Foster. A council was held, the evidence heard, and the members requested to return, which they did, since which time the church has been quiet.

In 1743 James Foster was chairman of the committee to build the new meeting house. It cost £3567 s10 d11. This meeting house was enlarged in 1795.

Adm. of estate of Elisha Foster, late of Dorchester, dec'd, intes., granted to Sarah, relict widow. Elisha died Oct. 16, 1682. Adm. granted at county court held Nov. 30, 1682. In agreement for distribution, widow to have use of whole estate, while remaining widow. If she change her condition, to have all household stuff and half of estate at her disposal, other half to go to relatives of deceased Elisha. Signed by Sarah, James, Comfort, Standfast Foster. Lib. 9, Fol. 107-8.

3588. CAPT. STANDFAST FOSTER (Hopestill, Richard, Thomas), b. Dorchester, Mass, Sept. 3, 1660; m. Abigail Holman. She d. June 22, 1713; m., 2d, (pub. at Boston, May 27, 1714) Sarah ——, b. 1668; d. Aug. 1, 1727. He was a freeman in 1690, was captain, selectman. In 1712. Standfast Foster and eleven other citizens of Dorchester agreed to build the Wharf at Wales' creek, and thus their heirs should enjoy it forever.

Adm. of estate of Standfast Foster, late of Dorchester, malster, dec'd, granted to his son Comfort Foster, of Dorchester, glazier, Dec. 4, 1727. Lib. 26, Fol. 24-5.

He d. Nov. 11, 1727. Res., Dorchester, Mass.

3949. i. COMFORT, bapt. June 29, 1689; m. Eleanor Woods and Abiel Withington.
3950. ii. ABIGAIL, b. March 18, 1692; d. Sept. 27, 1695.
3951. iii. ELISHA, b June 18, 1696; d. November, 1775.
3952. iv. MARY b. Oct. 31,, 1700; d. March 16, 1701.

3893. THOMAS FOSTER (Thomas, Thomas, Thomas), b., Cambridge, Mass., Aug. 1, 1663; m. there, Nov. 30, 1686, Experience Parker. She m. 2d, before 1719, Benjamin Geare, and in that year resided Voluntown, Conn. In regard to Thomas and Experience: he seems to disappear as Paige says in "Cambridge Hist." in 1715. In 1719 young Thomas is at Voluntown, Conn., with his mother. Experience who is married to a Gear or a Geary, is selling off rights in Stow that are not recorded till 1740 He d. before 1709. Res., Cambridge and Stow, Mass.

3953. i. THOMAS, b. Sept. 18, 1687; m. Mercy Gates.

3896. JONATHAN FOSTER (Thomas, Thomas, Thomas), b. Cambridge, Mass., Sept. 21, 1671; m. Abigail ——. She d. in Chelmsford, Mass., Jan. 8, 1759. In 1700 he was one of a committee for calling the minister. Stow was settled in 1650, but on account of the Indian depredations the settlers were obliged to retire in 1675. The place was then a wilderness. The town was incorporated in 1683, but the early town records were quite loosely kept and are very incomplete.

Middlesex Deeds, vol. 31, p. 284.—Margaret Stratton, of Chelmsford (a widow), Jacob Warren, of Littleton, and wife, Ruth; Joseph Adams, of Chelmsford, and wife, Mary; Jonas Whitney*, of Stow, and wife Margaret, for £350. sell to Jonathan Foster, of Stow, weaver, parcels of land and meadow in Chelmsford on the south side of Robins' Hill; first piece on road to Adams' mill; road from Stratton's house to highway, all buildings, orchard, etc. Second piece on south side of Adams' mill, near lands of John Burgess, Benjamin Parker, Deacon Joseph Warren, orchard, fences, buildings, etc. This was the old homestead probably and the heirs all sell Dec. 26, 1727.

Middlesex Deeds, vol. 102 p. 345—Jonathan of Chelmsford (called husbandman this time), for £170 from Joseph Foster, of Chelmsford (relation not stated), deeds one-third the homestead bought of Stratton heirs and Robins' Hill etc., April 10, 1738. His son, Joseph, b. 1714, was then twenty-four years old. Edward Foster, William Foster, Ephraim Warren, Joseph Spalding, witnesses.

He d. Jan. 5, 1755. Res., Stow and Chelmsford, Mass.

3954 i. JONATHAN, b. abt. 1698; m. Mary ——.
3955. ii. JOHN, b. abt. 1708; m. Eunice ——.
3956. iii JOSEPH, b. Aug. 24, 1714; m.——

Middlesex Deeds, vol. 58, p. 537.—Robert Fletcher, of Chlemsford, was appointed administrator of Joseph, Chelmsford, housewright, 1751—only 11 years after the deed to Elizabeth alludes to his appointment the year before (1750) and Joseph Mooars, who has been buying land on instalments or mortgaged land to Joseph, pays £40 and gets the land (a discharge) 13a, Feb. 14, 1752. Oliver and Ben Fletcher were witnesses.

3957. iv. ABIGAIL, b. abt. 1701; m. in Stow, Nov. 4, 1722, Jacob Osbon. of Winsor.
3958. v. ELIZABETH, b. ——. Was deeded half of her parents' homestead in 1740. She was not married then.

Middlesex Deeds, vol. 51, p. 310. Jonathan Foster, of

*Jonas Whitney was born in Stow in 1699; m., 1723, Dorcas Wood. She d. 1725 and he m. 2d 17[illegible], Margaret Stratton. He res. Stow and Harvard.—[Whitney Genealogy, by Fred C. Pierce.]

Chelmsford, husbandman, gives to Elizabeth Foster for £170 the other half of the homestead he deeded before to Joseph—evidently a daughter perhaps about to be married. This was Jan. 27, 1740. The deed was witnessed by John Foster and William Foster.

3899. HON. JOHN FOSTER (John, Thomas, Thomas), b. Marshfield, Mass., Oct. 12, 1666; m., 1692, Hannah Stetson, of Situate. John Foster, of Plymouth, owned all the land on the northerly side of Sandwich street, near the Arch bridge. It was granted to him in 1711 by the town. On this land he built a distillery on that part of it now occupied by Gales' block. He was a prominent citizen, deacon of the church, owned a distill house and represented Plymouth in the general court. He was very independent in his political conduct and would never accept an executive favor.

Will.—I John Foster of Plymouth in the County of Plymouth in New England being in the Seventy-fourth year of my age and at this time in usual health and of a Disposing mind and memory (Blessed be God for it) Do make and Ordain this my last Will and Testament in manner following—That is to Say I give and bequeath my Soul to God who gave it & redeemed it with the most precious blood of his Son Jesus C, I Give my body to the Earth to be buried in hope of a Glorious Resurrection, & Eternal Life through my Dear Lord & Saviour Jesus Christ—As for my Outward Estate Which God in his good providence has given me my mind & will is that it be disposed of as followeth—Imprimis I give and Bequeath to my beloved wife Hannah Foster she Resigning her Right of Dower the Sole use and improvement of my Home State during her natural life or widdow Hood (and no longer) Excepting the Blacksmith shop & warehouse & warfe which is to be set off beginning at the Path Ten feet westward from the Shop—I allso give unto my sd wife my best bed & furniture, my negro woman and one quarter part of my Household Goods with Liberty & and choosing her share.

Item. I Give and bequeath to my youngest son Seth Foster and to my Three Daughters viz Hannah Sarah & Mercy the three Remaining parts of my household goods & all my moveable and Personall Estate (Excepting what I Shall hereafter dispose off) To be divided equally among them.

Item. I Give and bequeath To my Eldest son Samuel Foster his Heirs and assigns forever One half of the Home Stall Houses & land (Excepting the Shop, warf and Warehouse & ye land below the Way ten feet Westward of the Shop as above) which he shall have after my wifes death or second marriage.

Item. I give and bequeath to my second son Thomas Foster his Heirs and Assign forever the One half of my meadow land at ye High pines within the bounds of Duxborough, and allso all my wearing apparell—and allso my Pine Lott of land at Billington Sea on ye Westerly side.

Item. I Give and bequeath to my Third son Nath'el Foster his Heirs and assigns forever my Blacksmith Shop with the Utensils thereunto belonging and the Warehouse & wharf & ye land to be Sett off ten feet Westward of the Shop as above. Allso ye other Half of the Home stall Houses & Land which he shall have after my wifes death or second marriage. Also my field & pasture Lying in Plymo. above Littletown with the Wood Lott at the head of it: Also my Sixty acres of Land at Gunners Exchange pond 40 acres on ye South & 20 acres on ye north side of sd. Pond allso my lott of land on ye beach with ye Blacksmith shop that stands on it with ye utensils. Allso one half of my meadow land at High Pines within the bounds of Duxborough. I allso give my sd. son Nathaniel my Negro Girl Nanne and whatsoever is due to me by Book. and I order him to pay all my debts and funeral Charges and to provide for & and support his mother Comfortably & Honourably as long as she Continues my widdow, or to give her yearly a certain sum of money for her support as my son Samuel and he Shall Agree. I allso order him to pay to my Grandson Eliphalett Bradford Ten pounds or let him have a good Cow and allso take care that sd. Eliphalet be learned the Smiths Trade or some other and when his time is up Give him two Suits of apparill one proper for the Lord, and the other for working days. Furthermore my Cedar Swamp at South meadows my sons Thomas & Nath'el shall have, one half to Thomas, his Heirs & Assigns and the Other half To Nath'el his Heirs and assigns. Finally I nominate and appoint my two sons Samuel & Nathaniel to be Joynt Executors of this my last will & Testament. In Witness hereof I have Hereunto Set my hand & Seal this ninth day of January Anno Dom. 1739-40

Signed Sealed & Declared this to be my last will & Testament in Presence of
Isaac Lothrop Junr.
Thomas Wetherell
Rebecca Wetherell

Memorandm. Thy words (my negro Girl Nane e) were Enterlined before Signing, &c

John Foster. [Seal]

Plymo. ss. Janr. 7 the 26, 1741 This will being Presented for probt. by the Execrs.. The above named Isaac Lothrop Junr.. Thomas Wetherell & Rebecca Wetherell made oath that they saw the above named John Foster sing & Seal & heard him declare this Instrument, to be his Last Will & Testamt. and that they at ye same time in ye Testators presence subscribed as witnesses & yt. he was then of sound mind.

Before me Jno. Cushing Judge of probt.

Recorded in Plymouth County Probate Records, Vol. 8, p. 466.

He d. Dec. 24, 1741. Res., Plymouth, Mass.

3959. i. HANNAH, b. July 25, 1694; m. William Bradford. She m., 2d, William Partridge. She d. Dec. 17, 1778. Bradford was son of John. Res., Plymouth, Mass. Ch: 1. James, b. 1717; m. Zerviah Thomas. 2. Zadock, b. 1719; m. Lucy Gray. Res., Duxbury. 3. Samuel, b. 1721. 4. Eliphalet, b. 1723; m. Hannah Prince. 5. Hannah, b. 1724; m. —— Spalding. 6. William, b. 1728.

3960. ii. SARAH, b. April 16, 1696; m. William Bartlett; m., 2d, Nathan Thomas. He d. Nov. 3, 1741; m., 3d, Oct. 24, 1743, Jedediah Brown She d. Feb. 7, 1788.

3961. iii. MERCY, b. ——; m., 1720, Capt. Ebenezer Morton, of Middleboro. Ch.: 1. Solomon, b. 1727. Captain Ebenezer was the gt.-gr.-father of Hon. Levi P. Morton, vice-president of the United States. Nathaniel Morton, son of Ebenezer and Mary Foster, b. 1735; d. November, 1826; m., 1757, 1st, Lucy Washburn; 2d, Rebecca Morton, dau. of Nathaniel and Martha Tupper Morton. Rebecca, b. in 1747; d. May 28, 1820, in Freetown, Mass. Lucy Washburn, m. 1757, d. 1766. The ch. were: Nathaniel, b. 1758; Tempe, b. 1762; Abraham, b. 1765. Rebecca Morton was married 1767. The ch. were: (a) Lucy Braley, b. Feb. 20, 1768; d. Aug. 13, 1852. (b) Abraham, b. Aug. 12, 1769; d. Sept. 27, 1821. (c) Ruth Braley, b. Jan. 13, 1771; d. Feb. 5, 1854. (d) Andrew, b. Dec. 26, 1772; d. 1805. (e) Ebenezer, b. Sept. 4, 1781; d. 1807. (f) Rebecca, b. Jan. 14, 1775; d. ——. (g) Martin Tupper, b. March 7, 1783; d. Sept. 25, 1841. (h) Hannah, b. Aug. 10, 1785; d. ——. (i) Deborah, b. Dec. 23, 1791; d. Aug. 21, 1854.

3962. iv. SAMUEL, b. ——; m. Margaret Tilden and Margaret Wadsworth.

3963. v. JOHN, b. Nov. 7, 1699; d. young.

3964. vi. THOMAS, b. Nov. 19, 1705; m. Lois Fuller and Mary Morton.

3965. vii. ICHABOD, b. Feb. 7, 1707; d. Aug. 8, 1707.

3966. viii. GRESHAM, b. Nov. 2, 1709; d. before 1741.

3967. ix. NATHANIEL, b. June 6, 1711; m. Mercy Thatcher and Mrs. Abigail (Woodman) Billings.

3968. x. SETH, b. Sept. 16, 1713. Was living in 1739, mentioned in his fatner's will. I think he went to Boston and was a grocer; m. Susanna Wait; d. intestate, September, 1753. Seth Foster, of Botson, grocer, dec'd. Inventory mentions widow Timothy Prout, Administrator, dated Sept. 14, 1753. Estate declared insolvent. Suff. Prob. Lib. 48, Fol. 559; Lib. 49, Fol. 505-6 His ch. were: 1. Mary, b. Oct. 18, 1734. 2. Hannah, b. March 26, 1739. 3. Thomas Wait, b. May 2, 1741. 4. Thomas Wait, b. Sept. 22, 1748.

3900. JOSIAH FOSTER (John, Thomas, Thomas), b. Marshfield, Mass., June 7, 1669; m. Sarah Sherman. She d. July 30, 1713; m., 2d, May 2, 1717, Ursula Rand. She d. Dec. 20, 1717. He settled in Pembroke, and appears to have been a farmer. He lived to be ninety years of age, as administration of his estate was granted to Isaac, his son, as late as April 4, 1757. The Plymouth County record shows that he married Sarah, dau. of Samuel Sherman, of Marshfield. His second wife was of Scituate. Josiah Foster, of Pembroke, Isaac Foster appointed administrator April 4, 1757; heirs not mentioned. He d. 1757. Res., Pembroke, Mass.

3972. i. MARY, b. Feb. 2, 1696; m., March 28, 1726, John Mackfarland, Jr.
3973. ii. ELIZABETH, b. November, 1698.
3971. iii. BARSHEBA, b. September, 1700.
3969. iv. JOSIAH, b. December, 1703; m. Mary Bonney and Elizabeth Carver.
3970. v. ISAAC, b. Aug. 5, 1705; m. Frances Joslyn.
3974. vi. DAVID, b. December, 1707.
3975. vii. NATHANIEL, b. December, 1710.
3976. viii. SARAH, b. July 10, 1713; m., Dec. 8, 1731, Isaac Mackfarland.

3902. JOSEPH FOSTER (John, Thomas, Thomas), b. Marshfield, Mass., 1674; m. Sept. 8, 1696, Rachel Bassett, of Sandwich; d. Dec. 12, 1744. He resided in Barnstable in 1696, where he married his wife. He soon after moved to Sandwich, where he died. She was b. Oct. 25, 1679; d. Dec. 12, 1744, dau. of William, 3d, and Rachel Willison, of Taunton. William, 3d, b. 1656, m., Oct. 9, 1675; son of William, Jr., and Mary, of Sandwich. He d. 1670, age abt. forty-five, son of William and Elizabeth, who came in Fortune 1621, and died 1667.

He d. April, 1750. Res., Barnstable and Sandwich, Mass.

3977. i. MARY, b. Sept. 1, 1697, at S.; m. Moses Swift, of S., Dec. 24, 1719.
3978. ii. JOSEPH, b. Sept. 19, 1698, at B.; m. Elizabeth Milton.
3979. iii. BENJAMIN, b. Nov. 16, 1699, at B.; m. Maria Toby, at Sandwich.
3980. iv. WILLIAM, b. March 31, 1702; m. Hannah Rider.
3981. v. THANKFUL, b. Nov. 3, 1703; m., Sept. 25, 1725, Nathan Toby, of Sandwich.
3982. vi. JOHN, b. April 12, 1705; m. Joanna Brown.
3983. vii. NATHAN, b. Jan. 3, 1707-8; m. Mary Lathrop and Mary (?) Smith.
3984. viii. ABIGAIL, b. Feb. 27, 1708-9; m., May 15, 1735, Zaccheus Swift.
3985. ix. DEBORAH, b. Jan. 18, 1710-11; m., Nov. 22, 1733, Isaac Freeman.
3986. x. EBENEZER, b. May 10, 1713.
3987. xi. SOLOMON, b. Sept. 4, 1714; m. Rebecca Nye.
3988. xii. RACHEL, b. Oct. 30, 1716; m., Dec. 10, 1743, Jonathan Churchill.
3989. xiii. SARAH, b. Sept. 23, 1721; m., Nov. 11, 1742, Nathaniel Nye.
3990. xiv. HANNAH, b. June 17, 1718.

3904. DEACON CHILLINGSWORTH FOSTER (John, Thomas, Thomas), b. June 11, 1680, in Marshfield, Mass.; m. Mercy, dau. of John Freeman, of Harwich (now Brewster), Mass. She d. July 7, 1720, ae. thirty-three. He m., 2d, Susannah, wid. of Nathaniel Sears, and dau. of John Gray. She d. Dec. 7, 1730. He m., 3d, Ruth, wid. of Samuel Sears, and dau. of William Merrick, Dec. 7, 1731. He settled in that part of Harwich, which is now Brewster. Like his father and grandfather, he was a blacksmith, and transmitted the mysteries of that craft to at least three sons. He was a deacon in the church from July 4, 1731, till he died. Was selectman nine years, town treasurer twenty-five years, town clerk twenty-eight years, representative eight years. He d. Dec. 22, 1764. Ruth d. Feb. 13, 1766, ae. eighty-two. At the time of his third marriage he had six children by his first wife, three by his second wife, and in his family also was the daughter of his second wife, by her former husband, ten in all, of whom only two were over twenty years of age. Nearly all these children were gathered under one roof, and constituted a very harmonious family.

From Probate records of Barnstable County, book 13, p. 87: I, Chillingsworth Foster of Harwich in the County of Barnstable and Province of the Massachusetts Bay in New England, Do make and ordain this my Last Will and Testament this Thirtyeth Day of September 1763. First, I recommend my soul to God that Gave it hopeing in his mercy thro' the merrits of Christ and my Body to the Earth in Decent Christian burial as to my worldly Estate I Give Demise & Dispose of the same in manner following

1st. I will that all my Just Debts Funeral charges & the Legacys Given in the Will be paid out of my real estate by my Executors hereafter named and ordained and I do hereby order and Impower my sd Executor to sell so much of my Real Estate as will be sufficient to Discharge the same for the most it will fetch & to give and execute good and lawful Deeds of conveyance to the Purchasers.

2lly I give to my beloved wife Ruth the free use and Improvement of one Third of my Personal Estate During her Life. I give to my son James Foster five shillings.

3lly. I give to my son Nathan Foster his heirs &c. the House he now lives in with my Land thereto adjoyning.

4thly. I give to my son Isaac Foster his heirs &c. my orchard & Land adjoyning to my Dwelling house bounded as follows, beginning at the southwest corner of sd orchard Thence Runing Easterly by the wayside till it comes to south of my front Door. Thence Northerly on a straight line Through the middle of the house to the Northeast corner of the Garden fence. Thence westerly as the fence now stands to sd Isaac Fosters Land and thence Southerly in the Range between this and sd Isaac's Land to the first specified Bound Reserving the Improvement of one-third of the Garden to my Daughter Jerusha as hereafter Exprest I also give my sd son Isaac my vice & Beeker in ye shop. 5ly. I give to my son Nathaniel Foster fifteen pounds in money.

CHILLINGSWORTH FOSTER PLACE.

6ly. I give to my Daughter Jerusha Foster the Feather bed that was her mothers with 2 pr sheets 1 pr blankets 2 coverlids 1 bolster & 2 pillows and one sixth part of the Remainder of my Indoors movables Further my Will is that my sd Daughter have the free use and Improvement of one Third part of the Garden and one Room in my Dwelling house either the Lower Room or Chamber as she shall choose so long as she remain unmarried & no longer I also give my said Daughter one Cow & Eight Pounds money. 7thly. I give all the Remaining part of my Estate both Real & Personal to my son & Daughters Chillingsworth Foster, Thomas Foster, Nathan Foster, Isaac Foster, Nathaniel Foster, Mary Paddock, Mercy Crosbie and Jerusha Foster to be Divided equally Between them their heirs & assigns forever.

And I ordain my son Chillingsworth Foster sole Executor to this my last will & Testament. In testimony whereof I have herunto set my hand & seal the Day & year above written. Signed sealed Pronounced & Declared to be his Last Will & Testament In presence of

Chillingsworth Foster,
(L. S.)

Barnabas Myrick
Nathl. Stone,
Hannah Stone.

A true copy. Attest: Freeman H. Lathrope, Register.

Mercy Freeman's ancestor was Edmund Freeman, who came over in the "Abigail," Captain Hackwell, master, 1635, and settled in Lynn, Mass., in 1635; was one of the grantees of Sandwich, Mass., April 3, 1637, and where he died in 1682, at the supposed age of ninety-two. He soon rose to distinction in the town and colony, and occupied many important positions. He was chosen assistant to the governor in 1640, and was reëlected yearly until 1646. There was no known relationship between him and Samuel, who came to Watertown. His wife's name was Elizabeth. Ch.: 1. Alice, b. 1618, in England; m. Deacon William Paddy, Nov. 24, 1639. 2. Edmund, b. 1620, in England; m. Rebecca, dau. of Gov. Thomas Prince. 3. Elizabeth, b. 1623, in England; m. John Ellis. 4. John, b. 1622, in England; m. Mercy, dau. of Gov. Thomas Prince. John was born in England; married Mercy, dau. of Gov. Thomas Prince and Granddaughter of Elder William Brewster, on the 13th or 14th of February, 1649-50. John early removed to Eastham; captian in 1675, and actively engaged in King Philip's war; was major in 1685; deacon in church; selectman ten years; when scarcely thirty years of age he was sent to the Colonial Court as deputy. He represented Eastham 1656 62-63-64-65-66. In 1667 he was chosen assistant to the governor and was reëlected yearly until the union of the Colonies in 1692. Sheriff of county under Andross' administration, and the first named judge of the Court of Common Pleas after the union of Plymouth and Massachusetts colonies. His grave-stone, at Eastham, bears the inscription: "Here lies the body of Major John Freeman. Died October ye 28th 1717 in ye 98th year of his age." His wife, Mercy, died Sept. 28, 1711, ae. eighty. There were few men in the colony of his day that bore a better reputation than Major Freeman. He was upright and impartial in all his acts while a public servant, and correct in his religious walks through life. Ch.: (a) John, b. Feb. 2, 1650-1; d. young. (b) John, b. December, 1651; m. Sarah Merrick. John was born in Eastham, m., March 1st, Sarah, dau. of William Merrick, Dec. 18, 1672, who died April 21, 1696. He m. 2d, Mercy, wid of Capt. Elkanah Watsen, of Plymouth. His children were all by his first wife. John resided near the line between Eastham (now Orleans) and Harwich (now Brewster), and his death. July 27, 1721, was recorded in both towns. His headstone is in Brewster. Mercy died Sept. 27, 1721, ae. sixty-two. Ch.: i. John, b. Sept. 3, 1674; d. young. ii. Sarah, b September, 1676; m. Edward Snow. iii. John, b. July, 1678; m. Mercy ——. iv. Rebecca, b. Jan. 28, 1680-1; d. young. v. Nathaniel, b. March 17, 1682-3; m. Mary Waters, of Plymouth; d. August, 1735. vi. Benjamin, b. July, 1685; m. Temperance Dimmick. vii. Mercy, b. Aug. 3, 1687; m. Deacon Chillingsworth Foster. viii. Patience, b. ——; m. Eleazer Crosby, Oct. 24, 1706. ix. Susanna, b. ——; m. John Mayo, Jr., Oct. 22, 1722. x. Elizabeth, b. ——; m. John Bacon, Jr., May 2, 1726. xi. Mary, b. abt. 1693; m. Judah Berry, 1713; she d. Aug. 19, 1719, ae. twenty-six. (c) Thomas, b. September, 1653; deacon, town clerk and town treasurer of Harwich. (d) Patience, b. ——; m. Lieut. Samuel Paine, Jan 31, 1682-3. (e) Hannah, b. ——; m. John Mayo, April 14, 1681. (f) Edmund, b. June, 1657. (g) Mercy, b. July, 1659; m. Samuel Knowles, December, 1679. (h) William, b. ——. (i) Prince, b. Feb. 3, 1665-6; d. young. (j) Nathaniel, b. March 20, 1669; selectman, town clerk of Eastham, justice of the peace, judge of county court; d. Jan. 4, 1670. (k) Bennett, b. March 7, 1670-1; m. Deacon John Paine, March 14, 1689. (5) Mary, b. ——, in England; m. Edward Perry.

3991. i. JAMES, b. Jan. 6, 1705 6; m. Lydia Winslow.
3992. ii. CHILLINGSWORTH, b. Dec. 25, 1707; m. Mercy Winslow.
3993. iii. MARY, b. Jan. 5, 1709-10; m. David Paddock, of Falmouth, Oct. 12, 1727. Rem. to South East, Dutchess Co., N. Y. He was b. Aug. 12, 1705, son of Zachariah, Jr., and Bethiah and gr.-son of Zachariah and Deborah (Sears), of Yarmouth, Mass.
3994. iv. THOMAS, b. March 15 1711-12; m. Mary Hopkins.
3995. v. NATHAN, b. June 10, 1715; m. Sarah Lincoln, June 14, 1739.
3996. vi. ISAAC, b. June 17, 1718; m. Hannah Sears.
3997. vii. MERCY, b. March 30, 1720; d. Aug. 28, 1720
3998. viii. MERCY, b. July 29, 1722; m. Isaac Crosby, Oct. 7, 1742.
3999. ix. NATHANIEL, b. April 17, 1725; m. Phebe Wing and Charity Knowlton.
4000. x. JERUSHA, b. Dec. 9, 1727; m. April 2, 1769, Capt. Solomon Bangs.
4001. xi. SON, b. and d. March, 1729.

3906. DEACON THOMAS FOSTER (John, Thomas, Thomas), b. Marshfield, Mass., 1686; m. Mrs. Faith (Oakham) White, wid. of Benjamin. She d. Dec. 26, 1758. He was a farmer, town clerk and deacon of the church. He inherited the homestead at Marshfield, where he died. Thomas Foster, of Marshfield, administrator, appointed April 3, 1758; no heirs mentioned. He d. Feb. 6, 1758. Res., Marshfield, Mass.

4002. i THOMAS, b. May 4, 1735; m. Mary Foster.
4003. ii. DEBORAH, b. March 10, 1736; m. in 1760, Anthony Waterman.

3914. THOMAS FOSTER (Joseph, Thomas, Thomas), b. Billerica, Mass., Feb. 11, 1681, m. Hepsibah ——. Res., Billerica, Mass.

4004. i. THOMAS, b Oct. 17, 1706.
4005. ii. JOHN, b. Jan. 11, 1708; m. Hannah ——.
4006. iii. SARAH, b. June 30, 1709; m. David Crosby, b. March 27, 1703. He was son of Joseph, of Billerica; rem. to Shrewsbury, Mass. None of the births of his children are on the town records in Shrewsbury. Ch.: 1. Hepsibeth, b. B., Oct. 17, 1727. 2. David, b. B., June 5, 1729. 3. Sarah, b. B., May 5, 1731. 4. Hannah, bapt. S., Jan. 7, 1733; m., July 3, 1751, Adonijah Rice. 5. Solomon, bapt. Dec. 29, 1735. 6. Persis, bapt. Nov. 14, 1736; m., Dec. 31, 1759. Daniel Forbush, Jr., of Westboro (see Forbes' Genealogy, by Fred C. Pierce). 7. Mary, bapt. March 4, 1739. 8 John, bapt. March 8, 1741. 9. Beulah, bapt. Nov. 7, 1742. 10. Relief, bapt. April 27, 1746. 11. Prudence, bapt. Aug. 17, 1748. 12. Rachel, bapt. Sept. 15, 1751. Hannah, the fourth of these children, was bapt., says the church record, "by virtue of her (the mother) having enjoyed that privilege at Billerica, where she lived." His wife, Sarah, was admitted to the Shrewsbury church in 1734, and he in 1741, and in 1743 he was dismissed to the church in the North Parish of Shrewsbury.
4007. iv. JOSEPH, b. April 8, 1711.
4008. v. HANNAH, b. Sept. 25, 1716.
4009. vi. OBADIAH, b. March 17, 1721. About 1740 he went with the naval expedition to the West Indies to assist in the war with America against Spain.

3921. JUDGE RICHARD FOSTER (Richard, William, Thomas), b. Charlestown. Mass., March 23, 1694; m. Sarah Emerson, b. 1695; d. Nov. 16, 1724; m., 2d, Oct. 21, 1725, Mary Foye, b. 1702; d. Oct. 26, 1774.

He was a sea captain and was quite a prominent citizen; held the office of high sheriff for Middlesex county for more than forty years; resigning which, he was in 1764 appointed justice of the Court of Common Pleas for the same county, in which office he continued until his death.

We also find in the old burying ground, at Charlestown, Mass., the tombstone with the arms of the wife of Richard Foster, Jr., 1724. He was grandson of William Foster, of Charlestown, 1650. Those arms, crest and motto, are those of the Fosters, or Forsters, of Brickhill county, Bedford, and the Boyne county, Lancaster, also reported by the Fosters of Jamaica, West Indies. Various ancient silver articles with the Foster arms are preserved in America. Among others, a large tankard, with the arms beautifully engraved, and the tinctures clearly indicated. It is in possession of Edward Ingersoll Browne, of Watertown.

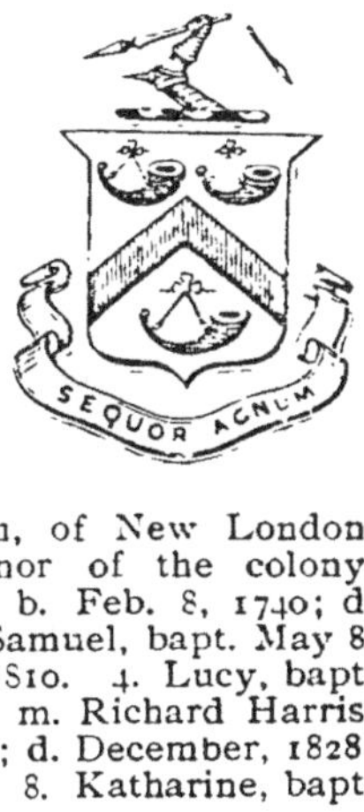

Crest An arm in armor embowered, holding in the hand a broken tilting spear, proper.

Motto: Sic fractus fortis. "If broken, still strong."

He d. Aug. 29, 1774. Res., Charlestown, Mass.

4010. i. SARAH, b. May 4, 1718; m., March, 22, 1738, Samuel Bradstreet. She d. February, 1702. He was son of Rev. Simon, of New London, and gr.-son of Governor Simon, governor of the colony. Res., Charlestown, Mass. Ch.: 1. Sarah, b. Feb. 8, 1740; d. young. 2. Sarah, bapt. May 24, 1741. 3. Samuel, bapt. May 8, 1743; merchant in Boston; d. unm. July 4, 1810. 4. Lucy, bapt. June 1, 1746. 5. Lucy, bapt. June 12, 1748; m. Richard Harris, of Marblehead. 6. Mary, bapt. April 7, 1751; d. December, 1828; unm. 7. Richard Foster, b., twin with K. 8. Katharine, bapt. May 20, 1753; d. June 6, 1837, unm.
4011. ii. RICHARD, b. Oct. 8, 1720; d. Jan. 22, 1722.

4012. iii. MARY, b. Nov. 4, 1722; m. June 18, 1741, John Breed; m. 2d, April 25, 1765, John White. Breed was son of Ebenezer, distiller. Res., Charlestown. White was born in Charlestown. Ch. by Breed: 1. Ebenezer, b. July, 1742. 2. Mary, b. March 25, 1744. 3. John, b. April 20, 1746. 4. Hannah, b. Dec. 28, 1747; m. Nov. 1, 1786, Rev. David Osgood. He was b. Andover, Mass., Oct. 14, 1747; was grad. Harvard College. 1771. He d. Dec. 12, 1822. He was the third minister in Medford, and was born within half a mile of the Tewksbury line. His father was Captain Isaac, who lived to an advanced age on the farm where his father, Mr. Stephen Osgood, resided. David's mother was Elizabeth Flint, the daughter of a respectable farmer in Reading. David worked on his father's farm until nineteen years of age; he taught school and entered Harvard. He sustained a high rank in his class. After his graduation he studied for the ministry, and settled in Medford in 1774. He was a true patriot and a learned and effective preacher, and held in the highest esteem by all who knew him. 5. Sarah, bapt. May 6, 1750. Ch. by White: 6. John, bapt. Sept. 14, 1766. Res., Billerica.

4013. iv. KATHARINE, b. Aug. 16, 1724; d. ae. five months.

4014. v. ELIZABETH, b. Sept. 17, 1726; m. Dec. 9, 1748, David Cheever; d. before 1760, for he m. 2d, that year. Res., C. Ch.: 1. Mary, bapt. June 20. 1751. 2. Mary, bapt. Feb. 17, 1753; m. Ephraim Hale. 3. David, bapt. Sept. 22, 1754.

4015. vi. RICHARD, b Feb. 17, 1728; probably died young, as he is not named as an heir.

4016. vii. PARNELL, b Aug. 24, 1729, m. Oct. 13, 1763, Richard Boylston, Jr.; he was a brazier. She d. July 28, 1796, his second wife. He d. June 30, 1807. Six ch. by first wife. Ch.: 7. Parnell, bapt. Dec. 23, 1764; m. 1786, Thomas Brooks. 8. Hannah, bapt. April 20, 1766; d. July 7, 1804.

4017. viii. HANNAH, bapt. Feb. 28, 1731; m. Nov. 22, 1753, Capt. Eben Kent, son of Captain Ebenezer; he enlisted in the Revolutionary war, 1780; was sergeant and captain. She was admitted to the church July 21, 1754. She d. s. p. before 1757, for he then m. again.

4018. ix. WILLIAM, bapt. Dec. 17, 1732; probably died young, as he is not named as an heir.

4019. x. MARGARET, b. May 19, 1734; d. Dec. 15. 1789; unm.

Margaret Foster's Will, 1790—In the name of God Amen I Margaret Foster of Charlestown in the County of Middlesex and Commonwealth of Massachusetts Spinster, being in perfect memory and understanding and knowing that I must quickly lay down this earthly tabernacle do make and appoint, this my last Will and Testament.

I commit my Soul into the hands of my dear Redeemer and my body to the dust to be buried with a decent burial, and after all my just debts and funeral expenses are paid—

I give and bequeath all my wearing Apparil to my three sisters namely to Parnel Boylston wife of Richard Boylston, to Ann Austin wife of John Austin Junr, and to Abigail Codman wife of Isaac Codman all of Charlestown aforesaid, to be equally divided between them, and all the Rest and Residue of my Estate I give and devise to Parnel Boylston for her particular use one fifth part, to Mary Hall wife of Ephraim Hall of Medford one fifth part and to the heirs of my late sister Katherine Sprague of Lancaster, deceased, namely to Sarah Sprague, to Ann Austin Sprague and to Samuel John Sprague, one fifth part to be equally divided between them, and I do hereby appoint Richard Boylston, John Austin Junr, and Isaac Codman all of Charlestown aforsaid to be my sole executors of this my last Will and Testament hereby Revoking all former Wills by me made in Witness whereof, I have hereunto sett my hand and seal this fourteenth day of

December Anno Domini One thousand Seven hundred and Eighty nine.

her
Margarit X Foster
mark

Signed Sealed published and Declared by the within named Margaret Foster, to be her last Will and Testmenat, in the presence of us, who in the presence of the Testator, and of one and other subscribers be as Witnesses
William Boylston
Rachel Monro
her
Mary X Gee   Prob. April 9, 1790.
mark
Hannah Austin witness to Mary Gee's mark

4020. xi. ANN, b. July 24, 1736; m. Oct. 29, 1767, John Austin, Jr. He was a merchant. Inspector of pot and pearl ashes. She d. Jan. 27, 1798. He d. Oct. 16, 1824. Res., C., s. p.

4021. xii. KATHARINE, bapt. March 19, 1738; m. (pub.), Nov. 21, 1772, John Sprague.

The Hon. John Sprague was a citizen of Lancaster from Sept. 1, 1770, to the 21st of September, 1800, the time of his death. The town was much indebted to him for the correctness of their municipal proceedings, and the unanimity with which their affairs were conducted. He was born at Rochester, in the county of Plymouth, then province of the Massachusetts Bay, on June 21, A. D., 1740, O. S., corresponding to the 2d of July, N S. He was the son of Noah Sprague, Esq., by Sarah, his wife, who was a lineal descendant of Elizabeth Penn, the sister of Sir William Penn, who was an admiral under Cromwell, and the father of William Penn, the proprietor of Penn. Her husband was William Hammond, of London. Benjamin, their son, removed from London to Sandwich, in the colony of Plymouth; married there in 1650, and thence removed to Rochester. John Hammond, the second son by this marriage, married Mary Arnold, daughter of the Rev. Samuel Arnold, the first minister of Rochester, and Sarah, a daughter by this marriage, was Mr. Sprague's mother. Judge Sprague began to prepare for College in December, 1760, and entered therein at Cambridge at the end of the summer vacation, after, viz., A. D., 1761. Having pursued his collegiate studies with reputation, he graduated in 1765, and soon after took charge of the grammar school in Roxbury; commenced the study of physics there, and pursued it under the instruction of the late Dr. Thomas Williams for a short time, viz: until May, 1766. In that month he removed to Worcester, abandoned the study of physics and entered as a clerk in the office of Col. James Putnam, an eminent barrister at law, and kept a private grammar school there. At the May term of the Court of Common Pleas, 1768, he was admitted as attorney of that court. Removed thence to Rhode Island, and in the following September was admitted an attorney in the Superior Court in the county of Providence, colony of Rhode Island, etc , and opened his office in Newport; there he remained without the prospect of much business, in the diligent pursuit of his professional studies until May, 1769, when he removed to Keene, in the county of Cheshire, then province of New Hampshire, where he pursued the practice of law until Sept. 1, 1770; made himself acquainted with the people and the business of the courts there, and by his talents, industry and fidelity acquired a reputation which long afterward afforded him extensive professional employment in the interior counties of that province. Inclined to take up his permanent abode in his native province, he then removed from Keene to Lancaster, in the county of Worcester, and opened an office in partnership with Abel Willard, Esq., a respectable counselor at law, for the term of ten years, beginning the 21st of the same month. This partnership was interrupted by the war with Great Britain. Mr. Willard, adhering to the king, left Lancaster in March, 1775, and never returned. In April, 1772, he was admitted an attorney of the Superior Court of Worcester. In December, 1772, he married Catharine Foster, of Charlestown, the twelfth child and ninth daughter of Richard Foster, Esq., sheriff of Middlesex. By this marriage he had one son and two daughters. He was occupied in extensive professional employment, till arms silenced the law; then he shared in the burdens and privations common to his neighbors and fellow citizens in the eventful period of the Revolution. Having purchased a small farm in the center of the town, he labored upon it as a farmer, dismantled himself of his linen and ruffles and other appropriate habiliments, and assumed the garments of labor, which were then the checkered shirt and trousers. He was resorted to for counsel in all cases of difficulty which occurred, and toward the close of the Revolution, when our government was formed, and business revived, he was one of the principal counselors and advocates in our courts of justice. His legal learning was so well combined with and aided by common sense and a sound discretion that he was considered one of the most safe, discerning and upright counselors in the commonwealth. As an advocate he was not the most eloquent, but such was the fairness of his statements and force of his arguments, that conviction seemed their natural result.

He was cotemporary with the two Strongs, the late Governor, and the late Judge, both of the county of Hampshire, and the late Hon. Levi Lincoln, of Worcester, and divided with them the multiplied business of advocating causes and collecting debts in the counties of Hampshire, Worcester and Middlesex, and in the counties of Hillsboro and Cheshire, in New Hampshire. In May, 1732, he was elected a representative of the town to the General Court, and in the January session following, a vacancy in the Senate occurring, being a candidate, voted for by the people, was elected by the legislature to fill that vacancy, and was again elected to the Senate by the people in 1785. In February, 1783, he was first commissioned a justice of the peace and quorum for the county of Worcester. So high was he held in the estimation of the judges of the Supreme Judicial Court, as a lawyer, that at the February term of that court, in Suffolk, 1784, he was made a barrister at law, and was called to that distinction by the first writ that issued for barrister in the commonwealth; the mode of admission preceding the Revolution having been without writ. He was to have been admitted before the Revolution, but the tumults in the country interrupted the courts. He was elected to represent the town in the General Court in 1784 and 1785.

In 1786 Mr. Sprague was selected by the government as the law adviser of Major-General Lincoln, to attend him in his expedition against Daniel Shays and his adherents, who had excited a rebellion in the commonwealth. May 5, 1787, he was bereaved of his wife, and in the latter part of the same year he married Mary Ivers, widow of Thomas Ivers, Esq., late treasurer of the commonwealth and eldest child of Mr. John Cutler and Mary, his wife, of Boston, who survived him. In 1788 he was elected a member of the convention for ratifying the Constitution of the United States. The town was opposed to the ratification, and by a committee of seven gave him instructions to vote against it. Having confidence, however, in the intelligence and rectitude of their delegate, they so qualified the instructions as to leave him to vote as he should think proper. He was one of the seven out of fifty members from the county who voted in the affirmative. In the winter of the same year he was appointed sheriff of the county of Worcester, in the place of William Greenleaf, Esq., who was removed from that office. He was punctual and faithful in the performance of his official duties; reduced the former irregularities in the administration of the office to order and system and resigned it in 1792.

He returned to the practice of law and continued in it until 1798. He represented the town in the General Court from the year 1795 to 1799 inclusive. In 1798 he was appointed chief justice of the Court of Common Pleas for the county of Worcester. It was a new and valuable acquisition to have a learned lawyer at the head of the judicial administration of the county, whose integrity and talents fitted him for the station, and whose justice and impartiality would insure the confidence of all engaged in the business of the court.

In this office he continued until his death. His historical and legal knowledge, the accuracy of his mind, and its adaptation in the choice of language to express it on all subjects, rendered him a very useful member of the legislature, and he was looked to as a safe adviser and guide in the political and local concerns of the commonwealth. He was a lover of peace, and possessed a happy talent at reconciling jarring interests and harmonizing discordant feelings. Such were his mental qualities, so strong his sense of justice and honorable dealings that he was selected, before he was on the bench, a commissioner or referee, to adjust the numerous controversies which prevailed to an alarming degree in the then District of Maine, between those who, without title, had settled on the lands of the commonwealth, of the Waldo Patent and Plymouth Company on the one part, and the lawful proprietors of them on the other. By his coöperating agency, together with the enactments thereon by the legislature, such a settlement of the contending claims was effected as restored peace and contentment to the parties.

In the course of his professional career many young gentlemen of liberal education entered his office as students in law and shared from him the requisite instruction. Of the distinguished men now living who were his pupils are the Hon. Edward H. Robbins, late lieutenant-governor of the commonwealth, now Judge of Probate for the county of Norfolk; the Hon. Nathaniel Paine, Judge of Probate for the county of Worcester; the Hon. Artemas Ward, Chief Justice of the Court of Common Please for the commonwealth of Massachusetts, and John M. Forbes, Esq., now Charge d'Affaires, at Buenos Ayres.

Res., Lancaster. Ch.: 1. Samuel. 2. John. 3. Sarah. 4. Ann Austin.

Copy of an epitaph in old burial field, Lancaster:

Mrs Katharine Sprague
the amiable Consort of ye
Honble John Sprague, Esqr.
And a daughter of the late
Richard Foster, Esqr.
Died May 5th A D. 1787.
in the 49th. year of her age,
And is here interred.
Blessed are the pure in Heart,
for they shall see God.

4022. xiii. ABIGAIL, bapt. Jan. 27, 1739; m., Sept. 22, 1768, Isaac Codman. He was son of John. Ch.: 1. Abigail, b. Feb. 13, 1770.

4023. xiv. JOHN, bapt. April 5, 1741; probably d. young, as he is not named as an heir.

4024. xv. MARTHA, bapt. June 27, 1742.

3925. CAPTAIN ISAAC FOSTER (Richard, William, Thomas), b., Charlestown, Mass., Jan. 30, 1704; m., Aug. 24, 1732, Eleanor Wyer, dau. Captain William, b. July 14, 1714; d. March 5, 1798 of "cramp in stomach." He was a sea captain, making frequent voyages between Boston and Europe; in 1765 he was called merchant; he was quite a prominent citizen of Charlestown and his name often occurs in Frothingham's history of the town. No probate of his estate.

Will—Isaac Foster, of Charlestown; merchant; wife, Eleanor Foster; two children, Isaac Foster and Eleanor Foster. Dated April 26, 1775. Prob. March 11, 1783. Called Capt. Isaac Foster. Lib. 82; fol. 471-2-3.

Eleanor Foster, of Boston; widow, appointed guardian unto Eleanor Foster, a minor, above fourteen years of age, daughter of Isaac Foster, late of Charlestown, deceased. March 30, 1787. Lib. 86; fol. 147.

He d. Dec. 27, 1781. Res., Charlestown, Mass.

4025. i. WILLIAM, b. May 27, 1733; graduated at Harvard University in 1752; was styled Doctor on various deeds, etc. He died Dec. 3, 1759. Administration on his estate was ganted to his father Isaac, merchant, Oct. 29, 1765.

4026. ii. ISAAC, bapt. May 28, 1738 d. young.

4027. iii. ISAAC, b. Aug. 28, 1740 m. Martha Mason and Mary Russell.

4028. iv. THOMAS, b. Dec. 27, 1741; probably d. young. not being named in 1751 as an heir of his grandfather, William Wyer

4029. v. EDWARD, bapt. May 6, 1744; probably d. young, not being named in 1751 as an heir of his grandfather, William Wyer.

4030. vi. ELEANOR, b. Aug 4, 1746; m., Oct. 30, 1769, Dr. Nathaniel Coffin, of Portland, Me.

4031. vii. RICHARD, bapt. Dec. 4, 1748; probably d. young, not being named in 1751 as an heir of his grandfather, William Wyer.

3932. CAPT. HOPESTILL FOSTER (Hopestill, Hopestill, Richard, Thomas), b. Boston, Mass, 1670; m., at Cambridge, Nov. 15, 1705, Elizabeth Phipps, dau. of Solomon and Mary (Danforth), of Charlestown, b. Jan 2, 1683; d. Feb. 15, 1732. Hopestill Foster (1694), of Boston, shopkeeper (some say housewright), son of Capt. Hopestill Foster (1673) and grandson of Capt. Hopestill Foster (1642), of Dorchester was born about 1670. He was a constable of the town in 1705 and 1731; clerk of the market in 1710 and 1720; tithingman in 1710, 1715, 1717, and 1722, and held other town office in 1720, and from 1725 to 1733, except in three years. He had a son, Hopestill, a bookseller in Boston. Hopestill (1694) was identified with the militia, and, like his father and grandfather, rose to the grade of captain.—[Hist. Ancient and Honorable Artillery Co.] He seems to have held office in Boston—constable, 1705; clerk of the market, 1710; tithingman, 1710, 1715, 1717. He became a shopkeeper at some date after 1715. By Suffolk deeds, vol. 37, fol. 128, Hopestill Foster, shopkeeper, and wife Elizabeth mortgage lands to Eben Maudsley, of Dorchester He died in his own house; see Sewall's Diary iii, 333. His widow, b. Jan. 2, 1683-4; d. Feb. 15, 1732, and aged fifty-one years (King's Chapel Epitaphs) Suffolk Wills, Oct 1735; Estate of Hopestill Foster, shopkeeper, viewed at request of Hopestill Foster, bookseller. The children were Elisha, Hopestill, Elizabeth, and Mary.

Will—Elizabeth Foster, of Boston, widow and shopkeeper, two daughters, Elizabeth and Mary; two sons, Hopestill and Elisha. Dated Jan. 10, 1733. Prob. Feb. 27, 1733 Suff. Prob. Lib. 30; fol. 158 and 185.

Administrator of estate of Hopestill Foster, late of Boston, shopkeeper, deceased, granted to Hopestill Foster, of Boston, stationer, Sept. 10, 1735. Suff. Prob. Lib. 32; fol. 219-234-252.

He d. April 21, 1724. Res., Boston, Mass.

4032. i. ELIZABETH, b. Aug. 26, 1707; d. Sept. 15, 1707.

4033. ii. HOPESTILL, b. June 28, 1708. He was of Boston, a bookseller (Suffolk Deeds, vol. 50, p. 55. dated Jan. 4, 1734), Elisha Foster and Elizabeth to our brother Hopestill Foster, bookseller, executor of our mother Elizabeth Foster, widow and shopkeeper. Mary Foster wills her rights to her brother Hopestill, bookseller, by deed of September, 1836. Suff Deeds, vol. 54; fol. 3.

Hopestill Foster, of Boston, bookseller, was made guardian of sister Mary Foster, aged about twenty years, daughter of Hopestill Foster, late of Boston, shopkeeper, deceased, granted Sept. 17, 1734. Lib. 30; fol. 364.

4034. iii. ELIZABETH, b. June 28, 1708.

4035. iv. ELISHA, b. May 25, 1711; m. Elizabeth Shepard.

4036. v. MARY b., Aug. 29, 1715.

4037. vi. DANFORTH, b. July 27, 1717; d. Aug. 14, 1717.

3933. SAMUEL FOSTER (Hopestill, Hopestill, Richard, Thomas), b. Dec. 27, 1676; m. Rebecca Brisco, dau. of Joseph. She m., 2d, Oct. 13, 1709, Thomas Morrise, and m., 3d, Dec. 25, 1718, William Scorch. Samuel Foster died at Boston

March 10, 1702. His widow married 2d, Thomas Morrise, Oct. 13, 1709; 3d, William Scorch, married Dec. 25, 1718. Suffolk Deeds, vol. 21, fol. 150, Samuel Foster made a trust deed, dated March 9, 1699-1700, describing himself as son of Hopestill Foster, the soap boiler—for love of now wife Rebecca, daughter of my father-in-law, Joseph Brisco, and also love of only child, Rebecca. In 1724, Suffolk Deeds, vol. 39, fol. 68, Samuel Foster, of Boston, periwig maker, and wife Rachel; Rebecca, wife of John Best, tanner; also Rebecca, widow of Samuel Foster and then wife of William Scorch, of Boston, cooper, make deed. He d. March 10, 1702. Res., Boston, Mass.

4038. i. REBECCA, b. April 10, 1699; m., pub. Aug. 31, 1721, John Best.
4039. ii. SAMUEL, b. June 25, 1701; m. Rachel Kneeland.

3940. JOHN FOSTER (James, Hopestill, Richard, Thomas), b. Dorchester, Mass., Feb. 9, 1688; m. Mary ——. He was a blacksmith. Administrator of estate of John Foster, late of Boston, blacksmith, deceased, granted to son Edward Foster, of Boston, blacksmith, Nov. 4, 1746. Suff. Prob. Lib. 39; fol. 230. He d. in 1746. Res., Boston, Mass.

4040. i. JOHN, b. April 10, 1713; m. Mary Fish.
4041. ii. MARY, b. Feb. 16, 1714.
4042. iii. ANNA, b. Dec. 26, 1716.
4043. iv. MARY, b. Feb. 4, 1718.
4044. v. EDWARD, b. Sept. 20, 1720. He was a blacksmith.
4045. vi. JAMES, b. Feb. 14, 1723. He d. unm. in 1747-8. Administrator of estate of James Foster, formerly belonging to his Majesty's ship Cambridge, but late of his Majesty's ship Rippon, deceased, granted to his mother, Mary Foster, of Boston, widow, Jan. 10, 1748. Suff. Prob. Lib. 42; fol. 103.
4046. vii. EBENEZER, b. Aug. 30, 1729.
4047. viii. MARY, b. Aug. 30, 1731.

3944. CAPT. JAMES FOSTER (James, Hopestill, Richard, Thomas), b. Dec. 8, 1698, Dorchester, Mass.; m. Priscilla ——, b. 1692; d. March 16, 1739; m., 2d, Oct. 9, 1740, Mrs. Elizabeth Pimer, b. 1696; d. May 25, 1771, ae. seventy-five.

Will—James Foster, of Dorchester, esqr., considering advanced age; wife Elizabeth, daughter Priscilla Topliff, daughter Mary Foster, son James Foster, executors; daughter Anna Low, grandson James Topliff, grandson James Foster. Dated, July 21, 1762. Prob. Jan. 21, 1763. Suff. Prob. Lib. 61; fol. 350-1. Lib. 72; fol. 229.

Will—Elizabeth Foster, of Dorchester, widow; son-in-law James Foster, daughter-in-law Mary Foster; other children-in-law, the children of my deceased husband, James Foster, Esq.—James Foster, Priscilla Topliff, and Anna Low; brother-in-law Capt. Hopestill Foster, executor Dated May 3, 1763. Prob. June 28, 1771. Lib. 70; fol. 344-5-6.

He d. Jan. 8, 1763. Res., Dorchester, Mass.

4048. i. PRISCILLA, b. Nov. 18, 1722; m., May 29, 1744, Ebenezer Topliff.
4049. ii. BEULAH, b. Oct. 27, 1725; d. Aug. 18, 1741.
4050. iii. MARY, b. June 3. 1727; unm. in 1763.
4051. iv. ANNA, b. Aug. 4, 1729; m., June 1, 1758, Obadiah Low, of Boston.
4052. v. JAMES, b. March 31, 1732; m. Mary Robinson.

3946. CAPT. HOPESTILL FOSTER (James, Hopestill, Richard, Thomas), bapt. Feb. 15, 1701, Dorchester; m., Nov. 11, 1724, Sarah Allen, b. 1702; d. September, 1772. His record of officeholding is similar to that of his cousin Hopestill, the gunsmith, but begins ten years later.

Will—Hopestill Foster, of Boston, gentleman, son Hopestill Foster, daughter Ann Swift, granddaughter Hanners, daughter Sarah Fearsey (in account of estate spelled Hearsey; in warrant spelled Mearzey,) daughter Mary Prince. Dated, Oct. 13, 1772. Prob. Jan. 1, 1773. Lib. 72; fol. 311-12-13-14. Inventory mentions him as Capt. Hopestill Foster. Lib. 73; fol. 3-4. Lib. 83; fol. 125, 136, 771-2. Lib. 79; fol. 290-1.

In division daughter Mary Prince, wife of Christopher Prince; Hopestill Foster only son, daughter Sarah Hearsy. Oct. 27, 1786 Lib. 85; fol. 742-3-4-5.

He d. December, 1772. Res., Boston, Mass.

4053. i. SARAH, b. Oct. 3, 1725; m., Aug. 17, 1749, George Hanners; m., 2d, —— Hersey May 27, 1762.

4054. ii. BENJAMIN, b. May 27, 1727; d. Aug. 30, 1747.
4055. iii. ANN, b. Oct. 3, 1729; m. Samuel Swift.
4056. iv. MARY, b. Dec. 19, 1731; d.——.
4057. v. CHILD, b. and d. Dec. 4, 1733.
4058. vi. MERCY, b. March 4, 1735; m. Col. Christopher Prince. They went from Boston to Annapolis, N. S.,, in 1770, and he was an United Empire Loyalist The family resided in Nova Scotia ever after.
4059. vii. ELIZABETH, b. Feb. 20, 1739; d. young.
4060. viii. HOPESTILL, b. June 29, 1744; m. Susannah Wood.

3949. COMFORT FOSTER (Standfast, Hopestill, Richard, Thomas), b., bapt. Dorchester, June 29, 1689; m., July 22, 1712, Eleanor Woods. She d. and he m. 2d, May 12, 1726, Abiah Withington, b. ——; d. March 23, 1810. He was a glazier.

Administrator of estate of Comfort Foster, late of Dorchester, glazier, deceased, granted to his widow, Abiah Foster, of Dorchester, March 9, 1735. Suff. Prob. Lib. 32; fol. 386, 475. Lib. 33; fol. 375.

He d. Jan. 30, 1735. Res., Dorchester, Mass.

4061. i. JOSEPH, b. July 3, 1712; d. January, 1727.
4062. ii. ABIGAIL, b. Jan. 8, 1713; m., June 21, 1733, Joshua Sevor, Jr.
4063. iii. THOMAS, b. March 21, 1715; m. Mary Lyon.
4064. iv. COMFORT, b. Aug. 30, 1718; d. Nov. 30, 1718.
4065. v. ELEANOR, b. Aug. 30, 1718.
4066. vi. MARY, b. July 29, 1721.
4067. vii. WILLIAM, b. April 24, 1727; m. Elizabeth Hunt.
4068. viii. JOHN, b. Dec. 26, 1733; m. Hannah Downs.

3953. THOMAS FOSTER (Thomas, Thomas, Thomas, Thomas), b. Cambridge Mass., Sept. 18, 1687; m. in Preston, Conn., July 3, 1711, Mercy Gates. He went from Cambridge to Preston and thence to Voluntown, Conn., with his mother Experience Foster, who had married for a second husband Benjamin Geary. This is all there is on Voluntown vital records. Thomas and mother Experience, 1709 (vol. 42, p. 142) Middlesex court, he a husbandman, like his father Thomas, of Stow (Thomas, Thomas of Weymouth). His wife was a Mercy; sold to Joseph Heald 10 acres house lot granted to father Thomas by town of Stow. March 3, 1709. I have searched the Voluntown, Conn., land records through, and the following is all that I can find of Foster: First Phillip's Bill, of Groton, Conn., deed to Thomas Foster, of Preston, Conn., dated March 3, 1714.

Res., Preston and Voluntown, Conn.

4069. i. SILAS, b. Voluntown, March 7, 1721; d. Dec. 8, 1721.
4070. ii. STEPHEN, b. Preston, April 20, 1712.
4071. iii. SARAH, b. Preston, July 31, 1717.

3954. JONATHAN FOSTER (Jonathan, Thomas, Thomas, Thomas), b. Stow, Mass., abt. 1698; m. Mary ——.

Middlesex Co. Deeds—vol. 28; 110. Jonathan of Shrewsbury, yeoman, for £8 from Gersham Keyes, 40 acres in Shrewsbury, drawn by William Johnson, Jr., Sept. 19, 1720 (Abraham Moulton and Thomas Hall), witnesses. He was married to his Mary and gone to Shrewsbury before his father made the move to Chelmsford.

From Ward's history of Shrewsbury: "Foster, Jonathan, on house lot No. 44, in 1729; ad. to chh. here in 1727; wife's name Mary, and ad. to chh., 1735. Their ch., as recorded here, were: 1. Jonathan, b. June 6, 1719, and ad. to chh. here in 1743; 2. Mary, b. Nov. 24, 1721. 3. Benjamin, b. March 1, 1724; bapt. at his father's house in 1727, and d. the same year, say the chh. records. 4. Thomas, b. Sept. 2, 1726. 5. Hezekiah, b. Aug. 28, 1728. 6. Beulah, b. Feb. 13, 1731; 7. Jemima, bapt. July 8, 1733. 8. Kezia, bapt. June 4, 1736. There is no death on the town record of the name of Foster for the family was set off to Lancaster." I found the record of Jonathan's admission to the church, but there is no record of his death or removal. I think that previous to 1724 there was no complete record kept, except of marriages, additions and baptisms. From the records of the church in Shrewsbury the following is taken: "Nov. 5, 1727. Jonathan Foster was admitted to full church privilege."

Jonathan Foster with others, at their request in 1752, were set off from Shrewsbury to Lancaster. This property also joined Holden.

Will—In the name of God Amen this Fourteenth day of December Anno Domino one thousand seven hundred and forty three I Jonathan Foster of Shrewsbury in the County of Worcester In the Province of the Massachusetts Bay in New

England Husbandman being at this time of sound mind and memory praised be God. But knowing myself in a mortal state as to my body. Wherefore I do make and ordain this to be my last will and Testament. Principally and first of all I commit my Immortal soul into the hands of God that gave it. And my body I Recommend to the Earth to be buried in a Christian manner nothing doubting but at the General resurrection I shall receive the same again by the mighty power of God. And as such worldly Estate God has bestowed upon me I give demise and Dispose of in the following manner and for once. First I order that my just debts and funeral charges be paid.—— Imprimis, I give unto Mary my dearly beloved wife the Improvement of all my Estate so long as she remains my widow —— Item. I give unto my son Jonathan Foster five shillings. Item. I give unto my son Thomas Foster Twenty pounds. Item. I give unto my son Hezekiah Foster Five pounds. Item. I give unto my daughter Mary Foster Five pounds Item. I give unto my daughter Beulah Foster Five pounds. Item. I give unto my daughter Jemima Foster Five pounds. Item. I give unto my daughter Keziah Foster Five pounds. Furthermore it is my will that if after this distribution is made any Estate be found that was mine that it be equally divided among the Heirs; and that if there be not enough for each to receive what is assigned, then an abatement to be made upon each according to their proportion given. And I do hereby constitute, authorize make and ordain my trusty and well beloved wife Mary Foster of Shrewsbury in the county and province above said to be sole Executrix to this my last will and settlement, and do hereby utterly disallowe, revoke, and disannul all, and every other former settlement, Legacies and Bequests, and Executors by me in any way before named willed and Bequeathed, Ratifying and confirming this and no other to be my last will and Testament. In witness whereof I have here unto set my hand and the day and year above written

Signed Sealed published Pronounced.
and declared by the said Jonathan
Foster as his last will and
testament in the presence of us
John Baker S Jonathan Foster
her
Judith I. Baker
mark
Job Cushing S

He d. in S. in 1743. Res., Shrewsbury, Mass.

4072. i. JONATHAN, b. June 6, 1719; m. Mrs. Bathsheba Crosby, Betty Hazen, Thankful Harington and Mercy Towne.
4073. ii. MARY, b. Nov. 24, 1721.
4074. iii. BENJAMIN, b. March 1, 1724; bapt. 1727, and d. 1727—church records.
4075. iv. THOMAS, b. Sept. 2, 1726.
4076. v. HEZEKIAH, b. Aug. 28, 1728; m. Hannah ——
4077. vi. BEULAH, b. Feb 13, 1731.
4078. vii. JEMIMA, bapt. July 8, 1733.
4079. viii. KEZIAH, b. June 4, 1736.

3955. JOHN FOSTER (Jonathan, Thomas, Thomas, Thomas), b. Stow, Mass., abt. 1705; m. Eunice ——.

Of all the branches of the Foster family this one, of which John and Eunice are the head, have caused me more trouble than any other half dozen lines. The first that was known of John, before his connection with the main line was made out, was his appearance in Stow, Mass., with Eunice. There he had three children born, Joseph, John and Abigail. The records of deeds of Middlesex county, at East Cambridge, show that about this time he was disposing of his property there on the Marlboro line, with water power privileges, given to John Wilt, of Marlboro (old Lynn family). The highway and adjoining estates he parts with to Thomas Gibson, and the same reservations and Hapgood's walls seem to point to an original estate, which probably formerly was his wife's estate in Stow, where the new project to start mills, perhaps iron mills, on the Marlboro line, by Hathorn and John Wilt, was on tap. In looking up Hathorn's for a Baltimore merchant lately, I struck the plans of the Lynn blacksmiths, some of which go to Wilmington, some to Marlboro, and John Wilt and a Goodale have land owned in Stow and Marlboro, on what was called the Alcock plantation. I find our John and Eunice had sold to John Wilt, by some reference in one deed I handled, for the purpose of improving a mill privilege on the land bordering the Assabet brook (Elizabeth river) property. When he sold, in 1733 was it, he reserves those rights. The iron business had a boom in that section in connection with William Russell and others, about that date, and farmers, gave up good land to pay assessments in a new concern, in all sorts of supplies, and the paper of the company seems to get into court later when they couldn't pay up. I have a long list of the Hathorn associates somewhere that include many Marlboro and Stow names later.

Stow town clerk, July 29th, in a letter, says he has looked the proprietors' books through and found no land at all owned by the name of John Foster. So it is inevitable that he bought of Cornet John Darby the two rights he sold to Gibson, and he must have lost the rights in any land owned by Thomas Foster.

John and Eunice next appear in Hassanamisco, incorporated that year, 1735, as Grafton, Worcester county, which was settled by many people from Stow and towns in that vicinity. The first record there is on the old Hassanamisco church book and reads as follows:

"Sept. 12, 1736, he was received in full communion by the Grafton church. His wife, Eunice, was admitted Feb. 17, 1742." He was selectman 1736-7-8, while he resided there, and was a prominent resident,* for in "seating the meeting-house," that is, in assigning seats in the church edifice, which was done by a committee appointed for that purpose, he was given the second seat, which shows that there were but few others more prominent. Two more children were born to the couple, and are found of record in the church and town books in Grafton—viz.: Jacob and Lydia. About 1736 there was quite an exodus from Grafton to Hardwick, then known as Wombernesiscook by the Indians, where he was one of the first settlers. There he owned 200 acres of land, part of which is located where the bridge now stands and where the woolen factories are located in that part of Hardwick,† incorporated twenty-four years after the present town was incorporated—in 1761—as Ware, Hampshire county. Thus it will be seen that his property was located in two towns. At this time the property in Hardwick was in Hampshire county, incorporated in 1662, and later in Worcester county, incorporated in 1731. On moving to Hardwick he took a prominent part in the affairs of the town and church. In 1740 and 1741 he was chosen selectman and town clerk. He seems to have returned to Grafton, and the vacancies in office were filled Nov. 23, 1741; but he bought land again in Hardwick Sept. 9, 1742, and is described as of Hardwick in the inventory of his estate Feb. 27, 1745-6, which estate was divided Aug. 4, 1751, between his children, Joseph, John, Jacob, Jonathan, Abigail and Lydia.

One branch of the family remained in the vicinity of Ware, and they state|| that their ancestor "Jacob" (this is a mistake, it should be John), "one of the first settlers in Ware, was born in Bridgewater. He lived in Ware, just over the bridge, near where the woolen factories are now. He was descended from the Pilgrims. He owned 200 acres of land near where Ware Village now stands. He raised a family of two sons and three daughters. His eldest son, Joseph, left his father and settled in the north part of the town on a farm. There he remained about thirty years; had four sons and moved to Barnard, Vt., where the family was well received and held responsible positions. John, his eldest son, was captain; another captain, and another representative for thirteen years."

I have endeavored to ascertain the exact date of death of John Foster. The town records of Grafton, Ware, Hardwick and Brookfield, have been examined but without success. Frederick D. Ruggles, of Hardwick, subsequently made a very thorough investigation and wrote as follows:

"I have looked for John Foster and wife, Eunice. I find by looking over old deeds wherein he bought land in the southwest part of Hardwick, near Ware, on his second return to Hardwick, which you are probably advised of. No record of his death I am able to find in Ware, or by any other tradition, or in the old Baptist Church yard, near his possessions. John Foster seems to be a man of mark in our early settlement. He was a town clerk and selectman; T. C. in 1740-41, and selectman at the same time."

Joseph Foster, aged about sixteen; Lydia Foster, aged fourteen; Abigail Foster, aged thirteen; Jacob, aged nine; John Foster, aged about fifteen; Jonathan Foster, aged five, children of John Foster, late of Hardwick; guardian appointed; does not give the mother's name. Joseph Wilder, Judge of Prob., 1745, Hardwick. —Worcester Probate Records.

* See History of Grafton, by Fred C. Pierce, the writer.
† See Paige's History of Hardwick, Mass.
|| Frank B. Foster, Riverside, Mass.

He d. in Hardwick, in 1745. Res., Stow, Grafton and Hardwick, Mass.

4080. i. JOSEPH, b. Stow, June 3, 1730; m. Susannah Roberts.
4081. ii. JOHN, b. 1731.
4082. iii. JACOB, b. Sept. 18, 1737, in Grafton. He was not in Rev. army from Mass.
4083. iv. LYDIA, b. Sept. 17, 1735, in Grafton.
4084. v. ABIGAIL, b. 1732; m., Feb. 28, 1754, in H., Jacob Pepper, of North Brookfield.
4085. vi. JONATHAN, b. in Ware, Aug. 18, 1740; m. Hannah Thayer.

3962. SAMUEL FOSTER (John, John, Thomas, Thomas), b. Plymouth, Mass., m., 1722, Margaret Tilden, dau. of Nathaniel; m., 2d, Margaret Wardsworth.

Samuel Foster, of Kingston, administrator; appointed Sept. 7, 1778, estate set off to Samuel Foster (son of John Foster, late of Kingston, deceased, who was the eldest son of the said Samuel, deceased), Charles Foster, Robert Foster, Margaret Foster, Sarah Tilden, widow of Joseph, late of Scituate, deceased, and Lydia Foster; no further relationship given.—Plymouth Probate.

In 1742 he purchased the estate of Joshua Drew, administrator of the estate of his father, Nicholas Drew. After having possession of it for one year he again resold it to Joshua. He d. 1778. Res., Plymouth and Kingston, Mass.

4086. i. JOHN, b. 1724; d. young.
4087. ii. SAMUEL, b. 1726.
4088. iii. MARGARET, b. 1728; unm. in 1785.
4089. iv. CHARLES, b. 1730; m. Sylvina Delano.
4090. v. HANNAH, b. 1732; d. before 1778.
4091. vi. SARAH, b. 1735; m. Joseph Tilden. Res., Scituate. He d. before 1778.
4092. vii. ROBERT, b. 1737; m. Elizabeth ——.
4093. viii. LYDIA, b. 1739; d. unm. 1795. Lydia Foster, of Kingston, single woman; will proved Oct. 5, 1795; written Aug. 2, 1781; all the estate given to her sister, Margaret Foster.

3964. JUDGE THOMAS FOSTER (John, John, Thomas, Thomas), b. Plymouth, Mass., March 19, 1705; m., Nov. 25, 1725, Lois Fuller, dau. of Jabez, of Barnstable; m., 2d, 1744, Mary Morton, of Plymouth.

Like his ancestors, he learned the trade of blacksmith, and was a deacon. He represented Plymouth in the General Court many years, commencing in 1741. He was a justice of the peace and quorum, and a judge of the Court of Common Pleas.

He died of small pox in 1777. He was a deacon of the church, and often speculated in real estate. He represented Plymouth for many years in the General Court, and in 1765 received instructions from his constituents to govern his action on the exciting questions of that time. At the beginning of the Revolution he continued loyal to the crown, and according to Sabine went with the British army to Halifax. He must have returned the following year, for his death is recorded in 1777. Many other citizens of Plymouth sympathized with Mr. Foster, as the records show.

In 1752 he secured the Silas West property on an execution, but soon sold it. In 1739 he owned fifty feet of land, having purchased it of Nicholas Drew. He sold it the same year to Judah West. In 1734 he purchased of his brother John the lot of land on which the Plymouth Rock House, now stands, and erected a house thereon. In 1743 he purchased property of Winslow S. Holmes, and sold it in 1757 to James Carver. The same year (1743) he purchased a residence of Ebenezer Doggett, and sold it the following year to John Kempton. In 1743 he purchased a lot of James Shurtleff and sold it in 1766 to Abiel Shurtleff. In 1762, for assisting in building the causeway and bridge, he had given him a parcel of land, which he sold that year to Barnabas Hedge.

Sabine, in his "Loyalists," says: "Foster, Thomas, Esquire, of Plymouth, Mass. He represented that town in the General Court several years, and in 1765 instructions were furnished him to govern his course on the exciting questions of the time. Aside from his political preferences, he was esteemed by his townsmen for his attention and fidelity to the municipal and civil concerns intrusted to his care. His father, Deacon John Foster, was also a representative from Plymouth, and pursued an independent line of conduct in that relation, never accepting of executive favors. His son, Thomas, was a graduate of Harvard University, and instructed a school at Plymouth. His grandson, Thomas, was an officer of a bank at Charleston, S. C., and died there in 1808, aged fifty-eight. Branches of his family settled in Middleboro and Kingston, Mass., and in Norfolk, Va. Mr. Foster accompanied the British army to Halifax in 1776."

Mary Foster, of Plymouth; will probated Dec. 12, 1781; written July 27, 1780 She gives to the children of her daughter, Elizabeth Jackson, deceased, and her daughter, Salome Dimon; daughters Mary and Eunice, sons Seth and Philemon. She appoints her daughter, Mary Foster, executrix.

He d. 1777. Res., Plymouth, Mass., and Halifax, N. S.

4094. i. THOMAS, b. 1727; m. Mercy Witherell.
4095. ii. ELISHA, b. 1730.
4096. iii. GERSHOM, b. Sept. 23, 1733; d. young.
4097. iv. LOIS, b. 1735; m. Josiah Sturtevant and Samuel Savery.
4098. v. DEBORAH, b. 1737; m., 1756, Samuel Doggett, son of Ebenezer. Ch.: 1. Deborah, b. 1758.
4099. vi. JOHN, b. 1739.
4100. vii. GERSHOM, b. 1740.
4101. viii. HANNAH, b. 1742.
4102. ix. MARY, b. 1745; d. young.
4103. x. ELIZABETH, b. 1747; m., 1768, Nathaniel Jackson. He was son of Thomas, senior. Ch.: 1. Nathaniel; m. Deborah Harlow. 2. Hezekiah, b. 1770; m. Sarah Nicolsen. 3. Betsey; m. William Harlow. 4. Henry, b. 1774. The wife, Elizabeth, died, for in 1776 he m. Martha Bartlett.
4104. xi. SALOME, b. 1749; m. Thomas Dimon.
4105. xii. MARY, b. 1751; unm. in 1781.
4106. xiii. SETH, b. 1753; d. young.
4107. xiv. JOB, b. 1755.
4108. xv. EUNICE, b. 1757.
4109. xvi. SETH, b. 1758; m. —— ——.
4110. xvii. PHILEMON, b. 1760.
4111. xviii. SUSANNA, b. 1762.
4112. xix. EUNICE, b. 1764; m., 1780, James Prince, son of Thomas Prince. Res., Providence, R. I. Ch.: 1. Polly, b. 1784. 2. Thomas, b. 1786. 3. Lydia, b. 1788.

3967. NATHANIEL FOSTER (John, John. Thomas, Thomas), b. Plymouth, Mass., 1711; m., 1735. Mercy Thacher, of Middleboro, Mass., dau. of Peter; m., 2d, December, 1748, Mrs. Abigail (Woodman) Billings, of Little Compton. She was dau. of Edward and Margaret Billings, of Little Compton, and m. at Little Compton, R. I., Sept. 22, 1734. Richard Billings, b. 1674; d. Nov. 20, 1748. Abigail was b. Aug. 23, 1714.

He sold his double lot, with the old house on it, to Samuel Ellis, who occupied the easterly half of it, in 1771. In 1734 he purchased what is known as the Durfey house of Nathaniel Morton.

Nathaniel Foster, of Middleboro; will probated Nov. 20, 1793; written May 7, 1791; sons, Nathaniel and Gershom; children of son John Foster, deceased, namely, William and Peter Foster and Elizabeth Dunham. (This grandson, William, is called Jr. in the papers.) He also mentions his daughters, Mary Foster, Mercy Russell and Abigail Bushope. He also mentions his grandchildren, children of his daughter Terry, deceased, also daughter, Martin. He appoints his sons Nathaniel and Gershom executors. In another paper, filed wtih the case, I find that James Washburn, attorney and guardian of Betsey Terry, Luther Washburn and Hannah, his wife; Abiel Perry, grandchildren and heirs to said Nathaniel Foster, appeals from a certian decree, filed in this case.—Plymouth Probate.

He d. October, 1793. Res., Middleboro, Mass.

4113. i. MARY, b. 1736; m., 1757, Thomas Foster, of Marshfield (see).
4114. ii. MERCY, b 1737; m., 1757, John Russell, and 2d, 1798. William Sever. He (Russell) came from Scotland and settled in Plymouth where he married. Ch.: 1. John, b. 1758. 2. James, b. 1760. 3. Thomas, b. 1761. 4. Mercy, b. 1763; m. William Jackson. 5. Abigail, b. 1766. 6. Nancy, b. 1767; m. John Sever, of Kingston. 7. Nathaniel, b. 1769. 8. Jane, b. 1773; m. James Sever, of Kingston. 9. George, b. 1776. 10. Charles, b. ——. Russell died, and Mercy m., 2d, 1798; Sever was son of Nicholas.
4115. iii. NATHANIEL, b. 1740; d. before 1751.

4116. iv. HANNAH, b. 1743; d. before 1749.
4117. v. PETER, b. 1745.
4118. vi. JOHN, b. ——; m. Elizabeth Rider.
4119. vii. HANNAH, b. 1749; d. before 1755.
4120. viii. SARAH, b. 1750; m. —— Martin.
4121. ix. NATHANIEL, b. Sept. 28, 1751; m. Lydia Barnaby.
4122. x. ABIGAIL, b. 1753; m. —— Bishope.
4123. xi. GERSHOM, b. 1754.
4124. xii. HANNAH, b. 1755; m. Luther Washburne.
4125. xiii. BETTY, b. 1757; m. —— Terry.

3969. JOSIAH FOSTER (Josiah, John, Thomas, Thomas), b. Pembroke, Mass., m., July 29, 1725, Mary Bonney. She d.; m., 2d, Marshfield, Mass., Feb. 10, 1756, Elizabeth Carver. She d. 1802. Joseph Foster, of Pembroke, will probated March 25, 1780, written Aug. 23, 1779; wife Elizabeth. He bequeathed money to the children of his daughter, Sarah Chamberlain, deceased; daughter, Mary Mackfarland; children of his daughter, Margaret Crooker, deceased; children of his daughter, Abigail Whitten, deceased; grandson, Nathaniel Chamberlain. He appoints Nathaniel Chamberlain, his grandson, his executor.

Elizabeth Foster, widow of Pembroke; will written Jan. 14, 1784; probated June 28, 1802.. She mentions in her will her sister, Lydia Phillips and her (Lydia's) daughter, Lydia; sister, Huldy Sampson, wife of Abraham Sampson; niece, Hipthsada Sampson (Gideon Sampson's daughter): sister. Keziah Sampson. She mentions Mary Bates, wife of Gamaliel Bates, the daughter of her brother, Reuben Carver; she also mentions her three nieces, Lydia Rickett, Abigail Fuller and Mercy King, daughter of her late sister, Deborah King. She appoints Amos Phillips, son of her sister, Lydia Phillips, executor, but he declines.

He d. 1780. Res., Pembroke, Mass.

4126. i. SARAH, b. ——; m. Nathaniel Chamberlain. Nathaniel Chamberlain who m. Sarah Foster, of Pembroke, located in East Bridgewater, where she d. 1765. She was b. 1725; d. 1814. Ch. by Sarah: 1. Nathaniel, b. 1745; m. Eleanor Whitman. 2. Sarah, b. 1747. 3. Ruth, b. 1751. 4. Mercy, b. 1754. 5. Lydia, b. 1756. 6. Joseph, b. 1761. 7. Benjamin, b. 1762. Rem. to Maine. 8. Josiah, b. 1764; m. Lucy Pratt. Res., Pembroke.
4127. ii. MARY, b. ——; m. —— McFarland.
4128. iii. MARGARET, b. ——; m. ——Crooker.
4129. iv. ABIGAIL, b. ——; m. ——Whitten.

3970. ISAAC FOSTER (Josiah, John, Thomas, Thomas), b. Pembroke, Mass., Aug. 5, 1705; m. July 6, 1732, Frances Joslyn. Res., Pembroke, Mass.

4130. i. DAVID, b. ——; m. Experience Randall.

3978. JOSEPH FOSTER (Joseph, John, Thomas, Thomas), b. Sandwich, Mass., Sept. 19, 1698; m. Elizabeth Milton, dau. of Edward and Sarah (Mantor), b. Jan. 6, 1701. Res., Tisbury and Barnstable, Mass.

4131. i. MILTON, b. April 10, 1728; m. Jean ——.
4132. ii. EDWARD, b. Oct. 22, 1729; m. Martha ——.
4133. iii. WILLIAM, b. Nov. 7, 1733; m. Deborah Lewis.
4134. iv. NATHANIEL, b. abt. 1740; m. Lydia Frisbee.
4135. v. JOSEPH, b. abt. 1744; m. ——.

3979. BENJAMIN FOSTER (Joseph, John, Thomas, Thomas), b. Sandwich, Mass., Nov. 16, 1699; m., Dec. 31, 1724, Mina Tobey, at Sandwich. He d. ——. Res., Tisbury, Mass.

4136. i. ELIZABETH, b. Jan. 26, 1726.
4137. ii. REMEMBER, b. Sept. 22, 1728.
4138. iii. THANKFUL, b. Sept. 12, 1733.
4139. iv. JONATHAN, b. Aug. 2, 1735.
4140. v. BENJAMIN, b. July 9, 1748; m. Anna Dunham.

3980. WILLIAM FOSTER (Joseph, John, Thomas, Thomas), b. Sandwich, Mass., Nov. 31, 1702, m., 1726, Hannah Rider. Res., Sandwich, Mass.

4141. i. WILLIAM, b. ——.
4142. ii. JOSEPH, b. ——.
4143. iii. MARY, b. ——.

3982. JOHN FOSTER (Joseph, John, Thomas, Thomas), b. Sandwich, Mass., April 12, 1705; m., in Sandwich, Mass., Joanna Brown, b. 1696; d. Feb. 9, 1771.

Will—From probate records of Barnstable Co., book 13, p. 449. In the Name of God, Amen. I, John Foster of Sandwich in the County of Barnstable in the Province of the Massachusetts Bay in New England, Sadler. Being under decay of Body but thro' divine Goodness of sound mind and memory, and mindful of approaching Death Do make this my Last Will and Testament and first I recommend my soul to the mercy of God thro' Jesus Christ, & my Body to a decent Burial at the discretion of my Executrix hereafter named, and as to my Worldly Estate I give Devise & dispose as follows: Imprimis. I give and bequeath to my Beloved wife Joanna Foster and to her heirs & assigns forever, my Dwelling house & all my other Buildings & all my Lands and all my Real Estate whatever & wherever and all my Cash Credits Bonds Notes of hand, Quick stock, Household Goods & all other my Personal Estate whatever & whersoever she paying my Just Debts and funeral charges.

Finally. I constitute and appoint my wife Joanna Sole Executrix of this my Last Will and Testament hereby revoking all former Wills by me at any time heretofore made. & declaring this to be my last Will & Testament. In witness whereof I have hereunto set my hand & seal this fourteenth day of April A. D. 1769 thousand seven hundred and sixty-nine.

Signed, sealed Published
& Declared by the sd — John Foster. (L. S.)
John Foster as and for his
last Will & Testament
in presence of us.
Nathaniel Bassett.
N. Bourn.
Abr. Williams.

Probated Sept. 27, 1769.

A true copy of the record.

He d. Sept. 14, 1769, ae. sixty-five. Res., s. p. Sandwich, Mass. These deaths are from Sandwich grave stones. He was a saddler by trade.

3983. NATHAN FOSTER (Joseph, John, Thomas, Thomas), b. Jan. 3, 1708, Barnstable, Mass. Nathan Foster resided in the Timothy Crocker house at West Barnstable. He was a hair dresser and wig maker by trade, and died aged. He married 1st, Mary Lothrop, May 21, 1753; 2d, Mercy Smith, 1766. Ch. b. in Barnstable. His will is dated Oct. 19, 1814; mentions his daughter Mercy, the widow of Ephraim Crocker; sons Nathan and John, daughter Elizabeth, and the heirs of his three children, Thomas, James and Mary Crocker, all deceased. He d. 1814. Res., New Barnstable, Mass.

4144. i. ABIGAIL, b. Sept. 24, 1756; d. young.
4145. ii. JOHN BURSLEY, b. June 11, 1758; d. young.
4146. iii. MARY, b. Oct. 4, 1765; m. —— Crocker.
4147. iv. JAMES, b. Feb. 8, 1767; m. ——.
4148. v. MERCY, b. March 7, 1768; m. Ephraim Crocker.
4149. vi. THOMAS, b. March 4, 1771; m. ——.
4150. vii. NATHAN, b. March 19, 1773; m. ——.
4151. viii. ABIGAIL, b. Jan. 4, 1775; d. young.
4152. ix. JOSEPH, b. July 16, 1776; d. young.
4153. x. JOHN, b. July 15, 1778; m. ——.
4154. xi. ABIGAIL, b. May 6, 1780; d. young.
4155. xii. ELIZABETH, b. Feb. 16, 1783; unm. in 1814.

3987. SOLOMON FOSTER (Joseph, John, Thomas, Thomas), b., Barnstable Mass., Sept. 4, 1714; m. in Sandwich, July 15, 1739, Rebecca Nye. He was town clerk and much engaged in public affairs at Sandwich, and later moved to Brookfield, Mass., where he died. His will is on file in the Worcester Probate Court office. He was of Brookfield, probated Dec. 27, 1791; mentions, wife Rebecca, sons Bryant, Elisha, Lemuel, and daughter Abigail Dow. He d. in Palmer, December, 1791. Res., Sandwich and Brookfield, Mass.

4156. i. BRYANT, b. July 5, 1741; m. Thankful Blackwell.
4157. ii. ABIGAIL, b. Dec. 30, 1750; m. —— Dow.
4158. iii. WILLIAM, b. Feb. 4, 1753; prob. d. before 1791, not mentioned in father's will.

4159. iv. ELISHA, b. Oct. 14, 1759; m. Eunice ——.
4160. v. LEMUEL, b. April 14, 1762.

3901 DEACON JAMES FOSTER (Chillingsworth, John, Thomas, Thomas) b. Jan. 6, 1706, in Harwich, Mass.; m., July 10, 1729, Lydia, dau. of Major Edward Winslow, of Rochester, Mass. She was b. Sept. 8, 1709; d. Jan. 7, 1770, ae. sixty. He m., 2d, Phoebe Axtell, of Berkley, published May 11, 1771. James, like his ancestors, was a blacksmith and deacon. He was also selectman, town clerk and town treasurer, resided in Rochester till 1774, when he removed to Athol with his son, John, and died there about 1788.

Will—I James Foster of Athol in the county of Worcester and commonwealth of Massachusetts gentleman being advanced in years but through God's goodness of sound and Disposing mind and memory and calling to mind the uncertainty of life do make and ordain this my last will and testament recommending my Soul to the hands of a merciful God that gave it and my body to be buried in a decent and Christian manner after my decease at the discretion of my executor hereafter named —as to such worldly personal estate wherewith it hath pleased God to bless me with in this world I give and dispose of the Same in the following manner Imprimis I give and bequeath to my beloved wife Phebe all the goods of all Sorts and kinds that she brought to me after marriage with me & that to be in room and stead of her thirds in my personal estate which is only on condition that she quit her right in my personal estate—Also I give to my wife Phebe the lawful right of dower. Item I give & bequeath to my three Daughters in Equal viz Mercy Rider, Mary Paige and Lydia Haskell all my indoor moveables except those before mentioned goods belonging to my wife Phebe—Also I give to my Daughter Mercy Rider three pounds four shillings lawful money to be paid by my executor after my decease Item I give to my three Sons Chillingsworth, James and Edward Foster Six shillings Each in full of their portion; Also I give to my son Nathan Foster six pounds eight shillings lawful money in full or his portion Item I give my wearing apparel to my five sons to be equally Divided amongst them after my decease. Item I give and bequeath to my son John Foster all my personal Estate Whatsoever or wheresoever the same is or may be found, that I have not in this my will Disposed of; also my Debts, Dues or Demands that shall be Due to me at my Decease and I order my kind son John to pay all my Debts and funeral charges and the charge of settling my estate Likewise I appoint my son, John Foster, as my executor to this my last will and testament. In witness whereof I have hereunto set my hand & Seal this Sixth Day of October Anno Domini 1784 and Eighth year of the Independence of America. James Foster [Seal]

(Edward and Magdalin Winslow, parents of Kenelm Winslow, of Droitwich, Worcestershire, England, had five sons and three daughters. The sons all came to this country. 1. Edward, b. Oct. 19, 1594; m., May 16, 1618, Elizabeth Barker, who died at Plymouth, March 24, 1621. He and his wife came on the "Mayflower" in 1620 to Plymouth. He m. 2d, May 12, 1621, Susanna, widow of William White, of the "Mayflower." (She was sister to Edward and Dr. Samuel Fuller who came of the "Mayflower.") 2. John, b April, 1596. Came in the "Fortune" November, 1621; m. Mary, dau. of James Chilton (a Mayflower passenger). Removed to Boston; was a merchant there, March 1655 and d. there, 1674, ae. seventy-eight. 3. Eleanor, b. April, 1598. 4. Kenelm, b. April 29, 1599; m. Elinor Newton, widow of John Adams. 5. Gilbert, b. October, 1600. Came with his brother Edward in the "Mayflower;" went back to England and died there before 1660. 6. Elizabeth, b. March 8, 1601. 7. Magdalin, b. Dec. 26, 1604. 8. Josiah, b. Feb. 11, 1605-6. Came to N. E. with his brother Kenelm; m. Margaret, dau. of Thomas Brown; settled in Marshfield. He d. 1674 and his widow d. 1683.

The descendants of Kenelm Winslow are as follows: Kenelm Winslow, son of Edward and brother of Governor Edward Winslow, of Plymouth, was born in Droitwich, Worcestershire, England, April 29, 1599, and came to New England in 1629, resided at Plymouth until about 1641, when he went to Marshfield. He m. June, 1634, Elinor, widow of John Adams, whose maiden name was Elinor Newton. She d. Dec. 5, 1681. He was a farmer and joiner; represented Marshfield at General Court 8 years and held sundry minor offices. He d. at Salem, Mass., Sept. 12, 1672, ae. seventy-three ("He resorted to Salem for medical aid having been long sick.") Ch.: (a) Kenelm, b. abt. 1636; m. Mary Warden, dau. of Peter Warden, of Yarmouth who d. Sept. 22, 1688, in her forty-eighth year. He m., 2d, Demaris ——, who survived him. He d. Nov. 11, 1715, in the seventy-ninth year of his age, in Harwich and his headstone stands in a cemetery near his home but within the easterly border of Dennis, Mass. Ch.: b. in Harwich. 1. Kenelm, b. abt. 1667; d. at Harwich, March 10, 1729, ae. sixty-one. 2. Josiah, b. Nov. 7, 1669. Captain, d. at Freetown April 3, 1761. 3. Thomas, b. abt. 1672; d. April, 1689 at sixteen. 4. Samuel, b. abt. 1674. 5. Mercy, b. abt. 1676; m. Melitiah White, of Rochester; m., 2d, Thomas Jenkins, of Barnstable. 6. Nathaniel, b. abt. 1678. Res., Rochester, Mass.; Little Compton, Mass.; Middleboro, Mass., and removed to Maine. 7. Edward, b. Jan. 30, 1681; m. Sarah ——. He resided at Rochester, was a farmer and egnaged in making and forging of iron; he was a selectman, town clerk, town treasurer, justice of the peace and of the quorum; also major of militia and was generally designated by his militia title. He d. June 25, 1760. Sarah d. Oct. 11, 1767, at eighty-five. Ch.: 1. Edward, b. Nov. 6, 1703; m., Hannah, dau. of his Uncle Kenelm Winslow, of Harwich, Dec. 14, 1728, who d. Sept. 23, 1745. He m., 2d, Rachel, dau. of his Uncle Josiah Winslow, of Freetown, May 1, 1746, who d. May 1, 1746. He m., 3d, Mrs. Susanna Winslow, of Dighton, pub. Aug. 9, 1767. He d. May 7, 1780. 2. Mehitable, b. May 6, 1705; m. Col. Thomas Winslow, son of her Uncle Kenelm, of Harwich, Feb. 12, 1722-3. 3. Sarah, b. 1707; m. Thomas Lincoln, who d. June 15, 1730; m., 2d, James Whitcomb, May 31, 1731. Removed to Western (now Warren), and was living there in 1771. 4. Lydia, b. Sept. 8, 1709; m., Deacon James Foster, July 10, 1729. 5. Mercy, b. Sept. 11, 1712; m. Chillingsworth Foster, Esq. 6. Thankful, b. April 2, 1715; m. Josephus Hammond, April 10, 1735. 8. Demaris, b. ——; m. Jonathan Small, of Harwich, July 30, 1713. 9. Elizabeth, b. ——; m. Andrew Clark, of Harwich, Aug. 9, 1711. 10. Eleanor, b. ——; m. Shubach Hamlin, of Barnstable, March 25, 1719. 11. John, b. abt. 1701; deacon in Rochester church and d. there 1755. (b) Ellen, b. abt. 1638; m. Samuel Baker, 1656; d. Aug. 27, 1676. (c) Nathaniel, b. abt. 1639. (d) Job, b. abt. 1641.]

4161. i. MERCY, b. July 4, 1730; m. Seth Rider, of Rochester; pub. May 2, 1747. Their daughter Thankful m. Oct. 27, 1774, Antipas Rice, of Hardwick, Mass.

4162. ii. MARY, b. April 11, 1732; m. Col. Timothy Paige, of Hardwick, Oct. 24, 1754; d. July 2, 1825, ea. ninety-three. Paige was b. May 24, 1727, and was son of Deacon Christopher and Elizabeth (Reed), of Hardwck. Christopher Paige, Feb. 10, 1691, was the first deacon of Hardwick, where he d. March 10, 1774; was son of Nathaniel Paige, who was in Roxbury in 1686, but removed to Billerica in 1688, and was also one of the purchasers of Hardwick, Mass. He d. Aug. 22, 1791, at Hardwick, although the date on his gravestone is Aug. 26, 1791. He was a representative to the General Court of Boston in 1781, and was Col. of the Fourth regiment of local militia of Worcester county, Ebenezer Newell being lieutenant-colonel and Asa Danforth major. Their ch. were: 1. Lydia, b. Sept. 15, 1755, Hardwick; d. July 8, 1810; m., November, 1778, Deacon Thomas Fuller, farmer. Removed to Hardwick, Vt. They had a son, Hon. Austin Fuller, of Saratoga, N. Y. 2. Timothy, b. Feb. 16, 1757; d. Oct. 29, 1821. He was a civil magistrate, selectman eighteen years; assessor, twenty-four years; delegate to the convention at Concord, October, 1779; member of committee of correspondence, inspection and safety in 1777 and 1779; justice of the peace May 9, 1803; representative to the General Court, seventeen years, viz: from 1805 to 1821; and delegate to the convention held in Boston, November, 1820, for revising the constitution of Massachusetts. He was in the Revolutionary war. He married at Hardwick, Jan. 20, 1780, Mary Robinson, b. Dec. 3, 1758, Hardwick, dau. of Thomas and Mary Warner, of H. She d. March 29, 1836, at Hardwick Their son was Rev. Lucius Robinson Paige, D.D., b. March 8, 1802, Hardwick, Mass.; commenced preaching in 1823 and was ordained as Universalist minister in 1825; settled in Springfield in 1826, Rockport in 1830, and Cambridge in 1832, where he remained till 1839, when he resigned his pastoral charge and engaged in literary pursuits. He received the honorary degree of A. M. from Harvard in 1850, and of D. D. from Tufts college in 1861. The following is list of his literary works as given in Allibone's Dictionary. 1. Selections from Eminent Commentators, 1833, 12mo. 2. Address at the Centennial Celebration at Hardwick, Mass.,Nov. 15, 1838. 3. Questions on Select Portions of the Gospels, 1838. 4. Commentary on the New Testament, 6 vols., 12mo; i. 1844, Gospels; ii. 1845, Gospels; iii. 1848, Acts; iv. 1857, Romans; v. 1867, I. and II. Corinthians; vi. Galatians to Jude. 5. Address before Amicable Lodge Oct. 18, 1855; Papers in the Universalist Expositor, Universalist Quarterly, etc.

Mr. Paige was for some years employed upon a history of Cambridge, Mass. He has been a civil magistrate since 1843; was elected town clerk of Cambridge in 1839, and was city clerk from 1840 to 1855, when he resigned that office and became cashier of the Cambridge bank, which office he also resigned in 1860; was reëlected in 1863, but again resigned in 1864. He was treasurer of the Cambridge Savings Bank, 1855 to 1871. He married at Brookfield, Mass., Sept. 14, 1826, Clarinda Richardson, b. June 28, 1805, Brookfield, dau. of Ezekiel and Sarah (Rice), of B. She d. Aug. 29, 1833, Cambridge, Mass. He m., 2d, at Cambridge, Oct. 5, 1834, Abby Riggs Whittemore, of Charlestown, Mass, b. in that town Oct. 22, 1807, dau. of Joseph and Comfort (Quiner) and sister of Rev. Thomas Whittemore, D. D. She d. Dec. 23. 1843, Cambridge. He m. 3d, at Brookfield, Mass., Oct. 22, 1845, Lucy (Comins) Richardson, b. March 19, 1799, Massachusetts, dau. of Barnabas and Mary (Bacon), of Charlestown, and widow of Solomon Richardson, of Brookfield. She d. Jan. 3, 1864, Cambridge. He m., 4th, at Worcester, Aug. 2, 1866, Ann Maria (Peck) Brigham, b. Sept. 21, 1806, Portland, Mass. (now Maine), dau. of Robert Maynard and Ann (Allen), of Worcester, and widow of Hon. David Trowbridge Brigham, of Keokuk, Iowa. Her mother was dau. of Hon. Joseph Allen, and sister of Chief Justice Charles Allen and Rev. George Allen, all of Worcester, Mass. For Allen family, see Joseph Parson's Memorial. Res., 1874, Cambridgeport, Mass., where he died. 3. Mary, b. Oct. 19, 1759; d. March 27,, 1834, Stockbridge, Vt.; m., Aug. 23, 1778, Daniel Fay. Res., Hardwick, Vt. They had a son, Cyrus Paige Fay, of Columbus, Ohio. 4. Foster, b. Aug. 29, 1761: d. June 22, 1843; m. Amittai Paige. Res., Bakersfield, Vt. 5. Reed, b. Aug. 30, 1764; d. July 22, 1816: m. Hannah Paige, Hancock, N. H. He graduated at Dartmouth college, 1786 and also received the degreee of A. M. from the same college; read divinity with Rev. Dr. Emmons of Franklin, Mass.; was ordained Sept. 21, 1791, as the first minister of the Congregational church at Hancock, N. H., and continued there till his death. The following is a list of his published discourses as found in Allibone's Dictionary: 1. Ordination Sermon, 1796 2. Ordination Sermon, 1803. 3. Election Sermon, 1805. 4. Fast Sermon, 1812. 5. Sermon, 1815. 6. Oration Fourth of July. He m. at Bedford, Mass., Dec. 25, 1794, Hannah Paige, b. March 11, 1773, Bedford, Mass., dau. of David and Abigail (Jones), of B. 6. Moses, b. Dec. 12, 1765; d. Dec. 28, 1765. 7. Moses, b. Feb. 16, 1767; d. Dec. 5, 1818; m. Lucy Aiken; m., 2d, Mary Aiken. 8. Rebecca, b. Nov. 28, 1768; d. August, 1795; m. Capt. Seth Pierce. She married as second wife, Dec. 22, 1793. Captain Seth Pierce, b. about 1747, son of Ebenezer and Mary (Haskins), of Middleborough, Mass. He d. Feb. 25, 1809, Hardwick, and was buried there. His death occasioned by accidentally sticking a penknife into his knee. He was a private in the company of minute man at Middleborough, commanded by Capt. Nathaniel Wood, and promptly responded at the Lexington alarm; and he afterward commanded a company in the patriot army of the Revolution, which company w s raised in the towns of Northfield, Shutesbury, Leveritt and New Salem. At the reorganization of the militia, in 1781, he received the commission of captain of the local or standing company of infantry at Shutesbury. He was one of the selectmen of Shutesbury four years, and representative to the General Court from Hardwick in 1806. [Pierce Family, p.

70.] He was married four times; first to Huldah Sampson, by whom he had five children; second [name of wife unknown;] third, to Abigal Hinckley, by whom he had one daughter; and fourth, to Mary McFarlin, who survived him; Hardwick, Mass. Child: ——, died in infancy. 9. Thomas, b. Nov. 7, 1770; d. Nov. 21, 1770. 10. Thomas, b. April 20, 1772; d. June 16, 1855, ae. eighty-three, at Compton, C. E; m. June 17, 1798, Susan Warner, b. Oct. 30, 1776, New Braintree, Mass., dau. of Warham, of New Braintree. She d. Dec. 9, 1863, Compton, C. E. Res., Hanover, N. H., New Braintree, Mass., and in 1836 removed to Lenoxville, Canada East, afterward to Compton, C. E. Children born at Hancock, N. H., with the exception of the last three, who were born at New Braintree, Mass. (a) Susan Warner, b. Aug. 10, 1800. Res., 1870, Worcester, Mass.; unm. (b) Hannah Ware, b. June 22, 1802; m., Compton, C. E., Feb. 9, 1843, Samuel Wood, b. in Brattleboro, Vt. He d. Jan. 24, 1848, ae. sixty-one. He was a farmer; removed to Farnham, C. E., when a young man, and resided there the rest of his days; was a magistrate forty years, and member of the provincial parliament. She resided, 1870, Worcester, Mass. (c) Daniel Waldo, b. Feb. 11, 1804, hotel keeper. Res., 1870, Lenoxville, P. Q. (d) George Washington, b. May 18, 1806. Res., Rochester, Mass. (e) Almira Clark, b. Feb. 7, 1808; d. March 11, 1838, Lenoxville, P. Q. (f) Prudence Maria, b. May 15, 1811; m., Worcester, Mass., April 5, 1831, Samuel Allen,Porter, b. Oct. 30, 1807, W., son of —— and Sarah (Patch), of W. Carpenter s. p. Res., 1870, Worcester, Mass. (g) Sophia Foster [1130], b. March 4, 1815; m. March 15, 1836, Austin Willard Bixby. (h) Leticia Duncan, b. May 2, 1817. Res., 1870, Worcester, Mass. (i) Thomas Reed b. June 1, 1821; d. May 25, 1836, Lenoxville, P. Q.; was killed by the kick of a horse the day after the arrival of the family at Lenoxville, at the residence of his brother, Daniel Waldo Paige. (j) Harriet Antoinette, b. July 2, 1825; d. May 5, 1827, New Braintree, Mass. 11. George Washington, b. Aug. 24, 1775; d. Sept. 10, 1834, Coldchester, N. Y.: m. —— Cunningham. Physician s. p. Res., Coldchester, N. Y.

4163. iii. CHILLINGSWORTH, b. Dec. 8, 1733; m., 1st, Margaret Pope, of Dartmouth; m., 2d, Mrs. Sarah Freeman, of Rochester.

4164. iv. JAMES, b. April 17, 1735; d. May 29, 1735.

4165. v. LYDIA, b. April 13, 1736; m. Nathaniel Haskell, of Hardwick; pub. April 3, 1757. He was b. Feb. 26, 1732; d. July 16, 1821. He was a farmer and cordwainer and resided in the northwestern part of Hardwick. Ch: 1. Prince, b. April 26, 1758; d. March 23, 1841. He m. in Hingham, Miss Leah Wilder; removed to Barnard, Vt., and later to Peru, Ohio; was a farmer. Had 10 ch. 2. George, b. April 23, 1761; d. May 25, 1837; was a farmer and shoemaker; inherited the homestead, and d. in Waldoboro, Me.; m. Comfort Knowlton, b. 1761; d. March, 1837. Had 13 ch. 3. Nathaniel, b. July 15, 1762. Res., Brookfield, N. Y. 4. Mary, b. July 1, 1765. 5. David, b. 1769; d. Feb. 22, 1850. Res., Shutesbury, Mass. 6. Lydia, b. ——; m., (pub.), Dec. 24, 1788, Jeremiah Powers. Res., Greenwich, Mass. 7. Jesse, b. ——; m.; had 4 ch. Res., Vermont and Ohio.

4166. vi. JAMES, b. April 12, 1737; m. Mary Lewis.

4167. vii. EDWARD, b. July 3, 1738; m. Deborah Bangs.

4168. viii. NATHAN, b. April 4, 1740; d. Oct. 28, 1742.

4169. ix. JOHN, b. Aug. 5, 1742; d. Sept. 9, 1742.

4170. x. NATHAN, b. Jan. 26, 1743-4; m. Hannah Haskell.

4171. xi. JOHN, b. July 30, 1745; m. Rebecca Paige.

3992. HON. CHILLINGSWORTH FOSTER (Chillingsworth, John, Thomas, Thomas), b. Dec. 25, 1707, Harwich, Mass.; m. Oct. 10, 1730, Mercy Winslow, dau. of Edward, Esq., of Rochester; b. Sept. 11, 1712; d. Jan. 25, 1757; m. 2d, July 7, 1757, Sarah Freeman, of Harwich. He was a son of Chillingsworth and Mercy (Freeman), of Harwich, and brother of Deacon James Foster, who m. Lydia Winslow. He was a blacksmith and resided generally in Harwich, now Brewster, but seems to have been in Barnstable a few years, where two of his children were born in 1735 and 1737. He was selectman of Harwich two years; representative ten years; justice of the peace, and special justice of the Court of Common Pleas. His will is dated Dec. 28, 1776.

Will—From Probate Records of Barnstable county, vol. 20, p. 415: I, Chillingwh Foster of Harwich in the County of Barnstable do make and ordain this my last Will and Testament this 28th Day of Decr. Anno Domini 1776 first I recommend my soul to God that Gave it hoping in his Mercy through the Merits of Christ and my body to the Earth in Decent Christian burial as to my worldly Estate I Give demise and dispose of the same in manner following.

My will is that all my Just Debts & funeral charges be paid by my Executor hereafter named and ordained.

Imprimis. I Give to my Daughter Sarah Waterman her heirs &c two acres and a half of upland & swamp lying on the Southerly side of the Country Road between said Road and the pond to be measured of to her of on ye westerly part of my land adjoining to Winslows land.

Item. I Give to my said Daughter Waterman my grandson Jeremiah Mayo and my Grand daughter Thankfull Freeman to their Heirs &c. to be divided in Equal thirds among them the woodlot I bought of Thomas Clark lying to the Southward of Sequastones way.

Item. I also Give to the said Sarah Jeremiah and Thankfull the land and meadow that I now own that was formerly my Grandfather John Freeman Deceased to them their Heirs &c to be divided Equally between them three.

Item I also Give to the said Sarah Waterman Jeremiah Mayo & Thankfull Freeman all my indoor movables and all my neat cattle & swine Excepting my best pair of oxen.

Item, I give my Grandson Jeremiah Mayo my chaise horse.

Item. I Give to my Daughter Sarah, my Grandson Jeremiah Mayo and my granddaughter Thankfull Freeman liberty to sett in my Pew in the meeting house from time to time as they shall have occasion.

My will further is that if both or either of my aforesaid Grand children shall die without issue in that case such part of the Estate as is Given to them or either of them in this will shall be to my Daughter Sarah Waterman her heirs &c forever.

Item. I Give to my son Chillingwh. Foster his heirs &c forever all my Estate both Real and personal Goods and Chattels not heretofore disposed of in this my Last will & Testament he paying all my Just Debts & funeral charges and faithfully performing what is injoined him in this will.

And I do constitute Ordain & appoint my son Chillingsworth Foster Sole Executor to this my last will and Testament. In Testimony whereof I have hereunto sett my Hand & Seal the day & year before written. Signed, Sealed Pronounced & declared to be his last will and Testament.

In Presence of us. Chillingwh. Foster. (L. S.)
Isaac Foster.
Joseph Snow.
Thomas Stevens. Proved June 9, 1779.

A true copy of the record.

He d. 1779. Res., Harwich, Mass.

4172. i. THANKFUL, b. June 14, 1733; m. Oct. 23, 1755, Joshua Freeman; had dau. Thankful.

4173. ii. MERCY, b. May 2, 1735, Barnstable, Mass.; d. May 4, 1760; m. Dec. 30, 1756, Hon. Solomon Freeman.

4174. iii. CHILLINGSWORTH, b. July 17, 1737, Barnstable; m. Nov. 15, 1759, Sarah Freeman, b. 1741; d. July 26, 1823. He d. Jan. 2, 1815. Res., Barnstable, Mass.

4175. iv. MEHITABEL, b. April 18, 1746; m., Nov. 25, 1762, Joshua Mayo of Eastham; had son Jeremiah.

4176. v. SARAH, b. Nov. 25, 1747; m. Jan. 8, 1767, Samuel Waterman, of Wellfleet.

3994. THOMAS FOSTER (Chillingsworth, John, Thomas, Thomas), b. March 15, 1711, Harwich, Mass.; m. July 11, 1734, Mary Hopkins, dau. of Joseph, of Harwich; gr. dau. of Stephen, of the Mayflower.

Thomas Foster, with his wife and four children, emigrated from Harwich, Mass., to the "Oblong," now Southeast, Duchess county, N. Y., some time before

1749, as his wife, Mary, was granted a letter of dismission from the church in Harwich to the church in Oblong, Aug. 20, 1749. Family tradition puts the removal several years earlier, probably soon after 1740. Four children were born after the family settled in the Oblong. Two daughters (of whom I have no record, save that Thomas had three sisters) and two sons, Tilly and Seth. Thomas Foster settled on a farm in the present town of Southeast, now occupied by his great-great-grandson, Alfred Crosby Foster (Alfred C., Joshua Crosby, James., Jr., James, Thomas), a bachelor. Three of his sons, Joseph, Tilly and Thomas, as they grew to manhood moved further up the Oblong, and into what is now Dutchess county, possibly further; traces of the last two are lost.

He d. 1790. Res., Harwich, Mass., and Oblong, N. Y.

4177. i. JOSEPH, b. March 27, 1735; m. Desire Hopkins.

4178. ii. THOMAS, b. June 22, 1736; m. and res. Southeast, N. Y.

4179. iii. JAMES, b. Feb. 18, 1737; m. Thankful Sears and Bathsheba Hall.

4180. iv. MARY, b. July 18, 1740; m. in Southeast, N. Y., Prince Hopkins. He was b. in Harwich, Mass., April 28, 1735, son of Stephen Hopkins. Ch.: 1. Chillingsworth, b. Aug. 27, 1774; m., March 12, 1798, Eunice Tucker, b. April 9, 1778; d. Hamilton, N. Y., Sept. 3, 1845. She d. Feb. 25, 1861. A dau. was Phebe, b. Sept. 13, 1799; m., April 16, 1821, Jabez B. Pomeroy, b. April 5, 1794; d. Feb. 26, 1879. She d. Sept. 10, 1870. Their ch. were b. in Lockport, N. Y., viz.: (a) Norton, b. May 12, 1823; m. Jane Chipman, of Kalamazoo, Mich., May 8, 1851. She d. Feb. 11, 1870. He m., 2d, wid. Mary E. Pomeroy, of Lewiston, N. Y., Jan. 11, 1872. He d. July 19, 1893. (b) Hopkins Chillingsworth, b. May 14, 1825; m. Mary C. Dean, of Glens Falls, N. Y., May 3, 1860; d. in Lockport, N. Y., Aug. 25, 1890. Mary C. Pomeroy d. Dec. 15, 1895. (c) Sarah C., b. Feb. 23, 1827; m. William D. Holt, of Rockford, Ill., March 12, 1857. (d) Jabez Davis, b. July 24, 1829; unm. (e) Orphia L., b. Aug. 26, 1831; m. Edwin F. Farley, of Lockport, N. Y., Dec. 11, 1855; d. in Flint, Mich., May 7, 1858. (f) Caroline, b. Nov. 30, 1833; m. Wardell Guthrie, of Chicago, Ill., Dec. 11, 1855. (g) L. Sherrill, b. Oct. 16, 1836; m. Mary E. Byrne, of Lewiston, N. Y., April 7, 1863; d. in Lockport, N. Y., Nov. 11, 1868. (h) Myron, b Aug. 5, 1836; m. Ariette Farley, of Wilson, N. Y., Dec. 23, 1864. Airette H. Pomeroy d. April 21, 1889. (i) Daniel W., b. Jan. 14, 1845; m. M. Louisa Weaver, of Lockport, N. Y., May 16, 1872. 2. Benjamin, b. 1763; m. Rebecca Goodrich. 3. Prince, Jr., b. ——; m. Jemima Tucker. 4. Thomas, b. ——. 5. Mary, b. ——. 6. Stephen, b. in Warren, Conn., Oct. 19, 1787. Prince, Sr., d. in Warren, Conn., March 16, 1805, ae. seventy years. Mary, his wife, d. in Warren, Conn., Nov. 30, 1813, ae. seventy-three years. Edward Tanner Hopkins (great-grandson of Benjamin), address, Station A, W. Winsted, Conn. Arthur T. Benson (great-grandson of Prince, Jr.), address, Dover Plains, N. Y.

4181. v. SETH, b. April 11, 1761; m. Huldah Ragan and Mrs. Elizabeth (Townsend) King.

4182. vi. TILLY, b. ——.

4183. vii. TWO more daughters.

3995. NATHAN FOSTER (Chillingsworth, John, Thomas, Thomas), b. Harwich, Mass., June 10, 1715; m., June 14, 1739, Sarah Lincoln, of Harwich. Res., Harwich, Mass.

4184. i. JENNY, b. April 12, 1740; m., Nov. 8, 1762, Isaac Davis.

4185. ii. JOHN, b. May 25, 1742; m., Dec. 14, 1765, Hannah Gould.

4186. iii. SARAH, b. Sept. 6, 1744; m., Jan. 23, 1766, Samuel C. Crosby.

4187. iv. SUSANNA, b. Jan. 21, 1746; m., March 23, 1769, Joseph Gould.

4188. v. MARY, b. July 13, 1749; m., Dec. 20, 1777, Gideon Clark.

3996. ISAAC FOSTER (Chillingsworth, John, Thomas, Thomas), b. Harwich, Mass., June 17, 1718; m., Nov. 2, 1738, Hannah Sears, of Harwich, dau. of Samuel and Ruth (Merrick), dau. of Isaac's stepmother. She d. Oct. 31, 1760. She was a direct descendant of Giles and Stephen Hopkins of the "Mayflower." He res. on the homestead and was a blacksmith. The graves of both are to be seen in the old grave yard in Brewster. He d. Sept. 10, 1777. Res., Harwich, Mass.

4189. i. ISAAC, b. May 29, 1739; m. Eunice Freeman, Almira —— and Rebecca Wing.
4190. ii. SAMUEL, b. May 31, 1741; m. Lydia Thacher.
4191. iii. DAVID, b. March 24, 1742; m. Phebe Freeman.
4192. iv. LEMUEL, b. Feb. 24, 1744; d. young.
4193. v. SETH, b. March, 1747; m. Sarah Cobb.
4194. vi. HANNAH, b. March 4, 1749; m. John Gill, of Boston.
4195. vii. NATHANIEL, b. April 8, 1751; m. Mary Hopkins.

3999. NATHANIEL FOSTER (Chillingsworth, John, Thomas, Thomas), b. Brewster, Mass., April 17, 1725; m. in Harwich; m. pub. June 21, 1746, Phebe Wing, b. Jan. 20, 1720; d. ——; m., 2d, Charity Knowlton.

Many of Chillingsworth's children went to New York and settled around Southeast, in the year 1750. Among them, Nathaniel, b. April 17, 1725, who was also a blacksmith and followed his trade a part of the time after he came. When he purchased his farm there, presumably, soon after his arrival, he is mentioned in the deed as "Nathaniel Foster, blacksmith." He had many children. His eldest son, Nathaniel, Jr., married, so the old folk say, a Crosby; and they also say she was known to the still older folk as Aunt Lydia, in her old age. A Joshua Crosby, of this vicinity, in his will, mentions his daughter, Lydia Foster. Among the other children of Nathaniel Foster, Sr., was a daughter, Ruth, who married Abner Crosby, from whom my wife is descended also. This Ruth was born 1750 and died Oct. 1, 1816. Her eldest son, Thomas Crosby, married Hannah Snow. Their eldest child, Esther, married Peter Waring.

He was a member of the committee appointed in 1777 to represent the Southeast precinct in the general committee, and his name appears on a military order of Col. John Field to Lieut. Jonathan Crane, to organize the persons named into a guard for the protection of the inhabitants of that quarter, dated Oct. 8, 1777. His name also appears prominently in the records of the early church, as does that of his son, Nathaniel, Jr. Both occupied places of prominence in the community.

I have no copy of a will of Nathaniel Foster, Sr., but I have an abstract thereof. It is the first will recorded in the Duchess county surrogate's office (what is now Putnam county, was, until 1812, a part of Duchess). Nathaniel Foster, Sr., according to the Harwich records, had recorded intention of marriage to Phebe, daughter of John and Rebecca (Vickery) Wing. The marriage, however, is not of record in Harwich. He was a prominent man in the town and church of his section during his life, and also served on the Revolutionary war committee of this town; these matters appear in the records of the town, a part of which had been incorporated in a history of the county, but were later destroyed by fire. His will, dated April 13, 1787, and proved May 15, 1787, mentions wife, Charity; sons, John, Nathaniel, David, Samuel; daughters, Thankful, Ruth, Phebe, Jerusha, Susanna; also son Robert Knowlton Foster, under age. Executors appointed were sons Nathaniel and Samuel, and Abner Crosby (the latter married the daughter Ruth, from whom many are descended). This son, under age, was born nine years before his father's death, and as he is the only one mentioned as under age, and Foster's wife, when he died, was Charity, I assume that he was twice married, at least, and I believe that this second wife must have been a Knowlton; of this I am not sure. There were families of that name near here, and the names Charity and Robert seem to have appeared often among them. The old church records are destroyed or stolen, or these points might be cleared up now.

His first wife was daughter of John Wing and his third wife, Rebecca (Vickery), of Brewster. Wing's property was on Crane Pond Neck. His second wife was probably a dau. of Ephraim and Charity Knowlton.

He d. 1787. Res., near Danbury, Conn., at Southeast N. Y.

4196. i. JOHN, b. Nov. 15, 1751; m. Deborah Elwell.
4197. ii. THOMAS, b. in 1756; m. Hannah Bliss.
4198. iii. DAVID, b. in 1758; m. Lydia White.
4199. iv. NATHANIEL, b. 1748; m. Lydia Crosby.
4200. v. SAMUEL, b. ——; m. Lucy ——.
4201. vi. ROBERT KNOWLTON, b. in 1775; m. Martha Conklin.
4202. vii. RUTH, b. 1750; m. Abner Crosby. She d. Oct. 1, 1816. Her son, Thomas, m. Hannah Snow. Abner Crosby, son of David and Reliance (Hopkins) Crosby, was born Dec. 25, 1744, and died May

5, 1813. Ch.: 1. Lowhama, b. 1766; m. Isaac Crosby. 2. Thomas, b. 1768; m. Hannah Snow. 3. Reliance, b. 1769; m. William Burrhus. 4. Ruth, b. 1772; m. Enos Marshall. 5. Stephen, b. 1774; d. young. 6. Stephen, b. 1778; m. Lydia Sears. 7. Eleazor, b. 1781; m. Prudence. 8. Zenas, b. 1783; m. Sarah Chapman. 9. Nathaniel Foster, b. 1788; m. Eunice Wakeman. 10. Naomi, b. 1790; m. Charles Birch. 11. Jane, b. 1793; m. Charles C. Crosby. 12. Phebe, b. 1786; m. John Snow. Of above children, Thomas and Hannah (Snow) Crosby (she was dau. of William Snow and Lydia Wixon), were married Feb. 12, 1786; he d. Feb. 16, 1844; she d. Feb. 24, 1853, ae. eighty-three. They had nine children, the eldest being Esther, b. Dec. 16, 1786; d. July 16, 1831. She m., March 23, 1805, Peter Waring, son of John and Mary (Elwell) Waring. He was b. Dec. 14, 1782, and d. July 16, 1831. They had ten children, among them being Charles Rundell's wife's mother, Catharine A., b. Aug. 2, 1828. She m. Levi H. Roberts, as shown elsewhere. Mrs. Rundell is descended through two lines from Nathaniel, Sr. There were many of the Foster and Crosby names in Southeast and Brewster, N. Y., early, and intermarriages between the families were frequent. Nathaniel had a brother, Thomas, who went to that section at the same time.

4203. viii. THANKFUL, b. ——.
4204. ix. PHEBE, b. ——.
4205. x. JERUSHA, b. ——.
4206. xi. SUSANNAH, b. ——.

4002. THOMAS FOSTER (Thomas, John, Thomas, Thomas), b. Marshfield, Mass., May 4, 1735; m., 1757, Mary Foster. He was a blacksmith and inherited the homestead in Marshfield, which he sold to Nathan Thomas (his cousin) and rem. to Middleboro. Res. Marshfield and Middleboro, Mass.

4207. i. THOMAS, b. April 16, 1758.
4208. ii. JOHN, b. Feb. 3, 1760.
4209. iii. PETER, b. July 16, 1761.
4210. iv. NATHANIEL, b. June 15, 1763.

4005. JOHN FOSTER (Thomas, Joseph, Thomas, Thomas), b. Billerica, Mass., Jan. 11, 1708; m. Hannah ——. His name disappears from the Billerica tax list after 1734. Res., Billerica and Tewksbury, Mass.

4211. i. NATHANIEL, b. Nov. 11, 1730.
4212. ii. PARKER, b. March 6, 1732. I think he went to Kittery, Me., and with his son, Parker, Jr., was in Rev. war. See Rev. soldiers.
4213. iii. JOHN, b. Aug. 28, 1733; m. —— ——.

4027. DR. ISAAC FOSTER (Isaac, Richard, William, Thomas), b. Charlestown, Mass., Aug. 28, 1740; m., July 4, 1765, Martha Mason, dau. of Thaddeus, of Camb, b. 1743; d. Sept. 21, 1770; m., 2d, Sept. 8, 1771, Mary Russell, dau. of Richard, of Camb, at Boston. She m., 2d, John Hurd (his second wife), June 8, 1783. She was b. 1749; d. Jan. 14, 1786. Hurd d. July 19, 1809, ae. eighty-two. Foster graduated at Harvard University in 1758. He then began the study of medicine under Doctor Lloyd, of Boston, and completed his studies in England. In his profession he achieved considerable reputation; had a large practice and numbered among his pupils Doctors Bartlett, Welch and Eustis. He was a staunch patriot and prominent in the town meetings of the day, his name appearing on several committees. He was elected a delegate to the convention in county of Middlesex, in August, 1774, and a member of the first Provincial Congress of Massachusetts, in October of the same year. In 1775 he was appointed a surgeon; was for some months at the head of the military medical department, while General Ward held command in Cambridge. After the battle of Concord he gave up a large private practice to attend to the wounded. He was appointed by the committee of safety to attend the men wounded at the battle of Bunker Hill. Soon after was appointed surgeon of the State Hospital. General Washington, on the discovery of the treachery of Doctor Church, appointed him, in October, Director General pro tem. of the American hospital department. In 1777 the office of Deputy Director General of Hospitals was established, and he was chosen by Congress to this office, having charge of the eastern department. This office was abolished in 1780, and, of course, Doctor Foster was left out of service. His health had suffered so much by fatigue and exposure that he lived but a short time longer.

"Foster, Isaac, physician, b. in Charleston, Mass., about 1740; d. in February, 1781. He was graduated at Harvard in 1758; studied medicine in this country and abroad, and settled in Charlestown, where he practiced for several years. He was a delegate to the convention of the county of Middlesex, in August, 1774, and

to the first provincial Congress of Massachusetts, in October of that year. Doctor Foster was appointed a surgeon in 1775, and was for some months at the head of the military medical department, while General Ward commanded at Cambridge, and before the arrival of General Washington. On April 20th, the day after the battle of Concord, by urgent request of General Ward and Doctor Warren, he attended the men who had been wounded, and gave up his private practice, which was very large. On June 18th, the day after the battle of Bunker Hill, he was appointed by the committee of safety to attend those who had been wounded there, and was afterward given the post of surgeon of the State Hospital, then just opened. In October he was appointed by General Washington director general pro tem. of the American hospital department. Congress shortly afterward appointed Doctor Morgan to that place, but Doctor Foster was still the oldest surgeon in the hospital. Again, in 1777, General Washington appointed him to take charge of the hospitals in the eastern department. He retired from public life in 1780, being in feeble health, but did not resign his commission. Several men, eminent in the medical profession, studied with Doctor Foster, among them William Eustis and Josiah Bartlett, the younger."—Am. Biography.

In the Atlantic Monthly, for May, 1859, under the title of "A Bundle of Old Letters," there is given a short sketch of his life and public services, together with over a dozen letters written by him, from various places, 1776-79, principally to his wife, in which reference is made to the state of affairs, and many incidents of the day are recorded. He lived on the northwest corner of Main and Henly streets, Charlestown, Mass. His will is dated Aug. 1, 1780, and proved April 19, 1782, Suffolk Probate records.

Will—Isaac Foster, of Boston, physician; wife, Mary Foster; eldest daughter, Eleanor Foster; my late wife, Martha Foster, deceased; daughter, Polly Beal Foster; youngest daughter, Nancy Foster; brother-in-law, Nathaniel Coffin. Aug. 1, 1780. Prob. April 19, 1782. Lib. 81, fol. 56-57-58-59-60. Lib. 83, fol. 1093. William Pratt, of Charlestown, mariner, admitted administrator cum. testamento annexo on the estate of Isaac Foster, late of Boston, physician, deceased. Feb. 9, 1796. Lib. 94, fol. 187.

He d. Feb. 27, 1782. Res., Charlestown, Mass.

4214. i. MARTHA, b. May 11, 1766; d. May 4, 1768.
4215. ii. ELEANOR, b. Nov. 4, 1767.
4216. iii. MARTHA, b. Sept. 19, 1769; not mentioned in her father's will.
4217. iv. NANCY, b. ——.
4218. v. MARY BEAL, bapt. Aug. 23, 1774; m. William Pratt, of Boston; mariner.

4035. ELISHA FOSTER (Hopestill, Hopestill, Hopestill, Richard, Thomas), b. Boston, Mass., May 25, 1711; m. there Elizabeth Shepard. She d. May, 1773.

Will—Elisha Foster, of Boston, merchant; wife, Elizabeth, executrix. Dated, March 27, 1766. Prob. May 16, 1766 Lib. 65, fol. 229-230.

Will—Elizabeth Foster, of Boston, widow; nephew, Nathaniel Shepard, and niece Catharine Shepard, children of my late brother, Nathaniel Shepard, deceased; nephews Thomas Shepard and Nathaniel Shepard, children of my late brother, Thomas Shepard, deceased; nephews Benjamin Thomas, and Nathaniel Thomas;

niece Susanna Blanchard. Dated, Sept. 13, 1771. Prob. June 4, 1773. Lib. 72, fol. 625-6-7.

He d. April, 1766. Res., s. p., Boston, Mass.

4039. SAMUEL FOSTER (Samuel, Hopestill, Hopestill, Richard, Thomas), b. Boston, June 25, 1701; m. (pub.), March 28, 1721, Rachel Kneeland. He was a periwig-maker. A deed, in 1724, Suffolk deeds, vol. 36, fol. 68, mentions him and wife, Rachel. Res., Boston, Mass.

4219. i. JOHN, b. in 1722; m. Jane ——.

4040. JOHN FOSTER (John, James, Hopestill, Richard, Thomas), b. Boston, Mass., April 10, 1713; m. there Mary Fish. After his death she m., 2d, —— Holmes.

Will—John Foster, of Boston, mariner; wife, Mary Foster; son, John; daughter, Mary; brother-in-law, William Fish. Dated, Jan. 4, 1734-5. Prob. Sept. 16, 1735. Suff. Prob. Lib. 32, fol. 226-227-236. In warrant for dower, Mary Holmes, formerly widow of John Foster, mariner, deceased. Dated, Aug. 30, 1754. Approved, Oct. 4, 1754. Lib. 49, fol. 594.

He d. in 1735. Res., Boston, Mass.

4220. i. JOHN, b. ——.

4221. ii. MARY, b. ——.

4052. CAPT. JAMES FOSTER (James, James, Hopestill, Richard, Thomas), b. Dorchester, Mass., March 31, 1732; m., July 4, 1754, Mary Robinson.

Mary Foster, widow, and James Robinson, gentleman, both of Dorchester, appointed administrators of estate of James Foster, late of Dorchester, gentleman, deceased, intestate. John Robinson, of Dorchester, victualler, bound with them. Oct. 25, 1771. Lib. 70, fol. 509. Lib. 71, fol. 75. Account of money paid in settling estate of Capt. James Foster by James Robinson, mentions Capt. Hopestill Foster, of Boston. Feb. 5, 1773. Lib. 72, fol. 350-1. James Robinson and Mary Foster, widow, petition for right to sell pasture land. Feb. 19, 1773. Lib. 83, fol. 46-7. Further account of Mary Foster and James Robinson, administrators, mentions money paid William Foster. Feb. 13, 1784. Lib. 83, fol. 110-111. Also mentions property destroyed by the enemy. (Their house was situated on Dorchester Neck, and was burned by the British.) Warrant for division mentions four children. July 8, 1788. Lib. 87, fol. 366. Division of real estate settled on daughter Susanna, wife of Abraham Gould; mentions Stephen Foster, eldest son; other children, Mary Foster and Benjamin Foster. July 15, 1788. Lib. 87, fol. 367. Bond to administrator mentions Stephen Foster, physician of Bath, in county of Lincoln; Abraham Gould, yeoman; Jonathan Bird, gentleman; legal representatives of Benjamin Foster and Elizabeth Foster Rice, both of Dorchester. July 18, 1788. Lib. 87, fol. 568-9. Further account of estate mentions money paid to Will Foster's estate. April, 1785. Lib. 87, fol. 351.

He d. June 4, 1771. Res., Dorchester, Mass.

4222. i. ELIZABETH, b. March 18, 1755; d. July 28, 1775.

4223. ii. JAMES, b. Jan. 15, 1757; d. April 17, 1771.

4224. iii. STEPHEN, b. Oct. 17, 1758; m. and res. Bath, Me. Was a physician.

4225. iv. MARY, b. March 8, 1760.

4226. v. BEULAH, b. Jan. 8, 1762; d. May 23, 1782.

4227. vi. JOHN, b. May 18, 1764; d. Sept. 11, 1765.

4228. vii. SUSANNAH, b. April 27, 1766; m. Abraham Gould. The great-great-grandmother of Abraham Gould, who married the above Susannah Foster (1766-1837), was Patience Foster, who died in Sudbury, Mass., August, 1706, ae. fifty-nine. She was wife of Maj. Thomas Brown, of Sudbury.

Abraham and Susannah's dau. m. Henry Robinson, b. Dorchester, Jan. 30, 1785. Their son, Edward Frederick Robinson, b. Worcester, Dec. 8, 1813; m., Boston, Sept. 5, 1837, Sophia Bigelow Easte, b. South Boston, Sept. 5, 1818. Is living. Ch.: 1. George Henry Robinson, d. in infancy. 2. Susan Sophia Robinson; m. John Freeman Nickerson. 3. Frederick Henry Robinson, m. Emma Colesworthy; no issue. 4. Francis Edward, b. Feb. 14, 1850; m., in Boston, October, 1873, Susan Lois Harlow and Grace Towle. He is Sec. Boston, Mass., Mutual Fire Ins. Co. Ch.: (a) Francis Walter, b. Aug. 10, 1874. Res., Boston; P. O. Box 1362. Purchasing agent Industrial Improvement Co., treasurer Tennessee Northern Ry. Co.; assistant treasurer Cumberland Coal & Iron Co.; clerk Brockton St. Ry. Co., Taunton & Brockton St. Ry. Co., Lowell, Lawrence & Haverhill St. Ry. Co. (b) Edward Frederick, b. Sept. 27, 1878. (c) Henry Eustis, b. Oct. 5, 1890.

4229. viii. RUTH, b. June 6, 1768; d. Aug. 7, 1783.

4230. ix. BENJAMIN, b. April 13, 1770. Jonathan Bird, of Dorchester, gentleman, nominated guardian of Benjamin Foster, a minor above fourteen years of age, son of James Foster, late of Dorchester, gentleman, deceased. Stephen Foster, of Bath, in the county of Lincoln, physician, bound with said Jonathan. July 7, 1788. Lib. 87, fol. 350-1. Discharge to his guardian, now arrived at lawful age. May 2, 1793. Lib. 92, fol. 272-3.

4066. CAPT. HOPESTILL FOSTER (Hopestill, James, Hopestill, Richard, Thomas), b. Boston, Mass., June 29, 1744; m. Nov. 2, 1769, Susanna Wood, dau. of David, of Charlestown, b. 1749; d. June 2, 1819.

Will—Hopestill Foster, of Boston, gentleman.—wife Susanna Foster, surviving children, Benjamin W. Foster; James Foster; Sukey, wife of Elisha Adams; Sally Foster; Hopestill Foster, Jr.; Ruth Foster; John H. Foster. Dated, Aug. 1, 1799. Prob., Feb. 15, 1802. Lib. 100; fol. 37-8.

Susanna Foster, of Boston, widow, admitted administratrix of will of Hopestill Foster, late of Boston, gentleman, deceased; Benjamin Wood Foster, merchant, and Elisha Adams, cabinet-maker, both of Boston, bound with her. Feb. 15, 1802. Lib. 100; fol. 49-151.

He d. December, 1801. Res., Boston, Mass.

4231. i. BENJAMIN WOOD, b. July 14, 1770; m. Hannah French and Mrs. Davison.

4232. ii. JAMES, b. Feb. 7, 1772; d. unm., 1800.

4233. iii. SUSANNA, b. April 18, 1774; m. Elisha Adams, of Medfield. Elisha was b. Medfield, Dec. 14, 1774. She d. Jan. 21, 1828. He was a cabinet-maker and resided in Dorchester. Ch.: 1. Susan Foster, b. Nov. 12, 1798; m. Stephen Turner, b. 1794. She d. in 1870. 2. Elisha, b. March 24, 1801; m. Caroline Boyden, of Walpole. 3. Isabella, b. Sept. 24, 1802. 4. Henry, b. April 18, 1804; d. Aug. 3, 1831. 5. William, b. Nov. 28, 1805; d. June 30, 1808. 6. Abigail, b. June 23, 1808. 7. William, b. April 5, 1810. 8. Maria, b. June 9, 1811; m. her cousin James E. Adams.

4234. iv. DAVID, b. April 30, 1776; d. Sept. 27, 1777.

4235. v. SARAH, b. Feb. 18, 1778; m. Thomas Forbes, of Groton.

4236. vi HOPESTILL, b. Aug. 14, 1780; m. Susan Sawyer.

4237. vii. RUTH, b. Sept. 28, 1783; m. Nathan H. Bartlett.

4238. viii. JOHN HANCOCK, b. May 30, 1785; m. Elizabeth Allen.

4066. THOMAS FOSTER (Comfort, Standfast, Hopestill, Richard, Thomas), b. Dorchester, Mass., March 21, 1715; m., Sept. 27 1737, Mary Lyon. She d. May 4, 1774. He d. April 14, 1776. Res., Dorchester, Mass.

4239. i. JOSEPH, b. July 27, 1738.

4240. ii. JACOB, b. May 30, 1737; d. June 1, 1739.

4241. iii. MARY, b. Feb. 2, 1741.

4242. iv. ELINOR, b. July 27, 1743.

4243. v. THOMAS, b. Feb. 15, 1745.

4244. vi. ABIGAIL, b. Nov. 4, 1746.

4245. vii. ANN, b. Aug. 24, 1750.

4246. viii. LUCY, b. Sept. 30, 1754.

4247. ix. ELISHA, b. Sept. 21, 1756.

4067. WILLIAM FOSTER (Comfort, Standfast, Hopestill, Richard, Thomas), b. Dorchester, Mass., April 24, 1727; m. July 19, 1749, Elizabeth Hunt. She d. May 16, 1800.

Elizabeth Foster, of Dorchester, widow, admitted administratrix of the estate of William Foster, late of Dorchester, cordwainer, deceased, Jan. 30, 1784. Lib. 83; fol. 53. Lib. 83; fol. 107-8-9-10.

He d. Jan. 30, 1784. Res., Dorchester, Mass.

4248. i. ELIZABETH, b. Oct. 1750; d. Oct. 22, 1750.

4249. ii. JOSIAH, b. Dec. 25, 1751; d. same day.
4250. iii. CHILD, b. and d. same day, Dec. 9, 1753.

4068. JOHN FOSTER (Comfort, Standfast, Hopestill, Richard, Thomas), b. Dorchester, Mass., Dec. 26, 1733; m., Oct. 9, 1755, Hannah Dowes. She d. March, 1787. He d. Nov. 7, 1784. Res., Dorchester, Mass.

4251. i. JOHN; b. Aug. 5, 1756; d. Oct. 26, 1786.
4252. ii. COMFORT, b. March 21, 1758.
4253. iii. WILLIAM, b Jan. 1762; d. May 20, 1763.
4254. iv. WILLIAM, b. July 11, 1763; m. Mary Maxfield.

4072. JONATHAN FOSTER (Jonathan, Jonathan, Thomas, Thomas, Thomas), b. Haverhill or Dunstable, Mass., June 6, 1719; m. in Shrewsbury, Mass., Aug. 2, 1741, Mrs. Bathsheba (Newton) Crosby, b. 1698; d. soon after marriage; m., 2d, Betty Hazen. Both wives d. s. p. m., 3d, abt. 1757, Thankful Harrington. d. January, 1779; m., 4th, Mason, N. H., Nov. 30, 1779, Mercy Towns, b. 1751. She d. in Townsend, Mass., in 1844. He lived to be 102 years of age. The Shrewsbury, Mass., records of the Congregational church there have this of Jonathan Foster, Jr.'s first marriage: "Jonathan Foster, Jr., married Aug. 2, 1741." In a note, Rev. Job Cushing, who married them, and by whom the records were kept, says: "Bathsheba Crosby, a widow more than twice his age. An unequal yoking together." Bathsheba was born in Marlboro, in September 1698, dau. of Joseph and Abigail. She married in Marlboro, Jan. 23, 1721, John Crosby from Billerica, one of the founders of the church in Shrewsbury, Mass., in 1723. They lived on house lot No. 13, in 1729; he d. in Shrewsbury, Dec. 5, 1738, ae. 43-48-50. They did not have any children and his widow married young Foster but soon died.

Hon. J. L. Davenport, of the Bureau of Pensions, Washington, D. C., writes as follows: "Jonathan Foster made an application for pension on May 1, 1818, at which time he was ninety-five years of age and residing at Mason, N. H., and his pension was allowed for three years' actual service as a private in the Massachusetts troops, Revolutionary war. He served under Captain Shattuck and Colonel Greaton. Place of his enlistment not stated. His widow, Mercy, made application and received a pension for the service of her husband as above set forth. He died March 31, 1821. The names of their children are not stated."

He d. March 31, 1821. Res., Mason, N. H.

4255. i. JONATHAN, b. Nov. 15, 1759. Was in Revolutionary war.
4256. ii. NATHAN, b. July 15, 1762. Served in Revolutionary war.
4257. iii. RICHARD, b. Nov. 28, 1764; m. Hannah Edwards.
4258. iv. ANDREW, b. July 5, 1768.
4259. v. BETTY, b. March 12, 1771.
4260. vi. DANIEL, b. Dec. 4, 1773; m. Abigail ——.
4261. vii. SAMUEL, b. March 18, 1776.
4262. viii. JOSEPH, b. May 28, 1780; a son resides at Bedford, Mass., a dau., Hannah F., m. Leonard Read. She d. 1876; he d. 1832. 1. Hannah Read, b. March 28, 1822; d. June 1, 1841. 2. Charles Theodore Read, deceased, b. Feb. 16, 1833; left two sons; their address is Charles Melvin Read and Fred Read, all of No. 279 Park avenue, Woonsocket, R. I. 3. Maria Read, b. Aug. 5, 1827; m.; her P. O. address, Mrs. Melvin, S. Litchfield, North Scituate, Mass. 4. Ford Foster Read, b. March 18, 1830, and is married; P. O. address, Greenville, N. H. 5. Leonard Rodney, b. June 25, 1825; m., June 15, 1876, Mrs. Eliza Dockham, b. Nov. 21, 1838. Res., Townsend, Mass. Ch.: Harrison L. Read, b. Sept. 15, 1877. Res., W. Townsend, Mass., P. O box 173.
4263. ix. STEPHEN, b. April 27, 1782; d. unm.
4264. x. ELISHA, b. ——; d. unm.
4265. xi. GARDNER, b. March 31, 1785; m. Mary B. Fuller.
4266. xii. WILLIAM, b. ——; a son is Charles H. Foster, of Nashua, N. H., P. O. box 688.
4267. xiii. SALLY, b. ——.
4268. xiv. LYDIA, b. ——.

4076. HEZEKIAH FOSTER (Jonathan, Jonathan, Thomas, Thomas, Thomas), b. Stow, Mass., Aug. 28, 1728; m. Hannah ——; m., 2d. ——. The only information I have concerning Hezekiah Foster, of Salisbury, N. H., is that he took the

Associational test before the Revolutionary war. He d. ——. Res., Shrewsbury, Mass., and Hopkinton and Salisbury, N. H.

4269. i. HANNAH, b. May 6, 1747 in Shrewsbury, Mass.
4270. 1½. RICHARD, b. 1762; m. Sarah Greeley and Esther Jewell.
4271. ii. ABIGAIL, b. ——; m. —— Stevens. Res., Claremont, N. H.
4272. iii. JACOB, b. ——; m. Lucy Bartlett. Res., Coos Co., N. H.
4273. iv. JONATHAN, b. ——; m. Mary Greeley.
4274. v. SARAH, b. ——; m. —— Bean.
4275. vi. DAU, b. ——; m. —— Stickney.
4276. vii. DAU, b. ——; m. —— Godfrey.
4277. viii. MEHITABLE, b. ——; m. —— Ward.
4278. ix. MARY, b. ——; m —— Judd.
4279. x. CALEB, b. ——. Res., Baltimore, Md.

4080. HON. JOSEPH FOSTER (John, Jonathan, Thomas, Thomas, Thomas), b. Stow, Mass., June 3, 1730; m. (pub.) Feb. 9, 1751, Susannah Roberts, of Brookfield, Mass., b. Billerica, 1730; d. Barnard, Vt., May 18, 1800. He was born in Stow, Middlesex county; moved in infancy to Grafton, Worcester county, and finally settled with his parents in Hardwick in that part incorporated in 1761 as Ware. He was the eldest son and was given in the division of the estate part of the 200 acres originally purchased by his father. He remained on the farm for thirty years; was a prominent and respected citizen and held the highest offices in the town, which shows he was a "man of character and influence."*

He was a delegate to the Provincial Congress from Ware, Mass., in 1774 and 1775. The church record contains this in relation to him, April 19, 1757: "Voted to hire preaching for this summer; voted to raise upon the polls and estates the sum of £13-6-8 for preaching and boarding ministers and going after ministers; voted Joseph Foster to go after ministers." In 1775, Joseph Foster was allowed £3-9-6 for expenses to the Provincial Congress. He was captain of a company in Col. Ruggles Woodbridge's regiment, which marched on Lexington alarm, April 19, 1775, and did other services during Revolutionary war. Soon after the war he moved with his family to Barnard, Vt., where many people from Hardwick had previously settled. In his new home he commanded the esteem and respect of the people. One son, John, was captain in the local militia, justice of the peace, deacon of the church and was elected representative for thirteen consecutive years. Another son was brigadier-general of the militia and another, Peter, was also captain. Deacon Joseph was selectman in Barnard in 1780-81-83-91-92-94. Joseph Foster's will made in 1798, presented for probate at Woodstock, Vt., June 2, 1807. Name of wife Susanna Foster. Names of children, who were all legates, John, executor; Joseph, Asa, Peter; Eunice, m. Emerson; Susanna, m. Lawton; Anna, m. Tucker. Each of these children had one-seventh of the property after provision for the widow. He d. May 10, 1807. Res., Ware, Mass., and Barnard, Vt.

4280. i. ASA, b. Oct. 11, 1761; m. Ruth Chedle.
4281. ii. JOSEPH, b. Sept. 10, 1759; m. Deborah Tracy and Dolly Parmenter.
4282. iii. JOHN, b. Sept. 3, 1757; m. Experience Gray and Mrs. Rachel (Richmond (Myrick) Chamberlain.
4283. iv. PETER, d. May 31, 1764; m. Sarah Herriden and Susanna Henry.
4284. v. ANNA, b. April 20, 1766; m. in Barnard, Sept. 10, 1789, Robert Tucker. She d. in Barnard, Vt.; he m. 2d, Sarah Foster, a niece of his first wife, Anna; b. May 13, 1787; d. December, 1846, in Irwin, Ohio. He d. in Irwin, Oct. 2, 1842, ae. seventy-five. Ch.: 1. Elvira, b. January 12, 1805; m. in Barnard, Hon. Ebenezer Atwood, b. March 29, 1802; was a farmer and d. in Malone, N. Y., Jan. 23, 1870. She d. April 17, 1871. Ebenezer Atwood came from best old Pilgrim and Puritan stock. His ancestors have always been people of influence, filling responsible positions in church and state. Ebenezer himself was a farmer, yet found time for much public service, always holding important town offices—selectman, assessor, etc. He served two terms in the state legislature. He raised a large family. Three of his sons were in the civil war, two of them sacrificing their lives. While he kept many of the sterner qualities or characteristics of his early ances-

*Hyde's Historical Address, Ware, Mass., 1847.

tors, he was a most genial friend and respected citizen. Ch.: (a) Joseph Foster Atwood, b. ——; d. Malone, N. Y., May 19, 1895. (b) Seth, d. in infancy. (c) Thomas Hammond, b. ——; d. Sept. 20, 1872. (d) George Alexander, b. ——; d. Nov. 2, 1856. (e) Elizabeth Penn, b. ——; d. Dec. 12, 1861. (f) Charles was ass't editor of Chicago "Tribune," and d. in California in 1880. Ch.: 1. Eleanor F., unm. 2. Charles Edward, b. Aug. 16, 1869: m. Oct. 21, 1897, Corrilla C. Dreutzer, res. 6541 Lafayette av. Ch.: Carl Edward, b. Sept. 30, 1898; with J. W. Doane & Co. 3. Joseph Foster, b. Jan. 6, 1873; m., June 15, 1899, Ruby Teasdale, res. 4619 Woodlawn avenue, Chicago. 4. Elizabeth Penn, unm. 5. Ebenezer, b. November 25, 1879, unm., resides Chicago. (g) Joel Tucker, b. ——; d. Feb. 4, 1854. (h) Nancy Ann, b. Sept. 3, 1837; m. in Royalton, Vt., Sept. 29, 1862, Albert Arnold Sprague, b. May 19, 1835, of Sprague, Warner & Co. Res., 2710 Prairie av., Chicago. Albert A. Sprague, the founder and senior member of the great wholesale house of Sprague, Warner & Co., was born in Randolph, Vt., May 19, 1835. His father, Ziba Sprague, was a well-to-do farmer and trader in his native town, and gave his children good educational advantages. Obtaining his preliminary education in the public schools, he fitted for college at the Meriden, N. H., seminary. Entering Yale, he was graduated in 1859. It was his intention to qualify for the legal profession, but on account of pulmonary troubles, he was obliged to forego a professional life. Returning to Vermont, he remained for three years and regained his health. In 1862, he came to Chicago, intending to engage in business, but with no settled plans as to what particular line he would engage in. Finding an excellent opportunity to embark in the wholesale grocery trade, he formed a partnership and began under the firm name of Sprague & Stetson. The business gradually increased and was soon one of the recognized leading commercial houses of Chicago, the firm name b ing changed to Sprague, Warner & Co., and under which name the business is still conducted. Under Mr. Sprague's personal management, ably aided by hundreds of employes, the house has had a wonderful and substantial growth, until to-day it is recognized as the largest exclusively wholesale grocery house in America, with one exception in New York. He is unselfish and retiring; never sought political office, though often importuned, and prefers a quiet place in the background rather than the glamour of publicity. He is one of the most successful merchants in America to-day, and is the soul of honor and integrity. He is an important factor in many commercial movements and is actively interested in a number of well known corporations; is a member of several of the leading clubs, and no man in Chicago in better known, more earnestly sought or justly esteemed. Ch.: 1. Elizabeth Penn, b. Oct. 30, 1864; m. Frederic Shurtleff

ALBERT ARNOLD SPRAGUE.

Coolidge, of Boston, Mass., Nov. 12, 1891; address 2636 Prairie avenue, Chicago. ii. Carrie Arnold, b. Oct. 15, 1866; d. Sept. 9, 1874. iii. Susy, b. June 7, 1869; d. Nov. 29, 1873. (i) Oliver Augustine, b. ——; res. Oyster Bay, L. I. (j) Ebenezer, b. ——; d. 1864, in war. (k) Irving Herbert, b. ——; d. 1864, in war. (l) Myron Winslow, b. Nov. 28, 1846; m., Sept. 10, 1873, Emeline Rice Swazey, dau. of Rev. Arthur Swazey; res. 4324 Ellis av. Ch.: 1. Eliza Weld, b. June 11, 1881. 2. Ella Marie, b. Oct. 30, 1883. Senior member of the firm of Atwood & Steele, 18 River st. (m) Lucia Elvira, b. May 24, 1849; living; m. Otho Sylvester Arnold Sprague. Res., Pasadena, Cal. Ch.: Mary Amelia Sprague, b. July 30, 1872; m. Adolph Casper Miller, professor at University of Chicago; res. 6018 Stony Island av., Chicago. Albert Arnold Sprague, 2nd, b. May 13, 1874, unm.; is connected with Sprague, Warner & Co. Gr. Harvard College class '98. Nancy Atwood Sprague, b. Aug. 8, 1876, unm.; at School in Cambridge, Mass. Lucy Sprague, b. July 2, 1878, unm.; at school at Cambridge. Otho Sylvester Arnold Sprague, Jr., b. Dec. 24, 1880, d. July, 1893. Arnold Sprague, b. Nov. 25, 1882, d. April 1, 1888. 2. Seth, b. Sept. 20, 1796. 3. Joel, b. Sept. 24, 1794. 4. John, b. Sept. 3 1798. 5. Laban, b. May 6, 1803. 6. Oliver, b. Dec. 29, 1789 7. Anna, b. March 24, 1801. 8. Aurora, b. May 8, 1824. 9. Seth Morton, b. Sept. 6, 1829. 10. Robert, b. Aug. 11, 1792. 11. Lavinia, b Feb. 22, 1811. 12 Stillman, b. Nov. 1, 1812. 13. Chauncey, b. Nov. 25, 1814. 14. Elmira, b. Feb. 24, 1817. 15. Calista, b. March 22, 1819. 16. Emily, b. Dec. 14, 1821. These children all lived and died in the west, except Aurora, who m. John Reynolds and resides in Crookston, Minn.; Seth m. and resides in Kansas. A son of Stillman is Rev. Joseph Foster Tucker, a Congregational clergyman in Tewksbury, Mass. Oliver went to Stockholm, N.Y., m. Nancy Newton, March 14, 1815, and d. there Feb. 23, 1874, and had eight daughters. 10. Robert resided in Stockholm; 2 ch. living, Elvira Ann and Robert. 3. Joel m. in Bridgewater, Vt., Lucia A. Hammond, who d., and he m. 2d, Elizabeth Orvis. Res., in Port Huron, Mich. He was a merchant. 2. Seth, never married and d. young. 4. John m., May 20, 1823, Betsey H. Atwood and resided in Barnard. 7. Anna, d. Malone, N. Y., June 27, 1867. 5. Laban, d Oct. 10, 1870, was a physician at Port Huron, Mich., and later at Rochester; m. Lucy Ballin, who d. in R. in 1863; he went east and m.; d. in Hartford, Vt.

4285. vi. EUNICE, b. April 18, 1753; m., Oct. 25, 1781, Asa Emerson. Res., Barnard, Vt. Ch.: 1. Abigail, b. July 15, 1782. 2. Luke, b. July 9, 1784. 3. Asa, b. March 14, 1786. 4. David, b. May 28, 1788. 5. Eunice, b. Nov. 14, 1790. 6. Susannah, b. Jan. 26, 1792. 7. Daniel, b. Aug. 25, 1794.

4286. vii. SUSANNAH, b. Sept. 5, 1755; m., (pub) Sept. 1, 1774, Jacob Lawton. Jacob, son of James and Joanna (Mark) Lawton, b. abt. 1752; m. his wife in Ware, Mass.; pub. Sept. 1, 1774. She d. at Barnard, Vt., Nov. 27, 1819 ae. sixty-four. Ch.: 1. Christopher Jacob, b. Oct. 2, 1778. 2. John, b. Aug. 14, 1780. 3. Joseph, b. Feb. 5, 1784. 4. Cyrus, b. April 10, 1786. 5. Susanna, b. Aug. 5, 1788. 6. Joanna, b. Jan. 4, 1793. 7. Lydia, b. June 14, 1795. The last three, born in Barnard. Jacob Lawton removed to Barnard abt. 1787, and d. there Aug. 23, ae. eighty-four.

4287. viii. ABIGAIL, b. Sept. 18, 1768; d. before 1798; prob. unm; not mentioned in her father's will.

4085. JONATHAN FOSTER (John, Jonathan, Thomas, Thomas, Thomas), b. Hardwick, Mass., Aug. 18, 1740; m. Hannah Thayer. He was the youngest son of John and Eunice, and settled in the north part of the town of Ware. This town originally extended from the northwest parish of Rutland, now Barre, on the north, to the Quabaug river, in Warren, covering Hardwick, parts of Ware, Palmer and Brookfield, and that part of Warren north of the river. Jonathan was always a farmer, and lived to the age of sixty-nine, giving his property to his only son, Moses. He was a soldier of the Revolution. Was a selectman for the town of Ware during the years 1782-3. He d. Nov. 24, 1805. Res., Ware, Mass.

4288. i. MOSES, b. June 22, 1768; m. Anna Joslyn.

4289. ii. HANNAH, b. Aug. 3, 1770; m., Nov. 29, 1787, Nehemiah Newcomb. He was b. Wellfleet, Mass., Nov. 16, 1762; rem. to Oxford, 1762, to Greenwich, 1782, in that part incorporated as Enfield, in 1816; was a farmer; committee on schools; assessor and surveyor of highways. He d. Nov. 26, 1852. She d. Sept. 9, 1843. Ch.: 1. Foster, b. Jan. 26, 1789; m. Hannah Latham and Fanny Collins. A grandson is Arthur E. Newcomb, of Ware. 2. Moses, b. Aug. 31, 1790; m. Susanna Thayer. 3. Ruth, b. Dec. 3, 1792; m., Dec. 31, 1814, Samuel Babbitt, Jr. 4. Betsy Collins, b. Nov. 20, 1796; m. in Ware, Elkannah Babbitt. 5. Isaiah, b. July 26, 1799; m. Betsy Fuller and Mrs. Lucina (Danforth) Cary. 6. Hannah Thayer, b. Jan. 20, 1802; m. Peter A. Joslyn, of Hardwick. 7. Alanson, b. Dec. 4, 1804; d. Aug. 3, 1807.

4089. CHARLES FOSTER (Samuel, John, John, Thomas, Thomas), b. Plymouth, Mass., 1730; m., 1752, Sylvia Delano.

Charles Foster, of Kingston; will written Nov. 22, 1804; probated May 7, 1805; wife mentioned in the will but name not given; also grandson, James Foster; daughter-in-law, Fear Foster, and sons of his late brother, namely, Charles, Nathaniel, Joseph and Samuel. He d. April, 1805. Res., Kingston, Mass.

4290. i. LUCY, b. 1753; d. young.

4291. ii. LUCY, b. 1756.

4292. iii. JAMES, b. 1758; m. Fear Washburn.

4092. ROBERT FOSTER (Samuel, John, John, Thomas, Thomas), b. Plymouth, Mass., 1737; m. Elizabeth ——. Robert Foster, of Kingston; administrator appointed Nov. 7, 1791; wife, Elizabeth; Elizabeth and James Foster appointed administrators. He d. 1791. Res., Kingston, Mass.

4293. i. ROBERT, b. abt. 1760; m. Elizabeth ——.

4294. ii. NATHANIEL, b. 1774; m. Abigail Adams.

4295. iii. CHARLES, b. 1769; m. Sarah Cook.

4296. iv. JOSEPH, b. ——; m. Lydia Cook.

4297. v. JOHN, b. ——.

4298. vi. SAMUEL, b. ——.

4094. THOMAS FOSTER (Thomas, John, John, Thomas, Thomas), b. Plymouth, Mass., 1727; m., 1747, Mercy Witherell, dau. of Thomas, b. 1727; d. 1796.

He was graduated at Harvard College in 1745. Soon after he assumed the charge of the Central School in Plymouth. Thomas Foster, of Plymouth; Mercy Foster appointed administratrix, July 17, 1778; wife, Mercy; heirs not mentioned. He is mentioned in one place as Thomas, Jr.; died insolvent.—Plymouth Probate.

Mercy Foster, of Plymouth, widow; will probated Oct. 19, 1796; written March 7, 1793; daughter, Mercy May, wife of John May; grandson, Samuel Bartlett; sons, Thomas Foster and George Foster. William LeBaron was appointed executor. Mercy was the widow of Thomas Foster. He d. in 1777. Res., Plymouth, Mass.

4299. i. HANNAH, b. 1748; prob. d. before 1796.

4300. ii. LUCY, b. 1750; prob. d. before 1796.

4301. iii. THOMAS, b. 1751. He went to Charleston, S. C., and was president of a bank there.

4302. iv. PRISCILLA, b. 1753; pub., m. —— Bartlett. Had son Samuel.

4303. v. GEORGE, b. 1755.

4304. vi. MERCY, b. 1758; m., 1778, John May, Jr., of Plymouth. Ch.: 1. John, b. 1778. 2. George, b. 1782. 3. Lucy, b. 1784. 4. William, b. 1788. 5. Charles, b. 1791. 6. Edwin, b. 1793. 7. Sally, b. ——. 8. Thomas, m. Cordelia Howard.

4109. SETH FOSTER (Thomas, John, John, Thomas, Thomas), b. Plymouth, Mass., in 1758; m. —— ——. Res., New Burnswick.

4304¼. SETH, b. abt. 1783; m. Mary Daniels.

4118. JOHN FOSTER (Nathaniel, John, John, Thomas, Thomas), b. ——; m., 1767, Elizabeth Rider. He d. before 1793. Res., Plymouth county, Massachusetts.

4304⅓. i. WILLIAM, b. ——.

4304½. ii. PETER THACHER, b. ——.

4304¾. iii. ELIZABETH, b. 1770; m., 1788, William Dunham. He was son of William, of Plymouth, b. 1765. Ch.: 1. John Foster, b. ——. 2. Betsy, m. John Lewis and Benjamin Barnes.

4305. iv. JOHN, b. 1768; d. before 1793.

4121. NATHANIEL FOSTER (Nathaniel, John, John, Thomas, Thomas), b. Plymouth, Mass., Sept. 28, 1751; m. Lydia Barnaby, b. 1761; d. July 14, 1829. He d. Jan. 21, 1823. Res., Middleboro and New Braintree, Mass.

4306. i. JAMES R., b. Feb. 24, 1798; m. Nancy Henry.

4307. ii. LUCINDA, b. Dec. 24, 1782; m. in Middleboro, Mass., Perez Dickinson. Perez was son of Nathan, of Amherst; d. Aug. 20, 1815, ae. fifty; m., June 28, 1787, Ruth, dau. of Reuben Dickinson. She d. March 25, 1798, ae. thirty-five; m., 2d, Lucinda Foster, who d. in Knoxville, Tenn., Dec. 12, 1855. Ch.: 1. Betsy; 1½. Electa, m., Oct. 31, 1815, Horace Gates, of Belchertown. 2. Fanny, m. Seneca Holland, of Belchertown and Amherst. 3. Ruth d. unm. Jan. 9, 1843, ae. forty-nine. 4. Nancy, bapt. May 11, 1806; m. 1822, Joseph Estabrook. 5. Appleton, bapt. March 27, 1808; grad. Amherst College, 1825. 6. Lucinda, b. April 18, 1811, bapt. June 2, 1811; d. April 27, 1849. 7. Perez, b. Feb. 25, 1813, bapt. April 25, 1813. Lucinda, dau. of Perez, b. April 18, 1811; d. at Knoxville, Tenn., April 27, 1849; m. James H. Cowan, Nov. 25, 1830. Ch.: 1. Margaret. 2. Mary. 3. James Dickinson. 4. Lucinda Foster. 5. Cowan Finegan. 6. Child. 7. Nancy Estabrook. 8. Perez Dickinson. 9. Susan Penniman. 10. Joseph. 11. Isabella White.

The immigrant ancestor was Nathaniel Dickinson, who m. Anna Gull, landed at Boston about 1630, and probably settled at Watertown for a little while, and settled in Wethersfield, Conn., in 1637; removed to Hadley, Mass. (Norwottuck), 1659; freeman, 1661; deacon, and first recorded; d. in Hadley, June 16, 1676.

Colonel Perez, Jr., b. 1813; m. in Boston, April 10, 1835, Susan Penniman, b. 1823; d. Aug. 9, 1846. Ch.: 1. Lucy P., b. July 1, 1846; d. Oct. 13, 1846. Res., Knoxville, Tenn.

The Knoxville, Tenn., paper says: "To-day marks the anniversary of the birth of a man who is honored and loved by everybody in Knoxville. Four score and five years ago Perez Dickinson was born in the State of Massachusetts. When a young man, he came to Tennessee, and has since made his home in Knoxville, where by diligence in business, integrity that commands universal confidence and a high order of ability, he has succeeded in accumulating a handsome fortune. At the age of eighteen he was graduated from the old East Tennessee University, in 1831. Soon afterward he became a partner in the mercantile business with the late James H. Cowan. The firm was universally popular and prospered. Back in the 50's he, with others, organized the great wholesale firm of Cowan, McClung & Co., in which establishment he still maintains an interest. To write of the reputation of this house would be words wasted, as it is known by everybody, and stands in the very front rank of the great business establishments in the United States. It will be considered no reflection upon the other able men interested in the house to say that none have contributed more to its well-merited popularity than Col. Perez Dickinson.

When he came to Knoxville, it was a small village. He has seen it grow into a large city, and he and his host of friends have the proud satisfaction of knowing that he has contributed much to its growth. He has made an impression upon Knoxville in various ways. His active business life, lasting for three score years, was marked by a strictness of integrity that left no room for question. It has been said in the past, by leading business men in New York and other great commercial centers, that the fact of a man being in business in Knoxville was prima facie evidence of his title to credit. No one is entitled to more credit for this high standard than Col. Perez Dickinson. A man of con-

COL. PEREZ DICKINSON.

stant integrity himself, he impressed, unconsciously perhaps, this virtue upon the minds and hearts of his associates, and hence it is a fact that excites pride in the bosom of every Knoxvillian that the business men in the city are trusted and honored and respected all over the land.

Beginning back at a time when the memory of most readers of the Journal runneth not to the contrary, Colonel Dickinson has been reckoned as the very soul of warm-hearted, generous hospitality. Strangers coming to the city from every state in the Union, presidents and other high officials; men great in their professions and men who have distinguished themselves in business; great preachers, great lecturers, and those who have shed brilliancy on the pages of American literature, all have been hospitably entertained at his table and around his fireside. And not these, only, for thousands who are less conspicuous, have been made happy by his attentions. Many years ago he purchased the famous Island Home farm, which was beautified regardless of expense, and for years it has been visited by our own people and by thousands of strangers, until it is as widely known as Knoxville itself.

He has made an impression upon Knoxville that has been a beneficent influence, that has been manifested for years and will be for an indefinite time in the future. He has always been punctilious in the observance of those conventionalities that do so much toward making smooth the rough places of life's journey, things that are too often overlooked in the rush and hurry of the fast age in which we are living. He has never been too busy and rarely too severely indisposed to remain away from the funeral of a deceased friend. Always a lover of flowers, in the cultivation of which he has taken constant pleasure, his floral contributions have found their way to the house of affliction and bereavement, not only to the mansions of the rich but also to the cottages of those upon whom fortune has smiled less benignly.

In his youth and early manhood on up to his maturer years, he always found time to take an active interest in public affairs. In the days of the whig party he was an ardent whig. He was an admirer and supporter of the grand men who lived and ruled during the golden era of Tennessee's political life. He knew them well and entertained many of them at his hospitable board. He exercised a good influence on the voters of the country adjacent to Knoxville, his advice being often sought, wisely given and willingly heeded. Without being an office-seeker himself in any sense, he exercised a wide influence in political affairs.

4308. iii. NATHANIEL, b. Jan. 26. 1795; m. Sally Salsbury.
4309. iv. SALLY, b. ——; m. —— Hudson.
4310. v. LYDIA, b. ——.
4311. vi. FANNY, b. ——.
4312. vii. HANNAH, b. ——.
4313. viii. BETSY, b. ——; d. unm. June 5, 1843.
4314. ix. SAMUEL, b. 1791; d. unm. Oct. 27, 1850.

4130. DAVID FOSTER (Isaac, Josiah, John, Thomas, Thomas), b. Pembroke, Mass., m. there Experience Randall. She d., Hanson, 1858. David, of Pembroke; widow, Experience Foster; she was appointed administratrix, Oct. 13, 1806. He d. 1806. Res., Pembroke, Mass.

4315. i. JOHN BUNYAN, b. Feb. 1804; m. Bathsheba H. Everson.
4316. ii. DAVID H., b. ——; m. Deborah ——.
4317. iii BETSY, b. ——.
4318. iv. SYBIL, b. ——.
4319. v. BETSY, b. ——; m. Ira Drake.

4131. MILTON FOSTER (Joseph, Joseph, John, Thomas, Thomas), b. Tisbury, Mass., April 10, 1728; m. Jean ——. Res., Tisbury, Mass.

4320. i. RACHEL, b. July 13, 1753; m., July 12, 1773, Stephen Cushing.
4321. ii. KETURAH, b. Aug. 30, 1755; m., June 14, 1778 Samuel Hovey. She d. Feb. 14, 1790.

CPSIA information can be obtained at www.ICGtesting.com
Printed in the USA
LVOW01s0150110114

368941LV00005B/830/P

9 781290 660174